T0417774

The Routledge Handbook of English Language Teacher Education

The Routledge Handbook of English Language Teacher Education provides an accessible, authoritative, comprehensive and up-to-date resource of English language teacher education. With an overview of historical issues, theoretical frameworks and current debates, this handbook provides unique insights into a range of teacher education contexts, focusing on key issues relating to teacher and learner priorities, language and communication, current practices, reflective paractice, and research.

Key features include:

- a cross-section of current theories, practices and issues, providing readers with a resource which can be used in a variety of contexts;
- the use of data, transcripts and tasks to highlight and illustrate a range of practices, including examples of 'best practice';
- 'snapshots' of ELTE from a number of contexts taken from all around the world; and
- examples of current technological advances, contemporary thinking on reflective practice, and insights gained from recent research.

This wide-ranging and international collection of chapters has been written by leading experts in the field. *The Routledge Handbook of English Language Teacher Education* is sure to be core reading for students, researchers and educators in applied linguistics, TESOL and language education.

Steve Walsh is Professor of Applied Linguistics in the School of Education, Communication and Language Sciences, Newcastle University, UK and visiting professor at Hong Kong University. He has been involved in English language teaching and teacher education for more than 30 years in a range of overseas contexts. His research interests include classroom discourse, teacher development and second language teacher education.

Steve Mann (Associate Professor) currently works at the Centre for Applied Linguistics at the University of Warwick, UK. He has experience in Hong Kong, Japan and Europe in both English language teaching and teacher development. Steve supervises a research group of PhD students who are investigating teachers' education and development. His research interests include action research, reflective practice, classroom discourse, and the role of video in language teacher education.

Routledge Handbooks in Applied Linguistics

Routledge Handbooks in Applied Linguistics provide comprehensive overviews of the key topics in applied linguistics. All entries for the handbooks are specially commissioned and written by leading scholars in the field. Clear, accessible and carefully edited *Routledge Handbooks in Applied Linguistics* are the ideal resource for both advanced undergraduates and postgraduate students.

THE ROUTLEDGE HANDBOOK OF ENGLISH AS A LINGUA FRANCA
Edited by Jennifer Jenkins, Will Baker and Martin Dewey

THE ROUTLEDGE HANDBOOK OF LANGUAGE AND SUPERDIVERSITY
Edited by Angela Creese and Adrian Blackledge

THE ROUTLEDGE HANDBOOK OF LANGUAGE REVITALIZATION
Edited by Leanne Hinton, Leena Huss and Gerald Roche

THE ROUTLEDGE HANDBOOK OF SOCIOCULTURAL THEORY AND SECOND
 LANGUAGE DEVELOPMENT
Edited by James P. Lantolf and Matthew E. Poehner with Merrill Swain

THE ROUTLEDGE HANDBOOK OF STUDY ABROAD RESEARCH AND
 PRACTICE
Edited by Cristina Sanz and Alfonso Morales-Front

THE ROUTLEDGE HANDBOOK OF TEACHING ENGLISH TO YOUNG
 LEARNERS
Edited by Sue Garton and Fiona Copland

THE ROUTLEDGE HANDBOOK OF SECOND LANGUAGE RESEARCH IN
 CLASSROOM LEARNING
Edited by Ronald P. Leow

For a full list of titles in this series, please visit www.routledge.com/series/RHAL

The Routledge Handbook of English Language Teacher Education

Edited by
Steve Walsh and Steve Mann

Routledge
Taylor & Francis Group

LONDON AND NEW YORK

First published 2019
by Routledge
2 Park Square, Milton Park, Abingdon, Oxon OX14 4RN

and by Routledge
52 Vanderbilt Avenue, New York, NY 10017

Routledge is an imprint of the Taylor & Francis Group, an informa business

British Library Cataloguing-in-Publication Data
A catalogue record for this book is available from the British Library

Library of Congress Cataloging-in-Publication Data
Names: Walsh, Steve, 1959– editor. | Mann, Steve, 1960–, editor.
Title: The Routledge handbook of English language teacher education / edited by Steve Walsh and Steve Mann.
Description: London ; New York, NY : Routledge, 2019. | Series: Routledge handbooks in applied linguistics | Includes bibliographical references and index.
Identifiers: LCCN 2019000994| ISBN 9781138961371 (hardback) | ISBN 9781315659824 (e-book)
Subjects: LCSH: English language—Study and teaching—Foreign speakers. | English teachers—Training of.
Classification: LCC PE1128.A2 R685 2019 | DDC 428.0071—dc23
LC record available at https://lccn.loc.gov/2019000994

ISBN: 978-1-138-96137-1 (hbk)
ISBN: 978-1-3156-5982-4 (ebk)

Typeset in Bembo
by Apex CoVantage, LLC

MIX
Paper from
responsible sources
FSC
www.fsc.org   FSC™ C013985

Printed in the United Kingdom
by Henry Ling Limited

To all teacher educators

Contents

Contents

Contents

Contributors

Maria Isabel Azevedo Cunha is a retired English teacher from CAp/UFRJ, a laboratory school in Rio de Janeiro, Brazil. She has acted as language teaching consultant to schools and NGOs and coordinates a *lato sensu* post graduate English language course (*Curso de Especialização em Língua Inglesa*), at the Pontifical Catholic University of Rio de Janeiro (PUC-Rio). She has also been working with the Rio de Janeiro Exploratory Practice Group in the development and dissemination of Exploratory Practice and Practitioner Research.

Nick Baguley is an educational consultant based at the British Council in Cairo, Egypt. Since 1992 he has worked as an English language teacher, recruitment consultant, teacher trainer and academic manager in schools across Europe, the Middle East, Africa and Asia and has extensive experience of mentoring newly qualified teachers. He holds an MA in Professional Development for Language Education, is a Joint Chief Assessor for the Cambridge Assessment English CELTA award and writes regularly for a variety of EFL publications. He is currently a part-time student on the MPhil/PhD in Applied Linguistics programme at Canterbury Christ Church University, UK, where he hopes to conduct research on the career development of newly qualified English language teachers.

Darío Luis Banegas is an EFL secondary school teacher, teacher educator and curriculum developer with the Ministry of Education in Chubut, Argentina, and an associate fellow of the University of Warwick, UK. Darío coordinates an initial English language teacher education (IELTE) programme in Esquel, Argentina, where he also teaches Research in ELT, Introduction to Linguistics, and Sociolinguistics. In Latin America, he is a visiting lecturer on CLIL, ELT pedagogies, and teacher research at universities in Argentina, Colombia, and Ecuador. He is actively involved in teacher associations in Argentina and is the founding editor of the *Argentinian Journal of Applied Linguistics*. His main interests are: pre-service teacher education, CLIL, and action research. He is currently doing research on the impact that different IELTE modules have on student-teachers' professional identity and preparation.

Gary Barkhuizen is Professor in the School of Cultures, Languages and Linguistics at the University of Auckland, New Zealand, and Research Fellow at the University of the Free State, South Africa. His research and teaching interests are in the areas of language teacher education, teacher identity, and narrative inquiry, and he has published widely on these topics. His latest book is *Reflections on Language Teacher Identity Research* (Routledge, 2017). Gary has taught English at high school and at college level, and has been involved in teacher education in South Africa, New Zealand and the United States.

Helen C. Barrett has been researching strategies and technologies for implementing electronic portfolios since 1991. She maintains an internationally recognized website <http://electronic portfolios.org>, has contributed chapters in several books on electronic portfolios, and numerous articles. A former Staff Development Coordinator for the Fairbanks School District, she was a pioneer in Alaska, USA on the early implementation of technology in education. In 2005, Dr Barrett retired from the faculty of the College of Education at the University of Alaska Anchorage, USA. She was on loan to the International Society for Technology in Education between 2001 and 2005, providing training and technical assistance on electronic portfolios for teacher education programs throughout the US under a federal PT3 grant. During that period, she observed the emergence of online ePortfolio tools specifically developed to support accreditation in teacher education.

Heather Buchanan has been a teacher trainer since 1993. She is an experienced Cambridge CELTA and Delta trainer, and is also involved with tailored training courses for primary and secondary teachers from Europe, Asia and Central America. In her current role at Leeds Beckett University, UK, she leads the MA English Language Teaching and Cambridge Delta courses. Her interests include the role of experience and intuition in teaching and the development and adaptation of materials. She is co-author of the ELT textbook *Navigate B1+* (2015) and co-editor of the *Routledge Handbook of Materials Development for Language Teaching* (2020).

Brian Clancy lectures in academic writing and research methods at Mary Immaculate College, University of Limerick, Ireland. His research work focuses on the blend of a corpus linguistic methodology with the discourse analytic approaches of pragmatics and sociolinguistics. His primary methodological interests relate to the use of corpora in the study of language varieties and the construction and analysis of small corpora. His published work in these areas explores language use in intimate settings, such as between family and close friends, and the language variety Irish English. He is author of *Investigating Intimate Discourse: Exploring the Spoken Interaction of Families, Couples and Close Friends* (Routledge, 2016) and co-author, with Anne O'Keeffe and Svenja Adolphs, of *Introducing Pragmatics in Use* (Routledge, 2011).

Mark A. Clarke is Professor Emeritus of Language, Literacy, and Culture in the School of Education at the University of Colorado at Denver, USA. He has lived in Costa Rica, Egypt, Saudi Arabia, and Spain, and he has taught and conducted teacher preparation workshops in Latin America, Europe, the Middle East, and Japan. He has served as an officer of COTESOL and TESOL. He is the author of *Common Ground, Contested Territory,* and *A Place to Stand: Essays for Educators in Troubled Times* (2007), and a co-author of *Reader's Choice and Choice Readings* (1996; with Sandra Silberstein and Barbara Dobson). Clarke received his BA at the University of Colorado, his MA at the American University in Cairo, Egypt, and his PhD at the University of Michigan, USA.

Fiona Copland is Professor of TESOL at the University of Stirling, UK, where she is also the Associate Dean Research in the Faculty of Social Sciences. Fiona has taught English in Nigeria, Hong Kong and Japan and has worked in teacher education in the UK for over 20 years. She has published widely including *Linguistic Ethnography: Collecting, Analysing and Presenting Data* (2015; with Angela Creese) and *The Routledge Handbook of Teaching English to Young Learners* (Routledge, 2018; with Sue Garton).

Magdalena De Stefani obtained her Diploma in TEFL in 1996. Since then, she has been working in a variety of contexts in Uruguay as teacher, teacher educator, lecturer and researcher. At present, she works as a university lecturer and is also Head at a primary school in Montevideo. From the beginning of her career she has been exploring different aspects of professional development. Her doctoral thesis (University of Manchester, 2012) focused on issues of teacher development and blended learning, and in the last few years she has turned her attention to leadership and its impact on teacher development and identity, institutional culture and change processes. As a researcher, she has integrated local and international research teams working on a variety of fields, from intercultural communication to teacher research.

Jo-Ann Delaney is an English language teacher and teacher trainer. She has worked on pre- and in-service teacher education programmes in Higher Education and in the private sector. She currently works freelance, mainly on Cambridge Assessment Teaching Awards (CELTA and Delta). Her research interests include the pedagogy of teacher education, and assessment and discourse analysis in relation to teaching reading and writing. She is based in France.

Oumar Moussa Djigo is a former Hornby scholar and member of the Association of Teachers of English in Senegal (ATES). He holds an MA in English language teaching with a specialism in teacher education and development from the University of Warwick, UK. He started teaching in 2005 in a local state school as a volunteer teacher before being officially trained at the Faculty of Education and training of Cheikh Anta Diop University, Senegal. He currently teaches English as a second language at Abbe Fridoil secondary school and English for specific purposes at the English Language Institute of Dakar. Oumar is actively involved in teacher education and development through ATES and his local pedagogic cell, and is particularly interested in the inclusion of technology in ELT in his context. He has recently published articles related to the use of technology tools and learner autonomy in low-resource classrooms for the ATES national convention and conducted research on the feasibility of the Flipped classroom approach in the Senegalese ELT context.

Helen Donaghue is a senior lecturer at Sheffield Hallam University, UK. She teaches on MA TESOL, EdD, PG Cert. in Higher Education and EAP courses. Her research interests lie in the fields of pragmatics and discourse analysis with a particular interest in institutional interaction in educational settings. She is currently interested in linguistic ethnography as a way to investigate contextualised talk, looking at aspects such as the negotiation of identity and face, the use of laughter, and the way interactants navigate socially delicate talk.

Teti Dragas is an Associate Professor in ELT and Teacher Education at Durham University, UK. She began language teaching in 1998, gaining experience with a wide range of international students working within GE, ESP and EAP. In 2006 she trained as a CELTA trainer and has since worked on and developed various bespoke teacher education courses for international pre-service and in-service teachers. She was Director of the MA TESOL programmes at Durham from 2010–2018, leading a curriculum development, which included the design of a number of modules, three of which she talks about in this book. Her interests lie in methodology and teacher education with particular emphasis on reflective practice.

Martha Epperson is an ELT teacher and teacher-educator who has worked in North America, Europe, the Caribbean, and South America, where she collaborated extensively with the Chilean Ministry of Education on professional development for public-sector ELT teachers. Previously, she worked in US public schools to support English as Second Language teachers and content area teachers. She is currently pursuing her PhD in the Teaching and Teacher Education Program at the University of Michigan, USA.

John F. Fanselow is professor emeritus at Teachers College, Columbia University, USA and a faculty member of the International Teacher Education Institute – iTDi. His main interest has been observation and analysis of interactions, both inside and outside of classrooms. His publications reflect this interest. In 'It's Too Damn Tight!' he illustrated major differences in how we talk about objects inside and outside of classes and used some common spoken words for the first time in the *TESOL Quarterly*. 'Beyond Rashomon' and 'Let's See', two of his seminal articles in the *TESOL Quarterly* led to *Breaking Rules* (1987) and *Contrasting Conversations* (1992). *Small Changes in Teaching, Big Results in Learning – Videos, Activities and Essays to Stimulate Fresh Thinking About Language Teaching and Learning* (2017) illustrates practices he has been exploring since his first teaching job in 1961 in Nigeria. In addition to teaching and writing, he has been active professionally, serving as second vice president and president of TESOL and president of New York TESOL. In 2005, John received the Distinguished Alumni Award from Teachers College, Columbia University.

Fiona Farr is Associate Professor of Applied Linguistics and TESOL at the University of Limerick, Ireland. Her key areas of expertise are teacher education, reflective practice, continuous professional development, applied corpus linguistics, and technology-enhanced language learning. She has been published widely in high impact journals in her field and is author of *Teaching Practice Feedback: An Investigation of Spoken and Written Modes* (Routledge, 2011), *Practice in TESOL* (2015), and *Social Interaction in Language Teacher Education* (2019, with A. Farrell and E. Riordan). She is co-editor (with Joan Cutting) of the *EUP Textbooks in TESOL* Series and co-editor (with Liam Murray) of the *Routledge Handbook of Language Learning and Technology* (Routledge, 2016). She has recently been Visiting Research Scholar at Lancaster University as part of a large ESRC-funded research project 'Corpus Approaches to Social Science'. She has also led a large-scale national project funded by the National Forum for the Enhancement of Teaching and Learning on 'Enhancing Digital Literacies for Language Learning and Teaching', and is currently part of the EU-funded 'Shout 4HE' project team, led by Cardiff Metropolitan University, UK.

Thomas S.C. Farrell is Professor of Applied Linguistics at Brock University, Canada. Professor Farrell's professional interests include reflective practice, and language teacher education and development. Professor Farrell has published widely in academic journals and has presented at major conferences worldwide on these topics. A selection of his most recent books include *Teaching Practice: A Reflective Approach* (2011; with Jack Richards); *Reflecting on Teaching the Four Skills* (2012); *Reflective Practice* (2013); *Reflective Writing for Language Teachers* (2013); *Reflective Practice in ESL Teacher Development Groups: From Practices To Principles* (2014); *International Perspectives on English Language Teacher Education: Innovations From The Field* (2015); *Promoting Teacher Reflection in Language Education: A Framework for TESOL Professionals* (Routledge, 2015); *From Trainee to Teacher: Reflective Practice For Novice Teachers* (2016); *Reflecting on Critical Incidents in Language Education* (2017; with L. Baecher); and *Research on Reflective Practice in TESOL* (Routledge, 2017). His webpage is: www.reflectiveinquiry.ca.

Donald Freeman is Professor of Education at the University of Michigan, USA, where his work focuses on designing and researching equitable professional development opportunities in ELT that are accessible across teaching circumstances and contexts. He directs the *Learning4Teaching Project*, a series of national research studies of ELT public-sector teachers' experiences in professional development conducted in Chile, Turkey, and Qatar, and is author, most recently, of *Educating Second Language Teachers* (2016). He is senior consulting editor on *ELTeach*, an online professional development program (National Geographic Learning).

Jo Gakonga works at Warwick University, UK, on the MA in TESOL and CELTA. She has taught English and trained teachers in countries including Taiwan, Australia, the Czech Republic, and Switzerland and in a range of contexts; state and private sectors, EFL and ESOL. She is committed to experiential learning and runs an MA-level practical teaching module and a mentor training programme to enable novice mentors to reflect on and improve their skills. The latter is the focus of the PhD she is pursuing in the field of teacher education and mentoring. She is a CELTA assessor and Joint Chief Assessor for Cambridge English and co-author of IELTS Foundation. She is interested in the potential of the internet for teacher training and development and runs a website at ELT-Training.com where she provides video-based courses and online support for language teacher trainees and novice teachers as well as CPD for more experienced teachers, trainers and mentors.

Sue Garton is a Reader in English Language (TESOL) at Aston University, UK where she teaches on both undergraduate and postgraduate programmes as well as supervising doctoral students. She has extensive experience of English language teaching in Italy and the UK and has been involved in teacher education for 20 years, working with teachers in China, Russia, Ukraine, the USA and Uzbekistan, amongst others. Her research interests are in language teacher education, language teaching materials and language policy and practice. She has written and edited books and articles including *The Routledge Handbook of Teaching English to Young Learners* (Routledge, 2018) and *TESOL Voices: Young Learner Education* (2018; both with Fiona Copland). She is series editor, also with Fiona Copland, of the 15-volume series *International Perspectives on ELT*, for which she also edited *International Perspectives on Materials in ELT* (2014; with Kathleen Graves).

Alex Gilmore is Associate Professor (English for Academic Purposes) in the Department of Civil Engineering at the University of Tokyo, Japan. He has worked as a language teacher, teacher trainer, and applied linguistics researcher in Spain, Mexico, Saudi Arabia, England and Japan. He has a Cambridge University Diploma in Teaching English as a Foreign Language to Adults (DTEFLA), MA in English Language Teaching and PhD in Applied Linguistics (both from the University of Nottingham, UK). He has worked as a teacher trainer on CELTA courses in the UK and Japan and also as an examiner for Cambridge English FCE, CAE and IELTS examinations. His research interests include authenticity in language learning, discourse analysis, corpus analysis, materials design and language pedagogy and he has published widely on these topics. In his free time, he enjoys mountain climbing, travelling and flying (with a private pilot's license for gyrocopters).

Paula R. Golombek is Clinical Professor of Linguistics and Robin and Jean Gibson Term Professor at the University of Florida, USA, where she helped to develop and supervises the Undergraduate Certificate in Teaching English as a Second Language Program. Her research interests include teachers' narrative inquiry as professional development, teacher learning in second language teacher education, and sociocultural research and perspective on teacher professional development. She is author of *Mindful L2 Teacher Education: A Sociocultural Perspective on Cultivating Teachers' Professional Development* (2016; with Karen E. Johnson), *Research on Second Language Teacher Education: A Sociocultural Perspective on Professional Development* (2010; with Karen E. Johnson); and articles published in *TESOL Quarterly, Modern Language Journal, Teachers and Teaching: Theory and Practice*, and *Teaching and Teacher Education*, which represent her engagement with Vygotskian sociocultural theory in language teacher education as praxis. She has a long-standing commitment to making language teachers' voices public through her scholarly writing, such as her co-edited volume *Teachers' Narrative Inquiry as Professional Development* (2002; with Karen E. Johnson), through her national and international professional development activities, and through her editorial board work.

Kathleen Graves is Professor of Education Practice at the University of Michigan, USA where she teaches courses in educational linguistics, curriculum development and educational inquiry. She has worked on curriculum renewal and language teacher education in the US, Algeria, Bahrain, Brazil, Japan, and Korea. Her research focuses on how a language curriculum is designed and enacted and the role of teachers in curriculum renewal. She is interested in helping teachers to 'think curricularly' and to develop a reflective practice both individually and collaboratively. She is the editor/author of two books on course design, *Teachers as Course Developers* (1996) and *Designing Language Courses: A Guide for Teachers* (1999). She is the Series Editor of TESOL's Language Curriculum Development series and co-edited *Developing a New Curriculum for School-Age Learners* (2009) for the series. She is co-editor of *International Perspectives on Materials in ELT* (2014) and co-author of *Teacher Development Over Time* (2018).

John Gray is Reader in Languages in Education at UCL Institute of Education, University College London, UK. He has published in *Applied Linguistics, ELT Journal, Gender and Language, Language and Intercultural Communication, Language Teaching Research* and the *Journal of Multilingual and Multicultural Development*. He is the author of *The Construction of English: Culture, Consumerism and Promotion in the ELT Global Coursebook* (2010) and the edited volume *Critical Perspectives on Language Teaching Materials* (2013). He is co-author of *Neoliberalism and Applied Linguistics* (2012; with David Block and Marnie Holborow), and of *Social Interaction and English Language Teacher Identity* (2018; with Tom Morton).

Nusrat Gulzar has worked as a researcher at the Centre for Applied Linguistics, University of Warwick, UK, where she completed her MA in English Language Teaching with a specialism in Teacher Education. She is a contributor to the British Council-funded ViLTE project (Video in Language Teacher Education) which seeks to investigate good teaching practices in terms of video use in language teacher education. She is working as lecturer at the Department of English at the University of Dhaka, Bangladesh, where she mostly teaches English academic writing courses, English for Professional Purposes and discourse analysis. She also has an MA in Applied Linguistics and English Language Teaching from the same university. Her research interests include ICT in English language teaching, reflective practice, and language teacher development.

Graham Hall is Associate Professor of Applied Linguistics/TESOL at Northumbria University, UK. He is the author of *Exploring English Language Teaching: Language in Action* (Routledge, 2011; 2nd edition, 2017), which was the winner of the 2012 British Association for Applied Linguistics (BAAL) book prize. He also edited the *Routledge Handbook of English Language Teaching* (Routledge, 2016), and was editor of *ELT Journal* from 2013–2017.

David Hayes is an Associate Professor at Brock University, Canada, and an independent education consultant. He holds a PhD in Applied Linguistics from the University of Birmingham, UK. He has been involved in the continuing professional development of English language teachers and teacher educators for many years in Sri Lanka, Thailand and other countries and has published widely on this topic. His other research interests include second language education and peace-building, English language education in primary schools, and social attitudes towards English. He is the author of *Factors Influencing Success in Teaching English in State Primary Schools* and editor of *Innovations in the Continuing Professional Development of English Language Teachers* (both 2014). He was also lead researcher on the 2016 British Council/Department for International Development study 'Social attitudes to the English language in Bihar' (British Council, Kolkata). Other recent publications on students' attitudes to English and primary English language teaching have appeared in the *Asia Pacific Journal of Education* (2016, 2017).

Jaeyeon Heo is an instructor and researcher of English Education Department at Cheongju National University of Education, South Korea. She has taught students with diverse English language levels as well as pre-service teachers and has been involved in teacher training programmes for in-service teachers in public schools and university lecturers in Korea and several other Asian countries. She gained an MSc in TESOL from the University of Bristol and a PhD in English Language Teaching and Applied Linguistics from the University of Warwick, UK. Her doctoral research focused on team teaching and team teachers in Korean contexts and her research interests include team teaching, NEST schemes, English educational policy, and teacher training and development.

Takaaki Hiratsuka is an associate professor at Tohoku University in Sendai, Japan, where he teaches various English language courses and organises faculty development seminars for language teachers and educators. Prior to his current position, he had worked, as an English teacher, at public high schools in Japan for a decade. He had also worked at the University of the Ryukyus in Okinawa, Japan, where he taught undergraduate and graduate school courses such as English teaching methods, sociocultural theories, and qualitative research methods in the field of applied linguistics. He received his PhD in language teaching and learning from the University of Auckland, New Zealand. His research and teaching interests lie in the areas of teacher education, teacher research, and qualitative research methods (in particular, narrative inquiry and action research approaches). His work has appeared in *Accents Asia*, *ELT Journal*, *JALT Journal*, *System*, *The Language Teacher*, *New Zealand Studies in Applied Linguistics*, and other journals. He has recently contributed a chapter to Barnard and Ryan *Reflective Practice: Voices from the Field* (Routledge, 2017).

Julia Hüttner is Professor in English Language Education at the University of Vienna, Austria, having moved there from the University of Southampton, UK in 2018. Her main research interests lie in Content and Language Integrated Learning (CLIL), English Medium Instruction (EMI) and language teacher cognition. She also addresses the use of video resources to foster teacher learning and is producer of the web-based resource VELTE (Videos in English Language Teacher Education, www.southampton.ac.uk/velte). Her publications include a monograph, edited volumes and numerous journal articles and she is co-editor of *The Language Learning Journal*.

Karen E. Johnson is Kirby Professor in Language Learning and Applied Linguistics at The Pennsylvania State University, USA. Her research focuses on teacher learning in second language teacher education, the knowledge-base of second language teacher education, and the dynamics of communication in second language classrooms. Her most recent books include *Second Language Teacher Education: A Sociocultural Perspective* (Routledge, 2009); *Research in Second Language Teachers Education: A Sociocultural Perspective on Professional Development* (co-edited with P. Golombek; Routledge, 2011) and *Mindful L2 Teacher Education: A Sociocultural Perspective on Cultivating Teachers' Professional Development* (with P. Golombek; Routledge, 2016). She has presented papers and given workshops for second language teachers and teacher educators in Brazil, Chile, Germany, Hong Kong, Japan, New Zealand, Turkey, Singapore, South Africa, and throughout the USA. She has served as the associate editor for Practitioner Research for the journal *Language Teaching Research*. In the MA TESL and the PhD in Applied Linguistics Program, she teaches courses in Applied Linguistics, Teaching English as a Second Language, Communication in Second Language Classrooms, and Theory and Research in Language Teacher Education.

Thom Kiddle is Director at NILE (Norwich Institute for Language Education), UK, where he has worked since 2011 after moving from Chile where he was head of academic research and educational technology at the Chilean-British University. He has previously worked in Portugal, the UK, Australia and Thailand in language teaching, teacher training and language assessment, and published on digital language learning materials, online tests of spoken language proficiency, evaluating teaching resources, and language learning motivation. He is the creator and Academic Director of NILE Online professional development courses for language teachers and trainers, and works on strategic management, project management and quality assurance, as well as teaching and training online and in the bricks-and-mortar classroom. Thom is also treasurer and founding director of AQUEDUTO (the Association for Quality Education and Training Online); webmaster for the Testing, Evaluation and Assessment Special Interest Group of IATEFL; part of the Accreditation UK Advisory Group; and Vice Chair of Eaquals.

Richard Kiely is Reader in TESOL Applied Linguistics at the University of Southampton, UK, where he carries out research, supervises research students and teaches on undergraduate and postgraduate courses. He has extensive experience as a teacher, teacher-trainer, researcher and curriculum developer in English as a second language contexts such as Poland, Hungary, Mexico, South Africa, Hong Kong, Malaysia, and Zambia. His research interests include language programme evaluation, language teaching and teacher development. He supervises PhDs in programme evaluation, classroom interaction, and teacher learning research themes. He has published in a range of journals (*TESOL Quarterly, ELT Journal, Innovation in Education and Teaching International, Language Teacher Research, Modern Languages Journal, Language Awareness, Innovation in Language Learning and Teaching*, and the *Journal of Second Language Teaching and Research*, among others). He is the author of *Programme Evaluation in Language Education* (with Pauline Rea-Dickins; 2005); *Investigating Critical Learning Episodes* (with Matt Davis and Eunice Wheeler; 2010); and *Exploratory Practice: An Innovative Approach to Language Teacher Development* (with Assia Slimani-Rolls; 2018).

Kuchah Kuchah is Lecturer in Language Education at the University of Leeds, UK. He has been involved in English language education for over 20 years, serving as English language teacher, teacher trainer, coursebook writer and policy maker with the Ministry of Education in his home country of Cameroon. Kuchah has also been involved in a range of teacher education and materials development initiatives in sub-Saharan Africa, South East Asia and Europe. More recently, he has served as a consultant with the Council of Europe in Albania and with Windle Trust International and ELT Consultants in South Sudan. He is one of TESOL International Association's '30 Up and Coming Leaders' in ELT and President of IATEFL. Kuchah's research and publications are in the areas of teaching English to young learners, English Medium Instruction, Context-appropriate methodology and language teacher education. He is co-editor of *International Perspectives on Teaching English in Difficult Circumstances* (2018; with Fauzia Shamim).

Martin Lamb is a Senior Lecturer in the School of Education at the University of Leeds, UK, having previously worked as a teacher/trainer of English in Sweden, Indonesia, Bulgaria and Saudi Arabia. At Leeds, he teaches undergraduate and postgraduate courses and supervises doctoral students in various aspects of language education. His main research interest is in learner and teacher motivation and he has published articles on this topic in several academic journals including *TESOL Quarterly*, *Language Learning* and *Language Teaching*, as well as one on in-service teacher training in *ELT Journal*. He is the co-editor of a collection of articles on a large-scale educational project in the Sultanate of Oman, *International Collaboration for Educational Change* (2010), which is where he met his co-author Mark Wyatt – and he is currently chief editor of a *Handbook of Motivation for Language Learning* (forthcoming).

Li Li is a Senior Lecturer at the Graduate School of Education in the University of Exeter, UK. She has been involved in English language teaching for nearly 20 years and has worked in different cultural and educational contexts. Her research interests include language teacher cognition, classroom discourse, developing thinking skills and the use of new technologies in language learning. She has published widely on these topics, including over 30 scholarly articles and a co-edited handbook on thinking skills. She is also the author of *Social Interaction and Teacher Cognition* (2017) and *New Technologies and Language Learning* (2017).

Amy Lightfoot is currently the Regional Education and English Academic Lead for the British Council in South Asia. With nearly 20 years' experience working in the education sector, Amy has expertise in language education, in-service teacher education programme design, the use of technology to support teacher and student learning, assessment and monitoring and evaluation. She has experience working as a teacher, teacher trainer, multimedia materials developer, project manager and evaluator in primary and secondary school sectors in Portugal, the UK, India and across South Asia, and as an associate lecturer for undergraduate programmes in the UK. She holds an MA in Education and International Development from the UCL Institute of Education, UK and an MA in English Language Teaching from the University of Bath, UK.

Michael McCarthy is Emeritus Professor of Applied Linguistics, University of Nottingham, UK; Adjunct Professor of Applied Linguistics, University of Limerick, Ireland; and Visiting Professor in Applied Linguistics at Newcastle University, UK. He is author/co-author/editor of 53 books, including the textbook series *Touchstone* and *Viewpoint*, *The Cambridge Grammar of English* (2006), *English Grammar Today* (2011) and *From Corpus to Classroom* (2003), as well as titles in the *English Vocabulary in Use* series. He is author/co-author of 110 academic papers. He is co-director (with Ronald Carter) of the CANCODE spoken English corpus. He has lectured in 46 countries and has been involved in language teaching and applied linguistics for 52 years.

Inés K. Miller holds a Master's in TESOL from UCLA, USA, a PhD in Applied Linguistics from Lancaster University, UK and has completed post-doctoral research at Warwick University, UK. As Associate Professor at the Pontifical Catholic University of Rio de Janeiro (PUC-Rio), Brazil, she researches the reflective discourse of learners, teachers and teacher educators. She mentors the Rio Exploratory Practice Group and has been engaged in the development and dissemination of Exploratory Practice. With Simon Gieve (formerly of Leicester University), she co-edited the book *Understanding the Language Classroom* (2006). She publishes widely in Brazilian and internationally edited books.

Tom Morton is Honorary Research Fellow in the Department of Applied Linguistics and Communication, Birkbeck, University of London, UK. His research mainly focuses on content and language integration in bilingual education, including such topics as students' language and literacy development, classroom interaction, and teacher knowledge and identity. He has co-authored two books on CLIL: *The Roles of Language in CLIL* (with Ana Llinares and Rachel Whittaker; 2012), and *Applied Linguistics Perspectives on CLIL* (with Ana Llinares; 2017). He is also co-author of *Social Interaction and English Language Teacher Identity* (with John Gray; 2018).

Anne O'Keeffe is Senior Lecturer in Applied Linguistics at Mary Immaculate College, University of Limerick, Ireland. Her research output includes papers, chapters and books on corpus linguistics, pragmatics and media discourse. These include *Investigating Media Discourse* (Routledge, 2006), *From Corpus to Classroom* (with Michael McCarthy and Ronald Carter; 2007); *English Grammar Today* (with Ronald Carter, Michael McCarthy and Geraldine Mark; 2011); *Introducing Pragmatics in Use* (with Brian Clancy and Svenja Adolphs; Routledge, 2011). She also co-edited the *Routledge Handbook of Corpus Linguistics* (with Michael McCarthy; 2010). Her most recent research on the Cambridge Learner Corpus has led to the online resource, the *English Grammar Profile* (with Geraldine Mark; 2017). She has also guest edited a number of international journals, most recently, *Corpus Pragmatics*, and she is co-editor of two Routledge book series, *Routledge Corpus Linguistic Guides* and *Routledge Applied Corpus Series*.

Amol Padwad is currently Professor and Director, at the Centre for English Language Education (CELE), Ambedkar University, Delhi, India. He is currently the Secretary of Ainet Association of English Teachers (AINET, India) and has been the National President of English Language Teachers Association of India. He has been a tertiary teacher, teacher trainer, ELT consultant and research mentor for over 30 years. Besides helping teachers working in difficult circumstances and low-resource classrooms, he is actively involved in promoting English Teachers' Clubs – self-help teacher development groups – especially in rural India, and is associated with several teacher networks and associations. His areas of interest are teacher networks, teacher development and education, ESL, teacher research and history of ELE. His recent publications include *Continuing Professional Development* (with Rod Bolitho; 2019) and *Teaching in Low-resource Classrooms: Voices of Experience* (with Richard Smith and Deborah Bullock; 2017). He is a member of IATEFL Research SIG and co-edits *ELT Research*.

Jon Parnham has worked in the field of English language teaching as a teacher, trainer and manager since 2001. He has worked in Taiwan, Hong Kong, India and Egypt. From 2014–2017 he worked as the British Council Senior Academic Manager for West India, responsible for the design, delivery and monitoring and evaluation of large-scale teacher development projects in partnership with the Governments of Maharashtra and Gujarat. He is currently based in Egypt where he works for the British Council on teacher development projects for primary and secondary school teachers across the country. This role has a particular focus on supporting teachers to form communities of practice in their local districts in order to practise their English together and learn new teaching skills and techniques. His areas of interest include the use of technology to support teachers' professional development, teacher networks and the monitoring and evaluation of projects. He has a diploma in English language teaching and an MA in Applied Linguistics.

Pascual Pérez-Paredes is a lecturer in Research in Second Language Education at the Faculty of Education, University of Cambridge, UK. His main research interests are learner language variation, the use of corpora in language education and corpus-assisted discourse analysis. He has published research in journals such as *CALL*, *English for Specific Purposes*, *Language, Learning & Technology*, *System*, *ReCALL*, *Discourse & Society* and the *International Journal of Corpus Linguistics*. He is the overall coordinator of the Research Methods Strand in the MEd in Education at the University of Cambridge, UK, and a member of the Editorial board of *Register Studies* and *ReCALL*.

Tony Prince is Academic Director at NILE and has spent the last 20 years involved in the management of English language courses; running a language school in Oxford, UK before moving to Norwich, UK, first at the University of East Anglia, then at NILE. He is module leader on the Teaching English for Academic Purposes module of the NILE MA in Professional Development for Language Education. His experience has included developing a content integrated Pre-sessional programme for students at the University of East Anglia, as well as Departmental In-sessional support across the University and he has been involved in a wide range of international consultancy projects, including running courses, workshops and presentations. He is also involved in teaching training related to materials development and ELT management. Tony is a keen proponent and user of technology in education. He spends a good deal of his time in work and out exploring the opportunities of different App ecosystems, Virtual Learning Environments and online provisions.

Pia Resnik is professor of ELT Research and Methodology at the University College of Teacher Education, Vienna/Krems, Austria, and teaches courses in linguistics and language competence at the English department of the University of Vienna. Her research interests include all aspects surrounding LX users of English, with a particular focus on emotions in multilingual contexts. She is the author of the book *Multilinguals' Verbalisation and Perception of Emotions* (2018).

Ayşegül Sallı is Assistant Professor at Eastern Mediterranean University, Northern Cyprus. She received her PhD in English Language Teaching in 2018 with a dissertation on the contribution of blogging interactions to pre-service English language teachers' reflections and construction of teacher identity. She has been working as an English language teacher and teacher trainer/mentor for more than 15 years. Currently, she is the coordinator of the Teacher Training and Professional Development Unit at the Foreign Languages and English Preparatory School, Eastern Mediterranean University. Her academic interests include technology integrated language teaching, pre-service teacher education, continuous professional development and language teacher identity.

Ali Fuad Selvi is an Assistant Professor of TESOL and Applied Linguistics in, and the Chair of the Teaching English as a Foreign Language Program at Middle East Technical University, Northern Cyprus Campus. His research interests include Global Englishes and its implications for language learning, teaching, teacher education and language policy/planning; issues related to (in)equity, professionalism, marginalization and discrimination in TESOL; and second language teacher education. He is the Area Editor for NNEST volume of the *TESOL Encyclopedia of English Language Teaching* (2018), co-author of *Teaching English as an International Language* (with Bedrettin Yazan; 2013) and co-editor of *Conceptual Shifts and Contextualized Practices in Education for Glocal Interaction* (with Nathanael Rudolph; 2018). In addition to his scholarship in these areas, he was recently recognized as one of TESOL International Association's '30 Up and Coming Leaders' in recognition of his potential to 'shape the future of both the association and the profession for years to come'.

Olcay Sert is Senior Lecturer in the School of Education, Culture and Communication at Mälardalen University, Sweden. He is the editor-in-chief of *Classroom Discourse* (Routledge) and the author of *Social Interaction and L2 Classroom Discourse* (2015). His book has been shortlisted for the BAAL Book Prize and AAAL First book award. His articles have appeared in international peer-reviewed journals such as *Journal of Pragmatics, TESOL Quarterly, System, Language and Education* and *Computer Assisted Language Learning*. His main research approach is conversation analysis and his research deals primarily with classroom discourse, interactional competence, and language teacher education.

Navaporn Snodin is an Assistant Professor of Applied Linguistics at Kasetsart University, Thailand. She holds a PhD degree in Educational and Applied Linguistics from Newcastle University, UK. She was a visiting scholar at the Department of English and American Studies, the University of Vienna, Austria, under the scheme of the ASEA-UNINET Staff Exchange. She was a holder of a Newton Advanced Fellowship from the British Academy. Her research focuses on world Englishes, English language education, and Internationalisation of Higher Education. She has published articles in journals including *World Englishes, Asian Englishes, System, Computers & Education* and the *RELC Journal*.

Russell Stannard is the founder of www.teachertrainingvideos.com. He has won several awards for his work in screen capture technology including the British Council 'Technology Award', the Times Higher 'Outstanding Innovation Award' and the University of Westminster 'Excellence in Teaching' award. He trains educators in the use of technology all over the world. Russell was previously a Principal Teaching Fellow at the University of Warwick and the University of Westminster, UK. His current role is with the Norwich Institute for Language Training where he runs online courses on the Flipped Classroom and tutors on the MA programme. He is widely published and writes a regular column called 'Webwatcher' for the English Teaching Professional that has been running for nearly 17 years.

Betelhem Taye is a former Hornby scholar and an active member of the Ethiopian English Language Professionals' Association (EELPA). She graduated from the University of Warwick, UK in 2017 with an MA (with Distinction) in English Language Teaching, specializing in Teacher Education and Development. For over nine years, Betelhem has been engaged in teacher training and education, English teaching, conference organization and hosting, news article production and translation works. She has had valuable experiences of working with governmental and non-government organizations like the Ethiopian Broadcasting Cooperation (EBC) as a newscaster and journalist, the British Council as a teacher trainer and Fhi 360 as an ESL trainer. Currently, she works as an English language specialist in a private school in Addis Ababa,

Ethiopia, and is responsible for managing English language teaching and learning in the school. More specifically, her role is to plan and develop systems and procedures that improve the intensity and quality of English teaching.

Scott Thornbury has written a number of books on language and language teaching, including *The New A–Z of ELT* (2017) and *30 Language Teaching Methods* (2017). He has taught and trained extensively in several continents, and currently teaches for The New School, New York, USA, on their MA TESOL program. He is also the series editor of the Cambridge Handbooks for Language Teachers.

Ivor Timmis is Professor of Applied Linguistics at Leeds Beckett University, UK. He has around 30 years' experience in teacher education and has taught extensively on MA in ELT, Cambridge Delta and Cambridge Celta courses. It is through work on these courses that he developed a strong interest in classroom management. In addition, he has worked on teacher development courses at Leeds Beckett with several groups of Spanish, Italian and Chinese teachers. Through the British Council he has also worked on CPD courses with teachers in Hong Kong, Thailand and Georgia. His other major areas of academic interest are materials development and corpus linguistics. He has been part of materials development projects for primary schools in China, teachers in Ethiopia and secondary schools in Singapore. In the field of corpus linguistics, his focus has been on research into spoken language and its relevance to ELT. More recently, his research has taken an historical turn with a focus on what we can learn about spoken language of the past through documentary archives from the 1930s and from mid-Victorian England.

Luis S. Villacañas de Castro is Associate Professor in the Language and Literature Education department at the Universitat de València, Spain, where he lectures and researches on critical pedagogy, multimodality, and ELT. Both his research and his teaching are premised on the understanding of English as an imperial language and on the belief that English teachers can and should draw on critical and participative pedagogies to make the English learning experience a more empowering one. Luis relies on action research as an engine of professional development so, together with other lecturers in his department, he coordinates an action research team that experiments with multicultural, multiliteracies, and multilingual orientations to ELT aimed at underprivileged school children in Valencia.

Anne-Coleman Webre has taught English as a Foreign Language to adults in Germany, and English as a Second Language and Social Studies in middle schools in Virginia and Maryland, USA. She is completing her PhD in Teaching and Teacher Education at the University of Michigan, USA, where she also prepares preservice teachers to work with English Language Learners and in research on teaching.

Mark Wyatt is an Associate Professor at Khalifa University, UAE. He has worked as a teacher and teacher educator in Thailand, Nepal, Oman, the UK and the UAE. This experience includes supporting teacher development on a University of Leeds, UK BA TESOL programme for in-service teachers in Oman and a University of Portsmouth, UK BA TESL programme for Malaysian pre-service teachers in the UK. He has published on teacher motivation in the *International Review of Education*, while his research into language teachers' self-efficacy beliefs has appeared in various journals: *Australian Journal of Teacher Education, Educational Action Research, Educational*

Review, International Journal of Qualitative Studies in Education, International Journal of Research and Method in Education and *System.* He has also contributed a chapter on language teachers' self-efficacy beliefs to *Language Teacher Psychology* (edited by Mercer and Kostoulas; 2018). Other professional concerns include supporting practitioner research. He is a member of the IATEFL Research SIG and he co-edits *ELT Research.*

Advisory Board

Fiona Copland
Tim Phillips
Eunice Tang
Graham Hall
Julian Edge

Acknowledgements

We have a number of people to thank in relation to this Handbook. First and foremost we would like to thank the contributors. They have been committed to delivering a collection that represents a contemporary and comprehensive vision of language teacher development. We'd like to thank them for their insights, deadline keeping and encouragement in what has been an exciting and challenging journey. Without your professionalism, perseverance and patience, this publication would never have seen the light of day! The dialogue between an editor and a writer always takes us to new points of interest and articulation. We would like to also thank our advisory board (Tim Phillips, Fiona Copland, Eunice Tang, Julian Edge and Graham Hall) for their advice and support.

In a book about teacher education development it is important to recognize those who have shaped our sense of the values and priorities of working with teachers. For Steve (M), Keith Richards and Julian Edge have been important touchstones, particularly because of their enthusiasm for working with teacher learners in collaborative and data-led ways. Jane and Dave Willis, Tony Wright and Tom Farrell have always been a source of great support and inspiration too. For Steve (W), Tony Young, Anne O'Keeffe and Mike McCarthy have been enormously supportive over the years. Tom Morton and John Gray have been important fellow travellers on the journey.

We have valued our engagement with some excellent MA and PhD students in recent years, and a good number of them have contributed to the book and its rationale in various ways. As we have supervised dissertations and theses on various aspects of teacher development, training and education, we have appreciated the range of contexts, processes, constraints and opportunities involved. The following is a list that recognizes the debt we owe these people and fellow teacher educators. There would be no book without them. There are too many to make clear the precise nature of their contribution, but many of them are cited in the following chapters. And so, we would like to thank Flori Dzay-Chulim, Bushra Ahmed Khurram, Wayne Trotman, George Skuse, Mohammad Manasreh, Tim Phillips, Ema Ushioda, Jane Spinola, Georgina Ma, Joan Sim, Jennifer Heo, Samiah Ghounaim, Timi Hyacinth, Iman Shamsini, Manuel Herrera Montoya, Daniel Xerri, John Knagg, Roy Cross, Shefali Kulkarni, Bulara Monyaki, Daniela Bacova, Reem Doukmak, Mike Solly, Jose Alberto Fajardo Castañeda, Amir Hamidi, Muhammad Fitri Bin Ahmad, David Block, Andrea Luci, Keith Richards, Andy Harris, Audrey O'Grady, Bede McCormack, Peter de Costa, Dario Banegas, Willy Renandya, Ezra Ora, Parwiz Hussain, Marwa Masood, Fareeha Manzoor, Victoria Inwang, Laurent Ahishakiye, Elya Menglieva, Mohammad Abdeirahman, Fiona Copland, Tom Farrell, Fiona Farr, Gokce Kurt, Hansung Waring, Heather Buchanan, Ivor Timmis, Simon Smith, Claudia Harsch, Armin Hottman, Joel Josephson, Teresa MacKinnon, David Falvey, Sal Consoli, Ged O'Connell, Masuko Miyahara, Atsuko Watanabe, Veronica Crosbie, Angela Creese, Saleha Ian Nakamura, Jade Blue, Jo Ann Delaney, Jo Gakonga, Andrew Davidson, Lara Walsh, Li Li, Marisela (Brasil), Mark Brooke,

Acknowledgements

Laura Baecher, Ross Crighton, Ian Clifford, Mark Wyatt, Mike Chick, Mohammad Aldhaen, Olcay Sert, Hatice Ergul, Olly Beddall, Paul Slater, Phillip Saxon, Jason Anderson, Rana Yildirim, Rezvan Rashidi, Richard Pinner, Joe Winston, Russell Stannard, Sandra Morales, Sarah Banks, Adam Edmett, Andy Gau, Tom Bloor, Sarah Haas, Gerald Talandis Jr., Peter Brown, Pat Chauhan, Claudia Bustos Moraga, I-Chen Hsieh Maricarmen Gamero, Natalia Dura Gatti, Wimansha Abeyawickrama, Saleha Mersin, Babita Chapagain, Abdou Dieng, Suzuki Koda Fuentes, Jennifer Joshua, Jingli Jiang, Tilly Harrison, Penny Mossavian, Lynnette Richards, Evelina Jaleniauskiene, Neil Murray, Sagun Shrestha, Oumar Djigo, Tran Phan, Mirian Fuhr, Betelhem taye Tsehayu Noel Franco, Mehdi Gholikhan, Komila Tangirova, Saifa Haque Julius Daniel Jayatha Ratnayake, Annamaria Pinter, Mala Palini, Sukhbir Atwal, Claudia Rodríguez, Duncan Lees, Teti Dragas, Judith Hanks, Matt Carty, Christine Tudor Jones, Jiamei Chen, Mohammed Bashir, Allwyn D'Costa, Larissa Goulart Da Silva, Urmila Khaled, Sol Loutayf, Vuyokazi Makubalo, Erkin Mukhammedov, Alireza Safar, Seetha Venunathan, Sefalane Shaike, Pipit Suharto, Aom Wongchaiwa, Betelhem taye Tsehayu and Abdalla Yousif.

In truth, there are many other students we have worked with at Aston University, Queen's University Belfast, the University of Birmingham, Newcastle University and the University of Warwick who have helped shape many of these ideas. In all these institutions, we have learned a great deal from working with such committed teachers and researchers.

We are grateful for Routledge's support in publishing this book and we would particularly like to thank Hannah Rowe, Eleni Steck, Elizabeth Cox, Victoria Brown and Louisa Semlyen for their advice patience, good humour and commitment. Special thanks too to Rosie Copland-Mann and Lara Walsh, who helped enormously with checking and formatting references. A special mention goes to Andy Davidson for his technical help at a crucial stage.

Steve Walsh
Ovingham, Northumberland
Steve Mann
Alrewas, Staffordshire

Introduction

Steve Walsh and Steve Mann

The main rationale for this handbook is to provide a comprehensive overview of English Language Teacher Education (ELTE), drawing on perspectives from the related fields of Applied Linguistics, Education and TESOL. The handbook seeks to identify, discuss and raise awareness of key issues and practices in education, training and in teacher development. The 39 papers assembled here offer insights into the range and detail of current practices in ELTE and associated research. We hope that the handbook offers a resource for teacher educators and researchers interested in the design, implementation and support of teacher-learners (TLs) in teacher education provision.

Our association and professional collaboration extends over 30 years. During this period, we have often been in contact to share and discuss ideas about teaching and teacher development. More recently, we have shifted our focus to writing and research, resulting in a series of publications (see, for example, Mann and Walsh, 2013, 2017 and Walsh and Mann, 2015). During this collaboration we have made contact with ELTE professionals who have been important in our own development as 'educators'. We have also re-connected with previous collaborators and mentors. This has made the process both collaborative and rewarding. The excellent contributions made by authors in this volume have enabled us to offer here what we believe to be a significant resource for ELTE and ELTE research. At this point, we would like to extend our sincere thanks to all the authors who have helped to shape, refine and polish our collective thinking and writing. Without them, this volume simply would not have been possible.

There are, we believe, a number of unique features in this collection. In all chapters, there is some reference to data: regarded as any evidence drawn from the classroom or training context and which enhances understandings of professional practice. Examples in this handbook include video recordings, transcripts, tasks, vignettes and so on. We could extend this range to include a piece of material, a conversation with a student, a test score; in short, anything which comes from an educational context and which can help us to reflect on and improve our practice. The chapters all include specific steps, procedures, frameworks, tools, and tasks for involving teachers in professional development. By including data, we aim to encourage new thinking and innovation and to make strong connections between the theory and practice of ELTE. The guidelines we offered to contributors encouraged them to make explicit such connections in their ELTE processes and to make the detail of their innovations clear; contributors were asked to focus on concrete processes or practices, to pay attention to how they work with teachers, and to high-light which topics and resources they used.

A second feature of the handbook is an attempt to move away from 'survey only' type chapters. While surveys certainly have their place, and many handbooks make extensive use of surveys of the field and state-of-the-art reports on a particular topic, we have included other approaches. In addition to the use of data in many of the chapters, we incorporate examples of materials, extracts from teacher training curricula, tasks, frameworks, examples of reflective tools, and so on. In this way, we hope to have made the processes and practices of ELTE as transparent and vivid as possible for our readers.

Any research or professional practice concerning ELTE cannot ignore context. A third feature of this handbook is to offer a cross-section of ELTE in a range of contexts and using a variety of approaches and practices. We hope that readers will gain valuable insights into the ways in which English Language Teacher Education 'gets done' around the world. A quick look through the list of contributors gives some idea of the range of contexts featured in this handbook. Contributions were sought from both established and early career writers who work in ELTE around the world; readers will notice that more established authors are often paired with less experienced researchers in order to offer a range of insights into a particular issue or topic. We also sought out those teacher educators who we believe are working at the cutting edge of teacher education and taking the field forward.

In this way, we anticipate that the readership will be truly international, as the handbook is useful both to professionals working in established geographical settings such as the USA and Europe, but also in lesser represented contexts such as, for example, South East Asia, Africa and South America. Our broad aim is to offer both a 'snapshot' of language teacher education around the world, while, at the same time, pursuing key issues which have relevance in any context. The upshot of this approach is that this handbook will hopefully have broad appeal and offer something for any professional engaged in ELTE or ELTE research.

Organising principles

This handbook follows three sets of organising principles. The first, and most obvious, are the six thematic Parts that give the resource its structure. The second is a number of key 'strands' that run through the whole book and inform each chapter. These strands are based on what we believe to be fundamental to contemporary second language teacher education. The third set are the guidelines given to authors to provide cohesion within each chapter while maintaining coherence and a certain amount of flexibility across the handbook.

In terms of the first set of principles, by organising the 39 chapters into six distinct thematic Parts we wanted to achieve the feel of a journal special issue for each Part. The most obvious way of understanding this handbook is through the six thematic Part headings which unpack 'ELTE'. It took us some time to arrive at these organising themes in attempting to do justice to the range of knowledge, skills, practices and research in our field. We are aware that there are other ways of 'cutting the cake' but we feel that this range of perspectives represents the key dimensions of the field. We begin with an overview of current debates, paradigms and trends, followed by the core contexts for teacher education. We then differentiate various perspectives on language before moving on to focus on pedagogic knowledge and the processes and practices of teacher education. In the final Part, we unpack the 'T' in ELTE, with a sustained focus on the teacher.

In addition to these six themes, we believe that one of the important strengths of the handbook are the key 'strands' that run through the whole book and inform each chapter:

- *The language learner.* The first priority is the centrality of the language learner in the process of ELTE. This is fundamental and each contribution needed to consider how teacher education actually relates to language learners.
- *Reflective practice.* This is crucial for us (see Mann and Walsh, 2017), as we believe that teacher educators should support and scaffold RP.
- *Data-led.* We have already highlighted this as a 'unique feature' of the book, but it is also one of the strands which runs right through each chapter.
- *The use of technology.* Making clear the ways in which technology is having an impact on the teacher training process and language learning in and outside the classroom.
- *The processes of working with teachers.* We take it as given that when something is being 'taught' in teacher education, there is always one eye on language learners in the actual classroom. This 'loop' aspect is particularly important for areas of teacher knowledge and classroom methodology.
- *Critical perspectives.* Many of the chapters adopt a critical stance on a particular issue, highlighting current debates and dichotomies in an effort to provide readers with a more balanced perspective.

In order to maintain the coherent and cohesive structure outlined above, we provided the contributors with a suggested template, connecting existing research to specific ways of working with teachers. We invited contributors to follow these sub-sections:

- Survey: current perspectives on a particular theme or issue, based mainly on the existing literature.
- Research: where appropriate, extracts of data are used to illustrate the chapter focus and highlight the main issues in ELTE.
- Applications: a more practically oriented section that considers the practical issues relating to the chapter focus and includes data and evidence.
- Further reading: three to five key texts are highlighted and annotated, along with useful web links.

Structure and content

In writing a handbook on ELTE, it is clearly impossible to include everything and do justice to the various bodies of literature which inform the discipline. We have tried to balance core or established topics and approaches with the recognition that the ELTE field is changing. Although the majority of writers are well known (and in some cases actually retired), we have also included innovative contributions from relatively new voices in our field. We hope that this has helped to maintain a balance between some of the better-established and widely accepted theories and practices of ELTE in addition to providing space for some new, and perhaps controversial, ideas. This is particularly relevant in the way new technologies (e.g. screencapture, ePorfolios, digital video tools) are creating new possibilities in ELTE. The six Parts, together with the chapters which make up each one, are now summarised below:

Part 1

The overview Part has seven chapters covering a range of themes which we consider to be central to ELTE. The opening chapter (Freeman, Webre and Epperson) was actually one of the last to be written. The question addressed in Chapter 1 is: What constitutes the knowledge base of ELTE? In particular, the authors argue that the prevailing 'ELTE-packaging' view of knowledge needs to be re-thought; rather, we need to know what constitutes the knowledge base for both teachers and teacher educators, and develop understandings of how the process of curating these ideas operates.

Much of the work in the handbook is located in a sociocultural theoretical (SCT) framework, as outlined by Golombek and Johnson in Chapter 2. Their Vygotskyan SCT (VSCT) perspective on ELTE provides an overview of key principles and concepts to demonstrate how VSCT might be used to inform the practices and interactions of ELTE programmes in systematic ways.

One of the key strands of the handbook is Reflective Practice (RP). In Chapter 3, Farrell discusses how SLT educators can encourage learner teachers to become reflective practitioners. The chapter outlines how educators can make use of technology, critical friendships, team-teaching, peer coaching, dialoguing, service learning, writing, action research and analysis of critical incidents to encourage learner teachers to engage in reflective practice. Another key strand running through the handbook is the use of technology, something taken up by Lightfoot (Chapter 4), who focuses on teachers and teacher educators using technology to facilitate professional development. The chapter explores the various benefits, issues and challenges associated with the use of ICT.

In what he calls 'critical language teacher education', Gray (Chapter 5) considers how neo-liberalism, marketization and the conditions of labour in neoliberal capitalism have affected LTE. Specifically, the chapter looks at the ways in which marketization has impacted an initial teacher preparation programme in the UK: the state sector Post Graduate Certificate of Education in Modern Foreign Languages (PGCE-MFL).

Of concern to anyone involved in ELTE are the ways in which programmes are evaluated, a theme taken up by Kiely in Chapter 6. This chapter describes the ways programme evaluation has developed in recent decades, and considers how this has shaped understanding, activity and research in the context of ELTE.

In Chapter 7, the final chapter of Part 1, in conversation, Fanselow and Hiratsuka reach a shared and collaborative understanding of key elements of language teacher education and develop several suggestions for teacher educators, including the development of autonomy, using classroom interaction transcripts and attending to small details in changes to practice.

Part 2

This Part allows us to focus on context, considered as fundamental to the development of successful and appropriate training, education and development. The opening chapter (Kiddle and Prince) provides an overview of the challenges and opportunities that digital technology presents for teacher educators and details practical examples and explanations of digital and online tools and platforms. Given the importance attached to technology, Chapter 8 provides us with a starting point to consider important variables such as design and structure, timing, and platforms and tools.

We then have three chapters that consider core contexts for training (pre-service/initial, in-service, and CPD). Chapter 9 (Baguley) focuses on the pre-service teacher training context (e.g. CELTA) and considers why the first year of teaching can be challenging. He considers the role of teacher trainers, academic managers, supervisors and mentors in helping the transition to the classroom.

Dragas then focuses on in-service Teacher Training (INSET) within ELT in Chapter 10. She highlights key future possibilities for INSETT courses in light of recent research in this area. One aspect of this chapter that is particularly relevant for Part 2 is the importance of putting socio-cultural context at the centre of the enterprise. This promotes teacher agency and, by embedding reflective practice, encourages the development of local understandings.

Hayes (Chapter 11) presents a perspective on continuing professional development (CPD), highlighting the relevance of teachers' professional contexts and their personal circumstances, as well as 'local' and professional needs in any CPD design process. His discussion of key issues in CPD provides a framework of reference for effective practice in CPD, for teacher educators and administrators as well as for teachers.

In Chapter 12, Morton looks across all three contexts (pre-, in-service education and continuing professional development) at content-based approaches to language teaching. Morton considers training implications for teachers who teach academic content through English in contexts where English is not the first language of the majority of the students.

Selvi brings this Part to close with an important set of issues which concern all teacher education contexts. In Chapter 13, he makes clear that ELTE has an important role in promoting a refined understanding of teacher identity, ownership of language and instructional competencies that move beyond oversimplified, essentialized and idealized categories. With this in mind, the chapter offers important practical suggestions and directions for us in ELTE.

Part 3

Moving on from a discussion of the contexts of ELTE, Part 3 focuses on the linguistic knowledge of ELTE, presented in five chapters which look at discourse, classroom discourse, world Englishes, SLA, and the use of corpora.

In Chapter 14, McCarthy and Clancy challenge some of the prevailing accepted wisdom of regarding language as either skill or system. In an attempt to shift the focus to discourse, they consider how 'meanings in context' might be created. Following an extensive discussion of the current obsession with grammar and lexis, they exemplify the types of activities that encourage discourse awareness and discuss how teachers can monitor the success of discourse-level teaching.

Continuing the focus on the 'language' of ELTE, Sert (Chapter 15) shifts the focus to the study of classroom interaction. His chapter looks at the close relationship between classroom interaction and teacher development. Using research evidence from both initial and in-service teacher education, the chapter makes a case for a technology-enhanced, reflective, and microanalytic teacher education framework.

In Chapter 16, Snodin and Resnik consider the ways in which the global status of English has challenged the very subject matter of our discipline, asking how should English be taught in light of the changing needs of its users? Their chapter offers a critique of the principles and practices of the range of Englishes currently being used in ELTE, and discusses the challenges faced by educators and researchers alike. Continuing in the same vein, Pérez-Paredes (Chapter 17) provides us with an introduction to Second Language Acquisition (SLA) and its relevance for ELTE. The aim of the chapter is twofold: to expose the complexity of L2 learning research as a multifaceted phenomenon that transcends local practices, and to encourage language teachers and language educators to survey and embrace such complexity as part of a much-needed transdisciplinary approach.

Farr and O'Keeffe's concern in Chapter 18 is to provide teachers and teacher educators with appropriate tools with which to analyse language. They propose the use of corpora and corpus linguistics as a means of facilitating teacher development in terms of content, pedagogy, technology, and research. Based on many years of research, the authors argue that corpora continue to play a minor part in much teacher education, but are a resource with much potential.

Part 4

While Part 3 deals with the linguistic knowledge of ELTE, Part 4 focuses on the pedagogic knowledge of our discipline with a review of some of its main elements. The Part includes six chapters which look at teaching methods, materials and authenticity, classroom management, teacher cognition and expertise, difficult contexts, teacher development.

No volume on ELTE would be complete without some discussion around teaching methodology. In Chapter 19, Hall explores the place of language teaching methods within ELT education programmes. The chapter asks what, if anything, a focus on methods brings to ELTE, and how methods might be explored in practice on teacher education programmes and courses, if, as is claimed, methods are 'dead' and ELT has entered a 'Postmethod' era.

Gilmore (Chapter 20) explores the complex issue of authenticity in language learning and outlines some of the reasons for its growing importance in the field. By way of exemplification, sample materials are provided to illustrate how *some* of the principles of authenticity highlighted in the chapter can be realized in a genuine classroom context.

For Buchanan and Timmis (Chapter 21), a major issue on teacher education courses is the ill-defined area of classroom management. In their chapter, the authors demonstrate how the construct is treated variously across a range of contexts (including on CELTA and Delta Programmes). They conclude that ELTE needs to be aware of methodological assumptions when looking at certain aspects of classroom management; for example, they suggest that factors such as establishing rapport and classroom presence might need to be revisited.

Of particular interest to the discipline for some years now is the field of teacher cognition, which promotes understandings of classroom instruction, pedagogical effectiveness and teacher development. In Chapter 22, Li considers how the research in teacher cognition might advance our understandings of teacher expertise. Particular attention is paid to raising teachers' awareness of their own teacher cognitions with a view to developing teacher expertise.

Extending our knowledge of ELTE into lesser-known contexts, Kuchah, Djigo and Taye (Chapter 23) examine the range of constraints on English language teacher education and professional development in developing world contexts, focusing mainly on sub-Saharan African (SSA) countries. Drawing on examples of existing collaborative initiatives in SSA, the authors argue for greater institutional recognition and support of bottom up teacher efforts to ensure sustainable quality teacher education in these contexts.

The final chapter in this part of the handbook (Chapter 24) considers the complex realities teacher educators face in developing thoughtful and local programs of professional development. Clarke draws on an ecological framework and principles to balance the perspectives of research and practice. This is an illuminating insight into the work of a committed group of teachers working towards responsive teaching and innovative approaches to complex problems of practice.

Part 5

Part 5 considers core processes in ELTE. The first two chapters consider the vital dimension of feedback. Delaney considers the role of assessment of teaching and giving feedback in promoting teacher development. In Chapter 25, she explores issues around assessment of teaching and providing feedback and shows how these processes can play an important role in teachers' learning.

Copland and Donaghue (Chapter 26) focus specifically on the nature of feedback in the post-observation conference. They discuss a number of key issues inherent in such post observation feedback. As well as focusing on the linguistic characteristics, purposes and value of the feedback conference, they also suggest ways of helping participants better understand feedback.

Any teacher education process needs to help teachers to become effective materials users and developers. Graves and Garton (Chapter 27) identify key areas that need to be addressed in ELTE. They focus on learning to adapt/develop materials to meet the needs of language learners and using technology to extend learners' language and interactions within and beyond the classroom.

The Part then continues with two kinds of collaborative teacher development processes: mentoring and team-teaching. Good quality mentoring can support the transition to becoming a confident and competent teacher. Gakonga begins Chapter 28 by considering different aspects of mentoring and discusses how mentors might be prepared for the role. She discusses examples of mentoring in education, including where a mentee is assigned to a cooperating teacher in their practicum and also when a novice teacher is given a mentor in order to support their initiation into the profession. Heo (Chapter 29) then provides an overview of professional learning and development in team teaching schemes. She presents a data-led understanding of the dynamic nature of team teaching and identifies key factors contributing to successful team teaching practices and relationships.

The last three chapters in this Part develop the technology strand of the handbook by looking at the increasing use of screen capture, video and e-portfolios in ELTE. Stannard and Salli (Chapter 30) focus on screen capture technology (SCT), a tool that is increasingly being widely used in teacher education and language training. The chapter provides examples of how SCT is used in ELTE through a range of case studies.

In Chapter 31, Hüttner presents an overview of the way video resources can be integrated into ELTE. Video is increasingly being used to provide a record of teaching practice for feedback and reflection. It is also used in other important ways (e.g. providing input on alternative practices). Hüttner provides guidance on how video can be used effectively as a resource for the development of 'professional vision'.

The last chapter in this Part features another tool which offers a great deal of promise for ELTE. After reviewing research, Gulzar and Barrett detail the affordances that ePortfolios can provide as a learning and assessment tool in ELTE. Chapter 32 provides a guide to the process of working effectively with ePortfolios and shows that technology can help support reflective processes in teacher education.

Part 6

Part 6 puts the teacher learner in focus. The chapters consider core dimensions of a teacher's growth (knowledge and development, motivation and identity). The Part then looks at alternatives for the support and development of teachers. We begin with the importance of teacher networks and then look at two forms of practitioner research (action research and exploratory practice). The final chapter gives us a view on the importance of leadership in creating the right conditions for teacher development.

Thornbury considers the role of teachers' guides ('methodology texts') in the construction of teachers' practical knowledge, as they make a transition from novice to expert teacher

Chapter 33 also includes interesting insights from methodology writers considering their role as 'mediators' across the research–practice divide.

Lamb and Wyatt make a convincing case for renewed consideration of the importance of teacher motivation for language teachers and their learners, especially as low teacher motivation is often a cause for concern. Chapter 34 provides an argument that protecting and enhancing teacher motivation should be an inherent goal of language teacher education and also make practical suggestions for how this might be achieved.

Barkhuizen focuses on language teacher identity (LTI), particularly on how it is theorized, constructed and negotiated in ELTE. The chapter also includes data from English teacher educators and explores the link between LTI and language teacher educator identity (LTEI). Chapter 35 also includes directions for future research in the field.

Chapter 36 looks at the importance and nature of teacher networks in the wild as alternative paths for professional development. Padwad and Parnham discuss the value of teacher networks in creating a community that supports teachers and encourages collaboration and the sharing of knowledge. The chapter discusses the value of four different kinds of teacher networks (teacher associations, teacher activity groups, teacher clubs, and digital communities of practice) and how these networks are created and sustained over time.

The next two chapters provide insights into the value of practitioner research. Chapter 37 gives an overview of action research (AR). Banegas and Villacañas de Castro provide support and guidance for teacher educators who want to encourage AR in ELTE (English language teacher education). In doing this, they share examples from teacher educators involved in supporting AR.

Miller and Azvedo Cunha (Chapter 38) put the focus on the value exploratory practice (EP) as an alternative inquiry-based framework for pedagogy or research that prioritizes working to understand local puzzles, as well as ethics and criticality. They describe how exploratory practitioners engage in work to understand what goes on in their learning/educational/professional environments. They also address the challenges practitioners face in the process.

The final chapter is an important insight into how leadership and language teacher development need to be related. In Chapter 39, De Stefani considers the relationship between leadership practices and teacher development, describing leadership practices that involve collaboration and cooperation. She puts particular value of 'flexible collaborative partnerships' and 'cooperative development'. The chapter draws on her own experience as well as the experience of other language teacher educators around the world.

Using the handbook

We anticipate that the main audience for this handbook will be teacher educators and teacher trainers working in a range of contexts around the world and engaged in PRESET, INSET, teacher support and development, mentoring and CPD. We would anticipate there also to be considerable interest among established and early career researchers involved in teacher education research. We also see potential readers as students on MA TESOL and taught doctorate degrees; most of these programmes include at least one module on language teacher education.

Different readers will have different expectations of the handbook, affecting the way in which the book is used. For experienced teacher educators, the resource offers new perspectives and new insights from a range of different contexts. Less experienced trainers and educators will also find value in this handbook, as they try to establish the materials, priorities and choices available to them in the ELTE enterprise. In addition, those involved in teacher education planning and evaluation (including ministries and publishers) might consider provision in light of the contributions in this handbook. Last, it can be used by the individual teacher or researcher as a resource, or as the starting point for a research project. There is clearly some overlap between these four potential readerships, but in what follows we offer suggestions as to how the handbook might be used across a range of contexts.

Teacher educators working on MA programmes, Diplomas and INSET might be teaching a module that includes aspects of training development. The handbook offers a wide range of different contexts and education perspectives that would enable individual students to choose articles relevant to their contexts and interests. In this way, the handbook adds to available teacher education literature (e.g. Richards and Nunan 1990; Bartels 2006; Burns and Richards 2009; Tedick 2013; Crandall and Christison 2016) and we hope that our international, comprehensive and data-led collection will be useful to future educators in ELTE.

The book could be used by less experienced trainers to get a sense of what is involved in delivering a quality and comprehensive course or module. Such a teacher might gain insights into the processes, rationale and operationalization of a data-led approach to teacher education. Most chapters have usable and practical suggestions that would provide the basis for training sessions or indeed a whole module.

We also think experienced trainer educators have much to gain from this collection. We have certainly learned a great deal about different approaches, technologies and areas of focus. It has certainly made us think about the balance of courses and modules we run. It has given us fresh ideas and data and examples that we can weave into our sessions.

We envisage that chapters could be used in different ways as a teacher education resource. Obviously, chapters could be set as core reading, but they might be used as flipped content too. In other words, teachers read an article and come to a subsequent class with views, ideas and critiques of the article. In a more limited but just as potentially interesting way, teachers might be directed just to the data and examples within specific chapters as the basis for discussion. If a chapter is selected for all the group to read, they might then use the suggestions for follow-up reading to compare what new perspectives are offered.

We also think this resource could be the basis for designing, redesigning or evaluating a teacher training curriculum (PRESET, INSET or CPD). This might have particular value in evaluating the coverage and processes of existing provision. The handbook provides answers to a range of questions. What knowledge about language needs to be included? What kind of technology improves the education experience for teacher learners? How can I make the training collaborative and encourage sharing? How can I make the training relevant to the teachers' needs and contexts? These questions related to the design and content of an ELTE curriculum are particularly relevant for teacher educators designing a programme which extends over three or four years, for example.

We also think that individual researchers interested in teacher education will find this book a useful springboard as a starting point for one of the various topics covered in the book. The first half of most chapters begins with a state-of-the-art overview of the area with key recent contributions. The suggestions for further reading provide considered selections to those resources that the experts in that area would recommend. Other sections in each chapter offer insights into what constitutes data and how that data might be analysed; in short, the handbook is a useful resource for anyone engaged in ELTE research.

Summary

In this Introduction, we have offered some insights into the thought processes which have informed the rationale, structure and organisation of the handbook in order to give readers some sense of how it was designed and compiled. Our aim was to make the process of putting together such a collection as transparent as possible so that readers can engage fully with the chapters. We have highlighted the organising principles, described what we consider to be the key features and unifying strands of the handbook and offered an overview of the six Parts. Finally, we have suggested how readers might use the collection in their professional lives. We hope that you enjoy the final product and look forward to hearing your views – both positive and negative – on what has been an enormously challenging endeavour.

References

Bartels, N. (2006) *Applied Linguistics and Language Teacher Education* (Vol. 4). Dordrecht: Springer.

Burns, A. and Richards, J. (2009) *The Cambridge Guide to Second Language Teacher Education*. Cambridge: Cambridge University Press.

Crandall, J. and Christison, M. (eds) (2016) *Teacher Education and Professional Development in TESOL: Global Perspectives*. Abingdon: Routledge.

Mann, S. and Walsh, S. (2013) 'RP or "RIP": A Critical Perspective on Reflective Practice'. *Applied Linguistics Review*, 4(2) 291–315.

Mann, S. and Walsh, S. (2017) *Reflective Practice in English Language Teaching: Research-Based Principles and Practices*. Abingdon: Routledge.

Richards, J. C. and Nunan, D. (eds) (1990) *Second Language Teacher Education*. Cambridge: Cambridge University Press.

Tedick, D. J. (ed.) (2013) *Language Teacher Education: International Perspectives on Research and Practice*. Mahwah, NJ: Lawrence Erlbaum Associates.

Walsh, S. and Mann, S. (2015) 'Doing Reflective Practice: A Data-Led Way Forward'. *ELT Journal*, 69(4) 351–362.

PART 1

Second language teacher education

An overview

1

What counts as knowledge in English language teaching?

Donald Freeman, Anne-Coleman Webre and Martha Epperson

Introduction: defining communities and their knowledge

A handbook is a sort of community statement. It is a socio-professional endeavor in defining what counts as worth knowing in and to a particular professional community. It puts a public face on the knowledge and understandings that community sees as central to its work. Compiling a handbook involves determining who is asked to contribute, about which topics and how these topics are organized, all of which reflect decisions about the knowledge that is seen as important in the professional community. These determinations are, by their nature, interested, by which we mean they represent a point of view. They will include some topics and miss others; they will mention certain views and overlook counter-examples. The point being that there is no perfect set of choices. However, examining the choices as choices – not with the intent of challenging or changing them – can offer insights into the state of mind of the community.

In this case, there are two communities involved in English language teaching[1]: the ELT[2] community and the group that is concerned with teacher education. How this second group, the English language teacher education community (known in this handbook as ELTE), relates to the first, the ELT community, is central to understanding what counts as knowledge in English language teaching as a field. While there is give-and-take between ELT teachers and the ELTE community, ultimately the teacher education community selects and curates what ELT teachers are expected to learn and know. By publishing and presenting professional information, by consulting on and contributing to national polices and professional standards, by determining what is (or is not) included in preparing ELT teachers, the ELTE community defines knowledge in ELT. The teacher education community, as it prepares people to teach English to learners across a wide variety of settings and circumstances, and as it supports them in doing so through professional development, functions as a sort of gate-keeper and sustainer of what counts as worth knowing in ELT.

This view of ELTE as curating the knowledge of ELT teaching differs from the more commonly exercised one in which ELT knowledge exists and ELTE simply 'packages' it for teachers to learn. These two views – of 'curating' versus 'packaging' what ELT teachers need to know – contrast in important ways, particularly in how each frames the role of the ELTE community. In the packaging view, it is unclear where (or how) the knowledge comes from. Content is grouped, usually by theme or topic, to be delivered into courses and modules. This packaging is more historically based than rigorously systematic. As a socio-professional practice, teacher education is a conduit for inducting people into ELT teaching. In the curating view, teacher education is seen as playing a central role in selecting, promoting, and downplaying the content of what ELT teachers need to know. This gate-keeping role exposes questions of which socio-professional institutions – from universities to examination boards, from professional associations to governmental bodies – are contributing to determining what the knowledge base of ELT is.

Inasmuch as the first move in teaching anything is to choose what is being taught, examining what is selected as knowledge in ELTE exposes these choices. Based on this reasoning, we argue that the curating function represented in the development of this handbook provides a view of what counts as knowledge in ELTE. It offers a snapshot of ELTE knowledge at this particular moment in time. A handbook is a synchronic view of what is being taken as important to know. This knowledge is clearly not static, however, especially in a global undertaking like English language teaching. The knowledge is produced by people and used interactively in a variety of socio-professional contexts. Capturing the broad snapshots like those compiled here can offer a sort of archeology of how past thinking fits into current knowledge. The topics of the handbook offer this form of evidence of what the ELTE community (as reflected by the editors, entry authors, and publisher) see as important and worth knowing.[3]

This chapter uses the abstracts for chapters in this handbook to examine what counts as knowledge in English language teacher education. We acknowledge that these abstracts are, by their nature, condensed forms and authors may address knowledge differently in the longer chapter. That said, the abstract is what the author chooses to foreground; it highlights the content readers will encounter in the chapter itself. It is part of a socio-professional exchange that offers a succinct preview of the text. In organizing these abstracts into categories, we examined the versions of ELT teaching knowledge each abstract presents. We started from a framework of knowledge generations (Freeman, 2016), described in the next section.

Initially we anticipated this analysis would focus on the knowledge of classroom ELT teaching. However, this focus was substantially less than abstracts about knowledge in ELTE teacher education. Our first move was to decide whether the abstract primarily addressed knowledge of ELT, which nine abstracts did, or knowledge of ELTE, which 27 abstracts did. After making this determination, we applied the same *a priori* coding approach to both domains, taken from the knowledge-generations framework. In doing so, we are arguing that, as with ELT, knowledge in ELTE is not randomly organized, but that there are shared views across the ELTE community. We expand this argument subsequently in this chapter.

In doing this analysis, we assert three interrelated premises. First, we argue that connections between ELT teaching knowledge and ELTE deserve careful examination. Second, the prevalent view in which ELT teaching knowledge is simply a subset that defines the content of ELTE practices is problematic. This 'subset' view reduces a complex set of teacher-learning opportunities and processes to the problem of how to 'package' content referred to above. Third, we argue that this 'ELTE-packaging' view of knowledge needs to be rethought. We need to examine what is proposed as important to know for both teachers and teacher educators in English language teaching, and how the process of curating these ideas operates.

The knowledge-generation framework

To identify versions of knowledge, we use the framework of knowledge generations from Freeman (2016) who defines knowledge-generations as 'patterns in how ideas about thinking and

Table 1.1 Knowledge generations

Generation	Key issue	Versions in ELT
Disciplinary knowledge *(what)*	If this is *the knowledge needed to teach languages,* **how is the knowledge used?**	1.0: linguistics + psychology 1.1: + literatures 1.2: + sociology & anthropology
Knowledge of pedagogy *(how)*	If this is *how to teach languages,* **are differences in teaching deficits in knowledge evidence of individuality?**	2.0: + 'innovative methods' & SLA 2.1: + Communicative Language Teaching 2.2: + eclectic teaching; 'best methods'; 'post-method condition'
Knowledge-in-person; in-place *(who* and *where)*	If this is *how individuals use knowledge in teaching, if personal experience and context shape what they do,* **what do language teachers have in common?**	3.0: PPK & identity 3.1: PCK & transforming subject matter in teaching 3.2: knowledge as 'contextual, contingent, and developmental'
Knowledge-for-teaching *(why)*	If this is *how knowledge works in the process of teaching …*	4.0: Knowledge-for-teaching languages 4.1: English-for-teaching

Source: Freeman (2016, p. 115).

about knowledge in language teaching have been understood' (p. 115). The generations are summarized in Table 1.1.

As *de facto* socio-professional agreements, these generations characterize broadly defined – if tacitly held – consensuses. They evolve in time through a process akin to software development. Similar to a new software version, each iteration or generation replaces the existing version, usually for one of two reasons. Either it is in order to remedy a defect (or problem in the existing knowledge) or it is to introduce new features (or understandings). A new knowledge generation addresses shortcomings in the one it subsumes; these shortcomings arise out of new insights into, or changes in, English language teaching. It is important to note, as Freeman (2016) argues, that the generations are not intended to be read as a history of English language teaching, but rather as 'patterns of ideas' that develop over time. In this sense, the framework is meant to chart how socio-professional perceptions of what matters in ELT have shifted and changed over time.

The first generation: disciplinary knowledge

The first generation centered its focus around 'the what' of teaching knowledge with linguistics and psychology playing central roles. Knowledge in these domains served to specialize language teaching knowledge. Influenced by behaviorist theories, for example, the Audio-lingual Direct Method (ALDM) translated the psychology of the day into the classroom. Over time, as new teaching methodologies developed, the field began distancing itself from notions of language teaching in which disciplinary knowledge alone served as the basis. Less emphasis was placed on *what* was taught and more on *how* it was taught. The 'parent' disciplines of linguistics and psychology gave rise in ELT to the fields of applied linguistics and second language acquisition respectively. These shifts led to the second-generation focus on the *how* of language teaching.

The second generation: teaching knowledge-as-pedagogy

In moving beyond language teaching as the simple application of disciplinary knowledge to classrooms, the next generation centered on 'the how' of teaching. A range of so-called 'innovative methodologies' emerged (e.g. Community Language Learning, the Natural Approach, the Silent Way, Suggestopedia) (e.g. Blair 1982). Each methodology represented a self-contained system of belief and action with its own set of social facts. Teaching using a particular methodology meant subscribing to its definitions of learning and language. Responding to the mutually exclusive – and sometimes competing – views of language teaching promoted by the different methodologies, Communicative Language Teaching (CLT) emerged as a common language. Propelled by increasing global use of instructional ELT materials (e.g. textbook series such as *Interchange* and *Headway*, among others), CLT moved classroom practices from belief-based to more generic principles of teaching. The net effect was for teachers to assert greater agency in individual decision-making based on their students, their classrooms, and their context.

The third generation: teaching knowledge as in-person, in place

The third generation sought to reconcile the parochial notions of closely aligned belief and action found in the different innovative methodologies with the catholic views of teacher decision-making. In doing so, the generation focused on the relational nature of language teaching in the classroom, and it served as a basis for teacher decision-making. Supported by conceptual developments in general education, notably Shulman's (1986, 1987) work on pedagogical content knowledge, or PCK, the third generation positioned teachers as knowers – of their students, their content, their classrooms, and their teaching contexts. This view recognized that teachers made decisions based on *who* (the students in their classrooms) and *what* (the specific content), and that expert teachers drew on such knowledge to transform content into something meaningful for their students. Thus, the *what* and the *how* of language teacher knowledge became dependent upon the *who* and the *where*. Inasmuch as teaching was shaped by how teachers' approaches interacted with their contexts, the notion of identity – both students' and teachers' (e.g. Kanno & Norton 2003) – developed as an important aspect of research in second language teaching. Ultimately, this knowledge generation pushed back against notions of teaching as simply idiosyncratic, contending instead that classroom practices varied precisely because they were socially situated and relational.

The fourth generation: knowledge-for-teaching

Attention to cross-cutting commonalities began to develop within this focus on individuality and teaching context. These commonalities focused on student learning and examining both *how* and *why* teaching decisions are made. The new generation shifts the focus away from teachers and their contexts, to the knowledge needed to teach for student learning. Conceptually, the fourth generation builds off Shulman's work on PCK, drawing from frameworks for knowledge-for-teaching (e.g. Ball et al. 2008 in elementary mathematics teaching) that organize teaching knowledge into two main categories: subject matter and pedagogical knowledge. Applying this framework to language teaching (Freeman 2016), subject-matter knowledge can be seen as being made up of common content knowledge (e.g. teacher command of English language) and specialized content knowledge (language awareness and applied linguistics), while pedagogical knowledge is subdivided into knowledge of second language acquisition, language teaching methods, and curriculum, materials, and assessment. Conceptualizing knowledge-for-teaching in language teaching, however, underlines differences between teaching languages and other subject matters. The central distinction between knowledge-for-teaching versus subject-matter and pedagogy begins to unravel when one considers the multiple roles that language plays in the ELT classrooms. In ELT, language serves as both the content and the means for organizing and teaching that content (Freeman et al. 2015). Beyond the classroom, the content – English – then provides the professional discourse and means of interacting in the global ELT teaching community.

Knowledge generations as a framework for socio-professional analysis

The knowledge-generations framework provides a lens for examining the development of socio-professional views of ELT teacher knowledge. In this analysis, we have taken the abstracts in this handbook as a loosely curated group of socio-professional statements. Using the knowledge-generation framework as a set of *a priori* codes, we conducted a content analysis. The four framework categories can be used to situate the ideas broadly, which allowed us to locate the focus of each chapter abstract and to surface patterns in how the abstracts represent central concerns. Two authors reviewed each chapter abstract holistically to identify themes and key words which they then categorized according to the generations framework. In the rare instances of disagreement, they conferred to come to a consensus. A primary focus was identified for each abstract. These are categorized based on the generational distinctions outlined above and in Table 1.1. For example, an abstract on teacher identity and its role in ELT would align with the third generation, knowledge-in-person, in-place, in addressing questions *who* and *where*, and how 'personal experience and context shape what [teachers] do' (Freeman 2016, p. 183).

It is important to clarify that the intent in the review was to generate a broad snapshot of the knowledge captured in this handbook as a socio-professional undertaking. We identified a main theme for each chapter abstract for example, and did not probe those that might be seen to have multiple or overlapping themes. Such a full, in-depth content-based analysis would have been another undertaking.

This analysis surfaced interesting differences in the abstracts focused primarily on ELT and those focused on ELTE. The following discussion outlines these distinctions and suggests how they may reflect the emerging focus on what counts as knowledge in English language teaching and teacher education.

Treatment of ELT teaching knowledge (ELT-focused contributions)

Abstracts of nine chapters in this handbook focus on ELT teaching knowledge; four of them address concerns of the first two knowledge generations. They do not focus on the disciplinary knowledge or teaching methodologies prevalent in ELT from the 1960s to 1980s. Rather, they categorize as disciplinary knowledge new additions to the ELT content and methods. For example, McCarthy and Clancy (Chapter 14) discuss the knowledge teachers need regarding authentic materials, while Pérez-Paredes (Chapter 17) outlines the knowledge of second language acquisition thought to be important to ELT teachers.

The middle two generations, knowledge as pedagogy and knowledge-in-person, in-place, which are unshaded in Table 1.2, are represented by one abstract each.[4] The abstract which was coded as knowledge as pedagogy focuses on teaching teachers about classroom interaction and research on interaction (Sert, Chapter 15). The chapter abstract coded knowledge in-person, in-place speaks to ELT teacher identity and the 'native/non-native speaker' distinction

Table 1.2 ELT-focused abstracts by knowledge generation (N = 9)

	Number of abstracts coded as	*Example*
Generation 1 *Disciplinary knowledge*	3	McCarthy & Clancy Pérez-Paredes
Generation 2 *Knowledge as pedagogy*	1	Sert
Generation 3 *Knowledge-in-person, in-place*	1	Barkhuizen
Generation 4 *Knowledge-for-teaching*	4	Padwad & Parnham Li Li

The remaining four abstracts, which are shaded in Table 1.2, address concerns of knowledge-for-teaching. These abstracts address topics such as how teaching knowledge can be shared over networks (Padwad & Parnham, Chapter 36) or how teacher cognition research can support the development of teacher expertise (Li, Chapter 22). They seem to anticipate concerns about the various dimensions of participation in professional learning, and how the virtual world is redefining opportunities to build and share knowledge. Table 1.2 displays how the nine ELTE abstracts are grouped.

To summarize, the treatment of ELT knowledge in this handbook includes concerns that span all four knowledge generations. However, just over half focus on the latter two generations: knowledge-in-person, in-place and knowledge-for-teaching. Notions of disciplinary knowledge, grounded in the first generation, extend definitions beyond grammatical knowledge and into areas of knowledge of language acquisition and ways of using linguistic knowledge. However, these topics are still treated as knowledge, as information based in academic disciplines that ELT teachers should know. Knowledge as pedagogy, the focus of the second generation, is discussed here in only one abstract, suggesting it is not a central concern. Taken together, these abstracts' foci on first and second generational issues suggest modified definitions of *what* ELT teachers should know with *how* they can use that knowledge. How knowledge is used in teaching – the focus of the fourth generation – is the subject of four abstracts. These abstracts seem largely grounded in the larger assumptions of social practice theories.

Treatment of ELTE teacher education knowledge (ELTE-focused contributions)

In contrast to the treatment of ELT teaching knowledge, there are three times as many abstracts that address ELTE teacher education knowledge. This picture of professional knowledge is different in the ELT-focused contributions. These are dominated by abstracts focusing on knowledge as teacher education pedagogy as indicated in Table 1.3.

Of the 27 abstracts, 14 (or just over half, shaded in Table 1.3) focus on methodology for conveying the ELT knowledge to teacher-learners. They include such topics as the role of assessment of teaching practice (e.g. Delaney, Chapter 25), the use of technology (e.g. Kiddle & Prince, Chapter 8), or how to use reflection in teacher education (e.g. Farrell, Chapter 3), This emphasis on the *how* of ELTE is indicative of the focus on educative practice within the larger teacher education community. The remaining 13 abstracts deal with the concerns aligned with the other three generations.

It may be that the content of ELTE is widely accepted, that there is a socio-professional expectation that ELTE educators are fully conversant with the applied linguistics and second

Table 1.3 ELTE-focused abstracts by knowledge generation (N = 27)

	Number of abstracts coded as	Example
Generation 1 *Disciplinary knowledge*	3	Buchanan & Timmis
Generation 2 *Knowledge as pedagogy*	14	Delaney Kiddle & Prince
Generation 3 *Knowledge-in-person, in-place*	8	Hayes
Generation 4 *Knowledge-for-teaching*	2	Graves & Garton

language acquisition knowledge that the teacher-learners need to know. In this sense, these first-generation concerns of disciplinary knowledge – defined as knowledge of the applied linguistics and second language acquisition – essentially 'pass through' from being an ELT teacher to being an ELT teacher educator. Therefore, the focus is on pedagogical questions of *how* to teach this disciplinary content to teacher-learners. This *de facto* consensus about the disciplinary content of ELTE certainly promotes a globally recognized ELT knowledge base, with the professional benefits that come to those who master it, even though it obscures attention to differences in what and how various ELT teachers learn. Do we assume, for example, that the linguistic knowledge of a CELTA trainee must be the same as a pre-service ELT teacher entering the public-sector in Germany, or as a pre-service ESL or EAL teacher entering teaching in Australia or the United States? Is the content knowledge a teacher needs the same regardless of the context and students they are teaching?

The third generation focus on knowledge-in-person, in-place is the second most frequent category of ELTE knowledge, represented in just under a third, or eight out of 27 entries. These abstracts speak to two principle issues: ELT professional development (e.g. Hayes, Chapter 11), or the need to recognize contextual influences on teacher education (e.g. Snodin & Resnik, Chapter 16). Other topics may fall into this category such as a chapter on using a particular teaching model in a given context (e.g. team teaching: Heo, Chapter 29), or how teacher educators can include teacher motivation in training (Lamb & Wyatt, Chapter 34).

There are three abstracts that address ELTE disciplinary knowledge (generation one). The specifics of how their foci are situated in this socio-professional landscape are instructive, however. The abstracts refer to what teacher educators need to know about the experiences of English language teachers, such as classroom management techniques they may need (Buchanan & Timmis, Chapter 21) or about the disconnect between new teachers' experiences and their training (Baguley, Chapter 9). The two abstracts grouped in the fourth generation, shaded in Table 1.2, speak about the wider use of teacher education knowledge for selecting materials (Graves & Garton, Chapter 27) and evaluating teacher education programs (Kiely, Chapter 6).

In summary, the ELTE-focused abstracts are squarely concerned with various ways of doing teacher education; over half of them were categorized as focusing on second generation concerns about how to teach ELT teachers. This emphasis introduces an interesting question, one that goes to the heart of how ELT teaching knowledge fits into ELTE. Framed broadly as 'knowledge as pedagogy', the second knowledge-generation is defined as 'the knowledge entailed in making pedagogical choices' (Freeman 2016, p. 166), which includes 'the specific protocols of the various innovative methods and ... the idea of pedagogical choice' (p. 170). From an ELT perspective, this knowledge is about *how* to teach in the classroom. When it is incorporated into ELTE however, 'knowledge as pedagogy' can take two different meanings. It can refer to content – in other words, information about how to use particular teaching methodologies, along with skills in doing so. Or it can refer to the pedagogy of teacher education itself. To separate the two, we could call the first, knowledge *as* pedagogy, and the second, knowledge *for* pedagogy.

The intermingling of the two has been a central concern in ELTE since the 1980s, when Woodward introduced the term 'loop input', which she defined as 'aligning process and content' to 'achieve a congruence, a consistency between what we say as trainers and what we do' (1991, p. 43). She described loop input as:

> [A]ligning process and content [so that] … trainees can experience techniques for themselves without moving to the work site (that is, to a language classroom), without entering into a lengthy apprenticeship with an experienced teacher …, and without taking on the artificial role of the student who is studying content unrelated to the trainee role.
>
> *(p. 43)*

From the perspective of the third-generation, the training technique has become widely practiced in ELTE to create knowledge in-person, in-place.

A topical overview

In the preceding section, we described chapter abstracts using the knowledge-generations framework. The aim was to overview the content, and the resulting analysis reflects the broad contours of ELT-focused and ELTE-focused knowledge found in this handbook. To give some more specificity and texture to the analysis, we then looked at the focus of the abstracts. We reviewed titles and abstracts for what we saw as the main content words in each chapter abstract. Here again, we emphasize that our aim was holistic. With the topics organized by the knowledge generation, we wanted to gain a sense of some of the terms used by chapter authors about their topics. For example, we had categorized Graves and Garton's abstract (Chapter 27) as ELTE-focused. Within that general area, they write about 'materials' – selecting them, understanding them, using them. Thus we saw the key word for their chapter abstract as 'materials.' These content words are laid out in Table 1.4 by knowledge generation.

In using the authors' own words, the table provides a broad look at the terms that mark current preferences in the discourse of English language teaching. The ELT abstracts identified as first generation include established terms like 'SLA' as well as more recent terms such as 'corpus linguistics', both of which reflect disciplinary knowledge. Notably, terms do not make overt reference to English or language teaching. Terms like 'cognition' and 'teacher networks' are examples that characterize the fourth generation. Again, these terms refer to what could be called generic aspects of teaching; they do not focus on the specificities of language as content or on English. In the ELTE-focused abstracts, this generic focus of content terms is widespread. Here the balance of topics address teaching generally, perhaps assuming English, and teaching *language* as a backdrop.

The breakdown of topics by knowledge generation, presented in Tables 1.2 and 1.3, show the type of knowledge that is being put forward as important for the English language teaching community to recognize. In each generation, however, there are topics privileged within that knowledge, presented in Table 1.4. In this sense then, the range of topics provides a view of the specifics of explicit content within the generation, while the generational categories offer a

Table 1.4 Abstract topics by knowledge generation (number of corresponding chapters in brackets)

	Generation 1	Generation 2	Generation 3	Generation 4
ELT-focused	Discourse teaching (1) Second language acquisition (1) Authentic teaching (1)	Interaction teaching (1)	Identity (1)	Cognition (1) Teacher networks (1) Content-area teaching (1) Methodology texts (1)
Number of chapter abstracts	**3**	**1**	**1**	**4**
ELTE-focused	Classroom management research (1) Novice teachers' experiences (1) Overview of teaching methods (1)	Technology (5) Action research (1) Mentoring/ leadership (2) Learning labs (1) Corpus linguistics (1) Exploratory/reflective practice (2) Teacher education methods (1) Assessment (1)	Professional Development in context (2) Team teaching (1) Motivation (1) Socio-cultural theory (1) Neoliberalism (1) Englishes (1) Teacher identity (1)	Evaluating TE programs (1) Materials (1)
Number of chapter abstracts	**3**	**14**	**8**	**2**

synchronic look at the focus of the English language teaching community's attention. This focus of attention differs between the ELT and ELTE communities.

Comparing ELT-focused and ELTE-focused knowledge

In view of the handbook's focus on teacher education, one might expect a greater number of chapters and topics to address ELTE particularly. At one level, one can argue that, ELTE educators simply need to know and do what the ELT teachers they are educating should know and do. This could be the essentialist position. It is the analogue to the cliché that '*If you can speak a language, you can teach it.*': '*If you can teach a language, you can teach others to teach it.*' The emerging counter-argument is that ELTE, like any form of teacher education, is itself a form of teaching, and as such has its own distinct knowledge base. 'Distinct' here may not mean entirely different, as the analysis discussed above shows; rather the distinction may have more to do with the purpose – ELTE involves teaching (language) teaching (Freeman 2016), while ELT involves teaching language.

When the abstract topics organized by generation are displayed side-by-side, as they are in Figure 1.1, some intriguing patterns emerge.

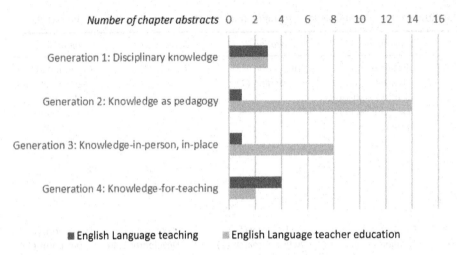

Figure 1.1 ELT- and ELTE-focused abstracts by knowledge generation

Abstracts that focused on the ELT knowledge base are a quarter of the total (nine out of 36 abstracts), and cluster around first-generation concerns of disciplinary knowledge and fourth-generation concerns about knowledge-for-teaching. These two categories name the content (Generation 1) and how it is used (Generation 4). The first group includes ELT-related terms, while the fourth uses terms from general education. In contrast, the chapter abstracts that focus on ELTE cluster around teacher-education pedagogy and the second generation's concern for how to teach (language) teachers. It seems at least from this analysis that concerns in ELTE focus principally on how ELT teaching knowledge is presented, conveyed, and practiced by those who are learning to teach it.

What it all means – thinking about the implications

This chapter has put forward a series of interrelated premises about what counts as knowledge in English language teaching. We began by stipulating an overarching field of activity, English language teaching, within which two knowledge domains co-exist. One is the domain of classroom practice, referred to here as ELT; the other focuses on educating and supporting teachers in ELT. This is the domain of ELTE, the subject of this handbook project. Mapping the terrain in this way accomplishes three important things. First, it raises questions of how the two domains interrelate. These questions go beyond the packaging view in which ELTE knowledge is simply concerned with conveying ELT teaching knowledge as content.

Second, treating the two domains as potentially separate allows a clearer focus on how they are distinct. For example, the distinction could lead to a closer examination of how professional learning works in each instance. In teacher learning in ELT, processes of learning to teach are now regularly studied and documented; but in teacher educator learning in ELTE, processes of learning to teach teaching have not yet generated this type of attention. What we generally refer to as 'training of trainers', activities that are intended to move individuals from their roles as teachers to new ones as teachers of teaching, assume a type of learning process that has not been researched.

There is a third benefit to the mapping of ELT and ELTE as separable domains within the superordinate activity, English language teaching. This is a benefit that has surfaced through the analysis of these handbook abstracts. Using the framework of knowledge generations as a scaffold lets us locate the primary foci in each domain. ELT teaching knowledge seems to bifurcate between the first and fourth generations, with attention to new additions to disciplinary knowledge on the one hand and to generic issues of teaching on knowledge-for-teaching on the other. ELTE teacher educator knowledge seems focused on methods for teaching new knowledge of ELT. This predominant focus in ELTE on second-generation concerns of pedagogy suggests that ELTE is caught up in how to deliver content. There is a certain irony, in that while ELTE has historically been more diverse and pragmatic than teacher education in other content areas (Freeman 2016), here it seems to be focused on how to teach its content.

English in the world is changing very rapidly, which is redefining the world of English language teaching, both in ELT and in ELTE. Perhaps not surprisingly, what counts as knowledge in ELT is evolving, driven primarily by these changes in the nature and role of English, and the recognition of who is teaching it. While public-sector education has always been the primary provider of ELT around the world, its critical role has often been eclipsed within arguments about language as content. Kachru's 1982 argument about the diversifying geo-political locus of English, and the role of 'first, outer, and expanding' circle countries in 'defining' what English is, are case-in-point. These arguments have linked the primary pedagogical identity of ELT teachers (as 'non-native') to political and economic forces of global geography and definitions drawn from colonial history. They have supported a dichotomous categorization in teaching knowledge between 'native' and 'non-native' speaking teachers, based on a designation which has no clear definition in linguistics or psychology. Kachru's ideas played an invaluable role in deconstructing notions of a single standard for English, however. In fact, one could further build out his initial framework to now include a fourth, 'virtual circle' of English use. Propelled by social media and the internet, this circle includes interactions and language uses that are firmly anchoring a new version of English as a *lingua franca* form of communication.

These dramatic changes in ELT are not directly reflected in the curated knowledge of ELTE, as represented in these chapter abstracts. What counts as knowledge in ELTE is caught up in second-generation concerns of pedagogy and how to teach this evolving ELT teaching knowledge. Using the analogy between evolving knowledge generations and updating software versions, it seems like ELTE is running older software on current hardware. It is getting the job done for now, but it is running more slowly and missing features that the new hardware can and does support. The ELTE professional community provides the software which is fundamentally important for the daily hardware that is English language teaching around the world. How these two communities address the alignment is a key challenge.

Notes

1 In this discussion, we are using the phrase 'English language teaching' to refer to the superordinate activity that includes ELT (see note 2) and ELTE.

2 In the acronym, ELT, we include teaching English as a second, additional, or foreign language. We acknowledge distinctions for teachers teaching in settings that are 'target-language embedded' (i.e. 'English as a Second or Additional Language' classrooms) versus 'target-language removed' (i.e. English as a Foreign Language' classrooms) (Graves 2008), particularly in aspects of teacher preparation and in-service support, but we contend nonetheless that there is an emerging global knowledge base which blurs this distinction (see for example, *Language Teaching Research*, 2018). We recognize the redundancy when 'ELT' is used as an adjective, as in 'ELT teaching' for example. We mean the term to refer to the knowledge base, and not simply the activity.

3 One could also examine the dynamism in how ELTE knowledge changes over time, diachronically, however that would entail a different approach, reviewing handbooks from different points in time.

4 The hyphenation in these two terms is intentional; it reflects the sense that the knowledge is instantiated in the person and place of the context (knowledge *in-person*, *in-place*, third generation) or in the activity (knowledge-*for-teaching*, fourth generation).

References

Ball, D. L, Thames, M. H. and Phelps, G. (2008) 'Content Knowledge for Teaching: What Makes it Special?'. *Journal of Teacher Education*, 59(5) 389–407.

Blair, R. W. (ed.) (1982) *Innovative Approaches to Language Teaching*. Rowley, MA: Heinle/Newbury House.

Borg, S. (2003) 'Teacher Cognition in Language Teaching: A Review of Research on What Language Teachers Think, Know, Believe, and Do'. *Language Teaching*, 36(2) 81–109.

Burns, A., Freeman, D. and Edwards, E. (2015) 'Theorizing and Studying the Language Teaching Mind: Mapping Research on Language Teacher Cognition'. *Modern Language Journal*, 99(3) 585–601.

Freeman, D. (2016) *Educating Second Language Teachers: The Same Things Done Differently*. Oxford: Oxford University Press.

Freeman, D. (2018). 'Arguing For a Knowledge-Base in Language Teacher Education, Then (1998) and Now (2018)'. *Language Teaching Research* (advance online publication).

Freeman, D., Katz, A., Garcia Gomez, P. and Burns, A. (2015) 'English-for-Teaching: Rethinking Teacher Language Proficiency for the Classroom'. *English Language Teaching Journal*, 69(2) 129–139.

Golombek, P. (1998) 'A Study of Language Teachers' Personal Practical Knowledge'. *TESOL Quarterly*, 32(3) 447–464.

Graves, K. (2008) 'The Language Curriculum: A Social Contextual Perspective'. *Language Teaching*, 41(2) 147–181.

Kachru, B. (1982) *The Other Tongue: English Across Cultures*. Champaign-Urbana, IL: University of Illinois Press.

Kanno, Y. and Norton, D. (eds) (2003) Special issue, '*Language Research*: Imagined Communities and Educational Possibilities'. *Journal of Language, Identity, and Education*, 2(4) 241–249.

Shulman, L. (1986) 'Those Who Understand: Knowledge Growth in Teaching'. *Educational Researcher*, 15(2) 4–14.

Shulman, L. (1987) 'Knowledge and Teaching: Foundations of the New Reform'. *Harvard Educational Review*, 57(1) 1–22.

Woodward, T. (1991) *Models and Metaphors in Language Teacher Training: Loop Input and Other Strategies*. Cambridge: Cambridge University Press.

2

Materialising a Vygotskian-inspired language teacher education pedagogy

Paula R. Golombek and Karen E. Johnson

Introduction

One of the challenges of working from a Vygotskian Sociocultural Theory (VSCT) stance in the field of language teacher education (LTE) is enacting the dialectic logic upon which the theory is based. Rather than being grounded in Aristotelian logic, which sets up dichotomies such as individual/social and theory/practice, VSCT is grounded in dialectics – the synthesis of seemingly opposite and contradictory sides or ideas. Understanding how dialectic logic is conceptualised in key principles and concepts of VSCT is essential to understanding how VSCT is used to inform the practices and interactions of LTE programs in systematic ways. Furthermore, for Vygotsky, educational practice is a form of scientific research: it is the laboratory where the principles of the theory are to be tested. Thus, when asked to organise our chapter according to the subheadings *research* and *applications*, we were unable to separate research from application because they are, from a VSCT perspective, two sides of the same coin. For over two and a half decades, our work as teacher educators has centered on the design and enactment of LTE practices using the principles and concepts of VSCT to promote the development of second language (L2) teacher/teaching expertise. Over that same period, our work as researchers has centered on empirically documenting the consequences of implementing educational practices intentionally derived from VSCT to support L2 teacher learning/development. Our scholarship and that of other VSCT-informed teacher educators/researchers not only employs VSCT as a theoretical lens to understand the development of L2 teacher/teaching expertise but intentionally deploys specific principles and concepts of the theory in/through systematically organised LTE practices to promote it. This scholarship therefore embraces a dialectical unity of theory and practice – praxis – in which theory guides practice while practice shapes theory. For VSCT-informed teacher educators/researchers, what we do as teacher educators is informed by our theory, and what we uncover as researchers is informed by what happens in our LTE practices.

We devote this chapter to VSCT-informed scholarship that originates in a dialectical approach to theory/practice in the specific social activities of LTE that take place in a myriad of sociocultural, historical, political, economic, and institutional contexts. We begin this chapter with an overview of key principles and concepts of VSCT. We then highlight recent VSCT-informed LTE scholarship that illustrates the practices and interactions in which teacher educators have challenged teachers' everyday concepts, developed teachers' conceptual thinking, and promoted teachers' enacting conceptual teaching in both pre-service LTE programs and in-service professional development. We show throughout how these teachers/researchers have made their LTE pedagogy explicit and documented the influence and consequences of LTE practices and interactions on the professional development of the L2 teachers with whom they work.

Key principles and concepts in Vygotskian sociocultural theory

A key principle in VSCT is that the development of an individual's mental processes is social in origin. According to Vygotsky (1978), an individual's mental functions appear 'twice', first in interaction with more knowledgeable others, the social plane, and then within the individual, the mental plane (p. 57). Such gradual qualitative transformation of innate mental functions to culturally shaped higher mental functions, originating in and emerging from social activity/interaction to individual higher mental processes, has been characterised as *internalisation*. As individuals interact with the physical world and with others, they are mediated. *Mediation*, the central concept in VSCT, shapes those interactions (occurring through written and verbal dialogue) and the qualitative transformations that occur in the processes of mental development. Explaining mediation can be knotty because different kinds of mediation and mediational tools exist (and we use 'mediation' as a noun, adjective, and a verb). For example, as we engage in the activity of lesson planning, the powerful semiotic tool of language, as well as concepts such as task-based teaching, mediate our thinking and activity while we write the lesson plan (itself both a physical and conceptual tool) on a computer (a physical tool). Dialogic interactions are social not only in terms of the relationships they involve, for example beginning teacher and teacher educator, but because those interactions are part of the larger historical cultural practices of the groups to which they belong, for example as part of an LTE program. Within those interactions, *a zone of proximal development* (ZPD) can emerge. For us, the ZPD is both a metaphoric space where individual cognition originates in the social collective mind, emerging in and through engagement in social activity; and an arena of potentiality, a space where we intentionally support individuals to perform beyond their current levels of competence and comfort. What makes mediating at an individual's upper limits challenging is that individuals have their own *social situation of development* – the historical and immediate conditions, including affordances and constraints, of their lived experiences. Through mediation, and by acting in and on the social situations in which they are embedded, individuals transform what is relevant for their own motives and contexts of use.

Vygotsky considered formal schooling (for us, language teacher education programs) as the fundamental setting in which educators are to work intentionally to develop the conceptual thinking needed to transform our everyday concepts. Developing conceptual thinking enables us to take purposeful control over our minds and actions, and our worlds. *Everyday concepts*, observations we make through the concrete experiences of daily life, are typically inaccurate, superficial, implicit, and unanalysed, whereas *academic concepts* are based on systematic study of entities and phenomenon around us. Everyday and academic concepts interact dialectically in that everyday concepts form a basis from which to understand and interact with academic concepts, and academic concepts have the potential to re-structure our everyday understandings. Academic concepts, as part of an organised system of knowledge and formal instruction, need to be materialised as a tool – externalised through language and/visuals – which individuals use in social activity, and increasingly, to self-regulate their thinking and activity. For example, teachers lacking academic concepts connected with American English phonetics might answer questions as to why American pronunciation of the word 'butter' sounds like 'budder' with 'that's just how

Americans say that word'. This inability to explain phonetic concepts stems, in part, from teachers' everyday experiences as speakers of English. In LTE programs however, teachers may learn the environmental conditions that distinguish the phoneme /t/ from the allophone [ɾ], the flap. Their explanation to students for the American pronunciation of 'butter' would be grounded in a systematic phonetic characterisation that would be presented preferably in a student-friendly manner.

From a VSCT-informed stance, LTE programs are therefore charged with providing the kind of intentional, well-organised instruction needed for the systematic learning of L2 teaching. Knowledgeable and intentional language teacher educators (*expert others*) are essential to mediate teacher development, externalising the kinds of pedagogical knowledge and academic concepts that language teachers need, and creating spaces for teachers to engage with pedagogical knowledge and concepts in a range of teaching activities. Thinking about LTE programs in this manner represents an alternative to the kind of rote memorisation that Vygotsky criticised and that is not uncommon in LTE programs. To accomplish these goals, LTE programs must create *structured mediational spaces* (Johnson & Golombek, 2016: 92) in which teachers are encouraged and supported as they externalise their everyday concepts of teachers and teaching, engage with materialised academic concepts, and critically reflect on and analyse these concepts through their own beliefs, identities, reasoning and teaching practices. Such structured mediational spaces and the teacher/teacher educator dialogic interactions that emerge in these spaces must also create opportunities for teacher educators to make their expertise explicit to identify the upper levels of teachers' potential as they attempt to enact teaching in ways that are beyond their current levels of competence and comfort (ZPD), and to adapt responsively to teachers' immediate understandings, needs and/or concerns. As teachers make their everyday concepts explicit, academic concepts can restructure them, mediating, or shaping teacher thinking and activity, so that teachers have increasing control over their thinking and teaching (they become *psychological tools* or *thinking in concepts*). Thinking in concepts for teachers emerges as academic concepts are repeatedly applied to concrete teaching experiences and concrete teaching experiences are repeatedly abstracted through a process of generalisation, which we illustrate in varied ways in the following sections. As is the case for all professional domains, concept development and conceptual thinking serves as the basis for expertise in the teaching profession.

Challenging everyday concepts

VSCT-informed teacher educators/researchers have infused VSCT-informed practices intentionally into their courses in LTE programs or workshops in varied instructional contexts to challenge everyday concepts of teachers and teaching. Through their knowledge of and experiences working in specific sociocultural and institutional contexts, teacher educators first identify everyday concepts that typically re-enforce axiomatic ways of thinking about language and language teaching and then the germane academic concepts to restructure them. When a language teacher educator challenges teachers' taken-for-granted assumptions about language learning and teaching, they need to create a safe environment because teachers may feel vulnerable in terms of what they do not know and, thus, emotionally exposed. By creating structured mediational spaces in which teachers externalise their everyday understandings and engage with the academic concept through varied activities, teacher educators try to identify the upper limits of teachers' abilities and offer both cognitive and emotional support. This requires teacher educators to be intentional (conscious about and explicit to themselves and their teachers) about the goals, quality, and manner of the mediation that they enact.

Challenging teachers' everyday concepts is demanding as they are rooted in tacit sociohistorical cultural beliefs and practices. Verity (2011) describes how she intentionally infuses key VSCT principles into a pedagogical grammar class in an MA TESOL program at a Japanese university, so students engage with grammar and teaching grammar 'in ways that encourage reflective, metacognitive, and self-regulated exploration and evaluation' (p. 154). She challenges students' everyday concept of grammar as a 'catalogue' of right answers that they teach to their students (p. 154), a concept rooted in their experiences as students taking high-stakes tests, by introducing the concepts of 'grammar as choice' and as 'a continuous activity of knowing' (p. 155). Many of the assignments and activities require that students collaboratively and individually practice talking about grammar' (p. 160). Because students typically fear not having 'the right answers' to explain grammar, she thoughtfully enables them to express and manage their emotions through the assignments and activities, sometimes in low-stress fun activities, including language play and reflective journals.

Verity incorporates two major collaborative assignments – two structured mediational spaces – in which students rehearse and re-design grammar explanations, experiencing grammar as 'a continuous activity of knowing'. To illustrate, in the Lesson Plan Assignment, students independently create a lesson for a specific group of students, collaboratively talk through/about it with their classmates, and then, if they desire, talk through/about it with the instructor. Students can integrate peer and teacher feedback before handing it in. In doing this assignment in which cognition is distributed across class members, she is also challenging students' everyday understanding that only teachers have the right answers. Students come to appreciate the collaborative feedback. For example, one student expressed gratitude for the 'important suggestions' she received from her classmates that some of her activities were 'teacher-centered'. After her peer collaboration, she could detail the reasoning behind the student-centered activity she created: 'students can review the content of their speech and the right use of past tense for themselves' (p. 161).

The way that VSCT-infused practices and interactions in Verity's pedagogical grammar course initiate students' processes of internalising the academic concepts 'grammar as choice' and of 'languaging' is evident as they describe having a 'sea change, a revolution, in how I think about grammar specifically and language generally' or respond to one of their own students' grammar questions to 'think about it in terms of meaning and use' (p. 164). Though Verity's course took place within a more traditional LTE program, she nonetheless emphasises 'how a relatively traditional classroom can be a setting for informed and principled sociocultural praxis' (p. 154). This kind of cognitive development may not result in internalisation of the academic concepts, but 'can set in motion a variety of developmental processes that would be impossible apart from learning' (Johnson, 2009: 76).

In another MA TESOL program in Japan, Yoshida (2011) likewise challenges Japanese EFL teacher-learners' everyday concepts – in this case, of curriculum as what is 'contained in the textbook'. He designed eight interconnected assignments (see p. 140) through which teachers worked through the academic concept of Graves' (2000) model of curriculum, as well as the contrasting metaphors of curriculum as 'learning the landscape' (Greeno, 1991) and 'the rutted path' (National Research Council, 2000). The assignments were uploaded to a Moodle site, a structured mediational space that allowed for Yoshida and the teachers 'to create and maintain a virtual conversation, where teachers were encouraged to explore, exchange, and confirm their emerging conceptualizations of curriculum' (p. 151), and Yoshida was able to prompt and support their externalised thinking.

The first assignment required teachers to brainstorm their concept of curriculum through a concept map in class, and then to further detail their concept, typically expressed through metaphor, in a paper. Yoshida challenged their everyday concepts by having them read about contrasting metaphors of curriculum, and write a reaction paper. Next, students read about and discussed Graves's (2000) model of curriculum design, and then wrote a reaction paper. Yoshida made the abstract notions of *articulating beliefs* and *defining one's own context*, emphasised in the model, concrete by having students externalise their implicit beliefs about language teaching as shaped by the Japanese sociocultural and political context, and scrutinise that context. Students then worked collaboratively to apply this concept of curriculum design in a 3-year task-based syllabus. In the final assignment, students referenced all previous assignments as they traced the development of their concept of curriculum over the course of the semester, enabling them to 'develop a metacognitive awareness of their own learning' (p. 151).

Students struggled as they engaged with their everyday concepts and the academic concepts of curriculum. For example, one student, Katsunori, began by explaining his understanding of extrinsic and intrinsic factors affecting students learning as 'many students stop eating this boiled-egg before teaching its yolk' (p. 148). What this meant was that students studied English for tests (the white) due to the Japanese educational context, but not for what he hoped, the joy of learning another language (the yolk). Later in the semester, he described ways that students might eat both the white and the yolk of the egg if the teacher could address the stress level students feel studying English for exams. Yoshida's results show that while students did not fully internalise academic concepts over the course of one semester, 'this struggle and these contradictions actually became a springboard for them to question their everyday experiences and problematise their instructional contexts' (p. 151). Awareness of and grappling with contradictions can represent an initial step in transforming concepts. What is clear from both Verity and Yoshida's efforts to engage students with academic concepts in structured mediational spaces over a semester-long course is that they still need extensive and extended engagement with concepts in the concrete activities of teaching, especially within the constraints and affordances of their actual instructional setting.

Providing opportunities for teachers in a course or workshop to engage with academic concepts in the activity of teaching is not always possible but certainly crucial for teachers to begin to use conceptual thinking. Feryok (2009) documented how Malaysian mathematics and science teachers learned to use tasks as a language-teaching practice in their English medium content teaching through participation in a 20-week program in New Zealand. She designed the program to be 25 per cent lecture with one experiential activity, and 75 per cent experiential activities performed first as students and later as teachers, or role reversal. These activities were configured intentionally as structured mediational spaces to enable teachers to imitate in instructional activities as teachers the kinds of activities in which they participated as students. To transform their teaching of English medium science and mathematics instruction by engaging in conceptual thinking, Feryok first introduced the academic concept of 'task-based teaching' using criteria established by Ellis (2003). In her day-to-day teaching activity, she repeatedly referred to these criteria as she modelled a variety of task-based activities based on them, focusing on how to create a gap in task-based design. In these tasks, teachers participated as students. For example, in a multi-step content-based activity, the teachers transformed a graphic organiser activity from a biology textbook into two modified versions representing variations of task-based activities: a task with shared information and optional two-way interaction and a task with split information requiring one-way interaction from teacher to students, which could have an optional two-way interaction (with student questions). Then, teachers completed a microteaching experience in which they designed tasks for students, after which they received 1 hour of feedback from the teacher and peers. After being immersed in the role of 'interaction' in task-based teaching and 'task conditions that stimulate interaction' (p. 284), teachers performed a second microteaching session, again receiving feedback.

Results showed that teachers successfully imitated more of the task criteria in the second microteaching than the first, but continued to struggle with certain ones, such as creating a 'gap' and a need for achieving the outcome communicatively. In other words, teachers had incomplete images of task-based teaching and were often mediated influentially by their prior experiences as learners and teachers of mathematics and science, as well as the academic concept. Consistent with Verity and Yoshida, Feryok cautions that although two microteaching sessions can initiate some changes in cognition and activity, teachers need to engage with academic concepts in the concrete activity of teaching numerous times over time to develop conceptual thinking and transform their teaching activity. Teachers also need to attach their own motive to the concept, for example linking their instructional intentions and goals to task-based teaching when teaching in their own classes, as opposed to using task-based teaching because of institutional mandates to do so.

Promoting conceptual thinking

VSCT-informed research in LTE has also focused on how teacher educators/researchers and teachers promote conceptual thinking to better understand the nuances of teachers' own teaching. We again highlight the dialectic unity of theory/practice, praxis: the teacher educators/researchers model and promote conceptual thinking in their professional development practices with teachers; by researching these practices and interactions, they simultaneously document the quality and character of those practices and interactions and their influence on the teachers. The intentions behind these practices are to create safe meditational spaces where teachers are encouraged to make their everyday concepts explicit, to reflect on and critique them, and to externalise their current understandings of what, how, and why they teach the way they do. At the same time, talking through and about concepts creates opportunities for teacher educators/researchers to make their expertise explicit, to model conceptual thinking, and to introduce relevant academic concepts that will assist teachers as they begin to think conceptually about how and why they make particular pedagogical decisions while teaching.

A common practice that is designed to promote conceptual thinking in both pre-service and in-service LTE programs is the post-observation conference. Dialogue about a lived classroom experience, between a teacher and a teacher educator, an administrator, or even a more experienced teacher, is assumed to not only benefit practicing teachers, but any benefits are expected to translate into quality instructional practices in classrooms. Harvey (2011) and later Harvey and Vasquez (2015) offer a window into how a mentor teacher models conceptual thinking during a series of post-observation conferences with two novice ESL teachers, Pepa and Rick. Working from a VSCT-informed stance, Harvey (2011) focused on not only the quality and character of the verbal mediation that emerged in these post-observation conferences but on its role in the development of conceptual thinking in the novice teachers. She identified, a priori, several VSCT principles that informed the quality and character of her verbal mediation during the post-observation conferences (Wertsch, 1991; Lantolf & Aljaafreh, 1995). The mentor and teacher must have similar expectations as to the conduct and outcome of the conference. Likewise, the nature of the verbal mediation must be dialogic where both mentor and teacher are active and vocal participants in the interaction, co-constructing solutions to problems, and making their reasoning visible through talk. While the mentor, acting as an expert-other, both uses and encourages the use of professional discourse to link the concrete teaching activities of the lesson she just observed to relevant academic concepts, the mentor must also be sensitive to the teacher's emerging ZPD and thereby provide assistance that is graduated and contingent on the teacher's immediate needs. By enacting these key VSCT principles in the moment-to-moment interactions between herself and the teachers, the mentor could see how Pepa and Rick were conceptualising their teaching, while simultaneously creating a space for her to make visible how expert teachers think conceptually. Pepa's discourse during the post-observation conferences reflected her emerging ability to think about her teaching at a conceptual level (i.e., scaffolding students' learning) while also indicating she was still in the process of enacting some of the concepts (i.e., task- and content-based teaching) discussed during their conferences. Rick's discourse showed less evidence of conceptual thinking about how his students were learning (i.e., grammatical concepts), yet the post-observation conferences allowed him to externalise his inner thoughts and feelings (i.e., struggling with the grammatical concept he was expected to teach) and indicated a sincere willingness to open up his teaching experience for inspection and analysis.

Harvey and Vasquez (2015) elaborated this work by offering a taxonomy of how the mentor modelled conceptual thinking during these post-observation conferences along a continuum from the 'contextualised nature of lived experience' to the 'decontextualised nature of generalizations and principles' (p. 101). On the contextualised end of the continuum, the mentor offered a concept or idea behind a single context-bound lived experience, such as when she ideated the features of an activity that Pepa had devised for her students in the words; 'it's this defined manageable achievable task' or commented on a single teaching strategy; *you were student oriented*. On the decontextualised end of the continuum, the mentor modelled conceptual thinking by making generalisations about events that occurred during instruction. For example, Rick's description of an activity in which his students were 'all working on it and talking about it' was generalised by the mentor as *they liked the intellectual challenge of that*.

A striking feature of the mentor's modelling of conceptual thinking was that it was emergent and contingent on what was being talked about, who these teachers are, where they are teaching, and how they are responding/reacting to the mentor's discourse. Ultimately, it is this reflexive interaction that shifts the contextualised ideation of lived experiences toward decontextualised generalisations and principles and therefore captures how conceptual thinking is represented in post-observation conferences.

The mediational role of talking through and about concepts to better understand the nuances of one's own teaching is also illustrated in Fagan's (2015) study of an experienced ESL teacher's interactional responses to learner inquiries. Using the conventions of conversation analysis (CA), Fagan provided the teacher, Ann, with transcripts which made visible her own talk-in-interaction when both problematic and unproblematic learner inquiries arose. During stimulated recall sessions and interviews, he asked Ann to externalise her understanding of how and why she made particular pedagogical decisions while teaching. Throughout this dialogic process of talking through her interactional responses, Ann became consciously aware that she managed unproblematic learner inquiries by what she came to see as *doing answering*, in other words, either answering directly or delegating the answer to another learner if there was evidence that the nominated learner could successfully address the inquiry. She was surprised by how often she found herself *doing answering*, even at the expense of limiting student participation. These emerging insights led her to articulate a pedagogical rationale for *doing answering*, stating that maintaining the clarity and flow of an activity helps to promote learner talk in subsequent interaction, an issue she 'never thought about … at least not consciously' (p. 82).

When faced with learner inquiries that could not be readily addressed, Ann found that she tended to *model exploration*, displaying her thought processes as she attempted to decipher how to answer a learner's inquiry. When asked about the appropriateness of the phrase *assertive communication*, or if *gun laws exist in NYC*, or how to express *the effect* over time, Ann first displayed a thinking stance during silence:

> (3.0) ((*Ann looks up, as if contemplating*)), then began to verbalize her thought processes; – *yeah. i see what you mean. and i-i-i don't' know if I would say it quite like that*, and then searched for resources for reaching an answer; *[google it. that's a good question.]* (4.0) *and it's such a good question that i want you to do some research.*

Again, seemingly unaware of such consistency in her interactional responses to problematic learner enquiries, Ann began to formulate a rationale for *modelling exploration*; to promote learners as knowledge-holders, to demonstrate how to think through genuine enquiries that students may not have answers to, and to give herself a glimpse into how her students were thinking.

In these structured mediational spaces, the CA transcripts themselves and Ann's dialogue with the researcher about them, worked in consort to mediate the development of a more nuanced, more conscious awareness of her own interactional responses to learner inquiries. In doing so, she was able to articulate pedagogically sound reasoning for the ways in which she used talk-in-interaction to promote learner autonomy in her teaching. Ann claimed:

> *I never thought about looking at my teaching so intricately: the nonverbal, the pausing, all of it. And I really had no idea that I was so systematic or that I could be systematic and organic at the same time. … I need to explore my own understandings of what it means to teach and reconsider what learner autonomy means to me… I'm glad to know that there are still things I'm learning about myself.*
> (p. 86)

Fagan's research makes a compelling case for professional development interventions that pay attention to the intricacies of the interactional work (made visible by CA) that goes on in the activity of actual teaching. Moreover, the mediational spaces created to assist Ann in understanding the quality and character of her own instructional practices emerged through dialogue with the researcher/teacher educator.

Developing conceptual teaching

VSCT-informed research in LTE has also focused on a key principle in VSCT-inspired pedagogy: how teacher educators/researchers intentionally insert relevant academic concepts into their work with teachers with the goal of enabling teachers to develop conceptual teaching. The particular academic concept or concepts are typically new to teachers, and thus learning to teach through these concepts requires that teachers come to internalise these concepts in the activities of actually teaching through them. The intentions behind the practices that foster conceptual teaching, like others we have described here, are to create safe meditational spaces where teachers play with their emerging understandings of the academic concepts to which they have been exposed as they try to restructure their teaching activities through those concepts. And to reiterate our position on the dialectic unity of praxis, the practice of intentionally engaging teachers with relevant academic concepts through which they come to re-envision and restructure their teaching activities informs theory on how academic concepts and teacher/teacher educator verbal mediation assists and supports the development of conceptual teaching (and dialectically, theory on practice).

As language teacher educators, we know that there is a difference between knowing the subject matter content and teaching someone else how to know and do something of substance with that content. This is compounded when teachers are asked to teach subject matter content that they themselves have not fully internalised. This was the case for Worden's (2015) study of an experienced ESL teacher who was asked to teach the academic writing genre of the analytic essay during her first semester of teaching a post-secondary L2 composition course. Not only was the analytic essay new to this teacher, it was new to the curriculum of the ESL composition program, and thus few resources were available to assist her in planning, teaching, or assessing this genre. Building on the theoretical construct of *pedagogical content knowledge* (Shulman, 1987), or the specialised content knowledge that teachers use to make the content they are teaching accessible and useable for students, Worden traced this teacher's developing pedagogical content knowledge of the analytic essay while she was engaged in the activities of teaching it. The VSCT-informed practices that made up the design of Worden's study included five semi-structured interviews in which the teacher, Sonja, was asked to draw concept maps of her emerging understanding of the analytic essay. Video recordings were taken of Sonja teaching the entire analytic essay unit followed by three stimulated recall sessions in which Sonja and the researcher discussed selected excerpts where she was explaining content, the students made contributions or asked questions about content, and any apparent moments of confusion for her or her students. Near the end of the semester, an additional stimulated recall session was conducted in which Sonja was asked to select high, middle, and low-quality students' analytic essays and comment on strong and weak elements of each essay. While Worden was clearly positioned as the researcher rather than a teacher educator in this study, the practices she employed were intended to create safe mediational spaces in which Sonja was able to externalise her thinking, verbalise her emerging conceptualisation of the analytic essay, and critically reflect on her attempts to make the essential elements of this genre accessible and usable for her ESL writers.

While Sonja's initial conceptualisation of the analytic essay was vague and unelaborated (*when you take an issue (.) that is clearly controversial, or debatable, or (.) just doesn't sit well with people, and you explicate it, you learn all you can about it*), as she taught the unit, the concept of *points of analysis* emerged as a pedagogically appropriate representation for how to help her students conceptualise the essential elements of this unfamiliar genre. Throughout the teaching of this unit, this concept, *points of analysis*, became more fully elaborated (*parts of an issue, from different perspectives, taking a microscopic view*) which allowed Sonja to develop a more systematic and easily generalised conceptualisation of the genre itself and as a more workable pedagogical tool to teach it. As the meaning of this concept of *points of analysis* emerged through use, both concretely with her students and through dialogue and guided reflection with the researcher, her concept maps became more elaborate and coherent, her instructions and explanations became more detailed and targeted, and she was better able to consciously and reflectively direct and regulate her own teaching activities.

Worden's research suggests that the development of pedagogical content knowledge for teaching is emergent, dynamic, and importantly mediated by the teacher's interactions with her students. It also illustrates in real-time what and how teachers learn as they engaged in the activities of teaching, as well as how what they learn gets instantiated in how they teach. Finally, it speaks to the design and enactment of VSCT-informed practices in which teachers engage in guided reflection and dialogue with an expert other about their own teaching as they develop conceptual teaching.

An additional example of VSCT-informed research that focused on developing conceptual teaching centered around a widely used professional development strategy known as *instructional coaching* (Knight, 2009). Designed to foster conceptual thinking and conceptual teaching through dialogue with an instructional coach, instructional coaching entails creating ongoing, collaborative, mediational spaces for teachers to focus on subject matter content, teaching activities, and student learning. Teemant et al. (2011) and Teemant and Hausman (2013) have taken up instructional coaching as a VSCT-informed practice to mediate individual teacher development by linking it to six standards for effective pedagogy for K-12 content-area teachers who work with English language learners (ELLs). Informed by the tenets of VSCT and critical pedagogy, the standards conceptualise *learning* as inherently social, *teaching* as offering appropriate assistance to facilitate students' learning, *knowledge* as co-constructed and culturally formed, and *taking action* to remedy societal inequities in students' lives and communities. For their teachers, the six standards (*joint productive activity, language & literacy development, contextualisation, challenging activities, instructional conversations, critical stance*) functioned as manageable and transparent academic concepts that they came to understand and eventually enacted by assessing their own pedagogical effectiveness through guided reflection and dialogue before, during, and after a series of lessons with an instructional coach. Additionally, the instructional coaching sessions focused on helping teachers working to change the ways in which they organise instruction (small groups), attend to the quality and character of their interactions with students (instructional conversations), and create opportunities for civic engagement (inclusive learning communities).

In a series of mixed-methods studies, Teemant and her colleagues established links between K-12 content-area teachers' engagement in instructional coaching around the six standards for critical sociocultural pedagogy, observable transformations in teachers' pedagogical practices, and increases in student academic achievement. Notably, Teemant and Hausman (2013) empirically demonstrated that teachers who participated in a 30-hour workshop followed by seven cycles of individualised instructional coaching were not only better able to enact the standards of critical sociocultural pedagogy, but their students, in particular ELLs, showed marked gains in academic achievement. Additionally, participation in instructional coaching was found to foster teacher creativity and ownership of the curriculum and a renewed sense of professional agency.

In our most recent work (Johnson & Golombek, 2016), we detailed how we challenge teachers' everyday concepts, promote conceptual thinking, and develop conceptual teaching by examining the motives, processes, and goals imbue behind our VSCT-inspired LTE practices. We empirically documented our interactions with our teachers as they unfolded within our own sociocultural and institutional contexts (see Chapters 5–9 for detailed practices and interactions). We propose responsive mediation as a psychological tool for teacher educators to orient and enact an intentional and systematic pedagogy that supports the development of L2 teacher/teaching expertise, as well as to examine the quality and character of the dialogic interactions that develop through the specific practices of our pedagogy. We place the teacher educator–teacher relationship/interaction at the center of this concept in that we teacher educators need to be mindful of who our teachers are (present), have come to be (past), and aspire to be (future); as well as where they are cognitively, affectively, and experientially as they experience being and becoming a teacher. We need to make explicit to ourselves and our teachers our motives, intentions, and goals when designing, sequencing, and enacting our pedagogy so we intentionally direct what happens inside our practices. As we interact with our teachers, responsive mediation should then emerge in the specifics of what a teacher is experiencing, the challenges and possible contradictions faced, along with a range of emotions experienced. As we engage with these specifics, we try to identify the upper limits of teachers' potential and provide the kind of support that teachers need and can exploit. Responsive mediation also involves moving back and forth between the academic concepts that we have inserted to restructure teachers' everyday concepts, through extensive and extended participation in talking through and enacting those concepts their teaching activity.

Future directions

Our chapter has demonstrated how various language teacher educators/researchers have infused VSCT-grounded practices into their LTE programs and professional development activities, thereby creating the kinds of structured mediational spaces in which L2 teachers are exposed to academic concepts that challenge their everyday understandings of language teaching and learning, and are supported – mediated – as they try to enact budding teacher identities and alternative instructional practices. This research, embodying Vygotsky's call for praxis, demonstrates how professional development programs and activities function as 'laboratories' where VSCT can be used as a theoretical lens to understand the development of L2 teacher/teaching expertise, as well as can be intentionally applied in appropriately organised LTE practices to promote L2 language teacher/teaching expertise.

Much research on teacher cognition has focused on what Kubanyiova and Feryok (2015) have recently conceptualised as the *ecologies of teachers' inner lives* without considering how this connects with student academic achievement. Future research needs to explore this connection between L2 teacher learning and student learning, what Freeman and Johnson (2005) have described as a 'relationship of influence'. The relationship of influence between teacher development and student learning, from a VSCT stance, is viewed as being in a dialectic in which they mutually shape each other as they interact within various teaching-learning activities. We echo our call (Johnson & Golombek, 2018) for exploration of this relationship of influence by encouraging teacher educators/researchers to trace the internal activity of teacher professional learning as it is unfolding, to detail the mediational means shaping teacher learning, accounting for how and why teachers re-shape their instructional thinking and activities while concomitantly determining how student engagement in such activities influences what and how they learn. We also believe methodological ingenuity that can capture, for example longitudinal studies of teacher development and in-process teacher thinking and teacher-student interactions, can be useful in informing our understandings of how teachers and students learning shape each other.

Language teacher cognition offers a relationship of influence as well when it comes to the quality and character of L2 teacher education pedagogy. In this chapter, we have shown how VSCT-inspired teacher educators/researchers have made their LTE pedagogy explicit and explored the influences and consequences of LTE practices and interactions on the professional development of L2 teachers. Future research should continue to empirically document teacher/teacher educator interactions as they unfold within the located contexts in which they occur. In doing so, we come to understand the consequences of our practices as teacher educators on the teachers for whom we are responsible, re-shaping our expertise in that process.

Further reading

Johnson, K. E. (2009) *Second Language Teacher Education: A Sociocultural Perspective*. New York: Routledge.
  Overviews the theoretical underpinnings of a Vygotskian SCT perspective and what it offers the field of L2 teacher education.
Johnson, K. E. and Golombek, P. R. (eds) (2011) *Research on Second Language Teacher Education: A Sociocultural Perspective on Professional Development*. New York: Routledge.
  Fourteen original SCT/AT informed research articles that document the complexities of L2 teachers' professional development in diverse L2 teacher education programs.
Johnson, K. E. and Golombek, P. R. (2016) *Mindful L2 Teacher Education: A Sociocultural Perspective on Cultivating Teachers' Professional Development*. New York: Routledge.

Demonstrates the meaningful role that L2 teacher educators and L2 teacher education play in the professional development of L2 teachers through systematic, intentional, goal-directed theorised L2 teacher education pedagogy.

Lantolf, J. P. and Poehner, M. E. (2014) *Sociocultural Theory and the Pedagogical Imperative in L2 Education*. New York: Routledge.

Explicates the full implications of a praxis-oriented language pedagogy – the pedagogical imperative.

References

Ellis, R. (2003) *Task-Based Language Learning and Teaching*. Oxford: Oxford University Press.

Fagan, D. S. (2015) 'When Learner Inquiries Arise: Marking Teacher Cognition as it Unfolds "In-the-Moment"'. *Ilha do Desterro*, 68(1) 75–90.

Feryok, A. (2009) 'Activity Theory, Imitation and their Role in Teacher Development'. *Language Teaching Research*, 13(3) 279–299.

Freeman, D. and Johnson, K. E. (2005) 'Towards linking teacher knowledge and student learning', in Tedick, D. J. (ed.) *Language Teacher Education: International Perspectives on Research and Practice*. Mahwah, NJ: Lawrence Erlbaum Associates: 73–95.

Graves, K. (2000) *Designing Language Courses: A Guide for Teachers*. Boston, MA: Heinle & Heinle.

Greeno, J. G. (1991) 'Number Sense as Situated Knowing in a Conceptual Domain', *Journal for Research in Mathematics Education*, 22(3) 170–218.

Harvey, J. S. (2011) 'A sociocultural-theory-based study of the impact of mediation during post-observation conferences on language teacher learning. Unpublished thesis, University of South Florida, USA.

Harvey, J. S. and Vasquez, C. (2015) 'Preparing for the Complexities of Teaching: Modeling Conceptual Thinking in Post-observation Conferences'. *Ilha do Desterro*, 68(1) 91–103.

Johnson, K. E. (2009) *Second Language Teacher Education: A Sociocultural Perspective*. New York: Routledge.

Johnson, K. E. and Golombek, P. R. (2016) *Mindful L2 Teacher Education: A Sociocultural Perspective on Cultivating Teachers' Professional Development*. New York: Routledge.

Johnson, K. E. and Golombek, P. R. (2018) 'Making L2 teacher education matter through Vygotskian-inspired pedagogy and research', in Lantolf, J. P. and Poehner, M. E. with Swain, M. (eds) *Handbook of Sociocultural Theory and Second Language Development*. New York: Routledge: 443–456.

Kubanyiova, M. and Feryok, A. (2015) 'Language Teacher Cognition in Applied Linguistics Research: Revisiting the Territory, Redrawing the Boundaries, Reclaiming the Relevance'. *The Modern Language Journal*, 99(3) 435–449.

Knight, J. (ed.) (2009) *Coaching: Approaches and Perspectives*. Thousand Oaks, CA: Corwin Press, Inc.

Lantolf, J.P. and Aljaafreh, A. (1995) 'Second Language Learning in the Zone of Proximal Development: A Revolutionary Experience'. *International Journal of Educational Research*, 23(7) 619–632.

National Research Council (2000) *How People Learn: Brain, Mind, Experience, and School*. Washington, DC: National Academy Press.

Shulman, L. (1987) 'Knowledge and Teaching: Foundations of the New Reform'. *Harvard Educational Review*, 57(1) 1–23.

Teemant, A. and Hausman, C. S. (2013) 'The Relationship of Teacher use of Critical Sociocultural Practices with Student Achievement'. *Critical Education*, 4(4) 1–19.

Teemant, A., Wink, J. and Tyra, S. (2011) 'Effects of Coaching on Teacher use of Sociocultural Instructional Practices'. *Teaching and Teacher Education*, 27(4) 683–693.

Verity, D. (2011) 'The reverse move: enriching informal knowledge in the pedagogical grammar class', in Johnson, K. E. and Golombek, P. R. (eds) *Research on Second Language Teacher Education: A Sociocultural Perspective on Professional Development*. New York: Routledge: 153–167.

Vygotsky, L. S. ([1930–1931] 1998b) 'Development of thinking and formation of concepts in the adolescent', in Rieber, R. W. (ed.) *Collected Works of L. S. Vygotsky: Volume 5. Child Psychology*. New York: Plenum: 29–81.

Vygotsky, L. S. (1978) *Mind in Society: The Development of Higher Psychological Processes* (M. Cole, V. John-Steiner, S. Scribner and E. Souberman, eds). Cambridge, MA: Harvard University Press.

Wertsch, J.V. (1991) *Voices of the Mind: A Sociocultural Approach to Mediated Action.* Cambridge, MA: Harvard University Press.

Worden, D. (2015) 'The Development of Content Knowledge Through Teaching Practice'. *Ilha do Desterro,* 68(1) 105–119.

Yoshida, T. (2011) 'Moodle as a mediational space: Japanese EFL teachers' emerging conceptions of curriculum', in Johnson, K. E. and Golombek, P. R. (eds) *Research on Second Language Teacher Education: A Sociocultural Perspective on Professional Development.* New York: Routledge: 136–152.

3

Reflective practice in L2 teacher education

Thomas S.C. Farrell

Introduction

Second language teacher education (SLTE) programs that basically consist of foundation courses followed by a teaching practicum are designed to prepare learner teachers for a teaching career. However, when they begin their teaching careers, what usually happens is that many soon realize there is something of a mismatch between the contents of their SLTE programs and their lived experiences as novice teachers (Farrell, 2012, 2015a, 2017). They discover that some of their theory focused SLTE courses have little to do with practice and some of their methods (or practice) courses have not enough theoretical conceptualizations of teaching and learning a second/foreign language (Farrell, 2016). Thus, many learner teachers have a difficult time adjusting to life in real classrooms and feel that they have not been adequately prepared for the reality of their teaching careers. Consequently, SLTE programs must be able to prepare teachers, as noted by Darling-Hammond and Bransford (2005: 359) to 'become professionals who are adaptive experts within the context in which they teach.' One way of nurturing learner teachers to become adaptive practitioners is to develop teachers as reflective practitioners who can make their own informed decisions about their practice based on such reflection (Farrell, 2015b).

This chapter discusses how SLT educators can encourage learner teachers to become reflective practitioners. The chapter outlines how SLT educators can make use of technology, critical friendships, team teaching, peer coaching, dialoging, service learning, writing, action research and analysis of critical incidents to encourage learner teachers to engage in reflective practice. The chapter first discusses the concept of reflective practice and second language teacher education and then outlines the reflective activities that can help teachers to reflect on their practice. In addition, it should be noted that the reflective activities outlined in this chapter should be viewed from a collaborative, cooperative, sharing, personal experience and peer-feedback dialoguing position rather than practiced in isolation; as Dewey (1933) noted, reflective practice is best practiced in the company of others.

Reflective practice and SLTE

Over the past 30 years or so SLTE programs worldwide have developed courses that are designed to prepare language teachers (L2 teachers) for future teaching careers. However, early research (e.g. Freeman, 1994; Tarone & Allwright, 2005) cautioned that we may not be preparing L2 teachers for the reality they would face in real classrooms, yet over the ensuing years, L2 programs have continued to deliver academic and theoretical content in courses that were arguably not serving the needs of the teachers (Faez & Vaelo, 2012; Wright, 2010). Indeed, as is often the case, when learner teachers are presented with any new teaching innovation in SLTE, they are slow to incorporate these when they enter real classrooms; as Tang, Lee, and Chun (2012: 91) noted, 'there is often a disparity between the suggested new practice [in SLTE] and its quality and frequency of use in the real classroom.'

This issue remains a major challenge for SLTE programs today and as Johnson (2013: 76) has noted, it is the responsibility of SLTE programs to present concepts they think are important to teachers, 'but to do so in ways that bring these concepts to bear on concrete practical activity, connecting them to everyday concepts and the goal-directed activities of everyday teaching.' Recently a number of SLT educators have begun to take notice of this theory/practice gap in their programs and have suggested that reflective practice can provide a context whereby learner teachers can make these connections between theory and practice. SLT educators can incorporate various reflective activities so that both pre-service and inservice language teachers can engage in self-reflection in order examine their prior beliefs and practices so that they can begin to question these and (re)consider what is best for their students' learning (Tang et al., 2012). As Tang, Lee, and Chun (2012: 105) point out, 'through self-reflection and questioning of the old practices, new ideas will be able to emerge.'

Technology and reflective practice

With advancements in technology, SLTE programs now have many more delivery and discussion formats at their disposal that can be used to encourage teachers to engage in reflective practice. For example, Faez et al. (2017) have noted a shift from providing solely traditional face-to-face instruction to delivering courses, or components of courses, on online interactive forums. They noted that these technology-enhanced environments are becoming a popular way of promoting discussions beyond the classroom, and increasing opportunities for languaging (or verbalizing thoughts for enhanced learning) and collaborative dialogue (problem-solving dialogue between two or more people) as participants attempt to engage in knowledge building. Faez et al. (2017) used Google Docs, an online collaborative word processor, as a platform to determine whether such a forum can provide a favorable space to facilitate rich discussions in language teacher education programs. Although they reported that they all felt that using an online platform for further discussions was a useful pedagogical tool, they also noted that such a platform did not lead to discussions that were as effective as their face-to-face communications, and concluded that it has limitations if using it as a sole means of classroom interaction in teacher education programs because although they believed that languaging occurred through their online contributions, chances for collaborative dialogue to form new knowledge were actually limited. Thus, the Faez et al. (2017) study indicates that the key to using online interactive forums effectively is finding an appropriate balance between these online collaborations and the more traditional face-to-face interactions in order to provide optimum opportunities for collaborative learning.

Advancements in communications technology also open SLTE programs to more virtual environments where mentors, instructors and supervisors participate in support with meaningful exchanges of ideas so that pre-service teachers can reflect through online collaborations. Mann (2015) outlined how supervisors can use such online collaborations when providing feedback on academic writing tasks and assignments in teacher education programs so that they become more dialogic. Mann (2015) detailed how supervisors can provide audio feedback

Thomas S.C. Farrell

through screen capture software (in this case *Jing*). This method of providing feedback in teacher education programs he noted, allows a supervisor to simultaneously provide a visual focus and an auditory commentary that provides a more scaffolded and dialogic process. This provides a type of reflective feedback loop input (see Woodward, 2003) where their experience (receiving both written and spoken feedback) enables more dialogue and reflection by both tutors and learners and enables discussion about the process of receiving feedback in this form.

Reflection in SLTE programs can also be enhanced with the compilation of blog-based teaching portfolios because they create opportunities for discussion, inquiry, feedback and reflection in a social networking environment and enable collaborative learning and information sharing among participants (Farr, 2015; Farr & Riordan, 2017; Tang & Lam, 2014). Such blogging technology according to Tang and Lam (2014) who used them successfully in a Hong Kong language teacher education context, allows teachers to record personal voice, critical thinking and reflection which creates an online learning community (OLC). Studies of these blog-based teaching portfolios have shown positive results in scaffolding reflection, mediating teacher education reform, fostering teacher competencies, and having a positive impact on teacher professional development as well as having an overall positive impact on the institutional environment (Tang & Lam, 2014). Tang and Lam (2014) reported that as long as members of the online learning communities remain active they can obtain continuous feedback and support from peers and mentors and discussion and resources can be stored and retrieved at any time, thus providing a powerful tool for the professional development of language teachers. As Farr and Riordan (2017: 24) maintain, such blogs and e-portfolios in SLTE programs are 'good mechanisms to promote individual and collaborative reflective practices.'

Critical friends and reflective practice

Critical friends (sometimes called critical friends groups (Bambino, 2002)) are two or more teachers who collaborate in a mode that encourages discussion and reflection in order to improve the quality of language teaching and learning. Teacher critical friendships entail entering into a collaborative arrangement with other teachers 'in a way which encourages talking with, questioning, and even confronting, the trusted other, in order to examine planning for teaching, implementation, and its evaluation' (Hatton & Smith, 1995: 41). Farrell (2014) outlined an example of a critical friendship in TESOL where three teachers reflected on their practice over one semester of teaching as critical friends. The teachers reported that they really enjoyed collaborating with each other, and suggested the isolated nature of the job of teaching. As one of the teachers explained, 'So often you are out on your island: "Here I am by myself". Am I the only one having this issue?' However as a result of her discussions with her colleague, she began to see her colleague 'in a whole new role' as a 'critical friend'; she said that her colleague 'clicked into almost a mentor mode because she had taught speaking so much more than I have recently and then she came up with these [teaching] ideas.' This critical friendship made her realize the value of colleagues collaborating; she continued: 'It just started to hit me that as we were talking that we could do more together than this; that's what you need between colleagues to get this kind of thing going' (Farrell, 2014: 51). In addition, Farrell (2013: 88) has suggested that critical friendships provide teachers with opportunities to 'reflect on and consolidate their philosophical and theoretical understanding of their practices and if they desire, can even lead to further and more detailed exploration of different aspects of teaching through detailed action research projects.' Thus, teacher education programs and courses should consider adding critical friendships into various activities, tasks, joint assignment and collaborative work so that learner teachers can realize that they are not alone when they begin their teaching careers.

The usual composition of critical friends as a pair of teachers reflecting together outlined above has been extended to a Critical Friends Group whose composition is ultimately decided by its members and can consist of two to 12 members. Dunne, Nave, and Lewis (2000: 9) define the goal of critical friendships as 'to identify student learning goals that make sense in their schools, look reflectively as practices intended to achieve these goals, and collaboratively examine teacher and student work in order to meet that objective.' These groups meet usually with the help of a facilitator who manages the reflective process. As Johnson (2009: 101) has noted, 'Critical Friends Groups although differing in the way they form or are used, all share common elements: sharing the question or dilemma, inviting questions from the participants, giving and receiving feedback, and promoting self-reflection.'

Research by Vo and Nguyen (2010) has noted the sensitivity of culture on Critical Friends Groups as they reported the learner teachers were initially hesitant to offer any criticism for fear of hurting others, but as the participants gained more trust, they became more comfortable contributing to the group. Vo and Nguyen (2010: 210) observed that Critical Friends Groups offered novice TESOL teachers 'opportunities to learn from colleagues' as they developed a sense of community and this ultimately led to improvement in their teaching. In a similar conclusion, Lakshmi (2014: 200) also links the collaboration involved in such arrangements as beneficial to their overall empowerment as teachers: 'Teachers realized the need for collaborative work, and sought advice from their senior colleagues to solve their classroom problems and for their self-evaluation'.

Team teaching and reflective practice

Team teaching is another type of critical friendship arrangement whereby two or more teachers cooperate as equals as they take responsibility for planning, teaching and evaluating a class (Richards & Farrell, 2005). Team teaching moves reflection beyond the usual practices adopted in many teacher education programs during the teaching practice (or field experiences) components such as student teachers observing lessons before obtaining the responsibility to teach a class alone. Team teaching involves developing a collaborative partnership between two or more teachers in order to develop a lesson to teach and evaluate, thus moving reflective practice from an individual pursuit to a more collaborative and dialogic process (see below for more on dialoging). Typically in such a collaboration the 'team' share responsibility for planning a class and/or course, then teaching the class/course, completing follow-up work (i.e. evaluations/assessments), and making various decisions and outcomes. Teachers usually cooperate as equals, though some elements of coaching (see below) may occur (DelliCarpini & Alonso, 2015; Richards & Farrell, 2005). Such team teaching collaborations better prepare the teachers for the transition to real classrooms. Central to team teaching collaboration is the sharing of experiences and reflective dialoging (see Mann & Walsh, 2017, and below for more).

Implementing team teaching in SLTE during field experiences can occur within five different models: the *observation model*, the *coaching model*, the *assistant teaching model*, the *equal status model* and the *team teaching model*. In the *observation model* one teacher observes (with a pre-agreed observation protocol) the other teacher teaching and collects information about the lesson and has no interaction with the students. Both teachers analyze and reflect together after the lesson (Badiali & Titus, 2010). In the *coaching model*, besides observing as in the previous model, the coach is expected to provide suggestions, assistance and support in a kind of mentoring capacity (Goker, 2006). In the assistant team teaching model, one teacher takes the lead, and the other teacher becomes an assistant, providing support to learners when necessary during the lesson (Badiali & Titus, 2010). The *equal status model* as the name suggests is a collaborative team teaching arrangement where both teachers have an equal status with all aspects of planning, delivery and evaluation (Dugan & Letterman, 2008). Finally, in the *team teaching model*, both teachers work collaboratively and share planning, delivery and evaluation equitably; however, unlike the models above, here both teachers are in front of the class together taking turns leading a discussion, while the other demonstrates something in front of the learners (Badiali & Titus, 2010). This model is more elaborate than the other three as it takes more time to set up as both teachers need to learn more about each other's teaching style (Badiali & Titus, 2010). Thus a wide variety of team teaching models (many of which can be combined) are available that promote reflection in SLTE.

In TESOL Yang (2013) conducted an ethnographic study during a graduate-level internship which included team teaching and noted that such an approach can develop cooperative working relationships, interpersonal networks and intercultural communication skills. Because the learner teachers get feedback from their co-teachers and supervisors, they can, as Yang (2013) observed, attempt to put TESOL theories learned in teacher education programs into practice as they gain practical and in-context teaching experience to improve their team teaching in the sessions that followed. The team teaching arrangements allowed the learner teachers to divide up what needed to be done and as a result, Yang (2013) reported the teachers found it more effective and easier to manage the challenges that many learner teachers initially face.

Gan (2014) also reported the positive effects of team teaching arrangements similar to a combination of the *observation model* above, for learner teachers mostly because of the impact of immediate feedback the teachers obtained from their peers and an increase in self-confidence. As Gan (2014: 136) says, 'Sharing among the fellow student teachers, most likely developed confidence in "self as a newcomer" and the timely feedback of peers contributed to valuing of personal experience in capacity to generate knowledge for teaching.' Aliakbari and Nejad (2013) explained that their encouragement of team teaching arrangements resulted in collaboration and consensus between the co-teachers as they all determined every issue of the teaching process, including evaluations at the end. However, they also note that students can sometimes become confused because team teaching is a novel approach for many given that some cultural expectations of teaching will differ depending on the context. Thus, Aliakbari and Nejad (2013) point out these team teaching arrangements will require consensus and planning and careful consideration of cultural background that includes such variables as the gender composition of the teams. Thus incorporating team teaching into SLTE programs can encourage and develop collaborative reflective practices among learner teachers.

Peer coaching and reflective practice

As mentioned in the section above in the coaching model of team teaching, peer coaching is another collaborative arrangement between teachers in SLTE that can promote collaborative reflection. Peer coaching is defined as 'the process where teams of teachers regularly observe one another and provide support, companionship, feedback, and assistance' (Valencia & Killion, 1988: 170). However, it is different from the team teaching arrangements discussed above as it is intended to improve specific instructional techniques of one of the peers, usually the observed teacher, in a supportive environment.

Within SLTE, peer coaches can enrich teaching practice (field-based programs) where peer coaches observe and record the performance of their peers, provide feedback on the observed teaching practice, and help the teacher correct any perceived deficiencies and thus improve instruction. Peer coaching is also important in inservice education whereby a more experienced peer teacher provides constructive feedback in a safe learning environment so that the observed teacher (less experienced) can develop new knowledge and skills and a deeper awarness of his or her own teaching. Thus the more experienced teacher can take on a mentoring role but both teachers view themselves as peers and equals. Arslan and Ilin (2013) outline the positive effects in terms of changes to their practices related to classroom management skills of a peer-coaching activity where teachers were in pairs and observed one another's lessons, exchanged feedback and repeated the process in a 3 week cycle. Indeed, they reported its success, in that the peers were willing to participate because it was tailored to their particular needs.

Thus, there are different types of peer coaching arrangements such as *technical coach* where a teacher seeks the assistance of another teacher who is experienced and more knowledgeable in order to learn new teaching methods/techniques (Richards & Farrell, 2005). Another type is a *collegial coach* where two teacher-peers focus on refining their existing teaching practices (Richards & Farrell, 2005). Yet another type of coach is a *challenge coach* where a problem arises and two teachers work jointly to resolve the problem (Richards & Farrell, 2005).

Within a US context, these different types of peer coaching arrangements can also be used in combination as attested to in research by Artigliere and Baecher (2017) and DelliCarpini and Alonso (2015). Artigliere and Baecher (2017) is an example of how different combinations of co-teaching arrangements in the US can become complicated for novice ESL teachers when they have to navigate different and sometimes competing models of content-based instruction (CBI) such as a *push-in* model where the ESL teacher provides instruction inside the students' content or grade-level classroom; a *pull-out* model where students receive ESL instruction in small groups in another location; and/or a *team teaching* model where the ESL and classroom or content teacher jointly provide instruction to English language learners (ELLs). As a result, these teacher educators instituted a policy in their teacher education course where the candidates had to deliver at least one co-taught lesson during their practicum (for more on the practicum, see section below).

DelliCarpini and Alonso (2015) in a US context also noted that their TESOL learner teachers were struggling with the demands of content where the content is that of the academic program in which their English language learner (ELLs) students were enrolled and where content teachers had a lack of awareness and understanding of the needs of ELLs in the mainstream classroom. They realized that this was an issue related directly to ESL teacher preparation so they devised what they call a two-way content based instruction (CBI) that extends teacher collaboration and traditional CBI. As a result they restructured their teacher education program and implemented coursework specifically designed to prepare pre-service teachers to effectively engage in Content Based Instruction that is tied to the academic curriculum through two-way CBI and teacher collaboration. Thus, 'teams' (English, Science, Math) developed and collaboratively worked from discussing relevant issues related to teaching to co-planning and actual co-teaching as the pre-service teachers learned how to develop both language and content for ELLs in both the ESL and mainstream settings. Two-way CBI promotes collegiality, alleviates the feeling of isolation, and also lowers student-teacher ratios in classrooms so that learner teachers can have more opportunities to develop their reflective skills and teaching repertoires.

Dialog and reflective practice

Teacher educators can encourage learner teachers to engage in reflective dialogue either face-to-face or in an online mode. As Mann and Walsh (2017: 8) point out, reflection benefits from such dialogue because it 'is a crucial part of the reflection-action-further-action cycle, since it allows for clarification, questioning and ultimately enhanced understanding.' Reflection is enhanced when operated through dialogue with a peer or more experienced colleague, mentor or teacher educator (see critical friends, team teaching, and peer coaching) or groups. These can be called teacher support groups and/or development groups, and/or reflection groups, and/or online chat groups and so on, where teachers come together in a mutual aid type collaboration in which they explore various issues that either directly impact their teaching and/or their practice in general including their professional identity outside the classroom (Farrell, 2014). They can be informal gatherings and at the same time they can engage in small-scale projects (action research or the like—see below).

Engaging in discussions with other professionals increases the likelihood that teachers will learn something from each other because each individual teacher will bring a different perspective to the discussions. In such a manner, entering into a discussion with another teacher or group of teachers can result in gaining new knowledge, new perspectives and new understandings that would have been difficult for teachers reflecting alone. As Mann and Walsh (2017: 8) point out, learner teachers can 'be "scaffolded" though their "Zones of Proximal Development" (ZPD) to a higher plane of understanding through the dialogues they have with other professionals.' Mann and Walsh (2017) also maintain that discussions with other teachers can be enhanced if artifacts are included such as video analysis and other such recordings of teaching to promote more systematic dialogue.

Research in TESOL supports the use of such dialogue in groups to enhance reflection. Chick (2015) for example, looked at dialogic interaction and exploratory talk during post-teaching practice discussions and examined the ways in which such an approach may help promote long term reflective practice involved in developing pedagogic expertise. Chick (2015: 302) reported that dialogic interaction and exploratory talk provided 'the space for learner teachers to externalize their understandings of the teaching process and thus facilitate mediation by the educator.' As a result, Chick noted that the learner teachers could learn from each other as they began to uncover their implicit beliefs regarding classroom actions, probe their emerging understandings, and encourage exploration of the teaching and learning process. Chick concludes that reflective conversations can mediate the development of learner teachers as they learn to teach. In another study, Kabilan et al. (2011) looked at teacher's use of an online discussion forum/board to discuss participants' (both preservice and inservice) video recorded teaching and also reported teachers' enhanced reflections. As Kabilan et al. (2011: 110) reported, the sharing and exchanging of ideas, knowledge, experiences among students in a community of practice, 'assisted the teachers to reconfigure and refine their knowledge in a community of practice.'

Service learning and reflective practice

SLTE programs usually provide some kind of field experiences that attempt to give their learner teachers some teaching practice. However, some language teacher educators are now beginning to realize that candidates may only obtain a formulaic understanding of TESOL rather than have any authentic experience in real classrooms because these experiences are very limited (Farrell, 2017). Thus some SLTE programs in the US have implemented what they call 'service-learning' in order to provide more authentic teaching experiences. Service learning really moves field experiences to the 'field'; or from traditional campus-based and formulaic presentation of programs to providing more authentic teaching experiences for their teacher candidates. Service learning seeks to mutually benefit both providers (TESOL programs) and recipients (schools) and because learning occurs in a context, it provides authentic experiences for learner teachers about the sociopolitical nature of teaching. The authenticity of service-learning provides opportunities for teachers to reflect in, on and for action (Farrell, 2015). Service learning has the following basic principles (adapted from Tomaš et al., 2017):

- *Need*: projects or partnerships revolve around an authentic need perceived by a community-based partner—typically a school;
- *Reciprocity*: the developed service is mutually beneficial to both service provider (TESOL teachers) and the school;
- *Reflection*: service providers must reflect on the experience and connect practical experience with theoretical knowledge in order to gain maximum benefit;
- *Civic engagement*: service-learning foregrounds civic awareness and engagement.

In the US, many of these experiences attempt to provide authenticity in the form of service-learning in after school programs. Some programs have the service learning experiences embedded in the TESOL Methods course and immediately following the service-learning experiences the teacher educator conducts TESOL methods course at that school (Colombo et al., 2017). In such a manner learner teachers are better able to make sense of practice through theory and connect theory to practice because service-learning occurs in such authentic settings and in addition, the recursive nature of teachers' theorizing, and an awareness of and sensitivity to the sociopolitical issues allows the teacher candidates to notice the way the context influences teachers' decision-making (Tomaš et al., 2017). Thus when pre-service teachers engage in service-learning they can not only enhance their teaching skills, but also learn how to reflect critically about less visible aspects of teaching such as the socio-political culture of the context in which they are teaching.

Writing and reflective practice

The act of writing has a built-in reflective mechanism; teachers must stop to think and organize their thoughts before writing and then decide on what to write. After this they can 'see' their thoughts and reflect on these for self-understanding and development (Farrell, 2013). Such reflective writing can include written accounts of teachers' thoughts, observations, beliefs, attitudes, and experiences about their practice both inside and outside the classroom (Farrell, 2013). Teachers can include records of incidents, problems, and insights that occurred during lessons in order to gain new understandings of their own learning and practices. Thus, when teachers take the time to write about their practice they can express their opinions, hypothesize about their practice and of course reflect later on what actually happened during their practice and compare results.

There are different modes of writing for reflection, some of which include teacher journals, and online writing in blogs, chats and forums. When teachers are writing as reflection on their professional practice, they can either write for themselves and keep it, or they can share it after writing. When they write for themselves, they can include their personal thoughts and feelings as well as facts about their practice. They can read these for later reflection with the idea that they can look for patterns over time on the contents of their writing. When they reflect on the patterns they notice in their journal writing, they can become more aware of issues of interest in their practice.

Hernandez (2015) reported on the benefits of reflective journal writing for both preservice TESOL teachers and their teacher educators. Hernandez used regular reflective journals and a written report on an observed class to see how preservice TESOL teachers could better understand SLA theory and observed that reflective writing provided valuable information about the impact of course materials and class activities to raise student teachers' awareness of their perceptions on SLA and on their philosophy of teaching. As Hernandez (2015: 147) remarked: 'The use of reflective writings allowed documentation of participants' awareness of their role to bring about change in students' lives, thus confirming that personal practical knowledge has a moral and emotional dimension as well.' However, as Mann and Walsh (2017: 18) have pointed out, a common problem with writing as reflection is that 'the focus of attention becomes the actual writing itself', and one result of this is that they can be faking what they write because of the demands of a TESOL course and the grading of this writing. This is a continuous issue in TESOL courses and some teacher educators have stopped grading these journals. Golombek (2015) for example, used journals as a course requirement but the journals were not graded. The pre-service TESOL teachers were asked to write a journal each week and email it to the instructor who would respond to their individual journals via email. In this manner the instructor hoped to foster their reflections as well as learn about what they were thinking and experiencing as they wrote about their expectations of an internship they were about to take up and their strengths and concerns as they embarked on their learning-to-teach experience. Thus, when incorporating writing as reflective practice, teacher educators are faced with the dilemma of deciding how much of the writing is really critically reflective and how much is mere description. Perhaps, teacher educators will need to provide examples of what *they* consider reflective writing so that learner teachers will be able to use this reflective activity effectively.

Writing has also been expanded to include online formats such as blogs, chats and forums in part to alleviate the above issue. Such online formats are easy to use (does not require understanding of HTML or web scripting), interactive and can be continuously updated (Yang, 2009). Indeed, some TESOL teachers report that online writing formats are better than discussions because teachers can challenge peers online easier than when discussing issues face-to-face (Yang, 2009).

Action research and reflective practice

Action research has a reflexive relationship with reflection; as Wallace (1991: 56–57) has noted, action research is 'an extension of the normal reflective practice of many teachers, but it is slightly more rigorous and might conceivably lead to more effective outcomes.' Action research involves some kind of systematic collection of information or data in a planned manner (some may say planned interventions), followed by some form of analysis of what is revealed by the information or data, then a formal reflection on the implications of these findings for possible further observation and then action (Burns, 2009). The general stages (cyclical) of the action research process are: plan (problem identification); research (literature review); observe (collecting data); reflect (analysis); and act (redefining the problem). Action research then for language teachers suggests that it serves to address and find solutions to particular problems in a teaching and learning situation and so it is undertaken to bring about change and improvement to a particular teaching practice.

Sowa (2009) encouraged preservice TESOL teachers to conduct action research projects together with course work in order to help them learn more about their English language learners. She reported that the learner teachers felt conducting actions such as research projects had given them 'the tools to conduct small research projects in their classrooms and to share their ideas with colleagues' (Sowa, 2009: 1029). Action research projects, as Sowa (2009: 1031) has observed, can help teachers to 'start reflecting more critically about their practice, particularly with respect to strategies they teach in the classroom to help all students learn.' In such a manner, learner-teachers can develop skills needed to investigate and analyze challenges they may face in their classrooms in the future (Farrell, 2018).

Critical incidents and reflective practice

No amount of study in L2 teacher education programs can fully prepare language teachers for dealing with the full range of issues that language teaching involves (Farrell & Baecher, 2017). Indeed, it is a fact that most teachers will encounter various critical incidents in their teaching. When such a critical incident occurs, it interrupts (or highlights) the taken-for-granted ways of thinking about teaching, and by analyzing such incidents teachers can examine the values and beliefs that underpin their perceptions about teaching. Richards & Farrell (2011) have pointed out that some of these issues, incidents or unforeseen events may arise from working with learners of different cultural, linguistic, and educational backgrounds; some can result from the intrinsic difficulties learning a new language entails; and some may be the result of work-ing with learners who have had difficult life experiences or who have pressing educational and other needs. SLTE programs should integrate more of these critical incidents and vignettes into their courses and materials so that learner teachers can get a glimpse of the real-world classroom challenges they will most certainly face when they begin their teaching careers (Farrell, 2015b).

In the field of TESOL Farrell (2013) has noted the positive effects when teachers analyze critical incidents. As he reported, teachers develop more awareness of how real practices can conflict with expectations and outcomes and as a result they can begin to explore assumptions that underlie their practice. In addition, Kiely and Davis (2010) also reported positive outcomes in TESOL when they used what they called a 'critical learning episode' from teachers' own practice (among other reflective instruments) and analyzed in a series of interactive contexts: co-analysis with a Continuing Professional Development (CPD) leader and discussion with all participating teachers in a series of workshops and in 'buddy' groups of two or three teachers. Kiely and Davis (2010) concluded that the experience for the teachers was overwhelmingly positive (in the context of a CPD program) with the collaborative analysis of these critical incidents because they developed greater awareness not only of teaching but also of social and interpersonal dimensions of the classroom.

Conclusion

There is growing research evidence within SLTE that encouraging TESOL teachers to engage in reflection is making a positive impact on their careers because teachers recognize the devel-opmental value and transformative potential in reflective activities. SLTE educators have various pedagogical tools at their disposal at the program and course level in order to encourage the habit of reflection. These include the use of technology, critical friendships, team teaching, peer coaching, dialoging, service learning, writing, action research and analysis of critical incidents to encourage reflection. These reflective activities need to be embedded into courses, activi-ties and assignments in a collaborative manner so that learner teachers can be prepared to face future challenges they will encounter in their teaching careers. In addition, SLTE educators must themselves be aware of the nature of reflection and the required attitudes that go along with becoming a reflective practitioner. It is not enough to encourage reflection though as SLTE educators themselves must model reflection by examining their own practices. Indeed, recent research in TESOL has suggested that if SLTE educators want teacher learners to notice that they (teacher educators) are modelling a methodology they want their learner teachers to practice when they become teachers, then SLTE educators must make such links overt through modelling for this realization to take place (Hanington & Devi Pillai, 2017). I agree with Wright (2010: 267) that the goal of SLTE is to produce 'reflective teachers, in a process which involves socio-cognitive demands to introspect and collaborate with others, and which acknowledges previous learning and life experience as a starting point for new learning.'

Further reading

Farrell, T. S. C. (2015b) *Promoting Teacher Reflection in Second Language Education: A Framework for TESOL Professionals.* New York: Routledge.

Taking the concept and the practice of reflective teaching forward, this book introduces a well-structured, flexible framework for use by teachers at all levels of development, from pre-service to novice to the most experienced. The framework outlines five levels of reflective practice—Philosophy; Principles; Theory-of-Practice; Practice; Beyond Practice—and provides specific techniques for teachers to implement each level of reflection in their work. Designed to allow readers to take either a deductive approach, moving from theory-into-practice, or an inductive approach where they start from a practice-into-theory position, the framework can be used by teachers alone, in pairs, or in a group.

Farrell, T. S. C. (2018) *Research on Reflective Practice in TESOL.* New York: Routledge.

In this comprehensive and detailed analysis of recent research on encouraging reflective practices in TESOL, Farrell demonstrates how this practice has been embraced within TESOL and how it continues to impact the field. Examining a vast array of studies through his own framework for reflecting on practice, Farrell's analysis comprises not only the intellectual and cognitive but also the spiritual, moral, and emotional aspects of reflection. Reflection questions at the end of each chapter provide a jumping-off point for researchers, scholars, and teachers to further consider and reflect on the future of the field. Providing a holistic picture of reflection, this book is an original compendium of essential research on philosophy and principles, instruments used in studies, and theory and practice.

Barnard, R. and Ryan, J. (eds) (2017) *Reflective Practice: Voices from the Field.* New York: Routledge.

Barnard and Ryan's (2017) collection contains reflective practice studies of TESOL teachers (preservice and inservice) on topics such as (collaborative) lesson planning, classroom observation, lesson transcripts, post-lesson discussions, journal writing, reflection on action, reflection in action, critical friends, and focus groups. The aim of the book is to explain a range of options for implementing the reflective practice cycle in educational settings in various international contexts. Written by international academics, these studies show how reflection can be interpreted in different cultural contexts.

Mann, S. and Walsh, S. (2017) *Reflective Practice in English Language Teaching.* New York: Routledge.

Mann and Walsh's (2017) book outlines an empirical, data-led approach to reflective practice and uses excellent examples of real data along with reflexive vignettes from a range of contexts in order to help teachers to reflect on their practices. Mann and Walsh also note the importance of dialogue as crucial for reflection as is allows for clarification, questioning and enhanced understanding.

Watanabe, A. (2016). *Reflective Practice as Professional Development Experiences of Teachers of English in Japan.* Bristol: Multilingual Matters.

Atsuko Watanabe (2016) book outlines a study of the reflective practices of seven inservice TESOL teachers in a high school setting, in Japan. Beginning with a series of uncomfortable teacher training sessions delivered to unwilling participants, the book charts the author's development of new methods of engaging her participants and making use of their own experiences and knowledge. Both an in-depth examination of reflective practice in the context of Japanese cultural conventions and a narrative account of the researcher's reflexivity in her engagement with the study, the book introduces the concept of 'the reflective continuum'—a non-linear journey that mirrors the way reflection develops in unpredictable and individual ways.

References

Aliakbari, M. and Nejad, A. M. (2013) 'On the Effectiveness of Team Teaching in Promoting Learners' Grammatical Proficiency'. *Canadian Journal of Education*, 36(3) 5–22.

Arslan, F. and Ilin, G. (2013) 'Effects of Peer Coaching for the Classroom Management Skills of Teachers'. *Journal of Theory & Practice in Education*, 9(1) 43–59.

Artigliere, M. and Baecher, L. (2017) 'Sink or swim: aligning training with classroom reality in ESL co-teaching', in Farrell, T. S. C. (ed.) *TESOL Voices: Insider Accounts of Classroom Life—Preservice Teacher Education*. Alexander, VA: TESOL Press.

Badiali, B. and Titus, N. E. (2010) 'Co-Teaching: Enhancing Student Learning Through Mentor-Intern Partnerships'. *School-University Partnerships*, 4(2) 74–80.

Baecher, L. (2012). 'Feedback from the Field: What Novice PreK–12 ESL Teachers Want to Tell TESOL Educators'. *TESOL Quarterly*, 46(3) 578–588.

Bambino, D. (2002) 'Critical Friends'. *Educational Leadership*, 59(6) 25–27.

Burns, A. (2009) 'Action research in second language teacher education', in Burns, A. and Richards, J. C. (eds) *The Cambridge Guide to Second Language Teacher Education*. New York: Cambridge: 289–297.

Chick, M. (2015) 'The Education of Language Teachers: Instruction or Conversation?'. *ELT Journal*, 69(3) 297–307.

Colombo, M., Brazil, K. and White, L. (2017) 'Reflections on service-learning', in Farrell, T. S. C. (ed.) *TESOL Voices: Insider Accounts of Classroom Life—Preservice Teacher Education*. Alexander, VA: TESOL Press.

Darling-Hammond, L. and Bransford, J. (eds) (2005) *Preparing Teachers for a Changing World: What Teachers Should Learn and be Able to Do*. San Francisco, CA: Jossey-Bass.

DelliCarpini, M. and Alonso, O. B. (2015) 'Teaching everything to no one and nothing to everyone: addressing the content in content based instruction', in Farrell, T. S. C. (ed.) *International Perspectives on English Language Teacher Education: Innovations from the Field*. Basingstoke: Palgrave Macmillan: 51–73.

Dewey, J. (1933) *How We Think: A Restatement of the Relation of Reflective Thinking to the Educative Process*. Boston, MA: Houghton-Mifflin.

Dugan, K. B. and Letterman, M. R. (2008) 'Student Appraisals of Collaborative Teaching'. *College Teaching*, 56(1) 11–15.

Dunne, F., Nave, B. and Lewis, A. (2000) 'Critical Friends Groups: Teachers Helping Teachers to Improve Student Learning'. *Phi Delta Kappa International Research Bulletin (CEDR)*, 28 9–12.

Faez, F. and Valeo, A. (2012) 'TESOL Teacher Education: Novice Teachers' Perceptions of their Preparedness and Efficacy in the Classroom'. *TESOL Quarterly*, 46(3) 450–471.

Faez, F., Cooke, S., Karas, M. and Vidwans, M. (2017) 'Examining the effectiveness of online discussion forums for teacher development', in Farrell, T. S. C. (ed.) *TESOL Voices: Insider Accounts of Classroom Life—Preservice Teacher Education*. Alexander, VA: TESOL Press.

Farr, F. (2015) 'English language teachers in further education: reflective practice with Web 2.0 technologies', in Farrell, T. S. C. (ed.) *International Perspectives on English Language Teacher Education: Innovations from the Field*. Basingstoke: Palgrave Macmillan.

Farr, F. and Riordan, E. (2017) 'Prospective and practising teachers discuss the theory-practice divide through blogs and e-portfolios', in Farrell, T. S. C. (ed.) *TESOL Voices: Insider Accounts of Classroom Life—Preservice Teacher Education*. Alexander, VA: TESOL Press.

Farrell, T. S. C. (2012) 'Novice-Service Language Teacher Development: Bridging the Gap Between Preservice and In-Service Education and Development'. *TESOL Quarterly*, 46(3) 435–449.

Farrell, T. S. C. (2013) 'Critical Incident Analysis Through Narrative Reflective Practice: A Case Study'. *Iranian Journal of Language Teaching Research*, 1(1) 79–89.

Farrell, T. S. C. (2014) *Reflective Practice in ESL Teacher Development Groups: From Practices to Principles*. Basingstoke: Palgrave Macmillan.

Farrell, T. S. C. (ed.) (2015a) *International Perspectives on English Language Teacher Education: Innovations from the Field*. Basingstoke: Palgrave Macmillan.

Farrell, T. S. C. (2015b) *Promoting Teacher Reflection in Second Language Education: A Framework for TESOL Professionals*. New York: Routledge.

Farrell, T. S. C. (2016) *From Trainee to Teacher: Reflective Practice for Novice Teachers*. London: Equinox.

Farrell, T. S. C. (ed.) (2017) *TESOL Voices: Insider Accounts of Classroom Life—Preservice Teacher Education*. Alexander, VA: TESOL Press.

Farrell, T. S. C. (2018) *Research on Reflective Practice in TESOL*. New York: Routledge.

Farrell, T. S. C. and Baecher, L. (2017) *Reflecting on Critical Incidents in Language Education*. London: Bloomsbury.

Freeman, D. (1994) 'Knowing into doing: teacher education and the problem of transfer', in Li, D., Mahony, D. and Richards, J. C. (eds) *Exploring Second Language Teacher Development*. Hong Kong: City University Press: 1–20.

Gan, Z. (2014) 'Learning from Interpersonal Interactions During the Practicum: A Case Study of Non-Native ESL Student Teachers'. *Journal of Education for Teaching*, 40(2) 128–139.

Goker, S. D. (2006) 'Impact of Peer Coaching on Self-Efficacy and Instructional Skills in TEFL Teacher Education'. *System*, 34 239–254.

Golombek, P. R. (2015) 'Redrawing the Boundaries of Language Teacher Cognition: Language Teacher Educators' Emotion, Cognition, and Activity'. *Modern Language Journal*, 99(3) 470–484.

Hanington, L. and Devi Pillai, A. (2017) 'Bridging the theory-practice gap in teaching writing in pre-service teacher education', in Farrell, T. S. C. (ed.) *TESOL Voices: Insider Accounts of Classroom Life—Preservice Teacher Education*. Alexander, VA: TESOL Press.

Hatton, N. and Smith, D. (1995) 'Reflection in Teacher Education: Towards Definition and Implementation'. *Teaching and Teacher Education*, 11(1) 33–49.

Hernandez, L. J. (2015) 'Making Sense of SLA Theories Through Reflection'. *Lenguaje*, 43(1) 137–158.

Johnson, K. E. (2009) *Second Language Teacher Education: A Sociocultural Perspective*. New York: Routledge.

Johnson, K. E. (2013) 'Innovation through teacher education programs', in Hyland, K. and Wong, L. (eds) *Innovation and Change in English Language Education*. New York: Routledge: 75–89.

Kabilan, M. K., Adlina, W. F. W. and Embi, M. A. (2011) 'Online Collaboration of English Language Teachers for Meaningful Professional Development Experiences'. *English Teaching: Practice and Critique*, 10(4) 94–115.

Kiely, R. and Davis, M. (2010) 'From Transmission to Transformation: Teacher Learning in English for Speakers of Other Languages'. *Language Teaching Research*, 14(3) 277–295.

Lakshmi, B. S. (2014) 'Reflective Practice Through Journal Writing and Peer Observation: A Case Study'. *Turkish Online Journal of Distance Education*, 15(4) 167–189.

Luo, W. (2014) 'An Exploration of Professional Development Programs for Teachers of Collaborative Teaching of EFL in Taiwan: A Case Study'. *Asia-Pacific Education Researcher*, 23(3) 403–412.

Mann, S. (2015) 'Using screen capture software to improve the value of feedback on academic assignments in teacher education', in Farrell, T. S. C. (ed.) *International Perspectives on English Language Teacher Education*. Basingstoke: Palgrave Macmillan: 160–180.

Mann, S. and Walsh, S. (2017) *Reflective Practice in English Language Teaching*. New York: Routledge.

Richards, J. C. and Farrell, T. S. C. (2005) *Professional Development for Language Teachers*. New York: Cambridge University Press.

Richards, J. C. and Farrell. T. S. C. (2011) *Teaching Practice: A Reflective Approach*. New York: Cambridge University Press.

Sowa, P. A. (2009) 'Understanding our Learners and Developing Reflective Practice: Conducting Action Research with English Language Learners'. *Teaching and Teacher Education: An International Journal of Research and Studies*, 25(8) 1026–1032.

Tang, E. L-Y. and Lam, C. (2014) 'Building an Effective Online Learning Community (OLC) in Blog-based Teaching Portfolios'. *The Internet and Higher Education*, 20 79–85.

Tang, E. L-Y., Lee, J. C. and Chun, C. K. (2012) 'Development of Teaching Beliefs and the Focus of Change in the Process of Pre-Service ESL Teacher Education'. *Australian Journal of Teacher Education*, 37(5) 90–107.

Tarone, E. and Allwright, D. (2005) 'Second language teacher learning and student second language learning: shaping the knowledge base', in Tedick, Diane J. (ed.) *Second Language Teacher Education*. Mahwah, NJ: Lawrence Erlbaum: 5–23.

Tomaš, Z., Moger, N., Park, A. and Specht, K. (2017) 'Enriching graduate TESOL methods and materials courses with academic service-learning pedagogy', in Farrell, T. S. C. (ed.) *TESOL Voices: Insider Accounts of Classroom Life—Preservice Teacher Education*. Alexander, VA: TESOL Press.

van Lier, L. (1994) 'Action Research'. *Sintagma*, 6 31–37.

Valencia, S. W. and Killion, J. P. (1988) 'Overcoming Obstacles to Teacher Change: Direction From School-based Efforts'. *Journal of Staff Development*, 9(2) 2–8.

Vo, L. T. and Nguyen, H. T. M. (2010) 'Critical Friends Group for EFL Teacher Professional Development'. *ELT Journal*, 64(2) 205–213.

Wachob, P. (2011) 'Critical Friendship Circles: The Cultural Challenge of Cool Feedback'. *Professional Development in Education*, 37(3) 353–372.

Wallace, M. J. (1991) *Teacher Training: A Reflective Approach*. Cambridge: Cambridge University Press.

Woodward, T. (2003) 'Loop Input'. *ELT Journal*, 57(3) 301–304.

Wright, T. (2010) 'Second Language Teacher Education: Review of Recent Research on Practice'. *Language Teaching*, 43(3) 259–296.

Yang, S. (2009) 'Using Blogs to Enhance Critical Reflection and Community of Practice'. *Educational Technology & Society*, 12(2) 11–21.

Yang, P. (2013) 'Two Heads are Better Than One: Team Teaching in TESOL Internship'. *Kalbų Studijos*, 23 113–125.

4

ICT and English language teacher education

Opportunities, challenges and experiences

Amy Lightfoot

Introduction

In much the same way as ICT (Information and Communications Technology) provides opportunities to access high quality resources for language learning, it has enormous potential to support English language teacher education. However, perhaps not surprisingly, there is considerably more research and literature written about the uses and potential of technology for learning English (and other subjects) than there is about its effectiveness (or otherwise) for teachers' professional development.

Through a growing number of platforms (e.g. online, mobile, social media, TV and radio), teachers can access resources and tools to develop their skills and subject knowledge. This is of particular relevance for teachers working in countries where the standard of more traditional opportunities for CPD is of poor quality and does not sufficiently prepare teachers to effectively support learning in the classroom. Through a variety of mediums and platforms, technology has the potential to offer teachers access to high quality content and resources which may help to bridge the gaps in their learning and development (Aslam et al. 2016).

The use of technology to augment learning for both students and teachers is clearly articulated in several globally utilised frameworks of continuing professional development for English and other subject teachers. For example, the British Council's framework incorporates 12 'professional practices' in which teachers are expected to demonstrate competence and of these, two have direct relevance to this area of work. *Integrating ICT* largely focuses on the technical skills needed to be able to use ICT with learners, but also the knowledge needed to be able to identify and assess the quality of learning resources available online. The professional practice *Taking responsibility for professional development* specifically includes a reference to using technology for this purpose. In another example, the EQUALS European Profiling Grid (2013) incorporates *Digital media* as one of three 'enabling competences' for teachers, which focuses on the development of skills and knowledge to use technology with learners (and in later development phases to train other teachers to do the same). The Cambridge English Teaching Framework identifies *Using digital resources* as a sub-component of the broader area of *Teaching, learning and assessment*, focusing on supporting learners' language development in and outside the class. However, using technology is not explicitly mentioned in the framework's category of *Professional development and values*.

Gaible and Burns (2005: 2) refer to the potential for the use of ICT in teacher education to be 'a catalyst for new forms of teaching and learning' in and outside the classroom, with application for teachers working in any subject domain or sector. In this chapter, priority will be given to examples and commentary relating to English subject teachers working in public (government-funded) school education systems, as opposed to those working within private language institutes. However, in line with Gaible and Burns' assertion, it is anticipated that many of the principles will be transferable to different contexts.

When considering how technology is used in teacher education, we can identify three key areas worthy of investigation and comment:

1. Teachers or teacher educators **using technology to facilitate professional development**, i.e. providing access to content, resources and tools (referred to by Gaible and Burns as 'a delivery system' – 2005: 2).
2. Teachers **developing skills and knowledge which will enable them to appropriately incorporate technology in the face-to-face classroom.** This includes both the technical skills required and understanding of effective pedagogical application (Carlson and Gadio 2002).
3. Teachers **developing skills and knowledge to deliver teaching and learning through the medium of technology – usually at a distance – through online or other digital platforms** (e.g. Skype; Moodle; etc.) For example, Xiao and Zhao (2011) discuss the professional development needs facing teachers who utilise technology (in this case radio) to provide English language teaching to their learners.

This chapter will focus predominantly on the first of these areas, with some brief discussion on the crossover in skills development for the use of technology with students in the classroom (face-to-face or otherwise). It explores the various ways that ICT could be used to augment and support teacher development, alongside a summary of the benefits, key issues and challenges that are specific to these modes of engagement. Three case studies will be presented and discussed, exemplifying the various ways that technology can be utilised in this regard. Through these, we consider the enabling factors that might be prioritised by individuals, institutions and governments when considering the deployment of technology to facilitate teacher development, to increase potential impact on teaching and learning.

Benefits of ICT for professional development

Technology affords a range of benefits for teachers' professional development, regardless of the location in which they are living and working. While those in higher resource contexts will have the greatest opportunities for maximising its potential, there has been considerable focus on the advantages of using technology to provide access to high quality resources, content and development opportunities for teachers in otherwise low-resource contexts.

ICT provides access to content and curriculum-relevant resources, including 'multimedia simulations of good teacher-training practice'. It enables access to resources developed by and for teachers all over the world, but can also be used to provide and share content among local groups of teachers quickly and easily – providing the requisite ICT infrastructure is in place and accessible. The key benefits described here can be summarised according to the impact on a) access, flexibility and choice with regard to CPD; b) opportunities for collaboration, community and inclusion and c) technology's role in improving administrative processes and transferable digital skills.

Access, flexibility and choice

For many, technology removes barriers to accessing content which is no longer 'constrained to a particular time or place' (Ally et al. 2014: 48). Ally et al. (2014: 50) cite research in sub-Saharan Africa which has found that 'teachers who own laptops are likely to engage in informal learning at their own pace, on their own time.' As technology can enable professional learning to take place closer to the site of teaching, it also follows that teachers may be more likely to apply what they are learning in the classroom and to access solutions to challenges 'just in time' as opposed to 'just in case'. Gaible and Burns (2005: 15–16) refer to this as a shift away from 'standardised teacher professional development' towards that which is 'site-based' and 'self-directed'. They assert that 'site-based teacher professional development, since it addresses locally based needs and reflects local conditions, should be the cornerstone of teacher development across the education system' (ibid.) – although the process involved in making this shift should not be underestimated.

Technology can be plugged into existing programmes of teacher development, amplifying current provision – e.g. in a blended mode – and providing ongoing support beyond a face-to-face component (Aslam et al. 2016). Whether or not used in conjunction with face-to-face input, the use of technology can help to shift the power, control and agency to the teacher to make decisions about where to place their focus. For example, Iris Connect, Onvu Learning and others are working with schools and teachers to use video technology which can enable self-observation, reflection and developmental discussions with peers as well as mentors or supervisors. This shifts the power away from a single observer to the teacher and enables him/her to more easily reflect on his/her own practice. This is in line with recommendations in much of the literature on teacher education, which highlights the need to move away from a purely top-down approach, including where training is delivered in lock-step mode or without input or choice from the teachers (Acedo 2014). This also supports the professional practice of *Taking responsibility for professional development* as described earlier.

Collaboration, community and inclusion

Digital platforms are about much more than just access to repositories of content. They also enable significant opportunities for teachers to connect and collaborate (Ally et al. 2014). These platforms can enable more individualised trainer–trainee and peer collaboration within a fixed group but also much wider connections to other educators around the world (Carlson and Gadio 2002: 119). More traditional approaches to providing information to teachers arguably offer less of these opportunities. As Laurillard (2016: 2) writes, 'publishing a book is unquestion-ably an instructivist approach to professional development.'

While there is the potential for technology-mediated teacher education programmes to deny opportunities to those who do not have the necessary skills or ICT access, they can also function to improve the inclusivity of professional development. For example, ICT-based resources can be of particular benefit to women in countries where travelling away from home to attend residential development programmes challenges societal norms and expectations (Aslam et al. 2016). Teachers who have sensory or other impairments can also have greater access to development opportunities through these platforms, where adjustments can be made to the way content is delivered or displayed to accommodate differing needs. There is, however, a need for greater exploitation of these affordances by online CPD providers; currently very few offer accessibility options.

Improving administrative processes and transferable digital skills

Using technology to improve class administration and record keeping can enable a higher degree of accuracy, for example with inputting and analysing assessment results. It can also reduce the time spent on administration and reporting, leaving more time for focusing on processes and content that more directly improve the quality of teaching and learning that takes place in the classroom.

Utilising technology for the purposes of professional development also has the effect of improving teachers' digital skills in general which can lead to more appropriate and effective use of technology with their learners (Ally et al. 2014). In contexts where learners can be classified as 'digital natives', teacher familiarity with current technological practices and software can also help them to better understand this important dimension of their learners' lives.

Clearly there are a number of benefits to the use of technology for teachers' professional development, with more likely to emerge as technology advances (e.g. state or school systems more formally adopting CPD tracking systems which will credit teachers for their involvement in communities of practice or online webinars or courses, further incentivising their involvement). Overall, it enables access to a wider range of content, resources and fellow professionals, allowing greater choice and flexibility on the part of the teacher. However, there are several issues inherent in the shift towards a focus on technology. Some of these will be explored in the following section.

Key issues and challenges

Despite the many useful affordances and features that technology offers, it is not a silver bullet which will solve problems inherent within an existing teacher education system. It is important to recognise the variety of factors that will influence the uptake and success of any professional development programme, with or without the use of digital tools and platforms. These factors exist on multiple levels (system, school and personal) and are interrelated as depicted in Figure 4.1.

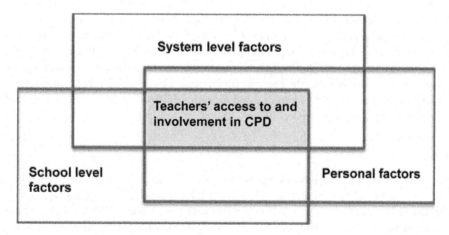

Figure 4.1   The interaction between factors affecting teachers' access to and involvement in CPD

Source: Adapted from content in Kwakman (2003); Cameron et al. (2013) and McMillan et al. (2016). First published in Lightfoot (2016).

Carlson and Gadio (2002: 119) remind us that 'designing and implementing successful teacher professional development programmes in the application of technology is neither easy nor inexpensive.' The complexity of issues surrounding if and how a programme will be undertaken, particularly with the use of technology, is an important reality check highlighting the need for individuals, institutional heads and government personnel not to succumb to the siren-like qualities of the use of ICTs, including the idea that its implementation will transcend related issues that beset any programme of CPD.

There are many accounts of where technology has been rolled out – often with significant financial investment – with very little return in terms of improvements in teachers' or students' knowledge or skills (see Trucano 2010 for an interesting list of worst practice in ICT integration). However, this presents an opportunity to learn from others' failures, by identifying how similar mistakes can be avoided in future. This section outlines a review of the various challenges reported in the literature that accompany the implementation of technology and summarises five areas where issues most commonly arise: access (or infrastructure), skills (or digital literacy), motivation, relevance and contextualisation.

Access

The challenge of access is arguably decreasing as computers, internet bandwidth and mobile technologies become more prevalent and less expensive. However, for teachers working in low-resource contexts and arguably with the greatest need for increased access to quality professional development opportunities, issues of access remain. These can vary from a complete lack of hardware, to being denied access to school-based hardware because of maintenance problems and further to poor bandwidth or outdated operating systems. Obondoh and Riechi (2013) and others refer to huge wastage in the procurement of ICT hardware which is then not used or is not maintained. It is important to note that issues with technology not working as intended (or not being available) are not confined to less developed contexts. Ally et al. (2014) report on projects in Europe where the introduction of classroom technology failed during the pilot because of poor connectivity and low skills in ICT.

Recently, there has been significant focus on the potential of mobile devices to bring professional development and other learning content to teachers and students, particularly in providing English language practice opportunities. Ally et al. (2014: 44) report that in some developing countries, people are 'bypassing the phases of personal computer and notebook ownership and moving directly to mobiles'. However, the same authors also highlight research indicating that people are not necessarily using their mobile for learning. This relates closely to the question of whether or not people have the awareness and necessary skills (or interest) to be able to exploit the technology for purposes such as CPD.

Skills

Research undertaken in South Asia suggests that some English language teachers lack the confidence and/or digital literacy skills to fully exploit the opportunities for professional development that technology affords or use it effectively with their students (British Council 2015). A similar picture has been found for teachers elsewhere, particularly – but not exclusively – in developing countries (e.g. Sadaf et al. 2016). Clearly there are some basic technical skills that are required to be able to locate and navigate through content available online or through any technology-enabled platform, and in some countries, teachers do not have (or have not had) an adequate introduction to the potential for these resources. Initial teacher training often contains little to no focus on the professional practice of *Integrating ICT* or digital literacy skills in general. Writing about teacher education in India, Bose (2013: 121) states that '[technology knowledge] is neither compulsory nor provided in a holistic manner [...] it is also not imparted in the context of pedagogy and content.' In addition to the more basic skills for using technology, there are also several 'soft' skills which are necessary for its effective use.

First, the quantity of resources available online is very large and increasing; this risks overwhelming teachers and teacher educators who need skills to filter through the content to identify quality and the appropriacy for their context. This involves critical thinking skills and an ability to be able to assess whether a source of information and ideas is credible. Some teachers – particularly those new to the profession or for whom the concept of CPD is less familiar – may struggle to ascertain what is and isn't good quality.

Second, the opportunity to seek out and work together with others to share ideas and learn is obvious on the surface, but again not always fully exploited. As highlighted earlier, there is significant potential of online courses and content to provide opportunities for collaboration and connection between groups of teachers. This is particularly important and useful for those who otherwise work in relative isolation. However, some research has shown that full engagement with these opportunities is relatively rare. Laurillard (2016) reports on evidence showing that the functions that enable discussion on MOOCs are much more often used for simple description as opposed to critical reflection and debate among participants. There is clearly a need to carefully construct tasks which foster this type of interaction, as opposed to assuming it will happen organically.

Similarly, Xiao and Zhao (2011) highlight that while establishing communities of practice is a good thing, it's important to recognise that they are not always used as the sites of learning that they are intended to be, with lots of 'small talk' and off-topic discussion taking place. This is supported by Parnham et al. (2018) who discuss similar issues in WhatsApp-based communities of practice established as part of a teacher development project in western India. Nevertheless, Parnham et al. (2018: 3) also highlight that this more social interaction can promote 'positive group dynamics' and 'build the trust and understanding within the group which [can be] useful in encouraging more members of the group to participate, share experiences and respond to others.' This is supported by Trust (2017) who discusses the complex sociocultural norms and rules which can govern the engagement (or otherwise) of teachers in an online learning environment.

Motivation

Motivation levels of teachers are a crucial factor in the uptake of any professional development initiative, whether or not it includes the use of technology. Guskey (2010, cited in McMillan et al. 2016: 152) referring to teacher education initiatives where little change in practice is seen, asserts that 'one of the reasons why teacher professional development has not resulted in changed classroom practice and student learning outcomes is that the factors which motivate teachers in their practice have not been considered.'

A teacher's motivation to participate in CPD can be influenced by a variety of issues including their social and cultural background and their beliefs about education in general. As Brinkmann (2015: 344) highlights, '[the promotion of] new pedagogical methods will only be effective if teachers have thoroughly accepted the assumptions underlying the innovation.' Where teachers have not previously been exposed to any form of technology as learners (i.e. at school or in higher education), immediate acceptance of it as a tool for their professional development (or for use in the classroom) is unlikely. It requires a considerable paradigm shift for teachers to accept new methodologies and ideas when they themselves have not experienced them (Banks and Dheram 2013). Similarly, if they are in general not aware or supportive of the concept of continuing professional development then ensuring participation in any programme that aims to enhance this is a key challenge – regardless of whether it utilises technology (UNESCO 2014).

Personal circumstances and competing demands on teachers' time are also highly significant factors affecting whether teachers will engage with a professional development programme mediated through technology or otherwise. Teaching is well-known to be a 'time poor' profession and clearly 'professional development needs time' (Xiao and Zhao 2011: 61). In many contexts, teachers undergo 'a constant negotiation […] between home and school activities' (Kirk 2013: 156), juggling the requirements of their role within teaching hours along with expectations to plan, mark, report, etc. outside of the school day.

There are also some further motivational issues which particularly arise when technology is introduced. In 2002, Carlson and Gadio suggested that these include a reluctance to change teaching and learning practices that teachers already feel comfortable with; not seeing the advantages or benefits that ICT integration can bring and feeling threatened by new ways of working. This is likely to still be a considerable obstacle for some teachers a decade and a half later. This may also be the case if the systems for technology-enabled CPD are in addition to other digital systems for marking or reporting, for example: another thing for teachers to have to accommodate.

However, it is also important to identify that there are several ways that the use of technology specifically can incentivise teachers in new ways and help to increase motivation for participating in CPD generally. For example, as outlined earlier, technology can enable choice more easily than face-to-face training modalities. A sense of agency in terms of deciding what topics they will focus on, when and where, is usually viewed positively by teachers (McMillan et al. 2016). The popularity of social media can also be leveraged for professional development – particularly in the formation of communities of practice. Being able to demonstrate as well as access expertise through these existing networks can be a motivating factor for teachers (Goodyear et al. 2014). Similarly, features of online platforms such as digital badges (which can be shared on social media platforms) and instant assessment on the completion of tasks can also encourage teacher participation.

Contextualisation

While much has been written about the potential for ICT to bring quality learning opportunities to those who need them the most (i.e. working in otherwise resource-poor contexts), evidence to date suggests that this ambition is some way from being realised. For example, Laurillard (2016: 1) reports that so far MOOCs are attracting 'highly qualified professionals', not the disadvantaged learners who could arguably benefit the most. This could be because of an interaction between some or all of the factors described above, but there are also concerns that because of the wide reach of technology-enabled initiatives, there may be a tendency or preference to take a 'one size fits all' approach. The time, skills and (often) money required to develop a high-quality online course cannot be underestimated. The return on investment for creating a resource like this will likely be greater the larger the numbers of teachers reached, and therefore the content will not necessarily be contextualised or relevant to the specific need and interests of the teachers within a niche group. It is also likely that the content creators and/or moderators will be operating remotely, and often asynchronously, without the face-to-face interaction that enables more immediate adaptation to the local context when needs arise.

In addition to considerations around the applicability of the content, assumptions around how the teachers will or won't engage, when and with whom, need to be reviewed according to the context in which they live and work. Programme providers also need to ensure that using technology to interact more directly with teachers doesn't reduce buy-in and support from other stakeholders within the system. School leaders and education officers are still key to the process for ensuring the programmes are successful (i.e. by resulting in measurable improvements in classroom teaching and learning), and the introduction of technology should not absolve them of this responsibility.

Despite the many and varied challenges that exist, there is still clearly a role for technology to play in improving access to quality CPD opportunities for teachers and others within the education system. As well as providing high quality but potentially impersonal input, technology also affords opportunities for high quality mentoring, coaching and tutoring – including through video-based observation platforms and online communities of practice. In the following section we will explore in more detail some of the different modalities available, illustrated by case studies of ICT-integration in teacher education programmes.

Modalities for teacher education through ICT

In 2005, Wagner lamented that 'when asked about the role of ICTs in the [Education for All] process, the consensus at most development agencies seems to be: there is no role' (p xi). Much has changed over the last decade, with increasing attention being paid by governments and funders to the potential role of ICT for teacher development. This is in part due to the growing prevalence of mobile technologies, reference to which was largely absent from Wagner's 2005 report.

There has been a significant shift over the last ten years to mobile technologies functioning as a repository of content and information, providing access to information and groups (communities of practice) and a multifunctional tool in itself which can be used in a variety of ways in the classroom or training room (e.g. video and audio recording). The proliferation of mobile phones has functioned as a significant leveller in terms of providing access to information and resources for teachers and others (Ally et al. 2014).

However, with the various challenges discussed earlier in mind, we cannot assume that mobile technologies in themselves offer us a quick solution. To be successful, any professional development programme will need to ensure high quality, accessible content, relevant to the context of the target teachers which requires flexible and adaptable design and multiple modes of delivery, integrated into a broader context and climate that supports teachers' CPD. As identified by Obondoh and Riechi (2013: 6):

> A comprehensive teacher training programme will […] make optimal blended use of print, audio/radio, video, television, computers, the internet, peer-group face-to-face contact and more traditional forms of classroom learning if they are to be successful.

A teachers' professional development is likely to operate in multiple modes, with technology supporting progress in different ways, at different points throughout the ongoing process. The following list describes the key ways that technology platforms and tools can support the professional development of English and other subject teachers.

- Technology for the assessment and evaluation of teachers' skills and knowledge.
- Digital content and resources for teachers' self-access (moderated or unmoderated; standalone resources or linked modules and courses).

- Digitally enabled repositories or portfolio tools.
- Digitally mediated remote one-to-one mentoring and support.
- Informal and formal collaborative learning networks or communities of practice (particularly to support geographically dispersed groups).

The following case studies exemplify how technology is being used in some of these ways and integrated into wider programmes of English language teacher development. While we are focusing on the specific uses of technology, it is important to note that in each case the digital tools augment a wider programme with higher level objectives around improving quality in the classroom.

Technology for the assessment and evaluation of teachers' skills and knowledge

Case study: The British Council's online self-assessment tool

The British Council's continuing professional development framework for teachers outlines 12 professional practices in which teachers are expected to demonstrate competence. The framework is used in teacher development projects around the world, with content and resources tagged to each area. As teachers gain experience, they have different needs and interests with regard to the 12 identified areas of focus. This is reflected by the use of four levels within the framework: *awareness, understanding, engagement* and *integration*. The framework design enables teachers to be placed at different levels against the different professional practices (resulting in a 'jagged profile'), moving away from a linear representation of teacher development.

A self-assessment tool has been developed to help teachers identify which levels they map against for nine of the professional practices. This tool is available online and via mobile, where the results enable the teachers to link through to appropriate content and courses on the British Council's websites (e.g. www.teachinigenglish.org.uk) It is also built into programmes such as the MOOC delivered in partnership with UCL Institute of Education on the FutureLearn platform: *Becoming a better teacher*, to facilitate the reflective practice that the course advocates.

At the end of 2017, over 8,000 teachers had used the self-assessment tool. Along with helping them to focus on their developmental needs, this has also provided a rich set of data that has been closely analysed. This data has provided useful insights into general perceptions of strengths and weaknesses in relation to the nine areas, along with how this interacts with teachers' backgrounds and contexts. For example, two areas where teachers generally have low confidence in their skills and knowledge is in assessing learning and promoting twenty-first-century skills (Borg and Edmett 2018).

The use of technology to enable the kind of reference point provided by the self-assessment tool is clearly appropriate. It enables both teacher reflection and support for navigating through the wide range of content available online and importantly provides data and evidence which can be used to shape future initiatives and programming.

Feedback from those taking the survey has been largely positive, but has also questioned how possible it is to create a framework and tool of this type which can have relevance and use in all the varied contexts around the world (Borg and Edmett 2018). This supports the need to promote the flexibility of the CPD framework – not all the professional practices need to be considered when working with groups of teachers, and in some cases some additional areas may also need to be included.

For further examples of technology-enabled assessment and evaluation tools for English language teachers see:

- Cambridge English Digital Framework: https://thedigitalteacher.com/
- Framework comparison: https://englishagenda.britishcouncil.org/continuing-professional-development/cpd-managers/continuing-professional-development-cpd-frameworks-english-language-teachers

Digital content and resources for teachers' self-access (moderated or unmoderated)

Case study: Teachers Online Professional Development Initiative (TOPDI)

In January 2018, the British Council conducted a pilot programme, offering 1,000 free places to government school teachers in India on myEnglish courses. myEnglish is a fully online course that is primarily offered to young aspiring adults who seek to improve their English language proficiency to improve their employment prospects. However, there is also a strong demand for English language development among school teachers in India, and widespread recognition of the need to find cost-effective and high-quality means to achieve this goal. The pilot offered the opportunity to test a model of online delivery.

It is important to highlight that teachers were offered places free of cost and with no link to official professional development requirements stipulated by the state government: both of these conditions may have had an effect on the pilot outcomes.

Teachers were offered the opportunity via channels of communication operated by the state governments where the British Council has previously been engaged in various programmes of continuing professional development. A total of 4,401 teachers registered their interest for the course by completing an online survey. This acted as an initial informal assessment of the potential participants' digital skills. One thousand and forty-four teachers reported the minimum level of access to technology that the course requires (stable internet connection; a laptop or PC) and enough time available to participate effectively. Of this subset, 1,159 teachers completed the online placement test and 571 were allocated a space on a course.

Courses ran for six weeks between February and April 2018, with a total of 299 teachers successfully completing their course. As 52 per cent of the total number of teachers placed onto courses, this compares favourably to reported industry standards for online learning. Teachers reported high degrees of satisfaction with the course, largely due to the quality of interactions with the course tutors.

A high proportion of the teachers reported increases in their confidence in terms of their own English language use and online study skills. In focus group discussions, there was some low-level evidence of learning transfer into classroom practice, but this is an area which needs further exploration in order to identify the extent to which participation in a programme of this type can positively impact on teaching quality.

For further examples of technology-enabled content and resources for English language teachers see:

- The online Oxford Teachers' Academy: https://elt.oup.com/feature/global/oxford_teachers_academy/?cc=global&selLanguage=en
- Teacher Training Videos: www.teachertrainingvideos.com and https://vilte.warwick.ac.uk
- British Council MOOCs aimed at English language teachers on the Future-Learn platform: www.futurelearn.com/partners/british-council
- TESSA and TESS India Open Educational Resources: www.tessafrica.net/ and www.tess-india.edu.in/

One-to-one mentoring and support

Case study: Ceibal en Inglés

Plan Ceibal is an initiative undertaken by the government of Uruguay to try to improve teaching and learning in schools. It includes uses of different technologies to achieve these goals, including the distribution of one laptop per child. One aspect of the programme – *Ceibal en Inglés* – has been developed and delivered in partnership with the British Council. In *Ceibal en Inglés*, classroom teachers are supported by 'remote teachers', specifically to improve English language learning. The remote teachers are language teaching experts based around the world, beamed into the Uruguayan classrooms in over 500 schools through video conferencing technology. A considerable investment has been made in hardware and much of the content is derived from British Council repositories. The remote teachers interact with their classes in real time, with the classroom teacher facilitating on the ground.

Importantly, there is a significant focus on the skills of the classroom teachers, working in collaboration with the remote cadre, including some development of English language proficiency. The remote and classroom teachers co-plan the lessons and the teachers work through moderated online courses, webinars, workshops and mentoring sessions to develop their content and pedagogical knowledge. Teachers are also observed by a 'quality manager' during the year with developmental and evaluative feedback. Results have shown comparable and, in some cases, improved levels of language learning for those participating students, relative to students whose classroom English teacher has the required level of language proficiency (Brovetto 2018). This project is unique in the way that it utilises technology to develop students' skills while at the same time facilitating the professional development of the teachers involved.

For further examples of technology-enabled mentoring and support for English language teachers see:

- The Open University/BBC Media Action's *English in Action* project in Bangladesh: www.open.ac.uk/about/international-development/ido-asia/EIA
- Examples of case studies and research about the use and impact of video-based observation: www.irisconnect.com/uk/impact/research/ and www.onvulearning.com/evidence

These case studies illustrate some of the possibilities for utilising technology for teacher education, in ways that augment existing programmes while taking into account the context, prior knowledge and specific needs of the target audience. Importantly, they involve technology to solve some of the challenges faced when trying to support professional development on the ground, providing opportunities for learning that would otherwise be out of reach. But given the various challenges that exist, what can we extrapolate from exploring why these initiatives have been largely successful? In the next section we will review some of these key facilitating factors.

Enabling conditions

So far in this chapter we have explored the various potential benefits and common challenges that relate to the use of technology for language teachers' professional development, along with several examples. In this section we will identify and summarise the factors which appear to create appropriate conditions for the effective use of technology. As Trucano (2005: 35) writes, 'the existence of ICTs does not transform teacher practices in and of itself. However, ICTs can enable teachers to transform their teacher practices, given a set of enabling conditions.' The use of digital tools and content can support professional development programmes if certain parameters are in place, many of which link back to the challenges outlined earlier.

Positive attitudinal shifts

Positive teacher attitudes towards using technology for professional development purposes is important for the success of any programme in which it is used. This can be supported by the use of technologies that are familiar to the teachers and by clear communication about the benefits of the chosen format, content or platform. Eshtehardi (2014) argues that teacher educators play a key role in inculcating teachers' positive attitudes towards ICT and technology in general and as outlined earlier, it is important that these attitudes are developed right from the pre-service training stage of a teacher's career.

Skill development

Teachers need to learn the skills for effective critical engagement using online and other digitally enabled platforms, in the same way that they will have learned appropriate interaction patterns and norms for effective engagement in the face-to-face training context. Furthermore, content designers need to actively build in tasks where teachers co-create outputs (Laurillard 2016). In the *Ceibal en Inglés* project described earlier, participating teachers (Classroom and Remote) needed to develop skills for co-planning and co-teaching through video-conferencing and other digital communication tools.

Importantly, it is not just teachers that need to learn new skills for engaging with professional development through digital platforms: teacher educators and course designers who may previously have excelled at creating or facilitating development opportunities need to ensure they stay up to date with the functionality of new platforms and tools. Similarly, technology developers who may be less aware of teachers' specific needs and contexts must not assume that they can adopt approaches for development that have worked for those in other professional sectors, or indeed with learners in the classroom.

Support and leadership

Shifting from a more centralised or standardised approach to professional development to one that is more personalised potentially puts greater onus on individuals to pursue and complete activities. To support this, it is imperative to have buy-in from stakeholders at all levels of the institution and education system. This includes school administrators, government education officers, school principals, teacher educators, teachers, parents and the learners themselves. Obondoh and Riechi (2013:5) also emphasise the need for 'strategic leadership' (at policy level) to make the integration of ICT and teacher education successful.

Carlson and Gadio (2002) suggest several extrinsic and intrinsic motivators to encourage teachers to engage more with technology for their professional development (and to develop their ICT skills for using technology in the classroom), all of which remain relevant today.

- Certification by the Ministry of Education (of both programmes as a whole and teachers who complete them – this certification can also be linked to salary and promotion).

- Formal allocation of time for completing professional development activities. This is of particular importance for those that are self-directed so that teachers do not assume that it should be completed in their own time.
- Highlighting the professional satisfaction that can be gained from connecting and collaborating with colleagues from elsewhere.
- Establishing pathways to enable teachers to become champions or trainers on technology-enabled professional development courses, or developers of content.

All of these factors underline the need to view any professional development initiative as a holistic process with many competing and interrelated factors affecting the success or otherwise of such a programme. Stakeholders at all levels of the system will need to adapt their thinking and behaviour whenever new platforms and modalities are introduced.

Conclusion

In the same way that technology is affecting the role of teachers in the classroom – driving a more facilitative role where content is curated and shared with their learners – so too is this a possibility for teacher education. Perhaps even more so for teachers than learners, technology allows the decentralisation of training and development and enables teachers to become architects of their own professional pathways – assuming they have the skills and infrastructure needed to access and navigate through the content.

Perhaps the biggest potential for ICT in teacher education lies not in providing alternative modalities for face-to-face training input, but rather in harnessing its affordances to enable new approaches to individualised teacher education. For example, by allowing new ways for teachers to reflect on and record their practice and development through video-based observation and providing access to new communities of practice and shared learning.

If we accept that there are considerable benefits to the use of technology as outlined throughout this chapter, then it is imperative that its use as an education tool is modelled and incorporated into teacher education programmes. This integration has the triple effect of 1) developing teachers own digital literacy and technical skills; 2) providing first-hand experience of learning using technology, enabling greater empathy with their learners who are likely to do the same; and 3) improving teachers subject and pedagogical knowledge as a result of experiences using these platforms.

Further reading

For more information about the British Council, Cambridge Assessment English and EQUALS frameworks of continuing professional development see here: www.teachingenglish.org.uk/sites/teacheng/files/joint_framework_statement.pdf.

For some examples of how teachers – usually in low resource contexts – are using technology for professional development and in their classrooms in India, see Motteram, G. (ed.) (2017) *Teaching and Technology: Case Studies from India*. New Delhi: British Council. www.britishcouncil.in/continuing-professional-development.

A series of guides to using technology for professional development and in the classroom, developed by the British Council: www.britishcouncil.in/teach/resources-for-teachers/technology-teachers-series.

References

Acedo, C. (2014) 'Mobile Learning for Literacy, Teacher Training and Curriculum Development'. *Prospects*, 44 1–4.

Ally, M., Grimus, M. and Ebner, M. (2014) 'Preparing Teachers for a Mobile World, to Improve Access to Education'. *Prospects*, 44 43–59.

Aslam, A., Naseer, F., Quereshi, J. and Bari, F. (2016) *Learning While You Teach – Integrating Technology into Teacher Training*. Lahore: SAHE.

Banks, F. and Dheram, P. (2013) 'India: Committing to change', in Moon, B. (ed.) *Teacher Education and the Challenge of Development*. Abingdon: Routledge: 76–90.

Borg, S. and Edmett, A. (2018) 'Developing a self-assessment tool for English Language Teachers'. *Language Teaching Research*, doi: 10.1177/1362168817752543.

Bose, S. (2013) 'Integrated Teacher Education Programme for Open Distance Learning: A Model for Development and Integration'. *Open Learning: The Journal of Open, Distance and e-Learning*, 28(2) 120–134.

Brinkmann, S. (2015) 'Learner-Centred Education Reforms in India: The Missing Piece of Teachers' Beliefs'. *Policy Futures In Education*, 13(3) 342–359.

British Council (2015) *Technology for Professional Development: Access, Interest and Opportunity for Teachers of English in South Asia*. Available online: <www.britishcouncil.in/sites/default/files/digital_teachers_report_final_low_res.pdf> (accessed 29 April 2017).

Brovetto, C. (2018) 'Ceibal en Inglés: integration of technology and pedagogy for equity in education in Uruguay', in Fernandez, J. and Ruiz, F. J. R. (eds) *Innovation for Systemic Improvement for Quality English Language Teaching in Latin America*. Mexico City: British Council.

Cameron, S., Mulholland, J. and Branson, C. (2013) 'Professional Learning in the Lives of Teachers: Towards a New Framework of Conceptualising Teacher Learning'. *Asia-Pacific Journal of Teacher Education*, 41(4) 377–397.

Carlson, S. and Gadio, C. T. (2002) 'Teacher professional development in the use of technology', in Haddad, W. D. and Draxler, A. (eds) *Technologies for Education: Potentials, Parameters, and Prospects*. Paris and Washington, DC: UNESCO and the Academy for Educational Development. Available online: <www.ictinedtoolkit.org/usere/library/tech_for_ed_chapters/08.pdf> (accessed 1 October 2017).

Eshtehardi, R. (2014) 'Pro-ELT: A Teacher-Training Blended Approach'. *Advances in Language and Literary Studies*, 5(5) 106–110.

EQUALS (2013) *EQUALS European Profiling Grid*. Available online: <http://clients.squareeye.net/uploads/eaquals/EAQUALS_TD_FRAM_-_November_2013.pdf> (accessed 5 November 2017).

Gaible, E. and Burns, B. (2005) *Using Technology to Train Teachers: Appropriate Uses of ICT for Teacher Professional Development in Developing Countries*. Washington DC: infoDev/World Bank.

Goodyear, V.A., Casey, A. and Kirk, D. (2014) 'Tweet Me, Message Me, Like Me: Using Social Media to Facilitate Pedagogical Change within an Emerging Community of Practice'. *Sport, Education and Society*, 19(7) 927–943.

Kirk, J. (2013) 'The lived experiences of women teachers in Karachi', in Moon, B. (ed.) *Teacher Education and the Challenge of Development*. Abingdon: Routledge: 150–163.

Kwakman, K. (2003) 'Factors Affecting Teachers' Participation in Professional Learning Activities'. *Teaching and Teacher Education*, 19 149–170.

Laurillard, D. (2016) 'The Education Problem that MOOCs Could Solve: Professional Development for Teachers of Disadvantaged Students'. *Research in Learning Technology*, 24. https://doi.org/10.3402/rlt.v24.29369

Lightfoot, A. (2016) 'Barriers and enablers for the continuing professional development of teachers in low-cost private schools in Delhi'. Unpublished MA dissertation, Institute of Education, University of London, UK.

McMillan, D. J., McConnell, B. and O'Sullivan, H. (2016) 'Continuing Professional Development – Why Bother? Perceptions and Motivations of Teachers in Ireland'. *Professional Development in Education*, 42(1) 150–167.

Obondoh, A. and Riechi, A. (2013) *PSIPSE Regional Themes and Challenges: The Use of Technology in Teacher Development in East Africa*. Centre of Social Sector, Education and Policy Analysis (CCSEPA)/Results for Development (RDA). Available online: <www.educationinnovations.org/research-and-evidence/psipse-regional-themes-and-challenges-use-technology-teacher-development-east> (accessed 10 October 2017).

Parnham, P., Gholkar, R. and Borg, S. (2018) 'Using WhatsApp for Peer Support in a Mentoring Programme'. *The Teacher Trainer*, 32(1) 2–7.

Sadaf, A., Newby, T. J. and Ertmer, P. A. (2016) 'An Investigation of the Factors that Influence Pre-Service Teachers' Intentions and Integration of Web 2.0 Tools'. *Education Technology Research Development*, 64 37–64.

Trucano, M. (2005) *Knowledge Maps: ICTs in Education.* Washington, DC: *info*Dev/World Bank.

Trucano, M. (2010) *Worst Practice in ICT Use in Education.* Available online: <http://blogs.worldbank.org/edutech/worst-practice> (accessed 30 October 2017).

Trust, T. (2017) 'Using Cultural Historical Activity Theory to Examine How Teachers Seek and Share Knowledge in a Peer-to-Peer Professional Development Network'. *Australasian Journal of Educational Technology*, 33(1) 98–113.

UNESCO (2014) *EfA Global Monitoring Report 2013/4 – Teaching and Learning: Achieving Quality for All.* Paris: UNESCO.

Wagner, D. A. (2005) 'Preface – ICT and EFA: why should we care?', in Gaible, E. and Burns, M. (eds) *Using Technology to Train Teachers: Appropriate Uses of ICT for Teacher Professional Development in Developing Countries.* Washington DC: infoDev/World Bank.

Xiao, J. and Zhao, C. (2011) 'Distance ELT Tutors in China's Radio and Television Universities: Professional Development'. *Open Learning*, 26(1) 51–66.

5

Critical language teacher education?

John Gray

Introduction

The fact that the title of this chapter (suggested by the editors) ends with a question mark is significant, as it makes what might be taken to refer to a particular kind of language teacher education appear literally questionable. And indeed, there are a number of questions that might be asked: What is critical language teacher education? Does it actually exist – and if so, what does it look like? If it doesn't exist, why is this the case? And by extension, what can be done about this? This chapter is an attempt to shed some light on these questions. In doing so I will give an account of what critical language teacher education is generally held to mean and suggest that it does indeed exist – but that it is marginal and that the forces arrayed against it globally, and indeed any kind of genuinely critical educational endeavour, are considerable, particularly at the present historical moment. In adding this caveat I am reminded of Didier Eribon's (2013: 121) lacerating assessment of these forces as they impact on schools:

> I cannot help but see an infernal machine in the school system, given the way it functions right in front of our eyes. [...] A war is going on against the underdogs and schools are one of the battlefields. Teachers do the best they can! But in fact there is little or nothing they can do when faced with the irresistible forces of the social order, forces that operate both in secret and in the light of day, and that impose themselves everywhere and on everyone.

This is a particularly bleak view of education and of the role of teachers – and while I share Eribon's anger, ultimately I take the view that his assessment is unduly pessimistic. That said, he draws attention to the importance of the field of education for the neoliberal project (discussed below) and its specific recalibration of education across much of the world from the late 1970s onwards. Although Eribon's comments were made with regard to the French educational system, they are nonetheless applicable to many educational settings globally. In the same way, although the examples focused on in this chapter relate to the UK, they can *mutatis mutandis* be seen as similar to what has happened to education in many other countries throughout what might be called the neoliberal era (i.e. late 1970s–present). The chapter begins with a discussion of neoliberalism as the main impediment to critical education in general and then moves to a consideration of data (from Gray and Block, 2012 and Block and Gray, 2016) in which these key issues can be seen to play out in a modern foreign languages teacher education programmes in the UK. Such an approach is necessary if it is to be understood why critical teacher education remains a marginal activity – and why the need for it is so pressing. The chapter then turns to a consideration of critical language teacher education as an alternative model of teacher preparation and development (Groenke and Hatch, 2009; Hawkins and Norton, 2009), and looks at how this is being attempted in one very particular English language setting – the education of ESOL (English for Speakers of Other Languages) teachers in the UK, and from which it is suggested mainstream teacher education has much to learn. Here I draw on interview data with a group of critical teacher educators – Dermot Bryers, Melanie Cooke and Becky Winstanley – whose work is based on Freirean principles (discussed below), and examples of the activities they advocate. The chapter concludes with consideration of the way forward for critical language teacher education.

The neoliberal project and the recalibration of teacher education

In discussions on the nature of neoliberalism, Philip Mirowski (2016) and Marnie Holborow (2018) retell the same joke which can be paraphrased as follows:

> Two young fish are swimming in the sea and as they swim along they meet an older fish heading in the opposite direction. The older fish greets them, saying 'Morning boys. How's the water?' The two young fish are baffled by this and continue swimming without speaking. Eventually one of them turns to the other and says 'What the hell is water?'

Their point is that we are often most oblivious to that which we are surrounded by and, by extension, that neoliberalism is now so pervasive a phenomenon that we can fail to recognise the extent to which our lives are saturated by it. But what is neoliberalism, and why has education been so important to it? Beginning with the first part of this question, we can say that in general neoliberalism refers to the form of market fundamentalism which has characterised the current phase of capitalism since the late 1970s. Although it exhibits regional variations and has been interpreted differently over time (Furlong, 2013), neoliberalism until now has tended to favour unrestricted free trade (although that may be changing under the Trump presidency), the privatisation of state assets, the dismantling or scaling down of institutions associated with welfare-statism, the deregulation of financial institutions, labour flexibility, and the marketisation of areas of life which were previously outside the market or which were seen as the preserve of the state. It has also tended to favour anti trade union legislation and low taxation of corporations and multinational companies.

Neoliberalism is also very much a project in the sense of being a collaborative enterprise which has been planned by individuals and propagated by institutions dedicated to its implementation – the most significant of which is the Mont Pèlerin Society founded in 1947. The society, which is an interdisciplinary global network of academics, journalists, business leaders and politicians, has been referred to by Mirowski (2013) as 'the neoliberal thought collective' – a term which is designed to capture the assiduousness of the society's members in disseminating their ideas globally through locally established groups and think tanks from its inception until the present.

At the same time, neoliberalism is also an ideology, understood here as an interested, class-based representation of the world, promulgated by the economically powerful through their political, business, academic and media allies as though it were common sense. Hence the circulation of ideas suggesting there is no alternative to the current economic order (Giddens, 2000); that economic austerity post-2008 is a necessity (Reinhart and Rogoff, 2010); that the poor are responsible for their own poverty (Murray, 1984); that social class is an outdated way of looking at contemporary society (Pakulski and Walters, 1996), indeed that society itself is a fiction misrepresenting the fact that there are only 'individual men and women' (Thatcher, 1987: npn); and that the market is the best and only guarantor of human liberty (Hayek, 1944). Discursively this has led to the proliferation of terms associated with the market being applied to more and more aspects of life. This has been referred to as a process of 'semantic stretching' (Holborow, 2007) in which students, hospital patients, passengers on public transport *inter alia* are reconfigured as *customers*, while teachers, nurses and doctors are recast as *service providers*, and universities, political parties, languages and even countries are talked about as *brands* (Holborow, 2012, 2015). Neoliberal discourse is also characterised by a rhetoric berating 'big government' and the notion of the intrusive state, while paradoxically relying on strong government to implement and monitor neoliberal policy, as well as being backed up by a robust carceral apparatus (Gottschalk, 2015).

With regard to the second part of the question as to why education has been so important to neoliberalism, two main reasons stand out. First, in those settings in which education had traditionally been mainly the preserve of the state, schools, colleges and universities were seen as ripe for the application of market principles, and competition for funding was introduced as a (supposed) mechanism for 'driving up standards'. Second, from the perspective of neoliberal government, the purpose of schools and other educational establishments is the production of citizens with the knowledge and dispositions appropriate for servicing the economy. In his overview of neoliberal reform of education in the UK, John Furlong (2013) shows that although British governments of different stripes from the Thatcher era onward adopted differing policies at times, overall they shared the view that education was central to economic development, and a belief in the need for the sector to be thoroughly subjected to market forces. This, as Furlong (2013: 40) states, had implications for teacher education which

> had to be reformed along neoliberal lines. [...] a new professionalism had to be developed to ensure that teachers would take on government-defined strategies and targets. The best way to ensure that the teaching profession did this was to maintain competitive markets among schools and providers of teacher education. While schools were required to meet targets, have inspections and be ranked on league tables, universities and other providers of teacher education were required to deliver teachers willing and able to embrace this centrally defined, target-driven culture.

But how exactly was this to be done? In the UK the first step was a sustained recalibration of what has been called 'the knowledge fit for teachers' (Cowen, 1995). This was characterised by the removal of subjects such as the sociology, philosophy and history of education from initial preparation courses – the presence of which were designed to produce a particular kind of teacher who was able to reflect on teaching in an academically informed way and capable of 'permanently re-examining the social fabric and social assumptions about the purposes of schooling within which he or she must daily practice' (Cowen, 1995: 21). Instead there was a new (and increasingly narrow) emphasis on subject knowledge, a focus on acquiring behaviours deemed 'best practice' which all teachers would have to demonstrate in regular government inspections, attention to classroom management and the administration of frequent rounds of high stakes pupil testing. At the same time, there was a move towards student teachers (known as trainees in the UK) spending more time in schools and less time in libraries and university lecture halls as part of their formation. Overall, this amounted to a redefinition of teacher professionalism and a politically motivated recalibration of teacher identity. These changes were memorably described by Bob Cowen (1995) as a shift from the model of the teacher as *reflective practitioner* to one of the teacher as *effective practitioner*. The aim, which amounted to a downgrading of the teaching profession, was to produce a narrowly educated and disciplined technician capable of implementing government policy (as opposed to the previously espoused model of the teacher as a broadly educated autonomous thinker – a model which was heavily influenced by the progressive education movement whose heyday had been the 1960s and early 1970s).

The consequences of this can be seen in the way in which the PGCE (Postgraduate Certificate of Education), which prepares teachers for the state school system in the UK, is currently structured. Although avenues into teaching have been pluralised, the PGCE course remains the most popular route. Student teachers on the PGCE-MFL (Modern Foreign Languages), who are required to have a relevant first degree (e.g. in subjects such as French, Spanish, German, etc.), spend 120 days of the 150-day course in schools learning on the job, where they have access to a mentor (a teacher already employed in the school and vetted by the university as someone capable of providing help and advice). The remainder of their time is taken up with lectures on topics such as the nature and principles of language teaching and learning, the place of languages in the school curriculum, effective and inclusive learning, teaching skills, classroom management, lesson planning, and continuing professional development. Although such courses have many virtues, their narrow remit and the short amount of time dedicated to the academic part of the course, where trainees could explore their experience of practice in the light of theory, can be seen as limiting. German and Spanish nationals taking the PGCE-MFL in the UK were interviewed by David Block (Gray and Block, 2012; Block and Gray, 2016) and their comments serve to highlight some of these problems. David was not a tutor on the course and the informants were aware that by being interviewed they were participating in a research project. In Extract 5.1, a trainee teacher pseudonymously named Harald describes his frustration with the course. Transcription conventions are listed at the end of the chapter.

Extract 5.1

many of the issues on the course seem to be determined by the government/or by the government/or by political or social services/and we're not allowed to talk about them (.5) which allows us to do what they want us to do (1) there seems to be one sort of model of teaching and how to do things/that's what the standards are/that's what we have to work towards /or we don't get the qualification (.5) there's not much diversity/no (.5) it's very much (.5) everything is done by objectives (.5) there's this one (.5) you identify targets/and you have this nice sheet with meetings and arrangements /and you have to identify targets every week (.5) in this week I'm working especially towards pronunciation/it's really silly /

(Block and Gray, 2016: 481)

The extract draws attention to the ways in which the teacher education course exerts control over what can and cannot be said (largely I would suggest on account of the limited time available to the teacher educators), the fact that only one way of doing things is seen as legitimate, and the way in which learning about teaching is framed within a highly instrumental discourse of standards, objectives and targets. The authors note similar constraints and lack of opportunity for discussion on the commercial CELTA (Certificate of English Language Teaching to Adults) course offered globally by Cambridge Assessment (Block and Gray, 2016) The CELTA is also a practicum-led qualification – but with the entire course lasting only 120 hours, opportunities for talking about teaching and learning are necessarily very limited.

In addition to the kind of frustration mentioned by Harald, Elena – a Spanish national – speaking in Spanish and English, drew attention to the problematic nature of the highly technical and bureaucratic way in which her learning had to be documented for subsequent inspection by the teacher educators running the PGCE-MFL course (who themselves in turn were subject to government inspection). Her use of Spanish with David (a Spanish speaker) may be seen as indicative of the rapport between them and her openness in criticising the course.

Extract 5.2

Original in Spanish	**English translation**
yo me pasé un día entero la semana pasada escribiendo la *evidence*/que son cosas de siete frases de decir *today I realised this and bla bla bla*/pero como está *evidence based*/en realidad (.5) podría perfectamente no haber hecho estas cosas y escribirlo igual (.5) te están pidiendo que crees la evidencia de la nada (.5) pero es totalmente posible/porque es una lista tan brutal/y lo dije a mi mentor/y me dijo/*well, do it/if you think by the end of the year you haven't produced evidence for everything/just fake it.*	I spent a whole day last week writing the *evidence*/which consists of seven sentences stating *I realised this* and bla bla bla/But because it's *evidence based*/actually (.5) I could very well not have done these things and written it [that I had] anyway/(.5) they're asking you to create the evidence out of nothing (.5) but it's completely possible/because it's such a long list/and I told my mentor that/ and he said/*well do it/if you think by the end of the year you haven't produced evidence for everything/just fake it.*

(Gray and Block, 2012: 130–131)

Here we see the mentor colluding with the trainee in recommending that the evidence of learning should be faked if necessary to comply with the requirements of the course. Such fakery allows the student teacher to demonstrate learning (however bogus), the mentor to be seen to be doing their job, and the teacher educators to satisfy the government inspectorate who require evidence-based demonstrations of learning. In such an environment, cynicism about education is inevitable, and no doubt partly responsible for the high dropout rate from teaching by young teachers – with almost a third of young teachers in the UK quitting within five years of qualifying (BBC, 2016). Studies of the reasons given by older teachers opting for early retirement noted that their sense of professional identity was perceived to be increasingly at odds with the new kind of effective practitioner identity valorised by the neoliberal state (Maclure, 1993). What we see in these examples is the opposite of what is generally understood by critical teacher education – to which I now turn. In the following sections we shall see that, despite its marginal status, critical teacher education offers a powerful alternative model of teacher preparation.

Critical language teacher education

In opposition to the neoliberal model of teacher education, critical (language) teacher education rests on a view of the teacher as a 'transformative intellectual', a theorising practitioner who

> exercises forms of intellectual and pedagogical practice which attempt to insert teaching and learning directly into the political sphere by arguing that schooling represents both

a struggle for meaning and a struggle over power relations. [...] [Such a teacher is some-one] whose intellectual practices are necessarily grounded in forms of moral and ethical discourse exhibiting a preferential concern for the suffering and struggles of the disadvantaged and oppressed. [...] Teachers who assume the role of transformative intellectuals treat students as critical agents, question how knowledge is produced and distributed, utilize dialogue, and make knowledge meaningful, critical, and ultimately emancipatory.

(Giroux and McLaren, 1986: 215)

From this perspective, schools – as well as teacher education colleges and universities – are seen as potential sites of social transformation, rather than as domains of social reproduction or organs of the 'ideological state apparatus' (Althusser, 1971) whose role (certainly as far as the neoliberal project with regard to education is concerned) is to service the economy though the production of 'human capital' (Becker, 1964). Critical (language) teacher education can be seen as the confluence of a number of distinct but related intellectual tributaries – on the one hand it is indebted to neo-Marxist critical theory (Marcuse, 1964) and its critique of the cultural aspects of consumer capitalism, and what would later be called the manufacture of consent (Herman and Chomsky, 1988); on the other hand, there is Paulo Freire's (1972) literacy work with peasants in the developing world which had an avowedly social emancipatory agenda, and which also saw knowledge as co-constructed rather than transmitted from teacher to students. At the same time, there is the uniquely North American post-1929 crash phenomenon known as social reconstructionism (Groenke, 2009), which had the declared aim of promoting alternatives to capitalism through teacher education. Spearheaded by a group of educationalists in Teachers College New York, the social reconstructionists took the view that capitalism had failed and that teacher education and schools should be at the forefront in helping to bring about radical social change. In *Dare the School Build a New Social Order?* George Counts (1932: 54), argued that teachers had to 'assume unprecedented social responsibilities' and abandon any pretence of neutrality with regard to the depredations of capitalism.

There is the fallacy that the school should be impartial in its emphases, that no bias should be given instruction. [...] My thesis is that complete impartiality is utterly impossible, that the school must shape attitudes, develop tastes, and even impose ideas.

(Counts, 1932: 19).

The charge of unwarranted imposition of ideas is one which would follow critical educational endeavours until the present (Gove, 2013) – however, the Freirean strand of what came to be known as 'critical pedagogy' (Giroux, 1983), and which predominates today (Auerbach, 1992; Cooke et al. 2018; Mallows, 2014; Shor, 1987), has consistently made a virtue of the absence of imposition in its approach, taking it as axiomatic that any kind of critical pedagogical intervention should revolve around dialogue and adopt as its starting point the interests, needs and concerns of those being taught. In his influential *Pedagogy of the Oppressed*, Freire (1972) argues against what he calls the banking model of teaching whereby the teacher's transmission of knowledge is seen in terms of metaphorical deposits which it is hoped will eventually be of use to the student. Such a model is seen as a negation of the necessarily dialogic nature of any genuine emancipatory educational encounter:

In the banking concept of education, knowledge is a gift bestowed by those who consider themselves knowledgeable upon those whom they consider to know nothing. Projecting an absolute ignorance onto others, a characteristic of the ideology of oppression, negates education and knowledge as processes of inquiry. The teacher presents himself to his students as their necessary opposite; by considering their ignorance absolute, he justifies his own existence. [...] The *raison d'être* of libertarian education, on the other hand, lies in its drive toward reconciliation. Education must begin with the solution of the teacher-student contradiction, by reconciling the poles of the contradiction so that both are simultaneously teachers *and* students.

(Freire, 1972: 46)

In addition, to the centrality of dialogue in which speaking rights are shared by teacher and students, Freire also proposes a pedagogy of problem-posing in which codes (explained in what follows) play a significant role. Problem-posing refers to the practice of exploring an issue of concern or relevance to students which may be approached though the generation of a code, namely a picture or some kind of graphic representation of an issue which is then discussed (decodified) – a process in which the teacher and students attempt to clarify what is at stake, how it affects them and what solutions there may be. This can also be combined (as shall see below) with techniques involving the use of drama.

In terms of teacher education, it can be a little difficult to establish what all this looks like in practice as it has been noted that there are few examples of data from critical language teacher education courses (Hawkins and Norton, 2009). However, one group of critical educators and researchers in the UK have been diligent in making the case for what they call 'participatory ESOL' and their publications provide a vivid blueprint for teachers who wish to educate themselves on how to go about implementing Freirean principles in the classroom (Bryers et al., 2013, 2014a, 2014b; Cooke et al., 2018). One member of the group, Dermot Bryers also runs a charity called *English for Action* which inducts teachers into the principles and practice of participatory ESOL. In the following section I look more closely at the work of this group of critical educators, and I begin by drawing on interview data with two of them.

English for Action

The following extracts are taken from an interview, recorded in 2014, in which members of this group and I discussed their views on social class in ESOL. The extracts include contributions from Dermot Bryers (DB) and Becky Winstanley (BW). In the course of our discussion, it emerged that *English for Action*, as well as running English language classes taught along Freirean lines, also provided training for teachers. Here I (JG) ask them to tell me about the way in which they prepare their teachers.

Extract 5.3

JG: how do you train the teachers for *English for Action*/I mean what/what do they need that a reg-/that a CELTA wouldn't give you/or I don't know whatever↓

BW: different things/erm I do completely different things with *English for Action* than I would do here for example

JG: Give me an example/I'm a complete outsider [...]/I mean what might you do in/ in something/in one of those sessions↑

DB: what was our last training session↑

BW: the last training session was about discussion (.)/and about using discussions/erm building up discussion skills with students/and using the forum of discussion to kind of talk about issues that were key to students/and how you do that in the classroom/how you set it up/what the pitfalls can be/you know what/what happens if something/a discussion arises where there's a bit of barney★ or/you know those kind of/so looking at training from that kind of view [JG: hmm]/erm rather than more technical teaching techniques [JG: hmm]/(.) does that make sense↑

★ *Informal British term for argument*

At the time of the interview Becky was also teaching on a PGCE in Literacy and ESOL in the institution in which the interview was taking place – hence her reference to 'here' in her first contribution. The point she is making is that the kind of input she provides 'here' is determined by the kind of externally determined constraints referred to earlier in this chapter in the discussion of the PGCE-MFL. It is significant that in her long turn on the *English for Action* training on how to manage discussions she contrasts this with 'more technical teaching techniques' which are eschewed – indirectly indexing the kind of teacher preparation associated with the PGCE model. That discussions should be focused on issues which are 'key to students' is in line with Freire's (1972: 68) view that

> We [...] must never provide the people with programmes which have little or nothing to do with their own preoccupations, doubts, hopes, and fears [...]. It is not our role to speak to the people about our own view of the world, nor to attempt to impose that view on them, but rather to dialogue with the people about their view and ours. We must realize that their view of the world, manifested variously in their action, reflects their *situation* in the world.

This principle emerges more explicitly when Dermot explains how drama is also used as a way of putting the students' experiences at the centre of a lesson. ESOL classrooms tend to be composed of migrants and asylum seekers, but as James Simpson (2015: 210) states the UK is a 'reluctant host state', where 'immigrants are needed', but paradoxically it is one in which they are 'not welcomed'. It is therefore not unexpected that discrimination reflects students' 'situation in the world' and that it should be used as an example of a theme for exploration. This extract is slightly longer than previous examples, but provides a rationale for the use of forum theatre and a clear indication of how it should be used in the classroom.

Extract 5.4

DB: next session/next session's on using forum theatre techniques in ESOL classrooms to build language

JG: hmm/what is that exactly↑

DB: so forum theatre is when you/it's/it's very similar to using role play/so you'd ask people to think about difficult situations where they've been in/where they felt erm/the/the original language was oppressed/which is from the theatre of the oppressed which was erm/Boal wrote/he was a contemporary of Freire in Brazil in the 70s and 80s

[some lines missing]

DB: yeah/but we don't really talk about oppressed/it just sounds/just sounds really dark in English/I think more than it does in Portuguese or Spanish or [J: hmm]/other languages/but anyway it's situations where you're/we say unfair (.)/erm I've used it before/where you've felt kind of/people treated you unfairly/and then people talk about being at the doctor/being disrespected by the receptionist/or doctors or/or their health professionals/or it could be anything/it could be the bus driver on a bus/and then people work in groups of threes and fours to kind of dramatise that/

make it into a role play/a three to five minute role play/perform it/the audience watch the role play/and then the teacher leads the/like problem posing/leads the erm group through an analysis of the situation/is it familiar to you↑/have you felt like this↑/who was the erm the/who was the victim in inverted commas↑/who was the person acting in an unfair way↑/why did it happen↑/you know/what systemic reasons are there for this↑/erm and then finally what can we do about it↑/ and when people start putting ideas towards what you could do/then they might say things like/she could say this/and you say no/don't tell me show me/and then you rewind the/the play to the beginning/you replace the protagonist who is the victim/sits down in the audience/and the audience member replaces the protagonist/ and then re-acts the situation with a more effective intervention

[some lines missing]

DB: and then you can challenge three or four audience members to get it better and better and better/until you then bring the original protagonist back in/and say now try it/and it really helps challenge like erm (.)/both sort of systemic unfairness and linguistic strategies to help deal with it

Here we see the problem-posing arising out of an initial dramatisation of a situation in which something perceived to be unfair took place. Overall the pedagogic cycle as outlined by Dermot (selection of a situation based on students' lived experience → dramatisation of what happened → problem-posing analysis of dramatisation in terms of feelings, characters, causes → re-enactments of the situation in which the unfairness is effectively challenged) can be seen as an example of what Freire calls *praxis*, namely the combination of reflection and action designed to challenge systemic unfairness. At the mention of this term, the following exchange takes place, which is a powerful reminder that critical language teacher education of this kind is a conscious political intervention, aimed not simply at producing teachers who can facilitate the building of language – but doing so in such a way that the language which is built can be used to resist and challenge the injustices faced by the students:

Extract 5.5

JG: what do you guys understand by systemic unfairness↑

DB: erm (.) well I suppose the *English for Action* analysis would be that erm London is an unequal city/with unacceptable levels of poverty and inequality/and that migrants are disproportionately affected by this/particularly migrants with English as a foreign language/so those three kind of steps mean that it's almost impossible to teach language in a vacuum without being aware of those two factors/and therefore it would be weird and unnatural not to have a level on which/if you've got twelve people in a room/that they they're not going to talk about these kinds of things

At the same time, the work of this group shows that issues affecting students do not only come from the host society, but can come from within the migrant communities themselves. In making this point, they highlight the importance of teachers listening to their students. In *Whose Integration?* (Bryers et al., 2013), an account of a research project designed to explore the trope of migrants failing to integrate in UK, they describe how a group of mainly Bangladeshi women in a class taught by all three of them introduced the topic of women riding bicycles and the (male) Bangladeshi community assessment of such women as having 'gone modern'. Their account of problem-posing from a code started with the introduction of the topic as one of concern to the students themselves. A code, which consisted of a simple line drawing of a woman with a headscarf riding a bicycle while being pointed at by male members of the community, was then introduced. The questions/instructions used for the problem-posing were as follows:

1. Describe the content – what do you see?
2. Define the problem.
3. Personalize the problem.
4. Discuss the problem.
5. Discuss the alternatives to the problem.

In their discussion of the wide-ranging discussion which followed this, Bryers, Winstanley and Cooke argue that the topic of gender created a sense of solidarity among all the women in the group, including the female teachers. Men in the group were challenged by the women and Dermot was questioned about the extent of his involvement in domestic chores in his own household. In their overall assessment of the activity they conclude:

> The discussion showed that the participatory ESOL class can be regarded as an important 'site' of integration, especially if integration means deeper understanding of 'the other' and an acceptance that the concept of 'the other' is fluid, not static. Discussions such as the one we describe here suggest that focusing primarily on identities other than the ethnic, national or religious can foster alliances based on categories such as gender, family and class, which may at times be more relevant. We came to see integration in this session, not as a state a person has reached or failed to reach, but as a *process* of fleeting and constantly shifting alliances, which we were involved in as much as the students.
>
> *(Bryers et al., 2013: 20)*

In concluding thus they make an important point about critical pedagogy in general. Not only is a classroom a real setting in the real world and not some kind of rehearsal space (although it can be that too), it is also a crucially a site of potential transformation for all concerned – teachers and students alike. Indeed a consistent feature of Bryers, Winstanley and Cooke's work is the extent to which they show themselves to be educated by their students – an important Freirean lesson for the teachers who turn to their work for a theorisation of critical language teaching and practical ideals on how to implement it.

Conclusion

What conclusions then can be drawn from this account of critical language teacher education and the forces arrayed against it? I began this chapter with a quotation from the sociologist Didier Eribon and his damning indictment of the influence on education of the 'irresistible forces' of the contemporary social order. While these are forces are considerable, I want to suggest that they are resistible – and indeed, as the work of groups such as *English for Action* demonstrate, they are being actively resisted. But in more mainstream settings, resistance *is* certainly difficult. The Freirean approach to teaching and teacher education does not sit easily with current neoliberal pedagogic regimes of pre-determined learning outcomes, cyclical testing, repeated government inspections and the generation of league tables. Its aims and its approach to achieving these aims are altogether different. As Freire (1972: 95) states:

> The important thing, from the point of view of libertarian education, is for men to come to feel like the masters of their thinking by discussing the thinking and views of the world

explicitly or implicitly manifest in their own suggestions and those of their comrades. Because this view of education starts with the conviction that it cannot present its own programme but must search for this programme dialogically with the people, it serves to introduce the pedagogy of the oppressed, in the development of which the oppressed must participate.

Such a view of education recognises the specific social, cultural and economic situatedness of the classroom, the unpredictability of teaching and the necessarily dialogic nature of a pedagogy which seeks to do more than provide students with the skills deemed necessary to service the needs of the economy. However, those of us who subscribe to the idea of critical language teacher education need to recall that *is* also being attempted in mainstream language teacher education courses as well. Susan Groenke and J. Amos Hatch (2009) provide some empirical evidence of what is being attempted by self-identifying critical teacher educators in the US. Using an online questionnaire sent to educationalists whose work espoused the values of critical pedagogy they received 65 responses to a number of prompts. These included:

1. The major issues I confront as I 'do' critical pedagogy in institution are …
2. Some ways I deal with these issues are …

(Hatch and Groenke, 2009: 63)

The responses make for interesting reading, with major issues being identified as student resistance, a lack of sympathy from colleagues, and institutional barriers. With regard to the first of these, the following comment gives an indication of the nature of this:

When it comes to working with students, the major issues are getting them to acknowledge their own privilege. [They] are convinced of the existence of individual and institutional racisms but are mostly sceptical of a systemic racism. All view issues of class from a lens that accepts capitalism as a natural political economy without alternatives. All readily agree that a student-centered pedagogy is important, but very few show enthusiasm for the radical edge that comes from Freire's problem-posing.

(Groenke and Hatch, 2009: 65)

Such views might be said to reflect the way in which the neoliberal worldview has succeeded (at least in some quarters) in eroding the concept of class and denying the reality of systemic disadvantage. That said, the data also suggest that graduate students with actual experience of teaching were more sympathetic to the notion of critical pedagogy than pre-service novices, who tended to think about teaching solely in terms of learning discrete classroom behaviours. As far as colleagues were concerned, the data suggest that many took the view that beginning teachers were either developmentally unready for critical pedagogy, or (like some students) that its social critique challenged their own privilege. And finally there was the obstacle of institutional barriers. For some informants, the neoliberal climate meant that the educational values they held were clearly at odds with the kind of teacher professionalism they were supposed to develop in their students. Others, mainly tenure-seeking informants, felt that they needed to be careful about the extent to which they openly espoused the values associated with critical language teacher education in their institutions as these might impact negatively on their own careers. This led in some cases to a somewhat softly-softly approach:

I quietly (sometimes) subvert the dominant discourse.

> I use my imagination to see where I can fit critical pedagogy into my work while flying under the radar.
>
> I just keep going ahead and not 'advertising' what I do.
>
> *(Groenke and Hatch, 2009: 76)*

There is therefore, I would suggest, some cautious grounds for optimism. In addition to continuing to work on the margins to keep counter narratives alive, those teacher educators committed to critical pedagogy might also consider making the links in their teaching between Freirean dialogism and other approaches such as sociocultural theory in which learning is also seen as co-constructed, and communicative and task-based approaches in which student talk is seen as central to learning. Ultimately however, significant structural change will only come about when neoliberalism itself is brought to an end. For that to happen, teachers and teacher educators must recognise that 'teaching and teacher education are inherently and unavoidably political' (Cochran-Smith, 2005: 3), and that they have no option but to become politically more active, forging links – as has been suggested elsewhere (Block and Gray, 2016) – with professionals and workers in other sectors of the economy in challenging the hegemony of this profoundly oppressive and anti-educational ideology and the system it supports.

Transcription conventions

(.)	very short silence (fewer than 0.5 seconds)
(.8)	duration of silence in seconds
wo-	cut-off
[ ]	overlapping talk
↑↓	significant rise or fall in pitch
/	chunk of talk

Further reading

Auerbach, E. R. (1992) *Making Meaning Making Change: Participatory Curriculum Development for Adult ESL Literacy*. Washington, DC: Center for Applied Linguistics/ERIC. Available online: <https://eric.ed.gov/?id=ED356688> (accessed 22 May, 2019).

Groenke, S. L. and Hatch, J. A. (2009) (eds) *Critical Pedagogy and Teacher Education in the Neoliberal Era*. New York: Springer.

Winstanley, B. and Cooke, M. (2016) Emerging Worlds. Papers 1–5. *English for Action*. Available online: <www.efalondon.org/esol/research-and-media> (accessed May 22, 2019).

References

Althusser, L. (1971) *Lenin and Philosophy and Other Essays*. New York: New Left Books.

Auerbach, E. R. (1992) *Making Meaning Making Change: Participatory Curriculum Development for Adult ESL Literacy*. Washington, DC: Center for Applied Linguistics/ERIC. Available online: <https://eric.ed.gov/?id=ED356688> (accessed May 22, 2019).

BBC (2016) 'New teachers: 30% of 2010 intake quit within five years'. Available online: <www.bbc.co.uk/news/education-37750489> (accessed 22 May, 2019).

Becker, G. (1964) *Human Capital: A Theoretical and Empirical Analysis, with Special Reference to Education*. Chicago, IL: The University of Chicago Press.

Block, D. and Gray, J. (2016) '"Just go away and do it and you get marks": The Degradation of Language Teaching in Neoliberal Times'. *Journal of Multilingual and Multicultural Development*, 37(5) 181–494.

Bryers, D., Winstanley, B. and Cooke, M. (2013) *Whose Integration?* London: British Council.

Bryers, D., Winstanley, B. and Cooke, M. (2014a) 'Participatory ESOL', in Mallows, D. (ed.) *Language Issues in Migration and Integration: Perspectives from Teachers and Students.* London: British Council: 9–18.

Bryers, D., Winstanley, B. and Cooke, M. (2014b) 'The Power of Discussion', in Mallows, D. (ed.) *Language Issues in Migration and Integration: Perspectives from Teachers and Students.* London: British Council: 35–54.

Cochran-Smith, M. (2005) 'The New Teacher Education: For Better or for Worse?'. *Educational Researcher,* 34(7) 3–17.

Cooke, M., Bryers, D. and Winstanley, B. (2018) '"Our Languages": Sociolinguistics in Multilingual Participatory ESOL Classes'. *Working Papers in Urban Language and Literacies.* King's College, London.

Counts, G. (1932) *Dare the School Build a New Social Order?* New York: The John Day Company.

Cowen, B. (1995) 'The State and Control of Teacher Education: The Knowledge Fit for Teachers', in Gardner, R. (ed.) *Contemporary Crises in Teacher Education.* Birmingham: British Association of Teachers and Researchers in Overseas Education: 18–34.

Eribon, D. (2013) *Returning to Reims.* Los Angeles, CA: Semiotext(e).

Freire, P. (1972) *Pedagogy of the Oppressed.* Harmondsworth: Penguin Books.

Furlong, J. (2013) 'Globalisation, Neoliberalism, and the Reform of Teacher Education in England'. *The Educational Forum,* 77(1) 28–50.

Giddens, A. (2000) *The Third Way and its Critics.* Cambridge: Polity Press.

Giroux, H. (1983) *Theory and Resistance in Education: A Pedagogy for the Opposition.* South Hadley, MA: Bergin & Garvey.

Giroux, H. and McLaren, P. (1986) 'Teacher Education and the Politics of Engagement: The Case for Democratic Schooling'. *Harvard Educational Review,* 56(3) 213–238.

Gottschalk, M. (2015) *The Prison State and the Lockdown of American Politics.* Princeton, NJ: Princeton University Press.

Gove, M. (2013) 'I refuse to surrender to the Marxist teachers hell-bent on destroying our schools: education Secretary berates "the new enemies of promise" for opposing his plans'. *The Daily Mail.* Available online: <www.dailymail.co.uk/debate/article-2298146> (accessed 27 March 2019).

Gray, J. and Block, D. (2012) 'The marketization of language teacher education and neoliberalism: characteristics, consequences and future prospects', in Block, D., Gray, J. and Holborow, M. (eds) *Neoliberalism and Applied Linguistics.* Abingdon: Routledge: 114–143.

Groenke, S. L. (2009) 'Social reconstructionism and the roots of critical pedagogy: implications for teacher education in the neoliberal era', in Groenke, S. L. and Hatch, J. A. (eds) *Critical Pedagogy and Teacher Education in the Neoliberal Era.* New York: Springer: 3–17.

Groenke, S. L. and Hatch, J. A. (2009) (eds) *Critical Pedagogy and Teacher Education in the Neoliberal Era.* New York: Springer.

Hawkins, M. and Norton, B. (2009) 'Critical language teacher education', in Burns, A. and Richards, J. C. (eds) *The Cambridge Guide to Second Language Teacher Education.* Cambridge: Cambridge University Press.

Hayek, F. A. (1944) *The Road to Serfdom.* London: George Routledge & Sons.

Herman, E. S. and Chomsky, N. (1988) *Manufacturing Consent: The Political Economy of the Mass Media.* New York: Pantheon Books.

Holborow, M. (2007) 'Language, Ideology and Neoliberalism'. *Journal of Language and Politics,* 6(1) 51–73.

Holborow, M. (2012) 'What is neoliberalism? Discourse, ideology and the real world', in D. Block, J. Gray and M. Holborow, *Neoliberalism and Applied Linguistics.* Abingdon: Routledge: 14–32.

Holborow, M. (2015) *Language and Neoliberalism.* Abingdon: Routledge.

Holborow, M. (2018) 'Education and the intercultural politics of global neoliberalism'. *Language and Intercultural Communication,* 18(5) 520–532.

Maclure, M. (1993) 'Arguing For Your Self: Identity as an Organising Principle in Teachers' Jobs and Lives'. *British Educational Research Journal,* 19(4) 311–322.

Mallows, D. (2014) (ed.) *Language Issues in Migration and Integration: Perspectives from Teachers and Students.* London: British Council.

Marcuse, H. (1964) *One-Dimensional Man.* Boston, MA: Beacon Press.

Mirowski, P. (2013) *Never Let a Serious Crisis Go to Waste: How Neoliberalism Survived the Financial Meltdown*. London: Verso.

Mirowski, P. (2016) This is Water (or is it Neoliberalism?). *Institute for New Economic Thinking*, 1–10. Available online: <www.ineteconomics.org/perspectives/blog/this-is-water-or-is-it-neoliberalism> (accessed 11 May, 2019).

Murray, C. (1984) *Losing Ground: American Social Policy 1950–1980*. New York: Basic Books.

Pakulski, J. and Walters, M. (1996) *The Death of Class*. London: Sage.

Reinhart, C. and Rogoff, K. (2010) 'Growth in a Time of Debt'. *American Economic Review*, 100(2) 573–578.

Shor, I. (1987) 'Action and Reflection, the Freirean Argument in ESL'. *Language Issues* 2/1, 2/2, in R. Bhanot and E. Illes (2009) *The Best of Language Issues: LLU+*, 83–99.

Simpson, J. (2015) 'English language learning for adult migrants in superdiverse Britain', in Simpson, J. and Whiteside, A. (eds) *Adult Language Education and Migration: Challenging Agendas in Policy and Practice*. Abingdon: Routledge: 200–213.

Thatcher, M. (1987) Interview for *Woman's Own*. Available online: <www.margaretthatcher.org/document/106689> (accessed 11 May, 2019).

6

Evaluating English language teacher education programmes

Richard Kiely

Introduction

In the last three decades, there have been two salient developments in LTE. First, there has been substantial growth in research into teaching, especially in the areas of teacher beliefs and conditions (Woods, 1996; Borg, 2006), and teacher identity, agency and lifelong learning (Freeman, 1998; Johnson, 2009). This perspective has prompted language teacher educators to look beyond the structure of English, and processes of second language acquisition in developing effective programmes (Ellis, 2010). Second, there has been increased awareness of the teacher as a key element in educational development: enhancement of programmes and learning opportunities have focussed on the development of teachers as autonomous thinking professionals, on whom the success of innovative techniques, methods, learning materials and tests depends. International policy initiatives have supported this direction of development. The OECD, for example, has underlined the significance of the development of teachers for effective education provision, for example in the Teaching and Learning International Survey (TALIS) programme (OECD, 2009).

In the context of programme implementation, teacher education has moved into the university sector in many countries, and programmes have benefited in terms of research activity which documented the complexity of the task of teacher education. The field has moved from a set of practices, established by tradition, and controlled by patriarchal authorities, to a vibrant amalgam of new and creative ideas about instruction and participation in classroom language learning, supported by challenging frameworks at the policy and regulatory levels. In a Special Issue of *Language Teacher Research* in 2009, the editors Gary Barkuizen and Simon Borg note that the common feature of the research articles is a focus on space. The focus of the research studies in the special issue is the ways teacher educators and teachers create and manage space for their own learning and development. The metaphor of space here underlines the importance of development and effectiveness in language teacher education programmes. Programme evaluation is the area of activity where these dimensions of our field can be understood.

This chapter examines the ways our understanding of effectiveness has developed over recent decades. The 'Survey' section provides an overview of developments in programme evaluation since its inception in the 1960s. The 'Research and applications' section examines a range of initiatives which have contributed to the conceptualisation of effectiveness of language teacher education, and which help identify the nodes in policy and practice which are relevant to further development to enhance effectiveness. The 'Further reading' section proposes a short list of readings which provide further insights into both PE and LTE.

Survey: programme evaluation and language teacher education

The field of programme evaluation (PE) has been an integral part of Applied Linguistics and language education since both fields developed in the 1960s. We can identify three major stages in the development of PE in the language education field since then. In this section, each is characterised by a representative definition, and discussion of the ways the approach has been influential in language education, and in particular in the field of language teacher education.

1. The age of alternatives

Early approaches focussed on comparing programmes and determining the most effective option, as evident from this definition:

> Educational evaluation is the process of delineating, obtaining and providing useful information for judging decision alternatives.
>
> *(Stufflebeam et al., 1971: 43)*

This approach to PE was based on the notion that a programme is a single, prescribed body of activity that can be implemented and empirically evaluated to determine its effectiveness. The evaluation was a service to policy makers, rather than practitioners such as teachers. In language education such evaluations were based on the notion of 'method', and a direct correspondence between learning outcomes on the one hand, and specific inputs and activities on the other. The methods evaluations, for example the Colorado Project (Scherer and Wertheimer, 1964) and the evaluation of the Bangalore Communicational language teaching project (Beretta and Davies, 1985), proved unhelpful. Greenwood (1985), for example, noted the lack of contribution of the evaluation to teacher learning and professional development: the lack of detail in terms of what the teachers actually did, and how this generated forms of classroom participation, meant that there were few lessons or insights for practitioners to develop programmes, and even fewer for the development of language teacher education programmes. The next generation of programme evaluations focus to a large extent on the contribution to the work of practitioners within programmes.

2. Evaluation for development

This approach to PE was characterised by an acceptance that the focus was not selecting between alternatives, but rather understanding the programme as it is, and identifying measures to enhance its operations and effectiveness. A key definition emphasises decision-making, but for establishing direction for development rather than selecting from alternatives:

> Evaluation is the principled and systematic (formal and informal) collection of information for purposes of decision-making.
>
> *(Rea-Dickins and Germaine, 1992: 36)*

PE in this period involved research and/or consultancy activity to identify strengths and weaknesses of a programme, and use these to set out directions and strategies for development. The approach was informed by utilisation-focused evaluation (Patton, 1982) in the US, by illuminative evaluation (Parlett and Hamilton, 1972) in the UK, and by a reform movement in UK schooling and education policy (Stenhouse, 1975; Macdonald, 1976). These approaches considered social and educational programmes as established contexts of investment and banks of knowledge which could not be replaced by an alternative, but which could be better understood and improved using evidence-based approaches. In the British context of ELT, this form of evaluation developed alongside aid programmes and British Council projects in the field of language teacher education. An example is the Nepal Baseline evaluation carried out in the context of a British Council project to enhance teacher knowledge and skills in Nepal (Weir and Roberts, 1994). As external evaluator, Weir designed an experimental study to compare the classroom teaching of trained and untrained teachers. The findings and discussion however, did not focus on the superior teaching of the trained teachers, and thus the effectiveness of the training programme: rather it focussed on development, improving the learning opportunities for all teachers, and thus their students. A key outcome of the evaluation was the need to involve the teachers, so that they had a stake and opportunity to invest in measures which had the potential to improve their teaching.

In the 1990s, in the context of a range of project contexts in Eastern and Central Europe, many of them focused on developing English language teacher education, the British Council established the Project Development and Support Scheme (PRODESS) to enhance stakeholder development of programmes, using the tools and process of programme evaluation (Kiely et al., 1995; Kiely and Rea-Dickins, 2005). The positive impact of this initiative is evidenced in retrospective, reflective accounts of project leaders who participated in PRODESS initiatives (Tribble, 2012; Komorowska, 2012; Wiseman, 2014).

The legacy of PE for development has been enduring. Two recent evaluations in LTE, published as research papers in *Language Teaching Research* and *TESOL Quarterly* illustrate this impact. Peacock (2009) presents an account of the evaluation of the 4-year pre-service language teacher education programme in Hong Kong. This study is located in the tradition of evaluation for development: the goal of the study was to identify strengths and weaknesses of the programme, with particular attention to the extent to which it met the needs of the students, and on that basis, to propose strategies for development of the programme. The approach to the evaluation is a broad-based stakeholder approach, with the purpose of identifying ways the programme can be improved, as well as set out a novel approach to PE in this field.

The second programme evaluation is Kiely and Askham (2012), an evaluation of the Trinity College London Certificate in TESOL which was commissioned and resourced by the owners of the programme. The purpose of the evaluation was an impact study – to understand better the impact in terms of teacher learning of the intensive (normally four to six weeks) pre-service programme. The focus of the research was to understand the work experience of graduates of the programme, and identify the ways the learning within the programme had an impact on that experience.

These examples make a contribution to our understanding of LTE in three ways: first, the research design and methodology are sufficiently rigorous to meet the requirement of peer review of academic journals. They are discussed further in the Research and Applications section below. Second, the evaluations look at the programmes as a whole: the programmes are contexts of learning experience of participants, and thus differ from many research studies in the LTE field which focus on particular theorisations of components of programmes. Third, both examples focus on the education of teachers of English, the language context which has been the context of growth and of research and enquiry in language education over recent decades (see Slimani-Rolls and Kiely, 2018 for discussion of programmes for the development of teachers of languages other than English). The next stage of PE in LTE is characterised by a greater level of involvement of programme participants – teacher educators, managers, teachers and trainees – and a reduced role for the external evaluation and research expert. In this way they achieve even greater integration into the processes of managing the implementation and ongoing development of programmes.

3. Evaluation as programme management

In a paper on language programme evaluation entitled 'Small answers to the big question' Kiely (2009) set out a definition to capture the complex and multi-faceted nature of PE in language education:

> Programme evaluation is a set of strategies to document and understand the programme. It involves research activity (conventional studies or action research by which teachers learn about and transform aspects of their practice) and assessment data (conventional measures of outcomes). In addition to these, evaluation has to engage with the social, cultural and historical identity of the programme, as a product of the institution, as a phase in the biographies of participants, and as a context of personal investments of individual stakeholders.
>
> *(Kiely, 2009: 114)*

The definition captures two particular features of PE as a tool of programme managers which are increasingly relevant to the field of LTE, particularly in English Language Teacher Education (ELTE). First, programmes are complex, with many separate components, and thus, many frameworks for understanding the relationships between programme experience and teacher learning. Second, a dimension of the complexity of programmes is shared ownership and the external specification which derives from this. For example, a pre-service teacher education programme such as the CELTA or TCL Cert TESOL, leads to an award by Cambridge ESOL or Trinity College London, is offered by a teacher education institution or university which may have its own quality management processes, and is led and taught by teacher educators who have their particular perspective on what is important. Evaluation in some form is likely to be carried out by each of these stakeholders, with each addressing particular aspects of learning and trainee experience. Macilwaine (2016) illustrates the complexity of ownership here: she describes an initiative by the organisation she works for, the Cochin International English Academy in Kerala, India. Her account is an evaluation in terms of how the programme facilitated personal investment by experienced and prospective teachers, and represented a vehicle for learning and career development for them. The account is of course a commentary on the effectiveness of the contribution of all stakeholders, including the more remote owners – Oxford TEFL and Trinity College London – even though the study is not initiated or managed by them. The answers to the big question – is the programme effective (Kiely, 2009: 99) – are small: they are not proposals for major changes, but rather tweaking local provision and practices based on emerging insights and creative ideas.

The outcomes of such evaluations do not always reach the public domain. However, conferences and professional publications are contexts where such evaluations are visible. Particularly important is the British Council, which has led on major developments in ELTE in a range of contexts, both as British Council programmes, and as partnership programmes with ministries of education and other education authorities. Two edited collections of papers – Edge and Mann

(2013) and Hayes (2014) – contain accounts of teacher education activity, by programme managers and teacher educators, which describe pre-service (Initial Teacher Training – ITT) and in-service (Continuing Professional Development – CPD). A particularly important theme in these accounts, is the value for programme participants, particularly programme managers and teacher educators, of having 'a space for considering how stakeholders have evaluated the innovation being reported' (Edge and Mann, 2013).

In Edge and Mann (2013) 14 accounts of practice provide evaluations and reflections of developing innovations in pre-service teacher education. The over-arching definition of innovation is 'new-in-context': a characterisation which addresses the core issues for practice in many contexts. Reflection is an abiding strand through the accounts, both as a core skill and disposition that teacher educators are seeking to develop in teachers, and also as a strategy that teacher educators and programme leaders use to develop their practices, and learn from experience. The accounts in the collection prioritise 'self-evaluation' as a strategy for effective teacher learning within pre-service programmes. The theme of handover, so that trainee teachers self-evaluate, and take responsibility for progressing their learning, is evident in many of the papers.

In Hayes (2014), many accounts describe teachers and teacher educators under pressure. For example Chang, Jeon and Ahn in South Korea note the challenge of establishing a space for teacher and teacher educator learning in the face of 'government-mandated quality control policies', and the 'competency rating system applied by the government officials' (2014: 272). What can be identified in this context are two forms of PE running in parallel. The official accountability-oriented evaluation focuses on outcomes and performance, while the reported study examines processes and evolutions of thinking which underpin changes in practice, and explain how teachers and teacher educators meet the challenges presented by policies and external drivers of their work. An important theme of the evaluations reported in Hayes (2014) is the way teachers and teacher educators cope with innovations in the field of information technology. Karavas and Papadopoulou (2014) and Woodward et al. (2014) provide evidence of success, but also provide insights and guidance relevant to other contexts, and to the overall task of our field in terms of understanding how teachers learn and change. The themes of diversity, practitioner investment, and reflection are also reflected in the accounts of Pickering and Gunashekar (2016), a collection of papers from the 2015 ELT conference in Hyderabad. The emphasis in these papers, generally written by teacher educators and programme leaders is the emergent, creative responses, based on both data analysis and personal experience, to deal with the challenges which emerge in teacher education programmes.

These conceptualisations of programme evaluation represent key shifts in recent decades which are particularly relevant to the development of ELTE programmes. The main direction of travel has been from programme evaluation as a well-defined activity with clear parameters of purpose and method, to a broad inclusive basket of activities which range from research-type studies, to quality assurance and enhancement activities and policy-oriented reviews, to exploratory and reflective aspects of practice. Increasingly, the evaluative and the reflective constitute a shared platform, as the development of programmes is led by practitioners who have a sense of ownership of, and investment in programmes.

The next section of this chapter examines the issues explored in language teacher education programme evaluation under four further questions:

- What is the focus of evaluating language teacher education?
- When is the evaluation carried out?
- Who does the evaluation?
- How are evaluations carried out?

Research and applications

1. The WHAT in evaluating language teacher education

Pre-service teacher education

A general trend has been towards the development of programmes which prepare teachers for an innovative communicative language teaching curriculum and a critical perspective of the teacher as an autonomous professional, and away from behaviourist, technique-based programmes which equip teachers to implement established routines, often in a transmissive and lock-step classroom. The accounts of pre-service programmes in Edge and Mann (2013) illustrate this trend. Cheng (2013) focuses on using materials, describing successful ways of getting trainees to adapt and augment set materials. Innovative components of programmes, particularly using technology, are documented: multi-media in the language classroom (Kurtoglu-Hooton, 2013), Corpus Linguistics (Özbilgin and Neufeld, 2013) and Knowledge about Language online (Gakonga, 2013). While we have a range of perspectives on these knowledge aspects of pre-service programmes, there is less on the ways target language proficiency affects teacher learning. A focus here is the affective impact: the ways levels of proficiency impacts on teacher's confidence and their capacity to teach and learn through teaching (Anderson, 2016). Hiver (2013) in a research study which examined the role 'possible selves' played in English language teacher development found a close correspondence between 'language self-efficacy' and 'teaching self-efficacy', a finding which would suggest that in that context (South Korean public sector schools) it is important for programmes to raise teachers' proficiency level and related confidence as users of English.

A trend which is evident in recent evaluation studies of pre-service programmes is the focus on reflection and collaboration in ELTE programmes (Mann and Walsh, 2013; Mann and Walsh, 2017). The role of reflection is explored as a skill and identity development node, and increasingly viewed as a way of implementing the approach first set out in Wallace (1991). Walsh and Mann (2015) focus on how this can be led by data from classroom interaction. Farrell in a series of papers has set out how this can be achieved: Farrell (2007) specifies how a reflective practice (RP) framework can map 'conceptual change' in language teacher education (2007: 221). In a review of 116 studies on RP (Farrell, 2016), he notes a shift in recent decades from a focus on RP as a set of skills and techniques developed in programmes, to a focus on reflexive practice, a process of 'teachers undertaking a self-analysis' (2016: 224). Gunn (2010) and Gün (2011) both describe the positive impact of linking reflection to the maintaining of a practicum journal in pre-service programmes. Nguyen and Ngo (2017) describe the success of integrating reflection into the practical component of a programme in Vietnam. Wherever a reflective component or strand is introduced and evaluated, it is found to be success: there may be an advocacy effect here, but as discussed below, this may not be problematic.

A major strand in pre-service programmes which arises from evaluation studies is the benefits for trainee teachers of collaborative learning, specifically being part of a supportive professional learning community (PLC). In a meta-analysis of the impact of PLCs on teacher learning and development, Vescio et al. (2008) found that they increased communication and collaboration in schools. The sense of being part of a PLC led to teachers sharing materials, peer observing, and engaging in critical friends groups, as well as leading to enhanced learning gains by students. In ELTE programmes, similar benefits have been reported (Kiely and Askham, 2012). Evaluations of induction programmes for teachers new to a given workplace are reported as having similar benefits (Fenton-Smith and Torpey, 2009). These studies focus on issues of transition and continuity between the training programme and the work context, which have been a challenge in language teacher education.

In-service teacher education

A key issue in in-service teacher education for language teachers is the continuity of professional learning, the CPD journey, as characterised in Hayes (2014). Evaluation studies of implemented initiatives illustrate the importance of a participant-led agenda: the focus of the training has to connect with a felt need on the part of teachers. Harland and Kinder (1997) in a seminal study of CPD impact in UK mainstream education emphasise the importance of relevance and agency in order to achieve positive outcomes of CPD initiatives. Morrow and Schocker (1993) note a similar situation in CPD for English language teachers: they propose 'process evaluation', so that the agenda of participating teachers shapes the direction and development of programmes. Kiely and Davies (2010), and Burns and Edwards (2014) also note that engagement by teachers in CPD programme derives from a sense of relevance to their work.

A key issue in CPD is the cultural transformation of practice, for example, shifting the English language curriculum from a knowledge-based approach, based on the intricacies of the grammatical system, and success in examinations based on this, to a skills-based approach where the focus is on language as communication. This has been an educational priority in many national systems over recent decades, and a focus for the design and implementation of teacher education programmes. A range of evaluation studies of CPD programmes engage with this issue. Pacek (1996) notes the benefit of 'negative evaluation': acknowledgement of (in her case) Japanese teachers feeling that the proposed ELT curriculum is not feasible for them in their contexts. More recent studies attest to the seriousness of this issue, as teachers from Outer Circle countries such as East Asia participate in CPD programmes in the Inner Circle, typically UK, Australia and US, as part of policies to transform English language teaching (Li and Edwards, 2013; Hunter and Kiely, 2016). Studies of similar programmes for Japanese teachers (Yukari, 2017) and Vietnamese teachers (Nguyen and Walkinshaw, 2018) found less positive impacts: in both cases the approach to teaching and the specific forms of practice encountered and promoted in training contexts in Inner Circle countries did not fit well with requirements and expectations in schools in Japan and Vietnam. While there has been an increasing focus on examining the impact on the work of teachers after the programme, there is still room to develop the evaluations of such programmes in two ways. First, evaluations can provide finer-grained distinctions between satisfaction with the experience of participating in a course in another country, and satisfaction with the experience of integrating novel strategies in their own teaching. Second, evaluations can provide more longitudinal accounts, so that the impact of such programmes is tracked over time, as part of teachers' lifelong learning.

In many contexts, in-service programmes have been structured along cascade models, where trained teachers lead CP sessions in their own schools and contexts. While there have been some evaluations, for example, Taylor (1992) and Hayes (2000), of aspects of cascading CPD, there are opportunities presented by theories of PLCs and communities of practice to examine the impact of such modes of in-service teacher education in establishing sustainable teacher learning through cascades.

2. WHEN to evaluate teacher education programmes

There are two main options in response to this question. First, evaluations can be carried out during and at the end of the programme. Second, the evaluation carried out after the programme, when teachers are in work. These evaluations can be characterised as focusing largely on *satisfaction* and *impact* respectively. In-programme evaluations are likely to capture aspects of the experience of participating and learning in the programme, while evaluations carried out when teachers are back at work are likely to capture perspectives on the usefulness of the training in terms of addressing challenges of classroom practice, and capacity to implement new policies and procedures. Kiely and Askham (2012) for example, collected evaluation data in months two and three of work after the end of the training programme, and then again in months five and six. The study of impact of an overseas intensive course for teachers of English in China (Li and Edwards, 2013; Hunter and Kiely, 2016) carried out the evaluation after the course, when teachers were back at work. Peacock (2009), carried out during and at the end of the programme, describes the lack of opportunity to gain substantial data sets from alumni of the programme and their employers as a limitation of his evaluation of a pre-service programme in Hong Kong.

Delayed evaluations of programmes are challenging in terms of design and resources, but are likely to become more important. We know from life history research of English language teachers for example, Hayes (2005) that change is continuous, and different learning experiences merge as teacher identity and transformative practice emerge. The initial period of work is often focused on survival, that is, managing classrooms and workload using the course book, without much attention to creative and transformative practice, reported by some novice teachers in Kiely and Askham (2012). Tribble (2012) contains a number of delayed evaluations, in the sense of reviews and reflections on projects designed to harness language teacher education programmes (pre-service and CPD) to the task of English language curriculum reform within national and university systems. Some note the lack of impact: Zikri (2012), reviewing the impact of a CPD programme implemented in Egypt from 1975–91, observes limited enduring impact largely due to inadequate needs analysis and engagement with the issues that concerned teachers. Many evaluations however, observe enduring transformations, both in terms of establishing innovative programmes and new institutions (for example, Komorowska, 2012), and in terms of establishing local champions of innovative approaches, who go on to have impact through their work as education leaders and teacher educators, for example, Dick (2012) and Wiseman (2014). The enduring success of these projects is due in part to the ways key stakeholders were persuaded that the innovative practices are worth investing in.

3. WHO evaluates language teacher education programmes?

There are two principal options here: external or internal evaluator. The former is supported by different discourses. In early programme evaluation theory, where the focus was on deciding between alternatives, there was a preference for external evaluators. They would be disinterested, and could be presumed to provide an objective assessment of the alternatives. More recently however, the role of internal evaluators has become more important: they are in a position to take forward to the development agenda, and lead the use of evaluation findings for the improvement of the programme, much as proposed by the principles of evaluation for development and the guidelines of the PRODESS initiative of the British Council in the 1990s (Kiely and Rea-Dickins, 2005). The issue which arises is that of *advocacy*: a concern that the success of the programme as represented by the evaluation findings might be due to the commitment or investment of the programme leaders, rather than to the philosophy, strategies or activities of the programme. The response to this question is acknowledgement that even the best designed programme does not work on its own: it requires implementation with commitment and creativity. The teacher educators is a part of the programme, and the learning within the programme is due in no small part from that investment and the notion of relationship developed, as within any professional learning community (PLC – see above).

In their introduction to the collection of papers Edge and Mann note that each account should have 'a space for considering how stakeholders have evaluated the innovation being reported' (2013: 11). The editors' call here is a recognition of on the one hand, the assumption that practitioners evaluate innovations within their programmes, and on the other, that such evaluations add to our understanding of both programme evaluation and teacher education.

4. HOW are language teacher education programmes evaluated?

Evaluation studies are normally carried out using the methods of social science research, particularly surveys and case studies. Surveys using questionnaires are particularly important, whether the focus is 'satisfaction' within or at the end of programmes. Such questionnaire-based evaluations are typically part of end-of-course evaluations within universities and other organisations. Surveys are also used to determine 'impact', when teachers document that ways training affects their teaching and other work routines (van Batenberg, 2013; Karavas and Popadopoulou, 2014). Cheng (2013) draws on the findings of two questionnaires to evaluate her innovative programme on materials evaluation: the regular, institutional student satisfaction feedback form, and a specially designed questionnaire to capture more specific accounts of participation in the materials initiative. Online platforms have made such surveys easier to manage (Ozbilgin and Neufeld, 2013). Two evaluations of pre-service programmes discussed above – Peacock (2009); Kiely and Askham (2012) – make extensive use of interviews rather than questionnaires. The rationale in both cases is the opportunity in interview contexts, to explore what has not been specified precisely in the initial question. In Kiely and Askham teachers were interviewed twice in the first six months in work (the budget included a small payment to participants who participated in two interviews). The focus of questions was the nature of work experiences, and the ways the components of the pre-service course prepared them for these experiences. The data show how the course input and experience was part of the reflection on and analysis of work experiences. One teacher for example, drew on advice from a tutor to manage his limitations in language analysis:

Interview extract

This was my weakest side (1) [...]
    I'm a lot better at selecting what I want to teach (1) and focussing on it [...]
    But the advice we were given, which I thought was very good, was if you're ever given a question you don't know the answer to, don't answer it (2) just take it on board and come back, come back later.

(Kiely and Askham, 2012: 509)

This evaluation also drew on documents from the programme, such as portfolios of materials and lesson plans and reflective commentaries on lessons. These were analysed thematically in terms of impact of the components of the programme. The analysis of the data in this study generated a conceptualisation of teacher learning as *furnished imagination*:

The construct represents what new teachers take to work. It illuminates the teacher learning that has taken place: understanding of key knowledge bases, procedural competence in planning for and managing lessons, a disposition characterised by enthusiasm and readiness, and a teacher identity—a sense of belonging in the world of TESOL.

(Kiely and Askham, 2012: 509)

Content analysis of course documents such as reflective journals is a data strategy used in many of the reports in Edge and Mann (2013). Focus groups are widely used, for example, Kurtoglu-Hooton (2013), and Gakonga (2013) combine forms of group discussion with a range of web-based tools – blogs, e-portfolio, and more traditional training processes. Oprandy et al. (2013) use group discussions, such as practicum conferences, combined with written reflections to capture the changing perspectives of trainees.

Classroom observations integral to practical teacher education programmes are also used, not only as a way to understand the impact of particular initiatives, but also for needs analysis and programme design (Woodward et al., 2014). Li and Edwards (2013) used classroom observation in their evaluation of an overseas in-service course. The observation focus was innovative practices which could be linked to the programme focus, and also 're-invention' of innovations for better alignment with contextual features.

Four points relating to evaluation methodology emerge. First, a great deal of routine information is used in evaluations, particularly in web-based programmes, with enhanced rigour in analysis used to determine the key valid messages. Second, interviews are used for large-scale surveys, and though short, these capture some aspects of the complexity of stakeholder views which might not be accessible by questionnaires alone. Third, essays, blogs and journals, written by the course participants are used as data, thus accessing the reflective responses of trainees and teachers to the programme. This strategy aligns with the Exploratory Practice tradition of understanding classrooms, where potentially exploitable pedagogic activities (PEPAs) become tools for understanding classroom processes (Allwright and Hanks, 2008; Slimani-Rolls and Kiely, 2018). Fourth, the intention to involve alumni, that is, teachers in work is a particularly challenging aspect of data collection, but particularly useful in understanding impact (Kiely and Askham, 2012; Li and Edwards, 2013). There are two directions for development of evaluation methods here: first, increase efficiency and validity by constructing routine information and processes as data. And second, explore the opportunity to pay or otherwise reward stakeholders such as alumni of programmes, as a means of securing their analyses and perspectives for understanding the programme, and as a recognition of the value of their learning experience over time for the ELTE field.

Conclusion

Programme evaluation is a test of effectiveness. In the context of language teacher education programmes, this means understanding on the one hand the ways the set curriculum works, and on the other understanding how the investments of the participants support teacher learning. A key feature of this learning is enhanced capacity to transform practice in classrooms and programmes so that students of English achieve greater success. There are many chains in the reasoning here, and the processes of understanding them are complex. Programme evaluations – quality assurance measures such as course satisfaction surveys, large-scale research studies, and local focused practitioner research studies – can make a contribution to understanding effectiveness. The evolution of the place, purposes and methods of programme evaluation in ELTE, as surveyed in this chapter suggests increasing levels of integration into practice, and greater use of evidence-based measures to improve programmes. There are areas where more PE activity is needed, for example, the relationship between English language proficiency levels and teaching effectiveness, the operation of cascade structures in CPD initiatives, and the long-term impacts of intensive courses in workplaces, or in transborder settings. The key to securing attention to these issues is more discussion in professional settings, and more publications which put PE activity in the public domain.

Further reading

Davis, J. McE., Norris, J. M., Malone, M. E., McKay, T. H. and Young, A-S. (eds) (2018) *Useful Assessment and Evaluation in Language Education*. Washington, DC: Georgetown University Press.

Edge, J. and Mann, S. (eds) (2013) *Innovations in Pre-Service Education and Training for English Language Teachers*. London: The British Council.

Hayes, D. (ed.) (2014) *Innovations in the Continuing Professional Development of English Language Teachers*. London: The British Council

Kiely, R. and Rea-Dickins, P. (2005) *Programme Evaluation in Language Education*. Basingstoke: Palgrave Macmillan.

References

Allwright, D. and Hanks, J. (2008) *The Developing Language Learner: An Introduction to Exploratory Practice*. Basingstoke: Palgrave.

Anderson, J. (2016) 'Initial Teacher Training Courses and Non-Native Speaker Teachers'. *ELT Journal*, 70(3) 261–274.

Beretta, A. and Davies, A. (1985) 'Evaluation of the Bangalore Project'. *English Language Teaching Journal*, 39(2) 121–127.

Borg, S. (2006) *Teacher Cognition and Language Education: Research and Practice*. London: Continuum.

Burns, A. (2005) 'Action Research: An Evolving Paradigm?'. *Language Teaching*, 38 57–74.

Burns, A. and Edwards, E. (2014) 'Introducing innovation through action research in an Australian national programme: experiences and insights', in Hayes, D. (ed.) *Innovations in the Continuing Professional Development of English Language Teachers*. London: The British Council: 65–88.

Chang, K., Jeon, Y. and Ahn, H. (2014) 'Investigating continuing professional development for teacher educators in South Korea: opportunities and constraints', in Hayes, D. (ed.) *Innovations in the Continuing Professional Development of English Language Teachers*. London: The British Council: 271–300.

Cheng, X. (2013) 'Cultivating expertise in materials design in pre-service English teacher education', in Edge, J. and Mann, S. (eds) *Innovations in Pre-Service Education and Training for English Language Teachers*. London: The British Council: 99–114.

Dick, L. (2012) 'The challenge of monitoring and evaluation in Sri Lanka', in Tribble, C. (ed.) *Managing Change in English Language Education: Lessons from Experience*. London: The British Council: 187–192.

Edge, J. and Mann, S. (eds) (2013) *Innovations in Pre-Service Education and Training for English Language Teachers*. London: The British Council.

Ellis, R. (2010) 'Second Language Acquisition, Teacher Education and Language Pedagogy'. *Language Teaching*, 432 182–201.

Farrell, T. S. C. (2007) *Reflective Language Teaching: From Research to Practice*. London: Continuum.

Farrell, T. S. C. (2016) 'Anniversary Article: The Practices of Encouraging TESOL Teachers to Engage in Reflective Practice: An Appraisal of Recent Research Contributions'. *Language Teacher Research*, 20(2) 223–247.

Fenton-Smith B. and Torpey, M. J. (2013) 'Orienting EFL Teachers: Principles Arising from an Evaluation of an Induction Program in a Japanese University'. *Language Teaching Research*, 17(2) 228–250.

Freeman, D. (1998) *Doing Teacher-Research: From Inquiry to Understanding*. New York: Heinle-Thomson.

Gakonga, J. (2013) '"Being there?": Comparing synchronous and recorded', in Edge, J. and Mann, S. (eds) *Innovations in Pre-Service Education and Training for English Language Teachers*. London: The British Council: 231–243.

Greenwood, J. (1985) 'Bangalore Revisited: A Reluctant Complaint'. *English Language Teaching Journal*, 39(4) 268–273.

Gün, B. (2011) 'Quality Self-Reflection Through Reflection Training'. *ELT Journal*, 65(2) 126–135.

Gunn, C. L. (2010) 'Exploring MATESOL Student "Resistance" to Reflection'. *Language Teaching Research*, 14(2) 208–223.

Harland, J. and Kinder, K. (1997) 'Teachers' Continuing Professional Development: Framing a Model of Outcomes'. *Journal of In-service Education*, 23(1) 71–84.

Hayes, D. (2000) 'Cascade Training and Teachers' Professional Development'. *ELT Journal*, 54(2) 135–145.

Hayes, D. (2005) 'Exploring the Lives of Non-Native Speaking English Educators in Sri Lanka'. *Teachers and Teaching: Theory and Practice*, 11(2) 169–194.

Hayes, D. (ed.) (2014) *Innovations in the Continuing Professional Development of English Language Teachers*. London: The British Council.

Hiver, P. (2013) 'The Interplay of Possible Language Teacher Selves in Professional Development Choices'. *Language Teaching Research*, 17(2) 210–227.

Hunter, D. and Kiely, R. (2016) 'The Idea as a Mechanism in Language Teacher Development'. *Journal of Second Language Teaching and Research*, 5(1) 37–61.

Johnson, K. E. (2009) *Second Language Teacher Education: A Sociocultural Perspective*. New York: Routledge.

Karavas, E. and Papadopoulou, S. (2014) 'Introducing a paradigm shift in EFL continuing professional development in Greece: the development of online communities of practice', in Hayes, D. (ed.) *Innovations in the Continuing Professional Development of English Language Teachers*. London: The British Council: 179–206.

Kiely, R. (2009) 'Small Answers to the Big Question: Learning from Language Programme Evaluation'. *Language Teaching Research*, 13(1) 99–116.

Kiely, R. and Askham, J. (2012) 'Furnished Imagination: The Impact of Pre-Service Teacher Training on Early Career Work in TESOL'. *TESOL Quarterly*, 46(3) 495–517.

Kiely, R and Davis, M. (2010) From Transmission to Transformation: Teacher Learning in ESOL. *Language Teaching Research*, 14(3) 277–296.

Kiely, R. and Rea-Dickins, P. (2005) *Programme Evaluation in Language Education*. Basingstoke: Palgrave Macmillan.

Kiely, R., Murphy, D. F., Rea-Dickins, P. and Reid, M. I. (1995) *PRODESS Evaluation Guidelines*. Manchester: The British Council.

Komorowska, H. (2012) 'The teacher training colleges project in Poland', in Tribble, C. (ed.) *Managing Change in English Language Education: Lessons from Experience*. London: The British Council: 147–153.

Kurtoglu-Hooton, N. (2013) 'Providing "the spark" for reflection from a digital platform', in Edge, J. and Mann, S. (eds) (2013) *Innovations in Pre-Service Education and Training for English Language Teachers*. London: The British Council: 17–32.

Li, D. and Edwards, V. (2013) 'The Impact of Overseas Training on Curriculum Innovation and Change in English Language Education in Western China'. *Language Teaching Research*, 17(4) 390–408.

MacDonald, B. (1976) 'Evaluation and control of education', in Tawney D. A. (ed.) *Curriculum Evaluation Today: Trends and Implications*. London: Macmillan Education: 125–136.

Macilwaine, H. (2016) 'Developing the Trinity College Certificate in Teaching English to speakers of other languages in India', in Pickering, G. and Gunashekar, P. (eds) *Ensuring Quality in English Language Teacher Education*. New Delhi: The British Council: 138–146.

Mann, S. and Walsh, S. (2013) 'RP or "RIP": A Critical Perspective on Reflective Practice'. *Applied Linguistics Review*, 4(2) 291–315.

Mann, S. and Walsh, S. (2017) *Reflective Practice in English Language Teaching: Research-Based Principles and Practices*. Abingdon: Taylor and Francis.

Morrow, K. and Schocker, M. (1993) 'Process Evaluation in an INSET Course'. *ELT Journal*, 47(1) 47–55.

Nguyen, H. T. M. and Ngo, N. T. H. (2017) 'Learning to Reflect Through Peer Mentoring in a TESOL Practicum'. *ELT Journal*, 72(2) 187–198.

Nguyen, X. N. C. M. and Walkinshaw, I. (2018) 'Autonomy in Teaching Practice: Insights from Vietnamese English Language Teachers Trained in Inner-Circle Countries'. *Teachers and Teacher Education*, 69 21–32,

Oprandy, R, Addington R., Brown, C. and Rutter, M. (2013) 'Fostering collaborative conversations between pre-service trainees and serving teachers through supervisory role plays', in Edge, J. and Mann, S. (eds) *Innovations in Pre-Service Education and Training for English Language Teachers*. London: The British Council: 81–98.

Organisation for Economic Cooperation and Development (OECD) (2009) *Teaching and Learning International Survey (TALIS)*. Paris: OECD.

Özbilgin, A. and Neufeld, S. (2013) 'iCorpus: making corpora meaningful for pre-service teacher education', in Edge, J. and Mann, S. (eds) (2013) *Innovations in Pre-Service Education and Training for English Language Teachers*. London: The British Council: 181–200.

Pacek D. (1996) 'Lessons to be Learnt from Negative Evaluation'. *ELT Journal*, 50(4) 335–343.

Patton, M. Q. (1982) *Practical Evaluation*. Thousand Oaks, CA: Sage.

Parlett, M. and Hamilton, D. (1972) 'Evaluation as illumination: a new approach to the study of innovatory programmes'. *Occasional Paper No 9*. Edinburgh: Centre for Research in the Educational Sciences.

Peacock, M. (2009) 'The Evaluation of Foreign Language Teacher Education Programmes'. *Language Teaching Research*, 13 259–278.

Pickering, G. and Gunashekar, P. (eds) (2016) *Ensuring Quality in English Language Teacher Education*. New Delhi: The British Council.

Reeves, J. (2010) 'Teacher Learning by Script'. *Language Teaching Research*, 14(3) 241–258.

Rea-Dickins, P. and Germaine K. (1992) *Evaluation*. Oxford: Oxford University Press.

Richards, J. C. and Nunan, D. (eds) (1990) *Second Language Teacher Education*. Cambridge: Cambridge University Press.

Samb, M. (2013) 'Formative assessment for a pedagogy of success', in Edge, J. and Mann, S. (eds) *Innovations in Pre-Service Education and Training for English Language Teachers*. London: The British Council: 33–46.

Scherer, G. A. C. and Wertheimer, M. (1964) *A Psycholinguistic Experiment in Foreign Language Teaching*. New York: McGraw-Hill.

Slimani-Rolls, A. and Kiely, R. (2018) *Exploratory Practice for Continuing Professional Development: An Innovative Approach for Language Teachers*. Basingstoke: Palgrave Macmillan.

Stenhouse, L. (1975) *An Introduction to Curriculum Research and Development*. London: Heinemann.

Stufflebeam, D. L., Foley, W. J., Gephart, W. J., Hammond, L. R., Merriman, H. O. and Provus, M. M. (1971) *Educational Evaluation and Decision-Making in Education*. Ithaca, NY: Peacock Press.

Taylor, R. (1992) 'The Production of Training Packs in In-Service Teacher Training'. *ELT Journal*, 46(4) 356–361.

Tribble, C. (ed.) (2012) *Managing Change in English Language Education: Lessons from Experience*. London: The British Council.

van Batenburg, E. (2013) 'Beyond theory and practice: Introducing praxis in pre-service language teacher education', in Edge, J. and Mann, S. (eds) *Innovations in Pre-Service Education and Training for English Language Teachers*. London: The British Council: 217–230.

Vescio, V., Ross, D. and Adams, A. (2008) 'A Review of Research on the Impact of Professional Learning Communities on Teaching Practice and Student Learning'. *Teaching and Teacher Education*, 24(1) 80–91.

Wallace, M. J. (1991) *Training Foreign Language Teachers*. Cambridge: Cambridge University Press.

Walsh, S. and Mann, S. (2015) 'Doing Reflective Practice: A Data-Led Way Forward'. *ELT Journal*, 69(4) 351–362.

Weir, C. and Roberts, J. (1994) *Evaluation in ELT*. Oxford: Blackwell.

Wiseman, A. (2014) '"My life changed when I saw that notice": an analysis of the long-term impact of a continuing professional development programme in Bulgaria', in Hayes, D. (ed.) *Innovations in the Continuing Professional Development of English Language Teachers*. London: The British Council: 301–315.

Woods, D. (1996) *Teacher Cognition in Language Teaching*. Cambridge: Cambridge University Press.

Woodward, C., Griffiths, M. and Solly, M. (2014) 'English in Action: a new approach to continuing professional development through the use of mediated video, peer support and low-cost mobile phones in Bangladesh', in Hayes, D. (ed.) *Innovations in the Continuing Professional Development of English Language Teachers*. London: The British Council: 227–248.

Yukari Takimoto, A. (2017) 'A Visit to Purgatory: Cultural Mismatch Between a Japanese International Teacher Candidate and her American Supervisors and Mentor Teachers'. *Teaching and Teacher Education*, 68 200–209.

Zikri, M. (2012) 'Redirecting a curriculum development project in Egypt', in Tribble, C. (ed.) *Managing Change in English Language Education: Lessons from Experience*. London: The British Council: 201–208.

7

Suggestions for teacher educators from a gentle iconoclast and a fellow explorer

John F. Fanselow and Takaaki Hiratsuka

For some, *iconoclast* has a negative connotation because it suggests attacking: breaking images. We hope the *gentle* before *iconoclast* makes the connotation less negative in our title (suggested by Alan Maley). Preceding *iconoclast* with *gentle* is a great example of an oxymoron. By using *gentle*, we hope to convey our intention is to explore everything, not to attack anything. If we do not question what we do and the results, we cannot make discoveries. Jacob Bronowski (1956) in *Science and Human Values* put it this way: 'In science and in art and in self-knowledge, we explore and move constantly by turning to the world of sense to ask, "Is this so?" This is the habit of truth, always minute yet always urgent' (p. 43).

I, John, have been writing, speaking about, teaching, analysing recordings of classes and conversations with teachers and exploring how we teach and how we prepare teachers for decades. I, Takaaki, am a member of the more recent 'seekers' who want to understand what we do in new ways by questioning accepted practices, changing them in small ways and comparing the results. Here is our interaction about teacher education:

Takaaki: *Though I want to discuss how you decided that we need to explore what we do and the results, I want to ask you first how you got involved in teacher development. As I recall, your first experience was working with teachers in Nigeria.*

John: Yes, my first experience preparing teachers was as a Peace Corps Volunteer in Nigeria, assigned to teach in a teacher training college. As background, The Peace Corps is an American organisation started by President John F. Kennedy in 1961 to send Americans to other countries to learn about them, to return to the US and share what they learned and try to make some useful contribution to the countries they were sent to. Many countries have similar organisations such as VSO in the UK and JICA in Japan.

Takaaki: *Did you apply to be a Peace Corps Volunteer in 1961 because you were interested in teacher preparation?*

John: No. I applied to the Peace Corps to improve my Spanish. I wanted to be a volunteer to learn. But there were no openings for me in Latin America in 1961. It would have been quite presumptuous of me to apply to a programme to prepare teachers since I had taught only one English and one Spanish class for one semester in a high school.

Takaaki: *What did you teach at the Teacher Training College in Nigeria?*

John: I taught English language and literature to raise the level of English of the teachers. And I used some methods in a demonstration classroom at the College that a British Council English Language Specialist, John Rogers, had demonstrated in my English classes. I also 'supervised' practice teachers when teachers went to primary schools to practice methods they were learning on campus. During practice teaching, no classes were held on campus. Staff met at the college with the practice teachers that they had visited to discuss lessons observed and plan lessons for the next day.

Takaaki: *Tell me some of the fundamental lessons from your experiences in Nigeria and a suggestion that grew out of them.*

John: My first lesson, and the theme of my teaching and writing for five plus decades, is that I see my role as a partner with those who take my classes or participate in my workshops or read what I write. In Uyo, Nigeria, I learned very quickly that my role was to jointly explore what questions each teacher had, jointly note what the teachers did, observe the results and then jointly generate another activity and compare the results. John Rogers, who observed my classes and demonstrated methods in my classes, was key to this idea. He did not say 'Do this because I said you should' but rather, 'Try this and let's compare what students wrote, said, read, etc. when we do X rather than Z.' He was a collaborator rather than a dictator.

Takaaki: *Sounds like the specialist was providing you what some call strategic mediation (Tharp & Gallimore, 1988; Wertsch, 1985) then. The kind of assistance that is tailored to meet trainees' needs and is adequately moderated. So, what else led you to see your responsibility as a joint exploration?*

John: Ignorance. I was being asked to supervise teachers who had two to 20 more years' experience than I had and who were teaching content that was unfamiliar to me. I knew less content than the teachers I was supposed to be supervising. And I was not familiar with any ESL methods until John gave us methods books and demonstrated in my classes many of the methods in the books. But I thought that if I understood their practices it would be easier for them to understand the alternative practices they had experienced in my classes. And it would be easier to find ways that alternative methods could supplement rather than replace the activities they were used to using.

Takaaki: *You said you knew less than the teachers, how did you translate this lesson into practice? I mean, how could you supposedly supervise them if you knew less about what they were teaching and how they were teaching than they did?*

John: In a few ways. Since I had never supervised a teacher in my life, I did not know what I was going to do when I visited the practice teachers. So, before the visits, I met with the practice teachers and asked them what they wanted me to do as their 'supervisor'. They said they wanted to learn activities that would interest students more, ways to teach grammar and vocabulary that were less boring, and activities that would improve the language skills of the students faster than the ones they had been using. They also wanted to learn how to spend less time planning lessons so they would have more energy for teaching. I have been hearing questions similar to these through my entire career.

I also asked them to write down activities they used that they thought were effective. Here there was some divergence of opinion. And when I noted this, I realised that one way to expand the range of activities in addition to using ones that John had introduced was to have teachers use each other's methods.

Takaaki: *And you did not have knowledge about what the primary students were learning?*

John: No. The Nigerian teachers were as you might expect teaching Nigerian history – what Lord Lugard did when he came to Nigeria and developed the constitution of 1914; Nigerian geography – the River Niger, groundnut and palm oil production, to name just a few areas I was totally ignorant of. They were not teaching American history or European history, which are courses I had taken. The fact that the teachers were teaching material that was completely unknown to me was an advantage because when I asked questions about the content I did not know the answer, I was exploring what they were teaching as well as how they were teaching.

Takaaki: *It was a kind of natural information-gap then. So, my question is how you managed to think about alternative ways of teaching which they had said they were interested in?*

John: Fortunately for me, there were two sections of each primary class, which met at the same time. The teacher in each section taught the same subjects at the same time in the school I was in. So, I was able to observe one teacher in one section for 20 minutes doing math and the other one for the next 20 minutes. As you might expect, each teacher taught slightly differently. When I observed the two sections, I wrote down what each had done.

   Some teachers gave directions aloud. Others wrote them on the board. Some teachers had their students copy sentences from the board and others asked their students to write what they said aloud and then wrote them on the board. When I met teachers at the end of the day, who both taught the same subject in two different streams, I would say, for example,

Okon, Benedict wrote his directions on the board. You said them aloud. Tomorrow, try writing them on the board. And Benedict, you wrote the directions on the board, tomorrow try saying the directions aloud.

Or,

Pius, you had your students underline the words they did not know and had them write a synonym above the unknown words. Okonkwo drew sketches on the board above words the students did not know. So tomorrow, try drawing a few sketches rather than writing synonyms. And Pius, have your students both draw sketches and write synonyms.

Takaaki: *So, a key lesson for you was the importance of comparing two different practices and having the teachers try alternatives. This reminds me of some of the emergent concepts in the field such as interthinking (Mercer, 1995) and dialogic praxis in teacher preparation (Bieler, 2010).*

John: I guess so, but I have not used those terms. They are new to me, but useful. And they resonate with how I described our role as teacher educators in *Contrasting Conversations* (Fanselow, 1992a):

I am going to observe you. Afterwards, when I look at excerpts from your lesson with you, I hope that through the analysis—playing with the words we use to discuss the lesson— we can see something we did not see before about our own teaching. Jointly comparing similarities and differences between your teaching practices and beliefs and my teaching is likely to reveal multiple interpretations of what we described. Let's explore teaching together. I came to your class not only with a magnifying glass to look carefully at what was being done, but with a mirror so that I could see that what you were doing is a reflection of much of what I do.

(p. 2)

Takaaki: *So, when you told Pius to draw sketches because his fellow teacher had, I guess you were starting a conversation rather than prescribing and suggesting that sketches are better than synonyms.*

John: I like to think my suggestions to teachers are different from prescriptions. Why? Because as I imply in the quote from *Contrasting Conversations* I just read to you, I make suggestions to provide opportunities to compare what teachers routinely do with alternatives, not for them to adopt the option because I suggested it. I want the teachers to determine whether they adopt the alternative based on their analysis of the results of contrasting activities. Teachers are tired of hearing me say, 'Don't believe anything I say, or what anyone else says; question everything.' These admonitions are not helpful unless I enable teachers to generate alternatives to supplement what they are doing.

Takaaki: *John, when many hear your name, they think of your advice to try the opposite, the title of your 1992 book (Fanselow, 1992b). Is this a way to enable teachers to generate alternatives?*

John: It is one way. But I have learned that the methods teachers create from doing the opposite are more powerful if we list some criteria for determining the likelihood that the opposite will be useful.

Takaaki: *Some criteria, huh? I'm intrigued.*

John: There are thousands of alternatives in teaching just as in medicine. Bloodletting was one used for hundreds of years in Western medicine but it killed more people than it helped. The criteria for this practice were based on a false premise that our body had four liquids.

If a teacher usually asks students to memorise ten word equivalents each day with no context, one alternative is 0 word equivalents; but another is 20 word equivalents. The 0 option would mean the teacher realises that students use words incorrectly when they match them with a word in their first language and that content words need to be integrated with function words and that words have meanings only in context. The 20 word equivalent option is based on the assumption that we learn languages by memorising lists of words out of context. This alternative is like bloodletting – based on a faulty assumption.

The following are criteria that I have developed through the years for generating alternatives. Alternatives should:

- be easy to try for teachers and students
- require thinking, problem solving or prediction
- be novel
- integrate grammar and vocabulary
- enable students to use language rather than listen to the teacher talk about language
- provide incomplete information rather than complete information
- provide chances for students to change mediums, for example give students opportunities to change sketches into language, printed words into spoken words, spoken words into printed words, gestures into spoken words, etc.
- integrate the four skills plus attend to the fifth skill, emotions
- personalise the language used

- make only small changes
- have students do activities that make use of what they already know.

Takaaki: *Can you tell me some alternatives that meet some of these criteria?*

John: Reading aloud while holding a text and looking at it is a universal practice. One of the most powerful alternatives to reading aloud is read and look up. Michael West (1960), one of the authors John introduced me to, suggested we have learners read sense groups silently, put the text on the desk, think about the meaning and then say as much as makes sense aloud. Both the student who reads the phrases plus the other students then write what was said. In Nigeria in 1961 of course I could not easily take a picture of the students doing the usual reading aloud and read and look up. But these days students can take selfies showing the differences between their usual practice and the alternative.

Look at the two freeze frames (Figures 7.1 and 7.2) from a video of the same students doing reading aloud (7.1) and read and look up (7.2).

Many teachers who have seen the videos have titled usual reading aloud (7.1) *torture* or *frozen in time* and read and look up (7.2) *engaging* or *animated*. Of course, others should not accept these interpretations but write their own.

Takaaki: *When I first did read and look up, though, I dictated sense groups like this: The three men / pushed the currach, from the beach / into the water. They got into the currach / and rowed to an island / one kilometre away. And my students always stopped at currach, or whatever word they were not familiar with. How can we get our students to move on to understand groups of words rather than get caught up with individual words?*

John: Students should be asked to do read and look up only with passages they understand at least 95 per cent of the words in. But even if they do not understand only one word, most students stop and focus on the word that is not familiar. While there are

Figure 7.1

Figure 7.2

many reasons for this, one is that an almost universal direction is to underline words students do not know. So, we teach students to ignore what is before and after words they are unfamiliar with. When teachers say, 'put a post it on words you do not know or cross them out and then look at the words you do know and write a word or draw a sketch on the word that stumps you', virtually all students demonstrate that they understood the meaning. In the case of *currach*, which is a word that hardly anyone will ever use, learners draw a small boat or write *boat* on the post it covering *currach*.

Takaaki: *I have been constantly amazed by how many words my students and I have been able to discover the meaning of. Of course word equivalents and definitions can be useful. But students cannot use dictionaries during exams so teaching them ways to discover meanings seems very important. On an unrelated point, I have seen some teachers use this method, but after a couple of weeks the students get tired of it. What should we do?*

John: *Homeostasis* is a fancy word for things returning to being stable. A central reason I urge teachers to constantly try the opposite is to enable them to continuously change what they do. If students are given a text in mirror writing (formed by writing in an opposite direction to the natural way: it appears normal when reflected in a mirror) a few weeks after they have become quite proficient in reading and looking up with a regular text, they see that they can do more with a more difficult format. Extending the time between silent reading and speaking and listening and writing also raises the ante.

Another idea to keep students engaged is to have students record what they say after they read lines silently on their cell phones. They then can compare what they think they had said and wrote with what they actually said. The students who tried this made remarkable discoveries about how they had misunderstood what they had read.

Takaaki: *I would like to hear an example of a discovery.*

John: One pair of students had said and written, 'The internet was originally developed for ordinary citizens. And...' But after they listened to what they had said three times and saw what they wrote and compared their words with the text they discovered that they missed the word *not* and *rather*. The sentence was 'The internet was not originally developed for ordinary citizens. Rather...' On the top of the page of the English textbooks, words such as *originally, developed, ordinary*, etc. were printed – all content words. No function or grammar words. I have not seen any textbook or observed any class in which teachers wrote so called key words that included words like *a, it, not*.

Takaaki: *I am fascinated by the possibilities of the use of technology and your point about grammar or function words or structural words. Tell me more.*

John: In Nigeria I could not record the teachers or myself. But these days with so many students having smart phones they can record themselves and compare how they do read and look up, on different days. They can see their progress. In the same way, these two students who compared what they had said and written discovered they had missed two grammar words – *not* and *rather*. I think that when students notice features of language together they are learning also ways to learn. And when teachers see what language students are having trouble with, they can see what to focus on in their teaching. I believe that a central part of teacher preparation is to teach teachers how to continue to develop their teaching on their own and with colleagues after they complete a course. In the same way, we need to show teachers how to show students ways to learn on their own and with peers.

Takaaki: *So you want teachers and students to take control of important aspects of their teaching and learning. Sounds like you consider teacher and learner autonomy (Benson, 2013) to be critical for their growth.*

John: I have taught workshops with *autonomy* in the title but I think we need to deal with this idea in *all* of our courses.

Takaaki: *You said earlier that trying the opposite with criteria to predict the degree to which students would be engaged was one way to expand the range of tasks teachers set. What is another way we can try to be more autonomous and responsible as professionals?*

John: Another way is to use a coding system. I introduced one in my article: 'Beyond *Rashomon* – conceptualizing and describing the teaching act' (Fanselow, 1977). I noted five characteristics of communications in the article but suggested we focus on just one or two at a time. One characteristic is the *medium* – spoken or written language, sketches, gestures, and silence, to cite a few. Another is the *content* that is communicated. One area is *language* with subcategories such as pronunciation, vocabulary, function or grammar words, and word order.

In sketches and photos of many nouns, the name of what is shown is printed without the article. Posters showing fruits, vegetables, animals, etc. around the world usually have labels under the pictures such as *apple, bean*, and *dog*. Ditto for the captions in dictionaries under sketches of *elephants, roses*, etc. Teachers usually write nouns on the board without the articles also.

Takaaki: *Again, function or grammar words are taken lightly!*

John: Yes and no. Teachers give rules for their use and textbooks also contain rules for the use of *the, an* and *a*. But knowing rules and using grammar correctly are two unrelated events. An alternative to rules that would enable students to more likely master the use of articles in English would be to combine grammatical information – the articles – with lexical or experiential information – *apple, rose*. Of course, you do not have to code the captions on posters or in dictionaries to generate the alternative of writing nouns that require an article with an article – *rose* and *a rose*. But if you code the *medium* – *linguistic visual, content vocabulary* you might notice that *content, grammar words* is not present – *rose* and *a rose*. Some teachers asked students to draw sketches for the grammar words – *a, an* and *the*, thus combining *grammar words content* with a *non-linguistic medium, sketches*. So many students drew the same symbols: one dot for *a,•*, two for *an,• •*, and a dot in a circle for *the*. We store written and spoken language and symbols in different parts of our brains. If students can access meanings from spoken and written meanings and symbols of the same meanings, they have three areas they can access rather than just one or two.

As teacher educators, I think we should provide educational philosophies to support alternatives or ask teachers we work with to find support in the fields of psychology or second language acquisition to give credence to different practices.

Takaaki: *These seem obvious but until you had pointed out that we should consider read and look up and integrating grammar and vocabulary I had not noticed that I was in fact making it difficult for my students to improve their reading or use articles. Coding pointed out details I had not seen.*

John: Gregory Bateson (1972), an English social scientist, once claimed that the obvious is difficult to see. This is one reason I think it is so crucial to record what we do and transcribe it with our students. Then we can generate alternatives by trying the opposite or by coding. There is no need for the students to learn a coding system. But for teachers it can be useful. Coding provides us with a more systematic way to expand the range of what we do and to check to see if in fact we have made the planned substitution of one category for another in the alternative.

Takaaki: *You said introducing a coding system was another way to prepare teachers to continue to develop on their own after they finish their degrees. You said you used your own coding system but that means there are others.*

John: There are many systems. In the heydays of classroom observation in the 1980s, Dick Allwright (1988) edited a collection of observation schemes, some of which were less complex than mine. In my classes some teachers found it easier to use FOCUS after they used other systems first.

Takaaki: *In class, I do not remember you ever mentioning how you became interested in coding or to use perhaps a less daunting word, grouping.*

John: Yes, *coding* and *classification* do not seem friendly to many. Grouping we all do. When we look at a menu we see food grouped as appetizers, soups, meat, fish, pasta, desserts, drinks – beer/alcohol, soft, coffee and tea. We do not see the food listed in alphabetical order or in the number of calories each food provides. But what is different about a menu and coding and classification is that these show relationships that are not obvious. In botany when I learned that strawberries and roses were in the same family I was ecstatic seeing relationships that are not that obvious. Of course, at the time I was not teaching so I saw no relationship between the taxonomies in botany and the grouping of foods on menus and observing teachers. But at Teachers College, a senior colleague, Arno Bellack and his team had published a book called *The Language of the Classroom* (1966).

Takaaki: *Since you used Bellack's system as a basis for FOCUS why didn't you title your book* The Language of the ESOL Classroom, *rather than* Breaking Rules?

John: First, my book was not a descriptive study as Bellack's was. Second, I wanted to encourage teachers to move beyond the usual interactions. Most classrooms are teacher centered and focus on facts for their own sake. The sub-title of the book is *Generating and Exploring Alternatives*. I think as teacher educators we have a responsibility to model ways for teachers to question accepted practices.

Takaaki: *O.K. So, how about you and small changes? When did you start to explicitly urge teachers to make small changes?*

John: Although I suggested over many years that teachers should try the opposite practices after understanding what they do by recording and transcribing their lessons,
it was not till my last book (Fanselow, 2017) that I highlighted that the changes that
teachers make when they try the opposite should be small. I mentioned this in my
previous publications but not so explicitly till I used the idea in my latest book.

Takaaki: *Why is this idea of small changes so important in the preparation of teachers?*

John: For a couple of reasons. First, teachers are busy, often teaching more than 100 students each day, and so they might not be able to manage large changes in their
daily teaching practices. Second, if there are big changes it is hard to see which of
the changes produced a different result. Some think that all I am suggesting is that
teachers make changes and then decide whether the changes work or do not work.
Unless the changes are small, we cannot determine what the it in 'It works' is. Nor can we
see what works means. When I told Pius to draw sketches and compare this with defining
words the change was small and it was reasonably easy to compare the results. I say reasonably easy because I had to depend on what I heard and wrote when I observed the two
practices. But these days we can record and see very precisely the effects of a small change.

Takaaki: *Can you give me another example of what you consider a small change? When I first heard
this suggestion, I did not really understand it.*

John: More recently I have made this mantra more accessible by inviting teachers to make
small changes. I asked them to write down or photograph or record small changes
in their lives that produce big results outside of classrooms. Teachers mention taking
vitamins to keep their blood healthy, Lipitor to decrease cholesterol, for example.
Others say that their flu shots inject a very small amount of vaccine but the liquid
prevents a lot of misery. A blister 1/2 inch in diameter can prevent us from walking.
Sunglasses can decrease the number of headaches we get on hot, sunny days.

Takaaki: *I know you have many more other references in your books. I would say you seem to strongly
believe that making small changes would lead to generating more creative teaching which
Maley and Kiss (2017) so strongly advocate. What are some other suggestions regarding how
to prepare teachers based on your experiences seeing lessons and reading about lessons?*

John: As I mentioned when you asked me what I taught, colleagues and I did demonstration lessons. There were desks for up to 40 primary school students in the front half
of the demonstration classroom and tiered seats for 40 to observe the lesson. We
taught a few lessons each week before practice teaching to show teachers activities they were not familiar with. A limitation of these 'demos' was that when we
discussed them we had to depend on memory and comments the observers made.
We had no data to analyse. In a 40-minute lesson there can be a few hundred communications made by the teacher and from 20 to 60 students. These days we can
have students record on their cell phones. We can make copies of the pages in their
notebooks to provide more data and we photograph what the teacher or students
did on the board.

Takaaki: *So, another suggestion is that those who prepare teachers should actually teach classes, in tandem with the teachers, to illustrate activities that you all read about. And you suggest we do
this by carefully paying attention to the details. I remember that during my MA courses you
always taught parts of some classes that we were teaching and we videotaped them.*

John: I have always taught classes of practice teachers I observed. If I were a soccer coach,
I think I could suggest movements and plays to players that I could not myself do
and the players would understand this. Coaches tend to be older than players and
less agile. But in the case of teaching, I think we need to try out what we suggest.

Teachers can then see that just as they might forget some steps or ignore some students so do we.

These days when we can record and then jointly view what we both did with the same students, teachers feel more relaxed about seeing themselves. When I visit a school the second or third time and teach a lesson or part of a lesson both the students and their teachers feel as if what we do is normal, not something special. The teachers see changes I make that are in some ways similar to ones they make.

Takaaki: *So, you have been following the model you experienced in Nigeria – students learned English with alternative activities they read about and saw you and others demonstrate, and they tried the activities and looked at your transcriptions of what they did and made small changes based on differences between what each and a colleague did.*

John: After I returned to the US from Nigeria, I was involved in Peace Corps training programmes at Teachers College. Almost all the trainees were native speakers but part of training was immersion in languages of the countries they were bound for. So, they experienced the methods as learners and as teachers and observed themselves and others on videos or listened to recordings.

Takaaki: *Now, I have read a lot about and conducted research on reflective teaching which to me is a key area of study in language teacher education. I have these on my notes in front of me: Farrell (2007, 2015), Gebhard (2017), Hiratsuka (2017), and Mann and Walsh (2017). To what extent has this field been important to you?*

John: Though I do not use the term much, I attach importance to many of the ideas and activities in that field. Many of the suggestions made by those who discuss reflective teaching are similar to some of my suggestions. My obsession with recording and transcribing and comparing what we usually do with small changes and constantly changing what we do are somewhat distinctive, though.

Takaaki: *To me, the few suggestions we just discussed seem somewhat unrelated to reflective teaching. Do you see a connection?*

John: I think there are some connections. When I ask teachers to generate alternatives I ask them to use these criteria to determine which alternatives are more likely to engage students. All of the suggestions focus on the joint analysis of detailed data – teachers, observers, supervisors, and those who prepare teachers. We must interpret the data from many perspectives by asking questions such as: 'What else might this indicate? What is another way we can see this as helpful or not helpful?'

We can only analyse detailed data if we have small amounts of it. I suggest a transcription that fits on one page of A4 paper. And we can only understand what is going on if we look at what we do on a regular basis, once a week I consider a minimum. Of course, teachers are busy, but as we analyse what we do we can simultaneously plan what to do the next day. Seeing what students produce decreases the need for preparing and grading tests.

Takaaki: *Yeah it makes sense and this is interesting. Now, I have always wanted to ask you this, but as somebody who has been a guru in our field, what do you think is lacking from current language teacher education programmes?*

John: As a teacher educator, I have always invited people to do workshops in various areas such as The Silent Way, Jazz Chants and Autonomy, to name a few. If I were asked to suggest to those establishing a new MA programme I would enrich the range of workshops a great deal. Here are a few areas that I think would broaden teachers' experiences of how we learn: phone applications, computer games, voice projection, mime, yoga, drama, dance, singing and directing singers, arts and crafts, cooking, knitting, guitar. Well, I could go on and on. But maybe a bit of a rationale, gleaned from comments from teachers who have experienced these activities. They said:

We are reminded of how many times we have to experience something to master it; that much of language learning is connecting language with experience; that experiences of our minds, bodies and language are interconnected; that some of us are good on one activity and not so good at another so we are reminded not to disparage students who cannot say, write, or spell but to tap what they are good at.

Takaaki: *I see. But your suggestion to language education programmes here involves only people outside the classroom conducting workshops for students in the programmes, though. I thought you learned in Nigeria that it was important for teachers to actually experience methods they were going to use later in their classrooms.*

John: Ideally, there would be opportunities for teachers to do mime in a class, record the event and discuss it with the person who did the mime workshop. But it would be very difficult to do so unless a teacher has private students or sponsors an English language club at school.

Takaaki: *Alright. On a different point, providing hands-on workshops as well as trying out mime, etc. sound very non-academic to me. Shouldn't teacher education programmes be a place to learn academic and scientific knowledge?*

John: They are indeed non-academic. I think the balance between doing and reading and writing in teacher preparation programmes has shifted away from doing these days. It seems to me that more hands-on experiences are necessary for the teachers. Reading about SLA, sociolinguistics, pedagogical grammar, etc. can be very intellectually stimulating. Discussing and writing about articles in such fields can be too. But teaching is not an intellectual activity and the influence reading and writing have on what we do is very small. When we do feel the need to read those texts in the field, I suggest that teachers read fewer but read them a few times. There is so much information in all of the areas in our field, much of it quite sophisticated. So, one reading is almost the same as no reading. Those who read fewer articles more but each more many times say they can apply some of the ideas better.

Takaaki: *We are almost there, but in the back of my mind and of many teachers, maybe often in the front of our minds is that there are so may constraints on what we can do that is different. As you know, there are texts we have to cover, tests to give, and external exams to prepare for that prevent us from trying to teach in different ways. Colleagues resent changes and students balk at things they are not used to. Clarke (2007) deals with other restraints in our contexts as well. What can we do about it?*

John: For the students who balk and colleagues who resent change, I have suggested that we spend five minutes on an alternative each day, selecting ones that students can use on their own outside of class to develop their English. Also, many schools have English clubs. In these, teachers can have students try out self-learning activities and get feedback from their teachers.

But read and look up, drawing sketches for words they are unfamiliar with, and symbols for grammar words over time students find them more engaging than the memorisation, fill in the blanks, talking about language or translation standard fare. They also see that they do better on tests after using English rather than memorising rules and definitions. So over time the five minutes can be extended.

Takaaki: *John, it has been such a refreshing conversation I have had with you.*

John: See how judgements come so easily to us. Let's let the readers decide if it was really a refreshing conversation.

Takaaki: *O.K. For me, though, it was truly an engaging conversation and maybe I can summarise some of what has been powerful for me in what you said. Through our conversation, I learned that we should be encouraged to: (a) make language teacher education a joint endeavour among the teacher educators, teachers and students; (b) generate teaching alternatives by trying the opposite and by using coding schemes; (c) cultivate teacher and learner autonomy by believing in their capacity – we can all do more than we think we can; (d) make small changes and attend to minute details; and (e) record and transcribe classroom interactions to see how what we think we did, what we actually did, and what we want to do are quite different events. Thank you, John. Any final suggestion for those of us especially in the younger generation in our preparation of teachers?*

John: You are one type of 'younger person' but children we can also think of as younger. And of course even people in their 80s and 90s can be young at heart. So, to me, a key feature of *young* is more than age. Now, let me read you a short quote from Thomas Huxley referring to a child: 'Sit down before what you see and hear like a little child, and be prepared to give up every preconceived notion, follow humbly wherever and to whatever abyss Nature leads, or you shall learn nothing.' A couple of insights I take from this. First, try everything. Two-year-olds often pick up snow the first time they experience it and put it in their mouths. Some around four seeing a straw for the first time put it in their drink and then their nose! Leonardo da Vinci put a straw in his ear to hear the sound of water at different depths. When children try things they often smile and laugh. They see jumping down three steps at a time as joyful. They run and laugh at the same time, thrilled by seeing they can do something they could not do a few days before. They have a playful spirit.

In preparing teachers as well as in our teaching of language learners a playful spirit, scepticism and openness to imagine all the possibilities are crucial. Alan Maley has, through the years both in his teaching and writing, exemplified this spirit of playfulness as much or more than any in our field. A model of playfulness.

Further reading

Gurrey, P. (1955) *Teaching English as a Foreign Language.* London: Longman.
Gurrey in his 1955 edition introduced a grid showing nine types of questions. He urged teachers to move beyond the predominant fact questions in the classroom (e.g., What is the longest river in Nigeria?) to inferential and experiential questions made up of either-or and yes-no questions (e.g., Does the longest river in Nigeria start with C?; Have you visited Onitsha and seen the River Niger?).

Barnes, D. (1976) *From Communication to Curriculum.* Montclair, NJ: Boynton/Cook.
Douglas Barnes analysed interactions in middle schools and introduced two different kinds of knowledge: 'school knowledge' and 'action knowledge'. According to him, school knowledge is the knowledge presented to us by someone else; whereas, action knowledge is the knowledge that is incorporated into our view of the world on which our actions are based. He encourages us to provide action knowledge, rather than school knowledge, in language teacher education so that we are able to better make sense of new experience by relating it to the old experience.

Fanselow, J. F. and Light, R. L. (eds) (1977) *Bilingual, ESOL and Foreign Language Teacher Preparation: Models, Practices, Issues.* Washington, DC: TESOL.
Fanselow and Light reflect the two differing perspectives in teacher education. One perspective maintains that guidelines and the time-honoured practices in teacher preparation would form a sufficient

base for the development of those teachers. The other argues that teacher preparation needs reforming and can only be carried forward effectively with a number of stipulations, for example, through a competency-based approach. After four decades, the perspectives and discussions in the book are still important and relevant in the world of language teacher education.

References

Allwright, D. (1988) *Observation in the Language Classroom*. London: Longman.

Bateson, G. (1972) *Steps to an Ecology of Mind*. Chicago, IL: The University of Chicago Press.

Bellack, A. A., Kliebard, H. M., Hyman, R. T. and Smith, F. L. (1966). *The Language of the Classroom*. New York: Teachers College Press.

Benson, P. (2013) *Teaching and Researching Autonomy*, 2nd edn. Abingdon: Routledge.

Bieler, D. (2010) 'Dialogic Praxis in Teacher Preparation: A Discourse Analysis of Mentoring Talk'. *English Education*, 42 391–426.

Bronowski, J. (1956) *Science and Human Values*. New York: Harper & Row.

Clarke, M. A. (2007) *Common Ground, Contested Territory: Examining the Roles of English Language Teachers in Troubled Times*. Ann Arbor, MI: University of Michigan Press.

Fanselow. J. F. (1977) 'Beyond Rashomon – Conceptualizing and Describing the Teaching Act'. *TESOL Quarterly*, 11 17–39.

Fanselow, J. F. (1992a) *Contrasting Conversations*. White Plains, NY: Longman.

Fanselow, J. F. (1992b) *Try the Opposite*. Tokyo: Simul Press.

Fanselow, J. F. (2017) *Small Changes in Teaching, Big Results in Learning: Videos, Activities and Essays to Stimulate Fresh Thinking About Language Learning*. Tokyo: iTDi.

Farrell, T. S. C. (2007) *Reflective Language Teaching: From Research to Practice*. London: Continuum.

Farrell, T. S. C. (2015) *Promoting Teacher Reflection in Second Language Education: A Framework for TESOL Professionals*. New York: Routledge.

Gebhard, J. G. (2017) *Teaching English as a Foreign or Second Language: A Self-Development and Methodology Guide*, 3rd edn. Ann Arbor, MI: University of Michigan Press.

Hiratsuka, T. (2017) 'Pair discussions for reflecting on action: Stimulated recall', in Barnard, R. and Ryan, J. (eds) *Reflective Practice: Options for English Language Teachers and Researchers*. New York: Routledge: 89–97.

Maley, A. and Kiss, T. (2017) *Creativity and English Language Teaching: From Inspiration to Implementation*. London: Palgrave Macmillan.

Mann, S. and Walsh, S. (2017) *Reflective Practice in English Language Teaching: Research-Based Principles and Practices*. New York: Routledge.

Mercer, N. (1995) *The Guided Construction of Knowledge*. Clevedon: Multilingual Matters.

Tharp, R. G. and Gallimore, R. (1988) *Rousing Minds to Life: Teaching, Learning, and Schooling in Social Context*. New York: Cambridge University Press.

Wertsch, J. V. (1985) *Vygotsky and the Social Formation of Mind*. Cambridge, MA: Harvard University Press.

West, M. (1960) *Teaching English in Difficult Circumstances*. London: Longman Green.

PART 2
Core contexts

8

Digital and online approaches to language teacher education

Thom Kiddle and Tony Prince

Introduction

Digital technology has a long history in language learning and teaching, and in language teacher education. In this chapter we address the challenges and opportunities that digital technology presents to teacher educators, exploring options available through online and blended provision, outlining decisions taken by providers to meet these challenges. After providing a brief historical perspective, we will consider variables such as time and timing; interaction; design and structure; pathways, platforms and tools; and assessment in evaluating providers' approaches to language teacher training and development.

From distance to online: a brief historical overview

We can trace the roots of much current practice in online and blended educational models to such early innovators as the Programmed Logic for Automated Teaching Operations at the University of Illinois, launched in 1960, with its forums, instant messaging, chatrooms, remote screen-sharing and online assessment (Wooley, 1994). The line continues through the Open University's move away from correspondence courses towards online courses in the late 80s and early forays by other universities into online Masters programmes. This includes teacher training providers reaching larger international teaching communities and individuals with online teaching qualifications, such as the Distance Delta from International House London. Organisations such as The Consultants-E, with fully online teacher training programmes launched in the early 2000s, moved the concept forward, and the rise in the mid-2000s of online teacher training websites and platforms (see, for example, Teacher Training Videos, and LessonStream) brought individual providers into the mix. The introduction of Massive Open Online Courses through pioneers at the University of Manitoba, and the famous 'Introduction to Artificial Intelligence' from Sebastian Thrun and Peter Norvig at Stanford (Ng & Widdon, 2014), led to rapid interest and growth and new players such as the OU's own FutureLearn, EdX, and Coursera, and MOOCs for language teachers and learners developed by Cambridge English and British Council among others. The launch of the Association for Quality Education and Training Online (AQUEDUTO) in 2014, the first quality assurance organisation specifically focused on the provision of online language teacher education further signalled the importance of online and blended delivery's presence, and its potential in the field with which this handbook concerns itself.

Alongside the omnipresence of digital technology in twenty-first-century life, there are specific pressures and opportunities which have led to online and blended approaches to language teacher education – in some cases to supplement, and in others to replace – traditional face-to-face classroom-based teacher training and teacher development activities.

One of these pressures has its roots in the wider educational context. Given that the international education community has pledged to achieve universal education by 2030 (which UNESCO estimates will involve recruiting 68.8 million teachers), it will be difficult to deliver the required number of teacher education programmes relying solely on traditional approaches.

Other relevant factors behind the drive for expanded provision include:

- The calls for reform prompted by international education comparisons such as the Programme for International Student Assessment (PISA) and the Trends in International Maths and Science Study (TIMMS);
- The changes in views of effective learning and teaching prompted by evidence based research (e.g. Yates & Hattie, 2013; Marzano et al., 2001);
- The development of educational tools (e.g. CAMTASIA, PowerPoint) or platforms (e.g. Blackboard, Moodle, Edmodo), and platforms co-opted for educational use (e.g. Facebook, SecondLife, Twitter).

Looking directly at language teacher education, we should add related factors such as:

- The rise in English as a Medium of Instruction in universities worldwide, bilingual schools curricula, and early-start English initiatives coupled with national bilingual and plurilingual policy drives;
- Frameworks in language teacher education such as those from Eaquals, the British Council and Cambridge University Press, which have heightened awareness of developmental pathways within a language teaching career;
- Interest in online and blended learning of languages (for example, Flipped Classroom models which move 'language input presentations' and controlled practice onto a pre-lesson, online, self-access platform).

Each of these exerts different forces on governments, education bodies, and institutions, such that they are not just concerned about training new teachers but retraining and developing existing ones. However, in many of these contexts, resources for teacher training are scarce. The capacity of these organisations to provide the specific focus, quality, breadth and depth of training needed is limited by cost, time, access to trainers and materials, among other factors.

Having outlined the demands driving alternative models of teacher education, we move on to look at a range of specific decisions facing teacher education providers, and how digital and online responses complement or contrast with face-to-face models.

Time and timing

The first factor is the staging of input and interaction within the training approach. From pre-service through to PGCEs and degrees programmes, input and interaction tend to be time-tabled and fixed. It is a similar story with in-service face-to-face teacher development – from

INSETT sessions through to Diplomas and Masters-level qualifications. Online and blended delivery models upend this rigidity, making input available not only on demand, but also available to be revisited, reviewed and recycled. For a related discussion, see the options outlined by Dudeney et al. (2013: 317–327) on integrating digital activities into the curriculum. Likewise, interaction patterns between peers take on a new character in the online space, with synchronous and asynchronous collaboration a core principle in online teacher education course design.

Second, we must consider reflection and response time. Face-to-face models typically base response to input within a timetabled session. Online and blended models allow for consideration of input and contextualised reflection (often based on implementation or experimentation). Participants can carefully construct responses often with the benefit of further reading and research. See, for example, the reflections on E-portfolio based learning from Hughes (in Sharpe et al., 2010: 199–211). This latter point we consider particularly important for the lower-language-proficiency teacher, who, when studying in the online context, has the time to formulate and proof their contributions.

A third consideration is time management. This is perhaps a blessing and a curse for the online and blended context. In our experience, an online/blended can offer significant benefits in terms of making studies fit around other professional and personal demands. However, the teacher educator must be aware that for those who struggle with time-management or are less committed, the online mode can provide the opportunity to 'disappear', thus creating more work for the trainer to chase and chivvy through messaging or mailing. Another commonly-heard complaint from participants in online teacher education programmes is 'It took longer than you said it would!', and this reflects the fact that by their very nature, web-based activities can lead to deeper and deeper expeditions 'down the rabbit hole' (see the recommendations from Salmon (2004: 210)).

Interaction

Interaction among peers and the tutor(s) in a teacher education context is an area in which the affordances of digital technology have added numerous options. Other chapters in this handbook discuss interaction in a face-to-face setting, and so we would like to focus on the flexibility which the online space offers.

The primary area of flexibility lies in multi-modality; in the choice afforded by interacting through voice, video, text, and image, and the consequent opportunities for personalisation and contextualised appropriacy. Tools such as the Talkpoint activity (see below), allow participants to respond to content through webcam, microphone or text. In contexts such as the Middle East, this can be significant in terms of allowing culturally/contextually appropriate interaction with course colleagues and tutors.

The area of contextualisation is also crucial here. For online and blended programmes where participants are contributing from their own professional context (rather than travelling to attend an intensive training/development event), the sharing of one's own situational reality, whether through video of the setting, images of teaching spaces, or voices from colleagues at one's own institution, adds a dimension often unattainable in a face-to-face setting.

Examples below demonstrate the further possibilities of a mix between synchronous and asynchronous interaction, but suffice to say here that the balance of live interaction with colleagues and tutors combined with considered, cumulative contributions across time, what Hockly and Clandfield (2010: 27–30) call 'liveware', is a valuable addition to all online teacher education programmes we have seen.

Design and structure

It is our contention that the online space has (r)evolutionised the design principles inherent in a previously linear approach, and allowed for participant-led navigation across content. The challenge lies with the provider to ensure that the varied pathways which may result, cover learning objectives. This may mean that multiple contextual instances, e.g. teaching at primary and secondary, are simultaneously available, and that the engagement with each one of those is determined by the participant (though necessarily tracked by the provider).

Multimodality not only applies to content delivery and interaction models, but also to assessment options and affordances for differentiation. Being able to review and consider participant responses, a tutor can personalise interventions more easily and effectively than when all participants are present in a face-to-face model.

Of course, all of these above claims are dependent not only on course design, but also the competence and awareness of the tutor. As the routes through the content (and the amount of content available), increase, so there is an increased need for guidance and support. Also, for principled decisions on issues such as anonymity, and 'lurking' (alternately known as 'legitimate peripheral participation'): the question of whether processing of content without active participation can count as engagement within an assessed programme. These are reasons behind a potential conflict between 'untutored' online models such as Massive Open Online Courses, and the level of quality assurance implied by frameworks like AQUEDUTO's, which have tutor competence in providing support as a key theme.

A final consideration for course design is the thorny issue of observed teaching practice. This has provoked the most scepticism in acceptance of online teacher education initiatives, most notably in pre-service settings. Currently, for example, the Online CELTA offered by Cambridge English still insists on assessed teaching practice being observed by a live assessor in the classroom. Defenders of the face-to-face setting claim that what can effectively be captured by video in a teaching practice activity is minimal compared to what we can reasonably expect a present observer to evaluate. For us, the jury should take time to consider their verdict on this. As will be explained below, this aspect of online teacher education is in its infancy, and is at the sharp end of issues of validity, reliability and practicality. Pilots and projects are underway, and it may well be an area in which digital technology needs to catch up with expectations before anything close to fully embracing the potential is possible.

In order to elucidate the above points, it will be most effective to look at the affordances of the online and blended setting, and illustrate the options and the decisions implied in the approaches that online teacher education providers have taken.

Pathways: adaptive learning; choice of content; timing; specialisation; deeper reading

Face to face, one of the main concerns of teachers is how to structure the content and the lesson, to support students' understanding and scaffold their progression. Those developing and delivering online courses have similar concerns. But as we shall see in this section, the opportunities provided by the online environment create significant tensions. As research into choice (Schwartz, 2004) has shown, while we may believe that more choice represents more freedom and personalisation, it often results in more frustration and confusion. The distance of online learning can magnify these issues, as the tutor is not immediately available to recognise or resolve them. Thus one of the main tensions of developing and delivering online courses is the extent to which we take advantage of the opportunity that online has to increase choice: through adaptive

learning, choice of what and when to study, through the depth and breadth of resources provided. Many of the resources discussed here are numbered and presented for easy reference in a
table at the end of the chapter.

For many teachers the simplest, and cheapest option for continuing online education is the
free resources available online. These may come through the news and opinions offered by corporate sites (e.g. edsurge.com) or via individuals (e.g. learningspy.co.uk). They may come via the
curation of images and information provided by others (e.g. pinterest.co.uk). They may come
through resources created by others, as information for lessons (e.g. TEDed.com) or as lessons
in themselves (e.g. Veritasium[1]). As can be seen from this list, the opportunities for learning are
significant. But, this opportunity is part of the problem. Not only is it difficult to know what to
choose, but it is also hard to identify where to go after you have made the initial choice. Linking
these resources into a pathway that leads to a clear learning goal requires time and knowledge.

The main advantage of an online course for many teachers is the structure it offers. At its
simplest, an online 'course' may be a series of hyperlinks, connecting resources that exist online,
perhaps with some introductory or explanatory text. Bloggers (e.g. gregashmanwordpress.com)
and institutional or corporate sites may provide such a service, linking to previous posts and
resources. On YouTube, vloggers have taken this a step further, providing series of lessons as a
course (e.g. crashcourse[2]). TEDed even provides activities to do while watching the videos, to
increase engagement and learning. Yet very few of these sites offer what might be recognised
as courses leading to continuing professional development. Part of the reason for this is the difficulty that comes when deciding on how to construct the pathway through the material.

From the perspective of the participant, at each branch – with each alternative – we run the
risk of dividing the community, diluting the knowledge and experience to be shared, reducing
the opportunity for interaction. A simple link to a series of articles that would deepen understanding, or allow individuals to explore specific interests, can lead to some participants feeling
that they are struggling with the content (due to the unfamiliarity with the topics) or are lagging behind others (due to the difficulty they have in commenting on the texts). It is possible
to reduce some of this tension by allowing the tutor more autonomy over what to link to and
when, but this increases the need for tutor involvement and knowledge of the content. In general, when thinking about how we construct pathways through courses we have to consider if
the gain to the individual from choice outweighs the gain to the community from cohesion. In
general, as the former increases so the latter will reduce (Salmon, 2013).

One method of reducing this issue is to require the results of all choice to funnel into one
product, in one place. For example a forum can be created on a core topic (e.g. Motivation).
A variety of links to the topic may be provided, but all participants are required to post their
findings into the forum, and perhaps to comment on the postings of others who have explored
different topics. Similarly, a wiki might act as a repository for the findings of research conducted
by participants into different areas (from different links), either as a collaborative exercise, or as
information for those who may be interested in, but not intent on this topic. Embedding these
tools into courses has been made relatively easy by paid-for services such as Blackboard, and
opensource platforms such as Moodle and BuddyPress (a plugin for wordpress sites). Examples of CPD courses built using these tools abound: using Blackboard to link institutions in a
global partnership (e.g. Laureate international Universities[3]), using Moodle to provide a range of
courses to global participants (e.g. NILE Online[4]), and using BuddyPress to provide a course to
participants from around the world (e.g. Learning Technologies in EAP[5]).

One problem encountered when creating an online course is that as we add options we also
increase the complexity of navigation. It can be difficult for participants to keep track of where
they are, even as they progress through a linear series of activities online. Designers must bear

in mind the need for tools to let the participant track their progress. Some online courses (e.g. at Futurelearn.com[6] or ELTjam.academy[7]) have eschewed both depth and breadth in favour of a flat single page hierarchy, with no link leading further than one task away from the main page. This allows participants to see very clearly where they last left the course. The more often participants enter and leave the course, or the longer between visits to the course – perhaps as a result of trying to fit it into other responsibilities – the more important consideration of such navigational concerns becomes.

Finally, as we increase depth of content, so we place more pressure on the participant to manage their time. The participant must be aware that the further they travel away from the main path, the faster they have to work in order to keep up with the other participants. Each resource takes time to consider, let alone consume or contemplate, and it should be remembered that a major attraction of online learning is fitting it around other responsibilities (England, 2012).

Thus far we have talked of design decisions as they affect the participant, but each choice has an impact on the tutor and the team supporting the course. Breadth and depth of content provided requires equivalent knowledge and experience on the part of the tutor, especially with regard to weaving comments into each other and waving participants to comments that may be of interest or use to each other. In weaving and waving, the tutor is drawing connections between points participants have made. This may be to highlight similarities of topics being discussed, of priorities expressed, of difficulties and issues faced across a range of participant contexts. It may also be to contrast points of view, to distinguish between solutions provided or options chosen. This not only has the intended outcome of strengthening group cohesion but extending what they are learning from each other, and from the course through revising and revisiting the topics, reflecting with new perspectives.

That said, if participants struggle to manage their time and become frustrated with the wealth of choice, it frequently becomes the responsibility of the tutor to help them back on track and to monitor their progress. More time spent keeping track of students may result in less time available for interaction. Thus, it is critical for those designing the courses to consider carefully the structure they use and options they provide. A significant number of those involved in online courses believe that teaching online takes longer than face-to-face (Allen & Seaman, 2013). It is important that this perception does not put tutors off the online experience.

Face-to-face courses in which participants have access to reliable online connections are increasingly blending their provision to include online components in different ways. One such option involves participants interacting in person in small groups, while keeping track of the activities of others in the larger group through online tools (Stein & Graham, 2014). Blended courses may also make use of techniques which seek to 'flip the classroom', placing emphasis on the time in class as opportunities for tutor support (e.g. clarification, differentiation) and for peer collaboration, rather than for tutor transmission of content (Talbert, 2017). For instance, it may be effective for participants to study online for three or four weeks, before coming together face-to-face for more hands-on or tutor interactive activities. Conversely, course design can front-load the face-to-face elements (e.g. where participants may need much more tutor support than is realistic online).

Discussion: fora, talkpoint, webinars

As Hammadou and Bernhardt (1987) note, 'In foreign language teaching the content and the process of learning are the same. In other words, in foreign language teaching, the medium is the message.' In this regard, online education has a number of benefits which those developing and delivering courses should be aware of. When study is asynchronous, it can benefit those who struggle to understand or to communicate. With activities which culminate in text-based forums, participants can make use of translation software and dictionaries (e.g. through curation sites such as Onelook[8]). They can consult more general sources of information on the topic (e.g. Wikipedia) or education related sites (e.g. The A–Z of ELT[9] or University English for Academic Purposes[10]). They can take their time to replay videos, to reread texts or comments in fora. When posting their responses, they have time to consider what to say and how to say it. These benefits accrue without participants needing to admit to language difficulties, or to feel that they are taking too long to respond (as may be the case face-to-face). In this way, those who may have struggled to join the community of discourse can more easily engage in discussion.

A second advantage of learning online is the variety of modes of communication afforded. An example of this can be seen in one of the main tools for enabling synchronous learning and teaching: the webinar. This allows students to be present in the same space – e.g. through Adobe Connect,[11] Zoom[12] or Skype – but in different ways. Participants can contribute by text only – giving them many of the advantages indicated in the previous paragraph. Similarly, limiting their contributions to audio can allow participants to ignore concerns about how they look, or interpreting the expressions of others, and focus on their words. At the same time, those who feel confident in their ability to understand and respond can use the video tools. Each of these choices can be made without anyone having to acknowledge the reasons for them.

It should be noted that such variety of tools available in webinars is not without its problems. As Hockly (2012) discusses, a great webinar requires the tutor to consider five ingredients: planning, engagement, interaction, variety and tech check. Each must be considered carefully if the tutor is to play to the advantages of the webinar. One example of this is in how students contribute to a discussion. By allowing participants to limit themselves to audio or text a tutor can give participants time to think and prepare. Thus, while some participants are interacting via video/audio, the more hesitant or linguistically concerned participant can participate via text. To make best use of these different modes, the teacher needs to structure opportunities for interaction differently, making it clear that those texting do not have to wait for their turn, and giving those on audio only (and therefore not so visible) the means of attracting or asking for attention (e.g. through text, by emoji). The tutor also needs to be conscious of waving and weaving between comments in a synchronous webinar, just as in an asynchronous discussion.

While the tools and techniques discussed above can be very effective in helping overcome some of the language issues in language teacher education, this is not their only, or even main role. In their review, tracking ten years of online courses in the USA, Allen and Seaman (2013) cite three main causes for high attrition rates: underestimating the amount of time needed, feelings of isolation, and lacking sufficient discipline to persist. Course designers can overcome many of these problems through the careful placement of activities requiring collaboration, or tools which facilitate communication between participants or with the tutor. One simple rule of thumb might be to offer more choice later in an activity or unit, rather than earlier, so that participants have more chance of staying on track and on time. Isolation may stem from feeling that you are the only one working on an activity, which may be more likely the more options are offered. Equally, regular 'funnel points' may be useful in an activity or unit, to bring participants together and allow them to discuss their reflections or reservations. Seeing or hearing what other people are doing, and having them comment on what you have done or thought can be a powerful incentive to continue. As such, a weekly webinar can be a powerful tool for group cohesion and individual motivation. Similarly, the placement of a forum at the end of a sequence of input or research can allow the participants to learn from each other, and to derive the benefit from having your ideas heard and acknowledged.

In this way then, online learning allows designers of courses to create a great deal of opportunity for interaction between participants. One crucial factor is the tutor's understanding of its intent, and of their own role in the course. For example, while a forum can provide an opportunity for participants to interact, it can also leave tutors feeling that they have to comment on each post. This can result in much of the interaction being between tutor and individual participants. One solution to this can be to train tutors in the 'waving and weaving' approach outlined in the previous section. Another, equally useful type of tutor interaction with participants is what we have termed 'Feeding, Seeding and Harvesting' on the NILE courses. In 'Feeding' the tutor is trying to develop ideas and interactions rather than responding to posts. One key technique for this is to pose questions, rather than make comments. These questions might be offered with regard to the posts of other participants (incorporating 'weaving and waving'). Alternately, 'Feeding' might involve 'Seeding', through a response based around a quote which challenges or contrasts with what the participant has said. The idea of 'Seeding' is to offer something more for the participant to consider. One of the benefits is that this can take the form of links to other resources – either in the course or outside of it. One further benefit of online (for the tutor) is that a bank of such links or resources can be built up over iterations of courses, so that the tutor can deploy them relatively quickly and easily. For the participant the 'seed' is no less useful for it having been used with others, or having been quickly found by the tutor. In the final type of tutor interaction – 'Harvesting' – the tutor is trying a) to provide the participants with a record of the key topics they have covered in a unit; b) to remind them of the points that they or others may have made; and c) to get them to reflect on both of these, further deepening the learning. The specific points made by participants are a key aspect of the summary and must be gathered from the tutor as they work through the unit, but these can be worked into a template of the unit topics and a style which encourages reflection that the tutor has built up over time. We have found that the tutor summary can offer a very important perspective and can model good practice. Participants may not keep track of what they have done simply because they do not know what 'good' practice looks like, or why it is good for them.

Use of video

In the early days of the internet, bandwidth speeds were such that text was the only content that could realistically be shared. Compression techniques, distribution methods and bandwidth increases have made video a realistic content option in many contexts. But if, as Anderson and Dron (2011) suggest, 'technology sets the beat and creates the music, while the pedagogy defines the moves' then we need to take care not only that the music can be heard (i.e. that the infrastructure is suitable) but that the music doesn't drown out or dominate the intention of the teacher or course designer. In the following section we will look at a number of key features of video in online learning: its efficacy in filling gaps in knowledge of technology that participants may have; its facility in generating and supporting group cohesion; its utility for course developers in managing time needed for input and for designers in creating input from everyday trainer/trainee output; its ability to bring the classroom into the online course and thereby reduce the distance between theory and practice, between the trainer supporting learning in the course and the participants learning in their classrooms.

One of the early stumbling blocks for many wanting to start learning online is their familiarity with the technology. As the futurist William Gibson put it, 'The future is here, it's just not evenly distributed'. Thus, while many participants may have heard of a 'forum', 'wiki' or 'webinar', fewer are likely to feel confident using them. In this regard, videos can be very effective instructional methods, giving demonstrations of how these tools are used, in the course. Such videos may be provided as course resources to be viewed when needed or can be incorporated into the course content, such that participants can share their experiences or their recommendations, posting their thoughts after viewing a video, or, as will be discussed later in this section, participant feedback may become part of the video itself.

Another early obstacle to participant engagement, and to longer-term learning, is the development of a group cohesiveness. Video allows the content designer to introduce the participants to the tutor and to each other, creating a sense of physical presence and familiarity online. It may be much easier to limit the tutor presence to text, but incorporating videos involving the tutor brings them closer and increases the sense of the tutor presence in the course – particularly important when a course may be delivered by a different tutor each iteration.

With the wealth of materials available online it can be tempting to link out to videos available elsewhere. These may be very effective, in terms of the authority of the person speaking (e.g. Hertzberg on Hygiene factors of motivation[13]), because of the production qualities of the video (e.g. Ken Robinson on TED[14]), or because of the specific methods being used to communicate information (e.g. RSA animate[15]). But, tools such as Camtasia[16] – which will be discussed later in this section in more detail – make it very quick and simple for the tutor to create content tailored to the course. Similarly, the ubiquity of video cameras on phones, tablets and laptops make it easier than ever before for the tutor to quickly record a response to a comment rather than typing it, making his or her response all the more immediate and potentially impactful. This also holds true for participants. While text responses may be quicker, video can be used to convey more information (e.g. about attitude) or to include more information (e.g. through visuals). Encouraging participants to post video responses rather than defaulting to text can be especially useful in the initial stages of a course, with those new to online study and with those widely separated by geographic distance.

Videos offer a number of tools to allow both the course developer and the participant to manage time effectively. For a course designer, video can allow input to be packaged into extremely short, dense and quite complex blocks, because images and animations can show or demonstrate more in a shorter amount of time than text. Videos can be quite short because those watching them can make them 'longer' by re-watching sections, or by slowing them down to examine parts in more detail, to ease cognitive load and increase processing time.

Many teacher educators will find that they have already created much of the material they need to construct a video. For example, a demonstration of how to give feedback on a text can be given much more effectively by videoing a tutor talk through that text, highlighting or annotating it as they go. This can be done on a computer, using a word-processing document and the annotation or review features, or on a tablet, using a PDF viewer and stylus. In each case the teacher would use screencast software such as Camtasia or Adobe Captivate on the computer, and Explain Everything[17] on the tablet, to capture a video of this. Tutorials of how to use such tools are available freely online (e.g. teachertrainingvideos.com[18]).

Similarly, with increasing availability of interactive whiteboards and data projectors in class more teachers are creating PowerPoints to deliver content more visually to the class. With screencast software such materials can easily be turned into videos. In this way, teachers can share classroom content with others in their online course, narrating what they would say with each slide or animated object. This allows the teacher to bring their class, and their classroom content, into the online course. Similarly, teachers may record their actual classes, using either video or audio, and then upload the results for the participants of their online course to view and comment on. Those doing so will need to be aware of laws regarding student privacy, obtaining the necessary permissions and being sensitive to how the video is to be used/shared. However, an increasing number of teacher training programmes are using videos of classroom instruction. A large-scale example of this is the work done by Doug Lemov with Uncommon schools, presented in his book Teach Like a Champion, and available online at teachlikeachampion.com.[19]

Footage of teachers in class forms the basis of most of the videos available on the website teachingchannel.org.[20] Both of these examples are making use of the 'thick slices' of classroom life that video offers. In their literature review of 'The Role of video in teacher professional development', Marsh and Mitchell (2014) cite one of the main advantages of video as its ability to provide dense, detailed representations of complex topics that are nevertheless accessible because of their concrete exemplification. Viewers can not only see what is being explained, but can review it, seeing more each time they watch. The developments in 360° video and audio capture will only extend this potential.

As the availability and use of video online has expanded, so have the number and variety of tools for interacting with that video increased. The aim of these tools generally is to increase the depth of engagement that participants have with the video. At the cheapest and simplest end of the spectrum of tools, Edpuzzle[21] allows tutors to add questions to a video, which can be shared with students for work outside class, or assigned to them as part of a course. Offering more tools, albeit for more money, Voicethread[22] allows participants to interact with a video, adding comments with text or video, annotating the images as you speak (with mouse or stylus). In this way participants can post questions, make suggestions, compare their reactions and reflections to those of others. This can make for a very rich input experience, with layers of responses as people coming later see the posts of those who have viewed earlier, responding and adding their own contribution. This has all the advantages of text-based forums for participants who are unsure of themselves (e.g. due to language level) – time for reflection and research – while offering a more immersive, media rich input. The NILE online courses make use of a purpose-built add-in for Moodle called VideoQuandA, which sits some way between EdPuzzle and Voicethread, allowing tutors to incorporate text questions into the videos they have uploaded, and participants to respond or post questions of their own. This tool is presented and discussed by Kiddle on the ViLTE website.[23]

As discussed by Gardner and Edge in 'Why be a learner online' (in England, 2012) the difficulty of such learning may lie in teachers transferring new ideas and techniques to their own context. Online learning allows teachers to extend the application of theory into their classroom and get immediate feedback. Video allows teachers to record this exploration and to discuss it with others, be that in the form of feedback on teaching techniques or in analysing classroom dynamics. In the latter area software/platforms such as Veo[24] are being developed to facilitate such conversations. Veo allows a teacher to tag a video of their classroom they have recorded, for example to highlight all the instances they can see of teacher talking time. They can then review this – adding a commentary – and either share this with a tutor/other participants, or compare their review to that done with the same video by others. As Sherin and Dyer (2017) explain, one of the key functions of such technology is helping teachers not just to understand the 'What' is happening in the classroom, but to understand the 'Why'.

Brainstorming: Padlet; community wall; chatrooms

Communication and critical thinking are often more effective and efficient when we can use tools to offload some of the cognitive strain, to reduce the number of things that we're trying to keep track of (Sweller, 1994). The more complex the goal we're trying to achieve, the more we need to make use of tools – e.g. notes, mind maps, charts – and the more tools we may need to make use of.

One advantage of using these tools online is that they allow for almost instantaneous consultation and collaboration. In class, participants may struggle to come up with ideas, and only start to progress towards their own ideas once they hear the results of others' thinking, at the feedback stage. Online, they can view what others are posting, or have posted. The designer can link to previous iterations of such activities, to spark ideas or encourage comparison, analysis and evaluation. Using a central virtual space, such as Padlet[25] a course designer can link to multiple documents, which participants can work through sequentially, or skip between as their interest, level or purpose dictates. Incorporating a collaborative text tool, such as Google Docs,[26] within the Padlet then allows participants to see the reactions/reflections of others and to compare these to their own. Such tools also allow the tutor a central point from which to monitor all interaction and respond where necessary. This in turn allows for differentiation:

- of support and scaffolding provided
- of time allowed and sequence/recycling
- of level of challenge and extension activities
- of role within the group

In NILE Online courses, much of the differentiation is left up to the tutor, with the courses designed to provide opportunities for tutor interaction with participants in a variety of ways. This in turn reflects the ethos of NILE that 'we teach participants, not courses': focusing on tailoring the content to participant needs. When creating online courses, it is vital for organisations to consider what their overarching aims and principles are, ensuring that the tools they use and the ways in which they use them reflect these.

Assessment: collaboration; grading; multimodality

We now turn from issues of content and interaction to the measurement of teacher competence in online language teacher education. A review of such programmes by Murray (2013) including case studies of 18 institutions, found a wide range of formative and summative assessment procedures and instruments in use, depending on the aims of the program. These included: a thesis or research portfolio, written assignments, examinations, participation in online discussion forums, participation in synchronous videoconference classes, f2f practicums (i.e. observed or video-recorded f2f teaching practice), internships (in one case study only), observations of video-recorded classes taught by experienced teachers, reflective journals and blogs, case studies, action research projects and action plans, and online quizzes and tests. Clearly, this breadth of options in assessment in teacher education programmes online shows how the affordances are already being explored and exploited – in particular, in the areas of collaboration, multimodality, and observation of teaching practice.

Collaborative submissions, where two or more course participants work on an assessed product together – whilst common in face-to-face situations (and a regular feature of *unassessed* activities in online teacher development programmes) were not commonly incorporated into assessment practices in a survey of online language teacher education providers (Hockly et al., 2016). This was reported as largely due to specific limitations and issues: the difficulty of measuring the output of individual participants, ownership of the product and more. Assessed collaborations which did exist included group project work, collaborative responses to assessed forum tasks, joint literature reviews, materials development projects and joint presentations. Approaches to address this in NILE Online courses include clear guidelines – defining roles, research necessary and how output could be shared – and self-reflection tasks following the assessment to add a formative, learner-training element to support the idea of collaborative assessment.

Multimodality in assessment practices closely mirrors the affordances of content and interaction on language teacher education programmes. Allowing a wider choice over the form that submission takes (e.g. using video instead of text) not only enables the teacher to bring more of their context and classroom into the assessment, but also embraces the diversity and the strengths of those being assessed. Online assessment submissions for the pilot of a new in-service teaching qualification, for example, included the options of video or audio recordings, peer observation forms, student feedback forms, and self-evaluation forms as data to support reflective teacher development.

Perhaps the elephant in the room in terms of assessment in online teacher education pro-grammes, is the issue of observed and evaluated teaching practice. Tools exist, as mentioned above, to video-record and live stream or subsequently upload teachers' lessons, and many of these tools, e.g. Veo, can be used so as to allow different views of what unfolds in the classroom. However, in our experience, and in initial, informal reports of projects which are underway to explore these tools (e.g. at Cambridge English, and the work on Virtual Reality in teacher training (Driver, 2017)), there is still a gulf between what can be captured using these tools and from having a live observer in the classroom. This has significant implications for the validity and reliability of assessment, and while it may prove to be very effective in formative, developmental assessment in the near future, we feel that certificated, summative, high-stakes assessed teaching practice via online video still has hurdles to overcome.

Conclusion

The drivers behind increases in provision of online and blended options in language teacher edu-cation mirror those in education generally, and language education specifically, fuelled particularly by pressures on governments to help language teacher education meet the demands of global demographic changes. Platforms, tools and approaches have developed over more than 50 years to lead us to a current situation where possibilities can quickly outstrip principles. In this chapter, we have explored what we feel to be some of the key considerations, current practices, and possible future developments, in provision and evaluation of language teacher education online.

The advantages are multiple, in our opinion, but must be weighed against practical realities within individual contexts, as well as pedagogical principles of what makes effective input, inter-action, reflection and output in a language teacher education programme. We have no doubt that these programmes are here to stay, and will grow in popularity as the above challenges are confronted and overcome, as both pre-service and in-service teacher education increasingly serve a teacher population which is itself familiar and comfortable with accessing and delivering education in multimodal, online spaces. We also believe this future is bright, and when online language teacher education is designed and facilitated in a principled and practical way, teachers will enjoy the benefits of programmes which meet their practical, economic, geographical and developmental needs and desires.

Recommended reading

Dirksen, J. (2015) *Design for How People Learn.* London: New Riders.
   A very accessibly written book with practical examples of design considerations to optimise materials, courses and interfaces for how people learn. A book that you'll refer to again and again throughout the designing and developing of online courses.
Dudeney, G., Hockly, N. and Pegrum, M. (2013) *Digital Literacies: Research and Resources in Language Teaching.* London: Pearson.
   This book offers an extensive introduction to the theory of digital literacies as well as practical advice and lesson plans for developing digital literacies with students.

Krug, S. (2013) *Don't Make Me Think, Revisited: A Common Sense Approach to Web Usability.* London: New Riders.

As the title indicates this book is focused on making online content as easy to access as possible. A thin book with a very useful set of principles for making your courses and content as early accessible as possible.

Salmon, G. (2013) *E-tivities: The Key to Active Online Learning.* Abingdon: Routledge.

This book contains a five-step process to build an online community within your courses, developing active online learning through the construction of knowledge through collaboration.

References

Allen, I. E. and Seaman, J. (2013) *Changing Course: Ten Years of Tracking Online Education in the United States.* Newburyport, MA: Sloan Consortium.

Anderson, T. and Dron, J. (2011) 'Three Generations of Distance Education Pedagogy'. *The International Review of Research in Open and Distributed Learning,* 12(3) 80–97.

Bergmann, J. (2012) *Flip Your Classroom.* Alexandria, VA: ASCD and ISTE.

del Carmen Contijoch-Escontria, M., Burns, A. and Candlin, C. N. (2012) 'Feedback in the mediation of learning in online language teacher education', in England, L. (ed.) *Online Language Teacher Education: TESOL Perspectives.* New York: Routledge: 22–38.

Driver, P. (2017) *A New Perspective: Virtual Reality and Transmedia Spherical Video in Teacher Training.* Cambridge University Press talk. Available online: <www.cambridge.org/elt/blog/2017/11/01/virtual-reality-spherical-video-teacher-training> (accessed 20 March 2018).

Dudeney, G., Hockly, N. and Pegrum, M. (2013) *Digital Literacies. Research and Resources in Language Teaching.* London: Pearson.

England, L. (ed.) (2012) *Online Language Teacher Education: TESOL Perspectives.* New York: Routledge.

Hall, D. and Knox, J. (2009) 'Issues in the Education of TESOL Teachers by Distance Education'. *Distance Education,* 30(1) 63–85.

Hammadou, J. and Bernhardt, E. B. (1987) 'On Being and Becoming a Foreign Language Teacher'. *Theory into Practice,* 26(4) 301–306.

Hockly, N. (2012) 'Webinars: A Cookbook for Educators'. *The Round.* Available online: <http://the-round.com/resource/webinars-a-cookbook-for-educators/> (accessed 11 May, 2019).

Hockly, N. and Clandfield, L. (2010) *Teaching Online.* Guildford: Delta Publishing.

Hockly, N., Dudeney, G. and Kiddle, T. (2016) *AQUEDUTO Members Assessment in Online Education Survey.* Internal AQUEDUTO publication.

Marsh, B. and Mitchell, N. (2014) 'The Role of Video in Teacher Professional Development'. *Teacher Development,* 18(3) 403–417.

Marzano, R. J., Pickering, D. and Pollock, J. E., 2001. *Classroom Instruction That Works: Research-Based Strategies for Increasing Student Achievement.* Alexandria, VA: ASCD.

Murray, D. (2013) *A Case for Online English Language Teacher Education.* Monterey, CA: The International Research Foundation for English Language Education.

Norton, B. and Nunan, D. (2002) 'Teaching MA-TESOL Courses Online: Challenges and Rewards'. *TESOL Quarterly,* 36(4) 617–621.

Ng, A. and Widdon, J. (2014) *Origins of the Modern MOOC.* Available online: <www.robotics.stanford.edu; www.robotics.stanford.edu/~ang/papers/mooc14-OriginsOfModernMOOC.pdf> (accessed 11 May, 2019).

Salmon, G. (2004) *E-Moderating: The Key to Teaching and Learning Online.* Hove: Psychology Press.

Salmon, G. (2013) *E-Tivities: The Key to Active Online Learning.* Abingdon: Routledge.

Schwartz, B. (2004) *The Paradox of Choice: Why Less is More.* New York: Ecco.

Sharpe, R., Beetham, H. and De Freitas, S. (2010) *Rethinking Learning for a Digital Age: How Learners are Shaping Their Own Experiences.* New York: Routledge.

Sherin, M. G. and Dyer, E. B. (2017) 'Teacher Self-Captured Video: Learning to See'. *Phi Delta Kappan,* 98(7) 49–54.

Stein, J. and Graham, C. R. (2014) *Essentials for Blended Learning: A Standards-Based Guide*. New York: Routledge.

Sweller, J. (1994) 'Cognitive Load Theory, Learning Difficulty, and Instructional Design'. *Learning and Instruction*, 4(4) 295–312.

Talbert, R. (2017) *Flipped Learning: A Guide for Higher Education Faculty*. Sterling, VA: Stylus Publishing, LLC.

Tesdell, L. S. (2003) 'Teaching MA-TESOL Courses Online: Challenges and Rewards'. *Technical Communication*, 50(4) 654–655.

The Open University (n.d.). *History of the Open University*. The Open University. Available online: <www.open.ac.uk/researchprojects/historyofou/> (accessed 11 May, 2019).

Willingham, D. T. (2009) *Why Don't Students Like School?: A Cognitive Scientist Answers Questions About How the Mind Works and What it Means For The Classroom*. Hoboken, NJ: John Wiley & Sons.

Wooley, D. R. (1994) 'PLATO: The Emergence of Online Community'. *Think of IT*. Available online: <http://thinkofit.com/plato/dwplato.htm> (accessed 11 May, 2019).

Yates, G. C. and Hattie, J. (2013) *Visible Learning and the Science of How We Learn*. Abingdon: Routledge.

Courses and resources referred to

1 Veritasium: www.youtube.com
2 Crashcourse: www.youtube.com
3 Laureate International Universities: www.laureate.net
4 NILE Online: www.nile-elt.com/online-courses
5 Learning technologies in EAP: www.sheffield.ac.uk/eltc/tesol/learning-technologies-eap
6 Preparing for Uni: www.futurelearn.com/courses/preparing-for-uni
7 ELT in the Digital Age: https://eltjam.academy/courses
8 Onelook: www.onelook.com
9 A–Z of ELT: https://scottthornbury.wordpress.com
10 University English for Academic Purposes: UEfAP.com
11 Adobe Connect: www.adobe.com/products/adobeconnect.html
12 Zoom: https://zoom.us
13 Hertzberg on Motivation: www.youtube.com
14 Ken Robinson: www.ted.com/talks/ken_robinson_says_schools_kill_creativity
15 RSA animate: www.wearecognitive.com/the-rsa
16 Camtasia: http://discover.techsmith.com/camtasia-brand-desktop/?gclid=Cj0KCQjw
17 Explain everything: https://explaineverything.com
18 Teacher training videos: www.teachertrainingvideos.com
19 Teach like a champion: http://teachlikeachampion.com/resources
20 Teaching channel: www.teachingchannel.org
21 Edpuzzle: https://edpuzzle.com
22 Voicethread: https://voicethread.com
23 Video in Language Teacher Education: https://vilte.warwick.ac.uk
24 VEO: www.veo-group.com
25 Padlet: https://padlet.com/dashboard
26 Google Docs: www.google.co.uk/docs/about

9

'Mind the gap'

Supporting newly qualified teachers on their journey from pre-service training to full-time employment

Nick Baguley

Introduction

Beginning to teach is generally recognised as a particularly complex stage of a teacher's career, with those joining the profession often describing this period as a time when just surviving is the main goal.

The main focus of this chapter is to consider why the first year of teaching can be so challenging and what teacher trainers, academic managers, supervisors and mentors might do to ease this burden. Much of the detail within this chapter will centre around internationally recognised pre-service teacher training courses such as the Cambridge Assessment English Certificate in Teaching English to Speakers of Other Languages (CELTA) and the Trinity Teaching English to Speakers of Other Languages (Cert TESOL) which prepare candidates to teach English as a foreign language in institutions such as private language schools or on University foundation programmes. However, many of the ideas discussed in this chapter could equally apply to other teacher training qualifications preparing participants for work in other contexts such as state school education, which is by far the biggest sector globally.

The chapter will begin by summarising the main discussions and debates, outlined in literature and research into this area, to explain why the first year of English language teaching can be so demanding. In particular there will be a focus on the issues caused by the disparity between what newly qualified teachers experience during their pre-service training and what they then find when they start full-time employment. This section will explore three possible reasons for this disparity. First, it will identify common features of pre-service training courses that are designed to support candidates but which are not always replicated in the real world. Second, it will identify some aspects of pre-service training courses which do not always help participants when they enter the teaching profession. Third, it will highlight elements of effective lesson preparation and classroom practice that are often missing from such training programmes but which would be useful for participants to experience before they start full-time employment. This section will finish by focusing on how newly qualified teachers often develop professionally over the first 12 months of employment.

The next part of the chapter will look at what can be done to deal with this disparity and outline three concrete solutions. First, those delivering pre-service training courses (referred to throughout this article as teacher trainers rather than the more widely accepted general term of educators) need to acknowledge from the outset that this gap exists. Second, teacher trainers need to consider what practical steps they can take both in terms of course design and delivery to help reduce this gap. Third, academic managers, supervisors and mentors need to focus on what can be done on school induction programmes, during probationary periods and over the first 12 months of employment to help bridge this gap and ensure that all newly qualified teachers are receiving the pastoral and pedagogic support they need to function as effectively as possible in the workplace.

TESOL: problems teachers often face during their first year

Researchers have put forward a variety of reasons to explain why the first year of teaching is often such a challenge. Veenman (1984) outlined several difficulties experienced by novice teachers including managing the classroom, dealing with individual differences amongst learners, coping with a lack of materials and supplies, assessing and evaluating students and motivating learners. Alexander and Galbraith (1997) focused on classroom management, teaching and learning, individual differences, resources and evaluation/assessment when researching how a group of student teachers in Queensland, Australia developed professionally in the first year of their career. McCann and Johannessen (2004) defined five major concerns of beginning teachers as: relationships with pupils' parents, colleagues and supervisors; workload/time management; knowledge of subject/curriculum; evaluation/grading; and autonomy/control. Similarly, MacKinnon (1987) found that although initial concerns centred on relationship with pupils, these soon gave way to issues with classroom management, teaching materials and methods of instruction. Melnick and Meister (2008) conducted a study of novice teachers and reported that dealing with behaviour issues and the diverse needs of students, time constraints, workload and a lack of communication skills when dealing with difficult situations were the most common concerns. Ryan (1986) suggested that coping with busy schedules, finding materials and organising and sequencing lessons were the main concerns of beginner teachers. Fantilli and McDougall (2009) highlighted how a novice teacher is expected to adjust to working in a new environment, become familiar with routines, procedures and school administration. In addition to teaching in the classroom, responsibilities as a teacher might involve keeping a record of attendance and work completed, writing reports, counselling students, doing placement testing and covering the lessons of absent colleagues at short notice. It is possible to argue that newly qualified teachers 'are expected to take on many job responsibilities which they are not yet ready for' (Gun et al., 2010: 1).

Whilst acknowledging the variety of contexts referred to in the studies outlined above, a common theme running through much of the literature is the notion that the realities faced by beginner teachers in the classroom are often very different to how they perceived the education profession to be (Inman and Marlow, 2004; Karatas and Karaman, 2013; Melnick and Meister, 2008; Veenman, 1984; Yuksel, 2014). According to Murshidi, Konting, Elias and Fooi, 'when beginning teachers enter the teaching force, they often encounter a reality shock as they confront the complexity of the teaching task' (2006: 266). Sometimes this reality or transition shock (Corcoran, 1981) is caused by the disparity between what teachers experience during their pre-service training and what they find in the real world (Mann and Tang, 2012; Nahal, 2010; Romero, 2013). Those with a good awareness of theory but little or no classroom experience will often be influenced by their own teaching experiences, beliefs and observations during the initial stages of a career (Calderhead, 1991; Richards and Lockhart, 1996). These ideas and beliefs can change once teachers gain experience and learn to 'develop and enrich their identity through reflection' (Yuksel, 2014: 3).

Another important consideration is the high level of support often provided to candidates on pre-service training courses. This might be both formal and informal input from experienced tutors as well as oral and written feedback on lessons observed. Such courses also place considerable emphasis on the need for participants to collaborate, share ideas and work effectively as a team. Mann and Tang (2012) and Nahal (2010) suggested that the support of colleagues is vital for novice teachers to feel accepted as 'a member of the learning community' and 'know the importance of being a staff member in the school or classroom' (Nahal, 2010: 7). Other researchers have highlighted the importance for novice teachers of getting practical support such as 'pedagogical ideas, teaching resources and logistical knowledge' (Karatas and Karaman, 2013: 12). Teachers who do not receive such assistance during their first year 'may experience a sense of abandonment and confusion' (Nahal, 2010: 3) leading to a lack of clarity about their role and even a sense of isolation.

Alexander and Galbraith (1997) questioned the effectiveness of some pre-service teacher education courses characterised by inflexible models of teaching to which the novice teacher is expected to conform. A prescriptive and outdated model of planning, which 'demands a linearity of thinking' (John, 2006: 483) is quite common on many pre-service courses. Yet this might not always fit with models used in schools, the course books and material teachers are expected to work from once employed and, most crucially, the needs, interests, motivation and learning preferences of the students within specific contexts. In addition, such frameworks, with their focus on lesson objectives, logical staging, procedures and the strict allocation of timings, often follow a linear structure and suggest quite a technical view of teaching (John, 2006). This is at odds with what many researchers believe effective classroom instruction to be.

On many pre-service training courses the success of a lesson 'is often thought to depend on the effectiveness with which the lesson was planned' (Richards, 2000: 103). As a result, course participants can spend hours producing an extremely detailed lesson plan often with considerable support from peers and a tutor, who will also observe the lesson and provide feedback. The completed lesson plan, with its focus on aims, is 'almost like a contract between teacher and observer rather than teacher and students' (Anderson, 2015: 231). There is some debate on the impact this has on teacher development. Liu's (2014) case study in Taiwan highlighted the importance of detailed lesson planning in terms of improving teacher confidence and reducing anxiety. Studies show that when a newly qualified teacher feels organised and prepared, the lesson runs smoothly and 'students are more likely to actively participate and listen' (Nahal, 2010: 9). Such teachers are also concerned about negative reaction from students and maintaining a sense of control within the classroom. Mann and Tang (2012) noted that when classes progressed as newly qualified teachers had planned, they were relatively comfortable and felt that they had been able to implement techniques learnt during pre-service education. Once newly qualified teachers feel confident that students are 'behaving and responding appropriately they will find better ways to present the materials for students to learn' (Nahal, 2010: 9).

However, others feel that 'there is a mismatch between the demands of the classroom and the prescriptive planning model' (Shavelson and Stern, 1981: 477). Newly qualified teachers often complete their pre-service training without being exposed to a range of strategies and teaching techniques that would enable them to respond or react more effectively to issues as they arise in the classroom (Romeo, 2013). Their desire to see a lesson progress as planned 'covering the essential material well and thoroughly' (Richards and Pennington, 1998: 186) means that such teachers are reluctant to trust their intuition and are often unable to move beyond what has been prepared in advance. Whilst such detailed lesson plans might look good on paper the 'negotiated nature of learning needs to be added to the planning equation if spontaneity and improvisation are to be allowed' (John, 2006: 487). The outcomes-based approach to planning used on many pre-service teacher training courses allows little room for participants to 'prepare for and respond to the unpredictable events, relationships and learning opportunities of the lesson itself' (Anderson, 2015: 229). Newly qualified teachers often graduate without 'a repertoire of pedagogical routines to cope with unexpected events arising during a class' (Mann and Tang, 2012: 481).

In terms of planning lessons effectively researchers have drawn attention to key elements which are often missing from pre-service training courses. Studies conducted by Alexander and Galbraith (1997) concluded that participants' priority was on being as well-organised as possible for individual lessons rather than considering each class as part of a series of learning events over time. This study also revealed that not enough attention is given on pre-service training courses to planning lessons that cater effectively for a wide range of student abilities. Fantilli and McDougall (2009) highlighted that those graduating from pre-service training courses were not introduced to useful concepts such as long-range planning and how to ensure that a series of lessons are clearly connected. There was also not enough focus on dealing with mixed ability and techniques for differentiation. Therefore, newly qualified teachers often find it difficult to deal with diversity within the classroom, which can lead to stress and a sense of feeling ill-equipped to engage effectively with every learner in the class.

Meyer (2004) conducted comparative case studies of novice and expert teachers and concluded that the former had an 'insufficient understanding of the importance of prior knowledge and its role in effective teaching' (Karatas and Karaman, 2013: 18). Other researchers have concluded that during the planning process newly qualified teachers can also struggle to anticipate problems of language, materials and learners and come up with possible solutions. Having failed to make predictions about student responses, they then 'have problems adjusting their practice according to the exigencies that they encounter' (John, 2006: 489). Perhaps most importantly of all given the considerable demands placed upon newly qualified teachers, pre-service training courses give little attention to how participants can prepare a lesson within a reasonable time frame.

It is unsurprising that on starting full-time employment many newly qualified teachers attempt to apply what they have learnt during their pre-service training course. In terms of lesson preparation this often leads to quite a procedural and information- based form of classroom instruction where teachers are comfortable if a lesson goes as planned (Karatas and Karaman, 2013). Romero points out that newly qualified teachers do not have 'a well-developed, automised collection of teachings strategies' (2013: 17). This argument is supported by Meyer (2004) who states that novice teachers depend on the lesson frameworks picked up during their initial training and are not especially skilled at responding, reacting or being intuitive. Hobbs argued that pre-service training courses focus mainly on practical teaching skills and 'does not support teacher autonomy or the ability to think critically about teaching or teaching contexts' (2013: 166).

How newly qualified teachers develop such skills and move away from the linear and transmission-based approach to lesson planning often used on pre-service training courses depends on several factors. The pedagogic support newly qualified teachers receive from academic managers, mentors and peers undoubtedly plays an important role. This should include a comprehensive induction programme and an on-going, in-house professional development scheme with opportunities for newly qualified teachers to plan lessons with both peers and experienced colleagues (Gun et al., 2010; Kidd et al., 2015). Hobbs believes that 'few employers, particularly in EFL, provide the professional development novice teachers require' (2013: 172). However, for schools that do invest time and resources in such a way, the long-term benefit can be continuity, staff retention and financial savings (Kidd et al., 2015).

Another key component is how newly qualified teachers respond to their classroom experiences throughout the first year of employment. Several researchers argue that as a teacher's confidence grows, the approach to lesson planning changes. Liu (2014) reported how an EFL teacher in Taiwan developed over a year from being nervous, teaching in a disorganised manner and spending too long preparing materials in the first year, to becoming more familiar with materials, taking less time to prepare and remaining calm when faced with unexpected issues in the classroom. There is also evidence to suggest that as newly qualified teachers become more familiar with the working environment and as their self-esteem starts to increase due to positive feedback from students, peers and experienced colleagues, they are better able to reflect on the teaching and learning process within their context. Osterman and Kottkamp, argued that reflection means 'developing a greater level of self-awareness about the nature and the impact of their performance' (1993: 19). Fox and Singletary (1986) stated that with continued support newly qualified teachers can become flexible, self-evaluative and competent therefore developing 'the ability to make informed choices' (Hobbs, 2013: 172) that many lack on completing their pre-service training.

TESOL: supporting teachers through their first year

The importance of dealing with the issue of disparity between 'learning to teach' and 'teaching in the real world' cannot be underestimated. Studies have consistently shown that whatever the context the number of teachers leaving the profession within the first five years of their career continues to rise. This has a clear impact on continuity, recruitment processes, staff morale and the allocation of resources. Perhaps the first step is to raise trainee teachers' awareness of how the training programme they enroll on is likely to differ from what they might experience when they start full-time teaching. Course literature, interview procedures and joining information needs to be clearer about what the course focuses on, what it does not provide and why. For example, courses such as the CELTA and Trinity Cert TESOL focus on the teaching of adult learners even though most graduates will be expected to teach Young Learners when they start work. These courses do not generally focus on how to teach large classes or complete beginners. Nor do they usually look at how to work with very demotivated learners or function effectively in very under-resourced schools. Teacher trainers could also be more explicit about why lesson planning documentation is so detailed on pre-service courses and acknowledge that in most teaching contexts it is unnecessary or impossible to replicate such an approach. In addition, tutors should explain that the support they provide to participants in the lesson planning process and the collaborative approach encouraged throughout the course, may not be so evident in the workplace. By being crystal clear about what each training scheme is designed to achieve and how some of the key components are delivered, educators could reduce any mismatch between product content and participant need, help manage expectations and therefore lessen the shock often experienced by graduates when they begin their first job.

In addition to acknowledging that this disparity exists, those working on pre-service training programmes might do more both in terms of course design and delivery to help reduce this gap. One option might be to ensure that the training schedule has as greater practical focus as possible. For example, including sessions on material light teaching, how to start and finish lessons in a variety of ways and techniques for extending or collapsing activities might provide participants with a range of useful ideas and techniques to make the lesson planning process more time efficient.

A second option might be to have lesson planning documentation, which enables participants to meet any assessed criteria but is, at the same time, less detailed and more user-friendly. Newly qualified teachers might then be more likely to continue using this template, which could include key indicators such as assumptions and timetable fit, when they start full-time employment. Indeed, tutors might even encourage participants to develop their own lesson planning proforma as long as it includes all elements of the assessed course lesson planning criteria. Another suggestion might be a greater focus on the importance of course planning. This element is rarely looked at in any depth on most CELTA or Trinity Cert TESOL courses. To help rectify this it could be that towards the end of the course tutors give an input session on this topic before asking participants to work together to produce a timetable of lessons. This might help newly qualified teachers to move away from planning lessons in isolation and see how looking at the 'bigger picture' can lead to recycling, revising and providing a better sense of connection between lessons for students. Finally, it would seem more useful for teacher trainers to demonstrate how participants can evaluate, adapt and supplement published material rather than place an emphasis on designing lessons from scratch. It is far more common for teachers to work from published materials once in employment, so to exploit existing materials well would appear to be a more practical skill to develop than consistently expecting those on training courses to create their own material, which is both time-consuming and difficult to do well with limited teaching experience.

The next logical step is for employers to do more in practical terms to help bridge the gap between pre-service training and employment as an English language teacher. Table 9.1 summarises the main differences between life on a pre-service training course such as the CELTA or Trinity Cert TESOL and what many teachers in a typical English language school face during their first year of employment.

Table 9.1 A summary of the main differences between pre-service training and full-time teaching

Course participants on a pre-service training course	Newly qualified teachers in their first year of employment
Usually teach around two hours a week	Often have a workload of around 20 to 25 contact hours a week
Usually teach lessons of no longer than 60 minutes	Can have classes of two hours or more
Often spend hours preparing for a lesson of no more than 60 minutes	Are unable to take such a time-consuming approach with a workload of around 20 to 25 contact hours a week
Often have considerable support from tutors and peers when preparing for a lesson	Do not always receive such structured and detailed support at work
Usually work with the same class for a limited period	Work with a class over time which often equates to a school term. This might be several weeks but in some contexts it could be an entire academic year
Often prepare lessons as 'single events' with no focus on course planning	Need to look at each lesson as part of a course syllabus and consider aspects such as timetable fit, recycling and revising
Rarely teach a lesson without any warning or sufficient preparation time	Are often part of a 'standby' rota where they might be asked to cover for an absent colleague with minimal notice/preparation time
Are not expected to assess formally the students they teach	Need to be familiar and comfortable with the assessment procedures used by the school

Table 9.1 (Continued)

Course participants on a pre-service training course	Newly qualified teachers in their first year of employment
Often work with classes of no more than 12 students	Might have classes of up to 25 students
Often teach a limited number of student levels	Might have to teach a variety of levels
Usually teach non-fee-paying students	Work with fee-paying customers who often have specific needs and expectations
Usually work with students who are generally patient, undemanding and very co-operative	Might have to deal with difficult situations such as failing students, persistent latecomers and customer complaints
Work with adult learners and receive little if any input on teaching Young Learners	Are often expected to teach classes of Young Learners despite having little or no training in this demanding area

From trainee to teacher: a case study

Having worked as a CELTA trainer since 1997, I have always been interested in how effectively pre-service training courses prepare participants for full-time employment as English language teachers. Since January 2008 I have been employed on a regular basis by a large private language school in Egypt both as a freelance CELTA tutor and a mentor for newly qualified teachers. As part of my recently completed MA in Professional Development for Language Education, I decided to investigate how three newly qualified teachers joining the school in September 2016 adapted to full-time employment. For the purposes of this article I shall use the names Mahmoud, Nour and Radwa throughout to protect the identity of the three teachers I worked with. This case study was conducted during the teachers' three-month probationary period which consisted of two seven-week adult terms and involved the following research tools:

1. A written questionnaire to encourage the participants to reflect on their pre-service training experiences.
2. Two face-to-face interviews, one at the start and the other at the end of the research period, to find out how the participants were adapting to full-time employment.
3. A journal, kept by each participant for a month in the middle of the case study, to allow for more personal reflections.
4. The submission of example lesson plans from both the pre-service training course and classes delivered at the school during the probationary period.

The in-depth interviews done at the start of the research period confirmed many of the concerns outlined in the table above. All three participants were extremely anxious about beginning full-time employment. Not only were they conscious of the demanding workload, but there was also the realisation that they would be teaching lessons of 150 minutes with up to 22 fee-paying students in a class. This was very different to their experiences on the CELTA course at the school where the maximum lesson length was 60 minutes and most classes contained around ten non-fee-paying learners all of whom appreciated that teachers were on a training programme. However, their anxiety about this change in context affected them in slightly different ways:

- Mahmoud admitted to being most concerned about getting through the course material stating that 'I would really like to consider student needs but because of the schedule I have to finish a unit every class and I find this hard to do.' At the start of the first term he often started the planning process by focusing on the learning aims of the lesson rather than student needs. His desire to cover everything in the course book often led to issues of time management with Mahmoud revealing 'I usually overrun. I hardly ever finish on time'. He was also worried about learner engagement so gave plenty of thought to lead-in activities, communicative purpose and a variety of interaction patterns 'to prevent boredom'.

• Nour stated that her main worry on starting full-time employment at the school was 'fear of running out of activities' and not knowing how to fill the remaining class time. This concern stemmed largely from not wanting 'to stand up in class with nothing. I wasn't at the point where I felt so confident to deal with that.' This led to her to preparing too many activities which she then tried to get through by rushing students.

• Radwa revealed that her main concern was how to be effective when teaching grammar. In her journal she wrote 'I have to admit my weakest point is when I teach grammar. My grammar lessons are dull as I just talk a lot and don't feel able to involve the students'.

None of these issues were addressed effectively during the school's week-long induction programme which the three case study participants felt lacked a practical focus. Mahmoud described the week as 'just the formalities with too great a focus on the organisation and not enough pedagogic support'. Radwa argued that what newly qualified teachers really need is help with 'lesson preparation and different activities to use in class rather than looking at facts and figures about the organisation'. They suggested that training sessions on planning the first class, how best to exploit the range of course books used at the school and where to find supplementary material easily would have been far more useful. They also indicated that on-going pedagogic support on how to prepare lessons quickly and effectively, ideas for starting and finishing a class, techniques for differentiation and further work on how to plan a series of lessons would have been more useful than some of the more theoretical training they received during the probationary period.

Having outlined the initial anxiety that existed amongst the case study participants, it is also important to recognise however just how quickly their confidence grew even within the relatively short three-month probationary period. There were several reasons for this. First, the teachers felt extremely supported by their mentors who were assigned to help them with pedagogic issues. In many ways the mentors replicated the role of a CELTA tutor making themselves readily available to provide advice, encouragement and practical ideas. Nour stated that her mentor 'was always available' adding that 'whenever I run out of ideas I just ask him and that is super helpful'. Radwa also worked closely with her mentor who was 'really helpful with lesson planning as she encouraged me to question the aim of each activity from the students' perspective'. Second, teaching techniques and activities, often presented during regular training sessions by more experienced teachers, gave them additional resources to use in class. Nour and Radwa also commented on the value of peer collaboration with the latter stating that exchanging ideas and materials with colleagues meant she 'never felt isolated'. Third, as they taught more lessons and developed their experience, each teacher admitted to becoming more comfortable within their new context. Consequently, anxiety levels dropped, their self-esteem grew and they appeared able to approach lesson planning in a more relaxed and reflective way. Towards the end of the case study Mahmoud wrote in his journal, 'I have come to realise that as a teacher you should always go for the student needs first when you're planning, then think of other things'. Nour commented that as her confidence improved she no longer spent hours looking for the 'killer activity', preferring to find something quickly and then taking time to consider how best to exploit it. Radwa revealed that her initial approach was 'to be in control for every minute of the class as that was good teaching'. However, more experience and advice from her mentor had shown 'that the more students are involved, it's so much better'.

There was also evidence to suggest that each newly qualified teacher then attempted to address the areas that had caused so much concern at the beginning of the first term. The most noticeable impact was how the focus of the lesson planning process shifted from the insecurities of the teachers to the needs of their students. For example, in his journal Mahmoud described reducing the scope of lead-in activities, planning his lessons from the final fluency task backwards and being less concerned about covering all the course book material to ensure that learners had sufficient time to practise language. Nour realised that planning too many activities and trying to rush through them all was simply 'a waste of time and energy'. She too became more selective in the second term when using course book material and tried to make better use of the activities she took into class. Radwa's experiences in the first term also led her to being more critical of teaching material and to look for activities that encouraged her students to do more of the work.

In addition, there was evidence that this increased confidence led to all three teachers feeling better able to react to students' needs within their lessons. Mahmoud referred to this change in his journal by describing an occasion when he taught a writing skills lesson, reflected afterwards on how he might have supported students more and then made changes before doing the same lesson with a different class later that day. During our second face-to face interview Nour mentioned how more classroom experience meant that 'if I've used all my material I know what to do. I wouldn't freak out'. In Radwa's journal there was evidence to support the view that during the second term she planned her lessons based, in part, on students' comments and was better able to make on-the-spot decisions in response to the needs of learners in class. Developing greater confidence also had an impact on the time spent planning lessons, with Nour and Radwa revealing that they spent considerably less time putting their lessons together during the second term. However, Mahmoud's planning time doubled. His decision not to rely solely on the course book material but to think a lot more about the needs of his students and how he could address these more effectively, meant that he needed longer to prepare classes. He revealed that much of this time was spent considering 'what students are going to do at every stage' and visualise each step to 'avoid undesired breaks in momentum as the result of unneeded surprises [sic]'.

An analysis of the research data also revealed some striking similarities amongst the case study participants in terms of their approach to writing lesson plans once they started full-time employment. It was interesting to note that none of them even attempted to use the lesson planning documentation introduced during their pre-service training. They immediately turned to a less detailed, more practical approach with key points written in a notebook. The evidence provided by these teachers suggested that staging, some referencing to page and exercise numbers and ad hoc reminders about course administration, how to transition between stages to keep students engaged and, on occasions, timings were considered the most important elements of a lesson plan to be written down. However, these notebooks contained little or no reference to key concepts such as overall lesson aims, stage aims, interaction patterns, anticipated problems and suggested solutions and procedural detail. Given the comments made by each case study participant about the number of hours needed to produce a written lesson plan and the perceived negative impact that producing such a document had on their classroom practice this development is, perhaps, understandable. Radwa commented that the amount of time spent during her CELTA course on producing a lesson plan was unrealistic given that 'in the real teaching world teachers rarely write lesson plans to that extent of details [sic]'. Nour revealed that having taken up to 6 hours to prepare each CELTA lesson, she then felt she 'should stick to the lesson plan no matter what, which made me sometimes overlook the needs of the students and move on to the next activity'.

The realisation that none of the newly qualified teachers continued with any form of written language research was far more surprising. This is a key component of the most pre-service training courses with candidates completing a detailed language analysis form, including anticipated problems and possible solutions. Nour and Radwa acknowledged that they were extremely anxious about teaching grammar and during the first term language research was often the starting point for their lesson preparation. However, their notebooks contained very little evidence of scripted language analysis. Most of the reviewed lesson plan notes made no reference to what the target language meant, how meaning would be conveyed or checked and what aspects of phonology would be highlighted. There was also very limited information on the form of the target language.

It was also noticeable that none of the newly qualified teachers wrote any reflections in their notebooks on their lesson plans to help to make future classes more effective and the lesson planning process less time-consuming. Most newly qualified teachers at the school are time-tabled for 'double ups' where they teach two classes of the same level on the same day to help reduce the stresses of lesson preparation. However, there was no training given during either the induction week or the probationary period on how to use lesson planning notes as a reflective tool. In addition, with no input on how to plan a series of lessons, there was little evidence to suggest that these teachers moved away from preparing lessons as one-off events and develop strategies for longer term course planning. Finally, all three case study participants mentioned the benefits of planning lessons at the school in terms of ready access to advice, computers and teaching resources, but complained how noisy the teachers' room was and the impact this had on time efficient lesson planning. They argued that the provision of a quiet workspace would help to alleviate this problem and go some way to ensuring that teachers could focus on lesson planning without their thought processes being disturbed.

Although providing some useful insights, there are several limitations to this study. First, the study focused on only three newly qualified teachers all of whom had done their pre-service training course at the school with the researcher as a tutor. The study was also limited in terms of time as it only focused on the participants' 12-week probationary period. In addition, the participants were all non-native English speakers, whilst two out of three had considerable English language teaching experience prior to taking the CELTA. Second, I started the data analysis at the end of the three-month research period rather than as an on-going process. This approach was taken to avoid asking the case study participants follow-up questions which might then have impacted on how their approach to lesson planning developed over the probationary period. For example, had I queried the lack of language analysis in teachers' lesson planning notebooks, they might then have included more detail in subsequent lessons plans. Third, the research tools did not include any lesson observations and, therefore, it was not possible to corroborate the teachers' actual use of their written lesson plans during the lessons or consider the impact of their approach to lesson preparation on student learning in class. Finally, there are a few inconsistencies between what some of the case study participants told me during the oral interviews and the evidence provided by them in written form. In particular, the copies of the lesson planning documents from both the CELTA course and teaching during the probationary period submitted by the case study participants do not match with what they reported during the oral interviews.

However, I firmly believe that this case study has the potential to form the basis of a more extended research project within the school. A study that involved newly qualified teachers who had completed their pre-service training at other institutions might provide a more comprehensive overview. A study that included native speaker teachers might offer a different insight into key areas such as language analysis. With participants who had considerable teaching experience prior to taking the CELTA, it might prove relevant to include questions during the face-to-face interviews to establish what impact, if any, this had on how their approach to lesson planning developed after the course. A longer study might also improve the depth of information provided and reveal how these teachers consolidated the initial changes made in their approach to lesson planning. Starting the data analysis sooner might allow the researcher to not only follow up on some of the more interesting information collated, but also allow any inconsistencies within the data to be explored with the participants immediately. Finally, incorporating lesson observations might enable a more detailed focus on how newly qualified teachers exploit their lesson plans in class and, possibly, provide scope for measuring the impact of their approach to lesson preparation on student learning.

Conclusion

I started working as an English language teacher in a private language school in Turkey in May 1992. During the first year I spent considerably more time planning lessons than teaching in the classroom. There were several reasons for this. First, I was determined to be an effective teacher but lacked knowledge and experience. Second, the four-week pre-service training course that I had completed two months prior to starting full-time employment proved insufficient preparation for life in the real world. And finally, with an extremely limited induction programme and virtually no pedagogic support or on-going professional development, I was left to get through those 12 months as best I could. For much of this period I felt isolated, lacking in confidence and stressed.

Over the last 26 years I have seen numerous newly qualified teachers go through a similar experience. However, in the school where I have worked for the last decade there is an in-house teacher development scheme designed to support newly qualified teachers. Following an induction week these teachers are assigned a mentor whose role is to provide pedagogic support especially in the key area of lesson planning. Over the next 12 months newly qualified teachers attend regular input sessions and observe both peers and experienced colleagues. Even within the limited three-month probationary period, it was noticeable how much this support helped to develop the confidence of the three newly qualified teachers who participated in the case study. The main impact of this increase in self-esteem was that they were much better able to put student needs, rather than their own, at the forefront of the lesson planning process.

The findings of this research have led me to consider what more could be done on pre-service training courses to better prepare participants for their first year of employment. If trainers can raise awareness of the gap between 'learning to teach' and 'teaching in the real world' and even reduce the disparity to some extent, newly qualified teachers might not be quite so anxious on starting work. In addition, if employers can provide the right kind of induction as well as on-going, practical professional development, newly qualified teachers are more likely to feel valued and supported. Inevitably, this requires time, as well as additional resources, planning and staffing. However, within the pro-active working environment created by this type of investment, the confidence of newly qualified teachers can grow quickly. Improved self-esteem appears to have a positive impact on new teacher development in terms of their approach to lesson planning. This can only be of benefit to the school, its newest members of staff and the students they teach.

References

Alexander, D. and Galbraith, P. (1997) 'Stories of Transition: From Students to Teachers'. *Queensland Journal of Educational Research*, 13 1–11.

Anderson, J. (2015) 'Affordance, Learning Opportunities, and the Lesson Plan Pro Forma'. *ELT Journal*, 69(3) 228–238.

Calderhead, J. (1991) 'The Nature and Growth of Knowledge in Student Teaching'. *Teaching and Teacher Education*, 7(5) 531–535.

Corcoran, E. (1981) 'Transition Shock: The Beginning Teacher's Paradox'. *Journal of Teacher Education*, 32(3) 19–23.

Fantilli, R. D. and McDougall, D. E. (2009) 'A Study of Novice Teachers: Challenges and Supports in the Early Years'. *Teaching and Teacher Education*, 25(6) 814–825.

Fox, S. M. and Singletary, T. J. (1986) 'Deductions about Supportive Induction'. *Journal of Teacher Education*, 37(1) 12–15.

Gün, B., Üstünlüoğlu, E. and Yürekli, A. (2010) 'Listening and Responding to Novice Teachers' Inner Voices'. *Humanising Language Teaching*, 12(3). Available online: <http://old.hltmag.co.uk/jun10/sart04.htm> (accessed 11 May, 2019).

Hobbs, V. (2013) '"A Basic Starter Pack": The TESOL Certificate as a Course in Survival'. *ELT Journal*, 67(2) 163–174.

Inman, D. and Marlow, L. (2004) 'Teacher Retention: Why do Beginner Teachers Remain in the Profession?' *Education*, 124(4) 605–614.

John, P. D. (2006) 'Lesson Planning and the Student Teacher: Re-Thinking the Dominant Model. *Journal of Curriculum Studies*, 38(4) 483–498.

Karatas, P. and Karaman, A. C. (2013) 'Challenges faced by novice teachers: Support, Identity and Pedagogy in the Initial Years of Teaching'. *The International Journal of Research in Teacher Education*, 4(3) 10–23.

Kidd, L., Brown, N. and Fitzallen, N. (2015) 'Beginner Teachers' Perception of Their Induction into the Teaching Profession'. *Australian Journal of Teacher Education*, 40(3) 154–173.

Kim, K. and Roth, G. (2011) 'Novice Teachers and Their Acquisition of Work-Related Information'. *Current Issues in Education*, 14(1). Available online: <http://cie.asu.edu/> (accessed 11 May, 2019).

Liu, Y. (2014) 'Perceived Problems of Novice English as a Foreign Language Teachers in Taiwan'. *International Journal on Studies in English Language and Literature (IJSELL)*, 2(5) 41–45.

MacKinnon, A. (1987) 'Detecting Reflection-in-Action Among Pre-Service Teachers'. *Teacher and Teacher Education*, 3(2), 135–145.

Mann, S. and Hau Hau Tang, E. (2012) 'The Role of Mentoring in Supporting Novice Language Teachers in Hong Kong'. *TESOL Quarterly*, 46(3) 472–495.

McCann, T. M. and Johannessen, L. R. (2004) 'Why Do New Teachers Cry?' *The Clearing House*, 77(4) 138–145.

Melnick, S. A. and Meister, D. G. (2008) 'A Comparison of Beginning and Experienced Teachers' Concerns'. *Educational Research Quarterly*, 31(3), 39–56.

Meyer, H. (2004) 'Novice and Expert Teachers' Conceptions of Learners' Prior Knowledge'. *Science Education*, 970–983.

Murshidi, R., Konting, M. M., Elias, H. and Fooi, F. S. (2006) 'Sense of Efficacy Among Beginner Teachers in Sarawak'. *Teaching Education*, 17(3), 265–275.

Nahal, S. P. (2010) 'Voices From the Field: Perspectives of First-Year Teachers on the Disconnect Between Teacher Preparation Programs and the Realities of the Classroom'. *Research in Higher Education Journal*, 8(1) 1–19.

Osterman, K. F. and Kottkamp, R. B. (1993) *Reflective Practice for Educators: Improving Schooling Through Professional Development*. Newberry Park, CA: Corwin Press.

Richards, J. C. (2000) *Beyond Training*. Cambridge: Cambridge University Press.

Richards, J. C. and Lockhart, C. (1996) *Reflective Teaching in Second Language Classrooms*. Cambridge: Cambridge University Press.

Richards, J. C. and Pennington, M. (1998) 'The first year of teaching', in Richards, J. C. (ed.) *Beyond Training*. Cambridge: Cambridge University Press: 173–190.

Romero, G. (2013) 'Sink or Swim: Surviving the First Years of Language Instruction'. *The LEC Journal*, 12–24.

Ryan, K. (1986) *The Induction of New Teachers*. Bloomington, IN: Phi Delta Kappa Educational Foundation.

Shavelson, R. J. and Stern, P. (1981) 'Research on Teachers' Pedagogical Thoughts, Judgements, Decisions and Behaviour'. *Review of Educational Research*, 51 455–498.

Veenman, S. (1984) 'Perceived Problems of Beginning Teachers'. *Review of Educational Research*, 54(2) 143–178.

Yuksel, E. (2014) 'How can Novice Teachers be Supported in the Early Stages of Their Careers in Turkish State Universities?'. *Humanising Language Teaching*, 16(5). Available online: <http://old.hltmag.co.uk/oct14/mart06.htm> (accessed 11 May, 2019).

10

Embedding reflective practice in an INSET course

Teti Dragas

Introduction

Recent developments in ELTE pedagogy have important implications for INSET course development and instructional design. These developments suggest a need for change, shifting our focus from the *what* or content of INSET courses, to a focus on the *how* we teach, making room for more 'reflective' (Wallace, 1991), 'responsive' (Hunter & Kiely, 2016) and 'experiential' approaches (Kolb, 1984) to ELTE pedagogy that employ reflective practices. Essentially, INSET requires a more democratic approach based on dialogic and collaborative inquiry that draws on everyone's experiences equally (Edge, 2011; Mann & Walsh, 2017). If the main aim of INSET is to enable teachers to build on their knowledge and skills in order to develop, teacher educators need to foster an environment where genuine development can occur. This chapter provides an example of how this broad shift in approach to ELTE pedagogy translates into practice through the examination of a UK MA TESOL programme adopted as an INSET case study. The chapter begins with a short review of current issues in reflective practice (RP) and teacher development, considering how RP might best be operationalised according to current research. The chapter then focuses on the case study, using data from the MA programme to demonstrate how RP has been embedded through the use of reflective activities and tasks, tools and practices. In the final part of the chapter, I offer a personal discussion and evaluation of the insights drawn from the data and highlight ideas for developments in pedagogy.

Key issues

Reflective practice (RP) has long been an established concept in teacher education and over the last two decades has become increasingly dominant within the ELTE landscape. Although there are varying definitions and models for reflection (see, for example, Dewey, 1933; Schön, 1983), most conceptions of RP centre on the fact that reflection brings about a change in understanding that is instigated by engaging cognitively and affectively with practical experiences with the view to learning and development (Brookfield, 1995; Osterman & Kottkamp, 2004). Reflection leads teachers to take responsibility for their practice, through the 'recognition, examination, and rumination over the implications of [their] beliefs, experiences, attitudes, knowledge, and values as well as the opportunities and constraints provided by the social conditions in which the teacher works' (Zeichner & Liston, 1996: 20). Because reflection is based *in practice* and is drawn out of practice, much in alignment with (self)-development, it must begin with(in) the teacher. In this sense, RP seems to fit perfectly with conceptions of teacher development: placing the teacher at the centre as they analyse and evaluate their own practice, initiate change, and monitor the effects of this change (Freeman, 2002; Richards, 2008; Wallace, 1991).

However, while RP is widely accepted in INSET as the prime means for promoting professional development, a number of concerns have been highlighted, particularly in relation to how RP 'gets done' (Mann & Walsh, 2013). Importantly, reflection demands 'not only a conscious awareness of the craft of practice, but also [...] an ability to articulate that knowledge' (Osterman, 1990: 138). In other words, there is a need for educators to create conditions in which teachers can explore aspects of their practice through written or spoken forms and make this knowledge explicit. Teachers need to become conscious of aspects of practice that they may not have noticed before, and then guided to articulate what they have noticed by naming it and exploring it further. This process can be seen in the diagram below.

Conscious awareness of aspects of practice = noticing

Articulation of knowledge = naming, talking/writing about

Conceptual understanding = comprehending, learning

(Dragas, 2017: 233)

It is this process from awareness to articulation that leads to a reshaping of practice or a 'theorizing from practice' which propels teachers' thinking forward and supports teacher development. However, although, it is natural for teachers to reflect at some level on their practice, without proper coaching and guidance, reflection can be 'uncritical' and closer to 'reaction' (Gün, 2011: 127), which means there is less potential to reshape knowledge and deepen the kinds of understanding encouraged by more critical levels of reflection. The fact that reflection can often be superficial or weak (Farrell, 2008) has led researchers to conclude that the process itself needs to be taught (Russell, 2005) and supported in a systematic way if it is to lead to genuine teacher growth (Korthagen & Vasalos, 2005).

Embedding RP

There are a number of supportive processes which need to be considered if RP is to be trained and supported in such a way that it facilitates professional development. For INSET course developers, these processes are summarised below in the form of tools, practices and activities that can help promote reflection.

One of the most popular tools for facilitating reflection is through reflective writing, which has been shown to have a number of benefits. Within teacher education, reflective writing is most often observed through the mode of diary writing or journaling and portfolios. Naturally autobiographical in nature, journals provide teachers with a personal biography and progressional history that helps them to map their development over time. However, written modes such as diary writing are a very self-reflexive, individual process that is often done in isolation and which can lead to distortion when it comes to being able to reflect critically (Larrivee, 2000). One way of dealing with this lack of criticality is to get critical checks provided from multiple lenses, such as others' perspectives, prompting teachers to see things differently, thus opening up new ways of understanding practice.

More recently, new forms of written reflection include audio, visual and online formats such as online blogging, collaborative forums and instant messaging, and social media applications. Some of these new modes move away from purely individual reflection and enable a more interactive, dialogic and collaborative review of practice that have proven to be more beneficial to practitioners than simply reflecting in isolation (Mann & Walsh, 2017). Dialogic and collaborative reflection is underpinned by socio-cultural theory (SCT), which highlights co-construction, interaction and mediation: new skills and knowledge are publicly derived and then privately internalised (Vygotsky, 1978). Dialogic, collaborative reflection (or 'learning by talking') can be done through both spoken and written modes, modes however, in order for this approach to be effective, it needs to be founded on trust, mutual understanding, empathy and listening (Dewey, 1933; Schön, 1983). When teachers feel free to express their own beliefs about teaching and learning without feeling constrained, judged or evaluated, it is more likely that real dialogue can occur (Edge, 2011); this, in turn, creates the conditions within which teacher development can arise (Kurtoglu-Hooton, 2010).

The importance of testing out and reviewing knowledge gained from the situated contextual reality of the classroom and the learners has been highlighted by socio-cultural approaches to teacher education (Johnson, 2009; Golombek, 2009). Contextual relevance, both in terms of how it informs teacher development, but also in terms of ensuring that a practitioners' espoused language teaching methodology is appropriate to a local sociocultural context where teaching takes place is, therefore, vitally important (Holliday, 1994). Given the centrality of context to teaching/learning and professional development, teachers need to be provided with enough guided opportunities to reflect on the differences between contextual realities and how these might varyingly be addressed by adopting appropriate pedagogies. However, this does not discount the notion that teachers may also find it useful to identify opportunities to reflect on practice in shared contexts with which they are all familiar. Reflection thus should ideally draw on varied (past) and familiar (present) contexts and be supported by both individual and collaborative reflection, using both written and spoken modes.

The understanding that all teaching is local (Canagarajah, 2005) means that 'one-size-fits all development' that packages knowledge without critical reflection risks being meaningless for teachers (Mann, 2005). Pennycook (2004) sees the teacher educator's role as paramount in seeking out and finding 'in small moments' the potential for a more critical perspective that moves teacher-learners to new spaces where development can happen. Teachers need to be encouraged to view knowledge through a critical but also personal lens drawing from their own experiences and teaching contexts in order for them to construct their own meanings. Engaging with theory as 'an idea' (Ellis, 2010) can further serve to support critical engagement; this engagement should move them to deepen their own understandings of (their own) practice and to develop an all-important critical stance, which gives their teaching plausibility (Prabhu, 1990).

An INSET case study: a UK-based MA programme

The following section provides an exemplar case study to demonstrate how reflection 'gets done' by drawing on data from a UK-based MA programme. In the section below, I demonstrate a) how reflective practice has been embedded on the programme; b) how these practices have helped teachers to reflect and move forward in their development. The data are taken from three core 10-week modules across four consecutive years. Data are taken from both written and spoken reflections and include analyses of both real-time data (such as audio recordings of collaborative class discussions), and *post ex facto* data (such as individual reflective written assessments and blog posts on a collaborative forum).

Context

According to a recent survey of MATESOLs worldwide (Stapleton & Shao, 2018), in 2014 there were over 300 programmes offered across 16 countries with the USA and UK being the dominant providers. Most of these programmes are 'taught' programmes that seek to meet the needs of the international ELT professional marketplace and support institutional and disciplinary employability agendas. Seen as the standard terminal degree in the profession (TESOL International Association, 2007), not only leads the MA TESOL to be most often associated with in-service teacher development (Richards, 2008), but also makes it the largest source of INSET internationally.

The MA under review here is a degree programme offered at a UK higher education (HE) institution. Entry requirements for the programme are an academic qualification with an accumulative GPA of 3.2 or above; IELTS 7.0 or C1; at least two years full-time teaching experience as an ELT practitioner. The degree is divided into modules in key content areas (see Table 10.1), each of which is allocated credits, with the overall degree equal to 180 credits. The programme runs across one full year from October to October.

The reflective curriculum

The inclusion of the practical module that provided space for the teachers to teach whilst on the programme was an important part of a recent MA programme curriculum development (2013–2014). Its inclusion came about as the result of two key drivers: first, there was a desire to provide teachers with a shared context in which reflective inquiry could take place; second to form a clear 'bridge' between theory and practice. By including the practice module (Advanced Teaching Practice), teachers were enabled and supported through collaborative, dialogic and individual reflection, to make connections between practice and theory (reflected on in the Language Teaching Methodology and Second Language Development modules), which is invaluable to supporting their development.

Table 10.1 MA Applied Linguistics for TESOL

Core Modules	Language for Teachers
	Second Language Development: Perspectives for Teachers
	Language Teaching Methodology
	Advanced Teaching Practice: The Reflective Practitioner
	Dissertation
Optional Modules	Discourse, Texts and TESOL
	ELT Materials Development and Evaluation
	English for Specific Purposes
	Evaluation and Assessment
	Global Englishes
	Pragmatics and the Language Classroom
	Second Language Teacher Education in Practice
	Teaching English for Academic Purposes
	Teaching Young Learners

Across the two key theoretical and practical modules on the programme specifically discussed here, a number of reflective tools and supportive practices are used which, collectively, both facilitate structured and systematic reflection, while providing evidence of how reflection 'gets done'. Examples include:

- *Reflective diary*: allows teachers to record individual reflections on issues that may have arisen in teaching and post-class reflection sessions.
- *Recordings of TP*: allows self-review of teaching and provides opportunities for educators to create tasks and questions for the group based on video recordings. These recordings could be 'clipped' into short sections (Dragas, 2016) for focused review that is both individual and collaborative (in class and on an online forum).
- *Observation tasks*: are provided in the form of a booklet with various focused observation tasks which teachers are encouraged to complete when observing TP as a means of gathering further 'evidence' for reflective review.
- *Collaborative lesson planning*: teachers teach sections of the lesson individually but are asked to plan together as a team promoting dialogic reflection and collaboration.
- *Reflective collaborative discussion sessions and online discussion forums*: is aimed at encouraging teachers to reflect as opposed to 'giving feedback' on practice and/or to learn from engagement with theory and research.
- *Reflective tasks and guided reflective questions*: tasks or questions aimed at promoting teachers to notice aspects of practice and articulate this, which they then bring to the discussion sessions or write about in discussion forums.

The first example we will look at is a set of reflective guided questions and reflective prompt tasks aimed at guiding teachers to do RP. On the ATP module, reflective questions and tasks follow teaching practice (TP) where teachers have either just taught a lesson or have been observers. In the short time that directly follows TP – which in many contexts is where 'hot feedback' is done (Bailey, 2006) – the teacher educator acts as a facilitator or mentor, rather than an expert or evaluator (Chamberlin, 2000), using the immediate post-lesson time to draw out key areas of focus from the lesson that can be used for more exploratory and critical reflection. The supervisor then builds upon these insights to write up a number of guided questions and tasks aimed at supporting teachers to do RP, that prompt both individual and collaborative reflection and draw on the use of a variety of reflective tools. These guided questions and tasks are then posted on the discussion forum on the VLE and work in collaboration with recordings of TP in order to enable reflective post-lesson review. Extract 10.1 is an example: the key area of focus was around post-activity 'feedback' though there were further tasks on this document which I have not included.

Extract 10.1 Post-lesson reflection

1. Tasks and feedback

Think back to specific lessons (including this one and others on the module and from your own practice) and reflect on the following questions. You can/should refer to literature where relevant to further reflect on and explore areas of interest.

- To what extent do you plan activities and feedback together?
- To what extent do you plan the timing of each of these?

- Do you always need feedback after a task?
- What kind of feedback do you plan? Does it follow the same pattern (e.g. open class? Ss–ss? Peer feedback? Student-centred?)
- What kinds of methods of giving feedback have you used/can you think of? (This was brought up in a previous reflective task)
- What should you give feedback on? How might this be different for skills based on language-based work?
- Does/should correction (always) have a place in feedback?
- What makes a successful task and feedback?
- When do you stop the task? (i.e. when the designated planning time is up? When the ss have finished? Other?) What should you take into consideration here?

Productive task and student language:

The specific language focus in this lesson was adjectives and modifiers and their use. In one of the later productive tasks, listening in to a few students, I picked up the following use of language. Students were clearly using the target language.

What do you notice about their language use? What could have been done to exploit this more in the lesson at the practice or 'authentic use' stage? What about correction?

To what extent do you notice/collect at monitoring stages student language? What do you do to exploit it?

SS LANGUAGE

(S talking about Prague castle in a group of four)

"It's absolutely fantastic place."

"When you're in Prague it's absolutely essential to go to Prague castle. Yeah and it's a really well-maintained castle."

"It's a very outstanding place"

(S talking about a place in Czech Republic)

"There is very important nature"

"It's really fantastic to wake up and see the snowy peaks"

"I think the view is breathtaking."

The document begins with a clear title 'post-lesson reflection' which is deliberately designed to move teachers away from the all-too-often ingrained expectation of post-lesson supervisory feedback and to remind them that instead they are 'doing RP'. The instructions are there to reinforce how 'doing RP' should be approached (which has also been supported throughout by module aims, introductions, supervisory approaches and verbal instruction and modelling), and there is a clear guide for teachers to draw on their own experiences and practice as well as to get ideas from the literature. Both focused areas – here, 'Tasks + Feedback' – are accompanied by a number of prompt questions which do not focus on one singular event or moment (from TP). Importantly, the questions are not meant to be answered one by one, nor should they necessarily all be answered: they are deliberately open-ended and exploratory serving as prompts to guide and support RP. The way the questions are constructed means that there is less of a focus on 'what you did in the lesson' or 'what you saw in the (particular) lesson' but more on 'what this means about practice', in other words, supporting 'reflection' not 'reaction'.

In Extract 10.2, we see an example of a discussion post written by one of the teachers on the collaborative discussion board. The writer, Susan, is a mature UK national who has had three years' teaching experience prior to beginning the MA. She began the module, referring to herself as a 'a baby teacher', but during the course of the module, grew in confidence, later referring to herself as having reached 'adolescence'. In the following example, Susan uses the prompt questions on feedback as a means for individual reflection on her own practice, an area that was clearly important to her development. The questions prompted her to look through her diary – another tool which is used on the module and is meant for noting individual reflections – and also to re-evaluate her teaching in light of thinking about this topic further.

Extract 10.2

I've just looked through my reflection diary, and 'feedback' comes up a lot!! This is clearly an area I need to focus on.

In this lesson, I failed to provide effective feedback for my activity. I've been trying to work out why this happened (and happens regularly).

Maybe there are a few reasons:

- Not having anything to feed back on. I don't have good methods for collecting information from students. In speaking tasks, sometimes I can't hear what students are saying, and when I do, I don't record it, so I can't remember the language they have used.
- Lack of planning – I have never considered feedback as an integral part of an activity. The word 'feedback' may appear on a lesson plan, but it is almost there to tick a box ("ah yes, I have included feedback"), with no thought behind it, or commitment to do it properly. Each activity should maybe have three elements: instructions, the task and feedback.
- Lack of clarity about the purpose of feedback – I need to be clearer as to what I want to achieve in the feedback section – what are we feeding back on? I guess this should relate to the aim of the activity. So maybe there should be an additional element in the activity plan – identify aim of the activity.
- Fear – for some reason I'm fearful! Why?

So, what can be learnt from this?

1. I would like to study "feedback" more to identify a range of methods that can be used – the subject of future posts?
2. It may be useful to take take a few activities in a lesson and try planning the four elements – aim, instructions, task and feedback. I don't have much opportunity to practise in a real class, but this would serve to practise planning.
3. Try and focus on this in our lesson on 8 December.

An analysis of Susan's reflections reveals how she is beginning to become more conscious of feedback in her practice: as she comments, she clearly 'needs to focus on feedback' as it 'comes up a lot'. The prompt questions led her to go back to other reflective tools – in this case the diary – and to become aware and notice feedback this as an aspect she hadn't thought about deeply before. Her post evidences both the noticing and articulation of this aspect of her practice and in identifying possible future directions she is learning to find solutions to 'problems' with her teaching; importantly, she shows that the process has helped her to do this autonomously. For example, she is able to identify that in her previous practice she did not really understand the purpose of feedback and/or plan for it accordingly. She describes doing feedback as 'a tick box' but without really understanding what she wanted to achieve and how it linked to aims. The reflections she makes are still at the exploratory stage for her, but as she has posted this on the collaborative forum, she shows she is willing to share and ask for others' ideas and reflections. She also clearly notes that she would like to 'study feedback in order to identify a range of methods that can be used' and invites others (though tentatively) to help: 'the subject of future posts'. Finally, she also identifies the need to put some of the ideas she collects into practice into her next lesson so that she can reflect on developments.

Reflection here, though clearly present, could still be seen as being more focused on technical aspects of practice, and therefore be construed as less critical. However, one of the important aspects of teaching or supporting RP is that teachers are given time to do RP systematically using multiple tools and processes which move them along a trajectory that prompts change and 'growth'. Extract 10.3 is taken from Susan's summative reflective assignment, submitted a couple of months after the module had finished, providing us with some evidence of this. The assignment is designed to encourage teachers to reflect through different lenses – self, peer, teacher, literature (Brookfield, 1995) – thus prompting teachers to consolidate learning from all the reflective activities that took place throughout the module. This extract provides evidence of Susan's developmental journey as she returns to the discussion of corrective feedback. It is also a good example of how her development was supported by doing RP; she describes how she has interacted with the varied reflective tools and reflective practices that were available to her on the module and has documented these throughout the extract.

Extract 10.3

Reflecting on our discussion about corrective feedback in a reflective session, my personal belief in the value of feedback has strengthened. I can see that I need to try to create an atmosphere where students feel comfortable experimenting with language. I would also like to improve my decision-making skills so that I know better when to provide feedback, how to do it effectively and what to give feedback on.

On viewing the recording, I have observed that I made some attempts to monitor the students but didn't keep any records. This meant that the feedback I did do focused on content only, missing the point of the lesson. It also couldn't be heard by all the students. Consequently, my attempt was of negligible value.

Reflecting on this, I identified a number a problems. First despite including feedback on the lesson plan, I didn't plan what to give feedback on and how to do it. Second I didn't have the means to be able to collect information on language points. Finally, I failed to appreciate the importance of this part of the lesson and on the day, almost gave up.

This led me to identify a number of planning solutions. From a lesson perspective, feedback needs to be given a more prominent place. For activities, a four-stage planning process (task aim, instructions, task and feedback) would ensure feedback is included. Finally, planning how to record evidence to feedback is essential. I was able to test these solutions on 8 December where I applied the four-stage planning model for the activity and ensured that I had paper with me to record language during the lesson. The result was positive, and I noticed a change in my own sense of self-efficacy, feeling more like a teacher

As we can see, we can map a reflective trajectory that begins with a 'personal belief' and ends with 'a change' in Susan's own self of 'self-efficacy', leading to a gain in confidence and further solidifying her identity as a teacher. This reflective trajectory is supported by a number of reflective tools that in turn help her to 'do' reflection and consequently, allow us to map the development of her thinking. Susan first refers to the collaborative discussion session, where feedback on teaching had clearly been discussed with the group. Discussion with the group gave her the confidence in her own beliefs, strengthening them, which in turn led her to explore further how these are played out in her practice. Here, video self-review (Tripp & Rich, 2012) allows her to do this efficiently both through a critical and personal lens, drawing from her own teaching context to construct new meanings. As a result of watching herself back, she is able to reflect on and identify 'problems' with her practice and importantly, is able to come to clear realisations as to why these happened. The final stage in this process reveals Susan's return to practice: having come up with 'solutions' that she is able to 'test out' in future lessons. It is here where she shows the kind of 'change' or 'growth competence' (Korthagen & Vasalos, 2005) that she has been able to achieve through systematic reflection.

In Extract 10.4 we have an example of a collaborative and dialogic in-class task. In this instance it is taken from the *Language Teaching Methodology* module, which begins with reflection on research or 'theory'. In this session, the pre-class task asked teachers to read four key papers and summarise for themselves key points of interest. Once in class, they were put into groups (that had been self-selected and named according to their own self-designated group personas) and asked to draw on their individual summaries and work together to complete an in-class collaborative writing task made available through an online platform which allowed teachers to write on the document simultaneously. The topic was focused on method and post-method debates, centring on the question: 'Are you a method-ist or a post-methodist?' Teachers were navigated to the online document and given the instructions shown in Extract 10.4.

Extract 10.4 Method and postmethod

In today's class, we are going to create a collaborative working document based on our reading of the four articles assigned for this week. Our aim, by the end of the class, is to understand what we mean by method and postmethod and to determine what this might mean for us as practising language teachers. You can then write a post on the blog – ARE YOU A METHOD-IST OR A POST-METHODIST?

To remind you of your groups:

Panda Lovers: Carla, Meilin: Prabhu (1990)
Behind the Mask: Fiona and Daisy: Kumaravadivelu (2002)
Caring Sharers: Gina, Janette and Susan: Bell (2007)
Four-eyed Chimera: Neil: Canagarajah (2005)

The class will be led like this:

1. In your groups and using your notes, draw out some salient quotes and key points about your article. Write them on this document in the relevant section.
2. Look at each other's sections and get an idea.
3. Write some questions in the 'questions section' about other people's papers.
4. Going back to your original group – answer the questions for the class in an open discussion.

Overall

What have we learnt about method and post method?
Collaborate and write some points in the conclusion section.

The teachers used their pre-prepared notes from their reading and worked together to complete the summaries, discussing and reviewing the literature and evaluating the ideas and principles in the light of their own practice and understandings. In the process of negotiating what to write, teachers were able to review and grapple with ideas in the articles they read, drawing on their own experience and knowledge and reformulating it in order to make it accessible to the group. Teachers were self-sufficient and highly engaged during the session and were deeply involved in their discussions and writing which allowed me to move away from the position of expert who was teaching them *about* theory. Instead, I was able to listen and engage in their co-construction of what these 'ideas' or 'theories' meant to them and their practice. In this way I was able to actively listen and facilitate the discussion where appropriate and as Pennycook (2004) notes above, use prompts to move teachers to more critical engagement when needed. On the whole, however, the task itself did this for me: teachers were able to negotiate meaning themselves and this was evident in the questions they wrote as a result of discussing and writing their summaries, which were prompted by the instructions on the document at the end of each section. When the summaries were complete, it was these group questions that formed the basis for a collaborative whole class discussion, where teachers were able to explore ideas together and relate them to their own practice. For example, Extract 10.5 shows the questions generated by a group who had summarised Prabhu's well-known paper 'There is no best method – why?' (1990):

Extract 10.5

Does 'sense of plausibility' mean engagement with teaching? Is he then saying that engaged teachers are good teachers? I don't think anyone would argue with that. What more has he to add!? Does this mean that each teacher has his/her own method? How do we ensure quality?

In the ensuing open class discussions, teachers were able to draw on their own experiences and examine their principles in the light of what they had read. The final question here 'how do we ensure quality?' shows that the teachers are reflecting on the concepts more deeply and trying to make the all-important connection from theory to practice. The fact that they were able to explore these concepts through discussion helped them to 'learn by talking' (i.e. dialogic reflection), enabling the kind of dialogic, collaborative reflection that helps to promote teacher learning.

Following the class, teachers were further encouraged to reflect and continue the discussion on the collaborative discussion forum. This provided a platform for individual reflection and allowed teachers to process knowledge for themselves: a movement from the 'public' to the 'private' under SCT theory. Extract 10.6 is a post by one of the teachers called Daisy, who was from China, reflecting further on the topic on the discussion blog.

Extract 10.6 Method? Postmethod?

There are always many ideas coming into my mind every time when we have methodology class, but I felt extremely inspired by the lecture given on Thursday. I have graduated and been teaching for nine years, and I was not major in teaching nor having huge theoretic systems to support my teaching. I still remember that I got my teacher's qualification through largely memorizing important contents of the textbooks and having an unskilful demo class in front of a number of professors. During my teaching career, I had many in-house trainings as well as a short TEFL course. My so-called 'teaching methods' were actually compressed information from the training or consisted of instant knowledge which may involve commercial and institutional purposes and then I put it into practice.

Perhaps I have created my own methods that work in my classroom which I was not aware of. However, I am very confused of what I have been doing and I have a strong sense of lost with all what happened. Kumaravadivelu (2002) mentions in his antimethod that teacher develop their own system during they teaching and they weight sequence of activities which is not necessarily related to any methods. There were many times I had terrible lessons and good ones, however I think it is the those lessons that make me, on one hand, rely on my intuitive ability and experiential knowledge, and on the other hand, feel I am hanging nowhere because I do not have something to support what I have been doing.

I think I know a bit why I am here studying, but I am still looking for more answers to help myself understand, and I see now it is not a personal issue and this happens to many teachers. What are methods? Are there ways that we get rid of methods? Do we have better solutions to deal with methods? What do I mean "something" to support me? Methods or theories?

This extract shows the impact that the collaborative discussion (dialogic reflection) had on this teacher personally. She makes a point in saying she 'felt extremely inspired' by the class (she calls it a lecture) and it prompts her to reflect on her own teaching and learning experiences as a teacher in a storied, narrative form (Golombek, 2009). On reflecting on her development, she acknowledges her lack of theoretical knowledge, identifying that she did not have a foundation on which to 'support' her teaching and brings up the example of how she 'memorizes important content from textbooks' in order to demonstrate her learning. Here, Daisy shows she is becoming metacognitively aware of how the way she learns teaching affects her practice; and through the reflection and narration of her experience she tries to come out the other side and make sense of it. In re-evaluating her experiences, she begins to 'think' but is still grappling with more questions, and these questions centre on how to bridge the gap between theory and practice: 'what do I mean I need something to support me? Methods? Theories?'. Despite not arriving at definitive answers, she has shown that she has begun to internalise these questions for herself, and as this has mapped a change in her thinking, it has also provided us with evidence of her development as a teacher.

Finally, it is worth noting that, as we have seen with Susan's extracts above, Daisy's final reflective assignment for this module documents the shift in the way she approaches learning to teach: from learning *about* teaching to learning *to* teach and to explore teaching by doing RP.

Extract 10.7

Reflecting on my past practice and also reading, I have been able to see who I was as a teacher, all my weaknesses and mistakes, and moreover, I have built my own opinions towards teaching and learning. The curiosity I did not have in the past has now started to grow. This is just the beginning of my career, not only as a teacher, but as a reflective practitioner.

In Extract 10.7, Daisy's final sentence reinforces the fact that she has found value in doing and being taught 'to do RP' and as a result she will continue to use it as an integral tool in her future development.

The final extract in this section (Extract 10.8) provides a few examples of written reflection in which Simon, a teacher with five years' experience who had been living and working in Korea prior to starting the MA, evaluates his teaching in the light of the learning and reflection he has done across the Methodology module. The assignment supported the reflective process as it asked teachers to write a letter addressed to the tutors in which they needed to evaluate their own previous practice as a teacher in the light of reading and reflective discussions on the module and then discuss possible methodological changes in their future practice. Teachers were asked to draw on any aspect of the module and reading they felt was important and that reflected this shift in thinking. Moreover, the fact that the letter was addressed to the tutors allowed them to write about their learning in a more personal way, which explicitly tapped into their beliefs and thus better supported RP. In this extract, Simon writes about some of the key ideas that helped him to re-evaluate his practice and develop over the course of the module.

Extract 10.8

I realise now that as the teacher I have the opportunity to create a classroom culture which fits with my preferred method of teaching. I would therefore like to look at ways of creating that culture, and using reflective practice effectively in whatever context I find myself in. I find it exciting that we don't have to be controlled by our context. We can form and grow our context by the way we teach and treat the students, and by using techniques and activities which can be put into play to create positive cultures. [...] This course is helping me to acquire the knowledge and tools to enable me to be more critical and create and modify activities to make them more cognitively effective. [...] Prabhu emphasises the need for 'submitting one's theory to an operational test, and sustaining or modifying it in the light of outcomes.' (1992:239) For me, reflective practice provides a starting point for this analysis.

Simon's reflections, much like Daisy's above, place reflection at the heart of his development as a teacher during the module. He recognises that 'the course' is providing him with 'knowledge and tools' that are enabling him to be 'more critical' and ultimately, more reflective. Interestingly, he makes a point of discussing 'culture' and context, which he has learnt to think about differently in the light of reflection. This is evident in the fact that he says he 'realises' that he is the person that can help to create a 'classroom culture', showing that he has become more aware of his own agency in the act of teaching. Crucially, he also realises that reflection starts with(in) the teacher who is the one that ultimately needs to 'test' theories and put them into practice, or the other way around.

Reflecting on reflective practice: a view from the 'outside'

The final section draws on data from an elective module on ELTE which was aimed at teachers who had an interest in teacher training and education and looks specifically at how teachers experienced reflection, as well as critically analysing the approach to instruction 'from the outside'. The module very much continued the approach taken in the Methodology module in terms of fostering a collaborative, critical and dialogic environment from which to explore ELTE and was taught solely by me to a small group of students. Building on the relationship and established trust I had gained as a result of teaching on the modules above, teachers allowed me to audio record the sessions from which I draw my data. Over the course of the module we looked at key areas in ELTE which included approaches to ELTE pedagogy. In one particular session we focused on exploring the reflective approach to ELTE and, as a way of engaging with the literature, we took the ATP module as a case study that we could evaluate and review in the light of our reading. What is noteworthy is that teachers moved between the positions of 'insider' and 'outsider' in their evaluation, operating as teachers who had directly experienced the approach the module was aiming to foster, and as future teacher trainers or curriculum reviewers who were evaluating the approach from outside the experience. The extracts in this section are taken from discussions in this session. Extract 10.9 shows the second part of the task, which gives the instructions for the session:

Extract 10.9 Pre-class preparatory task 2

We are going to use the ATP module as case study in thinking about reflective practice. Drawing on this week's reading and your table of principles (above):

To what extent does this module reflect the principles and approaches/tools that you have read about and identified in the reflective model?

- Make some notes drawing on at least three examples evaluating the module against these principles. (Think about input, course design, supervisory roles, tools, procedures, modes of inquiry).
- You can also draw on your own experience as a teacher in this process but also reflect on how this helps you to look at the module now as a teacher trainer.

The session involves four teachers and begins with definitions of RP in the literature but quickly moves towards teachers' own definitions and understandings of RP, which are drawn from their own experiences. In Extract 10.10, we observe Fiona, a teacher with two years' ELT experience and four as an English teacher in the British secondary school education system, talking about former experiences of reflective practice, in a previous teacher education programme, the Postgraduate Certificate in Education (PGCE).

Extract 10.10

I think I have a not very good view of being reflective because I was very much PGCE forced (.) very very forced. It's ridiculous. They took (...) They took reflective and reflective feedback to such an extreme that many of us were in tears. I was continuously criticised (.) and I got to the point where, I think I've said before (...) I wanted to know positives (...) I used to argue the case that we always tell students the shit sandwich ... I'd be told, well your timing is all wrong. And I'd be like: Where's the shit sandwich? What's going on? Where's my positive? I became so critical of myself.

Analysing Fiona's response to her experience of what she initially understood as 'reflection' or 'reflective feedback', leads to a number of key observations. First we can infer that the approach to supervision taken on the programme was 'prescriptive' rather than 'collaborative' (Wallace, 1991), an approach which is far removed from fostering the kind of reflection we have discussed above. The prescriptive approach is one where the supervisor, as expert, is the authority who judges the lesson, who very much has a blueprint of how lessons should be taught, and who gives advice and does the talking (Wallace, 1991). Fiona's experiences reflect this quite clearly. The supervisor's authority and expertise are expressed through her use of the third person pronoun 'they' and the passive 'I'd be told', illustrating the distance she feels to them and highlighting positions of power. Moreover, the fact that she felt judged – 'I was constantly criticised' – which led her both 'to tears' and to a situation where she became overly 'critical of herself' meant that she was unable to reflect on and learn from her practice. For Fiona, this approach, from which she craved 'positives', led to a loss of confidence in herself, and which, in turn, had a detrimental rather than positive effect on her development as a teacher.

Coming back to the focus of the session, which was to explore and evaluate reflective practice, in order to explore her understanding of reflection further, I asked Fiona to compare this to her experience on the ATP module, which strived explicitly to foster reflection through the employment of a more collaborative approach to supervision, as well as through specific strategies, processes and principles, many of which are discussed above. In Extract 10.11, we see in Fiona's response to the question, and note how her first observation interestingly relates to her expectation of supervision which was based on these prior formative experiences of reflection.

Extract 10.11

Tutor: is that being reflective though? Did it feel different on ATP?
Fiona: Yes! Yes. At first I did find it difficult for you not to question me. I sort of almost hankered for you to question me. To tell me… you know …

Fiona's response here reveals how her previous experiences on the PGCE had very much influenced her expectations of not only reflection, but of the role that the supervisor took in guiding her development. Fiona 'hankered' for a response that told her what her teaching was like: 'tell me'. However, the fact that she says 'at first' shows that this response slowly changed as she became more familiar and comfortable with the collaborative approach to supervision which was adopted on the module. Here, the supervisor is no longer an authority, but more so a colleague with whom the teacher co-shares expertise. Adopting a non-judgemental stance, the supervisor focuses on 'understanding' and 'listening' with the aim of developing teachers' autonomy and ability to self-evaluate (Wallace, 1991).

Fiona's need for feedback is not uncommon and is an expectation that has most likely been informed and influenced by the traditional supervisory cycle, which is very much a dominant part of the evaluation and appraisal practices that many teachers face in their working lives (Bailey, 2006). In this cycle, teachers are observed by a supervisor, discuss their teaching in a feedback session where 'problems' in their practice are identified, and then act on these as a means of improving future practice (Bailey, 2006). However, providing the space for teachers to discuss their experiences of these practices through critical reflection opens up new ways of looking at these positions with thus disbanding some of their 'negative' power.

In Extract 10.12, Frank, a male teacher and mature student with 20 years' experience reflects on this relationship to the supervisor. We had been talking about reflection and the importance of the supervisor in the process and about what it is the supervisor is really supporting. Frank, and other members of the group were recounting experiences of supervision, many of which which mirrored Fiona's initial reflections above. Supervisors were typically seen as very much the 'experts' who would 'tell' you whether your lesson was 'good' or 'bad' and give you feedback on your practice. The extract picks up on the discussion once we had collaboratively discussed, shared and evaluated these roles.

Extract 10.12

Frank: I think this very act of discussion is helpful, I think it's healthy as well. Because there will sometimes be that observer teacher, supervisor or whatever positioning.

And if you can unpack it a little bit, talk about it a little bit, think about it, then I think you change your view of those kind of things and what you can potentially get out of it rather than just see them as something that you've got to get through.

As we can see from the above examples of practice, on the ATP module this collaborative approach to supervision was further adapted and extended in order to focus teachers on reflection not reaction and the supervisor used various activities to support this. One such activity, as becomes apparent in the extracts below, left a powerful impression on the teachers: it involved initially taking both the teacher and the supervisor out of the equation in the post-TP reflection session to allow more room for listening and reflection as opposed to simply reaction. Directly following TP, teachers were asked to form groups of three: two members were observers and the other was the teacher who had just finished teaching the lesson. The observers were then instructed to have a discussion, reflect on the lesson, drawing out points of interest to them. During the discussion, the teacher was placed in the role of listener, and was not allowed to talk for the first ten–15 minutes. Instead, she had to listen to her peers' perceptions, making notes if she wished, which would help to form the basis of her own reflection on the lesson. When Fiona is asked whether her experience of reflection was different on the ATP module, she responds by recalling this particular activity which she describes in Extract 10.13.

Extract 10.13

Sometimes if you got us in groups ... that thing where we weren't allowed to talk. If you had been the teacher that lesson you were not allowed to talk for a while and you had to let the other two discuss you basically and what happened in the lesson for a while. (.) And you just had to sit there and listen. Now I found that was hard. (.) That was good because while it was hard but it gave you an opportunity...

When she was able to talk, after the ten–15 minutes of the observer-peers discussion was over, there was less opportunity for Fiona to justify the lesson and the teacher's pedagogic choices, freeing her from the need to answer back and defend her lesson. This, in turn, gave her an 'opportunity' to see aspects of it more objectively, from the outside. In addition, the fact that the supervisor was also absent (though monitoring) meant there was no opportunity for Fiona to receive the kind of evaluative feedback she was used to: there was now a shift from judging teaching performance, and whether the lesson was 'good' or 'bad', or 'okay', to reflecting on what was learnt and what it meant. This left space for the teacher to self-evaluate in the light of her own ideas and those of her peers, who were not there to judge her, but to discuss the lesson together.

At this juncture, a mature teacher with three years' prior teaching experience, joins the discussion. Extract 10.14 gives her contribution in which she explicitly refers to the notion of 'training' or teaching RP, recognising that this was vital in helping them to *do* it.

Extract 10.14

I think it's hard not to do the reacting. So I think if you're going to try and enable people to reflect you've got to give people training and some kind of guidance on how to properly (...) So you gave us structure by saying 'don't talk' giving us the instruction, so you're, you're kind of helping us, you were guiding us how to be reflective by doing that thing.

What is noteworthy in the teacher's response here is that she not only recognises the importance of offering supportive practices to guide RP from a theoretical perspective, but that she can back up this knowledge drawing directly from her own experience of an activity that sought to do this very thing on the ATP module.

Final reflections

In conclusion, my own understanding of the importance of RP in supporting teacher change has very much been informed by 'doing reflection' myself. Developing and teaching on the modules has meant experimenting and testing out how different processes tools and procedures work with different teachers and work for me, reading research on these areas and reflecting on all of this, both individually and with my colleagues in the light of experience. Most importantly, my understanding has involved collecting and analysing data some of which I evidence above, which in turn has helped me to evaluate and better understand how RP gets done and how it works. The analysis of the samples above, though by no means definitive, goes some way in evidencing this. Most importantly, it marks the shift in practices that see INSET courses focus less on *what* to put *in* them, and more on *how* one is to *do* them. For curriculum developers and teacher educators who are involved in designing and leading INSET courses, it means shifting the focus from expert to teacher and in so doing, it means disbanding these antagonistic positions in favour of a collaborative, democratic and sharing approach to ELTE which supports teacher learning and development. As the examples above have shown, it is an approach which is not only founded on RP, but embeds it through the various means and methods I have highlighted above, firmly into the curriculum.

References

Bailey, K. M. (2006) *Language Teacher Supervision: A Case-Based Approach*. New York: Cambridge University Press.

Brookfield, S. D. (1995) *Becoming a Critically Reflective Teacher*. San Francisco, CA: Jossey-Bass.

Canagarajah, S. A. (2005) *Reclaiming the Local in Language Policy and Practice*. New York: Routledge.

Chamberlin, C. R. (2000) 'TESL Degree Candidates' Perceptions of Trust in Supervisors'. *TESOL Quarterly*, 34(4) 653–673.

Dewey, J (1933) *How We Think: A Restatement of the Relation of Reflective Thinking to the Educative Process*, Boston, MA: DC Heath.

Dragas, T. (2016) 'Exploring in-house video training materials for "reflective" teacher development', in Pattison, T. (ed.) *IATEFL 2016: Birmingham Conference Selections*. Faversham: IATEFL: 232–233.

Dragas, T. (2017) 'Teacher development through bespoke video training materials: challenges and', in Pattison, T. (ed.) *IATEFL 2017: Glasgow Conferences Selections*. Faversham: IATEFL: 232–234.

Edge, J. (2011) *The Reflexive Teacher Educator in TESOL: Roots and Wings*. New York: Routledge.

Ellis, R. (2010) 'Second language acquisition, teacher education and language pedagogy'. *Language Teaching*, 43(2) 182–201.

Farrell, T. S. C. (ed.) (2008) *Novice Language Teachers*. London: Equinox.

Freeman, D. (2002) 'The hidden side of the work: teacher knowledge and learning to teach'. *Language Teaching*, 35(1) 1–13.

Golombek, P. (2009) 'Personal practical knowledge in L2 teacher education', in Burns, A. and Richards, J. C. (eds) *The Cambridge Guide to Second Language Teacher Education*. Cambridge: Cambridge University Press.

Gün, B. (2011) 'Quality Self-Reflection Through Reflection Training'. *ELTJ*, 65(2) 126–135.

Holliday, A. (1994) *Appropriate Methodology and Social Context*. Cambridge: Cambridge University Press.

Hunter, D. and Kiely, R. (2016). 'The Idea as a Mechanism in Language Teacher Development'. *Journal of Second Language Teaching and Research*, 5 37–61.

Johnson, K. E. (2009) *Second Language Teacher Education: A Sociocultural Perspective*. Abingdon: Routledge.

Kolb, D. A. (1984) *Experiential Learning: Experience as The Source of Learning and Development*. Upper Saddle River, NJ: Prentice-Hall.

Korthagen, F. and Vasalos, A. (2005) 'Levels in Reflection: Core Reflection as a Means To Enhance Professional Growth'. *Teachers and Teaching: Theory and Practice*, 11(1) 47–71.

Kumaravadivelu, B. (2003) *Beyond Methods: Macrostrategies for Language Teaching*. New Haven, CT and London: Yale University Press.

Kurtoglu-Hooton, N. (2010) *Post-observation feedback as an instigator of learning and change: exploring the effect of feedback through student teachers' self-reports*. Unpublished PhD thesis: Aston University, UK.

Larrivee, B (2000) 'Transforming Teaching Practice: Becoming a Critically Reflective Teacher'. *Reflective Practice*, 1(3) 293–307.

Mann, S. J. (2005). 'The Language Teacher's Development'. *Language Teaching*, 38(3) 103–118.

Mann, S. J. and Walsh, S. (2013) 'RP or "RIP": A Critical Perspective on Reflective Practice'. *Applied Linguistics Review*, 4(2) 291–315.

Mann, S. J. and Walsh, S. (2017) *Reflective Practice in English Language Teaching: A Data-Led Approach*. New York: Routledge.

Osterman, K. F. (1990) 'Reflective Practice: A New Agenda For Education'. *Education and Urban Society*, 22(2) 133–152.

Osterman, K. F. and Kottkamp, R. B. (2004) *Reflective Practice for Educators*. Thousand Oaks, CA: Corwin Press.

Pennycook, A. (2004) 'Critical moments in a TESOL praxicum', in Norton, B. and Toohey, K. (eds) *Critical Pedagogies and Language Learning*. Cambridge: Cambridge University Press: 327–346.

Prabhu, N. S. (1990) 'There Is No Best Method – Why?'. *TESOL Quarterly*, 24(2), 161–176.

Richards, J. C. (1998) *Beyond Training: Perspectives on Language Teacher Education*. Cambridge: Cambridge University Press.

Richards, J. C. (2008) 'Second Language Teacher Education Today'. *RELC Journal*, 39(2) 158–177.

Russell, T. (2005) 'Can Reflective Practice be Taught?'. *Reflective Practice*, 6(2), 199–204.

Schön, D. (1983) *The Reflective Practitioner: How Professionals Think in Action*. New York: Basic Books.

Stapleton, P. and Shao, Q. (2018) 'A Worldwide Survey of MATESOL Programs in 2014: Patterns and Perspectives'. *Language Teaching Research*, 22(1) 10–28.

TESOL International Association (2007) 'Position Statement on Terminal Degree for Teaching English as a Second, Foreign or Additional Language'. Alexandria, VA: TESOL International Association. Available online: <www.tesol.org/docs/pdf/10039.pdf?sfvrsn=2&sfvrsn=2> (accessed October 1, 2018).

Tripp, T. R. and Rich, P. J. (2012) 'The Influence of Video Analysis on the Process of Teacher Change'. *Teaching and Teacher Education*, 28(5) 728–739.

Vygotsky, L. S. (1978) *Mind in Society: The Development of Higher Psychological Processes*. Cambridge, MA: Harvard University Press.

Wallace, M. (1991) *Training Foreign Language Teachers: A Reflective Approach*. Cambridge: Cambridge University Press.

Zeichner, K. M. and Liston, D. P. (1996). *Reflective Teaching: An Introduction*. Mahwah, NJ: Lawrence Erlbaum Associates.

11

Continuing professional development/continuous professional learning for English language teachers

David Hayes

Introduction

Research tells us that successful continuing professional development (CPD) for teachers is multi-faceted, lifelong, can take place inside or outside the workplace and is influenced not just by the experience of the CPD activity itself but also by teachers' prior professional experiences, their beliefs and contexts (both instructional and socio-cultural) and their own personal circumstances. CPD can be mandated by others or teacher-initiated. When CPD is teacher-initiated it is typically in response to a need perceived by teachers themselves for additional knowledge or skills in a particular area of their practice, whether this is at the whole school level (e.g. developing strategies for more inclusivity across the curriculum) or at the classroom level (e.g. enhancing student involvement in English communication activities). When CPD is mandated, this is usually for policy reasons by superiors in an educational hierarchy, and often in response to government-sponsored changes in 'the role and functioning of schools […] and so what is expected of teachers' (OECD, 2009: 49). In such cases, CPD is normally sector-wide and designed, for example, to introduce a new national curriculum, teaching methodology, textbooks or assessment system. Mandated CPD programmes can arise from a deficit view of existing educational attainment and teachers' competences as well as in response to changing conditions in the wider society. A current instance of the latter is the growth in the use of digital technology in many areas of life with teachers 'increasingly expected to be adept at a variety of technology-based and other approaches for content delivery, learner support, and assessment' (Freeman et al., 2017: 30). This alters teachers' roles in the classroom and, hence, 'entails improving teacher training and professional development' in this area (ibid.: 31).

A great variety of factors can have an impact on CPD and how it is experienced by teachers. These range from conditions of teachers' work, which can either support or hinder efforts to promote classroom change, to teachers' personal dispositions towards their work. Their personal attitudes towards work may, in turn, be influenced by factors such as the stage they have reached in their professional careers and their moral commitment to teaching. At present teachers' conditions of work in many countries often seem to be inimical to effective CPD. Increasing demands for 'accountability' in education worldwide have led to greater bureaucratic control, more time spent on non-teaching tasks, less time for teachers to collaborate with each other in tightly scheduled school days and thus little time to invest in professional development activities. There is also a general lack of professional, financial, and technological resources for teachers and schools, according to an OECD study in 23 countries (Wang et al., 2011). Nevertheless, despite system constraints such as these, research into CPD indicates that teachers continue to strive to develop professionally and to do so in a variety of ways, both in collaboration with other teachers and as individuals. This chapter discusses successful instances of school-based professional development and technology-mediated CPD. Whatever form CPD takes and whether it is other or teacher initiated, consideration of its impact on professional learning is essential and the chapter also examines inter-related levels for evaluation of CPD.

As this chapter will show, in any education system, CPD is most likely to be successful if it is a shared enterprise. Teachers themselves need to be willing not just to critically engage in CPD activities which are mandated, but to actively seek out opportunities to enhance their professional practice in ways that are personally meaningful to them, alone and with other teachers. For their part, educational administrators at various levels, whilst making available at least some of the opportunities for CPD, must also develop the enabling conditions to ensure that teachers have the time, space and support to personalize, evaluate and implement learning from the CPD opportunities with which they engage. Teacher educators who have to lead CPD activities for teachers will find their own roles more effective – and satisfying – if they work with teachers to transform their practice rather than simply transmit others' knowledge about good practice. The discussion of key issues in CPD and learning points from the case studies, which follow in this chapter, provide what I hope will be a framework of reference for effective practice in CPD, for teacher educators and administrators as well as teachers.

Key issues in CPD/CPL

A central premise of this chapter is that CPD must promote continuous professional learning (CPL). Just having available or simply participating in opportunities for continuing professional development is no guarantee of continuing professional learning which impacts on practice. Hence in CPL the focus on 'learning' foregrounds 'the systematic and intentional maintenance, enhancement and expansion of the knowledge, skills and ethical values and behaviours necessary to ensure ongoing quality professional practice throughout a [teacher]'s career' (CEC, 2017: 4). The quality of the CPD experience in which teachers participate is critical to stimulating their professional learning. In this section, I examine key issues which feature in accounts of successful CPD and which seem most likely to promote the kind of CPL which has an impact on practice. It is particularly important for teacher educators that they take account of these factors in the development opportunities they provide for teachers.

Transmissive and transformational CPD

A comparative analysis of CPD for English teachers in Latin America and the Middle East (Howard et al., 2016) revealed that much of the CPD offered to teachers in these areas of the world is still provided by 'experts', either local or international. Top-down CPD of this type is usually transmissive and often primarily theoretical, designed to inform teachers of what they should be doing and why. It remains common worldwide. Wyatt and Ager (2017) discuss a recent example from Macedonia, and Gemeda et al. (2014) one from Ethiopia. Unfortunately, it has been known for many years that transmissive CPD results in primarily surface adoption by teachers of the rhetoric of reform whilst changes in actual classroom practice may be minimal. At the heart of this failure to impact practice is a lack of teacher investment in the programmes, which may not meet teachers' needs and in which they have had little or no say at the development stage (Gemeda et al., 2014). Sales et al. (2011: 911) note that it is 'teacher's critical capacity, professional self-esteem and degree of autonomy to innovate and be creative' that determines whether or not educational change will succeed, rather than top-down, power-coercive mandates for change. The obvious implication is that CPD is more likely to be successful if it promotes teachers' critical capacity to reflect on their own work, their self-esteem, their autonomy to innovate and their creativity – outcomes which transmissive CPD is neither designed for nor able to achieve.

This does not mean, of course, that teachers should reject the mandates of national education reforms as a focus for development; only that educational authorities are ill-advised to exclude teachers when developing, planning and implementing large-scale educational reform initiatives. Educational administrators need to take heed of research which indicates CPD is more likely to result in changes to classroom practice when it is managed by teachers at the local level, focused on teachers' own learning needs and enables collaborative work in a learning community or 'community of practice' which can foster both teacher and student learning. Paradoxically, education systems which introduce transmissive CPD programmes do not take account of the way teachers-as-adults learn, specifically in relation to making learning experiences personally meaningful (though this is often mandated as a curriculum objective for their students). Reinforcing the point that educational authorities need to involve teachers more in the design and development stages of CPD programmes is the fact that teachers themselves have clear ideas about what has most impact on their professional development. An OECD (2009) survey of professional development in 23 countries reported that teachers found the forms of development with the greatest impact to be 'informal dialogue to improve teaching', 'individual and collaborative research' and 'qualification programmes'. Both 'individual and collaborative research' and 'qualification programmes' had low participation rates, however, which may be indicative of their time-consuming nature and the consequent lack of space for them in most teachers' lives. A key challenge in the field of teacher education is thus how to make CPD more personalized, self-paced, relevant, context-appropriate, and sustainable.

Regrettably, the evidence from the research indicates that the type of CPD activities which are most likely to have an impact on classroom practices are not widely used. This is brought out in the OECD's analysis of their 'Teaching and Learning International Survey' (TALIS) data.

- Teacher professional development is deemed to be high quality when it includes opportunities for active learning methods, an extended time period, a group of colleagues, and collective learning activities or research with other teachers. The higher the exposure of teachers to high-quality professional development, the more likely they are to use a wide variety of teaching practices in the classroom.
- Professional development activities that focus on curriculum knowledge (rather than subject knowledge or pedagogy) and that involve collaborating with other teachers seem particularly well suited to enhancing teachers' classroom practices. However, these types of professional development are not those that are most widely used around the world.

(OECD, 2017: 1)

As we will see in the case studies of CPD discussed later in this chapter, school-based professional learning communities offer opportunities for transformational professional learning which has a direct impact on practice. However, for such communities to develop, time and space needs to be allocated at the institutional level for collegial working to take place and this needs to be combined with support from school leaders. Even then, deep-rooted changes at the classroom level will not occur overnight, but must be a longer-term objective.

Reflective practice and CPD

Implicit in the OECD's (2017) definition of high quality professional development cited above is for teachers to have a reflective orientation to their work. Indeed, discussion of any form of CPD in the twenty-first century does not seem to be complete without reference to the need for teachers to engage in 'reflective practice' for professional growth: as Walsh and Mann (2015) note, it is now an orthodoxy. Though research indicates that critical reflection is an intrinsic element in transformational learning, Day's (1993: 83) cautionary observation that reflection is 'a necessary but not sufficient condition for professional development' still holds true. Reflection in education needs to focus beyond what happens in the classroom in terms of technique and method, important though this is, and connect the classroom to structures in the school context, the wider community and the socio-economic environment. For example, teachers in state education systems in many parts of the world are both overworked and underpaid: simply to survive on a day-to-day basis they need to work in more than one school or work in a private tuition centre after school, often until late in the evening. Thus, for reflective practice to be truly transformational it needs to acknowledge that it is also 'political in the widest sense' and will 'necessarily subvert attempts to impose centralised or technocratic views of teaching or teacher education' (Ashcroft and Griffiths, 1989: 46).

However, the reality is that centralized and technocratic views of teaching have become more, not less, dominant worldwide in the intervening years since Ashcroft and Griffith's article was published, despite the status of reflective practice as an orthodoxy. Hence, I would argue that if English language teachers and teacher educators are to be truly reflective practitioners they need to take account of Zeichner and Liu's (2010: 73) standpoint that:

> All teaching actions have a variety of consequences which include (1) personal consequences – the effects of teaching on students' social and emotional development and social relationships; (2) academic consequences – the effects of teaching on students' intellectual development; and (3) political consequences – the cumulative effects of school experience on students' life chances. In our view, reflective teacher education needs to address all of these dimensions, and it should not be supported unless it makes a contribution to the making of a better society for everyone's children.

While the first two of these consequences feature in some discussions of reflective practice in English language teaching, the third is largely absent. The constraints on addressing political consequences of teaching actions will vary from context to context but in any context there will be scope for change to some degree. The case studies discussed later in this chapter indicate that, if headteachers and other administrators can be included in critical reflective practice, there is scope for at least the local organizational culture to become less hierarchical, more collegial and more teacher-centred in the sense of meeting teachers' learning needs and, in turn, improving their students' educational experiences and life chances. An essential element of CPD for teacher educators and the teachers with whom they work is thus to foster a capacity for identifying context-appropriate processes to effect change and collegial mechanisms to support it.

Evaluating the impact of CPD

The immediate beneficiaries of CPD are teachers but in the current age of 'accountability', it seems to be no longer sufficient for CPD programmes and activities to demonstrate an impact only on teachers. Teacher educators and teachers are increasingly asked to show the impact of CPD in terms of improved *student* achievement. This is problematic as establishing a causal link between any CPD activity and improved student learning is extremely difficult given the number of intervening variables and especially when the impact of any professional development programme is best measured in the long-term. Nevertheless, evaluation of CPD needs to be undertaken as much for the increased understanding it can bring to those who are participating in the CPD process as for demonstrating impact to outsiders to that process.

Guskey (2000), cited in Muijs and Lindsay (2008: 198–199), proposes five levels for evaluation of continuing professional development programmes:

Level 1: participants' reactions
Level 2: participants' learning from CPD
Level 3: organizational support and change
Level 4: participants' use of new knowledge and skill
Level 5: student outcomes

Level 1 is the level most often evaluated in CPD for teachers, especially in the transmissive, one-off workshops that are still so common. Typically, teachers are given formulaic, end-of-course questionnaires and asked to express their degree of satisfaction with various areas of the course or workshop. Questions such as *What did you learn from the workshop?* are, however, unlikely to provide much insight into what teachers will take from a workshop and make part of their own practice over time. Level 2 evaluation should, then, be a longitudinal process (and integrated with evaluation of Level 4). Level 3 – organizational support and change – is the level usually least considered in evaluation of professional development programmes for English language teachers, as if teachers are somehow dissociated from the contexts in which they work. Evaluation of Level 4 requires observation of what teachers actually do in the classroom and school over an extended period of time, coupled with investigation into the reasons why they change (or do not change) their practice as a result of a professional development experience. As we can see, student outcomes are not neglected in these levels but are the final level – and rarely evaluated. For example, Goodall et al. (2005) researched CPD in schools in the UK using Guskey's (2000) framework and found that while 100 per cent of the schools involved in the interview phase of their project evaluated Levels 1, 2 and 4, only 41 per cent evaluated Level 3 and just 25 per cent Level 5.

To improve the prospect of evaluation at Guskey's higher levels, Earley and Porritt (2014) argue that a CPD evaluation framework should allow for Level 5 assessment by articulating goals for improving student learning as the CPD programme is developed and by 'establishing an evidential baseline and impact picture that supports learning' (ibid.: 113). An evidential baseline in CPD impact studies is a rarity, however. Yoon et al. (2007) reviewed published studies on teachers' professional development and student outcomes but only found nine which met evidence standards. They suggest that substantial contact hours are a key variable in achieving any impact, though they were not able to determine the effectiveness of any particular type of professional development.

For student outcomes to be affected by CPD programmes for teachers, I would argue there needs to be a positive impact at all of the other levels. In essence, Levels 1–4 are enabling conditions for Level 5, student outcomes. To achieve change at Level 5 takes time and requires substantial contact hours. The tension between policy makers requiring immediate impact of CPD on students' achievement levels and the long-term nature of teachers' professional development needs resolution if demands for top-down 'accountability' and instant impact are not to severely limit or damage the CPD opportunities and experiences of teachers in school systems worldwide.

Learning from case studies of CPD

With the key issues of transformational CPD, reflective practice and meaningful evaluation in mind, in this section I discuss accounts of collaborative CPD in school-based learning communities and technology-mediated CPD which illustrate the issues in practice. As a whole, lessons from these case studies offer learning opportunities to teachers, teacher educators and educational administrators for successful CPD in their own contexts.

Collaborative CPD in school-based learning communities

As Level 3 of Guskey's (2000) evaluation framework referred to earlier indicates, professional development for teachers cannot take place without reference to the organization in which it takes place: 'As a social organization, a school is the locus for the interactions between administrators, teachers, students, parents, and communities' (Lee et al., 2011: 829). This concept of a school as a form of social organization, and here as a 'learning community', is not a new one and has been influential in other areas of education for some time but has only recently begun to have an impact in CPD for English language teachers (educational innovations are often first to be found in mainstream education and then filter down to English language teaching). Here, I discuss two examples of the development of successful learning communities for areas other than English, followed by an example of a collaborative action research project by English teachers in Argentina. All three case studies provide a stimulus for reflection on how collegial CPD for English teachers may be accomplished.

A school-based learning community for literacy teaching in Canada

Clausen et al. (2009) discuss the development of a learning community in a Canadian elementary school during one academic year. Four teachers participated alongside the school principal in a CPD project to improve student literacy outcomes. Ten characteristics of successful learning communities were identified from the research literature, against which the experience in the school was evaluated:

1. There exists within the community a constructed understanding of reality and learning.
2. The community is driven by a shared goal or purpose.
3. Informal power is shared amongst community stakeholders.
4. Flexibility is created within the organizational structure.
5. Through a balance of support and pressure, formal leaders show long-term commitment.
6. There is an open communication channel.
7. There is a group memory.
8. In-servicing becomes ongoing and internal.
9. Teachers begin to think in collegial terms.
10. A culture of trust and respect exists among stakeholders.

(Clausen et al., 2009: 445)

The typical nature of the institutional hierarchy in the school dictated that it was the principal who took the lead at the beginning of the project, with the teachers looking to her for guidance and direction. The principal herself then realized she would need to provide the impetus for the teachers to work more collegially rather than in their customary isolation. Just as important as this stimulus to work collegially was her recognition that other enabling conditions were necessary if the project was to succeed. Most importantly, as principal, she was able to allocate time in teachers' daily schedules for the collaborative CPD project work that, as she said, 'takes away some of their teaching pressure and [shows] that we value the professional learning that they're doing' (ibid.: 448). The principal was able to minimise the degree of her guidance as the school year went on, with the teachers correspondingly more self-directed. Relating teachers' experience in the year to the characteristics identified in the literature, Clausen et al. (2009: 451) concluded:

> It was only once they [the teachers] had been involved for a while that they began to show the more actualized characteristics of a learning community: with continued discussion in the meetings, they began to take the goals of the project to personal, shared levels (characteristics 1 and 2); they began to demand that they sit on each other's classes and act as mentors (characteristic 3); they began chatting about the project at lunch and outside of class (characteristic 6); began to think of internal inservicing (characteristic 8); began thinking like colleagues (characteristic 9); and trusting each other (characteristic 10).

It should not be surprising that a school-based learning community will take time to emerge. Teachers become used to working alone in their own classrooms and changing from individual to collaborative practice, opening up what happens in their classrooms to the scrutiny of their peers, is a radical change in professional behaviour. The process of building a learning community in the school was not just dependent on the interplay of the ten characteristics Clausen et al. (2009) identified, but was also reliant on someone in a position of authority – in this case the school principal – establishing the pre-conditions for growth and without which the project would not have been successful. This reinforces the importance of effective leadership in schools, which has been widely noted in general educational literature (see e.g. Liu and Hallinger, 2018).

Facilitated whole school action research for inclusive learning in Spain

While the Canadian case study offers evidence of the importance of an engaged school principal to the success of a CPD initiative, in this Spanish case study (Sales et al., 2011) the headteacher was not initially supportive of her teachers' project to develop a more intercultural and inclusive learning community in their primary school. The whole-school action research project developed from the school's annual plan for school-based CPD, which they were required to submit to their local Teacher Training and Resource Centre. Inclusivity was a major focus of the project as the school was located in a deprived urban area where the students were largely from the marginalized Roma community. Facilitators from a local university worked with the teachers but were not the instigators of the project, having asked to be included because of their prior knowledge of the school. It was the teachers who were always considered the 'leaders for change in school' whilst the teacher educator acted as a '"critical friend", a figure that encourages and accompanies teachers throughout the process of creating a professional learning community' (Sales et al., 2011: 912). In the beginning the teachers were 'pessimistic about any likelihood of change' (ibid.: 914) with self-evaluation showing that there were no shared values or framework on which to build a coherent conception of inclusive practice. Contributing to the pessimism was the headteacher who was considered excessively authoritarian, someone who did not respect or trust the teachers, rather than someone who saw her role as promoting the teachers' self-direction.

However, from an unpromising starting point, much was accomplished in a year. A 'Commitment Document' was negotiated 'in which all the teaching staff actively committed to the training process, which would be opened up to the whole school community' (Sales et al., 2011: 914). Recognizing that inclusivity in this context would need to involve the parents, not just the teachers and students, community assemblies were also held. Going beyond the school to the social organization of the community, the first assembly focused on obtaining the support of families 'with most authority in the community, who in turn appealed to the rest of the neighbourhood to participate in the project for change' (ibid.: 914). This approach was based on the practical reality that when children have poor attendance rates and suffer from high rates of failure, trust in schools is low and proposals for change need community leaders to advocate for them. Without the community assemblies, parents would have been sceptical that the school had either a genuine desire or the capacity to transform its practice. Community involvement continued throughout the year, with all committees including representatives of teachers, students and parents: a project with inclusivity as its pedagogic focus operated through inclusive participation.

Another important element of the project helped to ensure sustainability of change. All processes and decisions taken were clearly documented. This not only provided a written record of everything participants had agreed to but also validated the project's achievements. The inclusive approach also generated change in the attitude and behaviour of the school headteacher. Over time she became as committed to the process of change as the other stakeholders, delegating her authority and responsibilities to allow the project to become more democratic.

Based on this experience, Sales et al. (2011:918) offer five recommendations for school-based learning projects.

1. All stakeholders – headteacher, teaching staff, families – must recognise the need for change.
2. Space and time must be provided for 'collective reflection' at all levels, in the staffroom, classrooms and the community assemblies.
3. The action research process must develop 'tools and strategies to facilitate collaborative self-evaluation and democratic and dialogical decision making'.
4. While the teacher educators act as critical friends, teachers must retain their 'autonomy and responsibility […] to manage their own learning processes'.
5. Community participation 'fosters shared or distributed leadership, which is a key element in guaranteeing the sustainability of the change'.

School learning communities work best, then, when they are egalitarian and involve *all* stakeholders in the school community, going beyond managers and teachers to include the students as well as their parents, recognizing that it is local families that the school serves. Successful learning communities are genuinely collaborative and autonomous, responding to the needs of the school, its students and the community in which it is located. There is, of course, a place for outside involvement but when this occurs it should be in the capacity of 'critical friends', not initiators and leaders of the change. It is important, too, that the processes and outcomes be well documented so that there is a complete record of project achievements.

Collaborative action research by English teachers in Argentina

On a smaller scale than the whole-school project in Spain, the action research project described and evaluated in Banegas et al. (2013) involved a group of three teachers and a teacher-researcher in an Argentinian secondary school who decided to investigate their own teaching practices in response to perceptions that demotivation was rife amongst their students and having a negative impact on teaching and learning. Although only four teachers participated in the project, the cycles of research they proposed were not developed in isolation from other teachers but negotiated with them and with the school principal. In an institutional setting such as a government secondary school it is clearly important to have the approval, if not the direct participation, of authority figures and to keep those not in the project team – including other teachers – apprised of what is happening so that they do not work against it. As with the Spanish project, students' input, in this case in terms of their evaluation of their English programmes and making suggestions for content of the materials created during the project, was an essential element of the participatory process. Parental involvement, however, was restricted to approving their children's participation. In the first of the three action research cycles the results of classroom observations, student questionnaires and class student interviews were used to inform a change in direction of classroom materials; in the second cycle students provided feedback about teaching performance and further input on topic choice while there was inter-teacher classroom observation and feedback; and in the third cycle the materials development, observation and feedback continued alongside a return to the textbook to ensure grammar was also taught.

The teachers felt collaborative action research provided 'a space for professional development [...] for it helped us to work collaboratively on a common framework with shared aims even though each of us had different perceptions and motivations' (Banegas et al., 2013: 191). Whilst they all developed professionally, to different degrees in different domains, their common experience enabled them to revitalize their curriculum as 'we teachers identified ourselves as reflective–reflexive creators of knowledge from/for our context' (ibid.: 198). A collaborative process such as this is not without its challenges, of course, as teachers have to open themselves and their practices up to scrutiny, not just by their peers but also by their students. For many teachers this process can be daunting, even threatening, as they are used to working in cultures of isolation. Those teachers who do want to take this step might, therefore, want to begin by working out their own ground rules for collaborative activities, such as peer observations and reflective discussions, to help to establish the trust which is a necessary precondition for productive collaboration.

Technology-mediated CPD

The focus of the second group of case studies is on the role of technology in CPD. This is a rapidly growing phenomenon, an obvious reflection of the role of technology in most teachers' lives and not one restricted to more developed economies. The growth in mobile phone usage in South Asia, for example, has enabled users to access the internet without investing in desktop or laptop computers. Indeed, India leads all G20 nations in the percentage of users accessing the internet on their phones, at 79 per cent.[1] This has great potential for online CPD without the expense of hardware beyond the reach of many schools and individuals. In this section, then, I discuss a project in Bangladesh which uses material on SD cards in mobile phones to mediate CPD. I also discuss an example of online communities of practice in Greece where connectivity is greater and computer use in schools is more common than in an economically developing country like Bangladesh. Again, these examples provide many points for reflection for teachers and teacher educators who wish to use technology in CPD programmes elsewhere.

Mobile phones and CPD in Bangladesh

Woodward et al. (2014) discuss the use of mobile phones as a means to deliver training content in a major donor-funded project in Bangladesh.[2] In the context of a long history of large-scale educational projects, none of which have seemed to have had any enduring effect, the project team was concerned to maximize impact, reaching as many teachers as possible and, at the same time, develop a sustainable system of support for teachers. The scale of the task was challenging, with some 100,000 schools requiring assistance and the project working with 12,500 teachers. The solution seemed to be to use the form of ICT that was most readily available – mobile phones. Mobile phone usage in Bangladesh rose from 36 million users in 2008 to 116 million users in 2014, making it possible to reach the whole target group in this way. However, as the project team thought it unrealistic to expect teachers to fund their CPD through internet connection fees, they developed an approach which provided video training content on SD cards which teachers could view at their leisure. Woodward et al. (2014: 232) explain: 'Video on the mobile would offer an immediacy of impact and a degree of flexibility that much conventional training-room-based, trainer-led and time-bound input often could not match.'

Nevertheless, like other forms of input provided by trainers external to the school context, these materials needed mediation to be successfully used by the teachers. In this case, the mediation was provided by a Bangladeshi guide who became the 'face' of the trainers, exemplifying what research in human–computer interaction indicates is a key feature of an interface, i.e. that there should be a human presence. Project feedback indicates that teachers feel they 'know' the narrator as a kind of friend who speaks directly to them as individuals. Technology-facilitated training works best, it seems, when the importance of the human element is also recognized.

The importance of the human element is further acknowledged through peer support as two teachers from each school participate in the project, enabling on-site sharing of understanding of teaching practices introduced through the video materials and discussion of issues that may arise in implementation. Peer support is then extended via meetings with other pairs of teachers from ten–12 schools in their educational districts. These group meetings take place every six to eight weeks and are opportunities for teachers to maximise the sharing of experiences, offering a forum for collaborative learning which goes beyond individual schools. The professional learning communities built up in this way thus enable teachers to augment the professional development opportunities offered in video form on their phones. And, resonating with the experiences in Canada, Spain and Argentina discussed earlier, the project also recognises the need to secure the support of other key stakeholders in the education system – headteachers and both local and national level administrators – at the outset so that their positive attitudes promote a facilitative working environment for the teachers' CPD.

Online communities of practice in Greece

In the second of the technology-mediated case studies, Karavas and Papadopoulou (2014) discuss the development of online communities of practice, which provide CPD opportunities to Greek primary school teachers as a response to a policy decision to begin the teaching of English from Grade 1 rather than from Grade 3. Feedback on the initial introduction of this pedagogical innovation revealed that teachers wanted much more in-school practical support to help them teach learners of this age group as well as 'closer co-operation between teachers in dealing with the complexities of the innovation' (Karavas and Papadopoulou, 2014: 179). However, the Greek education system was considered to be 'one of the most centrally governed and managed education systems in Europe' (ibid.: 180) within which CPD was typically top-down and transmissive. These were unpromising conditions for the paradigm shift in CPD that the authors concluded was necessary to meet teachers' needs and ensure the sustainability of the innovation. The university project team in charge of the innovation decided that, as teachers had indicated that they favoured reflection on practice and collaboration with colleagues as their preferred modes of CPD, developing online communities of practice (CoPs) would be the best means to exploit their preferences. It was expected that the CoPs would enable teachers to exercise greater individual control in a centralized system in which adherence to its norms was expected and would allow for the kind of free expression usually denied space. Further, CoPs would account for the fact that 'professional growth and teacher learning are job embedded, collaborative, site-based and ongoing' (ibid.: 184).

The platform developed, called '2gather', integrated learning management systems and social networking features which research had indicated were important in online communities, including:

- a directory with members' avatars, profiles and professed areas of expertise
- tools for sharing experiences and introducing questions, including chatrooms, forums, blogs, comments and a direct messaging system
- a media library to deposit documents for the community knowledge base
- a search engine to enable members to easily retrieve all available information on specific topics

Recognizing that the online system, if it was to be successful, could not displace the INSET providers who had been important in the offline system, a space and roles were provided for the School Advisers who traditionally performed this function. However, the traditional roles of School Advisers as providers of top-down, one-off in-service workshops were reconfigured to allow them to function as facilitators of groups within their districts. This was important as School Advisers' place in the system had to be validated, albeit in different – and hopefully more effective – ways. In addition, the professional development needs of the School Advisers were met through their own online CoP group; another innovative feature of the project given that traditional INSET providers are rarely thought to have development needs of their own. Through their CoP School Advisers, just like teachers, were able to share information, knowledge and ideas, as well as finding out about developments in CoPs in areas of the country covered by their colleagues.

Evaluation of the small-scale pilot implementation of 2gather revealed that the platform was working as its designers had hoped. The CoP gave its users a sense of belonging to a group and broke down communication barriers between them. As Karavas and Papadopoulou (2014: 194) reported, teachers who used the platform agreed that their online community:

1. was mainly driven by the willingness of members to participate
2. helped them build relationships and network with others
3. motivated them to share work-related knowledge
4. provided an informal, welcoming social environment
5. helped them achieve better results in teaching projects
6. encouraged knowledge sharing and learning into work life
7. utilized a user-friendly social platform.

These successes in the pilot phase have led to larger-scale implementation of 2*gather* with other groups of teachers across the country. As Karavas and Papadopoulou (2014) caution, however, online communities – like other forms of community – take time to develop organically, to develop social norms, nurture leaders and become part of the dominant educational culture. Where space for this to happen is found, teachers become motivated to share their knowledge amongst new networks of supportive colleagues and the possibility of incorporating new understandings of teaching into their daily practice is heightened. Also important in the Greek context, and likely to be so in many others too, was the development of a structure which provided a place for the traditional INSET providers, School Advisors, to have their expertise validated and one which, moreover, provided opportunities for their own reflective and collegial development.

Conclusion

I have argued in this chapter that any form of continuing professional development (CPD) that we undertake as teachers must offer opportunities for continuous professional learning (CPL). This means that CPD opportunities need to go beyond the externally mandated face-to-face short course focusing on introducing a new curriculum or some other educational innovation, which is still the default mode for CPD in many parts of the world, to encompass a range of practices focused on the collaborative understanding of classroom issues which teachers identify as important to their own sense of self-efficacy as facilitators of their students' learning. By this means, we can conceive of CPD as a series of opportunities to understand better our workplaces – our classrooms, our institutions and the wider educational system. These opportunities need to be responsive to the professed needs of teachers and provided in ways that fit with the patterns of their working lives as 'Teacher learning is most likely to occur when teachers have influence over the substance and process of professional development' (King and Newmann, 2001: 86). Of course, impact on our students' learning must be considered a legitimate – if not immediate – outcome of CPD for teachers. However, if this is to be achieved everyone involved in the educational process, including policy makers and administrators, must recognise that 'where teachers are able to reflect, access new ideas, experiment and share experiences within school cultures and where leaders encourage appropriate levels of challenge and support, there is greater potential for school and classroom improvement' (Muijs and Lindsay, 2008: 195). The discussion of key issues and the case studies explored in this chapter reinforce this conclusion.

Notes

1 See https://qz.com/945127/internet-use-in-india-proves-desktops-are-only-for-westerners/.
2 See the project website at www.eiabd.com/.

Further reading

Avalos, B. (2011) 'Teacher Professional Development in *Teaching And Teacher Education* over Ten Years'. *Teaching and Teacher Education*, 27 10–20.
   This article reviews publications over the previous decade in a major educational journal. Themes identified include mediation of learning, conditions and factors which influence professional development, and effectiveness. The review concludes that prolonged interventions are more effective than short-term ones and emphasizes the power of collaborative learning amongst teachers.

British Council (2015) *Continuing Professional Development Frameworks for English Teachers,* London: British Council. Available as free download online: <https://englishagenda.britishcouncil.org/sites/default/files/attachments/joint_framework_doc.pdf> (accessed 11 May, 2019).

This document introduces key features of three CPD frameworks for use by teachers in any context, though emphasizing that teaching competence is context and culture specific. The three frameworks have been developed by the *British Council, Cambridge English* and *EAQUALS.* Links are provided to each of the frameworks for readers to explore them in detail.

Dadds, M. (2014) 'Continuing Professional Education: Nurturing the Expert Within'. *Professional Development in Education,* 40(1) 9–16.

This article criticizes delivery-focused and technocratic notions of CPD and places the development of teachers' own understanding of learning at the heart of education reform. Drawing on case stories of teachers engaged in enquiry-based CPD, it sees the nurturing of teachers' 'sense of voice, their judgement and their confidence' as essential to professional growth.

Hayes, D. (ed.) (2014) *Innovations in the Continuing Professional Development of English Language Teachers,* London: British Council. Available as free download online: <www.britishcouncil.in/sites/default/files/e168_innovations_in_cpd_final_web.pdf> (accessed 11 May, 2019).

This collection contains varied case studies of CPD worldwide at all educational levels. It showcases large-scale and individual innovations grounded in practice but also informed by theory. The chapters contain the authors' 'reflections' and 'learning points' from which readers are able to draw lessons for CPD innovation in their own contexts.

References

Ashcroft, K. and Griffiths, M. (1989) 'Reflective Teachers and Reflective Tutors: School Experience in an Initial Teacher Education Course'. *Journal of Education for Teaching,* 15(1) 35–52.

Banegas, D., Pavese, A., Velázquez, A. and Vélez, S. M. (2013) 'Teacher Professional Development Through Collaborative Action Research: Impact on Foreign English-Language Teaching And Learning'. *Educational Action Research,* 21(2) 185–201.

College of Early Childhood Educators (CEC) (2017) *Continuous Professional Learning Portfolio Cycle – Handbook 2017.* Toronto: College of Early Childhood Educators.

Clausen, K. W., Aquino, A-M. and Wideman, R. (2009) 'Bridging the Real and Ideal: A Comparison Between Learning Community Characteristics and a School-Based Case Study'. *Teaching and Teacher Education,* 25 444–452.

Day, C. (1993) 'Reflection: A Necessary but not Sufficient Condition for Professional Development'. *British Educational Research Journal,* 19(1) 83–93.

Earley, P. and Porritt, V. (2014) 'Evaluating the Impact of Professional Development: The Need for a Student-Focused Approach'. *Professional Development in Education,* 40(1) 112–129.

Freeman, A., Adams Becker, S., Cummins, M., Davis, A. and Hall Giesinger, C. (2017) *NMC/CoSN Horizon Report: 2017 K–12 Edition,* Austin, TX: The New Media Consortium.

Gemeda, F. T, Fiorucci, M. and Catarci, M. (2014) 'Teachers' professional development in schools: rhetoric versus reality'. *Professional Development in Education,* 40(1) 71–88.

Goodall, J., Day, C., Lindsay, G., Muijs, D. and Harris, A. (2005) *Evaluating the Impact of Continuing Professional Ddevelopment (CPD).* Research Report 659. Nottingham: Department for Education and Skills.

Guskey, T. R. (2000) *Evaluating Professional Development.* Thousand Oaks, CA: Corwin Press.

Howard, A., Basurto-Santos, N. M., Gimenez, T., Gonzáles Moncada, A. M., McMurray, M. and Traish, A. (2016) *A Comparative Study of English Language Teacher Recruitment, In-service Education and Retention in Latin America and the Middle East.* London: British Council.

Karavas, E. and Papadopoulou, S. (2014) 'Introducing a paradigm shift in EFL continuing professional development in Greece: the development of online communities of practice', in Hayes, D. (ed.) *Innovations in the Continuing Professional Development of English Language Teachers.* London: British Council: 179–199.

King, M. B. and Newmann, F. M. (2001) 'Building School Capacity Through Professional Development: Conceptual and Empirical Considerations'. *The International Journal of Educational Management*, 15(2) 86–93.

Lee, J. C., Zhang, Z. and Yin, H. (2011) 'A Multilevel Analysis of the Impact of a Professional Learning Community, Faculty Trust in Colleagues and Collective Efficacy on Teacher Commitment to Students'. *Teaching and Teacher Education*, 27 820–830.

Liu, S, and Hallinger, P. (2018) 'Principal Instructional Leadership, Teacher Self-Efficacy, and Teacher Professional Learning in China: Testing a Mediated-Effects Model'. *Educational Administration Quarterly*, 54(4) 501–528.

Muijs, D. and Lindsay, G. (2008) 'Where Are We At? An Empirical Study of Levels and Methods of Evaluating Continuing Professional Development'. *British Educational Research Journal*, 34 195–211.

OECD (2009) *Creating Effective Teaching and Learning Environments: First Results from TALIS*. Paris: Organization for Economic Cooperation and Development (OECD).

OECD (2017) *Teaching in Focus, 2017/16 – (April)*. Paris: Organization for Economic Cooperation and Development (OECD).

Sales, A., Traver, J. A. and Garćia, R. (2011) 'Action Research as a School-Based Strategy in Intercultural Professional Development for Teachers'. *Teaching and Teacher Education*, 27 911–919.

Walsh, S. and Mann, S. (2015) 'Doing Reflective Practice: A Data-Led Way Forward'. *ELT Journal*, 69(4) 351–362.

Wang, J., Lin, E., Spalding, E., Odell, S. J. and Klecka, C. L. (2011) 'Understanding Teacher Education in an Era of Globalization'. *Journal of Teacher Education*, 62(1) 115–120.

Woodward, C., Griffiths, M. and Solly, M. (2014) 'English in Action: a new approach to continuing professional development through the use of mediated video, peer support and low-cost mobile phones in Bangladesh', in Hayes, D. (ed.) *Innovations in the Continuing Professional Development of English Language Teachers*. London: British Council: 227–245.

Wyatt, M. and Ager, E. O. (2017) 'Teachers' Cognitions Regarding Continuing Professional Development'. *ELT Journal*, 71(2) 171–185.

Yoon, K. S., Duncan, T., Lee, S. W.- Y., Scarloss, B. and Shapley, K. L. (2007) *Reviewing the Evidence on How Teacher Professional Development Affects Student Achievement*. Issues & Answers Report, REL 2007– No. 033. Washington, DC: U.S. Department of Education, Institute of Education Sciences, National Center for Education Evaluation and Regional Assistance, Regional Educational Laboratory Southwest. Available online: <http://ies.ed.gov/ncee/edlabs> (accessed 11 May, 2019).

Zeichner, K. and Liu, K.Y. (2010) 'A critical analysis of reflection as a goal for teacher education', in Lyons, N. (ed.) *Handbook of Reflection and Reflective Inquiry.*, Boston, MA: Springer: 67–84.

12

Teacher education in content-based language education

Tom Morton

Introduction

There has always been content in language teaching. This content can be explicit knowledge about the language being taught, information about the target culture(s), literature, themes and topics chosen for their intrinsic interest and capacity to motivate students, or curricular content from other subjects. Content-based approaches to language teaching take this concern with content further by seeing content not just as a vehicle for language learning and use, but as knowledge to be learned, and in some cases, assessed. There are powerful arguments in favour of the inclusion of meaningful content in language lessons and courses, with most of them chiming with strongly communicative approaches to language pedagogy which emphasize the need for learners to be exposed to, and produce, language in meaningful contexts.

Content-based approaches to language education take on a wide variety of labels which reflect contextual and historical factors such as the roles in society of the language of instruction, the amount of exposure, and the extent to which there is an attempt to explicitly combine both types of instruction. They can also reflect different 'lineages' depending on whether their origins are in foreign language (FL) teaching, second language (SL) teaching or mother tongue (L1) teaching (Dale et al., 2017). A useful distinction is that between bilingual education programmes in which an L2 is used as a language of instruction for curricular content, with classes timetabled under their subject labels (history, science etc.), and second or foreign language programmes where content is introduced in language lessons timetabled as such.

Examples of bilingual education are immersion programmes in which 50 per cent or more of curriculum content is taught in an additional language, for example the French immersion programmes in Canada or Spanish immersion programmes in the US. In Europe, immersion programmes refer to those in which students study a large part (or all) of the curriculum in a minority language with the aim being to revitalize that language (examples being Basque, Irish and Welsh). Other bilingual programmes include those such as the Spanish ones, where up to 40 per cent of the curriculum is taught in English (or, less so, another FL such as French) in state primary and secondary schools.

Examples of the second type include content-based instruction (CBI) programmes in the US, where content is incorporated in the teaching of world languages (WL), both in K-12 and increasingly in tertiary education. Globally, however, perhaps the most popular term is content and language integrated learning (CLIL), which is used mainly to describe the combined teaching of a foreign or world language (such as English) with other curricular content. As such, CLIL is basically the same as CBI in the US context (Cenoz, 2015). Another term growing in popularity is English-medium instruction (EMI), which refers to the teaching and learning of curricular content in English, often at university level, and where often there is no attempt to integrate language learning, with the focus being strictly on the content (Dearden, 2015). For the purposes of this chapter, the umbrella term 'content-based language education' (CBLE) is used to cover both bilingual and non-bilingual contexts, with reference made to specific programme types where it is relevant to the discussion.

Whichever the label used, or the local contextual factors, a common concern in all content-based language education is the training and professional development of teachers. All teachers using a second/foreign language to teach other content need both a high level of linguistic and communicative competence in that language (as models for learners and for flexible use in dealing with content) as well as knowledge about how to integrate language and literacy with the subject content they teach. Teachers on these programmes will be either content teachers teaching and assessing their subject through an L2 in a bilingual programme, or language teachers introducing curricular content from other subjects into their language lessons. Thus, while both types of teachers face the pedagogical challenge of integrating content and language, the training and professional development needs for both types of teachers will have different emphases. Content teachers are likely to lack knowledge of language learning and language teaching methodology, while language teachers may lack sufficient subject matter knowledge to teach content effectively. However, both sets of teachers are likely to face uncertainty about what language to focus on, how to integrate it with content learning objectives, and how to deal with learners' output in providing feedback and assessing learning.

The chapter has the following overall structure. This introduction has given an overview of the current situation: the growing interest in approaches to world/foreign language education which combine content and language learning, and definitions of the different types. Section two moves on to the problematic issues and ongoing debates in teacher education for content-based language education. Section three provides illustrative examples of data drawn from a research project on CLIL teachers' knowledge and practices, with the analyses highlighting issues of importance for teacher education and professional development for these teachers. The final section focuses on implications and possible practical implications for teacher education and professional development in this type of language education.

Issues and ongoing debates

Current issues and debates in teacher education for CBLE revolve around the following key issues: a lack of initial and in-service teacher education provision; the need for greater understanding of teachers' training and professional development needs; a lack of research into teacher education programmes for CBLE and their processes and outcomes. On a more theoretical level, discussion has focused on the nature of teachers' knowledge: either of language or content knowledge taken separately, or of their integration. In line with the wider applied linguistics and TESOL fields, a recent trend has been a focus on content and language integration as a question of identity, particularly as teachers struggle to see themselves as responsible for both types of learning. Another key issue is the need for collaboration between content and language teachers in the different CBLE contexts, and the need for teachers to develop appropriate collaborative skills.

Many researchers and practitioners have pointed out that the explosion of interest in the different varieties of CBLE around the world has not been accompanied by adequate provision of teacher education and professional development. Over a decade ago, a Eurydice survey pointed out that 'there are virtually no initial and in-service training programmes devoted to methods used specifically to teach a subject in other than the normal language of instruction' (Eurydice, 2006: 52). Nine years later, the situation did not seem to have changed much, with a British Council seminar focused on the training needs for teachers in bilingual programmes in Spain concluding that there was still 'a lack of specific training programmes for bilingual education, and [a] lack of training for teacher educators to use adequate methodologies' (British Council, 2015, my translation). The situation does not appear to be better across the Atlantic, where Tedick and Wesely (2015) point out that 'Many if not most US immersion teachers do not benefit from pre-service preparation or in-service professional development focused on language and content integration' (p. 32). This situation continues to be a serious threat to the viability and maintenance of CBLE programmes, as they are not sustainable without adequate initial and in-service teacher education and professional development. As Pérez-Cañado (2016: 267) points out, 'The new – and increased – demands which the implementation of this approach places on teachers have been largely overlooked and insufficiently addressed.'

Not only is there a reported lack of teacher education provision for CBLE, there is also little research on what programmes do exist, or what teachers' training needs actually are. In the North American context, Tedick and Wesely observe that 'little research has addressed the process of preparing teachers for CBI contexts, either initially or in their professional development' (2015: 33). In the European context, Pérez-Cañado points to 'a conspicuous paucity of research into the analysis of teacher training needs across Europe' (2016: 268). One reason for this lack of research on teacher education needs, processes and outcomes may be that, to date, much research in CBLE has focused on its implementation. Studies have looked at the classroom practices of in-service teachers with the aim of understanding how content and language integration works in the classroom. While such studies continue to produce much useful knowledge that can feed into teacher education programmes, there is a clear need to focus on how teachers are prepared for such practices and what their needs are.

This gap is beginning to be filled by studies such as Pérez-Cañado's (2016) survey of CLIL teachers' training needs in Europe. This study focused on in-service CLIL teachers' reported needs in four areas: linguistic and intercultural competence, theoretical and methodological aspects of CLIL, materials and resources, and ongoing professional development. In contrast to previous studies, she found that the area where teachers claimed to have less need for training (where they were 'complacent' or 'optimistic' in Pérez-Cañado's terms) was in linguistic and intercultural competence. This may not be surprising given that in the sample of teachers, 82.16 per cent were language teachers (with B2 to C1 level of English). In fact, the content teachers in the sample did indeed identify a greater need for training in linguistic and intercultural competence. In the areas of methodology and materials the results are more mixed in that teachers' descriptions of their current levels of knowledge and their perceived training needs were not so evenly matched. This suggests that the in-service teachers in Pérez-Cañado's sample feel the need for more training and development in these areas even if they claim to already have some considerable degree of competence. This is unsurprising at least in the area of materials, which CLIL teachers identify as problematic in terms of the time needed to find and create them and the curricular and cultural appropriateness of existing materials (Morton, 2013).

The gap identified by Tedick and Wesely, that of a lack of research on the processes and outcomes of CBLE teacher education and professional development programmes, is also beginning to be addressed as new studies appear. These studies draw on constructs taken from the wider field of teacher cognition, such as different types of knowledge, belief, and increasingly, identity. Often, they track the progress of either individuals or small cohorts of teachers as they struggle to meet the challenges of combining language and content instruction. Irrespective of the specific CBLE context, whether immersion, EMI, CBI or CLIL, the same core issue emerges again and again: the need for teachers to have access to sound methodological principles and practices for the successful integration of content and language.

An important recent example of this tracking, or longitudinal, approach is Cammarata and Haley's (2017) study of what they describe as the professional development 'journey' of 15 grades 6–12 French immersion teachers in Canada, as they planned and implemented content instruction using pedagogic frameworks for content and language/literacy integration. Over a period of 18 months, the teachers in the study showed clear evidence of having learned to deliver rich and well-balanced lessons with a combined focus on content and language, but even so they still struggled with some aspects of content and language integration. One issue that emerged was that even when lessons had been carefully planned to incorporate a joint focus on content and language/literacy, sometimes the balance and integration were not seen in the lesson as it was taught, or other times some teachers were dissatisfied with the lesson even though observers evaluated it as having been successful. The findings of this study show the importance of professional development (PD) for content and language integration being embedded in teachers' contexts and worlds of practice, of having clear pedagogic models to guide them in integrating content and language, of using collaborative, learner-centred forms of PD such as Lesson Study, and having the opportunity to be part of a community beyond their immediate school-based environment, such as a University department.

In a Masters level teacher education context, Escobar Urmeneta (2013) studied the progression in knowledge of content and language integration of one student teacher (pseudonym Pilar) over an academic year. Adopting a reflective approach to teacher learning, the study sets out to track and characterise the stages in this teacher's developmental processes, both in terms of classroom practices and theoretical understanding of key issues in language learning relevant to this context. Using evidence from different data sources including video-recorded classroom interaction and Pilar's self-reflective reports collected over the academic year, the study shows how she was able to make increasingly sophisticated analyses of her own classroom practices. For example, in examining data from her own teaching, she shifts from a concern with her own performance to a greater focus on what the learners were doing. However, Escobar-Urmeneta's reconstruction of Pilar's progress in integrating content and language teaching shows that this is not an easy process, especially in meeting the double demands of learning to teach and using theory to reflect on teaching. Of course, this may be an issue common to all initial teacher education contexts – the cognitive demand of focusing on the challenges of classroom teaching as well as learning to articulate one's reflections using appropriate metalanguage drawing on theoretical principles. However, this may be even more challenging in CBLE contexts. It is difficult enough to learn to teach one subject alone (whether that subject is science or a foreign language), but combining the two in practice while learning to teach, and alongside this, reflecting on both the linguistic and content dimensions, is doubly challenging.

Recent studies of teachers in CBLE contexts have reflected a more general identity turn in studies of language teaching, as can be seen in special issues of *TESOL Quarterly* (2016) and *The Modern Language Journal* (2017), as well as books such as Barkhuizen (2017), Cheung, Ben Said and Park (2015) and Gray and Morton (2018). A key example is Cammarata and Tedick's (2012) study of three North American immersion teachers participating in a professional development (PD) programme aimed at enabling them to effectively integrate content and language instruction. Using a phenomenological approach, the study depicts the process of learning to integrate content and language as a 'multifaceted struggle' which deeply involved the teachers' identities as they moved from seeing themselves as primarily content teachers to seeing themselves as having responsibility for their students' language learning as well. Cammarata and Tedick argue that these teachers lacked the pedagogical content knowledge which would allow them to find ways of integrating language and content. Studies such as these show the strong inter-relation between the knowledge required for content and language integration and the formation of appropriate professional identities as content *and* language teachers.

The focus on language teacher identity is also clearly seen in Pappa, Moate, Ruohotie-Lyhty and Eteläpelto's (2017) study of Finnish primary CLIL teachers' negotiation of their pedagogical and relational identity. They use the concept of *identity agency* to theorise the relationship between teachers' pedagogical and relational identities, showing how they strive towards building a more encompassing professional identity both individually and through working with others. While the study does not take place in a teacher education context, the authors identify clear implications for CBLE teacher education and PD programmes. They argue that in these programmes, student teachers should have the opportunity to reflect on their own expectations and aspirations, with pedagogical theories used to help them to do so. They further argue that teaching practice should be seen as an opportunity for the enrichment of student teachers' experience by allowing them to develop a deeper awareness of the inter-relationships between their pedagogical beliefs and practical knowledge, their actions and the influence of these actions on their professional identities.

Dale, Oostdam and Verspoor (2017) draw on the construct of identity in framing their review of the literature on teacher education in CBLE with a view to establishing an analytical framework for the preparation of language teachers (LTs) working in these contexts. Apart from the construct of identity, the review addresses the thorny issue of focus in CBLE. Dale et al. identify five types of language focus and four types of content focus. The five types of language focus are: subject-specific, classroom, general academic, general everyday, and culture-specific. The types of content focus are school subjects, thematic content, cultural content and language as content. These foci can combine with four types of pedagogical theories derived from SLA, Systemic Functional Linguistics (SFL), Sociocultural theory, or Cultural theory. From these elements Dale et al. construct an analytic framework which depicts different identities available to CBLE teachers depending on whether they focus on content/meaning or language/form or whether they orient to culture-specific content, or content drawn from a specific subject.

Dale et al.'s review also touches on another key issue in CBLE teacher education: the need for content and language teachers to collaborate. They identify five topics in the literature on collaborative practices: teachers' lack of knowledge or skill, including knowledge of models of collaboration, different views on the content/language balance depending on whether the teacher is a language or content specialist, different understandings of pedagogy linked to disciplinary or subject identities, inequalities of power and status, and organisational factors. All of these have received attention in the literature, and studies all point to the centrality of teacher collaboration in CBLE, and the challenges faced by teachers in bringing about successful collaboration. It stands to reason, thus, that developing competence for collaboration needs to be a key focus in teacher education for CBLE.

All in all, then, this brief review suggests that teacher education in CBLE suffers from considerable shortcomings in two key areas: a lack of provision at both pre- and in-service levels, and a lack of research on the processes and outcomes of teacher education and professional development programmes. It is quite clear that where policy makers have supported the implementation of different forms of CBLE, they have underestimated the challenges for teachers in successfully integrating subject-matter content and language/literacy. While pedagogical and curriculum design frameworks for the integration of content and language/literacy exist (see Cammarata, 2016; Llinares et al., 2012; Lyster, 2007, 2016; Meyer et al., 2015), we still have very little understanding of the processes by which such frameworks are appropriated by different types of teachers in CBLE contexts, used in curriculum design and planning, and implemented in classroom practice. As Dale et al. put it, 'It is no surprise that LTs and their educators are struggling to find identity and focus as the literature does not provide a one-size-fits all guideline' (Dale et al., 2017: 14). While it may be over-optimistic and perhaps not desirable to have a 'one-size-fits-all guideline', there is an urgent need for both a firmer conceptual base for the knowledge upon which successful integration of content and language rests, and of the processes by which this knowledge is appropriated and used by teachers.

CLIL teachers' reflections on their practices

In this section I present data from a research project (Morton, 2012) which focused on CLIL teachers' planning and classroom practices, and their reflections on both. While the focus was on investigating teachers' cognitions and practices, the frameworks and procedures used, particularly stimulated recall-based reflections on video-recorded data, are very much in accord with a data-driven reflective approach to language teacher education (see Chapter 3 in this volume). The project was built around a tripartite conceptualisation of teachers' knowledge about language (KAL) for content and language integration: language as a curricular concern; language as a tool for content teaching and learning; language as a matter of learners' competence.

Language as a curricular concern focuses on the role of language in the content curriculum, particularly in terms of planning. The term is borrowed from Leung (2001) in which he argued that, in English as an additional language (EAL) contexts in the UK, language hardly figured as an object of curricular attention. Here, it is used to refer to the language features and skills that teachers may choose to focus on proactively (Lyster, 2007), incorporating them as objectives at the preactive (planning) stage of teaching. Language as a tool for content teaching and learning refers to how language is used in ongoing classroom interaction to meet curricular content learning goals. As such it is analogous to Walsh's (2011) construct of 'classroom interactional competence', at least how it is manifested in CLIL contexts (see Escobar Urmeneta and Walsh, 2017 for an example). Language as a matter of competence refers to teachers' conceptions about their learners' and their own levels of competence in the language of instruction (English). Thus, teachers' beliefs about what their learners are capable of or how well they accomplished an activity, in terms of language, may guide their decisions about the other two dimensions of language (what they plan for; and how they interact with students in class), and these can be the object of pre- and post-teaching reflection.

Four secondary CLIL teachers from a school which participated in a Spanish Ministry of Education/British Council Bilingual Education Project (see Dobson et al., 2010 for a description and evaluation) participated in the study. The subjects taught were biology, history, geography, design and technology, and the classes ranged from Year 7 (first year secondary in Spain) to Year 10. The teachers had relatively little formal training in Bilingual Education or CLIL methodology. This mainly consisted of short courses and workshops, including brief stays in the UK in which they visited schools and observed lessons and received some professional development in language teaching methodology.

Data were collected at three stages, each relating to one of the components of the tripartite view of language knowledge. To focus on language as curricular concern, the teachers filled in an instrument called a Content Representation or 'CoRe' (Loughran et al., 2004) in which they identified the key concepts and language features they planned to focus on in a topic they were about to teach. This document was used as the basis of a semi-structured interview, in which the teachers were able to reflect on their planning processes, particularly how language issues fitted into their view of the curriculum they were teaching. In order to focus on language as a tool for learning, for each teacher three lessons were video-recorded. Using a modified stimulated recall technique, brief clips in which issues discussed in the previous interviews emerged, or incidents which brought into sharp relief aspects of language as a tool for learning, were presented to the teachers for comment. The teachers' representations of language as a matter of competence (their students' or their own) emerged in both the pre- and post-teaching interviews, and were also evidenced in the classroom interaction data. In what follows, I present three illustrative examples – one for each component of the tripartite perspective on language for CLIL. The examples show CLIL teachers reflecting using two different types of data: the contents of the CoRe instrument, and instances of their own classroom practices, as recorded on video.

Teacher reflection on language as a curriculum concern in CLIL

Extract 12.1 comes from an interview with the science (biology) teacher based around the CoRe instrument she had completed. The interviewer (I) questions the teacher (T) about her general practices in relation to incorporating language into her planning of teaching sequences:

Extract 12.1 Maybe in English they do it that way ...

```
 1   I:   what about language,
 2        can language ever be erm a [factor=
 3   T:                              [( )
 4   I:   =in organising a [sequence=
 5   T:                     [mmm I'm afraid not
 6   I:   =of lessons or activities?
 7   T:   I ( ) say not.
 8   I:   mm
 9   T:   not in science
10   I:   mm
11   T:   maybe in English they do it that way
12   I:   mm
13   T:   but not in science (.) I mean it's the content that
14        leads me
15   I:   hm mm
16   T:   and then if I happen to find certain language points
17   I:   hm mm
18   T:   that I might think they're interesting (.) well then
19        I kind of mm focus on them a little bit more.
20   I:   mm
21   T:   but just just e::h just to follow my my science
22        contents
```

Perhaps showing an orientation to the identity of her interlocutor (a language specialist), this teacher constructs her negative response as a kind of apology (line 5). In any case, her response is clear: language is not used as a principle in organising teaching sequences, at least not in science.

The teacher quite sharply points out the division of labour in the bilingual education project in lines 11–14: identifying language goals is for English as a subject, not science. However, language is not totally ignored, as she does focus on 'certain language points' which she may 'happen to find'. The vague language with which this is expressed ('kind of', 'a little bit more') highlights the general attitude to language issues found among the teachers in the study – there is no systematic approach to language and such language attention as appears is usually incidental, it just 'comes up'. The main, almost exclusive, focus is on the 'science contents'. This was consistent across the study, as language hardly appears at all as a 'curriculum concern' in the teachers' planning and reflections. It highlights one of the issues highlighted in the literature review above: the need for teacher education and professional development to provide teachers with frameworks for the integration of content, language and literacy based on sound theoretical and methodological principles and practices.

Language as a tool for learning: reflection on classroom interaction

Extract 12.2 comes from a Year 9 (students are 14–15 years old) geography lesson on the concept of development. The students had carried out a small group activity in which they had to rank in order of importance factors which indicated that a country was more developed. The sequence below is from a longer stretch of discourse in which the teacher was conducting feedback on the outcomes of the activity, and is of interest because the teacher-led activity is at least partly 'taken over' by the students as an impromptu whole-class discussion breaks out:

Extract 12.2 Clean water

1	**T:**	number of people per doctor (0.2)
2		who chose that one (.) is was it you Cristina?
3	**S1:**	no
4	**S:**	Luis
5	**T:**	who chose that?
6	**S2:**	Irene
7	**T:**	Irene (.) ok so (.) why did you choose that (.) why
8		is that the main factor of development
9	**S3:**	because I think the wealth I think the wealth is the
10		most important because if you don't have – you don't
11		have –
12	**T:**	wealth or health?
13	**S3:**	(0.5) the::
14	**S:**	°health°
15	**T:**	health=
16	**S3:**	=health
17	**T:**	health? yes
18		(0.5)
19	**S3:**	because if you don't have (.) doctors (.) tha:t (.)
20		help you you don't know if the water is clean or
21		↑not (.)
22	**T:**	ah
23	**S3:**	an:d (.) >then< if you no – don't have any: doctor
24		(0.8) you can't=

25	**T:**	=hey, excuse me (.) are you listening?
26	**SS:**	yes
27	**T:**	hm hm very important (.) points yeah
28	**S3:**	you can't erm (2.5) erm clean the water or (.) .hh eh
29		see that this water is the – do is doing (0.9) is a –
30		is affecting you
31	**T:**	mm ok so you need a doctor as a supervisor for (.)
32		loads of activities in order to be healthy (.) ok
33		that's a good point (.) yes?
34	**S4:**	but you can know if water is clean or is not clean
35		but if you know it (.) you are not going to have
36		clean water (.) and,
37	**T:**	oh sorry sorry can you explain that again?
38	**S4:**	you can know that you can know that if you have clean
39		water or not=
40	**T:**	=you may know yeah
41	**S4:**	what what does it (1.0) what erm for what do you want
42		do you want to know if (.) if you have haven't got
43		clean water (.) because you are going to die?
44	**S3:**	( ) no (.) erm you can get a get sick (0.8)
45		because of –
46	**S4:**	yeah but you don't have the clean
47		water

The classroom interaction here follows the regular pattern for feedback following up a student-led task. The teacher asks individual students to call out their answers, and then asks them to expand on the answer by justifying it. This happens from lines 1–33. At times, the teacher scaffolds the students' language by initiating repair sequences as happens in lines 12–17. The sequence usually ends with the teacher accepting and summarising the student's response, often by highlighting the key point (31–33). However, at line 34 this sequence is interrupted by S4's objection to S3's choice of doctor as a more important factor than clean water. This leads to an extended sequence (not all shown here) in which the teacher takes a 'back seat' and a number of students take over in a discussion about whether having access to doctors or clean water are more important for health.

Extract 12.3 shows some of the teachers' reflections on this episode after watching the clip on video.

Extract 12.3 They feel confident to speak up

1	**I:**	what makes this kind of interaction happen.
2		when they start speaking sometimes to each other
3		and agreeing (.) disagreeing (.) arguing
4		and putting forward arguments (.)
5		what makes this happen, do you think.
6	**T:**	probably when they do know what they are talking
7		about, they have had time to be aware of that (.)
8		and they have had time to speak a little bit

9		with their partner so they feel confident
10		to speak up and place out their points of view.
11		so if there is this little process of working with
12		your partner or someone else and thinking (.)
13		then we get to a preliminary session to a big group
14		they feel more confident to express what they felt.

In her reflections, the teacher relates what happened in this interactional sequence to the activity they had done in small groups earlier, the ranking task. Having students do a task like this allows them to 'know what they are talking about' (lines 6–7), and gives them the chance to build their confidence by already having spoken with their partners (lines 8–9). In this teacher's reflections, we can see a relationship between the planning of lesson sequences and what can be expected in classroom interaction, especially in terms of students' spoken production. Having teachers explain and account for classroom episodes can allow them to 'get under the surface' to the methodological issues – in this case the potential for content-based activities in CLIL lessons to foster speaking skills. Here, the episode is a positive one, as a spontaneous discussion is what many teachers want to happen in their classrooms. However, such stimulated reflection can be even more useful and illuminating if the focus is on a more problematic incident, as may be more likely with novice teachers or teachers on teacher education courses.

Language as competence: reflection on students' ability

Extract 12.4 comes from the same CoRe interview with the science teacher as Extract 12.1. In this sequence, the teacher reflects on the differences in her interactional practices in relation to younger and older learners' competence in English:

Extract 12.4 I don't have to interact as much as I do with the little ones

1	**T:**	=so I'm having older students
2	**I:**	mm
3	**T:**	then it's not that different you see
4		because they are already a little bit more mature=
5	**I:**	hm mm
6	**T:**	=grownups so they are able to follow let's say
7		normal lessons
8	**I:**	hm hm mm (0.4) what do you mean by normal lessons=
9	**T:**	=normal lessons I mean normal lessons (laughs)
10		I mean I mean that they are able to follow
11		explanations and things they – I don't have to to mm
12		interact as much
13	**I:**	hm mm
14	**T:**	as I do with the little ones
15	**I:**	hm mm
16	**T:**	because of the language I mean (.) I interact because
17		of the science stuff
18	**I:**	hm mm
19	**T:**	you see not because of the language (.) with the

20		little ones that I know their English is not as good
21	**I:**	hm mm
22	**T:**	then I have to kind of do a lot of er language skills
23		and things focus a little bit more on language than
24		with the older ones
25	**I:**	yes
26	**T:**	because I think the older ones eh their level of
27		English is – is quite good to follow lessons entirely
28		in English
29	**I:**	hm mm

In her response to the interviewer's question about 'normal' lessons (line 8), the teacher explains that these are lessons in which she is free to focus on the science content ('I interact because of the science stuff' – lines 16–17), rather than scaffolding language skills as she does with the 'little ones' (Year 7 students), as she explains in lines 19–24. Thus, this teacher explicitly differentiates between two types of students in terms of their levels of competence in the L2, and constructs an account of how her classroom practices vary accordingly. In terms of what is acceptable CLIL practice, it is interesting that, for this teacher, 'normal' lessons do not include any language scaffolding as everything revolves around the content, and may also involve less interaction (lines 10–12). This kind of reflection around learners' competences and the implications for classroom practice can be used in CLIL teacher education and professional development to build an important component of teachers' knowledge: knowledge of learners as emerging bilinguals and its relation to other knowledge components such as instructional strategies and interactive practices.

Practical applications and future prospects

While research on teacher education and PD for content and language integration in CBLE is still relatively scarce, the studies reviewed above and the illustrative data extracts point to some clear implications and possible practical applications. These can be grouped in seven key themes: the time factor; the need for clear pedagogic models and frameworks; the need to build explicit meta-linguistic content knowledge of language; the need for situatedness and collaboration; the importance of data-driven reflection; the need to involve a wider range of participants; the need to build a strong and enduring professional identity. Each will be glossed in this final section.

Studies such as Escobar Urmeneta (2013) and Troyan et al. (2017) show clearly that teacher education and PD for content and language integration takes a long time. It is a slow-burning process built out of considerable frustration and trial and error. Even where teachers are given the opportunity to work with well-developed pedagogic models such as that provided by Cammarata (2016), they still struggle to find ways to craft effective and balanced lessons in which content and language/literacy goals are combined. This implies that teacher education programmes need to allow teachers many attempts to design and implement CBLE instruction.

All the existing pedagogic models for content and language integration, such as Cammarata, 2016, Llinares et al., 2012, Lyster, 2007 and Meyer et al. 2015, require high levels of metalinguistic knowledge, whether the focus is on language forms or aspects of literacy. If the focus is on language forms, as in form-focused instruction (FFI), teachers need to develop the required metalinguistic knowledge. In their study of FFI in a Spanish/English two-way immersion programme in the US, Tedick and Young (2017) concluded that 'teachers need to spend time understanding the linguistic forms and developing ways to explain those forms to different learners with clarity and consistency; materials also need to be clear and consistent' (p. 13). The teacher's reflections in Extract 12.1 also show a highly unsystematic and incidental approach to language in the context of content teaching. Thus, teacher education and PD programmes for CBLE need to devote considerable space to building up teachers' meta-linguistic knowledge, not just language forms for FFI, but also functional language for a more literacy-based type of instruction.

Content and language integration cannot be learned effectively outside situated moments of practice, whether these are adapting a piece of material, constructing a lesson plan, deciding on an assessment activity, or interacting with students in the classroom or online. As a corollary to this, neither can integration be learned and carried out in isolation from other teachers. As was seen in Extract 12.1, there is a tendency in CBLE contexts to highlight a division of labour in which strong boundaries are set up between the content and language specialists. To offset this, collaboration is an essential skill for CBLE teachers (Dale et al., 2017), and as such it should be embedded in teacher education and PD. In this respect, one model of great promise for achieving the dual aims of situating integration in the everyday tasks of teaching and ensuring collaboration is Lesson Study, as used by Cammarata and Haley (2018). This is an approach which is underexplored and underused in teacher education and PD for CBLE, and Cammarata and Haley's study is an important step in paving the way for its use. Teacher education programmes could, where the logistics permit, allow groups of content and language teachers to work together on integrating content and language objectives in lessons, observe these lessons (with a particular focus on how learners react), and engage in dialogic reflection on the lessons, with a view to improving their design, delivery and learner outcomes.

Where possible, reflective dialogue should take place around specific examples of practice, that is, it should be data-driven (Mann and Walsh, 2017). Examples of practice can be drawn from the teachers' own contexts, as seen in Extracts 12.2 and 12.3, or they can be fragments of teaching (on video and/or transcribed) from other contexts. The models of content and language knowledge (common and specialised) could be used by teacher educators to structure the reflections on these extracts, drawing attention to, raising awareness of, and aiming to build practical knowledge of, a range of uses of language to scaffold and promote content and language learning.

Turning to research on CBLE, Dalton-Puffer (2018) points out that most internationally-available research has been carried out by what she describes as 'language people'. There has been a lack of involvement of researchers from other subject areas. This can also be extended to research on CBLE teacher education and PD. Content and language integration cannot be left to just the language experts, but teacher educators and researchers in other subjects taught in CBLE programmes need to be involved. It is true that much of the research has identified shortcomings in language/literacy knowledge of content teachers (and language teachers too), but less attention has been paid to the content knowledge dimensions. It would be a disservice to the future prospects of successful CBLE programmes if the 'content' part is left to the experts in that discipline, while language knowledge and pedagogy are delivered in separate modules. Teacher education and PD for CBLE will be much more effective and enriched if it is embedded in contexts where teacher educators and researchers in both language and non-language subjects work together.

A consistent theme running through the research on CBLE teacher education and PD is the need for teachers to develop an identity which takes them beyond simply being a 'language' or 'content' teacher. They need to see themselves as professionals with a dual role: responsible for their students' achievement of content-learning outcomes and their language/literacy development. This also needs to be adapted to all stages of learning, to move away from the idea hinted at in Extract 12.4, that language learning is somehow 'finished' when learners are able to follow lessons. However, as was seen in Cammarata and Tedick's (2012) study, building a solid identity as a content *and* language teacher is a long struggle, and these inter-related changes to knowledge and identity do not come easily. Dale et al.'s (2017) framework provides a menu of choices which could be used by language teacher educators and student teachers for reflection on what kinds of identities are available to them, depending on their orientations to language (meaning/form) or content (culture/specific subject). Because it identifies four broad approaches to content and language integration, the framework can also act as a guide for the design of CBLE teacher education and PD programmes. For example, an approach which combines a focus on subject-matter as content and a focus on language as form, will prepare teachers to focus on subject-specific language.

To conclude, research and practice in teacher education and PD for CBLE can be said to be still in their infancy, although there has been a recent surge of interest. There is a need for an intensified effort in both practice and research and much more fluent channels of communication between them. Effective teacher education and PD for CBLE are not possible without clear pedagogic models and conceptual frameworks, and research-based knowledge of the processes by which the knowledge and professional identities required for content and language integration intertwine and develop together. However, these models need to be grounded in the everyday realities of teachers engaged in the tasks of integrating content and language in their instruction, and in those of teacher educators supporting their professional development. The popularity of the different forms of CBLE around the world shows no signs of abating. However, the main threat to the sustainability of these programmes is the shortage of suitably skilled teachers. This can only be addressed by a growth in the commitment to long-term, research-based, situated, collaborative, reflective and identity-fostering teacher education and professional development.

Further reading

Ball, P., Kelly, K. and Clegg, J. (2015) *Putting CLIL into Practice*. Oxford: Oxford University Press.
   This is a very useful tool for CLIL teacher educators as it provides much-needed practical advice and frameworks for the integration of content and language. It covers such important topics as lesson and unit planning, materials design, and assessment. It also stands out for its inclusion of a chapter specifically dedicated to teacher education in CLIL.

Cammarata, L. (ed.) (2016) *Content-based Foreign Language Teaching: Curriculum and Pedagogy for Developing Advanced Thinking and Literacy Skills*. New York: Routledge.
   This edited volume is extremely valuable for teacher educators in all CBLE contexts as it provides a wealth of ideas for curricular design and pedagogical practice and presents a vision of content and language integrated classrooms as cognitively stimulating environments where advanced thinking and academic skills are given equal status to language skills.

Genesee, F. and Hamayan, E. (2016) *CLIL in Context: Practical Guidance for Educators*. Cambridge/New York: Cambridge University Press.
   This book is an excellent overview of the key issues in content and language integration and is relevant to a wide range of CBLE contexts. It is a valuable resource for teacher educators in all CBLE contexts, who can draw on it to establish key principles, tools for planning content and language integrated lessons, and for advice on how to coordinate and integrate the different participants in CBLE programmes.

References

Barkhuizen, G. (ed.) (2017) *Reflections on Language Teacher Identity Research*. Abingdon: Routledge.

British Council (2015) 'Formación inicial para profesores de programas bilingües en inglés: políticas, prácticas y recomendaciones'. Seminar, University of Alcalá, 2–3 February.

Cammarata, L. (2016) 'Foreign language education and the development of inquiry-driven language programs: key challenges and curricular planning strategies', in Cammarata, L. (ed.) *Content-based Foreign Language Teaching: Curriculum and Pedagogy for Developing Advanced Thinking and Literacy Skills*. New York: Routledge: 123–143.

Cammarata, L. and Haley, C. (2017) 'Integrated Content, Language, and Literacy Instruction in a Canadian French Immersion Context: A Professional Development Journey'. *International Journal of Bilingual Education and Bilingualism*, 21(3) 332–348.

Cammarata, L. and Tedick, D. J. (2012) 'Balancing Content and Language in Instruction: The Experience of Immersion Teachers'. *The Modern Language Journal*, 96(2) 251–269.

Cenoz, J. (2015) 'Content-Based Instruction and Content and Language Integrated Learning: The Same or Different?'. *Language, Culture and Curriculum*, 28(1) 8–24.

Cheung, Y. L., Ben Said, S. and Park, K. (2015) *Advances and Current Trends in Language Teacher Identity Research*. Abingdon: Routledge.

Dale, L., Oostdam, R. J. and Verspoor, M. (2017) 'Searching for Identity and Focus: Towards an Analytical Framework for Language Teachers in Bilingual Education'. *International Journal of Bilingual Education and Bilingualism*, 21(3) 366–383.

Dalton-Puffer, C. (2018) 'Postscriptum: Research Pathways in CLIL/ Immersion Instructional Practices and Teacher Development'. *International Journal of Bilingual Education and Bilingualism*, 21(3) 384–387.

Dearden, J. (2015) *English as a Medium of Instruction: A Growing Global Phenomenon*. London: The British Council. Available online: <www.britishcouncil.org/sites/default/files/e484_emi_cover_option_3_final_web.pdf> (accessed 11 May, 2019).

Dobson, A., Pérez Murillo, M. D. and Johnstone, R. M. (2010) *Bilingual Education Project Spain: Evaluation Report*. Madrid: Gobierno de España Ministerio de Educación and British Council (Spain).

Escobar Urmeneta, C. (2013) 'Learning to Become a CLIL Teacher: Teaching, Reflection and Professional Development'. *International Journal of Bilingual Education and Bilingualism*, 16(3) 334–353.

Escobar Urmeneta, C. and Walsh, S. (2017) 'Classroom interactional competence in content and language integrated learning', in Llinares, A. and Morton, T. (eds) *Applied Linguistics Perspectives on CLIL*. Amsterdam: John Benjamins: 183–200.

Eurydice (2006) *Content and Language Integrated Learning (CLIL) at School in Europe*. Brussels: Eurydice.

Gray, J. and Morton, T. (2018) *Social Interaction and English Language Teacher Identity*. Edinburgh: Edinburgh University Press.

Leung, C. (2001) 'English as an Additional Language: Distinct Language Focus or Diffused Curriculum Concerns?'. *Language and Education*, 15(1) 33–55.

Llinares, A., Morton, T. and Whittaker, R. (2012) *The Roles of Language in CLIL*. Cambridge: Cambridge University Press.

Loughran, J., Mulhall, P. and Berry, A. (2004) 'In Search of Pedagogical Content Knowledge in Science: Developing Ways of Articulating and Documenting Professional Practice'. *Journal of Research in Science Teaching*, 41(4) 370–391.

Lyster, R. (2007) *Learning and Teaching Languages Through Content: A Counterbalanced Approach*. Amsterdam: Benjamins.

Lyster, R. (2016) *Vers une approche intégrée en immersion*. Montréal: Les Éditions CEC.

Mann, S. and Walsh, S. (2017) *Reflective Practice in English Language Teaching: Research-Based Principles and Practices*. Abingdon: Routledge.

Meyer, O., Coyle, D., Halbach, A., Schuck, K. and Ting, T. (2015) 'A Pluriliteracies Approach to Content and Language Integrated Learning – Mapping Learner Progressions in Knowledge Construction and Meaning-Making'. *Language, Culture and Curriculum*, 28(1) 41–57.

Morton, T. (2012) *Teachers' knowledge about language and classroom interaction in content and language integrated learning.* Unpublished thesis, Universidad Autónoma de Madrid, Spain.

Morton, T. (2013) 'Critically evaluating materials for CLIL: practitioners' perspectives and practices', in Gray, J. (ed.) *Critical Perspectives on Language Teaching Materials.* Basingstoke: Palgrave: 137–160.

Pappa, S., Moate, J., Ruohotie-Lyhty, M. and Eteläpelto, A. (2017) 'Teacher Agency Within The Finnish CLIL Context : Tensions And Resources'. *International Journal of Bilingual Education and Bilingualism,* 65 61–70.

Pérez Cañado, M. L. (2016) 'Teacher Training Needs for Bilingual Education: In-Service Teacher Perceptions'. *International Journal of Bilingual Education and Bilingualism,* 19(3) 266–295.

Tedick, D. J. and Wesely, P. M. (2015) 'A Review of Research on Content-Based Foreign/Second Language Education in US K-12 Contexts'. *Language, Culture and Curriculum,* 28(1) 25–40.

Tedick, D. J. and Young, A. I. (2017) 'Two-Way Immersion Students' Home Languages, Proficiency Levels, and Responses to Form-Focused Instruction'. *International Journal of Bilingual Education and Bilingualism,* 21(3) 303–318.

Troyan, F. J., Cammarata, L. and Martel, J. (2017) 'Integration PCK: Modeling the Knowledge(s) Underlying a World Language Teacher's Implementation of CBI'. *Foreign Language Annals,* 50(2) 458–476.

Walsh, S. (2011) *Exploring Classroom Discourse: Language in Action.* Abingdon: Routledge.

13

The 'non-native' teacher

Ali Fuad Selvi

Introduction

Over the past couple of decades, there has been a growing interest in understanding, problematizing and reconceptualizing dominant approaches describing the English language, defining English language teaching professionals, and informing the broader field of English Language Teaching (ELT). Scholars adopt diverse conceptual, theoretical and analytical frameworks to scrutinize the complexity of identity, instruction, use and interaction. The overarching purpose of this chapter is to showcase the intertwined discourses, ideologies and connections across these areas, and more specifically, to destabilize some of the perceived and ascribed knowledge, skills, behaviours and practices traditionally predicated upon 'native' and 'non-native' English-speaking professionals in ELT. Only then, I contend, will we be able to grasp the vitality of English language teacher education (ELTE) for ELT professionals from diverse backgrounds, and advance the professional stature of ELT profession(als) beyond such idealized and essentialized categories. Furthermore, in this complex picture, ELTE has a substantial role and importance in promoting systemic pedagogical and professional responses for a refined understanding of teacher identity, ownership of language and instructional competencies (Selvi, 2016).

English and English language teaching in a changing world

The global expansion of the English language is a result of several interrelated factors: the processes of cultural and economic globalization, broader power relationships (e.g., colonial exploitations, contemporary inequalities, and neoliberal ideologies), domain-specific implications (e.g., commerce, culture, technology, travel, and religion) and trajectories across boundaries (e.g., (in)voluntary migration, transnational mobility, border-crossing practices and intercultural communication) (Pennycook, 2016; Selvi, 2016). From a linguistic standpoint, English language is now characterized as 'the first truly global language' (Crystal, 2012), and even 'the zeitgeist' in today's globalizing world (Mauranen, 2009).

The present-day 'triumph' of the English language across the globe has several important manifestations:

- English, as a language of globalization, has a profound role, presence and impact in various spheres of life, and is conceived as an important asset in the participation in the interconnected/interdependent global economy;
- In addition to *de rigueur* portrayal of English as an idealized linguistic key to a better future, it is criticized as 'a language which creates barriers as much as it presents possibilities' (Pennycook, 2016: 26) whose global spread 'contribut[es] to significant social, political, and economic inequalities' (Tollefson, 2000: 8),
- In response to growing demands for English and English-medium education, governments and policy makers spearhead projects and educational reforms to equip individuals with stronger links to the English language (Ferguson, 2013); and
- Transnational and transcultural uses, users, teachers, contexts and functions of English in an increasingly superdiverse world (Blommaert & Rampton, 2011) have pluralized the language (from *the* English language to World Englishes).

Collectively, these interconnected manifestations resulted in an unprecedented demand for E(LT), and concomitantly (in)formed the prevalence of global flows of discourses shaping the knowledge base of ELT professionals (regarding the nature, use, teaching and learning of English) via the professional literature in linguistics, second language acquisition (SLA), and ELT methodology (Yazan, 2018).

Within the dominant worldviews and discourses underpinning globalized ELT, there has always been an ongoing debate on how language ownership, use and instruction are conceptualized. Traditionally, the fundamental pillars constituting ELT– as an activity, profession and *bona fide* area of scholarly inquiry – have been under the decisive and destructive influences of sets of binaries (e.g., 'us/them', 'local/expatriate', 'centre/periphery'. Perhaps, most significant and interesting of all these dichotomously juxtaposed constructs of being, becoming and doing is 'native speaker (NS)/non-native speaker (NNS)' (and concomitantly, 'native English-speaking Teachers (NESTs)/non-native English-speaking teachers (NNESTs)). These binary categories are value-laden, identity-shaping, and confidence-affecting *a priori* definitions and distributions of linguistic, cultural, and academic authority and superiority to one idealized group, and thereby othering the identity negotiations of individuals by establishing and reifying borders of identity about who individuals 'were', 'are', 'will', 'could' and/or 'should' be and become as learners, users, and professionals of English (Rudolph, 2012, 2016; Rudolph et al., 2015).

The origins of the 'NS' construct dates back to the era of 'nation-state/colonial governmentality' (eighteenth–nineteenth centuries) propagating *monoglossic language ideologies* and positioning *monolingualism as the norm*, and thereby idealizing the NS as someone who inherited a particular language as a birthright and was charged with the task of protecting it from contamination, as the exclusive owner of a national language (Flores & Aneja, 2017: 442). As an extension of the 'one nation, one language' doctrine, the imperialistic orientation to impose ways of being, becoming and doing upon individuals served as an ideological foundation on which ELT was predicated (Yazan & Rudolph, 2018). Parallel to the increasing need for language teaching professionals worldwide, yet another divisive binary burgeoned in the field of ELT–native English-speaking teacher (NEST)/non-native English-speaking teacher (NNEST).

The 'idealized NS' construct (and 'NEST') in ELT has traditionally been conceptualized as White, Western, (often) male, middle-class, (often) monolingual individual living in urban spaces and endowed with the uncontested privilege of linguistic, cultural and pedagogical authority to serve as the benchmark by which various facets of the ELT enterprise (e.g., theory, research, learning, teaching, publishing, instructional materials, assessment, teacher training and hiring practices) might be defined and/or measured (Kubota & Lin, 2009). By proxy, 'NNSs' (and concomitantly, 'NNESTs'), on the other hand, are referred to as individuals whose linguistic, cultural and pedagogical capabilities as language users and teachers are defined *vis-à-vis* their 'NS'/'NEST' 'other', perpetually confined into the prefix of 'non-', and therefore are often associated with discrimination and marginalization of professional identities and personas. In summary, the 'idealized NS' construct has a set of damaging consequences at the nexus of ELT and applied linguistics:

- places 'ownership of English' (Widdowson, 1994) and 'default expertise' (Canagarajah, 1999) in the hands of *an idealized native speaker-hearer* (Chomsky, 1965);
- prioritizes 'idealized NS' as the universal linguistic and cultural target for acquisition, use, and instruction irrespective of language teaching and learning context (Canagarajah, 2007);
- permeates into second language acquisition (SLA) theory and research (e.g., *interlanguage* and *fossilization* Selinker (1972); *comparative fallacy* (Bley-Vroman, 1983); *interaction hypothesis* (Long, 1983) and *ultimate attainment* (Birdsong, 1992));
- shapes pedagogical theory and research (e.g., *monolingual principle* (Howatt, 1984)), and forms the 'bedrock of transnationalized ELT' (Leung, 2005, p. 128);
- influences various aspects of the ELT enterprise, such as theory, inquiry, curriculum and materials development, assessment, instruction and professional development, as well as hiring practices (Llurda, 2016; Rivers, 2016; Ruecker & Ives, 2015; Selvi, 2010).

Each of these points is a building block towards what I call *compulsory native speakerism* – a term, similar to *compulsory heterosexuality* (Rich, 1980), which refers to the set of institutionalized practices, values and beliefs that normalize and impose the construction, maintenance and perpetuation of discourses that juxtapose language user ('NS'/'NNS'), and concomitantly, language teacher ('NEST'/'NNEST') status in various facets of the ELT enterprise. Consequently, this leads to a pervasive professional ideology serving as Damocles' sword hanging over the ELT profession(als) (Selvi, 2014), often based upon 'automatic extrapolation from competent speaker to competent teacher based on linguistic grounds alone' (Seidlhofer, 1999: 236). For many language teaching professionals, this may generate a set of pathological discourses, such as *inferiority complex* (Medgyes, 1994), *I-am-not-a-native-speaker syndrome* (Suarez, 2000), *Stockholm syndrome* (Llurda, 2009) or *impostor syndrome* (Bernat, 2009), all of which have damaging effects on teachers' persona, personal/professional self-esteem, and even in-class performance. This is also reflected in, what Phillipson (1992) called, the *NS fallacy*, or 'the belief that the ideal teacher of English is a native speaker' (p. 217), which may be seen an extension of *native speakerism*, 'an established belief that native-speaker teachers represent a "Western culture" from which springs the ideals both of the English language and of English language teaching methodology' (Holliday, 2005: 6).

Even though 80 per cent of the entire population of 15 million ELT professionals worldwide, estimated to be around 12 million, are considered to be 'NNESTs' (Canagarajah, 2005; Freeman et al., 2015), 'their identities, roles and contributions to the profession have, for the most part, been [still] marginalized' in ELT (Llurda, 2016: 51). Departing from this premise, over the past couple of decades, scholars, at the nexus of ELT and applied linguistics, began to interrogate the *de facto* authority and prestige ascribed to the 'NS as target' model for language learning and teaching, as well as the pervasive ideological chasm between 'NSs'/'NNSs' (and concomitantly, 'NESTs'/'NNESTs'). While some argued that 'the native speaker exists only as a figment of linguists' imagination' (Paikeday, 1985: 12) and pronounced it 'dead', others conceived it as 'a fine myth' that we need it 'as a model, a goal, almost an inspiration; but it is useless as a measure; it will not help us define our goals' (Davies, 1991: 157). Although 'it no longer makes any sense to differentiate between the native speaker and the nonnative speaker' (Swales, 1993: 284), and subscription to the 'idealized NS' benchmark is impractical, inappropriate, and unfair (Smolder, 2009), 'it happens to be nonetheless socially present, and therefore, potentially meaningful as an area of research in applied linguistics' (Moussu & Llurda, 2008: 316).

Responses to move beyond idealization and essentialization have traversed the existing borders of scholarly inquiry, and transformed itself into a professional movement, known as the *NNEST movement* (Braine, 2010; Kamhi-Stein, 2016), operationalized at theoretical, practical, and professional levels in ELT (Selvi, 2014). The NNEST movement is critically situated at the nexus of TESOL and applied linguistics with a motivation to reconceptualize the value-laden, ideology-driven and professionally imposing discourses of NSism defining the legitimacy in language learning and teaching. It acknowledges, supports, and promotes ethnic, racial, cultural, religious, gender, and linguistic diversity in TESOL, both as a profession (e.g., issues of professionalism, standards, teacher education, hiring, and workplace) and as an activity (e.g., benchmark for learning, teaching, assessment, methodology, and material development). More specifically, the movement resulted in skyrocketing of *research efforts* (e.g., manuscripts, research articles, opinion pieces, presentations, workshops, seminars and colloquia in conferences, and theses and dissertations), *policy and advocacy initiatives* (e.g., the establishment of the NNEST Caucus/Interest Section in TESOL International Association, advocacy groups within local TESOL affiliates such as the Washington Area TESOL NNEST Caucus (WATESOL) and the California TESOL (CATESOL) Non-Native Language Educators' Issues Interest Group, white papers and position statements), and *teaching activities* (e.g., integrating issues of language ownership, learning, use, instruction into in-/pre-service ELTE curricula by means of readings, discussions, tasks, and assignments). Parallel to the expansion of information technologies and social networking sites, new advocacy-orientated professional groups have begun to emerge in online environments (e.g., NNEST Facebook Group, TEFL Equity Advocates website, Multilinguals in TESOL Blog, among others).

These entities and online initiatives have been highly instrumental in generating institutionalized advocacy efforts and responses against inequity, marginalization and discrimination in the ELT profession. More specifically, TESOL International Association passed two resolutions entitled 'A TESOL Statement on Nonnative Speakers of English and Hiring Practices' (TESOL, 1992) and 'Position Statement against Discrimination of Nonnative Speakers of English in the Field of TESOL' (TESOL, 2006). In recent years, local teacher organizations in the United States (e.g., CATESOL), Canada (e.g., BC TEAL–British Columbia Teachers of English as an Additional Language) and Europe (e.g., TESOL Spain) have raised their voices against discrimination in ELT (TESOL Spain, 2016; BC TEAL, 2014; CATESOL, 2013). Although these institutionalized initiatives and responses contribute to the ELT profession defined by equity and professionalism for all, inequalities still remain as bitter realities of the ELT profession, directed at both NESTs (Houghton & Rivers, 2013; Rivers, 2016; Rudolph, 2012, 2018) and NNESTs (Mahboob & Golden, 2013; Selvi, 2010) alike.

English language teacher education in a changing world

In the multifaceted, complex, and messy situation surrounding ELT profession(als), ELTE has a vital role in developing teachers' professional knowledge-base and promoting their sociohistorically situated negotiations of identities and lived experiences as translinguistic/ transcultural professionals aligned with the needs of the present-day sociolinguistic realities of the glocalized world (Selvi & Rudolph, 2017). The idealization and essentialization of NS as a language teacher not only perpetuates the asymmetrical power relations by making predefined causal generalizations about what a teacher is (or lack thereof) and can (or cannot) do, but also pushes the field of ELT away from professionalism by adopting reductionist and simplistic ways to define teacher competencies and effectiveness in a decontextualized fashion. For this reason, it is imperative to prioritize teacher education and professionalism over nativeness. If we argue that 'people do not become qualified to teach English merely because it is their mother tongue' (Maum, 2002: 1), we should also argue that 'people do not become qualified to teach English merely because it is their second language' (Selvi, 2014: 589). If the former is *native speaker fallacy*, then the latter is the *nonnative speaker fallacy*.

In a time characterized by winds of change in the foundational pillars of ELT enterprise, it is more critical than ever to translate such idea(l)s into viable, sustainable, and contextually-sensitive practices for the development of in-service and pre-service teachers. This view is also highlighted by Galloway and Rose (2015) who underscored the vitality of teacher education as a potential barrier to achieving Kumaravadivelu's (2012) *epistemic break* from native English-speaking norms. Serving as an intellectual, professional and *praxization* bridge between teachers' past histories, present realities and future trajectories, ELTE programs have an important role in 'approaching learner, user and instructor identity, introducing inquiry and practice beyond the "idealized NS" construct, and addressing equity in ELT contexts around the globe' (Selvi & Rudolph, 2017: 247). In the remainder of this chapter, I will outline a set of practical suggestions that may be used to forge new pathways sensitive to teachers' sociohistorically situated negotiations of identities, lived experiences, and professional practices as translinguistic, transcultural, and transnational professionals. It is my hope that these suggestions will spearhead some positive changes in ELTE, which is recalcitrant to the discourses of multilingual turn in applied linguistics (Flores & Aneja, 2017), and therefore, characterized by the paucity of sustainable pedagogical practices for in-service and pre-service teachers (Matsuda, 2017).

Practical applications in/for ELTE

This section presents a set of major principles undergirding ELTE through the lens of teacher identity, followed by brief discussions refining how these principles inform specific practices, experiences and applications to foster individuals' diverse ways of being and becoming as teachers.

Promote reflexivity regarding subjectivity and positionality with regards to personal/professional identity

One of the overarching goals of ELTE programs, especially at the pre-service levels, should be identifying, externalizing and building upon individuals' preconceived notions about surrounding teaching, learning, students, teachers and schooling. Lortie (1975) used the term 'apprenticeship of observation' to describe teacher candidates' initial values, beliefs and practices developed through the extended experience during their prior education as students. In order to further understand their beliefs and values, teachers may engage in what Edge (2011) calls *retrospective reflexivity* (the effect of work on the person) and *prospective reflexivity* (the effect of the person on the work) through engaging in acts of externalization about their stance regarding 'NS'/'NNS' (and 'NEST'/'NNEST') constructs. For example, through writing their own narratives/autobiographies or responding to a set of guided questions from Kamhi-Stein (2014) (e.g., 'Who is a qualified teacher?', 'What are the personal/professional qualities of an effective teacher?', 'What is the relationship between language proficiency and language teaching?', 'How do you perceive yourself as a language user/teacher?' etc.), teacher candidates may be probed to reflect upon their own previous schooling and language learning experiences and establish a link between themselves, their identities and their own sociohistorical experiences. At the end of the semester/program, teacher candidates may also be given a chance to revisit their auto-biographies in the light of their experiences in the course/program, and asked to comment on their future professional goals and trajectories. Collectively, these narratives will afford spaces of contextualized and fluidly critical-practical negotiations of linguistic, cultural, and professional identity (Selvi & Rudolph, 2017). Another strategy to help concretize and problematize teacher candidates' stance on teacher identity is through utilizing Kamhi-Stein's (2014) discussion of various positions on 'NS' and 'NNS' labels, namely: (1) Native English Speaking (NES) profes-sionals and Non-Native English Speaking (NNES) professionals are different; (2) With difficulty, NNS professionals can become NS professionals; and (3) NS and NNS labels are perceived as problematic. Teacher educators may organize small/large-group discussions or reflection papers as a springboard for further discussion with regards to their professional identities. In sum, these positions may afford teachers with a framework in the enactment of their personal/professional stance, accompanied by their operational definitions and rationales.

Offer opportunities to encounter, problematize and deconstruct native speakerism

Teacher educators may carefully utilize case scenarios, job advertisements and vignettes (Cop-land et al., 2016) that showcase instances of compulsory native speakerism and destabilize these binary juxtapositions embedded in these contested labels and categories of identity. Below are some examples that showcase the fluidity of teacher experiences that may not be captured using the terms NESTs/NNESTs (Selvi, 2018):

- You have been living and teaching in Turkey for 12 years and feel yourself a part of the local context, both culturally and linguistically. Is it fair to call you an 'outsider'?
- You have professional experience and expertise in teaching all kinds of language skills. Is it fair to ask you to teach only 'certain skills'?
- You are described as an 'NNEST' but you are not even considered for a teaching position because you are neither 'local' (citizen), nor a 'NEST'. How would this make you feel?
- You are described as a 'NEST' with experience and expertise but another 'NEST' with no such background and credentials was given the exact same job. How would this make you feel?
- Your 'NEST' colleague is neither considered for a teaching position nor for a promo-tion because s/he is not 'local' (citizen). Is it still fair to argue that 'NESTs are universally privileged'?
- You are a 'NEST' with experience and expertise in teaching ELT but you are not consid-ered for a teaching position because you do not come from the US/UK. Is it still fair to argue that 'NESTs are universally privileged'?

Considering that the 'idealized NS' construct is taken for granted by many stakeholders compris-ing ELT enterprise (e.g., users, instructors, teacher educators) and (in)forming ELT practices (in the form of norms, benchmarks, instructional qualities of instructors), these vignettes may serve as powerful departing points for transformative journeys for teacher-learners in these programs. For example, teacher educators may organise in–class discussions/debates around these critical cases, ask teacher-learners to write reaction/reflection papers based on them or embed these vignettes in the snippets of lived experiences of ELT professionals to be discussed, deconstructed and re-appropriated. What lies at the crux of these practices is the transformative orientation destabilizing widely held beliefs about who individuals 'were', 'are', 'will', 'could' and/or 'should' be and become as learners, users, and professionals of English (Rudolph, 2012, 2016; Rudolph et al., 2015).

Create an alternative space for the negotiation of professional identity

Teacher educators may feel the necessity to empower teachers, both at pre- and in-service levels, with an alternative space, framework and discourse used in the negotiation of their professional identity. One example of such frameworks is Pasternak and Bailey's (2004) *continua of language proficiency and professional preparation* (see Figure 13.1), which offers an example of a theoretical framework that aims to move beyond the problematic labels of NS/NNS (and NEST/NNEST).

According to this model, teachers in Quadrant 1 are proficient in the target language and are professionally prepared, whereas teachers in Quadrant 4 are neither proficient in the target language nor professionally prepared as language teachers. Those teachers falling in Quadrant 2 are professionally prepared as language teachers yet not proficient in the target language, and teachers in Quadrant 3 are proficient in the target language but not professionally prepared as language teachers. What makes this model interesting is that it places key qualities of effective teachers (i.e. linguistic proficiency and professional preparation) on a continuum, without 'NS'/'NNS' (and 'NEST'/'NNEST') serving as endpoints.

This model may be introduced by teacher educators as an alternative to contested terms such as 'NESTs/NNESTs' and used to inform practices in ELTE programs. To be more specific, Pasternak and Bailey (2004) argue that being a native speaker of a language is not the same as competent in teaching that language, and that teachers, irrespective of their (problematic) labels, should be not only proficient in the language they are teaching but also professionally prepared as language teachers. Furthermore, they underscored the importance of both *declarative knowledge* (the knowledge about the target language, culture, and teaching) and *procedural knowledge* (the

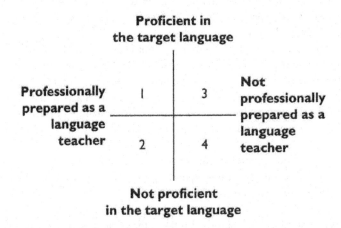

Figure 13.1 Pasternak and Bailey's (2004) continua of target language proficiency and professional preparation
Source: Kamhi-Stein (2014: 588).

knowledge about how to use the target language, to teach in culturally appropriate ways, and to behave appropriately in the target language) for language teachers to serve effectively in the classroom. Therefore, ELTE programs should support teachers' development in these areas through coursework (e.g., courses) and fieldwork experiences (e.g., teaching practices). As echoed by Doğançay-Aktuna and Hardman (2018), 'all teachers need to integrate training (pedagogical skill development) with disciplinary knowledge and understanding, which will be different for every type of teacher, as these qualities emerge from their particular contexts of teaching.'

Deal with ambivalence, resistance, reluctance, and indifference

Considering that ELTE is a collaborative activity distributed across various settings and stakeholders, it is quite plausible to come across individuals (teacher educators and teachers) with a wide variety of commitment, involvement and engagement to move beyond essentialized and idealized binaries of being, becoming, and doing (Selvi, 2016). Teacher educators may not be informed about essentialized binaries in ELT and/or their connection to ELTE (i.e. unawareness), may be in epistemological and conceptual disagreement with this paradigm (i.e. disagreement, rejection and resistance) or may be informed yet see no value within the scope of ELTE (i.e. ambivalance). As Matsuda (2017) acknowledges, the transformation may be found challenging and even threatening for teachers since 'in most cases, they are the successful products of English language and language arts curricula that are based on the traditional view of English' (p. xv). Therefore, it is imperative to scrutinize *institutional parameters* (e.g., curriculum, vision/mission of the program, programmatic rules, materials), and *actors* (e.g., teachers, teacher educators, mentor teachers, language learners) involved in ELTE programs. Any ambivalence, resistance, reluctance, and indifference (at the levels of professional dispositions and pedagogic practices) may be treated as a springboard to establish intellectual and professional dialogue and spaces for negotiation. Teacher educators may carefully scrutinize their immediate contexts and generate solutions for any ambivalence, resistance, reluctance, and indifference related to their practices. Below are some guiding questions for teacher educators:

- Who are my teacher-learners?
- How do they define their own identities?
- What is their position(ality) on these terms ('NESTs'/'NNESTs') and associated values and practices?
- Are they aware of problems associated with these terms ('NESTs'/'NNESTs')?
- Does my program offer alternative spaces and experiences for identity negotiations?
- How do/did my teacher-learners respond to moving beyond essentialized binaries?
- (If resisting against it) what are the reasons or rationales behind their viewpoints?
- What can I (as a teacher educator) or we (as an ELTE program) do more to sustain a more inclusive environment?

Integrate Global Englishes Language Teaching frameworks and approaches into the knowledge-base of teachers

It is recommended that ELTE programs adopt a non-deficit orientation to linguistic hybridity, variability and fluidity in a globalized world. This is an important step in expanding the sociocultural knowledge base of ELT professionals who are charged with the task of preparing language users who can successfully navigate within and across linguistic and intercultural borders and boundaries. Since 'idealized and essentialized NS-as-target' ideology is a common thread

Table 13.1 Differences between ELT and GELT

	ELT	GELT
Target interlocutor	NSs of English	NSs and NNSs of English
Owners	NSs of English	NSs and NNSs of English
Target culture	Fixed NS culture	Fluid cultures
Teachers	NESTs and NNEST (same L1)	NESTs and NNESTs (both same and different L1s)
Norms	NS and concept of standard English	Diversity, flexibility and multiple forms of competence
Role model	NSs	Successful ELF users
Materials	Native English and NSs of English	Native English, non-native English, ELF, and ELF communities and contexts
First language and own culture	Seen as hindrance and source of interference	Seen as a resource
Ideology	Underpinned by an exclusive and ethnocentric view of English	Underpinned by an inclusive Global Englishes perspective

Source: Galloway and Rose (2015: 208).

that runs through various strata of the ELT enterprise, teacher educators may adopt the principles of *Global Englishes (GE)* in language teaching, known as *Global Englishes Language Teaching* (GELT). GELT serves as a comprehensive pedagogical approach aiming to move beyond decontextualized and NS-centric discourses in ELT (see Table 13.1).

By promoting the shift from the traditional ELT to GELT through coursework and field practices, teacher educators may use these principles as overarching signposts to be used to re-examine and re-orchestrate existing practices, and inform future experiences and structures (e.g., curricula, course objectives and scope, tools of assessment, practicum experience, among others) in such a way as to promote equity, diversity and professionalism in the negotiation and construction of identity and practice. Today, teacher educators may actualize this transformation at various levels and utilizing various options (showcased in Matsuda, 2017):

- frameworks and approaches coalescing GEs with ELTE practices, e.g., 'situated meta-praxis model of EIL teacher education' (Doğançay-Aktuna & Hardman, 2017), 'ELF-aware teacher education' (Bayyurt & Sifakis, 2015) or paradigms with similar goals such as 'translanguaging' (García & Wei, 2014);
- ELTE programs orchestrated around the idea(l)s of GEs, e.g., *Program of English as an International Language* at Monash University, Australia (Sharifian & Marlina, 2012), and the *College of World Englishes* at Chukyo University, Japan (D'Angelo, 2012);
- courses dedicated to teaching GEs, e.g., *Global Englishes for Language Teaching* at the University of Edinburgh, Scotland (Galloway, 2017); *Global English* at Middle East Technical University, Northern Cyprus Campus, e.g., Galloway (2017); Selvi (2017);
- GEs-informed courses on another ELT topic, e.g., Rose (2017).

Promote teacher education, equity, and professionalism for all in ELT

Because the current level of professionalism in ELT is far from the desired state, it is imperative to infuse issues of inclusivity, diversity and professionalism into ELTE programs, both theoretically and practically (Selvi, Rudolph & Üzüm, 2016). On a theoretical level, teacher educators may align coursework, class discussions, activities and assignments with a particular focus on introducing models beyond categorical binaries (e.g., Pasternak and Bailey's 2004 model), problematizing uniform NEST/NNEST experiences (e.g., Rudolph et al., 2015), and scrutinizing the fluidity of privilege and marginalization beyond categorical binaries (Rudolph, 2018). On a practical level, a stronger commitment to the professionalism may be further promoted by encouraging all teachers to take active role in their immediate professional contexts as well as professional language teacher associations at local and international levels. First-hand involvement in these institutions (e.g., leadership roles and volunteer experiences) will boost a heightened sense of professionalism and an explicit commitment to innovation, incorporation, collaboration, and inclusivity in ELT. Advocating for equity, professionalism, experience and expertise over dichotomously juxtaposed and contested labels is a win-win for teachers and the professional stature of ELT. Therefore, teacher educators should promote issues of equity and professionalism for all in their courses, and actively encourage teacher-learners to take leadership roles (e.g., introducing the roles and functions of such organizations, inviting representatives of teacher associations to the program as guest speakers, nominating teacher-learners for various positions in such organizations, and supporting their applications by writing letters of recommendation and/or serving as professional mentors).

Develop teachers' professional language proficiency skills

Considering that 'general language proficiency' encapsulates assumptions about instructional qualities and effectiveness (and thereby perpetuate the 'non'-nativeness), and 'language fluency' traditionally acts as a marker of teaching competence (Freeman, 2017), there is a pressing necessity to reconceptualize the notion of 'language proficiency' for teaching and the 'language teacher/user' in the classroom. Departing from this premise, Freeman et al. (2015) developed *English-for-Teaching* (see Figure 13.2), a new model based on the 'reconceptualization of teacher language proficiency, not as general English proficiency but as a specialized subset of language skills required to prepare and teach lessons' (p. 129).

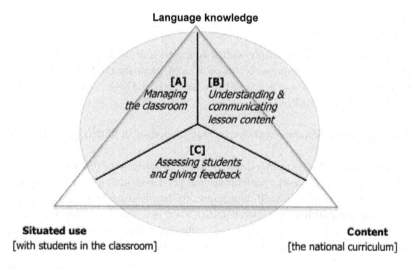

Figure 13.2 Functional areas of classroom language use in English-for-Teaching
Source: Freeman et al. (2015: 135).

This fresh perspective 'repositions English as a practical communicative tool to carry out certain defined responsibilities within a professional or work context, the language classroom' (p. 134), and is operationalized under three major areas, namely, managing the classroom (e.g., greetings and salutations, directions to students to settle down and begin work), understanding and communicating lesson content (e.g., activity instructions and explanations, definitions and explanations of new words, examples), and assessing students and giving them feedback (e.g., texts of various types as presented in students' instructional materials, feedback on target language). Teacher educators may adopt this model which bears the potential to reshape the notion of teachers' language proficiency by moving away from traditional and general language proficiency (often characterized by 'NS'/'NNS' divide) and anchoring it within the professional parameters.

As delineated by Quadrant 1 in Pasternak and Bailey's (2004) model, all teachers are expected to have advanced language proficiency in the target language and comprehensive professional preparation (i.e. teacher credentials, relevant experience at linguistic, intercultural and pedagogical levels). While the latter is widely recognized, the need to equip specialized language proficiency for teachers from all backgrounds and the specific roles of ELTE programs are expressed in the literature (Moussu & Llurda, 2008; Freeman et al., 2015). For this reason, it is important for ELTE programs to construe teacher identity beyond the 'idealized NS' norms by acknowledging and promoting the interwoven roles that ELT professionals embody – both as *a language teacher* and *a language user*. More specifically, ELTE programs should develop (or enhance) teacher-learners' awareness of the sounds, stress and intonation patterns of themselves and their students, and adopt a refined approach to pronunciation (teaching) beyond 'NS' ideals, based on such concepts as *intelligibility* (the ability to recognize words and utterances), *comprehensibility* (the ability to recognize meaning (locutionary force) attached to words and expressions) and *interpretability* (the ability to understand what the expression signifies (illocutionary force) in a particular sociocultural context) (Baker, 2014). Furthermore, teachers will also benefit extensively from, what Kamhi-Stein (2014) calls, conversational strategies (e.g., questioning strategies to seek clarification, turn-taking, etc.) through self-correction, peer and instructor feedback, which could be part a part of the (in)formal component of ELTE curricula.

Conclusion

The overarching premise of this chapter is that countering, destabilizing, and reconceptualizing discourses regarding identity, experience, (in)equity and interaction in ELT need to be interwoven into the knowledge-base and praxis of language teachers. This view underscores the vitality of the fundamental pillars of ELTE:

- *competent teacher educators* with experience, expertise in and commitment to critical approaches;
- *ethnolinguistically diverse teacher-learners* whose negotiation of (linguistic, cultural, ethnic, national, economic, academic, professional and gender-related) identity and agency is recognized, practiced and enhanced with respect to their instructional contexts; and
- *teacher education practices* orchestrated in such a way as to create a professional dialogic space building on teachers' past histories, present realities and future trajectories, as translinguistic, transcultural, transnational and transacademic border crossers (Selvi & Rudolph, 2017).

In this multifaceted picture, teacher educators have a critical role particularly because they are often responsible for organizing, implementing and (re)designing the programmes (or experiences) that prepare teacher-learners for their future professional tasks (Selvi, 2016). More specifically, they are charged with the task of examining macro- (e.g., vision/ mission of the program, curriculum, curricular aims, programmatic rules) and micro-level structures, artefacts and experiences (e.g., individual courses, course assignments, instructional materials, fieldwork experiences, extracurricular activities) as well as stakeholders involved in ELTE experiences (e.g., teacher educators, teacher-learners, mentor teachers, language learners).

In conclusion, ELTE has the potential to create a broader, deeper and more inclusive understanding and appreciation of translinguistic/transcultural identity negotiations of ELT professionals beyond oversimplified, essentialized and idealized categories ('NS'/'NNS' or 'NEST'/'NNEST'). The theoretical discussions and practical solutions delineated throughout this chapter are hoped to inform the future of ELTE and foster the alignment of ELTE practices/programmes with the present-day sociolinguistic realities of the glocalized world.

References

Baker, A. (2014) 'Exploring Teachers' Knowledge of L2 Pronunciation Techniques: Teacher Cognitions, Observed Classroom Practices and Student Perceptions'. *TESOL Quarterly*, 48(1) 136–163.

Bayyurt, Y. and Sifakis, N. (2017) 'Foundations of an EIL-aware teacher education', in Matsuda, A. (ed.) *Preparing Teachers to Teach English as an International Language*, Bristol: Multilingual Matters: 1–18.

BC TEAL (2014) *Position statement against discrimination on the grounds of nationality, ethnicity or linguistic heritage.* Available online: <www.bcteal.org/wp-content/uploads/2013/02/AGM-TEAL-StatementAgainst-Discrimination-passed.pdf> (accessed 11 May, 2019).

Bernat, E. (2009) 'Towards A Pedagogy of Empowerment: The Case of "Impostor Syndrome" Among Pre-Service Non-Native Speaker Teachers (Nnsts) of TESOL'. *English Language Teacher Education and Development Journal*, 11.

Birdsong, D. (1992) 'Ultimate Attainment in Second Language Acquisition'. *Language*, 68(4) 706–755.

Bley-Vroman, R. (1983) 'The Comparative Fallacy in Interlanguage Studies: The Case of Systematicity'. *Language Learning*, 33(1) 1–17.

Blommaert, J. and Rampton, B. (2011) 'Language and Superdiversity'. *Diversities*, 13(2) 1–20.

Braine, G. (2010) *Nonnative Speaker English Teachers: Research, Pedagogy, and Professional Growth.* New York: Routledge.

Canagarajah, A. S. (1999) 'Interrogating the "native speaker fallacy": non-linguistic roots, non-pedagogical results', in Braine, G. (ed.) *Nonnative Educators in English Language Teaching*, Mahwah, NJ: Erlbaum: 77–92.

Canagarajah, A. S. (2005) *Reclaiming the Local in Language Policy and Practice*, Mahwah, NJ: Lawrence Erlbaum.

Canagarajah, A. S. (2007) 'Lingua Franca English, Multilingual Communities, and Language Acquisition'. *The Modern Language Journal*, 91(5) 923–939.

CATESOL (2013) *CATESOL position paper opposing discrimination against Non-Native English Speaking Teachers (NNESTs) and teachers with 'non-standard' varieties of English.* Available online <http://catesol.org/nnest.pdf> (accessed 11 May, 2019).

Chomsky, N. (1965) *Aspects of the Theory of Syntax.* Cambridge, MA: MIT Press.

Copland, F., Garton, S. and Mann, S. (eds) (2016) *LETs and NESTs: Voices, Views and Vignettes.* London: British Council.

Crystal, D. (2012) *English as a Global Language.* Cambridge: Cambridge University Press.

D'Angelo, J. (2012) 'WE-informed EIL curriculum in Chukyo: towards a functional, educated, multilingual outcome', in Matsuda, A. (ed.) *Teaching English as an International Language: Principles and Practices.* Bristol: Multilingual Matters: 121–139.

Davies, A. (1991) *The Native Speaker in Applied Linguistics.* Edinburgh: Edinburgh University Press.

Doğançay-Aktuna, S. and Hardman, J. (2017) 'A framework for incorporating an English as an International Language perspective into TESOL teacher education', in Matsuda, A. (ed.) *Preparing Teachers to Teach English as an International Language.* Bristol: Multilingual Matters: 19–34.

Doğançay-Aktuna, S. and Hardman, J. (2018) 'Teacher qualifications, professionalism, competencies, and benchmarks', in Liontas, J. (ed.) *TESOL Encyclopedia of English Language Teaching*. Hoboken, NJ: Wiley/ TESOL International Association.

Edge, J. (2011) *The Reflexive Teacher Educator in TESOL: Roots and Wings*. New York: Routledge.

Ferguson, G. (2013) 'English, development and education: charting the tensions', in Erling, E. and Seargeant, P. (eds) *English and Development: Policy, Pedagogy and Globalization*. Bristol: Multilingual Matters: 21–44.

Flores, N. and Aneja, G. (2017) '"Why Needs Hiding?" Translingual (Re)Orientations in TESOL Teacher Education'. *Research in the Teaching of English*, 51(4) 441–463.

Freeman, D. (2017) 'The Case for Teachers' Classroom English Proficiency'. *RELC Journal*, 48(1) 31–52.

Freeman, D., Katz, A., Garcia Gomez, P. and Burns, A. (2015) 'English-For-Teaching: Rethinking Teacher Proficiency in the Classroom'. *ELT Journal*, 69(2) 130–139.

Galloway, N. (2017) 'Global Englishes for language teaching: preparing MSs TESOL students to teach in a globalized world', in Matsuda, A. (ed.) *Preparing Teachers to Teach English as an International Language*. Bristol,: Multilingual Matters: 69–86.

Galloway, N. and Rose, H. (2015) *Introducing Global Englishes*. Abingdon: Routledge.

García, O. and Wei, L. (2014) *Translanguaging: Language, Bilingualism and Education*. New York: Palgrave Macmillan.

Holliday, A. (2005) *The Struggle to Teach English as an International Language*, Oxford: Oxford University Press.

Howatt, A. P. R. (1984) *A History of English Language Teaching*. Oxford: Oxford University Press.

Houghton, S. A. and Rivers, D. (2013) *Native-Speakerism in Japan: Intergroup Dynamics in Foreign Language Education*. Bristol, Multilingual Matters.

Kamhi-Stein, L. (2014) 'Nonnative English-speaking professionals', in Celce-Murcia, M., Snow, M. A. and Brinton, D. (eds) *Teaching English as a Second or Foreign Language*. Boston, MA: Heinle Cengage: 586–600.

Kamhi-Stein, L. (2016) 'The Non-Native English Speakers in TESOL Movement'. *ELT Journal*, 70(2) 180–189.

Kramsch, C. (1997) 'The Privilege of the Nonnative Speaker'. *PMLA*, 112 359–369.

Kubota, R. and Lin, A. (2009) *Race, Culture, and Identities in Second Language Education: Exploring Critically Engaged Practice*. New York: Routledge.

Kumaravadivelu, B. (2012) 'Individual identity, cultural globalization and teaching English as an international language: the case for an epistemic break', in Alsagoff, L., McKay, S. L, Hu, G. and Renandya, W. A. (eds) *Principles and Practices for Teaching English as an International Language*. New York: Routledge: 9–27.

Leung, C. (2005) 'Convivial Communication: Recontextualizing Communicative Competence'. *International Journal of Applied Linguistics*, 15(2) 119–144.

Llurda, E. (2009) 'Attitudes towards English as an International Language: the pervasiveness of native models among l2 users and teachers', in Sharifian, F. (ed.) *English as an International Language: Perspectives and Pedagogical Issues*, Bristol: Multilingual Matters: 119–134.

Llurda, E. (2016) '"Native speakers", English and ELT', in Hall, G. (ed.) *The Routledge Handbook of English Language Teaching*. Abingdon: Routledge: 51–63.

Long, M. H. (1983) 'Native-speaker/non-native speaker conversation and the negotiation of comprehensible input'. *Applied Linguistics*, 4(2) 126–141.

Lortie, D. (1975) *Schoolteacher: A Sociological Study*. London: The University of Chicago Press.

Mahboob, A. and Golden, R. (2013) 'Looking For Native Speakers of English: Discrimination in English Language Teaching Job Advertisements'. *Voices in Asia Journal*, 1(1) 72–81.

Matsuda, A. (2017) 'Introduction', in Matsuda, A. (ed.) *Preparing Teachers to Teach English as an International Language*, Bristol: Multilingual Matters: xiii–xxi.

Maum, R. (2002) 'Nonnative-English-Speaking Teachers in The English Teaching Profession'. *CAL Digest*. Washington, DC: Center for Applied Linguistics.

Mauranen, A. (2009) 'Introduction', in Mauranen, A. and Ranta, E. (eds) *English as a Lingua Franca: Studies and Findings*. Newcastle upon Tyne: Cambridge Scholars Publishing: 1–7.

Medgyes, P. (1994) *The Non-Native Teacher*. London: Macmillan.

Moussu, L. and Llurda, E. (2008) 'Non-Native English-Speaking English Language Teachers: History and Research'. *Language Teaching*, 41(3) 315–348.

Paikeday, T. (1985) *The Native Speaker is Dead!*. Toronto: Paikeday Publishing Inc.

Pasternak, M. and Bailey, K. (2004) 'Preparing nonnative and native English-speaking teachers: issues of professionalism and proficiency', in Kamhi-Stein, L. D. (ed.) *Learning and Teaching from Experience: Perspectives on Nonnative English-Speaking Professionals*. Ann Arbor, MI: The University of Michigan Press: 155–175.

Pennycook, A. (2016) 'Politics, power relationships and ELT', in Hall, G. (ed.) *The Routledge Handbook of English Language Teaching*. Abingdon: Routledge: 26–37.

Phillipson, R. (1992). *Linguistic Imperialism*, Oxford: Oxford University Press.

Rich, A. (1980) 'Compulsory Heterosexuality and Lesbian Existence'. *Signs*, 5 631–660.

Rivers, D. J. (2016) 'Employment advertisements and native-speakerism in Japanese higher education', in Copland, F., Garton, S. and Mann, S. (eds) *LETs and NESTs: Voices, Views And Vignettes*, London: British Council: 79–100.

Rose, H. (2017) 'A global approach to English language teaching: integrating an international perspective into a teaching methods course', in Matsuda, A. (ed.) *Preparing Teachers to Teach English as an International Language*. Bristol: Multilingual Matters: 169–180.

Rudolph, N. (2012) *Borderlands and border crossing: Japanese professors of English and the negotiation of translinguistic and transcultural identity*. Unpublished doctoral dissertation, University of Maryland, College Park, USA.

Rudolph, N. (2016) 'Negotiating borders of being and becoming in and beyond the English language teaching classroom: two university student narratives from Japan'. *Asian Englishes*, 18(1) 1–17.

Rudolph, N. (2018) 'Education for glocal interaction beyond essentialization and idealization: classroom explorations and negotiations' in Selvi, A. F. and Rudolph, N. (eds) *Conceptual Shifts and Contextualized Practices in Education for Glocal Interaction*. Singapore: Springer: 147–176.

Rudolph, N., Selvi, A. F. and Yazan, B. (2015) 'Worldviews of Constructing and Confronting Native Speakerism: Orientations in and New Directions for the "NNEST Movement"'. *Critical Inquiry in Language Studies*, 12(1) 27–50.

Ruecker, T. and Ives, L. (2015) 'White Native English Speaker Needed: The Rhetorical Construction of Privilege in Online Teacher Recruitment Spaces'. *TESOL Quarterly*, 49(4) 733–756.

Seidlhofer, B. (1999) 'Double Standards: Teacher Education in the Expanding Circle'. *World Englishes*, 18(2) 233–245.

Selinker, L. (1972) 'Interlanguage'. *International Review of Applied Linguistics*, 10(2) 209–231.

Selvi, A. F. (2010) '"All Teachers are Equal, But Some Teachers are More Equal Than Others": Trend Analysis of Job Advertisements in English Language Teaching'. *WATESOL NNEST Caucus Annual Review*, 1 156–181. Available online: <http://sites.google.com/site/watesolnnestcaucus/caucus-annual-review> (accessed 11 May, 2019).

Selvi, A. F. (2014) 'Myths And Misconceptions about The Non-Native English Speakers in TESOL (NNEST) Movement'. *TESOL Journal*, 5(3) 573–611.

Selvi, A. F. (2016) 'The Role of Teacher Education at a Crossroads of Tensions and Opportunities'. *Asian Englishes*, 18(3) 258–264.

Selvi, A. F. (2017) 'Preparing teachers to teach English as an international language: reflections from Northern Cyprus', in Matsuda, A. (ed.) *Preparing Teachers to Teach English as an International Language*. Bristol: Multilingual Matters: 115–129.

Selvi, A. F. (2018) *Being an English language teacher: beyond labels and boundaries?* Plenary speech delivered at the 13th METU ELT Convention, Ankara, Turkey, May.

Selvi, A. F. and Rudolph, N. (2017) 'Teachers and the negotiation of identity: implications and challenges for second language teacher education', in Martinez Agudo, J. de D. (ed.) *Native and Non-Native Teachers in English Language Classrooms: Professional Challenges and Teacher Education*. Boston, MA and Berlin: De Gruyter: 257–272.

Selvi, A. F. and Rudolph, N. (2018) 'Introduction', in Selvi, A. F. and Rudolph, N. (eds) *Conceptual Shifts and Contextualized Practices in Education for Glocal Interaction*. Singapore: Springer: 1–14.

Selvi, A. F., Rudolph, N. and Uzum, B. (2016) 'Equity and professionalism in English Language Teaching: a glocal perspective', in Hastings, C. and Jacob, L. (eds) *Social Justice in English Language Teaching*. Alexandria, VA: TESOL Press: 83–96.

Sharifian, F. and Marlina, R. (2012) 'English as an International Language (EIL): an innovative academic program', in Matsuda, A. (ed.) *Teaching English as an International Language: Principles and Practices*. Bristol: Multilingual Matters: 140–153.

Smolder, C. (2009) 'ELT and The Native Speaker Ideal: Some Food for Thought'. *International House Journal of Education and Development*, 26(22). Available online: <ihjournal.com/eltand-the-native-speaker-ideal-some-food-for-thought> (accessed 11 May, 2019).

Suarez, J. (2000) '"Native" and "Non-Native": Not Only a Question of Terminology'. *Humanizing Language Teaching*, 2(6). Available online: <www.hltmag.co.uk/nov00/mart1.htm> (accessed 11 May, 2019).

Swales, J. (1993) 'The English Language and its Teachers: Thoughts Past, Present and Future'. *ELT Journal*, 47(4) 283–291.

TESOL (1992) 'A TESOL Statement of Non-Native Speakers of English and Hiring Practices'. *TESOL Quarterly*, 2(4) 23.

TESOL (2006) *Position Statement Against Discrimination of Nonnative Speakers of English in the Field Of TESOL*. Available online: <www.tesol.org/docs/pdf/5889.pdf?sfvrsn=2> (accessed 11 May, 2019).

TESOL Spain (2016) *Position Statement Against Discrimination*. Available online: <www.tesol-spain.org/en/> (accessed 11 May, 2019).

Tollefson, J. (2000) 'Policy and ideology in the spread of English', in Hall, J. K. and Eggington, W. G. (eds) *The Sociopolitics of English Language Teaching*. Clevedon: Multilingual Matters: 7–21.

Widdowson, H. G. (1994) 'The Ownership of English'. *TESOL Quarterly*, 28(2) 377–389.

Yazan, B. (2018) 'Contexts of English Language Teaching as glocal spaces', in Selvi, A. F. and Rudolph, N. (eds) *Conceptual Shifts and Contextualized Practices in Education for Glocal Interaction*. Singapore: Springer: 219–234.

Yazan, B. and Rudolph, N. (2018) 'Introduction', in Yazan, B. and Rudolph, N. (eds) *Criticality, Teacher Identity, and (In)equity in ELT: Issues and Implications*. Dordrecht: Springer: 1–19.

PART 3
Language perspectives

14

From language as system to language as discourse

Michael McCarthy and Brian Clancy

Introduction

Language as a system

When language is viewed as a system, we see it in terms of its component parts and how these interact. The three basic components are *substance*, *form* and *meaning*. *Substance* refers to the sounds the language uses (phonic substance), for example, its vowels and consonants, and the symbols used in writing (graphic substance). Next, we have three basic types of *form*: grammar, lexis and phonology. In the case of grammar, English forms include past-tense endings, modal verbs and prepositions, along with rules for putting these together (syntax). The lexical forms consist of words, which follow rules for vowel and consonant combinations, how they combine with other words in collocations, fixed expressions, etc. and how they interact with the grammar. Phonology gives us the forms for pronunciation, stress (the syllable with most intensity) and intonation (e.g. whether the voice rises or falls). The third component, *meaning*, refers to what the combinations of form and substance signify (the semantics). In English, the form *was speaking* signifies past time, *green* and *blue* signify particular colours and rising intonation often signifies a question. If we reverse this perspective, meaning is what we intend to say, form is how we assemble the message using appropriate words, grammar and sounds (or written symbols), and substance is what we actually say or write.

We find information on the system in reference grammars (for English, this includes reference grammars such as Biber et al., 1999; Carter and McCarthy, 2006), in dictionaries (e.g. Macmillan, 2002; Hornby, 2010), which usually give information on pronunciation. Works describing English intonation tend to be more specialised (e.g. Cruttenden, 1997; Tench, 2015).

Language as discourse

The system and its components form the raw material for the teaching and learning of languages. Every learner expects to be instructed in the pronunciation, grammar and vocabulary of the target language, and teachers and learners alike expect that major course books will have grammar charts and target vocabulary, listening and speaking sections where pronunciation and stress are practised, and reading and writing material where working with the graphic substance is on offer, for example, learning a new alphabet or learning punctuation rules. However, the system exists for a purpose, and that purpose is communication. Putting the system to work to enable communication means engaging in *discourse*, the creation of meaning in context. Cook (1989: 6) simply calls it 'language in use, for communication'. Gee and Handford (2012: 1), in their definition of discourse, refer to 'the meanings we give language and the actions we carry out when we use language in specific contexts'. The language we access within the system is transformed into *language as discourse* (McCarthy and Carter, 1994). This approach to language, therefore, is distinct from language as system, and may represent quite a new perspective on the raw material of their trade for trainee teachers. Language does not take place in a vacuum. However, language as system, often presented at sentence level and isolated from real world contexts, can be studied as if it does, and, at least up to the recent past, was the starting point from which many teacher education programmes approached the language elements of their syllabuses.

One of the major developments in recent decades has been a better understanding of the differences between speaking and writing, of how there is no one, single difference that accounts for everything (Chafe, 1982; Hughes, 1996: 6–15), and how speaking and writing often cross over or 'blur' in contexts such as lectures (often written-to-be spoken) and in the language of the internet (Crystal, 2006; Herring, 2010). Until relatively recently, many language courses, at secondary school and university level, focused primarily on the study of the great literature of the target language and on essay writing, with perhaps the occasional 'conversation class' and an oral examination tagged on. The model of the target language was typically a written one. Nowadays, thanks to our ability to record and store huge amounts of spoken and written data in corpora, we can observe significant differences between written and spoken discourse, and where they meet and create blends such as social media usage. In this chapter, we exemplify from several corpora of spoken data, for it is only by looking at attested data that we can begin to be objective about how discourse functions. The corpora we cite are the Michigan Corpus of Academic Spoken English (MICASE), the Limerick Corpus of Irish English (LCIE) and the British National Corpus (BNC). For more information on these corpora see Simpson-Vlach and Leicher (2006), Clancy (2016) or Aston and Burnard (1998), respectively. In all instances, we focus on spoken discourse to re-balance the past focus on writing and suggest ways in which pedagogy can move from knowledge of the system to the skills and strategies needed to create and participate in discourse. In doing so, we argue for language as discourse as an essential component in both pre- and in-service language teachers' repertoires. More specifically, we highlight the importance of a language as discourse approach and how to practically implement it in the language classroom through a discussion of methods, materials and classroom practices.

Beyond the sentence

In English, the sentence has been for centuries a powerful and dominant notion. Forming sentences requires attention to the rules as to how phrases and clauses combine in the system. However, Sinclair and Coulthard's (1975) pioneering work showed that it was possible to describe language in use without having recourse to the notion of sentences, while still showing how spoken language was structured and not randomly put together. They recorded lessons in English school classrooms and showed how the language of teachers and pupils followed set patterns during the process of teaching and learning. For example, in this exchange from the MICASE corpus, the lecturer asks a number of questions, students answer and the lecturer gives feedback, reinforcing the correct answer.

Extract 14.1

[Context: Taken from a Visual Sources lecture. S1 = lecturer, the other speakers are students. SU-f = unknown speaker, female; SU-m = unknown speaker, male; parentheses indicate uncertain speech]

S1:	listen to this. there is the Nile.
S5:	yes.
S1:	which is where?
S5:	in Egypt
SU-f:	Africa.
S1:	there's the Ganges.
S4:	India.
SU-m:	India
S1:	India. There's the Danube.
SU-m:	Turkey. no?
S1:	Danube. <SINGING> da da da da dum, bum bum, bum bum
SU-f:	none of us know it so you can just like tell us
SU-f:	Germany
SU-m:	yeah it's the Blue Danube. we know the song. (just tell me where it is)
S1:	where is the Blue Danube?
SU-f:	Austria.
SU-m:	(she's) got a correct answer.
S1:	Austria. Excellent. [continues]

(MICASE)

Notably, the teacher's feedback is withheld until the correct answer is given about the Danube. The example shows that teacher and students are both adhering to a set of conventions that are independent of sentences; we need not refer to sentences to understand what has happened. The pattern of teacher initiation (I), followed by a student response (R), then by teacher feedback, or follow-up (F), referred to as the IRF pattern, is a powerful and embedded structure which all the parties involved are accustomed to. The IRF pattern is a useful way of putting knowledge on public display and reinforcing learning. In non-classroom situations, we can see similar patterns, as in example (2), taken from family discourse.

Extract 14.2

[Context: Two siblings are trying to fix a computer printer. S1 = male, aged 24; S2 = female, aged 22]

S1:	So what's the problem?	**Initiation**
S2:	We needed to replace the print head.	**Response**
S1:	Oh right.	**Feedback**

(LCIE)

Here (I) is a question, (R) is a response to the question, and (F) acknowledges and accepts the response. This is what the speakers focus on; they know what to do to complete a satisfactory exchange. Studying language as discourse is not dependent on the notion of the sentence, or as Brazil (1995: 15) puts it, 'we do not necessarily have to assume that the consideration of such abstract notions as "sentences" enters into the user's scheme of things at all.'

Sinclair and Coulthard (1975) also showed how teachers marked the transition from one stage to another by using words and phrases such as *Right, Now, Well* and *Now then*, which are termed *discourse markers*. Alongside markers which organise phases or sections of a discourse, other markers point to degrees of shared knowledge (*you know, obviously, you see*). These markers are not part of the structure of sentences; they operate at the level of discourse (for general discussions, see Schiffrin, 1987; Jucker and Ziv, 1998: 1ff; Fraser, 1999; Fischer, 2006). A marker such as *I mean* or *actually* can modify a whole stretch of discourse consisting of a number of clauses and can exercise influence over not only the speaker's own turn but the contributions of others too. An example would be the way speakers use *anyway* in English to indicate 'I think we've both/all said enough on this topic', used as a pre-closing move, as in this extract from a radio phone-in show.

Extract 14.3

[**Context:**   Participants have been discussing tattoos as identifying marks for sailors. S1 = presenter; S2 = caller]

S2:   But the ehh the ehh they saw the tattoos were used extensively by sea captains to identify their their sailors. A lot of sailors and sea going men fell over. Excuse me I've a frog in my throat.

S1:   That's okay.

S2:   Emm a lot of sailors were lost at sea of course.

S1:   Right so. Obviously it would make an enormous amount of sense if there was a distinguishing mark like that. John thank you very much indeed for that. All sorts of other theories on why, when, where, how etc. **Anyway**, that's all from us for today, back with you tomorrow at the usual time until then a very good day to you.

(LCIE)

Fully to understand how the exchanges work in examples (1) to (3) above, we need to consider the following questions:

*   How do the speakers relate to one another?
*   Where are they?
*   What are they doing?
*   What are their goals?

We can see how this list of questions involves a complex perspective on how people utilise the system. We see how different *discourse roles* will affect what people say, how they respond to where they are and what they are doing, how they create and maintain relationships through what they say, and how they achieve their goals through verbal exchanges. To exemplify how the system can be exploited, we next look at examples of how grammar and lexis can be put to service in the creation of discourse.

Choices at the discourse level

Grammar as discourse

At the beginning of this chapter, we pointed to the role of grammar within the language system. English grammar consists of a finite set of rules and conventions that are largely deterministic: to express a meaning such as third person singular present tense indicative mood, it is predetermined that a lexical verb must end in -s (*she looks*, *he watches*, etc.). Equally, it is predetermined that in English the definite article will come before, not after, a noun. However, at the discourse level, grammar can be exploited to realise a variety of purposes, for example, to create and maintain good relationships or to indicate degrees of familiarity. In Extract 14.4, from a conversation between friends, we see how ellipsis (the non-use of an element of the grammar normally considered compulsory), contributes to informality and friendliness.

Extract 14.4

[**Context:** Friends in an Indian restaurant having a meal. S1 = unknown; S2 = female, student, aged 20; S3 = female, student, aged 20]

S1: **You finished**? Yeah.
S2: <laughing> No.
S3: Can I just finish this chi=?
S2: Huh!
S3: <laughing> Oh my God!

(BNC)

S1 says *You finished?* rather than *Have you finished?*, which the rules of English grammar normally require. Not saying *have* is a choice; it is not compulsory in the way the third person singular -s is on present tense indicative verbs. In informal contexts such as that of (4), the probability of ellipsis is greater than in formal settings (Caines et al., 2018). For this reason, Carter and McCarthy (2006: 6–7) refer to the 'grammar of choice' as being a feature of discourse. Speakers and writers choose to exploit the available grammatical resources in ways which are appropriate to their roles and to create the relationships that best enable them to achieve their goals.

Another, familiar, everyday strategy to exemplify the choices speakers make to create successful discourse is the telling of stories and anecdotes, where we often find speakers moving from the canonical past tense to the present tense (the so-called *present historic*) to heighten and intensify dramatic elements. In Extract 14.5, a speaker is recounting a story about someone who bought some very expensive prawns.

Extract 14.5

A: Tell Dad about the prawns Mary.
B: Grainne **bought** a small box of prawns for Kieran.
A: You know the prawns?
C: Yeah.

B: Kieran came out and he **was** like 'how much were the prawns?' She **goes** 'I don't know' and he **said** 'roughly how much are they?'. 'About two three or four euros. Two or three'. 'They were a tenner. It says a tenner here.'

C: And what **were** they?

B: A tenner. She **checked** them then when she **went** into Roches★.

(LCIE)

[★name of a well-known supermarket]

The story moves from the past to the present when the most important statement is quoted (*She goes 'I don't know'*), then back into the past. This is a choice; it is not a compulsory element of the system. The present tense is a marked choice; the past tense is the unmarked, most typical form in story-telling. Schiffrin (1981) shows how shifts from past to historic present are not random but are woven into the structure of narratives and relate to particular segments of a story (see also Rühlemann, 2007).

One striking aspect of how grammar operates at the discourse level is the way speakers co-construct grammatical patterns – in other words, clause combinations which in writing would qualify to be labelled as sentences may be jointly produced by more than one participant in a conversation. Speakers can expand on a potentially complete utterance by the addition of a subordinate clause. This is typically done using conjunctions such as *then*, *when*, *which*, or as is the case in (6), *if*.

Extract 14.6

[Context: Speakers are discussing having two phone lines in the house]

S1:   But in that case if you're going to have that, then you've a right to have two lines in the house

S2:   Exactly

S1:   and use one as a business line

S2:   Exactly

S1:   and one as a pleasure line

S2:   **Exactly and that's what I'm gonna do, exactly**

S1:   **if there's anything you can do** (unclear)

S2:   **Yep, I agree, exactly** and that's the only way you can do it …

(BNC)

S2 says *Exactly and that's what I'm gonna do, exactly*, which is syntactically complete. S1 then expands on this utterance with *if there's anything you can do*, effectively treating S2's utterance as a 'main clause' to which a 'subordinate' *if*-clause can be attached. This *if*-clause functions to qualify S2's statement of intent by suggesting that there may or may not be something that can be done about the present situation. This modification could prove to be interpersonally complex given, for example, the politeness issues involved in commenting on, qualifying or evaluating another speaker's utterance (see Ferrara, 1992). However, S2 responds to S1's modification with the unambiguously positive *Yep, I agree, exactly*. Clancy and McCarthy (2015) have shown how co-construction is an integral, largely unproblematic part of the turn-taking system and that, to account for this behaviour, we have to move beyond the sentence to a view that sees both syntax and meaning as a shared interactional resource (after Rühlemann, 2007). Rather than viewing syntax and meaning as static products of grammars and dictionaries, we should instead see them as emergent, as interaction unfolds in particular contexts, a concept which belongs in the realm of discourse and not system.

Lexis as discourse

What we have said about grammar can also be applied to lexis. Although the vocabulary of a language like English consists of a huge repertoire of words and phrases, presenting learners with a daunting task, there are significant areas where we can move away from seeing the lexicon as a component of the system towards seeing it as a strategic resource for the creation of discourse.

One such area is the choice of degrees of formality. Formality is concerned with making choices appropriate to the context and the relationship between the participants. Most words in English are neutral as to their degree of formality, but many words are conventionally associated with either formal or informal contexts. For example, phrasal verbs often convey greater informality than non-phrasal verbs that convey similar meanings. It is more informal to say *I screwed up*, rather than *I made a mistake/I did something wrong*. Similarly, idioms often convey a degree of familiarity, offering informal comments and evaluations of people and events (McCarthy, 1998: 131–140). Good dictionaries give guidance as to the level of formality associated with particular items. An allied question is whether descriptions of formal/informal language and formal/informal contexts can be applied across cultures or whether different cultures may view similar situations and relationships in different ways (see Irvine, 2009).

While most language teachers will have long been familiar with the notion of formality, it is only relatively recently that corpus analysis has revealed just how much of everyday discourse is composed of ready-made, multi-word units rather than single words. These multi-word units include familiar items such as phrasal verbs, idioms and prepositional phrases (e.g. *get up, feel under the weather, at the moment*). From the point of view of lexis as discourse, corpora show how frequent and important some multi-word strings (hereafter referred to as *chunks*) are in the structuring of discourse and the creation and maintenance of relationships. For example, many of the chunks in Table 14.1 are associated with *you* and *I*, demonstrating the interactive nature of the most frequent chunks.

The table contains a number of 'fragments' indicative of the syntactic system, e.g. *in the, it was, what do you* and *you want to*. However, it is interpersonal meaning that accounts for many of the items in the table. For example, *you know, I mean, I think* and *I don't know* are associated with linguistic politeness (see Fox Tree and Schrock, 2002). As Table 14.1 demonstrates, individual items like *know* and *think* provide us with the building blocks for different structures with interpersonal import, e.g. *I think → I don't think → I don't think I → I don't think I have*, etc. These 'frames', to which content is attached, demonstrate the routine nature of everyday spoken language routines which facilitate fluent, successful discourse.

Table 14.1 The ten most frequent two-, three- and four-word chunks in the spoken component of the BNC BABY

N	Two-word chunks	Three-word chunks	Four-word chunks
1	you know	I don't know	I don't know what
2	I don't	do you want	do you want to
3	do you	I don't think	no no no no
4	in the	you have to	I thought it was
5	I mean	a lot of	what do you want
6	I think	what do you	are you going to
7	is it	I mean I	I don't know whether
8	it was	I think it's	thank you very much
9	on the	do you think	have a look at
10	you got	you want to	I don't think I

Michael McCarthy and Brian Clancy

Also common in everyday spoken discourse are chunks such as *and things like that, that sort/ kind of thing* and *or whatever*, which operate beyond the sentence. These *vague category markers* are particularly significant in the way they project common ground among participants. The speaker who says, 'There's a whole new grammar for text messages and that sort of thing' assumes the listener(s) will mentally fill in the rest of the possible referents of *that sort of thing* (e.g., social media, blogs, emails, etc.) and does not need to have them explicitly listed. Vague category markers have been extensively studied and are seen as central to normal, efficient discourse, especially conversation (see Channell, 1994; Cutting, 2007; Vaughan et al., 2017). Vague language items and the other interactive chunks already discussed are best seen as 'big words' and should be considered as much a part of the vocabulary of a language as the thousands of single words needed to talk about people and things, and their place in the syllabus should be central if we are to move from system-based teaching to a discourse-based approach.

A further feature of lexis as discourse is seen in the way speakers pick up one another's vocabulary for strategic acts such as agreement or the negotiation of meaning. Carter and McCarthy (1988: 181–200) observed how speakers exploit features of the system such as synonymy and antonymy to show engagement with one another (see also Buttery and McCarthy, 2012). In Extract 14.7, we can see how S1 not only co-constructs the message by using a *which*-clause, but also uses a lexical strategy, picking up on the notion of 'difficulty' by using a synonym to agree with another speaker. This is an example of how meaning is negotiated rather than being fossilised in the semantic system.

Extract 14.7

S3: So I've no lectures. I've to do the research myself.
S2: You've to do it yourself.
S3: Which is **harder** like.
S1: Which would be very **difficult** I'd say.
S3: Yeah

(LCIE)

Teachers and learners may occasionally ponder why a language like English often seems to have more than one way of expressing the same idea, and many learners make notes to help them remember the meaning of a new word by listing any synonyms or antonyms they know. Here teaching can capitalise on a feature of the system and turn it into a useful strategy for communication. Simple pair-work activities where students agree with one another's statements using synonyms, or challenge one another using antonyms, are a natural context for putting the system into service to create discourse.

One final area where we see the lexicon serving the creation of discourse is in turn-taking behaviour. We know, from classic studies of turn-taking (e.g. Sacks et al., 1974), that speaking turns proceed smoothly, with one speaker ceding the turn to another as conversation unfolds. Corpus analysis enables us to see just how consistently and with what degree of regularity the vocabulary plays a role in smooth, natural turn-taking. McCarthy (2003 and 2015) showed, for example, that a relatively small number of lexical items are repeatedly used in different varieties of English to express reactions to, and engagement with, incoming talk without taking over the full speaking turn. These lexical items we refer to as *response tokens*, which often occur singly as in Extract 14.8, e.g. *Absolutely! Great! No way!* or often with *that* (*That's awful! That's wonderful!*).

Extract 14.8

S1: Hi Ann (pause) had a good
S2: Hello.
S1: week?
S2: Yeah lovely.
S1: **Great.**

(BNC)

Corpora often show that a large proportion of occurrences of words like *great* and *absolutely* do not come in the form of adjectives modifying nouns, or adverbs modifying verbs and adjectives, but are used to react to and engage with whole stretches of discourse. As such, they represent an important bonding mechanism between speakers. Tao (2003) and McCarthy (2010) also looked at turn-taking, this time considering how speakers begin their turns, and found that a relatively small number of items typically occurred as turn-openers (e.g. *well, so, right* and some of the response tokens already mentioned). Turn-openers attend primarily to what the previous speaker has just said, creating a smooth link between speaking turns, what McCarthy (ibid.) calls *confluence*, the feeling that a conversation is flowing, with a jointly constructed fluency.

Discourse pedagogy

In this section, we consider how materials, methods and classrooms can be conceived by language teachers in a way that operationalises the notion of language as discourse and weaves it into the pedagogical process. Thus far we have discussed discourse from the point of view of both grammar and lexis, both of which form a large part of day-to-day language teaching from the viewpoint of language as system. However, introducing the concepts of grammar and lexis as discourse furthers understanding of not just language form and function, but the processes, many of them unconscious, which facilitate better and more effective communication. The more teacher education programmes can create bridges and foster links across conceptual divides, the greater the level of language awareness teachers in training and professional development can achieve.

Discourse roles

One problem with abandoning the sentence as the core unit for teaching and moving instead towards notions such as discourse marking and responding or following up is that, in the traditional, teacher-led classroom, it is teachers who get to use markers like *Anyway, Right!* and *Now then!* and responses/follow-ups such as *Good!* and *That's great!* while students may get little or no opportunity to use them because of their limited, less powerful discourse roles. This is the kind of challenge we face in moving from language as system towards language as discourse. It is only one of many challenges, but it represents a prime example of what happens when we break free from seeing the sentence as the principal unit of communication. If markers and response tokens are common and central to the organisation of discourse, how can we create the conditions in the classroom where students themselves can take on roles where the use of markers and other discourse features traditionally the province of the teacher (e.g. initiating, using follow-up moves) become natural for them to use? Questions such as how to apportion discourse roles in the classroom affect not only the content of the syllabus, but also methodology and classroom practices.

The discourse syllabus

An important question is how to create a coherent syllabus which supports the transition from system to discourse in areas of language where the available linguistic repertoire is not closed or as well-described as, say, the tense system, the prepositions, the names of the days of the week, verbs of the senses, and so on. For example, in the case of discourse markers, scholars' lists of what to include differ greatly. Some researchers focus more on markers which support the coherent and logical inter-pretation of one piece of discourse in relation to another, such as *in other words, conversely* or *finally* (e.g. Fraser, 1990; Hyland and Tse, 2004), while others focus on markers we have already mentioned such as *well, you know* and *anyway* (e.g. Schiffrin, 1987; Aijmer, 2002). Furthermore, attempts to clarify exactly what discoursal competence means in second language contexts is often only vaguely defined (see the critique in Jones et al., 2018: 112–123). Defining and specifying content are recur-ring problems for anyone wishing to incorporate the world of discourse into an organised syllabus.

Another challenge lies in the fact that there is a bewilderingly wide range of contexts in which language use varies according to the situation and the participants. Sinclair and Coul-thard's work has been built upon by numerous studies that have looked at how verbal exchanges occur in contexts other than classrooms. These include service encounters (McCarthy, 2000; Félix-Brasdefer, 2015), workplaces (Vaughan, 2007; Koester, 2010), domestic settings (Blum-Kulka, 1997; Gordon, 2009; Clancy, 2016), academic settings (Farr, 2011; Evison, 2013), settings where people are engaged in action, e.g. assembling furniture, cooking (Carter and McCarthy, 1997) and many other contexts. They have all been examined through a discourse perspective, where the notion of the sentence has played a minor role, if any at all. In these varied studies, key features emerge time and time again as central to the creation of discourse. Areas of focus and insight in existing research where the syllabus can potentially bridge the gap between language as system and language as discourse include:

- Discourse roles
- Types of verbal exchange that are natural in different contexts;
- Natural turn-taking;
- Discourse marking;
- Creating and maintaining relationships;
- Goal-orientation.

Not all of these points offer ready-made linguistic repertoires that can be written into the syllabus. All require thought, planning and a reassessment of methods, materials, activities and classroom practices.

Materials

Some discourse items, for example discourse markers and response tokens, can be straightfor-wardly incorporated into materials as new vocabulary, or as new functions for known vocabu-lary, and can be graded in a coherent syllabus. For example, McCarthy et al. (2012 and 2014a) offer interactive activities promoting the use of the marker *actually* at two different CEFR levels. Its first occurrence in the material is at A2 level, with the functions of 'giving new or surprising information' and '"correcting" things people say or think' (2014a: 7). *Actually* is then recycled at B2 level with its function of giving new information, and, in the same unit of the material, the functions attributed to *actually* are repeated in the form of two new discourse markers, *in fact* and *as a matter of fact* (2012: 46–47). This process, from item to discourse function, then from the same discourse function to new item(s), is one way of building coherence and progression into the discourse syllabus. The process can be expressed diagrammatically as:

known item → new discourse function → known discourse function → new item

Perhaps the biggest challenge in connexion with discourse-based materials stems from teachers' and students' expectations as to what materials will contain and how teaching and learning will be conducted. For many years, the sequence *present, practise, produce* (often referred to as PPP) has provided a reliable routine. The materials, mediated by the teacher, present a structure or a set of new vocabulary, after which students do drills or controlled practice, followed by production, which could be anything from pair work to writing an essay. The discourse syllabus demands a different approach, in which building awareness is a central element. Awareness is fostered by *noticing* activities, on the basis that noticing is the first step towards understanding what might not always be familiar concepts for students (e.g. discourse marking, follow-up moves, co-construction). Noticing occupies a well-grounded position in research into language learning (see Schmidt, 1990). Shifting the emphasis away from PPP to a more awareness-based approach in materials and student engagement with them is discussed at length in McCarthy and McCarten (2018).

Presenting items in the context of their strategic use rather than their semantic meanings within the system is another key element in discourse-based materials. McCarthy et al. (2014b: 70–71) illustrate follow-up questions and follow-up prompts (e.g. *Really?*), along with using response tokens, in the context of reacting to new information. The response tokens include *that's great, that's interesting, that's terrible*. Students first do a noticing activity, there then follow listening activities (crucial for building awareness), controlled practice, and free practice with a partner, asking follow-up questions and responding to personalised items of news/interest. Students have considerable choice as to how they respond, with no one single 'correct' answer. All this is done at A1 level, and is feasible because the lexical items are simple, often already known, and the contexts are familiar, everyday conversational settings.

Materials are merely tools for the use of teachers and learners, and it is what happens in the classroom which ultimately underpins their success or failure. We now consider classroom practices in relation to moving from system-dominated approaches to an environment where the creation of discourse is a natural part of the teaching/learning process.

System and discourse in the classroom

Walsh (2006) sees the L2 classroom not as a static entity, but as a series of dynamic and complex contexts where interaction between participants is essential to teaching and learning. Through looking at classroom language as discourse, he identified four modes which characterise the interaction between teacher and learners: *managerial mode, materials mode, skills and systems mode* and *classroom context mode*. Each of these modes presents the teacher with opportunities to explore language as discourse in the classroom, regardless of the level the learners are at. The pedagogic purpose of *managerial mode* is the management of learning at the different stages of a lesson and is characterised by long teacher speaking turns, transition markers and little or no learner involvement. It may seem that this mode does not offer many openings to exploit in terms of fostering discourse; however, the teacher can model a range of frequently used organisational markers (*all right, ok, so, now,* etc.), as well as models for feedback of various kinds (*that's fine, excellent*) and the discourse role of manager/leader, which may then be assumed by certain students in pair and group work where tasks demand management and outcomes. The second mode, *materials*, is dominated by exchanges that emerge from language practice opportunities based on a piece of material, which we exemplified the 'Materials' section, where the materials cited first engage the teacher and students in dialogue to raise awareness of target items, then offer students opportunities to practise asking questions, or to react using response tokens, ask follow-up questions and so on, in natural contexts and where they can ultimately personalise the material and make the transition to *classroom context mode* (see below).

In the *skills and systems* mode, the pedagogical goal is to provide controlled, form-focused language practice in both systems (phonology, grammar, etc.) and skills (reading, listening, etc.). However, we propose that this focused practice of systems and skills be exploited to also include engagement in language as discourse. For example, past and present simple tenses could be explored through story-telling or through the use of tense-aspect choices for politeness and directness, utilising natural spoken texts. In addition, the teaching of conditionals might be broadened to include pair work where one participant produces a main clause and the other adds a subordinate one to model co-construction. This could then be extended to contexts where lexical strategies are employed to negotiate agreement and disagreement around these co-constructions. Finally, in *classroom context* mode, the defining characteristic is interactional space. In this mode, where the learners themselves co-construct the discourse, the emphasis is on providing opportunities for genuine communication and for extended, learner-led explorations of language as discourse. When practising speaking skills in classroom context mode, some prompts for language as discourse will naturally occur, given that the learners themselves will have control over the turn-taking system, allowing them the freedom to experiment with strategies such as holding the floor, changing topic and using natural turn-openers and responses. This, in turn, might be scaffolded by some post-activity feedback from the teacher that, instead of focusing on language form, focuses on concepts related to discourse such as (in)appropriacy or (im)politeness, concepts that are often culture- and/ or context-specific and part of communicative, rather than linguistic, competence (Hymes, 1972).

Conclusion

Walsh (2006) refers to his four modes of classroom talk under the umbrella label of SETT (Self-Evaluation of Teacher Talk). The choice of that label is not otiose: the teacher is seen as centrally responsible for the maintenance and monitoring of appropriate discourse in the classroom. It is important to acknowledge that English language teachers are faced with a unique teaching context, a 'unique art' (Hammadou and Bernhart, 1987: 305), where language is both the medium and intended outcome of instruction. Language teachers, in common with all teachers, strive to become experts in their field of teaching. However, language itself has been variously described as 'slippery and mutable' (Vaughan, 2008: 1) and 'as large and as complex as life' (Palmer, 1998: 2). Therefore, not everything in language teaching needs to be about the classroom; aspects of language teacher education, such as the understanding of language as discourse, should also be concerned with teachers becoming experts in their stock and trade, language. If our goal truly is to move from system to discourse, teacher education has to support teachers' professional development in not only gaining knowledge of discourse, but in becoming discourse analysts themselves, in their own classrooms, and constantly questioning the degree to which they seize upon and develop opportunities for creating the conditions that will lead to the emergence of natural discourse, whether it be in their interactions with students or in the interactions they set up among them. In order to successfully achieve this, input in the language classroom cannot be confined to language as system because this ignores the fact that language becomes a living, ambiguous, emergent, negotiated phenomenon once it leaves the classroom and enters the world beyond the classroom walls or beyond the screens of the virtual classroom. Indeed, it would be limited and limiting for language teaching professionals to simply base their teaching on what has been written in relation to language as system without considering the implications of using language in real life social and cultural contexts. Therefore, the materials must be supportive of, and reasonably transparent for, teachers who may not be familiar with discourse-oriented pedagogy, with non-patronising, helpful explanations and advice in teachers' manuals which accompany course materials (see also Farr and O'Keeffe, this volume). Ultimately, analysing language as discourse is a critical and fundamental part of any teacher education programme. However, teachers need to feel that time spent on fostering natural discourse is not time wasted and will pay dividends in greater fluency and higher achievement in assessment contexts, as well as increased student motivation and satisfaction.

Further reading

Baker, P. (2006) *Using Corpora in Discourse Analysis*. London: Continuum.
A comprehensive introduction to the intersection of corpus linguistics and language as discourse. Particularly strong with regard to the description of the potential of corpus linguistics for the analysis of authentic texts.

Carter, R. and Goddard, A. (2016) *How to Analyse Texts*. Abingdon: Routledge.
A great textbook and toolkit for analysing language in use. It provides the reader with a large amount of texts – spoken, written and multimodal – and a number of levels at which they can be analysed. It is an excellent classroom resource.

O'Keeffe, A., Clancy, B. and Adolphs, S. (2011) *Introducing Pragmatics in Use*. Abingdon: Routledge.
One of the first textbooks to apply a corpus approach to examining language in use. Chapter 8 is devoted entirely to the use of corpus materials to introduce features of language as discourse into the language classroom.

Gee, J. P. and Handford, M. (eds) (2012) *The Routledge Handbook of Discourse Analysis*. Abingdon: Routledge.
A comprehensive collection of articles by leading figures in discourse analysis. Parts III and IV pay particular attention to spoken language and to applications in education, including the classroom.

Walsh, S. (2011) *Exploring Classroom Discourse: Language in Action*. Abingdon: Routledge.
Walsh's work on interaction in second language classrooms, extensively quoted in the present chapter, is fully and clearly elaborated in this book, which looks at discourse in the classroom as a means towards achieving 'classroom interactional competence'.

References

Aijmer, K. (2002) *English Discourse Particles: Evidence from a Corpus*. Amsterdam: John Benjamins.

Aston, G. and Burnard, L. (1998) *The BNC Handbook: Exploring the British National Corpus with SARA*. Edinburgh: Edinburgh University Press.

Biber, D., Johansson, S., Leech, G., Conrad, S. and Finegan, E. (1999) *Longman Grammar of Spoken and Written English*. London: Longman.

Blum-Kulka, S. (1997) *Dinner Talk: Cultural Patterns of Sociability and Socialization in Family Discourse*. Mahwah, NJ: Lawrence Erlbaum.

Brazil, D. (1995) *A Grammar of Speech*. Oxford: Oxford University Press.

Buttery, P and McCarthy, M. J. (2012) 'Lexis in spoken discourse', in Gee, J. P and Handford, M. (eds) *The Routledge Handbook of Discourse Analysis*. Abingdon: Routledge: 285–300.

Caines, A., Buttery, P. and McCarthy, M. J. (2018) '"You still talking to me?" The zero auxiliary progressive in spoken British English, twenty years on', in Brezina, V., Love, R. and Aijmer, K. (eds) *Sociolinguistic Variation in Contemporary British English: Exploration of the Spoken BNC 2014*. Abingdon: Routledge: 209–234.

Carter, R. A. and McCarthy, M. J. (1988) *Vocabulary and Language Teaching*. Harlow: Pearson Education Limited.

Carter, R. A. and McCarthy, M. J. (1997) *Exploring Spoken English*. Cambridge: Cambridge University Press.

Carter, R. A. and McCarthy, M. J. (2006) *Cambridge Grammar of English*. Cambridge: Cambridge University Press.

Chafe, W. (1982) 'Integration and involvement in speaking, writing and oral literature', in Tannen, D. (ed.) *Spoken and Written Language: Exploring Orality and Literacy*. Norwood NJ: Ablex: 35–54.

Channell, J. (1994) *Vague Language*. Oxford: Oxford University Press.

Clancy, B. (2016) *Investigating Intimate Discourse: Exploring the Spoken Interaction of Families, Couples and Friends*. Abingdon: Routledge.

Clancy, B. and McCarthy, M. J. (2015) 'Co-constructed turn taking', in Aijmer, K. and Rühlemann, C. (eds) *Corpus Pragmatics: A Handbook*. Cambridge: Cambridge University Press: 430–453.

Cook, G. (1989) *Discourse*. Oxford: Oxford University Press.

Cruttenden, A. (1997) *Intonation*, 2nd edition. Cambridge: Cambridge University Press.

Crystal, D. (2006) *Language and the Internet*, 2nd edition. Cambridge: Cambridge University Press.

Cutting, J. (ed.) (2007) *Vague Language Explored*. Basingstoke: Palgrave Macmillan.

Evison, J. (2013) 'Turn Openings in Academic Talk: Where Goals and Roles Intersect'. *Classroom Discourse*, 4(1) 3–26.

Farr, F. (2011) *The Discourse of Teaching Practice Feedback: An Investigation of Spoken and Written Modes*. Abingdon: Routledge.

Félix-Brasdefer, J. C. (2015) *The Language of Service Encounters: A Pragmatic-Discursive Analysis*. Cambridge: Cambridge University Press.

Ferrara, K. (1992) 'The Interactive Achievement of a Sentence: Joint Productions in Therapeutic Discourse'. *Discourse Processes*, 15(2) 207–228.

Fischer, K. (ed.) (2006) *Approaches to Discourse Particles*. Oxford: Elsevier.

Fox Tree, J. and Schrock, J. (2002) 'Basic Meanings of *You Know* and *I Mean*'. *Journal of Pragmatics*, 34(6) 727–747.

Fraser, B. (1990) 'An Approach to Discourse Markers'. *Journal of Pragmatics*, 14(3) 383–398.

Fraser, B. (1999) 'What are Discourse Markers?' *Journal of Pragmatics*, 31(7) 931–952.

Gee, J. P. and Handford, M. (eds) (2012) *The Routledge Handbook of Discourse Analysis*. Abingdon: Routledge.

Gordon, C. (2009) *Making Meanings, Creating Family: Intertextuality and Framing in Family Interaction*. Oxford: Oxford University Press.

Hammadou, J. and Bernhardt, E. (1987) 'On Being and Becoming a Foreign Language Teacher', *Theory into Practice*, 26(4) 301–306.

Herring, S. C. (2010) 'Computer-mediated Conversation Part 1: Introduction and Overview'. *Language@Internet*, 7(2). Available online: <www.languageatinternet.org/articles/2010/2801> (accessed 5 December 2017).

Hornby, A. S. (2010) *Oxford Advanced Learner's Dictionary of Current English*. Oxford: Oxford University Press.

Hughes, R. (1996) *English in Speech and Writing*. London: Routledge.

Hyland, K. and Tse, P. (2004) 'Metadiscourse in Academic Writing: A Reappraisal'. *Applied Linguistics*, 25(2) 156–177.

Hymes, D. (1972) 'On communicative competence', in Pride, J. B. and Holmes, J. (eds) *Sociolinguistics*. London: Penguin: 269–293.

Irvine, J. T. (2009) 'Formality and informality in communicative events', in Duranti, A. (ed.) *Linguistic Anthropology: A Reader*, Chichester: Wiley-Blackwell: 172–189.

Jones, C., Byrne, S. and Halenko, N. (eds) (2018) *Successful Spoken English: Findings from Learner Corpora*. Abingdon: Routledge.

Jucker, A. H. and Ziv, Y. (eds) (1998) *Discourse Markers: Descriptions and Theory*. Amsterdam: John Benjamins.

Koester, A. (2010) *Workplace Discourse*. London: Continuum.

Macmillan (2002) *Macmillan English Dictionary for Advanced Learners*. Oxford: Macmillan Education.

McCarthy, M. J. (1998) *Spoken Language and Applied Linguistics*. Cambridge: Cambridge University Press.

McCarthy, M. J. (2000) 'Captive audiences. The discourse of close contact service encounters', in Coupland, J. (ed.) *Small Talk*. London: Longman: 84–109.

McCarthy, M. J. (2003) 'Talking Back: "Small" Interactional Response Tokens in Everyday Conversation'. *Research on Language and Social Interaction*, 36(1) 33–63.

McCarthy, M. J. (2010) 'Spoken Fluency Revisited'. *English Profile Journal*, 1. Available online: <http://journals.cambridge.org/action/displayAbstract?fromPage=online&aid=7908257&fulltextType=RA&fileId=S2041536210000012> (accessed 2 December 2017).

McCarthy, M. J. (2015) "'Tis mad, yeah": turn openers in Irish and British English', in Amador-Moreno, C., McCafferty, K. and Vaughan, E. (eds) *Pragmatic Markers in Irish English*. Amsterdam: John Benjamins: 156–175.

McCarthy, M. J. and Carter, R. A. (1994) *Language as Discourse: Perspectives for Language Teaching*. Harlow: Pearson Education Limited.

McCarthy, M. J. and McCarten, J. (2018) 'Now you're talking! Practising conversation in second language learning', in Jones, C. (ed.) *Practice in Second Language Learning*. Cambridge: Cambridge University Press: 7–29.

McCarthy, M. J., McCarten, J. and Sandiford, H. (2012) *Viewpoint. Student's Book 1*. Cambridge: Cambridge University Press.

McCarthy, M. J., McCarten, J. and Sandiford, H. (2014a) *Touchstone. Student's Book 2*. Cambridge: Cambridge University Press.

McCarthy, M. J., McCarten, J. and Sandiford, H. (2014b) *Touchstone. Student's Book 1*. Cambridge: Cambridge University Press.

Palmer, P. J. (1998) *The Courage to Teach: Exploring the Inner Landscape of a Teacher's Life*. San Francisco, CA: Jossey-Bass.

Rühlemann, C. (2007) *Conversation in Context: A Corpus-driven Approach*. London: Continuum.

Sacks, H., Schegloff, E. A. and Jefferson, G. (1974) 'A Simplest Systematics for the Organisation of Turn-Taking for Conversation'. *Language*, 50(4) 696–735.

Schiffrin, D. (1981) 'Tense Variation in Narrative'. *Language*, 57(1) 45–62.

Schiffrin, D. (1987) *Discourse Markers*. Cambridge: Cambridge University Press.

Schmidt, R. W. (1990) 'The Role of Consciousness in Second Language Learning'. *Applied Linguistics*, 11(2) 129–158.

Simpson-Vlach, R. and Leicher, S. (2006) *The MICASE Handbook: A Resource for Users of the Michigan Corpus of Academic Spoken English*. Ann Arbor, MI: University of Michigan Press.

Sinclair, J. and Coulthard, R. (1975) *Towards an Analysis of Discourse*. London: Oxford University Press.

Tao, H. (2003) 'Turn initiators in spoken English: a corpus-based approach to interaction and grammar', in Leistyna, P. and Meyer, C. F. (eds) *Corpus Analysis: Language Structure and Language Use*. Amsterdam: Rodopi: 187–207.

Tench, P. (2015) *The Intonation Systems of English*. London: Bloomsbury Publishing.

Vaughan, E. (2007) "'I Think We Should Just Accept…Our Horrible Lowly Status': Analysing Teacher-Teacher Talk Within the Context of Community of Practice'. *Language Awareness*, 16(3) 173–189.

Vaughan, E. (2008) *'Just say something and we can all argue then': community and identity in the workplace talk of English language teachers*. PhD thesis, University of Limerick, Ireland.

Vaughan, E., McCarthy, M. and Clancy, B. (2017) 'Vague Category Markers as Turn Final Items in Irish English'. *World Englishes*, 36(2) 208–223.

Walsh, S. (2006) *Investigating Classroom Discourse*. Abingdon: Routledge.

15

Classroom interaction and language teacher education

Olcay Sert

Introduction

Language teachers, like other teachers, perform constant multi-tasking in second/foreign/additional language (L2) classrooms while they are teaching. They manage materials, behaviours, content, discourse, and organise and co-construct (with the learners) learning environments at the same time. At the heart of this multi-tasking lies a process of instant decision making: they initiate turns, respond to student utterances, attend to linguistic mistakes within microseconds. Such responsive behaviour may become automatic as teachers gain more experience and acquire a level of expertise (not necessarily parallel to age). Successful teachers align their *'online decision making'* (Walsh, 2011: 220) with the pedagogical goal of the moment. As research in the last two decades has clearly documented, the convergence between *pedagogical goals* and *unfolding classroom interaction* (Seedhouse, 2004; Walsh, 2011; Sert, 2015) is perhaps one of the most important means of creating learning opportunities for students.

Opportunities for language learning are facilitated if interactional practices are fine tuned to the goal of teaching the L2. This requires a teacher's being responsive to the moment, also referred to as the principle of contingency (Waring, 2016); thus, closely related to the *awareness* teachers have with regards to language and interaction. Teacher Language Awareness (Walsh, 2003) is a facilitator of teacher development. It gradually and eventually transforms the more abstract construct of awareness into a set of skills that teachers develop, namely Classroom Interactional Competence (Walsh, 2006, 2011), described as the ability to mediate and assist classroom language learning.

Mainly using conversation analytic methods, researchers of L2 classroom interaction have documented the interactional manoeuvres of teachers so as to understand the microscopic details of instructed language learning and teaching. In this chapter, I first provide a review of classroom interaction research with a focus on the role of teacher talk in facilitating language learning opportunities. I then present how classroom interaction and teacher development are closely related by reviewing research in both initial teacher education and in-service teacher education, referring mainly to SETT and CIC (Walsh, 2006, 2011), and IMDAT (Sert, 2015). After presenting research on the longitudinal development of L2 CIC, I make a case for a technology-enhanced, reflective, and micro-analytic teacher education framework, present practical applications, and discuss future directions.

Current perspectives on L2 classroom interaction in teacher education

With its robust analytic tools that unpack social actions that teachers and students deploy in classrooms, conversation analysis (CA) has recently played a prominent role in describing micro-level details of teaching and learning events in L2 classrooms. The empirical findings evidencing *language learning* in conversation analytic studies of classroom interaction (e.g. Hellermann, 2008; Markee, 2008; Sert, 2017) as well as studies that describe pedagogical activities with a focus on interactional practices of teachers and students (e.g. Waring, 2009; Sert and Walsh, 2013; Matsumoto and Dobs, 2017) have huge potential to inform teacher education. However, to be able to reach out to teacher educators and teachers, we may need to go beyond what research from classroom interaction studies find. We need to (1) make practitioners aware of the importance of classroom interaction in relation to learning, (2) provide them with tools to integrate classroom interaction into teacher education, and (3) bring developmental evidence to illustrate change in teaching practices over time.

Teacher talk, classroom interaction, and language learning opportunities

In language classrooms, as Walsh (2006) claims, teachers 'play a much more central role than that advocated under both Communicative Language Teaching and Task-based Language Learning' (p. 3). The centrality of teacher-talk in facilitating or hindering student participation, and thus engagement, has been found to be key for creating opportunities for language learning (Walsh, 2002). Researchers have focused on different aspects of teacher talk. Waring (2008), for instance, shows that although explicit positive feedback (e.g. when an L2 teacher says 'very good' in response to a student answer) produced by a teacher may be sequentially and affectively preferred, pedagogically it may hinder learning opportunities. In a more recent study, Fagan (2014) illustrates that ESL teachers' positive feedback turns may maintain interactional flow and ensure 'information clarity with all learners in the class in relation to the goals of the immediate talk' (p. 45). In another important study, Jacknick (2011) illustrates instances of student agency when learners, rather than teachers, initiate turns in language classrooms, 'revealing students' ability to control sequences of talk in the classroom' (Jacknick, 2011: 49). Managing learner initiatives successfully (Waring, 2011) has been found to be an important teacher skill in language classrooms, and the ways teachers manage interaction in such sequences, as it has been reported, may be 'advancing learning' (Waring et al., 2016).

One of the most influential researchers that adopt a conversation analytic methodology to investigate L2 classroom interaction is Seedhouse (2004), who provides a detailed description of the interactional dynamics of L2 classrooms. Taking the position that any sort of generalisation is not comprehensive enough to understand local management of interactions in classrooms, Seedhouse (2004) has developed a variable perspective and showed that there are L2 classroom contexts 'each with its own pedagogical focus and corresponding organisation of turn taking and sequence' (p. 101). He proposes four L2 classroom contexts; namely, form-and-accuracy, meaning-and-fluency, task-oriented, and procedural. His work has contributed to our understanding of the dynamic nature of interactions in classrooms, and has brought evidence regarding the reflexive relationship between pedagogy and interaction. The variable approach taken by Seedhouse (see also Seedhouse, 2019) to the analyses of L2 classroom interaction has had growing impact on future work in this field.

Taking a variable approach to the analyses of classroom interaction, Walsh (2006, 2011) has developed the notion of Classroom Interactional Competence, defined as the ability 'to use interaction as a tool for mediating and assisting learning' (2011: 158). The concept of CIC encompasses the features of classroom interaction that make the teaching/learning process more or less effective. These features are (a) maximising interactional space; (b) shaping learner contributions (seeking clarification, scaffolding, modelling, or repairing learner input); (c) effective use of eliciting; (d) instructional idiolect (i.e. a teacher's speech habits); and (e) interactional awareness. It can be argued that all these interactional features become meaningful as long as they coincide with the pedagogical goal of the moment (Walsh, 2006). For instance, explicit corrections in a speaking activity when the focus is on meaning and fluency (i.e. what Walsh calls the classroom context mode) may be obstructive as it may be interruptive. This variable approach and the sensitivity towards local contingency in classroom talk has influenced more recent studies which have paid significant attention to multimodal and multilingual aspects of classroom interaction.

Sert (2015) builds on Seedhouse's classroom contexts and Walsh's notion of CIC to describe the ways epistemic, multimodal, and multilingual resources help us understand learning and teaching events in L2 classrooms. Using data that includes EFL classrooms in Luxembourg and Turkey, he examines the verbal and multimodal features of teacher–student interaction; including gaze, gestures, and orientations to classroom artefacts. It builds on the knowledge-base of L2 teachers' interactive skills by showing that the ways (1) teachers respond to students' use of first language(s), (2) manage interactional troubles, (3) visualise their actions through gestures, and (4) display awareness of unwillingness to participate have pedagogical and interactional consequences. Based on empirical findings, the book goes on to provide tips for teachers and extends these findings for investigating and enabling teacher development, which will be presented in the following sections.

In an attempt to theorize pedagogical interaction using conversation analysis, Waring (2016) argues that there are three main principles that revolve around what teachers do in classrooms. These three principles are competence, complexity, and contingency. The principle of competence includes teachers' sensitivity to competency concerns of students in interaction, while complexity is about the ways teachers manage to accomplish multiple actions by producing a single turn. The principle of contingency, on the other hand, is concerned with the idea that teaching requires being responsive to the moment. This principle goes in line with the findings of aforementioned studies (Seedhouse, 2004; Walsh, 2011; Sert, 2015) in that the responsive behaviours of teachers should converge with the pedagogical goal of the moment, closely tied to the skills teachers show in online (Walsh, 2011) interactive decision making (Walsh, 2011; Li, 2017).

Conversation analytic studies of L2 classroom interaction have been influenced by recent trends in micro-analytic research on (L2) interaction, including epistemics (Sert, 2013; Sert and Jacknick, 2015; Käänta, 2014; Lee, 2015; Rusk et al., 2016), multimodality (e.g. Käänta, 2012; Mortensen, 2016; Matsumoto and Dobs, 2017; Sert, 2015), and participation practices (e.g. Hazel and Mortensen, 2017; Evnitskaya and Berger, 2017). One of the important constructs in L2 classroom interaction research circles has been the development of L2 Interactional Competence (e.g. Cekaite, 2007; 2017; Hall et al., 2011; Pekarek Doehler, 2018), which has generally been dealt with from learners' perspectives. Studies that track longitudinal development of L2 interactional competence of students in various contexts (see, for instance, Watanabe, 2017 for EFL classrooms in Japan) have lots to offer us with regards to how the interactional resources students deploy change over time. Such studies can also be reinvestigated to reveal what teachers do to co-construct classroom learning opportunities, the results of which may in long term inform teacher education.

Published extracts from the studies that portray L2 classroom interaction can be used in teacher education. They can become useful materials to raise L2 teachers' awareness on classroom interaction, which may in turn inform future practices. Consider the extract that follows, for instance (see Appendix 1 for transcription conventions).

Extract 15.1 Mutter

1		**Tea:**	do you know what <u>mutter</u> ↑means. ((students avoid mutual gaze))
2	→	**Mar:**	°no:°.
3			+shakes her head
		Tea:	+turns his body towards Mar
4		**Tea:**	°you don't⁰ ↑know.
5		**Tea:**	it means almost to <u>whisper</u> to:: speak er: qui-
6			very quietly, and when you just hea::r,

#1#?#3

7	**Tea:**	er:::, (word here and there),
8	**Mar:**	+((imitates muttering sound))
9	**Tea:**	<u>ex</u>↑actly (.) then you are muttering.

Sert and Walsh (2013: 554)

This extract showcases how an EFL teacher in Luxembourg successfully manages a student's claim of insufficient knowledge and creates a learning opportunity evidenced by the display of understanding in line 8. In line 1 the teacher (TEA) asks the meaning of the word 'to mutter', which receives a no knowledge claim in line 2. From lines 5 to 7, the teacher deploys a resource to manage the student's knowledge gap, namely an embodied vocabulary explanation, by synchronising his bodily gestures with his explanation. In line 8, by producing a sound that resembles muttering, the student displays her understanding. Such an extract, with simplified transcriptions, can be integrated into a teacher education session in which the teachers discuss management of troubles in L2 classrooms. With written or oral instructions, the teachers in training can be asked to identify the problem in groups and discuss the ways this particular teacher resolves the problem.

Although such activities and tasks in teacher education programmes can be useful for teachers to increase their awareness on interaction, published extracts may not be as effective as video materials that provide rich audio-visual input. Furthermore, rather than reading an extract from previously published work, teachers may benefit more from recordings of their own contexts and by actively engaging in reflective dialogic processes (Mann and Walsh, 2017). In terms of practice, such an application requires reflection on recordings of own classrooms. In terms of research, it may require going beyond conversation analysis of classroom interactions only, and may necessitate other tools for qualitative data collection and analysis. In their research, Lazaraton and Ishihara (2005) argue that 'the microanalysis of classroom discourse and the teacher self-reflections complement each other by providing insights that neither method generated in isolation' (p. 529). In the following section, I refer to research that advocate 'reflection on classroom interaction' in teacher education programs.

Classroom interaction, reflection, and L2 teacher education

One line of research that has brought together conversation analysis methodology and teacher education is represented by studies on the interactional organisation of mentor/trainer – teacher talk (e.g. Kim and Silver, 2016; Waring, 2013, 2014, 2017) and collaborative post-observation feedback practices (e.g. Harris, 2013). Such research is important in teacher education because interactional events like post-observation feedback sessions create space for development through dialogic reflection and feedback, and they build a bridge from classrooms to reflective development, especially if classroom videos are also used in these sessions. Remembering that such encounters are also dialogic, the sensitive nature of advice giving, elicitation of reflection, and providing feedback have been subject to discursive research.

Based on 50 video-recorded post-observation meetings with English as a Second Language teachers in the US, Waring (2017) closely investigates the interactional dynamics of mentor-teacher talk. She argues that such settings necessitate delicate use of interactional resources as they entail pointing out problems and proposing solutions, both of which may challenge teachers' competence. Her findings reveal an interactional resource, namely *going general*, which promotes 'teacher alignment and facilitates professional socialization' (20).

In another recent study carried out in a teacher education context in Singapore, Kim and Silver (2018) show the ways professional roles of feedback-provider vs. facilitator of reflection are enacted in post-observation feedback sessions. They demonstrate that different sequential placement of queries by mentors may limit or facilitate affordances for reflection, and may, as a result, lead to teacher development. Such roles (feedback-provider vs. facilitator of reflection) or identities that emerge in these dialogic encounters are crucial in teacher development. Morton and Gray (2018) argue that trainers and trainees in teacher education contexts position themselves and others with 'an eye to roles and identities that cannot be separated from issues of knowledge and competence' (36). If competences enacted in classrooms are used together with the reflective dialogic processes in teacher education, there will be, I would argue, more room for development.

Using discursive methods, one of the early attempts to bridge what actually happens in classrooms in comparison to what is reported by teachers is Li and Walsh's (2011) study carried out in Chinese EFL contexts. The authors argue that a research methodology combining 'interview and classroom data is more capable of showing the very important relationship between stated beliefs and interaction' (53). Li and Walsh's study has informed studies that relate to teacher experience and teacher cognition in relation to teacher education (Fagan, 2012, 2017; Li, 2017). Using discursive methodologies, Li (2017) investigates both pre-service and in-service L2 teacher education settings and provides the bases for what she refers to as cognition-in-interaction. Her work is significant in that it challenges previous work on teacher cognition, moving teacher cognition from a quantitative and/or perception-based paradigm to a discursive, more dialogic one. Researchers have increasingly followed dialogic pathways in teacher education (Walsh and Mann, 2015; Mann and Walsh, 2017), and the field has now increasingly been witnessing classroom interaction based teacher education frameworks, including SETT (Walsh, 2006, 2011), IMDAT (Sert, 2015), and SWEAR (Waring, 2019).

SETT (Self Evaluation of Teacher Talk) is a teacher education framework that aims to contribute to teacher development through classroom interaction (Walsh, 2006, 2011, 2013), and initially emerged based on Walsh's (2006) study carried out in a UK university's English language centre. It developed out of teachers' reflections on their own interactional practices. SETT includes four classroom micro-contexts (known as modes), namely; (1) managerial mode, (2) materials mode, (3) skills and system mode, and (4) classroom context mode, each of which has its own distinctive *fingerprint* (Heritage and Greatbatch, 1989) identifiable according to the pedagogic goals in a given classroom moment and specific interactional features, known as interactures (see Walsh, 2011: 113 for a complete list). Driven by an applied conversation analytic framework, SETT provides teachers with a set of tools to engage in critical self-reflective practices based on their own classroom interactions and has inspired teacher educators around the globe. It facilitates teacher language awareness (Walsh, 2003) and helps teachers identify obstructive and constructive language teaching practices that promote or hinder learning opportunities.

SETT has been adopted in both researching classroom interactional practices and training L2 teachers. Howard (2010), for instance, adopts this framework to reveal the existence (or otherwise) of typical language classrooms and brings evidence to the existence of classroom modes. SETT has also been used to code classroom interaction data, for instance for understanding the impact of interactive whiteboards on teacher-student interaction in a Spanish context (Coyle, Yanez and Verdú, 2010). Furthermore, it has also informed methods of analysing classroom interaction. Yang (2014) uses SETT to investigate discourse markers in Chinese EFL classroom interaction using corpus linguistics in combination with a 'modes analysis', informed by SETT. As a tool for training teachers, the contexts it has been used in include and go beyond Hungary (Skinner, 2012), Iran (Ghafarpour, 2017), and Turkey (Aşık and Kuru Gönen, 2016; Ünal, Bozbıyık and Acar, 2018). In addition to shaping their teacher education programme using SETT, Aşık and Kuru Gönen (ibid.) investigate pre-service teachers' perceptions of the use of SETT and their development, revealing positive outcomes reported by EFL teachers in Turkey. SETT has been central to conceptualising L2 Classroom Interactional Competence, which was summarised in the previous section.

CIC includes a set of practices that help create more engaging L2 classrooms, e.g. maximising interactional space, shaping learner contributions, and effective elicitation. CIC is at the heart of IMDAT (Sert, 2015, 2019a), a teacher development framework that is micro-analytic and reflective. IMDAT involves a series of steps in teacher education that includes (I)ntroduction of CIC to teachers, (M)icro/initial-teaching experiences, (D)ialogic reflection on video-recorded teaching practices with the help of a mentor/supervisor/trainer, (A)nother round of teaching observed by a peer and (T)eacher collaboration for peer-feedback. IMDAT integrates visual experiences (through the use of videos) and micro-analyses into various forms of dialogic and written reflective practices driven by analyses of classroom interactions. Sert's IMDAT enables a longitudinal take on teacher education and expands SETT and CIC in its inclusion of multimodal (e.g. teacher gestures), multilingual (e.g. teachers' methods for handling L1 use, see Sert, 2019a; aus der Wieschen and Sert, 2018), epistemic (e.g. identifying and responding to knowledge gaps) and participatory (e.g. (un)willingness to participate) aspects of classroom interaction.

A very recent teacher education framework that incorporates classroom interaction into its pedagogical agenda has been proposed by Waring (2019). Waring takes heteroglossia as her point of departure in classroom interaction, arguing that classroom interaction, and in particular teacher talk, can be heteroglossic:

> a particular utterance can be saturated with more than one voice or achieve more than one goal, and a particular sequence can attend to multiple demands that the teachers manage on a daily basis: order, equity, learning, participation, progressivity, and inclusiveness. By deftly recruiting heteroglossia, teachers may succeed in, for example striking a delicate balance between exercising necessary control and fostering an open space for participation.

With its emphasis on student participation and engagement, SWEAR framework promises to help teachers to develop heteroglossia to manage paradoxes of classrooms. The framework consists of five stages that include (1) (S)ituating a problem, (2) (W)orking with a classroom recording, (3) (E)xpanding discussions, (4) (A)rticulating strategies, and (5) (R)ecording and repeating. Waring (ibid.) argues that the framework is best used 'as a way to enhance teachers' awareness of the challenges and possible solutions in classroom talk'.

Frameworks like SETT, IMDAT and SWEAR can be useful for language teachers as they encourage the use of recorded classroom interaction as well as dialogic reflection and feedback sessions, which facilitate awareness, criticality, and developmental points of departure that may inform future practice. Nevertheless, more research is required since identifying changes in teaching practices is a complex issue. In particular, longitudinal studies are required to be able to document the development of teachers who create more engaging classrooms. Discursive methods that combine analyses of classroom interactions with other qualitative data collection tools have proven to be useful so far, in particular in displaying the development of L2 Classroom Interactional Competence.

Research on the longitudinal development of L2 CIC

Although research on CIC in relation to teacher education has been around for a decade now, there is relatively little research which tracks the development of language teachers over time. One of the early examples is Escobar Urmeneta's (2013) study, which focuses on the development of a CLIL (Content and Language Integrated Learning) teacher in a Spanish context throughout one academic year, using multimodal conversation analysis and ethnographic content analysis. She shows how a student-teacher (who had been unable to promote student participation at the beginning of the year) – after recording, transcribing and reflecting on her own practice – starts using a more learner-convergent language, including a more efficient use of L1, showing signs of development in her CIC.

Based on an adoption of CIC to CLIL contexts proposed earlier by Escobar Urmeneta and Evnitskaya (2013), Escobar Urmeneta and Evnitskaya (2014) describe how CIC is enacted by participants while developing a teacher-led discussion based on data from a bilingual Catalan-Spanish secondary school classroom in Barcelona. Their findings reveal that teachers' deployment of multimodal resources favours learner initiated turns leading to sequences of mediation and remediation, 'providing the students with opportunities for the appropriation of language and content' (Escobar Urmeneta and Evnitskaya, 2014: 178).

In a Turkish EFL teacher education context, Sert (2015) tracks the development of pre-service language teachers over a year using analyses of teacher fronted classroom interaction as well as reflective writing and observation reports. The study documents how a novice language teacher becomes aware of a problem in facilitating student engagement in a speaking activity. The study then presents qualitative findings on this particular teacher's CIC, with a focus on a construct called *shaping learner contributions* (Walsh, 2011; Can Daşkın, 2015). This research provides empirical evidence for teacher development, showing how the same teacher becomes aware of this phenomenon and finally employs interactional resources that engage students, including embedded and embodied correction techniques in addition to embodied vocabulary explanations. Sert (2017) goes on to bring evidence based on the same teacher, this time not just for this teacher's effective management of interaction, but also the students' engagement as well as learning of a vocabulary item.

The stages of IMDAT (see Figure 15.1), as suggested in the previous section, has been found to help teachers develop teacher language awareness first, and eventually help them develop classroom interactional competence. More recently, video-tagging technology as well as other forms of reflection and feedback practices have been included in tracing the development of L2 CIC (Bozbıyık, 2017; Sert and Bozbıyık, 2017; Sert, 2016, 2019a), thus teacher development. Such an addition has boosted the micro-analytic and reflective nature of IMDAT with a practical technological element. The following section will present a guide for implementing this technology-enhanced, reflective, micro-analytic teacher education framework that combines classroom interaction with other tools, including stimulated recalls, trainer-teacher and teacher-teacher feedback sessions, as well as reflective writing.

A practical application to integrate IMDAT into L2 teacher education

In what follows, each phase of IMDAT will be described in some detail, using classroom excepts and other data based on reflections and feedback sessions to provide the readers with practical and data-driven insights. It should be noted that a video tagging software, VEO,[1] has also been integrated into this micro-analytic, reflective teacher education programme that was implemented at a Turkish higher education institution with pre-service English language teachers. The use of a video-tagging mobile application created affordances for data-led reflection and observation (see Çelik, Baran, and Sert, 2018). The data-led nature of reflection on interaction is suggested as a powerful endeavour in teacher education (Walsh and Mann, 2015), as observations get visually empowered when a video-tagging software is included (Haines and Miller, 2017).

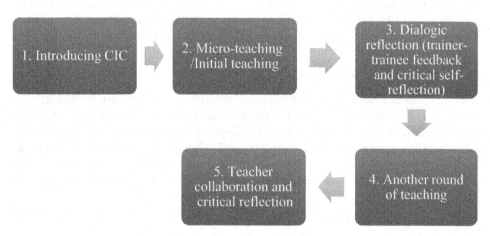

Figure 15.1 IMDAT: A classroom interaction driven, technology-enhanced and reflective teacher education framework

The initial stage, (I)ntroducing CIC, is meant to include short introductory hands-on sessions, aiming to introduce basic tenets of CIC using published extracts as well as accompanying videos where possible. The (M)icro-teaching/initial teaching phase requires teachers in training to prepare short teaching sessions, but can be as long as a full lesson if required. The session needs to be observed by a trainer/mentor, but can also be video-recorded using a video-tagging tool (e.g. VEO) or a camera. The third phase is a (D)ialogic reflection/feedback session between the trainer and the trainee teacher, followed by a critical self-reflection in written form. This part also requires the review of tagged moments if VEO is used. The fourth phase, (A)nother round of teaching, requires peer-observation. The final phase, (T)eacher collaboration and critical reflection, involves collaborative peer-feedback and another piece of reflective writing. The whole framework that involves an evolving 'teacher language awareness' (Walsh, 2003) and the development of L2 Classroom Interactional Competence can be described in detail as follows:

Step 1. Introducing CIC

In the initial phase of IMDAT, teachers in training receive a hands-on training, up to three sessions, so that they become familiar with the basics of L2 Classroom Interactional Competence and understand the importance of classroom interaction in teaching. This is an important requirement in that the introductory session gives candidates 'the language to be used' in reflections and peer-feedback, for instance different types of teacher questions and repair. The introduction should be designed exemplar-based by using published extracts from real classrooms, and if possible with sample videos (see Sert, 2019a for more on selecting these materials based on a comparative framework). If there are no videos available, then extracts in a variety of publications on CIC (e.g. Seedhouse and Walsh, 2010; Walsh, 2002, 2006, 2011, 2012, 2013; Walsh and Li, 2013; Sert and Walsh, 2013; Sert 2015, 2017) can be used while introducing the concepts. In an ideal three classroom-hour session, the first two can include the introduction of CIC concepts given below, with a whole class and hands-on workshop led by the trainer, while the third hour could include teachers' working on the transcripts together in pairs and groups. The following constructs can be introduced:

1a) Maximising interactional space

The teachers can be made aware that promoting extended learner turns is a significant indication of enhanced learner participation. This can be possible via increased wait-time, allowing planning time, and invitations for elaboration and additional learner participation.

1b) Shaping learner contributions

Examples of seeking clarification, scaffolding, and repairing learner input can be used. In repair sequences, both embedded corrections in meaning and fluency contexts and direct repairs in form-and-accuracy contexts can be illustrated. Extract 8.2 in Sert (2015) and how teachers' actions turn into opportunities for learning illustrated in Sert (2017) can provide good examples to teachers both for maximising interactional space and shaping learner contributions. Teachers can also be encouraged to study the relevant extracts in Walsh (2011) and Can Daşkın (2015).

1c) Effective use of eliciting

Teacher initiations that facilitate extended learner turns in both form focused and meaning based activities can be exemplified. Different resources like DIUs can be illustrated and discussed as hints in grammar focused (see Sert and Walsh, 2013: 556) or vocabulary-based (Sert, 2015: 102) episodes.

1d) Using goal-convergent language and interactional awareness

Being responsive to the moment in line with the pedagogical goal, namely mode-convergent language (Walsh, 2006, 2011), is extremely important. For instance, the ways student errors are treated (or not) can be illustrated using extracts 2.7 and 2.8 in Sert (2015). Teachers' responses to learner initiatives (Waring, 2011; Sert 2015, 2017) to deal with pedagogical shifts can be discussed using relevant extracts.

1e) Successful management of claims/displays of insufficient knowledge

Examples of different ways 'I don't knows' or very long silences are treated can be discussed using the extracts in Sert and Walsh (2013) and Sert (2013). The interactional resources that promote participation after these interactional troubles can be discussed, also considering different ways students display unwillingness to participate (Sert 2015, extracts 4.3 and 4.4).

1f) Effective use of gestures

The ways teachers employ gestures in correction (e.g. Sert, 2015: 94), elicitation (e.g. Sert, 2015: 102), and explanation sequences can be exemplified and discussed. How such resources lead to learning opportunities (Sert, 2017 for embodied and embedded repair and embodied explanations) need to be explicated, also using extracts in studies that focus on different aspects of language, including grammar (Matsumoto and Dobs, 2017).

1h) Successful management of code-switching

Different ways teachers respond to students' use of their first languages can be illustrated based on Chapter 6 in Sert (2015), and how a teacher can display dual orientations based on the pedagogical goals can also be shown, using extracts 6.9 and 7.1 in Sert (2015). Excerpts in Üstünel and Seedhouse (2005) and Üstünel (2016) may also be useful.

It would be ideal if teachers are encouraged to read relevant articles before and after the introduction sessions. Reading an introductory study before the session (for instance Walsh, 2012), and an optional article with a narrower focus (e.g. a focus on mother tongue use, or corrective feedback) after the session would be a good strategy to use. Upon completing this first step of IMDAT, the teachers should be asked to prepare a micro/initial-teaching session which will be observed by the trainer, preferably using a video-tagging tool.

Step 2. Micro/initial-teaching

The lesson to be observed by the trainer ideally includes the use of a video-tagging tool like VEO, considering different aspects of classroom interaction. The tagset (Figure 15.2) can include a variety of aspects of classroom interaction, like questions and corrective feedback types, L1 use of the students, and the use of body language. During the recording, the trainer can tag moments which will be of value for future reflection, and these tags can be accompanied by field notes.

Figure 15.2 VEO teacher tagset

Step 3. Dialogic reflection and trainer feedback

Post observation feedback right after a lesson ends is important for teachers, especially if they can immediately see what they have done in a specific lesson. Being able to go through a classroom video immediately with a trainer is possible through a video tagging software, using which a trainer has already identified points of reflection and feedback while observing. A dialogic reflection has to be carried out, during which the trainer walks the candidate through some features of classroom interaction observed. At this stage, VEO provides opportunities for stimulated recall. What follows is a sample trainer (TRA)-trainee (TEA) dialogue (translation in **bold**) in a post-observation session with VEO, based on data I collected recently in a Turkish pre-service teacher education setting:

Extract 15.2 VEO Enhanced feedback session, April 2017

01	**TRA:**	soru tiplerine bakalim (biraz)
		let's have a look at the question types
02		(13.6) ((VEO video playing))
03		şimdi şey guzel .hh <şimdi> did you vesaire gibi
04		yes no (0.3) type questionlarda bi <u>yes no</u>
05		geldikten sonra Ustune (.) aninda elaboration
06		question (0.1) burda yaptiğin gibs =
07	**TEA:**	=hihi=
		uh huh
08	**TRA:**	=err[sorman güizel bişey]

Now, It Is good. It's a [good thing that you ask] an elaboration question tight

after a yes or a no response that follows a yes no type question like "did sou"

09	TEA:	(hocam¹ bunda şeyden] şim- eer hocayi
10		gôzlemlediğimiz zamanlarda <fark ettim de> genellikle
11		bu simple past tense'i (0.4) genellikle
12		yes no questionlarla veriyo o yuzden=

[hocain It's because] now – I noticed when we were obserslng the (mentor)

teacher, generally (she) generally provides (examples of) simple past tense with

yes/no questions

13	TRA:	=hl[h1]

uh huh

14	TEA:	[kor] kutmamak için başta bi onla giriyim [dedim]

I thought I should start that was at the beginning not to [sra]re students

In this extract, the trainer brings in the topic of questions types (line 1) based on a moment in the lesson tagged using VEO. He then starts playing the video, illustrated in Extract 15.3, on the mobile device:

Extract 15.3 Tagged classroom moment

01	TEA:	bookshop yes↑ (0.5) did you go to the bookshop?
02		(0.3) murat?
03	STU:	°yes I did°=
04	TEA:	=yes (0.3) u::h which book (0.3) did you buy (0.5)
05		which book (0.1) remember?

The trainer provides a positive evaluation at the beginning of line 03 and in line 08 in Extract 15.2, considering the fact that when the teacher asked a yes/no question, she followed up with an elaboration question (line 03 to line 06). Since the teacher is also watching the video at the same time, this evidence-based feedback (Extract 15.3 is the episode they are talking about) elicits immediate reflection from the teacher. The teacher first refers to the mentor teacher (an experienced teacher) she has been observing before with this class, and argues that the mentor teacher generally provides examples of past tense using yes/no questions (lines 09–12). She justifies (line 14) her point by also adding that she did not want to scare the students by doing something different at the beginning of her first class.

As can be seen in Extracts 15.2 and 15.3, using a video tagging tool can facilitate evidence based feedback and reflection at this stage of IMDAT. The point here is not whether this feedback leads to 'good' teacher behaviours, but it is that it provides visual evidence for reflection during a feedback session, and therefore creates a data-led (Walsh and Mann, 2015) developmental experience. In addition to this dialogic feedback and reflection phase, this stage of IMDAT also includes 'critical self-reflection' in written form. The teachers can be asked to write a critical reflection (see sample guidelines in Appendix 2), focusing on examples in which they successfully engage students to the lesson, and in which they think they fail to do so. The process helps the teachers focus on micro details through repeated watching and reviewing the tags, thus facilitates critical reflection. The teacher who featured in the previous two extracts has written the following:

Extract 15.4 Critical reflective writing

firstly I asked a closed question like *Did you go to the bookshop before?* **at 02:58**. Then, to elaborate on their answers, I asked some open questions about their experiences in those places such as *Which book did you buy?, Have you ever read any English books before?, etc.* This was successful in terms of elicitation of vocabulary items and practice in speaking.

The teacher watches the same episode together with many other parts of her lesson video, and further reflects on the question type she used (closed questions vs. open questions) by referring to the teaching experience in minute level detail (**at 02:58**). She assesses her practices as successful, and argues that the strategies she has employed have been conducive to elicitation of vocabulary and to speaking skills of the students in general.

The next step of IMDAT is another round of teaching, to be observed by a peer rather than a trainer. The first reason to have a peer-observation and feedback practice is to balance the power relations in the training process, simply due to the potential dominance of a trainer or a mentor who assesses the teachers. Second having gone through the trainer-feedback process, the teachers have seen a model of feedback giving that they can selectively rely on in their own feedback giving reflective session. The use of VEO here is again very useful, as the videos shared on the video portal that is available through VEO app will be accessible by the trainer, and thus further trainer feedback will be possible.

Step 4. Another teaching session

Based on their experiences of preparing a lesson plan, teaching, being observed, getting feedback, and critical reflection, the teachers are asked to teach another lesson, preferably towards the end of a school semester. Before the teachers prepare their lesson plans, they should be encouraged to have a look at the lesson plan they prepared before their first teaching, and notice the differences between the plan and what actually happened in the classroom. This will help them to carefully consider issues regarding time management, activities carried out, and language used to encourage student participation. After they prepare their lesson plan, the trainer can provide feedback and make suggestions for changes. The lesson this time is observed, video-recorded, and tagged by another trainee, without the existence of a trainer in the lesson. The teachers are asked to critically watch each other's performances, by using the selected features of CIC and their previous experiences. Appendix 3 includes some of the guidelines used for this process with a group of teachers. This will prepare the grounds for the next phase.

Step 5. Teacher collaboration and critical reflection

Following on the previous step, the last phase of IMDAT involves an element of teacher collaboration. After the candidates observe each other's lessons, they repeat the stimulated recall cycle described in Step 3, this time without a trainer and following the guidelines in Appendix 3. The teachers are encouraged to discuss all the moments tagged by playing parts of their teaching sessions and referring to positive and problematic aspects of their teaching practices. Peer-feedback sessions, when a video-tagging software is used, can stimulate rich reflections and may facilitate critical thinking. One example of this, based on the data I collected in 2016, was provided as a vignette in Mann and Walsh (2017: 256). Another example comes from the same teacher (T1) who has featured in the last three extracts. In this extract, she receives feedback on how she responded to students' use of L1 (i.e. Turkish) from her peer (T2):

Extract 15.5 Peer-feedback on the use of L1

01	**T2:**	ya sorularx ingi- türkçe soruyorlar ama
02		sen ingilizce cevap verince (0.4) [iyi oldu]
		they ask the questions in en- Turkish but it was good when you responded in
		English
03	**Tl:**	[h1h1:]
04	**T2:**	instruction olarak=
		as instructions-
05	**Tl:**	=>ben zaten onlain< cevaplarini da çevirip
06		hani bir daha [ingi]lizce
07	**T2:**	[hmhm↑]
08	**Tl:**	olarak [söyledim]
		I, in the first place, translated their answers and said in English again
09	**T2:**	[evet işte] bu↑ çok güzel oluyor bence↑
		[yes you see] this is very good in my opinion

In lines 01 and 02, the peer teacher (T2) who observes T1's lesson provides a positive assessment (**it was good**) regarding the ways T1 responded in English to Turkish utterances produced by the students. This evidence-based (they are watching the episodes in VEO based on the tags) comment elicits reflection from T1, as she added that her L2 responses also included reformulations from L1 to L2. In line 09, T2 displays alignment and takes personal stance followed by an explicit positive assessment (**this is very good in my opinion**). What is important here is that the focus on classroom interactions and the whole teacher education framework generates evidence-based reflection. These reflections are based on an increased teacher language awareness and they enable the teachers in training to focus on various aspects of their lessons from a micro-analytic perspective. Whether the emerging and evolving teacher practices create learning opportunities for students or not requires an additional level of analysis, as documented in Sert (2017).

Conclusion and future directions

In this chapter, I have shown that empirical research on L2 classroom interaction in the last two decades has successfully documented teaching practices that can enhance engagement of students in L2 classrooms and that can facilitate learning opportunities. I have argued that the available classroom extracts and datasets from mediated language learning environments are rich resources that can be integrated into language teacher education. The attempts to help teachers with CIC, SETT, and IMDAT, all of which aim to help teachers to be aware of the value of interaction for creating learning opportunities, have been strengthened now with innovations in video and mobile technology, a point I have tried to develop in the previous section.

One possible future direction in the field of L2 classroom discourse and interaction is to start comparing findings from classrooms all over the world to be able to generate training materials for teachers. Markee's (2017) call for comparative reproduction research to investigate massively common teacher practices may help researchers of classroom interaction in many ways, especially in drawing conclusions for teacher education. Such a comparative agenda may feed into audio-visual materials development for teachers (see Sert 2019a). Emerging findings can be used to design video materials that facilitate evidence-based training. Issues including 'how teachers should manage L1 use', 'what kind of corrective feedback is more beneficial in a given activity', 'which elicitation techniques are more fruitful' are universal questions for teachers, and thus integrating such phenomena with visual materials into teacher education can be useful. Furthermore, how the language use of teachers and the development of interactional resources over time should also be considered as part of the research programme on 'L2 Interactional Competence' (Hall, Hellermann, Pekarek Doehler, 2011; Pekarek Doehler, 2018).

Video Enhanced Observation (VEO) in particular and integration of technology into teacher education in general require further research. We need to be able to facilitate visual reflective practices for teachers, and the use of flexible mobile technologies is the future, also considering the fact that what we understand from a word like classroom is going through a transformation. Online and technology enhanced training opportunities that put interaction in the centre of developmental agendas need to be created. VILTE (https://vilte.warwick.ac.uk/) and SETTVEO (https://englishagenda.britishcouncil.org/research-publications/elt-research-awards/eltra-winners/eltra-2016-winners) projects, both supported by the British Council, are important steps to relise such goals. These technological tools can facilitate self-reflection practices, which can be useful for action research and mentor education (Dikilitaş and Wyatt, 2017). A dialogue between researchers who focus on (1) classroom interaction from a conversation analytic perspective, (2) action research and teacher research, (3) reflective practice, and (3) teacher cognition has lots to offer to the future of language teacher education.

It should be noted that classrooms are not places with physical walls, but they are virtual or physical places where learning is mediated. This is why more research is required for investigating language learning practices in online environments (Balaman and Sert, 2017; Sert and Balaman, 2018) and online communication spaces designed for teachers. Classroom discourse research includes and is open to virtual environments. As an additional technological innovation in research, integration of eye-tracking technology to investigate teaching practices in teacher education is also important, since teacher gaze is an important element of student engagement (Sert 2019b), and engagement is key to learning (Walsh, 2006). There can be a future for artificial intelligence in education, but such a future requires massive amount of research documenting micro-level pedagogical practices that create learning opportunities. This is only one of the reasons why a micro-level analysis of interactional practices in teaching and teacher education has a never-ending potential.

Note

1 The integration of VEO software (Video Enhanced Observation) was possible thanks to an EU grant (Project code: 2015–1–UKO1-KA201–013414). Details of the VEOEuropa Project can be found online at: <https://veoeuropa.com/> (accessed 22 May, 2019).

Further reading

Sert, O. (2015). *Social Interaction and L2 Classroom Discourse*. Edinburgh: Edinburgh University Press.
Walsh, S. (2013). *Classroom Discourse and Teacher Development*. Edinburgh: Edinburgh University Press.

References

Aşık, A. and Kuru Gönen, S. İ. (2016) 'Pre-Service EFL Teachers' Reported Perceptions of Their Development Through SETT Experience'. *Classroom Discourse*, 7(2) 164–183.
aus der Wieschen, M.V. and Sert, O. (2018) 'Divergent Language Choices and Maintenance of Intersubjectivity: The Case of Danish EFL Young Learners'. *International Journal of Bilingual Education and Bilingualism*. Available online: <https://doi.org/10.1080/13670050.2018.1447544> (accessed 22 May, 2019).
Balaman, U. and Sert, O. (2017) 'Development of L2 Interactional Resources for Online Collaborative Task Accomplishment'. *Computer Assisted Language Learning*, 30(7) 601–630.
Bozbıyık, M. (2017) *The implementation of VEO in an English language education context: a focus on teacher questioning practices*. Unpublished MA thesis, Gazi University, Turkey.
Can Daşkın, N. (2015) 'Shaping Learner Contributions in an EFL Classroom: Implications for L2 Classroom Interactional Competence'. *Classroom Discourse*, 6(1) 33–56.
Cekaite, A. (2007) 'A Child's Development of Interactional Competence in a Swedish L2 Classroom'. *The Modern Language Journal*, 91(1) 45–62.
Cekaite, A. (2017) 'What Makes a Child a Good Language Learner? Interactional Competence, Identity, and Immersion in a Swedish Classroom'. *Annual Review of Applied Linguistics*, 37, 45–61.
Coyle, Y., Yanez, L. and Verdú, M. (2010) 'The Impact of the Interactive Whiteboard on The Teacher and Children's Language Use in an ESL Immersion Classroom'. *System*, 38(4), 614–625.
Çelik, S., Baran, E. and Sert, O. (2018) 'The Affordances of Mobile-app Supported Teacher Observations for Peer Feedback'. *International Journal of Mobile and Blended Learning*, 10(2) 36–49.
Dikilitaş, K. and Wyatt, M. (2018) 'Learning Teacher-Research-Mentoring: Stories From Turkey'. *Teacher Development*, 22(4) 537–553.
Escobar Urmeneta, C. (2013) 'Learning to become a CLIL teacher: teaching, reflection and professional development'. *International Journal of Bilingual Education and Bilingualism*, 16(3) 334–353.
Escobar Urmeneta, C. and Evnitskaya, N. (2013) 'Affording students opportunities for the integrated learning of content and language. A contrastive study on classroom interactional strategies deployed by two CLIL teachers', in Arnau, J. (ed.) *Reviving Catalan at School: Challenges and Instructional Approaches*. Bristol and Barcelona: Multilingual Matters and Institut d'Estudis Catalans: 159–183.
Escobar Urmeneta, C. and Evnitskaya, N. (2014) '"Do You Know Actimel?" The Adaptive Nature of Dialogic Teacher-led Discussions in the CLIL Science Classroom: A Case Study'. *The Language Learning Journal*, 42(2) 165–180.
Evnitskaya, N. and Berger, E. (2017) 'Learners' Multimodal Displays of Willingness to Participate in Classroom Interaction in the L2 and CLIL Contexts'. *Classroom Discourse*, 8(1) 71–94.
Fagan, D. S. (2012) 'Conversation analysis as a methodology for examining teacher knowledge in practice'. In Soneson, D. and Tarone, E. (eds) *Expanding Our Horizons: Language Teacher Education in the 21st Century: Selected Papers from the 6th and 7th International Language Teacher Education Conferences*. Minneapolis, MN: University of Minnesota, The Center for Advanced Research on Language Acquisition: 183–205.
Fagan, D. (2014) 'Beyond "Excellent!": Uncovering the Systematicity behind Positive Feedback Turn Construction in ESL Classrooms'. *Novitas-ROYAL (Research on Youth and Language)*, 8 45–63.
Fagan, D. S. (2017) 'Addressing Learner Hesitancy-to-Respond Within Initiation-Response-Feedback Sequences'. *TESOL Quarterly*, 52(2) 425–435.
Ghafarpour, H. (2017) 'Classroom Conversation Analysis and Critical Reflective Practice: Self-Evaluation of Teacher Talk Framework in Focus'. *RELC Journal*, 48(2) 210–225.
Haines, J. and Miller, P. (2017) 'Video enhanced observation: developing a flexible and effective tool', in O'Leary, M. (ed.) *Reclaiming Lesson Observation*. Abingdon: Routledge: 127–140.

Hall, J. K., Hellermann, J. and Doehler, S. P. (eds) (2011) *L2 Interactional Competence and Development*. Bristol: Multilingual Matters.

Harris, A. R. (2013) *Professionals developing professionalism: the interactional organisation of reflective practice*. PhD thesis, Newcastle University, UK.

Hazel, S. and Mortensen, K. (2017) 'The Classroom Moral Compass: Participation, Engagement and Transgression in Classroom Interaction'. *Classroom Discourse*, 8(3) 1–21.

Hellermann, J. (2008) *Social Actions for Classroom Language Learning*. Clevedon: Multilingual Matters.

Heritage, J. and Greatbatch, D. (1989) 'On the Institutional Character of Institutional Talk: The Case of News Interviews'. *Discourse in Professional and Everyday Culture. Linko ping, Department of Communication Studies, University of Linko ping, Sweden*, 47–98.

Howard, A. (2010) 'Is There Such a Thing as a Typical Language Lesson?'. *Classroom Discourse*, 1(1) 82–100.

Hutchby, I. and Wooffitt, R. (2008) *Conversation Analysis*, 2nd edition. Cambridge: Polity Press.

Jacknick, C. M. (2011) '"But This is Writing": Post-Expansion in Student-initiated Sequences'. *Novitas-ROYAL (Research on Youth and Language)*, 5(1) 39–54.

Kääntä, L. (2012) 'Teachers' Embodied Allocations in Instructional Interaction'. *Classroom Discourse*, 3(2) 166–186.

Kääntä, L. (2014) 'From Noticing to Initiating Correction: Students' Epistemic Displays in Instructional Interaction'. *Journal of Pragmatics*, 66 86–105.

Kim, Y. and Silver, R. E. (2016) 'Provoking Reflective Thinking in Post Observation Conversations'. *Journal of Teacher Education*, 67(3) 203–219.

Kim, Y. and Silver, R. E. (2018) '"What do you think about this?": differing role enactment in post-observation conversation', in Kunitz, S., Sert, O. and Markee, N. (eds) *Classroom-Based Conversation Analytic Research: Theoretical and Applied Perspectives on Pedagogy*. New York: Springer.

Lazaraton, A. and Ishihara, N. (2005) 'Understanding Second Language Teacher Practice Using Microanalysis and Self-Reflection: A Collaborative Case Study'. *The Modern Language Journal*, 89(4) 529–542.

Lee, Y. A. (2015) 'Negotiating Knowledge Bases in Pedagogical Discourse: Relevance of Identities to Language Classroom Interactions'. *Text & Talk*, 35(5) 621–642.

Li, L. (2017) *Social Interaction and Teacher Cognition*. Edinburgh: Edinburgh University Press.

Li, L. and Walsh, S. (2011) '"Seeing is Believing": Looking at EFL Teachers' Beliefs Through Classroom Interaction". *Classroom Discourse*, 2(1) 39–57.

Mann, S. and Walsh, S. (2017) *Reflective Practice in English Language Teaching: Research-Based Principles and Practices*. Abingdon: Routledge.

Markee, N. (2008) 'Toward a Learning Behavior Tracking Methodology for CA-for-SLA'. *Applied Linguistics*, 29(3) 404–427.

Markee, N. (2017) 'Are Replication Studies Possible in Qualitative Second/Foreign Language Classroom Research? A Call for Comparative Re-Production Research'. *Language Teaching*, 50(3) 367–383.

Markee, N. and Seo, M. S. (2009) 'Learning Talk Analysis'. *IRAL-International Review of Applied Linguistics in Language Teaching*, 47(1) 37–63.

Matsumoto, Y. and Dobs, A. M. (2017) 'Pedagogical Gestures as Interactional Resources for Teaching and Learning Tense and Aspect in the ESL Grammar Classroom'. *Language Learning*, 67(1) 7–42.

Mortensen, K. (2016) 'The Body as a Resource for Other-Initiation of Repair: Cupping the Hand Behind the Ear'. *Research on Language and Social Interaction*, 49(1) 34–57.

Morton, T. and Gray, J. (2018) *Social Interaction and English Language Teacher Identity*. Edinburgh: Edinburgh University Press.

Pekarek Doehler, S. (2018) 'Elaborations on L2 Interactional Competence: The Development of L2 Grammar-for-Interaction'. *Classroom Discourse*, 9(1) 3–24.

Rusk, F., Pörn, M. and Sahlström, F. (2016) 'The Management of Dynamic Epistemic Relationships Regarding Second Language Knowledge in Second Language Education: Epistemic Discrepancies and Epistemic (Im)Balance'. *Classroom Discourse*, 7(2) 184–205.

Seedhouse, P. (2004) *The Interactional Architecture of the Language Classroom: A Conversation Analysis Perspective*. Malden, MA: Blackwell.

Seedhouse, P. (2019) 'L2 Classroom Contexts: Deviance, Confusion, Grappling and Flouting'. *Classroom Discourse*, 10(1). Available online: <www.tandfonline.com/toc/rcdi20/10/1> (accessed 22 May, 2019).

Seedhouse, P. and Walsh, S. (2010) 'Learning a second language through classroom interaction', in Seedhouse, P., Walsh, S. and Jenks, C. (eds) *Conceptualising Learning in Applied Linguistics*. Basingstoke: Palgrave Macmillan: 127–146.

Sert, O. (2013) '"Epistemic Status Check"as an Interactional Phenomenon in Instructed Learning Settings'. *Journal of Pragmatics*, 45(1) 13–28.

Sert, O. (2015) *Social Interaction and L2 Classroom Discourse*. Edinburgh: Edinburgh University Press.

Sert, O. (2016) 'Transforming CA Findings into Future L2 Teaching Practices'. Paper presented at the American Association for Applied Linguistics Conference, 9–12 April, Orlando, USA.

Sert, O. (2017) 'Creating Opportunities for l2 Learning in a Prediction Activity'. *System*, 70 14–25.

Sert, O. (2019a) 'Transforming CA findings into future L2 teaching practices: challenges and prospects', in Kunitz, S., Sert, O. and Markee, N. (eds) *Classroom-Based Conversation Analytic Research: Theoretical and Applied Perspectives on Pedagogy*. New York: Springer.

Sert, O. (2019b) 'Mutual gaze, embodied go-aheads, and their interactional consequences in L2 classrooms'. In Hall, J. K. and Looney, S. D. (eds) *The Embodied Work of Teaching*. Bristol: Multilingual Matters.

Sert, O. and Balaman, U. (2018) 'Orientations to Negotiated Language and Task Rules in Online L2 Interaction'. *ReCALL*, 30(3) 355–374.

Sert, O. and Bozbıyık, B. (2017) 'A Technology Enhanced and Reflective Teacher Education Programme: Implications for Teaching L2 Interactional Competence'. *Interactional Competences and Practices in a Second Language (ICOP 2)*, 18–20 January, University of Neuchâtel, Switzerland.

Sert, O. and Jacknick, C. (2015) 'Student Smiles and the Negotiation of Epistemics in L2 Classrooms'. *Journal of Pragmatics*, 77(1) 97–112.

Sert, O. and Walsh, S. (2013) 'The Interactional Management of Claims of Insufficient Knowledge in English Language Classrooms'. *Language and Education*, 27(6) 542–565.

Skinner, B. (2012) 'Changing Identities: An Exploration of ESL Trainee Teacher Discourse in Microteaching'. *Classroom Discourse*, 3(1) 46–64.

Ünal, D. Ç., Bozbıyık, M. and Acar, Y. (2018) 'Almanca Öğretiminde Sınıf İçi Etkileşimsel Yetiye İlişkin Bir İhtiyaç Analizi ve Durum Tespiti' ['A Situation and Needs Analysis on Classroom Interactional Competence in German Language Teaching']. *Hacettepe University Journal of Education*. doi:10.16986/ HUJE.2018040663.

Üstünel, E. (2016) *EFL Classroom Code-Switching*. London: Palgrave.

Üstünel, E. and Seedhouse, P. (2005) 'Why That, in That Language, Right Now? Code-Switching and Pedagogical Focus'. *International Journal of Applied Linguistics*, 15(3) 302–325.

Walsh, S. (2002) 'Construction or Obstruction: Teacher Talk and Learner Involvement in the EFL Classroom'. *Language Teaching Research*, 6(1) 3–23.

Walsh, S. (2003) 'Developing Interactional Awareness in the Second Language Classroom Through Teacher Self-Evaluation'. *Language Awareness*, 12(2) 124–142.

Walsh, S. (2006) *Investigating Classroom Discourse*. New York: Routledge.

Walsh, S. (2011) *Exploring Classroom Discourse: Language in Action*. Abingdon: Routledge.

Walsh, S. (2012) 'Conceptualising Classroom Interactional Competence'. *Novitas-ROYAL (Research on Youth and Language)*, 6(1) 1–14. Available online: <www.novitasroyal.org/Vol_6_1/Walsh.pdf> (accessed 22 May, 2019).

Walsh, S. (2013) *Classroom Discourse and Teacher Development*. Edinburgh: Edinburgh University Press.

Walsh, S. and Li, L. (2013) 'Conversations as Space for Learning'. *International Journal of Applied Linguistics*, 23(2) 247–266.

Walsh, S. and Mann, S. (2015) 'Doing Reflective Practice: A Data-Led Way Forward'. *ELT Journal*, 69(4) 351–362.

Waring, H. Z. (2008) 'Using Explicit Positive Assessment in the Language Classroom: IRF, Feedback, and Learning Opportunities'. *The Modern Language Journal*, 92(4) 577–594.

Waring, H. Z. (2009) 'Moving Out of IRF (Initiation-Response-Feedback): A Single Case Analysis'. *Language Learning*, 59(4) 796–824.

Waring, H. Z. (2011) 'Learner Initiatives and Learning Opportunities in the Language Classroom'. *Classroom Discourse*, 2(2) 201–218.

Waring, H. Z. (2013) 'Two Mentor Practices that Generate Teacher Reflection Without Explicit Solicitations: Some Preliminary Considerations'. *RELC Journal*, 44(1) 103–119.

Waring, H. Z. (2014) 'Mentor Invitations for Reflection in Post-Observation Conferences: Some Preliminary Considerations'. *Applied Linguistics Review*, 5(1) 99–123.

Waring, H. Z. (2016) *Theorizing Pedagogical Interaction: Insights from Conversation Analysis*. Abingdon: Routledge.

Waring, H. Z. (2017) 'Going General as a Resource for Doing Advising in Post-Observation Conferences in Teacher Training'. *Journal of Pragmatics*, 110 20–33.

Waring, H. Z. (2019) 'Harnessing the power of heteroglossia in teacher talk' in Kunitz, S., Sert, O. and Markee, N. (eds) *Classroom-Based Conversation Analytic Research: Theoretical and Applied Perspectives on Pedagogy*. New York: Springer.

Waring, H. Z., Reddington, E. and Tadic, N. (2016) 'Responding Artfully to Student-Initiated Departures in the Adult ESL Classroom'. *Linguistics and Education*, 33 28–39.

Watanabe, A. (2017) 'Developing L2 Interactional Competence: Increasing Participation Through Self-Selection in Post-Expansion Sequences'. *Classroom Discourse*, 8(3) 271–293.

Yang, S. (2014) 'Interaction and codability: a multi-layered analytical approach to discourse markers in teacher's spoken discourse', in Romero-Trillo, J. (ed.) *Yearbook of Corpus Linguistics and Pragmatics 2014*. New York: Springer International Publishing: 291–313.

APPENDIX 15.1
TRANSCRIPTION CONVENTIONS

Adapted from Hutchby and Wooffitt (2008).

(1.8)	Numbers enclosed in parentheses indicate a pause. The number represents the number of seconds of duration of the pause, to one decimal place. A pause of fewer than 0.2 seconds is marked by (.)
[ ]	Brackets around portions of utterances show that those portions overlap with a portion of another speaker's utterance.
=	An equals sign is used to show that there is no time lapse between the portions connected by the equal signs. This is used where a second speaker begins their utterance just at the moment when the first speaker finishes.
::	A colon after a vowel or a word is used to show that the sound is extended. The number of colons shows the length of the extension.
(hm, hh)	These are onomatopoetic representations of the audible exhalation of air
.hh	This indicates an audible inhalation of air, for example, as a gasp. The more h's, the longer the in-breath.
?	A question mark indicates that there is slightly rising intonation.
.	A period indicates that there is slightly falling intonation.
,	A comma indicates a continuation of tone.
-	A dash indicates an abrupt cut off, where the speaker stopped speaking suddenly.
↑↓	Up or down arrows are used to indicate that there is sharply rising or falling intonation. The arrow is placed just before the syllable in which the change in intonation occurs.
Under	Underlines indicate speaker emphasis on the underlined portion of the word.
CAPS	Capital letters indicate that the speaker spoke the capitalised portion of the utterance at a higher volume than the speaker's normal volume.
°	This indicates an utterance that is much softer than the normal speech of the speaker. This symbol will appear at the beginning and at the end of the utterance in question.
> <, < >	'Greater than' and 'less than' signs indicate that the talk they surround was noticeably faster, or slower than the surrounding talk.

(would)   When a word appears in parentheses, it indicates that the transcriber has guessed as to what was said, because it was indecipherable on the tape. If the transcriber was unable to guess what was said, nothing appears within the parentheses.

£C'mon£   Sterling signs are used to indicate a smiley or jokey voice.

+   marks the onset of a non-verbal action (e.g. shift of gaze, pointing)

italics   English translation

APPENDIX 15.2

GUIDELINES FOR CRITICAL SELF-REFLECTION

1. Watch your video from the beginning to the end first, take notes based on your observation.
2. Go through the moments tagged in your lesson video.
3. Try to find the positive aspects and problematic aspects of your class.

Write a reflection

a. Briefly summarize your aim and classroom procedures that you planned for the lesson. Did your class go as planned? What are the differences between what you planned and what actually happened in the lesson?

b. Briefly describe a short segment in your lesson, which you found to be successful and engaging for your students. Refer to specific minutes and seconds where relevant.

c. Briefly describe a short segment in your class, which you found to be problematic and less engaging for your students. Refer to specific minutes and seconds where relevant.

d. Reflect on your and the students' use of L1 (i.e. Turkish), the questions you asked to the students, and the feedback turns. How did you manage student mistakes and correct answers? Think about what you did right after a student says something. What do you think about your own performance.

e. How did you manage troubles of communication? For example, long silences after you ask a question, or when a student shows that she does not know the answer, or displays unwillingness to participate.

f. What would you change in your next class?

APPENDIX 15.3
PEER FEEDBACK GUIDELINE

1. Record one of your peer's lessons and make sure they also record yours. While recording, use 'language learning and teaching' tagsets; you are free to choose the tags you want. Before you start recording, make sure that you can log in in advance. Put the name and surname of the teacher you are recording in the relevant text box, and also write which classroom you are recording (7C etc.).
2. After the lesson (immediately or sometime later) provide feedback to your peer. During the feedback session, do not just focus on 'feedback' giving, but remember that this is also a chance for your peers to reflect on their own classes.
3. Last, write a reflection paper on your performance during your second teaching. Refer to minutes and seconds and VEO tags where relevant. You may use the same categories/tags that you used in your first reflective paper if you like. Make sure that you also point out how things changed in the second teaching (or not).

16

WE, ELF, EIL and their implications for English language teacher education

Navaporn Snodin and Pia Resnik

Introduction

Even though the exact number of users of English in the world is difficult to state, recent estimates show that English is said to have approximately 1.2 to two billion users (see, e.g., Crystal, 2003; Graddol, 2006; Matsuda, 2012; Ostler, 2018), resulting in a great variety of World Englishes (see, e.g., Kachru, 1982, 1985, 1992; Kachru et al., 2009), the users of which have different needs. For a majority of those, English is not the L1 (first language). In fact, it is being used for different purposes and with different interlocutors, such as in EIL (English as an International Language) (Matsuda, 2012, 2017; McKay, 2002; Sharifian, 2009) and ELF (English as a Lingua Franca) (Jenkins, 1996, 2005, 2007; Seidlhofer, 2011; Mauranen, 2012) contexts, but also in EFL (English as a Foreign Language) and ESL (English as a Second Language) settings (e.g. Singapore). The line between these conceptualisations is not always clear-cut, as due to globalisation and, along with it migration, as well as the constant, dynamic intermeshing of users living side-by-side, the consequences are rapid changes of language use on societal and individual levels (Canagarajah, 2007). This diversity of English language users creates challenges, though, when it comes to ELT practices (Matsuda, 2012) and to training future teachers to successfully cater to the diverse needs of their learners. The aim of this chapter is to present, evaluate and critique the principles and practices related to the wide range of Englishes currently being used in English Language Teacher Education and to discuss the challenges faced by educators and researchers alike.

The chapter starts with a discussion of current perspectives on the great variety of users of English today and different conceptualisations of relevance in this context, the implications of which are linked to teaching contexts as a next step. In the following, findings from current research that acknowledges the current changing status of English will be presented. The third section discusses possible applications and elaborates on examples of actual practices. In a final step, the reader will be provided with an annotated bibliography of groundbreaking, as well as recent, publications on the topics discussed in the present chapter.

Current perspectives

Clearly, English has established itself as an international language (Matsuda, 2012) and 'is [often] the communicative medium of choice, and often the only option' (Seidlhofer, 2011. 7). Today, with non-native English speakers (NNES) outnumbering by far English native speakers (ENS), the long-held teaching and learning goal of being able to communicate with L1 users seems somewhat outdated, as it is 'only partially true, and thus pedagogy that introduces students only to the English varieties, people and culture of the Inner Circle countries is simply inadequate' (Matsuda, 2012: 5). It is, consequently, imperative to provide learners of English with an understanding of the variation explained above, which also implies equipping teachers with knowledge about and raising their tolerance towards World Englishes (Kirkpatrick, 2007). This helps depict a realistic picture as, more often than not, learners today engage in English conversations with people who do not share their L1 for mutual understanding to 'bridge communicative gaps' (Phillipson, 2008: 262).

Another highly controversial distinction, which is linked to the diversity of English users found these days, is the above-mentioned distinction between native speakers (ENS) and non-native speakers (NNES). Insisting on such a distinction often goes hand in hand with establishing a norm or standard, which also implies possible deviations from such a norm, and suggests a superiority of ENS varieties. In fact, it is not about deficit, but difference (Cook, 2016) and NNES, for instance, are language users in their own right and should be seen as such rather than as using a language in a restricted way of a(n idealised) monolingual native speaker of said language. Dewaele (2018) suggests overcoming this dichotomy by introducing new terms, such as 'LX user' instead of 'non-native speaker' (NNS). LX is a neutral label that can be used to refer to any foreign language user. Like Cook (1999, 2007), he aims at avoiding the dichotomy between NS and NNS because of their deficit-orientedness and implied inadequacy. What all LX users have in common is previous knowledge of (at least) their L1. As the languages a person knows mutually influence each other, and by definition no one can become an NS of anything other than one's L1 (Cook, 2012, 2016), the question arises as to why ENS still seem to be a highly important reference group in the EFL classroom. Frequently, their varieties are portrayed as the norm and absolute goal to be reached by NNES – a goal, which is strictly speaking elusive as it can never be reached by (at least a majority of) LX users (Cook, 2007, 2012, 2016). Moreover, ENS are no homogenous group themselves. Variation can be found in this group too, and their heterogeneity is not merely linked to regional variation as such, but also variation at the level of proficiency (Dewaele, 2018). The term 'native speaker' is often associated with high proficiency in this language, which is not necessarily the case. Research shows that language attrition can also affect the L1 (see, e.g., Schmidt, 2011). As multilingualism rather than monolingualism has become the norm in modern societies (Dewaele & Wei, 2013; Kirkpatrick, 2007), this also allows for questioning how realistic a monolingual native speaker norm in educational contexts is (see also Cook & Singleton, 2014). Knowing more than one language not only affects the knowledge and use of an LX, but research has also shown the opposite: multilinguals also use their L1s differently due to the mutual influence of the languages and cognitive processes in a speaker's mind. These influences may affect any skill, such as pronunciation (see, e.g., de Leeuw et al., 2012, 2013) or pragmatics (see, e.g., Dewaele, 2010, 2016a, 2016b). Dewaele (2018) consequently suggests using 'L1 user' instead of native speaker, as in this way, superiority or inferiority of any group is avoided, L1 users can also be LX users (which probably most of them are today) and no high proficiency in an L1 is implied.

The previous discussion shows that the concept of ENS standards in the foreign language classroom is actually idealistic and even unrealistic. Still, it seems to be highly valued by learners, and also by teachers themselves (Young & Walsh, 2010). It is debatable whether or not L1 users will cede as a reference group in educational settings, as language teaching- and learning-processes are model-oriented, and target varieties are also linked to prestige and learners' motivations and aspirations. Still, awareness-raising of English not being a 'static and monolithic entity'

(Matsuda, 2012: 3) is crucial in teacher training programmes. The Common European Framework of Reference for Languages (Council of Europe, 2001, 2017), for instance, has recently put a much stronger focus on plurilingualism and a holistic approach to LX users/learners by emphasising the importance of learner agency, plurilingual and pluricultural competence and translanguaging, 'the purposeful juxtaposition of the languages of input and output' (Farrell, 2015: 8). This is an important first step in empowering LX users and embracing plurilingualism and including these aspects may eventually also affect the long-held view of any 'deviations from "the" standard language' being 'marked as undesirable' (Kohn & Hofstaedter, 2017: 352). This would be much needed indeed, as the goal of ELT should not be to produce cloned native speakers (Cook, 2007) – a goal which is illusive.

Additionally, research has shown that learners often believe English belongs to its L1 users (Matsuda, 2003). This is not true when taking the great number of its LX users into account, which is still said to be increasing rapidly (Crystal, 2003; Graddol, 2006). Thus, awareness raising might also help overcome this misconception and foster teachers' and students' tolerance towards diversity of English language users and, consequently, linguistic hybridity. Also, LX users can 'make English their own' (Kohn, 2015: 37) when acquiring it, and they do so in the following way:

> by creatively constructing your own version of it in your mind, in your heart, and in your behaviour. Your ownership of a language is established through such a process of individual construction, influenced and shaped by what you are exposed to, where you come from, and where you want to go.
>
> *(Kohn, 2015: 37–38)*

According to Kohn (2015), users of English create 'their English' collaboratively with their interlocutors. This is their *own* way of using English, which is always different from a specific target model. This socio-constructivist approach to LX users' ownership of English implies that knowing a language is more than knowing the linguistic rules and applying them successfully. Acquiring and using English is also about expressing one's self and involves cognitive processes, but also emotional and behavioural ones (Kohn, 2015). LX acquisition is, thus, a 'fundamentally social process' (Morita, 2012: 26). As stated above, the diversity of owners and users of English, who also differ in their needs and wants regarding their own use of it, needs to be acknowledged. Learners' needs play an important role in successful LX acquisition indeed and, according to Kirkpatrick (2007: 3), they 'should determine the variety to be taught'. Thus, learners' reality needs to be taken into account in order to foster learning processes which requires local decisions (Seidlhofer, 2011). Acknowledging individual differences in LX learners of English makes generalisations regarding concrete pedagogical implications difficult, if not impossible. This, according to Matsuda (2012), often leaves teachers frustrated as they are made aware of the current teaching methods and conceptualisations being inadequate, but at the same time they are not given any concrete suggestions as to how to improve their teaching to prepare students for EIL contexts. Raising future teachers' awareness of the above-mentioned problems is an important first step in ensuring that students are not measured against native speakers and are made aware of differences to the latter not being a failure on their part, but constitutive of their multilinguality (Resnik, 2018). Furthermore, EIL describes a specific function, which English nowadays performs in multilingual contexts and there might not be one specific, best-practice model because of its context-dependence (Matsuda, 2012, 2017). Thus, there is a strong need for focusing on the specific context as well as individual learners' needs (see also Kirkpatrick, 2007).

Finally, the previous discussion also has clear implications for the question of who should teach English. In the past, native speakers were frequently seen as ideal teachers. This does not necessarily hold true of course, as sharing the cultural and linguistic background of a student, for instance, may facilitate the teaching and learning process, and teachers, who are LX users of English themselves, might have a better understanding of obstacles faced by students. Thus, instead of arguing against non-native teachers in ELT, it should be acknowledged that 'multilingual non-native teachers represent ideal teachers in many ELT contexts' (Kirkpatrick, 2007: 197).

All in all, much re-thinking has been done and needs to be done with regard to the goals of ELT, but also its underlying conceptualisations (Nero, 2012 cited in Galloway, 2017). New insights have clear implications for English Language Teacher Education as well. Before elaborating on these in great detail, the findings of current research in this context will be presented in the following section.

Current research

For decades, researchers have argued for a paradigm shift in English language teaching in order to meet the changing status of English, its diverse uses and needs of users of the language. There is an increasing number of studies that propose WE/EIL-informed curricula and materials (e.g. Bayyurt & Sifakis, 2017; D'Angelo, 2012; Matsuda & Duran, 2012; McKay & Brown, 2016; Sharifian & Marlina, 2012). In addition, both Dewey (2012) and Widdowson (2012) emphasise the need for teachers to reconceptualise the notion of English. Likewise, Galloway (2017) and Matsuda (2012) note the need for teachers of the English language to reconceptualise their teaching practice. However, according to Matsuda (2012) and Marlina (2014), these attempts remain at a theoretical level. Many English language teacher education programmes around the world still focus on linguistic theory and methodology, at the expense of preparing teachers who are adequately equipped for teaching in today's globalising world (Bayyurt, 2012; Dogancay-Aktuna, 2006; Govardhan et al., 1999; Sifakis, 2009; Sifakis & Sougari, 2005). A number of such programmes still hold on to the traditional conceptualisation of English and ignore the heterogeneity of the language by focusing on the Inner Circle or L1 varieties, evident through a strong attachment to native English norms and depending on a monolingual and monocultural vision of English (Phillipson, 1992; Floris, 2013; Llurda, 2015; Kiczkowiak et al., 2016). Teacher education is identified by Galloway and Rose (2015) as a major obstacle to achieving Kumaravadivelu's (2012: 4) 'epistemic break' from native English-speaking norms. In fact, during the past decade, there have been many attempts to update English language teacher education in various parts of the world. Table 16.1 reviews current research showcasing different approaches and pedagogical ideas in English language teacher education to respond to the changing norms and status of English, as well as the changing needs of the learners and users of the language.

Bayyurt and Sifakis (2015) recommended that an ideal EIL teacher education programme should include two vital components: (1) comprehensive information about the current role and status of English around the world, and (2) a change in student-teachers' attitudes fully in line with the changing landscape of English and a re-examination of their teaching practice. From their experiment on the ELF-aware teacher education called ELF-TEd, it was found that student-teachers responded differently and could be grouped into three categories: the supporter, the risk-taker and the sceptic.

Floris (2013, 2014) conducted research on pre-service teachers' beliefs toward EIL before and after joining a World Englishes class in order to detect any changes in the nature of these beliefs. She introduced the concept of EIL to preservice teachers by providing them with systematic opportunities to reflect on and articulate their beliefs. The student-teachers were asked to refer

Table 16.1 Studies of WE/ELF/EIL-informed teacher education

Study	Type of teacher training and pedagogy	Research setting	Details
Bayyurt and Sifakis (2015)	Preservice and in-service/ ELF-aware pedagogy	Boğaziçi University, Turkey	Student-teachers were exposed to the ELF/EIL construct by reading selections. Reflective questions were designed that guide their thinking through different aspects of the ELF construct. In online forums, they discussed issues related to reading.
Floris (2013, 2014)	Preservice/ EIL-incorporated curriculum	Petra Christian University, Indonesia	New courses believed to be consistent with the sociolinguistic realities of the spread of English as an international language were created, i.e., *World Englishes, Current Issues in Global Education,* and *Intercultural Teaching & Learning.*
Galloway (2017)	MSc TESOL/ GELT (Global Englishes language teaching)	The University of Edinburgh, UK	The *Global Englishes for Language Teaching* course was introduced to enable students who were TESOL practitioners to critically reflect on their teaching practice through a global Englishes lens. The teaching method used a mix of online and face-to-face delivery.
Hino (2017)	MA in English as a second language/ EIL Teacher Education	Osaka University, Japan	The *Education in Language and Culture: Principles and Practices of EIL Education* was created with an aim to train graduate students in Japan to be EIL teachers. The 'before and after' interviews were conducted to investigate the course outcome.
Kang (2017)	A grant-based teacher education programme for English teachers from the Expanding Circle countries	Bloomfield College, New Jersey, USA	An intensive course incorporating EIL pedagogy into sessions about SLA theories and methods.
Marlina (2017)	Master of Applied Linguistics (Teaching World Englishes for Intercultural Communication) for pre-service and in-service English teachers with zero or some teaching experience	Monash University, Australia	Student-teachers were required to complete tasks which engaged them in experiencing the practical aspects of teaching EIL through observation and teaching practicums.

to their own experiences, examine and reflect upon their own beliefs. It was found that having discussions and detecting incongruences within one's beliefs and comparing and evaluating them were very important for general conceptual change, which possibly leads to the development of a favourable attitude towards EIL.

In her monograph, Galloway (2017) suggests, in a teacher education context, that teacher training needs to be more aligned with the diverse linguistic reality of the twenty-first century, to be less prescriptive and to have more context-specific goals. She designed an 8-week course that focuses on revisiting the traditional TESOL methodology, curriculum concepts and theories in light of global Englishes research. There is a research plan in place to track the students if they implement GELT (Global Englishes Language Teaching) in their teaching contexts after graduation.

According to Hino's (2017) study, the outcome of the EIL-informed course was largely positive. After completion of the MA programme, some student-teachers developed a more positive attitude towards their own English and believed that it should be the primary model of English in class. This was perceived as the salient impact of EIL education. However, the author identified the main challenge which was the 'examination culture' of Japan as teachers were required to prepare their students for examinations, such as university entrance exams and standardised tests, which were based on native-speaker norms. This restrained teachers' attempts to translate the EIL theories into their teaching practice.

Kang (2017) described a short in-service teacher training programme in the US (four to eight weeks) for teachers from the Expanding Circle countries,[1] especially from China and South Korea. The training provides an overview of SLA theories, practices and research, along with the global status and varieties of English, multilingualism and the diverse needs of EIL learners. Some teachers demonstrated resistance. For example, some still believed that their students should learn standard Inner Circle Englishes and had negative attitudes towards themselves for their 'nonnative' English accent and limited communication skills. This study suggests that a short course might not be adequate to change long-held beliefs some teachers have about how they should teach the language.

Last, the students' feedback in Marlina (2017) was generally positive, and they highlighted its practical aspect as the strength of the course. However, the student-teachers in this study were not able to be completely independent from the native-speaker model when discussing their language proficiency. Therefore, it was suggested that teacher education programmes should dedicate more space for teachers to critically explore the construct of language teacher proficiency.

With insights gained from the above-mentioned research and the growing literature in WE, ELF and EIL, in the following section we argue for careful preparation of English language teachers in a variety of areas in order to equip them for dealing with the multiplicity of challenges that occur in the language classroom.

Applications

In recent years, at least two major English language teaching awards in two different continents have undergone a curriculum update to recognise the paradigm shift from TESL (Teaching English as a Second Language)/ TEFL (Teaching English as a Foreign Language) to include specific references to English as a global language and its fluidity and dynamic nature. They are referred to as the CertTESOL, which is administered in the UK, and Specialist Certificate in Teaching English as an International Language, which is administered in Southeast Asia by the Regional Language Centre (RELC) of Southeast Asian Ministers of Education Organisation (SEAMEO). Both are certificate qualifications for novice teachers who have little or no prior teaching experience. The CertTESOL, offered by Trinity College London, introduced ELF as a sub-requirement of the Language Awareness unit (see Dewey & Patsko, 2018) whereas the Specialist Certificate in Teaching English as an International Language is stated to have a curriculum informed by current literature on Teaching English as an International Language (TEIL) and includes the following as the expected outcome for the teacher trainees in the syllabus (available at www.relc.org.sg): 'to be a successful international/intercultural user and teacher of English in a wide variety of institutional settings and cultural contexts'. In principle, the inclusion of ELF and EIL in the aforementioned teaching awards is a good indicator that advances in the WE/ ELF/EIL research have started to have some influence towards changes in English language teacher education.

According to the current studies being reviewed in the previous section, there are other innovations with positive outcomes, some of which include online activities, classroom observation, and a teaching practicum. This section will discuss the integration of a WE/ELF/EIL perspective in the education of English language teachers, based on creative ideas and practices covered in the existing literature in light of growing WE, ELF, EIL research presented in the previous section. In our view, it is not enough that teacher education simply provides the knowledge on the sociolinguistic reality of English or relevant theories and research in WE, ELF and EIL. It is as crucial to provide opportunities for novice teachers to apply the theories into practice in an actual classroom during pre-service training. We would also like to recommend that student-teachers are made aware of possible post-qualification activities to make sure that they will be able to keep informed with the current developments in teaching practice, especially in relation to the changing landscape of the English language and its implication to teaching and learning. The proposed model of the WE/ELF/EIL-informed English language teacher education and professional development is illustrated in Figure 16.1.

Expanding knowledge base and increasing exposure to Englishes and cultures

It is vital to expose student-teachers to Englishes and cultures so that they will be aware of the sociocultural and political contexts of teaching English, as well as the changing roles of English

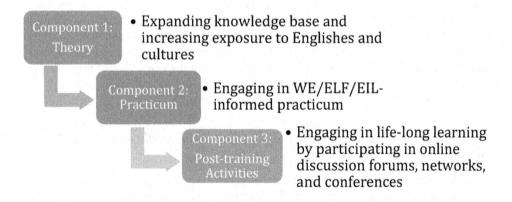

Figure 16.1 WE/ELF/EIL-informed English language teacher education and professional development

teachers, and then adjust their attitudes and teaching practices accordingly. Several studies suggest that teachers' normative mindset in many contexts is a result of their limited knowledge base. For example, in a study on global English teachers' beliefs, attitudes and practices by Young, Walsh and Schartner (2016), teachers in Thailand reported they had been taught either British or American English, or a mixture of the two, and there was a general consensus in that teachers would like to continue teaching the varieties they were taught, which was either American or British English. In other words, they chose to adopt the native variety of English in their teaching primarily because they were not aware of or familiar with other alternatives. Nguyen's research (2017) portrays the positive outcomes of introducing the student-teachers to English varieties and the global status of the language as the trainees' attention was shifted away from giving priority to L1 varieties of English and weakened feelings of inferiority towards native-speaker teachers.

Engaging in WE/ELF/EIL-informed practicum

To bridge the theory/practice gap, many scholars argue for an integration of a 'practical' component into English language teacher education programmes, rather than simply 'talking about' the current sociolinguistic reality of English (Bayyurt & Sifakis, 2015; Marlina, 2017). Student-teachers might be able to gain recognition of the diversity inherent in the use of English in the globalised world through courses such as WE, ELF, or EIL, but this is not a guarantee that this will affect their attitude or that they will be able to translate the theories into their teaching practice. In the case of student-teachers in the Sharifian and Marlina (2012) study, they reported that they were still entirely uncertain about how to apply such theoretical knowledge in an actual classroom. The course, POETIC ('Practices of Teaching Englishes for International Communication', which was developed in response to the limitation of English language teacher training in this regard serves as a good model how the practicum can be integrated into the teacher training programme (see Marlina, 2017). After the introduction of relevant theories and research, student-teachers should be given an opportunity to observe a WE/ELF/EIL-informed class taught by experienced practitioners, and then develop their own lesson plan, learning activities and materials that would be suitable for their teaching context which might have students who are from different lingua-cultural backgrounds. The practicum might also involve reviewing the existing ELT textbooks and adjusting them to be relevant to the student-teachers' own cultural contexts. By means of the practicum, student-teachers will be able to transform from transmitters of theoretical knowledge to learners or those whose assumption might be that the Inner Circle varieties, especially US or UK standard English, are the only legitimate instructional model, to reflection-oriented teachers who can assess the practicality of the traditional conceptualisation of English in ELT against the pedagogic teaching contexts they are going to be working in and the current use of English as a global language.

Engaging in life-long learning by participating in online discussion forums, networks, and conferences

As implied in the Current Research section, the change in teacher attitudes and teaching practices is a slow process. Several studies imply that one course for the whole teacher education programme might not be adequate to make a long-term impact on teaching practice; some student-teachers remained sceptic and show some resistance in changing their attitudes to be in line with the changing landscape of the English language. Longer engagement is essential to bring about understanding of WE/ELF/EIL issues to inform teaching practice. Some teacher educators engaged their student-teachers in online discussion forums outside of class which allowed student-teachers to reflect on the theories learned in class and related them to their own experiences and teaching contexts. However, such activities usually discontinue after the teacher training finishes. There are a number of platforms that we would like to recommend teachers to take up after post-qualifications to remain informed about up-to-date developments in English language teaching and learning relevant to the WE/ ELF/EIL growing research and its implication to teaching practice.

The most notable network in ELF is ELFReN (The English as a Lingua Franca Research Network) which is accessible at www.english-lingua-franca.org/forum/index and coordinated by Alessia Cogo and Marie-Luise Pitzl. The network currently includes 75 participants (from more than 20 countries) who have various areas of expertise within ELF research, and there is a number of posts in the online forum discussion that discuss ELF in ELT practice. Another network is called 'Teaching English & Teaching in English in Global Contexts' (www.globaleng lishes.education.ed.ac.uk/) coordinated by Nicola Galloway, Heath Rose and Jarek Kriukow. This newly established network has an aim to provide an online academic network with teaching resources, reading material, online seminars, blogs, a student/alumni section and a forum to foster collaborative projects in relation to teaching English in global contexts.

In addition to online discussion forums and networks, teachers may keep informed about current developments in the paradigm shift of the English language and ELT practice by a more conventional way such as attending and presenting at conferences. Other potential benefits include networking with other ELT professionals and sharing knowledge of ELT techniques. There are several international conferences, some of which attended by the wider ELT audience (e.g. TESOL in the US and IATEFL in the UK). There is a growing number of conferences with particular themes related to the global status of English, WE and ELF. They are, for example, the International Association for World Englishes Conference, the International Conference of English as a Lingua Franca,[2] and the biennial conference on Changing English (ChangE) at the University of Helsinki, Finland.

Conclusion

The status of English as a global language has challenged the fundamental principles of how English should be learned and taught. The current gap between the sociolinguistic realities of English and that some teacher education programmes are still dominated by native speakerism and Inner Circle bias and focus mainly on linguistic theory might influence student-teachers' sense of preparedness. Research into WE/ELF/EIL-informed teacher education demonstrates that teacher education could potentially strengthen teachers' beliefs about the linguistic diversity of English and leads them to question the native and non-native divide by incorporating the WE/ELF/EIL theories and research, together with providing the opportunities for the student-teachers to practice those theories in an actual classroom. English language teacher education is facing a dilemma of choosing to adopt either the native speaker model, or to adopt the English as an international language pedagogy. The former still seems to be a highly important reference group in most of the education of English language teachers around the world, which is ironic given that the aim of teacher education is to equip pre-service teachers with the skills needed to teach in today's globalised world. English language teacher education programmes should therefore offer students a broad range of relevant knowledge and skills to suit the changing landscape of English and the changing needs of professional teachers, and student-teachers should be encouraged to ask questions like how students in their context are likely to use English in the future and design their course to address their needs rather than depending on the native-speaker model as a one-size-fits-all prescriptive model. English language teacher education should facilitate their students' embracing a new way of thinking about English language teaching and learning, based on the paradigm shift in ELT. It is important that future English teachers understand what it means to teach English in the globalised world, and prepare themselves for the current and future use of English in which they use the language to communicate with people from various countries and cultures. English language teacher education plays an important role as it can potentially provide the first exposure to the idea of a paradigm shift in English language teaching and its diverse uses and users of the language, as well as providing scaffolding as student-teachers engage with and process the new conceptualisation of the English language to make it their own. One teacher educator and a paradigm shift made will affect student-teachers, each of whom will continuously affect their students leading to other innovations in light of the new demands and needs of English teachers, students and users today.

Notes

1 To better understand the use of English in different countries, Kachru (1992) conceived the idea of three concentric circles of the language: the Inner, Outer, and Expanding Circles. The Inner Circle represents the traditional bases of English: the UK, the US, Australia, New Zealand, etc. whereas the Outer Circle includes countries where English is not the native tongue but plays a part in the nation's institutions, for example, as an official language (e.g. India, Malaysia). The Expanding Circle encompasses those countries where English is used as a foreign language or lingua franca (e.g. China, Indonesia).
2 At the time of writing this chapter, the 24th International Association for World Englishes Conference was planned to be held in June 2019, at the University of Limerick in Limerick, Ireland, and the 12th International Conference of English as a Lingua Franca (ELF12) in Medellín, Colombia in 2019 (in Taiwan in 2020 and in Japan in 2021).

Acknowledgement

We would like to acknowledge the financial support from the Austrian Agency for International Cooperation in Education & Research (OeAD-GmbH) and the Office of Higher Education Commission, Ministry of Education of Thailand under the scheme of ASEA-UNINET Staff Exchange during the preparation of this chapter.

Further reading

Kirkpatrick, A. (2007) *World Englishes: Implications for International Communication and English Language Teaching*. Cambridge: Cambridge University Press.
    This book with accompanying CD can be a good resource for practitioners who want to explore varieties of World Englishes within the framework of English language teaching. The author also discusses implications of World Englishes to English language teaching and provides practical recommendations regarding teacher education in various contexts.
McKay, S.L. and Brown, J.D. (2016) *Teaching and Assessing EIL in Local Contexts around the World*. Abingdon: Routledge.
    This book provides the social and educational context of EIL classrooms and issues involved in teaching and assessing EIL which is an area that is not often touched in literature. What is particularly interesting about the book is the ways the authors illustrate how to integrate technology into EIL classrooms to raise cross-cultural exchanges and awareness.
Galloway, N. (2017) *Global Englishes and Change in English Language Teaching*. Abingdon: Routledge.

This book challenges the notion of an idealised monolingual native speaker norm in ELT classrooms, thereby stressing the need for a change of paradigm towards a holistic understanding of users of English. It is an invaluable contribution to our understanding of the crucial role of English learners and their attitudes in these processes, which are seen as a prerequisite for any innovations implemented in curricula. By including an emic perspective, this book gives insight into the complexities underlying (the shaping of) students' attitudes towards desired ('native') target varieties and suggests a framework for evaluating ELT curricula.

Matsuda, A. (ed.) (2017) *Preparing Teachers of English as an International Language*. Bristol: Multilingual Matters. This compilation of articles convincingly demonstrates that a powerful way of bringing about change in reconceptualising English in ELT practices is by means of preparing teachers of EIL in adequate ways. Not only does this book offer rich insights into theoretical perspectives, it also includes applications of EIL and concrete pedagogical ideas. It will thus appeal to language practitioners and researchers alike and is certainly a skilful attempt to foster dialogue across disciplines, such as ELF and WE.

References

Bayyurt, Y. (2012) 'Proposing a model for English language education in the Turkish socio-cultural context', in Bayyurt, Y. and Bektaş-Çetinkaya, Y. (eds) *Research Perspectives on Teaching and Learning English in Turkey: Policies and Practices*. Frankfurt: Peter Lang: 301–312.

Bayyurt, Y. and Sifakis, N. (2015) 'Developing an ELF-aware pedagogy: insights from a self-education programme', in Vettorel, P. (ed.) *New Frontiers in Teaching and Learning English*. Newcastle upon Tyne: Cambridge Scholars Publishing: 55–76.

Bayyurt, Y. and Sifakis, N. (2017) 'Foundation of an EIL-aware teacher education', in Matsuda, A. (ed.) *Preparing Teachers to Teach English as an International Language*. Bristol: Multilingual Matters: 3–18.

Canagarajah, S. (2007) 'Lingua Franca English, Multilingual Communities and Language Acquisition'. *Modern Language Journal*, 91 923–939.

Council of Europe (2001) *Common European Framework of References for Languages: Learning, Teaching, Assessment*. Cambridge: Cambridge University Press.

Council of Europe (September 2017) *Common European Framework of References for Languages: Learning, Teaching, Assessment. Companion Volume with New Descriptors (Provisional Edition)*. Available online: <https://rm.coe.int/common-european-framework-of-reference-for-languages-learning-teaching/168074a4e2> (accessed 1 October 2017).

Cook, V. J. (1991) 'The Poverty-Of-The-Stimulus Argument and Multi-Competence'. *Second Language Research*, 7(2) 103–117.

Cook, V. J. (1999) 'Going Beyond the Native Speaker in Language Teaching', *TESOL Quarterly*, 33 185–209.

Cook, V. J. (2007) 'The goals of ELT: reproducing native-speakers or promoting multi-competence among second language users?', in Cummins, J. and Davison, C. (eds) *Handbook on English Language Teaching*. Dordrecht: Kluwer: 237–248.

Cook, V. J. (2012) 'Multi-competence', in Chappelle, C. (ed.) *The Encyclopedia of Applied Linguistics*. New York: Wiley-Blackwell: 3768–3774.

Cook, V. J. (2016) 'Premises of multi-competence', in Cook, V. J. and Wei, L. (eds) *The Cambridge Handbook of Linguistic Multi-Competence*. Cambridge: Cambridge University Press: 1–25.

Cook, V. J. and Singleton, D. (2014) *Key Topics in Second Language Acquisition*. Bristol: Multilingual Matters.

Crystal, D. (2003) *English as a Global Language*, 2nd edition. Cambridge: Cambridge University Press.

D'Angelo, J. (2012) 'WE-informed EIL curriculum in Chukyo: towards a functional, educated, multilingual outcome', in Matsuda, A. (ed.) *Principles and Practices of Teaching English as an International Language*. Bristol: Multilingual Matters: 121–139.

de Leeuw, E., Mennen, I. and Scobbie, J. M. (2012) 'Singing a Different Tune in Your Native Language: First Language Attrition of Prosody'. *International Journal of Bilingualism*, 16(1) 101–116.

de Leeuw, E., Mennen, I. and Scobbie, J. M. (2013) 'Dynamic Systems, Maturational Constraints, and Phonetic Attrition'. *International Journal of Bilingualism*, 17 683–700.

Dewaele, J. -M. (2010) *Emotions in Multiple Languages*. London: Palgrave Macmillan.

Dewaele, J. -M. (2016a) 'Multicompetence and emotion', in Cook, V. J. and Wei, L. (eds) *The Cambridge Handbook of Linguistic Multi-Competence*, Cambridge: Cambridge University Press: 461–477.

Dewaele, J. -M. (2016b) 'Thirty Shades of Offensiveness: L1 and LX English Users' Understanding, Perception and Self-Reported Use of Negative Emotion-Laden Words'. *Journal of Pragmatics*, 94 112–127.

Dewaele, J. -M. (2018) 'Why the Dichotomy "L1 Versus LX User" is Better Than "Native versus Non-Native Speaker"'. *Applied Linguistics*, 39(2) 236–240.

Dewaele, J. -M. and Wei, L. (2013) 'Is Multilingualism Linked To Higher Tolerance Of Ambiguity?'. *Bilingualism: Language & Cognition*, 1–16.

Dewey, M. (2012) 'Towards a Post-Normative Approach: Learning the Pedagogy Of ELF'. *Journal of English as a Lingua Franca*, 1(1) 141–170.

Dewey, M. and Patsko, L. (2018) 'ELF and teacher education', in Jenkins, J., Baker, W. and Dewey, M. (eds) *The Routledge Handbook of English as a Lingua Franca*. Abingdon: Routledge: 441–455.

Dogancay-Aktuna, S. (2006) 'Expanding the Socio-Cultural Knowledge Base of TESOL Teacher Education'. *Language, Culture and Curriculum*, 19(3) 278–295.

Farrell, T. S. C. (ed.) (2015) *International Perspectives on English Language Teacher Education: Innovations from the Field*. New York: Palgrave Macmillan.

Floris, F. D. (2013) 'Exploring Beliefs of Pre-Service Teachers Toward English as an International Language'. *Thai TESOL Journal*, 1(1) 46–75.

Floris, F. D. (2014) 'Idea Sharing: Introducing English as an International Language (EIL) to Pre-Service Teachers in a World Englishes Course'. *PASAA*, 47 215–231.

Galloway, N. (2017) *Global English and Change in English Language Teaching*. Abingdon: Routledge.

Galloway, N. and Rose, H. (2015) *Introducing Global Englishes*. Abingdon: Routledge.

Govardhan, A. K., Nayar, B. and Sheorey, T. (1999) 'Do U.S. MATESOL Programs Prepare Students to Teach Abroad?'. *TESOL Quarterly*, 33(1) 114–125.

Graddol, D. (2006) *English Next?* London: British Council.

Hino, N. (2017) 'Training graduate students in Japan to be EIL teachers', in Matsuda, A. (ed.) *Preparing Teachers to Teach English as an International Language*, Bristol: Multilingual Matters: 87–99.

Jenkins, J. (1996) 'Changing Pronunciation Priorities for Successful Communication in International Contexts'. *Speak Out! Newsletter of the IATEFL Pronunciation Special Interest Group*, 17 15–22.

Jenkins, J. (2005) 'Teaching pronunciation for English as a Lingua Franca: a sociopolitical perspective', in Gnutzmann, C. and Intemann, F. (eds) *The Globalisation of English and the English Language Classroom*. Göttingen and Tübingen: Gunter Narr: 145–158.

Jenkins, J. (2007) *English as a Lingua Franca: Attitude and Identity*. Oxford: Oxford University Press.

Jenkins, J. (2009) *World Englishes: A Resource Book for Students*, 2nd edition. Abingdon: Routledge.

Kachru, B. B. (1982) *The Other Tongue: English Across Culture*. Urbana, IL: University of Illinois Press.

Kachru, B. B. (1985) 'Standards, codification and sociolinguistic realism: the English language in the Outer Circle', in Quirk, R. and Widdowson, H. G. (eds) *English in the World: Teaching and Learning the Language and Literature*. Cambridge: Cambridge University Press: 11–30.

Kachru, B. B. (1992) 'World Englishes: approaches, issues and resources'. *Language Teaching*, 25(1) 1–14.

Kachru, B. B., Kachru, Y. and Nelson, C. L. (eds) (2009) *The Handbook of World Englishes*. Oxford: Wiley-Blackwell.

Kang, S. -Y. (2017) 'US-based teacher education program for "local" EIL teachers', in Matsuda, A. (ed.) *Preparing Teachers to Teach English as an International Language*. Bristol: Multilingual Matters: 51–65.

Kiczkowiak, M., Baines, D. and Krummenacher, K. (2016) 'Using awareness raising activities on initial teacher training courses to tackle "Native Speakerism"'. *English Language Teacher Education and Development*, 19 45–53.

Kirkpatrick, A. (2007) *World Englishes: Implications for International Communication in English Language Teaching*. Cambridge: Cambridge University Press.

Kohn, K. (2015) 'A pedagogical space for ELF in the English classroom', in Bayyurt, Y. and Akcan, S. (eds) *Current Perspectives on Pedagogy for ELF*. Berlin: De Gruyter: 51–67.

Kohn, K. and Hofstaedter, P. (2017) 'Learner Agency and Non-Native Speaker Identity in Pedagogical Lingua Franca Conversations: Insight from Intercultural Telecollaboration in Foreign Language Education'. *Computer Assisted Language Learning*, 30(5) 351–367.

Kumaravadivelu, B. (2012) 'Individual identity, cultural globalization and teaching English as an international language: the case for an epistemic break', in Alsagoff, L., McKay, S. L., Hu, G. and Renandya, W. A. (eds) *Principles and Practices of Teaching English as an International Language*. New York: Routledge: 9–27.

Llurda, E. (2015) 'Non-native teachers and advocacy', in Bigelow, M. and Ennser-Kananen, J. (eds) *The Routledge Handbook of Educational Linguistics*. New York: Routledge: 105–116.

Marlina, R. (2014) 'The pedagogy of English as an International Language: more reflections and dialogues', in Marlina, R. and Giri, R. (eds) *The Pedagogy of English as an International Language: Perspectives from Scholars, Teachers and Students*. Cham: Springer International Publishing: 1–19.

Marlina, R. (2017) 'Practices of teaching Englishes for international communication training', in Matsuda, A. (ed.) *Preparing Teachers to Teach English as an International Language*. Bristol: Multilingual Matters: 100–113.

Matsuda, A. (2003) 'The Ownership of English in Japanese Secondary Schools'. *World Englishes*, 22(4) 483–496.

Matsuda, A. (ed.) (2012) *Principles and Practices of Teaching English as an International Language*. Bristol: Multilingual Matters.

Matsuda, A. (ed.) (2017) *Preparing Teachers of English as an International Language*. Bristol: Multilingual Matters.

Matsuda, A. and Duran, D. S. (2012) 'EIL activities and tasks for traditional EFL classrooms', in Matsuda, A. (ed.) *Principles and Practices of Teaching English as an International Language*. Bristol: Multilingual Matters: 201–238

Matsuda, A. and Friedrich, P. (2011) 'English as an international language: a curriculum blueprint'. *World Englishes*, 30(3) 332–344.

Mauranen, A. (2012) *Exploring ELF: Academic English Shaped by Non-Native Speakers*. Cambridge: Cambridge University Press.

McKay, S. L. (2002) *Teaching English as an International Language: Rethinking Goals and Approaches*. Oxford: Oxford University Press.

McKay, S. L. and Brown, J. D. (2016) *Teaching and Assessing EIL in Local Contexts around the World: English as an International Language*. Abingdon: Routledge.

Morita, N. (2012) 'Identity: the situated construction of identity and positionality in multilingual classrooms', in S. Mercer, Mercer, S., Ryan, S. and Williams, M. (eds) *Psychology for Language Learning: Insights from Research, Theory and Practice*. Basingstoke: Palgrave Macmillan: 26–41.

Nero, S. (2012) 'Languages Without Borders: TESOL in a Transient World'. *TESL Canada Journal*, 29(2) 143–154.

Nguyen, M. X. N. C. (2017) 'TESOL Teachers' Engagement with The Native Speaker Model: How Does Teacher Education Impact on Their Beliefs?'. *RELC*, 48(1) 83–98.

Ostler, N. (2018) 'Have we reached peak English in the world?'. *The Guardian*, 27 February. Available online: <www.theguardian.com/commentisfree/2018/feb/27/reached-peak-english-britain-china> (accessed 16 April 2018).

Phillipson, R. (1992) *Linguistic Imperialism*. Oxford: Oxford University Press.

Phillipson, R. (2008) 'Lingua Franca or Lingua Frankensteinia? English in European Integration and Globalisation'. *World Englishes*, 27(2) 250–267.

Resnik, P. (2018) *Multilinguals' Verbalisation and Perception of Emotions*. Bristol: Multilingual Matters.

Schmidt, M. (2011) *First Language Attrition*. Cambridge: Cambridge University Press.

Seidlhofer, B. (2011) *Understanding English as a Lingua Franca*. Oxford: Oxford University Press.

Sharifian, F. (2009) *English as an International Language: Perspectives and Pedagogical Issues*. Bristol: Multilingual Matters.

Sharifian, F. and Marlina, R. (2012) 'English as an international language: an innovative academic program', in Matsuda, A. (ed.) *Principle and Practices of Teaching English as an International Language*. Bristol: Multilingual Matters: 140–153.

Sifakis, N. C. (2009) 'Challenges in Teaching ELF in the Periphery: The Greek Context'. *ELT Journal*, 63(3) 230–237.

Sifakis, N. C. and Sougari, A. M. (2005) 'Pronunciation Issues and EIL Pedagogy in the Periphery: A Survey of Greek State School Teachers' Beliefs'. *TESOL Quarterly*, 39(4) 467–488.

Widdowson, H. G. (2012) 'ELF and the Inconvenience of Established Concepts'. *Journal of English as a Lingua Franca*, 1(1) 5–26.

Young, T. J. and Walsh, S. (2010) 'Which English? Whose English? An Investigation of "Non-Native" Teachers' Beliefs About Target Varieties'. *Language, Culture and Curriculum*, 23(2) 123–137.

Young, T. J., Walsh, S. and Schartner, A. (2016) *Which English? Whose English? Teachers' Beliefs, Attitudes and Practices*. London: British Council.

17

ELTE and SLA

Pascual Pérez-Paredes

Introduction

This chapter offers a short introduction to Second Language Acquisition (SLA) and its potential relevance for language teachers and language teacher educators by surveying existing practices and discussing the underlying motivations that explain the diversity of research approaches in this field. The aim is twofold: to expose the complexity of L2 learning research as a multifaceted phenomenon that transcends local practices and oversimplified approaches to language learning, and to encourage language teachers to examine and embrace such complexity as part of this much-needed transdisciplinary approach.

The chapter is divided into five sections. The next section will discuss the variety of epistemologies in SLA and recent turns in the field. In this section, a brief introduction to the themes and main constructs in SLA will be provided. Then I will discuss some areas of relevance for language teachers and L2 teacher education and, later, I will consider one recent area of research that can be of potential interest to L2 teachers: usage-based approaches. In this section, I will discuss why the notion of frequency and frequency distribution of language items is so important in language learning. I will also discuss how SLA can inform language teaching by offering a selection of papers of interest to language teachers that covers different areas of practice, themes and, more interestingly, research methods.

Survey: current perspectives on second language acquisition (SLA)

Defining the scope of SLA is extremely challenging as researchers hold widely different perspectives on both the ontology and the epistemology of the field. In other words, SLA researchers do not agree on *what* exactly is the purpose of SLA and *how* SLA research should be carried out; that is, they prescribe divergent methodologies for the investigation of the acquisition of second or foreign languages. Some have even proposed that SLA as a field is disintegrating (Dekeyser, 2010) or have claimed that the name of the field of inquiry, SLA, fails to recognize the fact that 'there is no common endpoint at which all learners arrive' (Larsen-Freeman, 2015: 503).

SLA is situated on a *fluid* ontology that is permeated by inquiries from other areas of knowledge such as psychology, education, cognitive sciences, linguistics and, among others, sociology.

The fluid nature of this area of study is a unique quality that tends to go unnoticed as trainees and language teachers are not usually presented with a problematized discussion of the wide variety of aims and methods underlying SLA. This lack of discussion may result in a fragmented understanding of the research and, potentially, a huge gap between researchers and language teachers. Furthermore, English Language Teaching (ELT) as a field has become an extremely complex area of practice that incorporates the concerns of 'business, service, profession, and disciplinary field […] operating within an international, multilingual, and multicultural environment' (Pennington and Hoekje, 2014: 174).

In the context of this chapter, I will align my discussion with the Douglas Fir Group (2016: 19) definition of SLA as a discipline that tries:

(1) to understand the processes by which school-aged children, adolescents, and adults learn and use, at any point in life, an additional language, including second, foreign, indigenous, minority, or heritage languages, (2) to explain the linguistic processes and outcomes of such learning, and (3) to characterize the linguistic and non-linguistic forces that create and shape both the processes and the outcomes.

This is an inclusive framework that will be of interest to most language teachers as it addresses language learning across the lifespan of individuals, focusing on the development of language learning from different instructional perspectives that take on board the experiences of language learners in different individual contexts.

In the following section, I set out to discuss two areas of SLA of interest to language teachers and teacher educators. The first addresses the different epistemologies that are embraced by researchers and how this may affect our understanding of the field. The second is concerned with two turns in SLA that have had an important impact on what is being researched in SLA and how it is being researched.

SLA research: a fluid field

SLA is an extraordinarily transdisciplinary field. As such, there are some underlying tensions that, while relevant to both researchers and language teachers, may not be immediately evident to different types of readers and users of SLA research. In particular, as pointed out by Ellis (2010), language teachers are more concerned with teaching than with *learning* and may possibly need help with theorizing the integration of learners and learning in instructed SLA. While I find Ellis's (2010) assertion a bit patronising, understanding these tensions and the discourses that surround them are necessary to gain an informed view of the aims and the results that we find in SLA research and how this research can be of interest to L2 teachers.

One or many epistemologies?

Some 25 years ago, Larsen-Freeman (1991) described SLA research as the attempt to explain the process of second language learning through the study of psycholinguistic entities such as input or transfer. By the end of the decade, a paper by Firth and Wagner (1997) challenged this mission and claimed that meaning is 'a social and negotiable product of interaction, transcending individual intentions and behaviours' (p. 290). Before the turn of the new century, it seemed as if SLA research was about to diverge into two independent disciplines.

For some SLA experts, the way in which research is done needs to conform largely to a limited set of methods that are considered as valid or, let us put it this way, *more* valid than others. Hulstijn (2013), for example, holds that SLA research needs to conform to the scientific cycle where empirical testing is crucial: 'if an academic discipline is characterized by too many non-empirical ideas and too few empirical ideas, it ruins the risk of losing credit in the scientific community at large (and in society)' (p. 515). Norris and Ortega (2003) have described the process underlying SLA research as one where *measurement* plays a crucial role, and where researchers are expected to collect data and transform it into evidence so that L2 language learning theory can be expanded. Under this lens, SLA research is perceived as a (post)-positivist discipline that through experimental – and semi-experimental – research designs can advance our understanding of language acquisition.

This post-positivist way of *doing* the kind of empirical research advocated in Norris and Ortega (2003) relies on defining the exact observable behaviours being measured, the *constructs*, and the theoretical assumption that they represent. For example, if we wanted to understand whether language anxiety plays a role in L2 language learning, we need to operationalise first the *construct* of language anxiety and decide how we would like to research it. This process, however, is never straightforward and requires time, long debates in research journals and resources. Even though the first major contribution to our understanding of language anxiety in L2 instructed contexts was both the Foreign Language Anxiety (FLA) construct developed by Horwitz, Horwitz and Cope (1986) and the corresponding instrument to measure it (the Foreign Language Classroom Anxiety Scale (FLCAS) (Aida, 1994)), FLA researchers still disagree on the exact nature of the construct. They, as a way of example, still debate whether the instrument is valid, its underlying dimensions, its psychometric properties and whether FLA varies across L1s and language skills (Park, 2014; Horwitz, 2016). Language teachers need to be aware of the dynamic nature of research constructs and methods as, it is often the case, research of a phenomenon implies different epistemologies across authors and time.

Other researchers, on the contrary, have proposed more open and inclusive SLA that embraces the process of *epistemological expansion* initiated in the 1980s. The Douglas Fir Group (2016) propose a transdisciplinary approach to SLA research that makes use of a wide range of methods that tap into 'the social-local worlds of L2 learners and then pose the full range of relevant questions—from the neurobiological and cognitive micro levels to the macro levels of the sociocultural, educational, ideological, and socioemotional' (p. 20). Coming back to language anxiety, some researchers are using other instruments to understand learners experiencing anxiety and make use of interviews and focus groups as complimentary instruments which can provide rich data and insight into the self-perceived cognition of learners. Tran, Baldauf and Moni (2013) looked at FLA in Vietnam in a sample of 419 non-English-major students and used both standard scales such as the FLCAS and learners' autobiographies and semi-structured interviews. This provided an ecological perspective that can rarely be obtained through quantitative methods only.

Some researchers dismiss the role of quantitative research methods in terms of relevance for language pedagogy as they fail to respond to the demands of individual students and pedagogy (Feryok, 2017). Accordingly, some research relies entirely on interview data or ethnographic studies when analysing, for example, language and identity. Norton (1997: 413) examined the language learning experience of Mai, a Vietnamese woman, following a course 'offered to adult immigrants in Canada, [who] continued taking ESL courses at night in order to improve her spoken and written English'. Norton claims that 'the teacher had not provided learners with the opportunity to critically examine experiences in their native countries in the light of more recent experiences in Canada or […] in the native country', which prevented Mai from making the most of the classroom activities and advancing her English language learning. This sort of insight necessitates shifting away from quantitative methods to qualitative, more interpretive research approaches to SLA.

Ellis (2010: 191), echoing Diane Larsen-Freeman, maintains that most basic research, as opposed to applied research, tends to appear as fragmented as 'researchers seek to promote and immunize their own preferred theories and epistemologies over those of their rivals'. This fragmentation needs to be understood and embraced by language teachers as part of a rich and intricate area of inquiry that tries to make sense of an extraordinarily complex activity: L2 language learning and use.

Recent turns

SLA research in the last 60 years has been largely influenced by both the application of Universal Grammar (UG) 'to the modelling of L2 competence' and cognitive perspectives that have examined learner language, the role of memory and attention and, among others, cognitive processing constraints (Mitchell et al., 2013: 286). These two approaches, particularly cognitive approaches, have dominated the agenda of researchers for decades. UG research has examined whether UG grammar, or at least some components, is available to L2 adult learners at all. The debate is exceptionally relevant. If UG grammar, that is, *the* hypothetical internal language acquisition device, is available to learners at adult age, the acquisition of languages is domain *specific* and different from the acquisition of other skills or *general* knowledge. Conversely, cognitive approaches have examined how our cognition mediates L2 learning by examining, among many other factors, the role of frequency of occurrence of linguistic features in learner input and the processing of linguistic structures. Mitchell, Myles and Marsden (2013: 127) stress that many of the cognitive accounts see language learning as an implicit process of 'calculation of the statistical properties of elements of language and how they relate to meaning and function'. Other areas of cognitive-based SLA are the study of memory, explicit and implicit knowledge and the role of attention. In a different manner, interactionist accounts of language learning have sought to explore how individual variables such as age, affect, etc. affect SLA in predominantly communicative language learning settings.

UG and cognitive approaches have placed the individual language learner at the centre of their focus and have tried to scrutinize how cognition interacts with language learning, either in naturalistic or in instructed settings. However, SLA research has seen two recent major turns. The first of these turns is the so-called *social turn*. Lantolf (1994), using Vygotskyan sociocultural theory, argues that language learning is a socially mediated process and suggests that SLA should look more closely at the role played by the social context. Advocates of this new paradigm highlight that more attention needs to be paid to how social interaction and language mediated behaviour cooperate in language learning:

> Mediation, whether physical or symbolic, is understood to be the introduction of an auxiliary device into an activity that then links humans to the world of objects or to the world of mental behaviour [...] conscious mental activity is distributed and jointly constructed in the dialogic interactions that arise between children and representatives of the culture [...] what is at one point socially mediated mental processing evolves into self- mediated processing.
>
> *(Lantolf, 1994: 418–419)*

Researchers adopting this perspective have shown evidence of the importance of private speech in L2 learning (Ohta, 2001) or, among other areas of interest, the usefulness of the L1 as a mediational tool for learners of EFL to structure and gain insights into the relationship between form and meaning in the L2 (Harun et al., 2014).

A more recent turn in SLA has shifted the attention of researchers from monolingual-biased research to multilingualism. Some SLA research in the past has predominantly studied the acquisition of a second language by monolingual speakers as a process where the mother tongue of the learner has been often attributed an interfering effect. This is what Ortega (2009, 2013) has framed as the monolingual bias in SLA, fed by the so-called *target deviation perspective* (Ortega, 2013: 2). The fact that a *deficit* perspective (Cook, 1999) has been given so much attention in SLA for so long has very likely affected our own perceptions of L2 learning in very negative ways.

In the next section I will touch on the notion of interlanguage. This construct exemplifies so well how SLA researchers, either consciously or unconsciously, are more often than not influenced by the prevailing, assumed views of mainstream research. Ortega (2013: 17) claims that 'a deficit approach to studying late bilingualism is a liability that limits the field's full potential for generating knowledge that is internally valid as well as valued and valuable beyond its disciplinary bounds'. Ortega blames this approach for the lack of disciplinary impact of SLA on other language sciences. Ortega (2013) and the Douglas Fir Group (2016), among others, have called for a bilingual turn in SLA that 'invests in a range of broader-looking, more positive framings of disciplinary goals for the field in the 21st century' (Ortega, 2013: 18). This call makes sense in a world which is not only more global and more connected than ever before, but also more likely to offer opportunities to use multiple languages through mobiles and communication technologies in ways which are unimaginable even today. The monolingual native speaker, once the golden standard of SLA, is now a blurred image, with half of the world population being bilingual and, for example, around 450 million learners of English in China alone:

> It is thus not surprising that in these superdiverse environments, transformed as they are by digital means for communicating across geographical boundaries and by expanding opportunities for learning and using additional languages, the once normative dichotomies in SLA of the 'second' and the 'foreign' (more recently applied as well to the 'heritage' and the 'indigenous') language context or the 'real world' and the 'classroom' setting become increasingly questionable.
>
> *(Douglas Fir Group, 2016: 23)*

The notion of multilingualism has only entered the SLA field and is beginning to bear fruit in the ways we see today the benefits of bilingualism on our health and our economy as well as holding less naïve and simplistic ways to understand how to study late bilingualism and language learning in the twenty-first century.

Research: SLA and L2 teacher education

SLA and language teaching: a brief survey

Much has been discussed about the gap between research and theory, between 'technical' and 'practical knowledge' (Ellis, 2010: 184) in SLA. The debate is by no means new. For over 70 years, linguists and applied linguists have tried to create links between SLA research and language teaching practice. Both Fries (1945) and Lado (1957) set out to bridge the gap between behaviourist accounts of human learning and teaching of languages. For them it was essential to contrast the L1 and the L2 and try to spot difficult areas for L2 learners as a way to facilitate acquisition. Contrastive analysis, widely spread in the 1960s and the 1970s, is still practiced, and many teachers, either consciously or not, refer to comparisons between L1 and L2 languages as a source to generate classroom activities and pedagogy. It is not rare to find such reflections, particularly in the Asian context where the distance between English and languages such as Mandarin or Cantonese is perceived as huge.

Later on, the analysis of learners' errors became a widespread practice that gave way to a new field of research that looked at the development in the acquisition of linguistic features such as morphemes or negation (Corder, 1967). A few years later, Selinker (1972) coined the term *interlanguage* and SLA researchers sought to explain how this unique *system* actually is built. Tarone (2006: 748) defined interlanguage in the following terms:

> The interlanguage system is clearly not simply the native language morphological and syntactic system relexified with target language vocabulary; that is, it is not the morphological and syntactic system that would have been evidenced had the learner tried to express those meanings in his or her native language [...] the interlanguage differs systematically from both the native language and the target language.

Interlanguage is still a widely used term but has adopted different meanings across different authors. Recent research has embraced alternative constructs to reflect theoretical perspectives that are consistent with recent, more complex views on language learning and, for example, some authors prefer to use the term *languaging* as it more suitable to understand 'the process of making meaning and shaping knowledge and experience through language' (Swain, 2006: 98). This approach highlights a dynamic view of L2 use which contrasts strongly with the more static perception of learner output back in the 1970s and 1980s.

Dulay and Burt (1973) provided evidence that only 3 per cent of errors of children learning an L2 can be traced back to their L1. This had a profound effect on the validity of Lado's (1957) contrastive hypothesis theory and opened up new ways to look at SLA and language teaching and situated error analysis as a major area of inquiry in SLA. Spada (2015: 71) maintains that most initial SLA research was influenced by L1 acquisition accounts and focused almost exclusively on 'accuracy order of grammatical morphemes, acquisition of grammatical features and the identification/explanation of l2 errors' operated on learners in naturalistic settings and not in classroom contexts.

In the 1980s, Long (1980) underscored the role of input and interaction in acquiring languages and Krashen (1981) formulated his monitor model that states that learning and acquisition are separate processes. Pienemann (1984) suggested that language items can only be learnt if the students have developed their interlanguage to a stage where a *teachable* item can be learnt, which is echoed in Krashen's (1985) input hypothesis. Swain (1985) stressed the role of learner output in developing various language skills and VanPatten (1996) developed a model that explains that learners process declarative knowledge (grammar, vocabulary and pronunciation) if they need it to retrieve meaning from a communicative situation. In the late 1980s, SLA researchers turned their attention to the role of individual differences (Skehan, 1989), including motivation, anxiety and personality traits as well as the role of memory and attention (Schmidt, 1990). As seen in the previous section, the social and the multilingual turns have introduced new research themes and ways to conceptualize language learning. In the next section, we will look at a very recent approach that uses language usage as the basis to understand how languages are learnt and used.

SLA and teacher education

Not all SLA research addresses language teaching and learning in classroom contexts. However, most of the research has implications for our understanding of the processes and the diversity of social and individual contexts involved in instructed learning. How these implications are discussed and highlighted will depend on the roles adopted by the different stakeholders in language teaching, including SLA researchers, classroom researchers, teacher educators and teachers. Language teacher educators and SLA researchers need to have conversations about the relationship between research and classroom practices in ways which facilitate better understanding of these *worlds*. A good example is Spada (2015: 78), who has rightly pointed out that there have been in the past 'misapplications of SLA research to L2 pedagogy' as findings from natural settings, for example migrants learning English in an ESL context, have been translated into L2 pedagogy in instructed settings, for example learners of EFL in secondary schools in Brazil. To illustrate this point, Spada uses a well known area of inquiry in SLA: implicit versus explicit knowledge. In short, these two types of knowledge can be characterized as follows (Table 17.1):

Table 17.1 Explicit vs. implicit knowledge

Explicit knowledge (EK)	Implicit knowledge (IK)
Analysed, conscious, declarative	Unanalysed, intuitive
Knowledge with awareness	Knowledge without awareness

Source: Spada (2015).

Spada maintains that the distinction between EK and IK is irrelevant to most EFL/ESL teachers that, in instructed settings where learners are adults or young adults, will use L2 pedagogy that is 'conscious, declarative and deliberate' (p. 78). Ellis (2010) has developed a framework for examining the SLA-language pedagogy nexus that conceptualizes at least three different roles for teacher educators. Language teacher educators can be transmitters of information about SLA and function as translators of theory into practice, mentors and awareness-raisers. These roles are necessarily shaped by the nature of the programmes where language teachers are gaining their qualifications and, to some extent, the orientation of the curriculum. Ellis (2010) highlights the need for teachers to make sense of how SLA theories and research impact language teaching and learning in classrooms. Moreover, teacher beliefs are of paramount importance in this process and, interestingly, have also been researched in the recent years. For example, Nassaji (2012) examined the influence of SLA research on L2 teaching by consulting 201 EFL and ESL teachers in Canada and Turkey. These teachers were 33 years old on average and had been teaching English for some eight years. This is a breakdown of the main findings in this study:

1. Most English language teachers (75 per cent) were familiar with SLA research as they had taken courses in their College years.
2. While 28 per cent had conducted research, only 4 per cent had published their results.
3. Most of them (79 per cent) agreed that knowing about SLA research improves second language teaching.
4. Most of them (60 per cent) agreed that SLA research is relevant to language teaching.
5. Few teachers (28 per cent) agreed that SLA research provides them with practical suggestions about how to teach.
6. Only 13 per cent of these teachers read research articles often and 48 per cent said that they rarely or never read them. 80 per cent indicated that they didn't read them because of lack of time.
7. 40 per cent indicated that research articles are difficult to understand.

Nassaji (2012) argues that there is a communication problem between researchers and teachers that needs attention. He believes that collaboration is necessary but warns that a top-down model where researchers colonize language teachers and impose their discourse will not be successful. Zand-Moghadam and Meihami (2016) conducted a similar research project in Iran with both language teachers with and without formal training in EFL. They found that these teachers were not, in general, familiar with SLA research methodology and, as in Nassaji's study, they lacked the time or the access to read SLA research. These studies lend support to R. Ellis's (2010) and N. C. Ellis's (1997: 238) view that different discourses may cause 'considerable resentment at what [teachers and some teacher educators] see as the hegemony of applied linguistics and SLA'. To bridge this gap, Ellis (2010) has put together a set of principles that may be useful in linking SLA theoretical knowledge and 'actual' (p. 195) language teaching. These principles try to underscore the active role of the language teachers as the developers of 'their own theory of how learners learn an L2 in an instructional setting' (p. 195). Ellis claims that such understanding can be achieved if, among other things, SLA courses cover topics that are relevant to language teaching and include classroom research rather than laboratory studies in a context where SLA theories and models are not imposed.

In the next section, I would like to explore how SLA can contribute to our understanding of how languages are learnt and used by the L1 community of speakers and how constructs such as frequency of use and distribution of frequency can affect L2 learning.

Application: usage-based accounts of language learning

SLA research can offer language teachers and language teacher educators opportunities to think about central issues in L2 learning and teaching that are not necessarily prominent in language teaching materials or other sources of information. For example, what is the role of frequency of occurrence of language constructions (words, phrases, interjections) in language learning? How do language material authors determine their selection of language items in coursebooks? What is the role of formulaic language in L2 learning? These are interesting questions to researchers and language teachers alike.

What are usage-based accounts of language learning?

In short, usage-based accounts of language learning (UB) explain how people learn languages while we engage in communication. The term *usage-based accounts* reflects the multi-theoretical nature of this group of theories as well as the relevance that language *usage* has for researchers in this area. Ortega (2013) sees in UB a reconceptualization of cognition into an embodied socio-cognitive system and Ellis, Römer and O'Donnell (2016: 23) frame usage-based theories as emerging from interaction when creating meaning:

> Usage-based theories hold that an individual's creative linguistic competence emerges from the collaboration of the memories of all the meaningful interactions in their entire history of language usage [...] Frequency of subsequent encounter strengthens [new symbolic] constructions, promotes implicit learning, and automatizes and tunes the system.

Researchers use methods from different disciplines to understand the nature of such constructions and how they are learned. Particularly, corpus linguistics, cognitive psychology and cognitive linguistics have informed UB (Figure 17.1).

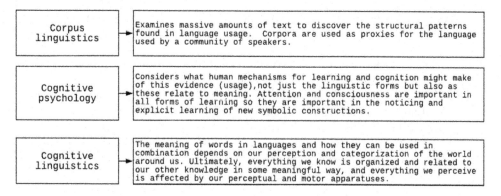

Figure 17.1   The role of corpus linguistics, cognitive psychology and cognitive linguistics in UB
Source: Ellis, Römer and O'Donnell (2016: 23–27)

UB researchers use language corpora to understand the role of the frequency of the constructions in any language. According to the Douglas Fir Group (2016: 29):

> What is attended to focuses learning, and so language is both constitutive of and constituted by attention. The functions of language in use determine its usage and learning [...] The more routine, frequent, and stable the occurrences of particular resources are in the interactions and the more L2 learners' attention is drawn to their form–meaning pairings, the more entrenched the resources become as cognitive–emotional representations of their experiences.

In the next subsections, I will briefly discuss why the frequency of occurrence of constructions determines usage and how L2 learning is impacted.

The role of frequency and its impact on L2 learning

When we use language, we access our stored inventory of constructions and information that links a given construction (a word, a string of words, the first line of a joke, part of a proverb) with the communicative situation in which it typically occurs, the role of the participants in the situation where that construction occurs, the formality or informality of the construction, etc. We do this with any language we speak but, it is clear that it is with our mother tongue or mother tongues that access to this wide range of information is immediate and intuitive. In technical terms, this type of implicit learning takes place in the neocortical system (Ellis, 2002). After conducting research on verb-argument constructions in L1 and L2 speakers (i.e. Verb + Direct object + Adverbial), Ellis and Ferreira-Junior (2009: 381) claim that 'frequency distribution in natural language [in the English language, for example] might [...] optimize learning by providing one very high-frequency exemplar that is also prototypical in meaning and widely applicable'. UB claims that the frequency, generality, prototypicality, and distinctiveness of a construction (i.e. *came to the conclusion, absolutely fine, fine, absolutely*, etc.) interact and are positively associated. These findings have clear implications for L2 teaching as the acquisition of linguistic constructions is affected by different factors that underscore the probabilistic nature of language usage, which according to Ellis and Ferreira-Junior (2009: 383) are:

1. the frequency, frequency distribution, and salience of the form types (the discrete units in the construction) of each construction;
2. the frequency, the frequency distribution, the prototypicality and generality of the semantic types, and their importance in interpreting the overall construction;
3. the reliabilities of the mapping between 1 and 2;
4. the degree to which the different elements in the construction sequence (such as Subj V Obj in a verb argument construction) are mutually informative and form predictable chunks.

UB research has shown that L2 learners acquire the most frequent, prototypical, and generic exemplars of a language: 'Learning is driven by the frequency and frequency distribution of exemplars within constructions and by the match of their meaning to the construction prototype' (Ellis and Ferreira-Junior, 2009: 384). Recent research has stressed the role of L1 frequency and chunking in providing relevant materials and exemplars to language learners, while teaching materials such as textbooks 'combined with a deductive emphasis will disrupt the sequence, at the extreme producing learners who compute by a mix of pedagogical rule, direct translation, and online declension' (Ellis, 2002: 320).

For UB, the main task for L2 learners is to learn the probability of the distribution of a construction and the mapping of form to meaning as conditioned by context. Understanding that there are units beyond the word (chunks, lexical bundles, collocations, etc.) and that grammar and lexis should not totally be seen as inseparable entities can help language teachers understand some of the conditions that govern L1 use and, consequently, explain the behaviour of potentially learnable constructions in L2 instructed contexts. As Ellis, Römer, and O'Donnell (2016) put it, formulaic language is comprehended and produced more readily by L1 speakers. Bringing formulaicity closer to the language classroom is one of the most fascinating challenges for all of us involved in L2 education. To do this, a reformulation of how we understand declarative knowledge is necessary.

In this section I have tried to show how UB is evolving our understanding of language learning by examining how human interaction with language and with people shape up our usage of language. This type of research has potentially a profound impact on how language teaching and learning will be understood in the forthcoming years. However, foreign language teaching (FLT) is complex and, arguably, a global phenomenon that is likely to be affected by a wide range of theoretical perspectives. In the next section, I will discuss some research that showcases the complexity and the wide scope of research that is found in SLA studies.

How can SLA research inform teacher education?

The following selection of papers examine different areas of research that are of potential interest to both trainee and in-service language teachers. Far from offering a complete picture of the field, they have been chosen as they are representative of different areas of inquiry and research methodologies where the gap between technical and practical knowledge can be bridged (Ellis, 2010). In short, they deal with the use of technology in L2 learning and teaching, teachers' attitudes to grammar teaching, the types and effectiveness of corrective feedback and a reconceptualization of the role of SLA research in multilingual societies.

Golonka, E. M., Bowles, A. R., Frank, V. M., Richardson, D. L. and Freynik, S. (2014) 'Technologies for Foreign Language Learning: A Review of Technology Types and Their Effectiveness'. *Computer Assisted Language Learning*, 27(1) 70–105.

Read this paper if you are interested in the use of ICT in language teaching.

Research methodology: systematic review of previous research. This paper reviews the evidence for the effectiveness of different types of technology and computer assisted language learning (CALL) in L2 learning and teaching. Review articles are extremely useful papers where the authors synthesize an area of research by applying a rigorous methodology in the selection, review and assessment of the research that has been carried out in a given topic or area. In this case, the authors used a categorial scale (Strong–Moderate–Weak) to assess the empirical support for claims of effectiveness of different technologies. With white boards, for example, language learners are expected to be more motivated and engaged in the process of learning. However, the research reviews in this paper failed to offer evidence of those claims or the evidence was weak because of research methodological flaws or lack of empirical data. On the contrary, research examining synchronous chats was able to provide strong evidence of their effectiveness. Chats facilitate 'communication and collaboration among students or between students and [other] speakers without constraints of distance or location' (p. 74), and according to the authors, chats seem to promote noticing and facilitate focus on form instruction.

Burgess, J. and Etherington, S. (2002) 'Focus on Grammatical Form: Explicit or Implicit?'. *System*, 30(4) 433–458.

Read this paper if you are interested in teacher beliefs, grammar teaching and English for Academic Purposes (EAP).

Research methodology: survey. This paper explores the beliefs, attitudes and the self-reported practices of 48 teachers teaching pre-sessional EAP classes in British universities regarding grammar teaching and learning. This research is interesting for two reasons: (1) it discusses different ways to teach grammar by looking at focus on form constructs, an important area of research in SLA during the last 20 years. In short, when it comes to teaching grammar SLA studies have researched three approaches, namely, Focus on FormS (explicit teaching of grammar points), Focus on Form (an occasional shift of attention to form in the context of meaning-oriented activities) and, finally, no attention to form or Focus on Meaning; (2) explores the self-reported practices of teachers and their interpretation of some relevant SLA constructs and, very importantly, places language teachers on the spotlight as relevant stakeholders in SLA. The paper also is very interesting from a methodological perspective as it offers an excellent discussion of how the survey was built. The researchers (p. 438) identified 'dichotomies and continua within the teaching of language and of grammar in particular [and] were incorporated into a framework for a consideration of grammar teaching'. These continua were: explicit vs implicit grammar teaching, analytic vs experiential and Focus on FormS vs Focus on Form differences. The results suggest that while language teachers seem to prefer the use of a Focus on Form approach, they seem to be aware that most of their students (in pre-sesional EAP UK university courses) prefer a more explicit, traditional approach to grammar teaching. An interesting paper to read is Russell and Spada (2006) meta-analysis on the efficacy of feedback on second language (L2) grammar.

Li, S. (2010) 'The Effectiveness of Corrective Feedback in SLA: A Meta-Analysis'. *Language Learning*, 60(2) 309–365.

Read this paper if you are interested in understanding and providing corrective feedback to language learners.

Research methodology: meta-analysis. This research examines 22 papers and 11 Ph.D. dissertations on the effectiveness of corrective feedback in language learning. Research on feedback has looked at different areas of interest to language teachers such as different types of feedback and their effects, the effect of recasts (the repetition of an 'error' back to the learner in a corrected form) as well as the learners' uptake of feedback. In general, recasts are the most frequent feedback type in the language classroom, seem to facilitate SLA and explicit feedback seems to be more effective than implicit feedback. In short, Li found that the most widely researched types of feedback are recasts, explicit correction, and clarification. Explicit correction showed substantially larger immediate effects than metalinguistic feedback and recasts. On long-delayed post-tests (weeks after the end of the experiment) implicit feedback seems to be more effective.

Meta-analysis research averages the effect size of research that makes use of quantitative methods across different populations. An effect size is 'a descriptive statistic that expresses the magnitude or strength of a relationship' (Loewen and Plonsky, 2016: 56) and it is used in this type of analysis as a proxy for the impact of the findings across different research studies. Reading meta-analyses is an excellent way to become familiar with the research in an area of interest for language teachers and can provide insight into the varied research methodologies used and groups of learners most frequently targeted by L2 researchers. In this meta-analysis, most research looked and younger adults and English language learners.

Douglas Fir Group (2016) 'A Transdisciplinary Framework for SLA in a Multilingual World'. *The Modern Language Journal*, 100(S1) 19–47.

Read this paper if you are interested in understanding contemporary accounts of SLA in the context of multilingual societies.

Research methodology: this is a position paper where distinguished SLA researchers reflect on the aims and practice of SLA. The framework proposed in this paper is the result of the collaboration of a group of 15 researchers with different theoretical roots, including (as featured in the original paper) sociocultural theory, language socialization theory, social identity theory, complexity and dynamic systems theory, usage-based approaches, the biocultural perspective, ecological and sociocognitive approaches, variationist sociolinguistics, systemic functional linguistics and conversation analysis. The authors claim that transdisciplinary work is needed to advance fundamental understandings of language learning and teaching, including understandings of linguistic development in an additional language, taking into account forces beyond individual learners and, among others, to promote the development of innovative research agendas for SLA in the twenty-first century. The framework is informed by a set of prominent themes (Han, 2016) in SLA during the early years of the twenty-first century:

- Language competences are complex, dynamic, and holistic.
- Language learning is semiotic learning.
- Language learning is situated and attentionally and socially gated.

- Language learning is multi-modal, embodied, and mediated.
- Variability and change are at the heart of language learning.
- Literacy and instruction mediate language learning.
- Language learning is identity work.
- Agency and transformative power are means and goals for language learning.
- Ideologies permeate all levels.
- Emotion and affect matter at all levels.

The framework displays three levels of relevance in L2 learning: a micro level of social activity, a meso level where sociocultural institutions and communities operate, and a macro level of ideological structures. This framework has been criticized by Han (2016), who thinks that the learner as an individual and *learning* are not well accounted. Han (p. 738), somehow poignantly, maintains that 'language learning is a complex, ongoing, multifaceted phenomenon' (p. 36) is a long-achieved understanding in SLA, not a newfound revelation'. However, the main value of this paper rests upon the recognition that no L2 learning theory or SLA research can fully explain language learning: 'language inextricably involves cognition, emotions, consciousness, experience, embodiment, brain, self, human interaction, society, culture, mediation, instruction, and history in rich, complex, and dynamic ways' (Douglas Fir Group, 2016: 39).

Further reading

Loewen, S. and Plonsky, L. (2016) *An A–Z of Applied Linguistics Research Methods*. London: Palgrave.
A very accessible introduction to the concepts and techniques used in applied linguistics research. This book examines both qualitative and quantitative research methods, sampling procedures, instrumentation and analyses found in applied linguistics research. Teachers will find in the examples provided plenty of research concepts and terminology that look at classroom based and instructed second language learning.
Mitchell, R., Myles, F. and Marsden, E. (2013) *Second Language Learning Theories*. Abingdon: Routledge.
One of the most informative and comprehensive books linking SLA theories and language learning and teaching stakeholders. The book will be of interest to language teachers worldwide across a wide variety of institutions and levels. This third edition includes a very useful timeline of second language learning theory development as well as an excellent glossary.
Ortega, L. (2009) *Understanding Second Language Acquisition*. London: Hodder Education.
A comprehensive introduction to second language acquisition that combines in-depth analysis of the major areas in SLA and practical knowledge about the learning process in different contexts.

References

Aida Y. (1994) 'Examination of Horwitz, Horwitz, and Cope's Construct of Foreign Language Anxiety: The Case of Students of Japanese'. *The Modern Language Journal*, 78 155–168.
Bialystok, E. (1978) 'A Theoretical Model of Second Language Learning'. *Language Learning*, 28 69–84.
Burgess, J. and Etherington, S. (2002) 'Focus on Grammatical Form: Explicit or Implicit?' *System*, 30(4) 433–458.
Cook, V. (1999) 'Going Beyond the Native Speaker in Language Teaching'. *TESOL Quarterly*, 33(2) 185–209.
Corder, S. P. (1967) 'The Significance of Learners' Errors'. *International Review of Applied Linguistics*, 5 161–169.
Dekeyser, R. M. (2010) 'Where is our Field Going?'. *The Modern Language Journal*, 94(4) 646–647.
Doughty, C. and Long, M. (2011) *The Handbook of Second Language Acquisition*. Malden, MA: Blackwell.
Douglas Fir Group (2016) 'A Transdisciplinary Framework for SLA in a Multilingual World'. *The Modern Language Journal*, 100(S1) 19–47.

Dulay, H. and Burt, M. (1973) 'Should We Teach Children Syntax?'. *Language Learning*, 23 245–258.

Ellis, N. C. (2002) 'Reflections on Frequency Effects in Language Processing'. *Studies in Second Language Acquisition*, 24(2) 297–339.

Ellis, N. C. (2003) 'Constructions, chunking, and connectionism: the emergence of second language structure', in Doughty, C. and Long, M. (eds) *The Handbook of Second Language Acquisition*. Malden, MA: Blackwell: 63–103.

Ellis, N. C. and Ferreira-Junior, F. (2009) 'Construction Learning as a Function of Frequency, Frequency Distribution, and Function'. *Modern Language Journal*, 93(3) 370–385.

Ellis, N. C., O'Donnell, M. B. and Römer, U. (2013) 'Usage-Based Language: Investigating the Latent Structures That Underpin Acquisition'. *Language Learning*, 63(1) 25–51.

Ellis, N. C., Römer, U. and O'Donnell, M. B. (2016) 'Constructions and Usage-Based Approaches To Language Acquisition'. *Language Learning*, 66 23–44.

Ellis, R. (2010) 'Second Language Acquisition, Teacher Education and Language Pedagogy'. *Language Teaching*, 43(2) 182–201.

Feryok, A. (2017) 'Sociocultural Theory and Task-Based Language Teaching: The Role of Praxis'. *TESOL Quarterly*, 51(3) 716–727.

Firth, A. and Wagner, J. (1997) 'On Discourse, Communication, and (some) Fundamental Concepts in SLA research'. *The Modern Language Journal*, 81(3) 285–300.

Fries, C. (1945) *Teaching and Learning English as a Foreign Language*. Ann Arbor, MI: University of Michigan Press.

Golonka, E. M., Bowles, A. R., Frank, V. M., Richardson, D. L. and Freynik, S. (2014) 'Technologies for Foreign Language Learning: A Review of Technology Types and Their Effectiveness'. *Computer Assisted Language Learning*, 27(1) 70–105.

Han, Z. (2016) 'A "Reimagined SLA" or an Expanded SLA? A Rejoinder to The Douglas Fir Group'. *Modern Language Journal*, 100(4) 736–740.

Harun, M., Massari, N. and Behak, M. (2014) 'Use of L1 as a Mediational Tool for Understanding Tense/Aspect Marking in English: An Application of Concept-Based Instruction'. *Procedia – Social and Behavioral Sciences*, 134(C) 134–139.

Horwitz, E. K. (2016) 'Factor Structure of the Foreign Language Classroom Anxiety Scale: Comment on Park (2014)'. *Psychological Reports*, 119(1) 71–76.

Horwitz, E. K., Horwitz, M. B. and Cope, J. (1986) 'Foreign Language Classroom Anxiety'. *The Modern Language Journal*, 70(2) 125–132.

Hulstijn, J. (2013) 'Is the Second Language Acquisition Discipline Disintegrating?'. *Language Teaching*, 46(4) 511–517.

Krashen, S. (1981) *Second Language Acquisition and Second Language Learning*. Oxford: Pergamon.

Krashen, S. (1985) *The Input Hypothesis: Issues and Implications*. Harlow: Longman.

Lado, R. (1957) *Linguistics Across Cultures: Applied Linguistics for Language Teachers*. Ann Arbor, MI: University of Michigan Press.

Lantolf, J. P. (ed.) (1994) 'Sociocultural Theory and Second Language Learning: Special Issue'. *The Modern Language Journal*, 78(4) 418–420.

Larsen-Freeman, D. (1991) 'Second Language Acquisition Research: Staking out the Territory'. *TESOL Quarterly*, 25 315–350.

Larsen-Freeman, D. (2015) 'Saying What we Mean: Making a Case for "Language Acquisition" to Become "Language Development"'. *Language Teaching*, 48(4) 491–505.

Li, S. (2010) 'The Effectiveness of Corrective Feedback in SLA: A Meta-Analysis'. *Language Learning*, 60(2) 309–365.

Loewen, S. and Plonsky, L. (2016) *An A-Z of Applied Linguistics Research Methods*. London: Palgrave.

Long, M. (1980) *Input, interaction and second language acquisition*. Ph.D. dissertation, University of California Los Angeles, USA.

Mitchell, R., Myles, F. and Marsden, E. (2013) *Second Language Learning Theories*. Abingdon: Routledge.

Myles, F. (2010) 'The Development of Theories of Second Language Acquisition'. *Language Teaching*, 43(3) 320–332.

Nassaji, H. (2012) 'The Relationship between SLA Research and Language Pedagogy: Teachers' Perspectives'. *Language Teaching Research*, 16(3) 337–365.

Nassaji, H. (2016) 'Research Timeline: Form-Focused Instruction and Second Language Acquisition'. *Language Teaching*, 49(1) 35–62.

Nation, P. (2018) 'Keeping it Practical and Keeping it Simple'. *Language Teaching*, 51(1) 138–146.

Norris, J. and Ortega, L. (2003) 'Defining and measuring SLA', in Doughty, C. and Long, M. H. (eds) *The Handbook of Second Language Acquisition*. Hoboken, NJ: Wiley: 716–761.

Norton, B. (1997) 'Language, Identity, and the Ownership of English'. *TESOL Quarterly*, 31(3) 409–429.

Ohta, A. (2001) *Second Language Acquisition Processes in The Classroom: Learning Japanese*. Mahwah, NJ: Lawrence Erlbaum.

Ortega, L. (2009) *Understanding Second Language Acquisition*. London: Hodder Education.

Ortega, L. (2013) 'SLA for the 21st Century: Disciplinary Progress, Transdisciplinary Relevance, and the Bi/Multilingual Turn'. *Language Learning*, 63 1–24.

Park, G. P. (2014) 'Factor Analysis of the Foreign Language Classroom Anxiety Scale in Korean Learners of English as a Foreign Language'. *Psychological Reports*, 115(1) 261–275.

Pennington, M. C. and Hoekje, B. J. (2014) 'Framing English Language Teaching'. *System*, 46 163–175.

Pienemann, M. (1984) 'Psychological Constraints on the Teachability of Languages'. *Studies in Second Language Acquisition*, 6 186–214.

Russell, J. and Spada, N. (2006) 'The effectiveness of corrective feedback for second language acquisition: a meta-analysis of the research', in Norris, J. and Ortega, L. (eds) *Synthesizing Research on Language Learning and Teaching*. Amsterdam: Benjamins: 131–164.

Schmidt, R. (1990) 'The Role of Consciousness in Second Language Learning'. *Applied Linguistics*, 11 129–158.

Selinker, L. (1972) 'Interlanguage'. *International Review of Applied Linguistics*, 10 209–231.

Skehan, P. (1989) *Individual Differences in Foreign Language Learning*. London: Arnold.

Spada, N. (2015) 'SLA Research and L2 Pedagogy: Misapplications and Questions of Relevance'. *Language Teaching*, 48(1) 69–81.

Swain, M. (1985) 'Communicative competence: some roles of comprehensible input and comprehensible output in its development', in Gass, S. and Madden, C. (eds) *Input in Second Language Acquisition*. Rowley, MA: Newbury House: 235–253.

Swain M. (2006) 'Languaging, agency and collaboration in advanced second language proficiency', in Byrnes. H. (ed.) *Advanced Language Learning: The Contribution of Halliday and Vygotsky*. London: Continuum: 95–108.

Tarone, E. (2006) 'Interlanguage', in Chapelle, C. A. (ed.) *The Encyclopedia of Applied Linguistics*. Wiley Online Library: 747–752.

Tran, T., Baldauf, R. and Moni, K. (2013) 'Foreign Language Anxiety: Understanding its Status and Insiders' Awareness and Attitudes'. *TESOL Quarterly*, 47(2) 216–243.

VanPatten, B. (1996) *Input Processing and Grammar Instruction: Theory and Research*. Norwood, NJ: Ablex.

Zand-Moghadam, A. and Hussein, M. (2016) 'TEFL Teachers' and non-TEFL Teachers' Perceptions on the Relationship Between SLA Research and Language Pedagogy'. *Journal of Language and Cultural Education*, 4(3) 233–256.

Zuengler, J. and Miller, E. R. (2006) 'Cognitive and Sociocultural Perspectives: Two Parallel SLA Worlds'. *TESOL Quarterly: A Journal for Teachers of English to Speakers of Other Languages and of Standard English as a Second Dialect*, 40(1) 35–58.

18

Using corpus approaches in English language teacher education

Fiona Farr and Anne O'Keeffe

Introduction: ELTE and corpora?

If language teaching is complex, then language teacher education is an incredibly complex endeavour. Supporting novice teachers in their preparation for the myriad of variables and influencing factors that will play a part in the success, or otherwise, of their own future students is a task that must be approached with the care it deserves. The many questions we ask ourselves as language teacher educators when considering course design, development and delivery are: how much content (language) should be covered? What theories should be included? Where is the practicum best integrated and how much is enough? What is the nature of the received wisdom the student teachers come with and how can that be best utilised, or should it perhaps be critiqued and discarded? How can the latest technologies be incorporated? What of teacher research – which methods, what kind of data and analytical skills are required? How can we imbue a strong commitment to ongoing professional development, so that the teacher education course is seen as the starting and not the finishing point? And what are the theoretical and practical frameworks needed to support this CPD? And then there are the philosophical stances that novice teachers have towards the nature of language, learning and teaching, also known as wisdom of practice (WoP) (Shulman, 2004). How can these be honed, critically developed and best aligned with the teacher's practice? Taking Shulman's original definition of content (knowledge about language), pedagogic (knowledge about teaching) and pedagogical content knowledge (transforming content knowledge into a format suitable for teaching) (Shulman, 1987, 1986), layering this with WoP (Chappell, 2017: 435), and adding technological knowledge (Mishra and Koehler, 2006) to give a TPACK (technological, pedagogic and content knowledge) acronym, goes some way to simplifying the complexity of the ELTE context. This is represented visually in Figure 18.1, as overlapping and integrated zones.

The aim of this chapter is to explore the ways in which corpus linguistics (CL) can facilitate teacher development in each of the spheres represented in Figure 18.1. Based on our own and other reported experiences of using CL in ELTE, we demonstrate the ways in which this approach is one of the ways teacher educators can more easily align their espoused theories (what they say they believe) with their theories in practice (what can be reasonably understood to be their beliefs based on direct observation of their practice) (Schön, 1987).

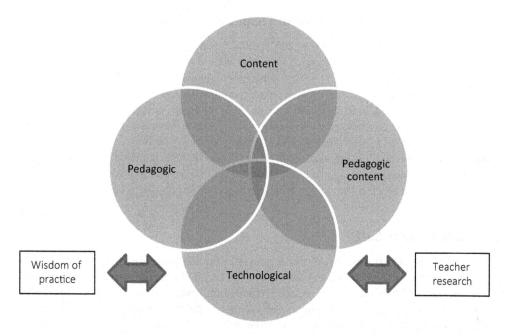

Figure 18.1 Teacher knowledge

In other words, so that they can practise what they preach in terms of supporting novice teachers to become independent, aware, critical, inquiring, reflective practitioners. We have long argued (e.g. O'Keeffe and Farr, 2003; Farr, 2010) that corpora continue to play a minor part in much teacher education but are a resource with much potential (see also Römer, 2006).

So, what do we mean by corpus linguistics? A simple definition is: the electronic analysis of a digital collection of naturally occurring spoken (in a transcribed format) or written language, potentially with additional contextual information. This analysis allows the user to get information such as frequency of use, patterns of use, collocations, range of use across texts, plus additional statistical information. A basic example of this is the *Google NGram Viewer*, which tracks the frequency of use of a word over time in its Google Books database and displays it on a line graph. And there are other easy to use interfaces such as Just-the-Word, based on the British National Corpus (BNC), which produces a list of the most common collocates of the search word, sorted by pattern. Such sites can be effective on shorter ELTE courses as an introduction to the concepts of CL, without the need for more serious technological upskilling (see Naismith, 2017 for examples of their use on intensive CELTA courses). On the other side of the cline is the full integration of CL approaches in ways that permeate all aspects of the teacher education programme, and this is usually more plausible in the context of an MA programme at university level, where time is less of an issue and the academic demands of the course are high. This potentially will allow detailed coverage of CL approaches (perhaps through following a MOOC, such as that offered by Lancaster on the FutureLearn platform), and the use of such approaches in each of the spheres identified in Figure 18.1, including as a research tool for an MA dissertation (see Farr, 2008 and Zareva, 2017 for such accounts in grammar courses).

Using corpus approaches: practical issues and considerations

In our 2003 article (O'Keeffe and Farr, 2003), we outlined some of the key decisions that need to be made when taking a CL approach in teacher education. It is timely to revisit these here, some 15 years later, to determine what has become redundant, what remains true, and what needs to be added to that list in order to take account of changes that have taken place during the interim period, both in terms of technology, information and pedagogic approaches. In 2003, using this terminology, we discussed building versus buying a corpus; spoken versus written data; small versus large corpora; native speaker versus learner or non-native corpora; and using handouts versus allowing students to work 'hands on' with the data. Below, we reframe some of these discussions in light of changes, such as ease of access, more advanced technology etc., that continue to affect the ways in which we integrate corpus use in ELTE.

To build or not to build?

It is slightly amusing that we began this section with the following statement: 'Many corpora are now commercially available and some can even be purchased for under $100' (O'Keeffe and Farr, 2003: 407). In fact, much of our effort at that time was spent on trying to secure funding to buy the few corpora that were available, either in disk format or through subscription. The question of 'buying' has now become all but redundant as there are a vast array of corpora readily and freely available online, representing many genres, varieties and registers. One prime example, is the Brigham Young collection of corpora, collated by Mark Davies (https://corpus.byu.edu), which contains freely available, searchable spoken and written corpora that run into billions of words and are reportedly accessed by 130,000 distinct users each month. Scott Thornbury has also produced a very useful video tutorial available on YouTube describing how to use COCA, the Corpus of Contemporary American English, which is part of the BYC (also available online: <https://scottthornbury.wordpress.com/2013/05/12/c-is-for-coca-corpus>). Murphy and Riordan (2016) provide an up-to-date broad overview of corpus types and uses. Their chapter outlines five types of corpora: general, parallel, historical, multimodal and specialised. In each section, they provide an overview of the corpus type, the key issues associated with the type as well as its applications in pedagogical contexts. So, the question of availability and cost have largely become irrelevant. This does not however, negate the need to consider whether it is desirable to build or collate one's own corpus. This can be a time consuming and complex task (see Reppen, 2016 for details of how to compile a corpus), and one which is generally undertaken by teacher researchers as part of an MA or PhD thesis project if they wish to examine a specific variety or genre that is not available to them from other sources (see below).

Spoken versus written

Direct access to spoken versus written corpora, although easier, continues to be a challenge in relative terms. But there has been a change:

> In comparison with written corpora, spoken corpora have not developed at the same rate [....] The reasons for this are largely to do with the huge costs and time involved in compilation and transcription, as well as access to recordable data. What has developed over the last 20 years, however, is an acknowledgement of the importance of spoken corpora in creating a fuller understanding of everyday spoken language, especially casual conversation.
>
> *(Caines et al., 2016: 348)*

McCarthy (1998) accounted for the dearth of spoken data in light of costs, access to appropriate and representative speech data situations, quality of recording, time involved in transcription, difficult decisions in relation to level of detail to include in transcription, and so on. Other than quality of recording, most of these considerations have become even more problematic. Stricter and tighter ethical protocols around data gathering and legal mandates around data storage have made it almost impossible to collect spoken language representation from some user groups (for example, children or vulnerable adults). These protocols are for the protection of individuals and are to be welcomed but they have brought a new reality to many interested in the compilation of spoken data. Having said that, where access is relatively straightforward, we have seen a growth, and a resultant discernible integration of the findings from spoken language research into materials development. In his 2015 article, Alex Gilmore examined the influence that discourse studies (including corpus linguistics) has had on language descriptions and task design in published ELT materials, and highlights that 'the "corpus revolution" (Rundell and Stock, 1992) has had a major and lasting impact on language learning materials in some respects' (Gilmore, 2015: 511). We now have two major grammar reference books which are corpus based (Biber et al., 1999 and more recently Carter and McCarthy, 2006), a range of course books, and many on-line materials. And it would be fair to say that not many, if any, publisher would dream of producing a dictionary which was not corpus based. This has meant that we are getting to a point where the spoken language descriptions and examples that are available to learners are much more reflective of real language use, both in substantial terms and as influenced by considerations of frequency and context of use. Therefore it is important that teacher education programmes also have a stronger focus on spoken language corpora and language awareness to equip teachers with the relevant conceptual frameworks to appropriately mediate published language learning materials.

Small versus large

Our arguments in terms of corpus size have not changed fundamentally and our original assertion 'whether to use a large, generalized corpus or a small, specialized corpus depends on the teacher educator's particular needs' (O'Keeffe and Farr, 2003: 409) still holds true. When using larger corpora, it is easier to discern repeated patterns of use and collocation, but smaller corpora are extremely useful for examining a specialised genre (Flowerdew, 2004). Small corpora are useful for introducing students to corpus techniques and methods, as they can sometimes feel overwhelmed by the sheer number of 'hits' they get for a particular search item in larger corpora. This is a more salient point amid today's world of billion word corpora. Small corpora can also allow the user to more readily access contextual information, where this is available, and this can be of great benefit if you are conducting pragmatic research (e.g. investigating the use of pragmatic markers in classroom discourse or power relations within spoken or written interactions – see O' Keeffe, 2018). Small contextualised corpora, which include a lot of information about the participants (i.e. metadata) are also of those interested in the corpus-based investigation of sociolinguistic variables (for example, Farr and Murphy, 2009, Murphy, 2010).

Learner corpora

Through research into learner language, CL has played a key role in maintaining the continuity of focus on learner interlanguage from the early 1990s. The pioneering International Corpus of Learner English (ICLE) project (Granger, 2002) brought a new intensity to the study of interlanguage because of the possibilities it opened up not just for the large-scale study of interlanguage but also for contrastive analysis (Tono and Díez-Bedmar, 2014). The main focus of early learner corpus research was on learner error analysis and, as noted by Gilquin (2008: 6), this allowed for systematic and contextualised analysis of learner language and enabled researchers investigate what learners get right, what they overuse and what they under use relative to native speakers.

Looking at current trends in learner corpora, we can say that they have enjoyed a relatively strong period of growth, and with this has come an expanded portfolio of use and usefulness (see Granger and Meunier, 2015 for a comprehensive overview). This has come at the same time as wider acceptance of outer circle Englishes as a continuously expanding realm (Kachru, 1992). In a very recent edited volume by Brezina and Flowerdew (2017), there are discussions of learner corpora for the investigation of learner language use (disagreement, self-repetitions, disciplinary genres, phrasal verbs, and figurative language). All of these investigations and their findings are likely to inform our discussions of variables on SLA and classroom practice in teacher education contexts. More interesting though, this volume also contains a section of three chapters on task and learner variables: the effect of task and topic on opportunity of use (Caines and Buttery, 2017); the effect of proficiency and background on phrasal verb usage (Marin-Cervantes and Gablasova, 2017); the effect of a study abroad period (Götz and Mukherjee, 2017).

Another important development in learner corpora in recent years, which has important implications for ELTE, is that they are increasingly basing their calibration of level on the Common European Framework of Reference for Languages (CEFR) as opposed to the learners' year of study (O'Keeffe and Mark, 2017). The *English Profile Project* (www.englishprofile.org) offers an important strand of new CEFR-based learner corpus research which is leading to pedagogical resource outputs. They are based on the Cambridge Learner Corpus (CLC), a 55 million-word collection of learner exam writing, of which over 30 million words are error coded. Apart from the ongoing body of research, the main resource outputs are listed below. These should all be of application in ELTE programmes as they will help bring more precision to materials selection, design and grading (in terms of choosing the right material for a given cohort and designing an appropriate task):

1. The *English Vocabulary Profile* (Capel, 2010) – [www.englishprofile.org/wordlists] this corpus-based resource profiles the CEFR level at which learners can use a given word and its meaning. For example, using the searchable interface, it tells us that the homonym *bark* can be used by B2 learners in the sense of the sound that a dog makes but learners cannot use it metaphorically, as in *His boss was barking at everyone in the office*, until C2 level and the sense the hard, outside part of a tree is also not acquired until C2 level. The resource can also be used to generate lexical sets around typical pedagogical topics (clothes, food, travel, etc.) and these can be used to design vocabulary lessons around lexical sets which are linked to the given level of the learners. Using this resource in ELTE, will bring attention to the importance of being aware of teaching level-appropriate vocabulary sets and it also underscores the importance of focusing on the polysemic nature of vocabulary where the most frequent 2000 words account for the up to 83 per cent of coverage in a given text (see O'Keeffe et al., 2007).

2. *Text Inspector* is a tool which uses corpus research into vocabulary acquisition across the CEFR, including EVP (as detailed above), and allows the user to copy and paste a text into its interface so as to instantly generate a lexical profile of that text. This will prove a very useful tool for ELTE as it allows for more precision in choosing texts that are appropriately pitched in terms of vocabulary level. This will be especially important when designing assessments so that texts that contain lexical items above the level of the test are not selected.

Word List	Types	Tokens
A1	53 (40.15%)	138 (61.06%)
A2	34 (25.76%)	42 (18.58%)
B1	14 (10.61%)	15 (6.64%)
B2	12 (9.09%)	12 (5.31%)
C1	1 (0.76%)	1 (0.44%)
C2	2 (1.52%)	2 (0.88%)
Unlisted	16 (12.12%)	16 (7.08%)

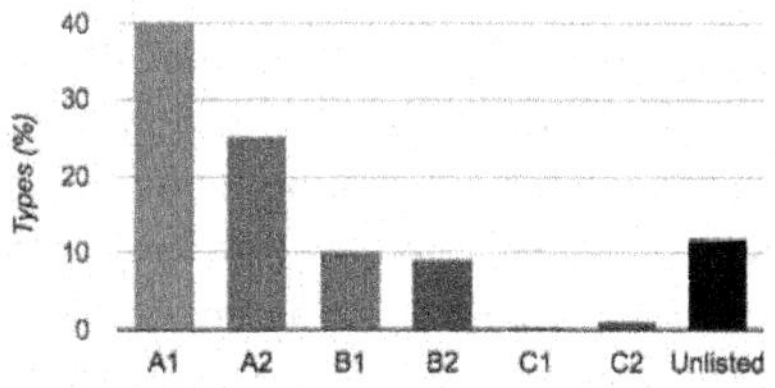

Figure 18.2 An example of how *Text Inspector* can be used to profile vocabulary of a given text, generated on www.englishprofile.org/wordlists/text-inspector

Figure 18.2 illustrates a lexical profile of a short extract from Bram Stoker's *Dracula*, by way of example.

3.   The *English Grammar Profile* (O'Keeffe and Mark, 2017) – [www.englishprofile.org/eng lish-grammar-profile] this resource profiles the grammatical competence of learners at each level of the CEFR. It outlines over 1,200 reference level descriptors, or 'can do statements' across the six competence levels. This resource marks a major shift of focus from learner error to learner competence. In the context of ELTE, this will prove an important reference point for syllabus and materials design in relation to grammar. It shows how learners acquire forms developmentally and how, as they grow in proficiency, they often continue to acquire new functions and pragmatic functions of syntax that they may have learnt at an early stage. An example of this is the Past Simple, which learners acquire at A1 level, in a limited way, but even at B2, they are still acquiring new uses, such as the examples below, which show learners at B2 using the Past Simple after *If* to show politeness:

It would be great if **you sent** me a free copy of the next edition of The Student Tourist Guidebook (B2, Korean).
I would be grateful if **you gave** me this job (B2, Greek).

(www.englishprofile.org/english-grammar-profile/egp-online)

Hand outs versus hands on

The discussion here relates to the direct versus indirect (mediated or moderated) access to language corpora, the major difference being the time and level of technical and analytical skills needed by the user for direct access in a data-driven learning (DDL) context (as discussed further below). As Boulton (2012: 152) underlines 'one of the most apparent obstacles to DDL is the use of the technology itself – the computer with its query software and interfaces for accessing electronic corpora'. Extensive training in corpus literacy is generally required for direct access on a computer or other electronic device (see for example, Farr, 2008; Heather and Helt, 2012; Zareva, 2017) to be able to do any meaningful analysis of the data. This needs to be considered in the context of the teacher education programme. Within our own institutional contexts, at MA level, we do integrate full direct access for our student teachers, and on some, but not all, of our shorter TESOL programmes at undergraduate level. Where direct access is not a viable option, 'the obvious question is whether the computer can be removed from the equation without losing the benefits of the overall approach' (Boulton, 2012: 152), and in our own practice we use learning materials that are corpus-based or corpus-informed, and at the very least the student teachers interact with a simple on-line corpus interface to get a sense of what is possible. Bouton's study compares a hands-on and hands-off approach with groups of language learners and found that, with some caveats, the paper-based option does represent a 'viable option'. We do remain true to our original contention in 2003 that even when adopting a direct access approach, it is usually very important to begin with some paper-based introductions in order to help develop conceptual frameworks before student teachers get distracted by the technology, overwhelmed by the volume of search return items, or diverted into statistical analyses that may be outside of their comfort zone. This sentiment is echoed in the research of Ebrahimi and Faghih (2017) on the reflections of MA TEFL students on their experience with using corpora for the first time.

Developing technological knowledge

Zareva (2017) reports on a questionnaire-based study of 21 TESOL trainee teachers enrolled on an MA Applied Linguistics, Teacher Education and Teacher Development programme in which she explored a number of research questions relating to the use of corpus linguistics within the programme. One of the key questions focused on the level of preparedness of the graduate students. Based on their self-reports within the surveys, only 43 per cent (n = 9) knew what a corpus was and only 29 per cent (n = 6) had ever used a corpus. To introduce a corpus literacy component to 'the already dense content of an English grammar course' (ibid.: 76) meant using five class periods over the first ten weeks of the semester. Feedback showed that teacher trainees felt this was very worthwhile. In fact, when asked whether they would recommend removing the corpus component from the grammar modules, they unanimously agreed that it should not be removed. While they felt that the preparatory input prepared them well, they had feedback on what needs to be improved. Two of the three of these related to technological knowledge: 1) dealing with technical difficulties (how to navigate a corpus, how to use wildcards in searches, restricting and filtering searches and getting to know the corpus interface), and 2) needing more hands-on practice in class. These concerns are consistent with other studies. Farr (2008), Heather and Helt (2012) and Ebrahimi and Faghih (2017) all cite user-related struggles with the technical side of using corpora, such as dealing with the interface, figuring out how it all works, interpreting findings. Interestingly, Zavera (2017) notes, the area that trainees found most challenging in the use of corpora within their English grammar module related to coming up with a project idea. In one sense, this is heartening as it is more a cognitive than a technical challenge. However, it points to an inter-related issue, namely the need for an understanding of the iterative process involved when using corpus interfaces to interrogate language. While technical processes and challenges can be explained and abated, an individual faced with a screen of concordance lines or a frequency list still has to find their own way in terms of following a querying pathway. In other words, the interactive processes of going from frequency lists to concordances, to sorting and resorting to follow up hypotheses about patterns of use is also a core skill. While on the one hand it requires a critical level of technical skill, it also requires an iterative thought process.

Developing language awareness (content knowledge)

In the aforementioned Zareva (2017) study, it is notable that one of the key themes from the teacher trainees who were surveyed on the use of corpus linguistics as part of their grammar modules was that they found that it heightened their awareness of grammar and that they saw the use of CL within this module as going hand-in-hand with acquiring a deeper cognitive understanding of language as a system. One informant summed this up as follows (Zareva, 2017: 75): 'It was a huge benefit to "see" the grammar we talked about in class being used in real-life language'. The same informant also noted the link to future practice through this statement: 'it was useful in understanding descriptive grammar and its relevance to ESL teaching' and s/he found an integrative benefit to the use of CL in the ELTE programme, 'it also offered a quantitative side to the class that helped reinforce the lectures.' These findings underscore those of Farr (2008). One of her informants reported that the use of CL on their MA programme helped to uncover 'functions and structures in language not found in grammar books' (ibid.: 36). Farr also notes that the fact that corpora represent 'real language use in context' was viewed as an asset in their awareness of language process.

What is heartening about Zavera's (2017) study is that participants cited 43 advantages in all to learning how to use CL in their programme and when these are collapsed into three overarching themes in terms of their gain in expertise they bode very well for not just present gain in language awareness and content knowledge but to future application and continuing professional development within the practice:

1. Language use and ESL teaching (74 per cent): they cited the many applications that they could envisage for using CL in their professional practice, including, *inter alia*, grammar teaching, academic vocabulary, vocabulary and collocations, developing writing skills, finding authentic examples, contrasting different language usage;
2. Research (16 per cent): for instance, they envisaged other opportunities to apply their new knowledge in other areas of their graduate studies;
3. Professional empowerment (10 per cent): often at a personal level, informants cited a sense of excitement and empowerment at about being able use their new skills to follow up their language queries and interests, summed up by the comment, 'it opens up a whole new world to me' (Zareva, 2017: 75).

Developing pedagogical knowledge

In addition to the more well-established use of corpus approaches in language awareness contexts, there are a number of ways in which small, local or personally constructed corpora can help facilitate improved pedagogic awareness of practice. Earlier research has described how the collection and analysis of corpora from the teacher education context can help us to understand it better (for example, the TP feedback context reported in Farr, 2010, or the construction of teacher identity in personal narratives and shared discussions in online modes reported in Farr and Riordan, 2015), and hence make informed decisions about how the process of teacher education can be made more effective. Such research has focused on how teacher educators can reflect on and improve their practices. The focus of the present discussion will be on how corpus-based evidence can be used to inform and improve the pedagogic practices of student and novice teachers undertaking a teacher education course. We situate this in the context of reflective practice (RP) as a framework for professional development, specifically as part of the practicum component of the course. Based originally on the work of Dewey and Schon (Farrell, 2012), much has been written on the usefulness of RP in teacher education, and it has established itself firmly as a developmental tool (for example, Mann and Walsh, 2017). One of the difficulties associated with it however is that it can be overly introflexive (looking inwards at oneself) and intuitive, and calls have been made to use more evidence as a basis for change and progression, where necessary (Akbari, 2007; Farr and Riordan, 2017; Mann and Walsh, 2013). To that end, we have implemented the use of the evidence-based PENSER (translates to think/reflect, from French) framework (Farr and Farrell, 2017) at our home university. This RP framework allows the student teacher to use and analysis corpus-stored evidence of classroom interactions, compared with other genres, where relevant, to inform their reflections and plans for change. The PENSER model proposes the following five-stage framework for novice teachers to assist their development during the practicum:

1. **Problem identification**: individual challenges are identified and articulated through observing and reflecting on personal practice.
2. **Embracing**: these challenges are accepted as issues in need of further investigation, understanding and improvement and there is a commitment to these actions.
3. **Noticing**: experienced teachers are observed to facilitate a better understanding of the challenge and to provide examples of practice to be considered for assimilation.
4. **Solving**: a solution for personal change to practice is proposed, planned and implemented.
5. **Exploring and Researching**: the solution is investigated and critically evaluated to determine if the challenge has been appropriately overcome or if further engagement is needed.

At each stage in this process, appropriate corpora of classroom data can provide a source of evidence for the decisions and focus of the RP undertaken. Such corpora can be transcribed spoken language, or multi-modal to include video recordings (see Adolphs and Carter, 2013 for details on building and using multimodal corpora). And while it would be far too time-consuming for an individual to build corpora of all of their own practice sessions, institutions can build up a library of such resources over time and make them available to their student teachers each year. At our home institutions we now have a range of classroom data in corpus format, and we build on this each year with contributions from students, teachers and researchers. Farrell (2015) provides good examples of how to explore individual awareness and use of regional and 'standard' language among cohorts of novice and experienced teachers as part of their professional development.

Developing wisdom of practice

Shulman (2004) developed the concept of teachers' Wisdom of Practice (WoP) to refer to the philosophical stances that frame their evaluation of what is going on in the classroom. In other words, their beliefs, their values, and their opinions, about language, how it is taught and how it is learned. This fits well with the work on teacher cognition that has triggered much understanding in the field of ELTE (for example, Borg, 2006; Li Li, 2017). Chappell (2017: 434) argues that 'finding ways to support teachers in articulating, interrogating, and developing their WoP is a powerful way to assist them in better understanding and developing their teaching practices'. He proposes a social and collaborative framework to develop teachers' WoPs (ibid.: 441). It involves the three stages of:

- Articulation: revealing the true nature of theoretical and philosophical stances
- Interrogation: comparison with other theoretical stances and comparison with actual classroom practice
- Change implementation: integrating the required innovations in practice to fit with the new theoretical orientations.

The use of corpus-data of classroom interactions, and other teacher-student interactions, can provide compelling evidence for stages two and three in this framework. Schön (1987) differentiates between espoused theories (what teachers say they believe) and theories in practice (what can reasonably be assumed to be a teacher's beliefs based on observing their practice), and using evidence from practice is one convincing way through which teachers come to realise any divergences or discrepancies between both, and initiate desired changes. In simple terms, this is about getting the walk to match the talk and vice versa.

Developing pedagogical-content knowledge

Pedagogical-content knowledge is about manipulating, mediating and developing content, English language in this case, so that it becomes useful for learners and learning contexts. This can happen in two ways. Indirectly, when corpus research findings 'get through' (Gilmore, 2015: 511–512) in the form of dictionaries, reference grammars, innovative approaches to textbook design or electronic resources as detailed above. There are not many corpus-based examples of all of these resources available to teachers, and although they have not been directly involved in their development, by preparing to teach and by mediating the materials for their students they can develop their own awareness of how corpus-based findings relevantly inform and direct pedagogic materials and how they might best be exploited for this purpose. Teachers can become more aware of notions of frequency of use, context-differentiated language use, and collocational language use, when using materials that are based on evidence from corpus-based research.

In a more direct way, teachers can engage in their own materials development, based on corpora. The use of smaller, often locally produced/gathered, specialised corpora is quite well-established to teach academic or professional English (for example, Flowerdew, 2004). Teachers are almost always de facto materials developers to some extent for their own students. The use of corpus materials with learners fits well with the SLA concept of 'noticing'. According to Mishan and Timmis (2015: 40):

> It is little surprise really that this field that depended on the 'noticing' of patterns (lexical, grammatical, discourse, pragmatic etc.) in corpus data conceived pedagogical applications that were a perfect 'fit' with this SLA theory. An early application was data-driven learning (DDL) (e.g. Johns, 1991), probably the closest pedagogically to CL research itself, which saw learners mining raw data (in the form of concordances) in order to expose grammatical patterns from which they could infer rules of use.

Mishan and Timmis provide much more detail on the principles and use of DDL in Chapter 5 of the same volume on Materials Development in TESOL. In fact, a word search for 'corpus' in that volume produced 71 occurrences, an indication of the growing importance of corpus data in the field of materials development. And, as discussed earlier, while DDL models, which allow learners to have direct access to corpora through computer interfaces, may not suit all learners or contexts, teacher mediation of corpus materials can be equally effective (Boulton, 2012).

Teacher as researcher

As recently as August 2017, in the ELT Journal, Peter Medgyes returns to the relationship between teacher and research in a context where he states that, 'It is a fact that a very low proportion of practising teachers are in the habit of reading ELT-related research papers' (Medgyes, 2017: 491), and goes on to discuss various reasons why this is the case, including the disparate nature of the two activities. From another angle, Borg (2009) identified a number of reasons why so few teachers are directly engaged in research activity (either reading or doing research), the most frequently cited being time constraints and limited access to books and journal articles. Those who did engage, did so primarily as part of a professional programme of study. Like Paran (2017: 501) we strongly believe that 'intuitions and beliefs are not reliable when complex issues such as teaching and learning are concerned. This is where a research-oriented or evidence-based approach comes into play'. Teacher education programmes are precisely the appropriate place to engender this spirit of enquiry, or research, if research is taken in its broad meaning. It is here that prospective teachers learn the tools of research, such as appropriate methodologies, how to survey the relevant literature and make sense of it, how to collect and analyse data and how to disseminate and report findings to others, or simply to implement changes to one's local practice. And it is in this realm of a teacher education programme that there is a place for corpus-based methodologies and principles. They can be used to systematically explore practice in a more formal manner than suggested in the previous two sections on pedagogic knowledge, or to explore language through a research lens. In addition, corpora provide the kind of data and evidence which are central to teacher development (Mann and Walsh, 2017).

Hockly (2017: 364) suggests that

> the term 'ELT researcher' is a broad one, taking in experienced academic researchers who are au fait with qualitative or quantitative research methods on the one hand, to 'teachers as researchers' on the other, that is practising English language teachers interested in carrying out more informal or ad hoc action research based on their classroom practice.

Whichever is the case, collecting or collating a corpus for research purposes is a very legitimate way to explore language in use from a variety of contexts. Data is everywhere and it is now easier than at any other time in the past to build a corpus by scouring the internet. A couple of hours of effort can easily yield a sizeable corpus ready for analysis and investigation to answer a specified set of relevant research questions. There are however a range of complex ethical considerations around digital or online data gathering and use. Consent and anonymity are not as straightforward as they might be in face-to-face contexts. The Association of Internet Researchers (AoIR) provide ethical guidelines which will help researchers steer clear of unethical pitfalls, inadvertent or otherwise.

Looking to the future

Returning again to our (2003) paper, we note our call at that time for the need to educate teachers who can manipulate language corpora for their own pedagogic ends, scrutinise and evaluate findings that are presented as 'facts', so that they will be better placed for the socio-cultural mediation and pedagogic recontextualisation of these resources and findings in their language classrooms of the future. In terms of looking to the future, we can say that so much amelioration has occurred technologically to allow this to happen. Corpora and software are freely available, online supporting training materials for their use abound, and so on. The conditions seem ripe for a future where the integration of corpus linguistics in ELTE will be a given. Yet, despite all of these affordances, we are mindful of Ebrahimi and Faghih's (2017: 121) caveat in relation to current practice, that, 'the reality is that they [corpora] are still rarely used by language teachers'. Collating ELTE practice-based evaluative studies of the use of corpus linguistics on MA programmes play a key role in addressing why this is so. The work of Farr (2008), Heather and Helt (2012), Ebrahimi and Faghih (2017) and Zareva (2017), among others, is crucial to informing the way forward because they put corpora to the test in ELTE and invariably expose both the highs and lows of their use. Evidence from these studies shows that student teachers are aware of the challenges in terms of technical skills, time and application but they invariably seem to enjoy the use of corpora and to see the benefit of having corpus linguistics skills as part of their 'toolkit' (Timmis, 2015).

The future of ELTE seems firmly set in the socialisation of teachers in a way that is dependent on a set of understandings (Freeman, 2016), and the central argument of this chapter is that using corpus-based evidence in qualitative or quantitative ways can help to develop these understandings in ways that are relevant, local and even personal to the individual. We have briefly illustrated the ways in which such an approach can enhance the various types of 'teacher knowledge' outlined in the introduction. We are not suggesting that this is the only valid approach, but it is one that we have found extremely effective when working with prospective teachers on our programmes, and one that can complement other tools and methodologies with ease.

Related topics

The language of the classroom/classroom discourse; Teacher knowledge and development; From language as system to language as discourse.

Further reading

Ebrahimi, A. and Faghih, E. (2017) 'Integrating Corpus Linguistics into Online Language Teacher Education Programs'. *ReCALL*, 29(1) 120–135.
 This paper reports on the intensive use of an online CL course within an MA TEFL in Iraq and gives insight into the benefits and challenges of this approach based on the reflections of 50 participants. It gives an interesting perspective on the challenges relating to using corpus linguistics in ELTE in a context where access to IT and internet is not a given or to use the authors' term, in technology-poor educational settings.
Farr, F. (2008) 'Evaluating the use of Corpus-Based Instruction in a Language Teacher Education Context: Perspectives From The Users'. *Language Awareness*, 17(1) 25–43.
 This research thematically surveys the responses of 25 MA TESOL students to the use of corpora in their ELTE programme over a two-semester phase. The longer duration of this period of use is perhaps an important variable.
Farr, F. and Murray, L. (eds) (2016) *The Routledge Handbook of Language Learning and Technology*. Abingdon: Routledge. Part IV: Corpora and data-driven learning.
 Part IV offers six chapters which provide practical and illustrated advice on the integration of corpus linguistics in language teaching contexts, most of which is also directly relevant to ELTE contexts.
Timmis, I. (2015) *Corpus Linguistics for ELT: Research and Practice*. Abingdon: Routledge.
 This book offers a very practical curation of the essentials of using CL for ELT research and practice. It includes step-by-step guidance on how to use CL to query language in use as well as illustrating some

very practical applications for ELT practice, for example how to use CL in English for Specific Purposes classes and materials design.

Zareva, A. (2017) 'Incorporating Corpus Literacy Skills into TESOL Teacher Training'. *English Language Teaching Journal*, 71(1) 69–79.
Another paper which surveys the incorporation of CL in an MA programme. This offers insight into the technical and conceptual challenges that were involved for the MA student but is hearteningly positive in its overall appraisal.

References

Adolphs, S. and Carter, R. (2013) *Spoken Corpus Linguistics: From Monomodal to Multimodal*. New York: Routledge.

Akbari, R. (2007) 'Reflections on Reflection: A Critical Appraisal of Reflective Practices in L2 Teacher Education'. *System*, 35(2) 192–207.

Biber, D., Johansson, S., Leech, G., Conrad, S. and Finegan, E. (1999) *Longman Grammar of Spoken and Written English*. London and New York: Longman.

Borg, S. (2006) *Teacher Cognition and Language Education: Research and Practice*. London: Continuum.

Borg, S. (2009) 'English Language Teachers' Conceptions of Research'. *Applied Linguistics*, 30(3) 358–388.

Boulton, A. (2012) 'Hands on/hands off: alternative approaches to data-driven learning', in Boulton, A. and Thomas, J. (eds) *Imput, Process and Product: Developments in Teaching and Language Corpora*. Blansko: Masaryk University Press: 152–168.

Brezina, V. and Flowerdew, L. (2017) *Learner Corpus Research: New Perspectives and Approaches*. Oxford: Bloomsbury.

Caines, A. and Buttery, P. (2017) 'The effect of task and topic on opportunity of use in learner corpora', in Brezina, V. and Flowerdew, L. (eds) *Learner Corpus Research: New Perspectives and Applications*. London: Bloomsbury.

Caines, A., McCarthy, M. and O'Keeffe, A. (2016) 'Spoken language corpora and pedagogical applications', in Farr, F. and Murray, L. (eds) *The Routledge Handbook of Language Learning and Technology*. Abingdon: Routledge: 348–361.

Capel, A. (2010) 'A1 – B2 Vocabulary: Insights and issues arising from the English Profile Wordlists project'. *English Grammar Profile Journal*, 1(1) 1–11.

Carter, R. and McCarthy, M. (2006) *Cambridge Grammar of English: A Comprehensive Guide to Spoken and Written Grammar and Usage*. Cambridge: Cambridge University Press.

Chappell, P. (2017) 'Interrogating your Wisdom of Practice to Improve Classroom Practices'. *ELT Journal*, 71(4) 433–444.

Ebrahimi, A. and Faghih, E. (2017) 'Integrating corpus linguistics into online language teacher education programs'. *ReCALL*, 29(1) 120–135.

Farr, F. (2008) 'Evaluating the use of Corpus-Based Instruction in a Language Teacher Education Context: Perspectives from the Users'. *Language Awareness*, 17(1) 25–43.

Farr, F. (2010) 'How can corpora be used in teacher education?', in O'Keeffe, A. and McCarthy, M. (eds) *Routledge Handbook of Corpus Linguistics*. Abingdon: Routledge: 620–632.

Farr, F. and Farrell, A. (2017) 'PENSER: A Data-Informed Reflective Practice Framework for Novice Teachers'. *The European Journal of Applied Linguistics and TEFL*, 6(2) 85–103.

Farr, F. and Murphy, B. (2009) 'Religious References in Contemporary Irish-English: "For the Love of God Almighty…. I'm a Holy Terror for Turf"'. *Intercultural Pragmatics*, 6(4) 535–560.

Farr, F. and Murray, L. (eds) (2016) *Routledge Handbook of Language Learning and Technology*. Abingdon: Routledge.

Farr, F. and Riordan, E. (2015) 'Tracing the Reflective Practices of Student Teachers in Online Modes'. *ReCALL*, 27(1) 104–123.

Farr, F. and Riordan, E. (2017) 'Prospective and practising teachers look backwards at the theory-practice divide through blogs and e-portfolios', in Farrell, T. S. C. (ed.) *TESOL Voices: Insider Accounts of Classroom Life. Preservice Teacher Education*. Alexandria, VA: TESOL: 13–26.

Farrell, A. (2015) 'In the classroom', in Farr, F. (ed.) *Practice in TESOL*. Edinburgh: Edinburgh University Press: 89–110.

Farrell, T. S. C. (2012) 'Reflecting on Reflective Practice: (Re)Visiting Dewey and Schön'. *TESOL Journal*, 3(1) 7–16.

Flowerdew, L. (2004) 'The argument for using specialized corpora to understand academic and professional language', in Connor, U. and Upton, T. (eds) *Discourse in the Professions: Perspectives from Corpus Linguistics*. Amsterdam: John Benjamins: 11–33.

Freeman, D. (2016) *Educating Second Language Teachers*. Oxford: Oxford University Press.

Gilmore, A. (2015) 'Research into Practice: The Influence of Discourse Studies on Language Descriptions and Task Design in Published ELT Materials'. *Language Teaching*, 48(4) 506–530.

Gilquin, G. (2008) 'Combining contrastive analysis and interlanguage analysis to apprehend transfer: detection, explanation, evaluation', in Gilquin, G., Papp, S. and Díez-Bedmar, M. B. (eds) *Linking Up Contrastive and Learner Corpus Research*. Amsterdam: Rodopi: 3–33.

Götz, S. and Mukherjee, J. (2017) 'Investigating the effect of the study abroad variable on learner output: a pseudo-longitudinal study on spoken German learner English', in Brezina, V. and Flowerdew, L. (eds) *Learner Corpus Research: New Perspectives and Applications*. London: Bloomsbury: 47–66.

Granger, S. (2002) 'A bird's-eye view of learner corpus research', in Granger, S., Hung, J. and Petch-Tyson, S. (eds) *Computer Learner Corpora, Second Language Acquisition and Foreign Language Teaching*. Amsterdam: John Benjamins: 3–33.

Granger, S. and Meunier, F. (eds) (2015) *The Cambridge Handbook of Learner Corpus Research*. Cambridge: Cambridge University Press.

Heather, J. and Helt, M. (2012) 'Evaluating Corpus Literacy Training for Pre-Service Language Teachers: Six Case Studies'. *Journal of Technology and Teacher Education*, 20(4) 415–440.

Hockly, N. (2017) 'Researching with Technology in ELT'. *ELT Journal*, 71(3) 364–372.

Johns, T. (1991) 'Should You be Persuaded – Two Samples of Data-Driven Learning Materials'. *English Language Research Journal*, 4 1–16.

Kachru, B. (1992) 'World Englishes: Approaches, Issues and Resources'. *Language Teaching*, 25(1) 1–14.

Mann, S. and Walsh, S. (2013) 'RP or "RIP": A Critical Perspective on Reflective Practice'. *Applied Linguistics Review*, 4(2) 291–315.

Mann, S. and Walsh, S. (2017) *Reflective Practice in English Language Teaching*. New York: Routledge.

Marin-Cervantes, I. and Gablasova, D. (2017) 'Phrasal verbs in spoken L2 English: the effect of L2 proficiency and L1 background', in Brezina, V. and Flowerdew, L. (eds) *Learner Corpus Research: New Perspectives and Applications*. London: Bloomsbury.

McCarthy, M. J. (1998) *Spoken Language and Applied Linguistics*. Cambridge: Cambridge University Press.

Medgyes, P. (2017) 'The (Ir)relevance of Academic Research for the Language Teacher'. *ELT Journal*, 71(4) 491–498.

Mishan, F. and Timmis, I. (2015) *Materials Development for TESOL*. Edinburgh: Edinburgh University Press.

Mishra, P. and Koehler, M. J. (2006) 'Technological Pedagogical Content Knowledge: A Framework for Teacher Knowledge'. *Teachers College Record*, 108(6) 1017–1054.

Murphy, B. (2010) *Corpus and Sociolinguistics: Investigating Age and Gender in Female Talk*. Amsterdam and Philadelphia, PA: John Benjamins.

Murphy, B. and Riordan, E. (2016) 'Corpus types and uses', in Farr, F. and Murray, L. (eds) *The Routledge Handbook of Language Learning and Technology*. Abingdon: Routledge: 388–403.

Naismith, B. (2017) 'Integrating Corpus Tools on Intensive CELTA Courses'. *ELT Journal*, 71(3) 273–283.

O'Keeffe, A. (2018) 'Corpus-based function-to-form approaches', in Jucker, A. H., Schneider, K. P. and Bublitz, W. (eds) *Methods in Pragmatics*. Berlin: Mouton de Gruyter: 587–618.

O'Keeffe, A. and Farr, F. (2003) 'Using Language Corpora in Language Teacher Education: Pedagogic, Linguistic and Cultural Insights'. *TESOL Quarterly*, 37(3) 389–418.

O'Keeffe, A. and Mark, G. (2017) 'The English Grammar Profile of Learner Competence: Methodology and Key Findings'. *International Journal of Corpus Linguistics*, 22(4) 457–489.

O'Keeffe, A., McCarthy, M. J. and Carter, R. A. (2007) *From Corpus to Classroom: Language Use and Language Teaching*. Cambridge: Cambridge University Press.

Paran, A. (2017) '"Only connect": Researchers and Teachers in Dialogue'. *ELT Journal*, 71(4) 499–508.

Reppen, R. (2016) 'Designing and building corpora for language learning', in Farr, F. and Murray, L. (eds) *The Routledge Handbook of Language Learning and Technology*, Abingdon: Routledge: 404–412.

Römer, U. (2006) 'Pedagogical applications of corpora: some reflections on the current scope and a wish list for future developments'. *Zeitschrift für Anglistik und Amerikanistik*, 54(2), Special Issue (Gast, V. (ed.)) 'The Scope and Limits of Corpus Linguistics – Empiricism in the Description and Analysis of English', XX 121–134.

Rundell, M. and Stock, P. (1992) 'The Corpus Revolution'. *English Today*, 30 9–14.

Schön, D. (1987) *Educating the Reflective Practitioner: Toward a Design for Teaching and Learning in the Professions*. San Francisco, CA: Jossey-Bass.

Shulman, L. S. (1986) 'Those Who Understand: Knowledge Growth in Teaching'. *Educational Researcher*, 15(2) 4–14.

Shulman, L. S. (1987) 'Knowledge and Teaching: Foundations of the New Reform'. *Harvard Educational Review*, 57 1–22.

Shulman, L. S. (2004) *The Wisdon of Practice: Essays on Teaching, Learning, and Learning to Teach*. San Francisco, CA: Jossey-Bass.

Text Inspector (2016) 'Online lexis analysis tool'. Available online: <textinspector.com> (accessed December 8, 2017).

Timmis, I. (2015) *Corpus Linguistics for ELT: Reserarch and Practice*. New York: Routledge.

Tono, Y. and Díez-Bedmar, M. B. (2014) 'Focus on Learner Writing at the Beginning and Intermediate Stages: The ICCI Corpus'. *International Journal of Corpus Linguistics*, 19(2) 163–177.

Zareva, A. (2017) 'Incorporating Corpus Literacy Skills into TESOL Teacher Training'. *ELT Journal*, 71(1) 69–79.

PART 4

The pedagogic knowledge of second language teacher education

19

Locating methods in ELT education

Perspectives and possibilities

Graham Hall

As, over the last 30 years, I have developed MAs in ELT, Applied Linguistics and TESOL in five different universities, I have struggled to develop an approach to methods which meets the needs of teacher education on the one hand, and Applied Linguistics on the other.

(UK-based language teacher educator)

Introduction

English Language Teacher Education (ELTE) lies at the interface between 'teaching in theory' and 'teaching in practice'. With the exception of short, introductory, and explicitly practice or practically oriented courses such as the Cambridge English Certificate in Teaching English to Speakers of Other Languages (CELTA; Thornbury and Watkins, 2007), most ELTE programmes seek to draw explicitly on disciplinary knowledge while developing the 'specialised kind of knowledge that teachers use to actually teach' (Johnson, 2016: 125), albeit to differing degrees and in differing ways.

Exploring the place of language teaching methods, 'theories translated into classroom applications' (Hinkel, 2005: 631), within ELTE thus brings together a number of key debates and perspectives drawn not only from the domain of language teacher education itself, but also from the broader field of English language teaching (ELT) and the related academic discipline of applied linguistics. Problematising the relationship between 'theory' and 'practice' and between 'theorists' and 'practitioners', these perspectives highlight the importance of teachers' experiences, beliefs and understandings of their own work and professional contexts in diverse settings around the world, and question the relevance and continued discussion of methods within ELTE programmes, if, as is claimed, methods are 'dead' (Allwright, 1991) and ELT is entering a Postmethod era (Kumaravadivelu, 2003, 2006, 2012).

This chapter seeks to navigate these issues. It first outlines 'traditional' understandings of 'method' and methods, and the substantial criticisms of these conceptualisations that have emerged since the early 1990s. The chapter then traces how thinking about language teacher education has developed over the same period, similarly moving away from top-down prescriptions for practice to an appreciation of the importance of teachers' own contextually based reflections and understandings for their professional development. Given these moves towards complexity and diversity in the field, the chapter then asks what, if anything, a focus on language teaching methods brings to ELT education, and how methods might be explored in practice on ELTE programmes. The discussion draws on and is illustrated by the perspectives of a range of ELT educators working in a variety of contexts and on a variety of ELT education courses around the world.

'Method', methods and Postmethod: concepts and critiques

Although the teaching of English has a long history (Howatt with Widdowson, 2004), ELT emerged as a distinctive and recognizable enterprise in the early twentieth century. According to many accounts of methods, therefore, for much of the last century, language educators sought 'to solve the problems of language teaching by focusing attention exclusively on teaching *method*' (Stern, 1983: 452 – emphasis in original; see also, for example, Kumaravadivelu, 2006; Richards and Rodgers, 2014). However, while this might have been true of largely UK and USA-based theorists and methodologists, we might question the extent to which such concerns were shared by *teachers* around the world, a point we shall return to later in the chapter.

And while some terminological distinctions emerged, including references to language teaching 'approaches', 'styles', and even 'ways' (for further discussion, see, for example, Hall, 2017; Richards and Rodgers, 2014) alongside the additional challenge of similar terms being used in differing ways (Bell, 2003), a method can typically be characterised by its perspectives towards:

a) The nature of language
b) The nature of second language learning
c) Goals and objectives in teaching
d) The type of syllabus to use
e) The role of teacher, learners and instructional materials
f) The activities, techniques and procedures to use

(Richards and Schmidt, 2002: 330)

As this framework indicates, 'the concept of method has the *potential* to provide links between theory, practical principles and practice' (Andon and Leung, 2013: 156; emphasis added). Method could thus be an appropriate focus for ELTE as it offers a possible route from theories to practices (moving from a) to f) in Richards and Schmidt's framework). Equally, starting from activities, techniques and procedures, i.e., 'the actual point of contact with the students' (Cook, 2016: 258), and moving from Richards and Schmidt's points f) to a), ELTE programmes could move from teachers' classroom practices to their theoretical foundations. (Such processes could, of course, be two-directional, moving from theories to practices, or practices to theories, and back again in an iterative cycle of analysis).

Yet the difficulties which surround methods soon become evident once the discussion moves from method as simply a concept or a framework for understanding to examine methods in practice; this might be methods as pedagogic practice (i.e., methods as implemented by teachers in their classrooms) or as a social practice (i.e., methods as both constituting and reflecting the professional relationship between theorists and methodologists on the one hand and teachers on the other). As Nunan (1991: 3) suggests, all methods in fact:

> assume that there is a single set of principles which will determine whether or not learning will take place. Thus they all propose a single set of precepts for teacher and learner

classroom behaviour, and assert that if these principles are faithfully followed, they will result in learning for all.

Contiguous with this perspective was the idea that a 'best' method could be identified. Indeed, it was the twentieth-century search for 'the best method' which resulted in the proliferation of methods which we can see in ELT today; Larsen-Freeman and Anderson (2011), for example, identify 11 methods, Richards and Rodgers review 16 methods and approaches, while Thornbury (2017) summarises 30 language teaching methods. Such methods include Grammar-translation, the Direct Method, the Audiolingual Method, 'Humanistic' approaches such as the Silent Way and Community Language Learning, Communicative Language Teaching (CLT), Task-based Language Teaching (TBLT), Content and Language Integrated Learning (CLIL) and Content-based Instruction (CBI), Competency-based Teaching and so forth.

From a pedagogical perspective, however, it is evident that individual methods have failed to justify the claims made on their behalf or have 'solved the problems' of language teaching; there is little evidence in favour of one method over another (Andon and Leung, 2013). It is also clear that teachers quite sensibly adapt and bring together aspects drawn from differing methods to accommodate contextual influences and their own personal beliefs (Prabhu, 1990). Meanwhile, the prescriptivism inherent in the notion of methods ('if these principles are faithfully followed…' see Nunan (1991), above) is said to create and maintain a hierarchical divide between (largely male) theorists and (largely female) practising teachers (Apple, 1986; Pennycook, 1989). 'Method' thereby frustrates teachers who are unable to fully implement and follow prescribed principles and resulting practices fully and consistently; values one-size-fits-all, 'scientific' or disciplinary knowledge over teachers' own local and contextual knowledge; and ultimately 'de-skills' teachers who are required to merely implement the ideas of others (Pennycook, 1989). Such concerns are also reflected in Holliday's 'Appropriate Methodology' critique (1994) of **B**ritish, **A**ustralian and **N**orth **A**merican (BANA) method-based thinking and practice, questioning its relevance to non-BANA contexts, while Phillipson's (1992) identification of endemic 'Linguistic Imperialism' within ELT suggests that methods, and a Centre-to-Periphery 'methods trade' from English-dominant 'Centre' countries such as the UK and USA to 'the Periphery', creates and sustains patterns of power and control which favour 'the West' over 'the rest' in English Language Teaching.

Although the discussion so far may already make us question the place of methods in ELTE, a final, arguably more 'existential' concern can be added to this critique. That is, while focusing on apparently very different issues – from little evidence in favour of any particular method in the classroom to the global politics of ELT – all share the fundamental perspective that a succession of methods can be identified and labelled across 'bounded periods of history' (Hunter and Smith, 2012: 430). While contemporary accounts have moved away from the 'progressive' histories of methods, in which successive methods represent continuous improvements in language teaching effectiveness over time (Pennycook, 1989; Andon and Leung, 2013) to now characterise methods as 'products of their times' and subject to 'fashions', 'in which no method is inherently superior to another; instead, some methods are more appropriate than others in a particular context' (Adamson, 2004: 605), this view of methods has itself been critiqued. Hunter and Smith (2012), for example, suggest that the application of simple labels such as 'Grammar-translation' do not really accommodate the complex range of practices that were (and still are) found around translation and explicit grammar teaching in the classroom; similar arguments might be made regarding the variety of ways in which 'Communicative Language Teaching' or 'Content and Language Integrated Learning' are interpreted around the world. For Hunter and Smith a 'mythology' has developed around methods which simplifies and stereotypes complex and contested practices (2012: 430–431) and, as we have noted, prioritises the understandings of Anglo-American methodologists at the expense of local teaching traditions and teachers' own experiences. From this perspective, therefore, the concept of method and subsequent discussion of methods is essentially 'reductive', as it does not satisfactorily outline what really happens in language classrooms (Pennycook, 2004: 278).

As such arguments have taken hold in ELT over the last 25 years, and the limitations of Method, both as a theoretical concept and in practice, have become clear, many methodologists (and, indeed, teachers) have started to talk of a 'Postmethod era' (Kumaravadivelu, 2004, 2006, 2012) or 'Postmethod Discourse' (Akbari, 2008) within the field. Building on notions of 'principled eclecticism' in which teachers purposefully bring together and plan varied practices which are appropriate to the aims and context of their classroom (Rivers, 1981), Kumaravadivelu (2012: 12–16) proposes three principles which underpin Postmethod pedagogy: *particularity* (i.e., pedagogy which is sensitive to the local institutional, social and cultural contexts of teaching and learning); *practicality* (i.e., the superiority of theorists over teachers ends, as teachers theorise from their own practices and put into practice their own theories); and *possibility* (i.e., the socio-political consciousness of teachers and learners is developed in the classroom so their personal and social identities can be transformed). Postmethod teachers thereby assume an 'enhanced' role in which they make 'informed decisions' based on local and contextual expertise, utilising a series of 'macrostrategies' including the promotion of learner autonomy, fostering language awareness, maximising learning opportunities, facilitating interaction between learners and so forth (Kumaravadivelu, 2003, 2006; see also Bax's (2003) discussion of a 'Context Approach' to language teaching).

It is perhaps here, therefore, that a link to ELT education might be identified, as, logically, teachers in a Postmethod era need to be 'better informed' in order to make 'sound' decisions (Waters, 2009: 112); we shall return to this issue later in the chapter. And yet, like method and methods, conceptions of Postmethod are also problematic: are teachers really free to pick and choose how they teach, or are they actually limited by government and institutional policies, social convention and learners' expectations (Crookes, 2009)? Do teachers have the time, resources and willingness to carry the responsibilities Postmethod pedagogy requires of them (Akbari, 2008)? And do, in fact, the principles and related macrostrategies of Postmethod perhaps even qualify it as yet another method (Larsen-Freeman, 2005)?

The discussion so far has mapped out the key concepts and the debates which surround methods. Tracing a shift in perspectives over time within the field (or at least within the theoretical and methodological literature) from a position of confidence in method to one of doubt, and from an era in which methods were seen as overarching 'solutions' to the difficulties of language teaching to one which more clearly recognises the importance of a myriad of factors relating to teachers, learners, resources, contexts and cultures, which interact with each other in complex and diverse ways, we might question the relevance of a focus on methods within ELT education. And it is within this context that we now turn to consider briefly the emergence and development of ELTE, in which we can trace a parallel repositioning from certainty and the transmission of 'expert knowledge' to teachers, to perspectives which hold teachers' own experiences and beliefs to be central to the experience and success of teacher education.

Parallel debates? The emergence of 'located' ELT education

The emergence of formal courses or programmes of ELT education is a relatively recent development (Borg, 2011; Johnson, 2016). Although some language teaching methodology courses had previously existed, responsibility for language teacher education in the USA moved from schools to universities in the mid-twentieth century (Labaree, 2004, in Johnson, 2016), while, in the UK, EFL training courses commenced in the 1960s under the auspices of John Haycraft at International House, leading to the eventual emergence of the Cambridge ESOL (now Cambridge English) CELTA and the Trinity Cert. qualifications (Borg, 2011).

At the same time, the 1960s saw the emergence of Applied Linguistics as a field of study offering 'a body of specialized knowledge and theory that provided the foundation of the new discipline. This knowledge was represented in the curricula of MA programs, which began to be offered from this time' (Richards, 2008: 159). The aim of these programmes was therefore to familiarise teachers with theory and research, on the assumption that this would improve their classroom pedagogy (Borg, 2011). As Johnson (2016: 121–122) puts it:

> teachers were considered to be 'doers' rather than 'thinkers', and the doing of teaching was conceptualized as a set of instructional behaviours that, if carried out systematically and efficiently, would ultimately lead to greater gains in student learning, regardless of institutional and/or social context.

There are evident parallels here with the traditional conception of method as a set of principles 'handed down' for teachers to follow (see above, Nunan, 1991) which was dominant during this period.

However, the early 1990s realisation that there are no universal certainties in language teaching which underpinned the critiques of method that emerged at this time also underpinned a shift in thinking about ELT education. Arguing for an end to 'wish lists of what is best for the teacher' (p. xi), Richards and Nunan summarised (1990) the change in perspective as 'a movement away from a "training" perspective to an "education" perspective and recognition that effective teaching involves higher-level cognitive processes, which cannot be taught directly' (p. xiii). This involved 'less emphasis on prescriptions and top-down directives' and more emphasis on 'bottom-up learning' in which teachers 'generate theories and hypotheses and ... reflect critically on teaching' (ibid.). Consequently, as in Postmethod thinking (indeed the roots of both the shift in thinking about methods and ELT education can be traced to the emergence 'the social turn' in applied linguistics (Block, 2003), and, more generally, to ideas associated with postmodernism (Crookes, 2009)), contemporary approaches to ELTE conceive of teacher learning as being constructed though teachers' experiences in specific social contexts, with their knowledge, thoughts and actions emerging from participation in specific classrooms and school environments (Johnson, 2016). In the context of the debates surrounding methods and Postmethod, therefore, this can be characterised as a move from the top-down transmission of product-oriented (i.e., method-oriented) theories to teachers, to the emergence of teachers' own methodological or Postmethod thinking, theories and practices.

Placing methods within the knowledge base of ELT education

As the discussion so far suggests, therefore, until the mid-1980s, the knowledge base of language teaching was conceptualised as comprising two components – knowledge of language and knowledge of teaching – through dichotomies such as: content/pedagogy, theory/practice, and knowledge/skills (Graves, 2009). As we have seen, from this perspective a focus on methods within ELTE programmes provided disciplinary knowledge about teaching approaches underpinned by theories of language and of learning. From the mid-1980s onwards, however, the increased recognition of both the importance of context in teaching, and the role of teachers' prior knowledge, experience, and ways of thinking (see above) has meant that the knowledge base of ELTE has been reconsidered, thereby necessitating a re-evaluation of whether and/or how methods might be dealt with on ELTE programmes.

As discussed elsewhere in this volume, the 1990s saw two significant attempts to re-conceptualise the knowledge base of language teaching. Richards (1998) and Roberts (1998) both moved beyond notions of the transmission of theoretical knowledge of language and of learning imparted to teachers, to see teachers as active agents in the development of knowledge and enhancement of teaching skills. Considering, respectively, six 'domains of content' and six 'types of language teacher knowledge', their models subsume knowledge of method within categories such as 'theories of teaching', 'pedagogical content knowledge', 'subject matter knowledge', and 'curricular knowledge'. Central to these approaches, however, is the idea that there is no universal 'wish list' of desired teacher knowledge; rather, the knowledge that constitutes each domain or type of knowledge, and the balance between these domains, varies according to context, and is dependent on who the learning-teachers and their teacher educators are, where and who they teach or will teach and so forth (Graves, 2009). Thus, as Graves continues:

> the issue is not *what* is relevant – almost anything can be made relevant to language [teaching] – but *who* makes it relevant, how and why. In other words, teachers themselves need to conceptualize the relevance in their practice (p. 120; original emphasis).

Why, therefore, given the problems which surround the notion of method and methods, and the ways in which teachers' own understandings about practice are now seen as central to ELT education, might teachers regard a focus on methods within ELT education as relevant to their practice and to their development as language teaching professionals?

'The case for methods' in ELT education: empowerment, reflection and professional development

The strong and valuable critique of language teaching methods outlined earlier in the chapter has, it is sometimes argued, led to a 'shunning' of method in the contemporary literature (Thornbury, 2017). And yet, while there has been an evident change in the way methods are talked and written about in the field – a shift which, as we shall see, reflects Postmethod thinking – numerous writers and contemporary texts still focus on and make the case for the study of methods in teacher education, and argue for their continued relevance to teachers' professional practice more generally. Texts designed to meet the needs of and be accessible to teachers, and which focus exclusively on methods include Larsen-Freeman and Anderson (2011), Richards and Rodgers (2014), and Thornbury (2017); meanwhile, numerous other teacher education volumes include a significant focus on methods alongside other aspects of language teaching (e.g., Cook, 2016; Hall, 2017; Johnson, 2017; Ur, 2012). Furthermore, a focus on methods continues within the papers of academic, yet practitioner-oriented publications such as *ELT Journal*.

Underpinning all these accounts is a recognition that local decision-making by teachers is central in the development of contextually appropriate teaching, both as a matter of principle (i.e., teachers *should* make decisions about how to teach) and of practice (i.e., teachers *do* make decisions about how to teach, shaping any method(s) in light of their own experiences and beliefs). Consequently, echoing Waters's call for 'sound' teacher decision-making in a Postmethod era (2009), methods are said to offer a range of pedagogical options which 'empower teachers to respond meaningfully to particular classroom contexts' (Bell, 2007: 141–142). In practical terms, therefore, the suggestion is that methods offer 'templates' which enable teachers to coherently bring together classroom activities and routines (Thornbury, 2017). Thornbury suggests that, for novice teachers, methods might be 'a lifeline' as they navigate the complexities of classroom life; meanwhile, they are a 'toolkit' which more experienced teachers can adopt, adapt and combine (we shall return to differences between novice and more experienced teachers below).

Drawing on these ideas, Larsen-Freeman and Anderson (2011: xi–xii) argue that studying methods in language teacher education is 'invaluable'. First, they suggest that focusing on methods provides a 'foil for reflection' which helps teachers understand what they already do in the classroom, making the tacit explicit (Freeman, 1991). By engaging with the principles and practices of particular methods, teachers become aware of *their own* beliefs and assumptions about teaching. Second, as their awareness of what they do in the classroom and why they do it develops, teachers can choose to teach in different ways to how they were themselves taught, drawing on the possibilities which are available; thus, 'they are able to make choices that are informed, not conditioned' (Larsen-Freeman and Anderson, 2011: p. xi). Change is not inevitable, however; teachers may decide that their current practices are effective and appropriate or they may face contextual constraints on what might be possible. However, change becomes a *possibility* as teacher understandings develop, and in accordance with their own 'sense of plausibility' (Prabhu, 1990). Furthermore, like Thornbury, Larsen-Freeman and Anderson also suggest that a knowledge of methods can expand a teacher's repertoire of classroom techniques and practices, leading to professional development and growth, and enabling them to deal more effectively with the 'unique qualities and idiosyncrasies of their students' (p. x).

Beyond this focus on the relationship between the study of methods and teachers' own beliefs and possible practices, however, a knowledge of methods is seen as 'part of the knowledge base of teaching' (Larsen-Freeman and Anderson, 2011: x), as noted above (see discussion of Richards, 1998, and Roberts, 1998). Thus, drawing upon key characteristics of method, Johnson (2016: 124) argues that 'gaining a deep understanding of the disciplinary knowledge that reflects the history and current debates that define what language is, how second languages are learned and how language can best be taught' is 'an essential element of becoming a professional language teacher' (Johnson also notes, however, that such knowledge is only one element of the range or kinds of knowledge that contribute to teacher professionalism; others include experiential knowledge and the practical knowledge that teachers actually use in the classroom).

From this perspective, therefore, the study and knowledge of methods can provide English language teachers with an overview of how the profession has developed (Richards and Rodgers, 2014), thereby seeking to address the 'short memory' of language teaching theory, which has left ELT subject to fashions and trends (Stern, 1983: 76–77). In effect, such knowledge may enable teachers to be more critical of the many products, packages and apparently new ideas which typify the field, and, of course, may also be intrinsically interesting to some teachers in and of itself! Furthermore, according to Larsen-Freeman and Anderson (2011: x–xi), it also provides teachers with a stronger sense of professional identity and enables them to participate more fully in the wider professional community, the connection with others leaving them 'less isolated in their practice'. Interacting with others and sharing ideas about the principles and practices of teaching may prove invigorating and help teachers avoid becoming 'stale'.

Thus, knowledge of methods is widely posited as enabling teachers to join more fully ELT's professional 'community of practice' (Wenger, 1998), and its related 'professional discourse community' (Snow, 2005), providing them with the professional or disciplinary concepts and also, importantly, the language through which to think and talk about language teaching in general and their own practices in particular (Larsen-Freeman and Anderson, 2011; Graves, 2009). Yet if, as Kerr (2005) outlines, many teachers see practitioners on the one hand and methodologists, theorists and writers on the other as belonging to separate professional communities within the broader field of ELT, the potential for both groups to come together in a single community of practice which talks the 'same language' may not be realised.

From methodologists' to teachers' perspectives

While the case for teachers' knowledge of and engagement with methods appears substantial, it is also evident that the vast majority of the discussion outlined above draws on the perspectives of ELT methodologists and writers, rather than identifying *teachers'* perspectives about the importance or otherwise of knowledge about methods and its place in ELT education – ironically, this could perhaps be evidence in support of the critical claim that method is a pre-occupation of theorists rather than teachers (see above). And certainly, there is a relatively limited number of professional and methodological publications which report or examine teachers' views on or ability and willingness to engage with the concept of method and methods, Bell (2007) and Andon and Leung (2013) being notable exceptions to this trend.

Working with both experienced and less-experienced teachers, and with 'native' and 'non-native' English speaker teachers, Bell's (2007) study found that few teachers were as negative about methods as postmethodologists might suggest, being open to any method that offers possible solution to the dilemmas and difficulties of their own teaching context. Echoing many of the arguments outlined above, teachers identified themselves as having an 'eclectic' approach in the classroom, which a knowledge of methods supported. From this perspective, such knowledge was seen to be 'empowering', 'pragmatic' and 'crucial to teacher growth' (p. 141–142). Meanwhile, in Andon and Leung's (2013) case-study, experienced teachers discussed their own personal teaching approaches and the principles which guided them, making extensive reference to methods as they did so. Again, the teachers did not follow a single particular method, but were more eclectic in their approaches. However, Andon and Leung emphasise how knowledge of methods not only supported these teachers as they developed their classroom practice, but also provided them with knowledge of the professional discourse, the language needed and the 'conceptual tools' (p. 174) to share experiences and beliefs with their colleagues, and to be responsive to the demands of teaching in their own professional context.

While these two papers can only offer a relatively limited insight into teachers' perspectives on and engagement with knowledge of methods, they seem to exemplify many of the issues raised by methodologists and Postmethodologists and which are outlined above. From a Postmethod orientation, these teachers do seem to teach 'eclectically' and no longer identify with or try to follow a single method; they reflect on what is and is not contextually appropriate, making pedagogical decisions for themselves where possible. However, they also engage with methods as sources of teaching practices, and as prompts for reflection and professional development, suggesting that, for these teachers at least, methods are not yet 'dead'. As Block (2001: 72) notes, therefore, it seems that:

> While method has been discredited at an etic level (that is, in the thinking and nomenclature of scholars) it certainly retains a great deal of vitality at the grassroots, emic level (that is, it is still part of the nomenclature of lay people and teachers).

Yet the 'vitality' with which teachers debate, affiliate to and disaffiliate with method and methods is less intense and less a matter of principle than for theoreticians (Bell, 2007); teachers' interest 'is determined by how far [methods] provide options in dealing with their particular teaching contexts' (p. 142). And it is with this in mind that we now turn to examine specific examples of

ELT education practice and the perspectives of ELT educators when reflecting on whether and how they locate language teaching methods in ELTE programmes.

Locating methods in ELT education: programmes and practices

This section draws upon the perspectives of English language teacher educators working in a variety of contexts around the world to uncover and illustrate the extent to which and how method and methods are focused upon in contemporary ELT education programmes. The views of 65 teacher educators, known to the chapter author and working on both pre- and in-service programmes in over 25 countries (including, for example, Algeria, Argentina and Australia; Israel and India; the UK, Ukraine and Uzbekistan) were collected via an online survey. Meanwhile, teacher educators from 26 UK-based university Master's programmes in ELT/TESOL (i.e. around half the total number of such courses in Britain, and again, both for pre- and in-service teachers) shared their perspectives with the author via email. Clearly, although discussing a range of contexts, such data provides illustration and insights into the role of methods within ELT education rather than full representation of the field.

Methods and pre-service short courses

As noted in the Introduction to this chapter, there is generally little place for a focus on methods in pre-service short courses; rather, as a US-based teacher educator notes, 'more useful to participants [are] practical skills in both teaching/learning and reflecting upon teaching/learning, along with a rationale for that. The in-depth discussion of methods [is] more a preserve of the MA programme'. Consequently, this teacher educator argues 'that the study of methods is more effectively placed in longer pre-service or in-service courses (BA or MA programmes, or the Diploma in Teaching English to Speakers of Other Languages (Delta))', while, a teacher educator from Argentina simply states that 'going over each individual method and analysing their characteristics does not help Newly Qualified Teachers (NQTs) much'.

This perspective is reflected in the Cambridge English pre-service CELTA syllabus (Cambridge English, 2015), which makes no reference to methods. That said, the lessons novice teachers prepare and deliver in the practicum element of the CELTA (and similar short courses) are usually based around published coursebook material (Thornbury and Watkins, 2007; Thornbury, this volume), which of course draws on and incorporates methodological principles and practices (most contemporary coursebooks follow what might best be described as a weak or eclectic form of CLT – or even, according to Ur, 2012, a 'post-communicative' approach – mixing pre-planned explicit attention on language with subsequent practice and skill development activities). Consequently, even if it is not explicit, 'methods work' does take place on pre-service short courses, socialising teachers into a broad set of assumptions which many, but not all, in ELT will share (Lightbown, 2000).

Inevitably, in a field as diverse as ELT, perspectives and practices on pre-service teacher education short courses do vary. Although an explicit focus on methods is unusual, CELTA trainers in Australia and Ireland report that time is found on their programmes to focus on a selection of methods 'to let trainees know how/why we do things the way we do, but also to let them know what other options are available' and 'help them prepare for "life after CELTA"'. Meanwhile, pre-service teacher educators in Spain, where CLIL is an increasingly specified approach, report focusing explicitly on the principles and practices of the 'CLIL umbrella', a term which serves as a reminder that not only are pre-service approaches to methods varied, but so are the ways in which methods are realised in practice.

Methods and longer-term pre- and in-service programmes

Amid the array of longer-term ELTE programmes that can be found around the world, arguably the most recognizable are postgraduate Master's programmes of one or two years' length for both pre- and in-service language teachers, and the Cambridge Delta qualification, an eight-to-ten-week programme (when studied fulltime) for experienced teachers which, although more limited in scope and more overtly a balance of theory and practice than the typical Master's degree, is accredited at Master's level. The discussion in this section will focus in particular on these programmes due to their focus on *language* teacher education. The tendency of three-or-four-year-long pre-service undergraduate teacher education courses around the world to embed language pedagogy within a general education framework, and the sheer variety of ways in which these programmes are subsequently designed, precludes their further investigation.

Turning first, therefore, to the Delta qualification, its syllabus (Cambridge English, 2015) aims to develop teachers' 'critical awareness of approaches and methodologies and the principles underpinning these used in a range of ELT contexts' (p. 2), and refers to illustrative examples such as grammar-translation, the Direct Method, CLT and TBLT, as well as what it terms 'non-mainstream' methods such as the Silent Way and Total Physical Response. Echoing perspectives raised throughout this chapter, central to the Delta's approach is the development of teachers' abilities to 'choose methods and approaches that are appropriate for the content and aims of the lesson' (p. 4).

In contrast to the Delta, teacher educators working on Master's programmes generally have far more autonomy in the design of their programmes' goals and syllabus. The ways in which methods are addressed on these courses thus reflects ELT educators' own perspectives, and, given the debates outlined in the chapter so far, it is perhaps unsurprising to find that an overwhelming majority of Master's programmes focus explicitly on method and methods, albeit in different ways and to differing degrees. In the UK, for example, the survey of contemporary UK Master's programmes for this chapter revealed that the vast majority of explorations of methods are embedded in the broader discussions of modules with titles such as 'The Principles and Practices of ELT', 'Approaches to teaching and learning', 'ELT methodology', 'Pedagogy and Curriculum in TESOL', and 'Second Language Teaching' (indeed, the titles of only two modules from the range of programmes surveyed straightforwardly referred to 'methods'). Within these programmes and modules, ELT educators seek to problematize methods, 'putting time into developing a critical and reflective framework for an evidence-based appropriate methodology' (UK-based teacher educator) which, as summarised by two teacher educators in Argentina, enables students 'to develop more context-sensitive methodologies' by 'making sense of decisions they will need to take in the future'. That said, while clearly trying to explore methods within a framework of 'principled eclecticism', in some cases through an overtly Postmethod perspective, and, in all cases with 'an awareness of the dangers of imposing methods … context should be the starting point' (UK teacher educator), Master's programmes do tend to highlight communicative or task-based approaches. These, as a UK teacher educator puts it, 'still have a great deal of contemporary resonance/relevance' in the field. A number of programmes also focus on CLIL. While ELT educators report exploring these methods 'critically', a key emphasis for some to encourage a shift 'from traditional to more student-centred' approaches which help 'transform the classroom into a more communicative space' (views from Spain, Ireland and Canada). We may therefore see a critical approach to methods *per se* taking place within a broader set of assumptions that highlight the role of communication and interaction in language teaching and learning, the assumption being that knowing about communication is a key part of the knowledge base of language teaching (see above, Richards, 1998, and Roberts, 1998).

The discussion so far has focused on *what* and *how* methods are addressed on Delta and Master's courses, and a rationale for their inclusion on such programmes is, of course, implicit throughout (i.e., the importance of context, criticality, eclecticism, and an awareness of Post-method thinking, alongside socialisation into a broadly communicative-oriented general professional discourse). Yet a range of further possible reasons explaining *why* methods remain a focus of ELTE programmes, especially those with the particular academic orientation found at Master's level, can be identified. First, methods seem to offer a framework through which teachers can reflect on *their own* experiences to 'talk about what they themselves do and how they think about teaching in their context', before looking at theories and research. From this perspective, the study of methods offers, in the words of UK-based teacher educators, 'a good starting point', 'a useful foundation', and 'a window' to 'ways of seeing language and language learning, and giving a framework for the decisions that teachers make'.

Additionally, as teacher educators based in the UK and Israel note, the discussion of methods offers 'a way in which theory and research are indirectly passed down to teachers', operating as way 'to understand the professional literature'. From this perspective, shared by many of this chapter's informants, an exploration of methods makes theory more accessible to practitioners, usually through reflection about the relevance of method or methods to their own professional experiences. Yet there is perhaps a danger, as some UK-based ELT educators caution, that methods might be included on MA programmes because 'they seem they seem to give a good "academic", university-appropriate kind of content', or because 'there is a "teachability" factor that makes methods suitable input at Masters level. It represents content, with theoretical foundations and fixed procedures, and is manageable for Applied Linguists who have not had much engagement with classrooms'. From this perspective, are methods simply included in ELTE 'because it has always been done that way'?

A focus on methods is also said, by many teacher educators, to provide a way in which teachers might 'engage with the history of ideas that have shaped language teaching', in order that they can 'become aware of the faddish history' of the field. From this perspective, 'if teachers don't know where [a method] has come from, they won't be able to judge if new developments are steps "forwards" or "back"'. Yet it is important to note the contested nature of ELT history, whereby unifying narratives are viewed 'with suspicion' (Canagarajah, 2006: 9; see also earlier in the chapter). Thus while history offers a possible source of understanding for language teachers to build on, the history (or histories) of methods offers 'not answers or solutions, but a rich array of realizations and perspectives' (p. 29); as we have seen, most ELT educators acknowledge this.

Clearly, a key consideration in all ELTE is the preparation of teachers 'to equip them for their future jobs' (UK-based teacher educator). Yet knowledge of the ways in which teachers take up, adapt or reject ideas about method and methods in their classroom practice following their studies remains rather vague; while there has been some research into teachers' post-ELTE practices (e.g., Li and Edwards, 2013; Nguyen and Walkinshaw, 2018; Sahin and Yildrim, 2016), most teacher educators seem to draw on anecdotal evidence and feedback from individual students they have worked with. Thus, many teacher educators tend to summarise as 'impressionistic' or 'speculative' their knowledge of how their programmes' explorations of methods impact on teachers' future practice, outlining their 'hopes' that teachers leave with better understandings, 'extended classroom repertoires', and the ability to 'build and act on' their methodological insights. However, there is a clear acknowledgement that 'much will depend on their teaching situation and the freedom they have to adopt new or different methodologies to those which are prescribed'. For many teacher educators focusing on methods during UK-based Master's programmes, there is a clear concern as to 'how well this prepares international students for their [home] teaching contexts'.

Yet to focus on teachers' post-ELTE method innovations *per se* is, perhaps to miss the point of locating method and methods on English language teacher education programmes – as a UK-based teacher educator notes reflecting much of the discussion outlined earlier in the chapter, to assume that method discussions will, can and should 'simplistically transfer to classroom and teaching is to mis-serve teachers'. Rather, as suggested by another, teachers' explorations of methods within a broader programme of reflective ELTE can be 'transformational in the way they see themselves as teachers and how they understand their context and learners'. It is this process of reflection, which facilitates the emergence of locally situated understandings of practice and theory (Smith and McLelland, 2018), rather than the focus on method and methods for their own sake, that many teacher educators report as being central to English language teacher education.

Conclusion

In exploring the place and relevance (or otherwise) of methods in ELT education, this chapter has traced changing conceptions of both language teaching method(s) and of English language teacher education itself over the last 30 years. The assumption that a knowledge of methods learned on ELTE programmes would inform teachers' practices in straightforward ways has been replaced by an acknowledgement of the importance of teachers' own contextually informed understandings, beliefs and sense of plausibility in implementing or adapting methodological ideas and shaping their classroom practices. Yet the place of teaching methods within the field of ELT generally, and on many ELTE programmes specifically, 'seems to have persisted because it serves a pragmatic purpose. It gives a public place to focus on the teaching/learning relationship, even though we recognise that there [is] more to this connection than what we can see' (Freeman, 2013: 278). As Klapper (2006) suggests, therefore, examining methods through ELTE focuses attention on the links between practice and theory, and is 'fundamental to the process of reflective continuing professional development' (p. 123), a central aim of language teacher education.

Yet a number of concerns endure. Despite the critiques of method and methods outlined in this chapter, knowledge of and research into 'non-Western', 'traditional' or 'indigenous' approaches (Crookes, 2009) to language teaching are almost absent from the field and its literature. Discussions of method remain wedded to the familiar 'packaged-up' methods listed earlier in the chapter, even if a critical or Postmethod perspective is taken. Thus, the 'knowledge-base' of methods within ELTE remains constrained, and potentially overlooks the array of practices from multiple contexts which could be a starting point for teacher reflection and understanding. Furthermore, the relative lack of insights into teachers' post-ELTE practice, and if and how knowledge of methods is taken forward in the classroom, arguably suggests that, while a rationale for the location of methods within ELTE seems reasonable, its effects, whether on classroom practice or teachers' subsequent development as language teaching professionals remain largely unknown. Consequently, while 'the case for' addressing methods within ELTE seems strong, and teacher educators' accounts provide ample evidence of methodological discussion as a springboard for more general reflection about teaching and learning, both further research and teachers' accounts of their own practices would be invaluable as we locate methods within English language teacher education.

References

Adamson, B. (2004) 'Fashions in language teaching methodology', in Davies, A. and Elder, C. (eds) *The Handbook of Applied Linguistics*. London: Blackwell: 604–622.

Akbari, R. (2008) 'Postmethod Discourse and Practice'. *TESOL Quarterly*, 42(4) 641–652.

Allwright, D. (1991) 'The Death of the Method', *CRILE Working Paper*, No. 10. Lancaster: Lancaster University.

Andon, N. and Leung, C. (2013) 'The role of approaches and methods in second language teacher education', in Ben Said, S. and Zhang, L. (eds) *Language Teachers and Teaching: Global Perspectives, Local Initiatives*. Hoboken, NJ: Taylor and Francis.

Apple, M. (1986) *Teachers and Texts: A Political Economy of Class and Gender Relations in Education*. New York: Routledge and Kegan Paul.

Bax, S. (2003) 'The End of CLT: A Context Approach to Language Teaching'. *ELT Journal*, 57(3) 278–287.

Bell, D. (2003) 'Method and Postmethod: Are They Really so Incompatible?'. *TESOL Quarterly*, 37(2) 325–336.

Bell, D. (2007) 'Do Teachers Think that Methods are Dead?'. *ELT Journal*, 61(2) 135–143.

Block, D. (2001) 'An exploration of the art and science debate in language education', in Bax, M. and Zwart, J-W. (eds) *Reflections on Language and Language Learning: In Honour of Arthur van Essen*. Amsterdam: John Benjamins: 63–74.

Block, D. (2003) *The Social Turn in Second Language Acquisition*. Edinburgh: Edinburgh University Press.

Borg, S. (2011) 'Language teacher education', in Simpson, J. (ed.) *The Routledge Handbook of Applied Linguistics*. Abingdon: Routledge: 215–228.

Cambridge English (2015) *CELTA: Certificate in Teaching English to Speakers of Other Languages: Syllabus and Assessment Guidelines*. Cambridge: Cambridge English Language Assessment.

Cambridge English (2015) *Delta: Diploma in Teaching English to Speakers of Other Languages: Syllabus Specifications*. Cambridge: Cambridge English Language Assessment.

Canagarajah, A. S. (2006) 'TESOL at Forty: What are the Issues?'. *TESOL Quarterly*, 40(1) 9–34.

Cook, V. (2016) *Second Language Learning and Language Teaching*, 5th edition. London: Hodder Education.

Crookes, G. (2009) *Values, Philosophies, and Beliefs in TESOL: Making a Statement*. Cambridge: Cambridge University Press.

Freeman, D. (1991) 'To Make the Tacit Explicit: Teacher Education, Emerging Discourse and Conceptions of Teaching'. *Teaching and Teacher Education*, 7 439–454.

Freeman D. (2013) 'A dilemma of prediction: how teacher education is "piped" to classroom teaching and student learning', in Arnold, J. and Murphey, T. (eds) *Meaningful Action: Earl Stevick's Influence on Language Teaching*. Cambridge: Cambridge University Press.

Graves, K. (2009) 'The curriculum of second language teacher education', in Burns, A. and Richards, J. (eds) *The Cambridge Guide to Second Language Teacher Education*. Cambridge: Cambridge University Press: 115–124.

Hall, G. (2017) *Exploring English Language Teaching: Language in Action*, 2nd edition. Abingdon: Routledge.

Hinkel, E. (2005) 'Introduction', in Hinkel, E. (ed.) *Handbook of Research in Second Language Teaching and Learning*. Mahwah, NJ: Lawrence Erlbaum: 631–634.

Holliday, A. (1994) *Appropriate Methodology and Social Context*. Cambridge: Cambridge University Press.

Howatt, A. with Widdowson, H. (2004) *A History of English Language Teaching*, 2nd edition. Oxford: Oxford University Press.

Hunter, D. and Smith, R. (2012) 'Unpackaging the Past: "CLT" through ELTJ Keywords'. *ELT Journal*, 66(4) 430–439.

Johnson, K. (2017) *An Introduction to Foreign Language Learning and Teaching*, 3rd edition. Abingdon: Routledge.

Johnson, K. E. (2016) 'Language Teacher Education', in Hall, G. (ed.) *The Routledge Handbook of English Language Teaching*. Abingdon: Routledge: 121–134.

Kerr, P. (2005) 'The Use of Jargon in Teacher Education: Online Forum Report'. *ELT Journal*, 59(2) 151–153.

Klapper, J. (2006) *Understanding and Developing Good Practice: Language Teaching in Higher Education*. London: CILT National Centre for Languages.

Kumaravadivelu, B. (2003) *Beyond Methods: Macrostrategies for Language Teaching*. New Haven, CT: Yale University Press.

Kumaravadivelu, B. (2006) *Understanding Language Teaching: From Method to Postmethod.* Mahwah, NJ: Lawrence Erlbaum.

Kumaravadivelu, B. (2012) *Language Teacher Education for a Global Society.* Abingdon: Routledge.

Labaree, D. (2004) *The Trouble with Education Schools.* New Haven, CT: Yale University Press.

Larsen-Freeman, D. (2005) 'A Critical Analysis of Postmethod: An Interview with Diane Larsen-Freeman by Zia Tajeddin'. *ILI Language Teaching Journal*, 1 21–25.

Larsen-Freeman, D. and Anderson, M. (2011) *Techniques and Principles in Language Teaching*, 3rd edition. Oxford: Oxford University Press.

Li, D. and Edwards, V. (2013) 'The Impact of Overseas Training on Curriculum Innovation and Change in English Language Education in Western China'. *Language Teaching Research*, 17(4) 390–408.

Lightbown, P. (2000) 'Anniversary Article: Classroom SLA Research and Language Teaching'. *Applied Linguistics*, 21(4) 431–462.

Nguyen, X. and Walkinshaw, I. (2018) 'Autonomy in Teaching Practice: Insights from Vietnamese English Language Teachers Trained in Inner-Circle Countries'. *Teaching and Teacher Education*, 69 21–32.

Nunan, D. (1991) *Language Teaching Methodology.* New York: Prentice Hall.

Pennycook, A. (1989) 'The Concept of Method, Interested Knowledge, and the Politics of Language Teaching'. *TESOL Quarterly*, 23(4) 589–618.

Pennycook, A. (2004) 'History: After 1945', in Byram, M. (ed.) *Routledge Encyclopedia of Language Teaching and Learning.* Abingdon: Routledge: 275–282.

Phillipson, R. (1992) *Linguistic Imperialism.* Oxford: Oxford University Press.

Prabhu, N. S. (1990) 'There is No Best Method – Why?'. *TESOL Quarterly*, 24(2) 161–176.

Richards, J. (1998) *Beyond Training.* Cambridge: Cambridge University Press.

Richards, J. (2008) 'Second Language Teacher Education today'. *RELC Journal*, 39(2) 158–177.

Richards, J. and Nunan, D. (eds) (1990) *Second Language Teacher Education.* Cambridge: Cambridge University Press.

Richards, J. and Rodgers, T. (2014) *Approaches and Methods in Language Teaching*, 3rd edition. Oxford: Oxford University Press.

Richards, J. and Schmidt, R. (eds) (2002) *Dictionary of Language Teaching and Applied Linguistics*, 3rd edition. Harlow: Longman.

Rivers, W. (1981) *Teaching Foreign Language Skills*, 2nd edition. Chicago, IL: The University of Chicago Press.

Roberts, J. (1998) *Language Teacher Education.* London: Arnold.

Sahin, I. and Yildrim, A. (2016) 'Transforming Professional Learning into Practice'. *ELT Journal*, 70(3) 241–252.

Smith, R. and McClelland, N. (2018) 'Histories of Language Learning and Teaching in Europe: Guest Editorial'. *Language Learning Journal*, 46(1) 1–5.

Snow, M.A. (2005) 'Key themes in TESOL MA teacher education', in Tedick, D. (ed.) *Second Language Teacher Education: International Perspectives.* Mahwah, NJ: Lawrence Erlbaum Associates.

Stern, H. (1983) *Fundamental Concepts of Language Teaching.* Oxford: Oxford University Press.

Thornbury, S. (2017) *Scott Thornbury's 30 Language Teaching Methods.* Cambridge: Cambridge University Press.

Thornbury, S. and Watkins, P. (2007) *The CELTA Course: Trainer's Manual.* Cambridge: Cambridge University Press.

Ur, P. (2012) *A Course in English Language Teaching.* Cambridge: Cambridge University Press.

Waters, A. (2009) 'A Guide to Methodologia: Past, Present and Future'. *ELT Journal*, 63(2) 108–115.

Wenger, E. (1998) *Communities of Practice: Learning, Meaning, and Identity.* Cambridge: Cambridge University Press.

20

Materials and authenticity in language teaching

Alex Gilmore

Introduction

A brief history of authenticity in language learning

The notion of authenticity has a long history in language teaching, starting as early as the nineteenth century when Henry Sweet, one of the first linguists, criticized the 'incessant repetition' of artificial systems, and compared them unfavourably to natural texts which 'do justice to every feature of the language' (Sweet, 1899: 177). However, it was probably the 'communicative turn' in the 1970s that marked the most significant change in language teaching methodology, as the emphasis shifted from abstract grammatical rules to actual, contextualized performance and the development of learners' overall communicative competence (Hymes, 1972). No longer was it considered sufficient to simply contrive random, isolated sentences to exemplify form or model substitution drills. Initiatives like the Common European Framework of Reference for Languages (CEFR) sought to describe the different communicative needs of European citizens, using real communication tasks to promote interaction amongst its member states. Meanwhile, the development of the tape recorder allowed researchers to begin transcribing and analysing natural speech, spawning new fields of enquiry such as discourse and conversational analysis and providing insights into real-time interaction that then began finding their way into language textbooks (Gilmore, 2015). *Advanced Conversational English* (Crystal & Davy, 1975: v), innovative in its time, notes in the preface, for example:

> Recent concern with the nature of discourse has called further into question the oral dialogues of many ELT textbooks which, because of their sentence-structure illustrating task and a lack of ready-to-hand criteria for the treatment of actual speech, have borne little resemblance to the hesitations, false starts, speed and volume changing characteristics of everyday conversation. As a result, learners have been handicapped in their powers of interpretation of *real* spoken data.

Today, advances in information and communications technology (ICT) provide materials designers, language teachers and learners with unfettered access to authentic input from across the globe, 'impelling the issue of authenticity of texts and interactions to the fore in language pedagogy' (Mishan, 2005: ix). The rich variety of multimodal media available on the Web can also effectively illustrate how different semiotic modes (text, images, gestures, sound, movement, etc.) are exploited, in various combinations, to communicate, which can facilitate the development of a range of competencies in language learners (linguistic, pragmalinguistic, sociopragmatic, strategic or discourse – see Box 20.1).

Authenticity and teacher training

Given the prominence of concepts of authenticity in the ELT research literature and the widespread use of authentic materials in language textbooks and classrooms, this is an area well worth focusing on in both initial teacher training and in-service courses. Key areas to consider in any discussions with teachers include: (i) A critical analysis of what authenticity in language learning actually *means*; (ii) What kinds of authenticity we most value in the classroom; (iii) Selecting authentic materials for the classroom; (iv) Ways to effectively exploit the rich potential of authentic materials. These topics will be addressed in the remainder of this chapter.

What *is* authencity?

The wide variation in definitions of authenticity that exist in the ELT research literature 'reflect both its significance and ambiguity' (Trabelsi, 2014: 670). Authenticity is a multi-dimensional concept and its various manifestations all have important implications for L2 materials design and language classrooms. It is therefore a valuable exercise in teacher training courses for teacher-learners (TLs) to attempt to tease apart and make sense of the tangled web of meanings for the term:

Authenticity relates to…

1. language produced by native speakers (NSs) for native speakers (e.g. Porter & Roberts, 1981);
2. language produced by a real speaker/writer for a real audience, conveying a real message (e.g. Morrow, 1977);
3. the ability to think or behave like a target language group in order to be recognized or validated by them (e.g. Kramsch, 1993);
4. the types of task chosen (e.g. Guariento & Morley, 2001; Mishan, 2010);
5. language assessment (e.g. Bachman & Palmer, 1996; Lewkowicz, 2000);
6. the qualities bestowed on a text by a reader/listener in a process of 'authentication' (e.g. Widdowson, 1978; Breen, 1985);
7. a personal process of engagement between teachers and students in the classroom (e.g. van Lier, 1996).

The first five definitions above each tend to project *outside* of the classroom, focusing on the kinds of target discourse communities that learners are likely to want to operate in and the language or communicative competencies they may need to be successful in their imagined future lives.

Authenticity as the language of 'native speakers'

Definition 1 may seem rather outdated now in a world that recognizes the importance of English as an International Language (EIL) and values varieties of English from Kachru's (1985) inner, outer and expanding circles. With the spread of the English language across the world, it has naturally evolved into a multitude of dialects which vary in terms of pronunciation, intonation patterns, grammar, vocabulary, spelling and conventions of use so that 'it becomes ever more difficult to characterize in ways that support the fiction of a simple, single language' (Strevens, 1980: 79). However, 'native speaker' (i.e. British, American or Australasian) varieties of English still tend to predominate in internationally marketed textbooks and language teachers and their students around the globe continue to display a preference for inner circle, 'standard' forms (e.g. Mishan & Timmis, 2015: 38). NS discourse also offers a rich and readily accessible source of multimodal language input for teachers to exploit in the classroom, which can extend lessons beyond the (necessarily) rather bland and restricted content of many course books. Of course, it isn't inherently more interesting than any other source of L2 input though; indeed, it is more likely to be culturally opaque and difficult for learners to 'authenticate' and so will require care in terms of text selection and task design. Teacher trainers and TLs can usefully consider questions such as: (i) What varieties of English are most appropriate for target learners in a particular context and why? (ii) What are the advantages/disadvantages of selecting inner-circle varieties of English over 'local' varieties such as Singlish, or indeed proficient L2 speaker models from the learners' own culture (which may represent a more achievable goal)? (iii) How can NS English input be made accessible to learners through principled text selection and task design?

Authenticity as language conveying a 'real message'

Definition 2 prioritizes the fact that language models, as a minimum requirement, should come from a genuine communicative event as opposed to being something deliberately created for the purposes of language teaching. Presumably, this stems from a concern that contrived language models often present learners with distorted or partial representations of the L2 for a wide range of discourse features, including lexicogrammatical choices, interactional features of contingent talk, pragmatics and generic structure (Gilmore, 2015). In this sense of authenticity, 'proficient users' (Paikeday, 1985) of English are valued equally to NSs, and in fact may be seen as providing better language models for the classroom (e.g. Cook, 1999) since: (i) they represent a more achievable goal for learners to aim at; (ii) the 'linguistic accommodation' (adjustment of verbal or non-verbal communication style according to other participants), often seen when interlocutors from different cultures interact, might result in more comprehensible input; and (iii) if the participants are from the learners' own culture, the topical content might be more accessible, relevant or interesting. In addition to the questions considered in the previous sub-section, it would be useful on teacher training courses to compare language models from course books with authentic interaction, to examine if/how they differ and what effects any differences might have on language learning (e.g. Gilmore, 2004).

Authenticity as intercultural communicative competence (ICC)

Definition 3 focuses on the concept of *communicative competence*, or a speaker's ability to communicate effectively in a variety of social situations. It is often seen as being composed of five distinct areas of linguistic or social competence, shown in Box 20.1. However, this has been criticized for overemphasizing a native speaker model of effective communication when the communicative needs of non-native speakers are often very different. Byram and Fleming (1998: 12) proposed that what language learners actually need is intercultural communicative competence (ICC), which they describe as 'the acquisition of abilities to understand different modes of thinking and living, as they are embodied in the language to be learnt, and to reconcile or mediate between different modes present in any specific interaction'. Rather than teaching the language stripped of its cultural associations, this approach recognizes the importance of 'cultural authenticity' and helping students see the world from different perspectives so that they are better equipped to mediate between their own culture and that of the target community. It moves beyond language to consider aspects such as non-verbal communication (e.g. interpersonal space, gestures) or sociopragmatics (e.g. politeness conventions, taboo topics), where misunderstandings can often lead to more serious consequences than any kind of linguistic problem (see Gilmore, 2007a). It is a useful exercise on teacher training courses to consider the different types of communicative competence that exist and which ones are actively developed in language learning materials (typically linguistic competence). If the course books being used in a particular context are seen as deficient in any way, TLs could be asked to analyse a piece of authentic discourse (such as a film extract) and discuss how it could help to develop other kinds of communicative competence.

Box 20.1 The communicative competence model

Communicative competence is generally seen as consisting of five components:

1. **Linguistic competence**: This refers to a speaker's lexical, morphological, orthographical, syntactical and phonological knowledge of the language and only deals with the literal meaning (or *locutionary force*) of utterances. This is the type of knowledge that has traditionally been the focus in ESOL classrooms, but in the current model of communicative competence it takes on a lesser role, seen as only one aspect of language proficiency.

2. **Pragmalinguistic competence**: This refers to a speaker's ability to understand or convey communicative intent appropriately in a given context, based on a knowledge of phrases typically used by native speakers in those situations. This kind of competence therefore describes a speaker's ability to interpret the *illocutionary force* of utterances, for example, understanding that 'Can you open the door?' is an informal request, rather than a question about someone's ability to perform an action.

3. **Sociopragmatic competence**: This refers to a speaker's knowledge of what is socially or culturally appropriate in a particular speech community, including an understanding of politeness or social conventions, or non-verbal behavior. For example, the knowledge that in Japan business cards should be exchanged at the beginning of an initial meeting, handed to the recipient with both hands and a slight bow is a kind of sociopragmatic competence.

4. **Strategic competence**: This refers to a speaker's ability to exploit verbal or non-verbal communication strategies when communication problems arise, compensating for deficiencies in other competences. These include four common types:

   a. *Avoidance or reduction strategies* such as topic avoidance or message abandonment to try to keep conversation inside areas where the speaker feels in control;

   b. *Compensatory strategies* such as circumlocution or mime when a word is not known;

   c. *Stalling strategies* such as using hesitation devices or repetition to hold the turn in conversation while a message is formulated;

   d. *Interactional strategies* such as asking for repetition or clarification where the speaker makes use of the linguistic resources of other interlocutors to maintain conversation.

5. **Discourse competence**: This refers to a speaker's ability to produce unified, cohesive and coherent spoken or written discourse of different genres. In writing this might include the knowledge of the correct layout for a letter or how to use anaphoric reference in a text. In speaking it would include how to develop a conversation naturally through 'topic shading' where a sub-topic from preceding talk is taken up and expanded into the main topic. It could also include knowledge of different generic structures such as narratives, gossip or jokes or discourse intonation.

Authenticity as task choices

Definition 4 is concerned with the authenticity of the *tasks* rather than *texts*, and the extent to which they mirror the (projected) real-world needs of students. Advocates of task-based language teaching (TBLT), for example, often propose a needs-based syllabus, where the course content is shaped by the kinds of tasks learners are likely to perform in the target domain. In this context, tasks such as ordering from a menu in a restaurant role-play or taking notes from a university lecture might be considered more authentic than substitution drills or controlled grammar exercises. However, this oversimplifies what is, in reality, a complex situation:

1. The classroom context creates its own authenticity and highly controlled pedagogic tasks can be justified as important intermediary 'skill-getting' steps in the journey towards 'skill-using' and the ultimate goal of intercultural communicative competence (see Rivers & Temperley, 1978: 4).
2. Predicting exactly what future tasks a particular group of students will need to perform is likely to be extremely difficult, unless it is a clearly defined ESP context such as 'English for air traffic controllers'.
3. It takes a rather utilitarian approach to language learning and tends to favour purely functional needs over learners' affective needs. Listening to, and understanding a song, for example, although of limited use could be a highly meaningful and enjoyable task for some students.

TLs might want to consider to what extent language learning tasks should replicate real-world tasks and how far the tasks seen in course books adequately prepare learners for their future lives.

Authenticity as assessment choices

Definition 5 relates the notion of authenticity to L2 assessment. It generally refers to 'situational authenticity' – the extent that test tasks mirror target language use (TLU) tasks, although it may also consider 'interactional authenticity' which focuses on the test participants' engagement with the task. It is quite possible to have one type of test authenticity without the other, as the example below from an oral proficiency interview clearly demonstrates (van Lier, 1989: 499). Here, a female test taker is asked about her family – a task that could be seen as having high situational authenticity. However, the interviewer's responses lack any of the empathy that might be expected in a genuine encounter of this nature and his aggressive interrogation technique and abrupt topic changes suggest a primary concern with generating language samples for assessment purposes:

INTERVIEWER:	Where is your mother? What does your mother do?
SUBJECT:	She's dead.
I:	Ah – she's dead. Very good.
I:	What's your father's name?
S:	[no response]
I:	What does your father do? Where does he work? Where does your father work?
	Come on girl, talk! Talk! Don't be afraid. Where does your father work?
S:	[no response]
I:	What do you do at home? Do you help your mother? What does your mother do?
S:	[no response]
I:	(into microphone) Doesn't talk.

Of course, the test environment is artificial to some extent since test-takers are expected to maximize their display of the required L2 knowledge and skills in a limited period of time, but nevertheless authentic assessment should aim to reflect 'real world' language use and interaction patterns as far as possible. Test characteristics (particularly with 'high stakes' tests) can have a powerful impact on classroom practices, as teachers teach for the exam – an effect known as 'washback'. Positive washback has been linked to the use of authentic texts and tasks along with direct assessment of the skills we want to foster:

> If we want people to learn to write compositions, we should get them to write compositions in the test. If a course objective is that students should be able to read scientific articles, then we should get them to do *that* in the test. Immediately we begin to test indirectly, we are removing an incentive for students to practise in the way that we want them to.
>
> *(Hughes, 2003: 54)*

Unfortunately however, there is a tendency to design tests on the basis of what is convenient to administer or grade, rather than focusing on the skills students actually need to develop for their future lives. This is certainly the case in Japan with the National Center Test for University Admissions, which uses multiple-choice questions to principally assess students' lexical or grammatical knowledge. A listening component, still using a multiple-choice format, was only introduced in 2006 and speaking skills are not tested at all (although this is due to change in 2020). As a direct consequence of these policy decisions, high school students entering Japanese universities typically have skewed communicative competence, with very poor speaking skills. It is therefore useful on teacher training courses to consider the forces shaping assessment choices in local contexts, and whether or not test characteristics encourage the kind of classroom practice which will be beneficial to learners in their future target discourse communities.

Authenticity as appropriate learner response

The final two definitions of authenticity focus more on the social reality *inside* the classroom. Definition 6 is closely associated with Widdowson's (1978: 80) distinction between 'genuine' and 'authentic' texts: 'Genuineness is a characteristic of the passage itself and is an absolute quality. Authenticity is a characteristic of the relationship between the passage and the reader and has to do with appropriate response'. In this sense, any (spoken or written) text, whether genuine or contrived, which learners can engage with and learn from can be seen as serving an authentic pedagogic purpose. Indeed, it may well be that materials contrived for a specific group of students, from a particular culture at a known proficiency level have a greater potential to be authenticated by them than genuine texts, originally intended for a native speaker audience, which because of their low frequency vocabulary, idiomatic language or culturally opaque references become 'pragmatically inert' (Widdowson, 1998: 710) for learners, not to mention the non-native English-speaking teachers (NNESTs) who make up the majority of trained EFL or ESL teachers around the world (Moussu & Llurda, 2008). Teacher trainers can usefully consider with TLs the value of this distinction between 'genuine' and 'authentic' and the extent to which text accommodation to (i.e. convergence with) students' culture or proficiency level is desirable.

Authenticity as a search for personal meaning

Definition 7 embraces a social constructivist approach to language learning (e.g. Williams & Burden, 1997), which sees knowledge and meaning as being socially situated and collaboratively constructed through interaction occurring in the classroom. Texts, tasks, learners, teacher and broader contextual (emotional, physical, social, political or cultural) factors all come together to create a unique, and constantly changing, environment where learning, we hope, can take place. In this sense, authenticity equates to the search for *personal meaning* from the experiences we encounter and is 'a context-bounded, multi-dimensional and dynamic process of interpretation, validation and (co)construction of a text, a task or a lesson in general' (Külekçi, 2015: 318). Any change in the components of the complex system that shape a particular classroom context will obviously influence the learning outcomes, and teachers play a pivotal role in facilitating this 'classroom authenticity' through, for example:

1. Careful selection of relevant and interesting input that meets students' perceived needs.
2. Effective 're-contextualization' of authentic materials from the real world so that they are accessible to the target learners.
3. Task design that provides the right balance of challenge and support (e.g. Mariani, 1997).
4. Varying interaction patterns in the classroom (individual study, pair or group work, plenary) according to the aims at particular stages of the lesson and students' social needs.
5. Responding to learning opportunities that arise spontaneously in the class – experienced teachers are more likely to go 'off-script' and deviate from the lesson plan to make activities more effective (e.g. Külekçi, 2015).
6. Engendering a feeling of trust and belonging in the class.
7. Maintaining their *own* enthusiasm for the class content and activities so that teaching does not become a mechanical process (selecting, designing and trialing your own materials is an excellent way to stay motivated).

Scaffolding (instructional techniques which move students towards greater skill or understanding) can take place at both macro and micro levels in the classroom: at the 'designed-in' level, careful selection and sequencing of materials and tasks by the teacher helps to ensure that learners can engage with the input, while at the 'interactional' level, as the lesson unfolds, teacher and students interact contingently and in less predictable ways, to co-construct meaning (Hammond & Gibbons, 2005).

Importantly, learners' L2 developmental trajectories are likely to be highly idiosyncratic, as they interpret the classroom input in different ways and assess its value in terms of their own goals and interests. Stimulus appraisal models of language learning (e.g. Schumann, 1997) hypothesize that learners assess input across five criteria: novelty, pleasantness, goal/need significance, coping mechanisms and self or social image. Positive appraisals of input are believed to encourage greater cognitive effort and greater engagement, leading to more learning, while negative appraisals result in avoidance. Thus, this final definition of authenticity tries to embrace the full complexity of the language learning process and to recognize that, while some aspects of a lesson can be controlled, many cannot. Video recordings or transcriptions of language lessons can be used with TLs to explore how classes often unfold in unpredictable ways and how learners also authenticate materials, tasks and classroom interaction in a personal manner so that any lesson, ultimately, means something different for each participant.

Authenticity and social constructivism

Of all the varied definitions of authenticity explored above, it is this final social constructivist perspective that seems most fitting to the concerns of language teachers, both in terms of its scope and the primacy it gives to the 'lived experience' of the classroom. Sociocultural approaches to learning and development were first developed by the Russian psychologist, Lev Vygotsky (1978), who envisaged two levels of development in the process of learning: (i) the 'actual level of development' is that already reached, where the learner is able to solve problems independently; (ii) the 'potential level of development', or *zone of proximal development* (ZPD), is that which learners are capable of reaching with guidance or collaboration from others. Learning is seen as taking place within the ZPD, when the challenge of a task is just above the learner's level of competence and can only be achieved with the support of a 'knowledgeable other' or meditational tools (Lantolf, 2011).

Much of the discussion above of authenticity in language learning can be framed within this social constructivist model of the developmental process. First, the actual level of development of any group of learners is likely to differ according to factors such as language aptitude, interest in the target language/culture, or previous experiences with the L2. Teachers try to provide input at the right level of difficulty to ensure that learners are working within the ZPD, but this can only ever be an approximation and may leave students under- or over-challenged. Any materials or tasks that are outside of the ZPD are unlikely to be engaged with or 'authenticated' by the learners (see Figure 20.1). Support for learning in the classroom can come from the teacher, other learners, or through the way tasks are designed or lessons staged. The types of input and tasks introduced into the class will obviously affect the direction of L2 development, so it is important to consider carefully what the learning goals should be. This may not be straightforward in a general English class, but some kind of needs analysis

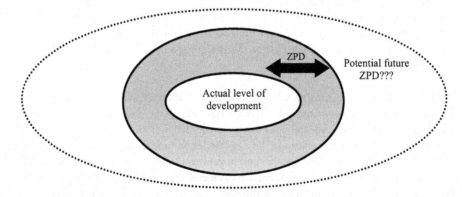

Figure 20.1   Actual and potential levels of development

and negotiation of course content between teacher and learners is more likely to ensure that learn-ers feel that they are developing their communicative competence and skills in an appropriate way and will therefore be more willing to engage with activities. 'Genuine' materials, originally produced for real communicative purposes outside of the classroom context, are often more motivating for learners precisely because they can see their practical relevance, as these comments from participants on a ten-month experimental course, using only authentic materials, suggest (Gilmore, 2007a: 228):

RI: All of the materials you gave me was practical [...]. Before participating in your class, my English was terrible! It was very Japanese English and quite unnatural. However, I really think that now I can speak English more naturally than before thanks to your lessons. You taught me how I should speak English for native English. It was very hard but quite useful for me. I like your teaching! Your lessons are unique, interesting and active!

YM: I learned a lot of things that I haven't know before! [...] I think that because I learned many techniques which make my English sound more natural. For exam-ple, it was great to learn 'listener responds' [reactive tokens], 'sign-posting languages' [discourse markers] and so on. Also, it was good to study polite English and formal English because I will definitely need them in the future.

TK: Today, we learnt how to close a conversation. For example, 'Well ... I've got to go', 'OK then, thank you for your help!' and so on. Actually, I was surprised that there were so many ending clauses. Now I know them, so I want to use them when I talk with foreigners!

Feedback from learners on materials or tasks such as this clearly shows how they are actively involved in evaluating the L2 input they receive in relation to their own communicative goals – something which is unlikely to be evident from in-class observations. Inexperienced teachers can benefit immensely from asking their students to submit 'learner diaries' which make explicit these thought processes (e.g. Gilmore, 2007a: 202).

As illustrated below, multimodal authentic materials also tend to provide a richer source of input than conventional textbooks, which allows learners to 'notice' (e.g. Schmidt, 1990) different L2 features, depending on their own particular stage of interlanguage development or interests, and to develop a wider range of communicative competencies. Exactly what gets noticed can be influenced to a certain extent through materials selection, task design, and the teacher's decisions on staging or delivery of the input, but ultimately learners will make their own personal mean-ings in the classroom – something that should be both encouraged and facilitated. TLs should consider what kinds of communicative competence are encouraged by the L2 input and tasks they select (or are obliged to use) in class and how far these match students' needs or interests.

Exploiting authentic materials in the classroom

The sample materials below illustrate how *some* of the principles of authenticity highlighted above can be realized in a genuine classroom context. As is always the case, the choice of materi-als and task design relate closely to the specific learning environment or learner profile (in this instance, students in the Japanese university system), so, although seen as successful here, they are unlikely to be appropriate to other learning contexts without adaption (or otherwise replaced completely). These examples represent 'unmediated' materials where there is no intervention between writer and learners, rather than 'mediated' materials where a range of stakeholders (e.g. editors, end-users, governmental bodies) might influence the end product (Timmis, 2014).

Teacher trainers working with teachers can use the materials here to demonstrate the process of text selection, task design, implementation and reflection possible with authentic materials

This could be followed up with activities where teachers are made aware of different potential sources of authentic L2 input and are then asked to select and try out samples of natural spoken or written language in their own classrooms. However, for this to be successful, teachers first need a solid foundation in discourse analysis, which can allow them to identify pedagogically useful features that are always present in any text but not necessarily obvious to the untrained eye (good entry points are McCarthy, 1991 and McCarthy & Carter, 1994).

'My secret life'

Target group: First year Japanese university writing skills class.

Lesson aims: (i) reading comprehension of an authentic newspaper article; (ii) vocabulary development (*cynical*, *eccentric*, *call the shots*, etc.); (iii) improving web search skills in English; (iv) question formation in English; (v) developing speaking skills (pair work interviews); (vi) developing writing skills (newspaper article); (vii) improving learning environment with familiarization activity for new university students.

Box 20.2   My Secret Life: Mark Watson, comedian, 31

Interview by Holly Williams, *Saturday, 16 April 2011*

1   **A life in brief...** Mark Watson was born in Bristol in 1980. He studied at Cambridge, and has
2   regularly appeared at the Edinburgh Fringe, on radio and TV, including hosting the panel
3   show Mark Watson Kicks Off. Watson is Chairman of Respect FC, aiming to unite fans and
4   players against the ugly side of football (respectfootballclub.com). He is the author of four
5   books; his novel Eleven is out in June, when he also embarks on a country-wide Request
6   Stops stand-up tour. Watson lives in London with his wife and son.
7   **My parents are ...** one of the most steady forces in my life.
8   I'm the first-born son, so I had the status of golden boy –
9   well, my siblings certainly thought so. Fortunately we are
10 quite a cynical family, so they are gently mocking in a
11 way parents should be.
12 **The house/flat I grew up in ...** was in Shirehampton in
13 Bristol. We had a really big garden which me and my
14 brother almost believed was an-all purpose sports stage.
15 I'm slightly resentful that whoever lives there won't be
16 using it as a cricket ground.
17 **When I was a child I wanted to ...** be a sports
18 commentator. It's a stereotypical wish to be a footballer; I
19 had the pragmatic dream of being someone who watched.
20 **If I could change one thing about myself ...** I'd like to be
21 more aggressively confident, without being a real idiot.
22 **You wouldn't know it but I am very good at ...** capital
23 cities, flags of the world, and geographical trivia like that.
24 **You may not know it but I am no good at ...** riding a
25 bike. It's quite embarrassing. I went to a local park with
26 the in-laws and I had to run alongside their bikes.
27 **At night I dream of ...** Embarrassingly, I do dream a lot about
28 football, and in really specific ways. My wife finds it incredibly uninteresting when I wake up and
29 say, 'Tottenham beat Arsenal 2–1'.
30 **What I see when I look in the mirror ...** Mostly I notice that I am alarmingly, unhealthily thin.
31 **I wish I'd never worn ...** I've always had fairly poor dress sense – now it's not a problem
32 because my wife calls the wardrobe shots. Anything I owned that was bad has been brutally

33 purged.
34 **I drive ...** nothing at all. I'm not really interested in cars or bikes.
35 **My favourite building ...** Flinders Street Station in Melbourne. It's not so much beautiful as
36 peculiar looking. It's covered in clocks – basically very eccentric.
37 **My secret crush is ...** Peggy Olson from Mad Men. She's irresistible, it's the intensity of her
38 eyes. Normally it's older women though, which means they have to stay secret because it gets
39 really embarrassing.
40 **Movie heaven ...** It's A Wonderful Life. Maybe not the best film ever made, but it is the film
41 that makes you feel warmest and most optimistic about mankind.
42 **A book that changed me ...** 1984, because I read it when I was about 14 and it made me
43 realise it was worth bothering to read adult books. It convinced me it's possible to write a book
44 that still has political resonance 50 or 100 years on.
45 **My greatest regret ...** On a day-to-day basis, I regret that I changed my phone to Orange.
46 They should spend less money on those cutesy black-and-orange adverts and more on pylons
47 so they have better signal.
48 **My real-life villains ...** The Pussycat Dolls. I'm pretty confident they are a force for evil; they
49 make terrible pop music, and are terrible examples for young girls.
50 They make me unhappy: it's just a step back for feminism, and for the world.
51 **The person who really makes me laugh ...** My brother, and my wife. It's not a coincidence
52 that the people close to you are the people who make you laugh the most.
53 **My five-year plan ...** The only plan that makes sense is to do what you're doing, better.
54 makes you look stupid if you have too definite plans.
55 **My life in six words ...** A good effort with some reservations.

<www.independent.co.uk/news/people/profiles/my-secret-life-mark-watson-comedian-31-2267228.html>

Commentary

This activity is based on a newspaper article series from the Independent called *My secret life* in which famous people reveal hidden aspects of themselves to readers. Newspaper articles have long been exploited for language learning since they provide a readily available source of topical material on an endless variety of subjects and, as 'stand-alone' texts, need little adaptation for the classroom. It is commonly recognized that authentic texts are naturally graded and interviews are towards the less challenging end of the cline because of their simple discourse structure (question–answer) and the limited number of 'elements' (interviewer–interviewee) they include. Even if students fail to understand isolated parts of the interview, they can therefore still grasp the basic global structure, and this, hopefully, gives them a sense of control over the task.

Learners start by reading the newspaper interview with a British comedian, Mark Watson, and answering comprehension questions designed to focus their attention on useful vocabulary or cultural information in the text, for example:

- What do we mean when we say somebody 'calls the shots' (line 29)? Check the Oxford Advance Learner's Dictionary online at: http://oald8.oxfordlearnersdictionaries.com/ (Hint: search for 'call the shots')
- Find some pictures of Flinders Street Station (line 31) on the Web and discuss your opinions of this building with your partner. Mark calls the station 'peculiar' and 'eccentric': Are these positive or negative adjectives here?
- What does it mean if you 'have a crush on someone' (line 33)? Do a Google search to find the answer (Hint: type 'have a crush definition' in the search box). Find Peggy Olson from *Mad Men* (line 33) on YouTube: Do you find her 'irresistible'?

Line references and web search hints are provided for support – an illustration of how materials designers can vary the level of challenge by altering the task rather than the text itself. The questions encourage learners to notice specific linguistic or cultural features that could benefit their L2 development; for example, Mark Watson (the interviewee) mentions that his favourite building is Flinders Street Station in Melbourne, saying, 'It's not so much beautiful as peculiar looking. It's covered in clocks – basically very eccentric'. Their attention is focused on the adjectives 'peculiar' and 'eccentric', which are used in a complementary sense in this context, although the Japanese translations 変 (hen) or 風変わりな (fugawarina) would tend to be seen as negative descriptions in what is a relatively homogenous society that emphasizes conformity (as the famous Japanese saying goes, '出る釘は打たれる' – 'The nail that sticks out gets hammered down'). Interestingly, Japanese often borrows words from other languages, which are marked as 'foreign' by being written in katakana (a different writing system), rather than kanji or hiragana. The word *eccentric* has been incorporated into the language as a loan word (エキセントリックな) and tends to have more positive connotations than its Japanese equivalents. The task also tries to elicit a personal (authentic?) response from learners with questions such as 'Do you find Peggy Olson from *Mad Men* irresistible?' to generate discussion and to make the target language more memorable. 'Culturally loaded' texts like this can therefore be used to heighten teachers' awareness of the importance of cultural differences in communication and also to demonstrate how students' intercultural communicative competence can be developed through principled materials selection and task design.

In the next stage of the activity, students are asked to produce question forms based on Mark Watson's interview responses, for example:

If I could change one thing about myself ... I'd like to be more aggressively confident, without being a real arsehole (idiot) » If you could change one thing about yourself, what would it be?

This task allows a focus on any problematical grammatical structures (here, the conditional use of *could* and *would*) and also primes learners for the upcoming pairwork oral interview by illustrating a range of possible questions. Notice the use of taboo language here, 'a real arsehole', which is a common feature in authentic texts. Teachers will need to decide just how much 'reality' they want to expose their students to – in this case, the decision was made to use the synonym 'idiot' given the level of maturity of the target group.

Students then brainstorm and share possible questions for the oral interviews, which gives them the opportunity to personalize the activity and ask questions that they themselves find meaningful, such as:

- If you imagine a colour for yourself, what is it?
- Which Olympic events do you most want to watch in 2020?
- If you could get one of Doraemon's belongings, which would you choose and why?

(Doraemon is a robotic cat from a popular Japanese manga series, who has a pocket full of gadgets including the 'bamboo-copter', a head accessory for personal flight, and the 'anywhere door', a door that opens onto any destination the user wishes to visit).

Finally, pairs interview each other and write up their notes for a class newspaper; attention is given to formatting features in the article, such as font style, the use of bold typeface or italics, and the choice of an image that can encapsulate the character of the interviewee. The 'published newspaper' is normally received with great enthusiasm by the class and avidly read since, being first year students, they are all new arrivals at university and are keen to find out more about each other's lives.

This kind of activity might also provide useful 'loop input' (e.g. Mann & Walsh, 2017: 89) in teaching workshops or initial teacher training courses, particularly where participants don't know each other well. After experiencing the task for themselves, teachers could be asked to identify the different stages included in the activity and the pedagogic rationale underpinning each step. They could also reflect on their own feelings about engaging with authentic texts or each other and the extent to which these types of activities have the potential to deepen the learning experience.

Reservoir Dogs (Quentin Tarantino, 1992)

Target group: Japanese university oral proficiency class.

Lesson aims: (i) understanding the structure of oral narratives; (ii) highlighting function of present historic tense in story-telling; (iii) non-verbal communication (NVC) in story-telling; (iv) vocabulary development (glove box, dashboard, etc.); (v) developing speaking skills (pair work discussion); (vi) developing listening skills (understanding a film scene); (vii) recounting personal stories effectively.

Commentary: Extracts from films or television programmes can be extremely motivating and excellent sources of multisensory input for language classrooms, but need to be selected with care, considering questions such as: (i) Is the scene interesting as a 'stand alone entity' and will it be comprehensible to students without excessive recontextualization work? (ii) Are there useful discourse features (lexicogrammatical, pragmatic, prosodic, non-verbal, etc.) for students to notice in the extract? (iii) Is the level of difficulty of the text appropriate for the target group (speech rates, accents, colloquial language, assumed cultural knowledge, etc.)? (iv) Are subtitles or transcripts readily available to support learning?

Oral narratives are extremely common in casual conversation and play an important role in building or maintaining relationships, providing speakers with 'a resource for assessing and confirming affiliations with others [...] in stories, values, attitudes and ways of seeing the world are created and represented' (Eggins & Slade, 1997: 229). They are, however, largely unrepresented in language teaching materials despite their crucial role in realizing a social identity.

The *Reservoir Dogs* extract was selected for its interesting content, with an American traffic cop recounting a story to a colleague of a dangerous incident when he pulled over a suspicious driver for questioning. It also highlights useful features of oral narratives, which students can incorporate into their own attempts at storytelling. The task begins by contextualizing the story visually, encouraging learners to develop relevant schemas and scripts around traffic violations in the USA and to activate key vocabulary arising in the listening activity. Students are then given an outline of the story and are asked to produce their own oral narratives first *before* they listen to the original scene, which encourages them to 'notice the gap' (Schmidt & Frota, 1986) between their own performances and that of the characters in the film and is thought to enhance language acquisition.

Telling stories

A. What is happening in this picture?
   1. What do you think the policeman is saying to the driver?
   2. What is 'police procedure' in your country when a car is stopped? How do you think it is different in America?
   3. What do people usually keep in their car's glove box in your country? How about in America?

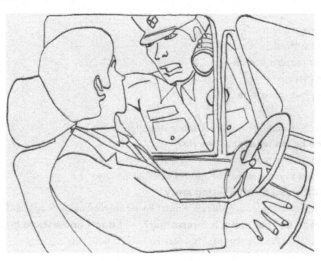

B. Work in pairs and imagine you are policemen in America. Policeman 1 is going to tell a story to Policeman 2. Try to make your story as interesting and funny as possible, Policeman 2 should try to sound interested in the story. Here are the details:

- The other day, you stopped a suspicious car with an American man (called Chuck) and an Asian woman in it, the man was driving.
- You parked behind the car and approached it with your gun drawn.
- You walked round to the driver's side and pointed your gun at the driver and told him not to move.
- The driver replied, 'I know, I know' but continued to move his right hand towards the glove box.
- You warned the driver again, saying you would shoot him if he didn't put his hands on the dashboard.
- The driver's girlfriend told him to listen to you and to put his hands on the dashboard.
- Finally, the driver put his hands on the dash but he was nearly shot by you!
- Chuck was trying to get his registration out of the glove box.

C. Write down your dialogue and practice acting it out in a natural way.
D. Now watch this scene from *Reservoir Dogs* (Quentin Tarantino). How was it different from your story? Think about:

1. the different parts of the story
2. the grammar patterns
3. the vocabulary
4. the intonation
5. the body language

The transcript below shows the interaction between two Japanese students attempting to reconstruct the story in Section B of the materials, and illustrates how they cooperate together to create their own personal meaning from the task, exploiting the materials and an electronic dictionary as mediational tools:

S1, S2: Male students
(...): Transcription remarks
[...]: Concurrent speech
italics: Japanese
bold: English translation

1 **S1:** *ha he ho ho nani ni shiyoka* A piece of paper
           ha he ho ho what shall we do?
2 **S2:** A piece of paper
3 **S1:** *sou nanka omoshiroi hanashi wo tsukurashite morauyo*
           Yes I'll make an interesting story
4 **S2:** *so omoshiroku shiyo omoshiroku naruka konna shinkokuna kore ga omoshiroitte iunara*
           Yes let's do that make it interesting?   I don't understand how we can make
5   *ore wa rikai dekihin* we don't understand what why this is funny

this serious story interesting

6 **S1:** What do we now here it's my it's my it's my car (S2 laughs) I'm sorry and I want to ride ride

7 pato car once finish (pato car = patrol car)

8 **S2:** (laughs) Oh really oh that's terrible

9 **S1:** *Patokaate nihongo patroruka ka?*

Is 'pat car' Japanese? Is it 'patrol car' in English?

10 **S2:** *Ah pata* Patrol car [**S1**: Patrol car]

Oh that's patrol car

11 **S1:** (Checking dictionary) Be available patrol car *rashii chuuka*

patrol car-ish or

12 Police car *no hou ga iissu*

Police car would be better

13 **S2:** Mm police car sq squad car

14 **S1:** *nani sore* squad car

What's squad car?

15 **S2:** *iya soo ya issho ni kangaete*

Can't we think about this together?

16 **S1:** *Pair yaro*

We're working as a pair aren't we?

17 **S2:** Pair *detan yaro kangaetekure*

If you're my partner please think of something

In line 6, S1 suggests a quick solution to the task, imagining the driver of the car simply apologizing to the policeman and explaining that his driving misdemeanors stemmed from his desire to ride in a police patrol car – a suggestion firmly rejected by S2 in line 8. The emergence of the expression 'バトカー' (*patoka*) in the discussion then initiates a series of turns from lines 9–14 where the two students negotiate with each other to arrive at a suitable English translation. They seem to be aware that, often, English loan words are shortened in Japanese (e.g. 'convenience store' becomes *konbini*) and this knowledge causes them to doubt (correctly in this case) the acceptability of *patoka* in English. S2 suggests 'patrol car' as a better alternative, but S1 appears to be unsure and searches his electronic dictionary for more examples. His search yields an alternative expression, 'police car', which generates a final suggestion of 'squad car' from S2. S1 appears to want to search for more information about 'squad car' in his dictionary, but this is curtailed by S2's impatience to continue with the dialogue construction task.

What is clear even from this short extract of classroom interaction is that the participants are both highly motivated and deeply engaged with the task, and in this sense the authentic materials appear to be facilitating language learning. However, the teacher's intended goal of preparing the learners for the follow-up listening task is somewhat undermined in this case as the pair 'go off script' and create their own original story from the outline. This illustrates the unpredictability inherent in 'authentic classrooms' where the act of authentication by participants inevitably takes the lesson in unexpected, and often interesting, directions (see Külekçi, 2015 for more on the important role of spontaneity in teaching).

For teacher trainers, this extract illustrates the potential value of recording, transcribing, and analyzing student interaction in the classroom. Effective teachers will often move around the class during activities, monitoring learners' progress with a task, but with communicative activities noise levels are often high and it can be difficult for teachers to catch more than random snatches of pair or group-work conversation. In this sense, as teachers, we can only ever have a rough sense of what is going on inside our classrooms – recording and analysing student interaction can deepen our understanding of these processes.

Students next act out their story scripts to other groups and usually enjoy seeing how each other's interpretations differ. They then watch the film version and compare the effectiveness of their own stories with the original, considering various discourse features such as the obligatory parts of an oral narrative, tense, vocabulary or prosodic choices, and NVC. A transcript of the scene is provided at the post-listening stage to allow for a closer analysis of the material:

1 Policeman 1: So hey, so, so anyway, I've got my gun drawn right?
2 And I've got it pointed right at this guy, and I tell him 'Freeze, don't fucking move'
3 and this little idiot's looking right at me, nodding his head yeah and he's saying
4 'I know, I know, I know' but meanwhile, his right hand is creeping towards the glove box.
5 And I scream at him, I go, 'Asshole, I'm gonna fucking blow you away right now!'
6 (story continues)

Students are introduced to the six stages normally included in a narrative (Labov, 1972):

i.   The *abstract* (e.g. 'Have I ever told you about the time…?') tells the listeners what the story is about and creates a 'storytelling space' in the conversation by suspending normal turn-taking patterns.
ii.   The *orientation* provides background information on the time, people and places relevant to the story.
iii. The *complicating action* provides the details of what happened and is temporally ordered.
iv.   The *evaluation* highlights the point of the story, warding off the question 'So what?' from listeners.
v.   The *result* or *resolution* describes what finally happened and brings the story to a satisfactory conclusion.
vi.   The *coda* acts as a bridge between the 'story world' and the 'real world' and signals the end of the narrative.

They compare these with the transcript to identify whether any parts are missing (in this case, the scene cuts straight to the complicating action) and try to imagine what might have been said in the omitted sections. They then focus on Policeman 1's verb choices in the complicating action and discover (inductively) how he shifts from past tense to historic present tense ('I tell him…') and progressive forms ('this little idiot's looking right at me, nodding his head…') in order to increase the story's dramatic impact – uses of tense that are rarely, if ever, illustrated in commercially produced textbooks. Other interesting discourse features evident in the transcript include the speaker's use of varied accents, speech rhythm and pitch to represent the different characters in the story, and his tendency to chain utterances together with the simple discourse markers *and*, *but*, or *so*, as is commonly the case in natural speech (e.g. Wardaugh, 1985). As we saw in the earlier example, the language in authentic materials can sometimes be rather risqué, but this provides a good opportunity to focus on the social role of swearing to amplify attitudinal meaning and claim group membership (particularly amongst males). A useful activity at this stage is for students to rewrite the dialogue in a more formal register, making lexical decisions in order to tone down the language to suit a different audience or context, where, in terms of power, relationships are more asymmetrical. As Wajnryb (1996) points out, examples of face-threatening acts (FTAs) are uncommon in language textbooks, and even when they do occur the opportunity for the 'facework' they provide is rarely exploited.

For teacher trainers, these materials provide a good example of the potential pedagogic value of even small extracts from films or other audio-visual materials. In workshops, teachers could be provided with the original scene and transcript from *Reservoir Dogs* and asked to brainstorm ideas for their use with L2 learners, before comparing their own ideas with the commentary here or finding and trialing their own film samples.

Finally, in a small group activity, students are asked to prepare and retell one of their own life stories in English, considering the typical features of oral narratives highlighted by the materials. This is a chance for them to review what they have learned and to personalize it, building relationships with classmates in a meaningful way. It is usually greeted with great enthusiasm and close attention from the audience – a grading sheet summarizing the key points for effective storytelling helps to keep the focus on the learning goals and gives students a stake in their own assessment.

Conclusion

It is probably clear from the discussion above that there are no easy answers to what authenticity actually is, or how it should best be encouraged in the classroom. The concept has been problematized and complexified considerably over the last few decades and its precise nature will always be determined by the context in which it is realized, shaped by local actors and conditions. For this reason, it is perhaps also best explored locally by practicing teachers themselves, through classroom investigations or action research cycles. Teacher trainers can begin by raising awareness of the many meanings ascribed to authenticity in the research literature and discussing with teachers which definitions they see as being most relevant and useful to their own practice and why. Only once this has been established can decisions be made in terms of what type of input or tasks are most likely to help educators achieve their teaching goals. Teachers should also be familiarized with the different types of spoken and written authentic texts readily available on the Web (newspapers, films, documentaries, soap operas, etc.) and consider, from a discourse perspective, what verbal or non-verbal features of the input could be exploited in the classroom to develop learners' communicative competence. When appropriate materials have been identified, teachers could practice adapting them to suit the needs of specific learner groups in their own contexts.

Further reading

Mishan, F. (2005) *Designing Authenticity into Language Learning Materials*. Bristol: Intellect.
  This is one of the first books to deal comprehensively with the complex issue of authenticity in language learning. Part 1 considers the theoretical underpinnings for using authentic materials, while Part 2 focuses on the practical implementation in the classroom, covering seven different 'cultural products': literature, broadcast media, newspapers, advertising, music, film, and ICT.

Gilmore, A. (2007b) 'Authentic Materials and Authenticity in Foreign Language Learning'. *Language Teaching*, 40(2) 97–118.

> This is a 'State-of-the-Art' article from *Language Teaching* (www.cambridge.org/core/journals/language-teaching) – in general, this thread in the journal provides an excellent starting point for an overview of many important areas in second-language teaching. The paper reviews some of the wide-ranging issues surrounding authentic materials and authenticity in language learning and has an extensive reference list.

Tomlinson, B. (ed.) (2011) *Materials Development in Language Teaching*, 2nd edition. Cambridge: Cambridge University Press.

> This is a very accessible edited volume, with contributions from 20 expert researchers/practitioners in the field. Impressive in its scope and consideration of materials development from multiple perspectives, it provides a strong link between theory and practice.

Mishan, F. and Timmis, I. (2015) *Materials Development for TESOL*. Edinburgh: Edinburgh University Press.

> This book, designed for use on TESOL programmes or self-study, aims to provide a comprehensive overview of the key theoretical and practical issues behind materials development. It is written in an accessible style and has practical tasks at the end of each chapter to encourage readers to consider the implications of the theoretical concepts or issues to their own teaching contexts.

References

Bachman, L. and Palmer, A. (1996) *Language Testing in Practice*. Oxford: Oxford University Press.

Breen, M. (1985) 'Authenticity in the Language Classroom'. *Applied Linguistics*, 6(1) 60–70.

Byram, M. and Fleming, M. (eds) (1998) *Language Learning in Intercultural Perspective: Approaches Through Drama and Ethnography*. Cambridge: Cambridge University Press.

Cook, V. (1999) 'Going Beyond the Native Speaker in Language Teaching'. *TESOL Quarterly*, 33(2) 185–209.

Crystal, D. and Davy, D. (1975) *Advanced Conversational English*. Harlow: Longman.

Eggins, S. and Slade, D. (1997) *Analysing Casual Conversation*. London: Cassell.

Gilmore, A. (2004) 'A Comparison of Textbook and Authentic Interactions'. *ELT Journal*, 58(4) 363–374.

Gilmore, A. (2007a) *Getting real in the language classroom: developing Japanese students' communicative competence with authentic materials*. PhD thesis, Nottingham University, UK.

Gilmore, A. (2007b) 'Authentic Materials and Authenticity in Foreign Language Learning'. *Language Teaching*, 40(2) 97–118.

Gilmore, A. (2009) '"The times they are a-changin'": strategies for exploiting authentic materials in the language classroom', in Rilling, S. and Dantas-Whitney, M. (eds) *TESOL Classroom Practice Series: Authenticity in Adult Classrooms and Beyond*. Alexandria, VA: TESOL Publications: 155–168.

Gilmore, A. (2015) 'Research into Practice: The Influence of Discourse Studies on Language Descriptions and Task Design in Published ELT Materials'. *Language Teaching*, 48(4) 506–530.

Guariento, W. and Morley, J. (2001) 'Text and Task Authenticity in the EFL Classroom'. *ELT Journal*, 55(4) 347–353.

Hammond, J. and Gibbons, P. (2005) 'Putting Scaffolding to Work: The Contribution of Scaffolding in Articulating ESL Education'. *Prospect*, 20(1) 6–30.

Hughes, A. (2003) *Testing for Language Teachers*. Cambridge: Cambridge University Press.

Hymes, D. (1972) 'On communicative competence'. In Pride, J. B. and Holmes, J. (eds) *Sociolinguistics: Selected Readings*. Harmondsworth: Penguin Books: 269–293.

Kachru, B. (1985) 'Standards, codification and sociolinguistic realism: the English language in the outer circle', in Quirk, R. and Widdowson, H. G. (eds) *English in the World: Teaching and Learning the Language and Literatures*. Cambridge: Cambridge University Press: 11–30.

Kramsch, C. (1993) *Context and Culture in Language Teaching*. Oxford: Oxford University Press.

Külekçi, E. (2015) *'Authenticity' in English language teaching and learning: a case study of four high school classrooms in Turkey*. PhD thesis, University of Warwick, UK.

Labov, W. (1972) *Language in the Inner City*. Oxford: Blackwell.

Lantolf, J. P. (2011) 'The sociocultural approach to second language acquisition', in Atkinson, D. (ed.) *Alternative Approaches to Second Language Acquisition*. Abingdon: Routledge: 24–48.

Lewkowicz, J. (2000) 'Authenticity in Language Testing: Some Outstanding Questions'. *Language Testing*, 17(1) 43–64.

Mann, S. and Walsh, S. (2017) *Reflective Practice in English Language Teaching: Research-based Principles and Practice*. New York: Routledge.

Mariani, L. (1997) 'Teacher Support and Teacher Challenge in Promoting Learner Autonomy'. *Perspectives*, 23(2) 1–10.

McCarthy, M. (1991) *Discourse Analysis for Language Teachers*. Cambridge: Cambridge University Press.

McCarthy, M. and Carter, R. (1994) *Language as Discourse*. Harlow: Longman.

Mishan, F. (2005) *Designing Authenticity into Language Learning Materials*. Bristol: Intellect.

Mishan, F. (2010) 'Task and task authenticity: Paradigms for language learning in the digital era', in Mishan, F. and Chambers, A. (eds) *Perspectives on Language Learning Materials Development*. Oxford: Peter Lang.

Mishan, F. and Timmis, I. (2015) *Materials Development for TESOL*. Edinburgh: Edinburgh University Press.

Morrow, K. (1977) 'Authentic texts and ESP', in Holden, S. (ed.) *English for Specific Purposes*. London: Modern English Publications: 13–17.

Moussu, L. and Llurda, E. (2008) 'Non-native English-speaking English Language Teachers: History and Research'. *Language Teaching*, 41(3) 315–348.

Paikeday, T. (1985) *The Native Speaker is Dead!* Toronto: Paikeday Publishing.

Porter, D. and Roberts, J. (1981) 'Authentic Listening Activities'. *ELT Journal*, 36(1) 37–47.

Rivers, W. M. and Temperley, M. S. (1978) *A Practical Guide to the Teaching of English as a Second Language*. New York: Oxford University Press.

Schmidt, R. (1990) 'The Role of Consciousness in Second Language Learning'. *Applied Linguistics*, 11(2) 129–158.

Schmidt, R. and Frota, S. (1986) 'Developing basic conversational ability in a second language: a case study of an adult learner of Portuguese', in Day, R. (ed.) *Talking to Learn: Conversation in Second Language Acquisition*. Rowley, MA: Newbury House: 237–326.

Schumann, J. H. (1997) *The Neurobiology of Affect in Language*. Oxford: Blackwell.

Strevens, P. (1980) *Teaching English as an International Language*. Oxford: Pergamon Press.

Sweet, H. (1899) *The Practical Study of Languages*. London: Oxford University Press.

Timmis, I. (2014) 'Writing materials for publication: questions raised and lessons learned', in Harwood, N. (ed.) *English Language Teaching Textbooks: Content, Consumption, Production*. Basingstoke: Palgrave Macmillan: 241–261.

Tomlinson, B. (ed.) (2011) *Materials Development in Language Teaching*, 2nd edition. Cambridge: Cambridge University Press.

Trabelsi, S. (2014) 'Towards a New Approach to Authenticity in ELT'. *US-China Foreign Language*, 12(8) 670–683.

van Lier, L. (1989) 'Reeling, Writhing, Drawling. Stretching. And Fainting in Coils: Oral Proficiency Interviews as Conversation'. *TESOL Quarterly*, 23(3) 489–508.

van Lier, L. (1996) *Interaction in the Language Curriculum: Awareness, Autonomy and Authenticity*. London: Longman.

Vygotsky, L. (1978) *Mind in Society*. London: Harvard University Press.

Wajnryb, R. (1996) *Death, taxes and jeopardy: Systematic omissions in EFL texts, or 'life was never meant to be an adjacency pair'*. Paper presented at the 9th Educational Conference, Sydney.

Wardhaugh, R. (1985) *How Conversation Works*. Oxford: Basil Blackwell.

Alex Gilmore

Widdowson, H. G. (1978) *Teaching Language as Communication*. Oxford: Oxford University Press.

Widdowson, H. G. (1998) 'Context, Community, and Authentic Language'. *TESOL Quarterly*, 32(4) 705–716.

Williams, M. and Burden, R. L. (1997) *Psychology for Language Teachers: A Social Constructivist Approach*. Cambridge: Cambridge University Press.

21

Classroom management

Art, craft or science?

Heather Buchanan and Ivor Timmis

Introduction

Classroom management (CM) is a commonly used term in teacher education and most people would agree that the skills involved are an essential part of any teacher's repertoire. Indeed, CM has been identified as a key factor in effective teaching (e.g. Marzano and Marzano, 2003), particularly as a minimum level of competence in CM may underpin development in other areas of pedagogy (Emmer and Stough, 2001). CM is described by Fowler and Saraplia (2010: 94) as the 'greatest concern of most teachers, especially those who have not yet begun their careers in education'. Significantly, Fowler and Saraplia (2010: 94) also argue that 'classroom management is just as important to students as it is to teachers'. To these observations we can add the quite startling claim by Wang, Haertel, and Walberg (1994, cited in Martin et al., 2007–2008: 11) that effective CM is at least as important as student ability in determining student achievement. However, while the importance of CM is generally recognised, it is often treated as an atheoretical aspect of teacher education, an aspect which merely involves practical techniques to maintain discipline and to organise learners and resources in the classroom. Perhaps because it is seen as an atheoretical aspect of teacher education, and perhaps also because CM is not measurable, there has been little research in the area (Martin et al., 2007–2008). Although CM may sometimes be portrayed as an atheoretical domain, little more than a 'bag of tricks', the argument of this chapter is that when we look closely at how CM is actually defined and described by different commentators, it becomes both more complex and more interesting. It can even be said that views of CM reflect methodological and perhaps broader educational beliefs. In this chapter we look first at definitions of CM and then at categorisations and inventories of CM skills. Following that, we present our own research into teachers' perceptions of CM skills and their views of whether these skills can be trained. Finally, we discuss how, in the light of the evidence, CM might be approached on teacher training courses.

Key issues

Defining classroom management

To show how views of the scope and nature of CM can differ, we now present six different definitions of CM with a brief commentary on the implications of each definition (we unashamedly use some internet sources, as a vox pop view of CM is important – we want to know how the term is generally understood).

Definition 1

Classroom management refers to the wide variety of skills and techniques that teachers use to keep students organized, orderly, focused, attentive, on task, and academically productive during a class. When classroom-management strategies are executed effectively, teachers minimize the behaviors that impede learning for both individual students and groups of students, while maximizing the behaviors that facilitate or enhance learning. Generally speaking, effective teachers tend to display strong classroom-management skills, while the hallmark of the inexperienced or less effective teacher is a disorderly classroom filled with students who are not working or paying attention.

(www.edglossary.org/classroom-management/)

This definition draws attention to the central role of CM skills in a teacher's repertoire. However, the phrase, 'When classroom-management strategies are executed effectively', seems to imply that there is a fixed set of techniques which simply need to be implemented. It is also interesting that the negative goal, 'minimize the behaviors that impede learning', appears before the positive goal, 'maximizing the behaviors that facilitate or enhance learning'. We see too the fear of a 'disorderly' classroom.

Definition 2

Classroom management is the term educators use to describe methods of preventing misbehavior and dealing with it if it arises. In other words, it is the techniques teachers use to maintain control in the classroom. Classroom management is one of the most feared parts of teaching for new teachers. For the students, lack of effective classroom management can mean that learning is reduced in the classroom. For the teacher, it can cause unhappiness and stress and eventually lead to individuals leaving the teaching profession.

(www.thoughtco.com/definition-of-classroom-management-773)

It would be difficult to find a more negative view of CM than this. CM is essentially seen as a set of preventive techniques to quell incipient rebellion. Fear, unhappiness and stress for the teacher loom large in this view. This definition strongly suggests that views of what constitutes CM are deeply influenced by the teaching context (e.g. primary, secondary or adult education). You will not need exactly the same set of skills to manage a class of unruly adolescents as you will to manage a class of well-motivated adults.

Definition 3

Classroom management is defined as the methods and strategies an educator uses to maintain a classroom environment that is conducive to student success and learning. Although there are many pedagogical strategies involved in managing a classroom, a common denominator is making sure that students feel they are in an environment that allows them to achieve.

*(http://education.gov.gy/web/index.php/teachers/tips-for-teaching/
item/1754-classroom-management-definition)*

This definition provides a stark contrast to Definition 2 above as it takes an enabling view of CM. It also refers to the potentially wide range of strategies a teacher can draw upon, stressing that the main role of such strategies is to promote learner achievement rather than simply keep order.

Definition 4

the actions teachers take to create an environment that supports and facilitates both academic and social emotional learning

Everstone and Weinstein (2006, cited in Rahimia & Asadollahia, 2012: 43).

As was the case with Definition 3, this definition sees CM as essentially a facilitative skill and with the phrase 'social emotional learning' adds an affective dimension to CM, a dimension you cannot approach armed only with mechanical techniques. In this approach, CM is used to shape students into emotionally intelligent and responsible citizens of the future.

Definition 5

Classroom management involves both decisions and actions. The actions are what is done in the classroom – e.g. rearranging the chairs. The decisions are about whether to do these actions, when to do them, how to do them, who will do them etc. The essential basic skill for classroom management is therefore to be able to recognize options available to you, to make appropriate decisions between these options, and to turn them into effective and efficient actions. As you grow in experience your awareness of possible options will grow.

Scrivener (1994: 9)

Scrivener's (1994) definition takes us beyond the notion of CM as a closed set of trained techniques, portraying CM as a complex decision-making process with a range of options available to the teacher. This range of options, Scrivener (1994) argues, is not a closed set – the range itself can evolve with experience. Scrivener (1994) goes on to make the following remark about CM:

Classroom decisions and actions are also greatly determined by the teacher's own attitudes, intentions, beliefs and values. What do you believe about learning? What is important for you in learning? What is your genuine feeling towards your students?

This comment suggests that, far from being a fixed, agreed, value-neutral set of behaviour management techniques, CM, and the decisions it entails, are value-laden. The way this view is expressed suggests that CM values are universal rather than context-related.

Definition 6

Classroom management refers to creating safe and stimulating learning environment (sic). This term combines the teacher's personality, his/her abilities and professional conduct designed to bring all of his/her professional roles, as well as the processes that take place in a group of students and the results of these processes.

(Djigic and Stojiljkovic, 2011: 820)

This is probably the broadest definition of all those we have considered thus far portraying classroom management as a multi-faceted domain of pedagogy. It is not quite clear what 'safe' means in this context, whether literally physically safe or emotionally secure, but it is particularly interesting that the teacher's *personality* is overtly brought into the equation, thus distancing us even further from a simple mechanistic view of CM. The notion of what constitutes CM is sensitive to teaching context and, as Thornbury (2017: 34) points out, how we conceive CM may depend on the kind of activities that take place in a particular classroom:

> Management is particularly important in large and diverse classes … and in lessons where the focus is on activities, such as tasks, as opposed to more lecture-type lesson formats.

The implication of this remark is that CM is sensitive to methodology. Given, for example, the role of varied activities in communicative language teaching, it can be argued that CM in language teaching may be particularly challenging in this context.

Broad and narrow views of classroom management

Through a consideration of various definitions, we have established that the scope of CM is difficult to pin down. It is possible to take a narrow view that CM is essentially about organising and controlling learners' behaviour, or a broad view that it is about fostering a classroom atmosphere optimally conducive to learning, or even to developing social and emotional skills in students. At its narrowest, CM is seen merely as a matter of maintaining order; it is, as the following definition by Doyle (1985: 31) clearly shows, problem-oriented: 'Classroom management refers to the actions teachers take to solve the problem of order in classrooms'. Narrower views of CM include, and may be limited to, obvious organisational techniques such as arranging the physical layout of the room and giving instructions for classroom activities. Arguably, however, even these basic techniques are not value-free. Clarity of instructions, for example, is obviously a *sine qua non* for any teacher of anything, anywhere, and so might appear at first sight to be value-free. There is, however, the question of the tone in which instructions are given: the same instruction can be given in a peremptory, engaging or hesitant manner. Tone, we would argue, relates to affective concerns of CM such as motivating learners, establishing rapport and maintaining discipline. The clearest of instructions are of little value if given with so little conviction that the learners are disinclined to enact them, or even listen to them. There is also the question of whether instructions are given in L1 or L2, which reflects the contentious issue of the role of L1 in the communicative classroom. Organising the layout of a classroom may at first sight seem to be a value-free CM skill, but even the basic configuration of the room, whether, for example, the classroom is arranged with a focus on the teacher (e.g. rows) or with students facing each other is indicative of methodology and underlying values. If we want to change the layout, it is probably to accommodate different activities, especially pair work, group work and kinaesthetic activities. This CM skill, in other words, carries tacit methodological values. Similarly, monitoring activities to help and prompt learners while they are engaged in some kind of activity is only an important skill if learners are involved in individual, pair or group work rather than just whole class work. There is again a tacit methodological statement: a 'chalk and talk' approach would be undemanding with regard to layout of the room and monitoring.

The broader view of CM is even more overtly value-laden than the narrow view. If we consider, for example, the chapter sub-headings below from Scrivener's (2012) book on CM, we can see that each one of them clearly implies certain pedagogic values:

Being yourself

Showing your real personality, rather than adopting a teacher persona, implies, we would argue, an egalitarian, humanistic classroom approach in an environment where discipline is not an issue. While it is certainly true that good teachers come in all shapes and sizes as far as personality is concerned, that is not the same as saying that any personality is suitable for teaching. It is also open to question how far anyone enacts his/her genuine personality in the classroom. There is an element of role play in teaching and the person who appears in the classroom is based on a true character, but perhaps with certain traits deliberately foregrounded and others temporarily concealed. In other words, teachers *perform* an identity in the classroom.

Establishing and maintaining rapport

Rapport is about establishing a warm working relationship, but are warm teacher–student relationships regarded as necessary in social contexts where teachers are seen as figures of authority? Being a figure of authority and having a good rapport with the class are not mutually exclusive, of course, but the two qualities may conflict.

A learner-centred approach

There are huge educational assumptions underpinning this principle, which may well conflict with local educational traditions where the teacher-fronted classroom is the norm.

Eliciting

Trying to draw contributions from learners is a core learner-centred technique in communicative language teaching, and a staple on pre-service teacher training courses such as the Cambridge CELTA, but it is not obvious that it is a core technique in contexts with large classes and a teacher-centred tradition.

Permitting emotion

This principle fits well with an affective, humanistic approach, but would be entirely inappropriate in many settings.

Other techniques

The following cluster of techniques and principles listed by Scrivener (2012) also implies a communicative approach to teaching in a learner-centred classroom: encouraging students to speak; making pairs and groups; encouraging quieter learners to speak in pairs and groups; encouraging students to use English; justifying pair and group work to students.

These remarks are in no sense a criticism of Scrivener's (2012) classroom management topics – they simply serve to reinforce the idea that it is difficult to talk about classroom management without implying certain pedagogic values.

Classroom management styles

We have thus far portrayed conceptions of classroom management as lying on a continuum running from narrow to broad. In terms of classroom management style, it has also been conceived as lying on a continuum, in this case running from non-interventionist to interventionist with an interactive style between these two poles. As described by Aliakbari and Heidarzadi (2015), interventionists are the most directive and much concerned with discipline, while non-interventionists are the least directive and least concerned with discipline. In between, we find the interactionists. The style of the interactionists is described by Djigic and Stojiljkovic (2011: 827):

> [The] Teacher who practices interactionist style encourages interaction and cooperation into the classroom, respects student's personality, appreciates the initiatives, interests and needs of students, uses teaching methods and materials that obtain full activity of the whole class during the lessons, designs activities well focused to learning goals, implement[s] procedures to build positive discipline based on self-control and responsibility of students.

Two other categorisations of classroom management techniques and qualities are summarised by Djigic and Stojiljkovic (2011). Watkins and Wagner (2000) described two categories of CM: integrative behaviour and directive behaviour. Integrative behaviour involves motivating the class to work towards common goals and ensuring that each member of the class has a stake in these goals. Directive behaviour involves techniques to conduct the learning activities which will lead to these goals. Four categories of CM are described by Bru, Stephens and Torsheim (2002: 1) providing academic support, 2) providing emotional support, 3) careful and simultaneous monitoring of the entire class, and 4) conflict management.

Inventories of CM

CM has been broken down even further into inventories of classroom actions. Two examples of this kind of inventory are *The Attitudes & Beliefs on Classroom Control Inventory (ABCC)* (Martin et al., 2007–2008) and *The Preferred Teacher's Management Styles Survey* (Fowler and Saraplia, 2010). The ABCC was originally divided into three domains: instructional management, people management, and behaviour management. These domains are described thus (Martin et al., 2007–2008: 11):

> Dimension one, instructional management, includes aspects such as overseeing seatwork, organizing daily routines, and distributing materials. The people management dimension pertains to what teachers believe about students as persons and what teachers do to develop the teacher-student relationship. Although similar to discipline, the behavior management dimension is different in that it focuses on pre-planned efforts to prevent misbehavior rather than the teacher's response to it.

However, on later reflection, Martin et al. (2007–2008) felt it was actually possible to collapse people management and behaviour management into one domain.

While there is quite an emphasis on behaviour management and discipline in both these inventories, it is striking that there are only three or four criteria in common, further evidence that views of what constitutes CM differ.

The 'trainability' of CM

The way we conceive CM must have a strong effect on how far we consider it is trainable. If, for example, we see personality as an important aspect of CM, we would presumably not see this aspect as trainable. A consideration of the literature has taken us in some respects well beyond a mechanistic view of classroom management. We can go even further: Marzano and Marzano

(2003: 6) describe teacher–student *relationships* as 'the keystone for all other aspects of classroom management'. It is, in other words, the affective which underpins the effective. For his part, Lutzker (2012), takes us about as far away from a mechanistic view of teaching as it is possible to get with his claim that teaching should be seen as an art form. The justification for this claim is that teachers' ability to take appropriate actions as classroom events unfold can reach the level of 'grace' if guided by a kind of informed intuition:

> The shifting, unpredictable dynamics of a classroom situation and the requisite abilities to make immediate and appropriate choices in such a manner that 'grace' in teaching can be achieved are invariably dependent on the human capacity for intuition.

It is intriguing that, in pursuit of this notion of 'grace' in teaching, the teacher development courses Lutzker (2012) describes require participants at a given point to improvise on stage armed only with a few simple props: a compulsory clown's red nose, a chair and a blanket. The effects of this novel form of teacher development are summarised by Lutzker (2012: 55) thus:

> The themes that consistently reappear are a heightened receptivity to the moment, a feeling of flow, new dimensions of contact with others, an acceptance of one's self, and a deep feeling of openness and liberation. Despite the fleeting and ephemeral qualities of such moments, participants were generally able to articulate what they had experienced.

While Lutzker speaks of 'grace', Atkinson and Claxton (2000) stress the important role of intuition in the classroom. Intuition in this context is defined by Claxton (2000: 49) as 'a loose-knit family of "ways of knowing" which are less articulate and explicit than normal reasoning and discourse'. Such intuition can, Claxton (2000: 50) argues, be developed through 'explicit teaching and modelling', but it is certainly one of the more intangible teaching qualities.

In terms of the trainability of CM, it seems reasonable to assume that concise and clear wording of instructions can be trained – we have certainly found this to be the case in our own experience of pre-service training. Similarly, adjusting the layout of the room for specific activities is little more than commonsense allied to a little experience. However, the clearest of instructions will be of no value if nobody is listening, and the optimum layout will not help if the learners are not engaged by the activity. A prerequisite for giving effective instructions is the ability to command attention, which in turn depends on the intangible, and probably less trainable, quality of classroom presence. Advice can, of course, be given about position in the classroom, voice projection and even posture, but there is certainly an argument that classroom presence is more than the sum of the parts. The question arises as to whether the X factor of classroom presence is trainable and, if it is, whether teacher educators are the best people to train it. In one or two cases in our experience of pre-service training we did not know how to help the teacher to develop the elusive quality of classroom presence and wondered whether a drama coach might have been better suited to the task.

The teacher also has to motivate the learners. Again, certain tips can be given e.g. use praise and encouragement; set manageable goals; personalise activities, but the ability to communicate commitment to and belief in what you are doing is a vital but perhaps less 'trainable' aspect of motivating learners. Closely related to the ability to motivate is the ability to establish rapport. We have found ourselves giving advice to teachers, particularly on pre-service teaching courses, on the following lines: make eye contact; smile; use learners' names; talk to the learners before the lesson. Such advice, we think, should lead to a reasonable working relationship between the teacher and the learners, provided, of course, that the learners understand and see the value of what they are learning. Will it, however, lead to a *productive* rapport where learners feel confident to take risks, to ask questions and to use the L2 in personal ways?

Our research

As we have seen, CM is a difficult construct to pin down, and its scope varies widely in the teacher education literature. But how is it seen by practising teachers and teacher trainers? To answer these questions, we examined a selection of teaching practice (TP) feedback sheets from pre-service (CELTA) and in-service (Delta) teacher training courses and also carried out a small-scale survey of practising teachers.

Teacher survey

Our survey aimed to find out what core skills teachers associated with CM and which CM skills they believed to be trainable. We compiled a list of 12 potential CM skills/ techniques, based on our experience of teaching, teacher training and the literature sources cited above. The link to our online survey was emailed to a range of (mostly experienced) teachers and teacher trainers in our professional networks. It asked participants to rank each skill or technique on a scale of 1 to 5 in terms of a) 'coreness' as a CM skill, and b) trainability, and to answer a small number of open questions in relation to:

- other skills or abilities included in the area of classroom management;
- the most important things participants learned about classroom management from their training and their experience;
- how far classroom management is influenced by a teacher's attitudes and beliefs.

We received 45 responses to our survey. We ranked the potential skills according to how core they were in the eyes of our participants. We imposed a 60 per cent cut-off point for our criteria: if more than 60 per cent of participants gave the skill a 4 or 5, it was considered core, or trainable. This cut-off point is, of course, arbitrary, but it seemed a sensible place to draw the line and enabled us to draw some tentative conclusions.

TP feedback sheets

The feedback sheets we had at our disposal were too numerous for us to analyse in detail in the time available; another problem was that many of these feedback sheets had been written by a small number of teacher trainers at one centre. Since we wanted to include feedback on a variety of trainees of varying abilities and at different stages in their teaching careers, at different centres, and written by a different teacher trainers, we used a purposive sampling technique (Cohen et al, 2000). This meant in practice that we looked at the selection of feedback sheets available to us and, using our experience and knowledge of the trainees, trainers and centres, selected feedback sheets representing as much variety as possible. We also deliberately chose feedback sheets from different stages of courses. We decided to concentrate on the summary section of the feedback sheets only, to avoid repetition and to focus on the areas prioritised by trainers.

Our purposive sampling resulted in a selection of 11 CELTA and 11 Delta feedback sheets; we coded the data in our feedback sheets against the 12 potential CM skills/techniques from our questionnaire and counted the number of comments related to each skill/technique. We also looked at the comments from a qualitative point of view.

There was clearly some overlap between some of our categories, for example, adopting different roles includes some of the other skills; for example, error correction overlaps with making on the spot decisions.

We inevitably had to make decisions about how broadly to interpret our categories before coding the data, and in some cases took a broad view. For example, we included comments regarding engaging students, personalisation and motivation in the 'rapport' category.

Results and discussion

Due to our small data sample, our results cannot be taken as conclusive or generalisable, but they raise a number of issues for teacher training/education, and highlight the need for future research in this area.

Table 21.1 presents our 12 potential CM skills/techniques, ranked according to their 'coreness', and presents the data related to each one. In column 1, percentages given are for the number of respondents who considered the skill/technnique to be a core aspect of CM. In column 2, percentages are given for the number of respondents who considered the skill/technique to be trainable. Column 3 gives the number of comments related to this skill/technique in the CELTA feedback sheets we sampled. Column 4 gives the number of comments related to this skill/technique on Delta feedback sheets.

Table 21.1 Twelve potential CM skills/techniques

Skill/ technique	% core	% trainable	CELTA 'mentions'	Delta 'mentions'
The ability to set up pair/groupwork	93	84	24	4
Monitoring activities effectively	91	64	9	1
The ability to keep discipline	87	38	3	1
The ability to establish rapport	87	51	9	8
The ability to make on the spot decisions in response to classroom events	85	18	6	11
The ability to elicit responses from the learners	80	68	11	2
An effective classroom presence/ teacher persona	71	18	7	1
Arrangement of physical features of the classroom	67	80	5	2
Giving praise and encouragement	67	58	0	1
The ability to adopt different roles in the classroom	65	18	3	0
Effective use of the whiteboard	51	87	6	1
Range of correction techniques	37	80	3	1

The ability to set up pair/groupwork

There is a near unanimous verdict that the ability to set up pair and group work is a core CM skill. What is interesting here is that one of the more methodologically loaded criteria, which seems to indicate a commitment to CLT, is seen as central by so many respondents. There is an unspoken assumption that pair and groupwork have an important role in the classroom. This probably reflects a strong but tacit privileging of CLT on CELTA and Delta courses and among our respondents, many of whom may have trained as teachers on such courses.

There were few specific comments in the qualitative data referring to setting up pair and groupwork, but it is no surprise that there are many comments which relate to giving instructions (which we included in our coding of this category) in CELTA feedback. As exemplified in the sample of CELTA and Delta feedback comments below, trainees are often encouraged to simplify instructions and to use instruction checking questions (ICQs).

- Use ICQs for simpler tasks and do examples for more complex ones
- You need to plan and script instructions for TP2…
- Slow down a little and try to use fewer words in your instructions

- Elicit examples and demonstrate activities, rather than wordy explanations (though you got better with this as the lesson progressed)

As this CM skill is seen as central, it is fortunate that the vast majority of respondents regard it as trainable, as indeed it has proven to be in our experience.

Monitoring activities effectively

Given the importance attached to pair and groupwork, it is to be expected that monitoring is regarded as a core CM skill. However, there is less certainty about whether it is trainable. As monitoring is a multi-purpose technique, it may well be that some aspects of it are seen as trainable while others are not. Monitoring to make sure learners are on task, for example, is fairly straightforward. Monitoring to make a note of errors or good examples of language use, however, requires 'on the spot' decision making, often involving a very good feel for both the level of the class and the individual learner. It is interesting in this respect that one respondent noted that she had learned from her CELTA course, 'To consider the purpose of classroom monitoring (why am I monitoring here, why am I putting them in pairs, etc)'. The two comments below from CELTA feedback involve both these aspects of monitoring: the simple procedure of confirming learners are doing what they are supposed to do and the more complex skill of differentiation in support and feedback:

- Sweep and zoom … do a quick 'sweep' first so you can be sure the ss have understood what to do.
- Your monitoring was good and you gave different help as ss needed it.

The ability to keep discipline

The ability to keep discipline would probably be rated as *the* core skill in some contexts e.g. teaching boisterous teenagers in a summer school, but even though most of our respondents taught adults it was still regarded as a key skill and drew a number of specific comments from respondents. One respondent, for example, commented that one of the most important things she had learned about CM from experience was, 'Maybe managing student interactions and behaviour – not letting a confident/able student dominate/making sure students are engaged and able/encouraged to contribute (not on phones)'. Another respondent stressed the need for teachers to have a conscious policy with regard to discipline:

'If dealing with students who are disruptive in class, it's important to have strategies in place to deal with different situations that might arise rather than just leaving this to chance'. There were very few comments in CELTA/Delta feedback relating to this issue, probably because the comments were made in an adult learning context.

There is a clear mismatch between perceived importance and perceived trainability for this facet of CM, although some respondents' comments could be interpreted as advice:

- Not applicable in many EFL contexts, but disciplinary/penalty system may be appropriate in a young learner context.
- To be firm but fair and allow follow through whether it's a promise or a threat/sanction.
- That the students don't have to 'like' you and it's okay to tell a student who is doing something that is not good for their/other students learning to stop it.
- I have learned the value of routines!

The ability to establish rapport

There is a very clear consensus that rapport is at the core of CM. A number of respondents stress the centrality of rapport to CM, as exemplified below:

- In some ways, I think a good rapport with the students is the key to good classroom management. If you have a good relationship with your students, they are more invested in the course and in the activities you are asking them to do.
- establishing rapport has by far been the most effective way for me to keep students both interested and working.

It was noticeable that respondents saw rapport not simply as a teacher–learner relationship but as vital among *the whole class* as part of group dynamics:

- managing classroom dynamics ... rapport between learners as opposed to building rapport with the teacher.

Another respondent drew attention to how complex the skill of developing constructive group dynamics can be, stressing the need to be 'a kind of UN mediator at times, especially in mixed nationality groups. Deflecting potential conflicts and engendering or creating an atmosphere of mutual respect and intercultural understanding and interest in class'.

Comments from CELTA and Delta feedback seem to reflect the fact that there are narrow and broad views of rapport. In the CELTA comments there are references to making small talk, personalisation, smiling, use of names and showing interest in the learners – aspects of rapport which all presuppose an informal relationship with learners. The Delta feedback comments below seem to reflect this broader view of rapport with references to inclusion and engagement of both groups and individuals.

- Rapport and inclusion of all the ss (strength)
- Responding effectively to learner contributions and showing a real interest in them.
- Full engagement of the learners ... both as a group and individually.

It is open to question whether these aspects would be feasible or desirable in cultural contexts where a certain distance is to be expected between the teacher and the learners. Class size might also have an impact on whether this informal kind of rapport can be achieved. That is not to say that a good rapport is impossible in such cases, but it may be different in kind and revolve more around motivation and mutual respect.

The rating for trainability (51 per cent) probably reflects that surface aspects of rapport *are* trainable e.g. use of names and smiling. Smiling sincerely and showing a genuine interest in learners are, however, obviously less trainable.

The ability to make on the spot decisions in response to classroom events

It is perhaps surprising, but also encouraging, to see this skill rated so highly as a key aspect of CM, as it is quite a sophisticated skill reflected in the fact there are more feedback comments at Delta level (where it is assessed explicitly) than CELTA level. The importance of developing the skill of responding flexibly in the classroom was noted by four respondents:

- Timing and pace are important aspects of classroom management – knowing when to stop an activity and when to keep it going.
- The ability to adapt. You might have planned a lesson, come in and the students just aren't in the right mood for that, and you have to change the way you're going to do things.
- The ability to deal with issues as they arise. Responding to learners' needs.
- Reacting to things as they arise – being flexible.

Many of the comments in CELTA and Delta feedback relate to adapting the plan and 'upgrading language' i.e. pushing learners to improve their output.

CELTA

- The main issue with the lesson was that there was not quite enough material to keep the faster ss purposefully busy, so think about how you could have extended the activities for them.

Delta

- Allow for more time to exploit learner output to further learning.
- Adapt the plan if required to help you implement it fully and allow more time for learner production and exploitation of learner output for consolidation.
- You noticed the learners' output and used it to upgrade their language.
- You were flexible with your plan when timing became a problem.

Despite being seen overwhelming as a core CM skill, and the fact that more comments were made in this CM category than any other on Delta feedback sheets, however, our respondents did not regard this key CM skill as trainable. One has to assume, then, that it is one of those skills which 'comes with experience'.

The ability to elicit responses from the learners

Elicitation is clearly seen as a central CM skill. In qualitative data, it is mentioned five times by respondents as a useful skill, but without any elaboration about what it entails and when it is useful. Elicitation was specifically mentioned 11 times in CELTA feedback. Though it appears to be a core part of a teacher's repertoire, there is arguably a danger that this technique can be both trained and applied indiscriminately, as illustrated in the CELTA feedback comment below in the phrase 'at every opportunity':

- Elicit even more at every opportunity rather than tell…

Respondents generally considered elicitation to be a trainable skill. As argued in the literature review, elicitation is a methodologically loaded technique as it presumes a learner-centred classroom rather than a teacher-fronted approach.

An effective classroom presence/teacher persona

We come here to another of the intangibles – classroom presence and persona. There is general agreement that is a core component of CM, and it is interesting that one respondent reported that she had developed the ability 'to *appear* confident'. There was great uncertainty, however, as to whether this quality is trainable. As with other skills with rapport, it may well be that this uncertainty reflects the idea that some aspects are trainable while others are not. We have found ourselves, for example, commenting in teaching practice feedback on position, posture and voice projection, which would all appear to be things that can be worked on. We also referred above to Lutzker's rather radical way of developing classroom presence through improvisation on stage. Nevertheless, respondents' uncertainty suggests that there is an X factor beyond the obvious points of advice we give.

Arrangement of physical features of the classroom

This CM skill, perhaps unsurprisingly, is regarded as quite important. One respondent commented on how the importance of this skill had become more apparent to her:

- I have come to realise more and more how important classroom layout and having easily movable furniture is. To be able to have a personalised learning environment and allow students their own spaces is wonderful.

It is interesting that two respondents saw the arrangement of physical features as linked with other classroom concerns:

- arrangement of groups and pairs according to students' needs, personalities, behaviours and relationships
- So, thinking about moving people into pairs/groups as well as thinking about why and what they will do in those situations.

Although the arrangement of physical features is a specific Delta criterion, it drew few specific comments in either Delta or CELTA feedback. Respondents saw this as a highly trainable skill.

Giving praise and encouragement

While this was a category closely associated with CM, it was not seen as a highly trainable skill, possibly because, like rapport, it is easy to train a teacher to say 'Well done' for example, but to give praise and encouragement with conviction and in response to an individual student's needs requires more skill and perhaps experience. Nevertheless, we were surprised to find only one brief comment at Delta level and no comments at all in the CELTA feedback summaries.

The ability to adopt different roles in the classroom

Most respondents agreed that the ability to adopt different roles in the classroom was a core CM skill, though there was also a distinct note of uncertainty among a significant number (29 per cent). There was little specific reference to different roles in the qualitative feedback, though there were two comments in response to the question about the link between attitudes/beliefs and classroom management.

- [classroom management] really does depend a lot on the teacher's belief of their role in the classroom and that of their learners
- ... teachers all manage their classrooms in different ways depending on how they perceive their and students' role

There were few explicit comments about teacher roles in CELTA or Delta feedback, apart from the following question in CELTA:

- What is your role as ss speak?

There was also a great deal of uncertainty as to whether this CM skill is trainable or not, with fewer than 20 per cent seeing it as definitely trainable and 56 per cent unsure.

Effective use of the whiteboard

This is another example of a CM skill which is regarded as highly trainable but not a particularly core skill. A number of feedback comments related to using the whiteboard for language focus work, for example:

- Think about how you can divide [the board] into sections, and use colour to mark stress, word class and so on.
- Useful vocab work ... marking word classes.
- Mark the stress on the items you write on the board.

Range of correction techniques

Given that error correction is a contested area even within CLT, it is not surprising that there is no consensus as to whether it is a core CM skill or not. A few respondents commented that they had improved their error correction techniques but they did not give any further details. One or two tutors stressed the value of delayed error correction.

- Delayed error correction. Good.
- Allow more time for ... delayed error correction.

Conclusion

Perhaps unsurprisingly, all but two of the categories were viewed as core CM skills, if we apply our 60 cut-off point. According to our data, there is no clear correlation between coreness and trainability, even if we take a narrow view of CM; many of the categories our respondents considered core were not considered trainable, for example, discipline, rapport, and presence/persona. However, we would argue that within each facet of CM, there may be *aspects* that are trainable (e.g. smiling, using names, making eye contact to establish rapport), and other more complex and less trainable aspects (e.g. responding genuinely to individual students, motivating students) which are linked to much wider emotional intelligence or interpersonal skills.

However, it is our experience that teacher trainers often shy away from tackling these less tangible, more complex aspects of classroom management, perhaps because they believe themselves to be ill equipped to deal with them (as we did when we considered drama coaching would be appropriate for some of our trainees), or perhaps because they consider these personality-related aspects of CM to be beyond the remit of the teacher trainer, or even fixed. However, it could be argued that these more complex, personality related aspects actually form the *basis* of the more easily trainable aspects – the *effective* depending on the *affective* – and for this reason, it is within our remit as teacher trainers. As one of our respondents put it, 'In some ways, I think a good rapport with the students is the key to good classroom management.' If this is the case, then the basis of CM consists of the complex, personality-based aspects, and the more straightforward mechanical techniques need to be built on this foundation.

More research is needed to investigate the trainability of CM skills, perhaps incorporating the use of a broader range of techniques not traditionally associated with ELT teacher training, such as drama techniques and voice coaching. However, if we were to train these affective aspects explicitly, training courses might need to be adapted, and many teacher trainers might themselves need further training.

It is impossible to confine CM to a 'bag of tricks', not least because teaching is a complex human activity and both context and beliefs about teaching will affect a teacher's management of the classroom. As one respondent put it, 'Regardless of what a teacher learns during training, he/she may interpret techniques differently depending on his/her attitudes and beliefs, which could include replicating the environment which he/she prefers as a student.' This has certainly been our experience as teacher trainers, and takes us back to the belief that CM is not, and cannot be, a value-free activity.

While there can be no doubt that some training in basic techniques can be beneficial for trainees, we have to ask ourselves whether it is useful to delineate CM from other aspects of teaching, or if CM is really about creating an optimum (context-sensitive) learning environment/ atmosphere. One respondent said 'the best is invisible'; our challenge as teacher trainers, educators and researchers is to find new ways to put the invisible under the spotlight.

Further reading

Evertson, C. and Winstein, C. S. (eds) (2011) *Handbook of Classroom Management: Research, Practice, and Contemporary Issues*. Abingdon: Routledge.

Lutzker, P. (2012) 'Developing Artistry in Teaching: New Approaches to Teacher Education'. *RoSE Journal*, 3(1) 52–58.

Scrivener, J. (2012) *Effective Classroom Management*. Cambridge: Cambridge University Press.

References

Aliakbari, M. and Heidarzadi, M. (2015) 'The Relationship Between EFL Teachers' Beliefs and Actual Practices of Classroom Management'. *Cogent Education*, 2 1–13.

Atkinson, T. and Claxton, G. (2000) 'Introduction', in Atkinson, T. and Claxton, G. (eds) *The Intuitive Practitioner*. Maidenhead: Open University Press: 1–13.

Ayse Canera, H. and Tertemizb, N. (2015) 'Beliefs, Attitudes and Classroom Management: A Study on Prospective Teachers'. *Procedia – Social and Behavioural Sciences*, 186 155–160.

Bru, E., Stephens, P. and Torsheim, T. (2002) 'Students' Perceptions of Class Management and Reports of Their Own Misbehavior'. *Journal of School Psychology*, 40(4) 287–307.

Claxton, G. (2000) 'The anatomy of intuition', in Atkinson, T. and Claxton, G. (eds) *The Intuitive Practitioner*. Maidenhead: Open University Press: 15–32.

Cohen, L., Manion, L. and Morrison, K. (2000) *Research Methods in Education*. London: Routledge.

Djigic, G. and Stojiljkovic, S. (2011) 'Classroom Management Styles, Classroom Climate and School Achievement'. *Procedia – Social and Behavioral Sciences*, 29 819–828.

Doyle, W. (1985) 'Recent Research on Classroom Management: Implications for Teacher Preparation'. *Journal of Education*, 36(3) 31–35.

Emmer, E. and Stough, L. (2001) 'Classroom Management: A Critical Part of Educational Psychology, with Implications for Teacher Education'. *Educational Psychologist*, 36(2) 103–112.

Erdogan, M. and Kurt, A. (2015) 'A Review of Research on Classroom Management in Turkey'. *Procedia – Social and Behavioral Sciences*, 186 9–14.

Fowler, J. and Saraplia, O. (2010) 'Telling ELT Tales out of School Classroom Management: What ELT Students Expect'. *Procedia – Social and Behavioural Sciences*, 3 94–97.

Harmer, J. (2007) *The Practice of English Language Teaching*. London: Pearson Longman.

Lutzker, P. (2012) 'Developing Artistry in Teaching: New Approaches to Teacher Education'. *Research on Steiner Education*, 3(1) 52–58.

Martin, N. K., Yin, Z. and Mayall, H. (2007–8) 'The Attitudes and Beliefs on Classroom Control Inventory Revised and Revisited: A Continuation of Construct Validation'. *Journal of Classroom Interaction*, 42(2) 11–20.

Marzano, R. and Marzano, J. (2003) 'The Key to Classroom Management'. *Educational Leadership*, 61(3) 6–13.

Rahimia, M. and Asadollahia, F. (2012) 'EFL Teachers' Classroom Management Orientations: Investigating the Role of Individual Differences and Contextual Variables'. *Procedia – Social and Behavioural Sciences*, 31 43–48.

Scrivener, J. (1994) *Learning Teaching*. Oxford: Heinemann.

Scrivener, J. (2012) *Effective Classroom Management*. Cambridge: Cambridge University Press.

Smith, C. and Laslett, R. (1993) *Effective Classroom Management*. London: Routledge.

Thornbury, S. (2017) *The New A to Z of ELT*. Oxford: Macmillan.

Wang, M. C., Haertel, G. D. and Walberg, H. J. (1994) 'What helps students learn?' *Educational Leadership*, 51(4) 74–79.

Watkins, C. and Wagner, P. (2000) *Improving School Behaviour*. London: Chapman.

22
Teacher cognition and teacher expertise

Li Li

Introduction

Over the past decade, research in teacher cognition has become an important agenda for second language teacher education (Johnson, 2009a; Li, 2017). This level of interest confirms that the field has changed from a relatively new and undeveloped area into an important and well-researched field of inquiry, which promotes understandings of classroom instruction, pedagogical effectiveness and teacher development (Li, 2017). In this chapter, I will provide a survey of the field of teacher cognition, focusing on the development of language teacher cognition research and approaches to the investigation of teacher cognition. I then move on to explore the construct of teacher expertise, drawing on theoretical and practical understanding of expert and novice. I will also discuss implications of teacher cognition research.

Teacher cognition research

Studying teacher cognition is important in understanding teachers' perceptions and decisions, teaching and learning, the dynamics of the classroom, effective pedagogy and teacher learning. Research suggests that teacher cognition directly affects both teacher perceptions and judgements of teaching and learning interactions in the classroom, which result in different behaviour in classrooms (Clark and Peterson, 1986; Clark and Yinger, 1987; Borg, 2006; Li and Walsh, 2011). More accurately, teacher cognition heavily influences the way teachers plan their lessons, the decisions they make in the teaching process and what kind of learning they promote in the classroom (Pajares, 1992; Li, 2012). To date, discussions have appeared in the literature on the degree of 'match' between learners' and teachers' beliefs (e.g. Peacock, 1999; Cohen and Fass, 2001); on beliefs about subject matters (for example grammar and grammar teaching; literacy) (e.g. Andrews, 2003, 2006, 2007; Svalberg and Askham, 2014); on changes in teachers' beliefs (e.g. Peacock, 2001; Mattheoudakis, 2007); on the influence of beliefs on teachers' classroom behaviour and the convergence of practice from beliefs (e.g. Breen et al., 2001; see Basturkmen, 2012 for a review); and on the influence of beliefs on both pre-service and in-service teacher education programmes (Busch, 2010). The recent development of teacher cognition research also sees more interests in intercultural competence (Llurda and Lasagabaster, 2010; Young and Sachdev, 2011) and technology integration (e.g. Brannan and Bleistein, 2012; Li, 2014).

Clark and Peterson's (1986) model of teacher thought process is perhaps the earliest framework tapping into the nature of teacher cognition and providing an agenda in researching this area. The model of teacher thought and action depicts two domains that are importantly involved in the process of teaching, namely teachers' thought processes, and teachers' actions and their observable effects. In Clark and Peterson's model of teachers' thought process, there are three main elements, namely teachers' planning (pre-active and post-active thoughts), teachers' interactive thoughts and decisions, and teachers' theories and beliefs. Research has shown a clear distinction between teachers' planning and teachers' interactive thoughts and decisions; in other words, the differences between what teachers think/plan to do and what teachers actually do when they are interacting with students in class (e.g. Bailey, 1996). So from this perspective, teaching is an 'improvisational performance' (Richards, 1998: 74; Li, 2013) that requires teachers to make constant interactive decisions. As a result of interacting with students and assessment of the activities they design and materials they use with students, they adjust their teaching accordingly.

Woods (1996) develops a multidimensional cycle of planning and decision-making within teaching. He further proposes a model to signify the evolving system of beliefs, assumptions and knowledge (BAK) that recursively informs/is informed by the context of teaching. Unlike others, Woods reduces the distinction between knowledge and beliefs rather than highlighting it, as he puts it 'in order to take appropriate action, people need to understand; and to understand they need knowledge about the world and specifically about the situation they are in' (ibid.: 59).

Borg (2006) proposes a framework of teacher cognition, how it develops and the interwoven and interactive relationships between cognition and teacher learning, as well as their classroom practices. Borg (2003: 81) terms teacher cognition the 'unobservable cognitive dimension of teaching – what teachers know, believe, and think'. This framework presents a schematic conceptualisation of cognition and its relationships with important factors in teachers' lives, including their schooling experience, their professional development, their classroom teaching and the specific contexts they are in, with a particular focus on the role of teacher (professional) learning and contextual factors in researching teacher cognition.

Approaches to the investigation of teacher cognition

Investigating cognition can be very difficult since personal theories may be subconscious so that teachers might be unable to articulate them. The difficulty also lies in the different understandings and conceptualisations of teacher cognition. As reviewed by Li (2017), a variety of terminologies have been used to describe teacher cognition, and therefore different methods were used to explore the concept, which result in different conclusions. So far, little work has been done to discuss methodological choices of teacher cognition research. Among the very few studies, Borg (2006) presents four categories of data collection: methods – self-report instruments, verbal commentary, observation, and reflective writing – and provides a detailed review of empirical studies following those methods. Borg (2012) compared research methods adopted in 25 articles published in 2011 on the focus of the study, context and participants, the research stance, data collection and analysis. Li (2017) reviewed relevant research studies and proposed four main strands of research methodologies employed in researching teacher cognition.

The cognitive approach is closely linked to a cognitive perspective on teacher cognition viewing the construct as fixed, prior-defined assumptions held by the teacher. Cross-sectional research or tests are often used to discover teachers' assumptions, beliefs and perceptions. The underlying position of such an approach is that teacher cognition is stable, fixed, and can be described or elicited by self-report instruments. This approach also indicates that beliefs or assumptions held by the teacher might be contradictory, therefore the motive of conducting research could be fixing teachers' understanding or illuminating misconceptions. Cross-sectional research often adopts Likert-scale questionnaires, like BALLI (Horwitz, 1985), the Beliefs Inventory (Johnson, 1992), or a scenario-based questionnaire (e.g. Borg, 2006), or tests to investigate teachers' knowledge (e.g. Andrews, 1999, 2003; Andrews and McNeil, 2005). Although in some research, qualitative methods such as interviews and diaries are used, it is very often used to explain the reasons for discrepancies and mismatch.

In recognition of the influence of contextual factors on teachers' beliefs, the contextual approach has become more popular in contemporary research. It adopts different methods of data collection including ethnographic classroom observations, diaries, discourse analysis and naturalistic interviews (see Bernat and Gvozdenko, 2005 for further discussion). Case study is the most frequently used methodology to explain 'why' and 'how' questions in researching teacher cognition. Despite the different methodological choices, many studies in this tradition still focus on exploring the differences between teachers' conceptions and their practice, with a particular emphasis on explaining why and how they differ. Farrell and Lim (2005) investigated and compared the beliefs with actual classroom practices of two experienced English teachers with regards to grammar teaching in a primary school in Singapore, using interviews, observation and students' written work. In both cases, they found that strong beliefs were held about the importance of grammar regarding writing, and also for both speech and listening comprehension. Li and Walsh (2011) compared the beliefs and classroom practices of a novice and an experienced teacher, using interviews and classroom interaction. Their study suggests that teachers' beliefs and their classroom practices exist in a complex and complicated relationship, a 'symbiotic relationship': beliefs both shape and are shaped by ensuing interactions.

Influenced by interactionist perspectives and discursive psychological views of cognition, ethnomethodology, including interactional analysis and CA are sometimes used. There are a few studies on teacher cognition investigating the concept through the lens of classroom interaction (e.g. Li and Walsh, 2011; Li, 2012; Li, 2017), adopting a broadly discourse analytic perspective. The discourse approach brings 'interaction' to the centre of teachers' professional lives and views teacher cognition as a context-specific and public-displayed understanding. Li and Walsh (2011) have argued the case for interactional analysis in researching teacher cognition. They claim:

> Teachers' stated beliefs (from the interview data) and their interactions with students (from the classroom observation data) were compared as a means of gaining insights into the complex relationship between what teachers report as belief and their interactions while teaching. Put differently, this procedure allowed us to compare what teachers say they do while teaching with what they actually do as evidenced in their interactions. The procedures used in this study also provided us with an opportunity to reflect on the extent to which classroom interaction data can enhance understandings of teachers' beliefs.
>
> *(2011: 44–45)*

Discursive psychology also uses conversation analysis to understand how, why and where everyday talk mobilises psychological concepts (memory, cognition, attitudes, affect, beliefs, identity, conception and motivation). In researching teacher cognition, Morton (2012) showed the participant teacher did not have the pre-existing belief that her students had 'misconceptions' but she produced and established this belief as the result of interaction with the researcher who was doing quite a lot of work in 'pressing' her. The analysis showed that this kind of belief or conception of students' conceptual status can be specified or partially re-specified as socio-interactive and discursive. Morton thus argues for the importance of raising teachers' awareness of the impact of their uses of classroom talk, 'from the broader level of a communicative approach to the more micro "action" level of specific interventions in teaching' (2012: 109). Li (2017) conceptualises teacher cognition as fluid and changing, which she terms cognition-in-interaction. It is a special kind of psychological reality – not the one defined by the mental state or process, but by the participants orienting practically in an ongoing interaction. Using conversation analysis, she shows how teachers display their understandings and conceptions during ongoing interaction with the people around them.

Having provided an overview of teacher cognition research, I will now focus on one aspect of teacher cognition, teacher expertise, for an in-depth treatment.

Teacher expertise

In recent years, teacher expertise has become an important agenda of teacher cognition research (Li, 2017). Expertise, according to Dreyfus and Dreyfus, is the ability of 'knowing how' to use knowledge one has to deal with cognitively demanding problems rather than 'knowing that' knowledge in de-contextualised situations (1986: 4). Understanding expertise has potential for teacher learning and development. In the literature on expertise, the most commonly associated topic is the study of experts. Tsui suggests that experts in their profession should possess certain qualities, such as 'being very knowledgeable in their field; being able to engage in skilful practices and being able to make accurate diagnoses, insightful analyses, and the right decisions, often within a very short period of time' (2003: 1).

As far as teacher expertise is concerned, research has differentiated experts from novices in task performance: novice teachers tend to follow context-free rules (Berliner, 1994), have difficulty in addressing issues emerging from interaction (Westerman, 1991), and have difficulties in bringing together theories and contemporary methodology in teaching (Tochon and Munby, 1993). In practice, novice teachers tend to deal with problems from a more superficial, short-term perspective, focusing on the 'here and now', while expert teachers are able to connect the problem at hand to a long-term goal and deal with it at a deeper level, bring learning theories to bear on their teaching, and are able to handle curricula demands (e.g. tests) (Li, 2013).

In order to understand the concept of expertise, the first step perhaps is to identity what expert teachers' attributes are and what those of novice teachers look like. Identifying novice and expert teachers is problematic as there is no reliable way of distinguishing them, and previous research has adopted different criteria to identify expert teachers. Work experience has been used to distinguish expert from novice. For example Gatbonton (2008) suggests that experienced teachers are those who have at least four to five years' work experience and novice teachers 'are those who are still undergoing training, who have just completed their training, or who have just commenced teaching and still have very little (e.g. fewer than two years) experience behind them' (ibid.: 162). Tsui (2003) used a combination of criteria which included experience, reputation, recommendation and classroom observation. In some cases, expert teachers were identified by educational authorities as well as by using additional criteria, such as student achievement, supervisor and peer nomination and recognition (e.g. Li, 2013). Li (2017) used similar criteria to differentiate expert and novice teachers in order to classify expertise. She argues that it is more meaningful and important to study how expertise is displayed in a situation rather than considering what expertise is in an abstract manner. Because of the close relationship between expertise and a particular situation, it is more appropriate to talk about distributed expertise as teachers engage in the interactions with the context (including colleagues, students and materials) to appropriate their knowledge and to apply their knowledge in different situations (Tsui, 2003). Equally, an expert teacher does not have expertise in every aspect of teaching and learning. For example, a novice teacher could have expertise in certain areas while remaining novice in most aspects of teaching (e.g. Tsui, 2003), and equally expert teachers could be a novice in an unfamiliar situation and become 'temporary novices' (Rich, 1993: 139).

The ability to manage classroom interaction and engaging students is termed Classroom Interactional Competence (CIC) (Walsh, 2011). Walsh argues that the construct CIC is vitally important for teaching and learning, telling us '[I]t puts interaction firmly at the centre of teaching and learning and argues that by improving their CIC, both teachers and learners will immediately improve learning and opportunities for learning' (2011: 158). There is a clear need to develop teachers' interactional competence to enable learners to participate and contribute to the class. In order to do that, teachers need to understand the role of classroom interaction in learning, and also develop their CIC in facilitating a learner-centred approach. In what follows, I will explain and explore distributed and multiple expertise in CIC using the principles of conversation analysis (see p. 235 in this volume for transcription conventions).

Extract 22.1 is an example where a novice teacher demonstrates expertise, in particular in the aspect of classroom interactional competence. This is from a relatively young teacher's classroom. She has been teaching these students for over a year and is considered by students as a good teacher. Although she is still at her 'launching' stage as a teacher, she demonstrates expertise in getting students involved and co-constructing ideas with her through the interactional work she does.

Extract 22.1

1	**T:**	em would you like to give some comments?
2		(4.0) and do you still remember the topic
3		(2.0) of her speech=
4	**SS:**	=((2.0 unintelligible))
5	**T:**	em would you like to give some comments
6		(3.0) ok in another word which sentence or
7		which expressions you remember=
8	**SS:**	=tomorrow is another day what we can do is
9		just to embrace this sunshine=
10	**T:**	=what else? What else? What else! ...
11	**S1:**	em I realize that er like during er (2.1) I
12		used to I used to say that a lot em
13		tomorrow is [another day]
14	**SS:**	[((laughing))]
15	**S1:**	now I realize em after that I realize its
16		like that tomorrow is another day all I
17		can do is to enjoy today's sunshine (1.3) I
18		realize that em (1.1) I realize that
19		yesterday is history tomorrow is history
20		and er today is gift er...you never
21		know what's happening tomorrow er what's
22		happened is accepted all we can do is try
23		to enjoy ourselves right now
24		and er try to treasure yourself and er all

25		you doing er I mean to enjoy yourself=
26	**T:**	=to enjoy yourself=
27	**S1:**	=yeah to enjoy yourself=
28	**T:**	=today and tomorrow (1.1) ok I don't I don't
29		know whether you know the sentence in a
30		famous movie called…
31	**SS:**	((2.0 unintelligible))
32	**T:**	ah no forest gum (1.0) [forest gum]
33	**SS:**	[forest gum] life is
34		a box of chocolate=
35	**T:**	=yes this is a very famous saying life is
36		a box of chocolate you never know which
37		one you will get but um whatever an-whichever
38		you will get I think you have to
39		love it you have to treasure it and try to
40		appreciate it right? ok and in her speech
41		one sentence er um left me a lot of
42		impression that (1.1) nowadays people are
43		chasing money :: fa :: me status um but people
44		forget their (2.1) health and their families

Li (2017) suggests that there is a strong link between classroom interactional competence and expertise. As shown in the extract, the teacher makes a great effort to involve students in the classroom by inviting contributions in lines 1, 5, 10 (*would you like to give some comments/would you like to give some comments/What else? What else? What else!*). These referential questions enable learner contributions as the focus is placed on personal meaning and opinions rather than testing memorisation. Alongside the two attempts for contribution invitation, extended pauses (lines 1 and 5) are evidently aimed at allowing students to reflect and construct ideas, maybe to rehearse the utterance before they speak publicly (Li, 2011). It is these attempts and space that the teacher creates that facilitate students' engagement with the topic. For example, when the teacher pushes hard in line 10 to elicit responses, S1 makes an attempt to express her opinion (line 11). The conversation between the teacher and S1 interests other students (as listeners), which is evident in line 14, when S1 repeats probably the most memorable sentence the speaker said in her speech *tomorrow is another day*. It is this non-verbal turn (line 14) that suggests learner participation and the skill of information collection and comprehension. In line 26, the teacher's echo summarizes and confirms the learner's contribution, and in lines 28–30 the teacher goes further to develop the topic by inviting students to make a link to a film.

These turn exchanges between the teacher and this student created an environment in which students may feel comfortable to share their ideas as the question posed did not seek any 'right' answers. This is also evident by the following statement the teacher made *I don't I don't know whether you know the sentence in a famous movie called…* As shown in data, as soon as the teacher suggested the name of the film, all students joined in with the famous line *life is a box of chocolate* (lines 33–34). The teacher, however, does not have any intention to let students elaborate the idea of *life is a box of chocolate* but took an extended turn (line 35–44). At face value, the teacher is trying to 'close down' the opportunity for learner contribution. However, if we consider the pedagogical goal of that moment, the teacher's intention is to draw students' attention to that day's topic: health. Again, it is the pedagogical goal and objectives that direct the conversation between the teacher and learners. So in this extract, the novice teacher displays her expertise in interactional competence and pedagogical competence.

Extract 22.2 is from another novice teacher's classroom, who has been teaching the students for two years. In this class, he is discussing some scientific facts about the moon with his students and one task is to ask students to judge whether the statements he provides are true or false. The teacher demonstrates expertise in subject and pedagogical knowledge and classroom inter-actional competence. Here, although the focus of the task is to comprehend the text and make judgements about statements, the teacher shows that his choice of topic focused more on using English as a medium to talk about other concepts, rather than learning English as a stand-alone subject through memorising vocabulary and grammar rules. His understanding suggests that he has an integrated knowledge of subject and appropriate pedagogical knowledge by designing an activity which involves students to use different subject knowledge in language acquisition and thinking possibilities and reason one's decision.

Extract 22.2

1	**T:**	a sunny day on the moon could kill you but
2		you can survive in the night
3	**SS:**	(1.0) false /false/false
4		((6.0 unintelligible))
5	**T:**	er (2.0) NAME
6	**S1:**	=it is false=
7	**T:**	=<u>it is</u> false why? (.)
8	**S1:**	because the temperature (1.0) on the moon is
9		very cold in the night (.) and you cannot
10		survive=
11	**T:**	=that means the temperature on the moon
12		is=
13	**S1:**	=can change=
14	**T:**	=yes is changeable right? (.) it changes
15		greatly (2.0) I learn during the day the
16		temperature is quite high during the
17		night is pretty low right even below zero
18		below zero

As shown in Extract 22.2, the teacher demonstrates expertise in classroom interactional com-petence in doing the task with students. In line 7, for example, after this student gave a brief answer *it is false* (line 6), the teacher confirms the student's contribution by echoing. However, the teacher does not simply complete his turn but asks a further question to guide the student in elaborating his answer. This feedback is closely followed by another initiation to develop a new learning cycle – the way the teacher handles the dialogue here is an important factor pre-venting it from becoming an IRF classroom discourse but a 'spiral IRF' (Panselinas and Komis, 2009). Following the teacher's cue, the student provides justification for his answer (lines 8–10). To help the student to make the point *the temperature on the moon is changeable*, the teacher takes a turn, where both of them are co-constructing the meaning (lines 11–13). It is important to note that the teacher uses different interactional strategies to close the conversation: summaris-ing and highlighting the point made. This summary and emphasis makes the whole conversation meaningful and relevant to the whole class. As shown in the data, the teacher-learner echo here shows the teacher's pedagogical goal of including the whole class and helping them to stay together (line 14). This extract shows two parallel considerations: on the one hand, the teacher modelled the students how they make their own judgements and suggestions by having information-seeking and reasoning questions; on the other hand, the teacher demonstrated how to direct the conversation to construct ideas by taking and giving turns.

Extract 22.3 is taken from an expert teacher's classroom and it shows that he becomes a temporary novice despite the different interactional strategies he uses. In this lesson, he is discussing a well-known novel with students: *Diamond Necklace*.

Extract 22.3

1	**T:**	Ok I have a question why WHY ((gestures student
2		to stand)) why didn't she Mathilde I mean have um
3		a diamond necklace (3.0)
4	**S1:**	°because she was not rich°
5	**T:**	it's very important she was not rich go on
6		((gestures for another student to stand))
7	**S2:**	on the way [home]
8	**T:**	[on on] her way home did she did she
9		take part in the PArty did she take part in the
10		BALL or in the PArty (.) did she take part in the
11		ball or in the party (.) yes or no (.)
12	**S2:**	yes ((nods))=
13	**T:**	=so tells us tell us something about party (.) do
14		you think ↑so?
15	**S2:**	er in the play er he:: he:: he may has pretty=
16	**T:**	=she might have been pretty at that day um at
17		that night ok on that night and then and did she
18		have a very good time (.) did she have a very
19		good time at the party in the party ok yes ok she
20		had a very good time (.) and her husband=
21	**S2:**	=and they have a very good time=
22	**T:**	=they had a very good time ok sit down go on
23		that's all go on (.)
24	**S3:**	but on her way home=
25	**T:**	=on her way home on THEIR way home
26	**S3:**	oh oh oh on their way home he find the the diamond
27		necklace was not around her neck=
28	**T:**	=good thank you

In this extract, the teacher's becoming 'temporary novice' is unfolding in his interaction with the students. At face value, the teacher posed a referential question, which could be categorised as creating a context for a dialogue (lines 1–3). However, such a question only requires from students that they retrieve information from the textbook rather than, for example, being asked to use their imagination or justify opinions. When a learner responded to the teacher's question in line 4, it could have been treated as an opportunity to develop student reasoning or imaginative skills, for example, by posing further questions that required students to reason their points or to imagine the character's life. Yet, the teacher closed down this opportunity by giving feedback *it's very important that she is not rich* (line 5) and inviting another student to answer his question using a gesture (line 6). This turn exchange demonstrates a typical IRF pattern and it focuses more on knowledge-retrieving rather than meaning construction. As the conversation carries on, the teacher seems to have missed another opportunity to involve students to make relevant contributions (lines 13–14). Here, the teacher interrupts the learner when he takes a turn to construct his story, by correcting grammar and providing an answer before the student attempts to complete the turn (lines 16–20). In this turn, the teacher seems to get in the way of student participation, which has a detrimental effect on meaning construction. Despite the teacher's interruption, this student still completes his turn (line 21), suggesting his self-confidence and competence in classroom task-based interaction as an independent learner, who is willing to control his turn and keeps his focus on the relevant part of the task. The teacher provides feedback by simply correcting his grammar and commenting on his contribution *that's all*, suggesting a possible obstruction to learner contribution. As the dialogue goes on, the third student provides the 'correct' answer the teacher expected, as the teacher upgrades his feedback to '*good*' (line 28) from not clear feedback to S1's input and '*that's all*' to S2's contribution. This illustrates strict boundaries given by the teacher for what is considered as a 'correct' answer, which might result in student non-participation in classrooms (Higgins et al., 2003). It's worth noting that the question emphasises information-retrieving process and all the students' contribution are somewhat an act of paraphrasing text from the book. This extract suggests several important features that is common in linguistic-focused and teacher-centred classrooms: 1) the interaction follows a simple IRF pattern and questions initiated by the teacher are usually to test students' knowledge and memorisation of the lecture or texts; 2) the teacher provides students with corrective feedback and the focus is placed on grammar or vocabulary (e.g. lines 8, 13, 22–23 and 25); 3) the students' turn are not necessarily brief but students are not encouraged to elaborate or reason their judgements; and 4) English is treated as an object rather than a tool.

Extract 22.4 is another example when a novice teacher demonstrates expertise in CIC and facilitates learning. In this extract, a learner's contribution is perceived as incorrect and dispreferred. Ringo (R), the teacher is teaching the student a topic on Frankenstein. The activity he asked students to do is a task together to answer questions pre-prepared by him.

Extract 22.4

1.	**R:**	eh (.) come to the front and
2.		tell us your answers ok?
3.		(0.8)
4.		((students applauding))
5.		Let's give him another hand
6.		((the teacher moves away from the platform))
7.		9 (8.0 student A is walking to the platform
8.		while other students are applauding) 0
9.	**A:**	Do you like sci-fi movies? (.)
10.		>yes< I like it (0.4)
11.		if you ↑do↓ which sci-fi movie is your favourite
12.		one ... My favourite sci-fi movie-s Harry Potter
13.		(3.0)
14.	**R:**	eh (.) <u>wait</u> a second (1.0)

15.   ((the student is moving towards the teacher))
16.   What is sci sci-fi me↓ans?
17.   **A:**   (0.2) um (0.3)
18.   **R:**   Science↑ (.)
19.   **S:**   Fiction=
20.   **R:**   =fiction (.)so↓ when it comes to <u>science</u> (1.3)
21.   Does Harry Potter qualify as science fiction↓
22.   你们觉得那个哈利波特算？它幻有幻想的部分
        (Do you think Harry Potter is? It has fantasy elements)
23.   但是它有科學的部分嗎
        (But does it have science elements?)
24.   **SS:**   算
        (yes)
25.   **R:**   Ok (.) you may have to rethink about the
26.   definition of sci sci-fi (.) ok? (2.0)
27.   ((Student A redirects his eye gaze towards the front))
28.   hh 其实 Harry Potter 应该比較算什嘛？(.)
        (What is Harry Potter more likely to be)
29.   **SS:**   奇幻=
        (fantasy)
30.   **R:**   =fanta↓sy
31.   **SS:**   ∘fantasy∘
32.   **R:**   Ok (.) ok (.)Good question

In this extract, Ringo invites students to come to the front to share their answers with the class. Here, he selects a particular student by drawing their numbers randomly. So in lines 1 to 4, he invites a student. Student A reads out the first question (line 9) and provides a relevant second pair part, an appropriate answer to the first pair part (line 10). After a brief pause, he reads out the second question (line 11), to which he again provides an answer (line 12). After a rather long pause, Ringo interrupts the student (line 14). Here the interruption suggests that Ringo treats the student's answer as a 'no-like', dispreferred response (cf. Liddicoat, 2007: 115). Ringo then follows up with a question, requesting clarification from the student regarding the definition of sci-fi. The student is uncertain, as suggested by the hesitation mark and a pause (line 17). Ringo provides a first part as elicitation (line 18), as indicated by a slightly rising tone, which is followed by another student, who provides a relevant and correct second part (line 19). Ringo then confirms the contribution and moves on to challenge student A by asking a specific question about *Harry Potter* (line 21). Then Ringo switches to L1 to ask the whole class about the question (lines 22 and 23), this time rephrasing the questions into two parts, with the first part asking whether *Harry Potter* is a sci-fi movie and the second part pointing out that it has elements of fantasy and questioning whether it has science elements. This can be considered a counter-question (CQ) strategy (Markee, 1995, 2004) to regain control. This question generates a relevant yet incorrect answer from Ringo's point view (line 24). Although he briefly acknowledges the students' contribution, he makes a suggestion to students to think about the definition of sci-fi (lines 25–26). Here, we see student A redirects his gaze toward the front 'home position' (line 27) (Sacks and Schegloff, 2002) and he is ready to get on with his next question but perhaps waiting for further instruction from the teacher. After a longish pause, Ringo initiates another turn, this time hinting to students to choose between fantasy and sci-fi for *Harry Potter* (line 28). Students agree that it is fantasy (line 29), which Ringo confirms (line 30) and moves on with the lesson (line 32).

In this extract, an unexpected contribution emerges when a student provides a relevant but incorrect answer. In order to clarify what sci-fi is, Ringo interrupts the student and engages with the whole class to discuss whether *Harry Potter* is sci-fi or fantasy. For Ringo, his pedagogical aim here is not only getting students to participate and contribute, but he shares relevant and correct information. So he makes an interactive decision to clarify the dispreferred contribution from student A. Again, Ringo used several interactional strategies, including: interrupting (line 14), asking questions (lines 16, 21 and 23), making suggestions (lines 25–26) and eliciting a preferred answer (line 28).

Applications

Researchers in SLTE have already taken teacher cognition as a source of experientially based professional 'know-how' which serves as a focus for both initial teacher education and reflective practice (Freeman and Richards, 1996; Farrell, 2013). Traditionally, SLTE has been centred on the learning of second languages to develop competent language teachers, rather than on teachers as learners of teaching (Freeman and Johnson, 1998). The focus of such an approach also looks at developing teachers' content knowledge and how content is learnt. Although the theoretical understanding of teacher learning has recently shifted from developing language teachers' knowledge, it is still clear that both teacher educators and trainee teachers focus on knowledge. Therefore, we see that much of the research in teacher cognition focuses on teacher knowledge, such as content knowledge, subject knowledge, pedagogical knowledge and personal knowledge. These areas are investigated in the manner that knowledge is treated as a concrete product which we are able to observe and examine. However, an adequate level of knowledge does not guarantee good teaching practice (Bartels, 2005; Johnson, 2009b).

A related point is Kumaravadivelu's call for more attention to the process, knowing, rather than the product, knowledge, in teacher education, 'as knowing is deemed to have greater significance than knowledge' (2012: 20). With regard to expertise, we see a close link to interactional competence. Specifically, teachers who demonstrate high levels of competence in interactional work are able to develop learning opportunities in class (see, for example, Walsh, 2002). When novice teachers demonstrate expertise, they do not follow rigid IRF patterns but use varied interactional strategies and resources. As shown in the data in this chapter, teachers who demonstrate expertise use different interactional strategies, such as confirmation checks, clarification requests, paraphrasing, elaboration, and so on, to push and shape learners' contributions. Clearly, when teachers demonstrate expertise in their teaching, they focus on learners' reactions in teaching and on teaching learners how to learn.

Because classroom interaction is central in understanding teacher cognition and CIC is a key feature of expertise, it is important to have CIC development as a key agenda item in teacher education. As Walsh (2013) claims, CIC is about good decision-making, and by examining CIC we come closer to understanding expertise. That is, expertise is no longer an abstract concept but practice teachers can identify in their actual teaching through examining their classroom interaction. In terms of developing teacher expertise, one useful way is to engage in a close examination of the moment where CIC is displayed and help teachers become conscious about utilising the interactional strategies outlined above in achieving their pedagogical goals, creating space for learner participation, and shaping learning. Expertise can be conceptualised as a quality or as a process. It is distributed, which is displayed in the talk-in-interaction. It is also multiple, which means it is not a certain characteristic which only exists in expert teachers, but is an ability which both novice and expert teachers can have at a given moment. Nishimuro and Borg argue that critical reflection informed by propositional knowledge might promote productive pedagogy (2013: 45). The critical reflection, which can be interpreted as deliberate practice, also contributes to developing expertise. Deliberate practice, as Ericsson et al. (1993) argued, 'would allow for repeated experiences in which the individual can attend to the critical aspects of the situation and incrementally improve her or his performance in response to knowledge of results, feedback, or both from a teacher' (p. 368). Therefore, it is within the rich experience of teaching that an individual can achieve expertise through purposeful and reflective engagement with the practice (Palmer et al., 2005).

Tsui (2003) proposes that teachers constantly construct and reconstruct their understandings of their work as teachers as a result of their interactions with the people in their context of work. Holliday (2005: 2) notes that '[I]t is people, not places, who have professions, prejudices and cultures', and the ideas and cultures that people bring to their interaction defines the nature of teaching and learning, the classroom order, the appropriate materials and language use in the classroom. For this reason, perhaps teacher education should place a strong emphasis on understanding the context and the influence of the local context on teaching practice. As we understand now, teachers develop their pedagogies within their professional contexts and through their interaction with the materials available to them, to their colleagues, to students and to influential parties (such as parents and school principals), and they engage in negotiation between macro-level educational policies and micro-level classroom realities.

Conclusion

Teacher cognition is a very important area for improving pedagogy, teacher learning and educational effectiveness. In researching teachers we must remember that teachers are active decision-makers who make interactive decisions in their local contexts. Therefore, it is vital to consider their cognition-in-interaction. Teachers are more likely to develop themselves as professionals and facilitate learning for their students if they engage in more meaningful reflective practice, such as examining their own cognition through analysing their classroom interactions. What this chapter demonstrates is an example of analysing one's understanding, conceptions and knowing in a specific situation from teachers' perspective. Of course, we have to remember that there is not a true or false cognition and teachers should not try to correct their cognitions, rather, they should try to understand their thinking in their local context by understanding that cognition is fluid, developmental and context-shaping. Therefore, learning to teach or teaching to learn is not just about teaching techniques, but is a process of teachers developing their expertise and identity. It involves personal experience, subject knowledge, contextual knowledge and pedagogical knowledge. Professional learning therefore should be continuous, long term and situated in teachers' practice contexts. Such learning should address the needs of teachers through exploring teachers' knowing, understanding, conceptualising and stance-taking. It has become clear through the examples illustrated in this chapter that cognition-in-interaction could well be used in professional development to enable teachers to conduct guided reflective practice, thereby improving pedagogy.

Further reading

Gatbonton, E. (2008) 'Looking Beyond Teachers' Classroom Behaviour: Novice and Experienced ESL Teachers' Pedagogical Knowledge'. *Language Teaching Research*, 12(2) 161–182.

Li, L. (2017) *Social Interaction and Teacher Cognition*. Edinburgh: Edinburgh University Press.

Tsui, A. B. M. (2003) *Understanding Expertise in Teaching*. New York: Cambridge University Press.

Tsui, A. B. M. (2005) 'Expertise in teaching: perspectives and issues', in Johnson, K. (ed.) *Expertise in Second Language Learning and Teaching*. Basingstoke: Palgrave Macmillan: 167–189.

References

Andrews, S. (1999) 'Why do L2 Teachers Need to "Know About Language"? Teacher Metalinguistic Awareness and Input for Learning'. *Language and Education*, 13(3) 161–177.

Andrews, S. (2003) '"Just like Instant Noodles": L2 Teachers and their Beliefs about Grammar Pedagogy'. *Teachers and Teaching*, 9(4) 351–375.

Andrews, S. (2006) 'The Evolution of Teachers' Language Awareness'. *Language Awareness*, 15 1–19.

Andrews, S. (2007) *Teacher Language Awareness*. Cambridge: Cambridge University Press.

Andrews, S. and McNeil, A. (2005) 'Knowledge about language and the "good language teacher"', in Bartels, N. (ed.) *Applied Linguistics and Language Teacher Education*. New York: Springer: 159–178.

Bailey, K. M. (1996) 'The best laid plans: teachers' in-class decisions to depart from their lesson plans', in Bailey, K. M. and Nuna, D. (eds) *Voices from the Language Classroom: Qualitative Research in Second Language Education*. Cambridge: Cambridge University Press: 15–40.

Bartels, N. (2005) 'Researching applied linguistics in language teacher education', in Bartels, N. (ed.) *Applied Linguistics and Language Teacher Education*. New York: Springer: 1–26.

Basturkmen, H. (2012) 'Review of Research into the Correspondence Between Language Teachers' Stated Beliefs and Practices'. *System*, 40(2) 282–295.

Berliner, D. C. (1994) 'The wonder of exemplary performances', in Margieri, J. N. and Block, C. C. (eds) *Creating Powerful Thinking in Teacher and Students' Diverse Perspectives*. Fort Worth, TX: Harcourt Brace College: 161–186.

Bernat, E. and Gvozdenko, I. (2005) 'Beliefs about Language Learning: Current Knowledge, Pedagogical Implications, and New Research Directions'. *TESL-EJ*, 9(1) 1–21.

Borg, S. (2003) 'Teacher Cognition in Language Teaching: A Review of Research on what Language Teachers Think, Know, Believe, and Do'. *Language Teaching*, 36(2) 81–109.

Borg, S. (2006) *Teacher Cognition and Language Education: Research and Practice*. London: Continuum.

Borg, S. (2012) 'Current approaches to language teacher cognition research: a methodological analysis', in Barnard, R. and Burns, A. (eds) *Researching Language Teacher Cognition and Practice: International Case Studies*. Bristol: Multilingual Matters: 11–29.

Brannan, D. and Bleistein, T. (2012) 'Novice ESOL Teachers' Perceptions of Social Support Networks'. *TESOL Quarterly*, 46(3) 519–541.

Breen, M. P., Hird, B., Milton, M., Oliver, R. and Thwaite, A. (2001) 'Making Sense of Language Teaching: Teachers' Principles and Classroom Practices'. *Applied Linguistics*, 22(4) 470–501.

Busch, D. (2010) 'Pre-Service Teacher Beliefs About Language Learning: The Second Language Acquisition Course as an Agent for Change'. *Language Teaching Research*, 14(3) 318–337.

Clark, C. M. and Peterson, P. L. (1986) 'Teachers' thought processes', in Wittrock, M. C. (ed.) *Handbook of Research on Teaching*, 3rd edition. New York: Macmillan: 255–296.

Clark, C. M. and Yinger, R. (1987) 'Teacher planning', in Calderhead, J. (ed.) *Exploring Teachers' Thinking*. London: Cassell Publications: 84–103.

Cohen, A. D. and Fass, L. (2001) 'Oral Language Instruction: Teacher and Learner Beliefs and the Reality in EFL Classes at a Colombian University'. *Journal of Language and Culture*, 6 43–62.

Dreyfus, H. L. and Dreyfus, S. E. (1986) *Mind Over Machine*. New York: Free Press.

Ericsson, K. A., Krampe, R. T. and Tesch-Romer, C. (1993) 'The Role of Deliberate Practice in the Acquisition of Expert Performance'. *Psychological Review*, 100(3) 363–406.

Farrell, T. S. C. (2013) *Reflective Practice in ESL Teacher Development Groups: From Practices to Principles*. Basingstoke: Palgrave Macmillan.

Farrell, T. S. C. and Lim, P. C. P. (2005) 'Conceptions of Grammar Teaching: A Case Study of Teachers' Beliefs and Classroom Practices'. *TESL-EJ*, 9(2) 1–13.

Freeman, D. and Johnson, K. (1998) 'Reconceptualizing the Knowledge-Base of Language Teacher Education'. *TESOL Quarterly*, 32 397–417.

Freeman, D. and Richards, J. (eds) (1996) *Teacher Learning in Language Teaching*. Cambridge: Cambridge University Press.

Gatbonton, E. (2008) 'Looking Beyond Teachers' Classroom Behaviour: Novice and Experienced ESL Teachers' Pedagogical Knowledge'. *Language Teaching Research*, 12(2) 161–182.

Higgins, C. M., Thompson, M. M. and Roeder, R. V. (2003) 'In Search of a Profound Answer: Mainstream Scripts and the Marginalization of Advanced-track Urban Students'. *Linguistics and Education*, 14(2) 195–220.

Holliday, A. R. (2005) *The Struggle to Teach English as an International Language*. Oxford: Oxford University Press.

Horwitz, E. K. (1985) 'Using Student Beliefs About Language Learning and Teaching in the Foreign Language Methods Course'. *Foreign Language Annals*, 18 333–340.

Johnson, K. E. (1992) 'The Relationship Between Teachers' Beliefs and Practices During Literacy Instruction for Non-Native Speakers of English'. *Journal of Reading Behavior*, 24(1) 83–108.

Johnson, K. E. (2009a) *Second Language Teacher Education: A Sociocultural Perspective*. New York: Routledge.

Johnson, K. E. (2009b) 'Trends in second language teacher education', in Burns, A. and Richards, J. C. (eds) *The Cambridge Guide to Second Language Teacher Education*. Cambridge: Cambridge University Press: 20–29.

Kumaravadivelu, B. (2012) *Language Teacher Education for a Global Society: A Modular Model for Knowing, Analyzing, Recognizing, Doing, and Seeing*. New York: Routledge.

Li, L. (2011) 'Obstacles and Opportunities for Developing Thinking Through Interaction in Language Classrooms'. *Thinking Skills and Creativity*, 6(3) 146–158.

Li, L. (2012) 'Belief Construction and Development: Two Tales of Non-native English Speaking Student Teachers in a TESOL Programme'. *Novitas-ROYAL (Research on Youth and Language)*, 6(1) 33–58.

Li, L. (2013) 'The Complexity of Language Teachers' Beliefs and Practice: One EFL Teacher's Theories'. *Language Learning Journal*, 41(2) 175–191.

Li, L. (2014) 'Understanding Language Teachers' Practice with Educational Technology: A Case from China'. *System*, 46 105–119.

Li, L. (2017) *Social Interaction and Teacher Cognition*. Edinburgh: Edinburgh University Press.

Li, L. and Walsh, S. (2011) '"Seeing is Believing": Looking at EFL Teachers' Beliefs Through Classroom Interaction'. *Classroom Discourse*, 2(1) 39–57.

Liddicoat, A. J. (2007) *An Introduction to Conversation Analysis*. New York: Continuum.

Llurda, E. and Lasagabaster, D. (2010) 'Factors Affecting Teachers' Beliefs about Interculturalism'. *International Journal of Applied Linguistics*, 20(3) 327–353.

Markee, N. (1995) 'Teachers' Answers to Learners' Questions: Problematizing the Issue of Making Meaning'. *Issues in Applied Linguistics*, 6 63–92.

Markee, N. (2004) 'Zones of Interactional Transition in ESL Classes'. *The Modern Language Journal*, 88 583–596.

Mattheoudakis, M. (2007) 'Tracking Changes in Pre-Service EFL Teacher Beliefs in Greece: A Longitudinal Study'. *Teaching and Teacher Education*, 23(8) 1272–1288.

Morton, T. (2012) 'Classroom Talk, Conceptual Change and Teacher Reflection in Bilingual Science Teaching'. *Teaching and Teacher Education*, 28(1) 101–110.

Nishimuro, M. and Borg, S. (2013) 'Teacher Cognition and Grammar Teaching in a Japanese High School'. *JALT Journal*, 35(1) 29–50.

Pajares, M. F. (1992) 'Teachers' Beliefs and Educational Research: Cleaning up a Messy Construct'. *Review of Educational Research*, 62(3) 307–332.

Palmer, D. J., Stough, L. M., Burdenski, T. K. and Gonzales, M. (2005) 'Identifying Teacher Expertise: An Examination of Researchers' Decision Making'. *Educational Psychologist*, 40(1) 13–25.

Panselinas, G. and Komis, V. (2009) '"Scaffolding" Through Talk in Groupwork Learning'. *Thinking Skills and Creativity*, 4 86–103.

Peacock, M. (1999) 'Beliefs About Language Learning and their Relationship to Proficiency'. *International Journal of Applied Linguistics*, 9(2) 247–263.

Peacock, M. (2001) 'Pre-service ESL Teachers' Beliefs About Second Language Learning: A Longitudinal Study'. *System*, 29 177–195.

Rich, Y. (1993) 'Stability and Change in Teacher Expertise'. *Teacher & Teacher Education*, 9(2) 137–146.

Richards, J. C. (1998) 'Teacher beliefs and decision making', in Richards, J. C. (ed.) *Beyond Training*. Cambridge: Cambridge University Press: 65–85.

Sacks, H. and Schegloff, E. A. (2002) 'Home Position'. *Gesture*, 2(2) 133–146.

Svalberg, A. M. L. and Askham, J. (2014) 'Student Teachers' Collaborative Construction of Grammar Awareness: The Case of a Highly Competent Learner'. *Language Awareness*, 23(1–2) 123–137.

Tochon, F. and Munby, H. (1993) 'Novice and Expert Teachers' Time Epistemology: A Wave Function from Didactics to Pedagogy'. *Teacher and Teacher Education*, 9(2) 205–218.

Tsui, A. A. M. (2003) *Understanding Expertise in Teaching*. New York: Cambridge University Press.

Walsh, S. (2002) 'Construction or Obstruction: Teacher Talk and Learner Involvement in EFL Classroom'. *Language Teaching Research*, 6 3–23.

Walsh, S. (2011) *Exploring Classroom Discourse: Language in Action*. Abingdon: Routledge.

Walsh, S. (2013) *Classroom Discourse and Teacher Development*. Edinburgh: Edinburgh University Press.

Westerman, D. A. (1991) 'Expert and Novice Teacher Decision Making'. *Journal of Teacher Education*, 42(4) 292–305.

Woods, D. (1996) *Teacher Cognition in Language Teaching*. Cambridge: Cambridge University Press.

Young, T. J. and Sachdev, I. (2011) 'Intercultural Communicative Competence: Exploring English Language Teachers' Beliefs and Practices'. *Language Awareness*, 20 81–98.

23

English language teacher education and collaborative professional development in contexts of constraints

Kuchah Kuchah, Oumar Moussa Djigo and Betelhem Taye

Introduction

The need for quality teacher education and development has been at the centre of discussions on education in developing world countries over the last two decades (see for example Akyeampong et al., 2007; UNESCO, 2005, 2013, 2015). This is because of the rising number of students in primary and secondary schools after the adoption of *Education for All* (EFA) policies in the 1990s (UNESCO, 1990, 2000) and because of the specific challenges these countries face in meeting quality benchmarks that are often set by international organisations (Coleman, 2018). Financial constraints in sub-Saharan African (SSA) countries have meant that governments are unable to provide sufficient resources for the growing number of students in state sector schools. This growth accounts for the rising need for qualified English language teachers in order to bridge the gap between the demographic and socioeconomic challenges that hinder quality education in SSA countries. It has also been suggested (e.g., by Jagusah, 2001; Kuchah, 2008; Okoth, 2016) that the top-down transmission-based approaches to teacher education and professional development often favoured by the ministries of education (MoEs) in these countries do not always meet the professional needs of teachers. In order to guarantee quality in-service training for all, English language teachers through active networks across the continent have set up bottom-up local initiatives wherein collaborative professional development programmes are designed to support teachers in contexts of constraints.

In this chapter, we focus on the organisational and pedagogical dimensions of English language teacher education and professional development in SSA with the aim of identifying key challenges and examining ways in which such challenges could be/are being dealt with. Although we mainly focus on in-service teacher education initiatives, we start by examining the constraints of initial teacher education, particularly in relation to recruitment, retention and motivation of teachers to show how this might affect their professional lives. Then we discuss the potential role of teacher collaborative initiatives in supporting and sustaining continuous professional development drawing examples from Senegal, Ethiopia and Cameroon.

Initial teacher education and the quality conundrum: from recruitment to retention.

In this section, we examine the conditions under which teachers become professionals as well as those factors that might affect their commitment to and engagement with continuous professional development. Teacher quality has continued to be highlighted as an important factor in the attainment of quality education (Bolitho, 2016; Wright, 2010), but at the same time issues of teacher shortage continue to be reported, particularly in state school systems in developing world countries (UNESCO, 2015). Bainton et al. (2016) have suggested that rapid expansion in secondary education in SSA following the implementation of EFA policies has placed demands on teacher recruitment, education and deployment.

There is evidence (e.g., Lewin, 2007; UIS, 2006) that the number of qualified individuals from which to recruit secondary school teachers is small compared to the population of students in school. Faced with this situation, there is a growing need for teacher education programmes to be able to provide quality teachers capable of dealing with the challenges, which come with the demographic and socioeconomic constraints of the school systems. Yet ensuring teacher quality in SSA, is often based on several variables including entry qualification, the content and nature of training, teacher motivation and other socioeconomic factors (see for example, Akyeampong and Stephens, 2002; Kuchah, 2013; Mtika and Gates, 2011). Bainton et al. (2016: 8) report that teacher education programmes in SSA, 'have a reputation for accepting less well qualified candidates, who could not compete for entry to more attractive programmes perceived to lead to more profitable careers and employment'. There is no doubt therefore that school teachers in such contexts often have language proficiency problems, although they may be competent in other subject content, and as a result, will require sustained language and pedagogic support throughout their careers if they choose to stay in the profession.

Even where higher entry qualifications are required such as for secondary level trainee teachers, there are other issues, which might affect teacher motivation and retention. Mtika and Gates's (2011) study in Malawi reveals that trainee teachers join teacher education as a result of a failure to follow their desired career choice. In Liberia, Lockheed and Verspoor (1991) showed that 75 per cent of trainee teachers joined the programme because they had no other option. This is exacerbated by the fact that education in SSA countries is generally under-financed and as a result, teachers' working conditions and salaries remain unattractive and teaching is perceived as a low status profession (UNESCO, 2015; Mtika and Gates, 2011). A possible result of this may be that more under-qualified and under-motivated people join the profession and in some cases, in fact, many might see teacher education as a springboard to a more lucrative career elsewhere (Mtika and Gates, 2011: 429) hence the high rate of teacher attrition observed with early career secondary school teachers (Bainton et al., 2016; Mtika and Gates, 2011; Mulkeen, 2010). For those teachers who are resilient to make teaching their career, there are other school and classroom based issues to grapple with, some of which we discuss below.

Context of teaching and learning

A major challenge that has been highlighted in the literature from sub-Saharan Africa (e.g., Focho, 2018; Komba and Nkumbi, 2008; Kuchah and Smith, 2011) is that of overcrowded classrooms. It has been suggested that the implementation of EFA policies such as free and compulsory basic education has meant an increase in enrolment into state primary and secondary schools with no concomitant increase in infrastructure (Kuchah, 2018). As a result, students in state primary and secondary schools in these contexts are often crammed in desks in crowded classrooms making it difficult for teachers to make use of recommended pedagogic practices such as group work, projects, differentiated learning and authentic assessment or even to pay attention to individual students (Focho, 2018).

Other school/classroom related constraints that have been extensively discussed in the literature include the lack of textbooks, lack of libraries, students' limited exposure to English language usage (see for example Kuchah and Smith, 2011; Muthwii, 2001; O'Sullivan, 2006) as well as low teacher proficiency (Krugel and Fourie, 2014; Nel and Muller, 2010). What is more, while technological advancements have been shown to enhance access to quality language education elsewhere (e.g., Gruba et al., 2016; Tyers and Lightfoot, 2018) challenges such as frequent power cuts in many SSA countries reduce access to the already very limited and basic internet and computer services in the few schools which might have them (Focho, 2018). As a result, a huge amount of ELT in these contexts continues to take place in situations that are far removed from the ideal world of pedagogical excitement and innovatory teaching that western ELT researchers and practitioners present in ELT materials and handbooks (Maley, 2001). These situations have been conceptualised as 'difficult' (West, 1960; Kuchah and Smith, 2011; Shamim and Kuchah, 2016; Kuchah and Shamim, 2018) and the constraints they pose can be further compounded, particularly in resource poor environments, where teachers may not have adequate English language and/or pedagogical skills (Shamim and Kuchah, 2016: 528).

In-service teacher education and continuous professional development: approaches and challenges

The aforementioned classroom constraints, together with problems of teacher shortage and lack of motivation, tend to limit the possibilities for teachers to engage in sustained professional development especially where in-service education mostly rests in the hands of the Ministry of Education (CONAP, 2008). Shamim and Kuchah (2016) explain that in most mainstream educational institutions in the developing world where large classes exist, teachers and even educational authorities can hardly afford time for sustained professional development opportunities. This is partly because teachers tend to focus more on the daily survival issues around their job and can hardly afford the time, energy or motivation to engage in any professional development activity (Focho, 2018). Even where teachers may be able to participate in available mandatory professional education, such opportunities are rare (Focho, 2018; Tchombe, 2010) and in some cases, some teachers might work for several years, sometimes a whole career, without having the opportunity to be supported by a teacher educator or pedagogic authority (Kuchah, 2008).

This resistance is evidenced in the policy-practice disconnections recorded in the research in SSA (e.g., O'Sullivan, 2006; Schlebusch and Thobedi, 2004; Weideman et al., 2003) and is often blamed on both the top-down transmission of, sometimes, inappropriate pedagogic ideas imported from otherwise privileged contexts (Rixon and Smith, 2010; Smith, 2011). The focus of language teacher education in SSA is still primarily on the theoretical aspects of learning, teaching and management (Bolitho, 2016) giving little room for teacher creativity, critical reflection and agency. It might therefore be argued that most teachers in these contexts are not adequately prepared to deal with the day-to-day conundrums of their classrooms such as how to teach and assess large, under-resourced classes, different age groups and abilities in one class (Samb, 2013; Smith et al., 2012).

Bottom-up constructivist approaches to teacher education and CPD

As suggested earlier, top-down transmission-based approaches to teacher education and professional development as promoted by MoEs in SSA sometimes fail to recognise the day-to-day challenges that teachers face in their classrooms. As a result, despite improvements in school enrolment and retention since the EFA declaration (UNESCO, 1990, 2000) there are still significant quality issues in education in SSA (UNESCO, 2015), which suggest that top-down transmissive initiatives to improve teacher quality might not be a viable way of promoting quality teacher development. Consequently, teachers may have to rely on alternative avenues to help them improve their practice and extend their professional knowledge base.

This is even more compelling in sub-Saharan Africa where governments are grappling with issues related to teacher recruitment and are sometimes unable to focus on the professional development of existing state school teachers (Bainton et al., 2016; Mtika and Gates, 2011; Mulkeen, 2010; UIS, 2016). As has been suggested, the strength of any educational system is to support and sustain teachers' professional development, to 'recognise the continuing needs of teachers as learners in a changing society and to foster practices which are responsive to the educational needs of all children' (Soler et al., 2001: 50). There is now agreement in the literature that teacher education needs to prepare teachers to be able to foresee eventual challenges in classroom practice and to be imaginative and skilful in addressing these challenges (Avalos, 2000; Kuchah and Shamim, 2018; UNESCO, 2000). Achieving this depends on creating opportunities for teachers to share knowledge and skills in ways that are enabling, rather than threatening.

In line with the above, Johnson (2006) explains that there has been a growing departure, over the last few decades, from the positivistic paradigm informing the transmission of new methodologies to teachers to the construction of individual knowledge through knowledge of the communities of practice (Wenger, 1998) but, and more importantly, the immediate social context within which the individual teacher works. In other words, the tradition of handing down recommended 'best' practices to teachers is now being replaced by approaches that promote the social co-construction of appropriate practices between teachers. This shift is particularly relevant in SSA where challenges such as rising enrolments, limited resources available to teachers as well as increasing demands for quality teaching are forcing teachers to rely on their own pragmatic responses to classroom realities, sometimes creating their own platforms for shared reflection on common challenges and solutions. One of such platforms is teacher associations (TAs) which serve as learning communities (Liebermann and Miller, 2011) where teachers can 'learn from each other in an environment that fosters collaboration, honest talk, and a commitment to growth and development' (ibid.: 16). The rising number of TAs in the continent now suggests that voluntary bottom up teacher-collaborative platforms can offer sustainable and durable opportunities for teachers to develop professionally.

The emergence and role of teacher network in sub-Saharan Africa

Language Teacher Associations have existed in many parts of the world for several decades, but it is only recently that they have become a subject of research interest. The recent publication of a special edition of the ELT Journal (Volume 70(2), April 2016) and an edited book dedicated to Language teacher associations (Elsheikh et al., 2018) show the rising role of TAs in the professional lives of teachers. This role can hardly be underestimated, particularly in contexts where MoEs are not sufficiently meeting the needs and aspirations of teachers.

Furthermore, the rapid spread of the English language into non-Anglophone African countries and the challenges discussed above, have led to a rise in TAs across Africa with a number of cross-national collaborations, e.g., between TAs in Rwanda, Uganda, Ethiopia and Tanzania in East of Africa; Nigeria and Cameroon in the West; and Gabon and Cameroon in Central Africa during the last decade. The creation of a Pan African network of TAs – Africa TESOL – in 2016 has since provided local TAs with an enabling environment for the pursuance of professionalism in language education and the sharing of research and good practice generated in contexts that are akin with those of its member associations (see http://africatesol.org/aboutus). Over the last three years, Africa TESOL has organised three annual conferences (in Sudan, Rwanda and Senegal) and has seen the number of affiliated national TAs rise from eight to 20, indicating a potential to reach out to and bring together teachers for a common purpose.

Some Africa TAs have also extended their networks beyond their sub-regions and Africa with 16 national TAs becoming Associates of IATEFL and 12 affiliated to TESOL International (this number includes eight TAs who are part of both IATEFL and TESOL). More importantly, collaborative endeavours within these TAs have shown that teachers can achieve a lot in terms of their own professional development where they can interact with each other in a non-hierarchical, non-threatening environment (Kuchah, 2008). We now turn to local examples of such collaboration from three countries to show the dynamics and role of TAs and pedagogic cells in promoting teacher education and CPD.

Bottom-up teacher networks in Senegal

Like in other SSA countries, in-service teacher training programmes are striving to offer quality education to a significant number of teachers scattered in remote areas in Senegal but continuing professional development still needs a more sustained support from the MoE. Because effective teacher development 'provides a focused and grounded way for teachers to share, develop, and understand practice in relation to how and what their students are learning' (Del Prete, 2013: 14), the association of teachers of English in Senegal (ATES) and pedagogic cells represent the two main pathways to teacher-led professional development that 'encourage, extend and structure professional dialogue' (Cordingley et al., 2003: 2).

The role of pedagogic cells

In Senegal, pedagogic cells which were initially set up by the MoE in 1984 to guarantee teachers' professional growth ultimately became bottom-up CPD opportunities run by teachers themselves in order to foster a sense of ownership. Though the coordinators of these cells are appointed by the ministry of education, professional development programmes are designed by teachers of each cell, and focus on the professional needs of the group because 'it is healthy for professionals to have an active role in their own development processes' (Mann, 2005: 104). These include the inclusion of the information and communication technologies in low-resource areas, issues related to the development of learners' oral skills in large classes, and other pedagogy-related issues that are not well addressed in teacher-training programmes. In so doing, teachers are empowered to take the lead by suggesting topics of interest that are related to the reality of their classroom. For example, classroom observation sessions offer teachers the opportunity to be observed in their classrooms and to receive objective feedback from their peers. In other sessions, teachers are invited to share effective and innovative self-initiated classroom practices that were designed to overcome common challenges related to ELT in large-size classes.

Online teacher collaboration has recently been introduced in our cell with the use of blogs as online platforms for asynchronous interactions. Our cell blog serves as a repository for video presentations, which were recorded during the sessions and posted online, of useful ELT articles, videos, and web links that can foster self-directed leaning skills. The use of screen-capture tools such as QuickTime player and Screencast-O-Matic enables tech-savvy teachers to post video tutorials so as to guide their peers on the use of technology tools that can foster learner autonomy and extend learning outside the classroom. Blogs are authoring tools that can be viewed on smart phones and tablets to guarantee easy access for busy teachers. The possibility to leave their comments creates interactions through questions and suggestions. Because teachers are not all intrinsically motivated to attend the pedagogic cell meetings, offering online support can mitigate the issue of low attendance and encourage online collaboration.

Pedagogic cells therefore provide 'an opportunity for teachers to meet collaboratively, to explore new strategies and to discuss how best to adapt them to suit their own contexts' (Cordingley et al., 2005: 3). Context-sensitive issues related to the national curriculum and its delivery in large and low-resourced classes are addressed in order to encourage teachers to reflect on their practice and become agents of change in their own classrooms. These cells are also viewed as platforms of exchange for beginner teachers to from more experienced peers while discovering basic classroom practices as stated below by a former president of ATES Dakar:

> I started teaching English 16 years ago without pre-service training. Attending the monthly meetings allowed me to learn basic things a starter teacher should know such as lesson planning, ways of teaching vocabulary, grammar, classroom management and most important how to foster learner collaboration through pair and group work activities. In addition, the positive feedback I received from senior colleagues after co- facilitating a session on communicative grammar during my second year permitted me to build confidence as a teacher.
> *Mamadou Kaly Diallo*

In addition to contributing to English language teachers' professional growth, pedagogic cells are believed to foster teacher collaboration through activities such as the harmonisation of lessons and assessments and the sharing of materials and teaching tips. Souleymane Ka, English language teacher in the North of Senegal shared this view:

> When I joined my new school in Saint Louis, I found the most dynamic English cell that I have ever known. We harmonise teaching and learning at all levels. Once the cell meets to plan what to teach in the next four months, tasks are shared, tests scheduled, and designs chosen. We have a group on WhatsApp for further discussions, sharing materials or proofreading of our productions before they are printed.

Despite the efforts of the ministry of education to appoint coordinators, no funding is provided to guarantee the success of these cells. Meetings are therefore held in different schools which offer the needed financial and material support.

The Association of teachers of English in Senegal (ATES)

Created in 1976, ATES also creates professional development opportunities for teachers across the country. The association started with the Dakar branch then extended its branches to many areas of the country with regional chapters which independently strive to provide members with in-service training programmes. Samb (2013: 36) explains that 'ATES organises its own annual convention and English language day (ELD) involving all decision-takers in the field of ELT, pulling together teachers, inspectors, teacher trainers and language experts from other parts of the continent' (Samb, 2013: 36). The annual convention is a platform of exchange where experienced and novice teachers share their expertise and set up new perspectives for teacher development. The ELD has become a popular event that enables teachers to 'experience a vast range of activities and interactions that can increase their knowledge and skills, improve their teaching practice, and contribute to their personal, social, and emotional growth' (Desimone, 2011: 28). As the current president of ATES mentions:

> Since 1976, ATES has been involved in teacher development and student improvement. Usually, the strategic plan starts in March with the ELD, English Language Day. It consists of four presentations under the umbrella of one theme. Each presentation is 45 minutes long. The second professional development activity is the National Seminar. It is organized in the regions and is often a workshop or based on Learning Stations. The third activity is the National Convention. It is the biggest event. It is based on a Keynote speech followed by concurrent presentations.
>
> *Mouhamadou Sadibou Diouf*

In 2015, the association started the idea of ATES generated manuals or teaching materials which aim at enhancing learners' basic skills and narrowing the gap between teacher-centered approaches and learner-centered ones. The ATES booklet entitled *On The Way* is a compilation of contextualised and well-adapted classroom activities designed by experienced teachers in collaboration with teacher educators and ATES members. The editorial committee of the first edition is a group of devoted teachers whose primary focus is to reach as many teachers as possible and help them 'to explore their own context, construct their own knowledge and understanding of what takes place in their classrooms' (Richards and Farrell, 2005: 13). While designing contextualised materials, ATES encourages teachers to reflect on their own practice and to address their learners' needs rather than using imported practices that do not necessarily fit their context.

The Ethiopian English Language Professionals Association (EELPA)

As was explained earlier, with the scarcity of in-service training or workshops for English language teachers' CPD, local TAs have become a viable network for professional growth. In this respect, TAs like the Ethiopian English Language Professionals Association (EELPA) play a pivotal role in filling such visible gaps. Though it was legally recognised in the country only since 2012 (IATEFL, 2013), EELPA was created more than a decade ago with the aim of providing professional development alternatives to English language teachers through substantial support from British Council Ethiopia. It was pioneered by a group of English language teachers from different educational establishments of the capital Addis Ababa. These teachers decided to meet every weekend at the premises of the British Council to informally share experiences and hold discussions on their respective development needs as a reaction to the extreme lack of appropriate professional development programmes in their schools, colleges and universities.

Through time, undertakings in the association began to grow to allow members to benefit not only from the experience sharing sessions but also from other renowned professionals in the field through training, workshops and annual conferences. Currently, members meet every fortnight on Saturdays, to follow presentations by colleagues or invited guests mostly from the British Council, VSO (Voluntary Service Overseas) and many other development partners. Areas of discussions or presentations vary, ranging from specific classroom concerns of individual teachers to national level English language teaching issues, which mostly are common to all teachers.

EELPA members are mostly self-driven professionals who believe the association is the only source of development, which provides the opportunity to establish professional networks, heighten their self-reflection and collaborative learning skill. Members like Teshale Seifesilassie who travels for hours to attend the association's regular sessions every fortnight express their opinions on the benefits they get from EELPA.

> As for me the reason why I chose to be a member of this association is just to improve my professional knowledge; just to grow professionally and personally. We meet some very good professionals here which can be a very good network.
>
> *Teshale Sefesilassie, EELPA member*

Teachers develop better when they take control of their own development and they also develop when empowered and encouraged to take the initiative in identifying and acting on their own needs through their co-existence with like-minded professionals (Borg, 2015b; Farrell, 2013). Daniel's testimony below reaffirms this:

> Every two weeks we come to this EELPA's session because, in this association, there is a very good culture of sharing. We share ideas. We share successes and failure stories and I learn from that and from others.
>
> *Daniel Mekonnen, EELPA member*

Ethiopian English language teachers have two major problems – absence of appropriate professional development endeavour in their schools and lack of adequate proficiency level in the language (Mijena, 2013; Heugh et al., 2007). These two setbacks are also recognised by the country's Ministry of Education (MoE, 2009; Birbiso, 2014). In this regard, EELPA has been so far recognised by its members for being a professional hub where these two major hindrances are being addressed. Abebe and Meron below respectively believe that the association is helping them develop their expertise in teaching the language and developing their proficiency level.

> As to me before I joined EELPA, I thought I was teaching English but I wasn't. Because I wasn't updated. I was maybe lecturing the whole day. You know once I finished my teacher education from my university, I was not exposed to any professional development endeavours like this one EELPA. So, before EELPA, I was like sitting alone with crossed legs and no one there to support me. But I started doing things for myself and joined this association.
>
> *Abebe Molla, EELPA member*

> I appreciate the fact that we use only English for communication in EELPA. You know the extent of how the language is never used in our environment. I think my English is improving because I get to use it regularly here.
>
> *Meron Lemma, EELPA member*

Being the only bottom-up initiative in the country thus far with sizable potential but very minimal recognition and support from the government, the association strives to impact the professional lives of more English language teachers despite many constraints it encounters. These constraints include:

- Lack of appropriate recognition from the ministry
- Financial constraints
- Teachers' extreme lack of interest or motivation to become members
- Frequent membership withdrawals

As a result, it can be argued that the association has not been influential in the country's national policy for English language teachers' professional development, yet EELPA has potential to influence practice positively and at scale, if it can eventually reach teachers outside its present confines in the capital city to English teachers based in the country's remote areas teaching in the most difficult circumstances.

The Cameroon English language Teachers Association (CAMELTA)

CAMELTA was created in April 2001 through the merging of local regional ELTAs in the country, some of which had hitherto existed for more than 20 years. Since its creation, the association has run more than 300 national and regional conferences for its membership of more than 1,500 members. More recently, CAMELTA has been involved in generating locally appropriate pedagogic ideas and practices through collaborative research initiatives.

The first phase of the CAMELTA research project started in August 2013 in Cameroon with 170 members writing down research questions they would want to investigate if they had the time and training to conduct research. These questions were then collated and categorised into research priority areas by members of the research and projects committee of the association and formed the basis for future decisions on conference and workshop themes as well as research and development project orientation. One significant project informed by the research questions was the 'Training of young teachers for leadership in ELT' project which won the IATEFL Projects Award in 2015. With support from an external researcher (Richard Smith) the committee designed a three-item open-ended questionnaire aimed at collecting stories of, and reflections on, successful lessons as well as narratives about members' challenges and how they had attempted to deal with these. In total, 504 questionnaires were returned and the responses as well as the initial research questions were collated and uploaded to the CAMELTA website. A preliminary analysis of the data revealed that despite a range of classroom challenges, teachers employed a variety of pragmatic strategies to motivate students and facilitate learning. Teachers' accounts included diverse classroom techniques and activities for selecting materials, organising and managing classroom interaction and encouraging student creativity (Smith and Kuchah, 2014; see also Ekembe, 2016 for a critical defence of the legitimisation of local pedagogies based on the CAMELTA research data). Further analyses of the data formed the basis for presented at the annual conferences in 2015 (by Kuchah) and 2016 (by Kuchah and Ekembe).

The second phase of the project started in September 2016 following the creating of a CAMELTA research group comprising of 34 TA members – most of whom were relatively novice teachers with up to five years' teaching experience – with a common interest in collaborative research. Ekembe and Fonjong (2018), themselves members of the group, report that after the first phase of the project, teacher identity, particularly amongst early career members of CAMELTA was still a critical issue as teachers perceived themselves as incapable of contributing to the local or global discussion on ELT. The research group sought to demonstrate to teachers that examples of their current practice could generate pedagogical reflections relevant both locally and globally. Following an initial identification and selection of research questions from the existing database of research questions which had been collected, categorised and prioritised earlier in the first phase of the project (see Smith and Kuchah, 2014), agreed on a set of thematic areas of mutual interest (See Ekembe and Fonjong, 2018). Over the last two years, the group has mainly focused on developing strategies and resources to foster learner motivation and have conducted a number of activities through WhatsApp, Facebook and face-to-face meetings. These activities have included article discussions, sharing and reflecting on stories of successful lessons, developing lesson plans collaboratively, collecting and analysing feedback from students, peer observation and feedback, as well as collaborative action research projects with the aim of developing principles for good practice in context (see Ekembe and Fonjong, 2018; Kuchah and Smith, 2018).

For members of the research group, the experience so far has been professionally enriching not just for their individual professional growth, but also in terms of their self-perception as can be seen from the following excerpt from a participant:

Excerpt 1

I have learned a lot through this group. First of all, I have learned that as a teacher, I need to be reflective in order to improve on my classroom practices. Secondly, I have learned that through Action Research, I can become a better teacher. I have also learned to share my shortcomings as a teacher and have learned from other colleagues. I have become more confident in preparing and delivering my lessons, moving from teacher-centered lessons to learner-centered lessons. I have also become conscious that I could document my lessons. Above all, I have become a better teacher and still strive to continue to grow personally.

Besides their own professional growth, involvement in the group has also given participants the confidence and ability to support their peers: as can be seen from the following two excerpts from the WhatsApp forum:

Excerpt 2

the activities we have had so far have given me more aptitudes to analyse classroom practices and coach younger colleagues in my department.

Excerpt 3

one of the most amazing benefits to me is that through this group, I am growing professionally and I feel like I am able to improve on ELT by empowering other close colleagues.

Despite the positivity within the group, there is still a danger that the lack of an institutional recognition of, and incentive for developmental projects such as this one may eventually experience burn out and lose motivation especially as, because of constraints on their time due to heavy workloads, they mostly carry out their activities during weekends and can barely squeeze time between their own work to observe colleagues in other schools. Like with the two examples from Ethiopia and Senegal above, the need for MoEs to recognise, support and reward teacher development initiatives is important and can be a powerful incentive (Focho, 2018).

Consolidating and expanding networks, looking to the future

The examples of teacher-led collaborative initiatives that we have presented above are only a tiny representation of the many bottom-up initiatives currently going on in SSA. The excerpts from teachers involved in the different teacher-led initiatives described in this chapter suggest that TAs and other teacher led collaborative platforms have the potential to serve as learning communities (Liebermann and Miller, 2011) where professional knowledge and expertise is co-constructed by members of the community and even shared with colleagues beyond the immediate group. While collaborative teacher development initiatives are increasingly common in a wide range of language teaching contexts (Johnson, 2009), the evidence from SSA shows that at least in some cases, they are the only available and/or viable means for teachers to develop context appropriate forms of pedagogy which respond to their specific contextual constraints. The examples in this chapter provide evidence that, for teachers in contexts of constraint, collaborative learning communities can inspire and energize and indeed constitute the most important factor in instituting change (Lassonde and Israel, 2009), if not directly on policy, at least in teachers' classroom practices. However, for these networks to be sustainable there is need for a committed membership and a leadership with a vision. In this regards, the Hornby trust has played a significant role in providing further education for professionals from developing world countries, which professionals have been at the centre of collaborative initiatives in otherwise under-privileged contexts. In fact a significant amount of the research that has informed our understanding of the important role of TAs has come to the limelight mainly through MA dissertations, doctoral thesis and other publications by, or including Hornby Scholars (e.g. Debacco, 2007; Dixit, 2007; Falcao, 2004; Gnawali, 2013; 2016; Padwad, 2016) who continue to play important leadership roles in their local TAs. Over the last two decades, Hornby alumni have had a dedicated slot on the IATEFL conference each year during which different alumni share developmental projects, which they have conducted with colleagues in their workplace or within their associations. Unfortunately, apart from individual publications in the IATEFL conference proceedings, there is yet no comprehensive documentation and evaluation of the impact of such projects over the years, which might provide more evidence of the value of collaborative bottom-up initiatives.

Conclusion

The challenges to the attainment of quality education in SSA are well known in the literature and include infrastructural, material, and human resources. In this chapter, we have examined how the fragile economic situations of SSA countries affects MoEs' ability to support teachers and how factors such as classroom challenges, low pay and reputation as well as lack of motivation on the part of teachers might be further exacerbated by existing top-down teacher education initiatives. Drawing from examples of bottom up teacher-led initiatives from three SSA countries as well as from other projects involving teachers as major stakeholders and decisions makers, we have shown that constructivist approaches which reinforce teacher agency and collaboration are more likely to support teacher professional development than existing top-down mandated training models favoured by MoEs in these countries. We thus understand that teachers are more likely to accept pedagogic ideas when these emanate from their peers than when such ideas are conveyed to them by MoE officials and outside experts to their collective realities. Looking at the examples from Ethiopia, Senegal and Cameroon, we suggest that because bottom up teacher-led initiatives may be a viable route to quality teacher education there is a growing need for these to be supported and incentivised by MoEs so that they may be sustainable. More importantly, given the range of expertise within TAs in SSA and the paucity of teacher-led research from the continent, it may be useful for African TAs and Africa TESOL to map out a research agenda which reflects the needs of their membership to initiate, encourage and support local inquiry-based collaborative projects.

Further reading

Elsheikh, A., Effiong, O. and Coombe, C. (eds) (2018) *The Role of Language Teacher Associations in Professional Development*. New York: Springer.

This book is a pioneering collection which examines the theoretical and research literature on language teacher education and professional development with a special focus English language teacher associations (ELTAs). The different contributions to the collection address a range of themes around the place and role of ELTAs in supporting and sustaining teacher education and professional development. The 24 chapters in this book are written by experienced professionals and experts with long standing involvement with national and international English language teachers association.

Kuchah, K. and Shamim, F. (eds) (2018) *International Perspectives on Teaching English in Difficult Circumstances: Contexts, Challenges and Possibilities*. Basingstoke: Palgrave Macmillan.

This book offers a holistic practitioner and research-based perspective on English Language Teaching and teacher education in difficult circumstances. The 12 chapters in this collection examine the challenges and problems that emerge from the complex current ELT environment, and present examples of contextualised inquiry-based strategies and interventions to address these challenges. The two chapters in section 4 of the book examine context-specific approaches to teacher development in contexts of constraint where opportunities for continuous professional development are scarce.

Smith, R., Padwad, A. and Bullock, D. (2017) *Teaching in Low-Resource Classrooms: Voices of Experience*. London: British Council. Available online: <www.teachingenglish.org.uk/publications>

This is an edited collection of stories of success and of teachers-inquiry authored by classroom practitioners from Bangladesh, India, Nepal and Pakistan through a collaborative developmental project organised by the Hornby Trust. The introduction describes the processes involved in this project and argues for a sustained collaboration between professionals within and across contexts. Each teacher account addresses a specific classroom challenge and the associated video materials provide a further stimulus for reflection.

References

Akyeampong, K. and Stephens, D. (2002) 'Exploring the Backgrounds and Shaping of Beginning Student Teachers in Ghana: Toward Greater Contextualisation of Teacher Education'. *International Journal of Educational Development*, 22(3–4) 261–274.

Akyeampong, K., Djangmah, J., Oduro, A., Seidu, A. and Hunt, F. (2007) *Access to Basic Education in Ghana: The Evidence and the Issues*. Brighton: University of Sussex, Centre for International Education.

Avalos, B. (2000) 'Policies for Teacher Education in Developing Countries'. *International Journal of Educational Research*, 33(5) 457–474.

Bainton, D., Barrett, A. M. and Tikly, L. (2016) *Improving secondary school teacher quality in Sub-Saharan Africa: framing the issues*. Bristol: University of Bristol. Working Papers in Education #03/2016.

Birbirso, D. T. (2014) 'Crisis in EFL Proficiency and Teacher Development in the Context of International Donation and Transformation Discourses'. *Australian Journal of Teacher Education*, 39(2) 1–20.

Bolitho, R. (2016) 'The ingredients of quality in teacher education', in Pickering, G. and Gunashekar, P. (eds) *Ensuring Quality in English Language Teacher Education*. London: British Council: 26–32.

Borg, S. (2015a) 'Researching teacher education', in Paltridge, B. and Phakiti, A. (eds) *Research Methods in Applied Linguistics: A Practical Resource*. London: Bloomsbury: 487–504.

Borg, S. (2015b) *Professional Development for English Language Teachers: Perspectives from Higher Education in Turkey*. Ankara: British Council.

Coleman, H. (2018) 'An almost invisible "difficult circumstance": the large class', in Kuchah, K. and Shamim, F. (eds) *International Perspectives on Teaching English in Difficult Circumstances: Contexts, Challenges and Possibilities*. Basingstoke: Palgrave Macmillan: 29–48.

CONAP (2008) *Contribution à la réflexion sur l'arrimage des reformes pedagogiques aux exigencies de la gouvernance educative*. Yaounde: Imprimerie Salvation Print.

Cordingley, P., Bell, M., Rundell, B. and Evans, D. (2003) *The Impact of Collaborative CPD on Classroom Teaching and Learning: Research Evidence in Education Library*. London: EPPI Centre, Social Science Research Unit, Institute of Education.

Cordingley, P., Bell, M., Evans, D. and Firth, A. (2005) 'The impact of collaborative CPD on classroom teaching and learning. Review: What do teacher impact data tell us about collaborative CPD?', in

Research Evidence in Education Library. London: EPPI-Centre, Social Science Research Unit, Institute of Education, University of London.

Debacco, D. (2007) *The role of teacher associations in INSET programmes in the public sector.* Masters dissertation, University of Warwick, UK.

Del Prete, T. (2013) *Teacher Rounds: A Guide to Collaborative Learning in and from Practice.* London: Corwin Press.

Desimone, L. M. (2011) 'A Primer on Effective Professional Development'. *Phi Delta Kappan,* 92(6) 68–71.

Dixit, K. (2007) *Towards a proposal for facilitator development for English Language Teachers' Clubs in India.* Master's dissertation, College of St. Mark and St John, University of Exeter, UK.

Ekembe, E. (2016) 'Do "resourceful" methodologies really work in "under-resourced" contexts?', in Murphy, A. (ed.) *New Developments in Foreign Language Learning.* New York: NOVA Science: 121–140.

Ekembe, E. E. and Fonjong, A. S. (2018) 'Teacher Association Research for Professional Development in Cameroon'. *ELT Research,* 33 28–31.

Elsheikh, A., Effiong, O. and Coombe, C. (eds) (2018) *The Role of Language Teacher Associations in Professional Development.* New York: Springer.

Falcao, A. (2004) *A Brazilian teacher association for teachers of English: organisational improvement through an international and comparative educational perspective.* Master's dissertation, University of Leeds, UK.

Farrell, T. S. C. (2013) *Reflective Writing for Language Teachers.* London: Equinox.

Focho, G. (2018) 'Towards a project-based approach to teacher development in difficult circumstances: the case of two English language teachers' professional development in Cameroon', in Kuchah, K. and Shamim, F. (eds) *International Perspectives on Teaching English in Difficult Circumstances: Contexts, Challenges and Possibilities.* Basingstoke: Palgrave Macmillan: 199–220.

Gnawali, L. (2013) *English language teacher education through professional associations: the NELTA way.* PhD thesis, Kathmandu University, Nepal.

Gnawali, L. (2016) 'English Language Teacher Development through Teacher Associations: The Case of NELTA'. *ELT Journal,* 70(2) 170–179.

Gruba, P., Hinkelman, D. and Cardenas-Claros, M. S. (2016) 'New technologies, blended learning and the "flipped classroom" in ELT', in Hall, G. (ed.) *The Routledge Handbook of English Language Teaching.* New York: Routledge: 135–149.

Heugh, K., Benson, C., Bogale, B. and Gebreyohannes, M. A. (2007) *Final Report Study on Medium of Instruction in Primary Schools in Ethiopia.* Addis Ababa: Ethiopian Ministry of Education.

IATEFL (2013) 'Linking, Developing and Supporting English Language Professionals Worldwide'. *IATEFL Voices,* 234 (September–October).

Jagusah, O. (2001) 'Educational Policy in Africa and the Issue(s) of Context: The Case of Nigeria and South Africa'. *International Education Journal,* 2(5) 113–125.

Johnson, K. (2009) *Second Language Teacher Education: A Sociocultural Perspective.* New York: Routledge.

Johnson, K. E. (2006) 'The Sociocultural Turn and its Challenges for Second Language Teacher Education'. *TESOL Quarterly,* 40(1) 235–257.

Komba, W. L. and Nkumbi, E. (2008) 'Teacher Professional Development in Tanzania: Perceptions and Practices'. *Journal of International Cooperation in Education,* 11(3) 67–83.

Krugel, R. and Fourie, E. (2014) 'Concerns for the Language Skills of South African Learners and their Teachers'. *International Journal of Educational Science,* 7(1) 219–228.

Kuchah, K. (2008) 'Developing as a professional in Cameroon: challenges and visions', in Garton, S. and Richards K. (eds) *Professional Encounters in TESOL: Discourses of Teachers in Teaching.* New York: Palgrave Macmillan: 203–217.

Kuchah, K. (2013) *Context appropriate ELT pedagogy: an investigation in Cameroonian primary schools.* PhD thesis, Centre for Applied Linguistics, University of Warwick, UK.

Kuchah, K. (2015) 'An Interim Report on the CAMELTA Teacher Association Research Project (Progress Report)'. *ELT Research,* 30 31–34.

Kuchah, K. (2016) 'ELT in difficult circumstances: challenges, possibilities and future directions', in Pattison, T. (ed.) *IATEFL 2015 Manchester Conference Selections.* Canterbury: IATEFL: 149–160.

Kuchah, K. (2018) 'Teaching English in difficult circumstances: setting the scene', in Kuchah, K. and Shamim, F. (eds) *International Perspectives on Teaching English in Difficult Circumstances: Contexts, Challenges and Possibilities*. Basingstoke: Palgrave Macmillan: 1–25.

Kuchah, K. and Shamim, F. (eds) (2018) *International Perspectives on Teaching English in Difficult Circumstances: Contexts, Challenges and Possibilities*. Basingstoke: Palgrave Macmillan.

Kuchah, K. and Smith, R. C. (2011) 'Pedagogy of Autonomy for Difficult Circumstances: From Practice to Principles'. *Innovation in Language Learning and Teaching*, 5(2) 119–140.

Kuchah, K. and Smith, R. (2018) 'An Invitation to Teacher Association Research'. *ELTED Journal*, 21 64–71.

Lassonde, C. A. and Israel, S. E. (2009) *Teacher Collaboration for Professional Learning: Facilitating Study, Research, and Inquiry Communities*. Hoboken, NJ: John Wiley & Sons.

Lewin, K. M. (2007) 'Diversity in Convergence: Access to Education for All'. *Compare*, 37(5) 577–599.

Liebermann, A. & Miller, L. (2011) 'Learning Communities: The Starting Point for Professional Learning is in Schools and Classrooms'. *Standards for Professional Learning*, 31(4) 16–20.

Lockheed, M. and Verspoor, A. (1991) *Improving Primary Education in Developing Countries*. Washington, DC: The World Bank and Oxford University Press.

Maley, A. (2001) 'The Teaching of English in difficult circumstances: who needs a Health Farm when they're Starving?'. *Humanising Language Teaching* 3(6). Available online: <www.hltmag.co.uk/nov01/martnov014.rtf> (accessed 20 June 2018).

Mann, S. (2005) 'The Language Teacher's Development'. *Language Teaching*, 38(3) 103–118.

Mijena, E. (2013) 'The need for professional growth of ELT teachers in Ethiopia'. *STAR Journal*, 160–168.

Ministry of Education (MoE) (2009) *Continuous Professional Development for Primary and Secondary School Teachers, Leaders and Supervisors in Ethiopia: The Framework*. Addis Ababa: Ministry of Education.

Mtika, P. and Gates, P. (2011) 'What do Secondary Trainee Teachers say About Teaching as a Profession of their "Choice" in Malawi?'. *Teaching and Teacher Education*, 27 424–433.

Mulkeen, A. (2010) *Teachers in Anglophone Africa – Issues in Teacher Supply, Training and Management*. Washington, DC: World Bank.

Muthwii, M. (2001) *Language Policy and Practices in Kenya and Uganda: Perceptions of Parents, Pupils and Teachers on the use of Mother Tongue, Kiswahili and English in Primary Schools*. Nairobi: Phoenix Publishers.

Nakabugo, M. G. (2008) 'Universal Primary Education for Growth? The Paradox of Large Classes in Uganda'. *Journal of International Cooperation in Education*, 11(1) 117–130

Nel, N. and Muller, H. (2010) 'The Impact of Teachers' Limited English Proficiency on English Second Language Learners in South African Schools'. *South African Journal of Education*, 30 635–650.

Okoth, T. A. (2016) 'Challenges of Implementing a Top-down Curriculum Innovation in English Language Teaching: Perspectives of Form III English Language Teachers in Kenya'. *Journal of Education and Practice*, 7(3) 169–177.

O'Sullivan, M. C. (2006) 'Teaching Large Classes: The International Evidence and a Discussion of Some Good Practice in Ugandan Primary Schools'. *International Journal of Educational Development*, 26 24–37.

Padwad, A. (2016) 'The Cultural Roots of Teacher Associations: A Case Study from India'. *ELT Journal*, 70(2) 160–169.

Richards, J. C. and Farrell, T. S. C. (2005) *Professional Development For Language Teachers: Strategies for Teacher Learning*. Stuttgart: Ernst Klett Sprachen.

Rixon, S. and Smith, R. (2010) *Directory of UK ELT Research 2005–08*. London: British Council.

Samb, M. (2013) 'Formative assessment for a pedagogy of success', in Edge, J. and Mann, S. (eds) *Innovations in Pre-Service Education and Training for English Language Teachers*. London: British Council: 33–46.

Schlebusch, G. and Thobedi, M. (2004) 'Outcomes-Based Education in the English Second Language Classroom In South Africa'. *The Qualitative Report*, 9(1) 35–48.

Shamim, F. and Kuchah, K. (2016) 'Teaching large classes in difficult circumstances', in Hall, G. (ed.) *The Routledge Handbook of English Language Teaching*. Abingdon: Routledge: 527–541.

Smith, R. (2011) 'Teaching English in difficult circumstances: a new research agenda', in Pattison, T. (ed.) *IATEFL 2010 Harrogate Conference Selections*. Canterbury: IATEFL: 78–80.

Smith, R. and Kuchah, K (2014) 'Teacher Association Research: An Innovative Form of Teacher-Research. *Voices*, 236 (January–February) 22–23.

Smith, R., Negash, N., França, V., Wang, Q., Phyak, P., Ajjan, M., Kuchah, H. K., Saleem, M., Sarwar, Z. and Coleman, H. (2012) 'Investigating large classes' (panel discussion), in Pattison, T. (ed.) *IATEFL 2011 Brighton Conference Selections*. Canterbury: IATEFL: 102–105.

Soler, J., Craft, A. and Burgess, H. (2001) *Teacher Development: Exploring Our Own Practice*. London: Paul Chapman.

Tchombe, T. M. (2010) 'Progressive Transformative Teacher Education in Cameroon: Policy, Training and Research for Sustainable Education'. *Journal of All India Association for Educational Research*, 22(2) 53–72.

Tyers, A. and Lightfoot, A. (2018) 'Using mobile to create low cost, high quality language learning opportunities: lessons from India and Bangladesh', in Kuchah, K. and Shamim, F. (eds) *International Perspectives on Teaching English in Difficult Circumstances: Contexts, Challenges and Possibilities*. Basingstoke: Palgrave Macmillan: 109–130.

UNESCO (1990) *World Declaration on Education for All and Framework for Action to Meet Basic Learning Needs*. Paris: UNESCO.

UNESCO (2000) *Dakar Framework for Action, Education for All: Meeting Our Collective Commitments, Expanded Commentary*. Paris: UNESCO.

UNESCO (2005) *Education for All: The Quality Imperative*. Paris: UNESCO.

UNESCO (2013) *Toward Universal Learning: Recommendations from the Learning Metrics Task Force*. Montreal and Washington, DC: UNESCO.

UNESCO (2015) *Education for All 2000–2015: Achievements and Challenges, Education for All Global Monitoring Report 2015*. Paris: UNESCO.

UNESCO Institute for Statistics (UIS) (2006) *Teachers and Educational Quality: Monitoring Global Needs for 2015*. Montreal: UNESCO Institute for Statistics.

UNESCO Institute of Statistics (UIS) (2016) *Education: Pupil-Teacher Ratio in Lower Secondary Education*. Montreal: UNESCO Institute for Statistics.

Weideman, A., Tesfamariam, H. and Shaalukeni. L. (2003) 'Resistance to Change in Language Teaching: Some African Case Studies'. *Southern African Linguistics and Applied Language Studies*, 21(1–2) 67–76.

Wenger, E. (1998) *Communities of Practice: Learning, Meaning and Identity*. Cambridge: Cambridge University Press.

West, M. (1960) *Teaching English in Difficult Circumstances*. London: Longmans, Green.

Wright, T. (2010) 'Second Language Teacher Education: Review of Recent Research on Practice'. *Language Teaching*, 43(3) 259–296.

24

Creating contexts for teacher development

Mark A. Clarke

Introduction

In this chapter I unpack the phrase 'professional development', arguing that we teacher educators need to adopt strategic, often political, approaches to changing the temporal, material, symbolic, and interactional contexts of teacher practice. I examine what it means for teachers, administrators, and mentors to confront the complex realities they face as educators and to collaborate in developing thoughtful responses to difficult situations.

Professional development occurs in a tangle of complexities. Teachers come to the sessions with their own issues and priorities. They often have families and mortgages and pressing concerns that overshadow the agendas of the individuals who have organized the activities. They are employed in particular situations – intensive English language programs that serve adults, public and private schools that serve a broad range of school-age students, immigrant programs in English speaking countries, English language programs around the world. Their classes may be large and diverse, with a wide variety of students whose interest in and commitment to learning English vary according to their life circumstances. The curriculum is often mandated and materials may be out-dated and/or sparse. School funding, and therefore salaries and job security, is often tied to enrolment. Governmental, administrative, parental, and community demands may play a significant role in the execution of one's duties. Roles, relationships, and responsibilities also vary. Teachers may be working at several institutions. They may be struggling under pressure from administrators to obtain professional certification and advanced degrees, with the attendant pressures of balancing the demands of being a student against the requirements of teaching. And, perhaps most importantly for the readership of this volume, the roles and responsibilities of teacher educators become complicated by the fact that the empirical realities of teachers loom larger than the scholarly concerns of professors. Our authority as scholars is tested against the growing experience of practitioners.

I argue that we teacher educators benefit by examining these factors closely, creating environments that support our own development as well as that of our students. I use an ecological framework and principles from systems theory, cultural-historical activity theory, and constructive developmental psychology to create a perspective that permits the operationalization of the aphorism, 'Think globally, act locally.' I draw on my work with an alternative high school in the United States to show how we approached this task. I describe in some detail the learning lab – a structured process of collaboration that emerged as part of a formal school–university partnership (Goodlad, 1994; Rhodes and Bellamy, 1999). The labs provided a coherent context for personal and professional reflection and collaborative action around specific problems of practice. A significant characteristic of this approach is that it balances the perspectives of research and practice, thereby illuminating the tensions that often arise between professors and teachers, permitting a context for both parties to make important discoveries about teaching, learning, and self.

English language teaching in troubled times

Teachers today face a daunting array of challenges both inside and outside the classroom:

- A world in frightening disarray – mass migration caused by extreme weather, drought, civil disorder, and violence.
- Dramatic shifts toward right-wing politics and validation of xenophobic policies that play to people's fears and suspicions of newcomers and reveal deep roots of racism and ethnocentrism.
- University/state regulations that privilege credentials rather than pedagogical accomplishments and commitments to professional responsibilities.
- The school as factory – assembly-line approaches to teaching that give priority to programs, curricula, textbooks, rather than authentic communication.
- High stakes testing and centralized decision-making driven by politics rather than empirically informed policy.
- Micro-managing administrators operating under pressure to become enforcers rather than leaders.
- School policies and procedures that reduce the discretion with which teachers teach.
- State and federal education policies that prioritize budgetary decisions based on narrowly defined criteria of learning.

The current state of affairs – unprecedented political, economic, and social chaos, compounded by instant globalized communication and narcissistic social media which feeds the illusion of entitled individualism – has its roots in a long history of colonialism, capitalism, and despotism (Mishra, 2017). The rise of neoliberalism has translated those broad-brush strokes of history into educational policies that privilege corporate-style management, quantitative achievement outcomes, and market-driven policies and practices. School funding, and perceptions of student success and teacher effectiveness, are shaped by the same power structures that drive the political and economic forces of the times (Eisenhart and Allen, 2016; Giroux, 2014; Harvey, 2005).

What is the role of teacher educators in this fearful scenario? How do we respond? How can we structure activities for learning and development that support teachers in their efforts at improving their practice?

The first step is to avoid the common mistake of thinking that we have solutions to the problems teachers face and that we can prescribe precise materials and activities. We want to escape the humiliation reflected in Richard Elmore's scathing characterization of conventional professional development activities:

I routinely work with schools that are asked to operate in systems that have completely, blatantly dysfunctional administrative structures, clotted with multiple levels and cross-functional relationships that, on their face, do not, cannot, and never will have a positive impact on learning. The main function of people who work in these organizations seems to be telling other people what to do – usually for things they themselves do not know how to do.

(Elmore, 2016)

There are no technical solutions for the problems that arise from the waves of human tragedy that brings students to English language classrooms today – no pre-packaged programs or checklists that will meet the requirements of the moment. What *is* required are adaptive responses – thoughtful, sensitive, authentic efforts that reveal an awareness of the trauma that students have endured (see Heifetz, 1994 for an elaboration on this distinction between technical and adaptive responses). Each student is unique, as are the circumstances of their life histories. Teachers cannot presume to truly understand what their lives have been like, so generic methods and materials will always strike discordant notes. For the same reasons, we must enter into the situation and collaborate with teachers in the search for appropriate responses.

Another requirement of the tumultuous complexity of the current era is that we acknowledge that a particular situation or event is an outcome of larger cultural, historical, and (inter)personal factors that have converged to become 'the problem of the moment.' For example, all teachers struggle with the issue of cheating, but the complexities are manifold – most obviously, cultural differences with regard to what sorts of behaviours are considered cheating. But teachers' efforts to promote classroom collaboration while emphasizing intellectual independence and creativity perplexes many students, who cannot be blamed for feeling that teachers are sending mixed messages by having them work in small groups on some occasions and requiring them to keep their work to themselves on others.

In other words, the problems facing teacher educators today entail the macro and micro dynamics of the cultural and the psychological, requiring novel approaches to problem solving. In the pages that follow I describe a year-long experiment with learning labs that constituted an attempt to create opportunities for personal reflection on, and organizational adjustment to, these sorts of problems. My central argument is that effective professional development activities require both individual and institutional identity work. I will elaborate on the theoretical premises of our approach, which provides a lens for examining our own assumptions about schooling even as we create opportunities for teachers' professional growth.

Learning labs as contexts for development

Learning labs are a community effort in which a group of teachers convene regularly to collaborate on a program of instructional improvement and professional development (Patterson and Tolnay, 2015). Working with university personnel, teachers identify pressing problems and negotiate a common focus that will permit them to mine professional literature to inform their effort, and to brainstorm ways of adjusting their practice or implementing new activities to improve learning. Figure 24.1 presents the cycle of activity of the lab.

The example described below is taken from my field notes during my work at New America School in Denver, Colorado. The first-person report reflects the immediacy of the work and maintains the ownership and personal bias of the description.

Learning labs emerged as an important feature of the school–university partnership between The New America School (NAS) and our research lab at the University of Colorado at Denver (UCD) (Clarke and Davis, 2007). NAS is a state-designated 'alternative high school' where 95 per cent of the students are classified 'at risk.' The school was founded some 15 years ago as a

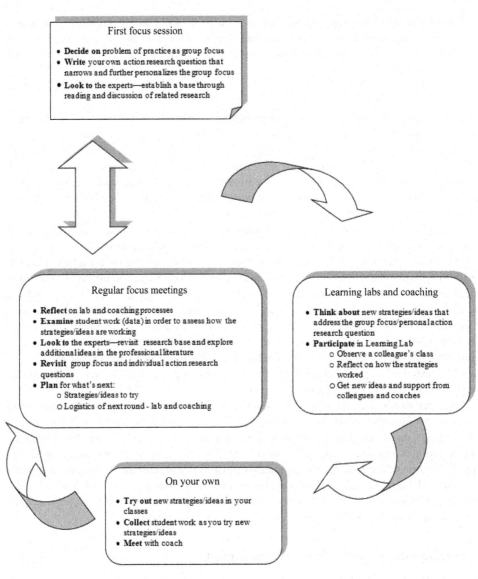

Figure 24.1 Learning lab cycle of activity

'newcomer school' designed to provide a safe haven and a secure learning environment for immigrants and refugees. English language instruction was to be integrated with the typical high school curriculum so that students would emerge with both a diploma and the language skills to succeed in their adopted country. However, funding exigencies caused by state educational policies forced the founders to include other students in their mandate. These are American-born youth whose difficulties in school reflect the failure of the educational system in the United States to serve low-income, minority, and marginalized learners (Darling-Hammond, 2010; Ravitch, 2010; Gandara and Contreras, 2009). The school, therefore, does not provide the best environment for the socialization of immigrants and refugees because many of their fellow students are considered at risk because of academic or behavioural problems they have had at other schools. NAS is, for them, a last-chance opportunity. Whether one considers them 'drop-outs' or 'pushed-outs', the reality is the same – they are at odds with the values and require-ments of the mainstream culture and they are openly resistant to the very norms that newly arrived immigrant and refugee students are attempting to master. The learning lab described here focused on English language learners. We were engaged in the delicate task of encouraging students' success in a new culture while helping them avoid emulating the raucous and counter-productive behaviour of many of their peers at the school.

Seven of us – four classroom teachers, two peer-coaches who were also English language teachers, and I, the university professor – gathered during the weekly professional development time slot to respond to the latest district mandate – the use of data teams to orchestrate a process of goal-setting, coordinated focus on particular instructional techniques, and centralized assess-ment intended to permit comparison across subject-matter and schools. At the first meeting we went around the table, everyone voicing their opinions about the appropriate focus for a problem of practice. Classroom management, technology integration, cheating, engagement, formative assessment, responding to administrative mandates were all nominated and discussed. Central administrators wanted a focus that would produce better test scores, and all of the afore-mentioned topics could be defended in that endeavour. However, after considerable discussion the problem of practice was articulated as 'academic integrity', which permitted teachers to continue work they had already begun and to also comply with the administrative mandate. Readings were identified (Martin, 2012; McCabe, 2005) and a schedule for observations and feedback sessions was developed.

We met as a group every week during the academic year, with the inevitable interruptions and abbreviated meeting times caused by high school dynamics. We developed a protocol to per-mit observed teachers to guide the conversation toward information they could use immediately to improve their instruction. Box 24.1 presents the protocol we used to guide our discussions.

Box 24.1   Learning lab negotiated protocol

Process

- Data team discusses up-coming observations and brainstorms with observed teacher around identified focus of lesson, problem of practice, etc.
- Teacher sends out brief description of the lesson, including his/her goals for the session.
- Teacher lists two or three things for observers to pay attention to (these can be differenti-ated – i.e., s/he might give different observers different things to watch for), reminders of brainstorming already completed.
- Observers take notes during session to support oral feedback.
- Debrief session follows protocol to make maximum use of time and to avoid judgmental or celebratory spirals that are not strictly data-based (need to be realistic about this – kind and collaborative support always welcomed):

  o   No excessive or elaborate expressions of admiration or approval or judgment.
  o   When we meet, observers go first, around the table, giving one noticing at a time. Teacher takes notes (observers read from their notes as they report, but hold on to them. We may not have time for all noticings to be voiced, so observers should prioritize).

- o Observers say, 'I noticed...' followed by descriptive statement (e.g., 'I noticed that you spoke to Juan seven times, to Maria two times, to Ngo zero times, to ... ' (etc. assuming that this is what the teacher asked observer to pay attention to).
- o Round and round, until observers have exhausted their noticings.
- o Teacher can ask clarification questions. No apologies or expressions of embarrassment or dismay or disagreement with what observers say. The point is to be clear on what others saw for reflection on what you intended and/or expected them to see.
- o At the end, teacher offers a brief tentative assessment of what s/he has learned from the process, and speculates on how s/he will use the information tomorrow.

Purpose of protocol

- To provide teacher with immediate feedback on what s/he was attempting to do so that s/he can adjust technique and materials for tomorrow's lesson.
- To maximize efficient use of time.
- To maximize collegiality and minimize congeniality.

Several aspects of the protocol merit attention, both to understand the functional dynamics of the activity and to illuminate the conceptual framework with which we were operating.

- The protocol was negotiated. Versions of learning labs had been used in NAS over the years, and staff had read and discussed the literature on them, but this document was very much a unique product of this group, reflecting the realities and priorities of the moment.
- The 'Purpose of protocol' bullets are grounded in Barth's distinction between 'collegiality' – honest critique – and 'congeniality' – friendly and flattering but not necessarily helpful observations (Barth, 1990).
- Classroom observations were key to the process, but an attitude of 'no judgment' was strictly enforced. We adhered to a rule of no 'suggestions for improvement' nor statements to the effect of 'here's how I would have done that', to prevent the feedback session from becoming a listing of advice. The assumption was that only the observed teacher knew all of the relevant information about the students and the lessons to date. The observers were considered 'legitimate peripheral participants' who reported descriptively on what they had been asked to observe. Observed teachers took what they could use, leaving the rest for another time. (Lave and Wenger, 1991).

Over the course of the academic year, we moved in and out of classrooms, observing, videotaping, taking notes, and convening for debriefing sessions. Although the feedback sessions were not aimed at prescriptions for improvement, they provided rich exchanges of information, insight, opinion, interpretation. Teachers reflected on what they had seen and discussed and the teachers who had been observed returned to their classrooms to adjust attitudes and activities in light of the conversations. Among techniques tried and reported on: novel ways of getting students' attention for instructions, of responding to individual problems, of negotiating differences of opinions among students. Teachers exchanged copies of classroom materials, adapted teaching techniques, and expanded assessment activities. One teacher produced a questionnaire on academic integrity that everyone used to orchestrate conversations with students. Another adopted an online program, Quizlet, to connect in-class and out-of-class learning activities and to foster independence of effort (https://quizlet.com/). A variety of techniques were developed and adapted for focusing student attention on personal growth rather than competitive assessment of learning. Box 24.2 presents an example of the email exchanges and notes around one observation.

Box 24.2   Learning lab email exchanges

From: Erin K
Sent: Monday, November 28, 2016 9:37:42 PM
To: Mark C
Cc: Erin G; Robert N; Colleen F; Kelly M; Lisa C; Annie T; Robert H; Christine L; Tracey M
Subject: Re: ELD Data Team Report

Hi,

I'm obviously interested in pursuing this since I brought it up. I also poked around on the internet and found a couple of articles: (http://library.uvm.edu/~pmardeus/honors/honorcode.pdf; www.aacu.org/publications-research/periodicals/it-takes-village-academic-dishonesty-and-educational-opportunity; www.mnsu.edu/cetl/teachingresources/articles/academicdishonesty.html)

One of the takeaways I had from what these said it that this is maybe larger than our own classrooms; that we would have to possibly address the whole culture of NAS to create one that discourages academic dishonesty. For example, a couple of years ago one of my young mothers copied and pasted an entire article and submitted it as her own work, but there was nothing in our handbook addressing academic integrity specifically. It makes it hard to have clear policies and clear consequences when we don't even have a clear policy around it.

Anyway, we can certainly discuss this in more depth later!
Erin K

From: Erin K
Date: Thursday, December 1, 2016 at 7:47 AM
To: Robert N
Cc: Erin G; Mark C; Colleen F; Kelly M; Lisa C; Annie T; Robert H; Christine L; Tracey M
Subject: Re: ELD Data Team Report

Hi,

So here's some information about my class for the observation. It's the first time I've delivered this particular week of instruction, so I'm not sure how the timing is going to play out ...

My objectives for the afternoon are two-fold; first, students are going to be able to demonstrate their mastery of the 20 vocabulary words we've been studying around film and TV genres on a computer-based quiz. Second, they are going to be able to interpret a bar graph of prime-time TV viewing habits and write about it using quantifiers (which we've been working on this week using pie charts). Ideally they will be creating a bar chart of their own to write about, but

---

that's where I'm not sure how the timing is going to work out, particularly because it is difficult to predict how long students will take to complete the test.

In terms of what I'd like y'all to look for, as I mentioned I've worked quite hard to find ways to try to encourage academic integrity while taking the test. Of course, several extra adults might be a deterrent, but I'd still like you to observe how independently students are working and to notice strategies they seem to use when they are struggling with an answer. I'd like you to also pay attention to how the transition between the test and coursework occurs and how the students who are continuing the test are working through it. Also, just generally helping me get a sense of how well they are able to achieve the goal of reading the graph and writing about it independently.

Cheers,

Erin

From: Mark C
Sent: Monday, Dec 5, 2016 10:39 AM
To: Erin G; Robert N; Colleen F; Kelly M; Lisa C; Annie T; Robert H; Christine L; Tracey M
Subject: ELD Data Team Report 12–1-16

ELD Data Team met during Panther Thursday, 3:30–4:15
Attending: Mark, Lisa, Newman, Colleen, Kelly
Next observation: Tuesday, 12/13, Lisa C @ 9:00
Swivl: We recorded the meeting using Swivl; continuing to experiment with the technology, also wanting a record for the Erins to consult.
Cheating/Academic Integrity
The topic was nominated by Erin K. and was the focus of our observations of her class at 12:50 that day.
We spent more time discussing the issue than we did on the observation; we should return to both next time we meet. Key points for further examination:

- Broad agreement that cheating can be operationally defined as submitting someone else's work as yours, with intent to deceive.
- Agreement also on the fact that our society and the school system encourages cheating by focusing on grades and high-stakes testing rather than emphasizing learning for learning's sake.
- School policy and school climate (i.e., informal norms among adults) needs to support individual teachers' efforts.
- Academic Integrity as cultural and developmental issue.

    o   Culture: No culture condones cheating, but definitions and sanctions vary widely across (and perhaps within) cultures.
    o   Developmental: Maturity plays a role in this. Two students from the same culture may differ considerably in regard to cheating depending on age.

From: Robert N
Date: Monday, December 5, 2016 at 10:49 AM
To: Mark C

Cc: Erin K; Erin G; Colleen F; Lisa C; Annie T; Robert H; Christine L; Tracey M
Subject: Re: ELD Data Team Report

Just to add the report, this week I'll be creating a survey for you to give your students (should you choose to do so) about their beliefs and attitudes around cheating. I'll share with you all for edits and additions before giving to students.
Robert N

This thread – just one of countless digital dialogues that punctuated our collaborations – provides a glimpse of work we were doing. It is representative of the dynamic in which we were engaged, and is self explanatory, with a few elaborations:

- We refer to the group as 'data team' because that is the phrase used by central administration for the activity.
- SWIVL is the video device we were using to capture classroom activities and record our meetings (www.swivl.com/).
- There are 11 people included in the messages – the seven of us participants in the learning lab and four administrators (the principal and assistant principals and the professional development coordinator). This is worth mentioning because the participation and support of the administrative team was vital to the success of the endeavour. They were included in most of our communications.
- The problem of practice as it first arose was simply stated as 'cheating', but expanded to 'academic integrity' as the discussion revealed a much wider and deeper range of issues.
- Notice that this email strand shows one teacher – Erin K – leading the discussion and doing a bit of legwork in identifying readings. This was common – different individuals assuming the lead at different times to move us along.
- Erin K also speculates about the range of behaviours we might encounter in the classroom and the potential impact of having several adults observing. This led to a discussion of how the learning lab process might become a topic of study in itself, revealing aspects of the 'observer's paradox' – we are always part of the problem as well as the solution (Bateson, 2000: 433–445).
- Not evident in the messages, but a significant factor in Erin K's planning and instruction is the size and diversity of the class: 35 students from Mexico, El Salvador, Somalia, and Myanmar, and a wide range of ages and educational experience.

The following bullet points summarize key elements of this radical revision of professional development activities.

- The Learning Lab format provided a safe environment for teachers to construct a productive response to a mandate from central administration that stipulated that all teachers were to adopt the same problem of practice and to use the same instructional methods and materials to address the problem.

The administrative goal of the process was to achieve higher levels of 'fidelity of implementation' (Dhillon et al., 2015) in instruction and assessment – a flawed concept that rests on causal assumptions that are of little value in a dynamic system such as school, where the complexities of student/teacher interaction coupled with the imperfections of school processes and communications make it difficult to predict precise outcomes.

The teachers were already several weeks into the semester when the memo came down the chain of command and each had developed materials and activities around goals they had established. They quietly set aside the mandate and negotiated a definition of a problem of practice that permitted them to continue with the work they had done without openly defying their superiors; they worked within the spirit, if not the letter, of the directive. By negotiating their participation in the endeavour and by aligning their own interests and agendas with the mandates, teachers were able to arrive at a 'principled enactment' of policy that maintained the goals of the initiative while addressing issues of immediate importance in their classrooms (Buxton et al., 2015). Baldly stated, this approach permitted a professional response to ill-considered and unrealistic administrative interference.

- The teachers acquired new instructional techniques, but on a deeper and more personal level, they were able to explore the contradictions they encountered in their own thinking and behaviour.

The consistent effort of observing others and analysing their own teaching and their reactions to others' teaching encouraged self-reflection and personal change. The culturally dominant default to confronting problems is defensiveness. We tend, naturally, to prefer our comfortable ways of thinking and acting, and when we observe others whose assumptions and behaviours are different from ours, we resort to our default response of judgment and critique that justifies our way of doing things. Because the rules of the learning lab formally proscribe the voicing of such reactions, we were forced to consider the merits of our colleagues' practice; we were given time and permission to examine new ideas and techniques in more depth (Edge, 2011, 2002). By recognizing that all significant and lasting change begins with oneself, we were able to shift the discourse in our study group from collective complaint to thoughtful analysis of factors that contribute to problems, including taking personal responsibility for our own short-comings (Kegan and Lahey, 2001).

- School administrators exercised leadership, rather than mere management – developing structures and processes to support productive collaboration in pursuit of enduring solutions to complex problems of practice.

Unlike many approaches to professional development, the learning lab requires significant investments of school resources, avoiding the implicit 'blame-the-teacher' perspective of most educational innovation, in which the dominant theme is a long list of changes required of teachers. Rather than adopt the stance that the appropriate response to problems is to fine-tune the directives for teachers to follow and to bear down with carrot-and-stick mandates, the principal and her assistants entered into the process as collaborators. In leadership meetings the administrative team followed the same protocols as those required of teachers, and they held themselves to the same standards in the examination of their own behaviours. They regularly polled staff for input on decisions, and they adjusted school policies, programs, and practices according to the response. They provided time and space for collaboration and they abandoned unsuccessful initiatives promptly (see Clarke and Edge (2009) and de Stefani, this volume), for elaboration on the role of leadership in innovative teacher education).

- Learning Labs created an egalitarian environment where teachers, administrators, and university staff all engaged in a democratic exchange of ideas.

Empirical and theoretical approaches to complex problems of practice were given equal weight, avoiding one of the major problems in education – the dysfunctions of the theory/practice divide (see Clarke, 1994). The distribution of power, both material and symbolic, in this approach encouraged creativity and innovation, and empowered individuals to exercise their freedoms regardless of their role in the school or the university.

- School administrators implemented an extended program of 'mindfulness' as a complement of/antidote to the barrage of 'innovations' being imposed on teachers.

The pressures for changes in instruction and assessment, coupled with demands on teachers to adopt quasi-parental roles and responsibilities with students, resulted in significant stress. By acknowledging that teaching at New America School required more of teachers than teaching at conventional high schools, the leadership team took responsibility for this stress and made a concerted effort at ameliorating it. By creating time and space in meetings for yoga and meditation, they endorsed thoughtful self-evaluation and calm contemplation as an important part of teachers' days (Kabat-Zinn, 1990).

Conceptual framework

Having described the sociopolitical situation in which teacher educators find themselves today, and elaborating with a detailed analysis of one response to the challenges of facilitating teacher development, I now need to clarify the conceptual principles on which that response is built.

We were operating on the belief that the scope and practice of teacher education must capture both the scale of a problem and the specificity of its occurrence in the everyday lives of teachers. It is not sufficient to elaborate theoretical principles; guidelines for implementing changes must also be provided. The learning lab was developed with this imperative in mind. The conceptual framework integrates three theoretical traditions – systems theory, cultural historical activity theory, and constructive developmental psychology – while the organization and operation of the activity conform to the realities of the school in which activities are orchestrated.

We conceive of schooling as an artefact of culture – a dynamic, emerging phenomenon – a network of complex patterns of thought and behaviour, nested social systems functioning toward stability, subject to constraints, and only partially susceptible to direct action (Bateson, 2000; Larsen-Freeman and Cameron, 2008; Capra and Luisi, 2014). We understand identity as micro-variations of culture, stable constellations of values and commitments as revealed in behaviour. Our images of self are fiercely protected through conscious and sub-conscious efforts that undermine change initiatives, even when we are the authors of the innovation (Kegan, 1994; Kegan and Lahey, 2009). We also acknowledge that schools are organizations that mediate cultural and individual identities (Cole, 1996; Holland et al., 1998; Engestrom, 2008). And, however modest our change efforts may seem, they approach conventional educational activity in unconventional ways, and therefore they threaten the status quo, for this is the nature of systems – to function toward stability. For this reason, we are alert to sources of resistance, including our own unconscious obstructions. Given these commitments, we have found it helpful to make explicit our understanding of key concepts, in particular, 'development', 'learning', 'context', and 'levels of the system.'

Development

'Development' is the primary pivot point of the essay. It is important that we move away from uttering the phrase 'professional development' with such superficial ease that it becomes code for 'sit and get' sessions of administrative fiat. Development involves a shift in consciousness, an adjustment in fundamental aspects of identity (Kegan, 1994). As with learning, it involves change – a change in understanding, of perspective, and ultimately, behavior – but, significantly, the change also involves coming to an understanding of oneself in relation to the world, which is why development entails a change in one's identity. Robert Kegan and his associates have identified three distinct stages in adult development, which they refer to as 'socialized, self-authoring, and self-transforming' mind (Kegan and Lahey, 2016: 57–64). Individuals operating at the socialized stage of development respond to their perception of what others expect of them. Self-authoring individuals operate according to a personal code of right/wrong. Self-transforming individuals are guided by an awareness of the possibility that their own perspective may be flawed or incomplete, and they bring a sense of dialectical playfulness to their assessment of situations and self.

The details of Kegan's research, developed over the course of some 40 years and countless studies, are beyond the scope of this chapter, but the crux of the distinctions between the stages and the importance for us in their perspective, lies in the pivotal fact that we humans make choices as we attempt to solve life's problems and these choices are always shaped by our theory of the world, our epistemology. 'Epistemology', a word that covers a complex array of philosophical tenets, can be understood as a matter of perception – the lens through which we apprehend the world and ourselves in it. The question is, to what extent are we aware of the lens that shapes our understanding? Kegan argues that this awareness is at the root of epistemology; he characterizes this as a function of the 'subject/object' tension: Are we able to distance ourselves from a point of view – are we able to see it as an object to be understood? Or are we subject to it, unable to disengage from the perspective and the emotions it engenders? All significant change efforts begin with an increasing awareness of one's own mental model. Growth in our way of knowing involves disturbing the balance, learning to look *at* that which we were previously looking *through*. These three qualitatively different levels of complexity – the socialized mind, the self-authoring mind, and the self-transforming mind – thus represent three distinct epistemologies (Kegan and Lahey, 2009: Chapter 2).

The metaphor of 'stepping back and stepping up' captures the essential insight of the analysis as it relates to decision-making in the maelstrom of the school day (Edge, 2011: 26–48). First we step back from the fray and examine the situation, then we determine how we want to act, and we own our actions. We avoid reacting impulsively; rather, we examine, reflect, and respond (Clarke and Edge, 2009). Humans act on the basis of authority, and the question we ask, not always consciously, is 'What is my justification for a particular stance on some issue? ...of an action? On whose authority am I acting?'

The learning lab environment encouraged teachers to shift from compliance with administrative directives, in which the source of authority was the external and hierarchical power dynamic of school politics, toward ownership of their decisions, in which the source of authority was their personal convictions and professional experience. The individual who is able to act on the basis of his/her personal convictions, who is able to take ownership for difficult or controversial decisions, is operating on a more complex developmental plane that one whose decisions depend on the ratification of others or of institutional rules and regulations, or on the authority of canonical figures in the academic pantheon. The lab gives people the experience of what it is like *not* to see someone else's practice as an object of critique, but instead to step back and see the bigger picture of themselves as a community of creative professionals with different talents and perspectives. This, in turn, helps them see their own practice as *not* fixed and in need of defense, but as emergent and ripe for continuing development.

Learning

Any enduring change in an individual's attitude, thinking, or behavior can be considered learning, so we have adopted 'change over time through engagement in activity' as a working definition. It has the virtue of conforming to scholarly perspectives (Engestrom, 2008; Rogoff, 2003; Lave and Wenger, 1991) but its most valuable asset is that it aligns with practical concerns; it encourages teachers to think of instruction as a matter of crafting activities focusing on what the *students* will be doing, rather than on their own behavior or the content of lessons.

Context

Context becomes a pivotal construct in this approach to teaching and learning. Ecologists remind us that the unit of analysis is always the individual plus the context. We cannot possibly respond effectively to a problem if we do not understand the factors that contribute to its occurrence. But, because the world is a mass of nested pulsating systems, dynamically (re)creating each other according to principles of patterned consistency, the constraints that produce a particular problem or event operate at different levels. We make choices for action based on our awareness of options available at different levels of the system. Thus, following Bateson (2000: 289) we define context as 'all the information we use to decide from among which <u>set</u> of alternatives to make the next move.' The word 'set' indicates that there are always many choices available, and that they cluster at different levels – decisions made at different levels have different consequences. Activities organized to promote teacher development will succeed to the extent that they encourage individuals to expand their field of vision beyond the immediate problem and the obvious cluster of options available. Significant problems are rarely solved at the level they are encountered.

Coupled with an awareness of participants' developmental capabilities, this approach encourages realistic decision-making; it requires us to broaden our understanding of roles and responsibilities – ours and other's – and to adopt a tentative, patient, and exploratory approach to our work as teacher educators. We find ourselves negotiating fundamental 'facts' of life and work, and rethinking our positions on heretofore unproblematic aspects of cognition, emotion, culture, and teaching/learning. Perhaps most unsettling, we find ourselves exploring the interconnections and co-constructions of individual and institutional identities.

Scale

These interconnections among systems of different sizes is addressed by what we refer to as 'levels' in a systems perspective. It is important to explain how we operationalized the construct in our implementation of learning labs. As a starting point we acknowledged that all open systems function according to the same basic principles: they function toward stability yet are constantly changing, responding to internal and external stimuli. By 'systems' we are referring to human beings, classrooms, schools, communities and societies, which are the nested and reciprocally co-constructing. As we work with individual teachers to improve their practice, we are aware that our behavior and our perceptions are collaboratively constructed and constantly influenced by many contexts. These range from the physical space and the immediate time frame in which we find ourselves to the institutions and community in which we live, and beyond – into the social and historical depths that preceded the moment. Obviously, we cannot construct a response to a problem that resolves of all these historical, cultural, and (inter)personal factors, but that does not diminish the importance of the fact that the constraints of all these material, symbolic, and temporal details impinge on the dynamics of the moment in which we find ourselves (Allen and Hoekstra, 2015; Capra and Luisi, 2014). There are two important takeaways from this mind-boggling scenario: First, that we cannot possibly understand everything that impinges on the present moment, but we can exercise patience and humility in our response; direct and decisive action does not translate into immediate and gratifying results. Second, we need to work for changes in the larger systems within which we live and work as well as focus on the immediate facts of 'the problem' as typically defined by institutional convention and personal convenience.

As we attempt to change the conditions of our work and the outcomes of our practice we focus on five distinct but overlapping and co-constructing 'pressure points.'

Pressure points for change

1. *Policy*, at both university and school, provides the formal arrangements and the authority for our work. We knew that our innovations would not last long if we were at odds with institutional policy; we therefore participated in the shaping of school and university policy.
2. *Programs* translate policy into practice and thereby constitute both affordances and constraints for the work. We participated in all textbook and curriculum decisions and we lobbied for flexibility of implementation.
3. *Realities of time and space* – university and school structures and the calendars and clocks of these institutions – shape the universe of our interactions and impinge on our perceptions of what is possible; these are often taken for granted, but they need to be constantly examined because they are pervasive shapers of thought and action. The NAS bell schedule and the use of professional development time were two significant areas where our input was felt.
4. *Roles and responsibilities* of professors, administrators, and teachers are powerful but implicit influences on thought and action, and they can inhibit effective collaboration. At NAS there was a marked flatness in the decision-making hierarchy, and people became comfortable with the challenging conversations that characterize such an organizational structure.
5. *Individual rhythms and routines*, willy-nilly shape the quality of interaction and the outcomes of collaboration; these are the visible manifestations of identity and often the most difficult to change. We struggled constantly with the demands of maintaining observation schedules and adjusting our preferred modes of teaching and communicating.

The learning lab required us to consciously work on all these aspects of organizational life. I contend that this approach to professional development is a radical departure from conventional professional development. Rather than being sessions in which school administrators and university personnel present information to staff, the labs become contexts for personal reflection and conscious efforts at changing practice that result in corresponding changes in how the school operates.

In other words, this approach requires significant change of all the participants (Kegan, 2000). Everyone – not just teachers – engaged in focused self-examination and honest change efforts. We all had to overcome the bias implicit in much of what we learned in our formal training – the pervasive assumption that there exist 'best practices', that all pedagogical problems have solutions, and that the authority for creative teaching rests with others – administrators, experts of various sorts, published materials, consulting agencies and so on (Clarke, 1984, 2007). Teachers had to overcome their reluctance to being observed, a big part of which is letting go of fears of judgment. Administrators learned to temper their preferences for control and to trust teachers' judgment. To do this they had to develop confidence in teachers' professionalism; this goes against traditional pressures for micro-management and cultural confidence in centralized decision-making. In this approach professors (re)enter the scrum of school life and learn to defer to practitioners, both teachers and administrators, when political realities override research-based recommendations. All of these points rest on acceptance of Kegan's subject/object psychology as the lens for examining self-in-action; it requires a fundamental commitment to the aphorism that 'Change begins with oneself.'

On a practical level, if this initial point of collective and individual effort at personal change has been conceded, it becomes necessary for the organizational realities of school and university to be adjusted to support the innovation. University criteria for tenure and promotion, for example, are severely strained by professors' dossiers that are heavier with service-based accomplishments than traditional research publications. The financial burdens of maintaining positions for non-traditional work in both institutions are significant. The learning labs at NAS required changes in daily school realities as well; schedules were adjusted, and staff responsibilities were modified to accommodate the innovations adopted because of the lab sessions. It will be noted that this is not a job that can be done by one person; collaboration across the two institutions and vertically within institutions is required.

The learning labs represented the culmination of an effort that was structurally and procedurally designed to nudge participants toward greater awareness of their own agency and to promote a sense of ownership of school-level decision-making – in other words, a conscious and collective effort to flatten the hierarchy of the school and increase the participant leadership of school staff.

Conclusions and speculations

New America School is a model of responsive teaching and innovative approaches to complex problems of practice. Within the local professional community the school is recognized as a healthy and exciting place to work; the defection of teachers from other schools to teach at NAS is indicative of this, as well as the lengthy tenure of staff at the school; they are committed to the mission of the school and dedicated to the students and their colleagues. They exercise their prerogatives as they participate in leadership decisions that extend their personal authority beyond the conventional boundaries of their position descriptions. Results have been positive in terms of conventional school measures; grades have improved, dropout numbers have gone down and graduation rates up. Local and international delegations have visited the school for observations and meetings with staff. The principal is in demand locally and internationally as a speaker and consultant.

However, it is important to acknowledge that, to many outsiders and some insiders, the investment of time, energy, and effort in collaborative decision-making has produced meager returns. For some the effort has been a failure, for others, a frustratingly unsatisfactory and inconclusive endeavor; test scores have not improved sufficiently, attendance remains an intractable problem, and in spite of herculean creative efforts, funding remains tenuous. Recently I bumped into an NAS administrator at a lunch counter. We had a brief catch-up and, as we parted, he asked about my research and the emerging publications, and wondered if there was a readership for 'dysfunctional schools involved in doomed innovations.'

Which brings us to a critical juncture – the acknowledgement of the difficulty of educational innovation and recognition that the conventional indicators of success do not adequately capture the accomplishments of collaborative initiatives such as learning labs. Schools are the tangible manifestation of a complex convergence of historical and political movements, and current efforts at creating humane environments for learners to explore their interests and exercise their freedoms rarely align with the harsh realities of cultural assumptions and financial constraints. The conditions required for authentic communication between human beings – in this case, between teachers and students and between teacher educators and teachers – do not lend themselves to rapid turn-around and digital displays of outcomes. It is not an exaggeration to assert that, as a culture, we bring a very narrow perspective to the implementation and assessment of educational initiatives, one which reflects our impatient nature and desire for clear-cut, bottom-line outcomes. The result, not surprisingly, is an emphasis on centralized decision-making, mandated curricula, and high stakes testing that short-changes marginalized students and the teachers dedicated to working with them (Darling-Hammond, 2010; Ravitch, 2010; Gandara and Contreras, 2009; Eisenhart and Allen, 2016; Giroux, 2014).

It is reasonable to assert that NAS's efforts at collaboration were a success for all the students who graduated during this time and who benefited from a more compassionate school experience than they had ever had. It was also a success for the staff who participated in a bold experiment and who therefore glimpsed a vision of leadership and an example of teaching and learning that goes beyond the conventional authoritarian and hierarchical versions of school that predominate today.

If we become discouraged by what appears to be limited impact and inconclusive results, we do well to remember that this is the way the world works; these outcomes are precisely characteristic of how change occurs in complex dynamic systems. Innovations do not change the system; they create local disturbances, perturbations that reverberate throughout the system. They are most noticeable at the local level, at the point of occurrence, but the waves wash out and affect larger circles. The extent to which they are recognized as important will depend on the awareness of the individuals doing the noticing. And if these individuals are in positions of power, they can act to create the contexts for sustainability. But the changes will always seem unsatisfyingly small and temporary, and individuals will always step back and take a break from the fray, perhaps just catching their breath, or maybe deciding that it is someone else's turn at the oars. This does not mean that we must lose hope; it means that we must learn to recognize hopeful events when we see them.

Further reading

Learning labs

Brancard, R. and QuinnWilliams, J. (2012) 'Learning Labs: Collaborations for Transformative Teacher Learning'. *TESOL Journal*, 3(3).
Patterson, A. and Tolnay, T. (2015) 'Bringing Teacher Learning to Life: Courageous Teaching Using Peer Learning Labs to Elevate Efficacy'. Available online: <www.pebc.org/wp-content/uploads/2016/07/PeerLearningLabs_web.pdf> (accessed 11 May, 2019).

These two articles provide a step-by-step description of learning labs, with examples and excerpts from actual labs. Brancard and QuinnWilliams were part of the UCD research team so their work constitutes an elaboration of the argument provided here. Patterson and Tolnay are part of the Public Education and Business Coalition, a Denver-based organization dedicated to improving public education and the originator of the concept of learning labs.

Systems theory

Bateson (2000); Capra and Luisi (2014); Larsen-Freeman and Cameron (2008).

Systems theory is a vast universe of scholarship with about 100 years of publications elaborating on key tenets. Capra and Luisi provide a very readable introduction to the topic. Larsen-Freeman and Cameron examine complex dynamic systems with the lens of applied linguists and make a concerted effort to apply systems principles to language teaching. Bateson's book is a collection of essays that have stood the test of time; he continues to be cited by scholars working in diverse fields.

Constructive developmental psychology

Kegan, R. (1994) *In Over Our Heads: The Mental Demands of Modern Life.* Cambridge, MA: Harvard University Press.

Kegan, R. and Lahey, L. (2009) *Immunity to Change: How to Overcome it and Unlock the Potential in Yourself and Your Organization.* Boston, MA: Harvard Business Press.

Heifetz, R. A. (1994) *Leadership Without Easy Answers.* Cambridge, MA: Harvard University Press.

This is where the rubber hits the road; if you do not acknowledge the importance of transformation and if you do not have the tools for creating an environment where transformation can occur, you will not make much progress in implementing the suggestions of this chapter. The place to start is with Kegan and Lahey (2009); this is a workbook with exercises that help you talk about your work in ways that will change the way you work. Caveat – it requires that you *work*, not merely read. Kegan (1994) is the scholarly foundation of subject/object psychology and Kegan and Lahey (2009) is a scholarly practitioner presentation of the argument that resistance to change is, in fact normal – cold comfort if you are a dedicated change agent, but strategically important information.

References

Allen, T. F. H. and Hoekstra T. W. (2015) *Toward a Unified Ecology,* 2nd edition. New York: Columbia University Press.

Barth, R. S. (1990) *Improving Schools from Within: Teacher, Parents, and Principals can Make a Difference.* San Francisco, CA: Jossey-Bass.

Bateson, G. (2000) *Steps to an Ecology of Mind.* Chicago, IL: The University of Chicago Press.

Brancard, R. and Quinn Williams, J. (2012) 'Learning Labs: Collaborations for Transformative Teacher Learning'. *TESOL Journal,* 3(3) 320–349.

Buxton, C. A., Allexsaht-Snider, M., Kayumova, S., Aghasaleh, R., Choi, Y-J. and Cohen, A. (2015) 'Teacher Agency and Professional Learning: Rethinking Fidelity of Implementation as Multiplicities of Enactment'. *Journal of Research in Science Teaching,* 52(4) 489–502.

Capra, F. and Luisi, P. L. (2014) *The Systems View of Life: A Unifying Vision.* New York: Cambridge University Press.

Clarke, M. A. (1984) 'On the Nature of Technique: What do we Owe the Gurus?'. *TESOL Quarterly,* 18(4) 577–594.

Clarke, M. A. (1994) 'The Dysfunctions of the Theory–Practice Discourse'. *TESOL Quarterly,* 28(1) 9–26.

Clarke, M. A. (2007) *Common Ground, Contested Territory: Examining the Roles of English Language Teachers in Troubled Times.* Ann Arbor, MI: University of Michigan Press.

Clarke, M. A. and Davis, A. (2007) *Professional Development Academies for Teachers of Immigrant Students.* National Professional Development Program CFDA #84.195N.

Clarke, M. A. and Edge, J. (2009) 'Building a communicative toolkit for leadership', in Murray, D. and Christensen M. (eds) *Leadership in English Language Education: Theoretical Foundations and Practical Skills for Changing Times.* New York: Routledge.

Cole, M. (1996) *Cultural Psychology: A Once and Future Discipline.* Cambridge, MA: Harvard University Press.

Darling-Hammond, L. (2010) *The Flat World and Education: How America's Commitment to Equity Will Determine Our Future.* New York: Teachers College Press.

Dhillon, S., Darrow, C. and Meyers, C. V. (2015) 'Introduction to implementation fidelity', in Meyers, C. V. and Brandt, W. C. (eds) *Implementation Fidelity in Education Research: Designer and Evaluator Considerations.* New York: Routledge: 8–22.

Edge, J. (2002) *Continuing Cooperative Development: A Discourse Framework for Individuals as Colleagues*. Ann Arbor, MI: University of Michigan Press.

Edge, J. (2011) *The Reflexive Teacher Educator in TESOL: Roots and Wings*. New York: Routledge.

Eisenhart, M. and Allen, C. D. (2016) 'Hollowed Out: Meaning and Authoring of High School Math and Science Identities in the Context of Neoliberal Reform'. *Mind, Culture, and Activity*, 23(3) 188–198.

Elmore, R. F. (2016) '"Getting to Scale … " It Seemed Like a Good Idea at the Time'. *Journal of Educational Change*, 17 529–537.

Engeström, Y. (2008) *Crossing Boundaries in Teacher Teams: From Teams to Knots*. New York: Cambridge University Press.

Gandara, P. and Contreras F. (2009) *The Latino Education Crisis: The Consequences of Failed Social Policies*. Cambridge, MA: Harvard University Press.

Giroux, H. A. (2014) *Neoliberalism's War on Higher Education*. Chicago, IL: Haymarket Books.

Goodlad, J. I. (1994) *Educational Renewal: Better Teachers, Better Schools*. San Francisco, CA: Jossey-Bass.

Harvey, D. (2005) *A Brief History of Neoliberalism*. Oxford: Oxford University Press.

Heifetz, R. A. (1994) *Leadership Without Easy Answers*. Cambridge, MA: Harvard University Press.

Holland, D., Lachitotte, W., Skinner, D. and Cain, C. (1998) *Identity and Agency in Cultural Worlds*. Cambridge, MA: Harvard University Press.

Kabat-Zinn, J. (1990) *Full Catastrophe Living: Using the Wisdom of Your Body and Mind to Face Stress, Pain and Illness*. New York: Delta Publishing.

Kegan, R. (1994) *In Over Our Heads: The Mental Demands of Modern Life*. Cambridge, MA: Harvard University Press.

Kegan, R. (2000) 'What "form" transforms? A constructive-developmental approach to transformative learning', in Mezirow, J. and Associates (eds) *Learning as Transformation: Critical Perspectives on a Theory in Progress*. San Francisco, CA: Jossey-Bass.

Kegan, R. and Lahey, L. (2001) *How the Way We Talk Can Change the Way We Work*. San Francisco, CA: Jossey-Bass.

Kegan, R. and Lahey, L. (2009) *Immunity to Change: How to Overcome it and Unlock the Potential in Yourself and Your Organization*. Boston, MA: Harvard Business Press.

Kegan, R. and Lahey, L. (2016) *An Everyone Culture: Becoming a Deliberately Developmental Organization*. Boston, MA: Harvard Business Review Press.

Larsen-Freeman, D. and Cameron, L. (2008) *Complex Systems and Applied Linguistics*. Oxford: Oxford University Press.

Lave, J. and Wenger, E. (1991) *Situated Learning: Legitimate Peripheral Participation (Learning in Doing: Social, Cognitive and Computational Perspectives)*. New York: Cambridge University Press.

Martin, J. (2012) 'Five Ways to Combat the Plague of Student Cheating'. *Arizona Republic*. Available online: <http://archive.azcentral.com/arizonarepublic/opinions/articles/20120518student-cheating-myturn.html> (accessed 22 May, 2019).

McCabe, D. L. (2005) 'It Takes a Village: Academic Dishonesty and Educational Opportunity'. Available online: <www.aacu.org/publications-research/periodicals/it-takes-village-academic-dishonesty-and-educational-opportunity> (accessed 22 May, 2019).

Mishra, P. (2017) *Age of Anger: A History of the Present*. New York: Farrar, Straus and Giroux.

Patterson, A. and Tolnay, T. (2015) 'Bringing Teacher Learning to Life: Courageous Teaching Using Peer Learning Labs to Elevate Efficacy'. Available online: <www.pebc.org/wp-content/uploads/2016/07/PeerLearningLabs_web.pdf> (accessed 22 May, 2019).

Ravitch, D. (2010) *The Death and Life of the Great American School System*. New York: Basic Books.

Rhodes, L. K. and Bellamy, G. T. (1999) 'Choices and Consequences in the Renewal of Teacher Education'. *Journal of Teacher Education*, 50(1) 17–26.

Rogoff, B. (2003) *The Cultural Nature of Human Development*. New York: Oxford University Press.

PART 5

The processes of L2 teacher education

25

Assessment and feedback

Jo-Ann Delaney

Introduction

The core purpose of language teacher education is to develop good teachers. As teacher educators we strive to help new and existing teachers to be better at the activity of teaching. There is a strong ethos of development and support in the work of the teacher educator, which is appropriate to the role. Yet part of what we do in promoting teacher development will also involve assessment of teaching and giving feedback, especially if we are working with trainees as part of a qualification, either pre or in-service. There are clearly tensions in the dual role of support and assessment. In this chapter we will explore issues around assessment of teaching and providing feedback and consider how underpinning principles and practice can actually help ensure that the activity of assessing plays and important contributory role in teachers' learning.

In this chapter, 'assessment' is used when we consider a formal judgement of teaching, whatever form it will take. The term 'evaluation' is used to identify the activity of thinking about a teaching event. In the context of a teacher education programme, trainee teachers might self-evaluate, whereas the tutor is both evaluating, but also making a judgement – assessing.

Discussions and debates about assessment and feedback

In this section we will look at some of the themes which arise in the literature about assessing teaching and providing feedback on teaching. The range of debate extends beyond the points addressed here and includes such questions as whether assessment of teachers and a focus on their performance is a valid one at all. The discussion below focuses on key points which may be useful to teacher educators when considering their practice.

What is being assessed?

It seems obvious to suggest that we are assessing 'teaching'. However, it is less straightforward to identify the knowledge which we are assessing. For some it is useful to think about knowledge and skills, as in the ability to deliver effective lessons (skills), but also knowing why the lesson was planned and delivered and why it was, or was not, effective (knowledge). This of course raises the question of whether both can be assessed in the same way and whether a teacher who seems most effective in one, but not in the other, is still an effective teacher. In a sense, we are looking at teachers' *knowing* and *doing* and attempting to assess both and, as assessors, make decisions about what this tells us in a more holistic way about the teacher's ability to teach effectively.

This duality of teacher knowledge is but one example of debates about knowledge in a more general sense which can be found as early as Aristotelian concepts of *Epistēmē* or scientific/theoretical knowledge, *Technē* or craft knowledge, which included action and the practical ability to produce something, and *Phronēsis*, the wisdom to know how to act. Thiessen characterises these divisions in relation to teacher knowledge as the inclusion of both the *doing* and *knowing* mentioned above. We should consider teaching behaviours or actions, but also the ability to theorise these actions. Behaviours are ... 'subsumed by more robust models of frameworks for making sense of, solving problems in, or making decisions about working with students' (Thiessen 2000: 527).

More recently, the merging of teacher actions and the decisions which underpin them has been considered under the concept of teacher cognition (Borg 2006), a term which refers to what teachers think, know and believe: the unobservable, which informs what teachers do. Through an understanding of what teachers are thinking about teaching, we can identify the knowledge that informs practice. Another useful model of what constitutes teacher knowledge is found in the concept of teachers' Personal Practical Knowledge (PPK). This model encompasses the teacher's acts in the classroom but also their ability to express the rationale of those acts: 'a teacher's theory about teaching that is contextualised in experience' (Golombek 1998: 448). Such a model recognises that we may be looking at a particular behaviour or act in the classroom but that any assessment also needs to take into account the 'capacity for intelligent and adaptive action' (Schulman and Schulman 2004: 263). Thus one of our considerations should be the teacher's rationale and their ability to take action either during teaching or for future lessons.

Most recognised English language teacher education programmes fully incorporate the different aspects of teacher knowledge in their assessment and have opportunities for assessing the range of teacher knowledge. Internationally valued programmes such as the Cambridge ESOL and Trinity Certificate and Diploma programmes have assessment of the practical activity of teaching in lessons, but also assess the thinking behind these actions through the assessment of planning and post lesson self-evaluations. Some exceptions exist. The Cambridge ESOL Teaching Knowledge Test (TKT), for example, deliberately focuses on declarative knowledge (Pratt 2015) and some university based teacher education programmes in the UK allow for ESL teachers to gain a qualification purely based on the achievement of the academic content and not the teaching practice.

Who is assessing?

Teachers working together in a teaching or course context form what could be called a 'Community of Practice' (Lave and Wenger 1991), where groups with different roles learn together. Lave and Wenger suggested that an important part of learning was observing a 'master' and gradually becoming engaged with the professional activities. For a teacher education context this community of practice usually consists of the trainee teachers (those teachers attending a course), their tutors and their learners. In a professional development context, this might be teachers, their learners and professional tutors delivering the training. Though the group may be learning together, it normally falls to the experienced member, the tutor, to carry out the formal assessment, since this is what leads to 'passing' the course and gaining professional recognition. The more established paradigm, therefore, is that the tutor carries out the assessment which decides the outcome for the trainee. In some cases there is one final observation carried out by an external person, who is normally a tutor at another institution.

Within the community of practice, the accepted paradigm of tutor assessment raises the issue of the relationship between tutor and trainee. A core value of most teacher education programmes is to be developmental, and by extension supportive. However, there is not an even distribution of power between participants (Barton and Tusting 2005; Hughes et al. 2007). Tutors can make assessment decisions which will significantly impact on the future of their trainee teachers. It is very likely then, that assessment will cause trainees to conform to the tutors' view of what good teaching is. Thus, tutor assessment will engender teacher behaviours which are congruent with tutor feedback and the opportunities for trainees to experiment are lessened. In many courses part of the feedback process is to invite trainees to self-assess, often before they hear their tutor's feedback. If we consider the power held by the tutor, it might be assumed that the trainee will self-assess in a way which conforms to what they believe the tutor would like to hear.

A less formal assessment role is often given to peers, who might observe the teaching practice of others on the course, particularly on the pre-service model such as CELTA or the Trinity Certificate course. As the outcome of this assessment does not necessarily carry weight towards the career success of the trainee teacher, it could be assumed that there is no pressure on the peers to conform to any perceived assessment or feedback model. Within the community of practice, however, peers may also be in competition, striving to get a more favourable result. A study of practices in sport shows the importance of competitive working both as a positive influence on learning and also the trigger of emotion and complex affective states that result from the 'comparative evaluation of self and other' (Owen-Pugh 2007: 89). Thus asking trainees to judge themselves in comparison to others, either other trainees or tutors, may cause them to feel strong, possibly negative emotions.

A self-assessment role can be given to the trainee teacher in the form of a post lesson self-evaluation or through reflective practice activities. In most teacher education programmes, verbal and written self-evaluations are commonplace and often form an important part of the course assessment. Trainees' lessons may be judged partially based on what they have identified in their own self-evaluation. The validity of using self-assessment as evidence in the overall assessment of teachers has been questioned (Hargreaves 2003; Delaney 2015). One drawback, for example, is that trainees 'choose only those reflections that fall within a professionally acceptable frame, or [choose] to fictionalise events.' (Hargreaves 2003: 200). Thus trainees will self-assess in a way which conforms to what they think the tutor will say in their assessment. Hobbs (2007) also concludes that teachers' reflections may be a false iteration of their true beliefs, which they express because they feel this is what is required. Brookfield has also considered the issue of 'impostorship' (Brookfield 2012: 222). When students are asked to be critically evaluative in front of the expert tutor, they experience difficulty and this can be both 'brutal and confusing' because they are being asked to identify errors and mistakes although they are not the experts within the learning group. Similarly, asking relatively inexperienced trainees to assess their own or peers' teaching in front of the expert tutors may be asking too much and result in rather invalid outcomes.

How is the assessment carried out?

It is intrinsically complicated to assess teaching because we are trying to assess inseparable aspects in isolation. Freeman, McBee Orzulak and Morrissey (2009) describe the changing focus of second language teacher assessment with different importance allocated to knowledge about language, personal language skills and language pedagogy. Each focus would determine the way the teacher is assessed. In some contexts the language teacher's own English skills would be of prime importance, suggesting a language test. In other contexts, the teacher's classroom practice would be the main focus and assessment would rely mainly on classroom observation. Freeman et al. argue for 'multiple sources of evidence to gauge teacher preparation and effectiveness' (2009: 87), suggesting that observation of practice on its own is not sufficient. This is reflected in many language teacher education programmes, where teachers produce written work in the form of academic assignments or written reflective pieces and such work forms part of their assessment.

Assessment of teaching is further complicated by the 'ephemeral' nature of the activity (Galaczi and Swabey 2015). We are seeking to capture events in the continuously fluctuating context of a classroom and make a judgement about them. As the assessment is usually carried out by an experienced tutor sitting in the lesson, the notions of subjectivity and the reliability of assessing while multiple events are happening are pertinent. To address the issue of subjectivity, many second language teacher education programmes use assessment criteria or standards (Galaczi and Swabey 2015; Katz and Snow 2009). These may be written in the form of 'can do' statements or may be a list of descriptors which are seen to typify the activities of a good teacher. The assessing tutor must then indicate how the teacher is exemplifying the criteria and thus justify the judgement they are making. While this promotes a more standardised approach to assessment, it can never rule out the issue of subjectivity as it remains the individual tutor's judgement as to whether a criteria or descriptor or standard has been achieved. Standardisation activities, for example, a number of tutors watching the same lesson and agreeing the assessment or the use of joint observations can promote reliability. However, the continued complex nature of teaching makes it difficult to assess regardless of the assessment process used.

What about feedback?

It is to be expected that any assessment would be followed by some form of feedback to the individual being assessed. Feedback on teaching may involve a grade or a judgement of standard. However, it is usual to have more detailed qualitative comment on the strengths and areas for development from an observed lesson provided in post-lesson verbal feedback and then in a formal written form.

Van Dinther, Dochy and Segers (2015) investigated the use of lesson observation as an assessment tool to develop self-efficacy; a feature of effective teaching. By considering trainees' views of effective lesson observation practice, features related to feedback most likely to lead to greater self-efficacy were identified. The first was whether the assessment was authentic, that is, had a 'resemblance of assessment to the future teaching assessment' (van Dinther et al. 2015: 46). The second related to the nature of the feedback given, which should be balanced and consist of 'affirming comments about what goes well combined with feed forward which identifies weak aspects of students' performance and providing suggestions for improvement' (van Dinther et al. 2015: 50). A final element of the mastery experience was the fact that great importance was attached by trainees to the notion of meeting a competence standard. These findings would suggest that trainees should be observed in a real teaching situation, they should be given feedback on both strengths and areas for development and should also be aware of how their teaching matches to an external standard, such as criteria or standards mentioned in the previous section.

The importance of how feedback is provided post lesson observation is discussed by Soslau (2015). Through a detailed discourse analysis of verbal feedback, successful strategies are identified. The findings indicate that of greatest importance is the opportunities for trainees to rationalise and justify their decision making. These opportunities are 'a key learning opportunity to develop adaptive teaching expertise' (Soslau 2015: 32). Adaptive expertise is an important tool for teachers as it allows them to make use of cues from the lesson as it develops and from learner reaction and feedback to theorise their practice further and implement new strategies (Darling-Hammond and Bransford 2005). Adaptive expertise also means that teachers can apply learning and insights from training programmes and professional development to a localised context.

The discussion in a previous section on who is assessing teaching is also pertinent to the issue of feedback. It is to be assumed that reflection activities, self or peer, will provide self and peer feedback. The questions raised around impostorship (Brookfield 2012), the potential fictionalisation of feedback (Hargreaves 2003) and the lack of experience of novice teachers (Delaney 2015) are all relevant to the issue of feedback. If the value of self and peer assessment remain a contested issue, then the value of feedback an individual teacher receives from their own thoughts and the reflections of their peers is also questionable.

Insights from practice

Practice on language teacher education programmes

Assessment practice by language teacher educators is likely to be heavily influenced by the assessment schemes of the programmes they are working on. Examples from the assessment schemes of programmes therefore make an interesting starting point to see how the issues discussed in the first part of this chapter are articulated in practice. Examples considered are from the internationally recognised Cambridge Assessment and Trinity College pre- and in-service qualifications. The fact that these qualifications are not contextualised in or bound by the teacher education regulations of a particular country allows for some more generic features to be discussed.

The Certificate qualifications (CELTA and Trinity Cert TESOL) are pre-service; designed for teachers with no prior experience. The practice element of the programmes is organised through teaching practice groups with volunteer learners. The trainees on the course teach in groups, observing and giving feedback on each other. The Diploma qualifications (Delta and Trinity Dip TESOL) are in-service programmes; students are already in employment and their practice is observed at their place of work by an experienced tutor. On both programmes, knowledge of pedagogy and of language is assessed through written assignments and, in the diploma, an exam.

Course assessment in each of the qualifications is described as being holistic in the sense that both practical teaching and theoretical knowledge elements both need to be passed in order to pass the qualification. Examples of the specific regulations for the assessment indicate that there are some interesting points in the articulations of the relative importance of classroom practice and theoretical knowledge. On the CELTA, for example, although the written work must be at a pass standard, the descriptors for attaining a higher grade lie with 'Candidates' planning and teaching' (Cambridge Assessment 2015: 14). Likewise in the Trinity Certificate, seven out of eight criteria for a pass refer to students' performance in teaching (Trinity College, London 2016: 27).

From these examples, it seems apparent that assessment of teaching should be focused on the practice elements. However, it is also clear that the practice elements should evidence an underpinning knowledge of both language and language pedagogy. This is evident in the list of assessment criteria as well as the fact the assessment of teaching should demonstrate trainees' understanding of both language and the pedagogy of language teaching. This is most explicit in

Jo-Ann Delaney

the modular Delta qualification, where one module assessment consists entirely of an exam, with exam questions focusing on the discussion of pedagogy. In addition, on Certificate programmes, where teaching is done in practice groups, the ability of students to reflect and comment on their peers' teaching also forms part of the assessment.

In the example questions from the Delta qualification, exam candidates are asked questions which focus both on their understanding of language and their knowledge of pedagogy. The first task shown requires them to show an understanding of specific language features and name them using correct terminology. The second task asks for a commentary on an extract from a methodology book. Exam candidates are expected to demonstrate their knowledge of classroom practice through their response.

Paper 1 Task Three (12 marks)

The extract for this task is the speaking activity below for pre-intermediate (CEFR B1) level learners.

In order to complete this activity successfully, learners at this level would need to use the following key language features:

- verbs and nouns relating to childhood activities, e.g. *go swimming, watch cartoons, play computer games*
- back-channelling and responding to others' contributions, e.g. *Oh, really?, Yes, I did that too!*

Identify a **total** of **three further key language features** learners at this level would need to use. Provide an example specific to this activity to support each choice.

Paper 2 Task Three (40 marks)

The text for this task is reproduced below. It is an extract from an article in an English language teaching journal.

Many teachers believe that they should at all times reduce their own talking time and increase that of their students.

a. What reasons are there for reducing teacher talking time and increasing student talking time?

b. How do learners benefit from teacher talking time in a lesson?

Write your answer in your answer booklet.

Cook, G. (2002) 'Breaking Taboos'. *English Teaching Professional*, 23(5).

Both of these tasks require the teacher to demonstrate their knowledge of effective language teaching through descriptions of language and pedagogy. In the first task the teacher shows that they would be able to prepare both a teaching task and their learners by recognising language features pertaining to an interaction type as well as to the level of learners. In the second task the teacher is asked to discuss a common area of language teaching methodology and provide a rationale for approaches to teaching. Both tasks assess the teachers' knowledge of language teaching. There is no assessment of whether the teacher would actually be able to carry out the teaching activity in the first task or would be mindful of the issues raised in the second task when in a classroom situation. These elements are, however, assessed in other modules of the qualification.

The practice of trainers and trainees: data and its origins

In this section we will look at the views of assessment from the point of view of those involved in the language teacher education process: trainees and tutors. The data were collected as part of a wider research project focusing on teacher knowledge and teacher learning on a pre-service teacher education programme from two groups of trainees and tutors. The first group of 12 trainees, pre-service, were interviewed while they were undertaking their pre-service programme at three stages in the course. These were semi-structured interviews. A group of eight pre-service tutors' views were gathered through an online survey. All were currently working on pre-service courses. The data from in-service trainees and tutors (three trainees, two tutors) was gathered though an online questionnaire. The in-service trainees had completed their programme within the previous year.

What is assessed?

Both trainees and tutors were in agreement that both the practical and the theoretical aspect of teaching were important to assess. The interplay between different aspects emerges from some of their comments.

The data below contains in part a summary of views and in part quotes from the trainee/tutor as an illustration of the views.

> *Extract 25.1*
>
> In service trainees were asked which element of their course played the largest role in the tutors' assessment of their teaching. They identified 'written assignments' as the most important. In service tutors identified 'classroom teaching' as the most important factor in assessing.
> In-service trainees and tutors were asked to agree or disagree with the following statements:
>
> a. You can only judge a teacher's understanding of pedagogy through watching them in the classroom.
> b. A teacher's ability to reflect on their teaching and express insightful comments is an indication of how good a teacher they are.
> c. Good teachers should able to discuss language and pedagogy in academic assignments or tests.
>
> Statement b) was agreed by less than half. The other statements were agreed by everyone.
> Tutors' comments also showed an ambivalence as to whether a trainee's ability to reflect on their teaching was evidence of their ability. Two views from the pre-service tutors are given below.
>
> *My instinct is that trainees who lucidly identify issues and strategies should be given credit.*
> *If they do a weak lesson but can pinpoint what went wrong and how they would improve it, it can count in their favour. If they can teach well but are not very perceptive I would not hold it against them.*
>
> Pre-service trainees identified the classroom practice as the most important element to be assessed. Comments included:
>
> *Actually it's been about the teaching and the actual teaching practice and the feedback from that.*
> *So we've got lectures, teaching practice – well I think whatever you do, if you're able to put it into practice, if you're able to do something, you know, rather than read it or whatever, I think that that's the most valuable.*

Commentary on Extract 25.1

Trainees and tutors fully recognise that assessing teaching requires a number of different elements to be taken into account. Pre-service trainees seem more focused on the practical aspect and this is likely to be because it is the area which is more unfamiliar and challenging to them. For in-service programmes there is recognition that all elements should play a role in assessment. The fact that trainees feel their written assignments play an important role may be because these are more challenging to an experienced teacher. However, the different perceptions between trainees and tutors also suggests that there could be a lack of transparency in the way assessment processes are made explicit to trainees. There may be assumptions on the part of tutors, who may have been involved in such programmes for a number of years, that assessment criteria are transparent, even though they may not be formally explained. Devoting time to discussing assessment at the start of, but more importantly, during each assessed element of the course would be a strategy which would facilitate a shared understanding of what was being assessed.

The reaction to the three statements about assessment indicate the view that theoretical knowledge and practical enactment in the classroom are intertwined and therefore we can and should assess both, as each is a reflection of the teacher's ability. The only doubt is expressed in relation to the assessment of reflection and whether this is actually evidence of teaching skill. Tutors seem to feel that it may be an indication of ability but if a teacher is less able to articulate an evaluation of their practice, this is not necessarily evidence of lack of ability as a teacher. The focus on written forms of reflective practice in many teacher education programmes can mean that 'assessment and evaluation distort the kind of reflection that individuals do' (Mann and Walsh 2013: 297).

Who assesses?

In the first section, the issue of the power relationship between trainee and tutor was highlighted. For trainees, not only does the tutor have the final say on the outcome of training, but they also derive their status from being more knowledgeable and more experienced. If we consider Brookfield's discussion of how students feel like imposters when asked to evaluate, then trainees consider their tutors as the non-imposter expert. This may not sit well with views of teacher education which emphasise the collaborative learning experience between trainees and tutors. That is not to say that trainees did not value the views of their peers. However, it is the tutor assessment which is 'proper', as explained by the comments in Data 2.

The views in Extract 25.2 represent those expressed by pre-service trainees when interviewed and asked to talk about their experience of feedback from both their tutor and their peers. Their experience is from the specific context of teaching in 'teaching practice groups', where trainees plan and co-teach a lesson and groups of trainees observe and provide feedback on peers' lessons

> Extract 25.2
>
> *It's been really, really useful having the feedback from the tutor, but also the feedback from the two other people in my group ... then I could try putting into practice those – the bits that they – the tutor points out ...*
>
> *The experienced person is the one who is assessing you, so he or she knows their stuff.*
>
> *The tutors are certainly more experienced, so I think I'd probably respect what they had to say. Each person needed to have their proper feedback from the tutor.*

For pre-service trainees who work together on teaching practice, an additional consideration was the fact that assessment by peers and by the trainees of themselves was influenced by the fact that trainees often said what they felt the tutor wanted to hear, a 'fake' reflection (Hobbs 2007). Since assessment was carried out in teaching practice groups, trainees felt that peers were more concerned with maintaining group cohesion and friendships with other trainees than making a realistic assessment. The comments in Extract 25.3 highlight the potential for falsehood to achieve these aims.

The views in Extract 25.3 are from the same group of pre-service trainees on their experience of teaching practice groups.

Extract 25.3

Trainee A

We try – rather bolster each other up than give – you know, because even if you try to give constructive criticism it can come across as negative.

Trainee B

I think it's very difficult as a novice maybe to give constructive criticism, and it might have come across not constructive or something.

Trainee C

So being asked to criticise them when generally speaking we're all saying to each other, 'No you're doing really well, you're doing really well', and then lo and behold in front of the teacher we go, 'Oh you could have done that' and it sort of feels wrong somehow.

In the process I felt like a bit of a – you know, a betrayer of the – because we have a – we have a bond between us.

When asked to comment on the veracity of trainees' assessment of their own and peers' teaching, they fully acknowledge some of the tensions between inviting reflective responses and simply asking trainees to second guess the tutor, whose job it is to assess and provide feedback.

The data below is from an online survey of tutors working on pre-service courses.

Extract 25.4

But there are so many other factors that play a role in what the trainees say in feedback: their rapport/ relationship with the trainer/each other; their general level of confidence, their previous educational experience (have they been able to be honest about their performance before or have they had to hide their real views?).

There is an understandable tendency for trainees to try to say what they think the trainer wants them to say to enhance their chances of a better evaluation. Again, this is very case dependent, though.

I think most are much more positive about their peers' lessons because they don't want to hurt their feelings, feel they are not in a position to 'judge' or think that is the trainer's job!

Commentary

The comments in Extracts 25.3 and 25.4 suggest quite a conundrum for language teacher educators in the use of peer and self-assessment, both as a pedagogic tool and as a way of reaching an overall assessment decision about a trainee. Trainees' ability to reflect on their teaching is enshrined in most teacher education courses as an important part of teacher ability. Yet it could be suggested that much of what trainees say or write in their self and peer assessment is influenced by their desire not to offend or show themselves up in a bad light, but more importantly, to be congruent with what they think the tutor wants to hear. In addition, the practice of self and peer assessment detracts from the fact that the tutor, as a more experienced and knowledgeable teacher, is in a better position to make a more reliable assessment and that this is what trainees believe and respect.

Feedback

Trainees were asked to describe what they felt were the key ingredients of effective feedback, but also to provide specific examples of feedback they received which had been very impactful on their development. In addition to the comments discussed below, the majority said that verbal feedback had a much bigger impact and that receiving feedback as soon as possible was important to its effectiveness.

The comments in Extract 25.5 were collected through interview (pre-service) and through online questionnaire (in-service). All the comments relate to describing feedback which impacted on practice.

Extract 25.5

Pre-service trainees

Trainee A

He gave us some … he just gave us some practical examples of, you know, 'this is something that you do. What you could do instead is this'. 'This is some … a way you present this material, but what you could do instead is this.' So that, it was really sort of specific to me and what I'd done in the past and what ways that I kind of … tendencies that I had towards certain, you know, methods in the classroom. So that was really useful.

Trainee B

I think what I've done is I've focused on very specific things to improve on and I think that's made me able to improve overall just by – instead of thinking, 'Oh I'm not that confident', or, 'I shouldn't be so worried', or kind of big general things like that, actually to try and focus on specific areas and improve on those.

In-service trainees

Trainee C

Asking questions e.g. why did u use that exercise. When criticising explain the reason behind it.

Trainee D

It regarded monitoring: what constitutes productive monitoring [of students working], and balancing between over-monitoring and being too 'hands off'.

Trainee E

Discussion of the negatives and positives but mostly on positives, and ending with positive feedback. The tutor asked me to reflect on my own teaching before giving me the feedback. The tutor discussed criticisms constructively and shared his/her own experience of teaching, informing what worked and didn't work so well.

Trainee F

Outline problems, guess the reasons, help with the solutions.

Commentary

A number of key themes are evident in the comments. The first is the importance of exploring the rationale behind events in the classroom. Trainees valued being asked for some of the reasons for what happened but also being given reasons for the suggestions made by their tutor. This point ties in with the notion of teacher knowledge comprising both the action of teaching but also of the understanding behind action. It is clear from the comments that trainees want to be assessed and receive feedback in a way that incorporates both.

A second theme is the focus on specific points and suggestions. Trainees appreciate feedback which looks at individual aspects of their teaching. They consider advice related to very micro aspects of the lesson to be extremely helpful. The final comment above is from a pre-service trainee who was reflecting on a lesson which had been assessed as a 'fail'. She felt that a changed focus to specific points in her teaching was the approach which helped her move on in her practice.

Trainees also feel they benefit from tutor feedback which includes specific suggestions which they can implement in their practice. Tutors are valued as experts who can provide detailed procedural and concrete proposals drawn from their own experience. There might be a concern that such suggestions might become too prescriptive, however, it seems that trainees like to hear what they 'could do' in some detail so that they have a palette of suggestions they might then choose from.

Moving practice forward

A number of areas have been highlighted thus far in relation to the assessment of teaching and providing feedback. In this part of the chapter we will look at some practical ideas which teacher educators could implement in order to address some of the issues raised in previous sections in relation to assessment.

Transparency of what is being assessed

Trainees and tutors are aware of the complexity of assessing teaching and the interplay between theory and practice. Often this is not as explicit as it might be, as in the example of trainees feeling their written assignments were more important than their classroom teaching (See Extract 25.1).

There are a number of ways that more transparency can be achieved. Some of these are generally implemented in course documentation: syllabus and assessment guidance, assessment criteria or course handbooks. Lists of criteria, for example, against which trainees can evaluate their progress are helpful. Possibly more important is an open and transparent discussion of where and how different elements are assessed. A suggested 'evidence sheet' might look something like this:

Table 25.1 Suggested evidence sheet

Criteria	We will look for evidence of this in
Manage groups of learners effectively	Teaching practice
Analyse language effectively for teaching	Lesson planning
	Assignments
Develop learners' pronunciation	Teaching practice
Identify areas for development in your teaching	Feedback on teaching practice
	Teaching practice
	Reflective log

It is not necessary to have this as a written document. Discussions during initial parts of a course could focus on raising trainees' awareness. In this way, trainees are clearer on how their theoretical understanding of, for example, language areas, is also evidenced in planning for lessons. An important area to open up to discussion is the notion of 'weighting'. Although it is impossible to provide quantitative measures of which aspects of the course are more important, it is vital that as tutors we at least acknowledge this concern and perhaps provide some reassurance.

Who is assessing: definition of roles

At the start of this chapter the dual support and assessor role of the tutor was discussed. These two roles can sometimes be difficult to unify, particularly when the tutor is working with a trainee who is struggling to meet the requirements of the course. There may also be a reluctance on the part of the tutor to emphasise their assessor role as this can seem to undermine their part in supporting and developing the trainee. For pre-service courses, in particular, trainees may be unaware of the assessment role of the tutor. Unfamiliarity with such programmes may mean trainees expect the 'teacher' to teach, set tasks and mark homework. It is questionable whether trainees are, or can be, made fully aware of the assessment expectations when they are being interviewed for their course.

However, trainees acknowledge and value the 'expert' role of the tutor. This would suggest that tutors should not be reluctant, where appropriate, to take the lead in feedback and in course documentation, to highlight the fact that their assessment decision is the one which actually carries weight in the course processes. It is a statement of honesty which will not automatically result in trainees contributing less in feedback. In fact, it might actually encourage trainees to comment on their teaching and their peers' lessons as they know that they do not carry the 'imposter' burden of assessment.

When peers are asked to evaluate teaching, the tendency is to either not say what they think because of worry about upsetting others or to say what they think the tutor wants to hear. On a teacher education programme which has a number of opportunities for peer assessment, some of this could be done without the tutor present. The group could then complete a collective, but anonymous, feedback summary which would then be discussed with the tutor.

Assessing the doing *and the* knowing

If teaching practice is the main focus of assessment, then it is important to capture teaching in a more permanent way so that they are not fleeting events and so that they can be used to interrogate underpinning understanding. The most obvious means of doing this is to video the lesson. There are a number of cheap and easy options to do this, including smart phone and tablet applications which allow for high quality recording. Once the lesson has been videoed, the issue of storage and access arises. Many institutional virtual learning environments (VLEs) are limited in storage capacity. There are many options to store videos in the cloud and to grant trainee and tutor access where appropriate. Options to engage in commentary on the videoed lesson through electronic posts or message functions allow opportunities for trainee and tutor to reflect in more depth. Trainees appreciate the opportunity to explain why they took various teaching decisions and this explanation allows tutors to assess their understanding of pedagogy rather than assessing the classroom practice from a subjective observer perspective.

Feedback

The elements of feedback highlighted as valuable by trainees included a focus on the detail of practice and a willingness of tutors to offer practical suggestions. A suggestion would be for tutors to reflect on whether they feel it is 'wrong' of them to lead the feedback and to input their viewpoint. Trainees seem to be able to differentiate well between suggestions and prescription and perhaps tutors could be less reluctant to provide concrete examples of things trainees could implement to facilitate their development.

Peer feedback

Feedback by peers can be facilitated by the use of a system of synchronous chat during teaching practice. This allows peers and tutors to engage in a dialogue about the ongoing lesson. The importance of dialogic reflection is highlighted by Mann and Walsh as it 'allows potentially richer articulation and analysis (Mann and Walsh 2017: 39). Tutors can prompt peers to reflect on what is actually going on at the moment of teaching. There are a number of online tools which facilitate this and which can allow a group of trainees to communicate, and the trainee who is teaching to read the ongoing comments after the lesson to help them with self-assessment.

An example of this is given below in an extract from a chat. Trainees are observing their peer trainee teach and are able to access the chat online as they watch. Rather than make notes which might be discussed after the lesson, they are able to engage in immediate and synchronous commentary on what they are observing, in a dialogue with other trainees and the tutor. Everyone can view the contributions. In the extract, trainees are noticing and assessing the lack of success of the teacher's instructions. Through prompting, the tutor is able to make them aware of better alternatives. The focus on specific teaching strategies as they happen allows the discussion to be more relevant and more memorable.

Extract 25.6

Trainee 1:   I'm not sure they understood that instruction… match the…
Trainee 2:   I don't think so either, those two in the corner are just reading the first sheet.
Tutor: What was the problem?
Trainee 1:   She said it too quickly?
Trainee 3:   She also had her back to them.

Tutor:	What would a better way be?
Trainee 2:	Hold up the sheet… hold up and point and then show match.
Trainee 3:	Or do one… an example.

Breaking the paradigm

One of the issues highlighted above is that trainees are likely to self and peer assess in the paradigm which they feel the tutor expects. One such paradigm is asking for 'strengths' and 'areas for development' thereby establishing a pattern which the trainee feels obliged to follow. There are some suggestions for breaking with this paradigm, which may encourage trainees (and tutors) to think a bit differently about how they frame feedback.

Feedback from the student perspective

Trainees could be asked to focus on one particular student during their lesson. They then give an evaluation (spoken or written) from the perspective of the student. This is also very effective if there are peers observing the lesson as they are in a better position to notice the reaction of a student. Feedback could then be done as a role play between the 'student' and the trainee. This strategy is particularly useful for highlighting issues around poor clarification strategies. Often the trainee may not notice when learners do not understand because they are focusing on their activities. Considering everything from the learner perspective can be very insightful. The trainee observer or the trainee can then write their feedback from the learner perspective. An example is given below.

Point of view (student)

The teacher seemed nervous tonight. He spoke very quickly at the beginning of the lesson. When he said the word 'grammar' I thought he was going to cry! When he was writing up the examples he didn't look at us at all. This doesn't usually happen. Normally he's very friendly. I put up my hand to ask him a question but he didn't seem to notice me. When my friend asked a question, he asked her. The answer he gave wasn't very clear, but then we did this game and by the end my friend and I understood the grammar.

Change the genre of written feedback

When writing feedback, trainees will often follow a prescribed formula, again usually following the 'strengths'/'areas for development' model. There are many examples of pro forma feedback sheets for both trainee and tutor which follow this model. Sometimes it is more effective to disrupt the pattern and perhaps arrive at a more honest feedback and this can be done by asking trainees to write in a different genre.

An example is given below. In a series of lessons the trainee struggled with using repetition as a strategy for developing learners' pronunciation. He was unable or unwilling to vocalise his discomfort with asking groups of students to chorally say words and phrases. When set the task of reflecting on his lesson in the form of a gothic novel, his discomfort is made evident.

Gothic story

The rain beat against the windows of the room. Inside were 10 victims sitting in a circle. They looked afraid. Their torturers sat at the back. One of them stood up and wrote some strange signs on the wall............ Then she said some strange words and made the victims repeat them. Except the victims couldn't get it right. Every time they got it wrong the torturer said it again faster and louder but it didn't make any sense.

Conclusion

The existence of prescribed programmes and assessment schemes can encourage us to follow a pattern of assessment and feedback which we assume is understood by our trainees. There are a number of questions about given patterns which have been raised in this chapter.

One question is the potentially disparate views as to what is being assessed. The kinds of knowledge which make up the concept of 'teaching' can influence an assessor's decision about a teacher. It is important that there is a shared understanding of what the assessor is considering and why. Another question raised is the extent to which the trainees' ability to demonstrate that they can reflect on their teaching to improve practice is considered. The problematic nature of assessing reflection has been highlighted in this chapter and needs to be considered by tutors so that they do not conflagrate a trainee's ability to talk *about* teaching and their ability to teach.

Strategies for assessing and giving feedback were discussed and trainees' views suggested the importance of a focus on procedural knowledge in feedback as a means to understand theories and concepts. Ideas for facilitating valid assessment were proposed and the importance of technology was highlighted. Technological tools provide both synchronous and asynchronous means of looking at teaching practice, providing both trainee and tutor with a way of expressing immediate and delayed views and promoting a more holistic reflection which is not as influenced by momentary contexts such as the presence of the tutor or the stressful situation of teaching practice.

It is unlikely that assessment will cease to be a part of teacher education. Qualifications, standards and evidence of professional development are all part of a teacher's professional life. This chapter has looked at ways of making this assessment better at promoting teacher learning and development, of making assessment a tool for learning.

Further reading

Poulter, M. and Wilson, R. (eds) (2015) *Assessing Language Teachers' Professional Skills and Knowledge*. Cambridge: Cambridge University Press.
    This is a selection of chapters of how language teachers are assessed across the range of Cambridge English Teaching Award programmes. Use is made of large scale data sets generated from an international candidature.

Howard, A. and Donaghue, H. (2014) *Teacher Evaluation in Second Language Education*. London: Bloomsbury.
    An overview of key themes, and controversies, in current practice in assessing teachers' practice in a range of contexts.

Jo-Ann Delaney

References

Barton, D. and Tusting, K. (eds) (2005) *Beyond Communities of Practice*. Cambridge: Cambridge University Press.

Borg, S. (2006) *Teacher Cognition and Language Education*. London: Continuum.

Brookfield, S. D. (2012) *Teaching for Critical Thinking*. San Francisco, CA: Jossey-Bass.

Cambridge Assessment (2015) *CELTA Syllabus and Assessment Guidelines*, 4th edition. Cambridge: Cambridge Assessment.

Cook, G. (2002) 'Breaking Taboos'. *English Teaching Professional*, 23(5) 5–7.

Darling-Hammond, L. and Bransford, J. (2005) *Preparing Teachers for a Changing World*. San Francisco, CA: Jossey-Bass.

Delaney, J. (2015) 'The "dirty mirror" of reflective practice: assessing self- and peer-evaluation on a CELTA course', in Wilson, R. and Poulter, M. (eds) *Assessing Language Teachers' Professional Skills and Knowledge*. Cambridge: Cambridge University Press.

Freeman, D., McBee Orzulak, M. and Morrissey, B. (2009) 'Assessment in second language teacher education', in Bruns, A. and Richard, J. C. (eds) *The Cambridge Guide to Second Language Teacher Education*. Cambridge: Cambridge University Press.

Galaczi, E. and Swabey, M. T. (2015) 'Capturing the ephemeral: standardising the assessment of teaching practice' in Wilson, R. and Poulter, M. (eds) *Assessing Language Teachers' Professional Skills and Knowledge*. Cambridge: Cambridge University Press.

Golombek, P. (1998) 'A Study of Language Teachers' Personal Practical Knowledge'. *TESOL Quarterly*, 32(3) 447–464.

Hargreaves, J. (2003) 'So How do You Feel About That? Assessing Reflective Practice'. *Nurse Education Today*, 24 196–201.

Hobbs, V. (2007) 'Faking it or Hating it: Can Reflective Practice be Forced?'. *Reflective Practice: International and Multidisciplinary Perspectives*, 8(3) 405–417.

Hughes, J., Jewson, N. and Unwin, L. (eds) (2007) *Communities of Practice: Critical Perspectives*. Abingdon: Routledge.

Katz, A. and Snow, M. (2009) 'Standards and second language teacher education', in Bruns, A. and Richard, J. C. (eds) *The Cambridge Guide to Second Language Teacher Education*. Cambridge: Cambridge University Press.

Lave, J. and Wenger, E. (1991) *Situated Learning; Legitimate Peripheral Participation*. New York: Cambridge University Press.

Lee, G. C. and Wu, C. (2006) 'Enhancing the Teaching Experience of Pre-Service Teachers Through the Use of Videos in Web-Based Computer-Mediated Communication'. *Innovations in Education and Teaching International*, 43(4) 369–380.

Mann, S. and Walsh, S. (2013) 'RP or "RIP": A Critical Perspective on Reflective Practice'. *Applied Linguistics Review*, 4(2) 291–315.

Mann, S. and Walsh, S. (2017) *Reflective Practice in English Language Teaching*. New York: Routledge.

Owen-Pugh, V. (2007) 'Theorizing sport as a community of practice: the coach-athlete relationship in British professional basketball', in Hughes, J., Jewson, N. and Unwin, L. (eds) *Communities of Practice: Critical Perspectives*. Abingdon: Routledge.

Pratt, M. (2015) 'TKT Testing knowledge about teaching', in Wilson, R. and Poulter, M. (eds) *Assessing Language Teachers' Professional Skills and Knowledge*. Cambridge: Cambridge University Press.

Schulman, L. and Schulman J. (2004) 'How and What Teachers Learn: A Shifting Perspective'. *Journal of Curriculum Studies*, 36(2) 257–271.

Soslau, E. (2015) 'Development of a Post-Lesson Observation Conferencing Protocol: Situated in Theory, Research, and Practice'. *Teaching and Teacher Education*, 49 22–35.

Thiessen, D. (2000) 'A Skillful Start to a Teaching Career: A Matter of Developing Impactful Behaviors, Reflective Practices, or Professional Knowledge?'. *International Journal of Educational Research*, 33(4) 515–537.

Tomlinson, P. (1999) 'Conscious Reflection and Implicit Learning in Teacher Preparation. Part 1: Recent Light on an Old Issue'. *Oxford Review of Education*, 25(3) 405–424.

Trinity College London (2016) *CertTESOL Syllabus*. London: Trinity College.

Van Dinther, M. Dochy, F. and Segers, M. (2015) 'The Contribution of Assessment Experiences to Student Teachers' Self-Efficacy in Competence-Based Education'. *Teaching and Teacher Education*, 49 45–55.

26

Post observation feedback

Fiona Copland and Helen Donaghue

Introduction

As chapters in this volume describe, teachers learn how to teach in different ways. In formal teacher education courses, there is often a practicum of some kind in which teachers in training ('trainees') practise their skills, either with peers (often called microteaching) or with real students (often called teaching practice). In these contexts, a teacher educator ('trainer') will normally be present and he/she will observe and afterwards will discuss the lesson with the supervisee. This discussion is called 'post observation feedback' or 'post observation conference' in the literature and, as we will show in this chapter, it can be both a useful and painful experience.

Employers may also introduce observation and feedback as part of a process of appraisal. Although teachers may have many years of experience and advanced qualifications in teaching, they may still be required to present a lesson for evaluation and discussion. In this context 'employer' and 'employee', share some similarities with the trainer and trainee. In this chapter, we use the generic term 'supervisor' for the trainer/employer role except where it is analytically relevant to refer to the trainer or supervisor. Trainees and employees are therefore 'supervisees'.

Our aim in this chapter is to provide an introduction to post observation feedback and to discuss a number of key issues in this area. In the first section we will describe features that are central to the feedback conference, including its linguistic characteristics, its purposes and its value. Next, we will consider key debates and current issues in feedback. In the third section we discuss ways of helping participants better understand feedback. Finally, we will look to the future and identify areas that are currently drawing researchers' attention, as well as other areas that would benefit from further research. Throughout, we will draw on data collected during our research on post observation feedback conferences in pre-service and employment contexts to illustrate our points.

Feedback: central features

The feedback conference described

The feedback conference happens after a lesson has been taught and observed. If the conference takes place immediately after teaching and observation (or after a short break) it is called 'hot' feedback and if it takes place after a delay, it is called 'cold' (or 'cool') feedback. The conference can last for any length of time but generally takes around 45 minutes to an hour. Usually the supervisor and supervisee(s) meet in a quiet, private space to discuss the lesson. Often the supervisor will have completed a standard observation form (usually based on assessment criteria) issued by the employer or designed by the institution or an awarding body, and this may be the focus of the discussion.

Feedback is a kind of 'institutional talk' (Drew and Heritage, 1992; Roberts, 2013) and tends to display the characteristics laid out by Drew and Heritage (1992). Specifically, it involves an orientation by participants to a goal (in the simplest terms, identifying the strengths and weaknesses of a lesson with a view to improving practice) and there are therefore constraints on how participants act and what they may say (for example, supervisors generally do not shout at supervisees and supervisees generally do not disagree with supervisors). At least one participant represents a formal organisation (Roberts, 2013), the supervisor in this case, and this means that he/she is in a powerful position. Institutional talk is also associated with 'inferential frameworks' and procedures specific to the particular context (Drew and Heritage, 1992: 22). In feedback conferences, this means that supervisors and supervisees orient their talk to assessment/developmental criteria (see *Purposes* below) and tend to use particular linguistic forms in their talk, for example, hedging to deliver criticism (see *Face* below). Power differentials make feedback conferences asymmetrical and 'there is a direct relationship between status and role, on the one hand, and discursive rights and obligations, on the other' (Drew and Heritage, 1992: 49). Supervisors ask questions, take long turns and deliver evaluations and advice; supervisees answer questions, listen, and demonstrate they have taken on board advice proffered. Given the institutional nature of the feedback conference, it is not surprising that researchers have been interested in identifying its generic features. Waite (1992), for example, identified three main phases in his research on dyadic feedback in an in-service context: supervisor's reporting phase; supervisee's response phase and a programmatic phase. Copland (2010) identified five phases in group feedback on a pre-service certificate programme: trainer feedback phase; trainee self-evaluation phase; peer feedback phase; other talk about teaching phase (Waite's programmatic phase) and questioning phase.

Most post observation feedback conferences are dyadic, featuring an observer (trainer, supervisor, mentor, or peer) and a teacher or trainee teacher. Reflecting this, much of the research focuses on dyadic feedback. However, a large number of trainees on initial TESOL certificate courses such as CELTA experience feedback in a group format i.e. one trainer and a group of trainees. In this scenario, trainees also observe each other. Interestingly, Copland (2012) found that group feedback rarely included multi-party discussions, with talk tending to be between the trainer and one trainee, with the other trainees positioned as listeners, and trainees directing both their talk and their attention to the trainer, who also had the right to self-select, interrupt, and nominate who will speak. Copland also found that peer feedback was a source of tension for some trainees who struggled to negotiate the 'rules of the game' of this particular type of discourse (Copland 2010).

Purposes

There are two main reasons for providing feedback on teaching: evaluation and development. In teacher education programmes, where there are criteria for the supervisee to meet during the lesson, such as 'gives instructions effectively' or 'provides useful practice activities', feedback will usually, in part at least, evaluate how well they were fulfilled. In Extract 26.1, taken from around halfway through a pre-service 120-hour CELTA (Certificate in English language teaching to adults) programme, the trainer explicitly focuses on the aims of the lesson, of which trainees are required to demonstrate an understanding (Trer = trainer and Tree = trainee; there are two other trainees present):

Feedback extract 26.1

1	**Trer:**	but let's think about your overall ai:ms for the
2		lesson cos I mean I know however people sort of hear
3		the =
4	**Tree:**	= mhm =
5	**Trer:**	= word aims and shudder but I mean that's the
6		starting point it's what I want my learners to
7		achieve what I want them to get better at what I
8		want them to take away from the lesson so what were
9		you hoping that your learners would get better at?
10	**Tree:**	Just like I was hoping that they would sort of be
11		able to get together and plan a role play together
12		(.) and use *((inaudible))*
13	**Trer:**	is being able to p1 *((quickly))* sorry to interrupt
14		is being able to plan a *((slowly))* ro:le play (.) an
15		appropriate aim for a language lesson?
16	**Tree:**	(.) mmm (.) no

Features of institutional talk outlined above are present in this extract. The participants are orienting to the task of identifying strengths and weaknesses in the lesson. Participants are ostensibly polite in that they orient to each other's face needs to a certain extent (the supervisor 'apologises' for interrupting the supervisee, line 13). The supervisor represents both the institution in which he/she works and the body which awards the teaching certificate. Furthermore, the talk is clearly asymmetrical: the supervisor asks the questions and delivers the evaluation (inherent in line 13ff). By the end of this short extract, the supervisor has made the point that planning a role play is not an appropriate aim for a language lesson and while the supervisee may not agree, he/she accepts the point. Kurtoğlu-Hooton (2016), calls this kind of negative feedback 'corrective' and suggests that it is akin to 'a gentle telling off' (p. 10). Nonetheless, it is common practice as Copland (2011), Louw et al. (2016) and Kurtoğlu-Hooton (2016) have shown.

When employees are observed, evaluation is paramount. As Donaghue (2016) points out, an unsuccessful observation can have serious consequences for employees in terms of keeping a job or being considered for a salary increase or promotion. In these contexts, employees will often meticulously prepare their observed lesson, ensuring that they do their best to demonstrate a range of high level teaching skills and to meet institutional criteria. Feedback often focuses explicitly on the criteria (see Extract 26.6) and the employee may need to challenge a negative evaluation or promise to seek support for their teaching if the feedback is not positive.

In teacher education contexts, supervisors will try to ensure that feedback is developmental as well as evaluative, although given time limits (see below) it is often difficult to do so. Developmental talk provides supervisees with the opportunity to discuss the lesson from their own point of view, explaining their decisions, impressions and feelings. Developmental talk is often connected to reflective practice, that is, an approach that situates the teacher at the centre of his/her own developmental trajectory (see Mann and Walsh, this volume, and Mann and Walsh,

2017). To encourage development through reflection, supervisors will often ask questions that focus on the supervisee's needs and interests rather than on the evaluative criteria or their own interests. In Extract 26.2, the supervisor works with the supervisee to help him/her work out his confusion about why a task has been successful.

Feedback extract 26.2

1	**Trer:**	What are you saying?
2	**Tree:**	I'm saying (.) they really liked it *((small laugh))*
3		and I'm really confused and I'm saying that I'm
4		struggling to reconcile my thoughts on my own
5		learning

As can be seen, the supervisor is not focusing on the mechanics of teaching or the evaluation criteria but working with the supervisee to develop his knowledge and understanding of TESOL pedagogy. Importantly, the question the supervisor asks (line 1) does not have a right or wrong answer and the supervisor does not know how the supervisee will answer. This is a feature of dialogic teaching (Nystrand et al., 1997) which can be an effective way to support supervisees' development.

Why is feedback important?

For many supervisees and employees, post observation feedback is a valuable educative experience. It can be informative and engaging, revealing to supervisees and employees why their teaching appears to be successful (or not) in different contexts. As Watson Davis (2015) explains, 'Observation plays a fundamental role in improving the quality of teaching and learning … it is a powerful way to inspire and motivate'. A number of researchers have noted the positive effect feedback has had on supervisees when they recognise and understand why their teaching has not been successful, for example Hyland and Lo (2006) (who call this 'a catalytic moment' p. 167), Copland and Mann (2010), and Kurtoğlu-Hooton (2016), who argues that change happens as the result of confirmatory feedback.

An important purpose of feedback is to introduce supervisees and employees into ways of doing things in the profession or institution so that they can play by the rules of the game (Bourdieu, 1977). Learning how to talk about teaching, through acquiring its vocabulary and behaviours, or learning the expectations of an institution, through developing an understanding of what is considered good practice, supervisees and employees can develop a feeling of belonging at the same time as becoming more easily guided or coerced by those in control of the game (i.e. awarding bodies and institutions). This double-bind can cause supervisees and employees to feel both empowered and threatened by feedback. Pre-service teachers often feel empowered as they gain teaching skills and begin to feel part of a community, although they may also be discouraged by the realisation there is a lot to learn. In contrast, employees can feel their teacher identities are under threat as their personal teaching values, often developed over many years, may clash with those of the institution.

Linked to socialisation into the field, feedback can also be used as a gatekeeping device. As Roberts (2013) argues, 'the notion of gatekeeping implies the "objective" assessment of applicants' (p. 86) to ensure they are able to carry out the roles and responsibilities of, in our case, an English language teacher. However, as Erickson and Schultz (1982) argue and Roberts and

Sarangi (1999) and Copland (2010) show, gatekeeping encounters are rarely neutral and supervisors reject or downgrade supervisees because they do not fit, either because of their interactional style or because they do not exhibit co-membership of a group or community. Gatekeepers, therefore, may reject or discourage applicants to the field based on their attitude rather than on their skills or potential. In Extract 26.3 from a pre-service certificate programme, a trainer is explaining her views on a trainee who has been negatively evaluated by all the staff.

Interview extract 26.3

> She never really convinced me that she was that interested actually in the learners, to be honest, or in teaching or in developing herself. Erm, and I found her quite closed-minded, in terms of what had happened in her sessions, or other people. I just don't think she was that interested and I think that came across in her own development.

As can be seen, the trainer seems not to be basing her judgement of the supervisee on the assessment criteria (such as giving clear instructions) but on her interpretation of her motivation for teaching. Copland (2010) suggests that this trainee's interactional style both in class and in the feedback conferences was the main reason she was negatively evaluated, although none of the supervisors identified these areas explicitly as issues. The supervisee passed the course but only marginally and her reference was therefore less than glowing.

In this section we have described features that are central to the feedback conference, including its characterisation as institutional talk, its purposes and its value. In the following section we will elaborate on some of these areas as we examine current issues in the research into feedback conferences.

Key debates and current issues

Models of feedback

Within the literature on post observation feedback, different models of supervision have been proposed (e.g. Freeman, 1982; Gebhard, 1990; Wallace, 1991; Farr, 2011 for detailed overviews). These models are often visualised on a continuum with prescriptive and collaborative styles (Wallace, 1991) at either end. In a prescriptive/directive approach, the supervisor is seen as an authority who will offer opinions and prescribe actions for the teacher to adopt. This model relies on the supervisor being able to identify and describe effective teaching as well as recognise influential contextual factors (Farr, 2011). A prescriptive model may hinder teacher reflection, experimentation and independence but teachers (especially novices) often value direction. A collaborative style of supervision involves the teacher and observer working together as equals to solve problematic classroom issues in a process of observation and discussion, exploration and resolution. This model may encourage teachers to reflect and take ownership of their teaching, but less experienced teachers may lack the knowledge and experience needed to make teaching decisions (Farr, 2011).

Vásquez and Reppen (2007) maintain that there has been a historical shift away from prescriptive or evaluative styles of supervision to models intended to promote teacher reflection. Farr's (2011) study, however, uncovers an ongoing tendency for supervisors to be directive, and this is supported by other recent empirical research (e.g. Copland et al., 2009; Hyland and Lo, 2006; Louw et al., 2016). Studies have also identified a divergence between supervisors' espoused beliefs about appropriate models of feedback and the way feedback is actually conducted. Most discrepancies involve supervisors professing to value a collaborative, reflective approach, but in practice adopting a directive approach (e.g. Donaghue, 2015; Delaney, this volume; Farr, 2011; Hyland and Lo, 2006; Louw et al., 2016). Instead of encouraging dialogue, observers prescribe and evaluate while teachers are passive, mostly contributing information and accepting tutors' comments. Thus, supervisors rather than teachers do the reflective work of '*noticing, unpacking and processing*' (Baecher and Beaumont, 2017: 66). The tendency to directive supervision prompts Farr to ask:

> As a profession, we need to ask ourselves why this is still the case after strongly directive supervision was first criticised as being inadequate and inappropriate over 30 years ago.
>
> *(Farr, 2011: 174)*

While supervisory models may offer practitioners a useful way of thinking about feedback, they are theoretical constructs which may not reflect 'real life' feedback with its complexity, constraints, and contextual variation. Factors such as teacher experience, classroom realities and differences, the purpose and expectations of feedback, the relationship between observer and observed, and teacher motivation, interests and anxiety will all influence how feedback plays out. For example, supervisory models assume that supervisors have more knowledge than the observed teacher and the choice of feedback style rests with the supervisor. In in-service contexts however, teachers as well as supervisors can affect the content, direction and goal of the feedback meeting, and the teacher often has more knowledge than the supervisor (Donaghue, 2016). Farr suggests that, as with language teaching, '*we are in a post model era*' (2011: 23), and recommends we move on to view feedback as situated, collaborative, co-constructed and mutually reflective.

Researchers have identified various factors which contribute to the dominance of directive feedback. One factor is a lack of training for observers (Copland, 2010; Farr, 2011). If training is available, the type of training observers receive may also influence how they conduct feedback. For example, Ma (2009) points out that because trainer training on initial certificate courses is done through mentoring and shadowing an experienced tutor, tutors in training may not be exposed to more dialogic or reflective examples of feedback. Contextual constraints such as lack of time and heavy workload also contribute to observers adopting a more prescriptive style (Copland, 2012; Donaghue, 2015; Farr, 2011). Kobayashi (in preparation) explains that the feedback conferences she observed with undergraduate students were open-ended. Videos of the lessons were played to support recall, and ample time was made for detailed discussion, ensuring that the conferences concluded when the participants were all sure that the main points had been covered. However, she also notes that this approach is unsustainable outside a research project as a supervisor's schedule could not usually accommodate either the time commitment or the flexibility. This is highlighted by the interview comment in Extract 26.4 from a supervisor whose duties include an annual 1-hour observation of each of the teachers in his large team.

Interview extract 26.4

The biggest constraint is time. Fitting them in, you know? For example, I've got something like 41 English teachers that I need to observe, but if you think each observation, if you're going to do it properly you'd look at their lesson plan and give them feedback on that before they went in, you'd then observe the lesson, write it up, have the feedback session. You could be looking at three or four hours per person. And obviously, if you multiply that by the number, that in itself would become almost a full-time job.

Hall (2017) suggests that the lack of time for feedback means that many tenets advocated in reflective practice, such as using data-led approaches (as recommended, for example, by Mann and Walsh, 2017) are not practical. In his research with Japanese in-service junior high school teachers in their first year of teaching, feedback conferences were nearly always snatched from time usually dedicated to other purposes (such as preparing classes) and rarely lasted longer than 30 minutes. This allows for a scant discussion only of the issues both the supervisor and supervisee bring to the table and no time at all for examining data such as diaries or transcripts.

Face

Many researchers come to their studies with an interest in how post observation feedback conferences seem to be effective or not, leading many to investigate the pragmatics of feedback. Previous research has recognised that there is often much at stake in the post-observation feedback conference and it is a challenging speech event to manage (Copland, 2008). Although feedback talk can be confirmatory i.e. recognising positive aspects of an observed lesson, it can also be 'corrective' (Kurtoğlu-Hooton, 2008) i.e. it can focus on weaknesses, and can include evaluation (Copland, 2008; Farr, 2011) and criticism (Wajnryb, 1994). This aspect of feedback is potentially face threatening. Within the growing body of empirically grounded research looking at the discourse of feedback, a recurrent focus of analysis is how observers manage giving critical feedback while taking into account the face needs of the observed teachers. Wajnryb (1994) was perhaps the first to work in this area: she identified how supervisors' concerns are reflected in the language that they use. Importantly, Wajnryb (1994) identified the importance of face in feedback talk and showed how supervisors worked hard to maintain supervisees' face needs despite having to deliver negative messages (for a full discussion of face, see Goffman, 1967; Arundale, 2010; and Donaghue, 2016). Indeed, Wajnryb (1998) suggested that supervisors found it difficult to walk the line between providing a clear message to supervisees and doing positive face work and warned that this ran the danger of 'fuelling misconceptions' (1998: 541) by giving supervisees' the option of not taking up negative appraisal. This finding has clear implications for the effectiveness of feedback: if it is equivocal, then the message may not be communicated. If it is too blunt (in face terms, bald on-record, Brown and Levinson, 1987) supervisees might be too affronted to assimilate and accept the message. Extract 26.5, from a feedback conference, demonstrates this tension (see too, Copland, 2011).

Feedback extract 26.5

1	**Trer:**	<u>I think</u>, it's *probably,* **I mean** three's okay but
2		*probably* pairs is ideal for comparing answers to a
3		listening or something cos it's least threatening
4		you know when you you can really feel stupid
5		sometimes can't you because sometimes you can't
6		understand something <u>you tend to</u> feel **a bit** <u>it can</u>
7		<u>make you</u> feel **a bit** stupid so having to **kind of**
8		reveal that to more people is **a bit** more threatening
9		so <u>I think</u> just sharing it with a partner is **just**
10		*probably* the least threatening way to do it.

The message the supervisor wants to give is this: students should compare answers before the teacher checks in plenary. However, the message is difficult to hear as it is mitigated by modal verbs (underlined), vague utterances (bold) and modal adverbs (italics). Tracy (2008) calls this kind of language work, 'positive jewelry' (p. 187) and suggests that it is used to mask a face threatening act (Brown and Levinson, 1987). The question is whether the trainee can see through the mitigation to the message or whether, as Wajnryb (1998) warns, the message is obscured by it.

Since Wajnryb's seminal work, Hyland and Lo (2006), Vásquez (2004), Copland (2010, 2011) and Donaghue (2016) have all found face a valuable analytical lens through which to examine feedback. Recent work has focused on how both supervisors and supervisees negotiate face on a turn-by-turn basis in order for feedback to proceed smoothly (Copland, 2011) and how identity can influence the ways in which supervisors and supervisees conduct face work (Donaghue, 2016). These studies have contributed to understanding the complexity of the interactional work that both supervisors and supervisees engage in so that feedback can move along effectively.

Power

Studies investigating post observation discourse have identified asymmetrical power relationships between feedback participants. Trainers or supervisors manifest power by typically initiating topics, controlling the floor and taking longer turns (Copland, 2008; Hyland and Lo, 2006; Vásquez, 2004; Waite, 1992) with trainee teachers often uttering only single minimal responses (Vásquez, 2004). Copland (2012) looked in particular at how topics and speaking rights are established and negotiated. Her study found that although trainees were always given the opportunity to comment on their own lessons, it was the trainers who controlled how topics were to be understood, and the trainers' views on language teaching pedagogy which were transmitted through practices such as statements regarding best practice and privileging trainers' opinions through self-selections, interruptions and long turns. Trainees were expected to listen to the trainers and accept their views. However, Copland (2008) also found that trainees sometimes resisted the hegemonic order. Trainers' power was contested by trainees sometimes refusing to take part or accept pedagogic practice, or challenging the trainers' view of classroom practice. Donaghue (2016) also identified instances of teachers enacting powerful identities by defending their classroom actions, resisting advice, demonstrating superior knowledge, and contesting supervisors' grades. However, Copland (2008) and Donaghue (2016) both found that trainers and supervisors responded to these challenges by negotiating back to powerful positions.

Identity

Despite a growing interest in language teacher identity (Barkhuizen, 2017), very little research has examined the negotiation of identities during feedback talk. This is surprising because the feedback conference gives 'recurrent opportunities for teachers to construct a sense of themselves in relation to their teaching environments' (Urzúa and Vásquez, 2008: 1936), and feedback talk has the potential to both facilitate and illuminate teacher identities. To our knowledge, only three studies to date have examined identity in feedback. In a pre-service context, Urzúa and Vásquez (2008) examined instances of novice teachers talking about the future and constructing identities involving power and expertise. Riordan and Farr (2015) investigated narratives during face to face feedback and online discussions between student teachers and trainers, and report that student teachers constructed identities of novice and knowledgeable/confident teachers as they recounted difficulties and discussed their mental states and thoughts.

Donaghue's (2016) study of in-service teachers and supervisors also revealed that feedback participants indexed identities involving power, expertise, and experience. Supervisors invoked the identities of manager, leader, assessor, advisor and institutional representative, while teachers projected identities of competent, experienced professional and responsive, reflective, committed teacher. As well as these positive identities, disvalued identities were also made relevant such as inexperienced teacher and unknowledgeable supervisor. Context influenced identity work as participants co-constructed identities which were institutionally valued such as technologically proficient and enthusiastic teacher and skilled classroom manager.

This section has discussed some of the issues of current interest to researchers of feedback. In the next section we look at ways of helping participants better understand and manage feedback with a view to helping participants make feedback more effective.

Understanding feedback

Helping teachers manage feedback

Observed teachers, especially those new to feedback, often have difficulties understanding the norms of self-evaluation practices and reflection (Copland, 2010). To help overcome this difficulty, Copland (2010) recommends using a variety of feedback modes (e.g. peer, trainer led, pairs, groups, formal, informal). In addition, she suggests introducing an induction session preparing trainees for feedback. Farr (2015) also offers useful advice to help prepare student teachers for feedback. She suggests teachers prepare by identifying a particular focus, reviewing relevant evidence such as lesson recordings, student feedback, peer discussions, or student work, and then producing a written reflection to take to their feedback meeting. Farr also recommends that the trainer and trainee negotiate the approach and content of the feedback meeting in advance, and that trainees record the meeting to examine their own contributions, noting ways they think they could increase the quantity and quality of their contributions.

A useful way of narrowing the focus of the feedback conference is for the observed teacher to select one or two 'critical incidents' to discuss. Critical incidents are significant or interesting moments (positive, negative or neutral) from the observed lesson. Iyer-O'Sullivan (2015) questions the standard practice of describing and reflecting on a whole lesson (often in chronological order), as well as general questions commonly used by tutors such as 'How do you think that went?' or 'What would you do differently?'. She maintains that these practices can result in feedback which is negative, shallow and descriptive, with a tendency to be initiated, led and controlled by the tutor. Iyer-O'Sullivan (2015) argues that inviting teachers to identify one event and helping them examine and analyse this event through guided questions can foster deeper reflection (see also Kobayashi *in preparation*).

Helping observers understand feedback

Supervisors/trainers/observers have limited opportunities for professional learning (Baecher and Beaumont, 2017), despite the fact that teacher learning and development depends on teacher educators. Teacher educators working in TESOL need opportunities to practise what they preach and show that they are themselves committed to reflective practice (Mann and Walsh, 2015). By promoting a spirit of inquiry and research, educators can act as role models but can also develop the ability to identify their own strengths and weaknesses and find ways to enhance their practice.

A number of researchers have suggested using data from feedback recordings to help trainers or supervisors become critically aware of their professional talk and help them shape their own practice (Copland, 2012; Copland et al., 2009; Farr, 2011; Vasquez and Reppen, 2007). In comparison to the considerable research into teacher talk in classroom settings, there has been relatively little examination of trainer or supervisor talk in teacher education contexts, including the feedback conference (Engin, 2013). Donaghue and Oxholm (2017) describe the *'uncomfortable, sometimes horrifying'* (p. 158) realisation gained from analysing transcripts from post observation feedback meetings that their own interactional practices often limited student teachers' opportunities for reflection: *'we talked too much, often interrupting students, putting words in their mouths, finishing their sentences and reflecting for them'* (p. 158). Analysing feedback talk helped these tutors raise awareness of and critique their own practice as well as put in place strategies for improvement. In a similar vein, Vásquez and Reppen's (2007) longitudinal study identified areas for supervisor/researchers to change and improve their practice by building and analysing a corpus of their feedback talk. Farr (2005) also used a spoken language corpus of dyadic feedback interactions between university-based ELT trainers and trainees as a data source for describing and reflecting on how trainers conducted feedback. Farr used the corpus to qualitatively examine types of interventions used in feedback and to quantitatively investigate participation frameworks. She adds, however, that corpora could be used in many other ways to enrich knowledge of trainers' professional practice.

One area of change identified by Vásquez and Reppen (2007) was the supervisors' deliberate decision to ask more questions, which increased teacher talk between semesters one and two. Trainer questions also feature in Engin's (2013) study of scaffolding trainees' understanding during feedback, with Engin offering a framework of different question types to elicit evaluation or reflection from trainees. Similarly, Mann and Copland (2010) and Copland (2015) argue that when trainers question rather than pass judgement, trainees can develop a better understanding of the weaknesses in their teaching practice and how it can be improved. Developing trainers' proficiency in asking questions (particularly those which encourage dialogic talk) is one important area for development in trainer training to support more effective feedback (Copland, 2015; Engin, 2013; Copland and Mann, 2010).

Understanding the influence of institutional documents

As a result of the rise in managerialism in education and the ensuing quality assurance focus, many institutions have attempted to operationalise a construct of 'good' or 'effective' teaching via institutional observation forms consisting of criteria which purport to describe 'best practice'. However, few researchers have examined or described the use and role of institutional documents or artefacts in feedback interaction (Engin, 2015). Engin (2015) discusses the benefits that artefacts such as teaching transcripts, lesson plans and self-evaluation forms can bring to feedback. However, although institutional documents can mediate thinking and discussion and prompt reflection, they can also constrain these aspects of development. Waite (1992) found that trainers' presentation of data from observation records during feedback meetings meant that trainees had little time left for discussion of topics not initiated by supervisors, or for reflection. Similarly, Donaghue (2016) found that an institutional observation often formed the basis and structure of feedback meetings, with supervisors spending time explaining the scores on the form, reading aloud written evaluative comments and 'typing aloud' additional comments, making talk predominantly evaluative and dominated by the supervisor. Extract 26.6 demonstrates this tendency.

Fiona Copland and Helen Donaghue

Feedback extract 26.6

1	**Sup:**	all right so let's start with the teaching
2		competencies em and what I do is I make little
3		comments for each bullet and you can read along (.)
4		eh as I go you had mostly threes and fours here (.)
5		em you you're obviously very competent in the use of
6		smartboard em you know you it just was (.) f- s-
7		seamless just moved along and the students even know
8		how to use it cos they came up and did some work on
9		it themselves (.) em you had the objectives listed
10		on the smartboard which a lot of teachers neglect to
11		do (.) em there were visuals (.) aah you did integr-
12		interactive paragraph building where the students
13		had to come up themselves and and eh use the board
14		(.) none of the technology was forced it just fit
15		with the lesson you know I don't like to go in and
16		see that people oh well here we're gonna use
17		technology now because it's required for the
18		observation but it fit the lesson and that's what
19		makes sense em you knew all the students
20	**Teacher:**	[mm
21	**Sup:**	[you always called on them by name you walked around
22		the <u>room</u> during eh the CLASS to see what they were
23		doing (0.1) and for foundations boys they were very
24		well behaved em and I liked how you discipline
25		because it didn't interrupt with the flow of the
26		class I don't know if you're aware of this but there
27		were three different things that you did that I
28		really stuck in my mind (.) I mean you call their
29		names yeah sure but then you also were gentlemen are
30		you <u>ready</u> which indicated to them that they were not
31		prepa- doing what they were supposed to be doing and
32		then the last one which was kind of interesting when
33		you stopped speaking and just look at look at them
34		and it took the longest it took was about four and a
35		half seconds but usually within three seconds they
36		were looking right back at you and they had stopped
37		talking and they were back on track ((*laughs*))

What is striking about this extract is the amount of talk from the supervisor, with the teacher virtually silenced. The supervisor is also speaking very quickly (note the lack of pauses) as he/she tries to fit in discussion of all criteria on a three-page document. The supervisor immediately orients to the set of assessment criteria on the observation form ('teaching competencies' lines 1–2) and to the scores (four being the highest). He/she then goes on to give a descriptive account of the lesson in order to explain his scores. This pattern is typical of all of this supervisor's feedback meetings which means the teachers he/she observes are given little opportunity for discussion, reflection and professional growth.

The institutional document dominated proceedings in these meetings and the form embodied and gave prominence to the supervisor's perception of the lesson. The observation form was an important presence in these feedback meetings, giving voice to the institutional document's discourse of quality, control, and power. Much of the literature seems to take institutional documents such as observation instruments for granted but these findings suggest that they should be examined more closely for the effect they have on feedback.

Having considered central topics in the field of post observation feedback research, in the next section we conclude our discussion by looking forward to future developments and areas of potential research.

New directions

Feedback in new contexts

Previous research on post observation feedback in ELT has been carried out almost exclusively in the context of a formal teaching course such as an initial teaching certificate (e.g. Copland, 2008) or degree courses in English language teaching (e.g. Farr, 2011; Vásquez, 2004; Vásquez and Reppen, 2007; Waite, 1992). In addition, most of the literature focuses on pre-service teacher education (e.g. Copland, 2010, 2011; Engin, 2013; Farr, 2011; Kurtoğlu-Hooton, 2008, 2016; Louw et al. 2016). However, observation and feedback also form part of the working lives of experienced teachers (and other professionals) in other settings. Recently, researchers have begun to examine these contexts and in doing so, are uncovering previously undiscussed areas and new avenues of investigation. Donaghue's (2016) work on the evaluations of in-service teachers by their supervisors in the Emirates is the first of its kind. Taking a linguistic ethnographic approach, Donaghue recorded feedback conferences and interviewed supervisors and supervisees about the feedback process. The findings from the study reveal the high stakes nature of observation and feedback in this context, where poor grades on observations can result in termination to employment.

Hall's investigation of the first year of junior high school teachers in Japan provides detailed information on how teachers are socialised into their new roles and how they reconcile their beliefs about English language teaching with the realities of everyday school and classroom life (Hall, 2017). Hall conducted feedback conferences with three teachers over the course of a year with a view to provide a safe space for teachers to voice and discuss their concerns. This unique study, informed by a CHAT (cultural-historical activity theory) analysis, revealed that feedback can be valuable for in-service teachers but that the teachers need to find solutions to their own problems, taking into account a range of contextual features, and the supervisor's input may not always be either useful or welcome.

New uses of technology

With the development of new technologies, studies experimenting with feedback in a digital medium are starting to emerge. For example, Kassner and Cassada (2017) investigated the quality and nature of small group digital feedback conducted in real time. An instructor and peers on a graduate education course for in-service teachers used an online chatroom to give immediate, real-time, simultaneous feedback. All observers were able to see and learn from the online discussion and their feedback was captured in a transcript, providing a written record for participants, including the observed teacher, to later reflect on. The transcript also allowed the teacher educators to examine students' understanding of their own and others' practice, and to review the depth of peer feedback offered. The authors conclude that the online chat tool promoted rich, high-quality feedback and a space to collaborate and exchange ideas, while improving engagement.

More and more use is being made of video in helping supervisees analyse and critique their teaching practice. Video is also being used for supervisor development. For example, Baecher and Beaumont (2017) piloted a trainer development scheme whereby a supervisor and colleague collaborated on analysing a video of a post observation conference and found that focusing on the video enabled both the supervisor and colleague to confront their beliefs and assumptions and start to consider ways of changing or experimenting with their practice (see also Kobayashi, *in preparation*).

Researchers are also starting to build small, targeted corpora of both spoken and written feedback and using concordancing software to analyse these data (e.g. Farr, 2011; Vásquez, 2004; Vásquez and Reppen, 2007). Farr's (2011) meticulous combination of bottom-up corpus investigation with qualitative discourse analysis demonstrates the affordances corpus linguistics brings to determining the defining characteristics of the feedback genre. Farr's analysis established a framework of four main feedback categories: direction, reflection, evaluation, and relational talk, and by looking at language features such as hedging and boosting, she gives a nuanced picture of the social processes (such as directing, scaffolding, and relationship building) involved in feedback.

Conclusion

Given its ubiquity, its potential for teacher development and growth, and its impact and consequences, post observation feedback remains an important area of research. In this chapter we have aimed to highlight key issues and debates from previous studies with a view to inspiring practitioners and researchers to further explore the rich and fascinating area of post observation feedback.

References

Baecher, L. and Beaumont, J. (2017) 'Supervisor Reflection for Teacher Education: Video-Based Inquiry as Model'. *European Journal of Applied Linguistics and TEFL*, 6 65–84.

Baecher, L. and McCormack, B. (2015) 'The Impact of Video Review on Supervisory Conferencing'. *Language and Education*, 29 153–173.

Barkhuizen, G. (2017) 'Language teacher identity research', in Barkhuizen, G. (ed.) *Reflections on Language Teacher Research*. New York: Routledge: 1–11.

Bourdieu, P. (1977) *Outline of a Theory of Practice*. Cambridge: Polity Press.

Brown, P. and Levinson, S. (1987) *Politeness: Some Universals in Language Usage*. Cambridge: Cambridge University Press.

Copland, F. (2008) *Feedback in pre-service English language teacher training: discourses of process and power*. Unpublished thesis, University of Birmingham, UK.

Copland, F. (2010) 'Causes of Tension in Post-Observation Feedback in Pre-Service Teacher Training: An Alternative View'. *Teaching and Teacher Education*, 26 466–472.

Copland, F. (2011) 'Negotiating Face in the Feedback Conference: A Linguistic Ethnographic Approach'. *Journal of Pragmatics*, 43(15) 3832–3843.

Copland, F. (2012) 'Legitimate Talk in Feedback Conferences'. *Applied Linguistics*, 33 1–20.

Copland, F. (2015) 'Evaluative talk in feedback conferences', in Howard, A. and Donaghue, H. (eds) *Teacher Evaluation in Second Language Teacher Education*. London: Bloomsbury: 135–150.

Copland, F. and Mann, S. (2010) 'Dialogic talk in the post-observation conference: an investment in reflection', in Park, G. (ed.) *Observation of Teaching: Bridging Theory and Practice through Research on Teaching*. Munich: Lincom Europa Publishing: 175–194.

Copland, F., Ma, G. and Mann, S. (2009) 'Reflecting in and on Post-Observation Feedback in Initial Teacher Training on Certificate Courses'. *English Language Teacher Education and Development*, 12 14–23.

Donaghue, H. (2015) 'Differences in supervisors' espoused feedback styles and their discourse in feedback meetings', in Howard, A. and Donaghue, H. (eds) *Teacher Evaluation in Second Language Teacher Education*. London: Bloomsbury: 117–134.

Donaghue, H. (2016) *The construction and negotiation of identity and face in post observation feedback*. Unpublished thesis, Aston University, UK.

Donaghue, H. and Oxholm, A. (2017) 'Engaging Student Teachers with Reflection Through Microteaching and Interaction'. *The European Journal of Applied Linguistics and TEFL*, 6 145–164.

Drew, P. and Heritage, J. (1992) *Talk at Work: Interaction in Institutional Settings*. Cambridge: Cambridge University Press.

Engin, M. (2013) 'Questioning to Scaffold: An Exploration of Questions in Pre-Service Teacher Training Feedback Sessions'. *European Journal Of Teacher Education*, 36 39–54.

Engin, M. (2015) 'Artifacts in scaffolding the construction of teaching knowledge', in Howard, A. and Donaghue, H. (eds) *Teacher Evaluation in Second Language Teacher Education*. London: Bloomsbury: 85–100.

Erickson, F. and Schultz, J. J. (1982) *The Counselor as Gatekeeper*. Cambridge: Academic Press.

Farr, F. (2005) 'Reflecting on reflections: the spoken word as a professional development tool in language teacher education', in Hughes R. (ed.) *Spoken English, Applied Linguistics and TESOL: Challenges for Theory and Practice*. Basingstoke: Palgrave Macmillan: 182–215.

Farr, F. (2011) *The Discourse of Teaching Practice Feedback*. Abingdon: Routledge.

Farr, F. (2015) *Practice in TESOL*. Edinburgh: Edinburgh University Press.

Freeman, D. (1982) 'Observing Teachers: Three Approaches to In-Service Training and Development'. *TESOL Quarterly*, 16 21–28.

Gebhard, J. (1990) 'Models of supervision: choices', in Richards, J. and Nunan, D. (eds) *Second Langauge Teacher Education*. Cambridge: Cambrdge University Press: 156–166.

Goffman E. (1967) *On Face Work. Interactional Ritual*. New York: Basic Books.

Hall, J. (2017) *A linguistic ethnography of learning to teach English at Japanese junior high schools*. Unpublished thesis, University of Stirling, UK.

Hyland, F. and Lo, M. (2006) 'Examining Interaction in the Teaching Practicum: Issues of Language, Power and Control'. *Mentoring and Tutoring: Partnership in Learning*, 14 163–186.

Iyer-O'Sullivan, R. (2015) 'From bit to whole: reframing feedback dialogue through critical incidents', in Howard, A. and Donaghue, H. (eds) *Teacher Evaluation in Second Language Teacher Education*. London: Bloomsbury: 69–84.

Kassner, L. D. and Cassada, K. M. (2017) 'Chat it up: backchanelling to promote reflective practice among in-service teachers'. *Journal of Digital Learning in Teacher Education*, 33 160–168.

Kobayashi, E. (in preparation) *The role of post-observation feedback talk in learning to teach English as a foreign language: a linguistic ethnographic approach*. PhD Thesis, University of Stirling, UK.

Kurtoğlu-Hooton, N. (2008) 'The design of post-observation feedback and its impact on student teachers', in Garton, S. and Richards, K. (eds) *Professional Encounters in TESOL*. Basingstoke: Palgrave Macmillan: 24–41.

Kurtoğlu-Hooton, N. (2016). *Confirmatory Feedback in Teacher Education: An Instigator of Student Teacher Learning*. Basingstoke: Palgrave Macmillan.

Louw, S., Watson Todd, R. and Jimarkon, P. (2016) 'Teacher Trainers' Beliefs About Feedback on Teaching Practice: Negotiating the Tensions Between Authoritativeness and Dialogic Space'. *Applied Linguistics*, 37(6) 745–764.

Ma, G. (2009) *An enquiry into the discourse of post-observation feedback on the TESOL Course at Wits Language School*. Unpublished thesis, University of Warwick, UK.

Mann, S. and Copland, F. (2010) 'Dialogic talk in the post-observation conference: an investment for reflection', in Park, G., Widodo, H. P. and Cirocki, A. (eds) *Observation of Teaching: Bridging Theory and Practice Through Research on Teaching*. Munich: LINCOM Europa: 175–194.

Mann, S. and Walsh, S. (2015) 'Reflective dimensions of CPD: supporting self-evaluation and peer-evaluation', in Howard, A. and Donaghue, H. (eds) *Teacher Evaluation in Second Language Teacher Education*. London: Bloomsbury: 17–34.

Mann, S. and Walsh, S. (2017) *Reflective Practice in English Language Teaching: Research-Based Principles and Practices.* Abingdon: Routledge.

Nystrand, M., Gamoran, A., Kachur, R. and Prendergast, C. (1997) *Opening Dialogue: Understanding the Dynamics of Language and Learning in the English Classroom.* New York: Teachers College Press.

Riordan, E. and Farr, F. (2015) 'Identity construction through narratives: an analysis of student teacher discourse', in Cheung, Y. L., Ben Said, S. and Park, K. (eds) *Advances and Current Trends in Language Teacher Identity Research.* Abingdon: Routledge: 161–174.

Roberts, C. (2013) 'Institutional discourse', in Simpson, J. (ed.) *The Routledge Handbook of Applied Linguistics.* Abingdon: Routledge: 81–95.

Roberts, C. and Sarangi, S. (1999) 'Hybridity in gatekeeping discourse: issues of practical relevance for the researcher', in Sarangi, S. and Roberts, C. (eds) *Talk, Work and the Institutional Order: Discourse in Medical, Mediation and Mangement Settings.* Berlin: Mouton de Gruyter: 473–503.

Tracy, K. (2008), '"Reasonable Hostility": Situation-appropriate Face-attack'. *Journal of Politeness Research*, 4 169–191.

Urzúa, A. and Vásquez, C. (2008) 'Reflection and Professional Identity in Teachers' Future-Oriented Discourse'. *Teaching and Teacher Education*, 24(7) 1935–1946.

Vásquez, C. (2004) '"Very Carefully Managed": Advice and Suggestions in Post-Observation Meetings'. *Linguistics and Education*, 15 33–58.

Vásquez, C. and Reppen, R. (2007) 'Transforming Practice: Changing Patterns of Particpation in Post-Observation Meetings'. *Language Awareness*, 16 153–172.

Waite, D. (1992) 'Supervisors' Talk: Making Sense of Conferences from an Anthropological Linguistic Perspective'. *Journal of Curriculum and Supervision*, 7 349–371.

Wajnryb, R. (1994) *The pragmatics of feedback: a study of mitigation in the supervisory discourse of TESOL teacher educators.* Uunpublished thesis, Macquarie University, Australia.

Wajnryb, R. (1998) 'Telling it Like it Isn't – Exploring an Instance of Pragmatic Ambivalence in Supervisory Discourse'. *Journal of Pragmatics*, 29(5) 531–544.

Wallace, M. (1991) *Training Foreign Language Teachers.* Cambridge: Cambridge University Press.

Watson Davis, R. (2015) *Lesson Observation Pocketbook.* Alresford: Management Pocketbooks.

27

Materials use and development

Kathleen Graves and Sue Garton

Introduction

The last decade has seen an abundance of publications on materials, especially monographs and edited collections, including Garton and Graves (2014), Harwood (2010, 2014), Masuhara et al. (2017), McGrath (2013), Mishan and Timmis (2015), Tomlinson (2008, 2013a), Tomlinson and Masuhara (2010). Moreover, a number of publications have seen new editions, which is an indication of their popularity and endurance (McDonough et al., 2013; McGrath, 2016; Tomlinson, 2011, 2013a). In spite of the current interest in materials, however, very little has been published that is directly concerned with how materials have been addressed in language teacher education, although there are a few exceptions (see, for example, Augusto-Navarro et al., 2014; Canniveng and Martinez, 2003; Tibbitts and Pashby, 2014). Tomlinson (2013a) traces the history of materials in teacher education, identifying the 1990s as the time when the importance of materials evaluation and development was recognised as essential to teacher development, rather than as a sub-section of methodology, so it would appear that materials are slowly becoming a part of teacher education programmes but they still lag well behind other areas such as methodology, second language acquisition, linguistics, research methods and even educational management, at least at MA level (Stapleton and Shao, 2018).

In this chapter, we begin by reviewing the current relationship between publications on materials and language teacher education, before identifying what we believe to be some of the key areas that need to be addressed in language teacher education. We then go on to consider the practical applications of materials in such programmes and suggest three interrelated skill areas that should be included as part of teacher education programmes so that teachers can become effective materials users and developers.

Key issues and debates

In this section we discuss the key issues and debates around materials design and evaluation as they relate to language teacher education programmes. We begin by looking at publications about materials that have been written for use in such programmes before considering research into how teachers can be prepared to evaluate, adapt and develop materials. We then go on to look at three areas of research into materials that are not usually associated with language teacher education but which, we believe, should be included if teachers are to develop the critical skills necessary for effective materials use: materials use in the classroom, critical views of materials and technology. We highlight the issues that are most relevant to teacher education, which we then discuss in detail in the subsequent section on practical applications.

Materials for use in language teacher education

Whilst there may be little written specifically about materials in teacher education, much of what has been published focuses on key areas that can usefully inform teacher education programmes, and many of the books are explicitly intended for use on such programmes. Thus there are a number of 'how to' books, with advice for teachers and for trainees on how to evaluate and adapt materials (see for example McDonough et al., 2013; McGrath, 2016; Mishan and Timmis, 2015; Tomlinson, 2011, 2013a).

Materials design and development is also a common theme with the majority of chapters in Tomlinson (2011) dedicated to this, together with McGrath (2016) and chapters in Harwood (2010) and Tomlinson (2013a). A number of books also have chapters on both evaluating and developing different types of materials, for different target groups, and from different geographical areas (Harwood, 2010; Tomlinson, 2008, 2013a).

In his preface to Harwood (2010), Jack Richards noted:

> The status of materials design is sometimes undervalued in graduate education, where it is regarded as a relatively trivial and theory-free activity. However, whereas materials design may seem an eminently practical activity, sound instructional materials cannot be created in a theoretical vacuum.
>
> *(Richards, 2010: ix)*

Gilmore (2012: 250) in a comparative review of four books on materials evaluation and design also notes that 'the focus is beginning to shift away from the largely pragmatic concerns of classroom teachers and publishers towards a more theoretical stance.' Books and articles with a more theoretical and research-based approach to materials include Garton and Graves (2014), Harwood (2010, 2014), Masuhara et al. (2017), Tomlinson (2012) and Tomlinson and Masuhara (2010). It is hoped that the move towards greater theorising of materials and efforts to link materials to applied linguistics theory will help to establish its place as a field in teacher education and especially graduate programmes.

Materials in language teacher education

As previously stated, while much has been written about materials for use on teacher education programmes, very little has been written about how such publications are actually used to prepare teachers to evaluate, develop and use materials.

Canniveng and Martinez (2003) make some general suggestions around principles for the inclusion of materials in teacher training at all levels and propose a model where materials development is seen as an outcome of the integration of SLA theory, teachers' cognitions and teachers' experiences.

Tomlinson (2013c) describes theoretical, developmental and practical aims of materials development courses he has run, as well as procedures for attaining these aims. He states:

> focusing on materials development is the most effective way of running a course in applied linguistics, as theory can be made relevant and meaningful by reference to practical procedures which are at the heart of the language teaching and learning process. It is also the most effective way of helping language education professionals to articulate and develop their own theories of language learning and to help them to develop the skills which they need in order to apply these theories in practice.
>
> *(Tomlinson, 2013c: 499)*

In one of the few publications to address materials in an actual teacher education setting, Augusto-Navarro et al. (2014) report on how they introduced pre-service teachers on a 5-year university teacher education programme to materials evaluation and adaptation. Their starting point was the importance of developing trainee teachers' understanding of the theories of language and of teaching-learning that underlie the coursebook so that they are better equipped to critically evaluate and appropriately adapt the materials. Taking approaches to grammar as the focus, they followed a six-step sequence of activities (ibid.: 243):

1. Raising awareness of teaching materials and grammar through eliciting the teachers' views in individual interviews.
2. Reading and summarising (using guiding questions) relevant articles or book chapters on both theoretical perspectives on materials and theories of grammar.
3. Sharing understandings of the readings through class discussion.
4. Presenting a materials analysis and proposing adaptations in pairs.
5. Peer and tutor evaluation of the analysis and presentation, offering opportunities for critical reflection.
6. Post-course interviews to verify whether there has been any change in views as a result of the theoretical readings and to give trainees the opportunity to reflect on any changes.

Augusto-Navarro et al. (2014) found that, by following this sequence, their student teachers were able to make more informed choices, in particular as they became far more aware of the need to consider learners in the evaluation and adaptation of materials.

Another notable chapter in that it focuses on materials development in a specific context is Tibbits and Pashby (2014). They report on how they used project-based learning to implement a materials development project on a 4-week training programme in the US for elementary school teachers from South Korea. Through a series of experiential workshops with titles such as Dramatic Reading, Realia, Story Comprehension, Reading Expression, Vocabulary and four pronunciation workshops (ibid.: 228), the teachers were given opportunities for reflection and practice. At the end of the programme, they constructed their own 20-minute story-based lesson. The story-reading project enabled teachers not only to develop story-based lessons appropriate for young learners but also to focus on their own language use through, for example, the reading aloud and pronunciation workshops.

So far in this section, we have focused on what has been published *about* materials design and evaluation, touching on *how* it has been or might be implemented in education programmes. However, there are a number of key issues and debates around materials in ELT that are rarely discussed in connection with teacher education and yet we feel should be included in such programmes.

Materials use in the classroom

Garton and Graves (2014) noted that, in spite of the growing attention to materials in ELT, there continues to be a lack of empirical studies on materials use in actual classrooms. This is potentially an important area of research for teacher education because knowing how teachers actually use materials in their classrooms, the reasons for their choices and the decision-making processes they go through, can inform more effective teacher preparation.

Investigations into how teachers use materials in classrooms, their insights and decision-making, as well as learner perspectives, including their attitudes towards, and use of materials have only recently begun to emerge. Opoku-Amankwa (2010), for example, focused on an urban primary school in Ghana, identifying a range of contextual factors that influenced the way the materials were used including class size, seating arrangements, and the teachers' interpretation of the school policy around learners' access to materials.

Two studies have looked at the introduction of new coursebooks and how they were used in the classroom by teachers (Humphries, 2014; Seferaj, 2014). While it is claimed that materials, and in particular coursebooks, can support teachers and lead to changes in practice (Hutchinson and Torres, 1994; Masuhara and Tomlinson, 2008), Humphries (2014) and Seferaj (2014) show that the relationship between materials, teachers and classroom practice is complex.

Humphries (2014) reports on the introduction of a new communicative coursebook in a Japanese *kosen* which required a major change in teaching approaches. Studying four different teachers, he identifies a range of factors that influenced the way that they used the new coursebooks, including socio-cultural factors, teacher uncertainty, perceptions of learner needs and preferences and limited training. He found that generally, the teachers adapted the new coursebooks to their previous grammar-translation methods, thereby showing that materials alone may have a limited effect on the way a teacher teaches.

Seferaj (2014) presents a case study of one very experienced teacher in Albania following the introduction of communicative methodology as part of national education reform. Sefaraj presents a complex picture of Miss Landa's decision-making and use of the new communicative coursebook. On the one hand, she expressed her belief in the importance of following the book, of using English in the classroom and she consistently followed the suggested activities for skills teaching. On the other, she introduced extra grammar material and did not use pair and group work for speaking activities. In all cases, however, she was able to clearly articulate the very good reasons why she adapted the new communicative materials she had been given rather than changing the way she taught.

Grammatosi and Harwood (2014) also report on one experienced teacher's radical adaptation of the required materials based on his own preferences, as well as his perceptions of students' needs and interests. The disparity in proficiency levels among students, his perception that the topics were not relevant, and the level of difficulty of the language led the teacher to replace and supplement a great deal of the textbook. Nevertheless, the teacher still felt guilty for not using the textbook (ibid.: 186).

Other studies that have looked at adaptation and supplementation of coursebooks by teachers include Tasseron (2017) who investigated the use of the language-focus (grammar) sections of a global ELT coursebook by 31 teachers at a college in Oman, of whom six were subsequently observed and five interviewed. The teachers adhered closely to these sections, possibly because both teachers and learners in Oman place a high importance on learning grammar. The teachers also adapted and supplemented the book to provide more relevant content and additional grammar work. However, they varied widely in their approach to cultural components that might be considered inappropriate for the context, with some addressing them and some replacing them. Abdel-Latif (2017) investigated the use of inductive grammar teaching materials by 12 Egyptian secondary school teachers and found that they largely used a deductive approach. Menkabu and Harwood (2014) examined the use of textbooks by seven teachers in an ESP course for medical students in a university in Saudi Arabia and found that each adapted the textbook, but for different reasons, such as learners' proficiency and motivation, class size, their knowledge of the content and teaching preferences, classroom contact time and an exam-oriented system. Similar to Humphries's teachers, Lucas studied four Brazilian public sector English teachers' conception and use of materials (Lucas et al., 2017) and found that they had little or no preparation in how to use materials.

Each of these qualitative studies is clearly small scale. However, taken together, they highlight the interconnected roles that a complex variety of factors play in how teachers use and adapt materials, and yield insights that can usefully inform teacher education. First is the simple fact that many of the teachers in these studies had little preparation in how to evaluate, use or adapt their materials. As a result, they fell back on a 'default' mode based on their beliefs about language learning and teaching, one often at odds with the approach in the materials. The studies also show how the typical pragmatic response from teachers to materials use in the classroom is to interpret and adapt the approaches according to their local context. However, many teachers, especially beginning teachers, may not have the confidence to challenge the authority of the coursebook by adapting it (Bosompen, 2014; Gray, 2000) leading potentially to confusion and feelings of guilt. Moreover, external constraints and socio-cultural expectations exert a strong influence on what teachers can do with materials. At the same time, some teachers do experiment with materials as long as their own expertise is not threatened. We discuss below how teacher education may use these insights in their programmes.

Critical views of materials

Recent years have seen an increase in the number of voices criticising English language teaching materials from an ideological point of view. While many of the publications on materials invite teachers to be critical in the sense of evaluating materials for adaptation purposes, they are still treating materials as 'curriculum artefact' and not as 'cultural artefact' (Gray, 2000, 2012, 2016). Building on the work of critical applied linguists such as Pennycook (1994) and Philipson (1992, 2009), Gray (ibid.) considers global coursebooks as cultural artefacts, which he defines as focusing '[o]n the meanings they seek to create for teachers and students, and the conditions of their production, circulation, and consumption' (Gray, 2016: 99).

He describes how ELT publishers focus on 'aspirational content' with frequent use of topics around personal and professional success, celebrities, cosmopolitanism and travel, all of which are believed to be motivating for language learners (Gray, 2012: 87) and with the underlying message that English equates with success (ibid.: 104). However, such images may not be motivating and may be resisted by learners (Canagarajah, 1993) or may leave them feeling inadequate (Masuhara and Tomlinson, 2008: 19).

Gray (2012: 111) calls for alternative articulations of English, a call that is reflected in more critical approaches to English language teaching in general such as those outlined by Igielski (2014) and López-Gopar (2019). Teacher education has an important role to play in developing a sense of criticality in teachers, including towards materials, so that they can make their own informed decisions and at least develop the sort of healthy lack of idealism found, for example, by Yakhontova (2001) and Zacharias (2005). We explore this in detail below.

Technology

It is no exaggeration to say that developments in digital technology have revolutionised language learning materials (see Macaro et al., 2012 for a review of computer assisted language learning in primary and secondary education). Publishers now regularly accompany coursebooks with companion websites and versions of their materials for the interactive whiteboard (IWB), while there are increasing reports of the use of Web 2.0 tools in language learning. The chapters in Thomas (2009) show the range of possibilities afforded by these tools with chapters on Skype, mobile phones, personal learning environments, social networking sites, podcasts, and weblogs, to name just a few. The use of technology can also lead to a radical shift in roles, by putting learners at the centre and making them active users or creators of materials (see, for example, Butler, 2015; Pereira, 2014) and by extending the learning process beyond the classroom through on-line projects, or key-pals, for example (see Copland and Mann, 2011).

However, the increasing emphasis on technology and its role in language teaching may have unintended consequences that it is important for language teacher education to address. Chapelle (2009) points out that the global spread of technology in language learning and the social, political and economic realities of learners around the world may not be compatible. Where teachers and/or learners do not have access to technology, teachers may feel inadequate, and there is a risk of believing that technology can represent a solution to many of the problems in English language teaching if only it were available (see, for example, Garton et al., 2011). Teacher education programmes need to prepare teachers for the digital world of electronic materials, whilst being realistic about their use and the role they can play. We explore this further in the next section.

Practical applications

Given the relative paucity of published work on teacher education and materials highlighted in the previous section, whether focused on conceptualisations of how it can be done (e.g. Canniveng and Martinez, 2003) or examples of how it has been done (e.g. Augusto-Navarro et al., 2014; Tibbits and Pashby, 2014), any consideration of practical implications needs to also refer to studies of how teachers have used, adapted and developed materials. We will use these to draw out implications for teacher education for both pre-service and in-service teachers, focusing as well on critical views of materials and technology. We will also address how to integrate a focus on materials in all teacher education courses, not just those that focus on materials evaluation and development.

A common complaint from teachers is that what is taught in teacher education courses is disconnected from the realities of what teachers encounter in their actual teaching contexts and so they feel unprepared for the complexities of teaching. An equally common lament from teacher educators is that teachers do not use what they have been taught in their practice. According to Johnson (2016: 123), for disciplinary knowledge to be relevant to teachers, it must be connected to their experience and grounded in actual teaching and learning activities.

Using, adapting and developing materials is a daily activity for a language teacher and is thus an ideal vehicle for the grounding of disciplinary knowledge in teaching that Johnson proposes. In that sense, 'materials represent the first stage in which principles are turned into practice' (McGrath, 2002: 217). Materials are mediating instruments of language learning and teaching – they are shared by both teacher and learner, albeit with different roles.

Johnson's conception of teacher learning as grounded in the activities and settings of practice resonates with Canniveng and Martinez's tripartite model for understanding materials (2003).

Their model, described earlier, includes teacher experience (as both teachers and learners), teacher cognition (their understandings, beliefs, and preferences regarding learning and teaching, both tacit and explicit) and theories of language learning. Using these concepts, we have identified three interrelated skill areas that teacher educators can help teachers develop in order to be effective users and developers of materials:

1. *Theories of language learning/disciplinary knowledge:*
   Developing informed understandings of the principles and assumptions that underlie materials.
2. *Teacher cognition and experience:*
   Understanding one's own beliefs and assumptions about materials.
3. *Grounding learning in the activities and settings of teaching:*
   Learning to adapt/develop materials to meet the needs of students in specific contexts.

We will also explore a fourth area related to the changing nature of materials and learners' relationship to them:

4. *Using technology to extend learners' language and interactions within and beyond the classroom.*

Developing informed understandings of the principles and assumptions that underlie materials

Language teacher education courses help teachers develop disciplinary knowledge and understandings of theories of language, language learning, language teaching, curriculum, assessment and so on. Materials, whether they are developed by teachers themselves or by others, represent views of language, how a language is learnt, how it should be taught, assessed and so on. In any course, regardless of the disciplinary focus (methodology, SLA, etc.), teachers-in-training can analyse materials to decide how they do or do not exemplify the principles being taught in that course, and how they could be modified to do so. Teachers can also be asked to (re) design materials and to microteach with materials in ways that exemplify those principles. By doing this, they both gain a better understanding of the principles and how to teach according to that principle.

Here we give some representative examples of integrating materials analysis into teacher education courses. When examining the role of culture in language learning, teachers can be asked to determine the extent to which materials help learners to, e.g. 'become aware of assumptions, values and attitudes of the self and others beneath utterances and behaviours' or 'interact effectively with people from different social groups' (Byram and Masuhara, 2013: 151). When studying learner variables in language acquisition, they can analyse materials according to whether and how they could cater for characteristics of different types of learners such as visual, kinaesthetic, field-dependent/independent, extrovert/introvert and so on (Lightbown and Spada, 2013). When learning about teaching reading, they can analyse materials for whether the comprehension questions focus on lower or higher order thinking skills, personal response or evaluative response and so on (Freeman, 2014).

Materials analysis can also extend to ideologies represented in materials as discussed earlier. This means guiding teachers-in-training to analyse the 'hidden curriculum' of materials – who and what is valued and represented, who is included and who is left out. An early example of this type of critical analysis was carried out by Auerbach and Burgess (1985). They found that materials written for adult immigrants portrayed entry level jobs rather than careers, and included language functions such as asking for approval, permission, and reassurance, rather than disagreeing, criticising, and praising. A recent example of this can be found in Igielski (2014), who studied culturally responsive pedagogy in her teacher preparation programme. One aspect of this pedagogy is to evaluate materials in terms of whether and how the cultures and ethnicities of one's students are represented in materials. This type of analysis enabled her to change how she approached her teaching so as to draw on and highlight her immigrant students' heritage, resources and languages.

Thus, a first step in teacher education programmes is to give teachers-in-training opportunities to analyse materials to uncover the principles and biases they represent. If teachers persist in using 'old ways' when they use materials, despite being taught 'new ways', as some studies of teachers' use of materials show, the problem may lie in the lack of grounding of the 'new ways' in both understanding the principles underlying the materials and actual practice trying out the activities in the materials. This grounding can be achieved through analysing materials, followed by redesigning activities, as needed, and then microteaching the activities to get a sense of how the principles are enacted in practice. Teachers can also be asked to develop materials based on disciplinary principles, teach with them, and reflect on their effectiveness in enacting the principles. It should be noted that using materials as a lens for understanding disciplinary knowledge places a responsibility on teacher educators to be familiar with published materials and to do this type of analysis themselves.

Understanding one's own beliefs and assumptions about materials

Several of the studies of teachers' use of materials point to the role that a teacher's beliefs and self-concept play in their use of materials. For example, Abdel-Latif (2017) found that the reason the teachers in his study spent 68 per cent of the time explaining grammar and only 32 per cent of the time using the inductive materials in the textbook was because of their conceptions that good grammar materials should be 'well organized and present grammar deductively, add concretely to students' grammar knowledge, and foster the teacher's active role' (ibid.: 283). Menkabu and Harwood (2014: 166) found that some of the ESP teachers' 'lack of in-depth knowledge' about some of the medical topics 'led to discomfort', thus causing them to either delete the topics or follow them to the letter. The teacher in Sefaraj's study (2014) was very clear about her belief that the teacher serves as the model of correct language input, which is one reason she eschewed pair work in favour of controlled teacher–student exchanges.

Teachers views of how materials should be used are thus shaped by their own experience in classrooms, their education, the context, and their years of experience. These assumptions are often tacit, and so teachers are not aware of them. For teachers to be able to change their practice to align with principles of effective language learning, they need to become aware of their conceptions and how they might be in conflict with these principles. An initial step, first described by McGrath (2006) is to ask teachers to provide metaphors for textbooks and to explain why they chose that metaphor. Teachers can also use metaphors to describe different kinds of materials, such as print and digital (Allen, 2015). The positive and negative metaphors that inevitably emerge are 'a useful heuristic to uncover teachers' views' (Menkabu and Harwood, 2014: 147) of the role of materials and can open a forum for examining those views in relationship to their experience and beliefs.

Teachers can be asked to make explicit their personal theories about how languages are best taught and learnt by creating a list, such as the one Tomlinson provides about his own theories (2013b: 24–25). Teachers can use sentence stems from his list such as 'Language learners succeed best if…', 'Language teachers tend to teach most successfully if…' 'Successful learning in classrooms depends on…' 'The most important thing that learning materials have to do is…'. The list can be converted into criteria for evaluating materials according to what teachers think is effective or not. For example, Masuhara (2006: 38) explains how a belief such as 'Learners only learn what they need or want to learn' can be converted to questions such as 'To what extent do the materials cater for learners' genuine needs/wants?' This type of reflection and analysis links teacher education with 'the experiential knowledge that teachers bring with them to LTE programmes' described by Johnson cited above.

At the same time, it is very difficult to change a belief system that has been years in the making and that provides a comfort zone for teachers. Providing teachers-in-training with opportunities to successfully experience effective alternatives can help them consider alternatives. Humphries (2014) states that for teachers to use textbooks effectively, they need support with new methodology, with being able to evaluate and to select textbooks. He writes,

> Many training courses, such as the ones in Japan, feature lectures and presentations preaching theories originating from BANA cultures. It is ironic that interpretation-based learner-centred approaches are explained to teachers in a transmission-based style, and no surprise that teachers then struggle to understand and implement what they hear. We need workshops where teachers can practice using new materials and discuss issues of methodology with colleagues and teacher-trainers.
>
> *(p. 265)*

In effect, teacher educators need to practice what they preach – to demonstrate how principles can be put into practice through loop-input (Woodward, 2003), and to invite teachers to challenge their assumptions, based on a shared experience.

Along similar lines, Tomlinson (2013c: 486) writes,

> I have found the most valuable way to start any materials development course is to demonstrate materials which are innovative, radical, different and potentially engaging in principled ways. … it can be a very effective way of opening up discussion of theories of language learning and principles of language teaching.

Tibbits and Pashby (2014) provide a clear example of having teachers experience materials use and development. As described earlier, the in-service teachers in their story-book project first experienced the approach as learners, then reflected on the experience in order to analyse and reconstruct it. Each teacher then chose another story book and designed a similar lesson, which they then taught to their peers. Participating teachers noted the importance of 'facing a challenging project but building confidence through scaffolded tasks while creating concrete products' (ibid.: 234).

Ability to adapt/develop materials to meet the needs of students in specific contexts

The ability to adapt or develop material to meet the needs of students in specific contexts is at the core of effective teaching. In order to use materials effectively, teachers must both be able to identify what needs to be adapted and why, and know how to adapt. This ability builds on the type of principled analysis described above, and extends it into real contexts.

Studies of teacher use of materials identify recurring and interrelated factors in their decisions to adapt. These areas were first identified by Hutchinson (1987), cited in Grammatosi and Harwood (2014). They include the textbook content, the teacher, the learners, the classroom and the school or institutional setting. These factors are always interconnected. For example, teachers adapt textbook content because it does not match the level of their students (e.g

Nuangpolmak, 2014), the cultural content is inappropriate for their students or they do not feel comfortable with it (e.g. Messekher, 2014), they do not feel knowledgeable about the subject matter (e.g. Menkabu and Harwood, 2014). They adapt how students use the material to interact because of the way the classroom furniture is arranged (e.g. Yan, 2007), they adapt the amount of time they spend on certain material so as to prepare students for exams (e.g. Lee and Bathmaker, 2007). Some of these adaptations are *ad hoc*, however, principled adaptation requires the ability to analyse materials to determine what will and will not work in one's context.

As described earlier, evaluating materials for different contexts has been addressed extensively in the literature (see for example, McGrath, 2013; Tomlinson, 2013a; Mishan and Timmis, 2015). All agree that evaluation should be based on specific and relevant criteria. One issue, discussed by Canniveng and Martinez (2003: 484) is that lists of criteria tend to be either superficial and not very useful or 'highly complicated and useful only under the supervision of someone more theoretically competent.' They suggest that teachers learn to create their own criteria based on reflection on their own experiences of what has or has not been successful. This is clearly appropriate for in-service teachers who can reflect on previous teaching experience. Pre-service teachers can reflect on their experiences as learners as well as experiences in their practicum (if they have one) that can help them create initial criteria for materials evaluation. McGrath (2016) suggests beginning with an analysis of the context – students, teacher and institution, and then creating a list of criteria for evaluating the content in relation to the context according to, for example, topics, language content, skills and methodology.

Wette (2010), cited in Menkabu and Harwood (2014: 168) suggests that teacher preparation programs include case studies of how material is adapted for different contexts in order to 'raise trainee's awareness of how their plans and materials will change according to classroom conditions.' Teachers in training can also be given materials and asked to evaluate their effectiveness for different contexts. Or they can be given an authentic text, such as an advertisement, and asked to design activities based on it for a context and group of learners of their choice. By comparing their choices with their peers', they learn that activities and their sequences vary according to who the learners are, their context, and how they define their needs (Graves, 2000).

Teacher education can also help teachers learn and use different forms of adaptation. Bosompen's study of Ghanaian teachers found that they were not necessarily aware of different ways to adapt materials (2014). Bosompen discusses four types of adaptation: addition, modification, replacement and rejection. These form a repertoire of ways for teachers to adapt, giving teachers options for how to address the mismatches they identify between their materials and their contexts as well as options for varying activities in the classroom. (See also McGrath, 2013, 2016; McDonough et al., 2013; Mishan and Timmis, 2015 for frameworks and examples of how to adapt materials.)

Teachers-in-training also need to be aware that teachers using the same material in the same context will use it differently (Menkabu and Harwood, 2014). Graves (2000) describes a teacher-training activity in which the trainees are all given a textbook unit, with the activities separated into a pile, with no indicators of where they occur in the unit. Trainees arrange the activities in the order in which they would teach them and explain why. Trainees see that sequences vary widely, but that they each have principled reasons for their sequence.

Use of technology to enhance and extend learners' language learning and use within and beyond the classroom

As described earlier, technology has markedly changed the landscape of materials and the roles of learners, in terms of access to content, content creation, and interaction. Despite the proliferation of tools, 'the teacher's chief roles remain those of scaffolding and setting pedagogically valid tasks' (Mishan and Timmis, 2015: 78). Teachers need principled ways to integrate technology, both as product/content and as process/tool, and to leverage the digital skills that students bring to the classroom (Kiddle, 2013; Mishan and Timmis, 2015).

A useful approach to integrating language learning and technology is as development of digital literacies, which Dudeney et al. (2013: 2) define as 'the individual and social skills needed to effectively interpret, manage, share and create meaning in the growing range of digital communication channel'. They outline a framework of digital literacies for language teachers that focuses on language, information, connections and (re)design and links the types of literacy to each focus and show practical ways to incorporate them into a coursebook syllabus. Teacher educators can use frameworks such as these to guide teachers-in-training in how to approach the use of technology. (See also Mann and Copland, 2015.)

Despite the need for digital literacies and the seemingly limitless possibilities for developing them, there has been an uneven focus on technology in teacher education, which Dudeney et al. (op cit.) attribute to the lack of technological training and skills of the trainers themselves. They point out that educators 'may be unaware of the importance of digital literacies, their increased role in mainstream educational curricula, and their value in language teaching' (ibid.: 335) and suggest that teacher educators use technology as part of their own practice to both learn and model ways to use technology. For example, teacher educators who use or design virtual learning environments in their courses can ask teachers to consider how to use such environments in their own courses. Teachers can be taught to use screen casting to provide feedback on learners' written work. Teacher educators can use text-manipulation tools such as a word cloud generator to display, for example, metaphors teachers use to describe coursebooks. Teachers can be shown how to exploit the possibilities that technology offers for language learning outside the classroom. For example, online collaborations and projects can be introduced into teacher education programmes using tools such as Wikis or Blogs, or by recording and uploading YouTube videos. Keypal projects can be set up with groups of trainees on other programmes or in other countries (see Copland and Mann, 2011). However, as not all teachers will teach in technology-rich contexts, it is important to explore alternatives that will work in low-resource contexts (Hockly, 2014).

The suggestion that teacher educators model technology use as part of their own practice underscores a theme in how teacher educators can prepare teachers to understand, use and develop materials – they themselves have to be comfortable and proficient in their own understanding, use and development of materials.

Conclusion

We agree with McGrath's assertion that:

> language learning materials are such a key element in the teaching-learning encounter that consideration of their selection, use and design cannot be consigned to the periphery of a teacher education programme, narrowly constrained within wide-ranging courses dealing with curriculum/syllabus or method, or labelled as optional: materials evaluation and design should be a central (core) component of both pre-service programmes and post-experience postgraduate programmes.
>
> *(McGrath, 2013: 100)*

Research on teacher education and materials is clearly needed. This includes research on how work with materials is addressed in pre and in-service teacher education; how it is integrated into different types of courses, e.g. linguistics, second language acquisition, methodology, and so on; and how it is taught in courses whose focus is materials use and development. We also would like to see research on how teachers use what they learn in teacher education about materials in their actual teaching. This type of research would also provide further examples of materials use, which could loop back into teacher education, for example as case studies of teacher's effective or ineffective use of textbooks 'which could be used as evaluative/reflective case studies in an attempt to develop pedagogical reasoning' (Grammatosi and Harwood, 2014: 200). Such research would also help teacher educators redefine their own practice in terms of the usability of the knowledge they wish teachers to gain.

Recommended reading

Garton, S. and Graves, K. (eds) (2014) *International Perspectives on Materials in ELT*. London: Palgrave.
    Brings together perspectives of researcher-practitioners from 14 different countries on topics including globalisation, technology, teacher education and materials in the classroom
Harwood, N. (ed.) (2014) *English Language Teaching Textbooks: Content, Consumption, Production*. London: Palgrave.
    Robust and well-written research on textbooks in language teaching from the perspective of textbook content, use, and how textbooks are produced.
McGrath, I. (2013) *Teaching Materials and the Roles of EFL/ESL Teachers*. London: Bloomsbury.
    Explores materials development, evaluation and use from the perspectives of teachers, teacher educators, learners and publishers with clear discussions and examples.
Tomlinson, B. (ed.) (2013) *Developing Materials for Language Teaching*, 2nd edition. London: Bloomsbury.
    This second edition has chapters on materials evaluation, materials development, materials for target groups, specific types of materials, and materials and teacher training.

References

Abdel-Latif, M. M. (2017) 'Teaching grammar using inductive and communicative materials: exploring Egyptian EFL teachers' practices and beliefs', in Masuhara H., Mishan, F. and Tomlinson, B. (eds) *Practice and Theory for Materials Development in L2 Learning*. Cambridge: Cambridge Scholars Publishing: 275–289.
Allen, C. (2015) 'Marriages of Convenience? Teachers and Coursebooks in the Digital Age'. *ELT Journal*, 69(3) 249–263.
Auerbach, E. and Burgess, D. (1985) 'The Hidden Curriculum of Survival ESL'. *TESOL Quarterly*, 19(3) 475–495.
Augusto-Navarro, E., de Oliveira, L. C. and de Abreu-e-Lima, D. M. (2014) 'Teaching pre-service EFL teachers to analyze and adapt published materials: An experience from Brazil', in Garton, S. and Graves, K. (eds) *International Perspectives on Materials in ELT*. London: Palgrave: 237–252.
Bosompen, E. G. (2014) 'Materials adaptation in Ghana: teachers' attitudes and practices', in Garton, S. and Graves, K. (eds) *International Perspectives on Materials in ELT*. London: Palgrave: 104–120.
Butler, Y. (2015) 'The Use of Computer Games as Foreign Language Learning Tasks for Digital Natives'. *System*, 54 91–102.
Byram, M. and Masuhara, H. (2013) 'Intercultural competence', in Tomlinson, B. (ed.) *Applied Linguistics and Materials Development*. London: Bloomsbury: 143–160.
Canagarajah, S. (1993) 'Critical Ethnography of a Sri Lankan Classroom: Ambiguities in Student Reproduction Through ESOL'. *TESOL Quarterly*, 27(4) 601–626.
Canniveng, C. and Martinez, M. (2003) 'Materials development and teacher training', in Tomlinson, B. (ed.) *Developing Materials for Language Teaching*, 1st edition. London: Bloomsbury: 479–489.
Chapelle, A. A. (2009) 'The Spread of Computer-Assisted Language Learning'. *Language Teaching*, 43(1) 63–74.

Copland, F. and Mann, S. (2011) *The Coursebook and Beyond*. Tokyo: ABAX Publishing.

Dudeney, G., Hockly, N. and Pegrum, M. (2013) *Digital Literacies*. Harlow: Pearson.

Freeman, D. (2014) 'Reading comprehension questions: the distribution of different types in global EFL textbooks', in Harwood, N. (ed.) *English Language Teaching Textbooks: Content, Consumption, Production*. London: Palgrave: 72–110.

Garton, S. and Graves, K. (2014) *International Perspectives on Materials in ELT*. London: Palgrave.

Garton, S., Copland, F. and Burns, A. (2011) *Investigating Global Practices in Teaching English for Young Learners: Project Report*. London: British Council.

Gilmore, A. (2012) 'Authentic Materials and Authenticity in Foreign Language Learning'. *Language Teaching*, 40(2) 97–118.

Grammatosi, F. and Harwood, N. (2014) 'An experienced teacher's use of the textbook on an academic English course: a case study', in Harwood N. (ed.) *English Language Teaching Textbooks: Content, Consumption, Production*. London: Palgrave: 178–204.

Graves, K. (2000) *Designing Language Courses: A Guide for Teachers*. Boston, MA: Heinle Cengage.

Gray, J. (2000) 'The ELT Coursebook as Cultural Artefact'. *ELT Journal*, 54(3) 274–283.

Gray, J. (2012) 'Neoliberalism, celebrity and "aspirational content" in English teaching textbooks for the global market', in Block, D., Gray, J. and Holborrow, M. (eds) *Neoliberalism and Applied Linguistics*. Abingdon: Routledge: 86–113.

Gray (2016) 'ELT materials: claims, critiques and controversies', in Hall, G. (ed.) *The Routledge Handbook of English Language Teaching*. Abingdon: Routledge: 113–126.

Hall, G. (ed.) (2016) *The Routledge Handbook of English Language Teaching*. Abingdon: Routledge.

Harwood, N. (ed.) (2010) *English Language Teaching Materials: Theory and Practice*. Cambridge: Cambridge University Press.

Harwood, N. (ed.) (2014) *English Language Teaching Textbooks: Content, Consumption, Production*. London: Palgrave.

Hockly, N. (2014). 'Digital Technologies in Low-Resource ELT Contexts'. *ELT Journal*, 68(1) 79–84.

Humphries, S. (2014) 'Factors influencing Japanese teachers' adoption of communication-oriented textbooks', in Garton, S. and Graves, K. (eds) *International Perspectives on Materials in ELT*. London: Palgrave: 253–269.

Hutchinson, T. and Torres, E. (1994) 'The Textbook as Agent of Change'. *ELT Journal*, 48(4) 315–328.

Igielski, J. G. (2014) 'Designing effective, culturally, and linguistically responsive pedagogy', in Garton, S. and Graves, K. (eds) *International Perspectives on Materials in ELT*. London: Palgrave: 141–158.

Johnson, K. (2016) 'Language teacher education', in Hall, G. (ed.) *The Routledge Handbook of English Language Teaching*. Abingdon: Routledge: 121–134.

Kiddle, T. (2013) 'Developing digital language learning materials', in Tomlinson, B. (ed.) *Developing Materials for Language Teaching*, 2nd edition. London: Bloomsbury: 189–206.

Lee, R. N. F. and Bathmaker, A-M. (2007) 'The Use of English Textbooks for Teaching English to Vocational Students in Singapore Secondary Schools: A Survey of Teachers' Beliefs'. *RELC Journal*, 38(3) 350–374.

Lightbown, P. and Spada, N. (2013) *Oxford Handbooks for Language Teachers: How Languages Are Learned*. Oxford: Oxford University Press.

López-Gopar, M. E. (2019) *International Perspectives on Critical Pedagogies in ELT*. Basingstoke: Palgrave Macmillan.

Lucas, P., Graves, K. and Navarro, E. (2017) 'Using the past to build the future: how teachers' conceptions of materials in their practice can (re)shape teacher preparation', in Lucas, P. and Rodrigues, R. (eds) *Temas y rumos nas pesquisas em linguística (aplicada), Vol. 2*. Campinas: Pontes Editores: 13–36.

Macaro, E., Handley, Z. and Walter, C. (2012) 'A Systematic Review of CALL in English as a Second Language: Focus on Primary and Secondary Education'. *Language Teaching*, 45(1) 1–43.

Mann, S. and Copland, F. (2015) *Materials Development*. New York: TESOL Press.

Masuhara, H. (2006) 'Materials development as a teacher development tool', in Mukundan, J. (ed.) *Readings on ELT Materials II*. Petaling Jaya: Pearson Malaysia: 34–48.

Masuhara, H. and Tomlinson, B. (2008) 'Materials for general English', in Tomlinson, B. (ed.) *English Language Teaching Materials: A Critical Review*. London: Continuum: 17–37.

Masuhara, H., Mishan, F. and Tomlinson, B. (eds) (2017) *Practice and Theory for Materials Development in L2 Learning*. Cambridge: Cambridge Scholars Publishing.

McDonough, J., Shaw, C. and Masuhara, H. (2013) *Materials and Methods in ELT*, 3rd edition. Oxford: Blackwell.

McGrath, I. (2002) *Materials Evaluation and Design for Language Teaching*. Edinburgh: Edinburgh University Press.

McGrath, I. (2006) 'Teachers' and Learners' Images for Coursebooks'. *ELT Journal*, 60(2) 171–180

McGrath, I. (2013) *Teaching Materials and the Roles of EFL/ESL Teachers*. London: Bloomsbury.

McGrath, I. (2016) *Materials Evaluation and Design for Language Teaching*, 2nd edition. Edinburgh: Edinburgh University Press.

Menkabu, A. and Harwood, N. (2014) 'Teachers' conceptualization and use of the textbook on a medical English course', in Harwood, N. (ed.) *English Language Teaching Textbooks: Content, Consumption, Production*. London: Palgrave: 145–177.

Messekher, H. (2014) 'Cultural representations in Algerian English textbooks', in Garton, S. and Graves, K. (eds) *International Perspectives on Materials in ELT*. London: Palgrave: 69–86.

Mishan, F. and Timmis, I. (2015) *Materials Development for TESOL*. Edinburgh: Edinburgh University Press.

Nuangpolmak, A. (2014) 'Multilevel materials for multilevel learners', in Garton, S. and Graves, K. (eds) *International Perspectives on Materials in ELT*. London: Palgrave: 121–140.

Opoku-Amankwa, K. (2010) 'What Happens to Textbooks in the Classroom? Pupil's Access to Literacy in an Urban Primary School in Ghana'. *Pedagogy, Culture & Society*, 18(2) 159–172.

Pennycook, A. (1994) *The Cultural Politics of English as an International Language*. London: Longman.

Pereira, J. (2014) 'Using interactive fiction for digital game-based learning', in Garton, S. and Graves, K. (eds) *International Perspectives on Materials in ELT*. London: Palgrave: 178–197.

Phillipson, R. (1992) *Linguistic Imperialism*. Oxford: Oxford University Press.

Phillipson, R. (2009) *Linguistic Imperialism Continued*. Abingdon: Routledge.

Richards, J. C. (2010) 'Series editor's preface', in Harwood, N. (ed.) *English Language Teaching Materials: Theory and Practice*. Cambridge: Cambridge University Press: ix–xi.

Sefarej, K. (2014) 'Coping with new teaching approaches and materials: an East-European teacher's interpretation of communicative teaching activities', in Garton, S. and Graves, K. (eds) *International Perspectives on Materials in ELT*. London: Palgrave: 89–103.

Stapleton, P. and Shao, Q. (2018) 'A Worldwide Survey of MATESOL Programs in 2014: Patterns and Perspectives'. *Language Teaching Research*, 22(1) 10–28.

Tasseron, M. (2017) 'How teachers us the global ELT coursebook', in Masuhara, H. Mishan, F. and Tomlinson, B. (eds) *Practice and Theory for Materials Development in L2 Learning*. Cambridge: Cambridge Scholars Publishing: 290–311.

Thomas, M. (2009) *Handbook of Research on Web 2.0 and Second Language Learning*. New York: IGI Global.

Tibbits, B. and Pashby, P. (2014) 'The story-reading project: integrating materials development with language learning and teaching for NNES teachers in training', in Garton, S. and Graves, K. (eds) *International Perspectives on Materials in ELT*. London: Palgrave: 219–236.

Tomlinson, B. (ed.) (2008) *English Language Teaching Materials: A Critical Review*. London: Continuum.

Tomlinson, B. (ed.) (2011) *Materials Development in Language Teaching*, 2nd edition. Cambridge: Cambridge University Press.

Tomlinson, B. (2012) 'Materials Development for Language Learning and Teaching'. *Language Teaching*, 45(2) 143–179.

Tomlinson, B. (ed.) (2013a) *Developing Materials for Language Teaching*, 2nd edition. London: Bloomsbury.

Tomlinson, B. (2013b) 'Materials evaluation', in Tomlinson, B. (ed.) *Developing Materials for Language Teaching*, 2nd edition. London: Bloomsbury: 21–48.

Tomlinson, B. (2013c) 'Materials development courses', in Tomlinson, B. (ed.) *Developing Materials for Language Teaching*, 2nd edition. London: Bloomsbury: 481–500.

Tomlinson, B. and Masuhara, H. (eds) (2010) *Research for Materials Development in Language Learning*. London: Continuum.

Woodward, T. (2003) 'Loop Input'. *ELT Journal*, 57(3) 301–304.

Yakhontova, T. (2001) 'Textbooks, Contexts and Learners'. *English for Specific Purposes*, 20 397–415.

Yan, C. (2007) 'Investigating English Teachers' Materials Adaptation'. *Humanising Language Teaching*, 9(4) 12–34.

Zacharias, N.T. (2005) 'Teachers' beliefs about internationally-published materials: a survey of tertiary English teachers in Indonesia'. *RELC Journal*, 36 (1) 23–37.

28

Mentoring and mentor development

Jo Gakonga

What is a mentor?

The scope of the term 'mentor' is potentially very wide, but it generally refers to a more capable teacher who provides professional or emotional support to another (Nguyen 2017). According to Malderez and Bodoczky (1999: 4), mentors may take the role of 'a model, a sponsor, an educator or [offer] support or acculturation' and mentoring can occur at any stage of teaching, from initial training or early career to much later stages of development. In this chapter, however, our focus will be the two most prevalent instances of mentoring in education. The first of these takes place in pre-service training when a trainee is assigned to a cooperating teacher in their practicum and the second, when a novice teacher is given a mentor, usually a colleague, in order to support their initiation into the profession. There is good evidence in both cases that mentoring can significantly reduce attrition, with Hobson and Malderez (2013: 92) suggesting that school-based mentoring is 'perhaps the single most effective means of supporting the professional learning and development of beginning teachers'. In addition to these benefits for the mentees, a mentoring relationship is, at its best, a reciprocal one and mentors may choose this role, not only as a way in which to contribute to the teaching profession but also as part of their own reflective growth (e.g. Stanulis 1994; Orland-Barack and Rachamim 2009).

In this chapter, we will begin by considering three different aspects of mentoring, the tensions between these and the ways in which mentors can foster reciprocal relationships which are developmental for both parties. In the second part of the chapter, we will examine how mentors might be prepared for the role. It is often the case that teachers are asked to become mentors with little or no preparation and being a competent, even excellent classroom teacher, does not guarantee success given that a different (although clearly related) set of skills to teaching are involved. An example of a near peer mentor training programme will be examined for illustrative purposes.

Qualities of a mentor

Traditionally, mentoring was seen as a top-down approach from an authority figure (e.g. Blackwell 1989). However, in the more recent past, the emphasis on an authoritative role has changed and the imperative for experience has given way to a greater focus on empathy and the potential for the relationship to be a two-way process (Orland-Barak 2012). It should be noted that terminology in this area (mentor, supervisor, cooperating teacher), is often used interchangeably, especially with pre-service mentoring (Malderez 2009), and a mentor's role may include formal or informal assessment as well as support, meaning that a range of skills is required. A number of studies have explored this skill set, seeking to identify exemplary mentoring or 'good practices' (e.g. Searby and Brondyk 2016). Orland-Barak suggests that these include:

> An articulated educational ideology … a strong correspondence between what mentors say they believe in and their enacted roles in practice … [and] highly developed organizational skills, interpersonal relationships, reflexivity, ability to integrate theory and practice, subject matter expertise, professionalism, leadership roles and the right combination of challenge, modelling, and support.
>
> *(Orland-Barak 2012: 4)*

This is an impressive list, but one which may look rather daunting and require some unpacking. In order to do this, we will begin by considering different aspects of the mentoring relationship and the tensions between them.

Mentoring can be seen to be composed of three elements. The first is to provide emotional support; an affective role in what may be a challenging situation as a novice teacher. The second is as a technical adviser; a more knowledgeable professional who acts as a learning resource. The third is as a facilitator of reflection; a person who can encourage and enrich the mentee's reflective practice. Some scholars in the area see these aspects of mentoring as alternative or competing models. Wang and Odell (2002) discuss a 'humanistic perspective', a 'situated apprenticeship model', and a 'critical constructive perspective' and Orland-Barak and Klein (2005: 395) suggest that mentoring is 'shaped by *competing* dominant narratives' (*my emphasis*), which they see as 'therapeutic, apprenticeship, and reflective collaborative' (2005: 381) approaches. Whilst historically and contextually, there has been greater or lesser emphasis on one of these aspects, to the detriment of the other two, all three (emotional support, technical support and support with reflection) can be viewed as forming a whole whose proportions are interdependent. The challenge of mentoring, then, is in balancing these aspects, all of which are influenced by factors such as the context, the relationship between the mentor and mentee and the stage of development of both. Figure 28.1 gives an illustration of the holistic nature of the relationship and the three aspects of support. There are also two main directions of tension. These lie between the emotional support role and the more pedagogic roles on one hand (being a 'friend' vs being a 'teacher') and between an authoritative and facilitative role on the other ('telling' vs 'encouraging self-reflection'). Each of these aspects will be considered separately.

Emotional support

Providing emotional support is arguably the foundation upon which all other aspects of mentoring rest. Teaching, especially as a novice or trainee teacher, can be a stressful experience with many demands on time and much to assimilate, and there is good evidence that providing affective support through this process can reduce attrition (Feiman-Nemser 2001a). For many mentors this is intuitive, an extension of the care that they extend to their learners, and they may position themselves as 'co-thinkers' (Feiman-Nemser 2001b) or 'role models' or even 'mother figures' (Bullough 2005) but there can be issues which can jeopardise this relationship. Perhaps the main factor that affects the emotional support that is given to a mentee is the power

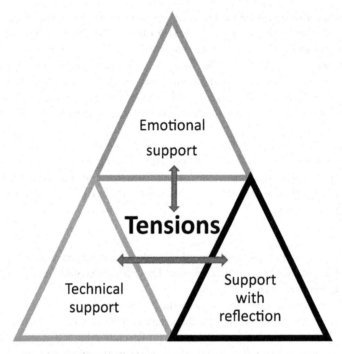

Figure 28.1 Aspects of mentoring and the tensions between them

differential between mentor and mentee. The relationship is most effective when the mentor has empathy and is 'an ally, a champion, an advocate for' their mentee (Hobson 2016: 100) but in many situations, especially that of cooperating teacher, the imperative to give formative feedback on lessons and a final evaluative report at the end of the practicum puts the mentor in a position of official authority which makes it difficult to provide unconditional support. Even in more informal situations, the mentor is often positioned as more powerful because of their greater experience or expertise and this may exert a strain on the relationship. There are many reports in the literature of mentors being negative or overly critical and Gratch's (1998) case study of a newly qualified teacher (Gina) and her mentor (Valerie) is a typical example.

> She [*Gina – the mentee*] believed that Valerie was very critical of her teaching but did not take the time to ask Gina why she chose to do the things she did. Valerie's criticism of Gina's teaching was not a critique that promoted self-reflection, but an attack on her method.
>
> *(Gratch 1998: 224)*

This kind of relationship which lacks empathy and is more evaluative than supportive is termed 'judgementoring' by Hobson and Malderez (2013) who found that this was common amongst mentors in their study. In a more recent follow up paper, Hobson (2016) proposes a methodology which he dubs ONSIDE mentoring. This has an overarching theme of the mentor being emotionally supportive and of the mentoring situation being:

- off-line (i.e. separated from line-management or supervision) and non-hierarchical;
- non-evaluative and non-judgemental;

- supportive of mentees' psychosocial needs and well-being;
- individualised – tailored to the specific and changing needs (emotional as well as developmental) of the mentee;
- developmental and growth oriented – seeking to promote mentees' learnacy and provide them with appropriate degrees of challenge;
- empowering – progressively non-directive to support mentees to become more autonomous and agentic.

(Hobson 2016: 101)

These are useful guidelines in an ideal situation, but, as has been stated above, official evaluation is often part of the mentor's role. In addition to this, there is evidence that the difficulties in the relationship may not always lie with the mentor and may be beyond their control. One example is Gratch's findings which suggest that in some cases, mentees enter the teaching profession 'already resistant to collaboration with other teachers' (1998: 225) and feeling that after their training they should be capable of teaching without support.

Providing effective and genuine emotional support is time consuming and mentoring cannot be done quickly (Malderez and Bodoczky 1999). Another frequent challenge, therefore, is the lack of resources allocated for the role. It is not uncommon that this is perceived as an additional duty for mentors, squeezed into an already full workload and often without financial remuneration (Walkington 2005). The role of cooperating teacher, for example, may be considered to be its own reward and a position given to experienced teachers who may have little choice in the matter. This may or may not be viewed as positive. One teacher interviewed by Mann and Tang (2012: 482), for example, reports her ambivalence; 'It's the school's decision … I wouldn't say I'm passionate about it'. In some situations, innovative solutions have been introduced to allow time to be allocated specifically for supporting teachers. One example of this is the mentoring scheme reported on by Bullough and Draper (2004) in which two newly qualified teachers were employed on full timetables but half salary, therefore freeing up the time of a full-time mentor teacher to support them. In theory, a scheme such as this provides an excellent opportunity for quality mentoring. However, tight school budgets often introduce constraints and in reality, the mentor teacher was only relieved of half of her timetable, limiting the amount of time that she had to interact with the mentors and with the university supervisor. Some teacher preparation courses (e.g. Walsh and Elmslie 2005) have teaching practicums in which paired trainees are placed in a class with a single cooperating teacher. This may help to even the power balance between mentor and mentees and this arrangement ensures that both trainees have practical support in the classroom, are able to collaborate with lesson planning and have the opportunity to observe other's practice. Another method of equalising the power structure with newly qualified teachers is to use a peer as a mentor. Whilst a teacher with experience seems intuitively to be a better choice, using a 'near peer' may be more effective (Mann and Tang 2012) since they have more recently been in the mentee's position and are able to empathise more easily.

An emotionally supportive relationship is crucial and without this, it is hard to envisage effective mentoring. However, the role of a mentor goes beyond a shoulder to cry on, with Wang and Odell suggesting that there is 'accumulating evidence' that emotional support alone does not 'guarantee that novice teachers will learn better teaching than they would have learned without mentors' (2002: 494). A mentor is a more experienced or knowledgeable professional in the field, and a significant part of the role is therefore that of providing technical support in the form of professional advice.

Technical support

'Technical support' is defined here as modelling of 'good practice' or giving advice, suggestions and practical tips and to a mentee. This originates from an apprenticeship model in which a novice learns from a more experienced practitioner by observation and replication of a tried and tested approach. Few teachers would suggest that copying techniques alone was an adequate recipe for development, but there is great value in learning teaching skills through critical observation and discussion of techniques with an expert practitioner. Mentees often state the importance of having a 'practical' approach that compliments the more theoretical stance that they may experience in a university setting (Bullough and Draper 2004), and there are a range of techniques which can offer support to novice teachers in their training and early stages of their career. An experienced, competent teacher as a mentor is potentially a good source of this kind of information and evidence from the literature and my own research with novice mentors suggests that there is often a strong desire on the part of a mentor to convey their accumulated knowledge of teaching to their mentee. The motivation for this is positive and has a basis in the desire to help. However, there are limitations of the mentor as 'advice-giver' which need to be considered, not least the definition of 'best practice'. Teaching and learning involve an interacting range of factors which includes the teacher, the learners, the immediate classroom setting and the wider educational environment and so, as Faneslow warns, to proffer advice on the precise course of action to take in any given situation implies a knowledge that 'one set of practices is consistently superior to another, [and] that we know what needs to be done in each distinct setting' (1990:196). There are few educators who would suggest that this is usually the case.

There are other challenges. Whilst mentor teachers have developed skills which allow them to operate effectively in the classroom, 'this knowledge base [...] is often tacit rather than explicit' (Murray and Male 2005: 126). An experienced teacher may instinctively know what works for them but may find this difficult to unpack and communicate and may need to develop the ability to articulate their own knowledge of teaching. In addition, a mentor, given the crucial nature of the relationship between them and their mentee, needs a good understanding of students or novice teachers as adult learners (Lunenberg 2002). Mentors usually come from a background of primary or secondary education and a significant change in approach, which may not be intuitive, is required when mentoring adults (Slaouti et al. 2013). Skill sets that are significantly different to those used in classroom teaching are required, including the ability to communicate and collaborate with mentees and in many cases, to evaluate them; skills which are not always necessarily transferrable from classroom practice, particularly if this has been with children. Even the culture of teaching itself is potentially detrimental to the development of mentoring skills. As Little (1990) points out, teachers tend to work alone in an environment of autonomy and often have little opportunity to observe their peers or even discuss their practice with others.

A further issue in the area of mentoring as technical support, perhaps particularly in the sphere of language teaching, is that although the mentor teacher may have experience and success in the classroom, their methodology may be at odds with a more communicative approach which is the usual priority of university-based input. This issue is one which is particularly pertinent to trainee teachers in classrooms with cooperating teachers and can be both confusing and frustrating for the mentee. A decision must be made about whether to follow the model that they see in the classroom (that which the mentor teacher will judge them against) or aim to practise the methods that their university tutors require as criteria for assessment. Bullough and Draper (2004) describe one such situation in which a mentee is required to negotiate diplomatically between her mentor and university tutor, positioning herself in such a way as not to be penalised in her assessments and thus having to consider, not her own judgement of best practice, but which practice would be most acceptable to her observer.

Support with reflection

As we have seen, two important dimensions of mentor practice are emotional and technical support, but alone, these have limitations. A mentee also needs to develop reflective practice that will allow them to continue to improve, to adapt to the different contexts that they teach in and to question established practice. Good teachers are reflective practitioners (Lunenberg 2002) but reflecting on a personal level requires different skills to encouraging, supporting and enabling reflective practice in novice teachers. These skills are not innate and need to be developed in mentors themselves to allow a dialogic approach which gives the mentee space and time to explore their practice. A common theme in the literature is that of mentors being directive or monopolising the conversation and this can easily lead to the mentee sitting 'like a sponge' in the words of one novice teacher (Hawkey 1998: 665). Advice and suggestions for classroom activities are often appreciated by pre-service teachers but taking an overly directive approach is unlikely to foster alternative approaches or reflection and may result in a lack of autonomous development and a tendency to adopt 'conventional norms and practices' rather than more 'progressive or learner centred methodologies' (Hobson and Malderez 2013: 92). Mentors are often revealed in the literature as taking this approach without wishing it or even being aware of it and the revelations of the mentor described in Stanulis (1994), on listening to recordings of her practice, are a good example of this. In her own words:

> I have to practice a lot, to not just tell. Because my way works so well for me! For me. You know, and I just think, oh, if I just told them how. I really don't want to try to develop student teachers who are carbon copies of me. I really don't.
>
> (Stanulis 1994: 34)

Maintaining an effective balance

The skill of effective mentoring lies in attaining an appropriate balance of the three aspects we have considered. The challenge is that the mentoring environment is constantly in flux, affected by characteristics of the mentor, the mentee, their relationship and the environment and also the micro-climate of a particular time and stage of development. My own experience in training mentors resonates with much of the literature, in that there is a particular difficulty in a balance between technical support and support with reflection; in offering advice and providing a more facilitative approach. An emphasis on the former potentially limits the mentee's autonomous development; an emphasis on the latter, taken to an extreme underplays the fact that 'some knowledge is widely agreed-upon and accepted' (Wang and Odell 2002: 498). In Feiman-Nemser's words, there is 'a central tension between encouraging personal expression and maintaining professional accountability' (2001a: 20) and in her description of an expert mentor, this was attained by becoming a 'co-thinker' with the mentees and providing a possible professional perspective without an expectation that this would be wholly accepted or reproduced.

Mentoring has been shown to be multi-faceted and challenging. Nevertheless, until recently, there has been very little attention paid to how novice mentors learn the skills that are necessary (Murray and Male 2005). In the next part of the chapter we will examine mentor development and some practical ways in which mentoring practice has been addressed.

Mentor development

Mentors are often asked to take on this role with little or no preparation (Tang and Choi, 2005) and being a competent or even expert teacher does not necessarily equate to good mentoring. There is, however, good evidence to suggest that the effectiveness of a mentor can be developed through explicit training (e.g. Langdon 2013). Mentors who have had training are reported to have better communication skills (Evertson and Smithey 2000) and better critical and reflective thinking. They also seem to be less prone to judgementoring (Fransson 2016) and the training is much appreciated by the mentors themselves (Stanulis and Ames 2009; Pohl and Révész 2014).

The process of developing as a mentor echoes that of developing as a teacher and a good mentor training programme will therefore also consist of emotional support, technical support and support with reflection. These will each be considered, followed by a description of a mentor training programme on an MA TESOL as an example of the way in which mentors' skills can be developed.

Emotional support

Emotional support in all areas of development is vital. The novice mentors may be experienced and confident in their teaching environment, but this does not necessarily mitigate the challenges of taking on a new role requiring reflection and the development of new skills. Emotional support usually involves peers and/or a mentor trainer and could take the form of regular discussion groups, team presentations, online forums (e.g. Pohl and Révész 2014) or one to one support.

Technical support

The fastest and cheapest methodology for mentor training focuses on tips and techniques, foregrounding 'technical support'. This can be implemented before or during mentoring and comprises discrete input, which may be delivered in a face to face or online environment. Areas covered might include methodology for different aspects of the mentoring process such as observation (having a pre-observation meeting, agreeing a focus, the use of different tools and techniques) and feedback (ways of conducting oral feedback, how to express written feedback). The training may also include role-play to simulate and practise mentor–mentee interactions. There are many examples in the literature of the success of such programmes (e.g. Ambrosetti 2014; Evertson and Smithey 2000) and these can also be delivered effectively online. A publicly available example is web-based mentor training http://mentormodules.com/ which includes videoed scenarios of mentor–mentee interaction and focusing questions to raise awareness of issues pertinent to mentoring practice.

This kind of training often includes an examination of mentee–mentor talk and suggestions for less face threatening discourse. An example is reported in Stanulis and Ames (2009) where sentence stems are provided for non-judgemental ways of engaging mentees and encouraging them to reflect more deeply. These include:

> Restating a mentee's contribution by saying, 'What I hear you saying is …' or 'As I listen, you seem to be saying…'
> Prompting clarification using: 'Can you give me an example to help me understand?'
> Helping novices to analyse: 'In what ways is this task well suited to your students? How do you know?'.

They also give ideas for language of suggestion and support: 'We could co-plan together so I can help you with…,' or 'You might want to consider….'

(Stanulis and Ames 2009: 33)

It is arguable that this methodology is rather prescriptive and therefore limited in allowing mentors to develop their practice autonomously. However, seen as suggestions and a framework for practice, and not as 'rules', this approach was reported as well received by the novice mentors.

Support with reflection

In addition to input there is a need for an approach which supports mentors' reflection on their practice and allows for more individually relevant and autonomous development. A reflective process gives novice mentors the opportunity to develop their own, critically subjective educational theories (Kelchtermans and Vandenberghe 1994) and to use the 'technical support' that they are also given in a manner which is appropriate for their personal context. The dominant methodology is for mentors to record (video or audio) their practice, reflecting on it by listening back, perhaps transcribing the talk and discussing this with a mentor-trainer. There are numerous case studies of mentors who have found this approach enlightening. One example is Orland-Barak and Rachamim's (2009) study, which describes a cooperating teacher, acting as a mentor to a trainee, video recording her mentoring interactions and reflecting on these in collaboration with a university-based researcher. The following comment is indicative of the way in which this process can allow a greater degree and depth of understanding of practice which can lead to development:

> Watching myself during the conversation makes me wonder whether I am controlling the discourse too much. For example, I noticed that I used a lot of language of telling … . As I watch myself I can even identify similarities between my controlling talk as a mentor and Chen's controlling talk as a teacher! This is certainly not what I thought I was doing…
>
> (Orland-Barak and Rachamim 2009: 602)

Mentor training programmes that have an element of reflective practice, especially when these are in-service, can be shown to have a positive effect. An example of this is Langdon's study with mentor teachers in New Zealand in which her findings show 'how difficult it is for mentors to move beyond a directive approach that favours telling, giving advice and affective support over a respect for the views of novices'. Her study followed 13 mentors of differing levels of experience over a 2-year period, who engaged in a professional development programme which included ten input sessions per year and a requirement to set mentoring goals, record and self-analyse their 'learning conversations' with their mentees using a framework they were given, reporting back annually on their progress. She found that all of the mentors on this programme exhibited some change in their practice, and for at least some (five of the 13 mentors), the programme had very positive results and resulted in 'fewer closed questions, interruptions, time spent telling/describing, speaking for the mentee and affirming comments' (Langdon 2013: 47).

A near peer mentoring programme on an MA TESOL

Successful development programmes for mentors take various forms, some of which have already been examined and in this final section, we will examine an example from my own research to illustrate common issues and highlight potentially useful aspects to include

With some notable exceptions (e.g. Pohl and Révész 2014) much of the mentor development in the literature refers to an in-service context where teachers are becoming mentors 'on the job'. However, university teacher training departments such as those which offer MA TESOL courses are a rich and currently underutilised context for mentor training in language teacher education. In the UK, these frequently combine cohorts of pre-service teachers and more experienced professionals, the latter of whom often wish to move in the direction of teacher education or management and need to develop practical skills in supporting teachers with planning and in feedback. An experiential approach to developing mentoring skills has great potential in this context and the programme at Warwick University has had excellent feedback from both the mentees (pre-service teachers) and the mentors (mid-career teachers) involved.

The programme takes place in the second term, when the pre-service teachers undertake a Professional Practice (PP) action research module in which they teach a group of peers, record, transcribe and reflect on this lesson and then teach for a second time a month later, with the aim of improving an element of their practice. Running parallel to this module is the mentor training programme for experienced teachers from the Teacher Education and Development (TED) module. These teachers are matched with and mentor students from the PP module, supporting their planning, observing their teaching and giving oral and written feedback over both cycles. There is no requirement for the mentors to assess the mentees and the relationship is beneficial to both parties, providing support to the pre-service teachers and enabling novice mentors to reflect on their practice, using this to inform their development. A summary of this can be seen in Figure 28.2.

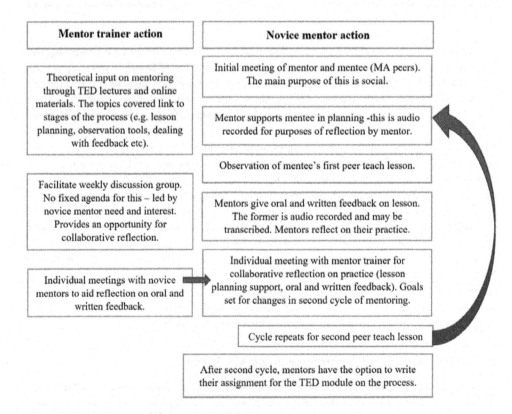

Figure 28.2 Summary of the mentor training programme

The primary focus of the mentor training is to encourage reflection on practice. For this to be effective, a systematic approach is necessary where reflection is collaborative and data-led (Mann and Walsh 2013). The mentors audio record their interactions with their mentees, listening back and reflecting on them as individuals but also theorising their lived experience through talk by sharing extracts with a mentor trainer and discussing their reflections with peers in an informal weekly discussion group. There are two cycles of peer teaching, a month apart, and this allows for two cycles of support providing an opportunity for the mentors to identify an area of their practice which they wish to improve from the first cycle and to work to do so in the second. There is also the option for the mentors to use the experience and their data as the basis for their assessed assignment on the TED module. The standard of these has been very high.

Working alongside the ongoing reflection to inform and scaffold the mentors' development, there are also elements of emotional support, provided by the mentor trainer and peers and technical support in the form of input and instruction. Input takes a blended approach with TED module lectures, covering aspects of mentoring and feedback and regular web-based input with a discrete area of focus. A new unit is released weekly with a short, introductory video giving an overview of the topic, an audio extract of practice from a previous mentor on the programme and a reflective task to complete whilst listening. These extracts include mentoring and feedback interactions, examples of mentors' written feedback and reflections of the mentors on their practice and on the process of the course. Academic papers related to the topic of each week are also provided to give a wider perspective. The areas that have been chosen as the focus of each unit have grown organically from the challenges of mentors in previous iterations of the programme and thus reflect the most pertinent of the issues which arise.

In the following section, four examples of these areas will be discussed to provide a taste of the course. Elements of the programme are also publicly available online in the free resources entitled 'Mentoring Resources' at www.elt-training.com/

Example 1   The balance of mentor to mentee talk in mentor meetings

As has been seen from other studies, finding an appropriate balance between technical support and support with reflection is a key tension in mentoring and this has proved to be the most challenging area for mentors on the programme with many of them realising that, although their advice is given with good intention, their mentees are not given any space for contribution. Recording interaction and transcribing a part of it is a powerful way to raise mentors' awareness of this as is listening to recordings of previous mentors with similar difficulties and mentors report that this has led to a more principled approach in the second cycle.

Example 2   How mentor's beliefs can affect their practice

Following on from the balance of talk, a related issue is that there is a discrepancy between the mentor's stated philosophy of education as a co-constructed event, and the actuality, especially when giving feedback. This is not uncommon in the literature (e.g. Louw et al. 2016) and often has roots in a mentor's previous experience of being a mentee. Where the norm in their context is a more authoritative or directive model, their experiences of this will inevitably be very powerful and influential on their own practice. A factor which is not often mentioned in the literature, but which has arisen on this mentoring programme is that some mentors have stated it is necessary for them to maintain this power differential in order to engender respect in their context. This reinforces the importance of a programme of this type not taking a prescriptive approach but aiming to raise mentors' awareness of their practice and thus allow the decisions that they make when mentoring to be purposeful and appropriate.

Example 3   Using questions to promote reflection

Questions are a way in which to increase mentee interaction. However, different types of questions can be more (or less) effective. Drawing explicit attention to the nature of response that open and closed questions will elicit, or whether questions are for display purposes or are of a more authentic nature can be useful. Novice mentors often use multiple, closed, display questions to 'shoehorn' a mentee towards the answer that they feel is appropriate. Bliss et al. (1996) call this 'bypassings' or pseudo-interaction and making mentors aware of this interaction pattern can support them to avoid this practice. One mentee noted:

> I asked a lot of questions and when I listen to the recording I got horrified ... because if you ask someone so many questions, the questions will make that person confused. I mean I felt that my mentee became more confused ... she realised that she wasn't in the right track because I was asking the same questions.

Reflecting on recorded interactions like this in addition to targeted input has been shown in my data to be a powerful way to increase awareness of questioning practice.

Example 4   Politeness theory and feedback

Introducing a theoretical lens such as politeness theory (Brown and Levinson 1987) can help to raise awareness of the language that mentors use, particularly when mentors are giving oral and written feedback. These acts are intrinsically face threatening but examining the mechanics of how feedback is structured can help to mitigate this and give mentors a wider range of linguistic tools to choose from. In the input of the programme, mentors are shown specific examples of both positive and negative politeness strategies, such as the examples shown in Tables 28.1 and 28.2.

Whilst training of this kind should not aim to be prescriptive, mentors have found that specific ideas of possible language to use and a framework for analysis is helpful.

The programme has been very successful, with a strong feeling of appreciation from the novice mentors for the opportunity to hone their skills experientially in a safe and supported environment. Mentors have commented that it has enabled them to 'see through their mentees' eyes' and thus be more empathetic as well as increasing their confidence.

Table 28.1 Negative politeness strategies (which reduce implied direction)

Using lower obligation modals and avoiding imperatives	e.g. 'You could....', rather than 'You should...' or 'Do this.'
Using forward facing modality to reduce implied criticism	e.g. 'You could do this...' rather than 'You could have done this...'
Modulating the assertiveness of statements using hedging devices.	e.g. 'Perhaps you could...' or 'The learners could be a bit more actively involved'

Table 28.2 Positive politeness strategies (which reduce implied criticism)

Using questions rather than statements	'What were the learners doing?' rather than 'The learners were doing...'
Avoiding contrastive conjunctions (mentees only tend to focus on what comes after the 'but')	'The lesson had a great pace. Some of the less able were struggling when...' rather than 'The lesson had a good pace but some of the less able were struggling when...'
Describing what happened in neutral terms and describing what the learners did rather than the teacher.	'The table of learners by the window are talking together in L1' rather than 'You need to make sure that all of the learners are on task'
Expressions of empathy	'It can be really challenging when...'

Conclusion

The metaphor of learning to dance with a partner to describe a successful mentoring relationship is useful (Fairbanks et al. 2000); the idea of a give and take process that requires knowledge of the 'steps' but also adjustment of both participants to the other's needs. In both cases, empathy is required and where the dancers are not in tune with each other, toes can be trodden on. In both cases, people need to work together and have a willingness to reflect and work towards a productive end. And in both cases, as I hope I have shown, some 'dance classes' can help to develop better skills.

Further reading

Feiman-Nemser, S. (2001) 'Helping Novices Learn to Teach: Lessons from an Exemplary Support Teacher'. *Journal of Teacher Education*, 52(1) 17–30.
   Whilst there is no 'perfect' mentor, this paper shows 'specific principles and practices' (p. 17) used by a mentor who was acknowledged by mentees and peers to be exemplary in his practice. The paper introduces the idea of 'educative' mentoring.

Hoffman, J., Wetzel, M., Maloch, B., Greeter, E., Taylor, L., DeJulio, S. and Vlach, S. (2015) 'What can we Learn from Studying the Coaching Interactions Between Cooperating Teachers and Preservice Teachers? A Literature Review'. *Teaching and Teacher Education*, 52 99–112.
   An overview of the literature in the area with a range of findings that are clear and useful for anyone becoming a mentor or training mentors.

Langdon, F. (2013) 'Evidence of Mentor Learning and Development: An Analysis of New Zealand Mentor/Mentee Professional Conversations'. *Professional Development in Education*, 40(1) 36–55.
   An account of a development programme, analysing the interactions of 13 mentors and their mentees over a two-year period, during which they were involved in cycles of 'learning conversations' to examine their practice. There is evidence of change in practice for all mentors, but to differing extents.

Malderez, A. and Bodóczky, C. (1999) *Mentor Courses: A Resource Book for Trainer Trainers*. Cambridge: Cambridge University Press.
   Included here because of its practical nature. The opening chapter of this book has an overview of mentoring and this is followed by a wide range of suggested activities for use with mentors to develop both skills and self-awareness.

References

Ambrosetti, A. (2014) 'Are You Ready to be a Mentor? Preparing Teachers for Mentoring Pre-service Teachers'. *Australian Journal of Teacher Education*, 39(6) 30–42.

Blackwell, J. E. (1989) 'Mentoring: An Action Strategy for Increasing Minority Faculty'. *Academe*, 75 8–14.

Bliss, J., Askew, M. and Macrae, S. (1996) 'Effective Teaching and Learning: Scaffolding Revisited'. *Oxford Review of Education*, 22(1) 37–61.

Brown, P. and Levinson, S. (1987) *Universals in Language Usage*. Cambridge: Cambridge University Press.

Bullough, R. (2005) 'Being and Becoming a Mentor: School-Based Teacher Educators and Teacher Educator Identity'. *Teaching and Teacher Education*, 21(2) 143–155.

Bullough, R. and Draper, R. (2004) 'Making Sense of a Failed Triad'. *Journal of Teacher Education*, 55(5) 407–420.

Evertson, C. and Smithey, M. (2000) 'Mentoring Effects on Protégés' Classroom Practice: An Experimental Field Study'. *The Journal of Educational Research*, 93(5) 294–304.

Fairbanks, C., Freedman, D. and Kahn, C. (2000) 'The Role of Effective Mentors in Learning to Teach'. *Journal of Teacher Education*, 51(2) 102–112.

Faneslow, J. (1990) '"Let's see": Contrasting conversations about teaching', in Richards, J. and Nunan, D. (eds) *Second Language Teacher Education*. Cambridge: Cambridge University Press.

Feiman-Nemser, S. (2001a) 'From Preparation to Practice: Designing a Continuum to Strengthen and Sustain Teaching'. *Teachers College Record*, 103(6) 1013–1055.

Feiman-Nemser, S. (2001b) 'Helping Novices Learn to Teach'. *Journal of Teacher Education*, 52(1) 17–30.

Fransson, G. (2016) 'Online (Web-Based) Education for Mentors of Newly Qualified Teachers'. *International Journal of Mentoring and Coaching in Education*, 5(2) 111–126.

Gratch, A. (1998) 'Beginning Teacher and Mentor Relationships'. *Journal of Teacher Education*, 49(3) 220–227.

Hawkey, K. (1998) 'Mentor Pedagogy and Student Teacher Professional Development'. *Teaching and Teacher Education*, 14(6) 657–670.

Hobson, A. J. (2016) Judgementoring and How to Avert it: Introducing ONSIDE Mentoring for Beginning Teachers'. *International Journal of Mentoring and Coaching in Education*, 5(2) 87–110.

Hobson, A. and Malderez, A. (2013) 'Judgementoring and Other Threats to Realizing the Potential of School-Based Mentoring in Teacher Education'. *International Journal of Mentoring and Coaching in Education*, 2(2) 89–108.

Hoffman, J., Wetzel, M., Maloch, B., Greeter, E., Taylor, L., DeJulio, S. and Vlach, S. (2015) 'What can we Learn from Studying the Coaching Interactions Between Cooperating Teachers and Preservice Teachers? A Literature Review'. *Teaching and Teacher Education*, 52 99–112.

Kelchtermans, G. and Vandenberghe, R. (1994) 'Teachers' Professional Development: A Biographical Perspective'. *Journal of Curriculum Studies*, 26(1) 45–62.

Langdon, F. (2013) 'Evidence of Mentor Learning and Development: An Analysis of New Zealand Mentor/Mentee Professional Conversations'. *Professional Development in Education*, 40(1) 36–55.

Little, J. (1990) 'The mentor phenomenon', in Cazden, C. (ed.) *Review of Research in Education*. Washington, DC: American Educational Research Association: 297–351.

Louw, S., Watson Todd, R. and Jimarkon, P. (2016) 'Teacher Trainers' Beliefs About Feedback on Teaching Practice: Negotiating the Tensions Between Authoritativeness and Dialogic Space'. *Applied Linguistics*, 37(6) 745–764.

Lunenberg, M. (2002) 'Designing a Curriculum for Teacher Educators'. *European Journal of Teacher Education*, 25(2–3) 263–277.

Malderez, A. (2009) 'Mentoring', in Richards, J. and Burns, A. (eds) *Cambridge Guide to Second Language Teacher Education*. Cambridge: Cambridge University Press.

Malderez, A. and Bodoczky, C. (1999) *Mentor Courses: A Resource Book for Trainer Trainers*. Cambridge: Cambridge University Press.

Mann, S. and Tang, E. (2012) 'The Role of Mentoring in Supporting Novice English Language Teachers in Hong Kong'. *TESOL Quarterly*, 46(3) 472–495.

Mann, S. and Walsh, S. (2013) 'RP or "RIP": A Critical Perspective on Reflective Practice'. *Applied Linguistics Review*, 4(2) 291–315.

Murray, J. and Male, T. (2005) 'Becoming a Teacher Educator: Evidence from the Field'. *Teaching and Teacher Education*, 21(2) 125–142.

Nguyen, H. (2017) *Models of Mentoring in Language Teacher Education*, 1st edition. Cham: Springer International Publishing.

Orland-Barak, L. (2012) *Learning to Mentor as Praxis*. New York: Springer-Verlag.

Orland-Barak, L. and Klein, S. (2005) 'The Expressed and the Realized: Mentors' Representations of a Mentoring Conversation and its Realization in Practice', *Teaching and Teacher Education*, 21(4) 379–402.

Orland-Barak, L. and Rachamim, M. (2009) 'Simultaneous Reflections by Video in a Second-Order Action Research-Mentoring Model: Lessons for the Mentor and the Mentee'. *Reflective Practice*, 10(5) 601–613.

Pohl, U. and Révész, J. (2014) 'Training to Become a Mentor: Hungarian EFL Teachers' Personal Discoveries'. *Working Papers In Language Pedagogy*, 8 116–131.

Searby, L. and Brondyk, S. (2016) *Best Practices in Mentoring for Teacher and Leader Development*. Charlotte, NC: Information Age Publishing, Inc.

Slaouti, D., Onat-Stelma, Z. and Motteram, G. (2013) 'Technology and adult language teaching', in Motteram, G. (ed.) *Innovations in Learning Technologies for English Language Teaching*. London: British Council.

Stanulis, R. (1994) 'Fading to a Whisper: One Mentor's Story of Sharing her Wisdom without Telling Answers'. *Journal of Teacher Education*, 45(1) 31–38.

Stanulis, R. and Ames, K. (2009) 'Learning to Mentor: Evidence and Observation as Tools in Learning to Teach'. *Professional Educator*, 33(1) 28–38.

Tang, S. and Choi, P. (2005) 'Connecting Theory and Practice in Mentor Preparation: Mentoring for the Improvement of Teaching and Learning'. *Mentoring & Tutoring: Partnership in Learning*, 13(3) 383–401.

Walkington, J. (2005) 'Mentoring Pre-Service Teachers in the Preschool Setting: Perceptions of the Role'. *Australian Journal of Early Childhood*, 30 28–35.

Walsh, K. and Elmslie, L. (2005) 'Practicum Pairs: An Alternative for First Field Experience in Early Childhood Teacher Education'. *Asia-Pacific Journal of Teacher Education*, 33(1) 5–21.

Wang, J. and Odell, S. (2002) 'Mentored Learning to Teach According to Standards-Based Reform: A Critical Review'. *Review of Educational Research*, 72(3) 481–546.

29

Professional learning and development in team teaching schemes

Jaeyeon Heo

Introduction

Along with rapid globalisation and the emergence of English as an international language, there has been an ever-increasing demand for competent teachers of English and native English-speaking teachers (henceforth NESTs) in public schools of Asian countries, resulting in the establishment of NEST schemes. This trend has clearly influenced other countries such as Columbia in South America and Oman in the Middle East, which have recently introduced schemes and are actively recruiting NESTs (Copland et al., 2016a). Within NEST schemes, team teaching practices have also become widespread in classrooms, where local English teachers (henceforth LETs) and NESTs work together. A number of studies have focused not only on the challenging issues of collaboration between team teachers but also on a wide-ranging discussion on how to improve current schemes and team teaching practices (Carless & Walker, 2006; Copland et al., 2016c; Heo, 2013; Jang et al., 2010; Liu, 2008). However, relatively little attention has been given to practical support for team teachers. If such schemes are to be run, constructive ways must be found to support teachers and make their experience collaborative and positive rather than arguments about whether such NEST schemes are effective or warranted. This chapter aims to consider this issue primarily from a teacher training and development perspective by seeking to understand the complicated dynamic nature of team teaching and the key factors contributing to successful team teaching practices and relationships. Drawing on interview data with team teachers, reflective essays, and policy documents, I will discuss feasible and sustainable suggestions to maximise the benefits and potential of team teaching.

Contextual background

This section presents a brief overview of NEST schemes. It then introduces the EPIK scheme in South Korea as this is my main focus for evaluating the research and issues on team teaching in EFL contexts.

NEST schemes

The perceived importance of communicative competence in English and a lack of proficient LETs in EFL classrooms have led to the establishment of NEST schemes. Similar NEST schemes are in operation in several different Asian countries: government sponsored ELT programmes are in operation such as the JET Programme in Japan, the NET Programme in Hong Kong, EPIK in Korea, and the FETIT Programme in Taiwan. Although these schemes have some differences (e.g. contextual background, scheme objectives, terms and conditions, or NEST's qualification requirements), there is a basic assumption that a form of collaborative team teaching between LETs and NESTs is an advantageous teaching model which best fulfils learners' needs in EFL contexts in these countries (Carless & Walker, 2006). Specifically, there are common purposes in these schemes as follows: to provide authentic language input in EFL classrooms, to facilitate cross-cultural communication, to enhance students' English ability, and to promote LETs' professional development (Carless, 2002, 2004, 2006a, 2006b; Liu, 2009; Tajino & Tajino, 2000; Tajino & Walker, 1998). Despite controversial issues pertaining to the dichotomous labelling of 'native and non-native speakers' or the debate on 'native speakerism' (see Selvi in Chapter 13 of this handbook), NESTs (mainly from the 'inner circle' countries) have been recruited, trained, and allocated to public schools. For example, the Ministry of Education in Korea (NIIED, 2017) reported that the largest number of NESTs recruited for EPIK from 2010 to 2017 were from the USA (56.7 per cent), followed by Canada (13.8 per cent), Britain (12.1 per cent), South Africa (9.8 per cent), Australia (3.1 per cent), Ireland (2.6 per cent), New Zealand (1.7 per cent) and Korea (0.2 per cent). However, scheme organisations and institutions have started to put more emphasis on NEST's qualifications than before and pay more attention to NESTs from 'outer circle' and 'expanding circle' countries. The JET scheme has recruited NESTs from 40 countries including expanding circle countries since 2012 and EPIK started recruiting well-qualified and experienced NESTs through strict policy and monitoring systems from 2015.

EPIK (English Programme in Korea)

Team teaching in Korean public schools has been mainly implemented through the two NEST schemes, EPIK (English Programme in Korea) and TaLK (Teach and Learn in Korea). EPIK (English Programme in Korea) is a government-funded scheme to recruit NESTs to teach in Korean primary and secondary schools in collaboration with LETs. It is co-sponsored by the Ministry of Education and the 17 Korean Provincial (Metropolitan) Offices of Education. EPIK was launched in 1995 with 54 NESTs from six countries including Australia, Canada, Ireland, New Zealand, the United Kingdom and the USA. Their nationwide implementation has been activated more systematically since 2007 and 13,249 new NESTs were mainly trained through onsite orientation programmes and assigned to public schools from 2007 to the first half of 2017 (NIIED, 2017). Despite the ongoing debate about NEST schemes, there have been sustained efforts and changes to improve and develop EPIK. From the fall of 2015, the Ministry of Education enhanced the recruiting policy to select EPIK applicants with higher standards as one of the mandatory requirements: as such, desired qualifications now include TEFL/TESOL/CELTA certificates, a Bachelor's in Education, a Master's in Education, a Major in an Education field, a Teacher's License, or one year of TaLK experience. According to policy documents (NIIED, 2017), 99.4 per cent of new NESTs involved in EPIK in 2017 had the stipulated certificates to meet the requirements. In addition, National Institute for International Education and Development (NIIED), an institute organising EPIK, has provided team teachers with training programmes including orientations, teachers' resources, good co-teaching samples selected in the annual EPIK co-teaching video contest and materials to share information, experience, knowledge, and life in different teaching contexts.

Team teaching issues in EFL contexts

The potential of team teaching is based on the assumption that team teachers can make a greater contribution than a teachers' individual work (Liu, 2008). Despite the challenges of demands on time and energy or achieving a balance between team teachers, team teaching has many benefits for teachers and students. Successful team teaching classes help create a more dynamic and interactive learning environment and provide students with more efficient instruction, effective monitoring and diverse input than what a single teacher can achieve (Bailey et al., 2001). Teachers are also able to take advantage of their individual strengths and 'their combined degree of knowledge and expertise' (Richards & Farrell, 2005: 160). Within these schemes, there is at least the potential for the complementarity of LETs and NESTs' skills to be exploited advantageously. As for the partnerships between LETs and NESTs, their strengths and weaknesses can be largely complementary (Medgyes, 1994). If a LET and a NEST harness their respective strengths and minimize their weaknesses, team teaching through a collaborative LET and NEST relationship can have a positive and effective impact on an EFL classroom (Carless & Walker, 2006). In spite of such advantages of team teaching, many researchers have identified the following obstacles or constraints that can limit the effectiveness of collaborative team teaching: lack of collaborative effort such as in lesson planning time, discussion and feedback before and after class (Kim, 2016; Park & Kim, 2000; Rutson-Griffiths, 2012), disagreement over division of work and workload between team teachers (Aline & Hosoda, 2006; Liu, 2009; Mahoney, 2004; Yanase, 2016) and tension exacerbated by different communication preferences (Chen, 2007; Chou, 2005; Tang, 2016), cultural differences and relationships (Carless, 2002; Choi, 2001; Heo, 2016; Khánh & Spencer-Oatey, 2016; Lin & Wang, 2016), and lack of teaching experience and training (Copland et al., 2016a; Heo & Mann, 2015; Kim, 2016). Copland et al. (2016a) also pointed out similar problematic issues and highlighted the importance of induction and training programmes for both LETs and NESTs, available time for planning and a joint endeavour between team teachers. In particular, such induction and training programmes for both LETs and NESTs have been rarely organised and provided systematically, practically, and consistently. I will further discuss this issue and focus on how to develop induction and training for team teachers later in the chapter.

Research design

This section reports on a further research project conducted in 2017, after my doctoral research which was based on the four team teaching cases between LETs and NESTs in Korean primary schools (2010–13). To gain a better understanding of team teaching practices and the dynamic relationship that exists between team teachers, a qualitative case study was designed and conducted based on 'detailed, in-depth data collection involving multiple sources of information' (Creswell 2007: 73). The procedures of data collection were divided into two stages. First, preliminary work involved collection of data through interviews with seven team teachers and an educational supervisor working for EPIK, essays written by LETs and NESTs, national documents and annual reports. The aims of this preliminary work were to explore the overview of current team teaching implementation, track its changes or development, if any, and raise new issues. In the second data collection stage, two team teacher cases were focused on and individual interviews were conducted with the teachers.

Participants

The main participants were the two pairs of team teachers who were assigned to conduct team-taught lessons in two different Korean primary schools on a regular basis in the 2017 school year. Background information on the two cases is briefly presented in Table 29.1. Additionally, in order to listen to more diverse voices of team teachers from different teaching conditions, some participants were involved in the preliminary work: there were three NESTs with teaching experience from four months to seven years and four LETs with teaching experience from one year to over 20 years in Korean primary schools. An educational supervisor who provided official documents (e.g. statistic data, annual reports, training programmes and plans regarding EPIK since 2015) was also interviewed.

Case 1

Lee was a very experienced English subject teacher with more than 18 years of teaching experience and she had completed an MA in TESOL while living in the USA for two years due to her husband's work overseas. She enjoyed teaching English and working with NESTs. Sonny, an inexperienced NEST, was a second generation immigrant with Korean parents, who was born and educated in the USA but could not speak a single Korean word at all when he came to Korea. He had been teaching English in this school since 2016 and renewed the contract because he wanted to learn more about Korea. He was in charge of organising two English classes for beginning and intermediate levels of Korean colleague teachers who were interested in learning English in this school.

Case 2

As a homeroom teacher, Kim took charge of teaching English and supporting a NEST in terms of, for example, official documents, housing, insurance, and bills. She was doing her MA

Table 29.1 Two cases of team teachers

	Case 1		Case 2	
Team teacher	Lee	Sonny	Kim	Michelle
Age	40s	30s	30s	20s
Gender	F	M	F	F
Nationality	Korea	USA	Korea	USA
Educational background	BA in Primary Education, MA in TESOL (USA)	BA in Journalism (USA)	BA in Primary Education, Ongoing MA in TESOL for young learners (Korea)	BA in Sociology (USA)
Certificate	Teacher's license in primary school, TEEM (Teaching English in English Master's certificate)	TESOL certificate	Teacher license in primary school	TEFL certificate
Teaching experience	18 years	18 months in Korea	Eight years	Two years in Thailand and Vietnam Two months in Korea

in TESOL with a focus on young learners in Korea and was willing to teach English in her school. Even though Kim gave a positive response to team teaching with a NEST, she thought everything a great deal depended on a NEST that she would meet and work with because of her previous experiences with two different NESTs. Michelle had two years of teaching experience in Thailand and Vietnam as a teaching assistant to support learners with special needs and as an English teacher in secondary schools respectively. Although Michelle had previous experience of living and teaching in other countries, she struggled to settle down in the new environment and work with several different team teachers of each grade in this school.

Data collection and analysis

There were two stages of data collection: preliminary work involved collection and analysis of interviews data, teacher essays, policy documents and annual reports. In order to examine the changes or development of the EPIK scheme and team teaching practices, 18 LETs and 40 NESTs' essays about their EPIK life posted on the EPIK website for five years (2009–2013), policy documents and annual reports on EPIK published by the Ministry of Education (2015–2017) were collected and examined. In the second stage, two team teacher cases were focused on and will be presented in this chapter. The interviews discussed here are active and locally accomplished events where 'ideas, facts, views, details and stories are collaboratively produced by interviewee and interviewer' (Mann, 2011: 8). To probe team teachers' perspectives and experience in their contexts, semi-structured interviews with two pairs of team teachers were individually conducted. Additional interviews were conducted online. Interview data and essays were analysed using a thematic analysis approach and the specific themes emerging were codified and categorised.

Findings and discussion

According to Copland et al. (2016a), each NEST scheme operates in different ways and contextual features greatly influence team teachers' roles and relationships. A number of elements affecting team teaching practices and relationships can be basically categorised in two ways: contextual factors which might not be easy for team teachers to change in their teaching contexts such as school atmosphere, member choice, the number of LETs and NESTs that they work with, and allocated time for solo or team taught classes. On the other hand, personal and interpersonal factors, largely dependent on individual team teachers, might be adjustable, flexible or changed through interaction between team teachers such as role sharing, communication, willingness to teach English and work together and building relationship. Along with some challenges that the team teachers experienced, the key factors underlying collaborative team teaching will be discussed in relation to the following three aspects: willingness and flexibility, mutual understanding and rapport, and awareness of cultural differences.

Willingness and flexibility for team teaching

As mentioned earlier, both LETs (Lee and Kim) were not only willing to teach English and work with NESTs but were also flexible in communication with NESTs and other LETs. The NESTs (Sonny and Michelle) also responded cooperatively to their counterparts when coping with problems. For example, while Sonny in Case 1 worked with Lee and another English subject teacher, Michele in Case 2 had to work with two English subject teachers, one English conversation instructor, and six homeroom teachers. Michelle was discouraged to implement collaborative team teaching with the homeroom teachers who seemed chiefly reliant on her.

Michelle said, 'I am the only NEST in this school and teach 11 different classes with nine different partners. Homeroom teachers are not likely to get involved in English classes and some don't help me.' The following extract from one NEST's essay revealed this variety clearly:

> As we learn very quickly when we begin teaching for EPIK, the co-teachers we have and our relationships with them vary. Some of us have only one co-teacher. Many of us have multiple co-teachers. Some work with their co-teachers on lesson planning, teach 50/50, and run the class together. Some take turns sharing the leading role while the other serves as support during the lesson. Some build great and close relationships with their co-teachers that extend far beyond the workday. Others have a mostly professional relationship with their co-teachers. Ask ten different native teachers for a description of their role and interactions with their co-teachers, and you will get ten very different responses.
>
> *(Essay, Dustin, 2013)*

As a team partner and coordinator, Kim explained the reason for less collaborative team teaching practices with some homeroom teachers: 'I fully understand Michell's difficulty. Some homeroom teachers taking charge of English classes for the fifth grade feel stressed and uncomfortable to teach English and even communicate with a NEST because of their lack of English competence and confidence.' Even though Yanase (2016) claimed that the homeroom teachers' English proficiency was not closely related to their involvement in team teaching, Heo and Mann (2015) reported similar difficulties that LETs experienced. Novice LETs had more challenges due to lack of confidence caused by a lack of teaching experience, perceived English deficiency and unwillingness to teach English. In many public schools where one NEST is likely to work with more than two LETs, LETs like Kim, as host teachers and coordinators, should be aware of NESTs' expected difficulties and help them share teaching materials with other LETs through casual meetings and discussions. In fact, two months later, Michelle and her team teachers found some solutions: they started a regular weekly meeting with all LETs and held 'teatime' with homeroom teachers after class, produced their own templates for lesson plans, shared them with all of the teachers, and posted updated events or any urgent changes on a monthly schedule board in the teachers' office.

As for teaching experience and expertise, Lee, a veteran teacher, revealed a different viewpoint, raising another issue from her previous working experience concerning teachers' qualifications. She argued that NESTs' strong sense of responsibility and flexible attitude towards the school and students were more important than their teaching experience and qualification as an English teacher. Lee expressed her opinions as follows:

> Whenever I have a meeting or workshop with other teachers from different schools, we talk about NESTs who we are working with. Simply, we describe our situation as 'heaven or hell' or 'luck or bad luck' because some could have really really nice NESTs whereas others don't. Two years ago, I had a terrible experience with one NEST who had lots of teaching experience before. Without any preparation, she was very good at teaching and managing classes. But she was quite opinionated and irresponsible. I was sick of her repeated absences because of her private matter I could not understand and finally she left the school before the contract. Personally, I prefer new NESTs keen to work with someone even though they lack teaching skills and experience. That's why I am happy to work with Sonny now. He didn't have any teaching experience, but he was willing to enthusiastically learn something new and considered this job serious.
>
> *(Interview, K – Case1)*

Although some researchers argue for the importance of NESTs' qualifications and experience (Choi, 2001; Kim, 2011; Kim, 2016), LETs with more than three years of team teaching experience in this research placed more emphasis on NESTs' serious attitudes towards a teaching job, flexibility and willingness to learn something new. Kim mentioned her positive experience with a previous NEST who was not only a well-prepared teacher with teaching experience of young learners but also a person eager to learn from and compromise with other LETs.

Mutual understanding and rapport

One of the key factors affecting team teachers was whether both team teachers could build and maintain rapport or a good relationship with each other (Carless, 2006a; Jang et al., 2010; Kim, 2011; Tsai, 2007). Copland et al. (2016c) pointed out that a positive relationship between team teachers was an essential feature of successful team teaching, which led to collaboration. According to Free and Griffin (2016: 42), this relationship is often likened to 'a marriage' which is frequently arranged, cross-cultural and difficult. In the same vein, the following extract from one NEST's essay revealed a similar analogy:

> I remember a training that was given for native teachers here in Seoul, when a lecturer called Nick came out and started talking about his wedding. He was giving us the details about meeting his wife, the wedding festivities, and then talking about their current daily life. Finally, he stopped and looked at us. He said, 'I'm telling you all this because you are all now married.' He then flipped his PowerPoint to an older, slightly severe looking Korean woman. 'This was my first co-teacher,' he said. 'You all have one, and I'm telling you right now that you are basically married to them' […] I could describe this teacher as my mom, my handler, my translator, my boss, my accountant, my guide, or even my personal assistant. Any one of these terms would be appropriate, but at the same time any one of these terms would fail to fully capture our relationship […] One day early during my time in Korea, I had to go to the bank to try to get things set up so I could transfer money home. Since no one at my bank speaks English, my co-teacher came with me. We were sitting there together, and my co-teacher was able to see every detail of my financial information, and was discussing it quite openly with the bank staff. She could see how much money I had, how much money I'd spent, and even line by line what I'd spent money on. I was definitely a little bit uncomfortable, but it really drove home the point about marriage.
>
> *(Essay, Dustin, 2013)*

As described above, it was true that most new NESTs relied on their LETs, particularly, coordinating teachers who tended to play multi-functional roles and handle multi-tasks beyond teaching. Without a reciprocal relationship between team teachers, it would be quite challenging to interact and work with each other. Lee stressed the importance of relationship management with a NEST, saying 'I've tried to know who my partner is whenever I meet a new NEST and make an effort to balance between being an intimate friend outside the classroom and maintaining a partnership in the school'. Lee said she often walked around school or went shopping with Sonny, talking about their daily routines or private life. Sonny was invited to Lee's house on special occasions such as Chuseok (Korean Thanksgiving Day), Christmas Eve, and her family gatherings or special events like her brother's wedding ceremony and her father's birthday. As Lee had lived in the USA for two years, she could thoroughly understand his situation and emotion as a foreigner who was easily isolated from national events or holidays in the host country. In addition, Lee wanted Sonny to experience and learn about Korean tradition and culture as much as possible while he was working in Korea, which encouraged Sonny to renew the contract for another year and stay at this school. While Kim described Michelle as 'the life of the party' in their class and teachers' office, which led them to communicate with each other in a better atmosphere, Michelle initiated Kim's nickname 'Miss Smile' as a way to indicate someone who was always hospitable and ready to help her. Kim helped Michelle to settle down in the new accommodation and spent almost every weekend guiding her to several sightseeing attractions in their province. One piece of advice for new NESTs often given by former NESTs was to stay active and take the opportunity to get to know co-workers and students, spending time with them (NIIED, 2017). Individual team teachers need to have interpersonal sensitivity (Carless, 2006a) to their partners and 'respect, equality, flexibility and empathy' (Luo, 2010: 273) in their teaching and relationship.

Awareness of cultural differences

A lack of intercultural understanding and cultural clashes have been identified as the main culprit in ineffectiveness of team teaching and conflicts between team teachers (Carless, 2002; Choi, 2001; Heo, 2016; Khánh & Spencer-Oatey, 2016). In 'intercultural team teaching' contexts (Carless, 2004: 345), team teachers need to explore not only cross-cultural aspects but also interpersonal ones. Each school has a different culture and each team partner responds to and solves the conflicts and problems in varying ways. The two cases of team teachers in my study did not face any serious conflicts or difficulties caused by cultural differences perhaps for the following reasons: first, both LETs and NESTs seemed ready to understand different cultures from their previous experience of living and learning in other countries. Second, LETs learnt the importance of a positive relationship with their NESTs from their previous team teaching experiences and NESTs had a careful attitude towards the host culture. At the beginning of the semester, Sonny was very confused about his identity as a second generation immigrant who had a Korean appearance but an American attitude and mind. Some Korean colleagues in the teachers' office treated him as a Korean teacher and they openly stated to him that he should have learnt the Korean language, which caused him to experience complicated unpleasant emotions. That was why he was reluctant to join some casual meetings or dinners with them at the beginning of his Korean life. Javier (2016) reported a similar challenging experience from a 'visible ethnic-minority' NEST who was not treated as a NEST by local teachers and even students because of being a non-white foreigner. However, through interacting with them more, Sonny got to understand they never intended to insult him and he learnt about the collective and hierarchical culture in Korea and senior teachers' concern and care about novice and junior teachers. Lee often mediated some misunderstanding or unexpected conflicts between Sonny and other colleagues working in the same office. EPIK integrates cultural contents into the training for new NESTs like Korean culture experience (six hours), Korean history and culture (two hours), cultural difference (two hours) and Korean language (two hours). These programmes provide basic cultural experiences including visiting national heritage sites or participating in cooking Korean dishes and helping NESTs get a general understanding of cultural issues. However, cultural training would be suitable for team teachers and other colleagues if they could share and discuss potential constraints and both negative and positive cultural experiences.

Implications for training and development

In this section I will discuss how to support team teachers in relation to the following three aspects: induction and training, materials development, and network and community.

Induction and training programmes

The argument for appropriate induction and training programmes for team teachers has been widely discussed (Copland et al., 2016a; Tang, 2016; Wang, 2012). In NEST schemes, most of the substantial induction training has been organised mainly for NESTs rather than LETs due to limited budgets and hectic schedules. For example, there are three different types of training programmes in EPIK: a 15-hour online pre-orientation programme which supports team teaching practices and team teachers; a 30–45-hour orientation as pre-service training designed for new NESTs who are new to Korea or to public school teaching; and a 15-hour online in-service training programme for both NESTs and LETs. Sonny and Michelle, LETs in this study, agreed that these programmes were supportive for them in glimpsing an unfamiliar world and settling down in new environments. According to the surveys on training programme satisfaction in EPIK from 2010 to 2016 (NIIED, 2017), NESTs answered they were satisfied with lectures in training programmes (4.54 on a 5-point Likert Scale) and cultural experience (4.47). In contrast to this positive feedback and answers from NESTs, some NESTs mentioned there were limitations of the training in how to implement team teaching with LETs appropriately. For instance, one inexperienced NEST reflected on his first day at school as a 'totally false start', saying 'I arrived at my school not knowing what to expect.' Lee (Case 1) argued that inexperienced team teachers might have more challenges to make up for a lack of knowledge and skills in ELT.

Most NESTs are allocated to schools and start their teaching job immediately without any observation or thorough preparation in advance. To support new NESTs and team teachers consistently, it is critical to place more emphasis on local school culture, norms and expectations in training programmes. As induction and orientation cannot meet their practical needs sufficiently in varying teaching contexts, each school needs to develop localised, contextualised and systematic programmes pertinent to different conditions. In addition, Copland et al. (2016a) have suggested joint training, that is, LETs should be involved in training and work together with NESTs. Regardless of teaching experience and skills, both LETs and NESTs need to know their students, schools and team partners, which can be an essential prerequisite for team teaching practice. To do this, it is necessary for team teachers to have an orientation course and preparation at school in advance before a new semester or during a vacation before they start working together. Given enough time, LETs and NESTs should have their own orientation and discussion regarding their team teaching contexts through local teaching communities and participate in and organise their own events to promote their learning and professional development.

To support these training programmes, first, the Ministry of Education and Provincial Offices of Education should discuss how to enhance and develop local induction and training programmes practically. Second, teachers should be given more opportunities to share and exchange new ideas and explore other cases of in-service and former team teachers through regular workshops and seminars by creating a network of other LETs and NESTs. Third, guidance or guidebooks should be appropriately designed and include the following content in training programmes: knowing the teaching contexts such as students, school culture, office, classroom and residential area, understanding cultural differences and personal tastes, sharing expected challenges when working together, how to prepare for team teaching practice from lesson plans to evaluation, how to clarify and share roles and responsibility, how to solve any conflicts or problems when they emerge, and how to communicate with other colleagues in an efficient way. This is closely related to material development which needs to be designed, developed and applied in varying ways in each team teaching context.

Materials development for team teachers

There has been little attention given to developing materials for team teaching and team teachers even though team teaching has been in operation for several decades. As mentioned above, teachers, trainers, practitioners, researchers and material developers should make an effort to design and develop more relevant materials and teaching resources for training programmes and team teaching practice. Copland et al. (2016b) published a set of useful materials, 'Introduction to Materials: Developing collaborative practice between LETs and NESTs', designed to support team teachers working in a range of different contexts. Considering the potential challenges, constraints and difficulties that team teachers have, the 12 different activities in this collection provide information aiming at helping LETs and NESTs to prepare to teach and work together or independently. Those materials were used in my classes for in-service LETs who were doing an MA in TESOL in Korea and in the workshop sessions for Vietnamese university lecturers who were working with NESTs in Vietnam. From my teaching and training experience of using these materials, they were beneficial for the in-service LETs and NESTs in that they developed a better understanding of team teaching and deepened their insights about cultural awareness and relationship. In addition, several activities were adapted to meet local teachers' needs and interest. As for teaching resources, team teachers in this study made good use of materials from other English teachers' blogs and online cafés, and free or paid online resources. They uploaded such materials to an e-board to share with colleagues in schools and developed their own workbook by modifying activities or games from other websites.

Network and community for teachers

Team teachers need to develop their own community and expand their teaching networks through various activities and social interaction with other LETs and NESTs. The former NESTs responded that they got valuable information on their teaching and daily life in the NEST local community through interaction with NESTs. For example, some NESTs explained how they overcame the obstacles as a NEST in EPIK and shared a variety of cultural events and experiences they participated in. These days some NESTs tend to be more active than before and play key roles in several national or international conferences such as KOTESOL in Korea or JALT in Japan by organising academic and social events and publishing newsletters. More NESTs tend to seriously think about their roles and positions as proactive English teachers not as simply visiting assistant NESTs. LETs also shared information with other LETs working in different schools in their community and had a casual meeting and events for LETs and NESTs. In fact, Lee and Sonny in Case 1 had a casual meeting with other team teachers working in different schools in their province. Both LETs and NESTs need to actively participate in teachers' groups and meetings in their community to share information, learn diverse teaching approaches and pursue professional development together. NIIED operates the EPIK-Newsletter and an e-press where NESTs involved in EPIK can share their teaching and living experience and information is given to potential EPIK applicants who may be interested in teaching. To recruit qualified NESTs, NIIED creates an English teacher resource pool, an alumni network of former NESTs and team teachers' community for new NESTs and novice LETs who need more support.

Suggestions for further research

There has been little research on current orientation and pre- and in-service training programmes and materials development for team teachers. As suggested, it is necessary to organise and conduct contextually specific training programmes for teachers relevant to their varying contexts and conditions. Along with the large scale orientation programmes implemented by the Ministry of Education, trainers, experienced coordinating teachers for team teaching and researchers need to investigate and develop training content to meet the needs of both team teachers and students.

To gain a greater understanding of team teaching practice and deeper insights of teachers' views, it is recommended to make a good use of the reflective practice approach in further research because 'it is small-scale, localised, context-specific, and private and conducted by teachers' (Walsh & Mann, 2015: 354). Based on a better understanding of teachers' experiences and life as team teachers, it is possible to enhance NEST schemes and team teaching practice, evaluate current schemes and discuss feasible solutions to support team teachers, trainers and educators.

Conclusion

Even though NEST schemes and team teaching have been implemented for several decades, little attention has been given to development of feasible suggestions for teacher training and professional development for team teachers. This chapter focused on how to support team teachers and team teaching practice practically and sustainably. From team teachers' perspectives and experiences, the key factors contributing to collaborative and successful team teaching practice were explored and three practical implications were discussed, such as induction and training, materials development and development and maintenance of a teacher community. If NEST schemes and team teaching are to operate effectively, it can be more valuable to seek to explore the successful cases of team teaching, learn from their experiences and find feasible solutions and support to develop team teaching and maximise its strengths.

Recommended reading

Copland, F., Davis, M., Garton, S. and Mann, S. (eds) (2016) *Investigating NEST Schemes Around the World: Supporting NEST/LET Collaborative Practices.* London: The British Council.
   A research project report on NEST schemes and useful recommendations for how LETs and NESTs can be best supported to make the most out of their collaborations.
Copland, F., Mann, S. and Garton, S. (eds) (2016) *LETs and NESTs: Voices, Views and Vignettes.* London: British Council.
   A book from teachers and academics working and researching in contexts where NESTs and LETs work on a daily basis with a range of perspectives, issues and practices.
Copland, F., Davis, M., Garton, S. and Mann, S. (eds) (2016) *Materials: Developing Collaborative Practice Between LETs and NESTs.* London: The British Council.
   A set of training materials for team teachers, trainers, and facilitators and even other teachers who can develop their own teaching alternatives and adaptations suitable for their own teaching and learning contexts.
The books above are free to download as a PDF file (British Council website).

References

Aline, D. and Hosoda, Y. (2006) 'Team Teaching Participation Patterns of Homeroom Teachers in English Activities Classes in Japanese Public Elementary School'. *JALT Journal*, 28(1) 5–22.
Bailey, K. M., Curtis, A. and Nunan, D. (2001) *Pursuing Professional Development: The Self as Source.* Boston, MA: Heinle & Heinle.

Carless, D. (2002) *Conflicts or collaboration: native and nonnative speakers' team teaching in schools in South Korea, Japan and Hong Kong*. Paper presented at the English in South East Asia Conference.

Carless, D. (2004) *JET and EPIK: Comparative respective*. Paper presented at Busan Chapter KOTESIL Conference, Korea.

Carless, D. (2006a) 'Good Practices in Team Teaching in Japan, South Korea and Hong Kong'. *System*, 34(3) 341–351.

Carless, D. (2006b) 'Collaborative EFL Teaching in Primary Schools'. *ELT Journal*, 60(4) 328–335.

Carless, D. and Walker, E. (2006) 'Effective Team Teaching between Local and Native-Speaking English Teachers'. *Language and Education*, 20(6) 463–477.

Chen, W. (2007) *A case study on the professional development of local and foreign English teachers in team teaching*. Unpublished PhD thesis, National Taiwan Normal University, Taiwan.

Choi, H. (2001) 'A Study on Team Teaching Between Native Teachers of English and Korean English Teachers in Elementary School'. *Studies in English Education*, 14(1) 161–189.

Chou, M. (2005) *A study of English Collaborative Teaching at elementary schools in Hsinchu City*. Unpublished Master thesis, National Taipei Teachers College, Taiwan.

Copland, F., Davis, M., Garton, S. and Mann, S. (eds) (2016a) *Investigating NEST Schemes Around the World: Supporting NEST/LET Collaborative Practices*. London: The British Council.

Copland, F., Davis, M., Garton, S. and Mann, S. (eds) (2016b) *Materials: Developing Collaborative Practice Between LETs and NESTs*. London: The British Council.

Copland, F., Mann, S. and Garton, S. (eds) (2016c) *LETs and NESTs: Voices, Views and Vignettes*. London: British Council.

Creswell, J. (2007) *Qualitative Inquiry and Research Design: Choosing Among Five Approaches*, 2nd edition. London: Sage.

English Programme in Korea (EPIK) in Korea. Available online: <www.epik.go.kr/EPIK> (accessed 22 May, 2019).

Foreign English Teachers in Taiwan (FETIT) Project in Taiwan. Available online: <http://english.moe.gov.tw> (accessed 22 May, 2019).

Free, M. and Griffin, M. (2016) 'Preparing to co-teach in a LET-NEST partnership with the experiential learning cycle', in Copland, F., Davis, M., Garton, S. and Mann, S. (eds) *Materials: Developing Collaborative Practice Between LETs and NESTs*. London: The British Council: 41–44.

Heo, J. (2013) A case study of team Teaching and Team Teachers in Korean primary schools. Unpublished PhD thesis, University of Warwick, UK.

Heo, J. (2016) 'Power, balance and identity', in Copland, F., Garton, S. and Mann, S. (eds) *LETs and NESTs: Voices, Views and Vignettes*. London: British Council: 169–183.

Heo, J. and Mann, S. (2015) 'Exploring Team Teaching and Team Teachers in Korean Primary Schools'. *English Language Teacher Education and Development*, 17 13–21.

Jang, H., Nguyen, B. H. and Yang, Y. (2010) 'Enhancing Pedagogical Roles of ESL/EFL Native and Non-Native Teachers through Team teaching: how to Make this "International Partnership" Successful'. *The International Journal of Learning*, 17(9) 249–257.

Japan Exchange and Teaching (JET) Programme in Japan. Available online: <www.jetprogramme.org> (accessed 22 May, 2019).

Javier, E. (2016) 'Almost native speakers: the experiences of Visible Ethnic-Minority Native English-speaking Teachers', in Copland, F., Garton, S. and Mann, S. (eds) *LETs and NESTs: Voices, Views and Vignettes*. London: British Council: 233–245.

Jeon, M. (2009) 'Globalisation and Native English Speakers in English Programme in Korea (EPIK)'. *Language, Culture and Curriculum*, 22(2) 231–243.

Khánh, T. and Spencer-Oatey, H. (2016) 'Managing relations in cross-national team teaching pairs: insights from rapport-sensitive incidents', in Copland, F., Garton, S. and Mann, S. (eds) *LETs and NESTs: Voices, Views and Vignettes*. London: British Council: 185–200.

Kim, M. (2011) 'Exploring Native English Speaking Teachers' Voices about Co-teaching'. *English Teaching*, 66(4) 27–52.

Kim, S. (2016) 'Native teachers' perspectives on co-teaching with Korean English teachers in an EFL context', in Copland, F., Garton, S. and Mann, S. (eds) *LETs and NESTs: Voices, Views and Vignettes*. London: British Council: 113–128.

Lin, T. and Wang, L. (2016) 'Native English-Speaking Teachers (NESTs) in Taiwan: policies and practices', in Copland, F., Garton, S. and Mann, S. (eds) *LETs and NESTs: Voices, Views and Vignettes*. London: British Council: 151–167.

Liu, L. (2008) 'Co-Teaching Between Native and Non-Native English Teachers. An Exploration of Co-Teaching Models and Strategies in the Chinese Primary School Context'. *Reflections and English Language Teaching*, 7(2) 103–228.

Liu, T. (2009) *Teachers' narrative understandings of the Taiwanese Foreign English Teachers Recruitment Project*. Unpublished PhD thesis, University of Manchester, UK.

Luo, W. (2010) 'Collaborative Teaching of EFL by Native and Non-native English-speaking Teachers in Taiwan', in Mahboob, A. (ed.) *The NNEST Lens: Non Native English Speakers in TESOL*. Newcastle Upon Tyne: Cambridge Scholars Publishing: 263–284.

Mahoney, S. (2004) 'Role Controversy Among Team Teachers in the JET Programme'. *JALT Journal*, 26(2) 223–244.

Mann, S. (2011) 'A Critical Review of Qualitative Interviews in Applied Linguistics'. *Applied Linguistics*, 32(1) 6–24.

Medgyes, P. (1994) *The Non-native Teacher*. London: Macmillan.

National Institute of International Education and Development (NIIED) (2017) Annual Report.

Native English Teacher (NET) Scheme in Hong Kong. Available online: <www.edb.gov.hk> (accessed 22 May, 2019).

Park, J. and Kim, D. (2000) 'Pedagogical Effects of Team Teaching Native Speakers: An Experiment to Compare Alternative Teaching Models'. *Foreign Language Education*, 7(1) 97–121.

Richards, J. C. and Farrell, T. S. (2005) *Professional Development for Language Teachers: Strategies for Teacher Learning*. New York: Cambridge University Press.

Rutson-Griffiths, A. (2012) 'Human tale recorders: curricular integration and team teaching in Japan', in *The Asian Conference on Education 2012 Official Conference Proceedings*. Nagoya: The International Academic Forum: 407–425.

Tajino, A. and Tajino, Y. (2000) 'Native and Non-native: What can they Offer? Lessons from Team Teaching in Japan'. *English Language Teaching Journal*, 54(1) 3–11.

Tajino, A. and Walker, L. (1998) 'Perspectives on Team Teaching by Students and Teachers: Exploring Foundations for Team Teaching'. *Language, Culture and Curriculum*, 11(1) 113–131.

Tang, E. (2016) 'Fostering better collaborative relationships between Native English Speaker Teachers and Local English Teachers for a more effective Native English Teacher (NET) Scheme in Hong Kong', in Copland, F., Garton, S. and Mann, S. (eds) *LETs and NESTs: Voices, Views and Vignettes*. London: British Council: 39–52.

Tsai, J. (2007) *Team teaching and teachers' professional learning: case studies of collaboration between foreign and Taiwanese English teachers in Taiwanese elementary schools*. Unpublished PhD thesis, The Ohio State University, USA.

Walsh, S. and Mann, S. (2015) 'Doing Reflective Practice: A Data-led Way Forward'. *ELT Journal*, 69(4) 351–362.

Wang, L. Y. (2012) 'Preparing NESTs and NNESTs for Team Teaching at the Pre-Service Level'. *Studies in Literature and Language*, 4(1) 32–37.

Yanase, C. (2016) 'From an assistant to a team member: a perspective from a Japanese ALT in primary schools in Japan', in Copland, F., Garton, S. and Mann, S. (eds) *LETs and NESTs: Voices, Views and Vignettes*. London: British Council: 201–216.

30

Using screen capture technology in teacher education

Russell Stannard and Ayşegül Sallı

Introduction

This chapter focuses on screen capture technology (SCT), a technology that is now being widely used in teacher education and language training. The chapter aims to make the reader aware of what SCT is and how it is used; bring the reader up-to-date on some of the research that has taken place in SCT; and provide a range of case studies around the use of SCT in education that could be applied to a teacher training context.

What is screen capture technology and how does it work?

SCT allows the user to record the screen of their computer as if a video camera was pointing at the computer screen. Anything the user opens onto the computer screen, their activities on the screen and voice can be recorded by the software and then turned into a video. For example, it is possible for a user to open up a PowerPoint presentation onto the screen, turn on the screen capture technology and record themselves talking over the presentation. Likewise, a teacher trainer could talk over a trainee teacher's lesson plan and give feedback on it, or perhaps talk over a diagram where they explain the principles of feedback in the learning cycle.

Screen capture technology (sometimes referred to as screen cast technology or screen cast software) is different from lecture capture technology. Lecture capture technology is used to record an actual lecture. In most cases, it includes some real video of the tutor delivering the lecture along with any slides that the tutor is showing to the audience. Lecture capture recordings tend to be longer and are achieved by such tools as TechSmith Relay (TechSmith, n.d.) or Echo 360 (Echo 360, n.d.). Screen capture technology is just a recording of the tutor's screen. It is possible to include a small head shot of the tutor but this is limited in size. Screen capture videos are normally shorter in length and often used for 'hands-on' training where the tutor takes the audience through a step-by-step process like how to create a blog or for short condensed lectures talking over a set PowerPoint slides.

Some examples of the uses of SCT include the Khan Academy (Khan Academy, n.d.) learning resources built almost entirely from SCT and used by thousands of students. A lot of the content that is used in flipped classroom is based on SCT, as suggested by Bergmann and Sams (2012). What is more, many of the Massive Open Online Courses (MOOCs) that are produced by organisations such as Future Learn (Future Learn, n.d.) and Coursera (Coursera, n.d.) also contain a lot of SCT video. In teacher education, www.teachertrainingvideos.com offers a collection of SCT videos showing teachers how to incorporate technology in their teaching (Stannard, 2018).

The versatility of SCT makes it possible for researchers and educators to implement screen capture technology in education in a range of ways. For example, Séror (2012) and Stannard (2017) experimented with using SCT to give feedback to students on their written work. Students' responses were very positive with the screencast feedback providing more detail, more personalised and clearer feedback than feedback provided in a written form. The early research into these ideas was based around English Language Teaching but then extended to other subject areas (West and Turner, 2016). The idea has more recently been applied in a teacher training context, where trainers used it to provide feedback to trainees on teacher training courses (Stannard and Mann, 2018).

A range of contexts

Due to the nature of SCT, it can be used in a range of creative ways. Here are just a few ideas, some of which we will look at in more detail in the later sections of this chapter.

- Teachers/Teacher trainers have used SCT to record themselves talking over a course assignment and providing oral and visual information about how to do the assignment. This is especially relevant in distance learning contexts but also where an assignment has several sections or options and needs clarification.
- Many schools and organisations have used SCT to create video guides that show students how to use the university library system, how to log onto the Moodle learning platform or even how to sign up for a particular course or module. The use of SCT can save time and money. For example, it can save money on costly induction days.
- Teachers have used SCT to record themselves talking through a marking scheme and explaining to students how a piece of work will be marked. This clearly has currency in a teacher training context, where more detailed information on marking schemes for teaching practice sessions or written work can be provided.
- Teachers have put SCT into the hands of students too. For example, students can develop their oral skills through recording themselves talking over a picture or a set of PowerPoint slides. In a teacher training context a trainee teacher can talk through their lesson plan and then send the resulting video to the teacher trainer.
- Students/Trainee teachers can also use SCT for recording their feedback and reflections on a lesson. So, for example after giving a practice lesson, trainee teachers can record their reflections on a lesson, perhaps writing out the key points in Microsoft Word and then turning on the SCT to record themselves talking about the points they have listed. This can then be shared with the trainer or with other trainees.

What is it about video?

There is an almost 'intuitive' belief that video is an effective way of delivering information. It is by far the fastest growing medium on the Internet and is an everyday part of most people's lives. Information that is passed through video is 'dual-coded' (Palvio, 1986). That is, a person watching the video is receiving both oral and visual information. This contrasts with reading or listening, where the information is only being passed through one channel. There has been a suggestion that this 'multimodal' form of delivery may lead to greater retention of information (Mayer, 2002). Mayer (2002) suggests that one possible benefit of video is that it may avoid cognitive overload. Someone who is looking at both a picture and reading text is actually working with only one channel, i.e., all the information is coming through the eyes, which can lead to 'cognitive overload' (sometimes described as visual overload). In contrast, information conveyed through a screen capture video uses two channels i.e., both visual and aural information is conveyed. The viewer hears the commentary and looks at the picture. This may reduce the possible impact of overloading the visual channel (Mayer and Moreno, 2003). Mayer's (2002) research shows that students who watch a series of pictures and listen to a commentary about the pictures recall more information than a similar group of students who look at the same pictures but have to read the text on the screen at the same time. In other words, the use of two channels, instead of one, leads to greater retention of information.

SCT is the ideal tool for producing the type of content that is delivered through two channels that Mayer (2002) highlights. Although Mayer does not claim that video is the only way to deliver information, he highlights the importance of the use of video within a well-designed series of activities. He emphasises that a well thought out video that includes certain features is likely to have a significant impact on retention. The following key principles (see Table 30.1) that Mayer (2002) put forward are a good guide for those who intend to make use of SCT.

Table 30.1 Summary of Mayer's key principles

Principle	Explanation	Link with screen capture technology
Coherence principle	It is important not to have distractors such as pictures not associated with the narration.	When the user records the screen, they can mark out a specific area that they want to focus on and avoid including all extraneous content.
Redundancy principle	People learn better from visuals and narration rather than visuals and text. Information may become redundant because it is not processed due to visual overload.	Screen capture records both the voice and the screen. The output is nearly always a combination of visuals and narration.
Temporal contiguity principle	It is important to present words i.e., narration and visuals simultaneously.	Screen capture allows the user to record their voice and the screen at exactly the same time. The whole process is synchronised.
Segmenting principle	Videos should be done in short segments rather than one continuous video.	Many screen capture tools (especially the free ones) only allow limited length videos. SCT is ideal for quick videos of between two to ten minutes.
Personalisation principle	It seems that people learn better if the narration is in a conversational style.	SCT allows the user to record their own voice. Many tutors choose not to script what they say but rather record their voice unscripted.
Voice principle	It is better if the voice is NOT a machine but a friendly human voice.	SCT uses real voice. The tutor can add their own voice along with the video recording.

(Mayer, 2002)

The principles outlined above focus on the delivery of information and concepts in a way that maximises retention of information. Mayer recognises that after the information is delivered, students need to process the new knowledge and engage in a series of activities to really internalise and own the knowledge. Therefore, he claims that video may be an effective way of delivering ideas and concepts to students. He is not claiming that delivering learning through video means that the information is internalised.

Bloom's taxonomy and creativity

Traditionally SCT videos in teacher training have tended to focus on delivering concepts and ideas. So for example there are literally hundreds of SCT videos on YouTube that explain what task based learning is, how summative and formative assessment differ or how to give feedback to students. These videos tend to be rather traditional in format and focus on explaining and summarising concepts and principles in teaching and learning. The learning tends to be very passive, with the viewer watching the videos and perhaps taking notes.

It is possible however, to use SCT technology in ways that make the learning more engaging and less passive. This usually requires trainers to be more creative in the ways they create the SCT videos or by passing the use of SCT over to the trainee teachers. For example, trainee teachers can record SCT videos where they go over a lesson plan they have produced and explain their plan and what they intend to do in the classroom. In this example, the trainee teachers are not passive receivers of SCT video produced by the trainer but rather actively process and analyse their lesson plan, reflecting on the rationale behind their choices and creating their own video.

In another example, trainee teachers might record themselves reflecting on a lesson they have just given, perhaps answering a series of questions that their teacher trainer has provided. The focus is on 'higher order thinking skills' as the trainee teachers analyse and reflect on their own lesson. It is often when we allow our trainee teachers to make use of SCT that we facilitate activities that support more active types of learning that encourage trainees to evaluate and analyse their work.

Taking creativity even further, it is possible to record a lesson with a standard video recorder, play the video back on a computer and use the SCT to record the lesson and comment on it. In this way, trainee teachers are able to analyse parts of their own lesson and comment on what they are doing, what they could do better and so on. The same could also be true of other trainee teachers on the same course i.e., using SCT for peer reflection. To illustrate, trainee teachers could record part of their own lesson and then provide this video footage to their peers. The peers could play back the video on a computer and then record themselves commenting on the lesson and providing feedback to the trainee teacher using SCT. These types of creative ideas require slightly more technical skills but in practice the only difference is that instead of screen capturing a PowerPoint presentation or a graph, teachers or trainee teachers simply screen capture a video that is playing on their screen. The only requirement would be a fairly modern computer.

Instructional design

How the SCT video is used will determine what type of impact it has on teacher education. Creative uses of SCT often lead to more trainee-centred approaches to learning, which often provide opportunities for trainee teachers to reflect, evaluate and apply their knowledge. However, we also need to consider how the video itself is designed. For example, a teaching video might start with an introduction to the topic before it moves onto the main content. There might be points in the video where questions appear on the screen or perhaps the video ends with a series of key points to consider. This is what we call the instructional design of the video. Loch and McLoughlin (2011) applied self-regulated learning (SRL) theory to the design of their videos and suggested a series of principles that might guide the organisation and staging of a video:

Table 30.2 Stages of self-regulation

1. Planning and goal setting	• Provide an overview of the concept being presented. • Activate prior knowledge.
2. Monitoring processes and metacognitive control	• Ask students to set a goal for the session. • Present questions and tasks to check for understanding, and to get students to actively engage in the problem-solving process.
3. Reflection on self-knowledge and task achievement	• Encourage students to reflect on the learning process and on their understanding of the concept. • Ask students to document areas of uncertainty and to prepare questions for their lecturer or tutor.

(Loch and McLoughlin, 2011)

There is a danger that watching a video can be a rather 'passive' type of activity like watching the TV. This is particularly the case where the video is essentially delivering basic summaries of key concepts and ideas. To eliminate this, Loch and McLoughlin (2011) suggest breaking up the videos into sections and providing opportunities to the viewer to reflect on the content of the video while viewing it (perhaps through questions that appear on the screen). They also suggest summarizing the key points or asking viewers to write down questions after watching the video.

The principles that appear in Table 30.2 could easily be applied to activities where the trainee teacher rather than the trainer is making a video. If a trainee teacher aims to record a reflective SCT video where they review a lesson they have just given, the video might include the following steps:

1. Set the context (level of group, objectives of lesson, etc.).
2. Focus on one aspect of the lesson that went well.
3. Focus on one thing that you weren't so pleased with.
4. Explain how you might improve it in the future.
5. What have you learnt from this process?

Providing a structure like this can help trainee teachers to organise their thoughts and produce more meaningful reflections that engage with the details and depth in their lessons. By thinking about the instructional design, we can make SCT videos much more engaging.

The following section demonstrates an example of how one of the authors of this chapter used SRL to develop reflection amongst his trainee teachers.

Authors' examples

Russell Stannard worked with a group of trainee teachers who participated in a Technology in English Language Teaching (ELT) module. In the course, trainee teachers were engaged in a number of classes where various technologies were used. After participating in the lessons, they were asked to reflect on the lessons and to comment on the contribution the technologies had made to the lessons. Instead of asking trainees to answer a questionnaire, the trainee teachers were sent a PowerPoint slide with questions to answer. These questions were structured so that specific issues and points would be raised using the principles of self-regulated learning. The trainee teachers were asked to open up the PowerPoint slides, record their answers to the questions using SCT and then, submit the resulting videos via Moodle. Stannard found that the recorded oral reflections were much more detailed than the reflections he had previously received in written form. In the subsequent lesson, he organised the trainee teachers into groups and asked them to listen to some of the reflections from other trainee teachers and comment on them.

Creating a video is very much like a 'blank sheet' and the actual content can vary widely (Sugar et al., 2010). For example, SCT seems to fit well with the instructional design of modelling answers or operations (Wouters et al., 2008). An example might be where a teacher trainer provides an example lesson plan on a task-based lesson and creates a screencast video that talks through the various stages of the lesson plan. This model video can then be provided to the trainee teachers who can make use of it to help them plan their own lesson. Another example might be a screencast video of a teacher trainer modelling presentation techniques that trainee teachers could consider using when giving a lesson. In both cases the screencast video provides trainee teachers with a model that they can follow. Again, the principles of instructional design can be applied to make the videos engaging and thought provoking.

Flipped classroom

The idea of the flipped classroom began to emerge from the United States of America about 12 years ago (Bergmann and Sams, 2012). It is loosely based on a previous idea known as the inverted classroom (Conley, 2013). Access to digital learning assets means that students can now access videos, articles, podcasts and a whole range of learning content outside the classroom. It is possible for example for a student to watch a video about the 'Fall of the Roman Empire' at home, prepare some key points and then come into class and engage in a group task to share ideas about why 'Rome fell'. One of the key principles underpinning the flipped classroom is that teachers do less teaching in the class and spend more of the class time on group work and task based activities. So in this example, the use of the video at home, takes some of the 'teaching' time out of the lesson and in theory allows more time for discussion and group tasks.

Flipped classroom can also be applied to teacher education. For example, we previously mentioned that one possible use of screencast video is through worked models. A trainer might produce a screencast video that takes trainee teachers through a model example of a task-based lesson plan. The trainee teachers watch the video at home and plan a task-based lesson. Then, in class, the trainee teachers are put into groups and asked to present their lesson plans to the rest of the group. The rest of the group discusses the strengths and weaknesses of the plan, and suggests improvements. The benefit of using SCT is that the teacher trainer does not have to use valuable class time explaining what a task-based lesson is.

Some of the data on the impact of the flipped classroom has been quite positive (Enfield, 2013). However, there is currently no such data on the impact of this in teacher training contexts. An example of where it has an impact on teaching and learning is when dealing with differentiation. There seems to be evidence that it may impact on weaker students who are able to play and replay the learning input at home to master the materials. Curtis et al. (2008) found that weaker students on database courses could work through the learning material and build up the basic core skills which then enabled them to move onto the more difficult concepts. In another study, the students reported that they had more opportunities in class to ask questions as the lesson time was more focused on doing task-based activities, which also gave the teacher time to move around the class to clarify points and deal with problems (Roehl et al., 2013). These points may also be applicable to teacher training contexts and it will be interesting to see if such studies emerge.

Open and distance learning

A real challenge in distance learning is teacher presence. On distance learning courses students often feel isolated and work through a course without really feeling the presence of their teacher (Olesova et al., 2011). This is particularly the case where an online teacher training course has lots of third-party materials from sources such as YouTube, Vimeo and blog posts. It can almost lead to a teacher being anonymous on a teacher training course since most of the material is not produced by the teacher trainer. Screen capture can help deal with this by facilitating the production of content produced by the teacher trainer. In this way the students can hear the teacher's voice and feel their presence on the course. Research evidence suggests that students expect to hear their teacher's voice on these types of courses and actually prefer it to third party material (Ladyshewsky, 2013).

Feedback

As mentioned earlier, SCT can easily be used as an innovative way of providing feedback to students. This area has been quite widely researched and more recently has been looked at in the context of teacher education (Stannard and Mann, 2018). Their work underpinned much of the previous research and highlighted the following benefits:

1. *Much more detailed feedback can be provided.* A person speaks at around 140 words a minute and so in a five-minute video, over 700 words of feedback can be provided as well as any visual information on the screen. This contrasts with the quite limited written feedback most trainers give.
2. *Trainees find it clearer.* Teacher trainers are able to provide much more context when giving feedback and this helps trainees to understand the feedback better. This contrasts with written feedback which tends to be in the form of short comments with little context or background information.
3. *Trainees value the voice.* Many trainees seem to like feedback delivered through the voice. Thompson and Lee (2012) suggested this might be to do with the use of hedging, which softens the feedback. Feedback provided through the voice tends to be chattier and makes use of modality and may feel less threatening.
4. *It is more motivating.* Trainees find the screencast feedback more motivating. This though, it likely not to be the case if the screencast videos are continually used as a mode of giving feedback. The suggestion is that the ideas should be used in key moments, perhaps for example before a trainee teacher is going to deliver a final paper or give a lesson.

Authors' examples

While at the University of Warwick, Russell taught on the MA in ELT specialising in the use of technology. Along with Tilly Harrison, they decided to ask the participants on the course to keep a reflective blog where the participants (mainly students preparing to become teachers) were asked to describe the different technologies they were exposed to on the course and how they might use them in their own teaching and learning. The reflective blog was an integral part of the assessment and it was decided to use screen capture to give the students feedback on the blogs they created. Giving feedback in written form can be laborious and it can be difficult to give comments concerning the layout, organisation or navigation of the blog. The problem is that the written comments are on a separate document to the blog. By using SCT the blogs can be opened on the screen and the tutors can record themselves going through the blogs pointing out issues around design, layout and organisation. The students can play back the video, listen, and watch their course tutor directly reviewing their blog.

This next example again concerns the use of feedback in a teacher training context. It highlights how the use of SCT can help provide feedback to newly recruited teachers on their observations and focuses on a number of interesting benefits while at the same time highlighting possible limitations.

Authors' examples

Ayşegül Sallı works as a teacher and a teacher trainer/mentor at the Foreign Languages and English Preparatory School, Eastern Mediterranean University in Cyprus. During the fall semester 2017–18, she mentored a group of newly recruited part-time English language teachers who were on the induction program. The program requires the part-time teachers to conduct two observed lessons. The classroom observation cycle includes pre-and post-observation meetings. In the pre-observation meetings part-time teachers and their mentors meet to go over the lesson plans the part-time teachers have produced. The part-time teachers receive feedback on their lesson plans and make modifications before conducting their lessons. After their lesson observations, the part-time teachers meet with the mentor to discuss the lessons and receive feedback.

Due to the busy work schedule of both Ayşegül and the part-time teachers, Ayşegül decided to provide feedback on part-time teachers' lesson plans via SCT rather than actually meeting them to talk through the plans. She hoped providing screencast feedback would:

a) reduce the dependency that the part-time teachers have on her;
b) allow the part-time teachers to listen to the screencast feedback in their own time and at their own pace;
c) provide them with the opportunity to play and replay the screencast video as much as they wanted to;
d) give them more time to absorb the information and make necessary changes to their lesson plans; and
e) save time.

When the part-time teachers submitted their lesson plans via Edmodo, Ayşegül used SCT to provide feedback on their lesson plans. Then, she shared the screencast videos on the Edmodo so that the part-time teachers could access the link to listen to their feedback, and make appropriate changes to their plans. A sample screencast video feedback can be reached from the following link: www.youtube.com/watch?v=LAUEUBfFwXw

At the end of the semester, Ayşegül prepared a survey that included seven open-ended questions on Google Forms to gather data about the part-time teachers' reaction to this way of receiving feedback on their lesson plans. She then posted the survey on Edmodo. The questions asked the part-time teachers to write about what aspects of screencast video feedback they liked, how they benefitted from it, list any advantages and drawbacks, and whether they would like to receive screencast feedback in the future. All of the participants responded to the questions.

The part-time teachers reported that they valued the screencast video feedback and highlighted a number of advantages. The main advantage highlighted by the part-time teachers was the opportunity to listen to the feedback when and where they wanted to. One of them reported that receiving screencast feedback on their lesson plans 'reduced the possibility of making a mistake' preparing the final lesson plan as it would be 'difficult to note everything down during a face-to-face pre-observation meeting'. Another new teacher commented: 'It can be hard to make changes on our lesson plan by just listening to the trainer once. Therefore, screencast feedback gave me the chance of listening to my feedback more than once.' This is an interesting point and highlights just how important it is to play and replay the screencast/video feedback. Crook et al. (2012) also reported on similar findings.

Clarity of feedback emerged as another finding. One of the part-time teachers stated that 'the trainer was to the point' in the SCT feedback video. Each point was clearly made with 'tips, suggestions or questions'. Another new teacher indicated that 'the trainer highlighted the areas' they needed to work on and this made following the feedback easier. Clarity was clearly a benefit.

On the other hand, the part-time teachers stated their preference for face-to-face pre-observation meetings due to the fact that they could 'ask questions' to the trainer on the spot while going over the lesson plan. One of the participants voiced their opinion as follows: 'Video feedback on lesson plans is fine but I definitely prefer face-to-face feedback on my lesson plan.' Therefore despite the merits of screencast feedback, face-to-face pre-observation meetings to discuss certain issues on lesson plans was preferred. Another trainee suggested that perhaps both have value:

> I would prefer both. However, face-to-face feedback may be better because it enables discussion but it will not be possible to meet face-to-face all the time. Video feedback on the other hand gave me the opportunity to access the feedback as many times as I wanted.

The quote above highlights that though the SCT can be an effective way of providing feedback to teachers, in this context it seems that they prefer face-to-face meetings to receive feedback on their lesson plans as it allows for more of a dialogue.

One key issue here is to look at ways of making the process more dialogic. Mann and Walsh (2017) suggest that when trainee teachers hand in their lesson plans, they could also hand in a form highlighting what specific issues and areas they would like feedback on. The trainer could then provide feedback on these specific issues and make the feedback much more specific to each student. Another way to build interaction might be through asking the students to respond to the video feedback by perhaps telling the tutor what feedback they have used or acted on.

Examples from other contexts: How are teachers around the world using screen capture technology?

So far we have discussed the general use of SCT in education and also looked at some specific uses of it within teacher education, mainly drawing on the research and work of the authors. In this section we want to take a broader look by looking at what other teachers around the world are doing with SCT. As we mentioned right at the start of this chapter, SCT is now beginning to be widely used in education. These examples reflect the flexible nature of SCT and various ways it can be used.

It is interesting to see the range of ways that SCT is being used. It can not only have an impact on the way that teaching and learning is delivered but it can even have an impact on the administration of courses and the way new teachers are recruited onto programmes. As we stated right from the start, SCT is being used in (see Table 30.3) a wide range of areas of education.

Table 30.3 Uses of SCT

Name	ICT use
Will Sutton	Uses SCT to make training videos for the teachers at his college. There is a continual need to offer CPD on a whole range of topics including training the teachers on the VLE, passing information about new systems and processes within the college as well as technical training etc. Making SCT videos frees up a lot of time, means there is 24-hour access to the training and allows for much greater flexibility in where and when the teachers access the content. It also saves money as there is less need for CPD sessions.
Sean Wordingham	Has used SCT to give trainee teachers feedback on their lesson plans. He commented: 'I also saw a real improvement in the lesson plans that I was sent. I feel this is because hearing my comments while watching me change aspects of the lesson plan is much more memorable for trainees.'
Ece Zehir Topkaya	Runs teacher training courses in Turkey and as part of the course actually trains the teacher trainees to use SCT. They have to make a learning asset like a pronunciation video, review of vocabulary, grammar lesson or video about organising an essay etc. The idea is that they learn to use SCT and learn its relevance in their teaching and learning. It is vital in the twenty-first century that new teachers know how to use SCT as it is technology that will continually come across in their teaching and learning.
Leigh Quadling-Miernik	Building an online M-level business programme. The 33 lecturers who are contributing content to the course have very different levels of knowledge of creating and uploading learning material for the course. Leigh has used SCT to make a video that shows the rest of the team how to upload their learning content into the Moodle site and create activities. This is a tremendous help as it means that Leigh doesn't have to get all the teachers together for a training session to learn how to use Moodle.
Henno Kotze	As the senior teacher, is involved in the process of teacher induction. This can be a very time-consuming process. Henno has produced SCT videos to help teachers learn a whole range of different tasks that they need to know when starting a new job. This includes things like 'How to check they have been paid' or 'How to access the school's virtual learning environment'. Videos have also been made on more specific tasks linked to teaching and learning. This saves considerable time when teachers are inducted into the school as new teachers can access this content in their own time.

Suggested tools and options to overcome possible challenges

We have described a number of case studies from different contexts and also provided examples of how SCT can be used in teacher training/education. Each one will have its challenges in the use of the technology as well as adapting to new ways of delivering learning and setting up tasks. The technical issues have become less challenging over time but teacher trainers will need to decide on a screencast software, learn to use it to make videos, save the resulting videos and upload them to the relevant repository for trainee teachers to access. The same challenge will confront any trainee teacher using SCT. We highly recommend that it is not only teacher trainers that should be using SCT but trainee teachers too.

One common question from all teachers is how the students/trainee teachers play back the videos and what software they need to do this. In nearly all cases the resulting videos made using SCT are immediately playable on any device. They can be uploaded onto YouTube, Google Drive, Dropbox, Moodle, Edmodo etc. or simply saved on the computer and shared via email. There is no need for the person playing the video to have any specific technology. What you do need of course is a fairly good internet connection or 4G network if you are watching the video from a phone.

In reality, what is actually the most challenging is simply getting used to a new form of delivering learning and receiving content from your trainee teachers. Thinking about how to make the optimal video that clearly delivers the content and material to the trainee teachers takes some time. However, as a teacher trainer becomes more proficient and organised in their approach to creating their videos, they are likely to change the format and way they design videos.

There are a huge number of screen capture software tools and many are actually free. A search on Google with the term 'screen capture software' or 'screen capture technology' will bring up a list of options. This is a list of the free and paid technologies (see Table 30.4) that the authors have been exposed to and used.

Table 30.4 Free screencast tools

Name	Description	Advantages	Disadvantages
Jing www.techsmith. com/jing-tool. html	Free tool downloaded onto their computers and then use very easily.	Free tool and easy to use.	Can only save videos online. Offline recordings are saved in a format that is not native to most computers. Limited to five-minute videos.
Cam Studio http://camstudio. org/	Free tool download onto a computer.	Free tool with capability to save resulting videos onto a computer. Can be downloaded onto a computer, so Internet access is not necessary.	Rather slow to use and limited options.
Screencast-O-Matic https://screencast-o-matic.com/	Free tool that can either be used online or by downloading the software onto a computer.	Can create videos of up to 15 minutes. Has a paid option too.	Can be tricky to use, especially the online version. Once mastered it is reliable but the videos are limited to 15 minutes.

Table 30.5 Paid screencast tools

Name	Description	Advantages	Disadvantages
SnagIT www.techsmith. com/download/ snagit/	Low cost option that allows for good quality recordings by downloading the application.	Has basic editing options and can be easily distributed to a variety of repositories. It also has a good image capture.	Requires a one-off payment of $30.
Camtasia www.techsmith. com/video-editor.html	Produces high quality recordings and allows a huge range of edits producing very professional outputs.	Has excellent edits. Lots of free assets included.	Expensive to buy ($169) and requires training to learn to use the editing options but can produce highly engaging videos with quiz options etc.

For free tools (see Table 30.5) our recommendation would be Screencast-O-Matic. It is sometimes a little tricky to use since the recorder opens as a separate app when you make a screen capture recording but once you have mastered that, it is reliable and offers a number of sharing options. For paid tools, our recommendation would be SnagIT. It is a one-off payment of $30 (single license education pricing). The cost may be prohibitive to some teachers but it is a reliable tool and one that offers a number of options for a teacher. The image capture facility is also very good. You can download SnagIT for free and trial it for two weeks.

Conclusion

This chapter has looked at the number of possible ways that SCT can be used in teacher training/education. As it is being widely used in education, we encourage teacher trainers to introduce this technology to their trainee teachers to make use of it.

SCT is often used to produce learning assets that deal with topics such as formative assessment, feedback, task-based approaches to learning and so on. Many of these can be found on YouTube. However, we have highlighted the point that if used creatively, the use of SCT can lead to videos that encourage active learning. Applying the principles of self-regulated learning, for example, can create much more compelling videos.

Do not forget that some of the most interesting and perhaps rewarding ways of working with SCT occur when we put the technology in the hands of our students or trainee teachers. It is ideal for reflection, discussions, presentations and sharing.

Just like any technology, the more familiar a teacher trainer or a trainee teacher becomes with using it, the more creative they will become with the way they use it. Based on our experience, it is probably best to build up confidence with the technology by producing material for trainee teachers first and then once a trainer is confident with the technology, introduce it as a tool so that trainee teachers can also use it.

There are a few challenges to overcome when using SCT but they are surprisingly few as technically this is a very simple technology to work with.

Remember also that this technology can be used way beyond the classroom. Newly recruited teachers can be provided with screen capture videos to learn all sorts of things like how to log on to the schools VLE or how to use the institution's email system. Libraries make extensive use of

SCT to provide help for students learning to search for journals on database systems. Wherever support and help is needed, SCT can play a vital role.

Further reading

In this section we are recommending some published articles and books in the area of technology integrated language teaching and learning and teacher development for further reading.

Li, L. (2017) *New Technologies and Language Learning*. London: Palgrave.

The book has three sections. The first section has two chapters that review seminal publications to give an overview of current research in the field. The second section, Chapters 3–6, focuses onto practices using new technologies to in different contexts. The last section from Chapters 7–10 focuses on feedback, materials, and teachers' attitudes. In this section, Chapter 7 is devoted to screencast feedback and assessment which also taps into possible challenges. Readers are provided with guidelines to follow regarding new ways of giving feedback. Among many others, one of the strength of the book is that it combines theory and practice and the tasks help the reader personalize information.

Zou, B. and Thomas, M. (2018) *Handbook of Research on Integrating Technology into Contemporary Language Learning and Teaching*. Hershey, PA: IGI Global.

This handbook aims to investigate the connection between language education and technology as well as the capacity of technological advances used to enhance language education. The book covers a wide range of critical scholarly articles on various topics from computer-assisted language learning, to flipped instruction, mobile technologies, and teacher education. Language teachers, teacher trainers, researchers and education professionals who search for relevant research on the improvement of language education through the use of technology can benefit from this handbook.

Nayar, K. A. (2018) *Teaching and Learning in Technology Empowered Classrooms—Issues, Contexts and Practices*. Gurgaon: Partridge Publishing.

This book focuses on not only the practical issues and case studies but also policy guidelines and features of policy frameworks that are affected by development and implementation of technology. The book describes different curricular research carried out in various contexts together with success and failures as well as the reasons. Furthermore, teachers can investigate the potentials of several technological tools for pedagogical implementation. This book may be a useful guide for teachers who are eager to integrate technology in lessons but have some doubts about how to do so.

Elola, I. and Oskoz, A. (2016) 'Supporting Second Language Writing Using Multimodal Feedback'. *Foreign Language Annals*, 49(1) 58–74.

The researchers report on a case study conducted with a group of Spanish language learners, who received both written and oral screencast feedback on their narrative essays. The results show that learners expressed their preference of oral feedback on the content, structure and organisation of their written work and the written feedback for form.

References

Bergmann, J. and Sams, A. (2012) *Flip Your Classroom: Reach Every Student in Every Class Every Day*. Washington, DC: International Society for Technology in Education.

Conley, L (2013) '7 Steps to Flipped Professional Development'. Available online: <www.gettingsmart. com/2013/01/7-steps-to-flipped-professional-development> (accessed 5 October 2017).

Coursera (n.d.). Available online: <www.coursera.org> (accessed:7 October 2017).

Crook, A., Mauchline, A., Maw, S., Lawson, C., Drinkwater, R., Lundqvist, K. and Park, J. (2012) 'The Use of Video Technology for Providing Feedback to Students: Can it Enhance the Feedback Experience for Staff and Students?'. *Computers and Education*, 58(1) 386–396.

Curtis, S., Love, M. and Uruchurtu, E. (2008) *Creation of reusable learning objects to support the teaching and learning of key introductory concepts in database systems*. Available online: <http://citeseerx.ist.psu.edu/ viewdoc/download?doi=10.1.1.571.6278&rep=rep1&type=pdf (accessed 17 September 2018).

Echo 360 (n.d.). Available online: <https://echo360.com> (accessed 12 February 2018).

Enfield, J. (2013) 'Looking at the Impact of the Flipped Classroom Model of Instruction on Undergraduate Multimedia Students at CSUN'. *TechTrends*, 57(3) 14–27.

Future Learn (n.d.). Available online: <www.futurelearn.com> (accessed 8 October 2017).

Khan Academy (n.d.). Available online: <www.khanacademy.org> (accessed 8 October 2017).

Ladyshewsky, R. K. (2013) 'Instructor Presence in Online Courses and Student Satisfaction'. *International Journal for the Scholarship of Teaching and Learning*, 7(1). Available online: <https://doi.org/10.20429/ijsotl.2013.070113> (accessed 29 October 2018).

Loch, B. and McLoughlin, C. (2011) 'An instructional design model for screencasting: engaging students in self-regulated learning', in Williams, G., Statham, P., Brown, N. and Cleland, B. (eds) *Changing Demands, Changing Directions*. Conference Proceedings of the ascilite Hobart 2011. Available online: <http://researchbank.acu.edu.au/cgi/viewcontent.cgi?article=2603&context=fea_pub> (accessed 18 January 2018)

Mann, S. and Walsh, S. (2017) *Reflective Practice in English Language Teaching*. Abingdon: Routledge.

Mayer, R. E. (2002) *Multimedia Learning*. Cambridge: Cambridge University Press.

Mayer, R. E. and Moreno, R. (2003) 'Nine Ways to Reduce Cognitive Load in Multimedia Learning'. *Educational Psychologist*, 38(1) 43–52.

Olesova, L. A., Richardson, J. C., Weasenforth, D. and Meloni, C. (2011) 'Asynchronous Instructional Audio Feedback in Online Environments: A Mixed Methods Study'. *Journal of Online Learning and Teaching*, 7(1) 30–42.

Palvio, A. (1986) *Mental Representations*. New York: Oxford University Press.

Roehl, A., Reddy, S. L. and Shannon, G. J. (2013) 'The Flipped Classroom: An Opportunity to Engage Millennial Students Through Active Learning Strategies'. *Journal of Family and Consumer Sciences*, 105(2) 44–49.

Séror, J. (2012) 'Show Me! Enhanced Feedback Through Screencasting Technology'. *TESL Canada Journal*, 30(1) 104–116.

Stannard, R. (2017) 'a genuine innovation in the delivery and form of feedback on student's written work', in Carrier, M., Damerow, R. M. and Bailey, K. M. (eds) *Digital Language Learning and Teaching: Research, Theory, and Practice*. New York: Routledge and TIRF: 179–187.

Stannard, R. (2018) 'Teacher Training Videos'. Available online: <www.teachertrainingvideos.com> (accessed 17 September 2018)

Stannard, R. and Mann S. (2018) 'Using screen capture feedback to establish social presence and increase student engagement: a genuine innovation in feedback', in Xiang, C. H. (ed.) *Cases on Audio-Visual Media in Language Education*. Hershey, PA: IGI Global: 93–117.

Sugar, W., Brown, A. and Luterbach, K. (2010) 'Examining the Anatomy of a Screencast: Uncovering Common Elements and Instructional Strategies'. *The International Review of Research in Open and Distributed Learning*, 11(3) 1–10.

TechSmith (n.d.). Available online: <www.techsmith.com/techsmith-relay.html> (accessed 9 October 2017).

Thompson, R. and Lee, J. L. (2012) 'Talking with Students Through Screencasting: Experimentations with Video Feedback to Improve Student Learning'. *The Journal of Interactive Technology and Pedagogy*. Available online: <https://jitp.commons.gc.cuny.edu/talking-with-students-through-screencasting-experimentations-with-video-feedback-to-improve-student-learning> (accessed 12 September 2018).

West, J. and Turner, W. (2016) 'Enhancing the Assessment Experience: Improving Student Perceptions, Engagement and Understanding Using Online Video Feedback'. *Innovations in Education and Teaching International*, 53(4) 400–410.

Wouters, P., Paas, F. and Van Merrienboer, J. G. (2008) 'How to Optimize Learning from Animated Models: A Review of Guidelines Based on Cognitive Load'. *Review of Educational Research*, 78(3) 645–675.

31

Towards 'professional vision'
Video as a resource in teacher learning

Julia Hüttner

Introduction

Over the last few decades, the use of video as a resource in teacher education has spread from being an innovation to becoming an increasingly established feature in both pre- and in-service teacher education (Brophy, 2004). Practitioner and research reports show that videos are used in educating teachers of all levels and subjects featured in education (Gaudin & Chaliés, 2015). The reason for this increased integration of video resources in teacher education lies in the specific affordances these offer. The most important of these are, first, the provision a lasting record of teaching practice, which can be viewed repeatedly and paused, so allowing for a selection of focus on the part of the student teachers and teacher educators, as well as a reduction of the demands of remembering a lesson observed or taught live. Second videos can be edited and collected, so that video libraries of teaching specific aspects can be created and made accessible. Finally, the use of videos allows for an observation of alternative practices, e.g. those in different contexts or following different curricula and/or frameworks, and so expands the range of pedagogical choices that (student) teachers are confronted with (Sherin, 2004). Additionally, the use of video resources can alleviate pressure on local schools in terms of visiting student teachers, and bypass any difficulties in accessing schools for lesson observation.

Despite many advantages, the creation and use of video resources for teacher education is not without its inherent difficulties. Curry (2012: 92) points out that the educationally positive fact of having a permanent record of a teaching event can 'heighten participants' sense of vulnerability in ways that [...] complicate the negotiation of relationships between researchers, subjects, and audience'. Additionally, the choices made during recording in terms of camera and microphone positioning, as well as later on during editing can restrict the viewers' observational options. Despite such drawbacks, video resources maintain a level of authenticity in reflecting the professional practice observed.

In line with Blomberg et al. (2011), I consider the use of videos in itself not a 'teacher education methodology' here, but see it as a relatively 'neutral' tool, which can be usefully linked to a variety of overarching models of language teacher education. Thus, the examples discussed in this chapter can be linked to aspects of competency-based or standards-based models of teacher education where, e.g. novice teachers aim to acquire the ability to perform certain aspects of language teaching or where established teachers aim to show conformity to required competencies to gain professional accreditation. Equally, and over recent years with increasing intensity, the use of video resources has been linked to reflective teacher education models, harnessing their potential to offer teachers a 'new' perspective on their own teaching and their own students' learning, a means to focus on specific educational cases or dilemmas, and finally, to reflect upon their individual growth and development. Given this variety of application, any positive effects on teacher learning from the use of video resources depends largely on their effective integration in an instructional framework rather than on any inherent qualities.

This proliferation of the practice of video use in teacher education, however, does not tally with an equally active research interest. In 2004, Sherin noted that:

> video has become a permanent fixture in teacher education. What is surprising, however, is that despite its extensiveness, the use of video in teacher education does not always reflect an understanding of precisely what it is about *video* that might provide support for teacher learning.
>
> *(ibid.: 10)*

The overviews of research into the use of video in teacher education by Gaudin and Chaliés (2015) and Marsh and Mitchell (2014) are clear evidence that the situation has since improved, and we can note that the potential of video resources to extend teacher learning has recently received increased attention in English language teacher education research (see, e.g. Eröz-Tuğa, 2013; Köhler, 2014; Kourieos, 2016; Mann, *forthc*; the VEO and SETTVEO projects). This is in contrast to the more established and vibrant research scene addressing video resources in teacher learning focusing on other subjects, especially science and mathematics (see e.g. Brophy, 2004; Calandra and Rich, 2015; as well as the body of work by Sherin and colleagues).

The present contribution aims at providing an overview of extant research on the use of video in English language teacher education and of research into the education of other subject teachers where there appears to be clear potential for transferability to ELT teachers. I will briefly discuss the main distinctions in types of video resources before then turning to the key findings and issues surrounding their use in language teacher education and their potential of enhancing specific teacher education practices. The final section will provide an outlook both in terms of potential new practices and new research endeavours.

Practicalities and types of video resources

As with the use of any technology-based innovation, the affordances and limitations of the actual technology affect their spread and use in practice. While teacher educators have integrated video since the 1960s (Brophy, 2004), recent technological advances have fostered an increased uptake and diversified use of video resources in teacher education. The tremendous developments in the ease with which classroom practices can be recorded and the videos edited, together with the quality of the final productions, are coupled with decreased costs. The management of teaching related videos in terms of storage, accessibility and sharing has equally improved. In addition to mainstream computer applications and web-based resources that are adapted to teacher education uses, there are now several dedicated programmes for educational uses of videos, such as VideoPaperMaker®, VAST (Video Analysis Support Tool, see van Es & Sherin, 2002) or the Observer Tool (Seidel et al., 2010). Most recently, the tool VEO (Video Enhanced Observation, see www.veo-group.com/) was launched, which is specifically aimed at facilitating recording and tagging on tablets. Most of these programmes allow teacher educators as well as students to easily select sequences that can be shared with either mentors or peers, and frequently allow for comments to be included in annotation panes alongside an integration of video clips in e-portfolios or hyperlinked papers.

Advances in technology have led to consistently rising levels of use of video resources in teacher education as well as to an increasing variability of formats of these resources. While there are no exact numbers or percentages for how many language teacher education courses have integrated the use of video resources, the surveys suggest that the average numbers of using videos as part of a course range from three times in a sample of 208 mostly US and Canadian teacher educators (Christ et al., 2017) to six times per course in a sample of 94 US teacher educators (Arya et al., 2016). These surveys also found a substantial variation in terms of individual video use in class, so that some teacher educators used several videos per session and others did not integrate video at all.

With regard to the second point, diversity, we find that video resources differ on four main production-related criteria. Two of these present as continua, namely, a) being edited and b) the quality of the recording. Criterion a) can affect the overall ratio of raw recording time to time on video and/or the selection of specific activities or other points of focus. The effects of editing in using video resources can be dramatic and make the 'difference between a piece of video that feels like a slice of life from the messy reality of classrooms to a slick performance that does not reflect the messiness of actual teaching' (Le Fevre, 2004: 238). Criterion b) covers both picture and sound quality, with the biggest variability found here in the quality of the recordings of student speech. The remaining criteria take an absent/present format and concern the free availability of the video resource and the availability of additional resources.

In addition to these production-related criteria distinguishing types of video resources, there are further important distinctions to be made in terms of the teaching practice being recorded. A key criterion here is whether the practice observed is the observer's own or that of another teacher. Both types of video are frequently used in language teacher education, with the first type, i.e. teacher-observer = teacher on video, most commonly found in reflective practice-based programmes for pre-service and, more rarely, in-service teachers, and the second type, i.e. teacher-observer ≠ teacher on video, either as part of group practices of viewing videos where all participants view each other's performances, or in competency-based teacher education programmes as items representing standard or ideal practices. Also, we can distinguish in terms of the time of the teaching event taking place vs. the time of viewing the video. Most of the video viewing activities take place in an asynchronous format, i.e. they are viewed after the teaching has taken place. There are, however, a number of projects that involve synchronous viewing via a link to a 'live' classroom (see e.g. Coyle, 2004; Marsh et al., 2010; Mitchell et al., 2010). While many of the affordances specific to using video, such as the 'luxury of time' (Rosaen et al., 2008, 349) in allowing for pausing, repeated viewing, rewinding, selection etc., an advantage suggested for synchronous use of video is to 'mitigate the "reality shock"' (Marsh & Mitchell, 2014) of teachers entering the practicum or, indeed, their first professional postings.

Linked to these are the final group of criteria according to which video resources can be classified which relates to the classroom practices represented. These can be roughly grouped into four categories, as shown in Figure 31.1.

These distinctions are to some extent abstractions, and in reality, there are overlaps and fuzzy boundaries; nevertheless, the potential of video use in teacher education partially depends on the affordances of the targeted type of classroom representation. The use of both ideal(ized) and innovative practice will be discussed below in connection with competency-based teacher

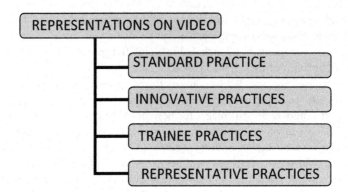

Figure 31.1 Types of classroom practices represented on video resources

education. All four types, especially trainee and representative practices, feature prominently as aids fostering teacher expertise, most notably so in reflective teacher education programmes.

Research overviews (Gaudin & Chaliés, 2015; Marsh & Mitchell, 2014), surveys of practice (Arya et al., 2016; Christ et al., 2017) and informal practice reports show that successful examples of teacher educators using the whole range of available videos, from unedited clips publicly available on platforms like Youtube to commercially produced, high quality and heavily edited videos. However, in light of the current variation in individual practices of integrating video resources, I concur with Arya et al. (2016) on a need to develop structures that foster an increased and more systematically varied use of video resources. The following section will provide an overview of the research findings from an integration of video resources in language teacher education programmes

Integrating video resources in language teacher education

Like many technological tools in education, video resources do not in themselves constitute a means of teacher education or development, but are a tool supporting and integrated into teacher education programmes. In this contribution, I suggest a broad distinction between the use of video resources in competency-based teacher education programmes, on the one hand, where videos might be used to exemplify a particular aspect of teaching, e.g. vocabulary. On the other hand, I will consider the use of video in teacher education programmes, that more generally aim at fostering greater expertise, such as Reflective Practice.

Video resources as part of competence-based teacher education

One of the frequent uses made of video resources in teacher education lies in their use as easy access points exemplifying specific, frequently isolated, aspects of language teaching. This can take place in the form of videos that – overtly or implicitly – suggest that the viewer should emulate the teaching presented on video in their own practices. Reasons for this vary, often the presumed viewer is a pre-service or novice teacher, but such use of videos has also been made when curricula or recommended teaching practice change.

One major use of videos in teacher education is as a means of presenting standard teaching practice, implicitly often assumed to be an ideal. This is the rationale underlying many commercially available teaching videos, such as the ones included in teacher training books (e.g.

Harmer, 2015; Thaler, 2012), produced by commercial language teacher training companies, such as the DVD series of the IH *International House London* or by national bodies like the *British Council*. A common feature of such resources is quite extensive editing, frequently cutting out or shortening any non-teacher-led activities, like group work. This predisposes the viewers towards a focus on the teacher and their actions. The resource creators explicitly brand these videos as showing examples of 'best practice' teaching, often focused on either quite general approaches or methods (e.g. Task-Based Language Teaching) or specific skills (e.g. listening), or uses of new technologies (e.g. interactive whiteboards). Bearing in mind the fact that all materials in teacher education can be used in a variety of ways and for diverse goals, we can stipulate that this specific representation implies two things; first, that teaching can be viewed as a set of competences which can be studied and acquired in isolation and, second, that student teachers should emulate these practices and learn through copying. A result, however, of the common editing is that the complexity of classrooms and the often eclectic practice of teachers in terms of methodology is removed from the viewer's sight, so that typically only the features in line with the focus of the video are maintained from a classroom. While time-efficient, the erasure of long periods of student activity downplays skills in classroom management, giving feedback and creating affordances of learning that might be enacted by the classroom teacher.

Despite these drawbacks, this use of video resources enjoys popularity especially in pre-service teacher education and on fast-track training courses. Overall, this particular representation of practice is used to provide a quick and accessible introduction of how to teach, very often by focusing on individual practices/elements. Despite the frequency of this use, it has not yet been given research attention. We might speculate, however, that the apparent slickness of the teaching portrayed might be a source of frustration for novice teachers encountering the messiness of real classrooms in their individual practices.

To some extent similar to the practice described above, video representing standard practices can be used in order to show examples of teaching adhering to specified curricular demands. This can be intended as a guide towards teachers, as in Strickland and Doty (1997), who show how teacher educators used videos to exemplify two expert teachers adhering to the guidelines from the National Council for the Teaching of Mathematics.

Showing standard practice on video is also linked to the assessment of teachers, both at pre- and in-service stages in their career. This can take the form of in-service teacher videos of own practice to accompany applications for diverse teaching qualifications. Examples of these are the US American *National Board for Professional Teaching Standards* (www.nbpts.org/national-board-certification/), which are available for English as a New Language (see www.nbpts.org/wp-content/uploads/ECYA-ENL.pdf) and for French and Spanish as foreign languages. Teachers are required to submit two 15-minute samples of their teaching plus accompanying commentaries to exemplify their adherence to the relevant standards. Brantlinger et al. (2011) show in their discussion of the preparations of these materials by a group of mathematics teachers that there does seem to be reflection on the part of the teachers in operationalizing these standards and applying them to their work. However, this reflection is subsumed under the overarching aim of showing themselves to be conforming to standard teaching practices in their classrooms. In a slightly different format, Wiens et al. (2013) show the use of a standardized video-based assessment of pre-service teachers' ability to identify effective teaching strategies in videos of other teachers' practice. Their initial findings suggest that their standardized tool VAIL (*Video Assessment of Interactions in Learning*) is reliable in measuring student teacher learning, although there is as yet limited evidence on the performance in this measurement to classroom behaviour. Admiraal et al. (2011) report on the use of a video portfolio in pre-service teacher assessment, where Dutch student teachers had to show their adherence to the national teacher standards, and the means to ensure reliability and validity of this assessment format. Their findings suggest clear benefits of using video recordings of student teachers' practice as they provide samples of behaviour necessary and so are more valid as performance-based assessment. This study also showed how the student teachers in their design of the portfolio were engaged in active reflection on their teaching and both Admiraal et al. (2011) and Wiens et al. (2013) make reference to 'video clubs' as a locus of reflections related to the production of these competency-oriented videos.

Sometimes, videos of as yet innovative practices are used in the context of a change in standard teaching practice, most frequently in relation to changes in the curriculum. Thus, videos may offer authentic examples of how to make (new) curricular requirements work in a classroom (Stickland & Doty, 1997).

Video resources as supporting teacher expertise

One of the targets long since identified in teacher education and development is a move towards greater expertise (Berliner, 1994). Research into teacher cognition (Borg, 2006) and teacher expertise (Tsui, 2003) shows that the specific knowledge and teaching processes applied by expert teachers are sophisticated, professionally specific and directly influential in the learning affordances provided by such teachers. What has also been noted is that expert teachers have a better developed 'professional vision' (Goodwin, 1994; Wipperfürth, 2015). Reflective practice (e.g., Mann & Walsh, 2017) has been accorded a pivotal role in fostering teacher expertise and there is a clear link between the ability to notice and analyse observed practice and the ability to reflect upon practice and integrate such reflections with theory. An aim of reflective practice is ultimately to improve teaching practice so that learners have a more fruitful educational experience. The concepts of teacher expertise, noticing, reflection, reflective practice and teacher development are distinct, but share certain underlying assumptions. In the study of video resources in teacher education, some studies have looked at several of these factors together while others have separated them. In the following, noticing, reflection, and teacher development will be addressed individually, while acknowledging that there are areas of overlap and fuzzy boundaries between these concepts. These teacher educational targets often make use of videos of representative practice in the context of teacher development and of trainee practices in the context of pre-service teacher education. It is important to note, however, that this constitutes tendencies rather than solid links between types of video and teacher educational frameworks.

A large body of work engaging with video-based teacher education has addressed the importance of teacher noticing, i.e. teachers' ability to select from the plethora of data surrounding them in the complexity of a classroom those elements they wish or need to attend to. The use of video data allows teachers to take time to review, reflect and re-direct their attention being freed from the need to react immediately. Sustained research activity in the field of mathematics teaching by Sherin, van Es and colleagues has addressed teacher noticing by linking it explicitly to the concept of teachers' professional vision (Sherin, 2007), i.e. 'the ability to notice and interpret significant features of classroom interactions' (van Es & Sherin, 2008). Two processes, *selective attention* and *knowledge-based reasoning*, are seen as constituents of this ability (Sherin & Russ, 2015), which Sherin (2001) views as generic to teachers, differentiated by levels of expertise. Blomberg et al. (2011), however, established effects of the subject-specific prior knowledge that student teachers had; unexpectedly, a comparison of the professional vision of student teachers from mathematics/science and social sciences/humanities subject clusters in their engagement with classroom videos of a range of subjects found that the latter group outperformed the mathematics/science group. This led the researchers to suggest that specific teaching subjects foster in their pre-service teachers shared, but distinct, ways of reasoning (Blomberg et al., 2011: 1139). This background knowledge and experience thus create 'lenses' through which teaching performances are viewed, specific aspects noticed and interpreted. Stürmer et al.'s (2013) research investigated the effect of teacher education courses at university on pre-service teachers' professional vision. Their findings show professional vision to be a heavily knowledge-guided process and conclude that, even without an element of active teaching, the engagement with teaching practice through a contextual video approach significantly supported student teachers' development of professional vision.

Linked to this development of professional vision is the use of video resources as facilitating reflection-based teacher development. Many current teacher education models embrace reflective practice (Mann & Walsh, 2017), which engages teachers in 'active, persistent and careful consideration of any belief or supposed form of knowledge' (Dewey, 1933: 118). Such educational programmes aim to lead teachers to extend their expertise through reflecting on their contexts, resources and actions, and raise awareness of the complexity of decision making in planning and in the classroom (Richards & Farrell, 2005). Engaging in such reflection should make 'the difference between the expert teacher, who actively seeks to become a better teacher, and the teacher who is merely more experienced than the novice teacher' (Burton, 2009: 299). Within reflective teacher education, the use of video resources has added a tool and enhanced practices by exposing teachers to varied and repeated opportunities of selecting and viewing an instance of classroom practice. This supports and expands the repertoire of artefacts and structures provided for (student) teachers to aid their reflective teacher learning, such as the use of diaries or portfolios, including the *European Portfolio for Student Teacher Learning* and, importantly, provides one of the few ways of not relying on written reflections (Mann & Walsh, 2013, 2017; Walsh & Mann, 2015).

As the ability to reflect in pre-service teachers has been linked to their future abilities to teach effectively, a number of research studies have focused on developing their reflective skills (Blomberg et al., 2014; Hiebert et al., 2007; van Es & Sherin, 2002). In outlining the differences between novice and expert reflections, Blomberg et al. (2014) summarise that novice reflections frequently are overly judgmental and focus on descriptions, rather than abstractions and interpretations which integrate prior knowledge. Such practices, conversely, are found in expert teachers, who also have a greater ability to differentiate according to levels of importance and to create both systematic and inter-connected layers of reflection, which make use of a whole range of approaches and types of reflection. These differences have been synthesized into a conceptualization of reflection as happening on three levels, i.e. 1) *description* of events 2) *evaluation* with regard to potential effects on students learning, and 3) *integration* of observed or experienced events with professional knowledge, leading to inferences on past and future action (see Blomberg et al., 2014; van Es & Sherin, 2002).

The largest body of research addressing the use of video resources in reflective practice is concerned with the education of future mathematics and science teachers (see, especially, Sherin and colleagues), but as there is clear transferability of some of the findings to language teacher education, the main points will be reported on here. Thus, mathematics teacher education has shown that pre-service teachers' reflections become more sophisticated in programmes employing video resources, leading them to move from descriptions towards analysis of classroom events and to a greater focus on specific aspects rather than an overly general response (Harford et al., 2010; Stockero, 2008; Star & Strickland, 2008; Sydnor, 2016). However, research within this discipline also shows the need for providing pre-service teachers with specific guidance in their use of video resources for such a positive effect to take place (Borko et al., 2008; Santagata & Guarino, 2011; Star & Strickland, 2008)

In terms of English language teacher education, research has addressed the issues faced by teachers preparing for an English as an Additional Language (EAL) context, especially in the US. In a multi-disciplinary study, Trip and Rich (2012) in their overview of the effects of the use of video in pre-service teacher reflections concluded that:

> using video to reflect was beneficial for helping teachers to evaluate their teaching. After using video to reflect, teachers were able to: (a) identify gaps between their beliefs about good teaching and their actual teaching practices, (b) articulate their tacit assumptions and purposes about teaching and learning, (c) notice things about their teaching that they did not remember, (d) focus their reflections on multiple aspects of classroom teaching, and (e) assess the strengths and weaknesses of their teaching.
>
> *(ibid.: 279)*

Their study included teachers of English Language Learners (i.e. EAL in the UK), and focuses on how the use of video triggered change in pre-service teachers' actions. The study involved students being video-recorded during their teaching practice and discussing their own and others' videos in a guided peer-group reflection. Students were able to annotate their video to highlight specific instances for discussion. The findings suggest that student teachers benefited from noticing areas for improvement by themselves rather than having to rely on their mentors' feedback solely and from the group input, and the resultant accountability to peers and them-selves, with regard to specific aspects that they wanted to develop. The two teachers summarized this in the following quotations (Tripp & Rich, 2012: 733).

> Without video I might have just gone the whole semester not really focused on anything specific and just kind of taught and tried to get better at teaching in general, but not really able to change anything specific.
>
> It gives you an opportunity to change specific things that you want to change, and it's not something that a mentor is telling you to change or something that a teacher is telling you to change, but it is something that you are really looking at in your own teaching and finding that you want to change.

Estapa et al. (2016) in their study of EAL teachers involved two novice teachers in the record-ing and analysis of their own teaching practice. The filming was conducted with both a fixed camera in the classroom as well as with head-mounted cameras on individual EAL children; the researcher conducted debriefing sessions with the teachers over a period of two years. The research focus lay on an analysis of the participants' practices of noticing as a vital step within reflection. Findings suggest a trajectory from the first step of noticing individual learners and describing their behaviour, towards making connections between specific behaviours and presumed reason-ing processes in the learners, and finally a move towards a clearer evaluation and interpretation of their own participants with a view towards improving their students' learning. One teacher linked a student's behaviour to his presumed internal reasoning processes, in this case relating to an arithmetic problem, leading her to observe the need for a change in her own teaching prac-tice to support EAL learners. Thus, the student teacher's comment '[b]ecause it was a three-digit subtraction, but I was glad that he asked for the blocks and sometimes you know he asks for the blocks and I know that I should work with them with the blocks more' (ibid.) offers both an explanation of behaviour and plan for adapting teaching practice. One example of a com-ment of the student teachers in the first year of the study was her saying 'I don't like it when she sits over there, she doesn't pay attention' (Estapa et al., 2016: 98), where we can note that an individual student is being focused on, but the reflection focuses on a description of the learner's behaviour. Later in the project, student teachers expanded their noticing patterns to explicitly comment on what they think the internal processes in the learners are vis-a-vis the behaviour observed and how their observations affect their planning for future teaching. The use of video resources to trigger reflections is linked to using video-stimulated-recall, both for purposes of research and for teacher development (see, e.g., Endacott, 2016; Wipperfürth, 2015), which can be used by a teacher educator to specifically guide student teachers towards particular sequences in teaching and so fostering, first, the noticing of specific actions and then, ideally, a reflection on these.

With regard to the scarce research addressing pre-service ELT teachers directly, Baecher (2011), Eröz-Tuğa (2013), Köhler (2014) and Kourieos (2016) focus on the effects of video-based reflections. Baecher (2011) and Eröz-Tuğa's (2013) student teachers were recorded during their practicum experiences at local schools and Kourieos (2016) recorded her students' micro-teaching sessions with peers. Köhler (2014) used trainee recordings during a practicum as bases for reflection, focusing largely on the use of non-verbal elements in language teaching. Various means of fostering reflection were used in these studies, including self-evaluation forms, the video recordings themselves, recorded reflections as data, both individually and as group discussions led by the teacher educator, written reflections and questions/letters to peers. Eröz-Tuğa's pre-service teachers only reflected on their own practice, whereas in the other studies both own and other practices were focused on. The findings from these studies show that the quality of students' reflections increased over time with the use of video recordings (see also Kuter et al., 2012; Lazarus & Olivero, 2009), and Kourieos additionally established an effect on the scaffolding provided by the teacher educator on the student teachers' analyses of teaching and reflective practice.

In terms of more ELT specific aspects, one issue Kourieos addresses are student teachers' attempts at applying a communicative approach to teaching grammar. Students' reflections highlight the gap between the competence they felt they had in designing such a lesson and their disappointment on viewing their teaching during video playback, commenting that 'at the time we felt we fully understand what that [i.e. teaching grammar communicatively] entailed', but 'we ended up using a more traditional approach which proved to be quite boring and unsuccessful' (ibid.: 74). Video-based reflections on these micro-teaching sessions enabled student teachers to shift their focus towards their peers, acting as learners, and also to engage more deeply with the effect of their own experiences or 'apprenticeship of observation' (Lortie, 1975), vis-à-vis their pedagogic knowledge, on their teaching practices.

While these issues of integrating methodological theories with practice are quite generalizable to a number of subjects, one topic of specific relevance to English language teachers arising in these reflections was classroom language, addressed by Kourieos, Köhler and Eröz-Tuğa. As English is the L2 of all the student teachers involved, one issue that arose was an increased awareness of their own performed language proficiency. Eröz-Tuğa's participant *Esra* commented on her difficulties in using English in general while another, *Meltem*, noted that her spontaneous language use was unsuccessful affecting her standing with the learners. Nine of Kourieos' 11 participants lowered their self-evaluation of their language proficiency after viewing themselves on video and, like *Meltem*, noted that the need to speak a foreign language spontaneously and under stressful circumstances affected their proficiency. Importantly, the student teachers also managed to turn their focus towards the effect this had on their learners, especially in terms of causing difficulties due to unclear instructions. Two student teachers explicitly mentioned that they had underestimated their need to prepare their actual language use, particularly in the context of giving instructions, despite having paid a lot of attention to their lesson planning in general. As one of them commented 'I am not particularly competent in English but I thought that introducing simple activities wouldn't be a problem. I was so wrong!' (Kourieos, 2016: 72)

In line with video-based reflections generally fostering an increased awareness of the learners' reactions, an additional aspect that featured in discussion was the appropriacy of the language used by the student teachers with regard to the level of the imagined learners. Thus, a highly proficient student teacher was criticized for his language use as 'both the vocabulary and tenses would be too advanced for [the envisaged learners] to understand' (Kourieos, 2016: 72). Similar comments were made regarding another student teacher, whose recasts were considered potentially unhelpful due to their advanced level; viz. 'the examples and alternative words he gave were quite hard even for most of us to understand … this wouldn't really work with young learners who are likely to become even more frustrated' (ibid.) This research on the effect of video-use in pre-service students is complemented by work addressing the supervisors' or mentor teachers' perspective. Within ELTE, Baecher et al. (2014) provide an overview of the practices of supervisors in the post-observation conference of integrating video to achieve intersubjectivity. This process involves aligning the perspectives of the video observed and so highlights some of the difficulties in successfully observing videos. Although experienced as a source of frustration by the supervisors, the fact that student teachers' observations and reflections are scaffolded seems to foster the development of their professional vision. Clearly, this study, like Orland-Barak and Rachamim (2009), suggests the need for providing guidance and training also to mentors and supervisors to ensure an optimal use of video resources.

In the context of in-service teacher education, one means of incorporating video that has received research attention is the 'video club', where teachers regularly meet to discuss videos of their own teaching in a group (Sherin, 2004; Sherin & van Es, 2009; Sherin & Russ, 2015). The majority of studies reported on above have used collaboration (either in a peer-group or with a mentor/supervisor) in the reflections related to the video observation.

Bringing it all together and looking to the future

In this section, I will show how some of the points raised in research discussed above come together if we consider a brief example of a reflective interaction of student teachers on a video-recorded lesson and then will conclude with a brief look at possible future research.

The data sample is taken from my ongoing work on integrating video in teacher education. Within a framework of reflective practice, I make use of the free online VELTE resource (www.southampton.ac.uk/velte) which features full-length recordings of English language lessons, accompanied by a reflective commentary of the teachers featured. Over the course of a year-long MA programme in English Language Teaching, students view these videos and engage with them in both individual and collaborative reflective tasks.

The following extract is taken from a discussion by three MA students with prior teaching experience after viewing a lesson taught for upper intermediate learners, focusing on the topic of fear.

> **S6:** one thing that I noticed that happened at different moments in the classroom it was that the teacher was trying to link the content (in hand) to the students' personal lives (.) even the […] activities they carried out was mostly about their lives and minute 13 he asks them 'is there anything you are afraid (of) if so why' and he asks 'do you know anybody who has phobia' it happened again in the minutes of 45 he said 'do you like to be hypnotized by this man' I think one good way to learn vocabulary and for students to remember then it's (linking) them to […]

S4: I noticed that when he [..] offered the story about the cable car [...] the students were fascinated to listen to that and really wanted to know, but they weren't so eager to divulge their own their own stories [...]

S3: don't you think that because he didn't allow extended enough extended time for example when he asked about the if one of them has a situation when he felt afraid or [...] so I think the time wasn't very wasn't enough for them to answer because maybe they feel shy because it's about phobia and about real life so, and then he moved to the imagination so imagine that blah blah blah so yeah I think it wasn't enough time for them

We can see here, I would argue, that the professional vision of the students is evident in that both S6 and S4 explicitly mention what they noticed and how they interpret it. It is worth pointing out that the affordances of using videos become quite apparent in S6 mentioning the exact time and formulation of instances of teacher talk that he is referring to (lines 6–9). The means for students to collaboratively reflect on the same instance of teaching allows for them to add further detail to the observation, as in highlighting student reluctance to answer the question (lines 15–17) and to offer alternative interpretations of the same event. Thus, S6 offers a positive evaluation of the teacher's behaviour of asking the students questions about their experience and interprets this as an instance of personalizing teaching, successful in terms of the lesson aims of expanding the learners' vocabulary knowledge in the semantic field of 'fear'. However, both S4 and S3 expand on that by offering a more critical view in terms of, on the one hand, referring to appropriate wait time and whether enough time was allowed for the students to answer this question and, on the other hand, whether it was at all an appropriate question to ask. Although this is only a very short extract, I believe it offers support to the affordance of using video in reflective tasks for improving the attention to and noticing of details of the observed lesson, the benefits of jointly developing foci of attention and, finally, of activating prior methodological knowledge.

To summarise this chapter, we find that, certainly in comparison with the work done in mathematics and science education, there is a strong mismatch in ELTE in the prevalence of the use of video resources in teacher education and research on its effects. I would suggest, however, that in addition to generic issues in teacher education, e.g. the improvement of professional vision or the increased depth of reflections, there are elements specific to ELT classrooms, where video resources are beneficial. An example of this are the studies by Kourieos and Eröz-Tuğa which show that classroom language in English as a foreign language is best understood in its detail with the aid of videos, which can then benefit teachers' development. This does tie in synergistically with previous work on the study of classroom language as a trigger for reflective practice in SETT (*Self-Evaluation of Teacher Talk*, see Walsh, 2006).

A final remark to make on the current state of video resources in ELTE is that there is a surprising dearth of structured integration of video in teacher education programmes. This constitutes a major drawback in my view, seeing that the research reviewed in this chapter shows unambiguously that video resources are only as effective as the overall programme into which they are integrated. On an optimistic note, there are very positive inroads in this area, and so Blomberg et al. (2013) outline principles for video use in pre-service teacher education, and Masats and Dooly (2011) as well as Admiraal et al. (2011) report on programmes and assessment of teacher education, which systematically integrate video resources.

Further reading

Baecher, L. and Connor, D. (eds) (2016) 'Video as a Tool in Teacher Learning'. *The New Educator* [Special Issue], 12(1).

Blomberg, G., Renkl, A., Sherin, M. G., Borko, H. and Seidel, T. (2013) 'Five Research-Based Heuristics for Using Video in Pre-Service Teacher Education'. *Journal for Educational Research Online*, 5(1) 90–114.

Calandra, B. and Rich, P. J. (eds) (2015) *Video for Teacher Education.* Abingdon: Routledge.

Gaudin, C. and Chaliés, S. (2015) 'Video Viewing in Teacher Education and Professional Development: A Literature Review'. *Education Research Review*, 16 41–67.

Marsh, B. and Mitchell, N. (2014) 'The Role of Video in Teacher Professional Development'. *Teacher Development: An International Journal of Teachers' Professional Development*, 18 403–417.

Suggested websites

IRIS Connect <www.irisconnect.com>
VELTE (Video Resources for English Language Teacher Education) <www.southampton.ac.uk/velte>
VEO (Video Enhanced Observation) <www.veo-group.com>
ViLTE (Video in Language Teacher Education) Project <https://warwick.ac.uk/fac/soc/al/research/vilte>

References

Admiraal, W., Hoeksma, M., van de Kamp, M. and van Duin, G. (2011) 'Assessment of Teacher Competence Using Video Portfolios: Reliability, Construct Validity, and Consequential Validity'. *Teaching and Teacher Education*, 27 1019–1028.

Arya, P., Christ, T. and Chiu, M.M. (2016) 'Video Use in Teacher Education: A Survey of Teacher-Educators' Practices Across Disciplines'. *Journal of Computing in Higher Education*, 28 261–300.

Baecher, L. (2011) 'Collaborative Video Inquiry in MA TESOL Coursework: Working Together to Improve Ourselves'. *ELTED*, 14 1–7.

Baecher, L, McCormack, B. and Kung, S. (2014) 'Supervisor Use of Video as a Tool in Teacher Reflection. *TESL-EJ*, 18(3) 1–17.

Berliner, D. C. (1994) 'Expertise: The wonder of exemplary performances', in Mangier, J. M. and Block, C. C. (eds) *Creating Powerful Thinking in Teachers and Students: Diverse Perspectives.* Fort Worth, TX: Holt, Reinhart & Winston: 161–186.

Blomberg, G., Stürmer, K. and Seidel, T. (2011) 'How Pre-Service Teacher Observe Teaching on Video: Effects of Viewers' Teaching Subjects and the Subject of the Video'. *Teaching and Teacher Education*, 27 1131–1140.

Blomberg, G., Renkl, A., Sherin, M. G., Borko, H. and Seidel, T. (2013) 'Five Research-Based Heuristics for Using Video in Pre-Service Teacher Education'. *Journal for Educational Research Online*, 5(1) 90–114.

Blomberg, G., Sherin, M.G., Renkl, A., Glogger, I. and Seidel, T. (2014) 'Understanding Video as a Tool for Teacher Education: Investigating Instructional Strategies to Promote Reflection'. *Instructional Science*, 42 443–463.

Borg, S. (2003) 'Teacher Cognition in Language Teaching: A Review of Research on what Language Teachers Think, Know, Believe, and Do'. *Language Teaching*, 36 81–109.

Borg, S. (2006) *Teacher Cognition and Language Education: Research and Practice.* London: Continuum.

Borko, H., Jacobs, J., Eiteljorg, E. and Pittmann, M. E. (2008) 'Video as a Tool for Fostering Productive Discussions in Mathematics Professional Development'. *Teaching and Teacher Education*, 24 417–436.

Brantlinger, A., Sherin, M. G. and Linsenmeier, K. A. (2011) 'Discussing Discussion: A Video Club in the Service of Math Teachers' National Board Preparation'. *Teachers and Teaching*, 17 5–33.

Brophy, J. (ed.) (2004) *Using Video in Teacher Education.* Bingley: Emerald.

Burton, J. (2009) 'Reflective practice', in Burns, A. and Richards, J. C. (eds) *The Cambridge Guide to Second Language Teacher Education*. Cambridge: Cambridge University Press: 298–308.

Calandra, B. and Rich, P. J. (eds) (2015) *Digital Video for Teacher Education*. Abingdon: Routledge.

Christ, T., Arya, P. and Chiu, M. M. (2017) 'Video Use in Teacher Education: An International Survey of Practices'. *Teaching and Teacher Education*, 63 22–35.

Coyle, D. (2004) 'Redefining Classroom Boundaries: Learning to Teach Using New Technologies'. *Canadian Journal of Educational Administration and Policy*, 32 45–67.

Curry, M. W. (2012) 'In Pursuit of Reciprocity: Researchers, Teacher and School Reformers Engaged in Collaborative Analysis of Video Records'. *Theory into Practice*, 52 91–98.

Endacott, J. L. (2016) 'Using Video-Stimulated Recall to Enhance Preservice-Teacher Reflection'. *The New Educator*, 12 28–47.

Eröz-Tuğa, B. (2013) 'Reflective Feedback Sessions Using Video Recordings'. *ELT Journal*, 67 175–183.

Estapa, A., Pinnow, R. J. and Chval, K. B. (2016) 'Video as a Professional Development Tool to Support Novice Teachers as they Learn to Teach English Language Learners'. *The New Educator*, 12 85–104.

Gaudin, C. and Chaliés, S. (2015) 'Video Viewing in Teacher Education and Professional Development: A Literature Review'. *Education Research Review*, 16 41–67.

Goeze, A., Zottmann, J. M., Vogel, F., Fischer, F. and Schrader, J. (2014) 'Getting Immersed in Teacher and Student Perspectives? Facilitating Analytical Competence Using Video Cases in Teacher Education'. *Instructional Science*, 42 91–114.

Goodwin, C. (1994) 'Professional Vision'. *American Anthropologist*, 96 606–633.

Harmer, J. (2015) *The Practice of Teaching English*, 5th edition. London: Pearson.

Harford, J., MacRuairc, G. and McCartan, D. (2010) '"Lights, Camera, Reflection": Using Peer Video to Promote Reflective Dialogue Among Student Teachers'. *Teacher Development*, 14 57–68.

Hiebert, J., Morris, A. K, Berk, D. and Jansen, A. (2007) 'Preparing Teachers to Learn from Teaching'. *Journal of Teacher Education*, 58 47–61.

Köhler A. (2014) 'Reflektierte strukturierte Videoanalyse als Mittel institutioneller Professionalisierung angehender Fremdsprachenlehrender: Fokus auf nonverbale Elemente', in Moritz, C. (ed.) *Transkription von Video- und Filmdaten in der Qualitativen Sozialforschung*. Wiesbaden: Springer VS: 523–543.

Kourieos, S. (2016) 'Video-Mediated Microteaching – A Stimulus for Reflection and Teacher Growth'. *Australian Journal of Teacher Education*, 41 65–80.

Kuter, S., Gazi. Z. and Aksal, F. A. (2012) 'Examination of Co-Construction of Knowledge in Videotaped Simulated Instruction'. *Journal of Educational Technology & Society*, 15 174–184.

Lazarus, E. & Olivero, F. (2009) 'Videopapers as a Tool for Reflection on Practice in Initial Teacher Education'. *Technology, Pedagogy and Education*, 18(3) 255–267.

Le Fevre, D. M. (2004) 'Designing for teacher learning', in Brophy, J. (ed.) *Using Video in Teacher Education*. Bingley: Emerald: 235–258.

Lortie, D. (1975) *Schoolteacher: A Sociological Study*. London: The University of Chicago Press.

Mann, S. (forthcoming) *Videos in Language Teacher Education (ViLTE)*. London: British Council.

Mann, S. and Walsh, S. (2013) 'RP or "RIP": A Critical Perspective on Reflective Practice'. *Applied Linguistics Review*, 4(2) 291–315.

Mann, S. and Walsh, S. (2017) *Reflective Practice in English Language Teaching: Research-based Principles and Practices*. Abingdon: Routledge.

Marsh, B and Mitchell, N. (2014) 'The Role of Video in Teacher Professional Development'. *Teacher Development: An International Journal of Teachers' Professional Development*, 18 403–417.

Marsh, B., Mitchell, N. and Adamczyk, P. (2010) 'Interactive Video Technology: Enhancing Professional Learning in Initial Teacher Education'. *Computers & Education*, 54(3) 742–748.

Masats, D. and Dooly, M. (2011) 'Rethinking The Use of Video in Teacher Education: A Holistic Approach'. *Teaching and Teacher Education*, 27(7) 1151–1162.

Mitchell, N., Marsh, B., Hobson, A. J. and Sorensen, P. (2010) '"Bringing Theory to Life": Findings from an Evaluation of the Use of Interactive Video Within an Initial Teacher Preparation Programme'. *Teacher Development*, 14(1) 15–27.

Orland-Barak, L. and Rachamim, M. (2009) 'Simultaneous Reflection by video in a Second-Order Action Research-Mentoring Model: Lessons for the Mentor and the Mentee'. *Reflective Practice*, 10 601–613.

Rosaen, C. L., Lundeberg, M., Cooper, M., Fritzen A. and Terpstra, M. (2008) 'Noticing Noticing: How Does Investigation of Video Records Change How Teachers Reflect on Their Experiences'. *Journal of Teacher Education*, 59 347–360.

Santagata, R. and Guarino, J. (2011) 'Using Video to Teach Future Teachers to Learn from Teaching'. *ZDM The International Journal of Mathematics Education*, 43 133–145.

Seidel, T., Blomberg, G. and Renkl, A. (2013) 'Instructional Strategies for Using Video in Teacher Education'. *Teaching and Teacher Education*, 34 56–65.

Seidel, T., Prenzel, M. and Kobard, M. (eds) (2005) *How to Run a Video Study: Technical Report of the IPN Video Study*. Münster: Waxmann.

Seidel, T., Stürmer, K., Blomberg, G. and Schwindt, K. (2010). *Observer: Videobasiertes Tool zur Diagnose Pädagogisch-psychologischer Kompetenzen bei Lehrpersonen*. Munich: School of Education, Technische Universität München.

Seidel, T., Stürmer, K., Blomberg, G., Kobarg, M. and Schwindt, K. (2011) 'Teacher Learning from Analysis of Videotaped Classroom Situations: Does it Make a Difference Whether Teachers Observe their Own Teaching or That of Others?'. *Teaching and Teacher Education*, 27 259–267.

Sherin, M. G. (2004) 'New perspectives on the role of video in teacher education', in Brophy, J. (ed.) *Using Video in Teacher Education*. Bingley: Emerald: 1–28.

Sherin, M. G. and Han, S.Y. (2004) 'Teacher Learning in the Context of a Video Club'. *Teaching and Teacher Education*, 20: 163–183.

Sherin, M. G. (2001) 'Developing a professional vision of classroom events', in Wood, T., Nelson, B. S. and Warfield, J. (eds) *Beyond Classical Pedagogy: Teaching Elementary School Mathematics*. Hillsdale, NJ: Lawrence Erlbaum: 75–93.

Sherin, M. G. (2007) 'The development of teachers' professional vision in video clubs', in Goldman, R., Pea, R., Barron, B. and Derry, S. (eds) *Video Research in the Learning Sciences*. Hillsdale, NJ: Lawrence Erlbaum: 383–395.

Sherin, M. G. and Russ, R. S. (2015) 'Teacher noticing via video', in Calandra, B. and Rich, P. J. (eds) *Video for Teacher Education*. Abingdon: Routledge: 3–20.

Star, J. R. and Strickland, S. K. (2008) 'Learning to Observe: Using Video to Improve Preservice Mathematics Teachers' Ability to Notice'. *Journal of Mathematics Teacher Education*, 11 107–125.

Stockero, S. L. (2008) 'Using a Video-Based Curriculum to Develop a Reflective Stance in Prospective Mathematics Teachers'. *Journal of Mathematics Teacher Education*, 11 373.

Strickland, J. F. and Doty, K. (1997). 'Use of Videotapes of Exemplary Mathematics Teaching for Teacher Preparation'. *Education*, 118(2) 259.

Stürmer, K., Könings, K. D. and Seidel, T. (2013) 'Declarative Knowledge and Professional Vision in Teacher Education: Effect on Courses in Teaching and Learning'. *British Journal of Educational Psychology*, 83 467–483.

Sydnor, J. (2016) 'Using Video to Enhance Reflective Practice'. *The New Educator*, 12 67–84.

Thaler, E. (2012) *Englisch unterrichten: Grundlagen, Kompetenzen, Methoden*. Berlin: Cornelsen.

Tsui, A. M. B (2003) *Understanding Expertise in Teaching*. Cambridge: Cambridge University Press.

Trip, T. R. and Rich, P. J. (2012) 'The Influence of Video Analysis on the Process of Teacher Change'. *Teaching and Teacher Education*, 28 728–739.

Van Es, E. and Sherin, M. G. (2002) 'Learning to Notice: Scaffolding New Teachers' Interpretations of Classroom Interactions'. *Journal of Technology and Teacher Education*, 10 571–596.

Van Es, E. and Sherin, M. G. (2008) Mathematics' Teachers Learning to Notice in the Context of a Video Club'. *Teaching and Teacher Education*, 24 244–276.

VEO Project. Available online: <https://veoeuropa.com> (accessed 24 May, 2019).

Walsh, S. (2006) *Investigating Classroom Discourse*. Abingdon: Routledge.

Walsh, S. and Mann, S. (2015) 'Doing Reflective Practice: A Data-Led Way Forward'. *ELT Journal*, 69 351–362

Wiens, P. D., Hessberg, K., LoCasale-Crouch, J. and De Coster, J. (2013) 'Using a Standardised Video-Based Assessment in a University Teacher Education Program to Examine Preservice Teachers Knowledge Related to Effective Teaching'. *Teaching and Teacher Education*, 33 24–33.

Wipperfürth, M. (2015) *Professional Vision in Lehrernetzwerken: Berufssprache als ein Weg und ein Ziel von Lehrerprofessionalisierung*. Münster: Waxmann Verlag.

32

Implementing ePortfolios in teacher education

Research, issues and strategies

Nusrat Gulzar and Helen C. Barrett

Introduction

With continuous innovations in technology, ePortfolios, as a means of digitally documenting and supporting collaborative learning, have gained prominence in both higher education and employment sectors (Hartnell-Young, 2007; Pengrum and Oakley, 2017). The emergence and development of ePortfolios has provided researchers and practitioners with the scope to explore their potential impact, uses and implementation in the field of teacher education as well. ePortfolios have the potential to bring considerable changes in key aspects of teacher education, including planning goals, self-development and representation, demonstration of transferable skills, continuous professional growth and successful employment (Cambridge, 2008). The success of ePortfolio use also depends on teachers and trainees' readiness, learning approach, ways to exploit the key features of the tool and the ability to document their impact on student-teacher development. Progress, therefore, should not be evaluated only in terms of end product, but the core skills involved in the development process e.g. 'collaboration', 'dialogues', 'reflection', 'self-evaluation' and 'continuous support' (Bhattacharya and Hartnett, 2007).

The first section of this chapter discusses current literature on ePortfolios in teacher education. The next section highlights the key affordances and challenges associated with ePortfolio use and initiation followed by an evaluation of the common uses and issues related to ePortfolios with reference to the views of teacher educators and graduates. The chapter concludes with the 'why' and 'how' of ePortfolio development and implementation, suggestions for planning, strategies for reflection, followed by some guidance for introducing ePortfolios using an open source platform like WordPress or Blogger.

Literature review

Chaudhuri and Cabau (2017: 4) define ePortfolios as 'a purposeful collection of student work that exhibits students' efforts, progress and achievements in one or more areas. Lorenzo and Ittelson (2005: 2) consider ePortfolios as a 'digitized' and illustrative collection of students' work that include audio, 'text-based graphics', video screencasts stored online and many more. The main elements in constructing portfolios are selecting, showcasing work and carrying out reflection

(Heinrich et al., 2007). In other words, ePortfolios function both as a reflective record and chronological archives of student evidence (van der Schaaf et al., 2016), which is both 'owned and operated' by learners themselves (Stefani et al., 2007: 41).

ePortfolios are considered 'a leading element' in a 'tectonic shift' in education providing a link for individual and community learning (Yancey, 2008 in Clark and Eynon, 2009). This strong claim comes after a decade of the widespread use of this digital tool in higher education and beyond. However, the methodologies involved in portfolio development have undergone some changes over time to meet the requirements of curricula and particular institutions. One key development is the growth of online interactive tools such as Wikis, blogs and other common web 2.0 applications (Heinrich et al., 2007; Woodward and Nanlohy, 2004). Boulton (2014) and Mason et al. (2004) recognize this gradual yet persistent shift from static paper folders to online interactive archives. They highlight the key characteristics of ePortfolios including their function as an artefact for representing trainee teachers' work. Digital showcasing of student artefacts has become a common means of observing student-teacher's growth (Wray, 2007) in recent decades, including for 'developmental', 'presentation' and 'assessment' (Mason et al., 2004: 717) purposes. The key aim of ePortfolio use is therefore, to help student-teachers grow as capable individuals with professional skills such as reflective practice, technical competence and strategies for lifelong learning.

The basic stages involved in ePortfolio development are interdependent; the phases of 'filing, learning, assessment and employment' provide a framework for student portfolio works in terms of organization, description and representation (Baume, 2003: 9). Composing and customizing ePortfolios requires learners to fully engage themselves in the tasks and the overall construction process and continue reflecting on information they share within the online space (Butler 2006 in van der Schaaf et al., 2016). To facilitate learners in learning to reflect, Moon (2013) highlights a few conditions, including time and space, strategies for guiding reflection, and most importantly, an emotionally conducive environment. Likewise, Lieberman and Miller (1984) argue for a collaborative environment wherein student-teachers will be flexible enough to exchange opinions on teaching issues. They term the exchanges 'authentic dialogues' (in Dzay-Chulim and Mann, 2017: 132).

The interactive tasks designed for ePortfolio-based learning generally require identification of gaps in learning, critical awareness regarding teaching practice and synthesis of the past records (Heinrich et al., 2007). Kurtoglu-Hooton (2013: 22) considers that providing the 'spark' or 'stimulus' through designed tasks can be a way to challenge student-thinking and foster reflection. She elaborates on the key functions of the online environment created on PebblePad (i.e. blogging as a 'supportive' platform for her trainees to negotiate their meaning-making process). As the approach is primarily student-led, the goal is not limited to building repositories of well-refined works but to developing core competencies such as self-regulative and reflective skills, leading to efficiency (Abrami et al., 2008; Boulton, 2014).

Reflective skill development is of significant value in teacher development (Oakley et al., 2014; Oner and Adadan, 2011; Farrell, 2012; Mann and Walsh, 2017) and is seen as the 'gateway' to deep and purposeful learning (Yancey, 2009). To exemplify Dewey's (1944) contributions to reflective practice, Rodgers illustrates four key criteria (i.e. 'meaning-making process', 'systematic, rigorous and disciplined way of thinking', 'needs to happen in a community', and 'requires attitudes that value personal and intellectual growth') that illustrate the concept of reflection (2002: 845). The critical task for trainees is to conceptualize and contrive meaning with a mature level of understanding of teaching. The continuous progression involves discovery and learning within a community and in interaction with others, where the emphasis is chiefly on the personal development of individuals. The key role of reflection thus is to form meaning and build connections between 'that experience and the experience', 'that knowledge and the knowledge produced by thinkers' (Rodgers, 2002: 848).

Barrett (2011) and Parkes et al. (2013) emphasize the cyclic process of reflection that students undergo while collating works on ePortfolios. Barrett (2011) connects the continuous learning process with two key theoretical frameworks, Gibbs's (1988) reflective cycle (i.e. description, feeling, evaluation, analysis, conclusion and action plan) and Kolb's (1976) (i.e. act, reflect, conceptualize and apply) experiential learning model. The processes entail phase-by-phase interactive learning journey which require students to show a considerable level of autonomy and critical awareness (Hughes, 2011). The results of engaging in such 'evidence-based' reflective process (showcased in trainee ePortfolios) can make trainees aware of their strengths and weaknesses. This view reflects Dewey's idea that teacher growth is enabled from the 'reconstruction of experience'(1933: 87 in Farrell, 2012). For instance, trainees get on-going constructive feedback which allows them to reflect, rebuild and redefine their pieces of ePortfolio work.

Learners engage themselves in continuous exploration where 'the conversation between the practitioner and the setting provides the data which then may lead to alternative meanings, further reframing, and plans for further actions' (Clarke, 1995: 245). Ehiyazaryan-White (2012: 175) conceptualizes the significance of dialogic communication in ePortfolio communities by referring to Salmon's (2012) five-stage model for collaborative online learning and Preece's (2000) notion of community as a 'process.' At developmental stages, it remains essential to motivate student-teachers to 'socialize online' to recognize the advantages of collaborative knowledge construction (ibid.). Again, getting support from peers is considered an important source of feedback (Sadler, 2010 in Yang et al., 2016). It encourages productive learning, enriches their knowledge base and teaches them to become self-reflective about their pedagogic actions. In ePortfolio discussions, as a result, students are expected to adopt 'interchangeable roles' of 'supportive fellow students' (Jones and Lea, 2008 in Ehiyazaryan-White, 2012: 175) to assist each other in their teaching endeavours. For instance, commenting on peers' blog posts, giving suggestions and stimulating each other's thinking on how to improve their current teaching practices are some common forms of assistance noticed in student-blogs on ePortfolios.

ePortfolio learning requires trainers to embrace new roles in achieving the pre-determined goals under a 'socially-mediated' process (Velikova, 2013: 203). As opposed to being strictly evaluative, trainers should adopt the position of a collaborator and a moderator whose active presence are likely to facilitate the development process (Elbow and Belanoff, 1997; Preece, 2000). Barnett (2007: 133) terms the idea of embracing new and challenging roles as 'pedagogical bungee jumping' for trainees should always be prepared to take risks, even 'amid uncertainty' (Hughes, 2011: 58). These risks could mean exposing oneself to a range of new technologies, pedagogical approaches and active discussions of critical incidents. Hughes assures us that integrated learning experiences formed through the 'dialogic and collaborative framework' of ePortfolios can help student-teachers grow as confident individuals (2011: 299).

The assessment process in ePortfolios can be considered as a specific form of authentic or performance assessment that attempts to measure higher order thinking skills including the ability to communicate clearly, to make judgments, and to demonstrate specific competencies (Miller and Legg, 1993). It is, therefore, crucial to provide timely help to students in reflection and setting a 'collegial environment' to reap the benefits from the process (Pecheone et al., 2005: 167). Moreover, grading reflective posts is deemed to be a challenging endeavour which requires trainers to defy strict objective evaluation techniques and focus on constructive feedback comments. Hodgson (2017) argues that grades can easily specify student achievements with reference to the 'holistic criteria', but it often does not interpret the student's cognitive knowledge, whereas Hobbs (2007) suggests reflections should not be assessed at the initial stages because trainees need enough flexibility to grow in confidence and awareness in a non-threatening and friendly environment.

Balancing collection and reflection on learning through ePortfolios

As discussed above, ePortfolios are implemented in many higher institutions for the purpose of data collection, accreditation, and assessment. In the US for instance, proprietary ePortfolio systems emerged in the early 2000s as a direct result of the accreditation requirements that the U.S. National Council for Accreditation of Teacher Education (NCATE) had in the year 2000. With the requirement of an electronic system to maintain data, institutions adopted a variety of proprietary systems that promised success in the accreditation process. However, the irony with proprietary ePortfolio systems has been the lack of relationship between the tools and strategies used in teacher preparation programs, and the subsequent use of ePortfolios. In practice, student-teachers were not learning to use ePortfolios in the same ways that could potentially be implemented with their own students once they have their own classrooms. This problem has been solved with some creativity by institutions that incorporated separate tools for collecting assessment data, allowing students to create representations of their own achievement using online tools. As examples, teacher educators at Ball State University (Stuve et al., 2010) created r Grade; Seattle Pacific University, University of Puerto Rico, Baylor University and Clemson University created their own systems for collecting evaluation data, while students maintained

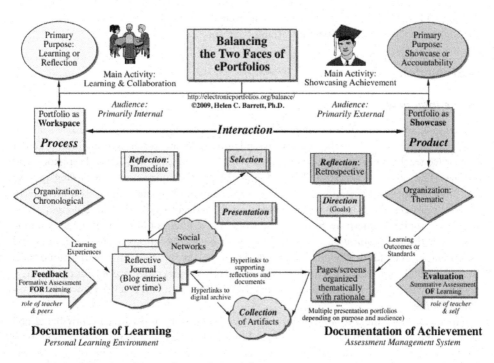

Figure 32.1 Balancing the two faces of ePortfolios

their portfolios using a variety of free online tools (i.e., WordPress, G Suite or Google powered tools for Education).

The primary motive of a learning portfolio is 'to improve student learning by providing a structure for students to reflect systematically over time on the learning process and to develop the aptitudes, skills and habits that come from critical reflection' (Zubizaretta, 2004: 15). For instance, an effective strategy in using technology for reflection is to have students create short digital stories or visual representations about their learning experiences e.g. using images and narration to document the learning activities or outcomes. Barrett (2011) further argues for balancing the two faces or the two different sides of ePortfolios, such as process vs. product, workspace vs. showcase and conversation vs. presentation:

Figure 32.1 represents the two 'faces' of ePortfolios, workspace (documenting day-to-day learning, collecting evidence and reflecting on learning) and showcase (presenting the results of learning at specific points in the learning process, selecting and organizing learning at specific points of time). It can be further explained with reference to Schön's reflective model (1983) and Killion and Todnem's (1991) categorization of reflection. Reflection occurs in three directions, at different times across the learning process: before (planning); during (doing), and after (reflecting). Reflection for action (before) involves forethought and influential processes which precede efforts to act and set the stage for actions. Reflection in action (during) involves processes that occur during action and affect attention and action. Last, reflection on action (after) involves metacognition and self-reflection, processes which occur after performance efforts and influence a person's response to that experience. Planning and implementing strategies provide an evaluation metric for learners to attribute successes or failures to evidence of their efforts rather than low ability (Abrami et al., 2008).

We now evaluate the above-discussed teacher development processes involved in ePortfolio learning with reference to some views and experiences gathered from targeted teacher educators and trainees working in different learning contexts.

(i) Evaluation

Online interviews

To examine current practices of ePortfolios in teacher education, interviews were conducted with seven experienced teacher educators and four graduate teachers from four different pre-service teacher training contexts (i.e. universities) namely, the UK, USA, Hongkong and Bulgaria. The objective was to understand and evaluate their experiences regarding specific uses of ePortfolios and their adopted strategies to accommodate and support new changes in teaching practices. The educators shared views on the reflective tasks they have designed (e.g. stimulating topics or questions to initiate collaborative dialogues online), the online communities built through communications on blogs and the modifications in methodologies and assessment for ePortfolios. They also shared views on the key functionalities of ePortfolio tools used (e.g. PebblePad, Mahara, WordPress, Blogger, and Google). The accounts of the teachers were equally useful in revealing their perspectives of reflection and teacher growth based on ePortfolio use.

The extracts provide a realistic picture of the ways ePortfolio tools are currently being utilized in different contexts in terms of their ability to encourage continuous reflection, peer collaboration and professional growth of pre-service trainees. The names appearing in the following transcripts are pseudonyms of the participants interviewed.

The extract below exposes teacher educator Emina's views on the useful functionalities of the ePortfolio tool PebblePad. She makes it clearer that critical engagement with relevant information available in different media promotes reflective thinking:

Extract 32.1 'Singing and dancing evidence of your fitness'

95	**Em:**	There is even in the portfolio which we now use,
96		store pebble, it's like an app where
97		they can capture reflections and send them to
98		their portfolios and stuff. I think
99		multimedia, which is not quite, I would say new,
100		because it was not used as much it
101		is now. ePortfolios allow you to have all singing and
102		dancing evidence of your fitness to practice.

In the extract above, Emina recognizes the value of capturing reflections on ePortfolios and favours using built-in applications (e.g., 'store pebble' on PebblePad) which allow trainees to creatively personalize their ways of sharing and embedding multimodal evidence with the audience. The process of reflection using digital means is not just 'text-based', but incorporation of audio files that make the representation much more meaningful, interesting and empowering.

The following extract illustrates the learning process and the changed roles of trainers involved in ePortfolio development. Juliana has been using PebblePad with her trainees for over a decade. She emphasizes practical teaching experience sharing among trainers and pre-service teachers and explains the importance of 'current' or the most updated knowledge that student-teachers construct, develop and share over time through the online platforms.

Extract 32.2 'It's about the democratic exchange in students'

142	**J:**	This isn't about us being so expert that we pour stuff into
143		them – we generate this together and I think,
144		that's because at the universities, we are out of practice
145		in that sector. Teachers are the most current, so
146		they are bringing the issues to discuss the practice. It's
147		about that democratic exchange in students
148		where you learn from them. Because they are bringing to you
149		the issues from practice that you might not thought about.
150		They learn to be teachers in practice and what we do is
151		scaffold some of the thinking around that.

The practice is influenced by the key principles of critical pedagogy. To Juliana, instead of a transmission approach ('pouring stuff' into trainees), the trainers and the curriculum itself should encourage opportunities for a more constructivist approach ('critical dialogues' or open discussions on the daily teaching incidents). These discussions are between the experts but 'out of practice' teachers and 'the most current' prospective teachers who serve as the representatives or 'agents' of new knowledge. The process echoes Freire's (1970: 79) concept of 'empty vessels' and 'problem-posing' which stands opposite to traditional teaching methods. The extract also recognizes the nature of teacher-student relationship outside the walls of classrooms and that ePortfolios are fundamentally collaborative and student-led.

In the following extract, teacher trainer Emina, who uses PebblePad with her trainees at a UK university recognizes the importance of having enthusiastic and motivated educators to assist and guide the trainees in their 'early days' of teaching practice where they undergo complex and intense phases of learning.

Extract 32.3 'The benefit of doing this ongoing reflection'

169	**Em:**	... especially in the early days when you are getting in the
170		transition of one thing to another. It had to have somebody
171		passionate driving you. From a student perspective, you got
172		to be able to convince them of the benefit of doing this
173		ongoing reflection. And how we try and kind of sell it here 174 sometimes,
		if you reflect on critical incidents or your
175		reflect on whatever it is, you will be reflecting on for
176		that particular example.

Emina's views make it clear that technical constraints can be effectively managed if the trainer herself is passionate about technology and believes in the potential of ePortfolios. To further inspire and foster their thinking and motivate them to continue reflecting on the critical incidents, 'students need to know that somebody is looking at their posts and that somebody cares that they are spending time on the ePortfolios'. Feedback and guidance are, hence critical to ePortfolio construction and further maintenance.

Consider the extract below, where trainer Nahla evaluates her experiences of providing feedback on-going through PebblePad. The purpose of her designed reflective tasks and feedback on the Gateway forum of PebblePad was 'to make students think further' and involve themselves more intensively in teaching practices:

Extract 32.4 'I think it was a novelty for them'

149	**M:**	I really wanted to go back to the feedback process. What was
150		the process of providing feedback?
151	**N:**	Let's say I am reading one of the critical analyses on the
152		pages via the Gateway, uh, I could read that and underneath
153		that I could type up my comments and if I click 'send' it
154		would automatically go to that person via email. It would
155		also let them see it if they logged in the system. So, it was
156		both. The system allows you to receive information via email...
157		I also told the students to log on to PebblePad at least once
158		everyday, because I said they can see what anybody has
159		written on the blog so it gives you a chance to comment, if
160		you have something to ask, you can then ask, so I said at

161 least once, I said 'set yourself a particular time which is
162 easy for you' and everyday go on it, which I think was
163 a novelty for them.

The interesting aspect of this extract is that it not only indicates the basic process of delivering online feedback to student-teachers but explains how the process itself is a 'novelty' for trainees (line 163), especially in terms of getting wider exposure to both tutor and peer comments. Through the Gateway, Nahla visits the hyperlinks and multimedia resources that her students embedded in the tasks. The feedback on each of these four tasks helped students to think ahead in terms of their progress.

As reflections are 'personal' in nature, there remains a concern as to whether they should be formally assessed with grades and marks and if so, then how and at which stage should the goals and learning outcomes be first introduced to trainees. Hobbs (2007) argues, reflection should not be assessed at initial stages because trainees need some space to gain confidence and personal strength before they expose themselves and their works to educators. This issue was prevalent in the interview conversations and provoked mixed opinions. For instance, the trainer, Vira, thinks, 'it is not fair to grade their first efforts and first attempts at teaching...' because learner growth and competency should be the key concern at that stage.

In defining the advantages of developing ePortfolios in teacher education, useful comments were made by the graduates during the interviews. For instance, graduate Viola thinks,

> Even though I felt miserable when I had to fill in those forms while I was so busy doing my teaching practicum, I still find that it is really useful for me because I not only evaluated on the strengths and weaknesses of myself, I also had become more aware of the progresses of my students.

Viola's account provides an overall evaluation of the long-term impacts of ePortfolios in teacher development and conveys a message to the educators that encouraging reflection at the initial stages should be at a minimum level to help teachers flexibly and simultaneously continue their teaching practice and develop ePortfolios. Ana, moreover, emphasizes the aspect of lifelong membership or sustainability in terms of the continuous process of professional development and revisiting past works through archives, 'it reminded me of the whole process and the effort that I put in. It helps to sustain my teaching career'. They both strongly value storing works digitally not only for the benefits of employability and future presentations but to nurture lifelong learning skills through community-based practices.

1) Strategies for implementation

How do we implement ePortfolios?

With specific goals and purposes, the transition from paper-based to electronic alternatives should be gradual and without major complexities; the process should be in line with the previously established or existing learning principles and frameworks (Woodward and Nanlohy, 2004) so that educators and trainees can easily follow the changes. This section will cover the following elements that institutions and educators need to take into account to implement ePortfolios:

a)   planning for ePortfolio implementation;
b)   selection from available ePortfolio tools;
c)   use of different devices that support the tools or in other words, ePortfolio processes with digital devices.

The last section includes an example of using WordPress as blogging tool in ePortfolio development process.

a) Planning for ePortfolio implementation

To encourage students and staff alike, it is important to 'sell the vision' (Strudler and Wetzel, 2005: 421) or in other words, to communicate the innovative rationale and the scope of the project to other stakeholders to establish the vision by 'spreading the enthusiasm'. Based on what has been discussed in the previous section, we suggest institutions consider the following five useful elements for implementation of ePortfolios:

1.   *Readiness*: It is crucial to establish whether teachers and students have access to computer or mobile hardware and software with adequate internet access and if the curriculum allows opportunities to develop artefacts that showcase learning outcomes or in other words, if the programme supports a culture of reflection.
2.   *Incentives:* Incentives for developing ePortfolios for teachers and students should be identified along with the benefits for implementing ePortfolios with students, emphasizing intrinsic motivation.
3.   *Vision:* Writing a clear vision statement that clearly identifies the rationale for creating ePortfolios for students is essential. In fact, the goals and purpose should be set from the very beginning which later can be revised or modified.
4.   *Skills and training:* In addition to basic technology skills, students and educators should develop specific portfolio skills. For students, the skills include collecting, digitizing, selecting, organizing, reflecting, goal-setting and finally, presenting. For educators, pedagogy includes facilitating portfolio processes, facilitating reflection, providing feedback, formative and summative assessment. Also, identifying useful resources, common technology tools and required assistance is important (see Table 32.2).
5.   *Stakeholders:* It is important to determine who is involved in the ePortfolio process and consider ways of introducing it to them. For instance, identifying stakeholders in the implementation process and developing an initial communication plan for each stakeholder group, such as students, teachers, parents, administrators and employers. Stakeholders can follow the four-level implementation plan shown in Table 32.1, to assess student progress.

The four stages given in Table 32.1 are interrelated. The first stage involves careful collection and selection of student artefacts to be displayed in the individual folios. This is followed by the next three stages which also require students to be meticulous, decisive and conscientious about the selections they intend to showcase and archive. It is necessary to be reflective at these stages in order to understand and communicate their refined works effectively. The assessment and evaluation stage remain the most important because educators should be mindful of the learning

Table 32.1 Four-level plan

Level 1 (Collection): Portfolio as storage
Structuring learning activities so that they result in digital documents or reflection on experience that
  can be stored in digital format as 'artefacts' of learning.

Level 2 (Collection and reflection): Portfolio as process or as workspace
Identifying the frequency of recording self-reflection on work/tasks/activities and achievement of goals.

Level 3 (Selection, reflection and presentation): Portfolio as product or showcase
Selecting the specific artefacts to demonstrate achievement of the portfolio's goals. Creating a
  showcase that is organized thematically, based on curriculum outcomes, goals, or standards.
  Employment portfolios should be organized around specific job requirements.

Level 4 (Assessment and evaluation)
Creating or adapting rubrics to evaluate the ePortfolios. Faculty may provide feedback based on
  learning outcomes, goals, or standards.

---

methods and programme aims to reach a transparent and effective assessment technique. Developing a well-thought-out evaluation plan and designing or adapting rubrics against the set goals can make the initiative a realistic one. Cleveland (2018) and Wray (2007) provide useful suggestions for using rubrics and guides as suitable alternatives to grades or marks in evaluating student improvement, more specifically, their reflection skills.

b) Selection of appropriate tools

Common free source ePortfolio tools provide useful features to compile works, assemble and comment on others' posts (Oakley et al., 2014). Most platforms include 'blogs' and 'Wikis' and these are key features that ensure space for reflective practice and experiential learning (Brown, 2011). There are stages of ePortfolio development (Barrett, 2011) and strategies for using technology tools at different levels:

LEVEL 1: EPORTFOLIO AS STORAGE

Using technology tools to create and upload text, images, audio, video, all resulting from academic or co-curricular activities. Office tools, G Suite tools, video editing software are useful to create artefacts. Online or cloud spaces such as, Google Drive, Dropbox, Microsoft's OneDrive etc. are helpful to store student artefacts; the built-in storage provided by commercial tools are equally user-friendly.

LEVEL 2: EPORTFOLIO AS WORKSPACE

Using online word processing or blogging apps such as *Blogger* can be used to provide reflective tasks and feedback, to collect, customize and organize student works chronologically. The tools can also be used for both goal-setting and formative assessment.

LEVEL 3: EPORTFOLIO AS SHOWCASE

The steps in editing online portfolios for showcase or summative assessment include selection, summative reflection and presentation, organized thematically by outcomes and goals, Below are the major examples of ePortfolio tools used in education for showcase and assessment portfolios:

Table 32.2 Common ePortfolio tools

- Commercial tools created specifically for ePortfolios in teacher education that include record-keeping to record and present assessment data. Most popular tools include LiveText and TaskStream (now Watermark), Chalk & Wire, Digication, PebblePad, Pathbrite.
- Commercial tool for ePortfolios in K-12 education: Seesaw.
- Online website authoring tools: Weebly, Google Sites, Wix.
- Open source ePortfolio platform: Mahara.
- Blogging medium: Blogger, WordPress or EduBlogs.
- Microsoft 365 including Word, Excel, PowerPoint, OneNote, OneDrive.
- G Suite and Google Classroom (i.e. Google Drive, Google Sites for publishing showcase ePortfolios).

There are pros and cons for each type of tool, including cost, continuity, and the ability for students to maintain their portfolios after they leave the educational institution and continue into professional life. Most commercial tools allow downloading an individual portfolio into HTML format. Maintaining the portfolio without the tool requires web server space, authoring software, and web authoring skills. Generic tools such as Microsoft, G Suite or WordPress allow the transfer of student portfolio data from institution hosting to individual accounts without learning new skills.

c) Facilitating ePortfolio processes with digital devices

Digital devices and the social software have the power to transform the learning environment and support a level of reflection we could only imagine a decade ago (see Figure 32.2). There are practical and financial considerations in different contexts including the developing world, where the humble mobile phone is the tool most widely available to students for electronically documenting their learning.

The first step in building an ePortfolio is the collection of artefacts (in text, images, audio, video) and reflection on experiences (in any of those same formats) by capturing the learning moment, which can be facilitated by almost every mobile or computer device:

With both mobile and computer devices, each of the following processes can be utilized:

- **Capturing and storing evidence**: This evidence of learning can be in the form of text, images, audio or video. This data can be stored online using free tools discussed above.
- **Reflecting**: Reflection can be captured in real time in different formats: writing, voice capture and voice-to-text conversion, video capture and digital stories. Most commercial ePortfolio software tools provide a structure for reflection. As discussed above in the evaluation section, students may need reflection prompts when using tools, such as WordPress or G Suite.
- **Delivering feedback**: There are a variety of strategies for facilitating this feedback. Commercial tools support built-in feedback delivery techniques. The major blogging platforms e.g. WordPress and Blogger have apps for posting entries while feedback can be provided by commenting.
- **Planning and setting goals**: A crucial part of the portfolio process is personal development planning and setting goals for achievement. Blogs can provide a powerful space for

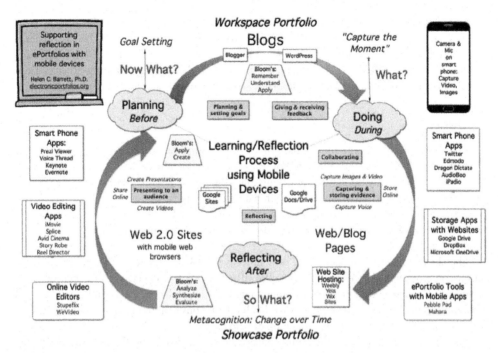

Figure 32.2   Supporting reflection in ePortfolios with mobile devices

posting goals, however, strategies for including goal-setting varies for each software or application.

- **Collaborating**: Some tools include the ability for collaborative editing. For example, this paper was collaboratively written using Google Docs across 13 time zones!
- **Presenting**: At specific points in the learning process, learners may put together presentations of their learning outcomes for an audience, either real or virtual.

ePortfolio based learning also support processes, such as digitizing, archiving, hyper-linking, embedding, storytelling, collaborating, publishing and so forth. As educators help students develop lifelong skills that will last after they graduate, they need to develop productive skills that can be applied in the 'real world' outside of formal education. Building on the tools that students are already using and considering intrinsic motivation factors that drive the use of social networking, those factors (i.e. autonomy, mastery and purpose) could also apply to the ePortfolio environment (Pink, 2009).

The section below discusses the practicalities of using WordPress as suitable and reliable ePortfolio tool. The description also refers to the experiences of trainers who used WordPress and Blogger as portfolios.

a)   How-to example: using Wordpress as an ePortfolio tool

Although commercially developed software tools provide structured framework for archiving and retrieving student artefacts and linking the contents with other sections, some institutions prefer developing their own system using open source tools such as, word processing software, web authoring tools etc. Free tools are particularly favoured as they allow more scope to customize the structure, artefacts and visual elements (Wray, 2007). For instance, Emisa (trainer) uses WordPress as an ePortfolio tool and specifically highlights the benefits of blogging in building online learning communities. She is impressed by the newly added 'buddy' feature of WordPress and believes it can effectively assist in initiating conversations on 'classroom management', 'academic issues and other issues related to their 'hard times':

Extract 32.5

103 **E:** (...) each student can have their own personalised erm,
104   teaching portfolios on WordPress, but then WordPress has
105   recently developed something called 'buddy' and that kind of
106   pastoral care can only be offered through talking online –
107   they are able to meet one another. They would discuss
108   classroom management, academic issues, their the hard times.

The above extract is an example of how reflective thinking as well as 'pastoral care' can be an outcome of online discussions using in WordPress. The experienced users or mentors assist relatively less-experienced trainees through suggestions, useful comments and guidelines on teaching practice within a democratic space. Such interactions help to promote a closer relationship among the community members (Tang & Lam, 2014).

Another experienced educator Hima explains how reflective journals are easily developed and maintained using WordPress and Blogger:

Extract 32.6

22 **H:** (...) so you have got reflective journal, which I think is
23   best done in a blog. You can incorporate blogging activities
24   into a variety of formats. I do like Blogger and I do like
25   WordPress – but in some other commercial ePortfolio sites
26   such as Mahara has a blog built-in. It has a social network 27 built-in for the
            group that is developed and has a
28   journal or a blog platform. The nice thing about the way the
29   blog is set up is that you can link to any individual entry
30   in the blog in your showcase portfolio.

The extract above recognizes blogging or reflective journaling as, perhaps, the most distinctive feature of digital platforms. The function of chronologically archiving entries with active links to different entries (lines 29–30) facilitates new meaning-making processes for students (Beetham & Oliver, 2010) as well as helping them 'showcase' their critical artefacts on teaching portfolios.

The diagram below demonstrates a step-by-step process for using the WordPress blogging tool to support ePortfolio development:

In this example, steps two, three and four represent an interactive process, using the blog to provide formative feedback on student work on a regular basis. The following guidelines can be useful for both trainers and students to initiate and continue ePortfolio learning:

• First, trainers need to identify appropriate ways of organizing the portfolio. The structure should consider outcomes, goals or standards.

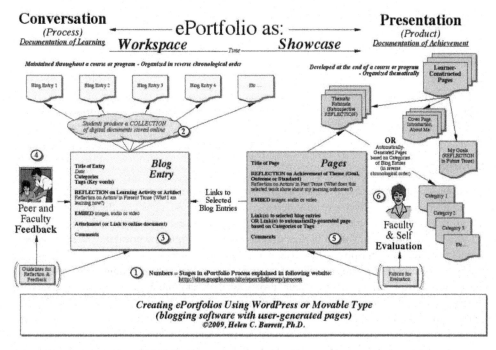

Figure 32.3 Using blogs and pages to create ePortfolio

- Based on the goals and other outcomes, students can set up a WordPress category for each major outcome required as part of the portfolio's purpose. Setting up a WordPress 'parent' page that will serve as the opening page to the portfolio and to the portfolio developer.
- For collection and classification, it is essential to understand the kind of artefacts to be included in their portfolios and the ways the entries will be classified. For students, creating a digital archive of work is the starting point. Using a local area network server or storing files online on the Internet using services such as Google Drive, Microsoft OneDrive, or Dropbox is recommended.
- Educators need to provide students with resources to support their reflection activities. For each learning activity or artefact, the key focus should be on students' reflections (see 'Further reading'). Again, students can write a blog entry with a reflection on each learning activity or artefact (e.g. what is the context in which this artefact was developed?) followed by classifying each entry with one or more WordPress categories and adding appropriate artefacts through hyperlinks or as an attachment to the blog entry. The viewers can click on the hyperlinks of each main category and visit a variety of artefacts which can also be shared in other posts through additional hyperlinks (Wray, 2007).
- As discussed in the evaluation section, the blog feature of posting comments can be useful to provide interactive feedback on the work posted in the ePortfolio blog entries. Along with guidelines and rubrics, students should be given the option of updating or modifying their works, based on the feedback they receive.

At the end of a programme, students can write a 'retrospective reflection' about the learning represented in the artefacts, selecting one or two examples that best represent their achievements. This writing looks back over the course and provides a meta-analysis of the learning experience as represented in the reflections stored in the blog entries. The self-assessment technique is helpful to build an overall impression of their portfolios for the audience. Furthermore, the final selections can include the evidence i.e. links of the appropriate sub-pages which can serve as a 'letter to the reader' and provides an explanation of the overall goals of the portfolio. Often the user has the freedom to decide what parts of the portfolio are to be made public. Last, according to what the trainers have highlighted, the final evaluation of portfolio can be assessed using a quantitative analytic rubric or a holistic rubric. Getting real-time access to students' posts is one of the prime features of ePortfolios as was mentioned by the interviewed teacher educators.

Summary

ePortfolio use is not limited to installing the platform and incorporating that into the regular teaching programmes. Success mainly depends on the purpose, aims and the projected learning outcomes which need to be comprehensive, integrative and well-explained to the staff and students before they are involved in the process. Studies highlight the possibility of dealing with 'conflicts' in terms of purposes and goals as one the few emerging issues in ePortfolio use in teacher education (Evans and Powell, 2007; Zeichner and Wray, 2001). Trainers emphasize making connections, building identities and professional development, whereas student-teachers mainly focus on the 'showcase' aspect of portfolios and how they can create a 'favourable' image to the future employers. These complications are in conflict with the main aims of using ePortfolios in teacher education discussed in the previous sections of this chapter. Again, being too directive or giving trainees the full onus of ePortfolio construction can often engender negative reactions as well as inauthentic reflections, less engagement or scarcity of teaching evidence (Zeichner and Wray, 2001). To balance the continuous practice of reflection, creative showcasing of student evidence and the degree of student-teacher agency, educators need to:

- Carefully receive and value the wealth of information (i.e. personal reflections, posts, comments, evidence of teaching practice) the student-teachers are sharing.
- Maintain sound communication with students and explain the skills that are desirable for them to acquire and develop throughout the programme.
- Remain technologically up-to-date and keep the trainees well-informed and motivated.
- Determine what is useful and should be harnessed to sustain teacher development and thereby, extend support and feedback.
- Establish the value of ePortfolios in trainees' learning journey, through guided and meaningful reflective tasks.

It is also necessary to identify the anticipated contextual challenges and take advantage of the potential of ePortfolios in further encouraging teacher reflection and professional growth (Zeichner and Wray, 2001). The following specific points should also be considered to tackle such obstacles:

- Not all students will have sound access to the internet and devices to continue ePortfolio learning and represent their tasks with different media facilities; therefore, it is suggested that institutions, as well as educators pay utmost attention to technical factors before introducing ePortfolio based learning. Regular 'drop-ins', 'tutorials' and online 'discussion forums' can be some practical options to keep trainees motivated and engaged in the process.
- To encourage staff, frequent workshops and reflective discussions could be an appropriate starting point where trainers will get chances to resolve any technical or teaching-related

issues in a collaborative environment while becoming more confident and professional about handling technology.

• It is beneficial to have clear assessment criteria and a set of realistic aims that include a balance of the process/product and theory/applications parameters.

Overall, developing as a professional requires a lifelong commitment to learning and research (Day, 1999). As ePortfolio learning shows a strong affinity with professional identity building and improvement of reflective skills, pre-service teachers can develop good teaching practices, make connections between theory and applications and sustain professional networks beyond the scope of the teacher education programme.

Further reading

Chaudhuri, T. and Cabau, B. (2017) *E-portfolios in Higher Education*. Singapore: Springer.
> Presents a diverse range of perspectives on ePortfolio use in higher education, for assessment and in building communities of practice.

Kurtoglu-Hooton, N. (2013) 'Providing "the spark" for reflection from a digital platform', in Mann, S. and Edge, J. (eds) *Innovations in Pre-Service Education and Training for English Language Teachers*. London: British Council: 17–32.
> This pertinent study discusses and evaluates the use of Pebblepad in promoting reflection in pre-service teacher education.

Stefani, L., Mason, R. and Pegler, C. (2007) *The Educational Potential of E-Portfolios: Supporting Personal Development and Reflective Learning*. Abingdon: Routledge.
> A comprehensive, well-written book on the key aspects associated with ePortfolio use and implementation such as, planning, sample ePortfolio tasks, challenges, affordances, assessment techniques as well as incorporation strategies.

Resources

Organizations

EUROPORTFOLIO European Network of ePortfolio Experts & Practitioners <www.eportfolio.eu>
ePIC, the International ePortfolio & Identity Conference <https://epic.openrecognition.org>
Electronic Portfolio Action Pac (EPAC) Community of Practice (free mail list): <https://mailman.stanford.edu/mailman/listinfo/epaccoplist>

Recommended sites

ePortfolios in teacher education: <https://warwick.ac.uk/fac/soc/al/research/vilte/resources/gulzar_thesis.pdf>
Reflection for Learning: <http://sites.google.com/site/reflection4learning/>
Mobile Devices in ePortfolio Development: <https://sites.google.com/site/mportfolios/>
ePortfolios in schools (GSuite): <https://sites.google.com/site/k12eportfolioapps/>
JISC <www.jisc.ac.uk/guides/technology-and-tools-for-online-learning/e-portfolios>

References

Abrami, P.W., Anne, C., Pillay, V., Aslan, O., Bures, E. M. and Bentley, C. (2008) 'Encouraging Self-Regulated Learning Through Electronic Portfolios'. *Canadian Journal of Learning and Technology*, 34(3) Available online: <www.cjlt.ca/index.php/cjlt/article/view/507> (accessed 22 May, 2019).

Barnett, R. (2007) *A Will to Learn. Being a Student in an Age of Uncertainty.* Maidenhead: Open University Press.

Barrett, H. (2011) 'Balancing the Two Faces of ePortfolios'. *Educação, Formação & Tecnologias*, 3(1) 6–14. Available online: <http://eft.educom.pt> (accessed 22 May, 2019).

Baume, D. (2003, May) *Supporting Portfolio Development.* Available online: <www.heacademy.ac.uk/system/files/id295_supporting_portfolio_development.pdf> (accessed 22 May, 2019).

Beethaam, H. and Oliver, M. (2010) 'The changes practices of knowledge and learning', in Sharpe, R. Beetham, H. and de Freitas, D. (eds) *Rethinking Learning for a Digital Age.* New York: Routledge: 155–169.

Bhattacharya, M. and Hartnett, M. (2007) 'E-portfolio Assessment in Higher Education'. *37th ASEE/IEEE Frontiers in Education Conference*, Milwaukee, 10–13 October.

Boulton, H. (2014) 'E-Portfolios Beyond Pre-Service Teacher Education: A New Dawn?'. *European Journal of Teacher Education*, 37(3) 374–389.

Brown, J. O. (2011) 'Dwell in Possibility: PLAR and e-Portfolios in the Age of Information and Communication Technologies'. *The International Review of Research in Open and Distributed Learning*, 12(1) 1–23.

Cambridge, D. (2008) 'Layering Networked and Symphonic Selves: A Critical Role for e-Portfolios in Employability Through Integrative Learning'. *Layering Networked and Symphonic Selves*, 25(4) 244–262.

Chaudhuri, T. and Cabau, B. (2017) *E-portfolios in Higher Education.* Singapore: Springer.

Clark, J. E. and Eynon, B. (2009) 'E-portfolios at 2.0-Surveying the Field'. *Peer Review*, 11(1). Available online: <www.aacu.org/publications-research/periodicals/e-portfolios-20—surveying-field> (accessed 22 May, 2019).

Clarke, A. (1995) 'Professional Development in Practicum Settings: Reflective Practice under Scrutiny'. *Teaching and Teacher Education*, 11(3) 243–261.

Cleveland, R. E. (2018) 'Using Digital Portfolios: Reflection, Assessment and Employment'. *TechTrends*, 62(3) 276–285.

Day, C. (1999) *Developing Teachers: The Challenges of Lifelong Learning.* London: Falmer Press.

Dewey, J. (1933) *How We Think.* Buffalo, NY: Prometheus Books.

Dewey, J. (1944) *Democracy and Education.* New York: Free Press.

Dzay-Chulim, F. and Mann, S. (2017) 'Collaborative and Dialogic Reflection in Second Language Teacher Education'. *European Journal of Applied Linguistics and TEFL*, 123–144.

Ehiyazaryan-White, E. (2012) 'The Dialogic Potential of ePortfolios: Formative Feedback and Communities of Learning within a Personal Learning Environment'. *International Journal ePortfolio*, 2(2) 173–185.

Elbow, P. & Belanoff, P. (1997) Reflections on an explosion: portfolios in the 90s and beyond', in Yancey, K. B. and Weiser, I. (eds) *Situating Portfolios: Four Perspectives.* Logan, UT: Utah State University Press.

Evans, M. A. and Powell, A. (2007) 'Conceptual and Practical Issues Related to the Design for and Sustainability of Communities of Practice: The Case of E-Portfolio use in Preservice Teacher Training'. *Technology, Pedagogy and Education*, 16(2) 199–214.

Farrell, T. S. C. (2013) 'Critical Incident Analysis Through Narrative Reflective Practice: A Case Study'. *Iranian Journal of Language Teaching Research*, 1(1) 79–89.

Freire, P. (1970) *Pedagogy of the Oppressed.* New York: Continuum.

Gibbs, G. (1988) 'Learning by Doing: A Guide to Teaching and Learning Methods'. Further Education Unit, Oxford Polytechnic.

Hartnell-Young, E. and Morris, M. (1999) *Digital Professional Portfolios for Change.* Victoria: Hawker Brownlow Education.

Hartnell-Young, E., Harrison, C., Crook, C., Pemberton, R., Joyes, G., Fisher, T. and Davies, L. (2007) 'The Impact of e-Portfolios on Learning'. The University of Nottingham. Available online: <www.research gate.net/publication/271509791_The_impact_of_e-portfolios_on_learning> (accessed 22 May, 2019).

Heinrich, E., Bhattacharya, M. and Rayudu, R. (2007) 'Preparation for Lifelong Learning Using ePortfolios'. *European Journal of Engineering Education*, 32(6) 653–663.

Hobbs, V. (2007) 'Faking it or Hating it: Can Reflective Practice be Forced?'. *Reflective Practice*, 8(3) 405–417.

Hodgson, P. (2017) 'Student E-Portfolios: Unfolding Transformation in University Life in General Education Program'. *E-Portfolios in Higher Education.* Singapore: Springer: 171–181.

Hughes, J. (2011) 'It's Quite Liberating Turning Up to a Classroom Without a Pile of Papers and Equipment: Pedagogic Bungee Jumping: A Strategy to Rethink Teaching in a Technology-Rich Age?'. *Management in Education*, 26(2) 58–63.

Killion, J. and Todnem, G. (1991) 'A Process for Personal Theory Building'. *Educational Leadership*, 48(7) 14–16.

Kitchen S (1999) 'An appraisal of methods of reflection and clinical supervision'. *British Journal of Theatre Nursing*, 9(7) 313–317.

Kolb, D. A. (1976) *The Learning Style Inventory: Technical Manual*. Boston, MA: McBer & Co.

Kurtoglu-Hooton, N. (2013) 'Providing "the spark" for reflection from a digital platform', in Mann, S. and Edge, J. (eds) *Innovations in Pre-Service Education and Training for English Language Teachers*. London: British Council: 17–32.

Leonard, P. and McLaren, P. (eds) (1993) *Paulo Freire: A Critical Encounter* London: Routledge.

Lieberman, A. and Miller, L. (1984) *Teachers: Transforming Their World and Their Work*. Alexandria, VA: Association for Supervision and Curriculum Development.

Lorenzo, G. and Ittelson, J. (2005) 'An Overview of E-portfolios'. *Educause Learning Initiative*, 1(1) 1–27.

McCaffrey, M. (2011) 'Why Mobile is a Must'. *T.H.E. Journal*. Available online: <http://thejournal.com/articles/2011/02/08/why-mobile-is-a-must.aspx> (accessed 22 May, 2019).

Mann, S. and Walsh, S. (2017) *Reflective Practice in English Language Teaching*. New York: Routledge.

Mason, R., Pegler, C. and Weller, M. (2004) 'E-portfolios: An Assessment Tool for Online Courses'. *British Journal of Educational Technology*, 35(6) 717–727.

Miller, M. D. and Legg, S. M. (1993) 'Alternative Assessment in a High Stakes Environment'. *Educational Measurement: Issues and Practice*, 12(2) 9–15.

Moon, J. A. (2013) *Reflection in Learning and Professional Development: Theory and Practice*. Abingdon: Routledge.

Oakley, G., Pegrum, M. and Johnston, S. (2014) 'Introducing E-Portfolios to Pre-service Teachers as Tools for Reflection and Growth: Lessons Learnt'. *Asia-Pacific Journal of Teacher Education*, 42(1) 36–50.

Oner, D. and Adadan, E. (2011) 'Use of Web-Based Portfolios as Tools for Reflection in Preservice Teacher Education'. *Journal of Teacher Education*, 62(5) 477–492.

Parkes, K. A., Dredger, K. S. and Hicks, D. (2013) 'ePortfolio as a Measure of Reflective Practice'. *International Journal of ePortfolio*, 3(2) 99–115.

Pecheone, R. L., Pigg, M. J., Chung, R. R. and Souviney, R. J. (2005) 'Performance Assessment and Electronic Portfolios: Their Effect on Teacher Learning and Education'. *The Clearing House: A Journal of Educational Strategies, Issues and Ideas*, 78(4) 164–176.

Pegrum, M. and Oakley, G. (2017) 'The Changing Landscape of e-Portfolios: Reflections on 5 Years of Implementing e-Portfolios in Pre-Service Teacher Education'. *E-portfolios in Higher Education*. Singapore: Springer: 21–34.

Pink, D. (2009) *Drive: The Surprising Truth About What Motivates Us*. New York: Riverhead Books.

Preece, J. (2000) *Online Communities: Designing Usability and Supporting Sociability*. New York: John Wiley & Sons, Inc.

Rodgers, C. (2002) 'Defining Reflection: Another Look at John Dewey and Reflective Thinking'. *Teachers College Record*, 104(4) 842–866.

Salmon, G. (2012) *E-moderating: The Key to Online Teaching and Learning*. Abingdon: Routledge.

Schön, D. A. (2017) *The Reflective Practitioner: How Professionals Think in Action*. New York: Routledge.

Sharpe, R., Beetham, H. and De Freitas, S. (2010) *Rethinking Learning for a Digital Age: How Learners are Shaping their Own Experiences*. New York: Routledge.

Stefani, L., Mason, R. and Pegler, C. (2007) *The Educational Potential of E-Portfolios: Supporting Personal Development and Reflective Learning*. Abingdon: Routledge.

Strudler, N. and Wetzel, K. (2005) 'The Diffusion of Electronic Portfolios in Teacher Education'. *Journal of Research on Technology in Education*, 37(4) 411–433.

Stuve, M., Noel, M. and Biddle, J. (2010) 'Using a rubric-based digital gradebook for performance assessment', in Gibson, D. and Dodge, B. (eds) *Proceedings of Society for Information Technology & Teacher Education International Conference 2010*. Chesapeake, VA: 222–223. Available online: <www.learntechlib.org/p/33339> (accessed 22 May, 2019).

Tang, E. and Lam, C. (2014) 'Building an Online Learning Community (OLC) in Blog-Based Teaching Portfolios'. *Internet and Higher Education*, 20 79–85.

van der Schaaf, M., Donkers, J., Slof, B., Moonen-van Loon, J., van Tartwijk, J., Driessen, E., Badii, A., Serban, O. and Ten Cate, O. (2016) 'Improving Workplace-Based Assessment and Feedback by an E-portfolio Enhanced with Learning Analytics'. *Educational Technology Research and Development*, 65(2) 359–380.

Velikova, S. (2013) 'Using the European portfolio for student teachers of languages (EPOSTL) to scaffold reflective teacher learning in English language teacher education', in Mann, S. and Edge, J. (eds). *Innovations in Pre-Service Education and Training for English Language Teachers*. London: British Council.

Woodward, H. and Nanlohy, P. (2004) 'Digital Portfolios in Pre-Service Teacher Education'. *Assessment in Education: Principles, Policy & Practice*, 11(2) 167–178.

Wray, S. (2007) 'Electronic Portfolios in a Teacher Education Program'. *E-Learning*, 4 40–51.

Yancey, K. B. (2009) 'Electronic Portfolios a Decade into the Twenty-first Century: What We Know, What We Need to Know'. *Peer Review*, 11(1) 28–32.

Yang, M., Tai, M. and Lim, C. P. (2016) 'The Role of E-Portfolios in Supporting Productive Learning'. *British Journal of Educational Technology*, 47(6) 1276–1286.

Zeichner, K and Wray, S. (2001) 'The Teaching Portfolio in US Teacher Education Programs: What We know and What We Need to Know'. *Teacher and Teaching Education*, 17 613–621.

Zubizarreta, J. (2004) *The Learning Portfolio*. Bolton, MA: Anker Publishing.

Zull, J. (2002) *The Art of Changing the Brain*. Sterling, VA: Stylus Publishing.

Zull, J. (2011) *From Brain to Mind: Using Neuroscience to Guide Change in Education*. Sterling, VA: Stylus Publishing.

PART 6
Teacher perspectives

33

Methodology texts and the construction of teachers' practical knowledge

Scott Thornbury

Introduction

Teachers' guides come in a range of formats and styles, and have a long (albeit largely undocumented) history. Typically, they take the form of the book (the 'teacher's book', although increasingly this may exist only in a digital format) that, as part of a package of materials for a language course, accompanies the 'student's book'. Its purpose is to guide and support the teacher's use of the student's book in the classroom. Alternatively, a teachers' guide (following Stern, 1983) is a free-standing monograph on methodology that (in the words of one of them) 'provides a complete introduction to teaching languages, for use in both pre-service or in-service settings. It can be used by groups of teachers working with a trainer, or as a self-study resource' (Ur, 1991: back cover). It is teachers' guides in this second sense – i.e. as free-standing monographs on methodology – that are the subject of this chapter.

As such, teachers' guides embody what Ellis and Shintani (2014: 2) call 'pedagogic discourse', i.e. one which 'is intended for teachers and thus is written in a form that is accessible to this audience. Its aim is to be 'practical' – to offer suggestions for what might work in the classroom'. This contrasts with 'research-based discourse', which 'is intended for fellow researchers and although it may propose a number of 'practical' applications, it is primarily directed at theory-testing or theory-building' (ibid.).

Harwood (2014: 9) comments that 'very little research has been done on ELT teachers' guides', and, while he is referring to the former type – i.e. those that complement specific coursebooks – the same might be said of methodology texts in general. This is perhaps surprising, given the key role that these texts often play, not only in terms of enshrining and perpetuating existing classroom practices, but in the construction of teachers' knowledge. Indeed, given many teachers' well attested reluctance to engage with 'research-based discourse', either by conducting research themselves or by reading the findings of other researchers (see, for example, Bartels, 2003; and Borg, 2009), methodology texts – especially those mandated on teacher training courses – may constitute one of their few sources of information as to how language teaching is conceptualized and practised. The principles that teachers subscribe to – either overtly or covertly – and which underwrite their pedagogical decision-making are more likely to have been derived from such texts than from primary sources. Hence, as Stern (1983: 478) notes, they 'form a valuable link between the "theoretic" … and the "practical"'. Indeed they may go some way towards bridging the 'dysfunctional' discourse between researchers and practitioners (Clarke, 1994). Carroll (1966: 97) likened this mediating role to that of the 'county agent':

> the person who by personal visitation communicates the findings of agricultural research … to the farmer right at his door. There could be an analogue of the county agent in education: the individual who makes a specialty of communicating the findings of research to the potential consumer, the teacher, teacher trainer, educational policymaker, or preparer of instructional material.

Survey

How effectively, then, do teachers' guides perform this bridging function? More specifically, to what extent – and how – do they transmute research-based discourse into pedagogic discourse, given that the former is frequently 'couched in language that is not accessible to outsiders' (Ellis and Shintani, 2014: 2). And, given their potential to shape teachers' pedagogical knowledge, how trustworthy are they? Do the writers of methodology texts represent and interpret the research-based discourse accurately and faithfully? Or do they cherry-pick the research findings, or otherwise simplify, or even distort them, in order to promote their own particular agendas – which, in the case of methodology writers, may often be a specific method?

In order to contextualize the way that the writers of contemporary methodology textbooks engage with these questions, a brief historical survey is in order. A glance, for example, at some leading methodology texts produced over the last 100 or more years suggests that writers have been less than consistent in terms of identifying and referencing the research evidence that might have informed their pedagogical recommendations. This reflects less a lack of probity on their part, perhaps, than the fact that, until relatively recently, there has been a dearth of research into language acquisition, and second language acquisition (SLA) in particular, on which to draw. (Ellis, 1997: 5, for example, chooses the 1960s as the date when SLA, as a research-driven discipline, 'was born').

However, the need to ground methodology on a principled base was expressed by Sweet as long ago as 1899. For Sweet, the multiplicity of existing methods could only be rationalized by an appeal to the then current psychological theory of associationism. For Harold Palmer, too, methodology needed to be based on scientific principles, as articulated in the title of his 1917 (1968) book, *The Scientific Study and Teaching of Languages*, regarding which Smith (1999: 60) notes:

> The book prefigures applied linguistics as constituted in the latter half of the twentieth century in proposing the establishment of a new "science of language-study" on the basis of insights from philologists, phonetics, grammarians, lexicologists, modern pedagogy and psychologists, with these insights 'placed in such order and with such observance of proportion that the inevitable conclusions will suggest themselves' (Palmer 1917: 22).

On the other hand, some writers of teachers' guides were sceptical as to the relevance of 'pure science' for classroom practice. Morris (1959: vi), for example, writes that

> while it would savour of impertinence to decry the application of scientific methods of investigation … it is permissible to question any attempt to treat the subject [i.e. language education] as a whole as though it belonged to the sphere of pure science. It must be borne

in mind that laboratory experiments of a pedagogic nature, however illuminating, can have only restricted validity, in view of the highly inconstant human factor.

In a similar vein, Brooks (1960) prefaces his influential methodology text with 'a word' about science. For Brooks, science is concerned with objective truths and verifiable facts, and is seemingly indifferent to issues of social responsibility. It sits uncomfortably, therefore, with the goals of education, especially of the young. He concludes,

> in this study we shall accompany the scientists as far as they wish to go; it will frequently be necessary to digress and to go further, for language is a private as well as public matter, and the world as it is is not the only world the young should contemplate.
>
> *(x–xi)*

This is a view argued much later by Widdowson (1990: 60) among others, i.e. 'that pedagogic research calls for the independent appraisal of ideas as a precondition to their application. That application cannot simply model itself on the procedures of empirical research.'

Generally, though, methodology writers steered a judicious, albeit at times unsteady, path between these two polarities, appealing on the one hand to their own experience, intuitions, and 'common sense', while, on the other, referencing the appropriate research literature – where it existed. Frisby (1957: 5), for example, asserts that his book 'is based on thirty-five years' experience of the teaching of English and study of the techniques involved', but he also acknowledges the influence of, among others, Charles Fries and Harold Palmer, and adds a book list which displays his debt to his predecessors. Chapman (1958) defers to commonly shared principles 'which have a general validity', although he gives no indication (e.g. in the form of footnotes or a bibliography) as to whence these principles were derived. Billows (1961: x) grants that his book is 'in some ways, a compendium of what other people have written and said about teaching', but adds

> a great deal more I have learned from particular teachers whom I have watched... My practice has been to observe success in learning, whether in my own classes or those of others, and try to abstract the cause of the success from the complex of what was done. From this I tried to establish a rule which can be generally applied.

Finally, he cautions that 'on some points I am disposed to be dogmatic'. More recently still, the methodology described by Haycraft (1978) is entirely practice-oriented, and based on the short intensive pre-service courses taught at International House, of which he was co-founder. However, at the end of each chapter, readers are referred to other contemporary resources, including Rivers (1968) and Byrne (1976). Byrne himself, in the preface to his book on teaching oral English, describes it as being 'the product of personal experience and of reflection on that experience' (1976: v), but does include 'suggestions and references for further reading' at the end of each chapter.

In prefacing a content analysis of a number of such texts, Stern (1983: 23) notes that 'one of the main problems which writers on language pedagogy have tried to contend with have been the continuous changes in the language sciences themselves.' This is often reflected in the number of editions that the more popular methodology texts rack up. A striking example of how two successive editions of a methodology text straddled a paradigm shift is Wilga Rivers' widely used text, *Teaching Foreign-Language Skills*, first published in 1968 and then revised in 1981. As Rivers herself wrote (in the second edition, 1981: xiii): 'Much water has flown under the bridge since the sixties'. Apart from being one of the few women in what at the time was an almost exclusively male-dominated field, Rivers is remarkable in not only embracing the transition into a communicative methodology, but, in some ways, being able to predict it. And, while thoroughly versed in developments in psycholinguistics, she also forestalls possible critics by appealing to the fact that she is 'an experienced teacher of languages' (ibid.).

In short, methodology writers over the last century have demonstrated a less than total allegiance to scientific method, appealing more often than not to their intuitions and personal experience. As Stern (1983: 478), in summarizing his own analysis of a number of contemporary teachers' guides (including Rivers, 1981), puts it,

> These guides commonly reflect the writers' experience as teachers or teacher trainers, their interpretations of the contemporary literature of linguistics, applied linguistics, and psycholinguistics, and their personal views on the method question.

But, less charitably, he adds:

> Looked at critically as a class, the guides frequently fail to make a clear distinction between firmly tested knowledge, research evidence, widely held opinion, personal views of the writer, and hypotheses or speculations to be tested. These books, therefore, are best treated as the personal language teaching theories of experienced and sophisticated theorists and practitioners.
>
> *(ibid.)*

However, on the positive side, Stern concurs that, as comprehensive sense-making exercises, they have a certain validity, and, in the end, '[t]hey are the most clearly defined global interpretations of language teaching at our disposal' (ibid.).

Arguably, the need for such 'interpretations' is more important than ever, given the exponential increase in research studies that have been undertaken in the last three decades, and given that the papers that directly report these studies 'do not seem to function well as a mechanism for communicating information for teachers' (Bartels, 2003: 737). This, at least, is the gist of McNamara's (2008: 304) defence of what he terms 'intellectual guides':

> As the various fields of theory develop and proliferate, the demands on those introducing theory to practitioners grow ever more complex. That is why intellectual guides to the whole area and its many perspectives are needed, as a resource for trainers and educators and as a way of demonstrating the richness of available perspectives to practitioners wishing to understand and develop their practice.

Research

With the aim of bringing this account up-to-date, as well as probing more deeply into the way these 'intellectual guides' are generated and informed, four leading writers of such texts were interviewed (by e-mail). They were Penny Ur (henceforth PU) author of (among many titles) *A Course in Language Teaching* (1991; 2012a); H. Douglas Brown (henceforth HDB), author of *Principles of Language Learning and Teaching* (2014) and *Teaching by Principles* (2007), among others; Jeremy Harmer (JH), author of many titles, including *The Practice of English Language Teaching* (2015), and *How to Teach English* (2007); and Jim Scrivener (JS), author of (among others)

Learning Teaching (2011) (all four authors have given their consent to be quoted in this chapter). While no accurate figures are available (and are probably jealously guarded by their publishers), a straw-poll of teacher trainers in a variety of contexts suggests that, between them, these four writers command a substantial share of the global market for methodology texts for use on ELT teacher training courses, both pre- and in-service.

Given the ongoing debate about the 'theory-practice divide, the questions that they were invited to address were the following:

1. How did you get into writing methodology texts?
2. How important is it, do you think, to link research and classroom practice?
3. How have you kept/do you keep abreast of new developments in research, e.g. SLA, corpus linguistics, neurobiology etc?
4. Given that most research is somewhat inconclusive, how do you select from – and prioritize – the research findings that inform your texts?
5. Do you feel you have an 'agenda', i.e. a bias towards a particular theoretical (or atheoretical) position? If so, do you think this matters?
6. Does it concern you that you might be 'dumbing down' or otherwise misrepresenting research findings? How do you guard against this?
7. To what do you attribute your success? (Don't be modest!)

In describing how they became writers of methodology texts, all four referenced their prior involvement in teacher education which had helped them articulate their own 'personal theories' of teaching and, at the same time, led them to identify a need in the market for practically-oriented texts written in accessible language. In their own words:

> Early in my career (mid-1970s) I found that no one current textbook fit my needs for assigned readings for courses, and considered writing my own book.
>
> *(HDB)*

> It started when I wrote notes to accompany/follow up my somewhat incoherent input on a teacher training course in Mexico many years ago. It turnout I was better at expressing myself in writing than speaking.
>
> *(JH)*

> I got excited about things that worked for me in the classroom, and wanted to share. First [I] talked to my colleagues at school, then started writing articles for a local teachers' journal, then a British one, and then I wrote something about ideas for task-centred oral fluency practice and got carried away…wrote an article full of teaching ideas that was too long for any journal to publish.
>
> *(PU)*

> I thought there was a real space in the market for a book that focussed on the "hows" a teacher needed when doing a short intensive practical course like CTEFLA (CELTA).
>
> *(JS)*

Often a fortuitous contact with another writer or publisher led to an invitation to submit a proposal: 'When a Prentice Hall rep came to my office asking if I had any books "up my sleeve," that was all the impetus I needed' (HDB).

On the question as to the importance of making connections between research and class-room practice, opinions varied, and, indeed, tended to reflect the range of positions adopted by previous generations of writers, as outlined in the survey above. JH, for example, argues:

> I simply fail to understand people who deny the role of research in helping us understand our practice and improve it. … Of course teacher intuition matters, and classroom experience is paramount, but unless, as teachers, we are open to listening to and evaluating other people's research we run the risk of thinking that we understand everything.

This is a sentiment echoed by HDB: 'Teachers need to *ground* their teaching in research-based findings and assumptions. And, more importantly, teachers themselves should not shrink from engaging in their own classroom-based "action research." It's an all-important interaction.'

PU, however, takes a more non-committal stance on the need to appeal to the research evidence, arguing that such evidence is 'not always essential, but often useful and enlightening'. And she adds, 'It's sometimes a useful support and can provide interesting insights, but it's certainly possible to write helpful and valid professional guidance for teachers with no research references whatsoever.' This echoes the opinion she had expressed in an earlier article on the relation between research and practice (Ur, 2012b):

> For the ELT practitioner the main source of professional learning is classroom experience, enriched by discussion with colleagues, feedback from students, and – for those teachers with the time and inclination – input through reading, conferences and courses, of which research is one important component. Research is not the primary basis of ELT knowledge for the practitioner, but it is a valuable supplement.

JS is more sceptical still: 'I've never found much formal "research" very helpful to my own classroom work. I am not "anti-research" but I do carry a suspicion of many statistical studies in teaching.' For him, research lacks what Clarke terms 'particularizability': 'The important question to ask is "To what extent can this information be made usable for particular teachers?"' (Clarke, 1994: 20). Or, as Han (2007: 392) puts it, 'researchers need to be ever mindful that as much as their studies are generalisable, pedagogy is largely local.'

Rather than relying on research, therefore, JS maintains that 'I learn more about my own teaching by watching and thinking about my own teaching. Other people's discoveries rarely feel applicable to me (being uniquely me), my context (being uniquely it) and my students (being uniquely them)'. He regrets that many practising teachers 'are rather in awe of supposed "experts" and quite wary of trusting their own experience and expertise', and his 'mission' is 'to encourage teachers to trust their own experience more and find hard-edged ways to learn from it.' For this writer, learning to teach is not only both situated and experiential, but is essentially *personal*, as revealed, for example, in the stories that teachers tell in order to make sense of their experience. As Golombek (2009: 155) notes, 'These stories are expressions of a dynamic and complex kind of knowledge – teachers' personal practical knowledge.'

In response to the question as to how these writers keep abreast of new developments in the field, there was again a diversity of opinion, reflecting the range of academic versus non-academic contexts in which they operate. Representing the more academic axis, HDB keeps up-to-date 'by teaching university courses myself and disciplining myself to set aside reading time. Purposeful reading of summaries of research in edited "state of the art" volumes helps to acquire information in subfields that are of interest but not in my central focus.' PU admits to the impossibility of keeping abreast of all current development in the field and that, despite reading as much as possible, she is sure she is missing some 'key publications'. 'But on the other hand things that are really important get cited by those I *am* reading, so sooner or later I think I get most of the major stuff. But certainly not all.' JH mentions three sources of input: reading (principally journals), attending conferences, and 'thirdly I keep my eyes and ears open through news media, magazines and, increasingly, social media where news of new research often breaks.' JS also mentions social media: 'For some years I think Twitter has been a very important sign-post to interesting articles and websites.' And he adds, 'In general, I have been more inspired by research in science areas (quantum physics, brain, astronomy etc) than by mainstream ELT/language learning research. *New Scientist* magazine is excellent in pointing towards science books worth reading.'

It is tempting to infer not just an academic versus non-academic divide here, but a geographical one: HDB works in a North American context, whereas the others are affiliated with British-based publishers. As Womack (1969) long ago noted: 'From the beginning, TEFL in the States has been closely tied to developments in linguistics, so closely that in the States we assume this relationship or collaboration. This does not universally seem to be the situation in Britain. Indeed, linguistics seems suspect among people in TEFL there' (cited in Rixon and Smith, 2017: 18.) Not just linguistics, perhaps, but SLA as well.

Asked about their criteria for selecting from the research evidence, HDB again positions himself within an academic and research-based discourse community, while also indicating a strong pedagogical orientation, effectively bridging the two discourses: 'The selection of findings to inform my writing is based on degrees of (1) *validity* through triangulation of findings, (2) *relevance* of findings to pedagogy, and (3) *practicality* of those findings for classroom teachers.' Similarly, PU looks for research that is 'well-designed and carefully executed, with convincing evidence and logical conclusions', and that, moreover, is not 'trivial' nor easily generalizable in terms of its practical applications. JH invokes Prabhu's (1987) 'sense of plausibility': 'I go for what seems plausible to me. But I have to be careful (and suspicious) of my own unreliable instinct.' And he adds, 'There IS an element of fashion in this too, of course. Readers of a general methodology book need to know what is most "current" as well as what has been'. Predictably, perhaps, JS takes a more experiential, even intuitive, stance: 'Mainly, I think I write what I do and what I see other teachers doing. Informed ideas that may or may not work for others. These need to fit in with my own internal schema for how I think people learn, study, behave etc.'

On the question of 'having an agenda', only JS expresses an allegiance to a specific theory of learning – what he describes as a '"muscular hard-edged humanism" based on honest, uncompromising feedback cycles', and influenced by the work of Carl Rogers in particular. The others are more circumspect, and aim for balance: 'Everyone has biases, but I try to be as fair-minded as possible in weighing relevant alternatives' (HDB); 'I really try hard in my own writing to be as objective as possible' (PU); 'In my case I write "general" methodology and I see it as my duty to try and present a balanced picture of what is going on – showing where alternative views of what is going on can be relevant' (JH).

JH gives an example of how he attempts to maintain a balance:

> A typical example is the issue of whether or not to use the L1 in the classroom. Different researchers/commentators have diametrically opposite views of this. So the job of a general methodology writer is to explain these two views and then, perhaps, draw a general conclusion – or perhaps that would better be described as a summary of what's going on.

However, even HDB confesses to a set of values that underpin his methodology, confirming the view that – as Johnston (2003: 5) insists – 'language teaching, like all other teaching, is fundamentally moral, that is, value laden':

> I firmly believe that language learning is a universal means for multicultural communication and reaching across national and linguistic borders, as well as appreciating and affirming diversity in points of view. I always remind my teachers that they have a social responsibility to appreciate that diversity among their students, to be nonjudgmental in responses to students, and to remind their students that language is a bridge to global peace. If that's a bias, so be it!

Asked whether they were concerned about 'dumbing down' or misrepresenting research findings, opinions differed. JH and HDB resist simplification and overgeneralization:

> I worry about dumbing down all the time. If I see it as my responsibility to give a general overview of our field; if I see it as a useful service make some complex ideas more accessible to practising teachers; if I see a kind of narrative flow as part of my trade – and I do see all those things – then the corollary is that I may (and almost certainly do) fall into the trap of oversimplification.
>
> *(JH)*

> I do not think we should "dumb-down" such findings, and I try to avoid it. Most "dumbing down" ends up as overgeneralization, which should be avoided at all costs. The best way to guard against it is to provide concrete examples and "show" (rather than "tell") how research informs pedagogical decisions and actions.
>
> *(HDB)*

On the other hand, JS and PU are more sanguine, and PU is refreshingly candid:

> I think there is a valid place for practical manuals for teaching that do not encumber the reader with all the background understanding the author has acquired.
>
> *(JS)*

> No, I don't think this worries me. Research which is very complicated and difficult I can't understand anyway, so I'm not about to dumb it down because I'm too dumb myself to deal with it in the first place. … Abridging, paraphrasing and simplifying are valid mediating strategies which enable a lot more people to get access to the findings; but this does not mean over-simplifying or diluting the essential facts and conclusions.
>
> *(PU)*

Finally, when asked to what they attribute their success, one theme recurred – their capacity to address practising teachers in language that is both accessible and personally engaging – i.e. that they have a distinctive 'voice':

> I avoid language that's pedantic and academically stuffy. I talk to my readers as I would in a classroom setting or sitting down with them in conversation.
>
> *(HDB)*

I seem to have found a writing "voice" that many teachers have found congenial. I think it's as simple as that.

(JH)

I'm seen as a sort of senior, experienced teaching colleague with lot of classroom experience rather than a university professor who is an "authority" on applied linguistics. At the same time, I can explain the underlying rationale and quote supporting research where appropriate, have "done my homework", as it were.

(PU)

I've been told that I sound like a real teacher – someone who quite obviously has taught a lot – talking to them – and this is compared with the voice they hear from many other books – that of some distant expert who is telling them what they should do, based on research – possibly without even having the relevant chalk face experience themselves.

(JS)

Discussion

While each of the writers interviewed might situate themselves at different points along a cline from purely research-based and academic to purely classroom-based and intuitive, all four share a number of features in common – features, what is more, that (as we have seen) are consistent with a tradition of writing about methodology that extends back more than a century. In writing about teaching they are:

- *principled* – the writers subscribe to a set of beliefs, or values, or principles that derive from research and/or their own experience, and which underpin the classroom practices that they endorse;
- *selective* – at the same time, they exclude or marginalize practices that are considered implausible, trivial, or not easily generalizable to a wide range of contexts, while, at the same time, they often advise teachers to be sensitive to contextual factors and, where possible, adopt a 'particularist' approach;
- *eclectic* – nevertheless, rather than promoting one single method or approach, the writers do draw on a variety of sources and describe a range of methods and techniques; they eschew prescriptivism or dogmatism, and aim for balance;
- *practical* – they all purport to provide practical advice and suggestions for classroom application, whether or not these are explicitly endorsed by research findings;
- *demotic* – they assume an informal, non-academic writing 'voice', appropriate to a pedagogic rather than a research-based discourse mode (Ellis and Shintani 2014).

In this sense, all four writers write guides that, in Stern's (1983: 478) formulation, 'offer a comprehensive and coherent interpretation of all aspects that the writer of the guide regards as important in language teaching.' On the other hand, all four – to varying degrees – might equally be liable to Stern's charge that they 'frequently fail to make a clear distinction between firmly tested knowledge, research evidence, widely held opinion, personal views of the writer, and hypotheses or speculations to be tested' (ibid.).

It is, after all, taken as axiomatic by most researchers – if not by many teachers – that 'firmly tested knowledge' is valued more highly than 'widely held opinion' and 'personal views'. As Long (2011: 385) insists, 'SLA research should obviously feature prominently in proposals for LT [language teaching]. SLA researchers study the very processes LT is designed to facilitate, after all.' It stands to reason (the argument goes) that teachers' guides should represent the research findings accurately, impartially and comprehensively.

However, given the popularity of these guides, it is tempting to suppose that their reluctance to feature SLA research 'prominently' may not in fact be a problem – that the guides fulfil an important function irrespective of their apparent lack of scientific rigour. This raises the vexed question as to how essential 'firmly tested knowledge' and 'research evidence' is for the purposes for which these guides are written, i.e. pre- or in-service teacher education. Some scholars, e.g. Freeman (1989: 29), might argue that they are not: 'Although applied linguistics, research in second language acquisition, and methodology all contribute to the knowledge on which language teaching is based, they are not, and must not be confused with, language teaching itself. They are, in fact, ancillary to it, and thus they should not be the primary subject matter of language teacher education.'

This is a view that has found support in case studies of teacher expertise, e.g. Johnson (1996), Woods (1996), Tsui (2003), which suggest that, in Johnson's words (1996: 166–167), 'what teachers know about teaching is not simply an extended body of facts and theories but is instead largely experiential and socially constructed out of the experiences and classrooms from which teachers have come'. It is knowledge, moreover, that is instantiated, developed and refined through reflection on practice: as Tsui (2003: 265) argues, 'one of the *critical* differences between expert and nonexpert teachers is the capability of the former to engage in conscious deliberation and reflection. Such engagement involves making explicit the tacit practical knowledge that is gained from experience'. Tsui refers to this process as 'the theorisation of practical knowledge' (ibid.).

Indeed, when teachers are asked to identify the sources of their expertise, they seldom appeal to 'firmly tested knowledge' or 'research evidence'. For example, Crookes and Arakaki interviewed 20 ESL teachers in an intensive teaching program in the USA over a 3-month period and found that 'accumulated teaching experience was the most often cited source of teaching ideas' (1999: 16). Other sources of ideas came from (in order) informal consultations with colleagues, 'pedagogically oriented printed resources (e.g., book series)' – presumably the kinds of books under discussion in this paper – 'spontaneous self-generation', preservice training, and in-house workshops. Crookes and Arakaki conclude (1999: 15):

> Many in the academic world of ESL might like to think that ideas come from research or research-based sources, but in the field of second and foreign language education, there is little evidence indicating whether such research is available, being used, or even appreciated as a source of teaching ideas by its intended audience of classroom teachers and program administrators.

Given this lack of 'appreciation', it is tempting to think that the popularity of the teachers' guides under consideration may be *due to* – rather than *in spite of* – their practical, experiential bias and their informal style. After all, knowledge that itself has been derived from, and is grounded in, the experience of teaching, or of observing teaching, or of talking with practising teachers, will arguably resonate more with practising teachers than knowledge which is derived directly from the applied linguistics literature, including second language acquisition research.

This need not discount the value of engaging with a research-based discourse entirely. Even Tsui (op. cit) acknowledges that teaching expertise 'also involves the transformation of "formal knowledge" to personal practical knowledge through personal interpretation of formal knowledge in the teacher's own specific context of work' (Tsui 2003: 265), where 'formal knowledge' is defined (by reference to Bereiter and Scardamalia (1993)) as 'publicly represented' and 'negotiable' knowledge.

Moreover, taking a sociocultural perspective on teacher education, a teacher's professional development involves aligning with the target discourse community – a process of acculturation – which involves learning how 'to talk the talk' – to publicly represent and negotiate their practical knowledge. As Freeman (1996: 238) argues, 'it may be that the role of teacher education lies less in influencing teachers' behaviour than enabling them to *rename their experience*, thus recasting their conceptions and reconstructing their classroom practice' (emphasis added). Teachers' guides might provide the material means by which this renaming process is facilitated: simply the act of putting into writing what teachers might otherwise talk about amongst themselves could serve to mediate the transition from 'other-regulation' to 'self-regulation' (Vygotsky, 1978).

This suggests ways in which these texts might best be used in teacher education contexts: as the vehicles by means of which teachers in training make sense of their experience and articulate their tacit theories of teaching and learning with respect to their own contexts. As Jourdenais (2011: 650) argues, 'the challenge may lie in assisting teachers to understand and interact with the research in such a way that they are able to assess theoretical relevance for their own context'. Johnson (1997: 779–780) gives a good example of how this might be expedited:

> When I ask my MA TESOL students to read about a particular theory, I ask them to reflect on how it may or may not be relevant to their own L2 learning and teaching experiences and to consider the extent to which the theory is consistent with their beliefs about how L2s are learned and should be taught…

And she adds,

> If we create opportunities for teachers to make sense of theory in terms of themselves, their students, their classrooms, and the broader social context within which they work, then theory becomes relevant for practice because teachers make it their own, and it becomes part of how they conceptualise, construct explanations for, and respond to the social interactions and shared meanings that exist within their classrooms.

Arguably, methodology texts play an important mediating role in helping teachers 'to make sense of theory in terms of themselves.' One way that they could do this is to incorporate the 'voices' of practising teachers, as they narrate critical incidents from their own experience, which might in turn trigger cycles of reflection and experimentation.

Conclusion

Given that a teachers' guide (of the type reviewed in this chapter) may be one of the few books on teaching that many teachers either read or consult – e.g. in the context of their pre- or in-service training – it has a potentially important impact on the way that teachers' practical knowledge is constructed. But it will only realise this potential if it is able to 'mesh' with the teacher's developing experience-based knowledge structures. Ideally, the writers of such texts, then, should themselves be experienced teachers whose writing is transparent and whose advice is plausible, but who also have a sense of how to leverage the inexpert teacher into the target discourse community – not necessarily by simply re-packaging the findings of SLA research and applied linguistics, but by inviting the teacher to map those findings on to their own experience, and, by 'renaming' them, gain ownership of them. As Woods (1996: 285) writes: 'While teaching to teach often focuses on the transmission of information about teaching, learning to teach can be seen as learning how to take advantage of experience so that acculturation as a teacher is enhanced.' Given that well-written teachers' guides enshrine the collective experience of others, they offer potentially powerful tools for mediating that acculturation process.

Further reading

Bartels, N. (2003) 'How Teachers and Researchers Read Academic Articles'. *Teaching & Teacher Education*, 19(7) 737–753.
  A study that suggests that research articles may need to align more closely with the discourse of teachers if their findings are to impact on classroom practice.
Clarke, M. A. (1994) 'The Dysfunctions of the Theory/Practice Discourse'. *TESOL Quarterly*, 28(1) 9–26.
  A critical perspective on the disconnect between the discourse of researchers and that of classroom practitioners.
Ellis, R. and Shintani, N. (2014) *Exploring Language Pedagogy through Second Language Acquisition Research*. Abingdon: Routledge.
  A comprehensive review of the pedagogical proposals found in teachers' guides, scrutinized through the lens of SLA research.

References

Bartels, N. (2003) 'How Teachers and Researchers Read Academic Articles'. *Teaching & Teacher Education*, 19(7) 737–753.
Bereiter, C. and Scardamalia, M. (1993) *Surpassing Ourselves: An inquiry into the Nature and Implications of Expertise*. Illinois: Open Court.
Billows (1961) *The Techniques of Language Teaching*. London: Longmans, Green.
Borg, S. (2009) 'English Language Teachers' Conceptions of Research'. *Applied Linguistics*, 30(3) 358–388.
Brooks, N. (1960) *Language and Language Learning: Theory and Practice*. New York: Harcourt, Brace and World.
Brown, H. D. (2007) *Teaching by Principles: An Interactive Approach to Language Pedagogy*, 3rd edition. New York: Pearson.
Brown, H. D. (2014) *Principles of Language Learning and Teaching*, 6th edition. New York: Pearson.
Byrne, D. (1976) *Teaching Oral English*. Harlow: Longman.
Carroll, J. (1966) 'The contributions of psychological theory and educational research to the teaching of foreign languages', in Valdman, A. (ed.) *Trends in Language Teaching*. New York: McGraw-Hill: 93–106.
Chapman, L. R. H. (1958) *Teaching English to Beginners*. London: Longmans, Green and Co.
Clarke, M. A. (1994) 'The Dysfunctions of the Theory/Practice Discourse'. *TESOL Quarterly*, 28(1) 9–26.
Crookes, G. and Arakaki, L. (1999) 'Teaching Ideas Sources and Work Conditions in an ESL Program'. *TESOL Journal*, 8(1) 15–19.
Ellis, R. (1997) *SLA Research and Language Teaching*. Oxford: Oxford University Press.
Ellis, R. and Shintani, N. (2014) *Exploring Language Pedagogy through Second Language Acquisition Research*. Abingdon: Routledge.
Freeman, D. (1989) 'Teacher Training, Development and Decision Making: A Model of Teaching and Related Strategies for Language Teacher Education'. *TESOL Quarterly*, 23(1) 27–45.
Freeman D. (1996) 'Renaming experience/reconstructing practice: developing new understandings of teaching', in Freeman, D. and Richards, J. C. (eds) *Teacher Learning in Language Teaching*. Cambridge: Cambridge University Press: 221–241.
Frisby, A. W. (1957) *Teaching English: Notes and Comments on Teaching English Overseas*. Harlow: Longman.

Golombek, P. (2009) 'Personal practical knowledge in L2 teacher education', in Burns, A. and Richards, J. C. (eds) *The Cambridge Guide to Second Language Teacher Education*. Cambridge: Cambridge University Press: 155–162.

Han, Z. (2007) 'Pedagogical Implications: Genuine or Pretentious?'. *TESOL Quarterly*, 41(2) 387–393.

Harmer, J. (2007) *How to Teach English*, 2nd edition. London: Longman.

Harmer, J. (2015) *The Practice of English Language Teaching*, 5th edition. London: Pearson.

Harwood, N. (2014) 'Content, consumption, and production: three levels of textbook research', in Harwood, N. (ed.) *English Language Textbooks: Content, Consumption, Production*. Basingstoke: Palgrave Macmillan: 1–41.

Haycraft, J. (1978) *An Introduction to English Language Teaching*. Harlow: Longman.

Johnson, K. E. (1996) 'The Role of Theory in L2 Teacher Education'. *TESOL Quarterly*, 30(4) 765–771.

Johnson, K. E. (1997) 'Comments on Karen E. Johnson's "The Role of Theory in L2 Teacher Education": The Author Responds'. *TESOL Quarterly*, 31(4) 779–782.

Johnston, B. (2003) *Values in English Language Teaching*. Mahwah, NJ: Lawrence Erlbaum.

Jourdenais, R. (2011) 'Language teacher education', in Long, M. H. and Doughty, C. J. (eds) *The Handbook of Language Teaching*. Oxford: Wiley-Blackwell: 647–658.

Long, M. H. (2011) 'Methodological principles for language teaching', in Long, M. H. and Doughty, C. J. (eds) *The Handbook of Language Teaching*. Oxford: Wiley-Blackwell: 373–394.

Morris, I. (1959) *The Art of Teaching English as a Living Language*. London: Macmillan & Co.

McNamara, T. (2008) 'Mapping the Scope of Theory in TESOL'. *TESOL Quarterly*, 42(2) 302–305.

Palmer, H. E. ([1917] 1968) *The Scientific Study and Teaching of Languages*. London: Oxford University Press.

Palmer, H. E. (1921) *The Principles of Language Study*. London: Harrap.

Prabhu, N. S. (1987) *Second Language Pedagogy*. Oxford: Oxford University Press.

Rivers, W. (1968) *Teaching Foreign-language Skills*. Chicago, IL: The University of Chicago Press.

Rivers, W. (1981) *Teaching Foreign-language Skills*, 2nd edition. Chicago, IL: The University of Chicago Press.

Rixon, S. and Smith, R. (2017) *A History of IATEFL*. Faversham: IATEFL.

Scrivener, J. (2011) *Learning Teaching*, 3rd edition. Oxford: Macmillan.

Smith, R. (1999) *The Writings of Harold E. Palmer: An Overview*. Tokyo: Hon-no-Tomosha.

Stern, H. H. (1983) *Fundamental Concepts of Language Teaching*. Oxford: Oxford University Press.

Sweet, H. (1899/1964) *The Practical Study of Languages*. Oxford: Oxford University Press.

Tsui, A. (2003) *Understanding Expertise in Teaching*. Cambridge: Cambridge University Press.

Ur, P. (1991) *A Course in Language Teaching: Practice and Theory*. Cambridge: Cambridge University Press.

Ur, P. (2012a) *A Course in Language Teaching: Practice and Theory*, 2nd edition. Cambridge: Cambridge University Press.

Ur, P. (2012b) 'How Useful is TESOL Academic Research?'. *The Guardian*. Available online: <www.theguardian.com/education/2012/oct/16/teacher-tesol-academic-research-useful> (accessed 22 May, 2019).

Vygotsky, L. S. (1978) *Mind in Society: The Development of Higher Psychological Processes*. Cambridge, MA: Harvard University Press.

Widdowson, H. (1990) *Aspects of Language Teaching*. Oxford: Oxford University Press.

Woods, D. (1996) *Teacher Cognition and Language Teaching*. Cambridge: Cambridge University Press.

34

Teacher motivation

The missing ingredient in teacher education

Martin Lamb and Mark Wyatt

Introduction

Despite the well-acknowledged importance of teacher motivation in effective pedagogy, and despite the abundant evidence that teacher motivation is a problem in almost all global settings, it is curious that the Second Language Teacher Education (SLTE) literature has hitherto given very little attention to the issue. A survey of the most well-known SLTE textbooks of the past two decades (e.g. Freeman & Richards, 1996; Malderez & Bodóczky, 1999; Randall & Thornton, 2001; Richards & Farrell, 2005; Malderez & Wedell, 2007; Burns & Richards, 2009; Johnson & Golombek, 2011; Farrell, 2015a) shows that it is either ignored altogether, or assumed to be just another beneficial outcome of effective SLTE (e.g. 'Workshops … can serve to rekindle teachers' enthusiasm for teaching' Richards & Farrell, 2005: 25). It is not explicitly included as being within the 'scope' of SLTE (Freeman, 2009), nor as part of the 'professional development of trainers' (Wright, 2009). Many writers do stress the importance of providing empathetic support for teachers during the change process, while others emphasize the need for teachers to reflect on (inter alia) their own motives and decision-making, but again these are treated as aspects of good quality SLTE rather than representing a serious attempt to engage with the professional motivation of the participant.

Moreover, it is evident from listening to teachers' voices that SLTE provision has sometimes ignored fundamental motivational principles. Farrell, for example, recalls being humiliated during a lesson observation by his Director of Studies during his early months of teaching, after which he 'felt like leaving the profession, thinking that maybe [he] was not suited to be a language teacher' (Farrell, 2015b: 2). Complaints are also heard from more experienced in-service teachers, such as those researched by Aboshiha (2013: 222), who report some antipathy towards teacher educators in academic settings, e.g.: 'I think these people, they lose touch with teaching EFL; they tell us how you should do this, this and this. And you think, how many years ago did you do this?'

Perhaps we should not be surprised by this lack of engagement with teachers' professional motivation; on the one hand, there has been a strongly cognitive orientation to the SLTE literature as trainers have been preoccupied with the key challenge of reconciling theory and practice in developing practitioner knowledge and skills, latterly informed by work on teacher cognition (e.g. Borg, 2006) and by sociocultural perspectives on teachers' knowledge construction (Johnson & Golombek, 2011). On the other hand, the field of teacher motivation itself has been under-developed, lagging well behind the advanced theoreticization of learner motivation (cf. Dörnyei & Ushioda, 2011).

On both these fronts, things are changing. First, there have recently been calls to broaden the focus of teacher education research and theory beyond teacher thinking, to include affect and desire (Korthagen, 2017). It is increasingly recognized that much teacher behaviour in class is triggered by unconscious motives; to understand these, in a bid to shape pedagogic practice, means giving serious attention to the feelings and wants, built up over years of classroom experience (as learner or teacher), that contribute to a teacher's moment-to-moment decision-making. In our own field, Kubanyiova and Feryok (2015) have argued that if teacher educators are to understand this decision-making – what socially oriented theorists have called 'emergent sense making in action' – their goals must go beyond the development of teachers' beliefs and knowledge and address teachers' inner lives, the self-concepts (present and future), the ethical concerns, the emotion-laden relationships and so on which inform their classroom practice, and which of course will also deeply influence their response to experiences of professional development. As Korthagen (2017: 399) puts it, the key question for teacher educators is not 'what do my participants need to know?' but 'what do the teachers think, feel, want, what are their ideals, what inspires them, what kind of teachers do they want to be?'.

Second, teacher motivation is now being theorized and researched with some of the same rigour with which learner motivation has been studied, indeed borrowing concepts and theories from that field as well as from the domains of management and occupational motivation. As Richardson, Karabenick and Watt (2014: xiii–xiv) describe:

> there has been a dramatic rise in the number of journal publications, special issues, and international conference papers addressing questions such as: What motivates people to choose teaching as a career? What are teachers' goals as they work with students in classrooms? And, how do intrinsic and extrinsic forces impact teachers' career experiences and trajectories?

In the rest of this chapter we will review some of the key findings of this emerging area of research, and then consider how they can inform the practice of teacher educators in both pre-service and in-service professional development. Our key argument is that teacher motivation matters because protecting and enhancing it should be an inherent goal of SLTE, and because the nature of participants' motivation will help determine whether they benefit from SLTE.

Review of theory and research on teacher motivation

Motives for joining the profession

As highlighted by Richardson and Watt (2014), only in the last decade has there been some agreement amongst researchers as to how to investigate motives for joining the teaching profession, although altruistic, intrinsic and extrinsic motives have been apparent to researchers for longer. Regarding altruistic motives, Dörnyei and Ushioda (2011: 161) emphasise that '"teaching" as a vocational goal has always been associated with the internal desire to educate people, to impart knowledge and values, and to advance a community or a whole nation'. Such idealism, apparent around the world, can be illustrated by the following quote:

> I want to become a teacher and help raise the falling standard of education in the country, especially in the remote area.
>
> *(Pre-service teacher in Ghana, quoted in Akyeampong & Stephens, 2002: 269)*

Intrinsic motives relating to stimulation derived from the educational process itself, working with children, and the subject matter to be taught (Dörnyei & Ushioda, 2011), are evident in statements such as the following (the last of which merges with the altruistic):

> I love kids. They are sincere and always smile.
>
> *(Pre-service teacher of English in Hong Kong, quoted in Gu & Lai, 2012: 50)*

> I loved English at that time. English was a miraculous thing to me.
>
> *(In-service teacher of English in China reflecting on being drawn to the subject, quoted in Gao & Xu, 2014: 159)*

> Through teaching my favourite subject, English, I will be more than happy if I can assist the growth of my young students on whose shoulders the future of our society lies.
>
> *(Pre-service teacher of English in Japan, quoted in Kumazawa, 2013: 50)*

Other new teachers, though, have more instrumental or extrinsic goals, i.e. viewing teaching primarily as a way of achieving separable utilitarian objectives, such as financial security, alternative employment for which teaching might be a stepping stone, or an exotic lifestyle. Statements that exemplify such perspectives include:

> Through teaching, one can become an officer (that is join the military) – and even enter politics to become a prominent person.
>
> *(Pre-service teacher in Ghana, quoted in Akyeampong & Stephens, 2002: 269)*

> In Hong Kong, the salary for teachers is relatively high. I can travel to other countries on my vacations.
>
> *(Pre-service teacher of English from mainland China being educated in Hong Kong, quoted in Gu & Lai 2012: 51)*

> My parents kept saying that teaching is an iron rice bowl (a stable job) and teachers had long vacations…
>
> *(In-service teacher of English in China, quoted in Gao & Xu, 2014: 159)*

Meanwhile, other teachers entering the profession might be amotivated (lacking motivation) since becoming a teacher had not been their goal. Failure in exams or bleak sociocultural factors had rather made the decision for them, as for this South African quoted in Shih (2016: 48): 'When I was growing up in South Africa, the only professions which were deemed, you know, fit for black people were maybe teaching, nursing, and being a policeman. So I didn't have much of a choice really'.

As to how these different motives influence what teachers subsequently do in the classroom and the ways in which they later engage professionally in their work, systematic research exploring these issues has emerged in the last 15 years, with the development of Richardson and Watt's (2006) 'factors influencing teaching choice' (FIT Choice) framework. Drawing on the 'expectancy-value' theory developed by Eccles et al. (1983), which holds that motivated behaviour can be explained by beliefs about likely success and the extent to which an activity is valued, Richardson and Watt (2006) developed, through their FIT Choice model, a psychometric scale applicable to exploring motives for entering teaching, i.e. tapping into altruistic, intrinsic, utilitarian, and also ability-related motives.

Drawing on this framework to analyse the motivation of a large sample of pre-service teachers of various subjects in their Australian context allowed Watt and Richardson (2008) to categorize these teachers as follows: 'highly engaged persisters' (those intrinsically motivated individuals with a passion for teaching), 'highly engaged switchers' (those restless spirits planning on putting effort into teaching in the short term but visualizing subsequent alternative careers) and 'lower engaged desisters' (those individuals already disaffected and looking for an escape route). Watt and Richardson's research suggests that the highly engaged persisters benefit much more from pre-service teacher education (being 'turned on' by it) than the lower engaged desisters, whose experience tends to be much more negative. Given that the latter group are also much less likely to stay in the profession, according to Watt and Richardson, there are economic as well as educational imperatives for addressing their needs during initial teacher training.

The FIT Choice model has been validated in various national contexts, as Suryani, Watt and Richardson (2016) report, with teachers of various subjects. Preservice English language teachers have been amongst the minorities sampled, but research applying the FIT Choice model specifically to this group is still needed. This could explore the extent to which the motivation of this group is distinct. Kubanyiova (2006: 8), for example, has suggested that some English language teachers might enter the profession with the 'wrong' kind of motivation, intrinsically motivated in terms of loving English, but desperate not to do the job of teaching. So it is possible that love of the language in European contexts such as Kubanyiova's is encouraging lower engaged desisters to enrol on English language teacher education programmes. Meanwhile, in other contexts, such as Indonesia, it is widely assumed that many English education graduates use their English to join other professions, such as interpreting for international companies (Suryani et al., 2016). So the problem of there being numerous lower engaged desisters on preservice courses may be particularly rife in our field. Nevertheless, as Watt and Richardson (2008: 426) point out, motivation can change and there may be ways of socializing lower engaged desisters 'into one of the other types' on a pre-service teacher education course (see below).

Motivation while teaching

While expectancy-value theory has been drawn upon by Watt and Richardson (2008) to understand the motivation of pre-service teachers, other major theoretical frameworks in motivation research have been applied to analysing the motivation of in-service teachers. These include self-determination theory, theories of self, principally self-efficacy beliefs, achievement goal theory, interest theory, flow theory, as well as theories relating to identity and ideal/ought-to/feared selves that are more fully treated in other chapters of this volume. These theories have received differing degrees of attention when re-applied from the study of students to teachers, as Urdan (2014) reports, with self-determination theory and, to an even greater extent, self-efficacy beliefs having been most influential with teacher motivation researchers.

Intrinsic and extrinsic motives in teaching

According to Ryan and Deci's (2000) 'Self-Determination Theory' (SDT), motivation to engage in work-related behaviour can be plotted on a cline from amotivation at one extreme through various forms of extrinsic motivation (from the externally to the internally regulated, i.e. from concerns with rewards and punishment, where outside forces are of paramount importance, to synthesis with organizational goals, where integration has taken place) to intrinsic motivation at the other end of the cline. From this perspective, educators can develop more internalized forms of motivation by satisfying students' psychological needs for competence, autonomy and relatedness. SDT has been drawn upon by a small but growing number of teacher motivation researchers (see Roth, 2014 for an overview). Recent studies have shown for example how more self-determined teachers, both in-service and novice, tend to teach in more autonomy-supportive ways (Roth et al., 2007; Korthagen and Evelein, 2016). In other words, teachers whose own needs for autonomy, competence and relatedness are satisfied are more likely to satisfy those needs in their learners, and so develop a healthy internalized motivation for their subject.

Teachers' self-efficacy beliefs

Bandura (1986: 391) defined self-efficacy beliefs as 'people's judgements of their capabilities to organize and execute courses of action required to attain designated types of performance' and argued that they play a central role in mediating the behaviour of individuals. Influenced by awareness of teachers' insecurities about their own language competencies in the face of native-speakerist discourses (e.g. see Chen & Goh, 2011), researchers are increasingly exploring language teachers' self-efficacy (LTSE) beliefs (Wyatt, 2018). Choi and Lee (2016), in a Korean context, for instance, suggest that self-perceived competence in English and LTSE beliefs can interact closely with each other, influencing the amount of the target language spoken in class. Low LTSE beliefs can be considered especially problematic if accompanied by fixed rather than growth mindsets (Dweck, 2000), i.e. when failings are self-ascribed to lack of ability rather than to insufficient effort, since the outcome of giving up rather than renewing effort might then be more likely (Wyatt, 2018). Of course it is also true that if LTSE beliefs are too high, classroom realities can cause such a shock that teachers may abandon the profession, while those teachers that continue in a state of inflated self-belief may be less open to continued professional development (Wheatley, 2002; Wyatt, 2015). In such a scenario, there is a need for teacher education that encourages 'efficacy doubts' (Wheatley, 2002) through reflective self-questioning.

Achievement goals

Achievement goal theory (Butler, 2014) holds that some teachers tend to be more mastery-oriented (investing effort to develop their knowledge and skills by actively setting themselves challenging tasks, monitoring their own progress and eliciting any needed help) while others are more ability-oriented (primarily concerned with displaying their innate abilities, measuring themselves through social comparison, avoiding the risk-taking that is part of learning). Yet others are more work-avoidant, aiming to complete required tasks with the minimum of effort. As Butler (2014) reports, more work-avoidant teachers tend to set their students easy tasks in class and give very little homework. In contrast, mastery-oriented teachers tend to be continually extending themselves and their students. These orientations also shape the achievement of relationship goals. A striking finding of Butler's (2014: 26) longitudinal research was that the more heavily teachers emphasized that they cared about creating positive relationships with their students at the beginning of a school year 'the more likely were not only the teachers, but also their students, to report that the teacher did indeed care' at the end of the year.

Possible selves theory

Dörnyei and others have hypothesized that people can be motivated to learn by their internal conceptions of who they are or want to be; the more vivid, accessible and realistic the vision, the more likely it is to regulate people's behaviour (Dörnyei & Ushioda, 2011); this theory, which has shed much light on the nature of learner motivation in the age of global English, is now being applied to the study of novice and experienced teachers (e.g. Dörnyei & Kubanyiova, 2014; Sahakyan et al., 2018). Just imagining a rosy future is not enough of course; Oettingen (2015) argues forcefully that, for motivation to be sustained over a longer period, wishes have to be accompanied by images of specific desired outcomes, of likely obstacles, and of plans for dealing with those obstacles. Her technique, acronymically named WOOP (Wish, Outcome, Obstacle, Plan), may well have applications on pre-service training courses (see the useful website below).

Other relevant motivational constructs

There is no space here to include all theoretical formulations of motivation that could contribute to enhancing teachers' professionalism. However, two constructs of particular value are 'Flow', which refers to periods of intense absorption in the task at hand during peak moments of experience, typically when teachers sense that learning is taking place (Tardy & Snyder, 2004), and 'teacher enthusiasm'. Kunter and Holzberger (2014) argue that there are two types of teacher enthusiasm which matter – for teaching and for the subject area – though it is enthusiasm for teaching which gains the most positive appraisals by students.

Teacher motivation in the practice of teacher education

We now consider how motivational principles should be incorporated in the design of SLTE, and give examples of practical activities that teacher educators could adopt. We discuss pre-service and in-service education separately because there are clearly some principles which apply more to one than the other, though some can apply to both.

Pre-service teacher education

As we have seen, research evidence suggests that teachers choose to enter the profession for different reasons, and this is likely to affect how they respond to initial teacher training. Broadly speaking, there are those who view it as a vocation and are intrinsically motivated from the beginning (Watt & Richardson's (2008) 'highly engaged persisters'), and there are those whose motives are much more ambivalent. Motivational practice in pre-service courses therefore has two distinct goals: to sustain the motivation of the former group, and to try to internalize the motivation of the latter such that they gradually do come to see teaching as their vocation. We deal with each in turn.

Sustaining the intrinsic motivation of those entering the profession for the 'right' reasons

Clearly many principles of motivational language teaching (Lamb, 2017) will also apply in the design and conduct of teacher training courses. Dörnyei's (2001) strategies for 'maintaining and protecting motivation', such as ensuring that students are aware of the purpose of tasks, are just as relevant for teacher training as for language learning. It is vitally important also that trainees get a chance to enjoy moments of 'flow'– too often the practicum consists of large periods of low challenge (observing others) combined with occasional moments of very high challenge (actual teaching), but there also needs to be times when the balance between challenge and skill is optimal, so the trainee can experience the joy of teaching.

The gradual development of 'novice teacher autonomy' is another important strategy for long-term professional motivation. Although there are many elements of pre-service teacher training courses that are non-negotiable, and indeed where trainees look for strong guidance from course leaders, there are many opportunities for developing trainee autonomy; here are three:

1. Ensuring that the novice teachers have plenty of choice throughout their training, from broad decisions about what topics to specialize in or what age groups to practise teaching with, to very specific practical issues like the format of their lesson plans, and the marking codes they employ. The key point is that when people choose, they are personally invested in that course of action.
2. Providing the means for the trainees to access new knowledge independently, both pedagogic understanding, for instance via resource centres, professional websites, webinars and online forums – and language skills, for example through tandem partnerships.
3. Encouraging various forms of peer and self-assessment, for example through analysing audio and video recordings of practice teaching according to (self-chosen) criteria. At the same time, it is important to protect novice teachers from damaging negative self-evaluations, especially during the often traumatic experience of the practicum. Research suggests that while stress levels are certain to rise during this component of the course, the relationship with a mentor can be crucial in maintaining or enhancing the novice teachers' self-efficacy beliefs, and enabling them to learn from the inevitable mistakes rather than be disheartened (Klassen & Durksen, 2014; see also Gakonga, Chapter 28 in this volume, on building constructive mentor relationships).

Internalizing the motivation of those entering teaching with extrinsic motives

As with language learning itself, teacher educators cannot assume that all pre-service teachers are there because they want to teach. Their task therefore includes, for these participants, 'creating the basic motivational conditions' and 'generating initial motivation' (Dörnyei, 2001). When teachers are asked what motivational strategies are most effective with their learners, one regularly comes top of the list: setting a personal example with your own behaviour (Lamb, 2017). The same principle probably applies in SLTE courses; that participants are profoundly influenced, subconsciously as well as deliberately, by their course leaders, who are assumed to represent models of successful pedagogues. The most fundamental quality of the effective teacher educator, then, is a love for teaching and a passion for communicating that to new generations of teachers. Dörnyei and Kubanyiova (2014: 161) cite an Italian proverb: 'Who shall kindle others must himself glow'.

There is also an important place in the pre-service curriculum for components which overtly aim to foster respect and enthusiasm for the teaching profession. Drawing on principles of positive psychology, Gregersen and MacIntyre (2017) suggest ways of doing this; these include linking teaching to the achievement of global needs (e.g. peace, environmentalism, non-discrimination), and encouraging trainees to view teaching as 'helping others' by doing informal teaching projects outside of class. Such practices encourage altruistic motives in novice teachers, and remind them of their higher calling as they learn the nuts and bolts of the profession.

Simultaneously, pre-service courses must work to develop novice teacher identities (see also Chapter 35 in this volume). From a motivational point of view, if trainees lack an aspirant teacher identity, they are also likely to lack a 'mastery orientation' (Butler, 2014) towards course content, instead focusing their efforts on satisfying course requirements, and avoiding the risk of failure. This is why activities like 'guided imagery' exercises can be so potent, in helping trainees to visualize themselves as future teachers. Among many practical ideas, Dornyei and Kubanyiova (2014) recommend asking trainees to do a writing exercise in which they describe their 'ideal classroom' – what the room looks like, what the learners are doing, what they are doing as the teacher, and how it all connects to their 'ideal society' of the coming decades. Having shared these ideas, the trainees should then consider what obstacles might lie in their path, and plan how they could overcome these in the early stages of their career.

In-service teacher education

In-service professional development for teachers takes many different forms and our aim here is not to suggest that one form is more motivating than another, rather to urge teacher educators to make participant motivation a central consideration in its design and implementation. Based on our review of teacher motivation above, we offer these selective (and overlapping) principles.

Don't force it

Following the principles of self-determination theory, teachers will only be truly motivated for Continuing Professional Development (CPD) – valuing it, investing effort, making a personal commitment to it over time – if it is offered as a benefit in its own right, rather than in return for some kind of reward (pace Shoaib, cited in Dornyei & Ushioda, 2011: 181). An example of how *not* to promote action research (AR) is found in Chang et al. (2013), which reports on a national context where AR was promoted as part of an incentive scheme for career advancement; any intrinsic motives teachers might have had for doing AR were crowded out by its extrinsic value, and as a result it was often conducted in perfunctory ways and rarely continued once the necessary 'career points' had been attained.

Make the process enjoyable

Too often the designers of CPD events think overly about the desired learning outcomes – usually in terms of changes in teacher beliefs or knowledge – without considering the process, and in particular participants' affective response to the event. If this is negative, it greatly reduces the likelihood of teachers changing their practice. As President Obama's biographer Jonathan Alter (2010: 140) wrote: 'logic can convince, but only emotion can motivate'. Motivational principles must inform the design, planning and preparation of training events (see Malderez & Wedell, 2007). For example, self-determination theory reminds us that, in addition to autonomy (satisfied partly through having a sense of choice and control – see above), educational courses must satisfy needs for relatedness and competence. Positive group dynamics are no less important among teachers than among learners, and Malderez & Bodóczky (1999) offer many suggestions to help groups bond and thrive, for instance through sensitively handled self-disclosure activities (e.g. 'I'm a person who…'; 'Once I had a class…'). Nowadays, of course, online social networking platforms mean that groups can continue to collaborate even after CPD events have finished, partly obviating the need to 'disband' groups.

Similarly, participants' sense of competence can be protected by not putting them in a position of deficit – 'you are here because you are ignorant of something important' – and instead framing the learning aims as additive and aspirational – 'you may be able to enhance your existing knowledge and skills in this way…'. Sociocultural approaches to teacher education derive their motivational power (even if 'motivation' itself is rarely cited as a benefit) by satisfying both these needs. First by stressing that all teacher learning derives ultimately from caring collaborative relationships. Second by their very deliberate attempt to work within teachers' 'Zone of Proximal Development', usually 'by encouraging teachers to verbalize their current understanding of whatever concept, skill, or disposition is the focus of study' (Johnson & Golombek, 2011: 8). Exemplifying such principles in practice is the rough plan of an SLTE programme provided by Malderez and Wedell (2007: 60); after group formation, there is a focus on 'getting out', sharing beliefs and past experience, before 'putting in'. Such an approach encourages the mediator to give respect to participants' existing competence while helping to ensure that CPD activities offer an appropriate level of challenge.

It is important to recognize that pleasure or other positive emotions are not the only source of motivation, however. Several commentators have argued that some form of emotional dissonance is necessary to push teachers towards new ways of thinking or behaving. This dissonance may be felt when CPD or other self-reflective activities confront teachers with contradictions or problems in their own work (e.g. Golombek & Johnson, 2004) or when they make more salient a discrepancy between their actual and ideal teacher selves (e.g. Kubanyiova, 2012). Seeking to support awareness in teachers of gaps between ideal- and reality-oriented cognitions, the teacher educator can adapt tools employed in teacher cognition research (Borg, 2006), e.g. observations together with pre- and post-observation discussions. This work can be non-judgemental, with the teacher educator collecting data to present to teachers for them to form their own interpretations and conclusions, so 'holding up the mirror' (Malderez & Bodóczky, 1999) to facilitate a collaborative reviewing of practice. Short-term discomfort might be the spark for long-term renewal, particularly if the teacher educator's support is sensitively attuned.

Foster the love of learning

There is evidence that many teachers begin to lose their motivation for teaching within a few years, for a variety of contextual reasons (Dörnyei & Ushioda, 2011), and in many global contexts there may be specific factors undermining the motivation of English language teachers. Drawn into the profession through a love of the language itself, or at least possessing relatively high self-efficacy beliefs, they find that years of repetitive classroom teaching not only dulls their enthusiasm for the subject but also lowers their self-confidence, deterring them from experimenting with new methods of teaching and initiating a vicious circle of demotivation as learners sense their teacher's lack of enthusiasm. With the spread of mobile technology, older teachers may also feel threatened by young people in their classrooms who are able to access new forms of English on the internet, undermining their position as sole authority on the language. It is perhaps not surprising then that, as Hiver (2013) has recently suggested, some English teachers' preferred form of CPD is actually language improvement, rather than pedagogical innovation.

Another reason for focusing CPD on language enhancement is that, if done well, it can remind teachers of why they fell in love with the language in the first place.

A different approach to fostering a love of learning is to enable teachers to create new knowledge for their learners, themselves and their colleagues through classroom research. Hanks (2016: 28) argues for the benefits of exploratory practice as 'creative, motivating, and "entirely relevant" work for learners, teachers, and teacher educators'. Meanwhile, Edwards described the transformative impact of AR on her own career trajectory in these terms:

> For me, the action research programme has achieved far more than improvements to my teaching, my students' learning, and the materials and syllabus used in my context. It has been a catalyst for my further academic study, for my involvement in other colleagues' professional development and for dissemination of my research through publications and presentations.
>
> *(Emily Edwards, in Burns & Edwards, 2014: 79)*

Reflect and prospect

'Reflection on practice' has become a staple ingredient in pre- and in-service teacher education in the last two decades. It has a strong pedagogic rationale – as the basis for teacher self-awareness and for provoking the kind of 'dissonance' that may, in turn, prompt change in beliefs and practice. Yet, it can be over-done through CPD experiences, leaving participants silently groaning at the prospect of yet another 'work in groups and discuss how you usually…' type of activity. Part of the problem is that, as Korthagen (2017: 394) argues, such reflection is often superficial, focusing only on actions and ignoring 'what is really going on during the lesson inside [the teacher] and her pupils in terms of the affective and motivational dimensions'. Mann and Walsh (2017) have argued for more use of data from teachers' own classrooms, like stimulated recall based on a video, or ad-hoc self-observation through audio recordings. Apart from their potential in expanding self-awareness and refining teacher's professional skills, these 'self-centred' activities are intrinsically motivating for the obvious reason that they relate directly to the individual concerned.

Successful SLTE activities need to motivate teachers to behave in more professionally efficacious ways, and that means encouraging them to 'prospect' as well as to reflect, i.e. to look forwards and identify actions they can take which will serve them and their learners better. As Husman et al. (2014) point out, just as students who lack a 'future time perspective' on their education tend to be just 'doing school', so teachers who cannot 'see' an enticing teacher future will tend to go through the motions of teaching. Dörnyei and Kubanyiova (2014: 189) suggest a number of activities for 'guarding the flame of teacher vision' as they put it, against the harsh winds of institutional pressures, unsympathetic managers, recalcitrant learners and so on. Many of these activities are visualizations which use a guided imagery script to help teachers see potentialities associated with positive emotions; though as Oettingen (2015) would remind us, the dreams must be accompanied by recognition of the obstacles, and developing practical plans for overcoming them to achieve the desired ends.

Conclusion

Graves (2009: 112) argues that 'teacher educators must "practice what they preach" and hold themselves accountable to the same criteria to which they hold teacher-learners'. Few would contest that enhancing pupils' motivation to continue learning is a criterial quality in education;

similarly, we should recognise that protecting and enhancing participants' desire to enter the teaching profession, to invest effort in their daily practice and to continue learning and developing as teachers should be a central concern of teacher educators. Our theoretical understanding of learner motivation has developed rapidly over recent decades, and many of the pedagogic implications that have emerged from this research have relevance for teacher educators. With the contemporary surge of interest among scholars in *teacher* motivation, teacher educators have even less excuse to ignore this fundamental element in their training or development curricula.

In this chapter we have offered an overview of some, but by no means all, of the links between teacher motivation and teacher education. An undeniably complex area, it deserves urgent empirical investigation, and we call in particular for studies on:

1. the impact of SLTE on teacher motivation; given the huge investment that countries make in teacher training and development, it is remarkable that so few studies have examined what effect it has on participants' short and long-term motivation to teach.
2. the impact of teacher motivation on SLTE; Kubanyiova's pioneering work (2012) suggests that the nature of teachers' pre-existing attitudes, self-concepts and motives can substantially influence how they respond to in-service training, and we can assume that the same is true for pre-service training.

We believe these considerations should form the basis of a developing research agenda.

Further reading

Dörnyei, Z. and Kubanyiova, M. (2014) *Motivating Learners, Motivating Teachers: Building Vision in the Language Classroom.* Cambridge: Cambridge University Press.
  Noting 'it is a curious fact that the role of teachers' unique personal talents and passions hardly ever features in L2 teacher education research or practice' (166), they offer a number of practical activities that encourage teachers to identify their personal strengths, values and goals, which will help them ride the bumpy contours of early professional experience.
Gregersen, T. and MacIntyre, P. (eds) (2017) *Innovative Practices in Language Teacher Education.* Dordrecht: Springer.
  An edited volume of chapters by a mix of experienced teacher educators and motivation experts. What the chapters have in common is an interest in the affective side of teacher education, in particular how insights from positive psychology can make the process more enjoyable, meaningful and productive.
Richardson, P. W., Karabenick, S. A. and Watt, H. M. G. (eds) (2014) *Teacher Motivation: Theory and Practice.* New York: Routledge.
  A state-of-the-art compendium of recent research and theory on teacher motivation in general education. The three sections deal with theoretical approaches, with motivation in day-to-day teacher activities, and with motivation and the long-term career trajectories of teachers.

Useful web links

<http://selfdeterminationtheory.org> – the official site of SDT, providing many free resources on different aspects of the theory.
<www.ted.com/talks/dan_pink_on_motivation> – the TED talk given by Dan Pink, author of (2009) *Drive: The Surprising Truth About What Motivates Us.* Edinburgh, Canongate.
See also the beguiling RSA animate presentation <www.youtube.com/watch?v=u6XAPnuFjJc>.
<http://woopmylife.org/woop-1> – Gabrielle Oettingen's website about her WOOP technique for achieving personal goals. Are there applications in teacher education?

References

Aboshiha, P. (2013) '"Native speaker" English language teachers: disengaged from the changing international landscape of their profession', in Ushioda, E. (ed.) *International Perspectives on Motivation*. Basingstoke: Palgrave Macmillan.

Akyeampong, K. and Stephens, D. (2002) 'Exploring the Backgrounds and Shaping of Beginning Student Teachers in Ghana: Toward Greater Contextualisation of Teacher Education'. *International Journal of Educational Development*, 22 261–274.

Alter, J. (2010) *The Promise: President Obama, Year One*. New York: Simon & Schuster.

Bandura, A. (1986) *Social Foundations of Thought and Action: A Social Cognitive Theory*. Englewood Cliffs, NJ: Prentice-Hall.

Borg, S. (2006) *Teacher Cognition and Language Education*. London: Continuum.

Burns, A. and Edwards, E. (2014) 'Introducing innovation through action research in an Australian national programme: experiences and insights', in Hayes, D. (ed.) *Innovations in the Continuing Professional Development of English Language Teachers*. London: The British Council.

Burns, A. and Richards, J. (eds) (2009) *The Cambridge Guide to Second Language Teacher Education*. Cambridge: Cambridge University Press.

Butler, R. (2014) 'What teachers want to achieve and why it matters: an achievement goal approach to teacher motivation', in Richardson, P. W., Karabenick, S. A. and Watt, H. M. G. (eds) *Teacher Motivation: Theory and Practice*. New York: Routledge.

Chang, M. C., Shaeffer, S., Al-Samarrai, S., Ragatz, A. B., De Ree, J. and Stevenson, R. (2013) *Teacher Reform in Indonesia: The Role of Politics and Evidence in Policy Making*. Washington DC: International Bank for Reconstruction and Development and The World Bank.

Chen, Z. and Goh, C. (2011) 'Teaching Oral English in Higher Education: Challenges to EFL Teachers'. *Teaching in Higher Education*, 16 333–345.

Choi, E. and Lee, J. (2016) 'Investigating the Relationship of Target Language Proficiency and Self-Efficacy Among Non-native EFL Teachers'. *System*, 58 49–63.

Dörnyei, Z. (2001) *Motivational Strategies in the Language Classroom*. Cambridge: Cambridge University Press.

Dörnyei, Z. and Kubanyiova, M. (2014) *Motivating Learners, Motivating Teachers: Building Vision in the Language Classroom*. Cambridge: Cambridge University Press.

Dörnyei, Z. and Ushioda, E. (2011) *Teaching and Researching Motivation*. Harlow: Pearson Education.

Dweck, C. (2000) *Self-Theories: Their Role in Motivation, Personality and Development*. Philadelphia, PA: Taylor & Francis.

Eccles, J., Adler, T. F., Futterman, R., Goff, S. B., Kaczala, C. M., Meece, J. and Midgley, C. (1983) 'Expectancies, values and academic behaviors', in Spence, J. T. (ed.) *Achievement and Achievement Motives*. San Francisco, CA: W. H. Freeman: 75–146.

Farrell, T. (ed.) (2015a) *International Perspectives on English Language Teacher Education*. Basingstoke: Palgrave Macmillan.

Farrell, T. (2015b) 'Second language teacher education: a reality check', in Farrell, T. (ed.) *International Perspectives on English Language Teacher Education*. Basingstoke: Palgrave Macmillan.

Freeman, D. (2009) 'The scope of second language teacher education', in Burns, A. and Richards, J. (eds) *Cambridge Guide to Second Language Teacher Education*. Cambridge: Cambridge University Press.

Freeman, D. and Richards, J. (eds) (1996) *Teacher Learning in Language Teaching*. Cambridge: Cambridge University Press.

Gao, X. and Xu, H. (2014) 'The Dilemma of Being English Language Teachers: Interpreting Teachers' Motivation to Teach and Professional Commitment in China's Hinterland Regions'. *Language Teaching Research*, 18 152–168.

Golombek, P. R. and Johnson, K. E. (2004) 'Narrative Inquiry as a Mediational Space: Examining Emotional and Cognitive Dissonance in Second-Language Teachers' Development'. *Teachers and Teaching*, 10 307–327.

Graves, K. (2009) 'The curriculum of second language teacher education', in Burns, A. and Richards, J. (eds) *The Cambridge Guide to Second Language Teacher Education*. New York: Cambridge University Press.

Gregersen, T. and MacIntyre, P. (eds) (2017) *Innovative Practices in Language Teacher Education*. Dordrecht: Springer.

Gu, M. and Lai, C. (2012) 'Motivation and Commitment: Pre-Service Teachers from Hong Kong and Mainland China at a Training Institute in Hong Kong'. *Teacher Education Quarterly*, Summer 2012 45–61.

Hanks, J. (2016) 'What might research AS practice look like?', in Dikilitaş, K., Wyatt, M., Hanks J. and Bullock D. (eds) *Teachers Engaging in Research*. Faversham: IATEFL.

Hiver, P. (2013) 'The Interplay of Possible Language Teacher Selves in Professional Development Choices'. *Language Teaching Research*, 17 210–227.

Husman, J., Duggan, M. A. and Fishman, E. (2014) 'The teacher time bubble: expanding teachers' imaginings of the future to support learning', in Richardson, P. W., Karabenick, S. A. and Watt, H. M. G. (eds) *Teacher Motivation: Theory and Practice*. New York: Routledge.

Johnson, K. and Golombek, P. (eds) (2011) *Research on Second Language Teacher Education*. New York: Routledge.

Klassen, R. M. and Durksen, T. L. (2014) 'Weekly Self-Efficacy and Work Stress During the Teaching Practicum: A Mixed Methods Study'. *Learning and Instruction*, 33 158–169.

Korthagen, F. (2017) 'Inconvenient Truths About Teacher Learning: Towards Professional Development 3.0'. *Teachers and Teaching*, 23 387–405.

Korthagen, F. A. J. and Evelein, F. G. (2016) 'Relations between student teachers' basic needs fulfillment and their teaching behavior'. *Teaching and Teacher Education*, 60 234–244.

Kubanyiova, M. (2006) 'Developing a Motivational Teaching Practice in EFL Teachers in Slovakia: Challenges of Promoting Teacher Change in EFL Contexts'. *TESL-EJ*, 10 1–10.

Kubanyiova, M. (2012) *Teacher Development in Action*. Basingstoke: Palgrave Macmillan.

Kubanyiova, M. and Feryok, A. (2015) 'Language Teacher Cognition in Applied Linguistics Research: Revisiting the Territory, Redrawing the Boundaries, Reclaiming the Relevance'. *The Modern Language Journal*, 99 435–449.

Kumazawa, M. (2013) 'Gaps Too Large: Four Novice EFL Teachers' Self-Concept and Motivation'. *Teaching and Teacher Education*, 33 45–55.

Kunter, M. and Holzberger, D. (2014) 'Loving teaching: research on teachers' intrinsic orientations', in Richardson, P. W., Karabenick, S. A. and Watt, H. M. G. (eds) *Teacher Motivation: Theory and Practice*. New York: Routledge.

Lamb, M. (2017) 'The Motivational Dimension of Language Teaching'. *Language Teaching*, 50 301–346.

Malderez, A. and Bodóczky, C. (1999) *Mentor Courses*. Cambridge: Cambridge University Press.

Malderez, A. and Wedell, M. (2007) *Teaching Teachers: Processes and Practices*. London: Continuum.

Mann, S. and Walsh, S. (2017) *Reflective Practice in English Language Teaching*. New York: Routledge.

Oettingen, G. (2015) *Rethinking Positive Thinking: Inside the New Science of Motivation*. New York: Penguin Publishing Group.

Randall, M. and Thornton, B. (2001) *Advising and Supporting Teachers*. Cambridge: Cambridge University Press.

Richards, J. and Farrell, T. (2005) *Professional Education for Language Teachers*. Cambridge: Cambridge University Press.

Richardson, P. W. and Watt, H. M. G. (2006) 'Who Chooses Teaching and Why? Profiling Characteristics and Motivations Across Three Australian Universities'. *Asia-Pacific Journal of Teacher Education*, 34 27–56.

Richardson, P. W. and Watt, H. M. G. (2014) 'Why people choose teaching as a career: an expectancy-value approach to understanding teacher motivation', in Richardson, P. W., Karabenick, S. A. and Watt, H. M. G. (eds) *Teacher Motivation: Theory and Practice*. New York: Routledge.

Richardson, P. W., Karabenick, S. A. and Watt, H. M. G. (eds) (2014) *Teacher Motivation: Theory and Practice*. New York: Routledge.

Roth, G. (2014) 'Antecedents and outcomes of teachers' autonomous motivation: a self-determination theory analysis', in Richardson, P. W., Karabenick, S. A. and Watt, H. M. G. (eds) *Teacher Motivation: Theory and Practice*. New York: Routledge: 36–51.

Roth, G., Assor, A., Kanat-Maymon, Y. and Kaplan, H. (2007) 'Autonomous Motivation for Teaching: How Self-Determined Teaching May Lead to Self-Determined Learning'. *Journal of Educational Psychology*, 99 761–774.

Ryan, R. M. and Deci, E. L. (2000) 'Self-Determination Theory and the Facilitation of Intrinsic Motivation, Social Development, and Well-Being'. *American Psychologist*, 55 68–78.

Sahakyan, T., Lamb, M. and Chambers, G. (2018) 'Language teacher motivation: from the ideal to the feasible self', in Mercer, S. and Kostoulas, A. (eds) *Language Teacher Psychology*. Bristol: Multilingual Matters.

Shih, S.-M. (2016) 'Why Do They Want to Become English Teachers: A Case Study of Taiwanese EFL Teachers'. *Perspectives in Education*, 34 43–55.

Suryani, A., Watt, H. M. G. and Richardson, P. W. (2016) 'Students' Motivations to Become Teachers: FIT-Choice Findings from Indonesia'. *International Journal of Quantitative Research in Education*, 3 179–203.

Tardy, C. M. and Snyder, B. (2004) '"That's Why I Do It": Flow and EFL Teachers' Practices'. *ELT Journal*, 58 118–128.

Urdan, T. (2014) 'Concluding commentary: understanding teacher motivation: what is known and what more there is to learn', in Richardson, P. W., Karabenick, S. A. and Watt, H. M. G. (eds) *Teacher Motivation: Theory and Practice*. New York: Routledge.

Watt, H. M. G. and Richardson, P. W. (2008) 'Motivations, Perceptions, and Aspirations Concerning Teaching as a Career for Different Types of Beginning Teachers'. *Learning and Instruction*, 18 408–428.

Wheatley, K. F. (2002) 'The Potential Benefits of Teacher Efficacy Doubts for Educational Reform'. *Teaching and Teacher Education*, 18 5–22.

Wright, T. (2009) '"Trainer development": professional development for language teacher educators', in Burns, A. and Richards, J. (eds) *Cambridge Guide to Second Language Teacher Education*. Cambridge: Cambridge University Press.

Wyatt, M. (2015) 'Using Qualitative Research Methods to Assess the Degree of Fit Between Teachers' Reported Self-Efficacy Beliefs and their Practical Knowledge During Teacher Education'. *Australian Journal of Teacher Education*, 40 Art 7 1–30.

Wyatt, M. (2018) 'Language teachers' self-efficacy beliefs: an introduction', in Mercer, S. and Kostoulas, A. (eds) *Language Teacher Psychology*. Bristol: Multilingual Matters.

35

Teacher identity

Gary Barkhuizen

Language teacher identity (LTI) has emerged as a legitimate field of research in English language teacher education. What is of particular interest is how LTI is theorised, how it is constructed and negotiated in contexts of teaching and teacher education, and how it relates to teaching practice and the work of teachers beyond the classroom. In the first section of the chapter I claim that LTI is difficult to define, and suggest that one of the reasons is that thinking about LTI includes multiple theoretical perspectives, some of which I address in the following section. I then comment on data extracted from interviews conducted with English teacher *educators*, thus making a relatively unexplored link between LTI and language teacher educator identity (LTEI). The teacher educators are experienced English teachers who are also students in a doctoral programme at a university in Colombia. Informed by what I see to be the most recent and current trends in LTI research, I conclude the chapter by suggesting directions for future research in the field.

Language teacher identity as an emergent field

As an English teacher and teacher educator I have always been interested in language teacher identity, both my own and of the teachers I work with. This interest became more focused when I began to explore through narrative inquiry the developing LTI of a pre-service English teacher who was a student in one of my graduate classes (see Barkhuizen, 2010, 2016). Doing so required me to search for relevant literature to inform my work. I came across two highly cited articles. One of these, reporting on one of the first studies to address English teachers' identities explicitly, was by Duff and Uchida (1997). Their 6-month ethnographic study investigated the identities of four teachers working in an EFL programme at a private educational institution in Japan. The aim was to understand the teachers' roles and identities as both language instructors and transmitters of (American) English culture(s). The researchers' ethnography delves deeply into the construction and continuous negotiation of the teachers' identities in close interrelationship with the particular sociocultural context in which they practised, and they include their own researcher identities in their interpretations. They conclude by suggesting implications for teacher education: 'a combination of biographical and contextual, practice-oriented reflection in ESL/EFL teacher education and in-service programs might enhance the development of teachers' cognitions with respect to their roles and their skills at negotiating these roles' (Duff & Uchida, 1997: 477).

The other influential journal article, and one that I will refer to in more detail later, is Varghese, Morgan, Johnston and Johnson (2005). Their article is the first to ask questions about theorising LTI. They do so by summarising three studies, each framed by a different theoretical perspective – social identity theory, situated learning and communities of practice, and a post-structural view of identity as image-text – and then undertaking a 'dialogue across paradigms' (p. 24) to illustrate commonalities and differences and to make the point that 'an openness to multiple theoretical possibilities, and more particularly a juxtaposition of those possibilities, allows us to keep in mind the complexity of what we are studying' (p. 38). They also state in the article that LTI is an emerging subject of interest in research on language teacher education and teacher development.

I would argue that LTI has now emerged as a legitimate field of interest and inquiry, and there is plenty of evidence to support this claim. In recent years almost every major applied linguistics or TESOL conference I have attended has included on the programme presentations that explicitly cover LTI. In the past ten years I have seen numerous graduate theses and dissertations appear (e.g., Castañeda, 2011; Jackson, 2015). I am aware of two edited books that deal exclusively with LTI, *Advances and Trends In Language Teacher Identity Research* (Cheung et al., 2015) and *Reflections on Language Teacher Identity Research* (Barkhuizen, 2017a), and a number of book-length studies, for example, *Language Teacher Identities: Co-Constructing Discourse and Community* (Clarke, 2008) and *English Language Teachers on the Discursive Faultlines: Identities, Ideologies and Pedagogies* (Menard-Warwick, 2014). Gray and Morton's (2018) monograph, *Social Interaction and English Language Teacher Identity*, provides a very readable and extensive coverage of the LTI field as a whole, both theoretically and methodologically, although the focus in their data-driven chapters is very much on the examination of social interaction in various language teaching contexts. And finally, English teacher identity studies and commentaries are scattered across the full range of journals regularly consulted by those working in TESOL, applied linguistics and language (teacher) education more generally.

So, there is plenty of evidence to show that scholars are engaging with LTI in English teacher education research. Why is this so? Varghese et al. (2005) remind us that perceptions of teachers as technicians who implement methods assigned by others have changed to one of teachers being viewed as thinking individuals who play a significant role in what happens in the classroom. Consequently, it became evident that the 'the teacher's whole identity was at play in the classroom' (p. 22). Who they are and how they become that way, and how that relates to what they do in classrooms, therefore, needed to be explored.

Defining exactly what LTI is, however, is not easy to do. Of the many definitions encountered in the literature, none appears to be completely satisfactory on its own. On reading these definitions, one can immediately think of something to add or delete or change in some way, for a number of reasons. First, LTI is a very broad concept. There are so many dimensions to what we do as English teachers. How is it possible to capture them all in a single definition? One of the more obvious dimensions, for example, is the variety of *roles* and associated functions that teachers perform in their relational work with others (see, for example, Xu, 2014, on becoming a teacher researcher, and Martel, 2017, on teachers as innovators). Another is teachers' *beliefs* and more generally their *theories* of language teaching (Kalaja et al., 2015). A related dimension is a teacher's *moral stance*. Morgan and Clarke (2011) comment, for instance, that the turn towards value-oriented, moral, and ethical dimensions is 'perhaps the most significant development in language teacher identity research' (p. 825). Closely tied to teacher beliefs and the moral dimension of LTI are teacher *emotions*. Barcelos (2015) reviews research and scholarly discussion in the fields of psychology, education and applied linguistics and concludes that little is known about the interrelationships among identity, beliefs and emotions in language teaching (see also Song, 2016). Wolff and De Costa (2017) have recently made the same claim about the intersection of *strategies*, emotion, and identity. Perhaps the most obvious connection with LTI is teachers' former *experiences* and their *histories*, which refer to their experiences of language learning (Benson, 2017), becoming and being a language teacher (Ruohotie-Lyhty & Moate, 2016; Trent, 2012), and their imagined experiences of language teaching in other (future) contexts (Barkhuizen, 2016; Pavlenko, 2003). Another facet is the actual *practice* of teaching, what teachers do as teachers – how they perform their roles in sociocultural contexts (Lee, 2013; Yuan & Burns, 2017). During the social process of practice, identities are negotiated and constructed in interaction with others – teachers, learners, managers. Teachers also interact with non-human objects in physical places, such as technological hardware and furniture in classrooms. As Porter and Tanghe (2016) put it, they are 'emplaced' in ecological spaces: 'an *emplaced identity* refers to relations between material settings, objects, and spaces, with particular respect to the ways they contribute to experiences of the self' (p. 773).

Another reason why LTI is difficult to define is that those interpreting the definitions come from a range of very different contexts, and thus any single definition will fall short of what they expect to find or what is currently applicable to their work. Teachers might possibly be looking for something quite different from academic researchers, and teacher educators might interpret a definition differently from graduate students searching for a dissertation topic. In addition, each of these categories is constitutively very diverse, and so it is unlikely that a satisfactory interpretation will be reached. Nevertheless, definitions abound and we use and re-shape them to inform our research and our work as teacher educators. A definition, of course, is not a theory, but it does represent a theoretical stance, of which there are many in LTI.

Conceptualising LTI

In a recent commentary by Varghese (2017), she first reiterates the argument from her co-authored 2005 article (Varghese et al., 2005) that 'any one theory limits one's perspective on language teacher identity, its formation, and its contexts' (p. 38), and that it is preferable to remain open to other theoretical possibilities not only to remind us how complex LTI actually is but to promote further exploration of the construct. She then goes on to re-state two theoretical positions that have dominated thinking about LTI in recent years. One of these is *identity-in-practice*, which refers to the close association between who teachers are and the work they do as members of particular groups: 'language teacher identity is seen to be constituted by the practices in relation to a group and the process of individual identification or nonidentification with the group' (Varghese et al., 2005: 39). In other words, teachers see themselves, as do others, as belonging to a professional group recognizable as language teachers.

Closely aligned with the idea of identification within groups is the now familiar concept of community of *practice* (Wenger, 1998), which emphasises identity formation as the negotiation of meanings while participating and engaging with others within a social configuration. A community of practice framework has been taken up with enthusiasm in LTI research. It was employed by Tsui (2007), for example, to examine the lived experiences of an EFL teacher in China. Tsui examined the construction of the teacher's multiple identities over a 6-year period, particularly that of a communicative language teaching (CLT) teacher, within the contexts of his institutional and personal experiences. Further examples include Trent's (2012) study of the discursive positioning of native-speaking English teachers in Hong Kong primary and secondary schools, and Liu and Xu's (2013) study of the learning trajectory of an English teacher and her associated identity changes during the process of pedagogical reform in the academic department of a Chinese university.

In Morgan's (2004) notion of *identity-as-pedagogy*, teachers' identities are understood to be a form of pedagogy; that is, their identities are pedagogical resources, intertextually interwoven within lessons (Morgan, 2017). As such, argues Morgan (2017: 206), they are 'a key source of agency for social change'. With an emphasis on the *negotiation* of identities within institutional discourses and the performance of a *transformative* pedagogical agenda, the link between identity and practice takes a decidedly post-structural turn. Zheng (2017) effectively draws on an identity-as-pedagogy perspective to frame her study of the practices of two international teaching assistants at a US university. She found that through reflection on and subsequent awareness of their translingual identities as resources they began to understand the link between identity and pedagogy. Only then were they able to utilize these identities to benefit both themselves and their diverse groups of students. Relatedly, Golombek (2017) adopts *identity-in-activity* to characterise her ideas about LTI and also to inform her practice as a language teacher educator. Identity-in-activity is grounded in Vygotskian sociocultural theory, uniting the 'many dichotomies so central to a sociocultural theoretical perspective, for example, the personal and social, the ideal (in the mind) and the concrete (in activity), and the diachronic and synchronic' (p. 154).

Varghese (2017) continues her commentary by locating *identity-in-discourse* firmly within a poststructural paradigm. In identity-in-discourse, identity is discursively constructed and thus 'agency is discursively constituted, mainly through language' (Varghese et al., 2005: 39). There could therefore be no singular definition of language teacher identity. Instead identities 'would vary according to the context and the set of power relations as well as the discourses available to the individual teachers and a community or network of teachers in that particular context' (Varghese, 2017: 46). As an example, Higgins and Ponte (2017) use Gee's (2000) four ways to view identity (nature-identity, institution-identity, discourse-identity, affinity-identity) as a framework to investigate the identities of a group of elementary school teachers who participated in a professional development project on multilingual language learners. Through analysing classroom observations, interviews, assignments and WebCT posts, they show how the teachers' own linguistic histories shaped both their views about multilingualism and their practice. Also significant in this study are its implications for language teacher education, demonstrating how identity, particularly reflection on identity, can become a valuable ingredient of professional development practices.

As a final example of a theoretical position on LTI, De Costa and Norton (2017) draw on the work of the Douglas Fir Group (2016) to propose an (all-encompassing) trans-disciplinarity approach to LTI. Their ideas are spelled out in the introductory article of a special issue of *The Modern Language Journal* (2016), which includes six contributions that cover topics such as how teacher identity intersects with the multilingual and translingual realities of contemporary classrooms, the investment of teachers in developing the semiotic repertoires of learners and a socially inclusive learning environment, and the emotions and ethical practices of teachers. Following a trans-disciplinarity agenda, and drawing on a range of different theories in conceptualising LTI, the studies take into account the highly inter-related macro, meso, and micro level dimensions of language teaching and learning. Respectively, these refer to ideological structures at the societal level, sociocultural institutions and communities, and social activity in micro spaces such as classrooms (see Barkhuizen, 2008, 2017b, who suggested similar levels or scales of context from a narrative perspective; *STORY, Story*, and *story*). The issue as a whole makes an important and productive contribution to our understanding of LTI by extending, as De Costa and Norton (2017) note, 'an important ongoing conversation about language teacher identity, transdisciplinarity, and social change' (p. 11). They go on to add that 'there is much evidence to support the view that language teaching is indeed "identity work" and that language teaching is enhanced by effective teacher training, both inservice and preservice' (p. 11).

In my edited book, *Reflections on Language Teacher Identity Research* (Barkhuizen, 2017a), I thematically analysed all the chapters, in which the 41 authors reflected on their perceptions of LTI in their area of scholarly expertise, to produce a composite conceptualisation of LTI – a broad 'definition' that aimed to capture the various theoretical perspectives on LTI drawn from the ideas in the chapters, and which is arguably applicable beyond the scope of the book as well. This conceptualisation captures much of what I have presented above, and perhaps serves as a summary of the discussion (Barkhuizen (2017c)):

> Language teacher identities (LTIs) are cognitive, social, emotional, ideological, and historical – they are both inside the teacher and outside in the social, material and technological world. LTIs are being and doing, feeling and imagining, and storying. They are struggle and harmony: they are contested and resisted, by self and others, and they are also accepted, acknowledged and valued, by self and others. They are core and peripheral, personal and professional, they are dynamic, multiple, and hybrid, and they are foregrounded and backgrounded. And LTIs change, short-term and over time – discursively in social interaction with teacher educators, learners, teachers, administrators, and the wider community, and in material interaction with spaces, places and objects in classrooms, institutions, and online.
>
> *(p. 4)*

I suggest in the book that my conceptualisation be interpreted variously from different theoretical perspectives as well as from different contextual realities (e.g., spaces where teacher education and language teaching are practised). From one particular theoretical perspective or set of contextual realities certain facets of the definition may be more or less relevant, and from other perspectives and realities other facets may be so. Different arrangements of the facets – their intersections and salience – would also reflect different theoretical perspectives and contextual realities. The conceptualisation, therefore, welcomes relative, situated reflection, interpretation, development and use by teachers and researchers.

Language teacher *educator* identity

This section considers some of the facets of the LTI conceptualisation described above with reference to data extracted from interviews conducted with English teacher *educators*, thus making a relatively unexplored link between LTI and LTEI. The teacher educators are experienced English teachers who are also students on a doctoral programme at a public university in Colombia. The interviews were conducted after their first year in the programme, and covered topics to do with their own English learning, their education, teacher preparation and experience, and their transition to becoming teacher educators. The aim of the study was to explore their developing identity as language teacher educators, particularly how it intersects with emotion and moral stance. To frame my brief commentary on the extracts, I draw on a narrative inquiry (Hacker, 2008) that examined the nature of language teacher educator learning (LTEL); that is, the experience of learning to become a language teacher educator in the particular contexts in which the learning takes place. The focus of Hacker's study was on *learning*, but in my view it has significant implications for language teacher educator *identity*. Drawing on the experiences of 15 language teacher educators working in New Zealand, Hacker inductively developed a conceptual framework of LTEL, with its core being a number of learning dimensions, which she calls the framework's *substance*. Hacker identifies a number of learning dimensions, the most salient being *teachers*, *teaching*, *professional position*, and *currency*. These dimensions apply to the learning of teacher educators, but it is very easy to see how they can equally apply to their identities, as I hope the following discussion makes clear.

Teachers and teaching

Teachers is the dimension concerned with language teacher educators' experiences 'relating to the people they teach or in some way assist to develop as promoters of language learning, and who are often referred to by the educators as their students' (Hacker, 2008: 140). As the LTI conceptualisation indicates, identities are discursively constructed and negotiated in social interaction with others, and for teacher educators the teachers they work with are their main contacts. Their relationship primarily involves the dimension of *teaching*, which is concerned with language teacher educators' experiences 'relating to any aspect of their own teaching in their work as language teacher educators in their contexts of practice' (Hacker, 2008: 139). In the following extract, the *teachers* and *teaching* dimensions are most salient, although there is also evidence of the *professional position* and *currency* dimensions as well, which is to be expected since all four are highly inter-related.

The teacher educator, Maria, is a very experienced teacher (about 25 years), having taught English from primary school level to university, often at the same time. She is currently a pre-service English teacher educator at a university. In this extract, she tells of an activity in which her students wrote autobiographical accounts of their English learning history, and her subsequent realisation that what they do together in the classroom may not be what they expect or want. She reflects on the implications of this finding for the class, her teaching, and the teacher education programme more generally.

Extract 35.1

1. well it's related to that subject that I told you
2. the one I'm teaching language society and culture
3. I started to ask my students to write their autobiographies as English learners
4. and I found very interesting issues about their life
5. which is very very interesting
6. and I thought 'okay this could be part of my research project at the doctorate programme'
7. and I find it very interesting
8. because first I found that it's a good opportunity to know my students better
9. and probably to make a contribution to the teacher education programme
10. in terms of giving the programme the opportunity to see what the students are really doing
11. what they are investing this investing in
12. because we give them the programme but
13. and we usually feel that that programme is okay
14. and we don't really ask 'is this what they really want
15. are they happy with what we are giving them
16. what are they expecting'
17. we don't know
18. we just assume that everything is okay
19. but in these autobiographies I found some aspects that are very interesting

20. and I see that sometimes the students are in your classroom
21. but they are not there
22. they have to be there
23. but they are not there
24. they want they are just like there because they have to
25. but what they are really doing outside the classroom is more interesting for them
26. than what they are doing in the classroom
27. I found that for example they think that in the classes the teachers are just using their board and teaching grammar
28. and doing things they say they have to do as future teachers
29. but it contradicts what they are teaching
30. and outside the classroom they for example enrol in paths where they can interact with native speakers
31. and in that way they improve their speaking skills
32. they use technology
33. they join online communities
34. and exchange written dialogues
35. and they speak as well
36. they read a lot
37. and I say 'wow this definitively has to do with something that we have to change in our classrooms'
38. and they say they learn more in that way
39. than what they do in class
40. and I said 'well probably probably'

Multiple identities emerge in this story. Most obvious is Maria's teacher educator identity ('I'm teaching', line 2). This is a story about her experience of working with pre-service teachers in the classroom, and through their practice together (i.e., the autobiography writing activity, line 3), getting 'to know my students better' (line 8). The key message she learns is that 'students are in your classroom/ but they are not there' (lines 20–21), meaning that they are physically in the classroom ('they are just like there because they have to', line 24) but are not engaged or invested in what is happening in the classroom. Maria points out that 'what they are really doing outside the classroom is more interesting for them' (line 25) than traditional methods whereby 'teachers are just using their board and teaching grammar' (line 27). Talking generally, Maria says that teacher educators, probably including herself, prepare the pre-service teachers to do 'things they say they have to do as future teachers' (line 28), but this contradicts the image the pre-service teachers have of their future selves. In addition, they may learn more by using technology and joining online communities (lines 32–33), for example, 'than what they do in class' (line 39). This raises questions for Maria regarding the students' learning, and there may be implications for the institution's 'teacher education programme' as well (line 9). These revelations unsettle somewhat Maria's teacher educator identity ('well probably probably', line 40) – her current teaching practice is threatened and as a result she contemplates other pedagogical possibilities. The identity dimensions *teachers* and *teaching* are foregrounded in Maria's story. Almost everything that happens in what she tells and reflects on involves her teaching and the pre-service teachers in her class. She does make reference though to her other identities; that of a PhD student and a researcher, the latter often associated with a teacher educator identity (Murray & Male, 2005). She considers using English learner autobiographies in her 'research project at the doctorate programme' (line 6), the topic of which she has still to determine.

Professional position and currency

In the following extract, the focus is on the *professional position* and *currency* dimensions, though, once again, *teachers* and *teaching* are also inter-related constituent dimensions in the teacher educator's identity. The *professional position* dimension is concerned with language teacher educators' experiences relating to their particular formal job descriptions: 'This involves the activities and requirements that educators are recommended or expected to engage in, perform and meet in their professional positions in their contexts of practice' (Hacker, 2008: 139). Aligned with these positions are particular roles and functions, and the positions are usually clearly visible to others in the workplace. By *currency* Hacker (2008) means language teacher educators' experiences relating to 'the most recent information available in the fields in which they have interests or responsibilities as language teacher educators' (p. 140). This may relate practically and/or theoretically to their teaching practice or research, or to other involvements they have in their capacity as language teacher educators, such as leaders or curriculum developers.

Carmen began teaching at an English language institute while she was still an undergraduate student. Immediately after graduating she got a job teaching at a primary school, followed by a short stint teaching Spanish in Asia. She returned to Colombia to the English institute and at the same time took up a position at a university where she now works. In this extract she reports on the challenges she faces finding a permanent university position as a teacher educator because of her perceived lack of research activity and publications. This prompted her decision to study towards a PhD.

Extract 35.2

1. well they opened they opened some posts
2. and I would apply for it
3. but then they said that I was not prepared
4. I mean I was not prepared because I didn't have research
5. because I didn't have this and that
6. 'because your only piece of research is the one that you did for your master's degree'
7. and I was like 'oh so I'm not enough
8. what I have done is not enough'
9. and so I said 'oh'
10. so I was thinking 'maybe I should study a PhD'
11. cause like having a master's will never be enough
12. if I want to work in a full time position in a university
13. I am aware that I didn't have time to carry out research
14. because like I was just able to work
15. like I was a language teacher despite I was
16. despite I was doing some training for teachers in action research and stuff
17. so when that happened I was like 'I should do research then as well
18. I should move'
19. so I said 'I'm going to do something
20. I'm going to do action research as well'
21. and so I started like 'what could I do
22. what could I research'
23. and I said 'well when I was a supervisor
24. teachers were not happy with the supervision system
25. and they would do things to comply'

26. and so I prepared a small scale action research about peer coaching
27. [describes peer coaching]
28. as I told you I couldn't get the position of full-time teacher at the university
29. and that was so disappointing for me
30. and I said 'I have to study again
31. I have to come back to research
32. otherwise no university will accept me'
33. because they expect that you are like publishing many things
34. and they want you to
35. 'how many articles have you published recently'
36. I wrote a letter of complaint to say 'how come you are not looking at me as a teacher
37. I mean the fact that I am not publishing or researching
38. that does not mean that I am not a good teacher'
39. and so they replied 'you don't have much research experience'
40. and so I was like 'so as soon as I can
41. as soon as I get a chance I will quit this job and then try to have a PhD programme'
42. cause I do want to become a full-time teacher somewhere right

Carmen's story starts with a job application for an English teacher educator position at a university. However, her application was unsuccessful 'because I didn't have research' (line 4). Like in many universities around the world, obtaining a full-time professional position as teacher educator requires research experience and a recognised publication record. Carmen has neither ('I am not publishing or researching', line 37), at least not to the extent required by the hiring institution. She does, however, have considerable experience as a language teacher (line 15), and in addition she 'was doing some training for teachers in action research and stuff' (line 16). In this story, Carmen's identity dilemma (Nelson, 2017) is reflected in her sarcastic outburst: 'Oh so I'm not enough/ what I have done is not enough' (lines 7–8). She knows she has adequate experience as an English teacher, which she foregrounds when telling the story, and some experience as a teacher trainer, but despite having done 'a piece of research' (line 6) for her master's degree and a small-scale action research project (line 20), her researcher identity was contested by the hiring university. She did not meet the requirements for the professional position they wanted filled. Perhaps their concern has to do with currency; that is, Carmen not being up-to-date with current developments in the field, which in their opinion research might have helped her achieve. Carmen formally complained about their decision ('I wrote a letter of complaint', line 36), declaring that even though she is not doing research it 'does not mean I am not a good teacher' (line 38). The university was not convinced, replying simply, 'you do not have much research experience' (line 39). In other words, the *professional position* they wanted filled required a researcher with adequate *currency*. To resolve this English teacher-teacher educator-researcher identity dilemma Carmen decides that the best course of action was to do a PhD ('maybe I should study a PhD', line 10). She realises that without the research experience and its associated symbolic capital 'no university will accept me' (line 32).

My brief commentary of Maria's and Carmen's interview extracts shows that Hacker's (2008) teacher educator learning dimensions, *teaching, teachers, professional position,* and *currency* can be usefully applied to examining identity in language education, most evidently for teacher educators, but, I would argue, for teachers as well. The dimensions offer points of departure for reflection on LTI in teacher education programmes, for example, or for planning an LTI-focused research project. More specific research areas and topics are covered in the next section.

Conclusion: topics and questions in LTI research

De Costa and Norton (2017) offer a three-way categorisation of the various theoretical positions with respect to LTI, namely, the ecological turn (a holistic approach to LTI within a complex ecology at micro, meso, and macro levels), teacher socialisation and investment (situated LTI development over time), and teacher affect (how teachers manage their emotions in the work they do). In addition, identities-in-practice, identities-in-discourse, and identities-in-activity serve as useful meta-labels for organising how we think about LTI, and my own composite conceptualisation presented above gives a perhaps even more inclusive heuristic for theoretical – and research – possibilities. These various theoretical perspectives on LTI, together with the need to address issues in language teacher education, have spawned an extremely diverse range of research topics that have been investigated over the past two decades. Norton and De Costa (2018: 94) suggest three interrelated sets of questions that chart the scope of identity research in language learning and teaching, but which equally apply to LTI. The questions address, respectively, social categories, social contexts, and research populations. To conclude this chapter, I provide a more comprehensive classification of current and potential research areas in LTI. I have arrived at this classification from my reading of the theoretical and empirical literature in the field of LTI, as well as an analysis of the 'Directions for future research' section which ended the chapters in my edited book, *Reflections on Language Teacher Identity Research* (Barkhuizen, 2017a). In these sections, authors were asked to look ahead to LTI-relevant research possibilities within their particular areas of expertise. My thematic analysis produced the following classification, which is by no means a definitive research agenda for LTI. Instead, it represents only one way of categorising the many topics that have currency in the field. For easy reference, the topic areas are captured in Figure 35.1. First six broad areas of LTI research describe the broad scope of current LTI research. For each of these topic areas, I provide two sample research questions taken from Barkhuizen (2017a) that suggest possible future research topics. Next, I list ten specific topic areas of LTI research, sub-categories of the six broad areas, and add to these a few topic suggestions of my own. Finally, seven new and emerging topic areas are proposed, with a short description of what these refer to.

Six broad areas of LTI research

1. LTI and pedagogy:

    i. How do trends in pedagogy and practice affect language teachers' identity, and what are the implications for language teacher education?

    (Nunan, 2017)

    ii. How do critical language teachers develop, alter, or rearrange their identities when they are confronted by ideological conflicts or other ethical challenges in the classroom?

    (Kubota, 2017)

2. LTI in neoliberal times:

    i. How are localised activity and institutional-level activity conditioned by the kind of economic regimes we live in?

    (Block, 2017)

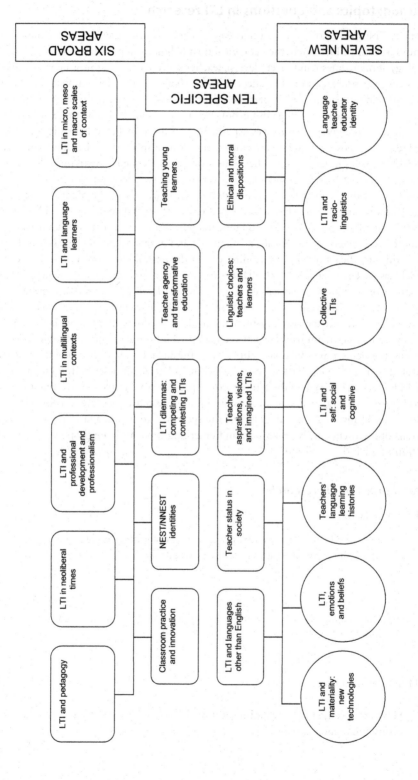

Figure 35.1 Thematic analysis of LTI-relevant research

    ii.   To what extent does the teacher educator encourage or allow for perspectives on the nation state – and on language teaching and learning – that facilitate critique or, conversely, reinforce the status quo?

(Morgan, 2017)

3.   LTI and professional development and professionalism:

    i.   What are the outcomes of our doctoral programmes on the professional identities of our graduates?

(Donato, 2017)

    ii.   How do schools and peers define 'collective teacher identities' and how do these influence the extent to which teacher research takes place?

(Borg, 2017)

4.   LTI in multilingual contexts:

    i.   What are the challenges in accommodating translingualism in academic writing and the role of multilingual teachers in facilitating this pedagogy?

(Canagarajah, 2017)

    ii.   How can L2 speakers be encouraged to see themselves as belonging to imagined communities of L2 users while participating in a study abroad programme?

(Jackson, 2017)

5.   Interplay between LTI and language learners:

    i.   What are language teachers' understandings of how their own or their students' language identities are produced in relation to such identity categories as race and nation?

(Motha, 2017)

    ii.   How do gender and age interact in the way students perceive their language teachers? Are older/younger female instructors less respected than older/younger male instructors?

(Vandrick, 2017)

6.   LTI in micro, meso and macro scales of context:

    i.   What motivates teachers to continue teaching amidst everyday occurrences of violence in conflict zones? What value do they feel an additional language has to their students in these situations?

(Hayes, 2017)

    ii.   How can we use the concept of LTI to advance our thinking through our roles in times of contestation, flux, and movement across borders?

(Leibowitz, 2017)

Gary Barkhuizen

Ten specific areas of LTI research

1. Classroom practice and innovation:

   i.   introducing new textbook or blended learning, or creating new materials
   ii. new forms of assessment imposed top-down

2. NEST/NNEST identities:

   i.   theorising NEST/NNEST identities and debating related issues
   ii. collective NEST/NNEST identities in a particular institution

3. LTI dilemmas: competing and contesting LTIs

   i.   negotiating LTI categories (e.g., sexuality, gender, age, religious) in the workplace
   ii. implementing policies and practices in multilingual contexts

4. Teacher agency and transformative education

   i.   enabling (critical) agency in teacher education programmes
   ii. developing teacher autonomy in the classroom and beyond

5. Teaching young learners

   i.   meeting the challenges of constant change in early language education
   ii. negotiating learner motivation and parent involvement

6. LTI and languages other than English

   i.   resisting competing pressures from English in non-English medium higher education
   ii. preparing teachers of other languages to teach in English dominant contexts

7. Teacher status in society

   i.   perceptions of language teachers as professionals
   ii. teachers' power to transform schools and communities

8. Teacher aspirations, visions and imagined LTI

   i.   relationship between teacher beliefs, emotions and imagined practices
   ii. investing in language teaching and teacher education for self and learners

9. Linguistic choices for teachers and learners
   i.   contesting linguistic standards in the curriculum, including assessment practices
   ii. teacher awareness of local linguistic practices and implications for pedagogy

10. Ethical and moral dispositions

    i.   teacher emotions and empathy in super-diverse working contexts
    ii. teacher commitment, workload and burnout

Seven new areas of LTI research

1. *Materiality and new technologies*: Materiality does not only refer to our relationships with objects and spaces in classrooms and schools, but to our connections with innovative digital technology, including social media. These new technologies have re-shaped the way we

conduct our language teaching, learning and teacher education, and how we connect to others globally. Teacher development occurs in times and spaces (e.g., the many webinars available through professional associations) quite different from just a few years ago.

2. *Emotionality and beliefs*: I've stated above that emotionality is receiving a lot of attention in LTI research, and interrelationships with beliefs and strategies are also being explored. There is much work to be done on this topic, especially if teacher learning is also to be taken into account.

3. *Teachers' language learning histories and teaching practice*: Not enough attention has been paid to the language learning experiences of language teachers, and how they relate to both their teaching practices and the development of their teacher identities. Often, such discussions are couched within NEST/NNEST debates (Ellis, 2016), but they could be considered more widely, and more seriously in my opinion.

4. *Self and identity – cognitive and social*: Conceptually, there is some confusion in the LTI field about how 'self' and 'identity' differ, and discussions often take on a cognitive versus social viewpoint. Suggesting this as an area of research is not an attempt necessarily to clear the confusion, but to explore the intersection of the concepts productively and from multiple disciplines to gain a fuller understanding of LTI.

5. *Collective LTIs*: The prevalent identities-in-discourse perspective in LTI, and associated research methodologies such as narrative inquiry, mean that our main research focus is on individual teachers, within particular social contexts. But what about the other teachers in those contexts? How do they develop distinctive collective identities as a group? There is always the danger of essentialising and simplifying identities when 'levelled out' as group characteristics, but with cautions in place, it would be interesting to see how these collective identities are formed and what impact they have on individual members of the collective.

6. *LTI and raciolinguistics*: This topic area addresses the interconnections among racial ideologies, language choices and use, and LTI. As Motha (2014) says, 'In a discussion of English language teaching, it would be naïve to attend to teachers' racial identities without addressing their linguistic identities … they are actually inextricable one from the other' (p. 499).

7. *Language teacher educator identity*: The stories of Maria and Carmen discussed in the previous section show that there are significant synergies between LTI and language teacher educator identity (LTEI). Many teacher educators continue to teach English at the same time, and it would be interesting to explore how these related identities are co-negotiated – how they are or become similar and different. But there are other educators who do not teach language, and some who have not even been in a classroom for years.

Kanno and Stuart (2011) claim that even though LTI has been part of research and debates on language education it 'rarely takes center stage' (p. 250). I would add that LTI is currently only loosely aligned with English teacher education policies and practices. I do believe, however, that with the recent and ongoing LTI research contributions evident in the field of English language teaching and learning, this situation will change. The broad array of research topics outlined above, and the many examples of already published research presented in this chapter, indicate that LTI as a topic of interest is thriving and that its contributions to our understanding and practice of English language teacher education will continue to grow.

References

Barcelos, A. M. F. (2015) 'Unveiling the Relationship Between Language Learning Beliefs, Emotions, and Identities'. *Studies in Second Language Learning and Teaching*, 5(2) 301–325.

Barkhuizen, G. (2008) 'A Narrative Approach to Exploring Context in Language Teaching'. *English Language Teaching Journal*, 62(3) 231–239.

Barkhuizen, G. (2010) 'An Extended Positioning Analysis of a Pre-Service Teacher's *Better Life* Small Story'. *Applied Linguistics*, 31(2) 282–300.

Barkhuizen, G. (2016) 'A Short Story Approach to Analyzing Teacher (Imagined) Identities Over Time'. *TESOL Quarterly*, 50(3) 655–683.

Barkhuizen, G. (ed.) (2017a) *Reflections on Language Teacher Identity Research*. New York: Routledge.

Barkhuizen, G. (2017b) 'Investigating Language Tutor Social Inclusion Identities'. *The Modern Language Journal*, 101(S1) 61–75.

Barkhuizen, G. (2017c) 'Language teacher identity research: an introduction', in Barkhuizen, G. (ed.) *Reflections on Language Teacher Identity Research*. New York: Routledge: 1–11.

Benson, P. (2017) 'Teacher autonomy and teacher agency', in Barkhuizen, G. (ed.) *Reflections on Language Teacher Identity Research*. New York: Routledge: 18–23.

Block, D. (2017) 'Journey to the center of language teacher identity', in Barkhuizen, G. (ed.) *Reflections on Language Teacher Identity Research*. New York: Routledge: 31–36.

Borg, S. (2017) 'Identity and teacher research', in Barkhuizen, G. (ed.) *Reflections on Language Teacher Identity Research*. New York: Routledge: 126–132.

Canagarajah, S. (2017) 'Multilingual identity in teaching multilingual writing', in Barkhuizen, G. (ed.) *Reflections on Language Teacher Identity Research*. New York: Routledge: 67–73.

Castañeda, J. (2011) *Teacher identity construction: exploring the nature of becoming a primary school language teacher*. Unpublished thesis, University of Newcastle, UK.

Cheung, Y. L., Ben Said, S. and Park, K. (eds) (2015) *Advances and Current Trends in Language Teacher Identity Research*. Abingdon: Routledge.

Clarke, M. (2008) *Language Teacher Identities: Co-constructing Discourse and Community*. Clevedon: Multilingual Matters.

De Costa, P. I. and Norton, B. (2017) 'Introduction: Identity, Transdisciplinarity, and the Good Language Teacher'. *The Modern Language Journal*, 101(S) 3–14.

Donato, R. (2017) 'Becoming a language teaching professional: what's identity got to do with it?', in Barkhuizen G. (ed.) *Reflections on Language Teacher Identity Research*. New York: Routledge: 24–30.

Douglas Fir Group (2016) 'A Transdisciplinary Framework for SLA in a Multilingual World'. *The Modern Language Journal*, 100 19–47.

Duff, P. A. and Uchida, Y. (1997) 'The Negotiation of Teachers' Sociocultural Identities and Practices in Postsecondary EFL Classrooms'. *TESOL Quarterly*, 31(3) 451–486.

Ellis, E. M. (2016) '"I May Not be a Native Speaker but I'm Not Monolingual": Reimagining all Teachers' Linguistic Identities in TESOL'. *TESOL Quarterly*, 50(3) 597–630.

Gee, J. P. (2000) 'Identity as an Analytic Lens for Research in Education'. *Review of Research in Education*, 25 99–125.

Golombek, P. (2017) 'Grappling with language teacher identity', in Barkhuizen, G. (ed.) *Reflections on Language Teacher Identity Research*. New York: Routledge: 151–157.

Gray, J. and Morton, T. (2018) *Social Interaction and English Language Teacher Identity*. Edinburgh: Edinburgh University Press.

Hacker, P. (2008) *Understanding the nature of language teacher educator learning: substance, narrative essence and contextual reality*. Unpublished thesis, University of Auckland, New Zealand.

Hayes, D. (2017) 'Narratives of identity: reflections on English language teachers, teaching, and educational opportunity', in Barkhuizen, G. (ed.) *Reflections on Language Teacher Identity Research*. New York: Routledge: 54–60.

Higgins, C. and Ponte, E. (2017) 'Legitimating Multilingual Teacher Identities in the Mainstream Classroom'. *The Modern Language Journal*, 101(S) 13–28.

Jackson, A. (2015) *Language teacher development: a study of ESOL preservice teachers' identities, efficacy and conceptions of literacy.* Unpublished dissertation, Georgia State University, USA.

Jackson, J. (2017) 'Second language teacher identity and study abroad', in Barkhuizen, G. (ed.) *Reflections on Language Teacher Identity Research.* New York: Routledge: 114–119.

Kalaja, P., Barcelos, A. M. F., Aro, M. and Ruohotie-Lyhty, M. (2015) *Beliefs, Agency and Identity in Foreign Language Learning and Teaching.* Basingstoke: Palgrave Macmillan.

Kanno, Y. and Stuart, C. (2011) 'Learning to Become a Second Language Teacher: Identities-in-Practice'. *The Modern Language Journal,* 95(2) 236–252.

Kubota, R. (2017) 'Critical language teacher identity', in Barkhuizen, G. (ed.) *Reflections on Language Teacher Identity Research.* New York: Routledge: 210–214.

Lee, I. (2013) 'Becoming a Writing Teacher: Using 'Identity' as an Analytic Lens to Understand EFL Writing Teachers' Development'. *Journal of Second Language Writing,* 22 330–345.

Leibowitz, B. (2017) 'Language teacher identity in troubled times', in Barkhuizen, G. (ed.) *Reflections on Language Teacher Identity Research.* New York: Routledge: 74–79.

Liu, Y. and Xu, Y. (2013) 'The Trajectory of Learning in a Teacher Community of Practice: A Narrative Inquiry of a Language Teacher's Identity in the Workplace'. *Research Papers in Education,* 28(2) 176–195.

Martel, J. (2017) 'Identity, innovation, and learning to teach a foreign/second language', in Barkhuizen, G. (ed.) *Reflections on Language Teacher Identity Research.* New York: Routledge: 87–92.

Menard-Warwick, J. (2014) *English Language Teachers on the Discursive Faultlines: Identities, Ideologies and Pedagogies.* Clevedon: Multilingual Matters.

Morgan, B. (2004) 'Teacher Identity as Pedagogy: Towards a Field-Internal Conceptualisation in Bilingual and Second Language Education'. *International Journal of Bilingual Education and Bilingualism,* 7 172–188.

Morgan, B. (2017) 'Language teacher identity as critical social practice', in Barkhuizen, G. (ed.) *Reflections on Language Teacher Identity Research.* New York: Routledge: 203–209.

Morgan, B. and Clarke, M. (2011) 'Identity in second language teaching and learning', in Hinkel, E. (ed.) *Handbook of Research in Second Language Teaching and Learning.* New York: Routledge: 817–836.

Motha, S. (2014) *Race, Empire and English Language Teaching: Creating Responsible and Ethical Anti-racist Practices.* New York: Teachers College Press.

Motha, S. (2017) 'Who we are: teacher identity, race, empire, and nativeness', in Barkhuizen, G. (ed.) *Reflections on Language Teacher Identity Research.* New York: Routledge: 215–221.

Murray, J. and Male, T. (2005) 'Becoming a Teacher Educator: Evidence from the Field'. *Teaching and Teacher Education,* 21 125–142.

Nelson, C. D. (2017) 'Identity dilemmas and research agendas', in Barkhuizen, G. (ed.) *Reflections on Language Teacher Identity Research.* New York: Routledge: 234–239.

Norton, B. and De Costa, P. (2018) 'Research Tasks on Identity in Language Learning and Teaching'. *Language Teaching,* 51(1) 90–112.

Nunan, D. (2017) 'Language teacher identity in teacher education', in Barkhuizen, G. (ed.) *Reflections on Language Teacher Identity Research.* New York: Routledge: 164–169.

Pavlenko, A. (2003) '"I Never Knew I Was Bilingual": Reimagining Teacher Identities in TESOL'. *Journal of Language, Identity, and Education,* 2(4) 251–268.

Porter, C. and Tanghe, S. (2016) 'Emplaced Identities and the Material Classroom', *TESOL Quarterly,* 50(3) 769–778.

Ruohotie-Lyhty, M. and Moate, J. (2016) 'Who and How? Preservice Teachers as Active Agents Developing Professional Identities'. *Teaching and Teacher Education,* 55 318–327.

Song, J. (2016) 'Emotions and Language Teacher Identity: Conflicts, Vulnerability, and Transformation'. *TESOL Quarterly,* 50(3) 631–654.

Trent, J. (2012) 'The Discursive Positioning of Teachers: Native-Speaking English Teachers and Educational Discourse in Hong Kong'. *TESOL Quarterly,* 46(1) 104–126.

Tsui, A. (2007) 'Complexities of Identity Formation: A Narrative Inquiry of an EFL Teacher'. *TESOL Quarterly,* 41(4) 657–680.

Vandrick, S. (2017) 'Feminist language teacher identity research', in Barkhuizen, G. (ed.) *Reflections on Language Teacher Identity Research.* New York: Routledge: 228–233.

Varghese, M. (2017) 'Language teacher educator identity and language teacher identity: towards a social justice perspective', in Barkhuizen, G. (ed.) *Reflections on Language Teacher Identity Research*. New York: Routledge: 43–48.

Varghese, M., Morgan, B., Johnston, B. and Johnson, K. (2005) 'Theorizing Language Teacher Identity: Three Perspectives and Beyond'. *Journal of Language, Identity, and Education*, 4 21–44.

Wenger, E. (1998) *Communities of Practice: Learning, Meaning and Identity* Cambridge: Cambridge University Press.

Wolff, D. and De Costa, P. I. (2017) 'Expanding the Language Teacher Identity Landscape: An Investigation of the Emotions and Strategies of a NNEST'. *The Modern Language Journal*, 101(S) 76–90.

Xu, Y. (2014) 'Becoming Researchers: A Narrative Study of Chinese University EFL Teachers' Research Practice and their Professional Identity Construction'. *Language Teaching Research*, 18(2) 242–259.

Yuan, R. and Burns, A. (2017) 'Teacher Identity Development Through Action Research: A Chinese Experience'. *Teachers and Teaching: Theory and Practice*, 23(6) 729–749.

Zheng, X. (2017) 'Translingual Identity as Pedagogy: International Teaching Assistants of English in College Composition Classrooms'. *The Modern Language Journal*, 101(S) 29–44.

36

Teacher networks in the wild

Alternative ways of professional development

Amol Padwad and Jon Parnham

Introduction

Teachers face many challenges and demands throughout their professional lives. Taking a proactive approach to continuing professional development (CPD) can help teachers deal with and find solutions to these challenges. Options for teachers to take control of their CPD include attending in-service teacher training (INSETT) provided by institutions such as Ministries of Education at the national and regional level or individual schools at the local level. INSETTs are often one-off events and can range from short 1-hour workshops to training that lasts several days. INSETTs usually come with systemic support and recognition and seem to be the most common and sometimes the only avenue to CPD followed by teachers, though there are many other ways and means of CPD which remain underexploited. While INSETTs that are well planned and designed can have a positive impact on teachers, research has shown that teachers also need access to other forms of regular, ongoing support in order to strengthen and make positive changes to their classroom practise (e.g. Cordingley et al., 2015; Gulamhussein, 2013). As well as this, teachers who work in remote or rural areas may find it difficult to attend training workshops that are held outside of their communities in far off locations due to family commitments or travel and accommodation costs etc. For these reasons, teachers may consider alternative ways of working together with other teachers for their professional development – by joining or forming a network with other teachers.

Networks can be established as top down initiatives set up by organisations at different levels in an education system from Ministries of Education as part of their teacher development strategy, to universities and schools. Networks can also be bottom up initiatives set up by teachers themselves. They can exist in different forms such as formal, organised teachers' associations to informal teacher clubs to online social media groups for teachers. They can be large networks with member teachers spanning districts, countries or internationally across the world. They can also be small, consisting of a handful of teachers from the same village or town. The aim of each different network though is similar: to create a community to support teachers and encourage the sharing of knowledge through collaboration in order to enhance students' learning experiences and quality in the classroom. In this chapter we will explore four different kinds of teacher networks that teachers can become involved in. These include:

- teacher associations
- teacher clubs
- teacher activity groups
- online communities of practice on platforms such as Facebook and WhatsApp groups.

In this chapter we will discuss each of these using examples from teacher development initiatives in India. We will outline what they are, how they are being used by teachers in practice, the benefits of joining these networks, as well as the opportunities, issues and challenges different stakeholders may face in integrating them into teachers' own professional development.

Teacher associations

Professional associations of teachers of English can be found in most countries of the world. IATEFL and TESOL, the two leading global affiliating associations, together list around 150 English teacher associations (TAs) spread over all continents. It is, however, interesting to note that the history of English teacher associations does not date back very long with the earliest associations coming into existence about 60 years ago. There has been a remarkable increase in the number of TAs and also in their membership in the past 25 years. This is largely linked to the rise of English as a significant economic and development contributor as the process of globalisation started taking the world in its stride (Phillipson, 2009). As more and more countries went for an early introduction of English, for English as a medium of instruction and for English across curriculums, there was a massive rise in the numbers of learners, and consequently teachers, of English in a short span. Amid the huge challenges of producing materials, equipping teachers, building resources and so on, TAs started emerging as an important source of professional networking, learning and exchange within and across countries. In the past two decades there has been significant rise in collaborations and interactions among TAs of different countries. For example, IATEFL and TESOL have begun to organise joint web conferences, while TAs in India, Nepal, Bangladesh, Sri Lanka and Pakistan have formed an informal regional network to exchange experiences and expertise and to support each other's international conferences.

Teacher associations – a profile

TAs are more formal organisations, usually with written rules of functioning, a management and/or leadership structure, stated membership criteria and privileges, and a range of activities related to its goals and objectives, which may not be always explicitly stated. There are associations small and large, some with a handful of members covering a small town or a district and some others with a few thousand members covering several countries. It is useful to distinguish between teachers' unions and associations, though sometimes organisations may possess mixed characteristics of both. Teacher unions are normally broader organisations, catering to teachers in general, while associations are normally subject-specific, catering to the teachers of particular subjects. Unions aim at protecting teachers' professional rights and engage in activities like lobbying, advocacy, agitations and opinion mobilisation. Associations are more academically oriented, strive for teachers' professional development, tend to be more close-knit and focused on the subject domain, and engage in activities like conferences, seminars, publication, projects and research (see Lamb 2012 for a useful discussion of types of teacher associations). Though there is little research on types or trends of TA activities, the typical activities of teacher associations seem to include the following:

- Conferences, seminars and workshops
- Newsletters
- Publications
- Special Interest Groups and discussion forums
- Information dissemination about CPD opportunities
  (Aubrey and Coombe, 2010; Borg, 2015a; Padwad and Dixit, 2015)

Seminars and conferences seem to be a common and central activity of many TAs. However, some TAs also organise a range of short- and long-term activities that aim at targeted professional development and capacity building of teachers (Odhiambo and Nganyi, 2007; Kolesnikova, 2011; Rixon and Smith, 2017). For example, both IATEFL and TESOL run programmes to help affiliated TAs to improve leadership and organisational management of their members. They also support TAs and/or teachers to undertake projects based on locally relevant issues. TESOL and IATEFL support online courses and webinars, where teachers can pick up knowledge and skills in specific areas. Many TAs in Europe and East Asia have their own online courses for teachers or support members to join those organised by others. AINET (India) runs rounds of a teacher research initiative in which it helps teachers undertake classroom-based research over a year and then present studies at its conferences.

Contribution to CPD

Lamb (2012: 287) calls TAs 'empowering spaces for professional networks', one aspect of which is their nature as collaborative communities of practitioners. This sense of community is particularly strengthened through the large-scale events like conferences, where teachers get to connect with old and new peers, fostering 'the feeling of belonging to a group that shares your passion, the knowledge we get from presentations, and interacting with our peers and experts in the field' (Malupa-Kim, 2011). They also offer a good forum for sharing of experiences, ideas and resources. In larger associations this kind of sharing happens across a great diversity of contexts of members, thus offering rich experience and exposure (Borg, 2015a). TAs are often the chief source of information for many members about the latest developments in the field, about new policies or technological advances and about interesting practices elsewhere. Participation in the activities and events of TAs offers useful opportunities to members to play different roles like presenters, researchers and writers or even learn bits of organisational planning and management. TAs also contribute to boosting networking among teachers, and foster small informal teacher development groups (Alacantara, 2010; Arega, 2012, Gnawali, 2016).

Opportunities and challenges

There is a range of opportunities and challenges TAs face in the present times. Thanks to the ICT revolution, it is now cheaper and faster for TAs to communicate and network with their members and other TAs. It is also easier to extend their reach to distant areas and engage members from large geographical regions. Online tools of meeting, conferencing and sharing offer an opportunity of reaching more people quickly and cheaply. They also offer powerful means of bringing global content to TA members, as also of actively engaging with the worldwide ELT community. Running a TA or collaborating with TAs from other countries is now relatively easier and cheaper. There is also greater awareness among ELT practitioners about TAs and their roles.

In this scenario, one challenge for TAs is to develop new kinds of services and products on the one hand and modify their visions and management strategies on the other. With the rapid proliferation of internet and smartphones, TAs need to develop online ways – especially smartphone-based – of, for example, sharing information, enrolling members and publishing newsletters, and holding events and activities. Change in vision and management is needed, for example, to encash opportunities of expansion offered by social media, particularly through virtual communities, which may potentially change the very nature of a TA.

Another key challenge for most TAs is to increase their reach and membership. As a general trend across countries, only a tiny percentage of English teachers actually join any TA. While the gains to be made from TA membership are fairly obvious and the numbers of attendees at TA events are often large, it is intriguing why membership figures are low. Costs of joining, low awareness about TAs, a feeling of limited relevance of TA activities to one's needs, etc. may be cited as possible reasons. Teachers may also need support to benefit from TAs, such as leave and/ or financial assistance from schools to attend conferences, recognition of (voluntary) TA work as professionally valuable, encouragement to organise and/or participate in TA events at local levels, and so on.

English teacher clubs

If TAs are large and loose communities of teachers spread over larger geographical area, English teacher clubs (ETCs) tend to be small and close-knit groups of teachers typically from the same town or locality. Though Allwright (1991) prefers to call such small groups teachers' micro-associations, there are some essential differences between ETCs and TAs as discussed below.

Examples of ETCs are found in many parts of the world with different degrees of functionality, reach and impact. Anecdotal evidence suggests that there exist numerous ETCs in many countries with a wide diversity of composition, characteristics and ways of functioning, but there is little information publicly available about them. Among the more successful and recent examples are Bhandara and Sewagram English Teachers' Clubs (BETC & SETC) operating in Maharashtra in central India (Padwad, 2005; Padwad & Dixit, 2015), while some older examples (under different labels) from other parts of the world include the Chia-Yi Study Group in Taiwan (Huang, 2007), LEADS group in the US (Shwartz-McCotter, 2001) and teacher development groups in Kenya (Moon & Wanjohi, 2000). Research into the functioning and impact of ETCs is still limited, though, in addition to above, studies like Little (2003), Dixit (2007) and Sen (2007) have attempted to explore teacher development groups.

What are ETCs?

The word 'club' is highly indicative of the nature of most English teacher clubs (ETCs), which are typically small close-knit groups of teachers, characterised by friendliness, informality, flexibility, an absence of hierarchy, and a mixture of amateur and professional interests. They are essentially voluntary groups of teachers coming together to help each other address their concerns and improve their own selves as teachers. Though examples like BETC, SETC, Chia-Yi

Group or LEADS show that ETCs come in different forms and types, they seem to have the following in common:

- They usually emerge 'bottom-up', out of the efforts and felt needs of members to come together. Though in rare cases an external mandate or prescription may work as a trigger, these clubs are built on voluntarism of members.
- They are normally small-scale, informal and non-hierarchical. They also tend to cover a small geographical area, as the close proximity of members fosters regular face-to-face meetings and interaction. Chia-Yi Group members were from the same school, and BETC or SETC members from the same towns.
- They are self-managed, with members taking decisions and responsibility for acting on them. There is also a sense of collective ownership among members.
- Most of their activities revolve around the particular needs of their members, and thus tend to be more relevant and purposeful. Activities like English speaking sessions and meeting native speakers (Huang, 2007) or workshops on grammar and collective study of examination papers (Padwad, 2005) are indicative of how specific localised needs drive the activities of ETCs.
- The most prominent mode of operation in ETCs is talking. Sharing of feelings and concerns, exchanging ideas and experiences, supporting with suggestions and advice are the essence of the co-existence and take a large amount of time and space in ETCs.
- There is usually a mixture of the personal and the professional; members' sharing, interaction and mutual support relate to both personal and professional concerns and needs. As bonding within the group increases, members are also found to discuss, for example, financial problems, family affairs or children's behaviour (BETC meetings: personal notes, Padwad 2006–2016).

What do ETCs members do?

One of the most important activities of ETCs is the frequent meetings and sharing among the members. Meetings are often not very structured and agenda-driven, yet they are valued by members as opportunities of sharing and mutual support. Some of the common objectives of joining an ETC are improving one's own English (speaking) proficiency, finding solutions to practical classroom problems and improving one's teaching. Activities are related to these needs, which in course of time may expand to include classroom experimentation and research, conference presentations, publication and developing as trainers and mentors. A representative list of common ETCs activities will include periodic face-to-face meetings, English speaking activities for members, sessions by 'experts' on specific teaching concerns (e.g. teaching of essay writing skills), visits (to ELT institutes, other schools, language labs, etc), attending and presenting at ELT events, networking with other ELT groups and associations and undertaking (online) courses for self-development.

Contribution of ETCs to CPD

Perhaps the most distinctive contribution of ETCs to their members' CPD is facilitating personalisation and individualisation of CPD, which is not possible in other large-scale avenues like INSET workshops or conferences. When a young primary teacher says 'I had no chance to talk about my little problems and worries before. I can do so now and it's very helpful' (Padwad, 2005: 20), she apparently points at the scope ETCs offer to get her individual concerns addressed. ETCs help members to evolve their personal understanding of CPD, identify their own CPD goals, work out personal action plans and also carry them out with the support of peers. ETCs seem to effectively cater to the diversity of individual notions of and expectations from CPD, and individual ways of working towards it. For instance, BETC and SETC members had various CPD goals ranging from improving their English to becoming conference present-ers (which kept changing over time) (Padwad & Dixit, 2015), while LEADS members wished to address individual issues of social justice in their classrooms (Shwarz-McCotter, 2001). In their collaborative groups they were able to understand and work towards these individual goals.

The activities which ETCs members engage in amount to various kinds of professional learn-ing – language enhancement (e.g. English speaking sessions, grammar workshops), improving peda-gogic content knowledge (collective study sessions) and skills (how-to-teach workshops, classroom experiments), learning new roles (materials designer, classroom researcher, conference presenter), deeper understanding of one's context (constant reviewing and critiquing of experiences) and many others. Since they usually emerge from concrete practical issues and concerns, they bring back immediate contribution to and impact on members' thinking and action as teachers. The activities and experiences in ETCs represent a process of 'accumulating skills, professional knowl-edge, values and personal qualities', which is not 'externally mandated or manipulated but built on individual motivation, initiative and efforts' (Vonk, 1991, in Mushayikwa and Lubben, 2009: 375).

ETCs membership has been found to promote a sense of autonomy and agency in members (Padwad & Dixit, 2008; Sen, 2007; Dixit, 2007). This is manifested in members' recognising that not all of their problems are immutable, that there is scope for some action even within a highly prescriptive system and that they have some competence and potential to take such action. In a comparative study (Padwad & Dixit, 2008) ETCs members were found to be more positive than non-members about their difficulties, and more willing to work with or work around them.

ETCs also offer a psychologically safe environment where members can talk freely about their concerns, be ready to expose their weaknesses, try out different possibilities and risk fail-ure. Whether trying to speak in English or sharing about a failed experiment in the classroom, one thing members' may not worry about in ETCs is the loss of face, a risk which they may encounter when trying to do these things elsewhere. There is a sense of reassurance in being with sympathetic peers who are ready to listen and share experiences of similar challenges and difficulties, thus providing emotional and professional support. One important advantage here is that '[T]eachers address tough problems of teaching through exchange among members rather than being talked at by experts. [...] Being a part of the discourse community assures teachers that their knowledge of their students and of schooling is respected' (Lieberman & McLaughlin, 1992: 674). Sharing in a trustful environment is empowering, as 'the time to tell these stories and share narratives, the chance to "unload" which is weighing on us, is a form of support in itself' (McCot-ter, 2001: 693). The affective safety and reassurance also stem from the fact that members usually belong to a common context and hence share common experiences, understanding, concerns and contextual knowledge. It is easier to interact and exchange, and to respond meaningfully.

Different kinds of gains, both personal and professional, have been reported from ETCs. The comparative study of members and non-members of ETCs mentioned above (Padwad & Dixit, 2008) showed how ETC members developed pragmatic attitudes and sense of agency in approaching common problems in their work. For example, while ETC members accepted large classes as a 'bitter unavoidable reality' and believed 'whether one likes it or not, one has to handle the situation in one way or the other', non-members dismissed them as a systemic problem about which they could do nothing: 'the government deliberately gives maximum students to the classes and this creates problems.' Several studies of teacher development groups like ETCs point out how by belonging to these groups teachers gain confidence in themselves and their work, feel motivated to experiment, enhance their learning, get ideas and support to cope with challenges, develop a sense of autonomy, have more job satisfaction and come to join larger professional communities (Huang, 2007; Lieberman, 2000; Lieberman & McLaughlin, 1992; Padwad & Dixit, 2008, 2015; Sen, 2007; Shwartz-McCotter, 2001;Vesico et al., 2008).

Issues and challenges

One of the basic challenges in promoting ETCs is that there is still no clear views on how ETCs may be purposefully promoted. Two such attempts to deliberately launch ETCs in several places did not meet with much success (Padwad, 2005; Padwad & Dixit, 2009). So far, the successful examples like BETC and SETC seem to have emerged on their own. The understanding of what triggers the process, and which factors may ensure effective and sustainable ETCs, is still rudimentary at best. Thus, while it is easier to demonstrate the empowering impact of ETCs, it is difficult to provide any 'recipe' of how an ETC may be created.

For many of those ETCs already running, sustainability is a major issue. This involves many aspects like difficulties of management, shortage of resources, member burnout, having effective coordinators, identifying and implementing ever-new activities and sustaining member motivation at optimum levels.

Since ETCs members are practicing teachers, they need various kinds of support to engage in and benefit from their membership. They need support from their institutions, education authorities, policy provisions and even from the society around them, including their families. Usually, such support is available in a very limited way, if at all, which makes it quite challenging to sustain ETCs over a long period.

A special kind of support is needed in the form of recognition – both formal, as a valid form of CPD undertaking with attendant credits for career progression, and informal, as a meaningful and purposeful engagement worth spending time and energy on. In most cases, such recognition is missing, forcing teachers to entirely fall back on their personal time, money and resources and to keep their ETCs work away from their normal routines. Another interesting challenge is mentioned by Little (1989: 22 quoted in Grimmet & Crehan 1992), who feels that the assumptions behind the claimed benefits of collegiality in ETCs need to be critically examined. There is a particular danger of members confirming each other in their own practice, reinforcing each other's beliefs and values without critically evaluating and modifying them, in the absence of meaningful reflection on and learning from their experiences.

Teacher activity groups

Teacher associations and teacher clubs, in their respective ways, can provide opportunities for teachers to access ongoing support through contact and interaction with other teachers. A recent innovation implemented in a government school teacher development programme in Maharashtra, India that aimed to provide this kind of ongoing professional development support for teachers was the establishment of Teacher Activity Groups (TAGs). In this section we will look at what TAGs are, how they have been used in a project in India and discuss the benefits, issues and challenges they present in teacher development projects.

What are TAGs?

TAGs are semi-structured meetings that focus on supporting teachers' professional development. They are a place where teachers can discuss issues, ideas and experiences related to teaching and learning. They take place on a regular basis, e.g. once a month, and are attended by the same teachers from the same locality. They are also formalised in that TAGs form a core part of a teacher development programme that is running in an education system. This could be a project running at the school level or as part of a large-scale national project run by the government. During the TAG meeting, teachers take part in a series of activities using resources and materials that they have collectively decided are most relevant to their needs. At the end of the TAG, the teachers choose one or two ideas from the TAG and make an action plan on how they will use these ideas in their own lessons before the next TAG meeting. After the TAG, the teachers put their action plan into practice and keep in touch with their TAG peers on a social media group such as Facebook or WhatsApp.

It may be useful here to make a comparison between TAGs and ETCs. Both are similar in the sense that they are small-size teacher development groups, cater to more localised needs and interests of their members and are largely self-managed by the members. However, there are some important differences between them. ETCs essentially emerge 'from the bottom' through some teachers' voluntary initiative, while TAGs are promoted 'from above' with the active involvement and support of education authorities and have emerged out of the efforts to sustain and extend the impact of a large-scale teacher training project. They are formally recognised by the state education system and accounted for in the responsibilities of those involved, while ETCs are not. TAGs are a large-scale systemic intervention (about 750 groups in Maharashtra, India), while ETCs are small-scale personal initiatives (about eight to ten ETCs in Maharashtra). At least in this initial phase of their existence, TAGs are more closely focused on effective curriculum delivery and follow uniform plans of action and modes of operation, while ETCs focus on the members' varied needs and interests, keep changing their agendas and have diverse modes of operation.

TAGs in practice: The Tejas project in Maharashtra, India

Tejas, which roughly translates as 'bright light' in Hindi, is a 3-year teacher development and capacity building project for government primary school teachers in Maharashtra, India. It has been developed and delivered by the British Council in partnership with the Government of Maharashtra and Tata Trusts. The aims of these TAGs are to support primary school teachers to develop their English language skills and teaching competencies. In Maharashtra, cascade training has been the traditional approach to reaching the large number of teachers across the state. Tejas represents an alternative approach to providing professional development for teachers by establishing 750 TAGs across nine districts in the state. These TAGs have been set up by 250 TAG Coordinators who received training from the British Council to prepare them to manage and facilitate three TAGs each. Each TAG is attended by around 25 teachers who all live and teach in schools in the same area or cluster. The ongoing nature of TAGs enables the TAG Coordinators and teachers to establish professional communities of practice where trust and rapport can be developed over time. This is important for teachers who previously may have only had limited access to professional development through one off training events. As one teacher from a TAG in the city of Aurangabad said in an interview about her experience of TAGs,

> At first teachers thought about whether they could understand English or not. But our TAG Coordinator said to us that you need to think that I can do anything whatever it is – we can speak in English, we can discuss in English. All the teachers discuss in English and all the teachers take part in the TAG meeting with enthusiasm.

What do teachers do during a TAG meeting?

In Tejas, TAG meetings are divided into the following several sections all of which are facilitated by a TAG Coordinator:

1. *Warmer/Review of the past month*

   During this stage the TAG Coordinator facilitates a group discussion where the teachers share what they have tried in the lessons over the past month and talk about any successes and challenges they experienced.

2. *Language development*

   The teachers work through English language practice worksheets and take part in short role play activities to help build their speaking fluency and confidence.

3. *Learning by reading*

   The teachers read and discuss an article related to teaching. The articles the teachers read may include topics such as using stories, teaching English through songs, and methods and approaches to teaching different language skills to children. After reading the article, the TAG Coordinator facilitates discussion using guided questions to help the teachers reflect on the ideas in the article and relate it to their own contexts.

4. *Learning by watching*

   In this section, the teachers watch a short video of a teacher teaching a lesson or part of a lesson. The teachers use a worksheet and guided discussion questions to help them reflect on the teaching ideas and techniques they saw in the video.

5. *Reflection and action planning*

   Finally, the TAG Coordinator supports the teachers to discuss their reflections from the whole meeting and to complete an action plan on what ideas from the TAG meeting they will try in their lessons over the coming month.

For more information about TAGs in the Tejas project, watch this short video about the project: https://youtu.be/ao4AikxaIeo

Benefits of TAGs

There are many benefits of TAGs that relate to current research on what aspects of continuing professional development are likely to have an impact on teachers' practice in the classroom (see for example Borg, 2015b; Cordingley et al., 2015; Walter & Briggs, 2012). They include

1. TAGs take place in the teachers' own local area. This means teachers don't have to travel far to attend the TAGs and meet other teachers. This makes TAGs more accessible to all teachers to attend, particularly those who would find it difficult to travel and be away from their homes and family for extended periods of time.
2. TAGs are collaborative and over time create a shared purpose amongst the teachers as they begin to see each other as part of a network where they can share experiences and get support.
3. TAGs have the potential for reach and scale that make them suitable for large education systems.
4. As TAGs take place on a regular basis, they provide teachers with an ongoing form of CPD which helps them to get into a rhythm of focusing on the development of their teaching practice.
5. As teachers get into a rhythm of attending TAGs and focusing on their professional development, the teacher development programme that initiated the TAGs is more likely to be sustainable as the TAGs can continue after the programme ends.

Issues and challenges

Policy makers and those involved in running teacher development programmes may want to consider the following issues and challenges when considering implementing TAGs.

1. A cadre of TAG Coordinators who can effectively facilitate TAG meetings needs to be developed. These Coordinators need a lot of support to develop their facilitation skills such as building rapport, asking questions and demonstrating and encouraging active listening which support learning and reflection, guiding interaction and moderating discussions. This can help to ensure that TAGs do not turn into short training sessions.
2. Good infrastructure and resources need to be in place and available so that teachers are informed about the TAGs, know where to go to attend their TAG and have the necessary materials to use during the TAG.
3. Teachers need to be given time to develop their reflection skills. It's important that TAG meetings don't just focus on teaching activities, but also include adequate time for reflection and action planning. On the Tejas project, for example, it was found in observations of TAGs that the *Reflection and action planning* stage was the shortest section of the TAG. For the ideas from the TAG to be transferred to the classroom, it's important that teachers spend time reflecting, discussing and making action plans on how they will use the ideas from the TAG in their lessons.
4. A robust monitoring and evaluation system needs to be in place that captures data on how often TAGs take place, the materials the teachers use and find useful, and how the teachers are implementing the ideas from the TAG in their own lessons. A system that shares learning from each TAG with other TAGs can help connect, build up and connect teachers to teachers in other TAGs, which in turns strengthens their network of support.

Online networks and communities of practice (CoPs)

As computers and smartphones become more affordable, the number of people who can access the internet is increasing rapidly. According to the website www.internetworldstats.com, as of 30 June 2017, there were over 3.8 billion internet users worldwide. Over 1.9 billion of these users are in Asia and 388 million were in Africa. According to the 2016 World Bank report 'Digital Dividends', the internet promotes development through inclusion, efficiency and innovation. This affects teachers positively in a variety of different ways. For example, as the costs of accessing information reduce digitally, and the availability of the internet reaches communities even in remote rural locations across the world, inclusion increases as more teachers can become part of the global network of internet users and can gain access to information about teaching and learning. As teachers get online, the number of websites, blogs, videos, forums, social media groups for teachers increases. This increases efficiency and makes it easier for teachers no matter where they are in the world to connect, share their experiences and learn from each other. Finally, as the internet develops and new websites, apps and platforms become available, teachers can find innovative ways to find other teachers with similar interests to communicate, form groups with and develop networks. In this section we will explore different ways that teachers are communicating with each other online and building sustainable networks to support their professional development.

What is an online CoP?

'Communities of practice are groups of people who share a concern or a passion for something they do and learn how to do it better as they interact regularly' (Wenger-Trayner & Wenger-Treyner, 2015). This idea of collaborative group learning has become prevalent in teacher education and online CoPs are starting to flourish as the internet becomes more and more accessible. Online or digital CoPs are groups that are set up and run by practitioners in a specific field in order to discuss and share knowledge, learning and experiences related to their area of interest and/or expertise. CoPs serve a specific purpose for the participants and online CoPs can also do the same. Blogs, wikis, forums, social media sites such as Facebook and Twitter, online group messaging platforms such as WhatsApp, and social learning platforms such as Edmodo, all allow their users to create, share and discuss content. As such, teachers can use these platforms to form groups and develop networks with other teachers. Access to these groups and networks can provide teachers with support that they might not have access to in their own local context. 'An online CoP can provide instant help, expertise, long-term apprenticeship in a safe social setting, and perhaps most importantly, emotional support for teachers isolated from their technological peers' (Hanson-Smith, 2013).

Examples of online groups, CoPs and networks

Twitter

Twitter is a social media platform where users can send, or 'tweet', pictures, videos, links and short messages. A useful feature of Twitter is the 'hashtag'. This allows users to give their message a specific 'tag' or label by placing the # or hash character before a key word. This makes it easy for others who are not following you to see your post. Many teachers have been taking advantage of this feature to form groups and have 'Twitter chats' or discussions using specific hashtags.

Examples of popular teaching and teacher education hashtags include:

#Edchat

A weekly Twitter discussion open for all teachers that covers a wide variety of topics relating to teaching and CPD. The chats take place on Tuesdays at midnight GMT.

#Edtechchat

This hashtag is used during a weekly discussion on educational technology. The chat takes place on Mondays at midnight GMT.

#ELTChat

This very popular hashtag is used by English language teachers across the world who are interested in CPD. A twitter chat is held once a week (currently Wednesdays at 12.00pm and 9.00pm GMT) where teachers discuss a topic that they have chosen. A summary of the discussion is posted on their website. See their website http://eltchat.org/wordpress/ for more details.

By searching for and using these and other education related hashtags, teachers can come into contact with other teachers interested in similar topics. Teachers can build their own Personal Learning Network (PLN) by 'following' other teachers who post Twitter messages on topics and areas that interest them. Once a teacher has followed a number of others, and a number of other teachers are following them, they have a support network that they can use to give and receive advice no matter where they are in the world. This is reflected in tweets from teachers from the Tejas project during their monthly Twitter chat using the #Tejas4Ed hashtag. During one of these Twitter chats on the theme of social media held in November 2017, teachers tweeted many ideas on how social media had helped them. Responses included how it enabled them to 'connect with movers and shakers in education', and how it 'helps me to study what others are doing and how I can improve myself'. This connectivity allows teachers to 'access knowledge' and 'become aware of many online courses some of which are free of cost.'

WhatsApp

In Tejas, the project in Maharashtra mentioned above, WhatsApp has played a central role in enabling the project participants to remain in touch and discuss issues related to their role on the project and topics that would support their professional development. As this project involved working with multiple stakeholders, a number of different WhatsApp groups were set up.

- One group for 30 government academic resource staff
- One group for 250 Coordinators who facilitated Teacher Activity Groups (TAGs)
- Over 400 groups set up by Coordinators for the teachers in the TAGs they facilitated.

Members of the British Council Tejas project team joined the first two of the above groups to act as moderators, encourage discussion and provide support in areas that were identified as areas of development through monitoring and evaluation activities. Overall, the majority of the messages posted were related to the project and focused on

- describing and sharing experiences that had happened to them on the project
- providing short reports of TAG meetings
- discussing questions about the English language, grammar and vocabulary
- providing support by asking and answering questions about TAGs
- posting pictures and videos of their TAGs
- sharing website links about teaching
- sharing information about events such as webinars, conferences and the monthly #Tejas4Ed Twitter chat
- sharing inspirational stories

The following example discussion from the TAG Coordinator WhatsApp group demonstrates how the participants used it to ask for and provide support:

TAG Coordinator 1: Hello all. I need your help … Will you please suggest me some tools and activities for developing 4th grade writing skills… One of my TAG members asked me about this… I want to suggest more and more activities to him… Please help me.

TAG Coordinator 2: You can use ABL cards (activity based learning). I have some writing PDFs. I'll send them to you. Please think which are useful for you. Take a print out and laminate them. Students can use them with a sketch pen and it's easy to remove.

TAG Coordinator 3: he motive of Tejas is to create self-support groups. It would be great if you could ask the members from the TAG to suggest tools.

Several more suggestions about books and procedures for a variety of activities were also provided by different TAG Coordinators. The TAG Coordinator then compiled all the suggestions into a PowerPoint presentation which were then shared with group.

TAG Coordinator 1: Thanks all of you for your valuable guidance. I made this PPT to send him all of your suggestions.

Facebook

The English language initiative for secondary schools (ELISS) project was a 4-year training and development project run by the British Council for 16,400 government secondary school teachers across Maharashtra, India. As part of this project 420 teachers were selected to be Master Trainers and school-based mentors. These Master Trainers were then trained to deliver cascade training and mentor teachers in schools near the areas they lived. As the Master Trainers were based across the state, a Facebook group was set up to provide them with a space to share their experiences and learning from the project and receive ongoing support from each other and the British Council. The Master Trainers used the group in a number of ways, including:

- sharing links to Facebook posts from other groups about teaching
- sharing pictures with short descriptions of classroom activities either they or their mentees had tried in their lessons
- discussing teaching techniques they had learnt and their experiences of trying them in class.

For example, in one post, a Master Trainer posted the following message:

Master Trainer 1: 55 students were divided into 11 groups, 5 in each group. A task of analysing a dialogue of 5 to 6 lines from the textbook was given. The groups then presented their work before the class.

The post was then accompanied by pictures showing the students sitting in groups of five and also of the students presenting their work to the class. Several members of the Facebook group responded by giving praise and asking questions about the activity. For example,

Master Trainer 2: Great. Which activity did u conduct?

Master Trainer 1:
(original poster): They were given the task of analysing 5/6 lines from the textbook. I gave them freedom to focus on the areas they wanted. 1 group focused on the vocabulary, one pointed out the grammar, one group decided to write an interview with the character in the dialogue. I guided wherever necessary.

Master Trainer 2: Oh great. A variety of activities promoting learner autonomy.

Master Trainer 3: Good keep it up.

In another Facebook post, a group moderator from the British Council asked a question about dictogloss, a listening and writing activity which had been introduced in a recent training course for Master Trainers.

Moderator: Dictogloss – Has anybody tried it in their classes yet? Can you describe what you did? How did you arrange the classroom? Did you have any class-room management issues? How did you solve them?

Following this, seven different Master Trainers responded and discussed the question.

Master Trainer 1: Yes, I tried it with listening texts. My students liked this activity though my class is large I don't need to arrange anything.

Master Trainer 2: I have tried this in my classroom for 9th grade and a little variation with the 6th grade too. They enjoyed it. But I want to repeat it in the next term and then…

Recent research (for example, Gulamhussein, 2013) has shown that teachers need ongoing support to implement new ideas in the classroom and may need to practise a new teaching skill up to 20 times before they are able to integrate it into their teaching practice. As well as this, teachers need to see success in the activities they do. The sharing and discussion such as the conversation above is very positive as it can help motivate others in the group as they can see the success others are having in implementing different teaching techniques into their lessons.

Benefits of participating in online networks and CoPs

Teachers can benefit from joining and participating in online networks and CoPs in a number of ways.

1. The nature of communication in online groups allows teachers to access and contribute to online discussions at any time from any location. Online discussions are often asynchronous and can take place over a number of hours and even days. This allows teachers to contribute at times convenient for them. Online discussions that are synchronous, such as Twitter chats, can still be accessed afterwards by teachers unable to join at the time of the discussion.
2. Teachers who live and work in remote or rural areas, or who don't have the time to commit to joining face-to-face meetings can benefit from joining and participating in online groups. This can reduce feelings of isolation for teachers who may not usually be able to meet with other teachers in their own areas.
3. As outlined above, many online groups for teachers make use of social media platforms. If a teacher has access to the internet, then they will have access to a social media platform that they can join and communicate with other teachers online. These platforms encourage users to keep messages short, share links, pictures and videos. This means that teachers do not need to spend a huge amount of time composing messages. They can quickly engage in discussions that support their own and others' CPD.

Issues and challenges

Policy makers and those involved in integrating online groups and CoPs into teacher development programmes will need to consider a range of issues and challenges.

1. Establishing an online group is simple. Getting the people within the group to use it frequently and purposefully is more challenging. A plan of how to engage and encourage teachers to participate is vital. A useful resource which can help those starting or managing online groups is the *Action Notebook* chapter in Wenger, White and Smith's 2009 book *Digital habitats: Stewarding technology for communities*. This is also available on their website to download for free at http://technologyforcommunities.com/excerpts/actionnotebook. While not aimed specifically at teachers, it provides templates and ideas that can be used to help gain a better understanding of the characteristics of the online community you want to work with and develop.
2. Teachers in online groups need to understand the purpose and mission of the group. If the purpose of the group is clear, understood and agreed upon by all members of the group, interactions and discussions will be more meaningful for the participants.

3. In order to maintain the purpose and momentum of the group, the selection and recruitment of moderators should be considered. Moderators can start discussions, encourage participation, guide discussions and ensure that they stay on track.
4. If teacher development initiatives are going to introduce online groups and CoPs as part of their programme, they should consider the data costs that teachers will have to incur to access and participate in these online groups. The costs of internet data plans are reducing, however, participants of online groups will soon eat into their data plans especially if they are sharing videos and pictures and teaching.

Conclusion

When teachers come together to collaborate, reflect and support each other, they are likely to have positive impact on teachers and their classroom practice (see for example Borg, 2015b; Walter and Briggs, 2012). One way teachers can take responsibility for their own professional development is by joining a teacher network.

In this chapter we have looked at four different kinds of teacher networks ranging from the larger and more formally organised ones, such as Teacher Associations, to smaller, voluntary and informal ones, such as teacher clubs, to somewhere in between, such as Teacher Activity Groups. We have also seen the huge potential for online groups and CoPs to support teacher learning and development. It is clear that each of the teacher networks we have explored in this chapter can play a significant role in a teacher's own CPD and that they connect strongly with current understanding of what makes effective CPD. With the increasing recognition among policy makers and teacher education providers of the importance of CPD avenues supplementing the traditional dependence on short-term training, it seems that teacher networks, like those discussed in this chapter, are going to play a much greater and more central role in teacher education/development initiatives in future. As Trust et al. (2016: 16) point out 'If teachers are to continually develop their practice then they could benefit from broad, holistic, and flexible networks as they navigate shifting professional landscapes.' There is also an urgent need of more extensive and intensive research into what different networks contribute to CPD and how various kinds of networks may be promoted and sustained, and what may be the implications of such promotion/ sustenance of teacher networks for the prevalent ELT policies and practices.

Further reading

Farell, T. (2013) *Reflective Practice in ESL Teacher Development Groups: From Practices to Principles*. Basingstoke: Palgrave Macmillan.
  Based on the insider experience of a teacher development group, the author offers a rich description of the professional learning journey the members went through and abstracts some key principles of teacher learning in TD groups.
Gulamhussein, A. (2013) *Teaching the Teachers: Effective Professional Development in an Era of High Stakes Accountability*. Washington, DC: Center for Public Education.
  This paper examines different forms of professional development made available to teachers and what the research says about the structure of professional development programmes that lead to changes in teachers' practice and the learning of students.
Stoll, L. and Louis, K. S. (eds) (2007) *Professional Learning Communities*. Maidenhead: Open University Press.
  This book offers a general discussion of PLCs and some frameworks to conecptualise the nature and role of PLCs in professional learning. It also discusses aspects of PLCs such as distributed leadership, dialogue, trust, inquiry and purpose in their relation to learning.

Wenger-Trayner, E. and Wenger-Trayner, B. (2015) 'Communities of Practice – A Brief Introduction' Available online: <https://wenger-trayner.com/introduction-to-communities-of-practice> (accessed 22 May, 2019). This paper explores what communities of practice are, what they look like in practice and how they are being used by people and organisations in a variety of different fields.

References

Alacantara, E. (2010) *A lonely rooster cannot bring on a new dawn: The role of a FL teachers' association in the professional development of its associates.* Unpublished MA dissertation, Universidade de Brasília, Instituto de Letras, Brazil.

Allwright, D. (1991) *Exploratory teaching, professional development and the role of a teacher association.* Invited paper for the Cuban Association of English Language Specialists (GELI), Havana, Cuba. *CRILE Working Paper no. 7.* Available online: <www.letras.pucrio.br/unidades&nucleos/epcentre/readings/cuba%20 91%20paper.htm> (accessed 22 May, 2019).

Arega, A. A. (2012) *Teacher development: English language teachers' associations impact on the professional development of English language teachers with a special reference to Addis Ababa English Language Teachers' Association (AAELTA), Ethiopia.* Unpublished MA dissertation, Lancaster University, UK.

Aubrey, J. and Coombe, C. (2010) 'The TESOL Arabia Conference and its Role in the Professional Development of Teachers at Institutions of Higher Education in the United Arab Emirates'. *Academic Leadership Journal,* 8(3).

Borg, S. (2015a) 'The Benefits of Attending ELT Conferences'. *ELT Journal,* 69(1) 35–46.

Borg, S. (2015b) *Contemporary Perspectives on Continuing Professional Development.* London: British Council, Available online: <https://englishagenda.britishcouncil.org/sites/default/files/attachments/contempo rary_perspectives_on_cpd.pdf> (accessed 22 May, 2019).

Cordingley, P., Higgins, S., Greany, T., Buckler, N., Coles-Jordan, D., Crisp, B., Saunders, L. and Coe, R. (2015) *Developing Great Teaching: Lessons from the International Reviews into Effective Professional Development.* London: Teacher Development Trust.

Dixit, K. K. (2007) *Towards a proposal for facilitator development for English Language Teachers' Clubs in India.* Unpublished MEd dissertation, College of St. Mark and St John, University of Exeter, UK.

Gnawali, L. (2016) 'English Language Teacher Development Through Teacher Associations: The Case of NELTA'. *ELT Journal,* 70(2) 170–179.

Grimmett, P. P. and Crehan, E. P. (1992) 'The nature of collegiality in teacher development: the case for clinical supervision', in Fullan, M. and Hargreaves, A. (eds) *Teacher Development and Educational Change.* London: Falmer Press.

Gulamhussein, A. (2013) *Teaching the Teachers: Effective Professional Development in an Era of High Stakes Accountability.* Washington, DC: Center for Public Education. Available online: <www.centerforpubliceducation.org/ Main-Menu/Staffingstudents/Teaching-the-Teachers-Effective-Professional-Development-in-an-Era- of-High-Stakes-Accountability/Teaching-the-Teachers-Full-Report.pdf> (accessed 22 May, 2019).

Hanson-Smith, E. (2013) 'Online communities of practice', in Chapelle, C. A. (ed.) *The Encyclopedia of Applied Linguistics.* Hoboken, NJ: Blackwell Publishing Ltd.

Huang, Y-C. (2007) 'How Teachers Develop their Professional Knowledge in English Study Group in Taiwan'. *Educational Research and Review,* 2(3) 36–45.

Kolesnikova, T. (2011) 'Use of appropriate tools in village teacher professional development', in Gunashekar, P., Padwad, A. and Pawelec, D. (eds) *Starting, Stimulating and Sustaining English Language Teacher Education and Development: A Selection of Papers Presented at the International Conference in Hyderabad in January 2011.* London: British Council: 123–127.

Lamb, T. (2012) 'Language Associations and Collaborative Support: Language Teacher Associations as Empowering Spaces for Professional Networks'. *Innovation in Language Learning and Teaching,* 6(3) 287–308.

Lieberman, A. (2000) 'Networks as Learning Communities: Shaping the Future of Teacher Development'. *Journal of Teacher Education,* 51(3) 221–227.

Lieberman, A. and McLaughlin, M. W. (1992) 'Networks for Educational Change: Powerful and Problematic'. *Phi Delta Kappa,* 73 673–677.

Little, J. (2003) 'Inside Teacher Community: Representations of Classroom Practice'. *Teachers College Record,* 105(6) 913–945.

Malupa-Kim, M. (2011) *Professional Development: Why Attending Conferences Counts.* Alexandria, VA: TESOL Inc.

McCotter, S. S. (2001) 'Collaborative groups as professional development'. *Teaching and Teacher Education,* 17(6) 685–704.

Moon, J. and Wanjohi, G. (2000) *Kenyan Teacher Development Groups: Co-ordinators' perceptions of their roles and of their relationships with their groups.* Paper presented at the joint IATEFL Teacher Trainer SIG/University of Leeds Conference on Training the Trainers, November, University of Leeds.

Mushayikwa, E. and Lubben, F. (2009) 'Self-directed Professional Development – Hope for Teachers Working in Deprived Environments?'. *Teaching and Teacher Education,* 25(3) 375–382.

Odhiambo, F. and Nganyi, D. O. (2007) 'Sharing Examples of Existing Successful Practice in ELT Associations in East Africa'. *English Language Teacher Education and Development,* 10(4) 63–68.

Padwad, A. (2005) *Final Report on English Teachers' Clubs (ETCs) Project* submitted to British Council, London (unpublished). Huntingdon: Mimeo.

Padwad, A. and Dixit, K. K. (2008) 'Impact of Professional Learning Community Participation on Teachers' Thinking About Classroom Problems'. *TESL E-Journal,* 12(3) 1–11. Available online: <http://tesl-ej.org/ej47/a10.html> (accessed 22 May, 2019).

Padwad, A. and Dixit, K. K. (2009) *Draft Report on British Council and Hornby Trust Supported Project on Consolidation and Replication of English Teachers' Clubs* (unpublished). Huntingdon: Mimeo.

Padwad, A. and Dixit, K. K. (2015) 'Exploring Continuing Professional Development: English Teachers' Clubs in Central India', in Wright, T. and Beaumont, M. (eds) *Experiences of Second Language Teacher Education.* Basingstoke: Palgrave Macmillan: 153–174.

Phillipson, R. (2009) *Linguistic Imperialism Continued.* Abingdon: Routledge.

Rixon, S. and Smith, R. (2017) *A History of IATEFL.* Faversham: IATEFL.

Sen, Sanghita (2007) *English Language Teachers' Clubs: a new option for ESL teachers' ongoing professional development in India?* Unpublished MA dissertation, Institute of Education, University of London, UK.

Shwartz-McCotter, S. (2001) 'Collaborative Groups as Professional Development'. *Teaching and Teacher Education,* 17(6) 685–704.

Trust, T., Krutka, D. G. and Carpenter, J. P. (2016) '"Together We Are Better": Professional Learning Networks for Teachers'. *Computers and Education,* 102 15–34.

Vescio, V., Ross, D. and Adams, A. (2008) 'A Review of Research on the Impact of Professional Learning Communities on Teaching Practice and Student Learning'. *Teaching and Teacher Education,* 24(1) 80–91.

Walter, C. and Briggs, J. (2012) *What Professional Development Makes the Most Difference to Teachers?* Oxford: Oxford University Press.

Wenger, E., White, N. and Smith, J. D. (2009) *Digital Habitats: Stewarding Technology for Communities.* Portland, OR: CPsquare.

Wenger-Trayner, E. and Wenger-Trayner, B. (2015) 'Communities of Practice – A Brief Introduction. Available online: <https://wenger-trayner.com/introduction-to-communities-of-practice> (accessed 22 May, 2019).

World Bank Group (2016) *World Development Report 2016: Digital Dividends.* Washington, DC: World Bank.

37

Action research

Darío Luis Banegas and Luis S. Villacañas de Castro

Introduction

Student-teachers, teachers, and teacher educators may ask themselves:Why should we do action research? Based on case studies and teachers' voices, Burns (2005) believes that, in terms of benefits, AR equips teachers with systematised reflections and rich data to transform, change, improve, and contest their own classroom practices. In addition, Edwards and Burns (2016a) suggest that AR can help teachers feel more confident about their teaching, feel more connected to their students, engage with research, and feel more recognised in their professional community. For the students, the impact is on the quality, reach, and significance of their learning. Thus, AR needs to be encouraged among teachers, and therefore it is in the hands of teacher educators in pre-service and in-service programmes and continuous professional development opportunities to provide student-teachers, teachers, and fellow teacher educators with awareness, knowledge, and experiences of AR.

Since our aim is to support teacher educators in disseminating the nature and power of AR, we organise this chapter from general aspects to examples from our own experience. First, we define AR and summarise its value, the role of teachers, and the crucial relevance of motivation and sustainability in AR engagement. Second, we discuss features and conditions of AR in its preparation, navigation, and socialisation. Finally, we share examples of teacher educators involved in teaching, doing, and supporting AR carried out with student-teachers, teachers and teacher educators across ELTE (English language teacher education). Readers may find that our recommendations can be helpful to both teachers and teacher educators given their role as empowerers.

AR: an overview

We refer to AR as an umbrella acronym which includes different realisations of teachers investigating their own practices (Stenhouse, 1975) to transform them, in line with Somekh's (2010: 104) emphasis on the educational dimension of all AR initiatives. 'Action research,' she says, 'is always a learning process, and in trying to bring about improvements in human interactions [...] the action researcher is always engaged in an educative process'. Framed in qualitative research,

AR involves investigating an issue present in a given context, most likely a classroom or an institution, with the aim of implementing and evaluating change. To improve a situation, teachers need to act, reflect, and act again until they can see a transformation in practice achieved through synergistic efforts between those involved, for example teachers and students. In this section we focus on the transformative value of AR, the role of teachers, and the place of motivation and sustainability for AR to be meaningful and a trigger for empowerment and social justice.

The essential trait of AR is not that the teachers do the research, nor that they investigate their own practices – other forms of teacher research comply with this too. Rather, the defining trait of AR would be that the teachers' fundamental beliefs and ideas about education are fully engaged in the research process. AR is and cannot be disconnected from the general (even philosophical) questions concerning the purpose of education or its role in society, nor from how the latter should tie to choices of academic subject matter or pedagogical and didactic orientations. Insofar as this is the case, we think that AR is always *critical*, to the extent that it goes against the progressive deskilling of teachers and their conversion into mere *technicians* in the present neoliberal regime.

The fact that teachers' essential ideas about education are inscribed in AR also places strict boundaries and qualifies the research dimension. Whatever are the beliefs they hold about education, most teachers will agree that it is their job to contribute to education through *teaching* and making pupils learn. In the same way as 'the physician cannot experiment without attempting to heal', for Stenhouse ([1979] 2012: 133), 'the teacher cannot learn [from AR] without undertaking that the pupils learn too'. That is why AR will always prioritize the action of teaching over research. 'The fundamental aim of action research', Elliott (1991: 49) claimed, 'is to improve practice rather than to produce knowledge. The production and utilisation of knowledge is subordinate to, and conditioned by, this fundamental aim'. Indeed, if knowledge must empower action in AR (and not the other way around), then it must do so *while* and *where* the action is taking place, i.e. while the teacher *teaches* and the learners *learn*, as well and as much as possible. This fact not only confers a context-bound nature to AR and the knowledge it may generate; it also implies that action researchers, i.e. teacher researchers, should always make sure that the intrinsic aims of education are not being neglected at any point during the research process. For example, Banegas (2017a) developed an AR project to help his student-teachers develop their English language proficiency and benefit from linguistics knowledge. With this aim in mind, student-teachers' education became central in the context of the study, and the data collected emerged from their regular lessons, e.g. student-teachers' exams and assignments or the tutor-developed materials. This example shows that teachers integrate research into the regular teaching and learning processes, thus making students, and possibly other teachers and principals, participate in the transformative dynamics that underpin AR. The transformations that AR generates impact directly on the teachers carrying out AR (Burns, 2005). However, the transformative value of AR is not circumscribed to a single classroom at a specific point in time. AR seeks transformation from the grassroots to larger systemic bodies and regulations (Somekh and Zeichner, 2009), yet transformative practices do not change overnight, and the findings of teachers' research need to be supported for some time in order for teachers and institutions to feel that their efforts pay off in the long run. Therefore, the power of transformation underpinning AR is linked to two aspects: motivation and sustainability.

Drawing on notions of teacher motivation (Ushioda, 2013), teachers' self-efficacy through teacher research (Wyatt and Dikilitaş, 2016), and the central role played by teachers in AR (Burns, 2010), it is often agreed that AR must be initiated by teachers themselves in response to an issue they feel curious about and are driven to explore. In order to support their motivation, teachers should not be left alone. Edwards and Burns (2016a: 14) remind us that 'a balance of bottom-up individual teacher motivation and top-down institutional support is crucial in ensuring the sustainability of the impact of AR over time'. In the Ethiopian context, Aga's (2017) AR study with teachers reveals that motivation to engage in AR is essential to counteract the effects of demotivating factors such as lack of time, bureaucratic processes and paperwork, funding opportunities, and teachers' lack of commitment to avoid accountability for their own practices. It follows that if motivation needs to be maintained, then sustainability in keeping a project running and sharing the outcomes must be secured. It is our understanding that the need for sustainability is a call for ELTE. Teacher educators are in an advantageous position to support AR since they may work with future and present teachers on different projects aimed at transforming practice and, ultimately, education. To increase sustainability, teacher educators can work on providing student-teachers and teachers with knowledge and awareness of AR not only by drawing on the literature but also by engaging them in AR within ELTE programmes. Research engagement goes hand in hand with collaboration and therefore AR is a collaborative enterprise as it can include colleagues and students. CAR (collaborative action research) stresses the collective and participatory nature of AR (Banegas et al., 2013), however power imbalance should be minimised to maintain motivation and sustainability (Yayli, 2012).

Whether teachers are doing AR alone or with colleagues, it is important to understand how AR can be prepared, navigated, and socialised. In the following section, we consider these three dimensions of AR.

AR: considerations

A brief glance at the literature shows that AR in ELT can be found across a wide range of contexts and with different participants such as:

- Young learners (Vaca Torres and Gómez Rodríguez, 2017)
- Undergraduate students in ELTE programmes (Banegas, 2017a, 2017b)
- Postgraduate students in ELTE programmes (Crawford Garrett et al., 2015; Halbach, 2016; Villacañas de Castro, 2014)
- Novice and experienced teachers (Burns et al., 2017; Castro-Garcés and Martínez Granada, 2016)

What all these contexts share is the way in which AR was carried out. There was initial planning, development, and socialisation of the experience. In this section we provide teacher educators with insights and suggestions about how to support AR in ELTE with student-teachers, teachers, and fellow teacher educators. These considerations apply to raising student-teachers' awareness and constructing knowledge about AR, empowering teachers to take full control of AR or supporting them through, for example, a university–school collaborative project.

Preparing for AR

As we have hinted above, an AR project starts with a practice-related issue or a question posited by teachers who wish to explore their own practices (Burns, 2010). AR should never be imposed on teachers. In arranging an AR project in ELTE, first, it is imperative to consider the aims, the resources, possible obstacles, the support available, and, most importantly, how the project derives from and feeds into teachers' situated practices and curriculum development so that the ecological, i.e. research from/for the context, and critical dimensions of AR are ensured. The critical dimension of AR responds to critical pedagogy, i.e. a type of pedagogy that seeks to challenge hegemonic practices by empowering and emancipating teachers and learners to become agents of change, thus bringing about social justice (Giroux, 2011). From critical pedagogy, it is also worth thinking outside the box and awakening teachers' pedagogical imagination with the notion of transforming education based on their context and their own images and dreams of how education and professional practices should be like. For example, Ruohotie-Lyhty and Moate (2016) carried out an AR study with foreign language student-teachers in Finland to help them reflect on their identity and think of ways in which they could exercise prominent agency as full-time teachers.

In preparing for AR, it is important to develop a sensible timeframe, for example, a month, a term, or a whole academic year. Such a timeframe is often organised around spiralling cycles with stages (Burns, 2010; Dikilitas and Griffiths, 2017). There is no prescribed number of cycles to follow. For example, there are AR projects containing one (Yan, 2017), three (Banegas, 2017a), or four (Edwards and Burns, 2016b) cycles. In order to record the history of an AR project whatever the number of cycles, it is advisable to keep a journal in which teachers describe, anticipate, and problematise their AR activities as they move from stage to stage and cycle to cycle. Below, we unpack the notion of cycles and stages focusing on what teachers need to plan ahead.

A cycle starts with an exploratory stage focused on initial investigations and reflections around the issue to address. Smith (2015) stresses the importance of understanding the context and issue with care before moving forward with an action plan to ensure that context-responsiveness is achieved. This first stage is followed by an action stage where the intervention to bring about change is carefully planned. At this stage, and preferably before, teachers need to think about how they will collect data to ensure that their project produces change. Then an intervention/implementation stage is put in place and it involves setting the planned course of action in motion and observing and exploring its impact. During this stage teachers can collect data through classroom observation, reflective journals, survey questionnaires, interviews, and learning and teaching artefacts (e.g. students' exams, teacher-made handouts). The data collected at that stage feeds into the following stage, that of reflection/evaluation of the intervention. Based on such reflections a new action stage begins with the aim of strengthening the intervention and ensuring the impact of the overall project. Although reflection/evaluation is usually placed at the end of a cycle, reflection occurs throughout the cycle as teachers need to be aware of what is happening in the classroom and what contextual factors may impinge on the overall project as it unfolds. Constant reflection is what makes AR iterative in nature; since the knowledge obtained in a first cycle shapes a second cycle (Banegas, 2017a; Edwards and Burns, 2016b). Finally, the reporting stage emerges as an opportunity to share the findings with, for example, those involved in the project, colleagues, and other professionals, and to further objectify and understand the educational subject matter, in turn. We return to this last stage further below.

Navigating AR

By *navigating* we mean enacting the AR project. In this dimension of AR, teachers need to be flexible and open to changes as their context and participants may inevitably suggest a different course of action. As suggested above, navigating AR with confidence and awareness requires that teachers continue recording their reflections, actions, and plans in their research journal, and sharing their experience with others. Such a writing activity will help them be systematic with the AR cycles and stages planned, while keeping an open attitude, so that a healthy balance between flexibility and structure is achieved. Teachers need to remember that this kind of research is not objective, but rather intersubjective and context-bound, which entails that they need to listen to the context, their own voice, and their participants'. As the cycles go by and teachers look back at the data they have slowly been able to gather, they are likely to be impressed!

Having clear aims within an ecological perspective helps teachers gather as much data as possible through observations, interviews, questionnaires, surveys, teaching artefacts, students' work, etc. For example, in Banegas (2017a), data were collected through student-teachers' reflective journals, the teacher educator's journal, group interviews, copies of the student-teachers' exams, and the worksheets developed by the teacher educator. Teachers can also collect data through photographs and videos (Basallo Gómez, 2016). Whatever the data collection instruments, it is necessary to have written consent form of those who are, for example, interviewed, or photographed. For ethical reasons (Banegas and Villacañas de Castro, 2015), we need to preserve the identity of the participants and make sure that, at least, confidentiality and anonymity are in place unless the participants explicitly state that, for example, they would like to appear with their real names in a report for publication. Another ethical issue has to do with making sure that the research methods do not conflict with the educational aims of the course, but rather to ensure that the students' learning and skills are measured and assessed within a context that is valuable and interesting for them – that is, within a situation that remains *educative*.

While navigating the project, teachers can start collecting and reading relevant books and articles which will provide them with the foundations and concepts of their project. AR may become more fruitful and navigable when findings are analysed as cycles shape other cycles.

Socialising AR

Research is dead if it is not shared with colleagues in the local as well as international context and this is why a reporting stage must be ensured in any AR project. Most of all, we should share the findings with those who participated and made the project possible. This reporting stage, in addition, provides further chances to objectify, analyse, criticise, and contrast the research through peer deliberation. Findings could be shared in multiple ways such as a short video which can be uploaded on a YouTube channel or institutional website, a poster hung at your institution, a staff meeting, or a presentation at a local, regional, national, or international conference. For example, the *Teachers Research! Conference* in Buenos Aires 2017 organised by the British Council, APIBA (Asociación de Profesores de Inglés de Buenos Aires), and FAAPI (Federación Argentina de Asociaciones de Profesores de Inglés) invited teachers to share their research projects through poster presentations. Some of these presentations are available online at the British Council Argentina YouTube channel for dissemination. Teachers can also think about writing a report to be published in a newsletter, a professional magazine, or regional or international journals which are well-known for promoting AR, such as *Profile* and *Educational Action Research*. In addition, *Language Teacher Research* accepts submission under a section called Practitioner Research. For example, in 2016, the *Argentinian Journal of Applied Linguistics* published a special issue on language learning and intercultural citizenship education guest-edited by Porto and Byram (2015); the articles were mostly written by teachers and teacher educators sharing their interventions and reflections.

While writing contributes to the dissemination of AR findings, it could be a daunting task. A good idea to avoid staring at a blank page is to start describing the context of the AR project, i.e. the institution, the programme, and the tutors and students involved. In addition, teachers may start by studying how articles are structured and worded. Copying phrases, reporting verbs and other features of academic writing can help teachers organise their notes and drafted findings. Once teachers start writing, they need to remind themselves that writing is a process through which there will be writing, deleting, rewriting, starting again, and producing different versions. In this process, looking for the support of a critical friend to provide feedback can become a tremendous learning experience.

Now that we have provided a succinct description of preparing, navigating, and socialising AR, we will attempt to share specific and detailed examples of how AR can be included in ELTE.

AR and ELTE

Since our main aim is to support teacher educators in their interest of spreading and supporting AR, we share below examples of teacher educators (1) teaching AR-based modules in IELTE, (2) doing AR projects on their practices in IELTE, and (3) supporting AR projects with (novice) teachers.

Teaching AR

In the province of Chubut, southern Argentina, a new four-year pre-service English language teacher education curriculum was introduced in 2014. With the aim of promoting teachers' identity as producers of school knowledge based in teacher research, especially AR, two modules were introduced. Both modules were two terms long and they involved the design and implementation of a research proposal in groups.

One module was called Educational Research (Table 37.1), delivered in Spanish through peer teaching, and it provided future teachers with an overview of educational research beyond

Table 37.1 Outline of an educational research module in IELTE

Module: Educational Research	
Two tutors: A teacher educator specialised in general education and research and a teacher of English with experience in research and academic writing	
Two terms (March–November)	
Two hours weekly	
Aims:	Help future teachers reflect on their practices.
	Encourage interdisciplinary research.
	Examine educational settings as complex social objects.
	Empower future teachers to generate classroom knowledge.
	Develop critical thinking skills and academic writing skills.
Term 1	Student-teachers attend lessons on epistemology, research paradigms and research methodology. They also have workshops on academic reading and writing. In groups, they collect and analyse research articles on educational issues from Argentina and Latin America. They make presentations which summarise and critique some of those articles.
Term 2	Lessons focus on designing a research project. In groups, student-teachers plan descriptive-exploratory studies which they implement in higher education or secondary education institutions. There are tutoring sessions so that the tutors in charge of the module provide them with specific feedback and support. They submit a report and make a presentation in front of their peers and teacher educators.

ELT. The core contents of the module were: situated professional practice and research, research paradigms, features of literature reviews and theoretical frameworks, sources of academic knowledge, research critique, and features of a research project.

This first module was significant because it helped student-teachers operationalise the results of systematic reflection and develop a research attitude in their development as future teachers. It was also a novelty, and a challenge for the teacher-educators in charge, as it was their first encounter with research through a module specifically designed to introduce educational research.

The second module was called Research in ELT (Table 37.2) and it was delivered in English. The module aimed at educating future teacher-researchers from a perspective based on empowerment, participation, criticality towards dominant ELT discourse, bottom-up processes, and the development of context-responsive answers to educational issues, even if their answers did not match mainstream ELT. The core contents were: action research and teacher research, ethics in AR, participatory action research, research methods, and reflection through AR.

The module usually received positive evaluation from the student-teachers as it featured a learning-by-doing approach through which they started thinking about their research topic and questions from the start and developed further awareness of ELT research while experiencing it first-hand.

Table 37.2 Outline of an AR module in IELTE

Module: Research in ELT	
One tutor: A teacher of English with experience in research and academic writing	
Two terms (March–November)	
Two hours weekly	
Aims:	Help future teachers reflect on their practices.
	Empower future teachers to generate classroom knowledge.
	To develop critical thinking skills and academic writing skills.
Term 1	Face-to-face
	Student-teachers outline an AR project to be carried out in their own settings as student-teachers. The F2F lessons will provide opportunities to discuss the rationale of AR and research methods and relate this framework to their own projects. There will be opportunities to read and discuss AR-based studies published in different settings. The tutor can ask student-teachers to make a short presentation on a study of their own choice.
	Projects will be implemented and will continue over the second term. Together with implementation, student-teachers will be asked to start drafting their rationale, context description, and other parts a research report may contain.
Term 2	Face-to-face meetings every two weeks + work online
	Lessons every two weeks together with online work through a platform which can channel student-teachers' concerns, experiences, and progress with their AR project. F2F lessons will also be used for student-teachers to share their work in progress.
	Ends with the student-teachers submitting a report and presenting their research. Their reports will be collected and edited and shared as an institutional pdf book through different platforms and social networks with the aim of socialising the student-teachers' first experience with doing and writing research.

Leading research modules as condensed in Tables 37.1 and 37.2 implies that teacher educators need to become acquainted with recent studies and reviews on educational and action research in their region and elsewhere. It also implies selecting suitable reading material for student-teachers who approach research for the first time in their trajectories as learners. Furthermore, it means making sure that there is a balance between theory and practice since modules of this nature aim at doing research at the educational institutions where the student-teachers may be completing their practicum experience.

Doing AR

We usually say that teachers are surrounded by data. Their classrooms, whether material or digital, contain a whole universe ready to be explored. This situation also runs true in ELTE settings where teacher educators can collect data with their student-teachers in their higher education classrooms. Below we share two examples of teacher educators carrying out research on their own practices in IELTE triggered by issues they noted and shared with the student-teachers. While the first example (Table 37.3) shows one teacher educator with his student-teachers, the second example (Table 37.4) illustrates CAR as it involved another teacher educator and their student-teachers.

Table 37.3 Teacher educator-led AR in IELTE

Issue:	What's the impact of this module on student-teachers' professional knowledge and English language proficiency?
	To what extent does the module respond to student-teachers' needs and expectations?
Module/Tutor	English Grammar (with a focus on systemic functional grammar) (Darío)
Timespan	Two terms

Cycle/stages	Activities
Initial investigations	Student-teachers read the syllabus and in pairs talk about what they expect from the module. They write a summary and hand it out to the tutor.
Action	The tutor starts a reflective journal to keep track of feelings and support for the development of materials.
	The tutor plans the lessons and prepares the materials for Unit 1 in the syllabus making sure that the student-teachers' expectations and needs have been included whenever possible.
Implementation	Lessons are delivered.
	The tutor scans the student-teachers' assignments and other evidence of learning (e.g. answers to tasks completed in class).
Evaluation & Reflection	At the end of the unit, the student-teachers are provided with a set of evaluation questions for individual reflection. In the following lessons, they answer them in groups and submit their collective answers by email.
	The tutor condenses their answers and shares them with the group to receive more specific feedback. He plans Unit 2.
	The cycle is repeated two more times.
Reporting	Based on the questions and data collected (tutor's reflective journal, and student-teachers' evaluations and learning artifacts), the tutor makes a Prezi presentation to his students and later shares the findings with his colleagues. A manuscript for potential publication is prepared.

Table 37.4 Teacher educator-led CAR in IELTE

Issue:	How can we ensure that our student-teachers cover assigned materials before each lesson?
Modules/Tutors	Introduction to Linguistics (Darío)
	English Language and Interculturality (Grisel)
Timespan	One term

Cycle/stages	Activities
Initial investigations	Record students' excuses for not reading the assigned material.
	Discuss with students how many hours should be devoted for 'home reading'.
	Both tutors keep separate journals of what happens at every lesson.
Action	The two tutors choose texts together (e.g. articles, videos) which students can relate to both modules for a month. The content could be linked to Introduction to Linguistics, and language use could be deconstructed in English Language and Interculturality.
	To promote purposeful reading, each text must be followed by a short activity (e.g. answer comprehension questions, summarise the text through a graphic organiser). Students will know that any of them can be asked to share their answers.
	In their journals, the tutors keep a record of their criteria for choosing texts and designing the text-based activities.
Implementation	At the beginning of each lesson, a student is asked to share the answers and ensures that their peers also complete the task. Each of these activities counts towards the final grade for each module.
	Students are asked how they found the text and the activities.
	The tutors keep a record of students' responses and rate of activity completion.
Evaluation & Reflection	At the end of the experience, the tutors lead a group interview (audiorecorded) where everyone discusses the impact of the activity. They share their reflections as written in their journals. The tutors note down strengths and weaknesses, and altogether agree on ways of going through another cycle to encourage reading.
Reporting	Based on the question and data gathered, the findings are shared with the student-teachers and later with colleagues at a staff meeting and institutional conference.

What implications can such experiences (Tables 37.3 and 37.4) have for teacher educators? First and foremost, they imply being open to sharing concerns, strengths and weaknesses with student-teachers and colleagues. Second, they imply being ready to receive negative feedback (sometimes worded without any hedging!). Finally, they involve active reflection and a research attitude in tandem with teaching as the data should be systematically collected and analysed as the project develops so that the findings are fed back into the learning process.

Supporting AR

The following collaborative action research (CAR) project gave two student-teachers (Ana Hortelano and Violeta Cano) the chance to refine their critical thinking on ELT as they transitioned from the last years of their university degree to the world of in-service education. Together with Luis, their university teacher (a lecturer and researcher working at the University of Valencia, Spain), they reflected on and devised alternatives to how the prevailing models of EFL teacher and learner identity constricted teachers and learners alike (Canagarajah, 2017), and to how ELT in Spain is still a 'signifier of social class privilege and access' (Vandrick, 2014: 88), meaning that learners from low and/or marginalised social, economic and cultural contexts find it harder to connect their own identities and cultural capital to English as a subject, and consistently obtain lower results than in any other subject (Anghel et al., 2016). In order to make English education more significant and less oppressive for these learners, the team experimented with concepts originally coming from fields other than ELT, and which remained distant from its mainstream theory and practice: funds of knowledge (González et al., 2006), funds of identity (Esteban-Guitart and Moll, 2014), and the notion of multiple, multimodal literacies as put forward by the New Literacy Studies (Pahl and Rowsell, 2012). As can be seen in Table 37.5, during three long research cycles the team assessed the affordances created by these concepts for EFL education with children who lived in an underprivileged neighbourhood in Valencia.

As might be expected of a 3-year CAR, the participants' situation changed both professionally and personally in the process: Ana and Violeta started off as university students but had already become in-service teachers by the final research cycles. As main researcher, Luis had to fight hard to find flexible ways to conduct the research and keep Ana and Violeta fully engaged. WhatsApp conversations, Facebook posts, or informal exchanges in front of coffee cups, all became essential to channel the team's reflections and exchanges, together with more formal and academic seminars in which the team shared, commented, and coded their research journals, thus creating a solid base of evidence for writing academic papers later on.

In terms of sustainability, even more important than the professional and personal changes just mentioned was how the CAR team was able to adapt itself, year after year, to a new academic setting. A new school management team was elected at the end of the first research cycle, which brought changes to the school's timetable that impacted on the feasibility of the project. Thus, from being first implemented in the context of Ana's and Violeta's practicum period (with Luis acting as a supervisor), by the second cycle the project was already restricted to a regular, weekly EFL lesson, and was finally bound to an extra-curricular workshop on Fridays. Despite the obstacles that these (and other) decisions can have on the stability of an AR project, action researchers need to adapt to the changing conditions that surround them, since this is the price to pay in order to work in real institutions under real circumstances, which is the only way to access and transform education as it is. As a result of the change that came up at the start of the

Table 37.5 AR cycles and projects.

Research cycle	Academic year	Academic context	Projects	Members' role
Cycle 1	2015/2016	Ana's and Violeta's practicum placement period	'Multimodal identities': pupils create multimodal self-portraits	Luis: university teacher as researcher Ana: student-teacher as researcher Violeta: student-teacher as researcher
Cycle 2	2016/2017	Regular EFL sessions	'If I were a giant in Nazaret': pupils create artistic interventions in the neighbourhood	Luis: university and school teacher as researcher Ana: school teacher as researcher
Cycle 3	2017/2018	Extra-curricular workshop	'Words matter/Palabras reales' project: pupils organize a community museum to display their multimodal and artifactual work	Violeta: school teacher as researcher

second cycle, Luis began to act as school teacher for the first time in his life, which posed manifold challenges but also new opportunities to the project.

The examples included in this section illustrate the extent to which teacher educators need to be aware of their fluctuating contexts and use creative and critical thinking to transform challenges into possibilities which gravitate between teaching and researching as a two-facet entity aimed at equipping those involved in AR with reflective tools for making their contributions meaningful and sustainable.

Conclusion

We have seen how the benefits of the AR initiatives that teacher educators put forward shape and are shaped by the contexts in which they are developed. Some of the issues we addressed through our AR projects found no viable alternatives coming from the prevailing ELT commonsense (Gitlin, 2008) or doxa-ruled practices espoused by our institutions, and some of our AR projects were even directed against ELT common-sense itself, which loomed as the problem from which we wanted to free ourselves. While dominant ELT discourse, as exerted through a powerful cultural, educational and testing industry, has contributed to providing strength and cohesion to the ELT field during decades, on the other hand it has often imposed decontextualised solutions and approaches in national school curricula and teacher education programmes (Guerrero, 2010).

Fifteen years ago, García Doval and Sánchez Rial (2002: 286) described ELT in Spain in the following terms: 'Somehow, the view of the primary school teacher as a technician has not changed very much: "Blind faith in the textbook! You don't need anything else!". In such a scenario, it is unlikely for English teachers to find enough institutional freedom to develop a strong sense of agency, or at least not of the kind that includes making decisions over curricular matters and push forward their own professional development (Stenhouse, 1975). Nor will there be much ground, either, for significant cases of AR projects to grow and mature. Accordingly, it may actually be inconsistent to call for further engagement with AR on part of English language teachers without encouraging them, also, to question the power dynamics that shape our professional and academic field. For the chances are that the former will hardly occur without the latter. This is something all of us working with AR in ELTE should remind ourselves of every now and then. It may well be the case that AR in ELT must become more critical if AR is to survive at all.

All in all, teacher educators working with others in AR in ELTE have to: (1) configure a professional identity that is characterised by acute awareness of their context, (2) develop creativity to respond to challenges opportunities, and (3) reflect on the ideologies that develop not only in a classroom, but in organisations, institutions, and curriculum development. In this way, the outcomes of AR can lead to further participation in educational processes and policies.

Further reading

Abdallah, M. M. S. (2017) 'Towards Improving Content and Instruction of the "TESOL/TEFL for Special Needs" Course: An Action Research Study'. *Educational Action Research*, 25(3) 420–437.

This article addresses a pressing issue: how to educate future teachers in special needs education. The context is a group of student-teachers at an Egyptian university and their tutors, and the article discusses their quest for understanding and implementing more systematic opportunities for learning how to teach English as a foreign language to learners with special needs. The article provides a wealth of information to teacher educators and practitioners.

Dikilitaş, K. and Griffiths, C. (2017) *Developing Language Teacher Autonomy through Action Research*. Basingstoke: Palgrave Macmillan.

This book is mainly characterised by its practical angle. The authors provide a succinct discussion of AR and other forms of teacher research before a careful elaboration of AR through examples of projects and other stories carried out by practitioners. The authors describe AR as a tool to empower teachers and help them develop professionally through research in/for/from the classroom and in their hands.

Mirra, N., García, A. and Morell, E. (2016) *Doing Youth Participatory Action Research*. New York: Routledge.

This volume looks at education from a broader and complex perspective. Therefore, it is helpful for those language teachers who are interested in examining education from a more integrative and bigger picture. The authors address AR from a participatory perspective which includes how learners can become active agents of change and co-researchers.

References

Aga, F. J. (2017) 'Motivating and/or De-Motivating Environments to do Action Research: The Case of Teachers of English as a Foreign Language in Ethiopian Universities'. *Educational Action Research*, 25(2) 203–222.

Anghel, B., Cabrales, A. and Carro, M. (2016) 'Evaluating a Bilingual Education Program in Spain: The Impact Beyond Foreign Language Learning'. *Economic Inquiry*, 54(2) 1202–1223.

Banegas, D. L. (2017a) 'Teaching Linguistics to Low-Level English Language Users in a Teacher Education Programme: An Action Research Study'. *The Language Learning Journal*, DOI: 10.1080/09571736.2017.1370604.

Banegas, D. L. (2017b) '"We Can Also Be Researchers": Teacher Research in Initial English Language Teacher Education'. *ETAS Journal*, 35(1) 31–33.

Banegas, D. L. and Villacañas de Castro, L. S. (2015) 'A Look at Ethical Issues in Action Research in Education'. *Argentinian Journal of Applied Linguistics*, 3(1) 58–67.

Banegas, D. L., Pavese, A., Velázquez, A. and Vélez, S. (2013) 'Teacher Professional Development Through Collaborative Action Research: Impact on Foreign English Language Teaching and Learning'. *Educational Action Research*, 21(2) 185–201.

Basallo Gómez, J. S. (2016) 'Adult EFL Reading Selection: Influence on Literacy'. *Profile. Issues in Teachers' Professional Development*, 18(1) 167–181.

Burns, A. (2005) 'Action Research: An Evolving Paradigm?'. *Language Teaching*, 38 57–74.

Burns, A. (2010) *Doing Action Research in English Language Teaching: A Guide for Practitioners*. New York: Routledge.

Burns, A., Dikilitaş, K., Smith, R. and Wyatt, M. (2017) *Developing Insights into Teacher Research*. Faversham: IATEFL.

Canagarajah, S. (2017) 'Multilingual identity in teaching multilingual writing', in Barkuizen, G. (ed.) *Reflections on Language Teacher Identity Research*. New York: Routledge: 67–73.

Castro-Garcés, A. Y. and Martínez Granada, L. (2016) 'The Role of Collaborative Action Research in Teachers' Professional Development'. *Profile. Issues in Teachers' Professional Development*, 18(1) 39–54.

Crawford Garrett, K., Anderson, S., Grayson, A. and Suter, C. (2015) 'Transformational Practice: Critical Teacher Research in Pre-Service Teacher Education'. *Educational Action Research*, 23(4) 479–496.

Dikilitaş, E. and Griffiths, C. (2017) *Developing Language Teacher Autonomy through Action Research*. Basingstoke: Palgrave.

Edwards, E. and Burns, A. (2016a) 'Language Teacher Action Research: Achieving Sustainability'. *ELT Journal*, 70(1) 6–15.

Edwards, E. and Burns, A. (2016b) 'Action Research to Support Teachers' Classroom Materials Development'. *Innovation in Language Learning and Teaching*, 10(2) 106–120.

Elliott, J. (1991) *Action Research for Educational Change*. Milton Keynes: Open University Press.

Esteban-Guitart, M. and Moll, L. C. (2014) 'Funds of Identity: A New Concept Based on the Funds of Knowledge Approach'. *Culture and Psychology*, 20(1) 31–48.

García Doval, F. and Sánchez Rial, M. (2002) 'EFL Initial Teacher Education for Primary and Secondary Schools in Spain'. *CAUCE. Revista de Filología y su Didáctica*, 25 281–298.

Giroux, H. (2011) *On Critical Pedagogy*. London: Bloomsbury.

Gitlin, A. (2008) 'Rethinking action research: commonsense and relations of freedom', in Noffke, S. and Somekh, B. (eds) *The SAGE Handbook of Educational Action Research*. Los Angeles, CA: SAGE: 442–452.

González, N., Moll, L. C. and Amanti, C. (eds) (2006) *Funds of Knowledge: Theorizing Practices in Households, Communities, and Classrooms*. New York: Routledge.

Guerrero, C.H. (2010) 'The Portrayal of EFL Teachers in Official Discourse: The Perpetuation of Disdain'. *Profile. Issues in Teachers' Professional Development*, 12(2) 33–49.

Halbach, A. (2016) 'Empowering Teachers, Triggering Change: A Case Study of Teacher Training Through Action Research'. *Estudios sobre Education*, 31 57–73.

Pahl, K. and Rowsell, J. (2012) *Literacy and Education*, 2nd edition. London: SAGE.

Porto, M. and Byram, M. (eds) (2015) Special issue, 'Developing intercultural citizenship education in the language classroom and beyond'. *Argentinian Journal of Applied Linguistics*, 3(2).

Ruohotie-Lyhty, M. and Moate, J. (2016) 'Who and How? Preservice Teachers as Active Agents Developing Professional Identities'. *Teaching and Teacher Education*, 55 318–327.

Smith, R. (2015) 'Exploratory action research: why, what, and where from?', in Dikilitaş, K., Smith, R. and Trotman, W. (eds) *Teacher-researchers in Action*. Faversham: IATEFL: 37–45.

Somekh, B. (2010) 'The Collaborative Action Research Network: 30 Years of Agency in Developing Educational Action Research'. *Educational Action Research*, 18(1) 103–121.

Somekh, B. and Zeichner, K. (2009) 'Action Research for Educational Reform: Remodelling Action Research Theories and Practices in Local Contexts'. *Educational Action Research*, 17(1) 5–21.

Stenhouse, L. (1975) *An Introduction to Curriculum Research and Development*. London: Heinemann.

Stenhouse, L. ([1979] 2012) 'Research as a basis for teaching', in Elliott, J. and Norris, N. (eds) *Curriculum, Pedagogy and Educational Research*. Abingdon: Routledge: 122–136.

Ushioda, E. (ed.) (2013) *International Perspectives on Motivation: Language Learning and Professional Challenges*. Basingstoke: Palgrave.

Vaca Torres, A. M. and Gómez Rodríguez, L. F. (2017) 'Increasing EFL Learners' Oral Production at a Public School Through Project-Based Learning'. *Profile. Issues in Teachers' Professional Development*, 19(2) 57–71.

Vandrick, S. (2014) 'The Role of Social Class in English Language Education'. *Journal of Language, Identity and Education*, 13 85–91.

Villacañas de Castro, L. S. (2014) 'Meta-action Research with Pre-service Teachers: A Case Study'. *Educational Action Research*, 22(4) 534–551.

Wyatt, M. and Dikilitaş, K. (2016) 'English Language Teachers Becoming More Efficacious Through Research Engagement at their Turkish University'. *Educational Action Research*, 24(4) 550–570.

Yan, C. (2017) '"You Never Know What Research is Like Unless You've Done it!" Action Research to Promote Collaborative Student-Teacher Research'. *Educational Action Research*, 25(5) 704–719.

Yayli, D. (2012) 'A Hands-on Experience of English Language Teachers as Researchers'. *Teacher Development*, 16(2) 255–271.

38

Exploratory practice

Integrating research into regular pedagogic activities

Inés K. Miller and Maria Isabel Azevedo Cunha

Introduction

In this chapter, we conceptualize Exploratory Practice as a principled inquiry-based framework for pedagogy or research that prioritizes work for understanding local puzzles, inclusivity among involved practitioners, as well as ethics and criticality. Exploratory Practice work has been developed through the integration of research into regular pedagogic and professional activities conducted in (language) classrooms in various educational institutions, teacher education programs or other professional contexts. We situate Exploratory Practice within the horizon of language Teacher Development, as a viable form of Practitioner Research, aligned with contemporary critical Applied Linguistics and in theoretical dialogue with other current modes of Practitioner Research, such as Reflective Practice and Action Research. We also describe how exploratory practitioners (teachers, students and other professionals) engage in work to understand what goes on in their learning/educational/professional environments and we address the challenges they face in the process.

Exploratory Practice within the horizon of teacher development

The seminal ideas of Exploratory Practice have been with us since the early 1990s, when Dick Allwright began to express his concern with what he later came to call 'third-party research'. Having been for years an academic classroom researcher himself, he realized that academic classroom research studies were, in a way, 'parasitic', since they extracted knowledge from the classroom to build theories about the classroom without involving teachers or learners in such theorizations (Allwright, 2003a). Aligned with the thinking of Stenhouse (1975) and other precursors of the Action Research movement, Allwright and Bailey (1991: 197) introduce the concept of 'exploratory teaching' as a way 'to help bridge the gap between research and teaching, and more particularly between teachers and researchers' (ibid.: 194). These two authors had the ambition 'to help language teachers understand better their own, and their learners', classroom lives' without promising 'short cuts to more effective language teaching' (ibid.: 196). As we can see, 'exploratory teaching' (and its later development into Exploratory Practice) has always prioritized understanding rather than problem-solving, proposing that learners be considered as agents capable of working with teachers in order to understand what goes on in their classrooms. Along these lines, and in a very close relationship with the work being developed by the Rio de Janeiro Exploratory Practice Group (Miller et al., in Allwright and Hanks, 2009), several of Allwright's papers written in this period addressed specific issues that concerned him at the time: integrating research and pedagogy (1993), bringing life into the classroom (1998), putting learning on the classroom agenda (1999), among many others. In these papers, Exploratory Practice (EP) was consistently proposed as a way for these issues to be addressed by teachers and students, during class time, via the integration of puzzling themes with the teaching and learning of the language.

Between 1990 and 2015, Exploratory Practice built an intense dialogue with such proposals for teacher development as Reflective Practice (Zeichner and Liston, 2006) and Action Research (Burns and Edwards, 2014). The more intense the dialogue became, the richer the points of convergence and divergence between these teacher development approaches emerged. In the text *The Major Processes of Teacher Development and the Appropriate Design Criteria for Developing and Using Them*, Allwright (2001) claimed the place of 'action for understanding', as an indispensable focus brought by Exploratory Practice that could complement or enrich the traditional 'action for contemplation', which characterizes Reflective Practice. Likewise, 'action for understanding' could postpone or displace the predominant 'action for change', a central orientation in Action Research. Putting 'understanding' in the limelight has helped the Exploratory Practice framework consider 'integration' as its main contribution to the dialogue among teacher development approaches. As discussed later in this chapter, we believe that integration constitutes the backbone of the principles of Exploratory Practice, as these propose an inextricable integration of the people involved, as co-practitioners, in the work for understanding the learning experience while it is going on.

From teacher research to practitioner research: a critical discussion within contemporary applied linguistics

In order to present the distinct identity of Exploratory Practice as a form of Practitioner Research, we start by establishing connections with issues that have been discussed within critical contemporary transgressive Applied Linguistics (Pennycook, 2006) and go on to highlight the notions of 'research' and 'reflection', as conceptualized in Exploratory Practice.

In our view, teacher research emerged as the chosen path to enrich teacher development, mainly understood as professional 'improvement', mostly oriented towards 'efficiency' and 'problem-solving'. This movement was compatible with a period in which Applied Linguistics focused on the improvement of society and/or the resolution of social problems (Davies, 1999). Yet, since Allwright had always claimed that 'understanding' was the *sine qua non* condition for teacher development, Exploratory Practice comes through as the modality that best encompasses this issue. In his text *Six promising directions for Applied Linguistics*, Allwright (2006) claims that teachers can work to: understand the quality of their classroom lives, become knowledge-makers in the field and, along with learners, come to be considered as developing practitioners. These seminal ideas are very much in tune with agency, autonomy, awareness, inclusivity, performativity, and empowerment, central notions to a contemporary, critical and transgressive Applied Linguistics. As part of this agenda for social transformation, this contemporary perspective strives to understand the human suffering of those living on the margins (Mushakoji, 1999). Aligning Exploratory Practice with these concerns, we claim that students and teachers, mostly framed as trouble-makers and trouble-shooters (Wright, 2006), have been living on the margins of hierarchical educational systems and have had their agencies subdued in most 'teacher research as improvement' processes.

As far as 'research' is concerned, we agree with Allwright and Hanks (2009: 142–143) when they argue that some teacher research initiatives appear to have missed a major opportunity of exploiting teachers' capacities for fully teacher-owned research. Unfortunately, 'the continuing influence of the third-party research model' and 'the focus on change and improvement, rather than understanding' (ibid.: 142) seem not to enable teachers to gain ownership or deeper understandings of their own professional practice. As research participants, teachers become data-gatherers and students tend to be kept in the position of data-providers – and 'not practitioners in their own right at all' (ibid.: 143). Allwright and Hanks insist, and we agree, that unless teachers and students are encouraged to think of themselves as practitioners or co-practitioners, as in Exploratory Practice, the opportunity to understand the nature of research itself seems to have been missed.

Regarding reflective processes, our position is that the reflection proposed by Exploratory Practice aims at problematizing the very essence of teaching and learning practices without the foremost intention of *improving* them. Working towards practitioners' enhanced understandings, Exploratory Practice revitalizes teachers' and students' needs to question the underlying principles of traditional pedagogic practices, facilitates the emergence of professional provocative questions and discourages the officially sanctioned drive for improving unquestioned practices. Working towards enhanced understandings, exploratory teachers and students favour 'why' questions such as the following: 'Why do we have homework?', 'Why do we cheat?', 'Why do we use nicknames?', 'Why is English important for you?', 'Why do we quit?', among many others analysed in Cunha and Miller (forthcoming).

As introduced earlier in the text, rethinking practitioner research has always been the main motivation for proposing and developing the ideas of Exploratory Practice. Allwright (2003a: 128) claims that

> The proper aim of practitioner research, as we see it, is best put as 'working to understand life', not trying to directly solve problems, but to step back from them and see them in the larger context of the life (and lives) they affect.

Allwright's *avant-garde* proposal for this field of study has been seeking to understand social issues instead of proposing research-based solutions. Inspired by the work of the Rio de Janeiro Exploratory Practice Group, we support the notion that classroom life can be reinvented to explore and develop students' and teachers' understandings of what goes on inside and outside the classroom. Most importantly, Exploratory Practice considers students and teachers as practitioners of learning and teaching. Along these lines, Allwright and Hanks (2009: 2) insist on the term practitioner to refer to students and teachers, since they want to make the students' role 'as importantly parallel to the role of the people we already happily see as "practitioners" – the teachers.'

Inspired by Freire (1970) and based on our practice as teacher educators (Miller and Cunha, 2016), we have come to understand that students *and* teachers (i) can notice what is going on in their lives, inside and outside the classroom, as practitioners of teaching and learning, (ii) are willing to reflect about these interpersonal relations, (iii) are capable of intensifying their attention towards issues that interest or puzzle them in a specific context, and (iv) can find it relevant to address (inter)personal and professional issues in order to understand them more deeply. An experienced Exploratory Practice teacher and two student teachers teaching English at a public sector school in Rio de Janeiro noticed that some adolescent students used derogatory nicknames with each other. They initially thought of adopting a punitive action, but decided to intensify their attention towards this puzzling issue, by integrating some 'action for understanding' with the topic and grammar points of the next lesson: Family Members, possessive adjectives and the verb 'to have'. Acknowledging the value of integrating students' lives inside and outside the classroom, the teachers proposed an exploratory pedagogic activity which invited students to draw a family tree and find out about their families' nicknames. Students promptly engaged in this investigative activity and later willingly reflected upon 'nicknaming' and spontaneously categorized nicknames into 'cute', 'funny', 'offensive', and 'useful'. Having researched this issue, the group understood more deeply the complexity of using nicknames in interpersonal relations (for the whole narrative, see Miller et al., 2015).

Another important contribution of Exploratory Practice to the reconceptualization of practitioner research has been to consider both students *and* teachers as lifelong learners. Wells and Claxton (2002: 10–11) invite us to look at 'lifelong learning, and the demands of the "learning society", in terms of a continuing process' that occurs not only in early childhood and school years but also in adulthood, in 'professional or work-based learning'. Clearly, this thinking is echoed in the Five Propositions about Learners (Allwright and Hanks, 2009: 7):

Proposition 1: Learners are unique individuals who learn and develop best in their own idiosyncratic ways.

Proposition 2: Learners are social beings who learn and develop best in a mutually supportive environment.

Proposition 3: Learners are capable of taking learning seriously.

Proposition 4: Learners are capable of independent decision-making.

Proposition 5: Learners are capable of developing as practitioners of learning.

In our view, these propositions stand as a *manifesto* in favour of both students and teachers as practitioners of learning. Operating on trust, Allwright and Hanks advocate for learners to be respected as serious and unique individuals who learn according to their own idiosyncrasies, in collaborative social settings. Based on our long-term experience with Exploratory Practice, we notice that students and teachers find it difficult to believe in themselves as fully fledged practitioners of learning, accepting society's mistrust in students' capabilities and in teachers' capacity to act as autonomous professionals. It is common in Brazil, for example, to find students who say 'We are unable to learn English because we cannot even speak Portuguese'. Likewise, it is sadly recurrent to see teachers who do not feel confident about their linguistic knowledge or their capacity to reflect independently about pedagogic matters.

The emphasis in Exploratory Practice work lies on helping learners – students and teachers – to raise their own puzzles or intriguing questions about issues that they wish to understand better and elaborate their own 'action for understanding'. This, we believe, is the strongest movement towards students and teachers enhancing their understandings of who they are and what they do as students and teachers, i.e., towards becoming practitioners regarding their learning and teaching practices.

Exploratory Practice enables the development of practitioner identities by purposefully avoiding a research attitude that interferes with what is going on pedagogically or, in other words, by avoiding transforming the pedagogic context into a research site. It is precisely by integrating students *and* teachers as well as the pedagogy *and* the work for understanding that Exploratory Practice has helped re-signify students and teachers as practitioners who are able to work critically, collegially and reflexively, in order to develop deeper understandings of their own personal practitioner lives. As we will discuss later, since this orientation is not commonly experienced in most educational or professional contexts, it can be challenging for teachers engaged in teacher development processes oriented by Exploratory Practice or for students being invited to participate in class in this way.

We sense that practitioner identities are more likely to be developed when students and teachers are respected both as practitioners and as learners and encouraged to search for deeper understandings about what they do, what they would like to do more of and even what they do not or cannot do in some contexts. An *ethos* of mutual respect can also generate possibilities for the co-construction of trust relationships among practitioners. In Allwright's (2009: 2) own words,

> The growth of trust in pedagogical relationships may not be, for administrators especially, a *substitute* for increases in quantitatively measurable achievement.
> BUT
> Like understanding, trust may well be a *pre-requisite* for sustainable, lasting progress on any measures, quantitative or qualitative.

Such inclusive reflexive processes, integrated with the learning and teaching practices that normally happen in classrooms at various levels of (language) education, have allowed students and teachers to become more aware of their own emotions (Zembylas, 2005), more 'invested' in their practices (Norton, 2013), and more conscious of the importance of negotiating the 'gift of confidence' in lifelong learning (Mahn and John-Steiner, 2002).

A principled view of Exploratory Practice: the issue of integration

We hope to have conveyed by now that integration is at the core of Exploratory Practice. We have, thus, decided to honor this integrative perspective by attempting to present the principles of Exploratory Practice as parts of an organically integrated whole, seeking to represent their fusion in the confusion of our life-world experience. We will momentarily stay away from the didactic discursive organization of the principles as they have traditionally been systematized in the Exploratory Practice literature.

First and foremost, Exploratory Practice recognizes the constitutive integration that exists between life inside and outside the classroom. Teachers and learners are valued as human beings whose lives cannot be 'split' but are lived as 'united wholes' (Palmer, 1998). Such a holistic conception of the people involved in teaching-learning communities – learners, parents, teachers, supervisors, coordinators, school psychologists, etc. – helps take integration on board rather than artificially ignore it or attempt to destroy it. As exploratory teacher educators in public and private professional contexts in the city of Rio de Janeiro, we have learnt that the desire to understand the quality of (classroom) life (Gieve and Miller, 2006) is, for some teachers and their students, more urgent than their classroom work or productivity. Such practitioner-based realization led us to agree that 'prioritizing the quality of classroom life' as well as 'working to understand it' are the principles that voice 'what' exploratory practitioners choose to focus on.

Building on integration at the human level, Exploratory Practice rekindles the affective connection between teachers, learners, and others in the community – the 'who' that co-construct their daily lives in educational contexts. Natural collegiality is thus regained, since exploratory practitioners perceive themselves as developing practitioners of learning and manage to integrate their work for mutual development.

Teachers and students, as co-workers, create classroom/school time and space to engage in pedagogic practices that reactivate their natural curiosities about various aspects of their lives (social, personal and academic) and work for understanding their local and situated puzzles in

Inés K. Miller and Maria Isabel Azevedo Cunha

an integrated and interdisciplinary way. In this sense, exploratory practitioners enhance their agencies in their own teaching and learning contexts and become knowledge-builders of their own teaching and learning practices. We can see that, working in this fashion, they also manage to integrate with the materials and equipment that *they* choose to use, instead of being used *by them*.

When working within the Exploratory Practice framework – the 'how' in Exploratory Practice – teachers and learners become more creative and agentive about course-books and other materials; they feel confident to suggest activities and transform exercises. In short, authorial use of materials emerges when practitioners bring together and integrate their pedagogic creativities. Once such integration is established among the people involved, the materials used and the collaboratively created practices, sustainability of practitioner research has a stronger chance in everyday practice over time.

Summarizing these seminal ideas, Allwright and Hanks (2009: 260) present the 'Seven principles for inclusive practitioner research':

> *The 'what' issues*
> 1. Focus on *quality of life* as the fundamental issue.
> 2. Work to *understand* it, before thinking about solving problems.
>
> *The 'who' issues*
> 3. Involve *everybody* as practitioners developing their own understandings.
> 4. Work to bring people *together* in a common enterprise.
> 5. Work cooperatively for *mutual* development.
>
> *The 'how' issues*
> 6. Make it a *continuous* enterprise.
> 7. *Minimise the burden* by integrating work for understanding into normal pedagogic practice.

We must admit that the notions of 'quality of classroom life' and 'work for understanding' have been challenging ones to work with. We align with Gieve and Miller (2006) when they argue that, whoever has been in a classroom knows what is meant by 'classroom life' – the affective and social interpersonal relations that are co-constructed in classrooms. The main difficulty lies in dissociating the notion of 'quality' in 'quality of classroom life' from a marketing conception. Most of the time, it has been necessary to deconstruct 'the quality of classroom life' as 'the nature of the life that we lead in classrooms', which can, of course, be 'good', 'less good', or 'bad'. Probably due to the use of the term 'quality' in the discourse of marketing, it has been traditionally associated with 'good quality'. In some efficiency-oriented educational contexts, 'quality of work' is what, unfortunately, counts the most; 'quality of life' does not seem to matter. Yet, as we mentioned earlier, our data-driven understandings (Lyra et al., 2003) show us that, when invited to reflect on what they wish to understand more deeply, teachers as much as learners raise 'why-questions' about interpersonal relations in the classroom.

In some cultural and educational contexts, where teaching and learning are generally not conceived of as critical or reflective practices, the notion of 'understanding' is hard to grasp. It is, also, hard to define. So, in our work, we have used intuitive and not theoretical definitions, in agreement with Allwright and Hanks (2009: 146) when they say that 'teachers, and especially learners, need understandings *now*, and they need particular understandings that are directly appropriate to their unique situations, not high-level generalisations.' Another difficulty comes from the apparently professional need that teachers have to work with *consensus* – in order to reach a common understanding, one that is static and shared by everybody in the group, one that will remain the same forever. Exploratory Practice has been working for the acceptance of plural and dynamic understandings (highlighting the need for teachers to learn how to work with *dissensus* – Menezes de Souza, 2011). Last, conveying the idea that we are or can all be working for understanding is another challenge. Due to personal traits or contextual professional circumstances, some teachers appear to resist the developmental aspect of their learners' and of their own learning. Also, the issue of power emerges so strongly here that Freire's (1970) claim to learn *from* or *with* the learner still seems to be an enormous challenge for many teachers. In this sense, Exploratory Practice has worked in the direction of social justice as discussed in Zeichner (2008).

Exploratory Practice in action

In this section, we present and discuss a typical EP workshop or course organized by us, as teacher educators in continuing teacher education contexts (Miller and Cunha, 2016). We usually start by asking practitioners to share their puzzles about their everyday situated experiences or react to a list of former practitioners' puzzles. We encourage participants to word these puzzles in the form of 'why questions' because we believe that this formulation fosters deeper reflection that tries to stay away from the more common 'how-to questions', which normally arise from a problem-solving attitude. We also exploit the writing and sharing of participants' narratives drawn from events of their own learning or teaching to unearth relations with personal, professional and institutional beliefs that underlie their normal practice. As potential action for understanding, these narratives can be read and collectively discussed in more or less depth according to the local needs and/or wishes of group participants, in a similar fashion as we do in this chapter.

Exploratory Practice practitioners have asked questions dealing with psychological and affective dimensions of language. Regarding language as something which goes beyond a mere 'instrument of communication' (Revuz, 1998: 217), some of their puzzles have been: 'Why do advanced young learners refuse to talk in English even when they are fluent?', 'Why are some of the students more reluctant or shy to ask questions in class?', 'Why do some people have the need to show off?'. There have been puzzles that reconsider the role of the learner, the input offered by the teaching context and the relation between the two (Renart, 2005: 1942): 'Why do we have to take tests?', 'Why do we have few English classes?'. Other puzzles have questioned the imposition of English as the dominant language to be learned (Phillipson, 1992: 47): 'Why is English the main language in the world?', 'Why is it important to know English?' and problematized the socio-political aspects embedded in a learning/teaching situation: 'Why does she feel disrespected?', 'Why do my students drop out of school?', 'What do adolescents think about violence?'. Questions that show a recurrent worry with teaching successfully, as 'How can a film be successfully used in a one-hour class?' and 'Why was this class successful?', can exemplify two different standpoints: the first one suggests a belief in ready-made solutions for teaching problems while the second one proposes to reflect upon the reasons that lead to a successful lesson.

With a view to deconstructing the questions raised, participants work towards refining the terms used in the formulation of their puzzles, trying to unearth beliefs and to formulate further related questions. Taking for example a puzzle formulated by a foreign language course teacher, 'Why do I feel I am not giving good English classes?', we notice that it can be scrutinized and more puzzle-related questions can be raised. In order to try to understand why she feels that she does not teach good lessons, the teacher can narrow down the scope of her question and address other aspects related to her puzzle. In relation to 'feel', she can try to define this feeling and what it tells her about her classes and students. Another part of the puzzle, 'I am not giving' can also be defined and the teacher can reflect upon the meaning of 'giving classes' and how this 'giving' happens. Finally, taking another element of the question, 'good English classes', can help her think about what she believes a good class to be. Sometimes, this exercise of unearthing ideas from the puzzle may lead to a refinement of the whole question itself.

It is worthwhile noticing that, in our continuing teacher education context, workshop participants are engaged in their regular teaching and have the chance to integrate the notions discussed in the course with their regular classroom practices. Participants are offered a selection of texts on the main notions of Exploratory Practice which help them become familiar with actions for understanding, such as puzzlement, monitoring, planning and working for understanding (Hanks, 1999; Allwright, 1996, 2003b; respectively). At various points during the workshop different tasks are assigned to encourage the teachers to bring their classrooms into the course. In this integrated way, they come to perceive that their own foreign language classes can offer opportunities for them and their learners to work within the syllabus and also ask questions about their realities inside or outside the classroom. Young students, who were exercising the grammatical structure for making questions, formulated why-questions like: 'Why is good excellent?', 'Why is learning English difficult?', 'Why do we judge people?', which later became the focus of group or individual student-initiated investigation.

The exploratory practitioner group is then invited to reflect on the characteristics of their regular activities and to try to adapt them so as to explore what goes on in their workplaces. This is how we introduce the notions of Potentially Exploitable Pedagogic Activities (PEPAs) and Potentially Exploitable Reflective Activities (PERAs). According to Allwright (2003a) they are 'discursive actions for understanding' since they are slight adaptations made to everyday activities with the intention of promoting reflection and digging for further understanding of puzzles and questions. In educational contexts, 'puzzle-driven' lessons, course modules, entire courses, group discussions, debates, readings, written or oral assignments, journals, grammar exercises, tests, sketches and plays, seminar presentations, lesson planning, classroom observation, microteaching, practicum reports, narratives, etc. can be adapted to foster understanding (Miller, 2013).

Emanuelle Souza, a 9th grade teacher at a state public school in Rio de Janeiro, Brazil, who allowed us to use her real name, describes in her narrative how she adapted grammar activities on the use of modals by asking students to write sentences about their perception of their English classes.

> I started thinking about my practice as a teacher and, based on a puzzle 'Why do I feel I am not giving good English classes?' I tried to develop an activity, a PEPA. They were studying modal verbs and we developed an activity where they could make sentences practicing the modal verbs while reflecting about our English classes. In this activity, they had the option to write in Portuguese or in English. Most of them wrote in English, only two students wrote in Portuguese, and after they did it we discussed the sentences. Some of the students' sentences were: 'Teacher of English could give class to the third year of school', 'It could have English classes during the week', 'I can go to another country to speak English', 'Must have English classes in the week', 'I could understand more what is said', 'The teacher could interact more in English and Portuguese', 'The English classes should have more hours', and 'I should understand more the English classes'. After reading these sentences, I started to realize that the classes were not as bad as I thought. They were the way they should be, according to the students' necessities.

As the students and the teacher integrated this exercise with the discussion of the sentences, they exploited the opportunity to practice a language point and to collegially understand the emerging plurality of their thoughts. By attentively listening to what was being said (monitoring in the Exploratory Practice sense) and not restricting her attention to the grammar point being practiced (monitoring for accuracy control), the integrative quality of this pedagogic activity helped Emanuelle understand her puzzle better.

Potentially Exploitable Pedagogic Activities (PEPAs), however, can also occur spontaneously as the teacher is inspired by an incident that happens unexpectedly in the classroom. Such is the case of Adriana Nóbrega, at the time a teacher in an English language institute, who had to work with 'Life in the future' as a topic and questions in the future tense, creatively shifted the activity by inviting students to ask 'wh-questions' about their own lives in the future. Some of the questions were: 'Will I be good?', 'Will we have food?', 'Where will I study?', 'What will be my grade?', 'Who will be my wife?', 'Will we live in space?', 'Where will I work?'. Having asked about 80 questions, Adriana's learners realised that their questions were mostly about themselves, their families, life, death and school. Then, they decided to group the questions and proudly helped the teacher organize a poster that many teachers and learners have found inspiring.

In the reflective narrative written by Beatriz Maciel, who also allowed us to use her real name, we find an English language teacher of 6th and 7th graders at a public school in Rio de Janeiro, Brazil, describing a reading comprehension activity that she had planned as a Potentially Exploitable Pedagogic Activity. Not only did she manage to address an issue she wanted to discuss in class but also integrate it with the evaluation activity required by the school. To contextualize Beatriz's story, it is important to say that the moment she is narrating happened right after a term-long teachers' strike.

As Beatriz herself admits, she initially resisted the alternative activity proposed by a student, immersed as she was in institutional bureaucracy.

> I was at the board, writing instructions for a reading comprehension exercise about teachers and students' perspective on the use of cell phones in classroom when a student right behind me said something like 'Teacher, why don't we interview people about it?'. I loved her idea, but I was so worried about time and presenting their grades that I said something like 'I love your idea! We can certainly try it in next opportunities ... ', but she insisted 'No, teacher, you don't get what I mean! Why don't we do it now, interview people about this topic?' and I finally realized I was not listening enough. That's when I understood I was being offered a gift from that 13- or 14-year-old girl, and decided to take it. I still requested the students to answer questions about the text, but told the whole group that Maria had given a brilliant idea, that I was willing to take and that could even replace our test, and asked the students for their opinion about it. Students were happy with the idea, especially because it could mean not taking the test.

Paradoxically, in the midst of institutional disputes among educators, we find echoes of the Learner Propositions in the teacher's and the students' attitudes. Both Beatriz and Maria show that they are 'capable of taking learning seriously' (Proposition 3) and of 'independent decision-making' (Proposition 4). Maria makes the individual and initial move of suggesting an alternative activity for the test, while Beatriz, institutionally a teacher but a learner from an Exploratory Practice perspective, recognizes the learning opportunity. But, at the risk of accepting such a creative suggestion and facing the challenge of having to adapt it to replace a test, she comes to understand that she can reconsider a previously planned assessment activity. However, Beatriz also feels that she needs to consult the whole group in search of 'a mutually supportive environment' (Proposition 2). Likewise, when Maria struggled for her voice to be heard and her suggestion attended to, she was also seeking mutual social support from the teacher and her colleagues.

As Beatriz's narrative unfolds, we can hear her reflecting upon her attentive listening attitude (Miller and Cunha, 2016) which allows her to listen intensively to her students and try to understand what they are saying about the use of cell phones in class and many other issues.

> [...] students interviewed people from the school (coordinators, cooks, teachers, kids' parents, classmates) and family members. We had interesting discussions, in which students expressed their opinions (and asked me for mine – again, this makes me think that, the more I listen to my students, the more they feel like listening back to me), mentioning the moments in which they believed cell phones helped in class (when doing an exercise, for example, students mentioned that listening to music on the cell phone helped them concentrate) and moments in which cell phones could become a problem. We also discussed how to deal with the moments in which cell phones would not be helpful but some students still insisted on using them. At this moment, the students suggested practices in which I would be the one in charge of the solution. Maybe this is a result of the fact that, as students also mentioned in this opportunity, they miss being more respected in their right to speak up in the school routine.
>
> This was a moment when the students and I reflected a lot, and it certainly was richer than if students had taken a test. Thank you, Maria, for your gift!

Beatriz notices that her students ask her to express her opinion about the issue under discussion and to be in charge of management solutions. Most importantly, she realizes that the more she listens to her students, the more they feel like listening back to her. Freire's (2005) insightful thought that it is important to learn 'to listen to ourselves while we are listening to others' could be helpful here to problematize the need that social beings feel to listen and to be listened to. Beatriz' students miss being listened to and 'miss being more respected in their right to speak up in the school routine.' Her narrative about a classroom situation and her reflection upon it illustrate how an Exploratory Practice attitude is capable of generating discursive space (PEPAs and PERAs) to address critical and ethical issues about life in a group, such as respect, trust, autonomy, inclusivity, and agentivity.

Paraphrasing Allwright's text (2013: 2), we could say that Emanuelle, Beatriz and Adriana exploited their normal teaching activities, and normal language content to investigate their own puzzles about their relationship with their students. They involved the students quite directly in working with them on the investigations, and the bonus was, through all the shared work for understanding, a much better understanding all round of how to work together. As part of their Exploratory Practice experiences, Emanuelle, Beatriz and Adriana have been sharing their understandings *beyond* their classrooms in practitioner research events and in their own writing.

Sharing collective understandings generated by the use of PEPAs and PERAs are a central part of an Exploratory Practice course, so that a special session is generally devoted to the creation and preparation of posters, videos, plays, and other modes of artistic production. Some participants manage to engage their students in the co-organization of multimodal presentations and encourage them to co-present at events. Others stimulate student independent authorship and autonomous presentations. Exchanging collective understandings is fostered during final course sessions, in events organized by teacher associations, language institutes, and schools or in the already traditional annual EP events, in which teachers, students, coordinators, teacher educators are the main protagonists.

Concluding thoughts

In more than two decades of Exploratory Practice work, we have been involved in innumerable practitioner development processes which have generated a wide range of 'effects' – demotivated teachers or learners have become invested in school life; similarly, already involved teachers and learners have become more conscious of their emotional involvement with school life and with life in general. Working within the Exploratory Practice framework stimulates practitioners to take a developmental view of personal professional identity (re)construction, of courage and confidence building, and of their responsibility as teaching and learning practitioners in search of social justice.

Far from only sharing an idyllic view of Exploratory Practice, we reflexively acknowledge to have faced challenges while working with its principled framework. Issues of control and resistance have emerged when practitioners come to realize, for instance, the criticality of such work, as it inevitably problematizes traditional power relations in educational contexts. In practitioner development processes, teachers as well as learners admit to have suffered from moments of anxiety on account of the Exploratory Practice attitude, which expects practitioners to heighten their level of reflexivity and to recognize the need to exercise their autonomy more fully.

Believing that integration is a forceful agenda within Exploratory Practice, we sense that the way practitioners understand and live integrative processes has a great deal to do with their developing work as exploratory practitioners. Given the integrative constitution of Exploratory Practice and the relationships it promotes, being an exploratory practitioner is necessarily living an organic and fluid process. We understand integration not only as inclusivity but, centrally, as an incessantly reflexive movement towards a joint and collaborative life attitude that presupposes respect for uncertainties, ambiguities, and diversity.

In closing, we wish to reinforce Allwright's (2003a: 137) idea that Exploratory Practice is 'work in progress' and that it 'must always remain in the process of development, as we learn from the different circumstances in which the framework is invoked.' By sharing our long-term experience with Exploratory Practice, we did not intend to 'save the reader from further thought about how participant research can contribute to language teacher, and learner, development', but instead 'hope to stimulate readers to even more thought, in the hope that together we will be able to do more than if we remain isolated.'

Further reading

Miller, I. K., Côrtes, T. C. R., Oliveira, A. F. A. and Braga, W. G. (2015) 'Exploratory practice in initial teacher education: working collaboratively for understandings', in Bullock, D. and Smith, R. (eds) *Teachers Research!*. Faversham: IATEFL: 65–71.
This co-authored chapter narrates a particularly interesting case of Exploratory Practice developed in a public school in Rio de Janeiro, Brasil. The collegial narrative focuses on the process of investigating a local puzzle and of co-constructing posters as Potentially Exploitable Pedagogic Activities.
Moraes Bezerra, I. C. R. and Miller, I. K. (2015) 'Exploratory Practice and New Literacy Studies: Building Epistemological Connections'. *Pensares em Revista*, 6 90–128. Available online: <www.epublicacoes. uerj.br/index.php/pensaresemrevista/article/viewFile/18426/18051> (accessed 23 May, 2019).
This article builds relevant connections between Exploratory Practice and the area of literacy studies. The reflective narratives present teaching-learning moments experienced by college students who were becoming exploratory practitioners.
Yoshida, T., Imai, H., Nakata, Y., Tajino, A., Takeuchi, O. and Tamai, K. (eds) (2009) *Researching Language Teaching and Learning: An Integration of Practice and Theory*. Bern: Peter Lang.
This volume brings together chapters that clarify philosophical connections between Exploratory Practice, Action Research, Narrative Inquiry, among other forms of currently developed research practices.

References

Allwright, D. (1993) 'Integrating "Research" and "Pedagogy": appropriate criteria and practical possibilities', in Edge, J. and Richards, K. (eds) *Teachers Develop Teachers Research: Papers on Classroom Research and Teacher Development*. Oxford: Heinemann: 125–135.

Allwright, D. (1996) *Monitoring*. Unpublished manuscript, Lancaster University, UK.

Allwright, D. (1998) 'Bring Classroom Language Learning to Life'. *GELI Newsletter (Grupo de Especialistas en Lengua Inglesa, Havana, Cuba)*, VI(1–4) 3–17.

Allwright, D. (1999) *Putting Learning on the Classroom Agenda: A Case for Learner-based Exploratory Practice*, invited plenary talk for the National Congress on English, Zeist, the Netherlands, January.

Allwright, D. (2001) 'Three major processes of teacher development and the appropriate design criteria for developing and using them', in Johnston, B. and Irujo, S. (eds) *Research and Practice in Language Teacher Education: Voices from the Field*. Minneapolis, MN: Center for Advanced Research on Language Acquisition: 115–133.

Allwright, D. (2003a) 'Exploratory Practice: Rethinking Practitioner Research in Language Teaching'. *Language Teaching Research Journal*, 7(2) 113–141.

Allwright, D. (2003b) 'Planning for Understanding: A New Approach to the Problem of Method'. *Pesquisas em Discurso Pedagógico: Vivenciando a Escola*, 2(1) 7–24.

Allwright, D. (2006) 'Six promising directions for Applied Linguistics', in Gieve, S. and Miller, I. K. (eds) *Understanding the Language Classroom*. London: Palgrave Macmillan: 11–17.

Allwright, D. (2009) *EP and the development of trust: Going beyond achievement measures*. Paper presented at the Exploratory Practice Event, Rio de Janeiro, Brasil, November.

Allwright, D. (2013) *Practitioner research in the classroom must be good pedagogy*. Paper presented at the University of Lancaster, UK.

Allwright, D. and Bailey, K. M. (1991) *Focus on the Language Classroom*. Cambridge: Cambridge University Press.

Allwright, D. and Hanks, J. (2009) *The Developing Learner: An Introduction to Exploratory Practice*. Basingstoke: Palgrave Macmillan.

Allwright, D. and Miller, I. K. (1998) *Exploratory Practice: Our underlying rationale*. Paper presented at the IATEFL Annual Conference.

Burns, A. and Edwards, E. (2014) 'Introducing innovation through action research in an Australian national program: experiences and insights', in Hayes, D. (ed.) *Innovations in the Continuing Professional Development of English Language Teachers*. London: The British Council: 65–86.

Cunha, M. I. A. and Miller, I. K. (forthcoming) *Studying Practitioners' Concerns Through Their Puzzles*. London: British Council Action Research Award Scheme, The British Council.

Davies, A. (1999) *An Introduction to Applied Linguistics. From Practice to Theory*, Edinburgh: Edinburgh University Press.

Freire, P. (1970) *Pedagogy of the Oppressed*. New York: Seabury Press.

Freire, P. (2005) *Pedagogia da Tolerância*. São Paulo: Editora UNESP.

Gieve, S. and Miller, I. K. (2006) 'What do we mean by quality of classroom life?', in Gieve, S. and Miller, I. K. (eds) *Understanding the Language Classroom*. Basingstoke: Palgrave Macmillan: 18–46.

Hanks, J. (1999) 'Enthusiasm, Puzzlement and Exploratory Practice'. *The International House Journal of Education and Development*, 7: 14–16.

Hanks, J. (2017) *Exploratory Practice in Language Teaching: Puzzling About Principles and Practices*. Basingstoke: Palgrave Macmillan.

Lyra, I., Fish, S. and Braga, W. (2003) 'What Puzzles Teachers in Rio de Janeiro, and What Keeps Them Going?'. *Language Teaching Research*, 7(2) 143–162.

Mahn, H. and John-Steiner, V. (2002) 'The gift of confidence: a Vygotskian view of emotions', in Wells, G. and Claxton, G. (eds) *Learning for Life in the 21st Century*. Oxford: Blackwell: 46–58.

Menezes de Souza, L.M.T. (2011) 'Towards a redefinition of critical literacy: conflict and meaning making', in Maciel, R. F. and Araujo, V.A. (eds) *Formação de Professores de Línguas: ampliando perspectivas*. Brasília: Paco Editorial. Available online: <www.researchgate.net/publication/260598029> (accessed 23 May, 2019).

Miller, I. K. (2013) 'Formação inicial e continuada de professores de línguas: da eficiência à reflexão crítica e ética', in Moita Lopes, L.P. (ed.) *Linguística Aplicada na modernidade recente: Festschrift para Antonieta Celani*, São Paulo: Parábola Editorial: 99–121, 257–266.

Miller, I. K. and Cunha, M. I. A. (2016) 'Exploratory practice in continuing professional development: critical and ethical issues', in Dikilitas, K. and Erten, I. H. (eds) *Facilitating In-Service Teacher Training for Professional Development*. Hershey, PA: IGI Global: 61–85.

Miller, I. K., Cunha, M. I. A. and Members of the Rio de Janeiro EP Group (2009) 'The "web of life" of the Rio de Janeiro Exploratory Practice group', in Allwright, D. and Hanks, J. (eds) (*The Developing Language Learner: An Introduction to Exploratory Practice*. Basingstoke: Palgrave Macmillan: 216–234.

Miller, I. K., Côrtes, T. C. R., Oliveira, A. F. A. and Braga, W. G. (2015) 'Exploratory practice in initial teacher education: working collaboratively for understandings', in Bullock, D. and Smith, R. (eds) *Teachers Research!*. Faversham: IATEFL: 65–71.

Mushakoji, K. (1999) 'Em busca de uma nova aliança anti-hegemônica', in Heller, A., Santos, B. de S., Chesnais, F., Altvater, E., Anderson, B., Light, M. T., Mushakoji, K., Appiah, K. A. and Segrera, F. L. (eds) *A crise dos paradigmas em ciências sociais e os desafios para o século XXI*. Rio de Janeiro: Contraponto.

Norton, B. (2013) *Identity and Language Learning. Extending the Conversation*. Bristol: Multilingual Matters.

Palmer, P. J. (1998) *The Courage to Teach: Exploring the Inner Landscape of a Teacher's Life*. San Francisco, CA: Jossey-Bass Publishers.

Pennycook, A. (2006) 'Uma Linguística Aplicada Transgressiva', in Moita Lopes, L. P. (ed.) *Por uma Linguística Aplicada Indisciplinar*. São Paulo: Parábola: 67–84.

Phillipson, R. (1992) *Linguistic Imperialism*. Oxford: Oxford University Press.

Renart, L. (2005) 'Communicative Competence in Children: Spanish-English Bilinguality', *4th International Symposium on Bilingualism*. Somerville, MA: Cascadilla Press: 1934–1944.

Revuz, C. (1998) 'A Língua Estrangeira entre o Desejo de um Outro Lugar e o Risco do Exílio', in Signorini, I. (ed.) *Linguagem e Identidade: Elementos para uma Discussão no Campo Aplicado*. Campinas: Mercado de Letras: 213–230.

Stenhouse, L. (1975) *An Introduction to Curriculum Research and Development*. London: Heinemann.

Wells, G. and Claxton, G (2002) *Learning for Life in the 21st Century*. Oxford: Blackwell.

Wright, T. (2006) 'Managing classroom life', in Gieve, S. and Miller, I. K. (eds) *Understanding the Language Classroom*. Basingstoke: Palgrave Macmillan: 64–87.

Zeichner, K. M. (2008) 'Formação de professores para a justiça social em tempos de incerteza e desigualdades crescentes', in Diniz-Pereira, J. E. and Zeichner, K. M. (eds) *Justiça Social – Desafio para a formação de professors*. Belo Horizonte: Autêntica: 11–34.

Zeichner, K. M. and Liston, D. P. (2006) *Reflective Teaching: An Introduction*, 2nd edition. New York: Routledge.

Zembylas, M. (2005) 'Beyond Teacher Cognition and Teacher Beliefs: The Value of the Ethnography of Emotions in Teaching'. *International Journal of Qualitative Studies in Education*, 18(4) 465–487.

39

Leadership and language teacher development

Magdalena De Stefani

Introduction

For over 20 years, I have been exploring and discovering the art of teaching and learning. Being a teacher of English has allowed me to learn about students, teachers and the learning process, but most of all, I have acquired a deeper understanding of myself as a lifelong learner. In my different roles as school teacher, university lecturer, academic coordinator and head, I have had to exercise my reflexivity in order to guide others in their processes of discovering how they can become the best version of themselves.

During this learning process, I have come to realise how leadership practices and beliefs are inextricably linked to teacher development schemes. I believe it is essential for teacher educators in managerial positions to be reflexive about their own styles, as these can have a key impact on the teacher development opportunities they offer. This reflexivity, understood as the ability to examine any situation from different standpoints, needs to be exercised within a deep knowledge of the local context that values the institutional culture and involves an empathetic understanding of the characteristics of each teacher. Without this knowledge of the context and sincere respect for the affective aspects, leadership cannot effectively promote teacher learning.

In this chapter I intend to theorise the relationship between certain leadership practices and teacher development. From an integrated perspective, I describe leadership practices that involve collaboration and cooperation, analysing how they facilitate professional development processes. I do this by drawing on the understandings that derive from my research, and by referring to the experience of other language teacher educators around the world.

The chapter is organised as follows. I start by discussing different affordances facing effective professional development from a leadership perspective. In the Research section, I focus on certain issues regarding the impact of leadership on teacher learning which have come to the fore as a result of my action research. I present two particular strategies, 'flexible collaborative partnerships' and Cooperative Development (Edge, 1992, 2002), as tools for effective professional development. I then draw on the voices of teacher educators from around the world in leadership positions to enhance the transferability of concepts across work environments, in the hope that they can be of use for other colleagues. I end by reflecting on some aspects of leadership and teacher development on which I would like to extend my knowledge.

Definitions

I will now briefly define some terms I will be using throughout the chapter. I would like to address the difference between the terms 'collaboration' and 'cooperation'. While cooperative processes imply working together and sharing resources and time, the focus is on each individual product or process. Meanwhile, collaboration entails working together towards a common, shared goal (Polenske, 2004; Misanchuk and Anderson, 2001). Both types of partnership are equally relevant to this chapter and are displayed in the data and ideas presented. For the sake of reader-friendliness, however, I will use the term 'collaboration' throughout the text.

Professional trust, defined by Frowe (2005) as a two-way process in which both employer and employee must develop certain qualities that allow them to forge a trusting relationship, is the basis of what I refer to as trusting leadership. Trust is an essential ingredient in a distributed leadership style, as it provides endless opportunities for teacher growth and is linked to school effectiveness (Moore, 2008). Within this professional trust framework, teachers are given enough 'responsible freedom' (De Stefani, 2014), thus being able to experiment, learn and collaborate in the knowledge that their employers are 'mentors' rather than 'tormentors' (Hargreaves and Fullan, 2000).

On the other hand, flexible collaborative partnerships refer to the idea of sustained, effective and varied teamwork, in which the voices of all those involved are a fundamental part of the forward-thinking system. In this ecosystem, different teams are built depending on needs at each time. For example, teachers may work with academic coordinators, with their peers, or with technicians such as psychologists or SEN specialists, to name a few. A variety of teams may be assembled at different times to solve problems, depending on teachers' and students' needs.

Another development strategy I address is Cooperative Development, a discourse framework created by Edge (1992, 2002), aiming to promote professional learning through a non-judgemental relationship between colleagues. The basis of Cooperative Development is the adoption of a particular discourse style, in which two professionals (Speaker and Understander), leave aside their professional status and interact in a non-judgemental fashion, with the aim of better understanding themselves and their colleagues. This is done for agreed periods of time, or 'sessions', in which individuals resort to their cognitive and emotional resources to interact purposefully. This collaborative framework leads to individuals learning more about themselves as professionals and increases collegiality (Edge and Attia, 2016).

In the following section I discuss some of the challenges and opportunities facing professional development from a leadership viewpoint, interweaving my understandings with voices from the literature in the field.

Survey: challenges, affordances and strategies in the provision of sustainable professional development

Being a leader in education is no easy task these days. It is unfortunately quite commonplace in my context in Latin America to find stressed, over-worked teachers, with diverse educational backgrounds, often being forced by economic circumstances to have multiple jobs (Vaillant, 2011, 2013). An added difficulty is that while some may have a clear teaching vocation, others may not. This is, in fact, similar to what happens with students; we are used to heterogeneous classes and different degrees of ability and motivation. As leaders, therefore, whether we are teaching students or leading staff, we have to find ways in which to open paths for learning that are effective and sustainable.

Effective leadership in the twenty-first century

The question of whether leaders are born or made has been endlessly discussed (e.g. Barker, 1997; Perkins, 2003; Bryman, 2007), and there is still an elusive feel to the issue of what effective leadership entails. I believe every leader is unique, as is each educational institution, and success lies in the awareness and reflexive capacity of the main leader, who needs to be able to respect the local culture, know the staff in depth and trust them so as to bring out everybody's strengths. Regardless of this artisan feature of leadership, it is indeed possible to articulate a list of strategies that are expected to be of use for professional development facilitators, irrespective – but always respectful of – the particularities of local contexts (MacGilhrist, n.d. in O'Donoghue and Clarke, 2009).

Effective leaders need an in-depth understanding of what learning in the twenty-first century means, since student learning depends on teacher learning (O'Donoghue and Clarke, 2009). If student learning is that which 'engages students intellectually, socially and emotionally' (Hargreaves and Fink 2004), then this is also relevant for teachers. Like with students, therefore, we need to foster in teachers the development of higher-order thinking skills such as analysing, synthesising, problem solving and creative thinking (Barak et al., 2007), for them to create the same conditions for their students. Equally fundamental for teachers and learners are the so-called 'soft skills' (Andrews and Higson, 2008) such as flexibility, openness to learning, self-regulation and a clear understanding of team-work.

This teacher and student learning occurring in parallel is a feature of professional learning communities (DuFour, 2004; Stoll and Louis, 2007; Hord, 2009), for which both skills development and collaboration are key elements. A professional learning community, according to Richmond and Manokore (2010: 545) is 'a group of teachers who meet regularly with a common set of teaching and learning goals, shared responsibilities for work to be undertaken, and collaborative development of pedagogical content knowledge'. A relevant question at this point is, 'What kinds of leadership do we need for this?' There are myriad terms and definitions, but in building my argument I focus on some views that I consider directly relevant to my understanding of what successful leadership entails.

An important characteristic of leadership that is crucial to the facilitation of teacher learning is the conception that it should be distributed among all those involved in professional development (Hord, 2009; Spillane and Orlina, 2005; Perkins, 2003). Distributed or shared leadership is often thought of as 'the network of both formal and informal influential relationships in a school' (Louis et al., 2010: 318). In this sense, a leader becomes a provider of opportunities for all teachers to be part of such a network, in which any member of staff may be a 'leader' or a 'follower' depending on the circumstances. As explained by Gibb (1978) in Gronn (2000: 324), it is important that both leaders and followers are seen as collaborators set to accomplish certain tasks. Therefore, exercising leadership should be more about enabling and facilitating, and less about prominence and authority.

Trusting leadership, according to Moore (2008), involves practices that promote the development of trusting relationships, while 'implementing change and empowering stakeholders to become leaders through collaboration' (Moore, 2008: 3). It is somewhat related to transformational leadership, characterised by an emphasis on supporting and stimulating teachers (Leithwood and Jantzi, 1999). Teachers who experience a transformational leadership style in their work context not only develop their skills, but also increase their commitment and productivity (Bass and Avolio, 1994; Burns, 1978 in Thoonen et al., 2011).

In parallel with these leadership styles, there are many affordances inherent in educational institutions that may act as barriers to effective professional development if not analysed critically and used constructively. I turn to these now.

Trust and affect

Trust refers to 'an individual's or group's willingness to be vulnerable to another party based on the confidence that the latter party is benevolent, reliable, competent, honest and open' (Cummings and Bromiley, 1996). Teachers who feel trusted as professionals will be more committed to the institution and its students, and therefore their own development (Louis et al., 2010; Moore, 2008).

Trust is also essential in building a collaborative learning environment (O'Donoghue and Clarke, 2009). Not only does it need to be present among colleagues, but it is also a fundamental factor in the employer-employee relationship. From a leadership perspective, trusting teachers will result in a higher degree of risk-taking and commitment, which will improve their practices and thus affect students' learning (Modoono, 2017).

Trust is an important aspect of professional learning communities because it helps teachers to cope with their uncertainties and vulnerabilities (Thoonen et al., 2011; Sorrentino and Short, 1986). Teachers who feel more certain or safe will be more open to learning and flexible in their approaches (Thoonen et al., 2011). Professional trust, as I have learned through research, involves a certain degree of 'responsible freedom' on the part of teachers, the downside of which may be a feeling of insecurity, as represented in Figure 39.1.

The diagram shows one of the potential dangers of professional trust, occurring when teachers interpret responsible freedom as insufficient supervision, or when there is actually too little feedback for teachers to remain motivated. In both cases, a vicious circle is fuelled, which may have a negative impact on staff and institutional well-being. Successful teams, on the other hand, encompass a combination of trust, collaboration and cooperation. Needless to say, the value assigned to trust is linked to each institution's culture.

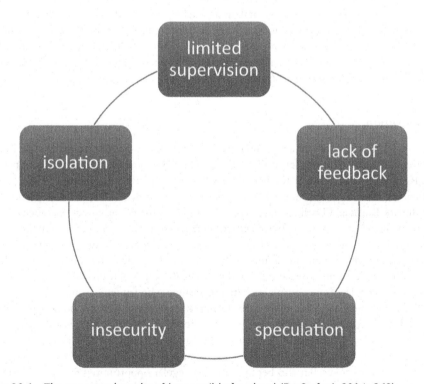

Figure 39.1 The unwanted results of 'responsible freedom' (De Stefani, 2014: 263)

Tradition and institutional culture

Leadership needs to be locally appropriate; therefore, it must be knowledgeable and respectful of the institutional culture and tradition, understood as 'the deeply embedded patterns of organizational behavior and the shared values, assumptions, beliefs, or ideologies that members have about their organization or its work' (Peterson and Spencer, 1991: 142, in Kezar and Eckel, 2002). Educational leaders should have insider knowledge of an institution's history, in order to understand its culture and make the most of it. This respect for tradition and institutional culture helps increase teachers' sense of belonging in the institution as well as their self-efficacy, as they internalise the institutional goals so that they become personal ones (Thoonen et al., 2011).

Regarding the effect of tradition and institutional culture on change, it is essential to understand that they will have a key effect on how change occurs. Respect for tradition must be balanced with innovation, for change to take place as harmoniously as possible. It is illogical to expect students to acquire transferable, lifelong learning skills, if the staff are not open to learning and change. However, there must be a balance between stability and change, as well as 'inclusiveness, connectivity, equity, prudence, and consistent attention to the needs of human beings' (Gladwin et al., 1995 in Stoll and Louis, 2007: 8).

During my research on professional learning, I focused on the change process involving the introduction of a phonics-based literacy programme in English in a school (2013–2015). In this institution, where there was great respect for tradition, the new literacy programme implied a significant impact for some teachers, who had to re-design their courses and be trained in this new methodology. For this move to have a positive effect, it was decided that teachers themselves would train one another and conduct peer observations and teaching. From a leadership position, it was essential to delegate and trust teachers while offering enough support and supervision. It was also fundamental, for a few years, not to introduce other significant changes, allowing the new programme to become part of the school culture. Trust is also, as will be explained below, an essential element in successful collaboration, and this also became evident in the aforementioned research process.

Collaboration

Collaboration is known to be an essential ingredient in the learning process, since it leads to the development of higher-order thinking skills and helps to strengthen teachers' interpersonal skills. Research has shown that teachers who work collaboratively can improve their practice and their reflective capacity, thus becoming better professionals (e.g. Hunter and Back, 2011). According to Burns and Darling-Hammond (2014), when there is an intentional focus on collaboration, the result is seen as better quality teaching and higher student achievement.

Successful collaboration requires clear guidelines and a certain amount of supervision to be sustainable. It is a skill for life, and a fundamental one for the professional life of teachers. It will allow teachers to learn from one another and from the dynamics of team-work, such as effective problem solving, tolerating constructive criticism, dealing with frustration and exercising empathy. All these elements also became visible during the introduction of the literacy programme explained above, resulting in an effective team that continue working closely to this day.

Interdisciplinary collaboration (Kaufman and Grennon Brooks, 1996) is also particularly important, as will be seen later on in the vignettes. It not only allows teachers to move away from their comfort zones, but also because offering regular opportunities for engaging in collaborative work with colleagues is essential for change to take place (Hargreaves and Goodson,

2006). Within this collaborative, interdisciplinary framework, action research is an essential form of reflective practice that needs to be conceived as a natural part of any teacher's professional life.

Having referred to some of the central challenges and opportunities inherent in promoting professional development from a trusting leadership standpoint, I now turn to specific strategies and practices I have experienced and theorised.

Research: creating a sustainable model for teacher development

In this section I focus on two strategies, which I have explored through my action research. The implementation of these strategies must be based on what Frowe (2005) calls professional trust, showing teachers that they are valued and counted on to make informed, responsible decisions. It requires clear institutional goals and guidelines, as well as clear boundaries. As a leadership strategy, trust is not easy to exercise. To begin with, teachers have to be sufficiently competent and reliable, whilst leaders need to have a significant amount of flexibility and enough self-esteem to delegate. Likewise, a clear authority is essential for trust not to be perceived by teachers as abandonment or institutional chaos, as shown in Figure 39.1.

According to my experience, professional trust can be represented in many different ways in different contexts. In a school context, it may imply allowing teachers to decide how to deal with discipline issues in each classroom, provided that they know the range of behaviours considered acceptable in the institutional culture. At university level, it could be exercised by letting each lecturer decide on the assessment criteria for their subject. In both the school and the university examples, short- and long-term objectives must be sufficiently clear, and support must be available.

I now describe the strategies that have emerged from my practice, in the belief that they could be relevant to colleagues in a variety of work environments.

Transferable strategy 1: Flexible collaborative partnerships

In this chapter, the idea of flexible collaborative partnerships is defined by the availability of opportunities for teachers to collaborate and cooperate with different professionals depending on their and their students' needs. Some of these partnerships last for years and turn into friendships, while others may last for days or weeks.

Insofar as teachers feel they are enabled to be part of this interdisciplinary work, their self-efficacy, self-esteem and motivation are enhanced. In this style of work, status is not a prerequisite for anybody's voice to be foregrounded, so much so that partnerships occur among staff members with different hierarchies. All opinions are heard, valued and considered. This professional learning community spirit is strong enough for teachers to know they can potentially reach out to different team members for collaboration.

Thanks to the flexible nature of these partnerships, teachers can choose to work with whom they feel more at ease. Also, if paired up with professional trust, a distributed leadership style and 'affective' teamwork, teachers are given the opportunity to alternate between leading and following, supporting and being supported at the same time. The inherent variability in this conception of teamwork is directly related to leadership, which is thus 'understood as a fluid and emergent, rather than as a fixed, phenomenon.' (Gronn, 2000: 324), which may simply last until a problem is solved.

To illustrate the notion more clearly, I draw on data gathered between February and October 2017, which evidence occurrences of flexible collaborative partnerships taking place at a bilingual school in Uruguay.

One of these was a planned partnership between a form teacher of English, the science coordinator and the academic coordinator in order to design a series of experimental lessons to motivate students. The form teacher, Inés, knew she could draw on the knowledge of both the subject specialist and the pedagogic leader. It is important to note that for this to operate as an instance of development for all those involved, professional respect and horizontality were essential. That is, even if the subject specialist and coordinator had a technically higher status than the teacher, within that partnership, nobody's voice was more important. In fact, the English teachers' 'local' knowledge of her students was fundamental.

Equally essential for the success of flexible collaborative partnerships are reflexivity, flexibility and trust towards others in different hierarchical positions. This became evident in another partnership that was formed among the director general, the psychologist, the SEN specialist and another form teacher, Sofia, in order to prepare parents' interviews. Both the pre-interview preparation and the post-interview reflection were essential learning opportunities for all those involved. This particular partnership required a significant amount of self-confidence, and the presence of trust was crucial in the building of rapport between Sofia and others in higher hierarchical positions, for them to actually function as a team.

Another interesting instance occurred when a group of Spanish and English teachers spontaneously agreed to work on the value of empathy, joining an international campaign entitled *en tus zapatos* ['in your shoes']. This shows how within a trusting leadership model, teachers will often take the initiative to collaborate, thus evidencing their gains in self-direction.

Transferable strategy 2: Cooperative Development as a tool for professional learning

Cooperative Development (Edge, 1992, 2002) is another valuable strategy for professional growth that involves collaboration. As a non-judgemental discourse framework, Cooperative Development requires two colleagues, Speaker and Understander, who will interact (not necessarily face-to-face or in real time) for an agreed period of time. The Speaker will articulate his/her thoughts, and the Understander will Reflect these back, always bearing in mind the non-judgemental nature of the interaction. This Reflection will allow the Speaker to see his/her thoughts from a different perspective in order to gain a deeper understanding of the issue at play.

Earlier in this year, Mariana, a 30-year-old teacher of English working with 5 and 6 year olds, expressed to me her unhappiness about her students' behaviour. Since she and I had worked through Cooperative Development several times since 2014, I offered my support from this perspective. As Speaker, Mariana tried to articulate her thoughts and feelings about the problem, and in my role as Understander, I attempted to Reflect her thinking non-judgementally.

She begins the session by highlighting the importance of collaboration, and the idea that her assistant is just as important as she is, which to me was a vivid representation of the idea of distributed leadership at the teacher level.

1 A great asset in class is that I work with an assistant
2 teacher, and it's always richer, and the other teacher
3 has always seen things that you haven't seen and
4 together we make an analysis of what has been going on,
5 of how we can try to make it work, and the strategies or
6 what we can do with the child at the moment in class.

She then expands on her views of why collaboration is important, highlighting the need for her to be part of a professional learning community, which she describes as 'professional team-work'.

7　　And I really, really believe in team-work, and the more
8　　the merrier, and once the problem has turned into
9　　something where the child or the parents or the
10　　classmates are suffering because of the child's
11　　behaviour it's something that you can't really do
12　　without professional team work.

She refers to the different sources of support she finds in the institution, showing her assertiveness and proactive nature when it comes to solving problems.

13　　Generally the first thing we try is that we try to solve
14　　the problem in the classroom and if it persists, then
15　　the first person I resort to is the head and the
16　　psychologist. I try to ask them to go to the class and
17　　see by themselves because it is much, much better than
18　　telling them myself – what has been going on. When you
19　　see a child and you understand what kind of behaviour
20　　the teacher is talking about, it's really, really more
21　　interesting to talk to someone once they've already seen
22　　the child.

Implicit in her discourse is a complaint about the psychologist, and perhaps myself, not having been to her class enough times; 'When you see a child and you understand what kind of behaviour the teacher is talking about it's really, really more interesting to talk to someone once they've already seen the child.'
　　She continues talking about her problem-solving strategies, telling me about the complex case of a boy whose behaviour she cannot really understand.

23　　Two days ago, I asked the sports teacher, because
24　　there's a boy that worries me a lot in terms of his
25　　behaviour and his understanding, and I asked the sports
26　　teacher what he thought about the child. And he told me
27　　that when he explained exercises, or how to do things in
28　　sports class, [the child] understands. The thing is that
29　　I know that he's a child who knows very well how to copy
30　　and imitate his friends, so I asked the sports teacher
31　　to collaborate with me, and we decided he could try and
32　　ask [the child] to demonstrate the exercise, as a means
33　　of checking instructions, before doing it. And I think
34　　this is going to be a great resource for me to see if he
35　　understands or doesn't.

As seen above, Mariana presents a clear example of how she spontaneously assembled a team for collaboration over a brief period of time, and how much she values interdisciplinary work.

She then goes back to the topic of collaboration, referring to this interdisciplinary work and to the professional learning community she feels part of.

36   Other staff members give you other perspectives, or
37   perhaps just a tip, it gives you another way of trying,
38   I don't know, it's rewarding, as a teacher it makes you
39   feel you can count on others working with you. It gives
40   you – for example, when I talk to the psychologist,
41   there is not one time that I don't go to a book and
42   read. It makes me want to know more, it makes me want to
43   read about what different people say about certain
44   things. I want to know so that the next child who comes
45   with something similar, I am way ahead than before.

In the above, Mariana clearly shows a desire 'not to go out the same way we came in', as expressed by Edge (2002: 1); 'so that the next child who comes … I am way ahead than I was before'. That is to say, she interprets the present situation as a learning opportunity.

Within the Cooperative Development framework, horizontality is exercised and no status difference is intended to exist between Mariana and me. This may be seen as impossible or idealistic, but if approached reflexively and with sufficient awareness, my experience is that one can establish a working framework within which the most complex issues can be approached. In fact, Mariana is able to express her concerns about issues that are directly my responsibility.

46   Sometimes I think that it's like parenting, you have to
47   lay some ground rules, and this doesn't happen that much
48   here … I think it's to do with how the institution works
49   – perhaps the coordinator is not sure about what is
50   expected of her. Sometimes you hear people talking about
51   things they shouldn't talk about, but perhaps it's
52   because they don't know what is expected of them.

In the extract above, she clearly expresses she thinks there is a lack of clarity in terms of roles. Outside the CD framework, it would be quite risky for her to question the management so straightforwardly. Yet, within the framework, and in an environment of professional trust, she feels she can say it openly, as it will entail no negative consequences.

I have been using Cooperative Development as a discourse framework for more than ten years, not just with peers, but mostly with others in both higher and lower hierarchical positions. I have witnessed how it fosters teachers' awareness of their professional selves, but also how it strengthens relationships. It is a strategy for professional development that requires trust, openness and honesty.

Voices from around the world

In order to continue exploring the intersection of leadership and teacher development, in this section I present vignettes written by colleagues from different backgrounds working in a variety of contexts, in answer to the question: 'What kind of leadership practices are needed to facilitate the professional development of teachers of English in your context?'

Rosana Glatigny, Teacher Educator, Argentina

Rosana highlights the need for interdisciplinary collaboration. She refers to the difficulties involved in working collaboratively and mentions some strategies she has applied in order to overcome them. Rosana believes that systematising interdisciplinary partnerships would be an asset in her context in Comodoro Rivadavia, Argentina.

> The three of them were [teaching] experiences in which we thought together (cooperation) but also they helped me grow because they taught me about their specific field, which in the end resulted in my personal and professional development. It was not an easy task because we [teachers] had different 'logics' so at the beginning we needed to put beliefs in common, we needed to exchange readings, points of view ... I learned a lot about Education, ITC, Pedagogy and Didactics, Psychology and what we call in Spanish el sujeto. My colleagues acknowledge the fact that they had the opportunity to go deeper into the field of Foreign Language Teaching and Learning and improve their knowledge of the language. I also think that more experienced teachers could cooperate and collaborate with new teacher both of them would gain knowledge. Why? Younger teacher may have more technological skills, be more motivated, bring new ideas/theoretical standpoints and more experienced teacher could share their experience. Comodoro Rivadavia is a growing city with few qualified teachers, there are a lot of non-graduate teachers, and if you look at a map, we are far away from big cities like Bs As or Córdoba. In my humble opinion, professional development could by achieved by organizing study groups in which teachers could grow by collaboration and cooperation by reading material, debating about it, etc.

Like Rosana, I have also experienced the power of interdisciplinary partnerships, and how collaboration leads to personal and professional growth by making teachers exercise their interpersonal skills.

Paul Breen, University of Greenwich, UK

Paul highlights the importance of fostering teachers' self-direction for effective professional learning and reflects on the role of the leader, citing the creation of informal communities of practice (Wenger and Snyder, 2000) as an effective leadership strategy. For these communities to flourish, Paul suggests the need for a particular style of leadership that involves trust, which he describes as 'a fine balancing act between hands-on involvement and a hands-off approach'.

> In the first instance teacher learning ought not to be bound and delivered, but rather activated (Wilson & Berne, 1999, p. 194). Such activation is triggered only when teachers come to an understanding of their own knowledge and reach the point of 'cognitive self-direction' espoused by Vygotsky (Manning & Payne, 1993, p. 369). Brockett & Hiemstra (1991, p. 29) define this as the 'characteristics of an individual that predispose one toward taking primary responsibility for personal learning endeavours.' This self-direction often occurs at the juncture of past knowledge and new experience (Vygotsky, 1978; Manning & Payne, 1993). In order for such self-direction to be triggered, reflection plays a crucial part. Thus, even though my approach to teacher education is essentially Vygotskian, I also believe that certain aspects of the developmental process are best fostered in constructive learning environments. One of the approaches that has worked best for me in cultivating such an environment is to draw upon the ideas of Wenger & Snyder (2000) in their suggestion

of creating informal communities of practice within the workplace. This is not easy and requires a form of leadership on the part of teacher educators that is a fine balancing act between hands-on involvement and a hands-off approach that allows the seeds of such a community to flourish. Again, going back to Vygotsky (1978), people learn through having their higher mental processes stimulated, and good leaders recognise how to achieve this. In my [doctoral] study, most of the teachers did become more self-directed and this suggests that such an approach works well.

Paul's reference to the creation of informal communities of practice relates to the idea of promoting flexible collaborative partnerships as a development strategy. For these to operate successfully, affective factors play a fundamental role, and it is these that I now focus on, through Mariam's voice.

Mariam Attia, Lecturer, University of Sussex, UK

Mariam focuses on the role of affect and collaboration in the professional development process, drawing on one of her recent publications (Edge and Attia, 2016). Like Paul, she mentions the importance of teachers attaining self-direction. She also refers to the role of trust in creating what she terms 'emerging teacher communities', specifically highlighting the importance of trust in collegial relationships.

In this short reflective piece, I wish to foreground the value of Cooperative Development — a discourse framework for practitioners as colleagues — in nurturing collaborative educational environments and supporting language teachers in their constant state of becoming. Whilst working as a language teacher at a private institution of higher education in Cairo, Egypt, my colleagues and I were informed that all our language classrooms were to be refitted with the latest educational technology. Naturally, the news sparked feelings of joy and excitement but when student laptops were installed, interactive whiteboards hung up, and satellite television tested, apprehension and anxiety started to creep in. Before long, we were all working in an educational environment of ubiquitous computing and networking. The transition was smooth for some and an uphill struggle for others. Reflecting on my teaching context back then, I think that supporting the use of Cooperative Development in workplaces can inspire effective bottom-up integration of information and communication technologies (ICT). First, because the approach promotes self-directed learning, it gives teachers responsibility for their own growth and helps them prioritise specific technology-related issues. Second, the approach allows teachers to experiment with different digital media at their own pace, to space out meetings with colleagues, and to integrate technology incrementally. Third, considering its non-judgmental non-defensive nature, Cooperative Development offers teachers a safe space in which to address sensitive issues related to integrating ICT, for instance, institutional constraints, lack of confidence, and fear of failure. Teachers may find it easier to speak to a trusted colleague about such issues than to others in their professional environment. Fourth, the approach is not only built on trust but can also enhance trust among colleagues over time. Such empathetic relationships are key to continuous teacher development in the use of ICT and to fostering emerging teacher communities in this area. Finally, considering the open and inclusive nature of Cooperative Development, teachers may appreciate a variety of benefits, which its adoption offers for effective technology integration.

Even though Mariam's experience at university is described through the ICT pedagogy lens, it is similar to my own experience in using Cooperative Development in a school context. This, I believe, highlights the relevance of the framework across educational settings.

All three vignettes foreground issues in leadership and teacher development that have been present throughout the chapter; the role of trust, the importance of collaboration, professional learning communities and leadership styles. This reinforces the idea that these concepts and strategies are relevant across a variety of teaching and learning contexts.

Applications

In this final section I reflect on what I have learned from my experience, my action research and from writing this chapter. I intend to theorise my own learning, hoping that it can be relevant for others wishing to enrich their understanding of how leadership and teacher development interact.

By seeing the professional development process through the leadership lens, learners, teachers and managers become part of a cycle of continuous learning in an era of constant change. As shown in the data, collaboration needs to be exercised at different levels, not only between colleagues, but also with others in different positions. This requires a clear sense of professional trust.

For teacher development to be sustainable and effective, we need a combination of leadership characteristics that include a deep understanding of the local and institutional culture, valuing the affective aspects of teacher learning, and trusting teachers enough to offer the necessary independence for them to flourish. Going back to the 'roots and wings' metaphor in Edge (2011), we need to give teachers the roots, in the form of affect and opportunities for collaborative learning, and also the wings to exercise their professionalism competently and confidently, in the knowledge that we trust them.

Trusting leadership will imply a constant state of seeking a balance between different forces. To begin with, in foregrounding the affective by making work a 'safe' place, as expressed in Mariam's vignette, we must not lose sight of effectiveness. Also, as pointed out by Paul, we need to seek a balance between a hands-on and a hands-off approach that allows teachers to grow. This means that self-direction must be actively promoted, without losing sight of the importance of clear guidelines and supervision. Finally, knowledge of and respect for the institutional culture and tradition must be present, without halting the change forces that make a professional learning community dynamic.

Further research is needed in order to consolidate the relevance of the collaborative practices and strategies discussed in this chapter. To begin with, it would be interesting to gain a deeper understanding of the role of trust in other collaborative professional development environments. In addition to this, I personally intend to further my understanding of the role of collegial and collaborative discourses on teachers' professional identity. Last but not least, I am convinced that the transformative power of Edge's (1992, 2002) Cooperative Development framework deserves to be acknowledged and disseminated by means of further research.

Further reading

With the aim of providing an inter-disciplinary understanding of the issues of leadership and teacher effectiveness, I suggest four texts that explore different aspects related to professional development and leadership.

Cameron, K., Bright, D. and Caza, A. (2004) 'Exploring the Relationships Between Organizational Virtuousness and Performance'. *American Behavioral Scientist*, 47(6) 1–24.

Cameron, Bright and Caza present a view of organizational effectiveness in which they place forgiveness, trust, integrity, optimism and compassion as fundamental factors. Although not strictly related to educational settings, I believe the theories espoused by the authors are very much related to the notions of leadership I have focused on throughout the chapter.

Edge, J. (2002) *Continuing Cooperative Development: A Discourse Framework for Individuals as Colleagues*. Ann Arbor, MI: University of Michigan Press.

Edge's known book is becoming more and more relevant in today's educational reality, in which there is often little space for reflection. Available online: <http://cooperative-development.com> (accessed 23 May, 2019).

Frowe, I. (2005) 'Professional Trust'. *British Journal of Educational Studies*, 53(1) 34–53.

In a high-quality academic article, Frowe provides an in-depth discussion of the notion of trust in educational environments, which is central to this chapter.

Modoono, J. (2017) 'The Trust Factor'. *Educational Leadership* 74(8). Available online: <www.ascd.org/publications/educational-leadership/may17/vol74/num08/The-Trust-Factor.aspx> (accessed 23 May, 2019).

Modoono presents her arguments for intentionally building trust as an integral part of an educational community, since it will favour collaboration and an essentially positive school culture, which will in turn result in favourable results for students. She offers a series of strategies in order to create this trust-centred school culture.

References

Andrews, J. and Higson, H. (2008) 'Graduate Employability, "Soft Skills" Versus "Hard" Business Knowledge: A European Study'. *Higher Education in Europe*, 33(4) 411–422.

Barak, M., Ben-Chaim, D. and Zoller, U. (2007) 'Purposely Teaching for the Promotion of Higher-order Thinking Skills: A Case of Critical Thinking'. *Research in Science Education*, 37 353–369.

Barker, R. (1997) 'How Can We Train Leaders if We Do Not Know What Leadership Is?'. *Human Relations*, 50(4) 343–362.

Bass, B. and Avolio, B. (1994) *Improving Organizational Effectiveness through Transformational Leadership*. Thousand Oaks, CA: Sage Publications.

Bryman, A. (2007) 'Effective Leadership in Higher Education: A Literature Review'. *Studies in Higher Education*, 32(6) 693–710.

Burns, D. and Darling-Hammond, L. (2014) *Teaching Around the World: What Can TALIS Tell Us?* Stanford, CA: Stanford Center for Opportunity Policy in Education.

Bush, T., Bell, L. and Middlewood, D. (2010) *The Principles of Educational Leadership and Management*. London: SAGE.

Cameron, K., Bright, D. and Caza, A. (2004) 'Exploring the Relationships Between Organizational Virtuousness and Performance'. *American Behavioral Scientist*, 47(6) 1–24.

Cummings, L and Bromiley, P. (1996) 'The Organizational Trust Inventory (OTI): development and validation', *Trust in Organizations: Frontiers of Theory and Research*. London: SAGE: 302–330.

De Stefani, M. (2014) 'Challenging traditions: constructing an identity through innovative teaching practices', in Breen, P. (ed.) *Cases on Teacher Identity, Diversity, and Cognition in Higher Education*. Hershey, PA: IGI Global: 258–286.

DuFour, R. (2004) 'What is a Professional Learning Community?'. *Educational Leadership*, 61(8) 6–11.

Edge, J. (ed.) (1991) *Action Research*. Alexandria, VA: TESOL Inc.

Edge, J. (1992) *Cooperative Development*. London: Longman.

Edge, J. (2002) *Continuing Cooperative Development: A Discourse Framework for Individuals as Colleagues*. Ann Arbor, MI: University of Michigan Press.

Edge, J. (2011) *The Reflexive Teacher Educator in TESOL: Roots and Wings*. New York: Routledge.

Edge, J. and Attia, M. (2016) 'Technology, communication, and collaboration for innovation', in Tajino, A., Stewart, T. and Dalsky, D. (eds) *Team Teaching and Team Learning in the Language Classroom: Collaboration for Innovation in ELT*. Abingdon: Routledge: 115–126.

Frowe, I. (2005) 'Professional Trust'. *British Journal of Educational Studies*, 53(1) 34–53.

Gronn, P. (2000) 'Distributed Properties: A New Architecture for Leadership'. *Educational Management and Administration*, 28 371–338.

Hargreaves, A. and Fink, D. (2004) 'The Seven Principles of Sustainable Leadership'. *Educational Leadership*, 61(7) 8–13.

Hargreaves, A. and Fullan, M. (2000) 'Mentoring in the New Millennium'. *Theory Into Practice*, 39(1) 50–56.

Hargreaves, A. and Goodson, I. (2006) 'Educational Change Over Time? The Sustainability and Non Sustainability of Three Decades of Secondary School Change and Continuity'. *Educational Administration Quarterly*, 42(3) 3–41.

Hord, S. (2009) 'Professional Learning Communities: Educators Work Together towards a Shared Purpose'. *Journal of Staff Development*, 30 40–43.

Hunter, J. and Back, J. (2011) 'Facilitating Sustainable Professional Development Through Lesson Study'. *Mathematics Teacher Education and Development*, 13(1) 94–114.

Kaufman, D. and Grennon Brooks, J. (1996) 'Interdisciplinary Collaboration in Teacher Education: A Constructivist Approach'. *TESOL Quarterly*, 30(2) 231–251.

Kezar, A. and Eckel, P. (2002) 'The Effect of Institutional Culture on Change Strategies in Higher Education: Universal Principles or Culturally Responsive Concepts?'. *The Journal of Higher Education*, 73(4) 435–460.

Leithwood, K. and Jantzi, D. (1999) *The effects of transformational leadership on organizational conditions and student engagement at school*. Paper presented at the Annual Meeting of the American Educational Research Association, Montreal, April.

Leithwood, K., Anderson, S., Mascall, B. and Strauss, T. (2010) 'School leaders' influences on student learning: the four paths', in Bush, T., Bell, L. and Middlewood, D. (eds) *The Principles of Educational Leadership and Management*. London: SAGE.

Louis, K. S., Dretske, B. and Wahlstrom, K. (2010) 'How Does Leadership Affect Student Achievement? Results from a National US Survey'. *School Effectiveness and School Improvement*, 21(3) 315–336.

Misanchuk, M. and Anderson, T. (2001) 'Building community in an online learning environment: communication, cooperation and collaboration'. *Teaching and learning: today's success, tomorrow's horizons*, Sixth Annual Mid-South Instructional Technology Conference, Murfreesboro, Middle Tennessee State University.

Modoono, J. (2017) 'The Trust Factor'. *Educational Leadership* 74(8).

Moore, R. (2008) *Trusting Leadership: Developing Effective Schools*. Glassboro, NJ: Rowan University, ProQuest Dissertations Publishing.

O'Donoghue, T. and Clarke, S. (2009) *Leading Learning: Processes, Themes and Issues in International Contexts*. Abingdon: Routledge.

Perkins, D. (2003) 'From Lordship to leadership', in Perkins, D. (ed.) *King Arthur's Round Table: How Collaborative Conversations Create Smart Organisations*. Hoboken, NJ: Wiley: 89–117.

Polenske, K. (2004) 'Competition, Collaboration and Cooperation: An Uneasy Triangle in Networks of Firms and Regions'. *Regional Studies*, 38(9) 1029–1043.

Richmond, G. and Manokore, V. (2010) 'Identifying Elements Critical for Functional and Sustainable Professional Learning Communities'. *Science Teacher Education*, 95 543–570.

Sorrentino, R. M. and Short, J.-A. C. (1986) 'Uncertainty orientation, motivation, and cognition', in Sorrentino, R. M. and Higgins E. T. (eds) *Handbook of Motivation and Cognition: Foundations of Social Behavior*. New York: Guilford Press: 379–403.

Spillane, J. and Orlina, E. (2005) 'Investigating Leadership Practice: Exploring the Entailments of Taking a Distributed Perspective'. *Leadership and Policy in Schools*, 4(3) 157–176.

Stoll, L. and Louis, K. (eds) (2007) *Professional Learning Communities: Divergence, Depth and Dilemmas*. London: Open University Press and McGraw Hill.

Thoonen, E., Sleegers, P., Oort, F., Peetsma, T. and Geijsel, F. (2011) 'How to Improve Teaching Practices: The Role of Teacher Motivation, Organizational Factors, and Leadership Practices'. *Educational Administration Quarterly*, 47(3) 496–536.

Vaillant, D. (2011) 'Preparing Teachers for Inclusive Education in Latin America'. *Prospects*, 41(3) 385–398.

Vaillant, D. (2013) 'Initial Teacher Training in Latin America: Dilemmas and Perspectives'. *Revista Española de Educación Comparada*, 22 185–206.

Wenger, E. and Snyder, W. (2000) 'Communities of Practice: The Organizational Frontier'. *Harvard Business Review*, 1 139–145.

Index

Page numbers in **bold** refer to tables; those in *italics* refer to figures; *a* indicates appendix.